*Essentials of Maternal-Newborn Nursing*

# Essentials of
# Maternal-Newborn

*Addison-Wesley Nursing*

*A Division of The Benjamin/Cummings Publishing Company, Inc.*
Redwood City, California ● Fort Collins, Colorado ● Menlo Park, California
Reading, Massachusetts ● New York ● Don Mills, Ontario ● Wokingham, U.K.
Amsterdam ● Bonn ● Sydney ● Singapore ● Tokyo ● Madrid ● San Juan

# Nursing

## Second Edition

*Patricia Wieland Ladewig, RNC, PhD*

Director, Program in Nursing
Regis College
Denver, Colorado

*Marcia L. London, RN, MSN, NNP*

Associate Professor and
Director, Neonatal Nurse Practitioner Program
Beth-El College of Nursing
Colorado Springs, Colorado

*Sally Brookens Olds, RNC, MS*

Associate Professor
Beth-El College of Nursing
Colorado Springs, Colorado

Sponsoring Editor: Debra Hunter
Developmental Editor: Jackie Estrada
Production Coordinator: Brian Jones
Text Designer: Detta Penna
Cover Designers: Rudy Zehntner, Detta Penna
Cover Artist: Joan Carol
Copyeditor: Jenny Hale Pulsipher
Proofreader: Melissa Andrews
Page Checker: Jeanne Heise
Indexer: Katherine Pitcoff
Photographers: Suzanne Arms Wimberley, William Thompson, George B. Fry III
Medical Illustrators: Jack P. Tandy, Charles W. Hoffman III
Compositor: G&S Typesetters, Inc.
Printer and Binder: Von Hoffmann Press

Credits for epigrams and photographs used throughout
the text appear after the Glossary.

Library of Congress Cataloging-in-Publication Data

Ladewig, Patricia A.
    Essentials of maternal-newborn nursing / Patricia Wieland
Ladewig, Marcia L. London, Sally Brookens Olds.—2nd ed.
        p.   cm.
    Includes bibliographical references.
    ISBN 0-201-13238-9
    1. Obstetrical nursing.   2. Neonatology.   3. Pediat-
ric nursing.   I. London, Marcia L.   II. Olds, Sally B.,
1940–  .   III. Title.
    [DNLM: 1. Neonatology—nurses' instruction.   2. Obstet-
rical Nursing.   WY 157.3 L154e]
    RG951.L33   1990
    610.73'678—dc20
    DNLM/DLC
    for Library of Congress                           89-17594
                                                           CIP

BCDEFGHIJ—VH— 93210

The authors and publishers have exerted every effort to ensure
that drug selections and dosages set forth in this text are in
accord with current recommendations and practice at the time
of publication. However, in view of ongoing research, changes
in government regulations, and the constant flow of information
relating to drug therapy and drug reactions, the reader is urged
to check the package insert for each drug for any change in
indications of dosage and for added warnings and precautions.
This is particularly important where the recommended agent is
a new and/or infrequently employed drug.

**Addison-Wesley Nursing**
A Division of The Benjamin/Cummings Publishing Company, Inc.
390 Bridge Parkway
Redwood City, California 94065

*We dedicate this book to parents*
*who give their children*
*the breath of life*
*and hold,*
*soothe,*
*comfort,*
*encourage,*
*nurture,*
*and love them,*
*and then*
*set them free to be.*
*And especially to our parents*
*Alice and Warren Wieland*
*Edna and Kenneth Brown*
*Naomi and Randall Brookens*

# Reviewers

# Preface

Today's nurses are client advocates and educators. They play a central role in a family's experience of birth. Women now have choices about how and where they will give birth and, in some cases, whether their care giver will be a physician or a nurse-midwife.

## Focus on Client Teaching and the Nursing Process

We feel strongly that one of the primary roles of the nurse is that of client teacher—helping people acquire the information and skills they need to meet their own needs. There is therefore a strong focus throughout this text on teaching. In addition, we firmly believe that it is essential for nurses to use the nursing process to provide high-level, effective nursing care. These two foci—client teaching and the nursing process—form the basis of the book's organization—and result, we believe, in a text that is as relevant and useful to practicing nurses as it is to nursing students.

## Why an "Essentials" Book?

In today's varied nursing curricula, the course in maternal-newborn nursing can range in length from 4 to 13 weeks—depending on the type of program and the availability of clinical facilities, among other factors. In response to requests from those nurse educators who do not have a full 12 or 13 weeks to cover this content, we developed *Essentials of Maternal-Newborn Nursing* as an alternative to our bestselling, more detailed and comprehensive *Maternal-Newborn Nursing*. This *Essentials* text, first published in 1986, was designed to meet the demand for a shorter text focused on the essentials of safe,

thoughtful nursing care. In this, the second edition of our *Essentials* text, not only have we updated content to make the book as current and accurate as possible, but we have also expanded coverage in certain areas and added new content in others—based on extensive reviews by nurse educators who are helping us to refine our definition of what is "essential" content.

## Organization

*Essentials of Maternal-Newborn Nursing* is comprised of five parts: *Basic Concepts, Pregnancy, Birth, The Newborn,* and *Postpartum.* Within each part, the sequence of chapters moves logically from normal to abnormal (or "at risk") coverage, while cultural aspects of the childbearing experience are integrated appropriately throughout.

## Content New to This Edition

Users of the first edition will immediately notice that this second edition is longer. In adding new material, we have been guided always by those nursing educators who used or reviewed the first edition and who had specific requests for additional material they needed to teach their students. We have added an entirely new chapter on *Women's Health Care* (Chapter 3), which covers such diverse topics as gynecologic issues, rape, and family violence; a new chapter on *Age-Related Considerations* (Chapter 9), which covers the special concerns of both adolescent pregnancy and the first-time pregnancy of an older couple; and a new chapter on *Newborn Nutrition* (Chapter 23). We have also increased the depth of coverage of such complications of the childbearing process as pregnancy-induced hypertension, diabetes mellitus, and AIDS.

## Nursing Process and the Role of the Maternity Nurse

While some books cover the role of the medical community in childbirth as a separate topic, our book gives an overview of *all* aspects of the childbearing process *with a specific emphasis on nursing care throughout pregnancy, labor and birth, and the postpartum period.* The nurse's role is clearly delineated, and is presented within the framework of the nursing process. Chapters are organized around the five steps of the nursing process: assessment, diagnosis, planning, implementation, and evaluation. And numerous special features reinforce the nursing process as a framework for learning and for nursing care. See, for example, the **Assessment Guides,** such as those on pages 186 and 197; the **Essential Nursing Diagnoses to Consider** boxes, such as those on pages 236 and 262; the **Nursing Care Plans,** such as those on pages 298 and 316; and **Procedures,** such as those on pages 192 and 359, which describe interventions specific to maternal-newborn nursing care in illustrated, step-by-step fashion. Throughout the text, we have used the most current nursing diagnoses, those approved following the 1988 NANDA Conference. And for easy reference in the clinical setting, we have included a handy list of the current NANDA diagnoses in detachable card format.

## Emphasis on Client/Family Teaching

A crucial responsibility of the maternity nurse that we emphasize and highlight more strongly than ever before is client and family teaching. Our focus here is on the teaching that nurses do at all stages of pregnancy and the childbearing process—including the important postpartum teaching that is done before and immediately after families are discharged from the hospital. Throughout the text, discussion of client/family teaching is highlighted by this apple logo in the margin. And in several places, a more detailed discussion of client/family teaching is summarized in a **Teaching Guide,** such as the one on *Sexual Activity During Pregnancy,* which starts on page 223, or the one on *What to Expect During Your Labor,* which starts on page 419. In addition, the **Client/Family Teaching Cards,** found opposite page 178, are handy tools for the student to use while studying or in the clinical setting for quick reference. Finally, a four-color chart (tucked into the back of the book) depicts maternal/fetal development month-by-month and provides specific teaching guidelines for each stage of pregnancy. Students can put this chart on their walls as a tool to use while studying—or they can save it for use as a reference tool in the clinical setting.

## State-of-the-Art Pedagogy

Instructors and students alike have praised the wealth of in-text learning aids included in our books. In this edi-

tion of our *Essentials* text, we have once again created a book that is both easy to learn from and easy to use as a reference. Each chapter begins with behavioral **Objectives** and a list of **Key Terms,** and ends with a summary of **Essential Concepts,** as well as lists of **References** and **Additional Readings.** Throughout the body of the text, we have included special boxes called **Essential Facts to Remember,** which students can use to review the material they've just read, and to be sure they understand the most important concepts. In addition, where appropriate, we have included **Drug Guides** for those medications commonly used in maternal-newborn nursing, to guide students in correctly administering medications. Finally, a glossary of terms commonly used in the field of maternity nursing can be found on the blue pages at the back of the book.

## Enhanced Visual Appeal

For today's visually oriented students, we have developed an attractive new two-color design that commands their interest at the same time it highlights the key information they need to learn. Students are brought closer to the childbearing experience through the use of dramatic photographs of women and families from many cultures. In particular, the photographs taken by Suzanne Arms Wimberley, an internationally renowned author and childbirth educator, reveal an extraordinary sensitivity to the needs, desires, and customs of a variety of women in a variety of cultures and settings. And opposite page 594, we have included a selection of four-color photos that vividly show particular visual aspects of pregnancy, childbirth, and the newborn.

## Complete Teaching/Learning Package

To complement this new second edition of *Essentials of Maternal-Newborn Nursing,* Addison-Wesley Nursing publishes a complete package of supplements for students and instructors. Students can improve their studying with *Maternal-Newborn Nursing Care: A Workbook,* Third Edition, which not only emphasizes factual knowledge but offers practice in clinical problem-solving as well. (If this workbook is not available in the campus bookstore, students can ask their bookstore to order it, or they can order it directly from Addison-Wesley Nursing by calling 1–800–447–2226.) Available to faculty only are several important tools to help with classroom presentations and the evaluation of students. An 800-item *Test Bank* is available both as a printed paperback and in computerized form for IBM and Apple personal computers. An *Instructor's Manual,* prepared by Virginia Kinnick, CNM, EdD, gives suggestions for covering necessary content in a logical, creative way. And a *Transparency Resource Kit* containing 40 two-color transparencies, including several illustrations not otherwise included in the text, is available at a substantial discount to course adopters. (For further information on these and other Addison-Wesley Nursing texts and supplements, instructors can contact their Addison-Wesley Nursing representative directly by calling 1–800–950–5544.)

## Acknowledgments

Our goal with every revision is to incorporate the newest research and latest information from the literature of nursing and related fields to make our text as relevant and useful as possible. This would not be possible without the support and encouragement of our colleagues. The comments and suggestions we have received from nurse educators and practitioners around the country have helped us make the text accurate and up-to-date. Whenever a nurse takes the time to write, or to speak to one of us at a professional gathering, we recognize again the intense commitment of nurses to excellence in practice. And so we thank our peers.

In publishing as in health care, quality assurance is an essential part of the process; that is the dimension our reviewers have added. Some reviewers assist us by validating the accuracy of the content, some by their attention to detail, and some by challenging us to examine our ways of thinking and to develop new awareness. Thus we extend our sincere thanks to all those who reviewed the manuscript for this book: their names and affiliations are listed separately right before this Preface.

We are also grateful to the contributors to the third edition of the larger text, *Maternal-Newborn Nursing: A Family-Centered Approach.* They include Joyce Boles, RN, MN, CPNP, Bellarmine College; Rena Brescia, RNC, MS, Nurses' Association of the American College of Obstetricians and Gynecologists; Sharon Glass, RN, BS, NNP, Eastern Oklahoma Perinatal Center; Effie A. Graham, RN, PhD, University of Alaska; Janet Griffith-Kenney, RN, PhD, College of New Rochelle; Louise Westberg Hedstrom, RN, CNM, MSN, North Park College; Patricia Hemak, RN, MS, Regis College; E. JoAnne Jones, RN, MEd, MSN, Norfolk State University; Lynette Karls, BS, MS, University of Wisconsin; Jo Ann Kilb, RN, MSN, NNP, St. Joseph Hospital; Stephen Kilb, RN, NNP, University of Arizona; Virginia Gramzow Kinnick, RN, CNM, EdD, University of Northern Colorado; Kathleen Knafl, RN, PhD, University of Illinois; Dietra Lowdermilk, RN, MEd, University of North Carolina; Nancy McCluggage, RN, CNM, MA, Yale University; Mary Ann Neihaus, RN, MSN, CEN, EMT-A, University of Cincinnati Hospital; Shannon Perry, RN, PhD, San Francisco State University; Lovena L. Porter, RN, MS, Colorado Springs Medical Center; Carol Hawthorne Rumpler, RN, MS, Franklin University; Madrean Schober, RNC, BGS, Bloomington Obstetrics and Gynecology, Inc.; Constance Lawrenz Slaughter, RN, BSN, University of Portland and Bess Kaiser Hospital; Deborah Sweeney, RN, CNM, MS, Medical College of Georgia; and Linda Ungerleider, RN, MSN, North Park College.

In addition, we want to thank nursing students everywhere. They challenge and stimulate us. Their questions, their insights, and their enthusiasm have helped make writing exciting and even, at times, fun. For this, we thank them.

A project of this scope requires the support and cooperation of many people. We would personally like to thank the following:

Debra Hunter, our sponsoring editor, has brought her considerable knowledge and expertise to the project. She is warm, supportive, and always committed to excellence. We have learned from her as from a new friend, and we value her ability to stay calm and supportive even during hectic times and short deadlines.

In beginning a project of this size, it is important to have a developmental editor to help sharpen the editorial focus of the text as a whole. Jackie Estrada guided us in the early stages as we worked to develop a consistent format. She reviewed early drafts and advised us thoughtfully and skillfully. We value her insights and recommendations, which helped make this book more internally consistent and more readable as well.

Brian Jones masterfully dealt with all aspects of production. His efficiency, keen eye for detail, and patience kept the project on target. We consider him a special friend.

Creative imagination is necessary to make a text look both contemporary and also warm. We firmly believe that a book on maternal-newborn nursing must not only be visually appealing but must also convey an appropriate caring attitude in order to help students learn. And so we thank Detta Penna for the text design and layout, Rudy Zehntner and Detta Penna for the cover design, and Joan Carol for her wonderful cover illustration.

We are honored that many of the photographs in the text were taken by Suzanne Arms Wimberley, who is justly renowned for her concern about—and her own work on—the childbearing family. The magic of her photographs is that they capture and convey so eloquently the essence of a moment in the life of a childbearing family.

Charles W. Hoffman III, a tremendously talented illustrator, has done a superb job with the tonal art. We think his work on the maternal-fetal development chart conveys the miracle of the developing infant exceptionally well.

Jack Tandy, another good friend, rendered most of the line art throughout the text. The great educational value of his drawings lies in their simple clarity.

Jenny Hale Pulsipher brought her skills as copyeditor to bear on the text, while Melissa Andrews brought hers as proofreader. Jeanne Heise checked the pages, and Katherine Pitcoff created the index. To all of them, we say thank you.

We are also grateful to Bill Grosskopf and the able staff of G&S Typesetters, Inc., for their fine work in typesetting, page makeup, and film preparation on this text.

Ginny Kinnick, CNM, EdD, has done all editions of the *Instructor's Manual* for our books. She has authored an academically sound and valuable tool for instructors everywhere. Her work reflects her strong academic and clinical base. We respect her ability and are delighted to work with her.

The children and families so beautifully pictured on the endsheets are members of the families of our reviewers, of those who contributed to the production of this text, and of the fine people at Addison-Wesley Nursing and The Benjamin/Cummings Publishing Company. We are grateful to all of them for sharing these important snapshots of their lives.

During the years the three of us have worked together to develop this text, our families have been steadfast in their love and support. We have watched our children grow and evolve as people. We have rejoiced in the steadfast love of our husbands, and we have developed deep friendships among ourselves. We are blessed to share the support of our families and of each other.

The comments and suggestions of those who used the first edition of this text have helped to shape its continuing development. We hope this second edition will be even more useful to faculty and students in communicating the power and wonder of the miracle that is birth.

Patricia Wieland Ladewig
Marcia L. London
Sally Brookens Olds

# Contents

# Special Features

## Assessment Guides

## Dx Essential Nursing Diagnoses to Consider

## Case Studies

## Essential Facts to Remember

*(continues)*

**Essential Facts to Remember** (continued)

# PART
# I
# BASIC CONCEPTS

# Contemporary Maternal-Newborn Care

When I started out in practice by myself, I didn't fully appreciate that when I went single-handedly to deliver babies at home—one midwife in the midst of at least three generations of a family—that I would be, in many respects, at their mercy. The qualities of their lives and relationships crowded in on the relatively simple act of birth, making it rich with possibilities, some beneficial, some not. (A Midwife's Story)

## Objectives

● Describe changes in childbirth practice in the twentieth century.

● Discuss the various nursing roles in maternal-newborn care.

● Describe some nursing strategies for caring for the family.

● Briefly discuss selected state-of-the-art advances in the care of the childbearing family.

● Contrast the arguments advanced for specific ethical issues affecting maternity care.

● Discuss selected tools used in maternity nursing practice.

● Contrast descriptive and inferential statistics.

## Key Terms

biopsychosocial
birth rate
certified nurse-midwife
certified registered nurse
client
client advocate
clinical nurse specialist
descriptive statistics
family-centered care
fetal death
inferential statistics

informed consent
maternal mortality
neonatal mortality
neonatology
nurse practitioner
nursing diagnosis
nursing process
perinatal mortality
perinatology
problem-oriented medical
   record (POMR) system
professional nurse

At the moment a child is born, the quality of his or her future depends on many genetic and environmental factors. Some of these factors are present at the time of conception; others become apparent as the child develops.

The actions and decisions of parents and health professionals have great impact on children's lives. Health professionals can improve a child's chances for a healthy future by providing expert care to the expectant family. Parents can provide a positive family environment for their children by living as healthfully as possible and seeking help from professionals when a family member's physical or psychologic condition is threatened.

This textbook is about the contribution of maternal-newborn nurses to the quality of a child's life. Since the psychologic and physical health of parents has a marked effect on their offspring, our focus is the childbearing family and the responsibilities of the nurse caring for that family. This chapter is an introduction to childbearing and maternal-child nursing in North America.

## ● CHILDBEARING IN THE TWENTIETH CENTURY

Before 1900, few infants were born in hospitals. Only very poor or unwed women went to a hospital for childbirth. As the scope of medical practice increased, hospital births gained acceptance from more affluent clients. By the middle of the twentieth century, most women were hospitalized for childbirth.

Until early in this century, newborns remained with their mothers after a hospital birth. Outbreaks of diarrhea, scarlet fever, diphtheria, and other communicable diseases, however, caused a large number of infant and maternal deaths. Physicians emphasized the need for separate care for mother and infant to prevent the spread of infection. Newborn nurseries became firmly entrenched, and an era of rigid management of pregnancy, labor, and birth began.

Labor and birth were treated as a medical problem, controlled by the obstetrician and hospital staff. Many types of analgesic agents were administered during labor, and general anesthetics were given for the birth. Some of these agents were harmful to the fetus. During labor and the birth, the father sat in the waiting room. After the birth, the father saw his child through the window of the nursery.

Frequently, the mother was separated from her newborn for hours after the birth. During the remainder of the hospital stay, maternal-newborn contact depended on hospital routine. Strict asepsis and scheduled formula feedings were accepted practices. Postpartal stays for mother and child usually lasted about ten days while the mother remained on bed rest, and infant-care classes were unknown. Little thought was given to the psychologic effects of these policies on the childbearing family.

In the early 1940s, social scientists and health care professionals began analyzing the effects of this rigid management of childbirth on family relationships and on individual members. Studies showed that the psychologic and social well-being of family members was affected by impersonal, rigid hospital practices.

By the early 1950s, it became clear to some that more personalized and family-oriented maternity care was essential. They began advocating changes in the care given during childbearing. These advocates included Grantly Dick-Read, who introduced the concept of preparing the mother and father for childbirth and allowing the father to participate in labor and the birth; Arnold Gesell, who supported the practice of rooming-in so that newborns could remain in the hospital rooms with their mothers; and John Bowlby, who described the tragic effects of maternal deprivation on children.

The movement toward **family-centered care** during childbirth was advanced in the late 1950s by the Family-Centered Maternity Care Program established at St. Mary's Hospital in Evansville, Indiana. This program was based on the concept that a hospital could provide professional services to mothers, fathers, and infants in a homelike environment that would enhance the integrity of the family unit.

The movement toward family-centered care received added impetus from families themselves. In the 1960s, when many people began questioning long-held beliefs about many areas of life, those pertaining to traditional medical practices and philosophies also came under scrutiny. The consumer, feminist, and self-help movements made people take a new look at childbearing and its medical management. Couples began demanding assistance, not control, from physicians and nurses. Women began realizing that the successful outcome of their pregnancy had more to do with their role and activities than those of the obstetrician. People began asking for complete information about medical practices—what, why, and how much—so that they could make their own decisions. Childbearing couples began seeking alternatives to traditional obstetric management, including home birth and midwives as birth attendants.

The health care system has responded to the demands of health care consumers and professionals. Hospital policies and practices have been modified, and alternatives to conventional institutional childbirth are being offered to women considered at low risk for complications.

Today's typical childbearing experience is characterized by its focus on the family. Fathers are participants during the birth, not passive bystanders. Even when cesarean delivery is necessary, the father usually can remain with the woman. Analgesic and anesthetic agents for pain relief are carefully monitored and used minimally, and special breathing patterns and other methods are used to relieve discomfort.

Unless the newborn is at risk and requires immediate care, he or she remains with the parents so that they can become acquainted. The newborn is usually fed on demand instead of on a schedule. The mother may have the baby in her room as much as she desires. The hospital stay for a healthy mother and newborn may be as brief as 12 hours.

Many hospitals offer alternative birth facilities to childbearing couples. Labor and delivery rooms have been remodeled to convey a homelike atmosphere. Some hospitals have established outpatient birth centers as well as birthing rooms within the hospital. In birthing rooms and birth centers, the father and others important to the mother are allowed to participate in the birth. Some birth facilities allow siblings to be present during delivery.

Occasionally, the birth center is established and managed by nurse-midwives, who are also in attendance during labor and delivery. If a complication arises, clients are transferred to a health care facility that is equipped to handle the situation.

The goal of the maternity staff in birth facilities is to promote a meaningful experience for the childbearing family as well as to ensure the health of mother and child. Most couples come away from their childbearing experience feeling satisfied with their maternity care.

## ● MATERNAL-NEWBORN GOVERNMENT PROGRAMS

More than 60 years ago, the United States government became involved in improving the quality of maternity care. The Sheppard-Towner Act of 1921 was the first federal legislation to provide funds for state programs in maternal and child care; this act was in force until 1929. In 1935, the Social Security Act was passed, which provides federal grants for health and welfare programs, with many services in the maternal-child health area.

In 1964, the Maternity and Infant (M&I) Care Projects were begun by the Public Health Service of the Department of Health, Education, and Welfare. These projects were started in 56 geographic areas where maternal and infant mortality rates were much higher than the national average.

The purpose of these projects is to provide high-risk women safe, effective maternity care with the goals of reducing maternal and infant mortality and preventing prematurity, birth trauma, and mental retardation. Services range from medical and dental care to infant care. These projects have been very effective.

Women, Infants, and Children (WIC), a supplemental food program, was established in 1975 to provide food and nutrition counseling to low-income families. WIC has been important in promoting the nutritional well-being of women and small children.

# ● MATERNAL-NEWBORN NURSING

Nurses who want to care for childbearing families can choose from a variety of career positions and settings. Depending on the nurse's qualifications, the nurse may *assist* the primary caregiver or *be* the primary caregiver during the pregnancy and birth. This section explores professional options for nurses as well as other issues arising from the expansion of nursing practice.

Underlying all maternity nursing care, no matter what the nurse's position, is a family-centered approach. A major goal of family-centered maternity care is to help each member of the expectant family become or stay healthy. The nurse who wants to care for childbearing families must understand family structures, roles of family members, and family processes. An in-depth discussion of the family unit is beyond the scope of this book, but there are many excellent books and articles on the subject. Later in this section, some general principles of nursing care for the family are provided.

## ● Roles and Settings

Maternity nurses are found in the obstetric departments of acute care facilities, physician's offices, public health department clinics, and any other setting where women seek maternity care. The depth of care provided by the nurse depends on her or his qualifications and scope of practice. A **professional nurse** has graduated from an accredited basic program in nursing, has successfully completed the nursing licensure examination, is currently licensed as a registered nurse, and is qualified to provide basic nursing care. A **certified registered nurse** (RNC) has shown expertise in a field by taking a national exam. A **nurse practitioner** (NP) has received specialized education in a master's degree program or a continuing education program and thus can function in an expanded role. Nurse practitioners often provide ambulatory care services to the expectant family, performing physical and psychosocial assessments and certain diagnostic tests and procedures. Nurse practitioners also work in normal or high-risk neonatal nurseries.

The **clinical nurse specialist** has a master's degree and specialized knowledge and competence in a specific clinical area. The **certified nurse-midwife** (CNM) is educated in the two disciplines of nursing and midwifery and possesses evidence of certification according to the requirements of the American College of Nurse-Midwives. The nurse-midwife is trained to manage independently the care of women at low risk for complications during pregnancy and birth and the care of normal newborns.

## ● Nurse-Midwifery

Throughout history, birth attendants or midwives have had an important place in most societies. Midwifery is an honored profession that has developed throughout the ages. Even today, eight of ten women in the world are attended in childbirth by a midwife.

Midwifery and nursing are distinct disciplines; in fact, the education, regulation, and practice of the professional midwife were instituted before organized professional nursing came into existence in 1871. They are complementary disciplines, however, and this has led to the development of the nurse-midwife.

The nurse-midwife practices within the framework of a medically directed health service in accord with the guidelines specified by the American College of Nurse-Midwives (ACNM). The basic beliefs and commitments of nurse-midwives are reflected in the following statement:

> Every childbearing family has a right to a safe, satisfying experience with respect for human dignity and worth; for variety in cultural forms; and for the parents' right to self-determination.
>
> Comprehensive maternity care, including educational and emotional support as well as management of physical care throughout the childbearing years, is a major means of intercession into, and improvement and maintenance of, the health of the nation's families. Comprehensive maternity care is most effectively and efficiently delivered by interdependent health disciplines.
>
> Nurse-midwifery is an interdependent health discipline focusing on the family and exhibiting responsibility for insuring that its practitioners are provided with excellence in preparation and that those practitioners demonstrate professional behavior in keeping with these stated beliefs (American College of Nurse-Midwives 1972).

Nurse-midwifery made a major advance in 1981, when Congress authorized Medicaid payments for the services of nurse-midwives.

## ● The Nurse and the Family

Because each person develops as a member of a family unit, the nurse must acquire understanding of the family to understand the individual. This is especially important in the maternity setting because the nurse is directly responsible for the well-being of two members of the same family—mother and child.

The family unit has been identified as critical for the

success of health care services for the following reasons (Friedman 1981):

1. In a family unit, a dysfunction of one or more family members generally affects each individual as well as the family unit. If the nurse considers only the individual, nursing care is fragmented rather than complete and holistic.

2. Assessing the family aids the nurse's understanding of the individual functioning within his or her own primary social context. With the childbearing family, the nurse is able to assist the prospective parents to prepare for the new family member.

3. There is a strong interrelationship between the health status of the family as a whole and that of its members. The nurse can have a positive effect not only on individuals but also on their families.

4. In considering the family as a whole, the nurse can identify potential risk factors and thereby prevent illness.

5. When illness occurs, the family is instrumental in seeking medical assistance and in determining their own attitude and that of the sick person toward the illness.

In family-centered maternity nursing, the nurse generally focuses on health promotion and maintenance and prevention of illness. The nurse uses a **biopsychosocial** approach, which recognizes the influence of the prenatal environment and the quality of parenting on the growth and development of the child. Nursing principles for the childbearing family include the following:

● An intimate relationship exists between family members. The woman receiving maternity care assumes a unique role within the family group, a role that must be acknowledged if the family is to function optimally.

● An ailing family member becomes dependent on others in the family, thereby increasing stress and perhaps temporarily or permanently impeding the ability of the family to perform its tasks. A pregnant woman or a woman who has just come home with a newborn baby is usually not ill, but she may need to rely on others in her family to perform activities that she previously performed. The nurse can help the other family members take on added responsibilities and find outside resources to support family functioning.

● Variables such as cultural beliefs, community resources, and health beliefs can significantly affect the family's response to health care.

To be effective, nurses must be aware of their own cultural beliefs and values and recognize their biases and beliefs about other cultures. The nurse must avoid generalizations and assumptions about families from a particular culture because there is diversity within every culture.

## ● Legal Considerations

The *scope of practice* is defined as the limits of nursing practice as set forth in state statutes. These statutes broadly describe the practice of professional nursing, which includes such activities as observing, recording, and administering medications and therapeutic agents. Many nurse practice acts identify functions and actions that are appropriate for nurses functioning in expanded roles such as nurse-midwife and OB/GYN or neonatal nurse practitioner. Such actions may include diagnosis and prenatal management of uncomplicated pregnancies (nurse-midwives may also manage deliveries), and prescribing and dispensing medications under protocols in specified circumstances. A nurse must function within the scope of practice or run the risk of being accused of practicing medicine without a license.

### STANDARD OF CARE

A minimum standard of care is required of all professional nurses. The standard against which practice is compared is the care that a reasonably prudent nurse would provide under the same or similar circumstances.

There are a number of examples of written standards of practice. The American Nurses' Association (ANA) has published standards of professional practice written by the ANA Congress for Nursing Practice. In addition, Divisions of Practice of the ANA have published standards including the standards of practice for maternal-child health. Specialty organizations, such as the Organization for Obstetric, Gynecologic and Neonatal Nurses, formerly called the Nurses' Association of the American College of Obstetricians and Gynecologists (NAACOG), and the Association of Operating Room Nurses (AORN), have developed standards for specialty practice. Agencies have policy and procedure books. Other guidelines for care include standardized procedures, that is, policies and protocols—developed through collaboration among administrators, physicians, and nurses within health care facilities—that cover overlapping functions of nurses and physicians. Nurses on units may develop standard care plans. Books and articles are another source of standards, as are common practice and those functions that have common acceptance. The identified standards range from those having the force of law to those that are suggestions or guidelines for care. Some standards may be goals to strive for; others may define minimums, violations of which may provide grounds for accusations of nursing negligence. Nurse managers have a responsibility to keep the policy and procedure books on their units up to date so that the written standards are consistent with current practice in their agency. And practicing nurses must follow the established policies and procedures. When a nurse acts outside the guidelines, he or she invites litigation and faces the difficult task of convincing a jury he or she was practicing competently.

## INFORMED CONSENT

**Informed consent** is a legal concept that has great significance for nurses. Basically, the policy protects a client's right to autonomy and self-determination by specifying that no action may be taken without that person's prior understanding and freely given consent. While this policy is usually enforced for such major procedures as surgery or regional anesthesia, it pertains to *any* nursing, medical, or surgical intervention. To touch a person without consent (except in an emergency) constitutes battery. In a normal, uncomplicated labor, when the woman has time to give consent, consent must be obtained. Consent is not informed unless the woman understands the usual procedures, their rationales, and any associated risks. To be a truly active participant in decision making about her care, she should also understand possible alternatives.

Just as the physician must, under the doctrine of informed consent, explain associated risks and benefits of any diagnostic or treatment activities performed (Cushing 1984), the nurse is responsible for education about any nursing care provided. Prior to each nursing intervention, the nurse lets the woman know what to expect, thus ensuring her cooperation and obtaining her consent. Afterward, the nurse documents the teaching and the learning outcomes in the woman's record.

The importance of clear, concise, and complete nursing records cannot be overemphasized. These records are evidence that the nurse obtained consent, performed prescribed treatments, reported important observations to the appropriate staff, and adhered to acceptable standards of care.

## ● Professional Issues

The maternity nurse faces the same job-related issues confronting other nurses, including the following:

### DIAGNOSTIC RELATED GROUPS PROSPECTIVE REIMBURSEMENT PLAN

The federal Diagnostic Related Groups (DRGs) were originally devised to contain Medicare costs and are now used by some insurance companies. The DRG reimbursement plan requires that hospitals change their per diem fee system in an attempt to control costs for hospital care. Under the DRG plan, illnesses, injuries, and surgical procedures are divided into diagnostic classifications. The cost of the care given to an individual with a specific diagnosis is established prior to hospitalization; this cost represents the average cost of care given to others with the same diagnosis. The DRG plan has important implications for nurses because it forces hospitals and nurses to quantify nursing services by time and cost. Proposed amendments to the DRG plan include a system tying nursing services to patient outcomes (Curtin 1983).

## NURSES AND PHYSICIANS

Nurse-midwives and nurse practitioners are becoming major providers of health services to childbearing families. These nursing professionals are establishing and operating family planning clinics, general health clinics, and birth centers. Such facilities are often independent of physician control, although women are referred to physicians when necessary.

The response of physicians to this trend has been mixed. Some physicians support independent nursing practice, while others have attempted to block moves by nurses for autonomy. The reason physicians usually give for their negative reaction is that these alternatives pose a threat to the safety of the childbearing woman. Other reasons for the negative reaction of physicians may exist, however. Some suggest that physicians may feel their professional status and financial well-being are being threatened by the potential loss of clients who choose the services of other health care professionals (Lubic 1981).

## ● Malpractice and the Cost of Insurance

One of the most significant influences on current maternity care involves the ever-increasing specter of litigation and the rising cost of malpractice insurance, especially in specialties such as obstetrics. In February 1986 in Massachusetts, hundreds of physicians refused to treat clients to protest a 68% rate increase that would result in malpractice insurance premiums of nearly $30,000 a year for some physicians, with the increase to be retroactive over the past two years (Boring 1986). In Georgia more than 1500 physicians gathered at the state capitol to urge the legislature to change the rules concerning malpractice suits. They were met by a contingent of attorneys and a group of people, many in wheelchairs, who said they were victims of malpractice (The malpractice mess 1986). The increases in rates have also affected many communities as more and more physicians drop the obstetrics portion of their practices or refuse to take new clients. In many areas family practitioners have given up obstetrics completely. Thus communities find themselves with no physician willing to perform deliveries. In some cases women must drive 100 miles or more to receive qualified obstetric care. The implications for the high-risk woman are profound and frightening.

What factors have contributed to this problem? Lander (1978) stated that three conditions are necessary for a malpractice action to occur: (1) an angry client, (2) an error by the physician or the hospital, and (3) injury to the client as the result of the medical intervention. Today's physicians suggest that a fourth factor must also be considered: the desire for money on the part of an attorney or a client. Physicians suggest that careful doctors must bear the financial burden for the mistakes of careless or negligent colleagues. However, physicians do relatively little to police their ranks and remove the incompetent or impaired. Attorneys suggest that physicians should pay for their mistakes because these mistakes have such a lasting impact. The phrase "doctors bury their mistakes" has become their battle cry. Although lawsuits can force physicians to pay for serious errors, one can also argue that many frivolous lawsuits are filed that waste the courts' time and cost the physician and insurance company time and money in preparation.

It is easy to focus on the physicians and attorneys and lose sight of the insurance companies. These companies claim their rate increases are financially necessary because of the large financial awards made to victims by the courts. However, outspoken critics of the insurance industry suggest the increases are necessary because of poor financial management. Thomas G. Goddard, a former official with the Association of Trial Lawyers, suggests that the cause is even more devious: Insurance companies claim financial necessity while spiriting profits away in tax write-offs and reserve funds (The malpractice mess 1986).

The problem has become so visible that many state legislatures are considering legislation to attempt to control it. It seems obvious that something must be done to keep the many people who need skilled medical care from being penalized because of the malpractice crisis that has developed.

Nurse-midwives also face a serious malpractice insurance crisis, not because of poor performance, but because of the general problem facing many health care providers. From 1975 to 1985 more than 60% of obstetricians and gynecologists had a suit filed against them. Although fewer than 6% of the members of the American College of Nurse-Midwives have ever had a claim filed against them, and less than 1% have lost suits, in May 1985 the ACNM was notified that their group policy would not be renewed (New insurers' consortium 1986). The American Nurses' Association attempted to help by offering coverage to nurse-midwives through its own policy. Unfortunately the ANA's insurer also revised its coverage to exclude CNMs. The very existence of nurse-midwifery as a profession in this country was threatened. Fortunately in the fall of 1986 Congress passed the Risk Retention Act. This enabled special groups to band together to self-insure. Although the cost will be far higher than previously (approximately $2500 to $3600 per year), it does permit CNMs to practice. In the future the cost of insurance will be influenced by the amount of money paid out as claims. Because of this, CNMs as a group must "give a high priority to the development of and adherence to standards for midwifery practice" (Sinquefield 1986, p 67). Sinquefield suggests that nurse-midwives are especially vulnerable in this insurance crisis because:

1. Nurse midwives are few in number and have rather limited assets.

2. Because most midwives attend deliveries, they are affected by the long-term disabilities that are often tied to childbirth. (Suits may be brought years after birth.)

3. As a profession CNMs are committed to cost-effective care. Thus CNMs find it difficult to justify passing on to clients as professional expenses the increases that occur.

Despite this vulnerability, some good for nurse-midwifery has come from the crisis. Nurse-midwives recognize the impact that each has on other CNMs. They have recognized anew the importance of maintaining positive, open relations with clients; of involving clients in decision making; of obtaining informed consent; and of carefully documenting their actions. In addition the ACNM has learned that the group can be a force; the members can mobilize, present a positive image to the public and to legislators, and make a difference politically (Sinquefield 1986).

## ● ISSUES IN MATERNAL-NEWBORN CARE

### ● Biomedical Technology

Tremendous strides have been made in maternal and newborn health care. These advances include the development of clinical and research specialties that focus on various aspects of fetal development, childbearing, and newborn care. **Perinatology** is the medical specialty concerned with the diagnosis and treatment of high-risk conditions of the pregnant woman and her fetus. **Neonatology** is the specialty that focuses on the management of high-risk conditions of the newborn.

New diagnostic and treatment methods have been developed that enhance a woman's chances for having a healthy baby. Some of these developments are listed here:

1. *Ultrasound.* Ultrasound examination is used to assess fetal status. High-frequency sound waves are directed into the maternal abdomen to identify fetal and maternal structures.

2. *Amniocentesis.* In an amniocentesis, amniotic fluid is removed from the amniotic sac for analysis. Amniotic fluid analysis provides information about the fetus's genetic makeup, well-being, sex, and maturity.

3. *Chorionic Villus Sampling.* Chorionic villus sampling is used early in the pregnancy to obtain a sample of tissue (chorionic villi) from the edge of the placenta. Testing may then be completed for genetic studies.

4. *Electronic fetal monitoring.* Electronic monitoring equipment can be attached to the pregnant woman or the fetus to measure the fetal heart rate (FHR). In conjunction with other procedures, electronic fetal monitoring can be used to determine fetal well-being and the fetus's ability to withstand the stress of labor before labor begins.

5. *Intrauterine surgery.* Intrauterine surgery is the surgical attempt to correct fetal problems while the fetus is still in the uterus.

6. *Infertility procedures.* Artificial insemination, in vitro fertilization, and embryo transplants are techniques used to treat infertility. *Artificial insemination* is the introduction of sperm into the vagina by artificial means. The sperm may be from the woman's partner or a donor. In *in vitro fertilization,* a mature ovum is collected from a woman whose ovaries are functioning but whose fallopian tubes are blocked. The ovum is fertilized in a petri dish by sperm collected from her partner. The embryo is then implanted in the woman's uterus. The *embryo transplant* procedure is used when the woman's ovaries are not functioning. An ovum from another woman is fertilized by sperm collected from the partner. The embryo is then transplanted into the infertile woman's uterus.

The benefits of these technologic advances are clear. Because of these advances, a healthy baby was delivered in a San Francisco hospital from a brain-dead mother whose body was kept functioning for over two months until the fetus was viable. Because of these advances, previously childless couples are having children. Yet concern is growing that the reliance on technology in maternal-newborn care is excessive and that in some cases the risks of certain procedures outweigh their advantages.

The controversy about electronic fetal monitoring is representative of the issue of technologic excess in obstetrics. Initially, electronic fetal monitoring was used to monitor high-risk labors. In the past few years, however, its use in low-risk pregnancies has increased. Electronic monitoring has gained widespread acceptance in some birth facilities because it can detect fetal distress in cases prenatally categorized as low risk.

But electronic fetal monitoring can have adverse effects on the laboring woman and fetus. For example, the increasing incidence of cesarean births has been attributed to the routine use of fetal monitoring. Cesarean delivery is performed when fetal distress, indicated by abnormal FHR patterns, is diagnosed. The data from the monitoring equipment, however, may be misleading, and the fetus may not be in distress at all. The woman is then subjected to an unnecessary surgical procedure.

Do intrapartal fetal monitoring and similar procedures in cases of low-risk labor and delivery constitute excessive medical intervention? Some argue that every pregnancy and delivery pose potential medical problems and that maternity clients should be managed intensively to prevent complications. To that end, the use of any medical intervention is justified. Others argue that pregnancy and childbirth are natural, normal processes and should not be monitored in the same rigorous way as diseases or high-risk conditions. Medical intervention is perceived as unnecessary and costly interference in low-risk cases.

Opinion is growing that clients receiving certain services should be more carefully screened. Because of the high cost and, as in the case of ultrasound, unknown risks, consumers and insurance companies are questioning the necessity of certain procedures.

### IMPLICATIONS

The idea that medical and nursing actions should depend on the pregnant woman's level of risk is gaining support from consumers and health professionals. To evaluate a woman's level of risk properly, nurses are being encouraged to develop their assessment skills. Each woman's physical and psychologic status should be monitored throughout pregnancy, labor, and delivery to detect changes indicating increased risk. The unnecessary use of assessment and diagnostic procedures, however, should be avoided. For example, the use of ultrasound for a pregnant woman at low risk is usually unnecessary, but its use is increasing. Although the woman may find "seeing" her baby exciting, ultrasound should be used only when necessary since its long-term effects are still unknown.

Advances in technology have affected the educational requirements for nurses. The knowledge needed by nurses who provide general health maintenance services to maternity clients is growing. Nurses must take continuing education courses and read more professional literature to keep up with the expanding and changing knowledge base.

The professional opportunities for nurses in maternal-newborn care have also grown as a result of biomedical advances. Nurses are specializing in perinatal and neonatal nursing. Other nurses are joining research projects or conducting research to expand perinatal knowledge.

## ● *Changes in Health Care Relationships*

For many years, the term *patient* was applied to the person receiving health care services. The relationship between the patient and health professional was one of dependence; the patient depended on the professional to make decisions about matters of health and sickness. The patient placed trust and faith in the professional's expertise, and the professional "took care" of the passive patient.

Over the past two decades, attitudes of those using health care services have changed radically. The patients of traditional medicine have become "consumers." The consumer and health professional are in a buyer-seller relationship. Satisfaction with services rendered determines the continuation of this relationship.

Health care professionals have recognized that the traditional patient–health professional relationship is no longer acceptable or desirable. The two parties should be in a collaborative relationship, not a dependent or even a buyer-seller relationship.

Many health professionals refer to those seeking and receiving services as **clients.** The term *client* implies an active role, not a passive one. In the client–health professional relationship, the client assumes responsibility for decisions about his or her health. The client seeks advice and assistance from individuals who have special skills and knowledge. It is understood that the client can choose not to accept the professional's advice and that the health professional cannot proceed with a plan of action without the client's consent.

## IMPLICATIONS

The nursing profession has been at the forefront in recognizing that people should take an active role in their own health care. Nurses involved in a maternity client–health care professional relationship must understand that it is their professional expertise that is being sought. They should not make decisions for their clients.

An important role for nurses is that of **client advocate** (Kohnke 1982). The maternity nurse advocate informs clients by clearly identifying all available options and the benefits and risks of each one, by explaining the nursing actions simply but completely, and by answering all questions with facts and not personal opinions. The maternity nurse advocate then supports the client's decision by adhering to it and ensuring that others do the same.

The nursing profession is meeting consumer and client demands in maternal-newborn care in important ways. Nurses are usually the instructors of prenatal and postpartal education classes. Nurse practitioners and nurse-midwives are the primary caregivers in many clinics and birth centers that emphasize family-centered health. Maternity clients and their families are finding that nursing's orientation toward education, self-care, and health maintenance meshes with their desire to participate in and make decisions about their birth experience.

## ● Ethical Issues

Although ethical dilemmas confront nurses in all areas, those involving pregnancy, birth, and the newborn seem especially difficult to resolve. These dilemmas result from conflicting social, cultural, and religious values and beliefs held by individuals.

Most of the ethical questions in maternity care are aimed at delineating and protecting the rights of the pregnant woman or couple, the fetus, and the newborn. Ethical issues related to childbearing include the following:

## ABORTION

Induced abortion is the purposeful termination of a pregnancy. In 1973, a decision by the United States Supreme Court made obtaining and performing abortions legal. Despite its legality, abortion continues to spur ethical and moral debate. Opponents of abortion, the "pro-life" group, support one moral principle: The unborn fetus is a human being with an undeniable right to life. For supporters of abortion, the "pro-choice" group, the primary consideration is the right of a woman to control her own body and reproductive activity.

## PASSIVE EUTHANASIA

Passive euthanasia occurs when someone is allowed to die because of inaction or lack of treatment. Some believe that a person's life should be preserved by any and all means, regardless of the wishes of that person or the quality of that person's life. Others believe that the quality of life is more important than simply preserving life and that one has the right to refuse extraordinary medical measures if he or she believes a meaningful life is not possible after treatment.

Maternity nurses are confronted with the issue of passive euthanasia when the decision is made to allow a severely handicapped newborn to die by withholding life-sustaining treatment, including nutritional support (Curtin 1984). Such a decision is usually made by the parents of the infant, in consultation with medical and religious authorities, who must determine whether their child's life will be improved or merely prolonged by extraordinary medical intervention. The President's Commission for the Study of Ethical Problems in Medicine and Biomedical and Behavioral Research (1983) has provided guidelines for making such decisions. In some cases, however, it is not always clear whether a medical intervention will be futile or beneficial, and the decision to provide or forego treatment can have legal consequences (Hubbard 1984).

## INTRAUTERINE SURGERY

Intrauterine surgery has many ethical ramifications. Does the fetus have the absolute right to treatment? Is the fetus a client? What are the rights of the fetus versus the rights of the pregnant woman and her partner? Can a woman be required to undergo surgery to ensure a better quality of life for her fetus? If the fetus dies or is injured during surgery, what are the legal implications for those performing the surgery?

## IN VITRO FERTILIZATION, EMBRYO TRANSPLANTS, AND SURROGATE CHILDBEARING

In vitro fertilization and embryo transplants were described previously. Surrogate childbearing occurs when a woman agrees to become pregnant for a childless couple. She is artificially inseminated with the male partner's sperm. If fertilization occurs, the woman carries the fetus to term and then releases the infant to the couple after delivery. These three methods of resolving infertility raise many ethical questions, including the problem of religious objections to artificial conception, the question of who will assume financial and moral responsibility for a child born with a congenital defect, the issue of candidate selection, and the threat of genetic engineering. With surrogate childbearing and embryo transplants, the rights of the surrogate mother and the woman donating the embryo must be considered.

## IMPLICATIONS

The complex ethical issues facing maternity nurses have many social, legal, and professional ramifications. Nurses must learn to anticipate ethical dilemmas and to develop some basic beliefs about the issues. To do so, they may read about bioethical issues or attend courses and workshops on ethical topics pertinent to their areas of practice. Further, nurses need to develop skills in logical thinking and critical analysis.

Nurses must thoughtfully assess their values and identify any clinical situations in which they feel they could not function. It may be difficult to help a client make decisions based on the client's needs when the nurse's values are in conflict with the client's. Nurses must remember that they are to act in the client's best interests, and not their own. This means "helping them [clients] clarify values and beliefs, to develop their understanding of self and of the situation, and to make decisions based on their own goals and wishes" (Benoliel 1983).

A nurse may be caring for a client who is faced with a problem with many ethical ramifications. The client may ask for assistance in resolving the dilemma. In the case of a severely deformed newborn, for example, the parents who are considering passive euthanasia may request information from the nurse about their child's chances for recovery and the quality of life their child can expect after treatment. The nurse can clarify her or his own ethical position as well as help the parents make their decision by using these guidelines (Kozier and Erb 1989):

1. *Establish a complete data base.* Find out all the information about the situation, including data about those involved; their physical, psychologic, financial, and support resources; the proposed action and the reason behind it; and the possible results of the proposed action.

2. *Identify the ethical conflicts created by the problem.* Determine what the ethical problems are for the clients, the health care agency, and the various health professionals involved.

3. *Outline various courses of action.* Present alternative solutions to the problem.

4. *Determine possible outcomes of the suggested actions.* What are the consequences of the various courses of action as well as the proposed action?

5. *Determine who "owns" the problem and who should make the decision.* The following factors must be considered: who will be affected by the decision, who is the decision being made for, whose moral principles or legal responsibilities are being affected, and what degree of consent is needed from those involved.

6. *Define the obligations of the nurse.* In situations requiring ethical decision making, nurses must determine their obligations both to the client and to themselves.

## ● TOOLS FOR MATERNAL-NEWBORN NURSING PRACTICE

Professional maternity nurses use a variety of "tools" in everyday practice that enable them to deliver high-quality nursing care. These tools are:

● Knowledge

● Nursing process

● Nursing diagnosis

● Communication

● Statistics

● Nursing research

This section is not designed to give a complete explanation of nursing tools but to highlight them and explore ways in which the maternity nurse may use them in practice.

## ● Knowledge Base

Current knowledge and theories from a variety of disciplines form the basis for nursing actions. The nursing knowledge base is subject to change as new discoveries are made, statistical analysis reveals new trends, and new technology is developed. The nursing knowledge base is continually expanding, presenting a challenge to nurses to keep current.

# ● Nursing Process

The **nursing process,** built on a comprehensive knowledge base, represents a logical approach to problem identification and resolution, and serves as the framework for nursing. Whether it consists of four or five steps (some authors combine the analysis/nursing diagnosis and planning phases), the nursing process is an analog of the problem-solving process used by nurses since Florence Nightingale.

## ASSESSMENT

The maternal-newborn nurse gathers both subjective and objective data about the health status of the childbearing woman. Subjective information may be obtained from the woman and family members and includes their perception of health status and of any health impairment or problem and its management. Objective data are measurable and include physical assessment findings and laboratory test results.

## ANALYSIS AND NURSING DIAGNOSIS

The second step in the process is the analysis, assimilation, and clustering of assessment data into relevant categories from which nursing diagnoses are derived. Each nursing diagnosis describes a specific health problem, either actual or potential; its etiology; and the associated signs and symptoms. The formulation of a nursing diagnosis is the crucial step in the process, for the resulting plan of care is based on the problems as the nurse perceives them. In contrast to the medical diagnosis, which generally remains the same throughout the woman's health problem, the nursing diagnosis will reflect the changing response of the woman as her condition improves or worsens, and as she and her family adjust to those changes.

The term **nursing diagnosis** represents both a process and an outcome. The process is the analysis, assimilation, and clustering of data just described. It is a problem-solving technique. The outcome is a classification system of diagnostic labels (Carpenito 1987). The nursing diagnosis is a two-part statement that includes the health problem and related etiology (Gordon 1987). The North American Nursing Diagnosis Association (NANDA) has developed a list of acceptable nursing diagnoses.

Consider the following nursing diagnosis: Knowledge deficit related to inadequate knowledge of normal anatomic, physiologic, and psychologic changes in pregnancy. The health problem, knowledge deficit, is presented with

specific knowledge deficit areas. Knowledge deficit is a client health problem that nurses clearly deal with, and it does not belong to the medical diagnosis realm.

Once established, nursing diagnoses serve to direct the nursing plan of care. Expected outcomes (goals) and priorities of care are identified. Nursing interventions necessary to achieve the specified goals are also identified. Nursing interventions are directed at altering or eliminating the etiological and/or contributing factors of the health problem, and the related signs and symptoms serve as a baseline for evaluation of the effectiveness of care.

Nursing diagnoses are incorporated in this text in various ways. In chapters that incorporate the nursing process, nursing diagnosis appears clearly as a part of the nursing process. A subheading identifies the nursing diagnosis section and examples of nursing diagnoses are provided. In addition, tables with Essential Nursing Diagnoses to Consider are incorporated into many of the chapters. The chapters devoted to high-risk situations present examples of nursing diagnoses that may apply to the specific problems being discussed. In addition, nursing diagnoses are emphasized in the nursing care plans, which focus on selected conditions or situations. These nursing diagnoses are used as the basis for organizing and directing nursing care.

## PLANNING

Once the analysis is completed and nursing diagnoses are formulated, the nurse establishes outcome goals. The nurse identifies interventions that will help the client meet the established goals and develops outcome criteria that will signify that the goals have been met. Lastly the nurse prioritizes the care needed. The beginning nurse usually works through this process step by step, while the more experienced nurse is frequently able to develop an intricate plan of care covering all the steps simultaneously.

## IMPLEMENTATION

In the fourth step of the nursing process, the identified plan of care and specific nursing interventions are implemented by the maternal-newborn nurse. The nurse uses many skills that are common to other areas of nursing, as well as many skills specific to the maternal-newborn setting. Common interventions include auscultation of FHR, Leopold maneuvers to determine fetal position in the uterus, measurement of the uterus to determine growth, sterile vaginal examinations to determine the woman's labor progress, and use of electronic monitors that provide continuous data regarding the fetal heart rate and uterine contractions.

## EVALUATION

The woman's progress or lack of progress toward the identified expected outcomes (goals) is evaluated by the woman and the nurse. These questions are asked: Have expected outcomes been met? Is reassessment needed? Are new problems present? Are changes in any part of the process necessary? Do new priorities need to be identified? Is revision of the plan of care required?

Evaluation is a logical end step, but it is also a continuous process throughout the whole nursing process. The nurse continually evaluates the assessments that have been made, the priorities of care, and the effectiveness of the nursing interventions as nursing care is delivered.

## ● *Communication*

The **problem-oriented medical record (POMR) system** allows for the systematic documentation and retrieval of information about the client's care and progress. Although originally intended for use with medical diagnoses, POMR can be adapted for documentation of nursing care using nursing diagnoses. POMR is a system of charting observations and interventions using the SOAPE format. The acronym SOAPE stands for the five components of each charting entry: subjective data, objective data, analysis (sometimes called assessment), plan, and evaluation. The subjective and objective data come from the nursing assessment (the first step in the nursing process) and are recorded under the appropriate problem number (each nursing diagnosis is listed numerically on a problem sheet kept on the chart). The analysis entry represents the nurse's conclusions about the client's progress based on the data collected. The plan of care is continued or changed in accordance with the data analysis. Finally, an evaluation of nursing care is added.

The importance of the POMR system for nursing is

---

## Application of the Nursing Process

The following brief example illustrates the application of the nursing process.

Sarah, a 16-year-old adolescent, comes to the school nurse's office and asks why she seems to be having trouble with her pregnancy. She states she doesn't have any energy and can't keep her weight down. She is in her sixth month of pregnancy and has gained 3 pounds. She exercises every day for one hour, smokes one pack of cigarettes a day, and has trouble sleeping because of the pressure of homework and a part-time job each evening.

The nurse applies the nursing process as follows:

*Assessment:* Subjective data—Sarah states "I have trouble with my pregnancy; I have no energy, have trouble keeping my weight down, and lots of trouble sleeping." Objective data—3-pound weight gain in six months of pregnancy (below recommended rate). Sarah appears underweight for her height, pale with dark circles under her eyes.

*Analysis/nursing diagnosis:* The objective and subjective data support problems with adequate nutrition and the statements regarding her weight suggest the need for information regarding nutritional needs during pregnancy. Sarah also needs to understand the need to obtain adequate rest and to clarify her perception of the role of exercise in pregnancy. The nurse ascertains that Sarah is going to the prenatal clinic on a fairly regular basis. The nurse decides the highest priority nursing diagnosis is knowledge deficit related to adequate nutritional needs during pregnancy. The nurse could have selected a nursing diagnosis directed toward the sleep disturbance or the potential for alterations in nutrition related to inadequate intake for pregnancy needs. But overall she decided that giving Sarah complete information about her pregnancy would address a number of problems.

*Planning:* The goals of care include: Client will be able to verbalize the nutritional requirements in pregnancy, will not lose any further weight, and will begin gaining at least 3 pounds per month.

*Implementation:* The nurse and Sarah plan sessions for the next few weeks during which there will be time for discussion and information to be shared. She gives Sarah some booklets designed for pregnant adolescents regarding nutritional and general care needs. The nurse obtains a current weight, and together they create a graph to record her weight each week. Sarah's interest in cartooning makes this a fun and creative project. The nurse asks her to keep a food intake record for three days and to drop it off at the end of the week.

*Evaluation:* As the relationship builds and they work together, the success of the interventions will be measured by Sarah's ability to verbalize nutritional needs and the objective data provided by her weight each week. The food intake record provides specific data to work with to encourage a diet to meet pregnancy needs.

The preceding example indicates the application of the nursing process. The nursing process can be used to provide logical, systematic care in any situation encountered in maternity nursing practice.

that the SOAPE format, when used correctly, provides readily accessible data and ongoing evaluation of the effects of nursing care. The response to treatment can be evaluated regularly and as frequently as the client's condition dictates, and the plan for nursing care can be altered as necessary.

The POMR system and SOAPE format for documenting information can be applied in the example just mentioned as follows:

After assessment of Sarah's situation, the nurse would analyze the data and determine a problem list that would include:

Inadequate weight gain

Insufficient information regarding nutritional needs of pregnancy

Inadequate rest

Presence of risk factors—age, inadequate weight gain, smokes one pack of cigarettes a day

A SOAPE entry regarding the problem of inadequate weight gain would appear as follows:

**S:** Sarah states she is just not hungry and if she cuts down on exercise she feels like she has no energy.

**O:** Three-day food intake reveals diet is below RDA in calories, calcium, iron, and folic acid. One pound weight gain this week.

**A:** Although Sarah does not feel hungry, she has been trying to improve the quality and quantity of foods each day. She is willing to continue the food intake record and is incorporating suggestions and ideas from counselor and nutrition booklets. One pound weight gain is a positive sign even though diet is still inadequate in RDA requirements. Sarah has not been willing to cut down on exercise to date.

**P:** Supplement information she is gaining on nutrition and support her efforts to improve her diet. Work with her in interpreting and evaluating her food intake records. Continue to offer support and praise for gaining weight. Continue one-on-one conferences to share information and provide support.

Provide additional booklets on nutrition for Sarah. Use booklets specific for adolescents.

Have Sarah weigh herself and help her develop a weight graph to record and follow weights over the next few weeks.

Encourage Sarah to modify her exercise program. Encourage Sarah to cut her exercise by five minutes each session, and substitute some low-impact movements for some of the high-impact movements.

**E:** Sarah continues to gain weight and decreases her exercise.

The nurse has used the SOAPE format to record assessment of subjective and objective data and analysis of the present situation, and to formulate a plan that identifies interventions to address the problem of inadequate weight gain. At each visit the nurse may record new information using the same format. Other identified problems may be SOAPE charted at the same time.

## ● *Maternal-Newborn Teaching*

The role of teacher is becoming increasingly important for nurses in the maternal-newborn area. In the prenatal period, expectant parents look to the nurse to assist them in gathering information to help them make informed consumer choices. The expectant mother seeks advice in learning self-care measures during the pregnancy. The new parents look to the nurse to assist them in learning to care for their new baby. The focus on teaching is indeed great.

The teaching process may be enhanced by approaching it in a systematic manner. The nursing process provides an excellent systematic approach that can easily be incorporated into a teaching plan. It provides a framework that begins with assessment of the knowledge base of the client and the information that the client would like to have. The analysis and nursing diagnosis phase then provides an opportunity to analyze the assessment findings and identify an appropriate nursing diagnostic statement. In the next phase, the nurse plans the content that will be included in the teaching session, and the most appropriate method to present the content. A small group presentation may be the best way to present baby bath classes; however, one-on-one teaching may be the best method to teach about contraceptives in the postpartum period. In the next phase, implementation, the nurse actually presents the content. During the last phase, evaluation, the nurse evaluates the learning that has been achieved and provides other information as needed.

In order to assist the nursing student in this important aspect of client teaching, a number of features have been incorporated into this text. Teaching guides based on the nursing process have been incorporated into Chapters 3, 4, 8, 10, 13, 16, 22, and 26. The teaching guides will focus on important areas of the teaching that the maternal-newborn nurse does in the clinical area. In addition, teaching directed toward self-care measures is incorporated throughout the text. Teaching for self-care and to provide client education has been identified with the symbol of an apple in the margin to highlight the content. The nursing care plans will also incorporate the need for teaching. This variety of approaches will hopefully assist student nurses in increasing their teaching knowledge base.

## ● *Statistics*

Nurses often overlook or underestimate the usefulness of statistics. Health-related statistics, however, provide an objective basis for projecting client needs, planning for use of resources, and determining the effectiveness of treatment.

There are two major types of statistics: descriptive and inferential. **Descriptive statistics** describe or summarize a set of data. They report the facts—what is—in a concise and easily retrievable way. Although no conclusion may be drawn from these statistics about *why* some phenomenon has occurred, certain trends and high-risk "target groups" can be identified and possible research questions generated. **Inferential statistics** allow the investigator to draw conclusions or inferences about what is happening between two or more variables in a population and to suggest or refute causal relationships between them.

Descriptive statistics are the starting point for the formation of research questions. Inferential statistics answer specific questions and generate theories to explain relationships between variables. These theories can be applied in nursing practice to help change the specific variables that may be causing or contributing to certain health problems.

In this section, descriptive statistics that are particularly important to maternal-newborn health care are discussed. Inferential considerations are addressed as possible research questions that may assist in identifying relevant variables.

### BIRTH RATE

**Birth rate** refers to the number of live births per 1000 people. Table 1.1 compares live births and birth rates by race from 1970 to 1988 in the United States. After reaching a peak of 25.0 for all races in 1955, the birth rate declined, reaching a low in 1975 and 1976 of 14.6 live births per 1000 people. The birth rate began increasing in 1977, except for slight drops in 1978, 1983, and 1984.

## Table 1.1   Live Births and Birth Rates by Race of Child: United States, 1970–1988

| | Number | Birth rate* | | | |
| | | White | All other | | All races |
| Year | All races | | Total | Black | |
|---|---|---|---|---|---|
| 1988 provisional | 16.0 | | | | |
| 1987 provisional | 15.6 | | | | |
| 1986 | 15.6 | | | | |
| 1985 | 15.8 | | | | |
| 1984 | 15.5 | 14.5 | 21.2 | 20.8 | 65.4 |
| 1983 | 15.5 | 14.6 | 21.3 | 20.9 | 65.8 |
| 1982 | 15.9 | 14.9 | 21.9 | 21.4 | 67.3 |
| 1981 | 15.8 | 14.8 | 22.0 | 21.6 | 67.4 |
| 1980† | 15.9 | 14.9 | 22.5 | 22.1 | 68.4 |
| 1975† | 14.6 | 13.6 | 21.0 | 20.7 | 66.0 |
| 1970‡ | 18.4 | 17.4 | 25.1 | 25.3 | 87.9 |

*Birth rates per 1000 population in specified group. Fertility rates per 1000 women aged 15 to 44 years in specified group. Population enumerated as of April 1 for census years and estimated as of July 1 for all other years. Beginning 1970 excludes births to nonresidents of the United States.
†Based on 100% of births in selected states and on a 50% sample of births in all other states.
‡Based on a 50% sample of births.

Source: Modified from National Center for Health Statistics: Advance report of final natality statistics, 1984. *Monthly Vital Statistics Report.* Vol. 35. No. 4, Supp. DHHS Pub. No. (PHS) 86–1120. Public Health Service, Hyattsville, MD July 18, 1986 and National Center for Health Statistics: Births, marriages, divorces, and deaths for December 1988. *Monthly Vital Statistics Report,* Vol. 37, No. 12. DHHS Pub. No. (PHS) 89–1120. Public Health Service, Hyattsville, MD.

## Table 1.2 Live Births and Birth Rates, Canada, 1980–1985

| Year | Live births* | Birth rate† |
|------|------|------|
| 1985 | 375,727 | 14.8 |
| 1984 | 377,031 | 15.0 |
| 1980 | 370,709 | 15.5 |

*Live births = per 1000 population
†Live birth rate = 1000 population

Source: Modified from *Vital Statistics*. Vol. I. Births and deaths. 1985. Canada Health Division Vital Statistics and Disease Registry. Cat. 84–204. Minister of Supply and Services. November 1986. Table 1, p 2.

Live births and birth rate for Canada are presented in Table 1.2. The birth rate there is slightly lower than in the United States.

Research questions that can be posed about the birth rates include the following:

- Is there an association between birth rates and changing societal values?
- Is the difference in birth rate between various age groups reflective of education? Or does it represent availability of contraceptive information?
- What factors might contribute to the differences in fertility rates between Canada and the United States?

### AGE OF MOTHER

In 1985, women 20–24 years of age had the highest birth rate for a first child (109.3 births per 1000 women of that age) in the United States (National Center for Health Statistics 1988). Women 25–29 years of age had the next highest rate for first births (106.7 births per 1000 women of that age). Teenagers in the 15–19 age group had a birth rate of 55 per 1000 females of that age for first births.

Of all age groups, the smallest increase in birth rate, less than 1%, occurred in teenage girls 15–17 years of age. Women 30–34 years old had a birth rate of 62.1 in 1985. The largest increase in births occurred in this age group—a 62% increase in 1985 from 1975.

The variables that affect the birth rate of different age groups may be identified by investigating the following research questions:

- Is there an association with changing societal values? With changing roles of women? With changing national economic conditions and financial status?
- Is there a correlation with years of education? With availability of contraceptive information for different age groups?

### INFANT MORTALITY

The *infant death rate* is the number of deaths of infants under one year of age per 1000 live births in a given population. **Neonatal mortality** is the number of deaths of infants less than 28 days of age per 1000 live births. **Perinatal mortality** includes both neonatal deaths and fetal deaths per 1000 live births. (**Fetal death** is death in utero after 20 weeks or more of gestation.)

Table 1.3 presents infant mortality rates in the United States for selected years, and Table 1.4 presents infant mortality rates in Canada for 1980 and 1985. Comparison of these statistics shows that Canada has a lower infant mortality rate. The United States ranked twentieth among nations in infant deaths in 1988 (fifteenth in 1980). Since 1940 neonatal and postneonatal deaths declined steadily in the United States, until 1987 and 1988, when the rate leveled and even began to increase.

Among the principal causes of infant death are congenital anomalies, sudden infant death syndrome (SIDS),

## Table 1.3 Infant Mortality Rates by Age: United States, 1950, 1960, 1965, and 1970–1988*

| Year | Under 1 year | Under 28 days | 28 days– 11 months |
|------|------|------|------|
| 1988 provisional | 10.1 | | |
| 1987 provisional | 10.1 | 6.8 | 3.7 |
| 1986 | 10.4 | 6.9 | 3.7 |
| 1985 | 10.5 | 7.0 | 3.5 |
| 1980 | 12.6 | 8.4 | 4.1 |
| 1975 | 16.1 | 11.6 | 4.5 |
| 1970 | 20.0 | 15.1 | 4.9 |
| 1965 | 24.7 | 17.7 | 7.0 |
| 1960 | 26.0 | 18.7 | 7.3 |
| 1950 | 29.2 | 20.5 | 8.7 |

*For 1980 and 1985 based on a 10% sample of deaths; for all other years based on final data. Rates per 1000 live births.

Source: National Center for Health Statistics: Annual summary of births, marriages, divorces, and deaths, United States, 1985. *Monthly Vital Statistics Report*. Vol. 34, No. 13. DHHS Pub. No. (PHS) 86–1120. Public Health Service, Hyattsville, MD September 19, 1986; National Center for Health Statistics: Advance report of final mortality statistics, 1984. *Monthly Vital Statistics Report*. Vol. 35, No. 6 Supp. (2). DHHS Pub. No. (PHS) 86–1120. Public Health Service, Hyattsville, MD September 26, 1986; National Center for Health Statistics: Births, marriages, divorces, and deaths for December 1988. *Monthly Vital Statistics Report*. Vol. 37, No. 12. DHHS Pub. No. (PHS) 89–1120. Public Health Service, Hyattsville, MD.

## Table 1.4 Infant Mortality (Total Infant Death Rate per 1000 Live Births): Canada, 1980, 1985

| Year | Under 1 year (infant) | Under 28 days (neonatal) | 28 days– 11 months (postneonatal) |
|------|------------------------|---------------------------|-------------------------------------|
| 1985 | 8.0 | 5.2 | 2.7 |
| 1980 | 10.4 | 6.7 | 3.8 |

Source: Modified from *Vital Statistics*. Vol. I. Births and deaths. 1985. Canada Health Division Vital Statistics and Disease Registry. Cat. 84–204. Minister of Supply and Services. November 1986. Table 22, p 54.

respiratory distress syndrome, and disorders related to preterm infants and those with low birth weights.

Some research questions raised by the infant mortality statistics include the following:

● Does infant mortality correlate with a specific maternal age?

● Is it associated with the time during pregnancy that the woman seeks prenatal care? With the number of prenatal visits? With the woman's diet?

● Is there a difference among racial groups? If so, is it associated with educational level? Availability of prenatal care? Socioeconomic level?

## MATERNAL MORTALITY

**Maternal mortality** is the number of deaths from any cause during the pregnancy cycle (including the 42-day postpartal period) per 100,000 live births. The maternal death rate in the United States has decreased steadily in the last 30 years (Table 1.5).

Factors influencing the decrease in maternal mortality include the increased use of hospitals and specialized health care personnel by antepartal, intrapartal, and postpartal maternity clients; the establishment of care centers for high-risk mothers and infants; the prevention and control of infection with antibiotics; the availability of blood and blood products for transfusions; and the lowered rates of anesthesia-related deaths. Additional factors may be identified by asking the following research questions:

● Is there a correlation between maternal mortality and age?

● Is there a correlation with availability of health care? Economic status?

## IMPLICATIONS

Nurses can use statistics to:

● Determine populations at risk.

● Assess the relationship between specific factors.

● Help establish a data base for different client populations.

● Determine the levels of care needed by particular client populations.

● Evaluate the success of specific nursing interventions.

● Determine priorities in case loads.

● Estimate staffing and equipment needs of hospital units and clinics.

● Determine whether a problem exists.

Statistical information is available through many sources, including professional literature; state and city health departments; vital statistics sections of private, county, state, and federal agencies; and special programs of family planning and similar agencies. Nurses who use this information will be better prepared to promote the health needs of maternity clients and their families.

## ● Nursing Research

Research is a vital step toward establishing a science of nursing as well as establishing nursing as a true profession with its own unique knowledge base. Research is also

## Table 1.5 Maternal Mortality Rate per 100,000 Live Births: United States, 1950–1987

| Year | Rate |
|------|------|
| 1987 | 7.1 (provisional) |
| 1986 | 7.2 |
| 1985 | 7.3 |
| 1980 | 9.2 |
| 1975 | 12.8 |
| 1970 | 21.5 |
| 1965 | 31.6 |
| 1960 | 37.1 |
| 1950 | 83.3 |

Source: National Center for Health Statistics: Advance report of final mortality statistics, 1986. *Monthly Vital Statistics Report.* Vol. 37, No. 6, Supp. (2). DHHS Pub. No. (PHS) 88–1120. Public Health Service, Hyattsville, MD September 30, 1988.

a means to improve client care by translating research findings into clinical practice.

Research by nurses can help clarify the relationships between the health professional and the client. Nursing research also can help determine the psychosocial and physical risks and benefits of nursing and medical interventions.

The gap between research and practice is being narrowed by the publication of research findings in popular nursing journals, the establishment of departments of nursing research in hospitals, and collaborative research efforts by nurse researchers and clinical practitioners. In addition, numerous journal articles giving "how-to" information for translating research into practice have been published in the last few years.

## ● Application of Tools for Nursing Practice

Each of the tools—knowledge, nursing process, communication, teaching, statistics, and nursing research—can exist separately, but in practice they overlap and complement each other. The maternity nurse can put each of these tools to use in a variety of ways. An example of just one possible situation is presented in the following case study.

## *One Nurse's Story*

*Two birthing center nurses express concerns to each other about the number of adolescents who have been giving birth in their unit. At the next staff meeting, they voice their concerns and raise questions about whether the number of teenage mothers seen in their unit is larger than normal. After discussion, the nurses decide they need to formulate a plan to gather more information. Each nurse volunteers to pursue a particular aspect of the plan of action.*

*Their plan includes the following activities:*

● *Contacting the local public health department for local and national statistics on this age group*

● *Investigating the availability of health care for adolescents in their community*

● *Checking the availability of prenatal education groups for adolescents*

● *Finding out whether their community has school health programs and what the program content is*

● *Determining the availability of family planning information*

● *Looking at national statistics that identify when adolescents seek prenatal care*

● *Talking with community nurse-midwives, physicians, and prenatal clinic personnel to see if the national statistics apply to their community*

● *Collecting information about legislative issues affecting adolescent health care*

● *Seeking further information about the needs of adolescents during pregnancy and childbirth by doing library research*

● *Looking for continuing education programs dealing with the pregnant adolescent client*

*At subsequent staff meetings, each nurse shares information, and other areas are investigated as the need is identified. How they evaluate the data and apply them will depend on the requirements of their maternity unit and the needs of their community.*

*Possible outcomes may include developing a research study, doing volunteer work in local adolescent clinics, developing and teaching prenatal classes for adolescents, volunteering to teach in community school health programs, organizing a continuing education program on the adolescent mother for community hospitals, and forming a network within their professional nursing organizations to stay informed about legislative issues pertaining to adolescents.*

*As the case study demonstrates, the application of tools for nursing practice helps define a problem, guides the collection of data, and provides a framework for intervention.*

● ● ● ● ● ● ● ● ● ● ● ● ● ● ● ● ● ● ● ● ● ● ● ● ● ● ● ● ● ● ● ●

## ESSENTIAL CONCEPTS

● **Contemporary childbirth is family centered, offers choices about delivery, and recognizes the needs of siblings and grandparents.**

● **Nurses in maternity care may function in a variety of roles and settings.**

● **The standard of care is that of a reasonably prudent nurse.**

● **Informed consent—based on knowledge of a procedure and its benefits, risks, and alternatives—must be secured prior to providing treatment.**

● **Today's contemporary nurse uses a variety of tools in everyday practice.**

● **A comprehensive nursing knowledge base forms the basis for nursing activities.**

● **The nursing process, composed of assessment, analysis and nursing diagnosis, planning, implementation, and evaluation, provides a systematic method of approaching nursing practice.**

● **Communication of nursing problems and care provided is an important aspect of nursing practice. Two methods to communicate client care data are POMR and SOAPE.**

● Nursing standards provide information and guidelines for nurses in their own practice, in developing policies and protocols in health care settings, in directing the development of quality care, and in promoting the accountability of nursing practice.

● Descriptive statistics describe or summarize a set of data. Inferential statistics allow the investigator to draw conclusions about what is happening between two or more variables in a population and to establish or refute causal relationships between them.

● Nursing research is vital to add to the nursing knowledge base, expand clinical practice, and expand nursing theory.

● ● ● ● ● ● ● ● ● ● ● ● ● ● ● ● ● ● ● ● ● ● ● ● ● ● ● ● ● ● ●

## References

American College of Nurse-Midwives: *Statement of Philosophy.* Washington, DC: 1972.

American College of Nurse-Midwives: *What Is a Nurse-Midwife?* Washington, DC: 1979.

Benoliel JQ: Ethics in nursing practice and education. *Nurs Outlook* July/August 1983; 31:210.

Boring NL: Health care ads—who pays? *US News & World Report* February 17, 1986; 73.

Carpenito LJ: *Nursing Diagnosis: Application to Clinical Practice,* 2nd ed. New York: Lippincott, 1987.

Curtin L: Determining costs of nursing services per DRG. *Nurs Management* April 1983; 14:16.

Curtin L: Should we feed Baby Doe? *Nurs Management* August 1984; 15:22.

Cushing M: Informed consent: An MD's responsibility? *Am J Nurs* 1984; 84:437.

Friedman MM: *Family Nursing Theory and Assessment.* New York: Appleton-Century-Crofts, 1981.

Gordon M: *Nursing Diagnosis: Process and Application.* New York: McGraw-Hill, 1987.

Hubbard R: Caring for Baby Doe. *Ms* May 1984; 84.

Kohnke MF: *Advocacy: Risk and Reality.* St. Louis: Mosby, 1982.

Kozier B, Erb G: *Fundamentals of Nursing,* 3rd ed. Menlo Park, CA: Addison-Wesley, 1989.

Lander L: *Defective Medicine: Risks, Anger and the Malpractice Crisis.* New York: Farrar, Straus, and Giroux, 1978.

Lubic RW: Alternative maternity care: Resistance and change. In: *Childbirth: Alternatives to Medical Control.* Romalis S (editor). Austin: University of Texas Press, 1981.

The malpractice mess. *Newsweek* February 17, 1986; 74.

National Center for Health Statistics: *Monthly Vital Statistics Report.* Vol. 37, No. 12, Supp. DHHS Pub. No. (PHS) 89–1120. Public Health Service, Hyattsville, MD, November 1988.

New insurers' consortium will cover nurse-midwives' practice. *Am J Nurs* September 1986; 1051.

President's Commission for the Study of Ethical Problems in Medicine and Biomedical and Behavioral Research: *Deciding to Forego Life-Sustaining Treatment.* Washington, DC: Government Printing Office, 1983.

Sinquefield G: The medical malpractice insurance crisis: Implications for future practice. *J Nurse-Midwife* March/April 1986; 31:65.

## Additional Readings

Aumann GE-E: New chances, new choices: Problems with perinatal technology. *J Perinat Neonatal Nurs* 1988; 1(3):1.

Chakrauarty SN, Weisman K: Consuming our children? *Forbes* November 1988; 222.

del Bueno D: The promise and the reality of certification. *Image* Winter 1988; 20(4):208.

Friede A, Baldwin W, Rhodes PH et al: Older maternal age and infant mortality in the United States. *Obstet Gynecol* 1988; 72(2):152.

Gerlach C, Schmid M: Second skill educational development of personnel for a single-room maternity care system. *J Obstet Gynecol Neonatal Nurs* November/December 1988; 17(6):388.

Green GJ: Relationships between role models and role perceptions of new graduate nurses. *Nurs Res* July/August 1988; 37(4):245.

Hogstel MO: Teaching student observational skills. *Nurs Out* March/April 1987; 35(2):89.

Huey FL: How nurses would change US health care. *Am J Nurs* November 1988; 88(11):1482.

Krysl M, Watson J: Existential moments of caring: Facets of nursing and social support. *ANS* 1988; 10(2):12.

Labun E: Spiritual care: An element in nursing care planning. *J Adv Nurs* 1988; 13:314.

Lynaugh JE, Fagin CM: Nursing comes of age. *Image* Winter 1988; 20(4):184.

Makuc DM, Freid VM, Kleinman J: National trends in the use of preventive health care of women. *Am J Pub Health* January 1989; 79(1):21.

Melnyk KA: Barriers: A critical review of recent literature. *Nurs Res* July/August 1988; 37(4):196.

Palmer ME, Deck ES: Teaching your patients to assert their rights. *Am J Nurs* May 1987; 87(5):650.

Popkin BM, Akin JS, Flieger W et al: Breastfeeding trends in the Philippines. *Am J Pub Health* January 1989; 79(1):32.

Sonstegard L: A better way to market maternal-child care. *MCN* November/December 1988; 13(6):395.

Weis D: Who are the working poor? *Am J Nurs* 1987; 87(11):1451.

Werley HH, Devine EC, Zorn CR: Nursing needs its own minimum data set. *Am J Nurs* December 1988; 88(12):1651.

# 2

# Reproductive Anatomy and Physiology

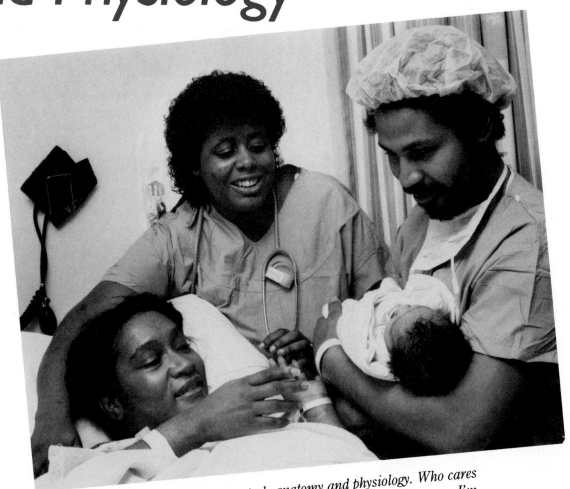

*I always thought it was so boring to study anatomy and physiology. Who cares how many bones there are in the pelvis, or the muscles involved. But now I'm with mothers having babies and now it all makes sense. (A nursing student)*

## Objectives

● Summarize the major changes in the reproductive system that occur during puberty.

● Identify the structures and functions of the female and male reproductive systems.

● Summarize the action of the hormones that affect reproductive functioning.

● Describe the menstrual cycle, correlating the phases of the cycle with their dominant hormones and the changes that occur in each phase.

● Explain the physiologic aspects of the female reproductive cycle.

● Describe the significance of specific female reproductive structures during childbirth.

Understanding childbearing requires more than understanding sexual intercourse or the process by which the male and female sex cells unite. One must also become familiar with the structures and functions that make childbearing possible. In this chapter, the anatomic, physiologic, and sexual aspects of the male and female reproductive systems will be considered.

The male and female reproductive organs are *homologous;* that is, they are fundamentally similar in structure and function. The primary functions of both the male and female reproductive systems are to produce sex cells and to transport the sex cells to locations where their union can occur. The sex cells, called *gametes,* are produced by specialized organs called *gonads.* A series of ducts and glands within both the male and female reproductive systems contribute to the production and transport of the gametes.

## Key Terms

ampulla
androgens
areola
breasts
broad ligament
cardinal ligaments
cervix
conjugate vera
cornua
corpus
corpus luteum
diagonal conjugate
endometrium
estrogens
external os
fallopian tubes
false pelvis
female reproductive cycle
    (FRC)
fimbria
follicle-stimulating
    hormone (FSH)
fundus
gonadotropin-releasing
    factor (GnRF)

graafian follicle
human chorionic
    gonadotropin (hCG)
infundibulopelvic ligament
innominate bones
internal os
ischial spines
isthmus
luteinizing hormone (LH)
myometrium
nidation
nipple
obstetric conjugate
oogenesis
ovarian ligaments
ovary
ovulation
ovum
pelvic cavity
pelvic diaphragm
pelvic floor
pelvic inlet
pelvic outlet
perimetrium
perineal body

perineum
polar body
progesterone
prostaglandins
pubis
round ligaments
rugae
sacral promontory
spermatogenesis
spermatozoa
symphysis pubis
testis
testosterone
transverse diameter
true pelvis
uterosacral ligaments
uterus
vagina
vulva
zona pellucida

# EARLY DEVELOPMENT OF REPRODUCTIVE STRUCTURES AND PROCESSES

Although the genetic sex of the embryo is determined at fertilization, sexual differentiation does not occur until the eighth week of pregnancy. The male gonad, the **testis,** develops between the seventh and eighth weeks. The female gonad, the **ovary**, is recognizable about the tenth week of fetal development.

The testis produces the male gametes, called **spermatozoa** or *sperm,* by a process called **spermatogenesis**, which is described in Chapter 5. Spermatogenesis of mature sperm does not occur until the onset of puberty.

Every egg available for maturation in a woman's reproductive life is present at her birth. During fetal life, the ovary produces *oogonia,* cells that become primitive ovarian eggs, called *oocytes,* by the process of **oogenesis**. No oocytes are formed after fetal development. About 143,000 oocytes are contained in the ovary at birth (Wallach 1988). Each oocyte is contained in a small ovarian cavity called a *primordial* or *primitive follicle.*

Every month during a female's reproductive years, one of the oocytes undergoes a process of cellular division and maturation that transforms it into a fertilizable egg, or **ovum**. During the reproductive years, at **ovulation**, the ovum is released. The remaining follicles and oocytes degenerate over time.

# PUBERTY

The term *puberty* refers to the developmental period between childhood and attainment of adult sexual characteristics and functioning. Its onset is never sudden, although it may appear so to parents or to the young person who is not prepared for the physical and emotional changes of puberty. Generally, boys mature physically about two years later than girls. In boys, the age of onset of puberty ranges from 10 to 19 years; 14 years is the average age of onset. In girls, the age of onset ranges from 9 to 17 years; 12 years is the average age of onset.

Puberty occurs over a period lasting 1½–5 years and involves profound physical, psychologic, and emotional changes. These changes result from the interaction of the central nervous system and the endocrine organs.

## Major Physical Changes

In both boys and girls, puberty is preceded by an accelerated growth rate called *adolescent spurt*. Widespread body system changes occur, including maturation of the reproductive organs.

The pattern of physical changes varies among individuals. Girls experience a broadening of the hips, then budding of the breasts, the appearance of pubic and axillary hair, and the onset of menstruation, called *menarche.*

The average time between breast development and menarche is 2.0 years (Speroff et al 1989). The physical changes of puberty manifest themselves differently in every person. The age at onset and progress of puberty vary widely, physical changes overlap, and the sequence of events can also vary from person to person. This diversity results from people's different degrees of response to hormonal stimulation.

Boys usually first note such changes as an increase in the size of the external genitals; the appearance of pubic, axillary, and facial hair; the deepening of the voice; and nocturnal seminal emissions without sexual stimulation (mature sperm are not usually contained in these earliest emissions).

## Physiology of Onset

Puberty is initiated by the maturation of the hypothalamic-pituitary-gonad complex (the *gonadostat*) and input from the central nervous system. The process, which begins during fetal life, is sequential and complex.

The central nervous system releases a neurotransmitter that stimulates the hypothalamus to synthesize and release **gonadotropin-releasing factor (GnRF)** (Wallach 1988). GnRF is transmitted to the anterior pituitary, where it causes the synthesis and secretion of the gonadotropins, **follicle-stimulating hormone (FSH)** and **luteinizing hormone (LH)** (Figure 2.1).

Although the gonads do produce small amounts of **androgens** (male sex hormones) and **estrogens** (female sex hormones) before the onset of puberty, FSH and LH stimulate increased secretion of these hormones. Androgens and estrogens influence the development of secondary sex characteristics. FSH and LH stimulate the processes of spermatogenesis and maturation of ova.

After puberty, a higher level of androgens and estrogens must be present to inhibit the production of GnRF and the initiation of the negative (inhibitory) feedback loop; therefore, the positive (stimulatory) feedback loop predominates (Wallach 1988, Ferin 1987). One theory is that the brain becomes less sensitive to the inhibitory effects of gonadal steroids on the gonadotropin secretion (Guyton 1986).

Other hormones are involved in the onset of puberty. Although less direct, their action is essential. Abnormally high or low levels of adrenocorticotropic hormone (ACTH), thyroid hormone, or somatotropic (growth) hormone (STH) can disrupt the onset of normal puberty.

# FEMALE REPRODUCTIVE SYSTEM

The female reproductive system consists of the external and internal genitals and the accessory organs of the

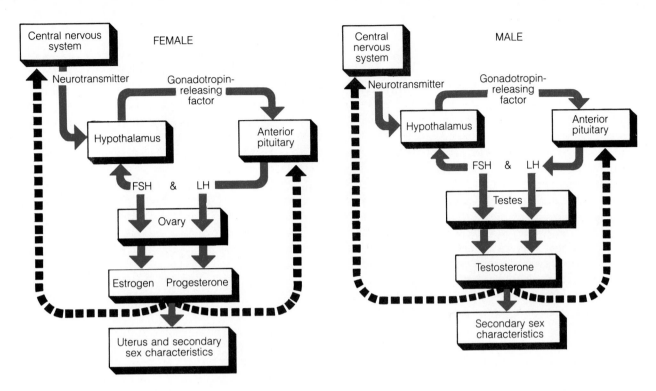

*Figure 2.1  Stimulation of hormone production is illustrated with solid lines, and inhibition is illustrated with a broken line. Through a neurotransmitter, the CNS stimulates the hypothalamus, which in turn produces a gonadotropin-releasing factor that causes the anterior pituitary to produce gonadotropins (FSH or LH). These hormones stimulate specific structures in the gonads to secrete steroid hormones (estrogen, progesterone, or testosterone). The rise in pituitary hormone production increases hypothalamus activity. Elevated steroid hormone levels stimulate the CNS and pituitary gland to inhibit hormone production.*

breasts. Also discussed in this chapter are the bony pelvis and its structure because of its importance to childbearing.

## • External Genitals

All the external reproductive organs, except the glandular structures, can be directly inspected. The size, color, and shape of these structures vary extensively among races and individuals.

The female external genitals, referred to as the **vulva** or *pudendum,* include the following structures (Figure 2.2):

- Mons pubis
- Labia majora
- Labia minora
- Clitoris
- Urethral meatus and paraurethral (Skene's) glands
- Vaginal vestibule (vaginal orifice, vulvovaginal glands, hymen, and fossa navicularis)
- Perineal body

Although not true parts of the female reproductive system, the urethral meatus and perineal body are considered here because of their proximity and relationship to the vulva.

The vulva has a generous supply of blood and nerves. As a woman ages, hormonal activity decreases, causing the vulvar organs to atrophy and become subject to a variety of lesions.

### MONS PUBIS

The *mons pubis* is a softly rounded mound of subcutaneous fatty tissue beginning at the lowest portion of the anterior abdominal wall. Also known as the *mons veneris,* this structure covers the front portion of the symphysis pubis. The mons pubis is covered with pubic hair, typically with the hairline forming a transverse line across the lower abdomen. The hair is short and varies from sparse and fine in the Asian woman to heavy, coarse, and curly in the black woman (Figure 2.2). The mons pubis protects the pelvic bones, especially during coitus.

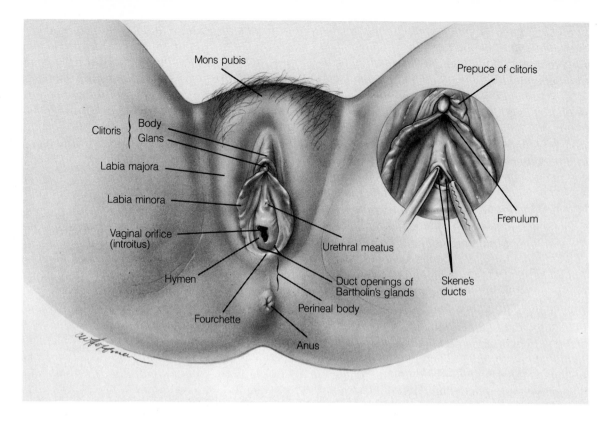

*Figure 2.2  Female external genitals, longitudinal view*

## LABIA MAJORA

The *labia majora* are longitudinal, raised folds of pigmented skin, one on either side of the vulvar cleft. As the pair descend, they narrow, enclosing the vulvar cleft, and merge to form the posterior junction of the perineal skin.

With each pregnancy, the labia majora become less prominent. The labia majora are covered by stratified squamous epithelium containing hair follicles and sebaceous glands with underlying adipose and muscle tissue. Under the skin the dartos muscle sheet is responsible for the wrinkled appearance of the labia majora as well as for their sensitivity to heat and cold.

The inner surface of the labia majora in women who have not had children is moist and looks like a mucous membrane, whereas after many deliveries it is more skin-like (Pritchard et al 1985).

Because of the extensive venous network in the labia majora, varicosities may occur during pregnancy, and obstetric or sexual trauma may cause hematomas.

The labia majora share an extensive and diffuse lymphatic supply with the other structures of the vulva. Understanding this supply is important in understanding malignancies of the female reproductive organs.

Because of the nerves supplying the labia majora (from the first lumbar and third sacral segment of the spinal cord), certain regional anesthesia blocks will affect them.

The chief function of the labia majora is protection of the structures lying between them.

## LABIA MINORA

The *labia minora* are soft folds of skin within the labia majora that converge near the anus, forming the *fourchette*. Each labium minus has the appearance of shiny mucous membrane, moist and devoid of hair follicles. The labia minora are rich in sebaceous glands. Because the sebaceous glands do not open into hair follicles but directly onto the surface of the skin, sebaceous cysts commonly occur in this area. Vulvovaginitis in this area is very irritating because the labia minora have many tactile nerve endings. Labia minora increase in size at puberty and decrease after menopause due to changes in estrogen levels.

The functions of the labia minora are to lubricate and waterproof the vulvar skin and to provide bactericidal secretions.

## CLITORIS

The *clitoris* is the most erotically sensitive part of the female genital tract and is a common site of masturbation. The clitoris, located between the labia minora, is about 5–6 mm long and 6–8 mm across. Its tissue is essentially erectile.

The clitoris consists of the *glans*, the *corpus* or *body*, and two *crura* (Figure 2.2) (Delancey 1987). The glans is partially covered by a fold of skin called the *prepuce*. This area often appears as an opening to an orifice, and, on visualization, may be confused with the urethral meatus. Attempts to insert a catheter here produce extreme discomfort.

The clitoris has very rich blood and nerve supplies. Overall, the clitoris has a richer nerve supply than the penis.

The clitoris exists primarily for female sexual enjoyment. In addition, it secretes *smegma*, whose odor may be sexually stimulating to the male.

## URETHRAL MEATUS AND PARAURETHRAL GLANDS

The *urethral meatus* is located 1–2.5 centimeters beneath the clitoris in the midline of the vestibule; it often appears as a puckered and slitlike opening. Urine passes out of the body from this orifice. The paraurethral glands, or *Skene's ducts,* open into the posterior wall of the urethra close to its orifice. Their secretions lubricate the vaginal vestibule, facilitating sexual intercourse.

## VAGINAL VESTIBULE

The vaginal vestibule is a boat-shaped depression enclosed by the labia majora and visible when they are separated. The vestibule contains the vaginal opening, or *introitus,* which is the border between the external and internal genitals.

The *hymen* is a thin, elastic membrane that partially closes the vaginal opening. Its strength, shape, and size vary greatly among women. The hymen is essentially avascular. The belief that the intact hymen is a sign of virginity and that it is broken at first sexual intercourse with resultant bleeding is not valid. The hymen may occasionally be broken through strenuous physical activity, masturbation, menstruation, or the use of tampons. Occasionally a woman about to give birth may still have an intact hymen.

External to the hymenal ring at the base of the vestibule are two small papular elevations containing the orifices of the ducts of the *vulvovaginal (Bartholin's) glands.* They lie under the constrictor muscle of the vagina. These glands secrete a mucus that is clear and viscid, with an alkaline pH, all of which enhance the viability and motility of the sperm deposited in the vaginal vestibule.

These gland ducts can harbor gonococci and other bacteria, which can cause pus formation and Bartholin's gland abscesses (Pritchard et al 1985).

The vaginal vestibule generally is not sensitive to touch. The hymen, however, contains many free nerve endings.

## PERINEAL BODY

The **perineal body** is a wedge-shaped mass of fibromuscular tissue found between the lower part of the vagina and anal canal. This area is also referred to as the **perineum.**

The muscles that meet at the perineal body are the external sphincter ani, both levator ani, the superficial and deep transverse perineal, and the bulbocavernosus. These muscles mingle with elastic fibers and connective tissue in an arrangement that allows a remarkable amount of stretching.

The perineal body is much larger in the female than in the male and is subject to laceration during childbirth. It is the site of episiotomy during delivery (see Chapter 19).

## ● Internal Genitals

The female internal reproductive organs—the vagina, uterus, fallopian tubes, and ovaries—are target organs for estrogenic hormones. These organs play a unique part in the reproductive cycle (Figure 2.3). The internal reproductive organs can be palpated during vaginal examination and assessed through use of a speculum, laparoscope, or culdoscope.

## VAGINA

The **vagina** is a muscular and membranous tube that connects the external genitals with the center of the pelvis (Figure 2.3). It extends from the vulva to the uterus in a position nearly parallel to the plane of the pelvic brim. The vagina is often referred to as the *birth canal* because it forms the lower part of the axis through which the presenting part of the fetus must pass during birth.

Because the cervix of the uterus projects into the upper part of the anterior wall of the vagina, the anterior wall is approximately 2.5 cm shorter than the posterior wall. Measurements range from 6 to 8 cm for the anterior wall and from 7 to 10 cm for the posterior wall.

In the upper part of the vagina, which is called the vaginal *vault,* there is a recess or hollow around the cervix. This area is referred to as the vaginal *fornix.*

The walls of the vaginal vault are very thin. This structure facilitates pelvic examination. Various structures can be palpated through the walls and fornix of the vaginal vault, including the uterus, a distended bladder, the ovaries, the appendix, the cecum, the colon, and the ureters.

When a woman lies on her back, the space in the fornix permits the pooling of semen after intercourse. The collection of a large number of sperm near the cervix in a favorable environment increases the chances of impregnation.

The walls of the vagina are covered with ridges, or

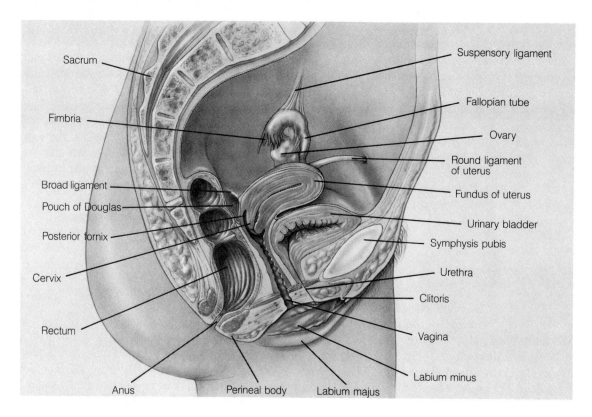

*Figure 2.3   Female internal reproductive organs*

**rugae**, crisscrossing each other. These rugae allow the vagina to stretch during the descent of the fetal head.

During a woman's reproductive life, an acidic vaginal environment is normal (pH 4–5). Secretion from the vaginal epithelium provides a moist environment. The acidic environment is maintained by a symbiotic relationship between lactic acid–producing bacilli (Döderlein bacillus or lactobacillus) and the vaginal epithelial cells. These cells contain glycogen, which is broken down by the bacilli into lactic acid. The amount of glycogen is regulated by the ovarian hormones. Any interruption of this process can destroy the normal self-cleansing action of the vagina. Such interruption may be caused by antibiotic therapy, douching, or use of vaginal sprays or deodorants.

The acidic vaginal environment is normal only during the mature reproductive years and in the first days of life when maternal hormones are operating in the infant. A relatively neutral pH of 7.5 is normal from infancy until puberty and after menopause.

The vagina's blood and lymphatic supplies are extensive (Figure 2.4).

The vagina is a relatively insensitive organ, with little somatic innervation to its lower third by the pudendal nerve and virtually no special nerve endings. Sensation during sexual excitement and coitus is minimal and pain during the second stage of labor is less than if somatic innervation were greater.

The functions of the vagina are as follows:

● To serve as the passage for sperm and for the fetus during delivery

● To provide passage for the menstrual products from the uterine endometrium to the outside of the body

● To protect against trauma from sexual intercourse and infection from pathogenic organisms

## UTERUS

Throughout the ages, the uterus, or womb, has been endowed with a mystical aura. As the core of reproduction and hence continuation of the human race, the uterus and its bearer have received particular attention and treatment. Numerous customs, taboos, mores, and values have evolved about women and their reproductive function. Although scientific knowledge has replaced much of this folklore, remnants of old ideas and superstitions persist. The nurse must be able to recognize and deal with such attitudes and beliefs so that nursing care can be effective.

The **uterus** is a hollow, muscular, thick-walled, pear-shaped organ lying centrally in the pelvic cavity between the base of the bladder and the rectum and above the vagina (Figure 2.5). It is level with or slightly below the brim of the pelvis, with the external opening of the cervix (the *external os*) about the level of the ischial spines. Its anterior and posterior surfaces are in opposition, making its cavity potential rather than actual. The mature organ weighs about 60 g and is approximately 7.5 cm long, 5 cm wide, and 1 to 2.5 cm thick.

The position of the uterus can vary, depending on a woman's posture, number of children borne, bladder and rectal fullness, and even normal respiratory patterns. Only the cervix is anchored laterally. The body of the uterus can move freely forward or backward. The axis also varies. Generally, the uterus bends forward, forming a sharp angle with the vagina. There is a bend in the area of the isthmus of the uterus; from there the cervix points downward. The uterus is said to be *anteverted* when it is in this position. The anteverted position is considered normal.

The uterus is kept in place by three sets of supports. The upper supports are the broad and round ligaments. The middle supports are the cardinal, pubocervical, and uterosacral ligaments. The lower supports are those structures considered to be the pelvic muscular floor.

The isthmus, referred to earlier in this section, is a slight constriction in the uterus that divides it into two unequal parts. The upper two-thirds of the uterus is the **corpus**, or *body*, composed mainly of a smooth muscle layer (myometrium). The lower third is the **cervix**, or *neck*. The rounded uppermost portion of the corpus that extends above the points of attachment of the fallopian tubes is called the **fundus**. The elongated portion of the uterus where the fallopian tubes enter is called the **cornua**.

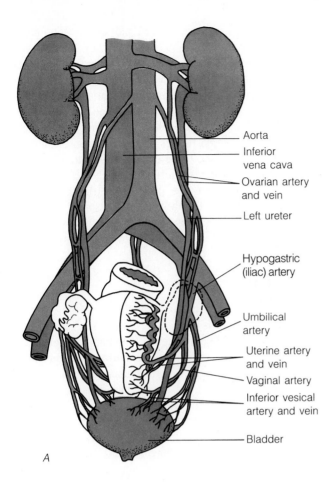

Aorta
Inferior vena cava
Ovarian artery and vein
Left ureter
Hypogastric (iliac) artery
Umbilical artery
Uterine artery and vein
Vaginal artery
Inferior vesical artery and vein
Bladder

*A*

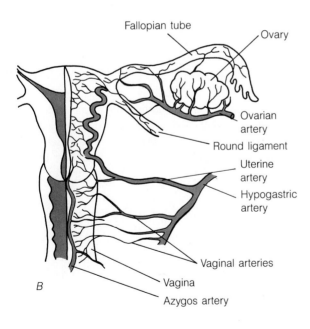

Fallopian tube
Ovary
Ovarian artery
Round ligament
Uterine artery
Hypogastric artery
Vaginal arteries
Vagina
Azygos artery

*B*

*Figure 2.4   Blood supply to internal reproductive organs: (**A**) Pelvic blood supply (**B**) Blood supply to vagina, ovary, uterus, and fallopian tubes*

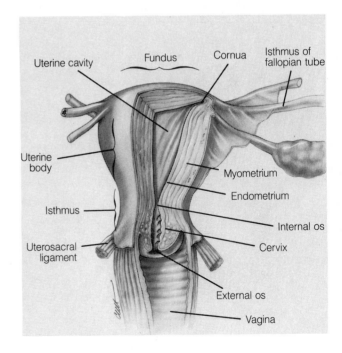

Uterine cavity
Fundus
Cornua
Isthmus of fallopian tube
Uterine body
Myometrium
Endometrium
Isthmus
Internal os
Uterosacral ligament
Cervix
External os
Vagina

*Figure 2.5   Structures of the uterus*

The isthmus is about 6 mm above the uterine opening of the cervix (the *internal os*), and it is in this area that the uterine endometrium changes into the mucous membrane of the cervix. The isthmus takes on importance in pregnancy because it becomes the lower uterine segment. With the cervix, it is a passive segment and not part of the contractile uterus. At delivery, this thin lower segment, situated behind the bladder, is the site for lower-segment cesarean deliveries (see Chapter 19).

The blood and lymphatic supplies to the uterus are extensive (Figure 2.4). Innervation of the uterus is entirely by the autonomic nervous system and seems to be more regulatory than primary in nature (Delancey 1987). Even without an intact nerve supply, the uterus can contract adequately for delivery, as illustrated by the fact that hemiplegic patients have adequate uterine contractions.

The function of the uterus is to provide a safe environment for fetal development. The uterine lining is cyclically prepared by steroid hormones for implantation of the embryo (**nidation**). Once the embryo is implanted, the developing fetus is protected until it is expelled.

Both the body of the uterus and the cervix are changed permanently by pregnancy. The body never returns to its prepregnant size, and the external os changes from a circular opening of about 3 mm to a transverse slit with irregular edges.

### The Corpus

The corpus of the uterus is made up of three layers. The outermost layer is the *serosal layer* or **perimetrium**, which is composed of peritoneum. The middle layer is the *muscular uterine layer* or **myometrium**. This muscular uterine layer is continuous with the muscle layer of the fallopian tubes and with that of the vagina. This helps these organs present a unified reaction to various stimuli—ovulation, orgasm, or the deposit of sperm in the vagina. These muscle fibers also extend into the ovarian, round, and cardinal ligaments and minimally into the uterosacral ligaments, which helps explain the vague but disturbing pelvic "aches and pains" reported by many pregnant women.

The myometrium has three distinct layers of uterine (smooth) involuntary muscles (Figure 2.6). The outer layer, found mainly over the fundus, is made up of longitudinal muscles, which cause cervical effacement and expel the fetus during birth. The middle layer is thick and made up of interlacing muscle fibers in figure eight patterns. These muscle fibers surround large blood vessels, and their contraction produces a hemostatic action. The inner muscle layer is composed of circular fibers that form sphincters at the uterine (fallopian) tube attachment sites and at the internal os. The internal os sphincter inhibits the expulsion of the uterine contents during pregnancy, but stretches in labor as cervical dilatation occurs. An incompetent cervical os can be caused by a torn, weak, or absent sphincter at the internal os. The sphincters at the fallopian tubes prevent menstrual blood from flowing backward into the fallopian tubes from the uterus.

Although each layer of muscle has been discussed as having a unique function, it must be remembered that the uterine musculature works as a whole. The uterine contractions of labor are responsible for the dilatation of the cervix and provide the major impetus for the passage of the fetus through the pelvic axis and vaginal canal at birth. The mucosal layer, or **endometrium,** of the uterine corpus is the innermost layer. This layer is composed of a single layer of columnar epithelium, glands, and stroma.

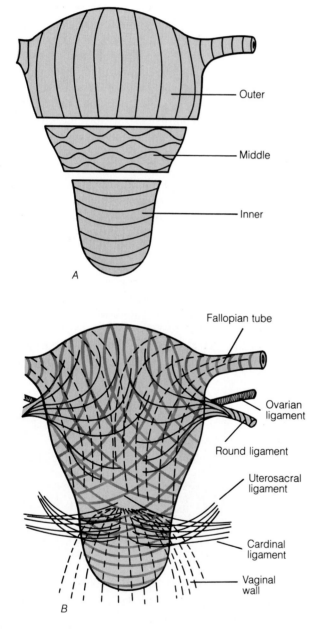

*Figure 2.6   Uterine muscle layers: (A) Muscle fiber placement (B) Interlacing of uterine muscle layers*

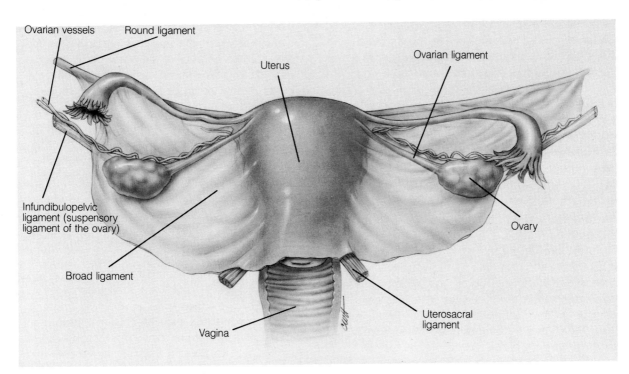

*Figure 2.7   Uterine ligaments (cardinal ligaments not shown)*

From menarche to menopause, the endometrium undergoes monthly degeneration and renewal in the absence of pregnancy. As it responds to a governing hormonal cycle and prostaglandin influence as well, the endometrium varies in thickness from 0.5 to 5 mm.

The glands of the endometrium produce a thin, watery, alkaline secretion that keeps the uterine cavity moist. This *endometrial milk* not only helps the sperm travel to the fallopian tubes but also nourishes the blastocyst before it lodges in the endometrium (Chapter 5).

The blood supply to the endometrium is unique. Some of the blood vessels are not sensitive to cyclic hormonal control, and others are extremely sensitive to cyclic hormonal control. These differing responses allow part of the endometrium to remain intact, while other endometrial tissue is shed during menstruation.

### The Cervix

The cervix is about 2.5 cm in both length and diameter. It is canal-like; its exit into the vagina is called the **external os**, and its entrance into the corpus is called the **internal os** (Figure 2.5).

The cervix is a protective portal for the body of the uterus as well as the connection between the vagina and the uterus. The cervix is divided by its line of attachment into the vaginal and supravaginal areas. The *vaginal cervix* projects into the vagina at an angle of from 45° to 90°. The *supravaginal cervix* is surrounded by the attachments that give the uterus its main support: the uterosacral liga-

ments, the transverse ligaments of the cervix (Mackenrodt's ligaments), and the pubocervical ligaments.

The vaginal cervix appears pink and ends at the external os. The cervical canal appears rosy red and is lined with columnar ciliated epithelium, which contain mucus-secreting glands. Most cervical cancer begins at this squamocolumnar junction. Its exact location varies with age and number of pregnancies.

Elasticity is the chief characteristic of the cervix. Its ability to stretch is due to the high fibrous and collagenous content of the supportive tissues and also to the vast number of folds in the cervical lining.

The cervical mucus has three functions:

● To lubricate the vaginal canal

● To act as a bacteriostatic agent

● To provide an alkaline environment to shelter deposited sperm from the acidic vagina

At ovulation, cervical mucus is clearer, thinner, more profuse, and more alkaline than at other times.

### Uterine Ligaments

The uterine ligaments support and stabilize the various reproductive organs. The ligaments shown in Figures 2.6 and 2.7 are described in this section.

1.  The **broad ligament** keeps the uterus centrally placed and provides stability within the pelvic cavity.

It is a double mesenteric layer that is continuous with the abdominal peritoneum. The broad ligament covers the uterus anteriorly and posteriorly and extends outward from the uterus to enfold the fallopian tubes. The round and ovarian ligaments are at the upper border of the broad ligament. At its lower border, it forms the cardinal ligaments. Between the folds of the broad ligament are connective tissue, involuntary muscle, blood and lymph vessels, and nerves.

2. The **round ligaments** help the broad ligament keep the uterus in place. Each of the round ligaments arises from the sides of the uterus near the fallopian tube insertion. They course outward between the folds of the broad ligament, passing through the inguinal ring and canals and eventually fusing with the connective tissue of the labia majora. Made up of longitudinal muscle, the round ligaments enlarge during pregnancy. During labor the round ligaments steady the uterus, pulling downward and forward so that the presenting part is forced into the cervix.

3. The **ovarian ligaments** anchor the lower pole of the ovary to the cornua of the uterus. They are composed of muscle fibers, which allow the ligaments to contract. This contractile ability influences the position of the ovary to some extent, thus helping the fimbriae of the fallopian tubes to "catch" the ovum as it is released each month.

4. The **cardinal ligaments** are the chief uterine supports, suspending the uterus from the side walls of the true pelvis. These ligaments, also known as *Mackenrodt's* or the *transverse cervical ligaments,* arise from the sides of the pelvic walls and attach to the cervix in the upper vagina. These ligaments prevent uterine prolapse and also support the upper vagina.

5. The **infundibulopelvic ligament** suspends and supports the ovaries (Figure 2.7). Arising from the outer third of the broad ligament, the infundibulopelvic ligament contains the ovarian vessels and nerves.

6. The **uterosacral ligaments** provide support for the uterus and cervix at the level of the ischial spines (Figure 2.7). Arising on each side of the pelvis from the posterior wall of the uterus, the uterosacral ligaments sweep back around the rectum and insert on the sides of the first and second sacral vertebras.

The uterosacral ligaments contain smooth muscle fibers, connective tissue, blood and lymph vessels, and nerves. They also contain sensory nerve fibers that contribute to dysmenorrhea.

## FALLOPIAN TUBES

The **fallopian tubes**, also known as the *oviducts,* arise from each side of the uterus and reach almost to the sides of the pelvis, where they turn toward the ovaries (Figure 2.8). Each tube is approximately 8–13.5 cm

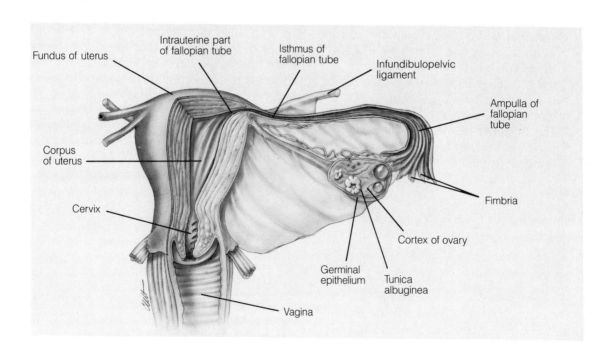

*Figure 2.8   Fallopian tube and ovary*

long. These tubes are not inert, rigid structures; they are dynamic and restless, constantly seeking the ovum to be released from the ovary. The fallopian tubes link the peritoneal cavity with the uterus and vagina. This linkage increases a woman's biologic vulnerability to disease processes.

A short section of each fallopian tube is inside the uterus; its opening into the uterus is only 1 mm in diameter.

Each tube may be divided into three parts: the isthmus, the ampulla, and the infundibulum or fimbria. The **isthmus** is straight and narrow, with a thick muscular wall and an opening (lumen) 2–3 mm in diameter. It is the site of tubal ligation, a surgical procedure to prevent pregnancy.

Next to the isthmus is the curved **ampulla**, which comprises the outer two-thirds of the tube. Fertilization of the secondary oocyte by a spermatozoon usually occurs here. The ampulla ends at the **fimbria**, which is a funnel-like enlargement with many projections, called *fimbriae*, reaching out to the ovary. The longest of these, the *fimbria ovarica*, is attached to the ovary to increase the chances of intercepting the ovum as it is released.

The wall of the fallopian tube is made up of four layers: peritoneal (serous), subserous (adventitial), muscular, and mucous tissues. The peritoneum covers the tubes. The subserous layer contains the blood and nerve supply, and the muscular layer is responsible for the peristaltic movement of the tube. The mucosal layer, immediately next to the muscular layer, is composed of ciliated and nonciliated cells with the number of ciliated cells more abundant at the fimbria. Nonciliated cells secrete a protein-rich, serous fluid that nourishes the ovum. The constantly moving tubal cilia propel the ovum toward the uterus. Because the ovum is a large cell, this ciliary action is needed to assist the tube's muscular layer peristalsis. Different types of prostaglandins cause proximal tubal contraction and distal relaxation (Marshall and Ross 1982).

A rich blood and lymphatic supply serves each fallopian tube (Figure 2.4). Thus, the tubes have an unusual ability to recover from an inflammatory process.

The functions of the fallopian tubes are as follows:

● To provide transport for the ovum from the ovary to the uterus (transport time through the fallopian tubes varies from three to four days)

● To provide a site for fertilization

● To serve as a warm, moist, nourishing environment for the ovum or zygote (Chapter 5)

## OVARIES

The ovaries are two almond-shaped structures just below the pelvic brim. One ovary is located on either side of the pelvic cavity. Their size varies among women and with the stage of the menstrual cycle. Each ovary weighs approximately 6–10 g and is 1.5–3 cm wide, 2–5 cm long, and 1–1.5 cm thick. The ovaries of girls are small but become larger after puberty. They also change in appearance from a dull white, smooth-surfaced organ to a pitted gray organ. The pitting is caused by scarring due to ovulation. Ovaries atrophy after menopause.

The ovaries are held in place by the broad, ovarian, and infundibulopelvic ligaments. These ligaments were discussed in detail earlier in the chapter.

There is no peritoneal covering for the ovaries. Although this lack of covering assists the mature ovum to erupt, it also allows easier spread of malignant cells from cancer of the ovaries. A single layer of cuboidal epithelial cells, called the germinal epithelium, covers the ovaries. The ovaries are composed of three layers: the tunica albuginea, the cortex, and the medulla. The *tunica albuginea* is dense and dull white and serves as a protective layer. The *cortex* is the main functional part because it contains ova, graafian follicles, corpora lutea, degenerated corpora lutea (corpora albicantia), and degenerated follicles. The *medulla* is completely surrounded by the cortex and contains the nerves and the blood and lymphatic vessels.

The ovary is a crucial component of reproduction. Even a small part of a functioning ovary will ovulate, providing an ovum for fertilization monthly.

The ovaries are the primary source of two important hormones: the estrogens and progesterone. *Estrogens* are associated with those characteristics contributing to femaleness including breast alveolar lobule growth and duct development. The ovaries secrete large amounts of estrogen, while the adrenal cortex (extraglandular sites) produces minute amounts of estrogen in nonpregnant women.

**Progesterone** is often called the *hormone of pregnancy* because its effects on the uterus allow pregnancy to be maintained. This hormone also inhibits the action of prolactin in α-lactalbumin synthesis, thereby preventing lactation during pregnancy (Pritchard et al 1985).

The interplay between the ovarian hormones and other hormones such as FSH and LH is responsible for the cyclic changes that allow pregnancy. Later in this chapter, the hormonal and physical changes that occur during the female reproductive cycle are discussed in depth.

When a woman reaches the age of 45–52 years, the ovary no longer secretes estrogen. Ovulatory activity ceases and menopause occurs.

## BONY PELVIS

The female bony *pelvis* has two unique functions:

● To support and protect the pelvic contents

● To form the relatively fixed axis of the birth passage

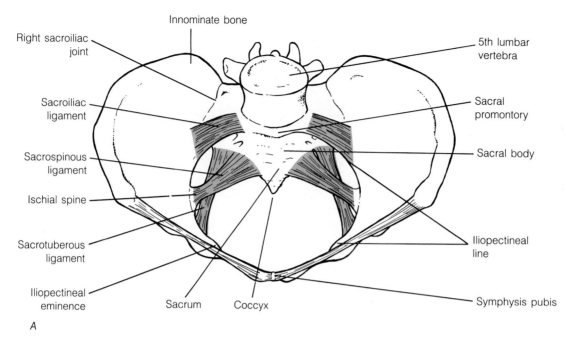

*A*

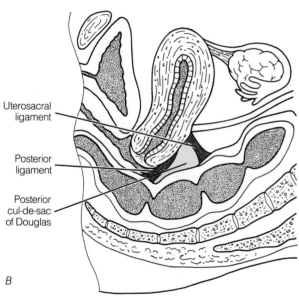

*B*

*Figure 2.9   Pelvic bones: (A) With supporting ligaments (B) Midsagittal view in supine position*

Because the pelvis is so important to childbearing, its structure must be understood clearly.

## Bony Structure

The pelvis is made up of four bones: two innominate bones, the sacrum, and the coccyx. The pelvis resembles a bowl or basin; its sides are the innominate bones, and its back is the sacrum and coccyx. Lined with fibrocartilage and held tightly together by ligaments, the four bones join at the symphysis pubis, the two sacroiliac joints, and the sacrococcygeal joints (Figure 2.9).

The **innominate bones**, also known as the *hip bones* or *os coxae*, are made up of three separate bones: the ilium, ischium, and pubis. These bones fuse to form a circular cavity, the *acetabulum*, which articulates with the femur.

The *ilium* is the broad, upper prominence of the hip. The *iliac crest* is the margin of the ilium. The *iliac spine*, the foremost projection nearest the groin, is the site of attachment for ligaments and muscles.

The *ischium*, the strongest bone, is under the ilium and below the acetabulum. The L-shaped ischium ends in a marked protuberance, the *ischial tuberosity*, on which the weight of a seated body rests. The **ischial spines** arise near the junction of the ilium and ischium and jut into the pelvic cavity. The shortest diameter of the pelvic cavity is between the ischial spines. The ischial spines can serve as a reference point during labor to evaluate the descent of the fetal head into the birth canal (see Chapter 14 and Figure 14.6).

The **pubis** forms the slightly bowed front portion of the innominate bone. Extending medially from the acetabulum to the midpoint of the bony pelvis, the pubis meets the other pubis to form a joint, the **symphysis pubis**. The triangular space below this junction is known as the *pubic arch*. The fetal head passes under this arch during birth. The symphysis pubis is formed by heavy fibrocartilage and the superior and inferior pubic ligaments. The mobility of the inferior ligament, also known as the *arcuate pubic ligament*, increases during pregnancy and to a greater extent in subsequent pregnancies than in first pregnancies.

The sacroiliac joints also have a degree of mobility that increases near the end of pregnancy as the result of an upward gliding movement. The pelvic outlet may be in-

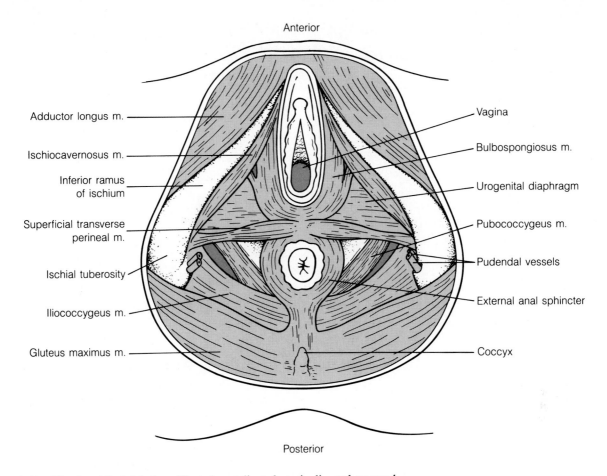

*Figure 2.10  Muscles of the pelvic floor. The puborectalis, pubovaginalis, and coccygeal muscles cannot be seen from this view.*

creased by 1.5 to 2 cm in the squatting, sitting, and dorsal lithotomy positions. These relaxations of the joints are induced by the hormones of pregnancy.

The *sacrum* is a wedge-shaped bone formed by the fusion of five vertebras. On the anterior upper portion of the sacrum is a projection into the pelvic cavity known as the **sacral promontory**. This projection is another obstetric guide in determining pelvic measurements. (For further discussion of pelvic measurements see Chapter 7.)

The small triangular bone last on the vertebral column is the *coccyx*. It articulates with the sacrum at the sacrococcygeal joint. The coccyx usually moves backward during labor to provide more room for the fetus.

### Pelvic Floor

The muscular **pelvic floor** of the bony pelvis is designed to overcome the force of gravity exerted on the pelvic organs. It acts as a buttress to the irregularly shaped pelvic outlet, thereby providing stability and support for surrounding structures.

Deep fascia and the levator ani and coccygeal muscles form the part of the pelvic floor known as the **pelvic dia-** **phragm**. Above it is the pelvic cavity; below and behind it is the perineum.

The levator ani muscle makes up the major portion of the pelvic diaphragm and consists of four muscles: ileococcygeus, pubococcygeus, puborectalis, and pubovaginalis. The coccygeal muscle, a thin muscular sheet underlying the sacrospinous ligament, helps the levator ani support the pelvic organs. Muscles of the pelvic floor are shown in Figure 2.10 and discussed in Table 2.1.

### Pelvic Division

The pelvic cavity is divided into the false pelvis and the true pelvis (Figure 2.11, *A*). The **false pelvis** is the portion above the linea terminalis. Its primary function is to support the weight of the enlarged pregnant uterus and direct the presenting fetal part into the true pelvis below.

The **true pelvis** is the portion that lies below the linea terminalis. The bony circumference of the true pelvis is made up of the sacrum, coccyx, and innominate bones.

This area is of paramount importance in obstetrics because its size and shape must be adequate for normal fetal passage during labor and at delivery. The relationship of

## Table 2.1 Muscles of the Pelvic Floor

| Muscle | Origin | Insertion | Innervation | Action |
|---|---|---|---|---|
| Levator ani | Pubis, lateral pelvic wall, and ischial spine | Blends with organs in pelvic cavity | Inferior rectal, second and third sacral nerves, plus anterior rami of third and fourth sacral nerves | Supports pelvic viscera; helps form pelvic diaphragm |
| Iliococcygeus | Pelvic surface of ischial spine and pelvic fascia | Central point of perineum, coccygeal raphe, and coccyx | | Assists in supporting abdominal and pelvic viscera |
| Pubococcygeus | Pubis and pelvic fascia | Coccyx | | |
| Puborectalis | Pubis | Blends with rectum; meets similar fibers from opposite side | | Forms sling for rectum, just posterior to it; raises anus |
| Pubovaginalis | Pubis | Blends into vagina | | Supports vagina |
| Coccygeus | Ischial spine and sacrospinous ligament | Lateral border of lower sacrum and upper coccyx | Third and fourth sacral nerves | Supports pelvic viscera; helps form pelvic diaphragm; flexes and abducts coccyx |

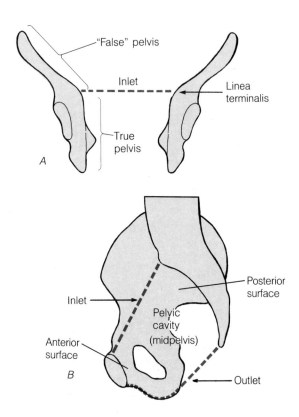

*Figure 2.11 Female pelvis: (**A**) False pelvis is shallow cavity above inlet; true pelvis is deeper portion of the cavity below inlet. (**B**) True pelvis consists of inlet, cavity (midpelvis), and outlet.*

the fetal head to this cavity is of critical importance.

The true pelvis consists of three parts: the inlet, the pelvic cavity, and the outlet (Figure 2.11, **A**). Associated with each part are distinct obstetric measurements that aid in evaluating the adequacy of the pelvis for childbearing. (For in-depth discussion see Chapter 7.)

The **pelvic inlet** is the upper border of the true pelvis. The size and shape of the pelvic inlet are determined by assessing three anteroposterior diameters. The **diagonal conjugate** extends from the subpubic angle to the middle of the sacral promontory. The diagonal conjugate can be measured manually during a pelvic examination. The **obstetric conjugate** extends from the middle of the sacral promontory to an area approximately 1 cm below the pubic crest. Its length is estimated by subtracting 1.5 cm from the diagonal conjugate. The fetus passes through the obstetric conjugate, and the size of this diameter determines whether the fetus can move down into the birth canal in order for engagement to occur. The true (anatomic) conjugate, or **conjugate vera**, extends from the middle of the sacral promontory to the middle of the pubic crest (superior surface of the symphysis). One additional measurement, the **transverse diameter**, helps determine the shape of the inlet. The transverse diameter is the largest diameter of the inlet and is measured using the linea terminalis as the point of reference. The female pelvic inlet is typically rounded.

The **pelvic cavity** is a curved canal with a longer posterior than anterior wall. The curvature of the lumbar spine influences the shape and tilt (inclination) of the pelvic cavity (Figure 2.11, **B**).

The **pelvic outlet** is at the lower border of the true pelvis. The size of the pelvic outlet can be determined by assessing the *transverse diameter,* which is also called the *bi-ischial* or *intertuberous diameter.* This diameter extends from the inner surface of one ischial tuberosity to the other. The pubic arch is also a part of the pelvic cavity. The pubic arch has great importance because the fetus must pass under it during delivery. If it is narrow, the baby's head may be pushed backward toward the coccyx, making extension of the head difficult. The clinical assess-ment of each of these obstetrical diameters is discussed further in Chapter 7.

## Pelvic Types

The Caldwell-Moloy classification of pelves is widely used to differentiate bony pelvic types (Caldwell and Moloy 1933). The four basic types are *gynecoid, android, anthropoid,* and *platypelloid* (Figure 2.12). The type of pelvis is determined by assessing the posterior segment of the pelvic inlet. Each type has a characteristic shape, and each shape has implications for labor and delivery. See Chapter 14 for further discussion.

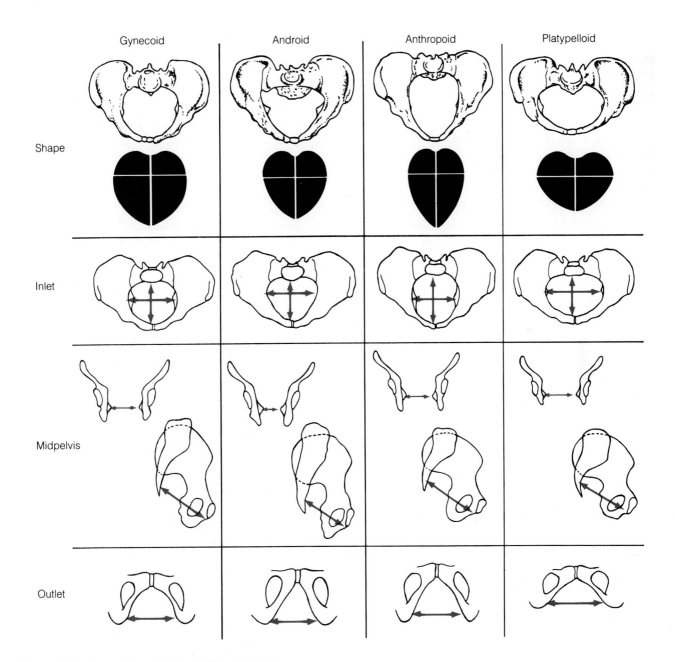

*Figure 2.12   Comparison of Caldwell-Moloy pelvic types*

## BREASTS

The **breasts,** or *mammary glands,* considered accessories of the reproductive system, are specialized sebaceous glands. They are conical and symmetrically placed on the sides of the chest. The greater pectoral and anterior serratus muscles underlie each breast. Suspending the breasts are fibrous tissues, called *Cooper's ligaments,* that extend from the deep fascia in the chest outward to just under the skin covering the breast. Frequently, the left breast is larger than the right.

In the center of each mature breast is the **nipple,** a protrusion about 0.5–1.3 cm in diameter. The nipple is composed mainly of erectile tissue, which becomes more rigid and prominent during the menstrual cycle, sexual excitement, pregnancy, and lactation. The nipple is surrounded by the heavily pigmented **areola,** 2.5–10 cm in diameter. Both the nipple and the areola are roughened by small papillae called *tubercles of Montgomery.* As an infant suckles, these tubercles secrete a fatty substance that helps lubricate and protect the breasts.

The breasts are composed of glandular, fibrous, and adipose tissue. The glandular tissue is arranged in a series of 15 to 24 lobes separated by fibrous and adipose tissue. Each lobe is made up of several lobules composed of many alveoli clustered around tiny ducts. The lining of these ducts secretes the various components of milk. The ducts from several lobules merge to form the larger ducts, called the *lactiferous ducts,* which open on the surface of the nipple (Figure 2.13).

The biologic function of the breasts is to provide nourishment and protective maternal antibodies to infants. They also are a source of pleasurable sexual sensation.

## ● FEMALE REPRODUCTIVE CYCLE

The monthly rhythmic changes in sexually mature females is usually called the *menstrual cycle.* A more accurate term is the **female reproductive cycle (FRC).** The FRC is composed of the ovarian cycle, during which ovulation occurs, and the menstrual cycle, during which menstruation occurs. These two cycles take place simultaneously (Figure 2.14).

*Menstruation* is cyclic uterine bleeding in response to cyclic hormonal changes. (Secondary sex characteristics associated with the hormonal changes are discussed earlier in this chapter.) Menstruation occurs when the ovum is not fertilized and begins about 14 days after ovulation in a 28-day cycle. The menstrual discharge, also referred to as the *menses* or *menstrual flow,* is composed of blood mixed with fluid, cervical and vaginal secretions, bacteria,

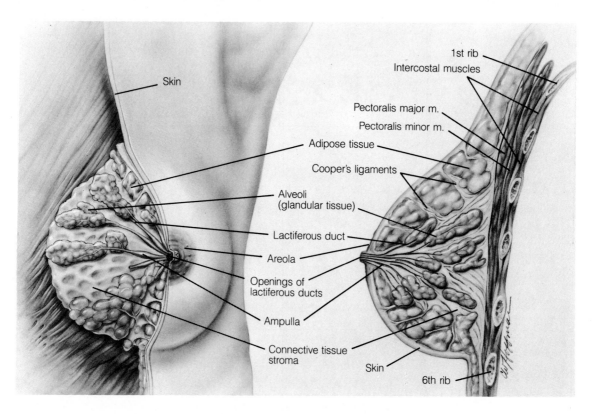

*Figure 2.13   Anatomy of the breast: **(A)** Anterior view of partially dissected left breast* **(B)** *Sagittal view (Adapted from Spence AP and Mason EB,* Human Anatomy and Physiology, *3rd ed. Menlo Park, CA: Benjamin/Cummings, 1987, p 830)*

mucus, leukocytes, and other cellular debris. The menstrual discharge is dark red and has a distinctive odor. It results from physiologic tissue death caused by lack of blood and oxygen to the endometrium.

*Menarche*—the onset of menstruation—usually occurs when a girl is about 12–13 years of age. Frequently, ovulation does not occur in early cycles; these are called *anovulatory cycles.* Early cycles also are often irregular in

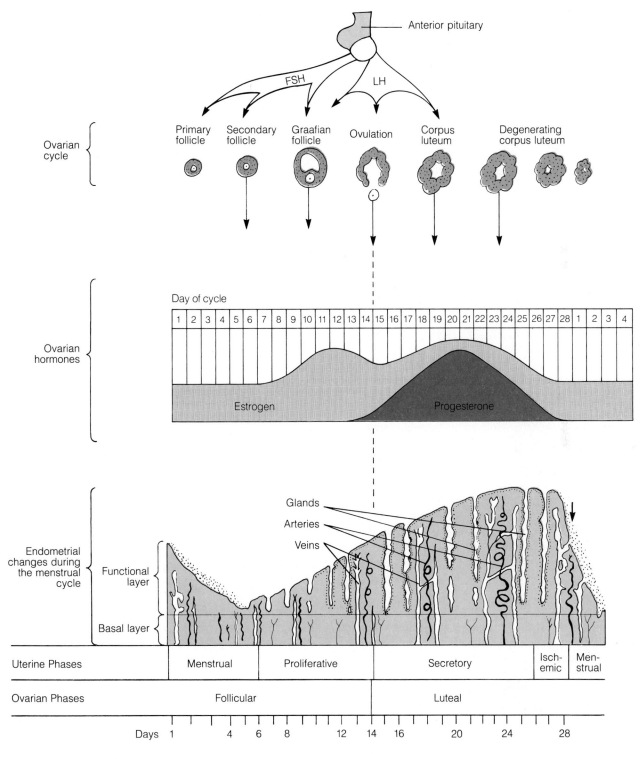

*Figure 2.14   Female reproductive cycle: interrelationships of hormones, the four phases of the uterine cycle, and the two phases of the ovarian cycle*

frequency, amount of flow, and duration. Within several months to two to three years, a regular cycle becomes established.

Menstrual parameters vary greatly among individuals. Generally, menstruation occurs every 28 days, plus or minus five to ten days. Emotional and physical factors such as illness, excessive fatigue, and stress or anxiety can alter the cycle interval. In addition, certain environmental factors such as temperature and altitude may affect the cycle.

The duration of menses is from two to eight days, with the blood loss averaging 30–100 mL and the loss of iron averaging 0.5–1 mg daily.

## ● Physiologic Aspects of the Female Reproductive Cycle (FRC)

### EFFECTS OF FEMALE HORMONES

After menarche, a female undergoes a cyclic pattern of ovulation and menstruation (if pregnancy does not occur) for a period of 30 to 40 years. This cycle is an orderly process under neurohormonal control: Each month one oocyte matures, ruptures from the ovary, and enters the fallopian tube. The ovary, vagina, uterus, and fallopian tubes are major target organs for female hormones. Each organ undergoes changes indicative of the exact point in time of any menstrual cycle.

The ovaries produce mature gametes and secrete hormones. Ovarian hormones include the estrogens, progesterone, and testosterone. The ovary is sensitive to FSH and LH. The uterus is sensitive to estrogen and progesterone. The relative proportion of these hormones to each other controls the events of both ovarian and menstrual cycles.

### Estrogens

*Estrogens* are associated with those characteristics contributing to "femaleness." The major estrogenic effects are due primarily to three classical estrogens: estrone, β-estradiol, and estriol. β-Estradiol is the major estrogen. Estrogens are secreted in large amounts by the ovaries in nonpregnant women.

Estrogens control the development of the female secondary sex characteristics: breast development, widening of the hips, and adipose deposits in the buttocks and mons pubis. Estrogens assist in the maturation of the ovarian follicles and cause the endometrial mucosa to proliferate following menstruation. The amount of estrogens is greatest during the proliferative (follicular or estrogenic) phase of the menstrual cycle. Estrogen also causes the uterus to increase in size and weight because of increased glycogen, amino acids, electrolytes, and water. Blood supply is augmented as well. Under the influence of estrogens, myometrial contractility increases in both the uterus and the fallopian tubes, and there is increased uterine sensitivity to oxytocin. Estrogens inhibit FSH production and stimulate LH production.

Estrogens have effects on many hormones and other carrier proteins. This explains, for example, the increased amount of protein-bound iodine in pregnant women and in women who use oral contraceptives containing estrogen (Little and Billiar 1980).

Estrogens may increase libidinal feelings in humans. They decrease the excitability of the hypothalamus, which may cause an increase in sexual desire.

### Progesterone

*Progesterone* is secreted by the corpus luteum and is found in greatest amounts during the secretory (luteal or progestational) phase of the menstrual cycle. It decreases the motility and contractility of the uterus caused by estrogens, thereby preparing the uterus for implantation after fertilization of the ovum.

Under the influence of progesterone, the vaginal epithelium proliferates and the cervix secretes thick, viscous mucus. Breast glandular tissue increases in size and complexity. Progesterone also prepares the breasts for lactation.

The temperature rise of about 0.35°C (0.5°F) that accompanies ovulation and persists throughout the secretory phase of the menstrual cycle is probably due to progesterone.

### Prostaglandins (PGs)

**Prostaglandins** (oxygenated fatty acids), which are also classified as hormones, have a varied action in the body. The different types of prostaglandins (PGs) are indicated by Roman letters and either numbers ($PGE_1$) or Greek alphabet letters ($PGF_{2\alpha}$). Generally PGEs relax smooth muscles and are potent vasodilators; PGFs are potent vasoconstrictors and increase the contractility of muscles and arteries. While their primary actions seem antagonistic, their basic regulatory functions in cells are achieved through an intricate pattern of reciprocal events. The discussion here will summarize their role in ovulation and menstruation.

Certain PGs are known to have a major role in the regulation of reproductive processes. For example, $PGE_1$ and $PGE_2$ appear to affect gonadotropin secretion by acting on the hypothalamus (Aten et al 1986).

Prostaglandin formation increases during follicular maturation, is dependent on gonadotropins, and is essential to ovulation. Extrusion of the ovum, resulting from the increased contractility of the smooth muscle in the theca layer of the mature follicle, is thought to be caused by $PGF_{2\alpha}$ (Wallach 1988). Significant amounts of PGs are found in and around the follicle at the time of ovulation.

While the exact mechanism by which the corpus

luteum degenerates in the absence of pregnancy remains obscure, $PGF_{2\alpha}$ is thought to induce progesterone withdrawal, the lowest point of which coincides with the onset of early menses.

Endometrium and menstrual fluid are known to be rich sources of PGs. One study (Vijayakumar et al 1981) suggests that the ratio of $PGF_{2\alpha}$ to PGE is a critical factor in the endometrial cycle.

During the late secretory phase the level of $PGF_{2\alpha}$ is higher than that of PGE. This event increases vasoconstriction and contractility of the myometrium, which contributes to the ischemia preceding menstruation. High concentration of PGs may also account for the vasoconstriction of the endometrium venous lacunae allowing for platelet aggregation at vascular rupture points, thereby preventing a rapid blood loss during menstruation. The menstrual flow's high concentration of PGs may also facilitate the process of tissue digestion, which allows for an orderly shedding of the endometrium during menstruation.

## ● Neurohumoral Basis of the Female Reproductive Cycle

The FRC is controlled by complex interactions between the nervous and endocrine systems and their target tissues. These interactions involve the hypothalamus, anterior pituitary, and ovaries; their functions are reciprocal.

The hypothalamus controls anterior pituitary hormone production by secretion of gonadotropin-releasing hormone (GnRH). This releasing hormone is often called both luteinizing hormone–releasing hormone (LHRH) and follicle-stimulating hormone–releasing hormone (FSHRH).

In response to GnRH, the anterior pituitary secretes the gonadotropic hormones FSH and LH. FSH primarily is responsible for the maturation of the ovarian follicle. As the follicle matures, it secretes increasing amounts of estrogen, which enhance the development of the follicle. (This estrogen also is responsible for the rebuilding/proliferation phase of the endometrium after it is shed during menstruation.)

Final maturation of the follicle will not come about without the action of LH. The anterior pituitary's production of LH increases sixfold to tenfold as the follicle matures. About 18 hours after the peak production of LH, ovulation occurs.

The LH is also responsible for the "luteinizing" of the theca and granulosa cells of the ruptured follicle. As a result, estrogen production is reduced and progesterone secretion continues. Thus estrogen levels fall a day before ovulation; tiny amounts of progesterone are in evidence. Ovulation takes place following the very rapid growth of the follicle, as the sustained high level of estrogen diminishes, and progesterone secretion begins.

The ruptured follicle undergoes rapid change; luteinization is accomplished and the mass of cells becomes the corpus luteum (Hatcher et al 1988). The lutein cells secrete large amounts of progesterone with smaller amounts of estrogen. (Concurrently, the excessive amounts of progesterone are responsible for the secretory phase of the uterine cycle.) Seven or eight days following ovulation, the corpus luteum begins to involute, losing its secretory function. The production of both progesterone and estrogen is severely diminished. The anterior pituitary responds with increasingly large amounts of FSH; a few days later LH production begins. As a result, new follicles become responsive to another ovarian cycle and begin maturing.

## ● Ovarian Cycle

The ovarian cycle has two phases: the follicular phase (days 1–14) and the luteal phase (days 15–28) in a 28-day cycle. Usually only the length of the follicular phase varies in menstrual cycles of varying duration because the luteal phase is of fixed length (Ferin 1987). During the *follicular phase,* the primordial follicle matures as a result of FSH. Within the follicle, the oocyte grows. A mature **graafian follicle** appears about the 14th day under dual control of FSH and LH. It is a large structure, measuring about 5–10 mm. In the mature graafian follicle, the oocyte is surrounded by fluid and enclosed in a thick elastic capsule called the **zona pellucida**.

Just before ovulation, the mature oocyte completes its first meiotic division (see Chapter 5 for a description of meiosis). As a result of this division, two cells are formed: a small cell called a **polar body** and a larger cell called the *secondary oocyte.* The secondary oocyte matures into the ovum (see Figure 5.2).

As the graafian follicle matures and enlarges, it comes close to the surface of the ovary. The ovary surface forms a blisterlike protrusion, and the follicle walls become thin. The secondary oocyte, polar body, and the follicular fluid are pushed out. Discharged near the fimbria of the fallopian tube, the ovum is pulled into the tube and begins its journey through it.

Occasionally, ovulation is accompanied by midcycle pain, known as *mittelschmerz.* This pain may be caused by a thick tunica albuginea or by a local peritoneal reaction to the expelling of the follicular contents. Vaginal discharge may increase during ovulation, and a small amount of blood (midcycle spotting) may be discharged as well.

The body temperature increases about 0.3–0.6°C (0.5–1.0°F) 24–48 hours after the time of ovulation. It remains elevated until the day before menstruation begins. There may be an accompanying sharp basal body temperature drop just before the increase. These temperature changes are useful clinically to determine the approximate time ovulation occurs.

Generally, the ovum takes several minutes to travel through the ruptured follicle to the fallopian tube opening.

## Essential Facts to Remember

### Signs of Ovulation

The cervical mucosa changes in the following ways:

- The amount of mucus increases.
- It appears thin, watery, and clear.
- Spinnbarkeit greater than 5 cm is present.
- A ferning pattern appears on microscopic examination.

Basal body temperature increases 0.3 to 0.6°C 24–48 hr after ovulation.

Mittelschmerz may be present.

Midcycle spotting may occur.

---

### Table 2.2   Characteristics of Menstrual Cycle and Ovulation

| | |
|---|---|
| Menstrual phase (Days 1–5) | Estrogen levels are low. Cervical mucus is scanty, viscous and opaque. Endometrium is shed. |
| Proliferative phase (Days 6–14) | Endometrium and myometrium thickness increases. Estrogen peaks just before ovulation. Cervical mucosa at ovulation: Is clear, thin, watery, and alkaline. Is more favorable to sperm. Has *spinnbarkeit* greater than 5 cm. Shows ferning pattern on microscopic exam. Just prior to ovulation body temperature drops and then at ovulation BBT increases 0.3 to 0.6°C, and *mittelschmerz* and/or midcycle spotting may occur. |
| Secretory phase (Days 15–26) | Estrogen drops sharply, and progesterone dominates. Vascularity of entire uterus increases. Tissue glycogen increases, and the uterus is made ready for implantation. |
| Ischemic phase (Days 27–28) | Both estrogen and progesterone levels fall. Spiral arteries undergo vasoconstriction. Endometrium becomes pale. Blood vessels rupture. Blood escapes into uterine stromal cells. |

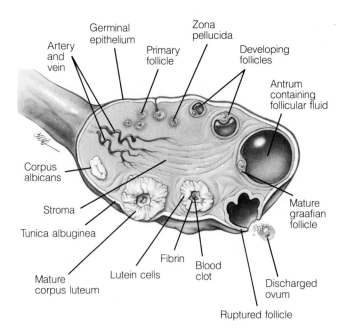

*Figure 2.15   Various stages of development of the ovarian follicles*

The contractions of the tube's smooth muscle and its ciliary action propel the ovum through the tube. The ovum remains in the ampulla, where it may be fertilized and cleavage can begin. The ovum is thought to be fertile for only 6–24 hours. It reaches the uterus 72–96 hours after its release from the ovary.

The *luteal phase* begins when the ovum leaves its follicle. Under the influence of LH, the **corpus luteum** develops from the ruptured follicle. Within two or three days, the corpus luteum becomes yellowish and spherical and increases in vascularity. If the ovum is fertilized and implants in the endometrium, the fertilized egg begins to secrete **human chorionic gonadotropin (hCG),** which is needed to maintain the corpus luteum. If fertilization does not occur, within about a week after ovulation the corpus luteum begins to degenerate, eventually becoming a connective tissue scar called the *corpus albicans*. With degeneration comes a decrease in estrogen and progesterone. This allows for an increase in LH and FSH, which trigger the hypothalamus. Approximately 14 days after ovulation (in a 28-day cycle), in the absence of pregnancy, menstruation begins. Figure 2.15 depicts the changes that the follicle undergoes during the ovarian cycle.

### MENSTRUAL CYCLE

The menstrual cycle has four phases: the menstrual phase, proliferative phase, secretory phase, and ischemic phase (see Table 2.2). Menstruation occurs during the *menstrual phase.* Some endometrial areas are shed, while others remain. Some of the remaining tips of the endo-

## Essential Facts to Remember

### Female Reproductive Cycle

#### Ovarian Cycle

*Follicular phase* (days 1–14): Primordial follicle matures under influence of FSH and LH up to the time of ovulation.

*Luteal phase* (days 15–28): Ovum leaves follicle; corpus luteum develops under LH influence and produces high levels of progesterone and low levels of estrogen.

#### Menstrual Cycle

*Menstrual phase* (days 1–5)

*Proliferative phase* (days 6–14): Estrogen peaks just prior to ovulation. Cervical mucus at ovulation is clear, thin, watery, alkaline, and more favorable to sperm; shows ferning pattern; and has spinnbarkeit greater than 5 cm. At ovulation body temperature drops, then rises sharply and remains elevated.

*Secretory phase* (days 15–26): Estrogen drops sharply and progesterone dominates.

*Ischemic phase* (days 27–28): Both estrogen and progesterone levels drop.

metrial glands begin to regenerate. The endometrium is in a resting state following menstruation. Estrogen levels are low, and the endometrium is 1 to 2 mm deep. During this part of the cycle, the cervical mucosa is scanty, viscous, and opaque.

The *proliferative phase* begins when the endometrial glands enlarge, becoming twisted and longer, in response to increasing amounts of estrogen. The blood vessels become prominent and dilated, and the endometrium increases in thickness sixfold to eightfold. This gradual process reaches its peak just before ovulation. The cervical mucosa becomes thin, clear, watery, and more alkaline, making the mucosa more favorable to spermatozoa. As ovulation nears, the cervical mucosa shows increased elasticity, called *spinnbarkeit*. At ovulation, the mucus will stretch more than 5 cm. The cervical mucosa pH increases from below 7.0 to 7.5 at the time of ovulation. On microscopic examination, the mucosa shows a characteristic ferning pattern (see Figure 4.4). This fern pattern is a useful aid in assessment of ovulation time. For in-depth discussion, see Essential Facts to Remember—Signs of Ovulation.

The *secretory phase* follows ovulation. The endometrium, under estrogenic influence, undergoes slight cellular growth. Progesterone, however, causes such marked swelling and growth that the epithelium is warped into folds.

The amount of tissue glycogen increases. The glandular epithelial cells begin to fill with cellular debris, become tortuous, and dilate. The glands secrete small quantities of endometrial fluid in preparation for a fertilized ovum. The vascularity of the entire uterus increases greatly, providing a nourishing bed for implantation. If implantation occurs, the endometrium, under the influence of progesterone, continues to develop and become even thicker (see Chapter 5 for an in-depth discussion of implantation).

If fertilization does not occur, the *ischemic phase* begins. The corpus luteum begins to degenerate, and as a result both estrogen and progesterone levels fall. Areas of necrosis appear under the epithelial lining. Extensive vascular changes also occur. Small blood vessels rupture, and the spiral arteries constrict and retract, causing a deficiency of blood in the endometrium, which becomes pale. This ischemic phase is characterized by the escape of blood into the stromal cells of the uterus. The menstrual flow begins, thus beginning the menstrual cycle again. After menstruation the basal layer remains, so that the tips of the glands can regenerate the new functional endometrial layer. See Essential Facts to Remember—Female Reproductive Cycle.

## ● MALE REPRODUCTIVE SYSTEM

The primary reproductive functions of the male genitals are to produce and transport its sex cells, sperm, through and eventually out of the genital tract into the female genital tract. The male reproductive system consists of the external and internal genitals (Figure 2.16).

## ● External Genitals

The two external reproductive organs are the penis and scrotum. The *penis* is an elongated, cylindrical structure consisting of a body, termed the *shaft*, and a cone-shaped end called the *glans*. The penis lies in front of the scrotum.

The shaft of the penis is made up of three longitudinal columns of erectile tissue: the paired *corpora cavernosa* and a third, the *corpus spongiosum*. These columns are covered by dense fibrous connective tissue and then enclosed by elastic tissue. The penis is covered by a thin outer layer of skin.

The corpus spongiosum contains the urethra. The urethra terminates in a slitlike opening, located in the tip of the glans, called the *urethral meatus*. A circular fold of skin arises just behind the glans and covers it. Known as the *prepuce*, or *foreskin*, it is frequently removed by the surgical procedure of circumcision (Chapter 22).

If the corpus spongiosum does not surround the urethra completely, the urethral meatus may occur on the ventral aspect of the penile shaft or on the dorsal as-

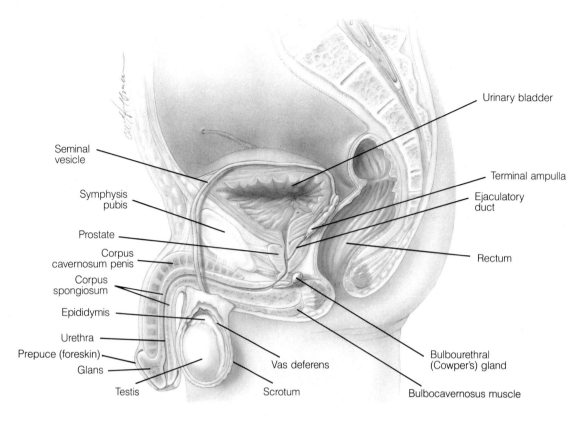

*Figure 2.16  Male reproductive system*

pect, conditions known respectively as hypospadias and epispadias.

Sexual stimulation causes the penis to elongate, thicken, and stiffen, a process called *erection*. The penis becomes erect when its blood vessels become engorged, a consequence of parasympathetic nerve stimulation. If stimulation is intense enough, the forceful and sudden expulsion of semen occurs through the rhythmic contractions of the penile muscles. This phenomenon is called *ejaculation*.

The penis serves both the urinary and reproductive systems. Urine is expelled through the urethral meatus. The reproductive function of the penis is to deposit sperm in the vagina so that fertilization of the ovum can occur.

The *scrotum* is a pouchlike structure that hangs in front of the anus and behind the penis. Composed of skin and the *dartos* muscle, the scrotum shows increased pigmentation and scattered hairs. The sebaceous glands open directly onto the scrotal surface; their secretion has a distinctive odor. Contraction of the dartos and cremasteric muscles shortens the scrotum and draws it closer to the body, thus wrinkling its outer surface. The degree of wrinkling is greatest in young men and at cold temperatures and is least in older men and at warm temperatures.

Inside the scrotum are two lateral compartments, each containing a testis with its related structures. The left testis and its scrotal sac usually hang lower than the right.

The function of the scrotum is to protect the testes and the sperm by maintaining a temperature lower than that of the body. Spermatogenesis will not occur if the testes fail to descend and thus remain at body temperature. Because it is sensitive to touch, pressure, temperature, and pain, the scrotum defends against potential harm to the testes.

## ● Internal Genitals

The male internal reproductive organs include the gonads (testes or testicles), a system of ducts (epididymides, vas deferens, ejaculatory duct, and urethra), and accessory glands (seminal vesicles, prostate gland, bulbourethral glands, and urethral glands). See Essential Facts to Remember—Male Reproductive Organ Functions.

### TESTES

The *testes* are a pair of oval glandular organs contained in the scrotum. In the sexually mature male, they are the site of spermatozoa production and the secretion of several male sex hormones.

## *Essential Facts to Remember*

### Male Reproductive Organ Functions

The testes house seminiferous tubules and gonads.

Seminiferous tubules contain sperm cells in various stages of development and undergoing meiosis.

Sertoli's cells nourish and protect spermatocytes (phase between spermatids and spermatozoa).

Leydig's cells are the main source of testosterone.

Epididymides provide an area for maturation of sperm and a reservoir for mature spermatozoa.

The vas deferens connects the epididymis with the prostate gland, then connects with ducts from the seminal vesicle to become an ejaculatory duct.

Ejaculatory ducts provide a passageway for semen and seminal fluid into the urethra.

Seminal vesicles secrete yellowish fluid rich in fructose, prostaglandins, and fibrinogen. This provides nutrition that increases motility and fertilizing ability of sperm. Prostaglandins also aid fertilization by making the cervical mucus more receptive to sperm.

The prostate gland secretes thin, alkaline fluid containing calcium, citric acid, and other substances. Alkalinity counteracts acidity of ductus and seminal vesicle secretions.

Bulbourethral (Cowper's) glands secrete alkaline, viscous fluid into semen, aiding in neutralization of acidic vaginal secretions.

---

Each testis is 4–6 cm long, 2–3 cm wide, and 3–4 cm thick. Each weighs about 10–15 g. It is covered by an outer serous membrane and an inner capsule composed of tough fibrous connective tissue. The connective tissue sends projections inward, dividing the testis into 250–400 lobules. Each lobule contains one to three tightly packed, convoluted *seminiferous tubules.* These tubules contain sperm cells in all stages of development, arranged in layers.

The seminiferous tubules are surrounded by loose connective tissue, which houses abundant blood and lymph vessels and *interstitial (Leydig's) cells.* The interstitial cells produce testosterone, the primary male sex hormone.

The many seminiferous tubules come together to form 20–30 straight tubules, which in turn form an anastomotic network of thin-walled spaces, the *rete testis.* The rete testis forms 10–15 ducts that empty into the duct of the epididymis.

Most of the cells lining the seminiferous tubules undergo spermatogenesis, a process of maturation in which spermatocytes become spermatozoa. (Chapter 5 discusses further the process of spermatogenesis.) Sperm production varies among and within the tubules, with cells in different areas of the same tubule undergoing different stages of spermatogenesis. The tubules also contain *Sertoli's cells,* which nourish and protect the spermatocytes. The sperm are eventually released from the tubules into the epididymis, where they mature further.

Like the female reproductive cycle, the process of spermatogenesis and other functions of the testes are the result of complex neural and hormonal controls. The hypothalamus secretes releasing factors, which stimulate the anterior pituitary to release the gonadotropins—FSH and LH. These hormones cause the testes to produce **testosterone,** which maintains spermatogenesis, increases sperm production by the seminiferous tubules, and stimulates production of seminal fluid (Guyton 1986).

Testosterone is the most prevalent and potent of the testicular hormones. Its target organs are the testes, prostate, and seminal vesicles. In addition to being essential for spermatogenesis, testosterone is responsible for the development of secondary male characteristics and certain behavioral patterns. The effects of testosterone include structural and functional development of the male genital tract, emission and ejaculation of seminal fluid, distribution of body hair, promotion of growth and strength of long bones, increased muscle mass, and enlargement of the vocal cords. The action of testosterone on the central nervous system is thought to produce aggressiveness and sexual drive. The action of testosterone is constant, not cyclic like that of the female hormones. Its production is not limited to a certain number of years, but it is thought to decrease in quantity with age.

In summary, the primary functions of the testes are to serve as the site of spermatogenesis and to produce testosterone.

### *EPIDIDYMIS*

The *epididymis* is a duct about 5.6 m long, although it is convoluted into a compact structure about 3.75 cm long. An epididymis lies behind each testis. It arises from the top of the testis, courses downward, and then passes upward, where it becomes the vas deferens.

The epididymis provides a reservoir where maturing spermatozoa can survive for a long period. When discharged from the seminiferous tubules into the epididymis, the sperm are immotile and incapable of fertilizing an ovum. The spermatozoa remain in the epididymis for 2–10 days, until maturation is complete.

### *VAS DEFERENS AND EJACULATORY DUCTS*

The *vas deferens,* also known as the *ductus deferens,* is about 40 cm long and connects the epididymis with the prostate. One vas deferens arises from the posterior border of each testis. It joins the spermatic cord and weaves over and between several pelvic structures until it meets the vas deferens from the opposite side. Each vas deferens then unites with a seminal vesicle duct to form the *ejaculatory ducts,* which enter the prostate gland, terminating in the prostatic urethra.

Prior to its entrance into the prostate, the vas deferens enlarges. This enlargement is called the *terminal ampulla* and serves as the primary storehouse for spermatozoa, which are still relatively immotile, and tubule secretions. The ejaculatory ducts serve as passageways for semen and fluid secreted by the seminal vesicles.

## URETHRA

The male *urethra* is the passageway for both urine and semen. The urethra begins in the bladder and passes through the prostate gland, where it is called the *prostatic urethra*. The urethra emerges from the prostate gland to become the *membranous urethra*. It terminates in the penis, where it is called the *penile urethra*.

## ACCESSORY GLANDS

The male accessory glands are specialized structures under endocrine and neural control. Each secretes a unique and essential component of the total seminal fluid in an ordered sequence.

The *seminal vesicles* are two glands composed of many lobes. Each vesicle is about 7.5 cm long. They are situated between the bladder and rectum and immediately above the base of the prostate. The epithelium lining the seminal vesicles secretes an alkaline, viscid, clear fluid rich in high-energy fructose, prostaglandins, fibrinogen, and proteins. During ejaculation, this fluid empties into the ejaculatory ducts and mixes with the sperm. This fluid helps provide an environment favorable to sperm motility and metabolism.

The *prostate gland* surrounds the upper part of the urethra and lies below the neck of the urinary bladder. Made up of several lobes, it measures about 4 cm in diameter and weighs 20–30 g. The prostate is made up of both glandular and muscular tissue. It secretes a thin, milky, slightly acidic fluid (pH 6.5) containing high levels of zinc, calcium, citric acid, and acid phosphatase. This fluid protects the sperm from the acidic environment of the vagina and the male urethra, which could be spermicidal.

The *bulbourethral* or *Cowper's glands* are a pair of small round structures on either side of the membranous urethra. The glands secrete a clear, viscous, alkaline fluid rich in mucoproteins that becomes part of the semen. This secretion also lubricates the penile urethra during sexual excitement as well as neutralizes the acid in the male urethra and vagina, thereby enhancing sperm motility.

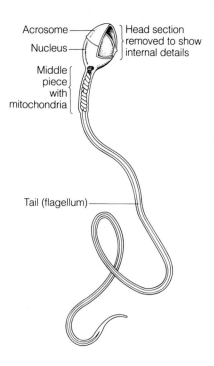

*Figure 2.17   Schematic representation of a mature spermatozoon*

The *urethral* or *Littre's glands* are tiny mucous-secreting glands found throughout the membranous lining of the penile urethra. Their secretions add to those of the bulbourethral glands.

### Semen

The male ejaculate, *semen* or *seminal fluid,* is made up of spermatozoa and the secretions of the bulbourethral glands, urethral glands, prostate, epididymides, and seminal vesicles. The seminal fluid transports viable and motile sperm to the female reproductive tract. Effective transportation of sperm requires adequate nutrients, an adequate pH (about 7.5), a specific concentration of sperm to fluid, and an optimal osmolarity.

A spermatozoon is made up of a *head* and a *tail.* The tail is divided into the middle piece and end piece (Figure 2.17). The head's main components are the *acrosome, nucleus,* and *nuclear vacuoles.* The head carries the haploid number of chromosomes (23), and it is the part that enters the ovum at fertilization (Chapter 5). The tail, or *flagellum,* is specialized for motility.

Sperm may be stored in the male genital system for a period of several to 42 days, depending primarily on the frequency of ejaculations. The average volume of ejaculate following abstinence for several days is 2–5 mL but may vary from 1–10 mL. Repeated ejaculation results in decreased volume. Once ejaculated, sperm can live only two or three days in the female genital tract.

## ● ● ● ● ● ● ● ● ● ● ● ● ● ● ● ● ● ● ● ● ● ● ● ● ●
# ESSENTIAL CONCEPTS

● Reproductive activities require a complex interaction between the reproductive structures, the central nervous system, and such endocrine glands as the pituitary, hypothalamus, testes, and ovaries.

● At puberty, an alteration in brain sensitivity leads to an increased release of GnRH, which stimulates LH and FSH, leading in the male to an increase in testosterone, and in the female to an increase in estrogen and progesterone.

● Estrogen is the principal cause of the events of puberty (maturation of ova, enlargement of the uterus and fallopian tubes, deposition of fat in the breasts and hips, and characteristic hair growth) in females.

● Puberty changes for the male (onset of spermatogenesis; enlargement of the penis, scrotum, and testes; voice changes; and characteristic hair growth) occur as a result of increased testosterone production by the testes.

● The female reproductive system consists of: the ovaries, where female germ cells and female sex hormones are formed; the fallopian tubes, which capture the ovum and allow transport to the uterus; the uterus, whose lining is shed during menstruation or is the implantation site for the fertilized ovum (blastocyst); the cervix, which is a protective portal for the body of the uterus and the connection between the vagina and the uterus (it must thin and dilate to allow passage of a baby); and the vagina, which is the passageway from the external genitals to the uterus and provides for discharge of menstrual products to the outside of the body.

● The female reproductive cycle is composed of the ovarian cycle, during which ovulation occurs, and the menstrual cycle, during which menstruation occurs. These two cycles take place simultaneously and are under neurohumoral control.

● The ovarian cycle has two phases: the follicular phase and the luteal phase. During the follicular phase the primordial follicle matures under the influence of FSH and LH until ovulation occurs. The luteal phase begins when the ovum leaves the follicle and the corpus luteum develops under the influence of LH. The corpus luteum produces high levels of progesterone and low levels of estrogen.

● The menstrual cycle has four phases: menstrual, proliferative, secretory, and ischemic. Menstruation is the actual shedding of the endometrial lining, when estrogen levels are low. The proliferative phase begins when the endometrial glands begin to enlarge under the influence of estrogen and cervical mucosa changes occur; the changes peak at ovulation. The secretory phase follows ovulation and under the influence primarily of progesterone the uterus increases its vascularity to make it ready for possible implantation. The ischemic phase is characterized by degeneration of the corpus luteum, fall in both estrogen and progesterone levels, constriction of the spiral arteries, and escape of blood into the stromal cells of the endometrium.

● The male reproductive system consists of: the testes, where male germ cells and male sex hormones are formed; a series of continuous ducts through which spermatozoa are transported outside the body; accessory glands that produce secretions important to sperm nutrition, survival, and transport; and the penis, which serves as the organ of copulation.

● ● ● ● ● ● ● ● ● ● ● ● ● ● ● ● ● ● ● ● ● ● ● ● ●

## References

Aten RF, Luborsky JL, Behrman HR: Prostaglandins: Basic chemistry and action. In: *Gynecology and Obstetrics*. Vol. 5. Sciarra JL et al (editors). Hagerstown, MD: Harper and Row, 1986.

Caldwell WE, Moloy HC: Anatomical variations in the female pelvis and their effect on labor with a suggested classification. *Am J Obstet Gynecol* 1933; 26: 479.

Delancey JOL: Anatomy of the pelvis. In: *Gynecology and Obstetrics*. Vol. 2. Sciarra JL et al (editors). Hagerstown, MD: Harper and Row, 1987.

Ferin M: The central nervous system–hypophyseal-ovarian axis and the menstrual cycle. In: *Gynecology and Obstetrics*. Vol. 5. Sciarra JL et al (editors). Hagerstown, MD: Harper and Row, 1987.

Guyton AC: *Textbook of Medical Physiology,* 7th ed. Philadelphia: Saunders, 1986.

Hatcher RA et al: *Contraceptive Technology: 1988–1989,* 14th ed. New York: Irvington, 1988.

Little AB, Billiar RB: Endocrinology. In: *Gynecology and Obstetrics: The Health Care of Women,* 2nd ed. Romney SL et al (editors). New York: McGraw-Hill, 1980.

Marshall JR, Ross J: Other aspects of the endocrine physiology of reproduction. In: *Obstetrics and Gynecology,* 4th ed. Danforth DN (editor). Philadelphia, PA: Harper and Row, 1982.

Pritchard JA, MacDonald PC, Gant NF: *Williams Obstetrics,* 17th ed. East Norwalk, CN: Appleton-Century-Crofts, 1985.

Speroff L et al: *Clinical Gynecologic Endocrinology and Infertility,* 4th ed. Baltimore: Williams and Wilkins, 1989.

Vijayakumar R et al: Myometrial prostaglandins during human menstrual cycle. *Am J Obstet Gynecol* 1981; 141(3):313.

Wallach EE: The mechanism of ovulation. In: *Gynecology and Obstetrics*. Vol. 5. Sciarra JL et al (editors). Hagerstown, MD: Harper and Row, 1988.

## Additional Readings

Chard T, Liford R: *Basic Sciences for Obstetrics and Gynaecology*, 2nd ed. New York: Springer-Verlag, 1986.

Cooper TG: *The Epididymis, Sperm Maturation and Fertilization*. New York: Springer-Verlag, 1986.

Embrey MP: Prostaglandins in human reproduction. *Br Med J* 1981; 238:1563.

Gardner J: Adolescent menstrual characteristics and predictors of gynaecological health. *Ann Hum Biol* 1983; 10:31.

Griffith-Kenney J: *Contemporary Women's Health: A Nursing Advocacy Approach*. Menlo Park, CA: Addison-Wesley, 1986.

Lierse W: *Applied Anatomy of the Pelvis*. New York: Springer-Verlag, 1987.

Lublanezki N et al: OTC-menstrual pain preparations. *Pediatr Nurs* November–December 1987; 13(6):435.

Mills JL et al: Early growth predicts timing of puberty in boys: Results of a 14-year nutrition and growth study. *J Pediatr* September 1986; 109(3):543.

Ryan KJ: Interpreting the controls of the menstrual cycle. *Contemp OB/GYN* 1985; 26(3):107.

Samples JT et al: The dynamic characteristics of the circumvaginal muscles. *J Obstet Gynecol Neonatal Nurs* May/June 1988; 17(3):194–201.

Shaver JF et al: Menstrual experience: Comparisons of dysmenorrheic and nondysmenorrheic women. *West J Nurs Res* November 1987; 9(4):423–39.

Simon JA et al: Variability of midcycle estradiol: Positive feedback evidence for unique pituitary responses in individual women. *J Clin Endocrinol Metab* 1987; 64(4):789.

Urban DJ et al: Nurse specialization in reproductive endocrinology. *J Obstet Gynecol Neonatal Nurs* May/June 1982; 11:167.

Yen SS, Jaffe RB: *Reproductive Endocrinology: Physiology, Pathophysiology and Clinical Management*, 2nd ed. Philadelphia: Saunders, 1985.

# 3

# Women's Health Care

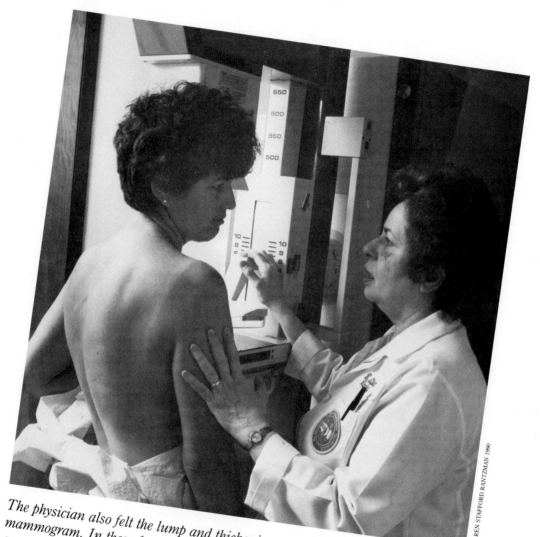

© KAREN STAFFORD RANTZMAN 1990

*The physician also felt the lump and thickening, and now I'm waiting for my mammogram. In these few days my thoughts and feelings have been a roller coaster. I'm 46, and I'm wondering if this is it. Am I dying? Now? I'm afraid as I have not been afraid since one of our children was very ill. Try as I may to fill my head with other thoughts, it keeps slipping back to this.*

## Objectives

● Summarize information that women may need to implement appropriate self-care measures in dealing with menstruation.

● Delineate the factors that influence the development of attitudes about sexuality.

● Compare the sexual responses of females and males as described by Masters and Johnson.

● Relate the basic content of preconception counseling to its rationale.

● Compare the various methods of fertility control with regard to advantages, disadvantages, and effectiveness.

● Contrast the common benign breast disorders.

● Develop a plan of care to meet the nursing needs of a woman with cancer of the breast.

● Describe the common sexually transmitted diseases.

● Summarize the health teaching a nurse should provide to a woman with a sexually transmitted disease.

● Discuss the physical and psychologic aspects of menopause.

● Describe the concept of the feminization of poverty.

● Identify environmental hazards present in the workplaces of childbearing women.

● Delineate the nurse's role in working with rape survivors.

## Key Terms

amenorrhea
cervical cap
coitus interruptus
condoms
contraceptive sponge
diaphragm
dysmenorrhea
dyspareunia
endometriosis
estrogen replacement therapy

fertility awareness methods
fibrocystic breast disease
intracervical devices
intrauterine device
mammogram
menarche
oral contraceptives
orgasm
Pap smear
pelvic inflammatory disease

premenstrual syndrome
situational contraceptives
spermicides
toxic shock syndrome
tubal ligation
vasectomy

Throughout her lifetime a woman's health care needs change. As a young girl she requires health teaching about menstruation, sexuality, and personal responsibility. As a teen she needs information about reproductive choices and safe sexual activity. During this time she should also be introduced to the importance of health care practices such as breast self-examination and regular Pap smears. The mature woman needs to be reminded of these self-care issues and prepared for physical changes that accompany childbirth and aging. The nurse can work with women to provide health teaching and information about self-care practices whenever possible—in schools, during routine examinations, during regular prenatal care, or as part of postpartum assessments. By educating women about their bodies, about their health care choices, and about their right to be knowledgeable consumers, nurses can help women assume responsibility for the health care they receive.

The contemporary woman is likely to encounter various major or minor gynecologic or urinary problems during her lifetime. These problems may provoke a variety of psychologic responses and physical concerns. The nurse can assist a woman in this situation by providing her with accurate, sensitive, and supportive health education and counseling. To meet the woman's needs the nurse must have up-to-date information about health care practices and about diagnostic and treatment options available.

This chapter provides information not only about physical conditions women often develop and the health information they need, but also about social issues that can affect them.

# ● MENSTRUATION

Girls today begin to learn about puberty and menstruation at a surprisingly young age. Unfortunately the source of their "education" is sometimes their peers, and thus the information frequently is incomplete, inaccurate, and sensationalized. Nurses who work with young girls and adolescents recognize this and are working hard to provide accurate health teaching and to correct misinformation about **menarche** (the onset of menses) and the menstrual cycle.

Cultural, religious, and personal attitudes about menstruation are part of the menstrual experience and, unfortunately, often reflect negative attitudes toward women. Historically many myths surrounded menstruation. Women were often isolated or restricted to the company of other women during their monthly flow because they were considered "unclean." Even today there is a tendency by some to regard the menstruating woman as vulnerable or less capable. Current customs include refraining from exercise and showers and hiding the fact of menstruation entirely. Cultural taboos against coitus during menses are of long duration. In reality, sexual intercourse during menses is common practice (Morris 1983) and not contraindicated; however, not all couples desire it. (The physiology of menstruation is discussed in Chapter 2.)

## ● Counseling the Young Girl About Menarche

Many young women find it embarrassing or stressful to discuss the menstrual experience, both because of the many taboos associated with the subject and because of their immaturity. However, the most critical factor in successful adaptation to menarche is the adolescent's level of preparedness. Information should be given to premenstrual girls over time rather than all at once. This allows time for them to absorb information and develop questions. Rierdan (1983) identified three areas in which girls require information:

- *Physiology of the experience.* Why does menstruation occur? How is it related to conception and childbirth? What anatomic and physiologic changes occur?

- *Menstrual hygiene.* What equipment is needed? How is it worn or used? Is it safe to take a bath or shower? What are the advantages and disadvantages of pads? Of tampons?

- *Concrete facts about the experience.* What color is the normal flow? What consistency? How does it smell?

The nurse should make it clear that variations in age at menarche, length of cycle, and duration of menses are normal, because girls are likely to become concerned if they are not "on time" as compared with their peers. Rier-

dan (1983) also reported that it is helpful to acknowledge the negative aspects of menstruation (messiness, embarrassment), as well as its positive role as a symbol of maturity and womanhood.

## ● Education for Self-Care

The nurse's primary role is to provide accurate information and assist in clearing up misconceptions so that girls will develop positive self-images and progress smoothly through this maturational phase.

### PADS AND TAMPONS

Since early times women have made pads and tampons from cloth or rags, which required washing but were reusable. Some women made them from gauze or cotton balls. Commercial tampons were introduced in the 1930s.

Today adhesive-stripped minipads and maxipads and flushable tampons have made life easier. Unfortunately, manufacturers have added deodorant to both sanitary napkins and tampons and have increased their absorbency. Both these "improvements" may prove harmful. The chemical used to deodorize can create a rash on the vulva and can damage the tender mucous lining of the vagina. Excessive or inappropriate use of tampons can produce dryness or even small sores or ulcers in the vagina.

Because the use of superabsorbent tampons has been linked to the development of toxic shock syndrome (TSS), they should be avoided. Regular absorbency tampons should be used only for heavy menstrual flow (during the first two or three days of the period), not during the whole period, and should be changed frequently. Since *Staphylococcus aureus,* the causative organism of TSS, is frequently found on the hands, a woman should wash her hands before inserting a fresh tampon.

In the absence of a heavy menstrual flow, tampons will absorb moisture, leaving the vaginal walls dry and subject to injury. The absorbency of regular tampons can vary. If the tampon is hard to pull out or shreds when removed or if the vagina becomes dry, the tampon is probably too absorbent. If a woman is worried about accidental spotting, she should check the diagrams on the packages of regular tampons. Those that expand in width are better able to prevent leakage without being too absorbent.

A woman should use tampons only during the day and switch to napkins at night to avoid vaginal irritation. Tampons should be avoided on the last spotty days of the period and should not be used for mid-cycle spotting or leukorrhea. If a woman experiences vaginal irritation, itching, soreness, or unusual odor or bleeding while using tampons, she should stop using them or change brands or absorbencies to see if that helps.

The choice of sanitary protection must meet the individual's needs, and she should feel comfortable using it whether it be napkins or tampons.

## VAGINAL SPRAYS AND DOUCHING

Vaginal sprays are unnecessary and can cause infections, itching, burning, vaginal discharge, rashes, and other problems. If a woman chooses to use a spray she should know that these sprays are for external use only and should never be applied to irritated or itching skin; nor should they be used with sanitary napkins.

Although douching is sometimes used to treat vaginal infections, douching as a hygiene practice is unnecessary since the vagina cleanses itself. Douching washes away the natural mucus and upsets the vaginal ecology, which can make the vagina more susceptible to infection. Douching with one of the perfumed or flavored douches can cause allergic reactions, and too frequent use of an undiluted or strong douche solution can induce severe irritation and even tissue damage. Propelling water up the vagina may also erode the antibacterial cervical plug and force bacteria and germs from the vagina into the uterus. Women should not douche during menstruation because the cervix is dilated to permit the downward flow of menstrual flow from the uterine lining. Douching may force tissue back up into the uterine cavity, which could create endometriosis.

The mucous secretions that continually bathe the vagina are completely odor free while they are in the vagina; only when they mingle with perspiration and hit the air does odor develop. Keeping one's skin clean and free of bacteria with plain soap and water is the most effective method of controlling odor. A soapy finger should be used to wash gently between the vulvar folds. Bathing is as important (if not more so) during menses as at any other time. A long leisurely soak in a warm tub will promote menstrual blood flow and relieve cramps by relaxing the muscles.

Keeping the vaginal area fresh throughout the day means keeping it dry and clean. After bathing or showering and patting herself dry a woman should powder her perineum with cornstarch or powdered natural clay (available at many health food stores) and wear cotton panties. She should make sure that her clothes are loose enough to permit the vaginal area to breathe. After using the toilet, a woman should always wipe herself from front to back and, if necessary, follow up with a moistened paper towel.

The most important thing to remember is that if an unusual odor persists despite these efforts, it may be a sign that something is awry. Certain conditions such as vaginitis produce a foul-smelling discharge.

## RELIEF OF DISCOMFORT

Some nutritionists suggest that vitamins B and E are helpful in relieving the discomforts associated with menstruation. Vitamin $B_6$ may help relieve the bloated feeling and cramping some women experience with menses.

Women are advised to take 100–200 mg of $B_6$ daily during menses and should continue for at least two menstrual cycles to determine effectiveness. However, excessive use has been associated with signs of toxicity such as nausea, headache, and depression, and with peripheral neurologic changes. Because the effectiveness of vitamin $B_6$ has not been confirmed, women should be warned of the potential complications and advised to avoid overdose (Glass 1988).

Vitamin E, a mild prostaglandin inhibitor, may relieve menstrual discomfort when taken in doses of 600 units/day.

Exercise can not only ease existing menstrual discomfort, but, if performed daily, also helps prevent cramps and other menstrual complaints. Aerobic exercises such as jogging, cycling, aerobic dancing, and fast-paced walking are especially helpful.

## ● Associated Menstrual Conditions

**Amenorrhea,** the absence of menses, is classified as primary or secondary. Primary amenorrhea is said to occur if menstruation has not been established by 18 years of age. Secondary amenorrhea is said to occur when an established menses (of longer than three months) ceases.

Primary amenorrhea necessitates a thorough assessment of the young woman to determine its cause. Possible causes include congenital obstructions, congenital absence of the uterus, testicular feminization, or absence or imbalance of hormones. Success of treatment depends on the causative factors. Many causes are not correctable.

Secondary amenorrhea is caused most frequently by pregnancy. Additional causes include lactation, hormonal imbalances, poor nutrition (anorexia nervosa, obesity, fad dieting), ovarian lesions, strenuous exercise (associated with long-distance runners with low body fat ratios), debilitating systemic diseases, stress of high intensity and/or long duration, stressful life events, a change in season or climate, use of oral contraceptives, the phenothiazine and chlorpromazine group of tranquilizers, and syndromes such as Cushing and Sheehan. Treatment is dictated by causative factors (Griffith-Kenney 1986). If the cause is related to such conditions the nurse can explain that once the underlying condition has been corrected—for example, when sufficient body weight is gained—menses will resume. Female athletes and women who participate in strenuous exercise routines may be advised to increase their caloric intake or reduce their exercise levels for a month or two to see whether a normal cycle ensues. If it does not, medical referral is indicated.

An abnormally short menstrual cycle is termed *hypomenorrhea;* an abnormally long one is called *hypermenorrhea.* Excessive, profuse flow is called *menorrhagia,* and bleeding between periods is known as *metrorrhagia.* Infrequent and too frequent menses are termed *oligomenorrhea* and *polymenorrhea,* respectively. An *anovulatory cycle* is one in which ovulation does not occur. Such irregularities should be investigated to rule out any disease process.

**Dysmenorrhea**, or painful menstruation, occurs at or a day before the onset of menstruation and disappears by the end of menses. Dysmenorrhea is classified as primary or secondary. *Primary* or *essential dysmenorrhea* usually appears within 12 months after menarche, occurs for the first one or two days of the menstrual flow, and has no pathologic cause. Dysmenorrhea does not occur if cycles are anovulatory. Nulliparous teens and women under 25 years of age experience it more often, and it usually disappears after the first pregnancy (Ganong 1985).

Hypercontractility of the uterus (as well as of the gastrointestinal tract) may result from excessive production of prostaglandins $F_2$ and $F_{2\alpha}$, which occurs following ovulation and peaks at menstruation. Dysmenorrhea usually corresponds to the secretory phase of the endometrium and indicates that ovulation has occurred. Treatment of physiologic primary dysmenorrhea includes hormonal therapy, such as low-dose oral contraceptives; nonsteroidal anti-inflammatory drugs or prostaglandin inhibitors such as ibuprofen; or cervical dilation. Biofeedback has also been used with some success.

Secondary dysmenorrhea is associated with pathology of the reproductive tract and usually appears after menstruation has been established. Conditions that most frequently cause secondary dysmenorrhea include endometriosis, residual pelvic inflammatory disease, and anatomic anomalies such as cervical stenosis, imperforate hymen, or uterine displacement (Fogel and Woods 1981). Because primary and secondary dysmenorrhea may coexist, accurate differential diagnosis is essential for appropriate treatment.

## PREMENSTRUAL SYNDROME

Progesterone withdrawal and a decreased progesterone-to-estrogen ratio with its resultant physiologic and metabolic changes in the late luteal/secretory phase may produce a cluster of symptoms known as **premenstrual syndrome (PMS).**

The syndrome has not yet been clearly defined as an entity by carefully designed studies, but it is real and has become part of the "menstrual mystique" for some women because of the recent publicity.

Women over 30 years of age are most likely to have PMS. Some or all of the following types of symptoms are often seen (Chihal 1982, Pariser et al 1985):

● *Psychologic:* irritability, lethargy, depression, low morale, anxiety, sleep disorders, crying spells, and hostility

● *Neurologic:* classic migraine, vertigo, syncope

● *Respiratory:* rhinitis, hoarseness, asthma

● *Gastrointestinal:* nausea, vomiting, constipation, abdominal bloating, craving for sweets

● *Urinary:* retention and oliguria

● *Dermatologic:* acne

● *Mammary:* swelling and tenderness

Most women do not experience all of these symptoms. The symptoms are most pronounced two or three days before the onset of menstruation and subside as menstrual flow begins, with or without treatment. It is less well known that some women experience feelings of heightened creativity, increased powers of concentration, and more productive mental and physical activity (Fogel and Woods 1981).

### Role of the Nurse

The nurse uses a self-care model to assist the woman in identifying specific symptoms and to support healthy behavior. After assessment, counseling for PMS may include advising the woman to avoid caffeine; restrict her intake of foods containing methylxanthines (eg, chocolate and coffee); restrict her intake of alcohol, nicotine, red meat, and foods containing salt and sugar; increase her intake of complex carbohydrates and protein; and increase the frequency of meals. Supplementation with B complex vitamins, especially $B_6$, and magnesium and zinc are also effective in some cases (Schaumburg 1984). Vitamin E supplementation to decrease food cravings has also been suggested. A balance between rest periods and a program of aerobic exercises such as fast walking, jogging, and aerobic dancing is suggested.

Two widely prescribed pharmaceutical treatments for PMS are progesterone supplementation by means of vaginal or rectal suppositories and spironolactone orally, but these treatments are under dispute (Griffith-Kenney 1986). Other drugs that may be advocated depending on symptomatology include prostaglandin inhibitors, psychoactive drugs, diuretics, and bromocriptine for treatment of breast discomfort (Pariser et al 1985).

An empathetic relationship with a health care professional to whom the woman feels free to voice concerns is highly beneficial. Encouragement to keep a diary may help the woman identify life events associated with PMS. Self-care groups and self-help literature both help women gain control over their bodies (Figure 3.1).

## ● HUMAN SEXUALITY

## ● Development of Sexuality

The stimuli, experiences, and relationships that are essential to the development of sexuality come into play at birth. The infant learns to find satisfaction through oral stimuli, through contact with another, and through cuddling and holding. Young infants learn to touch and stroke their genitals and seem to be capable of sexual arousal.

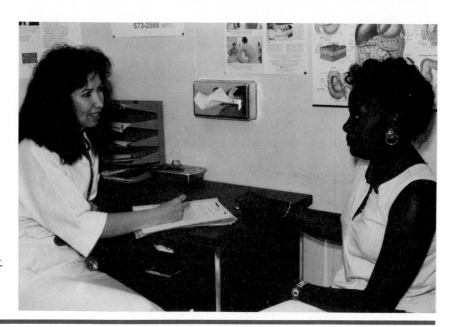

*Figure 3.1 A knowledgeable and caring nurse can help a woman identify effective self-help measures for dealing with symptoms of PMS.*

Toddlers facing toilet training become even more aware of their bodies and may more consciously practice masturbation although their parents often discourage it. By age 3 most children are aware of their sexual identity as a result of consistent parental and social reinforcement. During the childhood years, from 5 through 12, sexual activity and interest may be less apparent but it has not disappeared. Children show a preference for playmates of the same sex, although they may also show some romantic interest in members of the opposite sex.

Puberty and adolescence are a time of transition from childhood to adulthood. Adolescence finds sexually mature young people trying to cope with new situations and sensations while they are still psychologically immature. Sexual experimentation begins, and masturbation accompanied by fantasy is common. Homosexual experiences may occur, and mutual masturbation for boys is not uncommon. Heterosexual contacts progress over four or five years from initial kissing and fondling, to mutual body exploration and masturbation, to sexual intercourse.

With adulthood comes increased responsibility and choice. Because sexual expression in marriage has the most legitimacy in our society, many adults choose to marry. However, new life-styles, changing morality, and contraceptive choices have made available other situations in which sexuality can be expressed.

Attitudes about sex are influenced by a variety of factors. The home environment is one of the greatest influences. Children raised by parents who are comfortable with and open about sexuality will probably be more comfortable with their sexuality than children raised in more restrictive environments. Even if parents are not openly demonstrative, they can convey to children that sexuality is a natural, acceptable, and satisfying part of life by creating a positive home atmosphere.

Cultural background can profoundly influence the home and environment and thereby have a major impact on the child's socialization. Individuals raised in a male-dominated or strongly moralistic culture will usually have very different attitudes from those of individuals raised in a culture that views sexual expression as a shared experience between equals. People can reject cultural norms as adults, but doing so is often difficult and may cause stress. Thiederman (1986) describes the difficulties experienced by Indian and Pakistani women who have emigrated to Great Britain. Pressure from those trying to "educate" them about the value of self-reliance and independence has caused stress, anxiety, and emotional problems for these women.

Attitudes about sex are also influenced by education and socioeconomic level. People with more income and education tend to be more comfortable with a wider variety of sexual activities. Sexual attitudes can be profoundly affected by previous sexual experiences, especially very intense experiences such as incest, rape, or severe punishment for sexual experimentation.

The personal characteristics of the individual are also influential in the development of sexual attitudes. Although it is difficult to negate the influence of environment, people are born with different personality characteristics: some are shy, others more adventuresome, and so forth. Variations in sex drive or libido also significantly influence an individual's view of sexuality.

## ● Sexual Intercourse

Many terms are used to describe the mating of a sexually mature male and female, including coitus, sexual intercourse, copulation, making love, and the sex act. Coitus is defined as the insertion of the erect penis into the vagina.

After repeated thrusting movements of the penis, the man experiences ejaculation of semen concurrent with orgasm. **Orgasm** is the involuntary climax of the sexual experience, involving a series of muscular contractions, profound physiologic bodily response, and intense sensual pleasure. Orgasm may be achieved by other methods of sexual stimulation besides sexual intercourse, such as masturbation and oral stimulation.

Although the basic events of coitus are the same for all couples, wide variation exists in sexual positions, technique, duration, intent, meaning, and reactions among individuals.

## PSYCHOSOCIAL ASPECTS

Coitus is a personal act between two consenting individuals. It can signify a variety of feelings, beliefs, and attitudes.

The traditional purpose of coitus is procreation. However, with the availability of contraceptive methods and with changing social mores, sexual intercourse has become accepted as a pleasurable and personally gratifying experience in itself. The sexual union of two individuals may reflect their mutual commitment and caring, or it may be a more immediate interaction for the purpose of personal pleasure or merely temporary companionship. In our society, sexual intercourse ideally is the sharing by two persons of their emotions and bodies in the context of the larger sharing of their lives. Such sexual interactions are the result of mutual caring and love.

## PHYSIOLOGY OF SEXUAL RESPONSE

Masters and Johnson (1966) have identified and described the physiology of the sexual response in both females and males. All the responses can be classified as either vasocongestive or myotonic. *Vasocongestion* involves the congestion or engorgement of blood vessels and is the most common physiologic response to sexual arousal. *Myotonia*, a secondary physiologic response, is increased muscular tonus, which produces tension.

Sexual response occurs in four phases: excitement, plateau, orgasm, and resolution. Essentially, the sexual response of males and females is the same, involves the total body, and is continuous. Individual variations do occur.

The male physical response is relatively constant, resulting in orgasm if erection and sexual stimulation are maintained. Female sexual response varies considerably. Not all women experience orgasm consistently; they are influenced by their psychologic state, health, current sexual motivation, and environmental distractions. A woman may not experience orgasm during a particular act of coitus, or she may experience one or multiple orgasms of varying intensity. Such variation is usual in a woman of "normal" sexual activity, interest, and response.

Women and men exhibit several identical responses. The *sex flush* is a maculopapular rash that usually begins in the epigastric area and spreads quickly to the breasts. More than half of women experience sex flush, whereas less than half of men do. Heart rate and blood pressure increase in proportion to the degree of sexual excitement. Muscles tense beginning in the excitement phase. This tension increases during the plateau phase. Hyperventilation occurs just before and during orgasm. At orgasm, muscle tension is extreme. The face may contort, while muscles of the neck, extremities, abdomen, and buttocks contract tightly. Individuals may moan, murmur, or cry out and will experience a total surrender to bodily responses, accompanied by acute pleasure and relief.

## ● The Role of the Nurse

On occasion most people experience concern and even anxiety about some aspect of sexuality. Societal standards and pressures can cause people to evaluate and compare with others their sexual attractiveness, technical abilities, frequency of sexual interaction, and so on. Appearance and sexual behavior are not the only causes for concern; the reproductive implications of sexual intercourse must also be considered. Some people desire conception; others wish to avoid it at all costs. Health factors are another consideration. The increase in the incidence of sexually transmitted diseases (STDs), especially AIDS and herpes, has caused many people to modify their sexual practices and activities.

Because sexuality and its reproductive implications are such an intrinsic and emotion-laden part of life, people have many concerns, problems, and questions about sex roles, sexual behaviors, sex education, family planning, sexual inhibitions, sexual morality, and related areas. Women frequently voice these concerns to the nurse, who may need to assume the role of counselor on sexual and reproductive matters.

Nurses who assume this role must be secure about their own sexuality. They also need to know about the structures and functions of female and male reproductive systems.

Continuing education for the practicing nurse and appropriate courses in undergraduate and graduate nursing education programs may help nurses achieve this sense of self-security and the knowledge about aspects of sexuality. These courses can teach nurses about sexual values, attitudes, alternative life-styles, cultural factors, and misconceptions and myths about sex and reproduction.

Nurses today are often responsible for taking a woman's initial history. To be effective, the nurse must have good communication skills. Opening the discussion with a brief explanation of the purpose of such questions is often helpful. For example the nurse might say, "As your nurse I'm interested in all aspects of your well-being. Often women have concerns or questions about sexual matters, especially when they are pregnant (or starting to be sexually active). I will be asking you some questions about your sexual history as part of your general health history."

In addition, the nurse may find it helpful to use direct eye contact as much as possible and avoid writing during the interview. Open-ended questions are often useful in eliciting information. For example, "What, if anything, would you change about your sex life?" will elicit more information than "Are you happy with your sex life now?" The nurse should also clarify terminology and proceed from easier topics to those that are more difficult to discuss. Throughout the interview the nurse should be alert to body language and nonverbal cues.

After completing the sexual history, the nurse assesses the information obtained. If the nurse identifies a problem that requires further medical tests and assessments, he or she will refer the woman to a nurse practitioner, nurse-midwife, physician, or counselor as necessary. In many instances the nurse alone will be able to develop a nursing diagnosis and then plan and implement therapy. For example, if the nurse determines that a woman who is interested in conceiving a child does not have a clear understanding of when she ovulates, the nurse may formulate the nursing diagnosis: Knowledge deficit related to the timing of ovulation. The nurse could then evaluate the woman's knowledge through discussion and review and work with the woman to provide necessary knowledge. The nurse might also suggest that the woman keep a menstrual calendar and monitor basal body temperatures to identify the time of ovulation.

The nurse must be realistic in making assessments and planning interventions. It requires insight and skill to recognize when a woman's problem requires interventions that are beyond a nurse's preparation and ability. In such situations, appropriate referrals should be made.

## ● REPRODUCTIVE CHOICES

The decision to become sexually active marks a major turning point in a young woman's life. Some women choose to remain celibate until marriage; others become sexually active while single. In either case, if the teaching provided by the health care system has been effective, a woman will be knowledgeable about sexual activity, the risk of sexually transmitted diseases and ways of avoiding them, the possibility of pregnancy, and contraceptive options that are appropriate for her. Thus she can act as an informed consumer able to make the choices that are best for her.

### ● Preconception Counseling

Couples who choose to become pregnant generally want to do all they can to ensure that the child they have will be healthy. Consequently, they may seek advice about

actions they can take to achieve a successful outcome. Preconception counseling, often done by the nurse, should include information about:

*Preconception health measures.* The couple should avoid known or suspected health risks including alcohol. The woman is advised to cease smoking if possible or to limit her cigarette intake to less than half a pack per day. Because of the hazards of "second-hand smoke" it is helpful if her partner refrains from smoking around her. Since the effects of caffeine are less clearly understood, the woman is advised to avoid caffeine or limit her intake. Social and street drugs pose a real threat to the fetus and should be avoided. A woman who uses any prescription or over-the-counter medications should discuss the implications of their use with her health care provider. It is best to avoid the use of any medication when possible. Because of the possible teratogenic effects of environmental hazards in the workplace, the couple contemplating pregnancy should carefully determine whether they are exposed to any environmental hazards at work or in their community.

*Physical examination.* It is advisable for both partners to have a physical examination to identify any health problems so that they can be corrected if possible. If the couple is planning pregnancy when the woman is over age 35, the health care provider may suggest that the couple consider genetic counseling (see Chapter 4). Prior to conception the woman is also advised to have a dental examination and any necessary dental work.

*Nutrition.* Prior to conception it is advisable for the woman to be at a suitable weight for her body build and height. She should follow a nutritious diet that contains ample quantities of all the essential nutrients. Some nutritionists advocate emphasizing the following nutrients: calcium, protein, iron, B complex vitamins, vitamin C, folic acid, and magnesium.

*Exercise.* A woman should establish a regular exercise plan beginning at least three months before she plans to attempt to become pregnant. The exercise chosen should be one she enjoys and will continue. It should provide some aerobic conditioning and some general toning. Exercise improves the woman's circulation and general health and tones her muscles. Once an exercise program is well-established, the woman is generally encouraged to continue it during pregnancy. For a discussion of exercise during pregnancy see Chapter 8.

*Contraception.* Women who wish to conceive and who take birth control pills are advised to stop the pill two to three months before attempting to get pregnant. Women with intrauterine devices (IUDs) are advised to have them removed three months before attempting to conceive. During the three months, barrier methods of contraception (condom or diaphragm) are acceptable. Currently some clinicians are questioning the necessity of delaying pregnancy after discontinuing the pill or IUD. They suggest that if pregnancy occurs before the woman has a menstrual period, the gestation of the pregnancy can be determined with ultrasound.

*Conception.* Conception is a personal experience, and even if a couple is prepared they may feel some ambivalence about pregnancy. This is a normal response, but they may require reassurance that the ambivalence will pass. A couple may get so caught up in preparation and in their efforts to "do things right" that they lose sight of the pleasure they derive from each other and their lives together, and cease to value the joy of spontaneity in their relationship. It is often helpful for the health care provider to offer support and counseling for couples who seem to be very intent on achieving pregnancy.

## ● Contraception

The decision to use a method of contraception may be made individually by a woman (or, in the case of vasectomy, by a man) or it may be a decision made jointly by a couple. The decision may be motivated by a desire to avoid pregnancy, to gain control over the number of children conceived, or to determine the spacing of future children. In choosing a specific method, consistency of use outweighs the absolute reliability of the given method.

Decisions about contraception should be made voluntarily, with full knowledge of advantages, disadvantages, effectiveness, side effects, contraindications, and long-term effects. Many outside factors influence this choice, including cultural influences, religious beliefs, personality, cost, effectiveness, misinformation, practicality of method, and self-esteem. Different methods of contraception may be appropriate at different times in a couple's life.

### METHODS OF CONTRACEPTION
### Fertility Awareness Methods

**Fertility awareness methods,** also referred to as natural family planning, are based on an understanding of the changes that occur throughout a woman's ovulatory cycle. All these methods require periods of abstinence and recording of certain events throughout the cycle; hence, cooperation of the partner is important.

Advantages of fertility awareness methods include the following: the methods are free, safe, acceptable to many whose religious beliefs prohibit other methods, provide an increased awareness of the body, involve no artificial substances or devices, encourage a couple to communicate about sexual activity and family planning, and are also useful in helping a couple plan a pregnancy.

Disadvantages include the following: they require extensive initial counseling to use effectively; they may interfere with sexual spontaneity; they require extensive maintenance of records for several cycles prior to beginning to use them; they may be difficult or impossible for women with irregular cycles to use; and, although theoretically they should be very reliable, in actual practice they may not be as reliable in preventing pregnancy as other methods.

The *basal body temperature (BBT) method* to detect ovulation requires that a woman take her BBT every morning and record the readings on a temperature graph. After three to four months of recording temperatures, the woman with regular cycles should be able to predict when ovulation will occur. The method is based on the fact that the temperature sometimes drops just prior to ovulation and almost always rises and remains elevated for several days after. The temperature rise occurs in response to the increased progesterone levels that occur in the second half of the cycle. Figure 3.2 shows a sample BBT chart. To avoid conception, intercourse is avoided on the day of the temperature rise and for three days after. Because the temperature rise does not occur until after ovulation, a woman who had intercourse just prior to the rise is at risk of pregnancy. To decrease this risk, some couples abstain from intercourse for several days before the *anticipated* time of ovulation and then for three days after.

The *calendar method,* also referred to as the rhythm method, is based on the assumptions that ovulation tends to occur 14 days (plus or minus two days) before the start of the next menstrual period, sperm are viable for 48 to 72 hours, and the ovum is viable for 24 hours (Hatcher et al 1988). To use this method the woman must record her menstrual cycles for six to eight months, so that the shortest and longest cycles can be identified. The first day of menstruation is the first day of the cycle. The fertile phase is calculated from 18 days before the end of the shortest recorded cycle through 11 days from the end of the longest recorded cycle (Hatcher et al 1988). For example, if a woman's cycle lasts from 24 to 28 days, the fertile phase would be calculated as day 6 through day 17. Once this information is obtained, the woman can identify the fertile and infertile phases of her cycle. For effective use of this method, she must abstain from intercourse during the fertile phase.

The calendar method is the least reliable of the fertility awareness methods and has largely been replaced by the other, more scientific approaches.

The *cervical mucus method,* sometimes called the *ovulation method* or the *Billings method,* involves the assessment of cervical mucus changes that occur during the

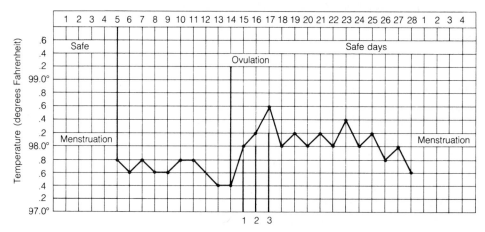

*Figure 3.2    Sample basal body temperature chart (Reprinted with permission from Crooks R, Baur K:* Our Sexuality, *4th ed. Redwood City, CA: Benjamin/Cummings, 1990.)*

menstrual cycle. The amount and character of cervical mucus change as a result of the influence of estrogen and progesterone. At the time of ovulation the mucus (type E) is clearer, more stretchable (spinnbarkeit), and more permeable to sperm. It also shows a characteristic fern pattern when placed on a glass slide and allowed to dry.

During the luteal phase the cervical mucus is thick and sticky (type G mucus) and forms a network that traps sperm, making their passage more difficult.

To use the ovulation method, the woman abstains from intercourse for the first menstrual cycle. Cervical mucus is assessed daily for amount, feeling of slipperiness or wetness, color, clearness, and spinnbarkeit as the woman becomes familiar with varying characteristics.

The peak day of wetness and clear stretchable mucus is assumed to be the time of ovulation. To use this method correctly, a woman is advised to abstain from intercourse when she first notices that the mucus is becoming clear, more elastic, and slippery, until four days after the last wet mucus (ovulation) day. Because this method evaluates the effects of hormonal changes, it can be used by women with irregular cycles.

The *symptothermal method* consists of various assessments that are made and recorded by the couple. This includes information regarding cycle days, coitus, cervical mucus changes, and secondary signs such as increased libido, abdominal bloating, mittelschmerz, and basal body temperature. Through the various assessments, the couple learns to recognize signs that indicate ovulation. This combined approach tends to improve the effectiveness of fertility awareness as a method of birth control.

### Situational Contraceptive Methods

**Situational contraceptive methods** also fall under the heading of natural family planning. These methods in-

volve no prior preparation by the couple but involve motivation to abstain from intercourse or to interrupt the sexual act.

**Coitus interruptus,** or withdrawal, is the oldest method of contraception. This method requires that the male partner withdraw from the female's vagina when he feels that ejaculation is impending. He then ejaculates away from the external genitalia of the woman. The method is available in any situation and requires no medication or devices; however, because of its high failure rate it is not recommended as a method of contraception. Failure tends to occur for two reasons: First, this method demands great self-control on the part of the man, who must withdraw just as he feels the urge for deeper penetration with impending orgasm. Second, some preejaculatory fluid, which can contain sperm, may escape from the penis during the excitement phase prior to ejaculation. Because the quantity of sperm in this preejaculatory fluid is increased after a recent ejaculation, this is especially significant for couples who engage in repeated episodes of orgasm within a short period of time.

*Abstinence* can also be considered a situational contraceptive and, because of changing values and the increased risk of infection with intercourse, is gaining increased acceptance as a viable alternative to intercourse.

### Mechanical Contraceptives

Mechanical contraceptive methods act either as barriers preventing the transport of sperm to the ovum or prevent implantation of the ovum/zygote. **Condoms** offer a viable means of contraception when used consistently and properly (Figure 3.3). Acceptance has been increasing as a growing number of men are assuming responsibility for regulation of fertility. The condom is applied to the erect penis, rolled from the tip to the end of the shaft, be-

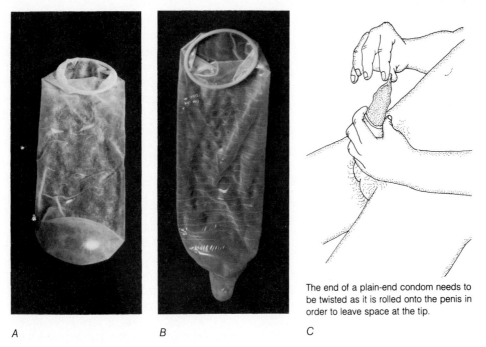

The end of a plain-end condom needs to be twisted as it is rolled onto the penis in order to leave space at the tip.

A        B        C

*Figure 3.3   Condoms: (A) Unrolled condom with plain end. (B) Unrolled condom with reservoir tip. (C) Correct use of a plain-end condom. (Reprinted with permission from Crooks R, Baur K:* Our Sexuality, *4th ed. Redwood City, CA: Benjamin/Cummings, 1990.)*

fore vulvar or vaginal contact. A small space must be left at the end of the condom to allow for collection of the ejaculate so that the condom will not break at the time of ejaculation. Vaginal jelly should be used if the condom or vagina is dry to prevent irritation and possible condom breakage. Care must be taken in removing the condom after intercourse. For optimum effectiveness, the penis should be withdrawn from the vagina while still erect and the condom rim held to prevent spillage. If after ejaculation the penis becomes flaccid while still in the vagina, the male should hold onto the edge of the condom while withdrawing to avoid spilling the semen and to prevent the condom from slipping off.

The effectiveness of condoms is largely determined by their use. The condom is small, lightweight, disposable, and inexpensive; has no side effects; requires no medical examination or supervision; offers visual evidence of effectiveness and protects against sexually transmitted diseases. Breakage, displacement, possible perineal or vaginal irritation, and dulled sensation are possible disadvantages.

The condom is becoming increasingly popular because of the protection latex condoms offer from AIDS and other sexually transmitted diseases. For women, infection with a sexually transmitted disease increases the risk of pelvic inflammatory disease and resultant infertility. Spurred on by the problem of AIDS, Surgeon General C. Everett Koop has advocated public education programs about the use of condoms. In addition, women are beginning to insist that their sexual partners use condoms and many women carry condoms with them. In fact, some manufacturers report that women are now buying 40% of all condoms (Connell 1988).

With their increasing popularity comes increased choice. Condoms are now available with ribbed sides or smooth sides, tapered or straight-sided, lubricated or unlubricated, with spermicide and without. Condoms called "skin condoms" made from lamb's intestines are also available and are preferred by some men, especially those who have difficulty tolerating latex. They are not considered as effective as latex condoms in preventing the spread of infection.

Currently a condom for women, the WPC-333, is being tested. This condom sheath fits in the vagina and has two rings: one stabilizes it in the vagina; the other remains outside the vagina. The manufacturer suggests that because the outer ring protects the labia and the base of the penis, it offers more protection from STDs than the male condom (Connell 1988).

The **diaphragm** (Figure 3.4) offers a good level of protection from conception, especially when used with spermicidal creams or jellies. The woman must be fitted with a diaphragm and instructions given by trained personnel. The diaphragm should be rechecked for correct size after each childbirth and if a woman has gained or lost 15 pounds or more.

The diaphragm must be inserted prior to intercourse, with approximately one teaspoonful (or 1½ inches from the tube) of spermicidal jelly placed around its rim and

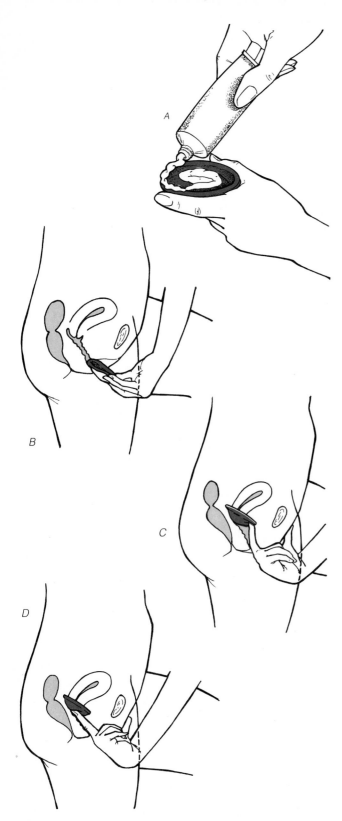

*Figure 3.4 (A) Diaphragm and jelly. Jelly is applied to the rim and center of the diaphragm. (B) Insertion of the diaphragm. (C) Rim of diaphragm is pushed under the symphysis pubis. (D) Checking placement of the diaphragm. Cervix should be felt through the diaphragm.*

in the cup. This serves as a chemical barrier to supplement the mechanical barrier of the diaphragm. The diaphragm is inserted through the vagina and covers the cervix. The last step in insertion is to push the edge of the diaphragm under the symphysis pubis, which may result in a "popping" sensation. When fitted properly and correctly in place, the diaphragm should not cause discomfort to the woman or her partner. Correct placement of the diaphragm can be checked by touching the cervix with a fingertip through the cup. The cervix feels like a small rounded structure and has a consistency similar to that of the tip of the nose. The center of the diaphragm should be over the cervix. If more than four hours elapse between insertion of the diaphragm and intercourse, additional spermicidal cream should be used. It is necessary to leave the diaphragm in place for six hours after coitus. If intercourse is desired again within the six hours, another type of contraception must be used or additional spermicidal jelly placed in the vagina with an applicator, taking care not to disturb the placement of the diaphragm. The diaphragm should be periodically held up to the light and inspected for tears or holes.

Some couples feel that the use of a diaphragm interferes with the spontaneity of intercourse. The nurse can suggest that the partner insert the diaphragm as part of foreplay.

Diaphragms are an excellent contraceptive method for women who are lactating, who cannot or do not wish to use the pill (oral contraceptives), or who wish to avoid the increased risk of pelvic inflammatory disease associated with intrauterine devices. They are also a good choice for older women who smoke but don't wish to be sterilized.

Women who object to manipulating their genitals to insert the diaphragm, check its placement, and remove it may find this method unsatisfactory. It is not recommended for women with a history of urinary tract infection because pressure from the diaphragm on the urethra may interfere with complete bladder emptying and lead to recurrent urinary tract infections (UTIs). Women with a history of toxic shock syndrome should not use diaphragms or any of the barrier methods because they are left in place for prolonged periods. For the same reason the diaphragm should not be used during a menstrual period.

The **cervical cap** is a cup-shaped device that fits over the cervix and stays in place by suction (Figure 3.5). The degree of suction depends on the tightness of fit between the cap and the cervix. Since the cap can be worn for extended periods (the manufacturer suggests up to three days), it offers a couple more spontaneity in their sexual activities. However, because of the risk of toxic shock syndrome associated with barrier methods and the tendency for odor to develop with prolonged wearing, the woman should be advised to limit wear to no longer than 24 hours (Hatcher et al 1988).

Since pregnancies have occurred without cup dis-

*Figure 3.5  Cervical caps (Reprinted with permission from Crooks R, Baur K: Our Sexuality, 4th ed. Redwood City, CA: Benjamin/Cummings, 1990.)*

placement, spermicidal jelly should be used in the cup. The cup does have disadvantages. The only cup currently approved for use in the United States—the Prentiff Cavity Rim—is only available in four sizes, so fitting may be difficult. (Other brands are available in Europe and may soon be approved for use in the U.S.) The cap is also more difficult for women to insert and remove (Connell 1988).

**Intracervical devices** made of either plastic or metal are under current investigation. Expulsion rates of current models are unacceptable, but new models offer promise.

The **contraceptive sponge,** available without a prescription, is a small pillow-shaped polyurethane sponge with a concave cupped area on one side designed to fit over the cervix. The sponge currently available, the Today Vaginal Contraceptive Sponge, contains spermicide. The sponge is moistened with water prior to use and inserted into the vagina so that the cupped area fits snugly over the cervical os (Figure 3.6). This decreases the chances of the sponge being dislodged during intercourse. The sponge may be worn for up to 24 hours. It should be left in place for six hours after intercourse. It is then discarded.

Advantages of the sponge are: professional fitting is not required; it may be used for multiple acts of coitus up to 24 hours; one size fits all; and it is both barrier and spermicide. Although data are limited, the sponge may provide some protection against chlamydia and gonorrhea. Problems associated with the sponge include difficulty removing the sponge, cost (approximately one dollar and fifty cents per sponge), and irritation or allergic reactions. Some women also report that vaginal dryness is sometimes a problem because the sponge absorbs vaginal se-

cretions. Women with a history of toxic shock syndrome should not use vaginal sponges (Hatcher et al 1988).

**Intrauterine devices** (IUDs) work primarily by producing a local sterile inflammatory reaction in the uterus. Consequently, even if fertilization occurs, implantation is inhibited.

Advantages include convenience, no coitus-related activity, and long duration of effectiveness. Possible adverse

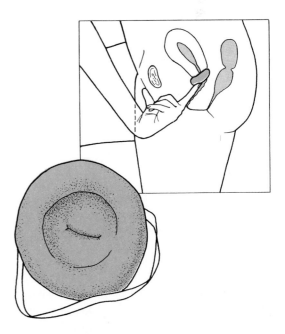

*Figure 3.6  Contraceptive sponge is moistened with water and inserted into the vagina with concave portion over the cervix.*

*Figure 3.7    The Progestasert T IUD (Reprinted with permission from Crooks R, Baur K:* Our Sexuality, *4th ed. Redwood City, CA: Benjamin/Cummings, 1990.)*

reactions to the IUD include discomfort to the wearer, increased bleeding during menses, pelvic inflammatory disease, perforation of the uterus, intermenstrual bleeding, dysmenorrhea, expulsion of the device, and ectopic pregnancy.

Because of numerous lawsuits major manufacturers have withdrawn their IUDs from the market. Only two IUDs are currently available—the Progestasert (Figure 3.7), which must be changed annually, and the Copper T380A (the ParaGard), a new IUD that was introduced in 1988 and is changed every four years. The new IUD is recommended only for women who have at least one child and are in a monogamous relationship, because they have the lowest risk of developing a pelvic infection. It is not recommended for women with multiple sexual contacts because they are at risk for STDs (Tatum 1988).

The IUD is inserted into the uterus with its string or tail protruding through the cervix into the vagina. It may be inserted during a menstrual period or during the four- to six-week postpartum check. After insertion, the woman should be instructed to check for the presence of the string once a week for the first month and then after each menses. She is told that she may have some cramping and/or bleeding intermittently for two to six weeks and that her first few menses may be irregular. Follow-up examination is suggested four to eight weeks after insertion.

## Oral Contraceptives

The use of hormones, specifically the combination of estrogen and progesterone, is a very successful birth control method. **Oral contraceptives** work by inhibiting the release of an ovum and by maintaining type G mucus, which is hostile to sperm. Numerous oral contraceptives are available. The "pill" is taken daily for 21 days beginning on the Sunday after the first day of the menstrual cycle. In most cases menses will occur one to four days after the last pill is taken. Seven days after completing her last pill, the woman restarts the pill. Thus the woman always begins the pill on the same day. Some companies offer a 28-day pack with seven "blank" pills so that the woman never stops taking a pill. The pill should be taken at approximately the same time each day—usually upon arising or before retiring in the evening.

Although highly effective, oral contraceptives may produce side effects ranging from break-through bleeding to thrombus formation. The majority of the side effects are related to the dosage. The use of low-dose (35 $\mu$g or less estrogen) preparations has reduced many of the side effects, but the threat of potential risk still deters some women from using oral contraceptives.

Contraindications to the use of oral contraceptives include pregnancy, previous history of thrombophlebitis or thromboembolic disease, acute or chronic liver disease of cholestatic type with abnormal function, presence of estrogen-dependent carcinomas, undiagnosed uterine bleeding, heavy smoking, hypertension, diabetes, pregnancy-induced hypertension (PIH), age over 40, lack of regular menstrual cycles for at least one to two years in adolescents, and hyperlipoproteinemia. In addition, women with the following conditions who use oral contraceptives should be examined every three months: migraine headaches, epilepsy, depression, oligomenorrhea, and amenorrhea. Women who choose this method of contraception should be fully advised of potential side effects. See Table 3.1 for side effects of oral contraceptives.

Following birth a nonnursing mother may begin taking oral contraceptives three to four weeks postpartum. This reduces the risk of thromboembolism associated with estrogen use in the early postpartal period. Mothers who have received bromocriptine to suppress lactation should start by the 14th day after birth because ovulation may occur earlier for them.

Because estrogen suppresses lactation and will cross into the breast milk, birth control pills are not the contraceptive of choice for nursing mothers. However, in 1981 the American Academy of Pediatrics issued a policy statement supporting the use of oral contraceptives for breast-feeding women after lactation is well established. Low-dose pills have been used by many women without apparent adverse effects on the infant or quantity of milk (Hatcher et al 1988).

A once-a-month oral contraceptive (RU486) that binds to progesterone receptors in the endometrium and blocks the action of progesterone is in early clinical trials.

Depomedroxyprogesterone acetate (Depo-Provera), an injectable progestin contraceptive approved for use in more than 80 countries around the world, is the most effective form of reversible contraception currently available (Rosenfeld 1985). The drug is given as an injection once every three months. The Food and Drug Administration (FDA) approved its use for women who could not use other forms of contraception but, after pressure from consumer groups, withdrew its approval pending further review. Major concerns involve reversibility and safety.

Women may take longer to conceive after using Depo-Provera, and breast cancer has been found in laboratory animals given the drug.

*Steroid implants* are biodegradable rods or microcapsules containing a sustained-release, low-dose progesterone. If they are approved for use, the safety of the currently available injectable forms of contraception will be a moot question. The drugs inhibit secretion of gonadotropins, including midcycle luteinizing hormone (LH) release.

### Spermicides

A variety of creams, jellies, foams, vaginal film, and suppositories, inserted into the vagina prior to intercourse, destroy sperm or neutralize vaginal secretions and thereby immobilize sperm. **Spermicides** that effervesce in a moist environment offer more rapid protection and coitus may take place immediately after they are inserted. Suppositories may require up to 30 minutes to dissolve and will *not* offer protection until they do so. The woman should be instructed to insert these spermicide preparations high in the vagina and maintain a supine position.

Spermicides are minimally effective when used alone, but their effectiveness increases in conjunction with a diaphragm or condom. They provide a high degree of protection from exposure to gonorrhea, and are also useful against chlamydia, trichomonas, and herpes organisms (Hatcher et al 1988). While some studies suggest that the use of spermicides at the time of conception or early in pregnancy may be associated with an increased risk of congenital anomalies, most researchers disagree (Digest 1988, Hatcher et al 1988). Further research is being done on the issue.

### Operative Sterilization

Before sterilization is performed on either partner, a thorough explanation of the procedure should be given to both. Each should understand that sterilization is not a decision to be taken lightly or entered into when psychologic stresses, such as separation or divorce, exist. Even though both male and female procedures are theoretically reversible, the permanency of the procedure should be stressed and understood.

Male sterilization is achieved through a relatively minor procedure called a **vasectomy.** This involves severing of the vas deferens in both sides of the scrotum. It takes about four to six weeks and 6 to 36 ejaculations to clear remaining sperm from the vas deferens. During that period, the couple is advised to use another method of birth control and to bring in two or three sperm samples for a sperm count. The man is rechecked at 6 and 12 months to ensure that fertility has not been restored by recanalization. Side effects of a vasectomy include pain, infection, hematoma, sperm granulomas, and spontaneous reanastomosis.

Vasectomy reversal resulting in pregnancy is possible in 29% to 85% of men and depends on the length of vas deferens removed, the use of coagulation methods during surgery, the length of time since the procedure, and the presence of sperm antibodies (Hatcher et al 1988).

Female sterilization is most frequently accomplished by **tubal ligation.** The tubes are located through a small subumbilical incision or by minilaparotomy techniques and are crushed, ligated, or plugged (in the newer, reversible procedures).

The postpartal period is an ideal time to perform a tubal ligation because the tubes are somewhat enlarged and easily located. Usually the woman remains in the hospital one extra day. Many hospitals require that the consent for tubal ligation be completed prior to admission for birth to avoid hasty, later-regretted decisions.

Complications of female sterilization procedures include coagulation burns on the bowel, bowel perforation, infection, hemorrhage, and adverse anesthesia effects. Reversal of a tubal ligation depends on many factors, including the portion of the tube excised, the presence or absence of the fimbriae, and the length of the tube remaining. With microsurgical techniques, a pregnancy rate of approximately 40% to 75% is possible (Hatcher et al 1988).

| Table 3.1 Side Effects of Oral Contraceptives | |
| --- | --- |
| **Estrogen component** | **Progestin component** |
| Altered carbohydrate metabolism | Acne |
| Altered clotting factors—thrombophlebitis | Amenorrhea |
| Altered convulsive threshold | Anabolic weight gain |
| Altered lipid metabolism | Breast regression |
| Breast tenderness or engorgement | Depression and altered libido |
| Chloasma | Fatigue |
| Edema and cyclic weight gain | Hirsutism |
| Excessive menstrual flow | Increased appetite |
| Headache | Loss of hair |
| Hypertension | Moniliasis |
| Irritability, nervousness | Oligomenorrhea |
| Leukorrhea, cervical erosion, or polyposis | |
| Nausea, bloating | |
| Venous or capillary engorgement (spider nevi) | |

## Table 3.2  Factors to Consider in Choosing a Method of Contraception

Effectiveness of method in preventing pregnancy

Safety of the method:
  Are there inherent risks?
  Does it offer protection against STDs or other conditions?

Client's age and future childbearing plans

Any contraindications in client's health history

Religious or moral factors influencing choice

Personal preferences, biases, etc

Life-style:
  How frequently does client have intercourse?
  Does she have multiple partners?
  Does she have ready access to medical care in the event of complications?
  Is cost a factor?

Partner's support and willingness to cooperate

Personal motivation to use method

### THE ROLE OF THE NURSE

In most cases the nurse who provides information and guidance about contraceptive methods works with a woman because most contraceptive methods are female oriented. Since a man can purchase condoms without seeing a health care provider, only in the case of vasectomy does a man require counseling and interaction with a nurse. The nurse can play an important role in helping a woman choose a method of contraception that is acceptable to her and to her partner.

In addition to completing a history and assessing for any contraindications to specific methods, the nurse can spend time with a woman learning about her life-style, personal attitudes about particular contraceptive methods, religious beliefs, personal biases, and plans for future child-bearing before helping the woman select a particular contraceptive method. Once the method is chosen the nurse can help the woman learn to use it effectively. Table 3.2 summarizes factors to consider while helping a woman or couple choose an appropriate method of contraception.

The nurse also reviews any possible side effects and warning signs of the method chosen and counsels the woman about what action to take if she suspects she is pregnant. In many cases the nurse may become involved in telephone counseling of women who call with questions and concerns about contraception. Thus, it is vital that the nurse be knowledgeable about this topic and have resources available to find answers to less common questions.

The Teaching Guide—Using a Method of Contracep-tion—provides guidelines for helping women use a method of contraception effectively.

### ● Surgical Interruption of Pregnancy

Although abortion was legalized in the United States in 1973, the controversy over moral and legal issues associated with it continues. This controversy is as readily apparent in the medical and nursing professions as among other groups.

A number of physical and psychosocial factors influence a woman's decision to seek an abortion. The presence of a disease or health state that jeopardizes the mother's life and serious, life-threatening fetal problems are frequently suggested as indications for abortion. In other instances, the timing or circumstance of the pregnancy creates an inordinate stress on the woman and she chooses an abortion. Some of these situations may involve contraceptive failure, rape, or incest. In all cases, the decision is best made by the woman or couple involved. A mother whose life is threatened by the pregnancy may choose to continue the pregnancy, while one with no obvious threat may choose abortion. Many feel this is as it should be because the decision must rest with the individuals who bear the impact of the continuance or termination of the pregnancy.

Abortion in the first trimester is technically easier and safer than abortion in the second trimester. It may be performed by dilatation and curettage (D & C), minisuction, or vacuum curettage. The major risks include perforation of the uterus, laceration of the cervix, systemic reaction to the anesthetic agent, and hemorrhage (Gabbe et al 1986). Second trimester abortion may be done using dilatation and extraction (D & E), hypertonic saline, systemic prostaglandins, and intrauterine prostaglandins.

Important aspects of nursing care include: provision of information about the methods of abortion and associated risks; counseling regarding available alternatives and their possible problems; allowance for verbalization by the woman; support before, during, and after the procedure; monitoring of vital signs, intake, and output; providing for physical comfort and privacy throughout the procedure; and health teaching regarding self-care, the importance of the postabortion checkup, and contraception review.

### ● THE FEMALE BREAST

In the United States today the breast is the primary symbol of female sexuality. Secondary sexual characteristics, especially the breasts, are vital to the adolescent female's concept of her body image. Because her primary sex organs are not visible, breast development provides visual confirmation that she is becoming a woman.

Like the uterus, the breast undergoes regular cyclical

*(Text continues on page 65.)*

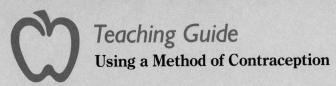

## *Teaching Guide*

### Using a Method of Contraception

***Assessment*** The nurse determines the woman's general knowledge about contraceptive methods, identifies the methods the woman has used previously (if any), identifies contraindications or risk factors for any methods, discusses the woman's personal preferences and biases about various methods, and discusses her commitment (and her partner's commitment if appropriate) to a chosen method.

***Nursing Diagnosis*** Knowledge deficit related to correct use of chosen method of contraception.

***Nursing Plan and Implementation*** The teaching plan will focus on confirming that a chosen method of contraception is a good choice for the woman. The nurse will then help the woman learn the method so that she can use it effectively.

***Client Goals*** At the completion of teaching the woman will be able to:

1. Confirm for herself that the chosen method of contraception is appropriate for her.

2. List the advantages, disadvantages, and risks of the chosen method.

3. Describe (or demonstrate) the ccrrect procedure for using the chosen method.

4. Cite warning signs that should be reported to the care giver.

## *Teaching Plan*

| Content | Teaching Method |
|---|---|
| Discuss the factors that a woman should consider in choosing a method of contraception (Table 3.2). Stress that different methods may be appropriate at different times in the woman's life. Review the woman's reasons for selecting a particular method and confirm any contraindications to specific methods. | *Contraception is a personal decision, so the discussion should take place in a private area free of interruptions.*<br><br>*The nurse should create a supportive, warm, and comfortable atmosphere by her or his attitude and communication style—both verbal and nonverbal.*<br><br>*The nurse needs to consciously recognize that her or his personal preferences about contraception may be very different from those of the woman she or he is counseling. The nurse has the responsibility to provide accurate information in an open, 'nonjudgmental way.* |
| Discuss the advantages, disadvantages, and risks of the chosen method. | *Focus on open discussion. It may help to have written information about the method chosen. If a signed permit is required (as with sterilization or IUD insertion), the physician should also discuss the advantages, disadvantages, and risks.* |
| Describe the correct procedure for using a method. Go through step-by-step. Periodically stop and have the woman review the information for you. If a technique is to be learned (as with inserting a diaphragm or charting BBT), demonstrate and then have the woman do a return demonstration as appropriate. (Note: If certain aspects are beyond the nurse's level of expertise, the nurse can review the content and confirm that a woman has the opportunity to do a return demonstration. For example, an office nurse who does not do cervical cap fittings may cover information on its use, have the woman try inserting the cap herself, and then have the placement checked by the nurse practitioner or physician.) | *Learning is best accomplished when material is broken down into smaller steps.*<br><br>*People learn best when multiple approaches are used, so it is helpful to have a model or chart to enable the woman to visualize what is being described. The nurse can also have a sample of the chosen method available: a package of oral contraceptives, an open IUD, or a symptothermal chart.* |

*(continues)*

## Teaching Plan (continued)

### Content

Provide information on what the woman should do if unusual circumstances arise: she forgets a pill, she misses a morning temperature, etc.

Stress warning signs that require immediate action on the part of the woman and explain why these signs indicate a risk. Carefully delineate the actions the woman should take: Should she contact her caregiver? Stop the method? and so forth.

Arrange to talk with the woman again soon, either on the phone or at a return visit to determine if she has any questions about the method and to ensure that no problems have arisen.

### Teaching Method

Provide a written handout identifying the warning signs and listing the actions a woman should take. The handout should also cover actions the woman should take if an unusual situation develops. For example, what should she do if she vomits or has diarrhea while taking oral contraceptives? What action should she take if she and her partner are using a condom and it breaks? and so forth.

The woman should know that she is free to call if she has questions or concerns once she starts using the method. This increases her comfort level and enables you to detect potential problems early.

changes in response to hormonal stimulation. Each month, in rhythm with the cycle of ovulation, the breasts become engorged with fluid in anticipation of pregnancy, and the woman may experience sensations of tenderness, lumpiness, and perhaps pain. If conception does not occur, the accumulated fluid drains away via the lymphatic network. *Mastodynia* (premenstrual swelling and tenderness of the breasts) is common. It usually lasts for three to four days prior to the onset of menses, but the symptoms may persist throughout the month.

In women who have never been pregnant, a degree of breast swelling may become chronic, with breast tissue assuming a lumpy texture that may remain even after menopause. After menopause, adipose breast tissue atrophies and is replaced by connective tissue. Elasticity is lost and the breasts may droop and become pendulous. The recurring breast engorgement associated with ovulation ceases. If estrogen replacement therapy is used to counteract other symptoms of menopause, breast engorgement may resume.

● *Breast Self-Examination (BSE)*

Throughout her lifetime a woman may experience a variety of breast disorders. Some, like mastitis, are acute conditions, while others, such as fibrocystic breast dis-ease, are chronic. In most instances, the initial discovery of a variation is made by the woman. If the woman is knowledgeable about her breasts because she does regular breast self-examination (BSE), she often is able to detect an abnormality earlier, or, on the other hand, recognize that a finding has been unchanged for years and is "normal" for her. Thus it is important for a woman to develop the habit of doing routine BSE as early as possible, and preferably as an adolescent. Woman at high risk for breast cancer are especially encouraged to be attentive to the importance of early detection through routine BSE.

In the course of a routine physical examination or during an initial visit to the care giver, the woman should be taught BSE technique and its importance as a monthly  practice. The effectiveness of BSE is determined by the woman's ability to perform the procedure correctly.

Breast self-examination should be performed on a regular, monthly basis about one week after each menstrual period, when the breasts are typically not tender or swollen. After menopause, BSE should be performed on the same day each month (the woman can choose the particular day).

The nurse is the woman's advocate in the community, industrial setting, hospital, or physician's office. Through routine health screening and assessment, the nurse has an opportunity to provide emotional support, evaluate the

---

## Procedure 3.1

## Breast Self-Examination—Inspection

Look at the breasts individually and in comparison with one another while standing in front of a mirror. Characteristics that should be reported to care giver are indicated.

Assess breasts in following positions: arms at sides; arms over head; arms on hips with muscles tightened, leaning forward.

### Size and Symmetry of the Breasts

1. Breasts may vary, but the variations should remain constant during rest or movement—note abnormal contours.

2. Some size difference between the breasts is normal. (The left is often larger.)

### Shape and Direction of the Breasts

1. The shape of the breasts can be rounded or pendulous with some variation between breasts.

2. The breasts should be pointing slightly laterally. Report changes in direction breasts point.

### Color, Thickening, Edema, and Venous Patterns

1. Report any redness or inflammation.

2. A blue hue with a marked venous pattern that is focal or unilateral may indicate an area of increased blood supply due to tumor. Report. Symmetric venous patterns are normal.

3. Skin edema observed as thickened skin with enlarged pores ("orange peel") may indicate blocked lymphatic drainage due to tumor. Report.

### Surface of the Breasts

1. Skin dimpling, puckering, or retraction (pulling) when the woman presses her hands together or against her hips suggests malignancy. Report.

2. Striae (stretch marks) red at onset and whitish with age are normal.

### Nipple Size and Shape, Direction, Rashes, Ulcerations, and Discharge

1. Long-standing nipple inversion is normal, but an inverted nipple previously capable of erection is suspicious. Note and report any deviation, flattening, or broadening of the nipples.

2. Check for rashes, ulcerations, or discharge and report.

woman's risk of developing breast cancer, and teach BSE. A return demonstration of BSE by the woman during a routine health examination facilitates understanding of the procedure and encourages the woman's commitment to her own health care. A method of record keeping also should be mutually determined by the nurse and the woman. On-going spoken feedback about the woman's performance of BSE should be part of the visit in which the technique is taught, as well as in subsequent visits. Nurse and client should review the woman's record of breast examination during follow-up visits to encourage establishment of a monthly pattern.

Breast self-examination is most effective when it uses a dual approach incorporating both inspection and palpation. Procedure 3.1 describes inspection of the breasts, while Procedure 3.2 and Figure 3.8 describe palpation.

## Procedure 3.2

## Breast Self-Examination—Palpation

| Objective | Nursing Action | Rationale |
|---|---|---|
| Provide instruction | Instruct woman as follows: | |

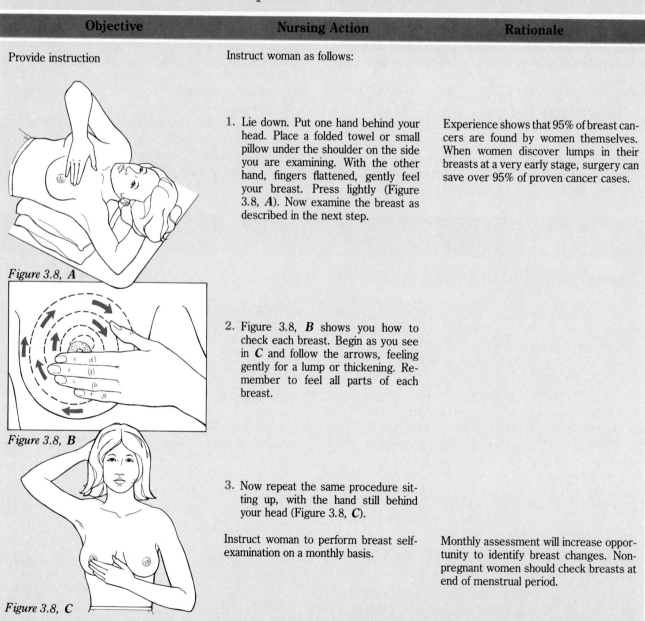

Figure 3.8, *A*

Figure 3.8, *B*

Figure 3.8, *C*

1. Lie down. Put one hand behind your head. Place a folded towel or small pillow under the shoulder on the side you are examining. With the other hand, fingers flattened, gently feel your breast. Press lightly (Figure 3.8, *A*). Now examine the breast as described in the next step.

Experience shows that 95% of breast cancers are found by women themselves. When women discover lumps in their breasts at a very early stage, surgery can save over 95% of proven cancer cases.

2. Figure 3.8, *B* shows you how to check each breast. Begin as you see in *C* and follow the arrows, feeling gently for a lump or thickening. Remember to feel all parts of each breast.

3. Now repeat the same procedure sitting up, with the hand still behind your head (Figure 3.8, *C*).

Instruct woman to perform breast self-examination on a monthly basis.

Monthly assessment will increase opportunity to identify breast changes. Non-pregnant women should check breasts at end of menstrual period.

Source: American Cancer Society: *Breast Self-Examination and the Nurse.* No. 3408 PE. New York, 1973.

# Care of the Woman with a Disorder of the Breast

**Fibrocystic breast disease** is the most common of the benign breast disorders and is most prevalent in women 30 to 50 years of age (Wynn 1983). Women with fibrocystic breast disease have an increased risk of developing cancer. Fibrosis is a thickening of the normal breast tissue. Cyst formation that may accompany fibrosis is considered a later change in the condition. Fibrocystic breast disease is probably caused by an imbalance in estrogen and progesterone, which distorts the normal changes of the menstrual cycle. The symptoms often increase as the woman approaches menopause, while the condition generally improves following menopause.

The woman often complains of pain, tenderness, and swelling that occurs cyclically and is most pronounced just before her menses begins. Physical examination may reveal only mild signs of irregularity, or the breasts may feel dense, with areas of irregularity and nodularity. Women often refer to this as "lumpiness." Some women may also have expressible nipple discharge.

If the woman has a large, fluid-filled cyst she may experience a localized painful area as the capsule containing the accumulated fluid distends coincident with her cycle. However, if small cyst formation occurs, the woman may experience not a solitary tender lump but a diffuse tenderness. A cyst may often be differentiated from a malignancy by its mobility and tenderness and by the absence of skin retraction (pulling) in the surrounding tissue.

Mammography, palpation, and fine-needle aspiration are used to confirm fibrocystic breast disease. Often, fine-needle aspiration is the treatment as well, affording relief from the tenderness or pain. Treatment of palpable cysts is conservative; invasive procedures such as biopsy are used only if the diagnosis is questionable.

Women with mild symptoms may benefit from restricting sodium intake and taking a mild diuretic during the week before the onset of menses. This counteracts fluid retention, relieves pressure in the breast, and helps decrease the pain. In other cases a mild analgesic is necessary. Other treatment approaches include the use of thiamine and vitamin E. In severe cases the hormone inhibitor danazol is the drug of choice.

Some researchers suggest that methylxanthines (found in caffeine products such as coffee, tea, colas, and chocolate; and some medications) may contribute to the development of fibrocystic breast changes and that limiting intake of these substances would help decrease fibrocystic changes (Minton et al 1981). Other research fails to demonstrate a clear association between methylxanthines and fibrocystic breast changes (Levinson and Dunn 1986).

In rare instances the condition can become so severe that the woman is incapacitated by pain and must undergo multiple biopsies for questionable masses. After careful evaluation and counseling the woman may elect to undergo simple mastectomy with or without implants. This is a drastic intervention and should never be undertaken without a second medical opinion.

*Fibroadenoma* is a common tumor seen in women in their teens and early twenties. It has not been significantly associated with breast cancer. Fibroadenomas are freely movable, solid tumors that are well defined, sharply delineated, and rounded, with a rubbery texture. They are asymptomatic and nontender.

If there are any disquieting features to the appearance of a lump, fine-needle biopsy and/or excision of the mass may be indicated. Caution is exercised when deciding upon biopsy because excision of the mass in a young girl may interfere with normal breast development. Watchful observation and possible surgical excision are the only treatments for fibroadenomas. Surgery is often deferred. When advisable, surgical removal of the fibroadenoma concludes its treatment.

*Intraductal papillomas* are tumors growing in the terminal portion of a duct or sometimes throughout the duct system within a section of the breast. They are typically benign but have the potential to become malignant (Havens et al 1986).

The majority of papillomas present as solitary nodules or, more frequently, as multiple lesions. These small ball-like lesions may be detected on mammography. The presence of a papilloma is often frightening to the woman because her primary symptom is a discharge from the nipple that may be serosanguineous or brownish-green due to old blood. The location of the papilloma within the duct system and its pattern of growth determine whether nipple discharge will be present. The tumor frequently is not palpable, although a small soft tumor in a central or peri-areolar portion of the breast can sometimes be palpated.

If the woman reports a nipple discharge, the breast should be milked to obtain fluid. The fluid obtained is sent for a Papanicolaou (Pap) smear. The diagnosis is confirmed if papilloma cells are present (Havens et al 1986). The lesion must be excised and histologically examined because of the difficulty in differentiating between a benign papilloma and a papillary carcinoma.

*Duct ectasis* (comedomastitis) commonly occurs during or near the onset of menopause and is not associated with malignancy. The condition typically occurs in women who have borne and nursed children. It is characterized by a thick, sticky nipple discharge and by burning pain, pruritis, and inflammation. Treatment is conservative, with drug therapy aimed at symptomatic relief. The major central ducts of the breast occasionally have to be excised.

Table 3.3 provides a summary of common breast disorders.

## NURSING ASSESSMENT

During the period of diagnosis, the woman may be anxious about a possible change in body image or a diag-

## Table 3.3  Summary of Common Breast Disorders

| Condition | Age | Pain | Nipple discharge | Location | Consistency and mobility | Diagnosis and treatment |
|---|---|---|---|---|---|---|
| Duct ectasis | 35–55 years; median age 40 | Burning around nipple | Sticky, multi-colored; usually bilateral | No specific location | Retroareolar mass with advanced disease | Open biopsy; local excision of diseased portion of breast |
| Fibroadenoma | 15–39 years; median age 20 | No | No | No specific location | Mobile, firm, smooth, well delineated | Mammography, xeromammography; surgical or needle biopsy; excision of the tumor |
| Fibrocystic breast disease | 20–49 years; median age 30 (may subside with menopause) | Yes | No | Upper outer quadrant | Bilateral multiple lumps influenced by the menstrual cycle | Needle aspiration; observation; biopsy if there is an unresolved mass or mammographic changes |
| Intraductal papilloma | 35–55 years; median age 40 | Yes | Serous or serosanguineous; usually unilateral from one duct | No specific location | Usually soft, poorly delineated | Pap smear of nipple discharge; biopsy; wedge resection |
| Mastitis | Childbearing years | Tenderness, pain | No | No specific location | Generalized redness of overlying skin | Antibiotic therapy; incision and drainage if mastitis progresses to an abscess |

Source: Modified from Fogel CI, Woods NF (editors): *Health Care of Women: A Nursing Perspective.* St. Louis: Mosby, 1981, p 337.

nosis of cancer. The nurse can use therapeutic communication to assess the significance the woman places on her breasts; her current emotional status, coping mechanisms used during periods of stress, and knowledge and beliefs about cancer; and other variables that may influence her coping and adjustment.

### NURSING DIAGNOSIS

Nursing diagnoses that may apply to a woman with a benign disorder of the breast include:

● Knowledge deficit related to a lack of understanding of diagnostic procedures

● Anxiety related to possible diagnosis of breast cancer

### NURSING PLAN AND IMPLEMENTATION

During the prediagnosis period the woman should be encouraged to express her anxiety, and misconceptions should be clarified. Once a diagnosis has been made, the nurse should ensure that the woman clearly understands her condition, its association to breast malignancy, and treatment options.

The nurse can also point out that frequent professional breast examination and regular mammograms are tools that help detect any abnormalities and that the woman who practices monthly BSE, follows her care giver's advice, and is examined regularly has taken positive action to protect her health.

### EVALUATION

Anticipated outcomes of nursing care include:

● The woman feels comfortable discussing her fears, concerns, and questions during the period of diagnosis.

● The diagnosis is made quickly and accurately.

● The woman incorporates monthly BSE into her personal routine.

### ● Care of the Woman with Carcinoma of the Breast

Approximately 123,000 cases of invasive breast cancer were diagnosed in the U.S. in 1986. An estimated one-third of these women will die from their disease (Feller

1988). Myths concerning the causes and treatment of breast cancer are commonplace. Concerted efforts on the part of health organizations and the media have begun to dispel myths, supplanting misinformation with health education.

The mastectomies of Betty Ford and Happy Rockefeller in September and October 1974 brought the importance of breast cancer, its detection, and its treatment to the attention of the American public. The feminist and consumer rights movements have also been instrumental in raising women's consciousness about their accountability for personal health care. As a result of this awareness, many women today expect a voice in any decisions made about their health and proposed treatments.

Within the medical profession, controversy persists regarding the treatment alternatives for breast cancer. What the physician recommends as the best treatment for a woman with a newly diagnosed breast cancer may not be what the woman wishes. The physician's major goal may be the attainment of cure, necessitating a more radical surgical treatment, whereas the woman may feel that the threatened loss of a valued body part is equally important.

Theories of causation include hormonal mechanisms, viral agents, and immunologic processes. The fact that breast cancer does not occur in the prepubertal female suggests that prior conditioning of the breast tissue by endogenous steroids may be essential for neoplastic development (Rickel et al 1982). The incidence of carcinoma of the breast increases in women after the age of 35. Most lumps (95%) are discovered by women themselves.

Factors placing women at risk for breast cancer have been studied extensively by epidemiologists and other clinical researchers. The risk factors associated with carcinoma of the breast in women are summarized in Table 3.4.

Although a complete discussion of breast cancer is beyond the scope of this text, screening methods, the condition itself, and its treatment will be summarized briefly.

## SCREENING AND DETECTION

The purpose of breast screening programs is to identify women who have no clinical signs of breast cancer but have covert signs suggesting the presence of the disease. The chances of cure improve dramatically when breast cancer is detected when the tumor is small and located in only one breast. In fact, the cure rate for noninvasive or minimally invasive cancers is greater than 95% (Donegan 1986).

The primary screening tools currently available include regular breast self-examination, examination by a health professional, and mammogram. Other screening methods include thermography and ultrasonography.

A **mammogram** is a soft tissue x-ray of the breast without the injection of a contrast medium. It can detect lesions in the breast before they can be felt.

Currently the American Cancer Society and the Ameri-

---

### Table 3.4  Risk Factors Associated with Increased Incidence of Breast Cancer

| Variable | High risk | Low risk |
|---|---|---|
| Age | Over 50 years of age | Under 50 years of age |
| Family history | Breast cancer in grandmother, mother, aunt, or sister | No family history of breast cancer |
| Marital status | Unmarried | Married |
| Medical history | Cancer in the other breast<br>Fibrocystic breast disease with dysplasia<br>Endometrial cancer<br>Other organ cancers<br>Lowered immunologic competence | No breast cancer<br>No fibrocystic breast disease<br>No endometrial cancer<br>No other organ cancers<br>No other systemic disorders |
| Menstrual history | Early menarche (before 12 years of age)<br>Late menopause (after 50 years of age)<br>More than 30 years of menstrual activity | Menarche after 12 years of age<br>Menopause before 50 years of age<br>Less than 30 years of menstrual activity |
| Nutrition | High fat intake<br>High protein intake<br>Low selenium intake | Low fat intake<br>Moderate protein intake<br>High selenium intake |
| Race | Caucasian | Non-Caucasian |
| Socioeconomic status | Upper middle class | Lower class |

Source: Scholtenfeld D, Fraumeni J (editors): *Cancer Epidemiology and Prevention.* Philadelphia: Saunders, 1982. Dunphy J, Way L: *Current Surgical Diagnosis and Treatment.* Los Altos, CA: Lange, 1980.

can College of Radiology suggest the following mammogram screening guidelines:

● Baseline mammogram between ages 35 and 40

● Mammogram every one to two years between ages 40 and 50

● Mammogram annually for all women over age 50

*Thermography* is a pictorial representation of heat patterns on the surface of the breast. Breast cancer tends to have a higher metabolic rate and may appear as a "hot spot" on the film. Because of its high incidence of false results, thermography has not gained wide acceptance.

*Ultrasonography* can distinguish cysts from solid masses but cannot differentiate between malignant and nonmalignant cells. Thus it is used primarily to determine the location of a cyst for needle aspiration.

## PATHOPHYSIOLOGY OF BREAST CANCER

The most common malignancy in women is breast cancer, which has its peak incidence prior to menopause. No method for preventing breast cancer is known. Cancer of the breast has an unpredictable course, with a long-term risk—20 years or more—of metastasis (Keyes et al 1983). A secondary rise in the incidence of breast cancer is observed following menopause. Practitioners tend to follow the informal rule that the older the woman, the greater the chance that malignant disease will appear.

A malignant breast neoplasm may originate either in a duct or in the lobular epithelium. It may be infiltrating (penetrating the limiting basement membranes) or noninfiltrating (nonpenetrating). All forms of breast cancer can spread locally by invasion. A breast tumor tends to adhere to the pectoral muscles or deep fascia of the chest wall beneath the breast and the skin overlying the breast. This adherence of the tumor can cause an appearance of skin dimpling and retraction in the later stages of the disease ("orange peel sign"). About 50% of all breast cancers originate in the upper outside quadrant and metastasize to the axillary lymph nodes. Approximately 25% of all breast cancers arise in the central portion of the breast and metastasize to the mammary lymph node chain (Rickel et al 1982).

Cancer of the breast is often discovered accidentally by the woman or her sexual partner. During the early stages of development, the lump is usually isolated, movable, and painless. A hard, circumscribed mass that is not freely movable also suggests malignancy. More advanced signs, such as fixation to the skin, skin edema, nipple retraction, or deep fixation, are further evidence of cancer.

## DIAGNOSIS

In diagnosing breast lesions, physical examination, radiographic or other diagnostic techniques, and biopsy are the most common procedures.

Surgical biopsy is performed on an outpatient basis with the woman under local anesthesia. The tissue sample obtained during biopsy is sent out as a permanent section, and a pathologist's report is sent to the surgeon within a few days. During a follow-up office visit to the surgeon, the woman is given the results and the opportunity to discuss the best breast cancer treatment alternative for her. This two-step approach to breast cancer treatment has gained a great deal of support from women and health care professionals alike. Participation in choosing treatment incorporates women, and possibly their families, as active partners. A decision made in this fashion is not as likely to be regretted later.

## SURGICAL TREATMENT ALTERNATIVES

As early as 1650, treatment of breast cancer involved removal of the affected breast (Weber 1983). The standard American surgical treatment was established in the 1890s when Halsted described the procedure now known as the Halsted radical mastectomy. This procedure entailed the removal of the entire breast, skin, pectoralis major and minor muscles, lymph nodes of the axilla, and surrounding fat tissue.

The unfortunate aspect of radical breast surgery is its mutilation. Breast cancer treatment has a significant emotional impact on the woman's integrity, body image, self-concept, and sexual identity. Because of the possibility of residual cancer cells after surgical intervention, many surgeons believe it is logical to remove the greatest amount of tissue in the hope of curative treatment. However, recent studies (Fisher et al 1985) have offered proof, in their study of 1843 women at five-year follow-up, that conservative breast surgery in early disease, combined with radiotherapy, gives survival results that are as satisfactory as the modified radical mastectomy. It is important for the nurse to realize that the aim of surgical breast cancer treatment is threefold.

1. To preserve the woman's life

2. To minimize recurrence

3. To provide the best cosmetic results possible

Currently available surgical approaches include various types of mastectomy, local wide excision, and breast reconstruction.

*Radical mastectomy* is the procedure described in the previous section. It is less commonly used today.

*Extended radical mastectomy* uses the Halsted radical mastectomy procedure plus the removal of the internal mammary lymph nodes.

*Modified radical mastectomy* involves removing the entire breast and the axillary contents; however, the pectoralis major muscle is preserved. Currently it is the surgical treatment of choice in many cases.

*Total (simple) mastectomy* refers to the surgical removal of the breast but not the pectoral muscle. This procedure is used for early-stage breast cancer and is usually followed by postoperative radiation of regional lymph nodes. Breast reconstruction can be combined with the mastectomy or done at a later time.

*Subcutaneous mastectomy* evolved as a procedure to complement breast reconstruction. The internal breast tissue is removed and the skin of the breast remains. An implant is then inserted to restore breast shape. It is best used in breast cancers that are noninvasive and located away from the nipple.

*Partial (segmental) mastectomy* removes the tumor and 2 to 3 cm of surrounding tissue. Some of the breast remains. Axillary node dissection and the removal of at least a portion of the nodes are recommended. Current trends support the use of both radiation and chemotherapy in women who have positive lymph nodes when segmental mastectomy is done (Margolese 1986).

*Local wide excision (tylectomy or lumpectomy)* removes only the tumor mass and a narrow margin of normal tissue surrounding the mass. In early breast cancer, simple excision followed by definitive radiation yields local tumor control and survival rates that compare favorably with those of other treatments (Wilson 1983). The procedure is done for cosmetic effect in women who are highly motivated to preserve the breast. However, many women are not suitable candidates for excision and radiation because of the stage or type of cancer they have.

*Breast reconstruction* may be done using a variety of implants and surgical approaches. Candidates for breast reconstruction are women with a mass less than 2 cm and fewer than three positive nodes. Women who have received a radical mastectomy or the extended mastectomy are not good candidates because they lack sufficient amounts of skin and muscle. Table 3.5 lists the advantages and disadvantages of reconstructive surgery.

## ADDITIONAL THERAPY

*Radiation therapy* to the breast and chest wall is generally recommended for women who have had local wide excision and is started one to two weeks following surgery (Feller 1988).

*Adjuvant chemotherapy* using a combination of drugs is recommended for premenopausal women with positive axillary nodes (Shingleton and McCarty 1987). For postmenopausal women with positive nodes, adjuvant chemotherapy using tamoxifen citrate (Nolvadex) is recommended (Feller 1988).

An assay of the breast cancer can be done to determine whether the malignant cells are estrogen receptor positive or negative. Additive hormonal therapy involves administering large doses of estrogen, androgen, or progestin in postmenopausal women. High doses of these hormones have been observed to cause tumor regression, although the exact mechanism of interaction is unknown.

## PSYCHOSOCIAL CONCERNS OF THE WOMAN WITH BREAST CANCER

Sometimes a woman does not seek medical attention following the discovery of a breast lump. Factors that appear to be significant in delay include: attempts to deny the presence of a lump, lack of knowledge about breast disorders, fear of mutilating surgery, fear of body image change, fear of relationship changes, and reluctance to submit to diagnostic and therapeutic procedures. Compared with women who seek treatment promptly, women who delay tend to believe more strongly that the condition is not serious, experience a greater sense of powerlessness, and use more avoidance defenses in coping. They are also more likely to be depressed. Related psychosocial problems of delaying women have included marital prob-

## Table 3.5  Advantages and Disadvantages of Reconstructive Breast Surgery

| Advantages | Disadvantages |
|---|---|
| Improved physical appearance | The reality that the reconstructed breast is never identical to the unaffected breast |
| An invaluable psychologic lift and improvement of body image | The expense and risk of further surgical procedures |
| The ability to wear normal clothing without worrying about exposing a prosthesis | The possibility of an unsatisfactory result or surgical complications |
| The opportunity to resume more strenuous activities (eg, sports) without being concerned about exposing a prosthesis | The fact that the reconstructed breast will never replace the lost one |

lems, rejection by family members, and a general sense of isolation related to living alone.

When a woman is confronted with a breast mass she initiates a decision-making process about her diagnostic and treatment options and her approach to her condition. The most consistent influence on a woman's decision making is her physician. Nevertheless, the woman is the only person who can decide what benefits of surgery are worth what personal risks. Despite the seriousness of the diagnosis, the time constraints, and the expense involved, the woman should be encouraged to seek a second opinion. Many third-party payment plans now pay for this.

The course of adjustment confronting the woman with breast cancer has been described as four phases: shock, reaction, recovery, and reorientation (Gyllenskold 1982).

In the shock phase, women make statements like "Everything is unreal" or "I can't understand what is happening to me." Shock extends from the discovery of the lump throughout the process of diagnosis.

Reaction occurs in conjunction with the initiation of treatment. As treatment begins, the woman is compelled to face what has occurred and begins to take in what has happened. Coping mechanisms become evident during this phase. Reaction extends for the length of treatment. During the phases of shock and reaction, the woman is completely absorbed with what has caused the problem. Treatment reinforces the diagnosis of cancer and the immediate consequences of the disease. Denial of breast loss and the reality of the illness is common during the periods of diagnosis and treatment. Denial protects the woman, making therapy tolerable and enhancing her compliance.

Recovery begins during convalescence following the completion of medical treatment. Anxiety about her illness diminishes and the woman looks to the future once more (Gyllenskold 1982). She turns outward and gradually resumes her former activities. Conversely, depression and social isolation occur if the woman is unable to negotiate this recovery phase successfully, and a chronic state of emotional and physical disability may result (Schmale 1979).

Reorientation follows recovery and is unending. It is accomplished when the woman can acknowledge that breast cancer is a part of her life; yet living, for her, has returned to or perhaps exceeded its former fullness and meaning.

## NURSING ASSESSMENT

The woman seeking health care following discovery of a lump is likely to be apprehensive. She may have misconceptions about breast cancer. Holistic health assessment should be conducted in an understanding, unhurried, emotionally supportive atmosphere.

Assessment of the woman facing a diagnosis of breast cancer must be an ongoing process that focuses on the woman's physical, mental, emotional, and social situation.

If a diagnosis of cancer is made and the woman elects to have a surgical intervention, nursing care is directed to the assessments and care typically indicated prior to any surgery, as well as the assessments indicated by the woman's diagnosis.

Nursing assessments during the postoperative period change as the woman progresses and adapts following surgery. The nurse assesses the woman's condition postoperatively to detect any potential complications. Vital signs are assessed regularly for evidence of change, and the nurse is alert to other signs that might indicate shock. The dressing is inspected and reinforced as necessary, and the quantity of drainage in the wound suction device (Hemovac) is monitored.

In addition, other routine postoperative assessments are made. The nurse auscultates the woman's lungs, assesses the abdomen for distention, evaluates urinary output, monitors the intensity of the woman's discomfort, and regulates the intravenous fluids.

After the immediate postoperative period, the nurse continues to assess the woman for evidence of infection, discomfort, and emotional problems. Throughout the postoperative period the nurse evaluates the woman's teaching needs and plans appropriate interventions.

## NURSING DIAGNOSIS

Nursing diagnoses that may apply during the diagnostic period include:

● Knowledge deficit related to the diagnostic procedures

● Fear related to the possibility of a diagnosis of cancer

Nursing diagnoses that might apply preoperatively include:

● Knowledge deficit related to the surgical procedure

● Anxiety related to possible change in body image following surgery

● Ineffective individual coping related to inability to accept the reality of the cancer diagnosis

Nursing diagnoses that may apply during the postoperative period include:

● Potential for infection related to surgical intervention

● Pain related to surgery

## NURSING PLAN AND IMPLEMENTATION

Nursing care for the woman with breast cancer changes as the woman progresses from the period of diagnosis to the recovery period.

### Period of Diagnosis

The nurse should explain the two-step procedure to assure the woman that she will be able to participate in decision making about her treatment once the biopsy results are known. Nursing advocacy involves supporting the woman's right to make the best decision for her. With the assistance of the nurse the woman can explore her fears, clarify her values, and identify the treatment options that would be personally acceptable. Once the woman has made an informed decision, the nurse's role becomes one of support. The woman and her partner should be told the treatment alternatives together once the results of the biopsy are known.

### The Preoperative Period

The nurse explains the routines and procedures that are pertinent to the woman's hospital stay, including preoperative preparation and the care and assessments that are done postoperatively. The nurse may also have the woman practice deep breathing and coughing and leg exercises. The nurse provides the woman and her family with opportunities to ask questions and express their feelings. It is important for the woman to feel that she is receiving care from individuals who are not only skilled technically but also concerned about her as a person.

### The Postoperative Period

Following surgery the woman receives appropriate postoperative care. This includes nursing actions to prevent respiratory and circulatory complications and to prevent infection. The nurse is alert to the woman's level of pain and uses medication and nursing techniques to help the woman be comfortable and obtain rest. The woman who has had lymph nodes removed as part of her surgical treatment is at risk of swelling and pain in the arm on her affected side. This is especially true if a radical or modified radical mastectomy was done. The nurse keeps the arm elevated, measures the circumference of the limb, and encourages the woman to use the affected arm for feeding, washing, and hair combing. The nurse also teaches arm exercises such as wall climbing, forward and lateral arm lifts, pendulum swinging, exaggerated deep breathing, and pulley exercises.

The nurse who assumes primary responsibility for helping the woman deal with the psychosocial aspects of her breast loss should provide the woman with opportunities to express her feelings about her breast and its loss. The nurse must be sensitive to the woman's cues as to when it is acceptable to involve the sexual partner in the observation of the woman's incision and in counseling about the woman's altered appearance. The nurse can also discuss the types of prostheses available if reconstruction is not possible or if the woman has decided against it. Even if the woman will be having reconstruction at a later time, she will probably be interested in using a prosthesis temporarily.

The nurse can help the woman plan the resumption of her normal daily activities and interests. Sexual activity can be resumed when the woman's energy level permits. The nurse can help the couple explore alternative methods of sexual expression if sexual intercourse is too difficult initially. The nurse can tactfully assess the woman's prior sexual activity and discuss modifications in sexual activity that may make sexual expression easier. These modifications may be as simple as changing the sides of the bed so that the partner can more easily caress the remaining breast or having the woman wear her prosthesis and an attractive nightgown to bed. Sexual or marital counseling is valuable for some couples and should be initiated if requested.

### Discharge Planning

Prior to discharge the woman should clearly understand her follow-up treatment and care. The nurse can collaborate with the physician regarding planned postoperative therapy so that the woman understands about any scheduled therapies such as chemotherapy. The woman should thoroughly understand the importance of preventive health care such as BSE and the need to comply with follow-up examinations.

Referrals to either a community health nurse or a "Reach to Recovery" volunteer should be initiated and the date of the visit confirmed with the woman. A "Reach to Recovery" volunteer from the American Cancer Society is invaluable in helping the woman adjust to her mastectomy. Each volunteer has had a mastectomy herself and often serves as a role model for the woman with a new mastectomy. The American Cancer Society volunteer can provide the woman with information about breast prostheses and guidelines for arm exercises and self-care.

### EVALUATION

Anticipated outcomes of nursing care include the following:

● The woman copes successfully with the diagnosis of breast cancer and the therapy she chooses.

● The woman clearly understands her diagnosis and treatment, her therapy, and her long-term prognosis.

● If she receives surgery, the woman has a successful recovery period. If complications do occur they are quickly recognized and treatment is begun.

● The woman participates in planning her recovery program.

● The woman completes planned exercises, activities, follow-up, and additional therapy.

# CARE OF THE WOMAN WITH A REPRODUCTIVE TRACT DISORDER

A variety of reproductive tract disorders exist. Some, like endometriosis, are chronic, while many others can occur as acute illnesses. Some are difficult to diagnose; others become obvious more quickly. Many pose a threat to a woman's health and fertility.

## Endometriosis

**Endometriosis** is a condition characterized by the presence of endometrial tissue outside the endometrial cavity. This tissue responds to the hormonal changes of the menstrual cycle and bleeds in a cyclic fashion. This bleeding results in inflammation, scarring of the peritoneum, and formation of adhesions.

Endometriosis may occur at any age after puberty, although it is most common in women between 30 and 40 and is rare in postmenopausal women. A familial tendency does seem to exist.

The exact cause of endometriosis is not known. One of the oldest theories suggests that endometriosis is caused by a reflux of endometrial cells through the fallopian tubes during menstruation and their implantation in the abdominal cavity. Another theory suggests that endometrial cells are carried to distant sites through the venous and lymphatic systems. Hormonal causes have also been suggested. To date, however, no single theory provides an adequate explanation (Garner and Webster 1985).

The most common symptom of endometriosis is pelvic pain, which is often dull or cramping. Usually the pain is related to menstruation. Dyspareunia and abnormal uterine bleeding are other common signs. The condition is often diagnosed when the woman seeks evaluation for infertility. Bimanual examination may reveal a fixed, tender retroverted uterus and palpable nodules in the cul-de-sac. Diagnosis is confirmed by laparoscopy.

Treatment may be medical, surgical, or a combination. If the woman does not desire pregnancy at the present time, she may be started on oral contraceptives. The woman who desires pregnancy and has been unsuccessful in her attempts to conceive is treated with a six-month course of danazol (Wedell et al 1985). Danazol alters estrogen production, which results in endometrial suppression. Side effects of danazol include fluid retention, weight gain, acne, hirsutism, depression, decreased breast size, rash, and deepening of the voice (Malinik and Wheeler 1985). (For further information see Drug Guide— Danazol.)

In more advanced cases surgery may be done to remove implants and break up adhesions. If severe dyspareunia or dysmenorrhea are symptoms, the surgeon may perform a presacral neurectomy (nerve excision). In advanced cases in which childbearing is not an issue, a hysterectomy with bilateral salpingo-oophorectomy may be done.

## NURSING ASSESSMENT

The nurse should be aware of the common symptoms of endometriosis and elicit an accurate history if a woman mentions these symptoms. If a woman is being treated for endometriosis, the nurse should assess the woman's understanding of the condition, its implications, and the treatment alternatives.

## NURSING DIAGNOSIS

Nursing diagnoses that may apply to a woman with endometriosis include:

- Pain related to dysmenorrhea
- Knowledge deficit related to a lack of understanding of the disease process
- Ineffective individual coping related to depression secondary to infertility

## NURSING PLAN AND IMPLEMENTATION

The nurse can be available to explain the condition, its symptoms, treatment alternatives, and prognosis. The nurse can help the woman evaluate treatment options and make choices that are appropriate for her. If medication is begun, the nurse can review the dosage, schedule, possible side effects, and any warning signs. Women are often advised to avoid delaying pregnancy because of the risk of infertility. The woman may wish to discuss the implications of this decision on her life choices, relationship with her partner, and personal preferences. The nurse can be a nonjudgmental listener and help the woman consider her options.

## EVALUATION

Anticipated outcomes of nursing care include:

- The woman clearly understands her condition, its implications for fertility, and her treatment options.
- The woman successfully copes with the discomfort and long-term implications of her diagnosis.

## Toxic Shock Syndrome (TSS)

Although **toxic shock syndrome (TSS)** has been reported in children, postmenopausal women, and men, it is primarily a disease of reproductive age women, especially women at or near menses or during the postpartum period. The causative organism is a strain of *Staphylococcus aureus*.

## 🏮 Drug Guide

# Danazol (Danocrine)

### Overview of Action

Danazol is a testosterone derivative with a mild androgenic effect. The drug has an antigonadotropic effect that results in the suppression of both follicle-stimulating hormone (FSH) and luteinizing hormone (LH). As a consequence, ovulation is suppressed and amenorrhea develops. Danazol also reduces levels of sex steroids by inhibiting the enzymes responsible for their production, and binds steroid hormone receptors on endometrial tissue implants (Hill and Herbert 1988). This results in atrophy of endometrial tissue implants and endometrium within the uterus. Progress of endometriosis is stopped and the woman's pain is relieved. May also be used to treat fibrocystic breast disease.

### Route, Dosage, Frequency

Endometriosis: 400 mg, orally, two times per day for three to six months. Therapy is begun if pregnancy test is negative or during woman's menstrual period. Treatment may be extended for nine months or restarted if symptoms recur.

Breast disease: 400 mg/day orally. Long-term effects of treatment not known.

### Contraindications

Pregnancy
Breast-feeding women
Impaired kidney, heart, or liver function
Undiagnosed abnormal vaginal bleeding

### Side Effects

| | |
|---|---|
| Vaginal bleeding | Clitoral enlargement |
| Vasomotor instability | Decreased breast size |
| Hirsutism | Irritability, depression |
| Acne | Sleep disorders, fatigue |
| Oily skin | Gastroenteritis |
| Weight gain | Signs of atrophic vaginitis |
| Reduced libido | Alopecia |
| Voice changes, hoarseness | |

Changed lab values including: reduced high-density lipoprotein (HDL); increased low-density lipoprotein (LDL); increased liver enzyme levels (serum glutamic-oxaloacetic transaminase [SGOT], serum glutamic-pyruvic transaminase [SGPT], creatinine phosphokinase [CPK], lactic dehydrogenase [LDH])

### Nursing Considerations

1. Inform woman about potential side effects; stress that menses and ovulation usually resume within two to three months after discontinuing therapy.

2. Continue routine breast examinations and report any enlarged or hardened breast nodules.

3. Obtain baseline and other liver function tests as ordered.

4. Voice changes should be reported immediately and the medication stopped to avoid permanent damage.

5. Observe woman for signs of virilization.

6. Since ovulation may not be suppressed, a back-up, non-hormonal form of birth control should be used if the woman wishes to avoid conception (Govoni and Hayes 1988).

The use of high absorbency tampons has been widely related to an increased incidence of TSS. However, occluding the cervical os with a contraceptive device such as a diaphragm or contraceptive sponge, especially if it is left in place for more than 24 hours, may also increase the risk of TSS (Connell 1985).

Early diagnosis and treatment are important in preventing a fatal outcome. The most common signs of TSS include fever (often greater than 38.9°C [102°F]); desquamation of the skin, especially the palms and soles, which usually occurs one to two weeks after the onset of symptoms; rash; hypotension; and dizziness. Systemic symptoms often include vomiting, diarrhea, severe myalgia, and inflamed mucous membranes (oropharyngeal,

conjunctival, or vaginal). In addition, disorders of the central nervous system, including alterations in consciousness, disorientation, and coma, may occur.

Laboratory findings reveal elevated blood urea nitrogen (BUN), creatinine, SGOT, SGPT, and total bilirubin, while platelets are often less than 100,000/mm³.

Women with TSS are generally hospitalized and given supportive therapy, including intravenous fluids to maintain blood pressure. Severe cases may require renal dialysis, administration of vasopressors, and intubation. Penicillinase-resistant antibiotics, while of limited value during the acute phase, do help reduce the risk of recurrence (Eschenbach 1986).

## NURSING ASSESSMENT

Nurses caring for women should ask about their clients' tampon-use practices. The nurse should pay special attention to women who customarily wear their tampons for extended periods of time or who leave a diaphragm or contraceptive sponge in place longer than six hours after intercourse. The nurse should also be alert for early signs of TSS and refer women with them to a physician for further evaluation.

## NURSING DIAGNOSIS

Nursing diagnoses that may apply to a woman with TSS include:

● Knowledge deficit related to ways of preventing the development of TSS

● Pain related to severe myalgia secondary to TSS

## NURSING PLAN AND IMPLEMENTATION

Nurses play a major role in helping educate women about ways of preventing the development of TSS. Women should understand the importance of avoiding prolonged use of tampons. Some women may choose to use other products, such as sanitary napkins or minipads. The woman who chooses to continue using tampons may reduce her risk by alternating them with napkins and by avoiding overnight use of tampons.

Postpartal women are advised to avoid the use of tampons for six to eight weeks after birth. Women with a history of TSS should totally refrain from using tampons (Eschenbach 1986).

Women who use barrier contraceptives such as diaphragms or contraceptive sponges should avoid leaving them in place for prolonged periods.

Nurses can also help make women aware of the signs and symptoms of TSS so that women will seek treatment promptly if signs occur.

## EVALUATION

Anticipated outcomes of nursing care include the following:

● The woman understands the cause of toxic shock syndrome and modifies any personal practices that might increase her risk of developing TSS.

● If a woman develops TSS, treatment is effective and any potential problems are quickly identified and corrected.

## ● Infectious Disorders of the Reproductive Tract

Many health professionals do not acknowledge the distinction between sexually transmitted diseases (STDs) and vaginitis, yet it is important to differentiate minor or recurring infections from those that can cause serious health problems. No matter how these infections are classified, women often feel anxious, guilty, embarrassed, or fearful when they have or suspect they have vaginitis or a sexually transmitted infection.

Vaginitis is an inflammation of the vulva and/or vagina. Symptoms of vaginitis and STDs include pain, discharge, foul odor, and/or pruritus. Vaginitis is sometimes but not always sexually related, whereas STDs include infections that are either definitely or potentially sexually related. Transmission of STDs can occur during various types of heterosexual or homosexual contact, including nongenital (eg, oral-genital) as well as genital contact. Often more than one sexually transmitted disease is found during evaluation.

Vaginitis and sexually transmitted infections are the most common reasons for outpatient treatment of women. Because vaginitis is a common, supposedly simple disorder, diagnosis and prescription of therapy are frequently done over the phone. Often clinicians fail to appreciate all aspects of these infections as they relate to discomfort and concerns of their clients.

Basic information applicable to infections that can be transmitted sexually is listed in Essential Facts to Remember—Information about Sexually Transmitted Diseases. Precautions specific to particular sexually transmitted infections are noted in the following discussion. The impact of these infections on pregnancy and on the fetus/neonate is discussed in Chapter 12.

### CANDIDAL VAGINITIS (MONILIASIS)

Moniliasis (often called "yeast infection") is the most common form of vaginitis affecting the vagina and vulva. Recurrences are frequent for some women. Factors that contribute to occurrence of this infection are use of oral contraceptives, use of antibiotics, frequent douching, pregnancy, diagnosed diabetes mellitus, and premenstrual factors that are unclear. A gram-positive fungus (*Candida albicans*) is the causative organism.

The woman will often complain of thick, curdy vaginal discharge; severe itching; dysuria; and **dyspareunia** (painful intercourse). A male sexual partner may experience a rash or excoriation of the skin of the penis, and possibly pruritus. The male may be symptomatic and the female asymptomatic.

On physical examination the woman's labia may be swollen and excoriated if the pruritus has been severe.

A speculum examination reveals thick, white, tenacious cheeselike patches adhering to the vaginal mucosa. Diagnosis is confirmed by microscopic examination of the vaginal discharge; hyphae and spores will usually be seen on a wet mount preparation (Figure 3.9).

Medical treatment of monilial vaginitis includes intravaginal insertion of miconazole or clotrimazole suppositories or cream at bedtime for one week. If the vulva is also infected, the cream is prescribed and may be applied topically.

Because *Candida* may be harbored in the folds of skin of the penis, it is important to treat the sexual partner to prevent recurrence of the vaginitis in the woman. Topical miconazole usually eliminates the yeast infection from the male.

If miconazole cream is being used by both partners, sexual intercourse is permitted and may assure the spread of the cream throughout the vagina. With other methods of treatment, abstinence is recommended until both partners are cured.

If a woman experiences frequent recurrences of monilial vaginitis, she should be tested for an elevated blood glucose level to determine whether a diabetic or pre-diabetic condition is present. A pregnant woman should be aware that infection at the time of delivery could cause thrush in the neonate.

### Nursing Assessment

The nurse caring for the woman should suspect monilial vaginitis if the woman complains of intense vulvar

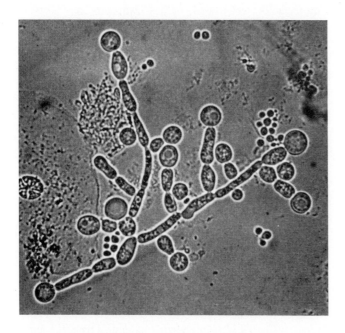

*Figure 3.9  The hyphae and spores of* Candida albicans *(Courtesy of Tortora G et al:* Microbiology, *3rd ed. Redwood City, CA: Benjamin/Cummings, 1989.)*

## Essential Facts to Remember

### Information About Sexually Transmitted Diseases

- The risk of contracting an STD increases with the number of sexual partners. Because of the extended periods of time between infection with the AIDS virus and evidence of infection, intercourse with an individual exposes a woman or man to all the other sex partners of that individual for the past five or more years.
- The condom is the best contraceptive method currently available (other than abstinence) for providing protection from STDs.
- Other contraceptive methods such as the diaphragm, cervical cap, contraceptive sponge, and spermicides also offer some protection against STDs.
- A person diagnosed with an STD has a responsibility to notify any sexual partners so that they can obtain treatment.
- Absence of symptoms or disappearance of symptoms does not mean that treatment is unnecessary if a person suspects an STD. She or he should be seen for evaluation and treatment. All prescribed medications should be taken completely.
- The presence of a genital infection may lead to an abnormal Pap smear. Women with certain infections should have more frequent Pap tests according to a schedule recommended by their care giver.

itching and a curdy, white discharge. Because women with diabetes mellitus during pregnancy are especially susceptible to this infection, the nurse should be alert for symptoms in these women. In some areas, nurses are trained to do speculum examinations and wet mount preparations and can, therefore, confirm the diagnosis themselves. In most cases, however, the nurse who suspects a vaginal infection reports this to the woman's health care provider. (See Essential Facts to Remember—Vaginitis.)

### Nursing Diagnosis

Nursing diagnoses that might apply to the woman with monilial vaginitis include:

- Potential impaired skin integrity related to scratching secondary to discomfort of monilial infection
- Knowledge deficit related to ways of preventing the development of monilial vaginitis

## Essential Facts to Remember

### Vaginitis

To distinguish among the common types of vaginitis and their treatments it is useful to remember the following:

*Moniliasis*
  Cause: *Candida albicans*
  Appearance of discharge: Thick, curdy, like cottage cheese
  Diagnostic test: Slide of vaginal discharge (treated with potassium hydroxide [KOH]) shows characteristic hyphae and spores
  Treatment: Clotrimazole vaginal cream or suppositories

*Bacterial vaginosis* (Gardnerella vaginalis *vaginitis*)
  Cause: *Gardnerella vaginalis*
  Appearance of discharge: Grey, milky
  Diagnostic test: Slide of vaginal discharge shows characteristic clue cells
  Treatment: Metronidazole

*Trichomoniasis*
  Cause: *Trichomonas vaginalis*
  Appearance of discharge: Greenish-white and frothy
  Diagnostic test: Saline slide of vaginal discharge shows motile flagellated organisms
  Treatment: Metronidazole

### Nursing Plan and Implementation

If the woman is experiencing discomfort due to the pruritus, the nurse can recommend gentle bathing of the vulva with a weak sodium bicarbonate solution. If a topical treatment is being used, the woman should bathe the area before applying the medication.

The nurse will also discuss with the woman the factors that contribute to the development of monilial vaginitis and can suggest ways to prevent recurrences, such as wearing cotton underwear and avoiding vaginal powders or sprays that may irritate. Some women report that the addition of yogurt to the diet or the use of activated culture of plain yogurt as a vaginal douche helps prevent recurrence by maintaining high levels of lactobacillus.

### Evaluation

Anticipated outcomes of nursing care include the following:

- The woman's symptoms are relieved and the infection is cured.

- The woman is able to identify self-care measures to prevent further episodes of monilial vaginitis.

## BACTERIAL VAGINOSIS (GARDNERELLA VAGINALIS *VAGINITIS*)

Many flora normally inhabit the vagina of the healthy woman. Some of these organisms are potentially pathogenic. In some women these bacteria begin to "overgrow," causing a vaginitis. The cause of this overgrowth is not clear, although tissue trauma and sexual intercourse are sometimes identified as contributing factors. The *Gardnerella vaginalis* organism (formerly referred to as *Hemophilus vaginalis*) has been found in the vast majority of cases, along with an increased concentration of anaerobic bacteria. The infected woman often notices an excessive amount of thin, watery, yellow-gray vaginal discharge with a foul odor described as "fishy." The characteristic "clue" cell is seen on vaginal smear (Figure 3.10).

The nonpregnant woman is generally treated with metronidazole (Flagyl). (See Essential Facts to Remember—Vaginitis.) Because of its potential teratogenic effects, metronidazole is avoided during pregnancy; 500 mg ampicillin every six hours for seven days is used instead.

## TRICHOMONIASIS

*Trichomonas* is a microscopic motile protozoan that thrives in an alkaline environment. Most infections are acquired through sexual intimacy. Transmission by shared bath facilities, wet towels, or wet swimsuits may be possible (Sonstegard et al 1982).

Symptoms of trichomoniasis include a yellow-green, frothy, odorous discharge frequently accompanied by inflammation of the vagina and cervix, dysuria, and dyspareunia. There is a wide variation of symptoms from woman to woman, including the symptomatic presence of *Trichomonas*. Visualization of *Trichomonas* under the microscope on a wet-mount preparation of vaginal discharge will confirm the diagnosis (Figure 3.11).

Treatment for trichomoniasis is metronidazole administered over seven days or in a single 2 g dose for both male and female sexual partners. Intercourse should be avoided until both partners are cured. (See Essential Facts to Remember—Vaginitis.)

The woman should be informed that metronidazole is  contraindicated in the first trimester of pregnancy because of possible teratogenic effects on the fetus. The woman and her partner should be cautioned to avoid alcohol while taking metronidazole; the combination has an effect similar to that of alcohol and Antabuse—abdominal pain, flushing, or tremors (Sciarra et al 1984).

The woman should be tested for other sexually transmitted infections such as gonorrhea and chlamydia.

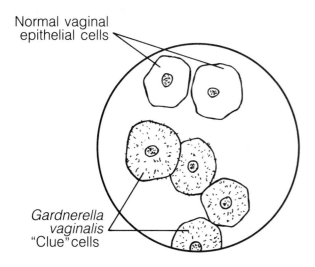

Normal vaginal epithelial cells

Gardnerella vaginalis "Clue" cells

*Figure 3.10   Depiction of the "clue cells" characteristically seen in bacterial vaginosis (*Gardnerella vaginalis *vaginitis)*

## CHLAMYDIAL INFECTION

*Chlamydial infection,* caused by *Chlamydia trachomatis,* is the most common STD in the United States. The organism is an intracellular bacterium with several different immunotypes. Immunotypes of *Chlamydia* are responsible for lymphogranuloma venereum and trachoma, which is the world's leading cause of preventable blindness.

Chlamydia is a major cause of nongonococcal urethritis (NGU) in men. In women it can cause infections similar to those that occur with gonorrhea. It can infect the fallopian tubes, cervix, urethra, and Bartholin's glands. Pelvic inflammatory disease, infertility, and ectopic pregnancy are associated with chlamydia.

Symptoms of chlamydia include a thin or purulent discharge, burning and frequency of urination, and lower abdominal pain. Women, however, are often asymptomatic. Diagnosis is frequently made after treatment of a male partner for NGU or in a symptomatic woman with a negative gonorrhea culture. Laboratory detection is now simpler due to the availability of a simple test to detect monoclonal antibodies specific for *Chlamydia.*

The usual prescribed treatment is tetracycline or doxycycline. Pregnant women should be treated with erythromycin ethyl succinate (Schachter 1986).

## HERPES GENITALIS

Herpes infections are caused by the herpes simplex virus. Because herpes is not a reportable infection, accurate incidence statistics are not available. Two types of herpes infections can occur: Type I (the "cold sore") typically occurs above the waist and is not sexually transmitted; type II is usually associated with genital infections. However, as a result of oral-genital contact, type I lesions

can occur in the genital area and type II lesions can occur around the mouth. The clinical symptoms and treatment of both types are the same when they occur in the genital area.

The primary episode of herpes genitalis is characterized by the development of single or multiple blisterlike vesicles, which usually occur in the genital area and sometimes affect the vaginal walls, cervix, urethra, and anus. The vesicles may appear within a few hours to 20 days after exposure and rupture spontaneously to form very painful, open, ulcerated lesions. Inflammation and pain secondary to the presence of herpes lesions can cause difficult urination and urinary retention. Inguinal lymph node enlargement may be present. Flulike symptoms and genital pruritus or tingling also may be noticed. Primary episodes usually last the longest and are the most severe. Lesions heal spontaneously in two to four weeks.

After the lesions heal, the virus enters a dormant phase, residing in the nerve ganglia of the affected area. Some individuals never have a recurrence, whereas others have regular recurrences. Recurrences are usually less severe than the initial episode and seem to be triggered by

*Trichomonas vaginalis*

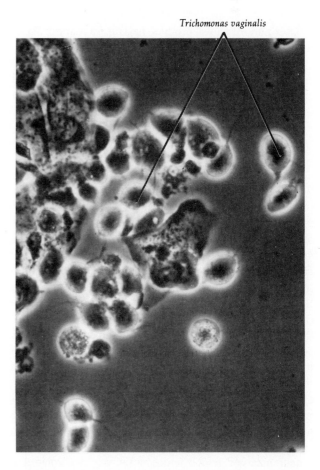

*Figure 3.11   Microscopic appearance of* Trichomonas vaginalis. *(Courtesy of Tortora G et al:* Microbiology, *3rd ed. Redwood City, CA: Benjamin/Cummings, 1989.)*

emotional stress, menstruation, ovulation, pregnancy, frequent or vigorous intercourse, poor health status or a generally run-down physical condition, tight clothing, or overheating. Diagnosis is made on the basis of the clinical appearance of the lesions, Pap smear or culture of the lesions, and sometimes blood testing for antibodies.

Studies suggest a possible link between genital herpes and dysplasia (abnormal cells) of the cervix or cervical cancer. This connection is still unclear. Women with a diagnosis of herpes should have yearly Pap smears.

There is no known cure for herpes. Prescriptive treatment is available to provide relief from pain and prevent complications from secondary infection. Women may apply acyclovir (Zovirax) ointment to reduce viral shedding and healing time of the lesions. Oral acyclovir can be prescribed for women with primary episodes and for recurrences.

Self-help suggestions include cleansing with povidone-iodine (Betadine) solution to prevent secondary infection and Burow's solution to relieve discomfort. Use of vitamin C or lysine is frequently suggested to prevent recurrence, although studies have not documented the effectiveness of these supplements. Keeping the genital area clean and dry, wearing loose clothing, and wearing cotton underwear or none at all will promote healing. Primary or recurrent lesions will heal without prescriptive therapies.

If herpes is present in the genital tract of a woman during childbirth, it can have a devastating, even fatal, effect on the newborn. For further discussion, see Chapter 12.

## SYPHILIS

Syphilis is a chronic infection caused by a spirochete, *Treponema pallidum*. Syphilis can be acquired congenitally through transplacental inoculation, and can result from maternal exposure to infected exudate during sexual contact, or from contact with open wounds or infected blood. The incubation period varies from 10 to 90 days, and even though no symptoms or lesions are noted during this time, the woman's blood contains spirochetes and is infectious.

Syphilis is divided into early and late stages. During the early stage (primary), a chancre appears at the site where the *Treponema pallidum* organism entered the body. Symptoms include slight fever, loss of weight, and malaise. The chancre persists for about four weeks and then disappears. In six weeks to six months, secondary symptoms appear. Skin eruptions called condylomata lata, which resemble wartlike plaques and are highly infectious, may appear on the vulva. Other secondary symptoms are acute arthritis, enlargement of the liver and spleen, non-tender enlarged lymph nodes, iritis, and a chronic sore throat with hoarseness. When infected in utero, the newborn will exhibit secondary stage symptoms of syphilis. If untreated, the client enters a latent period, which may last for several years. During the later latent phase immunity develops and the risk to the fetus is decreased to 10% (Eschenbach 1986). Tertiary or late syphilis may produce CNS or cardiovascular symptoms.

As a result of the disease's impact on the fetus in utero, serologic testing of every pregnant woman is recommended, and required by some state laws. Testing is done at the initial prenatal screening and repeated in the third trimester.

Diagnosis is made by dark-field examination for spirochetes. Blood tests such as VDRL (Venereal Disease Research Laboratories), RPR (Rapid Plasma Reagin), or the more specific FTA-ABS (fluorescent treponemal antibody absorption test) are commonly done. Blood studies may be negative if blood is drawn too early.

Syphilis is treated with intramuscular injection of benzathine penicillin G. If the woman is allergic to penicillin, erythromycin can be given. Maternal serologic testing may remain positive for eight months after treatment and the newborn may have a positive test for three months. If the mother is treated early in pregnancy the newborn is usually disease-free.

## GONORRHEA

Gonorrhea (popularly called "clap," "GC," "drip," or "dose") is an infection caused by the bacteria *Neisseria gonorrhoeae*. If a nonpregnant woman contracts the disease, she is at risk to develop pelvic inflammatory disease. If a woman becomes infected after the third month of pregnancy, the mucous plug in the cervix will prevent the infection from ascending, and it will remain localized in the urethra, cervix, and Bartholin's glands until the membranes rupture. Then it can spread upward.

The majority of women with gonorrhea are asymptomatic. Thus it is accepted practice to screen for this infection by doing a cervical culture during the initial prenatal examination. For women at high risk the culture may be repeated during the last month of pregnancy. Cultures of the urethra, throat, and rectum may also be required for diagnosis, depending on the body orifices used for intercourse.

The most common symptoms of gonorrheal infection include a purulent, greenish-yellow vaginal discharge; dysuria; and urinary frequency. Some women also develop inflammation and swelling of the vulva. The cervix may appear swollen and eroded and may secrete a foul-smelling discharge in which gonococci are present.

Treatment consists of antibiotic treatment with aqueous procaine penicillin G given intramuscularly to the infected woman. If the woman is allergic to penicillin, spectinomycin is given. Additional treatment may be required if the cultures remain positive 7 to 14 days after completion of treatment. All sexual partners must also be treated or the woman may become reinfected.

Women should be informed of the need for reculture to verify cure and the need for abstinence or condom use until cure is confirmed. Both sexual partners should be treated if either has a positive test for gonorrhea.

## HUMAN PAPILLOMA VIRUS (HPV) (CONDYLOMA ACUMINATA; VENEREAL WARTS)

Condyloma acuminata is a sexually transmitted infection caused by the human papilloma virus (HPV). Because of the increasing evidence of a link between HPV and cancer in both the female and male anogenital tract, the condition is receiving increasing attention. In a recent report, approximately 10% of women who tested positive for HPV progressed to an abnormal pap (cervical intraepithelial neoplasia, or CIN) within the first year (Symposium 1987). Because of this, women with a history of HPV should have Pap smears at least annually.

Often a woman seeks medical care after noticing single or multiple soft, grayish-pink, cauliflowerlike lesions in her genital area. The moist warm environment of the genital area is conducive to the growth of the warts, which may be present on the vulva, vagina, cervix, and anus. The incubation period following exposure is one to three months.

Because condyloma sometimes resembles other lesions and malignant transformation is possible, all large areas of genital warts should be biopsied and treatment should be instituted promptly (Ferenczy 1986). Small lesions can be treated with topically applied podophyllin, which the woman is instructed to wash off four hours after application. The drug is not used during pregnancy because it is thought to be teratogenic and in large doses has been associated with fetal death. If the woman is pregnant or if the lesions do not respond to podophyllin, trichloracetic acid, liquid nitrogen, or cryocautery may be used (Eschenbach 1986). Carbon dioxide laser therapy, performed under colposcopy, has a good success rate and is used if medical therapy has been unsuccessful or to treat large lesions. It is also safe to use for women who are pregnant (Holloway et al 1988).

## ACQUIRED IMMUNODEFICIENCY SYNDROME (AIDS)

Acquired immunodeficiency syndrome (AIDS) is a fatal disorder caused by a virus and occurs most commonly in homosexual or bisexual men, heterosexual partners of persons with AIDS, drug users, recipients of blood transfusions, Haitians, and Africans in Zaire. It can also be transmitted to a fetus in utero from an infected mother.

The care of a person with AIDS is primarily supportive, although some medications are being developed that seem to prolong life. The reader is referred to a medical-surgical text for a description of this care.

However, because the diagnosis of AIDS or the presence of the AIDS antibody has profound implications for a fetus if the woman is pregnant, AIDS is discussed in greater detail in Chapter 12.

## ROLE OF THE NURSE
### Nursing Assessment

The nurse working with women must become adept at taking a thorough history and identifying women at risk for sexually transmitted diseases. The nurse should be alert for signs and symptoms of sexually transmitted diseases and familiar with diagnostic procedures if STD is suspected.

While each STD has certain distinctive characteristics, the following complaints suggest the possibility of infection and warrant further investigation:

● Presence of a "sore" or lesion on the vulva
● Increased vaginal discharge or malodorous vaginal discharge
● Burning with urination

In many instances the woman is asymptomatic, but may report symptoms in her partner, especially painful urination or urethral discharge. It is often helpful to ask the woman whether her partner is experiencing any symptoms.

### Nursing Diagnosis

Nursing diagnoses that may apply when a woman has a sexually transmitted disease include:

● Altered family processes related to the effects of a diagnosis of STD on the couple's relationship
● Knowledge deficit related to the long-term effects of the diagnosis on childbearing status
● Personal identity disturbance related to difficulty in accepting the knowledge that the condition is sexually transmitted

### Nursing Plan and Implementation

In a supportive, nonjudgmental way the nurse provides the woman who has a sexually transmitted disease  with information about the disease, methods of transmission, implications for pregnancy or future fertility, and importance of thorough treatment. If treatment of her partner is indicated, the woman must understand that it is necessary in order to prevent a cycle of reinfection. She should also understand the need to abstain from sexual activity, if necessary, during treatment.

Some sexually transmitted diseases such as trichomoniasis or chlamydia may cause a woman concern but once diagnosed are rather simply treated. Other STDs may also be fairly simple to treat medically but may carry a stigma and be emotionally devastating for the woman.

The sensitive nurse can be especially helpful in encouraging the woman to explore her feelings about the diagnosis. She may experience anger or feel "betrayed" by a partner; she may feel guilt or see her diagnosis as a form of "punishment"; or she may feel concern about the long-term implications for future childbearing or ongoing intimate relationships. She may experience a myriad of differing emotions that she never expected. Opportunities to discuss her feelings in a nonjudgmental environment can be especially helpful. The nurse can offer suggestions about support groups if indicated and assist the woman in planning for her future with regard to sexual activity.

More subtly, the nurse's attitude of acceptance and matter-of-factness convey to the woman that she is still an acceptable person who happens to have an infection.

### Evaluation

Anticipated outcomes of nursing care include the following:

● The STD is identified and cured if possible. If not, supportive therapy is provided.

● The woman and her partner understand the infection, its method of transmission, its implications, and the therapy.

● The woman copes successfully with the impact of the diagnosis on her personal identity.

## ● Pelvic Inflammatory Disease (PID)

**Pelvic inflammatory disease (PID)** occurs in approximately 1% of women between 15 and 39, although sexually active young women between 15 and 24 have the highest infection rate (Eschenbach 1986). The disease is more common in women who have had multiple sexual partners, a history of PID, or an intrauterine device. It usually produces a tubal infection (salpingitis) that may or may not be accompanied by a pelvic abscess. However, perhaps the greatest problem of PID is that postinfection tubal damage is associated with a high incidence of infertility.

The organisms most frequently identified with PID include *Chlamydia trachomatis, Neisseria gonorrhoeae,* and *Mycoplasma hominis,* although other aerobic and anaerobic organisms that are often part of the normal vaginal flora have also been found in women with PID (Torrington 1985).

Symptoms of PID include bilateral sharp, cramping pain in the lower quadrants, fever, chills, purulent vaginal discharge, irregular bleeding, malaise, nausea, and vomiting. However, it is possible to be asymptomatic and have normal laboratory values.

Diagnosis consists of a clinical examination to define symptoms plus blood tests and a gonorrhea culture and test for chlamydia. Physical examination usually reveals direct abdominal tenderness with palpation, adnexal tenderness and cervical and uterine tenderness with movement (Chandelier sign). A palpable mass is evaluated with ultrasound. Laparoscopy may be used to confirm the diagnosis and to enable the examiner to obtain cultures from the fimbriated ends of the fallopian tubes.

Except in very mild cases, the woman is hospitalized and treated with intravenous antibiotics. Antibiotics such as doxycycline and cefoxitin are used if the causative organism is either *Chlamydia trachomatis* or *Neisseria gonorrhoeae,* while an abscess or the presence of anaerobes or gram-negative rods indicates treatment with clindamycin and gentamicin (Symposium 1987). In addition, supportive therapy is often indicated for severe symptoms. The sexual partner should also be treated. If the woman has an IUD, it is generally removed 24 to 48 hours after antibiotic therapy is started (Eschenbach 1986).

After the infection is treated, microsurgical techniques are sometimes used to release any adhesions and repair tubal damage.

### NURSING ASSESSMENT

The nurse is alert to factors in a woman's history that put her at risk for PID. Even though fewer IUDs are available, many women still have them, and the nurse should question the woman about possible symptoms, such as aching pain in the lower abdomen, foul-smelling discharge, malaise, and the like. The woman who is acutely ill will have obvious symptoms, but a low-grade infection is more difficult to detect.

### NURSING DIAGNOSIS

Nursing diagnoses that may apply to a woman with PID include:

● Pain related to peritoneal irritation

● Knowledge deficit related to a lack of understanding of the possible effects of PID on fertility

### NURSING PLAN AND IMPLEMENTATION

The nurse plays a vital role in helping to prevent or  detect PID. The nurse should spend time discussing risk factors related to this infection. The woman who uses an IUD for contraception and has multiple sexual partners should clearly understand the risk she faces. The nurse should discuss signs and symptoms of PID and stress the importance of early detection. Many care givers advocate treating the woman's sexual partners to prevent reinfection (Symposium 1987).

The woman who develops PID should understand the importance of completing her antibiotic treatment and of returning for follow-up evaluation. She should also understand the possibility of decreased fertility following the infection.

### EVALUATION

Anticipated outcomes of nursing care include the following:

● The woman clearly understands her condition, her therapy, and the possible long-term implications of PID on her fertility.

● The woman completes her course of therapy, and the PID is cured.

● ## *Care of the Woman with an Abnormal Finding During Pelvic Examination*

### ABNORMAL PAP SMEAR RESULTS

The purpose of the **Pap smear** is to detect the presence of cellular abnormalities by obtaining a smear containing cells from the cervix and the endocervical canal. Precancerous and cancerous conditions as well as atypical findings and inflammatory changes can be identified by microscopic examination. Regular Pap smears are important because in recent years the incidence of precancerous disorders of the cervix among teens has increased dramatically and the average age of women diagnosed with cancer of the cervix has decreased (Spitzer and Krumholz 1988).

Early detection of abnormalities allows early changes to be treated before cells reach the precancerous or cancerous stage. For this reason women should be encouraged to have regular physical examinations including Pap smears. Controversy exists about the frequency of Pap smears. The American Cancer Society has recommended a Pap smear every three years for low-risk women after three negative annual smears, while the American College of Obstetricians and Gynecologists recommends annual exams for all women.

Table 3.6 identifies Pap smears by class and description and specifies the appropriate response for each result.

Diagnostic or therapeutic procedures employed in cases of cellular abnormalities include repetition of Pap smears at shorter intervals, colposcopy and endocervical biopsy, cryotherapy, or laser conization. Decisions for management are based on the specific report.

Women who had first coitus at an early age, have multiple sexual partners, or a history of herpes, condyloma accuminata, or other STDs have an increased risk of abnormal cell changes and cervical cancer. Some researchers believe that precancerous cervical cell changes are more common in women who have been exposed to diethylstilbestrol (DES), but other researchers disagree.

### OVARIAN MASSES

Between 70% and 80% of ovarian masses are benign (Martin 1978). More than 50% are functional cysts occurring most commonly in women 20 to 40 years of age (Martin 1978). Functional cysts are rare in women who take oral contraceptives.

Ovarian cysts usually represent physiologic variations

## Table 3.6  Classification of Pap Smears

| Class | Description | Response |
|-------|-------------|----------|
| 1 | Negative for malignant cells<br>    with *Candida albicans*<br>    with *Trichomonas vaginalis*<br>    with inflammation | Repeat smear annually.<br>Treat with antifungal cream; repeat in three months.<br>Treat patient and partner with metronidazole; repeat in three months.<br>Culture for *Chlamydia trachomatis, Neisseria gonorrhoeae*; treat appropriately. |
| 2 | Inflammatory squamous or endocervical atypia<br><br>Koilocytotic or condylomatous atypia | Controversial—if possible refer for colposcopy and biopsy. Otherwise, treat the apparent source of inflammation and repeat in three months. If still atypical, refer for colposcopy.<br>Refer for colposcopy and biopsy. |
| 3 | Dysplasia—mild, moderate, or severe | Refer for colposcopy and biopsy. |
| 4 | Positive for in situ carcinoma | Refer for colposcopy and biopsy. |
| 5 | Positive for invasive carcinoma | Refer for colposcopy and biopsy. |

Source: Spitzer M, Krumholz BA: Pap screening for teenagers: A lifesaving precaution. *Contemp OB/GYN* January 1988; 31:33.

in the menstrual cycle (Sciarra et al 1984). Dermoid cysts (cystic teratomas) comprise 10% of all benign ovarian masses. Cartilage, bone, teeth, skin, or hair can be observed in these cysts. Endometriomas, or "chocolate cysts," are another common type of ovarian mass.

A woman with an ovarian mass may be asymptomatic; the mass may be noted on a routine pelvic examination. She may experience a sensation of fullness or cramping in the lower abdomen (often unilateral), dyspareunia, irregular bleeding, or delayed menstruation.

Diagnosis is made on the basis of a palpable mass with or without tenderness and other related symptoms. Radiography or ultrasonography may be used to assist or confirm the diagnosis.

The woman is frequently kept under observation for a month or two because most cysts will resolve on their own and are harmless. Alternatively, oral contraceptives may be prescribed for one to two months to suppress ovarian function. If this regimen has been effective, a repeat pelvic examination should be normal. If the mass is still present after 60 days of observation and oral contraceptive therapy, a diagnostic laparoscopy or laparotomy may be considered (Merrill 1986). Tubal or ovarian lesions, ectopic pregnancy, cancer, infection, or appendicitis also must be ruled out before a diagnosis can be confirmed.

Surgery is not always necessary but will be considered if the mass is larger than 6 to 7 cm in circumference; if the woman is over 40 years of age with an adnexal mass, a persistent mass, or continuous pain; and if the woman is taking oral contraceptives. Surgical exploration is also indicated when a palpable mass is found in an infant or young girl or in a postmenopausal woman (Merrill 1986).

Women who are taking oral contraceptives should be informed of their preventive effect against ovarian masses (Dickey 1983). Women may need clear explanations about why the initial therapy is observation. A discussion of the origin and resolution of ovarian cysts may clarify this treatment plan. If surgery should involve removal or impaired function of one ovary, the woman should be assured that the remaining ovary should take over ovarian functioning and that pregnancy is still possible.

## UTERINE MASSES

Fibroid tumors or leiomyomas are among the most common benign disease entities in women and are the most common reason for gynecologic surgery. Between 20% and 50% of women develop leiomyomas by 40 years of age (Sciarra et al 1984). The potential for cancer is minimal. Leiomyomas are more common in black women.

Smooth muscle cells are present in whorls and arise from uterine muscles and connective tissue. The size varies from 1 to 2 cm to the size of a ten-week fetus. Frequently the woman is asymptomatic. Lower abdominal pain, fullness or pressure, menorrhagia, metrorrhagia, or increased dysmenorrhea may occur, particularly with large leiomyomas. Ultrasonography revealing masses or nodules can assist in and confirm the diagnosis. Leiomyoma is also considered a possible diagnosis when masses or nodules involving the uterus are palpated on a pelvic examination.

The majority of these masses require no treatment and will shrink after menopause. Close observation for symptoms or for an increase in size of the uterus or the masses may be the only management most women will require. Routine repeat pelvic examinations every three to six months are commonly recommended unless there are other symptoms.

If a woman notices symptoms, or pelvic examination reveals that the mass is increasing in size, surgery (myomectomy, dilatation and curettage, or hysterectomy) will be recommended. The choice of surgery depends on the age and reproductive status of the woman and/or the significance of the noted changes. There are no medications or therapies to prevent fibroids.

## ROLE OF THE NURSE
### Nursing Assessment

Except for those nurses specially trained to do pelvic examinations and Pap smears, these procedures are not routinely done by nurses. In most cases, nursing assessment is directed toward an evaluation of the woman's understanding of the findings, their implications, and her psychosocial response.

### Nursing Diagnosis

Nursing diagnoses that might apply to a woman with an abnormal finding from a pelvic examination include:

● Anxiety related to the significance of the finding

● Fear related to the possibility of cancer

● Knowledge deficit related to the meaning of the diagnosis

### Nursing Plan and Implementation

The woman needs accurate information on etiology, symptomatology, and treatment options. She should be encouraged to report symptoms and keep appointments for follow-up examination and evaluation. The woman needs realistic reassurance if her condition is benign; she may require counseling and effective emotional support if a malignancy is likely. If the management plan includes surgery, she may need the nurse's support in obtaining a second opinion and making her decision.

### Evaluation

Anticipated outcomes of nursing care include the following:

- The woman understands the abnormal finding, the diagnostic procedures that are indicated, and the possible causes of the abnormal finding.
- The woman copes successfully with the stress associated with waiting for a definite diagnosis.

## CARE OF THE WOMAN UNDERGOING HYSTERECTOMY

**Hysterectomy,** the surgical removal of the uterus, is performed for a variety of reasons including cancer, severe uterine prolapse, large leiomyomas (fibroid tumors), severe pelvic infection, endometriosis, adenomyosis, and dysfunctional uterine bleeding (DUB). A *total hysterectomy* involves the removal of the entire uterus. When the uterus, fallopian tubes, and both ovaries are removed the procedure is called *a total abdominal hysterectomy with a bilateral salpingoophorectomy (TAH-BSO).*

The uterus can be removed through the vagina (*vaginal hysterectomy*) or through the abdomen (*abdominal hysterectomy*). An abdominal hysterectomy is used when exploration of the abdomen is anticipated, in the presence of severe infection, or if the uterus is very large. The vaginal route is used for cancer in situ of the cervix and for prolapse of the uterus. It may also be used for DUB.

When the uterus is removed the woman no longer has menstrual periods. If her ovaries remain, however, her hormonal secretions will not be changed. If the ovaries are also removed and the woman has not experienced menopause yet, estrogen and progesterone replacement therapy are often started to avoid the effects of a surgically induced menopause.

The personal significance of hysterectomy varies from woman to woman. Some women, especially those who have completed their childbearing and who have dealt with life-style limitations because of severe bleeding problems, are relieved by hysterectomy. Others may find the implications of loss of the uterus troubling and may experience problems with body image. Women whose hysterectomy was done because of malignancy must deal with the implications that a diagnosis of cancer has for them.

Physically, orgasm is still possible. If the surgery has resulted in a shortening of the woman's vagina, some dyspareunia may occur.

### Nursing Assessment

During the preoperative period the nurse assesses the woman's understanding of her diagnosis, its implications, and her feelings about surgery. The nurse also determines the woman's understanding of surgery and postoperative care.

Postoperative assessments are the assessments that are part of surgical nursing care. The nurse assesses vital signs, comfort level, hydration, urinary output, signs of infection, and presence of bleeding. The nurse auscultates the lungs to detect possible adventitious sounds, auscultates the abdomen for bowel sounds, and palpates the abdomen to detect distention. The nurse also assesses the status of the incision if an abdominal incision is done.

### Nursing Diagnosis

Examples of nursing diagnoses that may apply include:

- Knowledge deficit related to postoperative care and routines
- Fear related to the possibility of surgical complications
- Body image disturbance related to the loss of childbearing ability secondary to surgery

### Nursing Plan and Implementation

Based on the findings of the assessment, the nurse provides information about the woman's condition, the surgical procedure, and normal postoperative activities such as ambulation, coughing, and deep breathing. The nurse may have the woman practice breathing while supporting her abdomen if an abdominal hysterectomy is planned.

If a vaginal hysterectomy is scheduled an antiseptic douche may be ordered for the morning of surgery. In many instances the woman comes to the hospital early on the surgical day rather than the evening before, so the time available for teaching is limited.

Postoperatively the nurse provides care according to the woman's assessed needs. IV fluids are maintained, analgesics are administered, and any signs of complications are reported promptly and appropriate therapy is started. As with any situation, prevention of complications is an important aspect of nursing care. (For further discussion of postoperative care, please consult a medical-surgical nursing text.)

The nurse should be alert to the woman's response to the surgery and provide opportunities for discussion. Women who have a vaginal hysterectomy recover rapidly and are often discharged by the second postoperative day. Women with an abdominal hysterectomy are hospitalized somewhat longer.

### Evaluation

Anticipated outcomes of nursing care include the following:

- The woman is able to discuss her condition, her surgery, and the long-term implications of both.
- The woman recovers successfully from surgery and no complications develop. If complications do develop they are detected promptly and treated successfully.

# CARE OF THE WOMAN WITH A URINARY TRACT INFECTION

A urinary tract infection (UTI) may be a mere inconvenience or may reach life-threatening severity. Bacteria usually enter the urinary tract by way of the urethra. The organisms are capable of migrating against the downward flow of urine. The shortness of the female urethra facilitates the passage of bacteria into the bladder. Other conditions that facilitate bacterial entry are relative incompetence of the urinary sphincter, frequent enuresis (bedwetting) prior to adolescence, and urinary catheterization (Sciarra et al 1984). A habit of wiping from back to front after urination may transfer bacteria from the anorectal area to the urethra.

Voluntarily suppressing the desire to urinate is a predisposing factor. Retention overdistends the bladder and can lead to an infection. There seems to be a relationship between recurring UTI and sexual intercourse. General poor health or lowered resistance to infection can also increase a woman's susceptibility to UTI.

*Asymptomatic bacteriuria* (ASB) (bacteria in the urine actively multiplying without accompanying clinical symptoms) constitutes about 6% to 8% of UTI. This becomes especially significant if the woman is pregnant (Fantl 1986). Between 20% and 30% of pregnant women with untreated ASB will go on to develop cystitis or acute pyelonephritis by the third trimester (Whalley 1986). Asymptomatic bacteriuria is almost always caused by a single organism. If more than one type of bacteria is cultured, the possibility of urine culture contamination must be considered.

The most common cause of ASB is *Escherichia coli.* Other commonly found causative organisms include *Klebsiella* and *Proteus.*

A woman who has had a UTI is more susceptible to a recurrent infection. If a pregnant woman develops an acute UTI, especially with high temperature, amniotic fluid infection may develop and retard the growth of the placenta. Increased risk of premature labor exists if the infection occurs near term.

## Lower Urinary Tract Infection (Cystitis)

Because urinary tract infections are ascending, it is important to recognize and diagnose a lower UTI early to avoid the sequelae associated with upper UTI.

Symptoms of frequency, pyuria, and dysuria without bacteriuria may indicate urethritis caused by *Chlamydia trachomatis.* It has become a common pathogen in the genitourinary system.

When cystitis develops, the initial symptom is often dysuria, specifically at the end of urination. Urgency and frequency also occur. Cystitis is usually accompanied by a low-grade fever (101°F or lower), and hematuria is seen occasionally. Urine specimens usually contain an abnormal number of leukocytes and bacteria.

Oral sulfonamides, particularly sulfisoxazole, are generally effective against lower UTI. If the woman is pregnant these should only be used in early pregnancy since they interfere with protein binding of bilirubin in the fetus. Use in the last few weeks of pregnancy can lead to neonatal hyperbilirubinemia and kernicterus. Other drugs that are usually effective (and apparently safe for a fetus) are ampicillin and nitrofurantoin (Furadantin). Nitrofurantoin crosses the placenta, but no harm to the fetus has been demonstrated.

### NURSING ASSESSMENT

During each visit the nurse notes any complaints from the woman of pain on urination or other urinary difficulties. If any concerns arise, the nurse obtains a clean-catch urine specimen from the woman.

### NURSING DIAGNOSIS

Nursing diagnoses that may apply to a woman with a lower UTI include:

● Pain related to dysuria secondary to the urinary tract infection

● Knowledge deficit related to a lack of understanding of self-care measures to help prevent recurrence of UTI

### NURSING PLAN AND IMPLEMENTATION

The nurse should make sure the woman is aware of  good hygiene practices, since most bacteria enter through the urethra after having spread from the anal area. The Essential Facts to Remember—Information for Women on Ways to Avoid Cystitis—provides information on recommendations nurses can make to women to help them avoid cystitis. The nurse should also reinforce instructions or answer questions regarding the prescribed antibiotic, the amount of liquids to take, and the reasons for these treatments. Cystitis usually responds rapidly to treatment, but follow-up urinary cultures are important.

### EVALUATION

Anticipated outcomes of nursing care include the following:

● The woman implements self-care measures to help prevent cystitis as part of her personal routine.

● The woman can identify the signs, symptoms, therapy, and possible complications of cystitis.

● The woman's infection is cured.

## ● Upper Urinary Tract Infection (Pyelonephritis)

Pyelonephritis (inflammatory disease of the kidneys) is less common but more serious than cystitis and is often preceded by lower UTI. It is more common during the latter part of pregnancy or early postpartum and poses a serious threat to maternal and fetal well-being.

Acute pyelonephritis has a sudden onset with chills, high temperature of 39.6–40.6°C (103–105°F), and flank pain (either unilateral or bilateral). The right side is almost always involved if the woman is pregnant because the large bulk of intestines to the left pushes the uterus to the right, putting pressure on the right ureter and kidney. Nausea, vomiting, and general malaise may ensue. With accompanying cystitis, frequency, urgency, and burning with urination may be experienced.

Edema of the renal parenchyma or ureteritis with blockage and swelling of the ureter may lead to temporary suppression of urinary output. This is accompanied by severe colicky pain, vomiting, dehydration, and ileus of the large bowel. The woman with acute pyelonephritis will generally have increased diastolic blood pressure, positive fluorescent antibody titer (FA-test), low creatinine clearance, significant bacteremia in urine culture, pyuria, and presence of white blood cell casts.

Often the woman is hospitalized and started on intravenous antibiotics. In the case of obstructive pyelonephritis, a blood culture is necessary. The woman is kept on bed rest. After the sensitivity report is received the antibiotic is changed as necessary.

If signs of urinary obstruction occur or continue, the ureter may be catheterized to establish adequate drainage.

With appropriate drug therapy, the woman's temperature should return to normal. The pain subsides and the urine shows no bacteria within two to three days. Follow-up urinary cultures are needed to assure that the infection has been eliminated completely.

### NURSING ASSESSMENT

During the woman's visit the nurse obtains a sexual and medical history to identify whether she is at risk for UTI. A clean-catch urine specimen is evaluated for evidence of ASB.

### NURSING PLAN AND IMPLEMENTATION

The nurse provides the woman with information to help her recognize the signs of UTI, so she can contact her care giver as soon as possible. The nurse also discusses hygiene practices, the advantages of wearing cotton underwear, and the need to void frequently to prevent urinary stasis.

## Essential Facts to Remember

### Information for Women on Ways to Avoid Cystitis

- If you use a diaphragm for contraception try changing methods or using another size of diaphragm.
- Avoid bladder irritants such as alcohol, caffeine products, and carbonated beverages.
- Increase fluid intake, especially water, to a minimum of six to eight glasses per day.
- Make regular urination a habit; avoid long waits.
- Practice good genital hygiene, including wiping from front to back after urination and bowel movements.
- Be aware that vigorous or frequent sexual activity may contribute to urinary tract infection.
- Urinate before and after intercourse to empty the bladder and cleanse the urethra.
- Complete medication regimens even if symptoms decrease.
- Do not use medication left over from previous infections.
- Drink cranberry juice to acidify the urine. This has been found to relieve symptoms in some cases.

The nurse stresses the importance of maintaining a good fluid intake. Drinking cranberry juice daily and taking 500 mg vitamin C both help acidify the urine and may help prevent recurrence of infection. Women with a history of UTI find it helpful to drink a glass of fluid prior to sexual intercourse and void afterward.

### EVALUATION

Anticipated outcomes of nursing care include the following:

- The woman completes her prescribed course of antibiotic therapy.
- The woman is able to discuss factors contributing to UTI and methods of preventing UTIs.
- The woman incorporates preventive self-care measures into her daily regimen.

## ● Cystocele and Pelvic Relaxation

A cystocele is the downward displacement of the bladder, which appears as a bulge in the anterior vaginal wall. Arbitrary classifications of mild to severe are frequently given. Genetic predisposition, childbearing, obesity, and increased age are factors that may contribute to cystocele.

Symptoms of stress incontinence are most common, including loss of urine with coughing, sneezing, laughing, or sudden exertion. Vaginal fullness, a bulging out of the vaginal wall, or a dragging sensation may also be noticeable.

If pelvic relaxation is mild, Kegel exercises are helpful in restoring tone. The exercises involve contraction and relaxation of the pubococcygeal muscle. Women have found these exercises helpful before and after childbirth in maintaining vaginal muscle tone. Estrogen may improve the condition of vaginal mucous membranes—especially in menopausal women. Vaginal pessaries or rings may be used if surgery is undesirable or impossible or until surgery can be scheduled. Surgery may be considered for cystoceles considered moderate to severe.

The nurse may instruct the woman in the use of Kegel exercises. Information on causes and contributing factors and discussion of possible alternative therapies will greatly assist the woman.

## ● MENOPAUSE

**Menopause,** the time when menses cease, occurs near the end of middle age and is a period of transition for women, marking the end of their reproductive abilities. A variety of physiologic and hormonal changes occur during this period. Because many women will live one third to one half of their lives postmenopausally, there has been a tendency in current literature to address the stigma that was long associated with menopause. This trend should continue as the women of the "baby boom" generation approach menopause. These new attitudes are evident in the media as more actresses portray sexually appealing, strong-willed women who are middle-aged or older.

A woman's approach to menopause, or the *climacteric,* is influenced by social forces in her culture. It is important to determine if she has internalized Victorian beliefs about reproductive and sexual behaviors. Does she believe that sex should be limited to procreative purposes only? Is she intimidated by stereotypes of "older women"? These and other questions may help nurses understand a particular woman's response to this stage in her life. Spurred by the feminist movement, research is increasing in the area of adjustment and behaviors before, during, and after menopause. Of particular interest is a study by Uphold and Susman (1981). The results stress the importance of the quality of marital relationships as correlated with the reporting of climacteric symptoms. The most frequent and severe symptoms were reported by women whose marital adjustment was low. Symptoms were not related to the "empty nest" stage of childrearing as has often been assumed. Further research should consider the presence of and satisfaction with the support systems in women's lives.

## ● Physical Aspects

The physical characteristics of menopause are linked to the shift from a cyclic to a noncyclic hormone pattern.

Menopause usually occurs between 45 and 52 years of age. The age of onset may be influenced by nutritional, cultural, or genetic factors. The physiologic mechanisms initiating its onset are not exactly known. The onset of menopause occurs when estrogen levels become so low that menstruation ceases.

Generally ovulation ceases one to two years before menopause (the cessation of menses), but individual variation exists. Atrophy of the ovaries gradually occurs. Because the endometrium maintains a persistent state of proliferation, there is a tendency toward the development of uterine fibroids and endometriosis.

Many menopausal women experience hot flashes, a feeling of heat arising from the chest and spreading to the neck and face. The hot flashes are often accompanied by sweating and sleep disturbances. These episodes may occur as often as 20 to 30 times a day and generally last three to five minutes. Some women also experience dizzy spells, palpitations, and weakness. Most women deal with the hot flashes fairly well. Some report that using a fan or drinking a cool liquid helps. Still others seek relief from estrogen replacement therapy.

Long-range physical changes may include osteoporosis, a decrease in the bony skeletal mass. The bones become more brittle and can more easily be broken. This change is thought to occur in association with lowered estrogen and androgen levels, lack of physical exercise, and a chronic low intake of calcium. The occurrence of diabetes mellitus increases at this age. Loss of protein from the skin and supportive tissues causes wrinkling. Postmenopausal women frequently gain weight, which may be due to excessive caloric intake rather than to a change in adipose deposits.

Vulvar atrophy occurs late, and the pubic hair thins, turns gray or white, and may ultimately disappear. The labia shrivel and lose their heightened pigmentation. Pelvic fascia and muscles atrophy, resulting in decreased pelvic support. The breasts become pendulous and decrease in size and firmness.

The uterine endometrium and myometrium atrophy, as do the cervical glands. The uterine cavity constricts. The fallopian tubes and ovaries atrophy extensively. The vaginal mucosa becomes smooth and thin and the rugae disappear, leading to loss of elasticity. As a result, intercourse may be painful. This may be overcome with the use of lubricating gel or saliva. Dryness of the mucuous membrane can lead to burning and itching. The vaginal pH level increases as the number of Döderlein's bacilli decreases.

Women are still multiorgasmic and sexual interest and activity may even improve as the need for contraception disappears and personal growth and awareness increase.

## ● Estrogen Replacement Therapy

In the past, **estrogen replacement therapy (ERT)** was controversial, but currently health care givers view it with increasing favor for certain women. Estrogen replacement is helpful in stopping hot flushes and night sweats and in reversing atrophic vaginal changes. Perhaps its greatest value, however, lies in its ability to retard bone loss and decrease the fractures associated with osteoporosis.

Osteoporosis is a condition characterized by loss of bone mass, which puts an individual at risk for nontraumatic fractures. Osteoporosis is more common in women who are middle-aged or older. The following risk factors are also associated with osteoporosis:

● White or Asian
● Small-boned and thin
● Family history of osteoporosis
● Lack of regular exercise
● Nulliparous
● Early onset of menopause
● Consistently low intake of calcium
● Cigarette smoking
● Moderate to heavy alcohol intake

Pre- or postmenopausal women with four or more risk factors for osteoporosis should have bone mass measurements done. The woman's height should be measured at each visit because a loss of height is often an early sign that vertebrae are being compressed because of reduced bone mass (Miller 1988). A variety of conditions, including malabsorption syndrome, cancer, cirrhosis of the liver, chronic use of cortisone, and rheumatoid arthritis, can cause secondary arthritis, which resembles osteoporosis. If these secondary causes have been eliminated treatment for osteoporosis is instituted.

Prevention of osteoporosis is a primary goal of care. Women are advised to maintain an adequate calcium intake. Approximately 1000 mg of elemental calcium is recommended for premenopausal women and 1500 mg for postmenopausal women. To achieve this level most women require supplements (Bilezikian and Shane 1988). Vitamin D supplements are also recommended. Women are also advised to participate regularly in exercise, to consume only modest quantities of alcohol and caffeine, and to stop smoking. This is especially important because alcohol and smoking have a negative effect on the rate of bone resorption (Mezrow and Rebar 1988). Women with no contraindications to estrogen who are showing evidence of bone loss are good candidates for ERT.

When estrogen is given alone it can produce endometrial hyperplasia and increase the risk of endometrial cancer. Thus, in women who still have a uterus, estrogen is opposed by giving a progestin for a portion of the cycle. Currently opinion varies as to the number of days that progesterone (Provera) should be included. Typically estrogen is given the first 25 days of the month with 10 mg Provera added for days 13 to 25 (Mezrow and Rebar 1988).

| Table 3.7 Benefits and Risks of Estrogen Replacement Therapy (ERT) | |
|---|---|
| **Benefits** | **Risks** |
| Stops hot flushes and night sweats | Increases risk of endometrial cancer unless progestin is added |
| Reverses atrophic genital changes | May increase risk of cholelithiasis |
| Retards bone loss and decreases osteoporotic fractures | May worsen migraine headaches |
| Increases REM sleep | May increase risk of hypertension (idiosyncratic reaction) |
| May decrease atherosclerotic coronary artery disease (presumably by increasing HDL) | May increase risk of breast cancer (highly doubtful) |
| May protect against development of breast cancer | May increase risk of intravascular coagulation (highly doubtful) |
| May decrease risk of hypertension | May induce enlargement of existing fibroids |
| May decrease number and intensity of migraine headaches | May worsen existing endometriosis |
| May have beneficial psychologic and mental effects | May affect glucose tolerance adversely |
| May retard aging of skin | |
| May improve sexual relations | |
| May improve quality of life | |

Source: Mezrow G, Rebar RW: Tailoring ERT to fit the patient. *Contemp OB/GYN* April 15, 1988; 31S:51.

(Some care givers still prefer to add the Provera for days 16 to 25.) The benefits and risks of ERT are summarized in Table 3.7. While most women take estrogen orally in tablet form, some women prefer the transdermal estrogen skin patch.

A thorough history, physical examination including Pap smear, and baseline mammogram are indicated before starting ERT. An initial endometrial biopsy is no longer recommended for all women beginning ERT, but is indicated for women with an increased risk of endometrial cancer and in those with irregular vaginal bleeding. The frequency of endometrial biopsies for women on ERT is controversial at this time. Some recommend them every two years or after any episodes of abnormal bleeding (Mezrow and Rebar 1988).

Women taking estrogen should be advised to stop immediately if they develop headaches, visual changes, signs of thrombophlebitis, or chest pain.

Research to find additional therapies for osteoporosis is ongoing. Calcitonin inhibits bone resorption and has been approved for use by the FDA. However, it is expensive, requires daily injections, and the increased bone mass it promotes may level off after one year of therapy. Fluoride is inexpensive and effective in about half of users. However, it is not known yet if the quality of the bone produced following long-term fluoride use is as good as bone produced without fluoride supplementation.

## ● Role of the Nurse

Menopausal women may need assistance, in the form of counseling, to adjust successfully to this developmental phase of life. Reaction to menopause is determined to a large extent by the kind of life the woman has lived, by the security she has in her feminine identity, and by her feelings of self-worth and self-esteem.

Nurses or other health professionals can help the menopausal woman achieve high-level functioning at this time in her life. Of paramount importance is the nurse's ability to understand and provide support for the woman's views and feelings. Whether the woman expresses "relief and delight" or "tearfulness and fear," the nurse needs to use an empathetic approach in counseling, health teaching, or providing physical care. Touch and caring as nursing measures may enhance the self-actualization of both nurse and client.

Nurses should explore the question of comfort during sexual intercourse. In counseling the woman the nurse may say, for example, "After menopause many women notice that their vagina seems dryer and intercourse can be uncomfortable. Have you noticed any changes?" This gives the woman information and may open discussion. The nurse can then go on to stress that dryness and shrinking of the vagina can cause discomfort and difficulty during intercourse. Lubrication with a water-soluble jelly will help provide relief. Use of estrogen, orally or in vaginal creams, may also be indicated. Increased frequency of intercourse will maintain some elasticity in the vagina.

When assessing the menopausal woman, the nurse should address the question of sexual activity openly but tactfully because many woman in this age group may have been socialized to be reticent in discussing sex.

The crucial need of women in the perimenopausal period of life is adequate information about the changes taking place in their bodies and their lives. Supplying that information provides both a challenge and an opportunity for nurses. A woman at menopause looks forward to about 30 more years of life. As she accomplishes the developmental tasks of the climacteric period and adjusts to changes that her life brings, she can affirm her worth and go on to an exciting and challenging future (Figure 3.12).

## ● SOCIAL ISSUES AND THE CONTEMPORARY WOMAN

Because of political and social changes that have occurred in the Western world within the past two decades, women's options for personal and professional growth have expanded dramatically. Although many women still choose the traditional "women's" careers and become nurses, teachers, and mothers, others are entering occupations that until recently were filled almost exclusively by men. Women can be found in almost all occupations and are

*Figure 3.12    The postmenopausal years can be an enjoyable, exciting time!*

sharing in the benefits of these positions. Progress has its cost, however. For example, the woman with a career and a family may have difficulty maintaining both. As women become viewed as financially independent, the effects of "no fault" divorce often leave them without adequate financial support. Moreover, many of the diseases traditionally associated with men in high-stress occupations are now occurring more commonly in women.

A discussion of all the issues facing today's women is beyond the scope of this text. Here we will focus on a few selected issues: poverty, the environment, and rape.

## ● *Women and Poverty*

The economic plight of many women is reflected in the phenomenon referred to as the *feminization of poverty* (Pearce 1983). Simply stated, a growing number of women, especially single women with children, live on incomes at or below the poverty level. Projections indicate that by the year 2000 nearly all people living in poverty will be women and children (see Table 3.8).

The feminization of poverty has occurred primarily as a result of three factors:

1. *The increase in female-headed households.* The increase in the number of female-headed households is closely associated with divorce. As a result of divorce a woman's standard of living generally decreases approximately 73% while the male's increases by 41% (Leslie and Swider 1986). In addition, although women receive custody of the children in 90% of cases (Enrenreich and Piven 1984), only 35% of women receive child support, and only half of those who are granted child support receive the full amount (Pearce 1983).

2. *The inequities of the labor market.* In today's labor market the largest percentage of women work in low-paying, low-status occupations with few benefits and little chance for advancement (Leslie and Swider 1986). Sex discrimination and occupational bias also work to the detriment of women (Pearce 1983).

3. *The welfare system.* The welfare system does provide assistance to many women but the amount of assistance does not even raise the family to the poverty level. The elimination of work incentives and the incorporation of an earnings cap for Aid to Families with Dependent Children (AFDC) make it difficult to make ends meet (Zinn and Sarri 1984).

The effects of poverty on access to health care are extensive. Women living in poverty are frequently without any type of health insurance. Furthermore, since 1981 funding cuts have been made in AFDC, Medicaid, the food stamp program, and the Women, Infants, and Children (WIC) nutrition program. These cuts come at a time when the benefits of adequate nutrition and prenatal care have

### Table 3.8  Some Facts About Poverty in the United States

The rate of poverty in the general population is 15.2%.

78% of all the poor are women.

5% of male-headed couple households live at or below the level of poverty.

36% of female-headed households live at or below the level of poverty.

21% of white female-headed households live at or below the level of poverty.

51.7% of black female-headed households live at or below the level of poverty.

53.4% of Hispanic female-headed households live at or below the level of poverty.

Source: Leslie LA, Swider SM: Changing factors and changing needs in women's health care. *Nurs Clin North Am* March 1986; 21:111. Sidel R: *Women and Children Last.* New York, Viking, 1986.

been documented to save $2 to $11 for each dollar spent (Mundinger 1986).

The effects of poverty on women's health care require further investigation. Currently the status of mothers and babies is being studied by the Public Health Service Task Force on Women's Health Issues, which is considering not only childbearing but also other factors that affect women's health. They have identified general recommendations such as promoting a safe, healthful physical and social environment; providing services for the prevention and treatment of illness; coordinating research and evaluation; educating and informing the public; disseminating research information; and designing guidance for legislative and regulatory measures.

Nurses often work with women on welfare. They *see* the effects of poverty on childbearing families. Because of the limited resources of these women, nurses' efforts to provide quality care may be stymied. Nurses can take action to help ease the crisis resulting from the feminization of poverty by:

● Developing personal awareness and understanding of the impact of poverty on the childbearing woman and her family

● Learning to identify women at risk so that support, counseling, and referral can be provided

● Working with community organizations and planners to develop strategies to help women in need of assistance

● Being available to legislators as a resource person to help them become more knowledgeable about issues that affect women

● Supporting or instituting research to dispel myths associated with poverty

## ● *Environmental Hazards*

As more women enter the work force they are exposed to an ever increasing number of chemicals and environmental pollutants (Figure 3.13). A number of substances have been identified as potential dangers to childbearing women.

1. *Hazards of the microelectronic industry.* A link exists between the various substances used in this field and birth defects, spontaneous abortions, and other reproductive problems. Among the "high-tech" hazards are glycol ethers, arsenic, lead, and radiation (Hembree 1986).

2. *Heavy metals (lead and mercury).* Lead was one of the first agents found to cause adverse reproductive effects. Lead contamination causes an increased rate of spontaneous abortions, stillbirths, and prematurity; surviving children are more likely to have impaired growth and neurological damage (Bang et al 1983). These adverse effects have been found both in women who work in the lead industry and in wives of male workers (Hill 1984).

   Mercury was associated with an increased incidence of cerebral palsy when there was consumption of contaminated fish and shellfish in Japan from 1953 to 1960. The effects of occupational exposure are not yet clear, but mercury has been found to accumulate in the placentas of pregnant dental workers (Bang et al 1983).

3. *Vinyl chloride.* There is an increased incidence of spontaneous abortion and stillbirth in wives of workers exposed to vinyl chloride. The fetal death may be caused by chromosomal changes in the male germ cell (Bang et al 1983).

4. *Chloroprene.* Chloroprene is a liquid used to manufacture neoprene rubber. A study of wives of chloroprene-exposed males indicated a threefold increase in the spontaneous abortion rate (Bang et al 1983). Direct effects on the exposed female worker are not known at this time.

5. *Halogenated hydrocarbons.* Halogenated hydrocarbons are associated with a twofold increase in births of children with malignancies (Bang et al 1983). Polychlorinated biphenyls (PCBs) are the most widely known halogenated hydrocarbons and are used in the manufacture of plastics and as heat-exchange fluids in the electrical industry (Hill 1984). PCBs have been associated with the birth of babies who are smaller than expected and have cola-colored skin, premature tooth eruption (Bang et al 1983), and eye defects (Hill 1984).

6. *Pesticides.* Women who are exposed to pesticides through employment with tobacco or as cotton pickers are at increased risk for spontaneous

*Figure 3.13 Women may be exposed to dangerous substances in the workplace.*

abortion, stillbirths, premature birth, and some degree of mental retardation in their children (Bang et al 1983).

7. *Anesthetic gases.* Women who work in operating rooms are exposed to anesthetic gases. This exposure is associated with lowered fertility (Hemminki et al 1985), a threefold increase in spontaneous abortion, and low-birth-weight babies (Bang et al 1983).

8. *Antineoplastic drugs.* Nurses who administer antineoplastic drugs may have some increased risk during the childbearing years. A study of Finnish nurses exposed to antineoplastic drugs revealed an increase in spontaneous abortions and fetal anomalies (Selevan et al 1985).

9. Nurses have an occupational hazard in the exposure inherent in providing care for sick people.

Environmental hazards are increasing with the discovery and development of new products, and they exert their effect on all in that environment. Women are at particular risk while they are in the childbearing years. While no work environment is without risks, it is becoming more important for each woman to become knowledgeable about her own work environment. Information can be obtained from libraries, the Public Health Department, and special agencies that collect data regarding environmental hazards.

## ● Rape

**Rape** refers to any situation in which "a person is forced or coerced, physically or verbally, into any type of sexual contact with another person" (Ledray 1986, p 10). The term *sexual assault* is also used to label such acts. Legally, there are three preconditions for a valid charge of rape: 1) the use of threat, force, intimidation, or deception; 2) nonconsent of the victim; and 3) coitus or vaginal penetration, however slight.

Rape is not an act of sex but an act of violence expressed sexually—a man's aggression and rage acted out against a female. In the United States an estimated 330,000 to 810,000 women are raped every year (Ledray 1986). Of these women only 82,000 report their rapes. The National Center for the Prevention and Control of Rape estimates that one out of every three women will be raped at some time in her life.

Rapists come from all ethnic backgrounds and walks of life. More than half are under 25 years of age, and three out of five are married and leading "normal" sex lives. No single answer explains why these men rape. Freud viewed rape as an instinctual expression of male aggression usually blocked by society. Groth and Burgess (1977) found that 33% of rapists in their study had been sexually abused as children. Their assaults appeared to replicate their child-

hood experiences. Feminist theorists suggest that rape helps maintain patriarchy by keeping females dependent on males for protection (Brownmiller 1975). Early researchers suggested that rapists might have an abnormal chromosome pattern—the XYY phenomenon—resulting in elevated testosterone levels that lead to increased aggressiveness, but this finding has been invalidated.

Rape may be committed by a stranger, acquaintance, or spouse. It may be committed on impulse or it may be planned. Regardless of the style of attack, anger, power, and sadism are components of any rape.

### RAPE TRAUMA SYNDROME

Rape is generally a situational crisis. It is an unanticipated traumatic event that the victim is usually unprepared to handle because it is unforeseen. Following rape the survivor may experience a cluster of symptoms described by Burgess and Holmstrom (1979) as **rape trauma syndrome.** Originally this syndrome was described as having two phases: the acute phase and the adjustment or reorganization phase. Sutherland and Scherl proposed an intermediate "outward adjustment" phase (Golan 1978).

Rape survivors often enter the health care system through the emergency room. Thus the nurse is usually the first person to counsel them. Because the values, attitudes, and beliefs of a care giver will necessarily affect the competency and focus of the care given, it is important that nurses clearly understand their feelings about rape and rape survivors and resolve any conflicts that may exist. Table 3.9 describes the phases of the rape trauma syndrome and identifies appropriate nursing interventions for each phase.

### PHYSICAL CARE OF THE RAPE SURVIVOR

Because rape is a crime as well as a traumatic emergency, some aspects of medical care are governed by the need to collect and preserve legal evidence for use in prosecuting the assailant. In collecting evidence health care providers must respect the rights of the rape victim, which are summarized in Table 3.10. For the rape survivor who has already been violated and deprived of control, further invasion of her body for the collection of evidence can be traumatic. The nurse can assist her in coping with this procedure by carefully explaining what will be done and why it is necessary.

The survivor is offered prophylactic treatment for syphilis and gonorrhea. The woman is also questioned about her menstrual cycle and contraceptive practices. If she could become pregnant as a result of the rape, postcoital therapy is offered. Synthetic estrogens are most often used for this purpose. The initial dose of estrogen must be taken within 72 hours of intercourse to be effective. If the woman chooses not to be treated for the prevention of pregnancy, she may need information in the future about abortion or adoption agencies. She has the right to be informed of all alternatives.

## RAPE PREVENTION AS A COMMUNITY RESPONSIBILITY

Preventive education, often in the form of classes provided by community colleges or local rape awareness groups, may focus on increasing women's awareness of high-risk situations and preventive strategies. These classes may also provide information about what to do during and after a rape. Other classes may focus on changing societal attitudes about rape and rape survivors.

Communities also have a responsibility to provide rape crisis counseling. Often this is done through rape crisis counseling centers. Early crisis intervention often encourages a woman to seek professional assistance and treatment. This is especially important if the woman has decided to remain silent and not report the rape.

Legally rape is considered a crime against the state and prosecution of the assailant is a community responsibility. The survivor, however, must begin the process by reporting the assault and pressing charges against her assailant. In the past the police and the judicial system have been notoriously insensitive in dealing with rape survivors. Many communities, however, now have classes designed to help officers work effectively with rape survivors or have special teams to carry out this important task.

Unfortunately, many women who have sought to use the judicial process refer to it as a second rape. The woman repeatedly is asked to describe the experience in intimate detail, her reputation may be attacked, and the defense attorney will try to discredit her testimony. In addition, publicity may intensify her feelings of humiliation and, if the assailant is released on bail, she may fear retaliation.

The nurse acting as a counselor needs to be aware of the judicial sequence to anticipate rising tension and frustration in the survivor and her support system. They will need consistent, effective support at this crucial time.

## ESSENTIAL CONCEPTS

● **Girls and women should be provided with clear information about comfort issues, such as tampons (deodorant and absorbency); vaginal spray and douching practices; and self-care comfort measures, such as nutrition, exercise, and use of heat and massage during menstruation.**

● **Premenstrual syndrome occurs most often in women over 30, and symptoms occur two to three days before onset of menstruation and subside as menstruation starts with or without treatment. Medical management usually includes progesterone agonists and prostaglandin inhibitors. Self-care measures include improved nutrition (vitamin B complex and E supplementation and avoidance of methylxanthines, such as in chocolate and caffeine), a program of aerobic exercise, and participation in self-care support groups.**

● **Dysmenorrhea usually begins at or a day before onset of menses and disappears by the end of menstruation. Therapy with hormones such as oral contraceptives or the use of nonsteroidal anti-inflammatory drugs or prostaglandin inhibitors is useful. Self-care measures include improved nutrition, exercise, applications of heat, and extra rest.**

### Table 3.9 Phases of the Rape Trauma Syndrome

| Phase | Response | Nursing action |
|---|---|---|
| Acute phase | Fear, shock, disbelief, desire for revenge, anger, denial, anxiety, guilt, embarassment, humiliation, helplessness, dependency; survivor may seek help or may remain silent | Creating a safe milieu Explaining the sequence of events in the health care facility Allowing the woman to grieve and express her feelings Providing care for significant others |
| Outward adjustment phase | Survivor appears outwardly composed, denying and repressing feelings; for example, she returns to work, buys a weapon, adds security measures to her residence, and denies need for counseling | Providing advocacy and support at the level requested by the woman Providing assistance to significant others |
| Reorganizational phase | Survivor experiences sexual dysfunction, phobias, sleep disorders, anxiety, and a strong urge to talk about or resolve feelings; victim may seek counseling or may remain silent | Establishing a trusting relationship Assisting the woman to understand her role in the assault Clarifying and enhancing the woman's feelings Assisting the woman in planning for her future |

## Table 3.10   The Rights of the Rape Victim

The rape victim has the right:

1. To transportation to a hospital when incapacitated.

2. To emergency room care with privacy and confidentiality.

3. To be listened to carefully and treated as a human being, with respect, courtesy, and dignity.

4. To have an advocate of choice accompany her through the treatment process.

5. To be given as much credibility as a victim of any other crime.

6. To have her name kept from the news media.

7. To be considered a victim of rape regardless of the assailant's relationship to her.

8. Not to be exposed to prejudice against race, age, class, life-style, or occupation.

9. Not to be asked questions about prior sexual experience.

10. To be treated in a manner that does not usurp her control but enables her to determine her own needs and how to meet them.

11. To be asked only those questions that are relevant to a court case or to medical treatment.

12. To receive prompt, free medical and mental health services, regardless of whether the rape is reported to the police.

13. To be protected from future assault.

14. To accurate collection and preservation of evidence for court in an objective record that includes the signs and symptoms of physical and emotional trauma.

15. To receive clear explanations of procedures and medication in language she can understand.

16. To know what treatment is recommended, for what reasons, and who will administer the treatment.

17. To know any possible risks, side effects, or alternatives to proposed treatments, including all drugs prescribed.

18. To ask for another physician, nurse practitioner, or nurse.

19. To consent to or refuse any treatment, even when her life is in serious danger.

20. To refuse to be part of any research or experiment.

21. To make reasonable complaints and to leave a care facility against the physician's advice.

22. To receive an explanation of and understand any papers she agrees to sign.

23. To be informed of continuing health care needs after discharge from the emergency room, hospital, physician's office, or care facility.

24. To receive a clear explanation of the bill and review of charges and to be informed of available compensation.

25. To have legal representation and be advised of her legal rights, including the possibility of filing a civil suit.

Source: Adapted from Foley TS, Davies MA: *Rape: Nursing Care of Victims*. St. Louis: Mosby, 1983.

---

● **Attitudes about sex are influenced by a variety of factors including: family and home environment, culture, education, socioeconomic level, previous sexual experiences, and individual personality characteristics.**

● **Masters and Johnson (1966) have identified four phases to the human sexual response cycle: excitement, plateau, orgasm, and resolution.**

● **To be effective as a counselor on sexual matters nurses must be aware of and comfortable with their feelings and attitudes; have accurate, up-to-date knowledge; and be skilled in communicating.**

● **The nursing process can be used effectively when working with women concerned about sexual issues. The nurse must be insightful enough to recognize those occasions when a woman's problem requires more specialized intervention so that appropriate referral can be made.**

● **Preconception counseling focuses on factors to consider in deciding whether to have children (if this decision is morally acceptable to the couple). It also includes counseling about health measures, physical examination, nutrition, exercise, and contraception.**

● **Contraception is used by couples to decide when to have children and to help with the spacing of children.**

● **Fertility awareness methods are "natural," noninvasive methods often used by people whose religious beliefs keep them from using other methods of contraception.**

● **Mechanical contraceptives such as the diaphragm, cervical cap, contraceptive sponge, and condom act as barriers to prevent the transport of sperm. These methods are used in conjunction with a spermicide.**

● **The IUD is another mechanical contraceptive that works primarily by preventing the implantation of a fertilized ovum.**

● Oral contraceptives (the "pill") are combinations of estrogen and progesterone. When taken correctly they are the most effective of the reversible methods of fertility control.

● Spermicides are far less effective in preventing pregnancy when they are not used with a barrier method.

● A variety of experimental approaches to contraception are currently being tested.

● Permanent sterilization is accomplished by tubal ligation for women and vasectomy for men. Clients are advised that the method should be considered irreversible.

● The breasts function in a cyclic process that is regulated by nervous and hormonal systems. Thus many women experience breast tenderness and swelling premenstrually.

● In fibrocystic breast disease the cysts tend to be round, mobile, and well delineated. The woman generally experiences increased discomfort premenstrually. Because of the increased risk of developing breast cancer, women with FBD should understand the importance of monthly BSE.

● Factors that increase a woman's risk of developing breast cancer include: advancing age (most occur after age 40), family history of breast cancer (especially mother or sister), early menarche, late menopause, personal history of cancer in one breast, high levels of dietary fat, and high protein and low selenium diet.

● Recommendations for frequency of screening mammograms are:

Baseline mammograms between ages 35 and 40

Mammogram every one to two years between ages 40 and 50

Mammogram annually for all women after age 50

Diagnosis of a suspicious breast mass is made by fine-needle biopsy.

● A variety of surgical treatment alternatives now exist for women with breast cancer, including radical mastectomy, modified radical mastectomy, simple mastectomy, subcutaneous mastectomy, partial mastectomy, and lumpectomy. Breast reconstruction following surgery is becoming a more common alternative. Other treatment modalities for breast cancer include radiation therapy, chemotherapy, and endocrine therapy.

● A woman with breast cancer faces many psychologic concerns including fear of the diagnosis, altered body image, and the response of family and friends. She must also deal with the long-term prognosis and her physical response to the treatment she receives. Nurses play a vital role in providing information and psychologic support.

● Endometriosis is a condition in which endometrial tissue occurs outside the endometrial cavity. This tissue bleeds in a cyclic fashion in response to the menstrual cycle. The bleeding leads to inflammation, scarring, and adhesions. The prime symptoms include dysmenorrhea, dyspareunia, and infertility.

● Treatment of endometriosis may be medical, surgical, or a combination. For the woman not desiring pregnancy at present, oral contraceptives are used. Women desiring pregnancy are treated with a course of danazol.

● Toxic shock syndrome, caused by a toxin of *Streptococcus aureus,* is most common in women of childbearing age. There is an increased incidence in women who use tampons or barrier methods of contraception such as the diaphragm and sponge.

● Moniliasis, a vaginal infection caused by *Candida albicans,* is most common in women who use oral contraceptives, are on antibiotics, are currently pregnant, or have diabetes mellitus. It is generally treated with intravaginal miconazole or clotrimazole suppositories.

● Bacterial vaginosis (*Gardnerella vaginalis* vaginitis), a common vaginal infection, is diagnosed by its characteristic "fishy" odor and by the presence of clue cells on a vaginal smear. It is treated with metronidazole unless the woman is pregnant.

● Chlamydial infection is difficult to detect in a woman, but may result in PID and infertility. It is treated with antibiotic therapy.

● Herpes genitalis, caused by the herpes simplex virus, is a recurrent infection with no known cure. Acyclovir (Zovirax) may provide a reduction in symptoms.

● Syphilis, caused by *Treponema pallidum,* is a sexually transmitted disease that is treatable if diagnosed. The characteristic lesion is the chancre. Syphilis can also be transmitted in utero to the fetus of an infected woman. The treatment of choice is penicillin.

● Gonorrhea, a common sexually transmitted disease, may be asymptomatic in women initially but may cause PID if not diagnosed early. The treatment of choice is penicillin.

● Condyloma accuminata (venereal warts) is transmitted by a virus. Treatment is indicated because research suggests a possible link with abnormal cervical changes. The treatment chosen depends on the size and location of the warts.

● Nurses caring for women with a STD should discuss methods of prevention, signs and symptoms, and treatment alternatives in a supportive, nonjudgmental way.

● Pelvic inflammatory disease may be life threatening and may lead to infertility.

● Women with an abnormal finding on a pelvic examination will need careful explanation of the finding and techniques of diagnosis, and emotional support during the diagnostic period.

● The classic symptoms of a lower UTI are dysuria, urgency, frequency, and sometimes hematuria. Oral sulfonamides are the treatment of choice.

● An upper UTI is a serious infection that can permanently damage the kidneys if untreated. Generally the woman is acutely ill and may require supportive therapy as well as antibiotics.

● A cystocele is a downward displacement of the bladder into the vagina. Often it is accompanied by stress incontinence. Kegel exercises may help restore tone in mild cases.

● Menopause is a physiologic maturational change in a woman's life that may be associated with emotional attributes. It is a time of reflection on a woman's life up to this point and gives impetus to evaluate desired future directions. Physiologic changes include the cessation of menses and decrease in circulating hormones. The more common physiologic symptoms are "hot flashes," palpitations, dizziness, and increased perspiration at night. The woman's anatomy also undergoes changes such as atrophy of the vagina, reduction in size and pigmentation of the labia, and myometrial atrophy. Osteoporosis becomes an increasing concern.

● Current management of menopause still centers around estrogen replacement and calcium supplementation therapy.

● The number of women living in poverty is increasing at a rapid rate. Childbearing women seem to be at particular risk due to current trends in the divorce rate, the frequency with which the mother gains custody of children, and factors in the work environment that make it difficult for women to earn a good wage.

● The chemical compounds present in the workplace are numerous and are increasing each year. The implications of exposure during the childbearing years are known in some instances, and others are currently being investigated.

● A rape occurs every ten minutes, yet the majority of rapes are unreported. Following rape the survivor will usually experience an assortment of symptoms known as the rape trauma syndrome. Widespread education is still needed to abolish societal myths about rape.

● ● ● ● ● ● ● ● ● ● ● ● ● ● ● ● ● ● ● ● ● ● ● ● ● ● ● ● ● ● ● ● ● ● ● ● ● ●

## References

American Cancer Society: *Breast Self-Examination and the Nurse.* No. 3408 PE. New York, 1973.

Bang KM et al: Reproductive hazards in the workplace. *Fam Commun Health* May 1983; 6:44.

Bilezikian JP, Shane E: Osteoporosis: An update on risk factors and treatment options. *Female Patient* September 1988; 13:31.

Brownmiller S: *Against Our Will: Men, Women, and Rape.* New York: Simon and Schuster, 1975.

Burgess AW, Holmstrom LL: *Rape: Crisis and Recovery.* Englewood Cliffs, NJ: Prentice-Hall, 1979.

Chihal HJ: Painful periods and preludes. *Emergency Med* 1982; 14(17):33.

Connell EB: Which contraceptives *don't* cause TSS? *Contemp OB/GYN* October 1985; 26:127.

Connell EB: Reevaluating contraceptive needs. *Contemp OB/GYN* September 15, 1988; 32S:27.

Dickey RP: *Managing Contraceptive Pill Patients.* Durant, OK: Creative Informatics, 1983.

Digest: New studies find no link between spermicide use and heightened risk of congenital malformations. *Fam Plan Perspect* January/February 1988; 20:42.

Donegan WL: Diseases of the breast. In: *Obstetrics and Gynecology,* 5th ed. Danforth DN, Scott JR (editors). Philadelphia: Lippincott, 1986.

Enrenreich B, Piven FF: The feminization of poverty. *Discent* Spring 1984; 31:162.

Eschenbach DA: Pelvic infections. In: *Obstetrics and Gynecology,* 5th ed. Danforth DN, Scott JR (editors). Philadelphia: Lippincott, 1986.

Fantl JA: The urinary tract as it is related to gynecology. In: *Obstetrics and Gynecology,* 5th ed. Danforth DN, Scott JR (editors). Philadelphia: Lippincott, 1986.

Feller WF: Steps in evaluation of a breast mass. *Contemp OB/GYN* June 15, 1988; 32(s):11.

Ferenczy A: To contain the spread of condyloma: Treat your patient's partner. *Contemp OB/GYN* June 1986; 27:51.

Fisher B et al: Five-year results of a random clinical trial comparing total mastectomy and segmental mastectomy with or without radiation in the treatment of breast cancer. *New Engl J Med* 1985; 312(11): 665.

Fogel CI, Woods NF: *Health Care of Women: A Nursing Perspective.* St. Louis: Mosby, 1981.

Foley TS, Davies MA: *Rape: Nursing Care of Victims.* St Louis: Mosby, 1983.

Gabbe SG et al: *Obstetrics.* New York: Churchill Livingston, 1986.

Ganong WF: *Review of Medical Physiology,* 12th ed. Los Altos, CA: Lange, 1985.

Garner CH, Webster BW: Endometriosis. *J Obstet Gynecol Neonatal Nurs* 1985; 14(6)S: 10S.

Glass RH: *Office Gynecology,* 3rd ed. Baltimore: Williams and Wilkins, 1988.

Golan N: *Treatment in Crisis Situations.* New York: Free Press, 1978.

Govoni LE, Hayes JE: *Drugs and Nursing Implications,* 6th ed. Norwalk, CT: Appleton-Century-Crofts, 1988.

Griffith-Kenney J: *Contemporary Women's Health: A Nursing Advocacy Approach.* Menlo Park, CA: Addison-Wesley, 1986.

Groth AN, Burgess AW: Sexual dysfunction during rape. *New Engl J Med* 1977; 297(14): 764.

Gyllenskold K: *Breast Cancer: The Psychological Effects of the Disease and Its Treatment.* London: Tavistock, 1982.

Hatcher RA et al: *Contraceptive Technology 1988–89,* 14th ed. New York: Irvington Publishers, 1988.

Havens C et al: *Manual of Outpatient Gynecology.* Boston: Little, Brown, 1986.

Hembree D: High-tech hazards. *Ms* March 1986; 14: 79.

Hemminki K et al: Spontaneous abortions and malformations in the offspring of nurses exposed to anaesthetic gases, cytostatic drugs, and other potential hazards in hospitals based on registered information of outcome. *J Epidemiol Commun Health* June 1985; 39: 141.

Hill GA, Herbert CM: Endometriosis—Drug therapy or surgery. *Female Patient* October 1988; 13: 69.

Hill LM: Effects of drugs and chemicals on the fetus and newborn. (Part 2.) *Mayo Clin Proc* 1984; 59: 755.

Holloway RW et al: The $CO_2$ laser: A guide to its use in lower genital tract disorders. *Female Patient* August 1988; 13: 14.

Keyes HM et al: Breast cancer. In: *Clinical Oncology for Medical Students and Physicians.* New York: American Cancer Society, 1983.

Ledray LE: *Recovering from Rape.* New York: Holt, 1986.

Leslie LA, Swider SM: Changing factors and changing needs in women's health care. *Nurs Clin North Am* March 1986; 21: 111.

Levinson W, Dunn PM: Nonassociation of caffeine and fibrocystic breast disease. *Arch Inter Med* September 1986; 146: 1773.

Malinik LR, Wheeler JM: A practical approach to endometriosis: II. Treatment. *Female Patient* June 1985; 10: 15.

Margolese RG: Breast Ca treatment: Where do we stand? *Contemp OB/GYN* July 1986; 28: 39.

Martin I: *Health Care of Women.* Philadelphia: Lippincott, 1978.

Masters WH, Johnson VE: *Human Sexual Response.* Boston: Little, Brown, 1966.

Merrill JA: Endometriosis. In: *Obstetrics and Gynecology,* 5th ed. Danforth DN, Scott JR (editors). Philadelphia: Lippincott, 1986.

Mezrow G, Rebar RW: Tailoring estrogen replacement to fit the patient. *Contemp OB/GYN* April 15, 1988; 31S: 51.

Miller PD: Advances in osteoporosis management. *Contemp OB/GYN* December 1988; 32: 31.

Minton JP et al: Clinical and biochemical studies on methylxanthine-related fibrocystic breast disease. *Surgery* 1981; 90: 299.

Morris NM: Menstruation and marital sex. *J Biosoc Sci* 1983; 15: 173.

Mundinger MO: Health service funding cuts and the declining health of the poor. *New Engl J Med* July 1986; 13: 44.

Pariser SF et al: Premenstrual syndrome: Concerns, controversies, and treatment. *Am J Obstet Gynecol* 1985; 153(6): 599.

Pearce DM: The feminization of ghetto poverty. *Society* November/December 1983; 21: 70.

Rickel L et al: Solid neoplasms. In: *Medical-Surgical Nursing: A Conceptual Approach.* Jones D, Dunbar C, Jirovec M (editors). New York: McGraw-Hill, 1982.

Rierdan J: Variations in the experience of menarche as a function of preparedness. In: *Menarche.* Golub S (editor). Lexington, MA: Lexington Books, 1983.

Rosenfeld AG: Contraception: Where are we in 1985? *Contemp OB/GYN* February 1985; 25: 79.

Schachter J et al: Experience with routine use of erythromycin for chlamydial infections in pregnancy. *New Engl J Med* 1986; 314: 276.

Schaumburg H et al: Sensory neuropathy from pyridoxine abuse. *New Engl J Med* 1984; 309: 445.

Schmale A: Reactions to illness: Convalescence and grieving. *Psychiatr Clin North Am* 1979; 2(2): 321.

Scholtenfeld D, Fraumeni J (editors): *Cancer Epidemiology and Prevention.* Philadelphia: Saunders, 1982.

Sciarra JL et al: *Gynecology and Obstetrics.* Vol 1. New York: Harper and Row, 1984.

Selevan SG et al: A study of occupational exposure to antineoplastic drugs and fetal loss in nurses. *New Engl J Med* November 1985; 313: 1173.

Shingleton WW, McCarty KS: What you should know about breast pathology. *Contemp OB/GYN* February 1987; 29: 90.

Sonstegard L et al: *Women's Health.* Vol 1. New York: Grune and Stratton, 1982.

Spitzer M, Krumholz BA: Pap screening for teenagers: A lifesaving precaution. *Contemp OB/GYN* January 1988; 31: 33.

Symposium: PID: Best new routes to diagnosis and treatment. *Contemp OB/GYN* February 1987; 29: 156.

Tatum HJ: A new IUD offering more copper, better results. *Contemp OB/GYN* September 15, 1988; 32S: 36.

Thiederman SB: Ethnocentrism: A barrier to effective health care. *Nurse Pract* August 1986; 11: 52.

Torrington J: Pelvic inflammatory disease. *J Obstet Gynecol Neonatal Nurs* 1985; 14(6)S: 21S.

Uphold CR, Susman EJ: Self-reported climacteric symptoms as a function of the relationship between marital adjustment and child-rearing stage. *Nurs Res* March/April 1981; 30: 84.

Weber M: Breast cancer: Odds, options, arguments. *Vogue* August 1983, p 334.

Wedell MA et al: Endometriosis and the infertile patient. *J Obstet Gynecol Neonatal Nurs* 1985; 14(4):280.

Whalley PJ: Value of treating UTI during pregnancy. *Contemp OB/GYN* 1986; 27(5):134.

Wilson JF: Breast cancer treatment—current status. 3. Simple excision with radiation. *Postgrad Med* 1983; 74(3):151.

Wynn RM: *Obstetrics and Gynecology: The Clinical Case.* Philadelphia: Lea and Febiger, 1983.

Zinn DK, Sarri RC: Turning back the clock on public welfare. *Signs* Winter 1984; 10:355.

## Additional Readings

Brokaw A et al: Fitting the cervical cap. *Nurse Pract* 1988; 13(7):49.

DeNitto D et al: After rape: Who should examine rape survivors? . . . Nurse rape examiners? *Am J Nurs* May 1986; 86:538.

DeSantis L, Thomas JT: Parental attitudes toward adolescent sexuality: Transcultural perspectives. *Nurse Pract* August 1987; 12:43.

Dressel PL: Gender, race, and class: Beyond the feminization of poverty in later life. *Gerontologist* 1988; 28(2):177.

Ellerhorst-Ryan JM et al: Evaluating benign breast disease. *Nurse Pract* September 1988; 13:13.

Forrest JD: Women's five reproductive stages. *Contemp OB/GYN* September 15, 1988; 32S:12.

Lincoln R, Kaeser L: Whatever happened to the contraceptive revolution? *Fam Plan Perspect* January/February 1988; 20.

Mabray CR: Chronic candidiasis and polysystemic disorders: Study explores common features. *Female Patient* June 1988; 13(6):34.

McGregor JA, Todd JK: Toxic shock syndrome—still a threat. *Female Patient* July 1987; 12:32.

Reed A, Birge S: Screening for osteoporosis. *J Gerontol Nurs* 1988; 14(7):18.

Rice MA, Szopa TJ: Group intervention for reinforcing self-worth following mastectomy. *Oncol Nurs Forum* 1988; 15(1):33.

Riedmann GL: The fertility history card. *J Nurse-Midwifery* January/February 1988; 33(1):15.

Rutledge DN: Factors related to women's practice of breast self-examination. *Nurs Res* March/April 1987; 36:117.

Smith DH, Rosenthal MB: Sexuality and changes with aging. *Contemp OB/GYN* June 1988; 31:88.

Weaver CH, Mengel MB: Bacterial vaginosis. *J Fam Pract* 1988; 27(2):207.

Youngkin EQ et al: The triphasics: Insights for effective clinical use. *Nurs Pract* 1987; 12(2):17.

# 4

# Families with Special Reproductive Problems

*Thirty years ago the delivery of our first son went easily, but my husband failed to show up for visiting hours the next day. When he did come, he asked me to walk to the nurses' lounge. I was so excited about the baby that it didn't seem strange to be going there. When we were alone, he gently told me that our baby was "mongoloid." What an ugly word! Suddenly it felt as if torrents of black spiders were pouring over me. We cried together. A few days later we took our son home and began the long and tender process of parenting a Down syndrome child. It came to us with great clarity at the beginning that none of us has the right to expect our children to be more perfect reflections of ourselves. Each is an individual with a life to be lived to the fullest of its own possibilities. In thirty years we have seen a sense of humor, a love of music, and a loving disposition characterize the son some would call disabled.*

## Objectives

- Summarize the physiologic and psychologic effects of infertility on a couple.

- Identify the various tests done in an infertility workup.

- Discuss the indications for chromosomal analysis and genetic amniocentesis.

- Relate the significance of the Barr chromatin body to identifying sex chromosome abnormalities.

- Identify the general characteristics of an autosomal dominant disorder.

- Compare autosomal recessive disorders with X-linked (sex-linked) recessive disorders.

- Compare prenatal and postnatal diagnostic procedures that may be used to determine the presence of genetic disease.

- Explore the emotional impact on a couple undergoing genetic testing and/or the birth of a baby with a genetic disorder.

- Explain the nurse's responsibility in genetic counseling.

## Key Terms

| | |
|---|---|
| alleles | phenotype |
| autosomes | sex chromosomes |
| Barr body | Sims/Huhner test |
| basal body temperature recording (BBT) | somatic |
| | spinnbarkeit |
| chromosomes | sterility |
| ferning capacity | trisomies |
| genotype | Turner syndrome |
| haploid | ultrasound |
| heterozygous | |
| homozygous | |
| hysterosalpingography (hysterogram) | |
| infertility | |
| karyotype | |
| Klinefelter syndrome | |
| Mendelian (single-gene inheritance) | |

**M**ost couples who want children are able to have them with little trouble. Pregnancy and childbirth usually take their normal course, and a healthy baby is born. But some couples are not so fortunate and are unable to fulfill their dream of having a healthy baby because of special reproductive problems.

This chapter explores two particularly troubling reproductive problems facing some couples: the inability to conceive and the risk of bearing babies with genetic abnormalities.

## ● INFERTILITY

**Infertility** can be defined as the inability of a couple to produce a living child as a result of failure to conceive or of failure to carry the conceived baby to a viable state. The term *primary infertility* is applied to those women who have never conceived. *Secondary infertility* describes the client who has formerly been pregnant but has not conceived during one or more years of unprotected intercourse (Coulam 1982). The term **sterility** is applied when there is an absolute factor preventing pregnancy.

It has been estimated that one in six couples in the United States is infertile (Grimes and Richardson 1987). Today it is generally accepted that any couple who has tried unsuccessfully to achieve pregnancy for one year should have an infertility workup. Couples over 30 years of age should consider a workup after six months (Grimes and Richardson 1987).

The incidence of infertility appears to be increasing, which may be related to the following factors:

1. More couples are delaying marriage and postponing childbearing until they have passed the suggested age of optimal fertility in women (20–25 years of age).

2. Anovulation may be prolonged after using birth control pills, but this is rare with the low-dose pills.

3. Infections associated with intrauterine devices or following abortions can affect fertility.

4. Sexually transmitted diseases may cause obstructive disease of the male and female reproductive systems.

## • Essential Components of Fertility

Understanding the elements essential for normal fertility can help the nurse identify the many factors that may cause infertility. The following essential components must be present for normal fertility:

Female partner:

1. The vaginal secretions and cervical mucus must be favorable for survival of spermatozoa.

2. There must be clear passage between the cervix and the fallopian tubes.

3. Fallopian tubes must be patent and have normal peristaltic movement to allow ascent of spermatozoa and descent of ovum.

4. Ovaries must produce and release normal ova.

5. There must be no obstruction between the ovaries and the uterus.

6. The endometrium must be in a normal physiologic state to allow implantation of the blastocyst and to sustain normal growth.

7. Adequate reproductive hormone capacity must be present.

Male partner:

1. The testes must produce spermatozoa of normal quality, quantity, and motility.

2. The male genital tract must not be obstructed.

3. The male genital tract secretions must be normal.

4. Ejaculated spermatozoa must be deposited in the female genital tract in such a manner that they reach the cervix.

These normal findings are correlated with possible causes of deviation in Table 4.1. In addition to these necessary elements, certain general physiologic and psychologic conditions must be present to support conception.

With intricacies of timing and environment playing such a crucial role, it is an impressive natural phenomenon that approximately 85% of couples in the United States are able to conceive (Andrew 1984, Diamond 1988). Of the remaining 15%, for every 100 couples about 40 will show a male deficiency, 10 to 15 a female hormonal defect, 20 to 30 a female tubal disorder, 5 a cervical defect, and 10 to 20 couples have no discernible cause of their infertility (Coulam 1982). In 35 of the couples there are multiple etiolo-

## Table 4.1  Possible Causes of Infertility

| Necessary norms | Deviations from normal |
|---|---|
| **FEMALE** | |
| Favorable cervical mucus | Cervicitis, immunologic response ("hostile" mucus), use of coital lubricants, antisperm antibodies |
| Clear passage between cervix and tubes | Myomas, adhesions, adenomyosis, polyps, endometritis, cervical stenosis, endometriosis, congenital anomalies (for example, septate uterus) |
| Patent tubes with normal motility | Pelvic inflammatory disease, peritubal adhesions, endometriosis, IUD, salpingitis (for example, tuberculosis), neoplasm, ectopic pregnancy, tubal ligation |
| Ovulation and release of ova | Primary ovarian failure, polycystic ovarian disease, hypothyroidism, pituitary tumor, lactation, periovarian adhesions, endometriosis, medications (for example, oral contraceptives), premature ovarian failure, hyperprolactinemia, Turner syndrome |
| No obstruction between ovary and fimbria | Adhesions, endometriosis, pelvic inflammatory disease |
| Endometrial preparation | Anovulation, luteal phase defect, IUD, malformation, uterine infection |
| **MALE** | |
| Normal semen analysis | Abnormalities of sperm or semen, polyspermia, congenital defect in testicular development, mumps after adolescence, cryptorchidism, infections, gonadal exposure to x-rays, chemotherapy, smoking, alcohol abuse, malnutrition, chronic or acute metabolic disease, medications (for example, morphine, ASA, ibuprofin, and cocaine), marijuana use, constrictive underclothing, heat |
| Unobstructed genital tract | Infections, tumors, congenital anomalies, vasectomy, strictures, trauma, varicocele |
| Normal genital tract secretions | Infections, autoimmunity to semen, tumors |
| Ejaculate deposited at the cervix | Premature ejaculation, hypospadias, retrograde ejaculation (for example, diabetic), neurologic cord lesions, obesity (inhibiting adequate penetration) |

gies. Professional intervention can help 30% to 50% of infertile couples achieve pregnancy.

Couples are usually concerned about infertility following their inability to conceive after at least one year of attempting to achieve pregnancy. At the age of 25 years, which is identified as within the couple's most fertile time, the average length of time needed to achieve conception is 5.3 months. The average 20- to 30-year-old American couple has intercourse one to three times a week, a frequency that should be sufficient to achieve pregnancy if all other factors are satisfactory. In about 20% of cases, conception occurs within the first month of unprotected intercourse (Zacur and Rock 1983). Between 1975 and 1980 there was a 94% increase in the number of women who gave birth to their first child after the age of 30, and this trend is predicted to increase. Delaying parenthood appears to increase the risk to the success of each of the physiologic processes necessary for conception (Berg 1984).

## ● *Preliminary Investigation*

Evaluation and preliminary investigation should be available for couples seeking help for infertility. The easiest and least intrusive approach is used first. Extensive testing is avoided until data confirm that the timing of intercourse and the length of coital exposure have been adequate. The couple should be informed of the appropriate times to have intercourse during the menstrual cycle. Teaching the couple the signs of and timing of ovulation within the cycle and effective sexual techniques may solve the problem before extensive testing needs to be initiated (see Table 4.2). Primary assessment, including a comprehensive history and physical examination for any obvious causes of infertility, is done before a costly, time-consuming, and emotionally trying investigation is initiated. During the first visit for the preliminary investigation, the basic infertility workup is explained. The basic investigation usually includes assessment of ovarian function, cervical mucosal adequacy and receptivity to sperm, sperm adequacy, tubal patency, and the general condition of the pelvic organs, with examination of the sperm done first.

It is never easy to discuss one's sexual activity, especially when potentially irreversible problems with fertility may exist. The mutual desire to have children is the basis of many marriages. A fertility problem is a deeply personal, emotion-laden area in a couple's life. The self-esteem of one or both partners may be threatened if the inability to conceive is perceived as a lack of virility or femininity. The nurse can provide comfort to the client by offering a sympathetic ear, a nonjudgmental atmosphere, and appropriate information and instructions. Since counseling includes discussion of very personal matters, nurses who are comfortable with their own sexuality are more capable of establishing rapport and eliciting relevant information.

Health care interventions in cases of infertility are il-

### Table 4.2  Fertility Awareness

Avoid douching and artificial lubricants. Prevent alteration of pH of vagina and introduction of spermicidal agents.

Promote retention of sperm. The male superior position with female remaining recumbent for at least one hour after intercourse maximizes the number of sperm reaching the cervix.

Avoid leakage of sperm. Elevate the woman's hips with a pillow after intercourse. Avoid getting up to urinate for one hour after intercourse.

Maximize the potential for fertilization. Have intercourse one to three times per week at intervals of no less than 48 hours.

Avoid emphasizing conception during sexual encounters to decrease anxiety and potential sexual dysfunction.

Maintain adequate nutrition and reduce stress. Using stress reduction techniques and good nutrition habits increases sperm production.

Explore other methods to increase fertility awareness, such as home assessment of cervical mucus and basal body temperature recordings.

lustrated in Figure 4.1. Following the initial interview with the infertile couple, a comprehensive history (including a detailed sexual history) is taken and a physical examination is performed.

Following completion of the couple's histories, a complete physical examination of each partner is performed. See Table 4.3.

## ● *Tests for Infertility*

After a thorough history and physical examination of both partners, tests may be initiated to identify other causes of infertility. Infertility factors may be related to a female, male, or multifactorial problem.

More assessment tests have been developed for women than for men. At present, unless obvious pathology is identified in the male partner, male infertility assessments are usually limited to evaluating sperm production and viability and determining whether any obstruction interferes with ejaculation. Forty percent of all infertility problems are related to the male factor.

Four general areas are investigated to evaluate the anatomy, physiology, and sexual compatibility of the couple. The female's fertility assessments are discussed first. For review of female reproductive cycle characteristics see Table 4.4.

### OVULATORY FUNCTION

Ovulation problems account for approximately 15% to 20% of female infertility (Moghissi and Wallach 1983). The

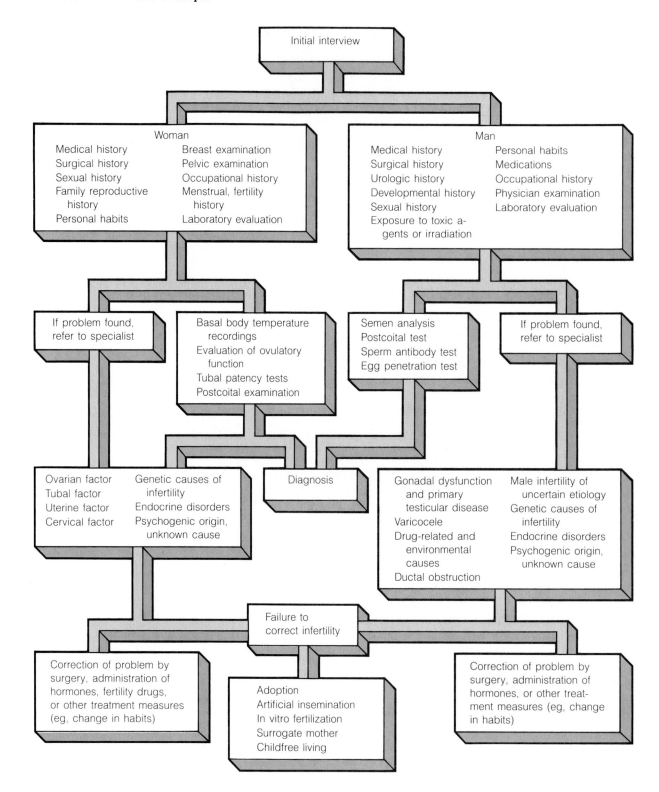

*Figure 4.1  Flow chart for management of the infertile couple*

## Table 4.3  Infertility Physical Workup

| Female | Male |
|--------|------|
| 1. Physical examination<br>  a. Assessment of height, weight, blood pressure, temperature, and general health status<br>  b. Endocrine evaluation of thyroid for exophthalmos, lid lag, tremor, or palpable gland<br>  c. Optic fundi evaluation for presence of increased intracranial pressure, especially in oligomenorrheal or amenorrheal women (possible pituitary tumor)<br>  d. Reproductive features (including breast and external genital area)<br>  e. Physical ability to tolerate pregnancy | 1. Physical examination<br>  a. General health (assessment of height, weight, blood pressure)<br>  b. Endocrine evaluation (for example, presence of gynecomastia)<br>  c. Visual fields evaluation for bitemporal hemianopia<br>  d. Abnormal hair patterns |
| 2. Pelvic examination<br>  a. Papanicolaou smear<br>  b. Culture for gonorrhea<br>  c. Signs of vaginal infections (see Chapter 2)<br>  d. Shape of escutcheon (for example, does pubic hair distribution resemble that of a male?)<br>  e. Size of clitoris (enlargement caused by endocrine disorders)<br>  f. Evaluation of cervix: old lacerations, tears, erosion, polyps, condition and shape of os, signs of infections, cervical mucus (evaluate for estrogen effect of spinnbarkeit and cervical ferning) | 2. Urologic examination (includes presence or absence of phimosis; location of urethral meatus; size and consistency of each testis, vas deferens, and epididymis; presence of varicocele) |
| 3. Bimanual examination<br>  a. Size, shape, position, and motility of uterus<br>  b. Presence of congenital anomalies<br>  c. Presence of endometriosis<br>  d. Evaluation of adnexa: ovarian size, cysts, fixations, or tumors | 3. Rectal examination<br>  a. Size and consistency of the prostate with microscopic evaluation of prostate fluid for signs of infection<br>  b. Size and consistency of seminal vesicles |
| 4. Rectovaginal examination<br>  a. Presence of retroflexed or retroverted uterus<br>  b. Presence of rectouterine pouch masses<br>  c. Presence of possible endometriosis | 4. Laboratory examination<br>  a. Complete blood count<br>  b. Sedimentation rate if indicated<br>  c. Serology<br>  d. Urinalysis<br>  e. Rh factor and blood grouping<br>  f. Semen analysis<br>  g. If indicated, testicular biopsy, buccal smear |
| 5. Laboratory examination<br>  a. Complete blood count<br>  b. Sedimentation rate if indicated<br>  c. Serology<br>  d. Urinalysis<br>  e. Rh factor and blood grouping<br>  f. If indicated, thyroid function tests, glucose tolerance test, 17-ketosteroid assay, 17-hydrocorticoid assay, urine pregnanediol level | |

most accurate ways of monitoring ovulation are recording BBT, observing cervical mucus changes, and obtaining endometrial biopsies.

One basic test of ovulatory function is the **basal body temperature recording (BBT),** which aids in identification of follicular and luteal phase abnormalities. At the initial visit, the woman is instructed in the technique of recording basal body temperature, which may be taken with a BBT thermometer. This special kind of thermometer measures temperature between 96°F and 100°F and is cal-

ibrated by tenths of a degree, thereby facilitating identification of slight temperature changes. The woman may choose the site to obtain the temperature. Possible sites include oral, axillary, rectal, or vaginal sites, and the same site should be used each time. For best results the thermometer should be kept beside the bed, and the woman should take her temperature upon awakening, before any activity. After obtaining her temperature, she shakes the thermometer down to prepare it for use the next day. This step is important, as even the activity of shaking the ther-

## Table 4.4 Female Reproductive Cycle (FRC)

FRC includes the ovarian cycle and the menstrual cycle.

OVARIAN CYCLE

*Follicular phase* (days 1–14): Primordial follicle matures under influence of FSH and LH up to the time of ovulation.
*Luteal phase* (days 15–28): Ovum leaves follicle; corpus luteum develops under LH influence and produces high levels of progesterone and low levels of estrogen.

MENSTRUAL CYCLE

*Menstrual phase* (days 1–5)
*Proliferative phase* (days 6–14): Estrogen peaks just prior to ovulation. Cervical mucus at ovulation is clear, thin, watery, alkaline, and more favorable to sperm; shows ferning pattern; and has spinnbarkeit greater than 5 cm. At ovulation body temperature drops, then rises sharply and remains elevated.
*Secretory phase* (days 15–26): Estrogen drops sharply and progesterone dominates.
*Ischemic phase* (days 27–28): Both estrogen and progesterone levels drop.

mometer immediately before use can cause a small increase in the basal temperature. Other factors that may produce temperature variation are sleeplessness, digestive disturbances, illness, fever, and emotional upset. Daily variations should be recorded on the temperature graph. The temperature graph shows a typical biphasic pattern during ovulatory cycles, whereas in anovulatory cycles it remains monophasic. The temperature graph and the readings are used for detecting ovulation and timing intercourse (Figure 4.2).

Basal temperature for females in the preovulatory phase is usually below 98°F (36.7°C). An ovulatory menstrual cycle is characterized by a biphasic basal body temperature pattern. As ovulation approaches, production of estrogen increases and at its peak can cause a slight drop then a rise in the basal temperature. When ovulation occurs, there is a surge of luteinizing hormone (LH), and progesterone is produced by the corpus luteum, causing a 0.5 to 1.0°F (0.3 to 0.6°C) rise in basal temperature. Figure 4.2, *B* shows a biphasic ovulatory BBT chart. Progesterone is thermogenic; therefore it maintains the tempera-

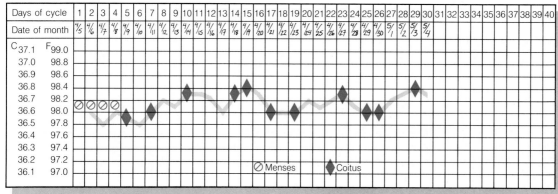

*A*

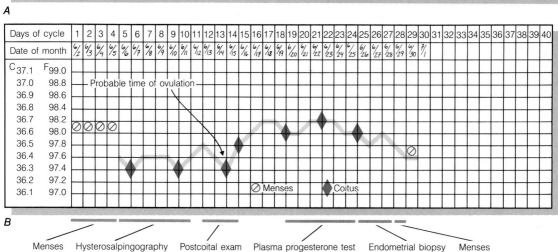

*B*

Menses  Hysterosalpingography  Postcoital exam  Plasma progesterone test  Endometrial biopsy  Menses

*Figure 4.2 (A) A monophasic, anovulatory basal body temperature chart (B) A biphasic basal body temperature chart illustrating ovulation, the different types of testing, and the time in the cycle that each would be performed*

ture increase during the second half of the menstrual cycle (luteal phase). Temperature elevation does not predict the day of ovulation but provides supportive evidence of ovulation about a day after it has occurred. Actual release of the ovum probably occurs 24 to 36 hours prior to the first temperature elevation (Coulam 1982).

With the additional documentation of coitus, serial BBT charts can be used to indicate if, and approximately when, the woman is ovulating and if intercourse is occurring at the proper time to achieve conception. A proposed schedule for intercourse based on serial BBT charts might be to recommend sexual intercourse *every other day* in the period of time beginning three to four days prior to and continuing for two to three days following the expected time of ovulation. See Teaching Guide—Self-Care Methods of Determining Ovulation.

Hormonal assessments of ovulatory function fall into two categories:

1. *LH assays.* Daily samplings of serum LH at midcycle can detect the LH surge. The day of the LH surge is believed to be the day of maximum fertility. LH assay testing can be done using a home urine test or radioimmunoassay (RIA) of an LH serum test. Normal serum values vary depending on the phase of the menstrual cycle:

   Proliferative phase: 5 to 15 mIU/mL

   Midcycle peak: 30 to 60 mIU/mL

   Secretory phase: 5 to 15 mIU/mL

   Enzyme immunoassay (EIA) techniques for urinary LH are becoming available with claims of 90% accuracy (Moghissi 1987). Collection of urinary LH is less cumbersome to the client.

2. *Progesterone assays.* Progesterone levels furnish the best evidence of ovulation and corpus luteum functioning. Plasma progesterone levels begin to rise with the LH surge and peak about eight days after the LH surge. Two blood samples, on days 8 and 21, showing an increase of from less than 1 ng/mL to greater than 5 ng/mL indicates ovulation. A normal serum progesterone level is 10 ng/mL or higher on day 21. Urinary pregnanediol reaches levels of 4 to 6 mg at 24 hours after ovulation; a level of 2 mg at 24 hours or greater indicates ovulation. Serum progesterone levels may be done instead of endometrial biopsy.

*Biopsy of the endometrium* provides information regarding the effects of progesterone produced after ovulation by the corpus luteum. The biopsy is usually performed two to six days before menstruation, since this is the time of the greatest luteal function. The woman should be informed that she will experience cramping similar to menstrual cramps at the time the actual specimen is taken.

A dysfunction may exist if the endometrial lining does not show the expected amount of secretory tissue for that day of the woman's menstrual cycle. Endometrial biopsies and serum progesterone assay may both be necessary to confirm luteal phase dysfunction.

**Ultrasound** is now also being used to detect ovulation and changes in follicular development to determine the best time for artificial insemination or in vitro fertilization.

## CERVICAL MUCOSAL TESTS

The cervical mucous cells of the endocervix consist mostly of water. As ovulation approaches, the ovary increases its secretion of estrogen and produces changes in the cervical mucus. The amount of mucus increases tenfold and the water content rises significantly. To be receptive to sperm, cervical mucus must be thin, clear, watery, profuse, alkaline, and acellular. As shown in Figure 4.3, the mazelike microscopic mucoid strands align in a parallel manner to allow for easy sperm passage (Poon and McCoshen 1985). The mucus is termed *hostile* if these changes do not occur.

Cervical mucus hostile to sperm survival can have several causes, some of which are treatable. For example, estrogen secretion may be inadequate for the development of receptive mucus. Therapy with supplemental estrogen for approximately six days before expected ovulation permits the formation of suitable spinnbarkeit. Cervical infection, another cause of mucosal hostility to sperm, can be treated, depending on the type of infection. Cone biopsy, electrocautery, or cryosurgery to the cervix may remove large numbers of mucus-producing glands and cervical crypts, creating a "dry cervix" inhospitable to sperm survival (Hammond and Talbert 1985).

The cervix can also be the site of secretory immunologic reactions in which antisperm antibodies are produced, causing agglutination or immobilization of sperm. A mucus-sperm contact or sperm penetration test has been developed in which initial interaction is observed microscopically (Bronson 1984). The most widely used serum-sperm bioassays are the gelatin agglutination test and the sperm immobilization test. Radioimmunoassays have been developed to detect specific classes of antibodies in serum and seminal fluid. Measures used to decrease antibody concentrations are:

● Corticosteroid therapy for immunosuppression to reduce IgG antibody concentration (Sogor 1986)

● Use of condoms for six months (when only the woman has the positive antibody titer) to decrease exposure to the antigen (McShane et al 1985)

Elasticity or **spinnbarkeit** increases and the viscosity decreases at ovulation. Excellent *spinnbarkeit* exists when the mucus can be stretched 5 to 6 cm or longer (Zacur and Rock 1983). This is accomplished by using two

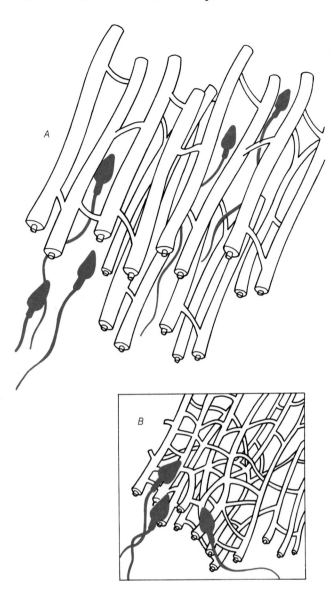

*Figure 4.3   Sperm passage through cervical mucus: (A) Receptive mucus under estrogen influence coincides with ovulation. (B) Nonreceptive mucus under influence of progesterone, endogenous or exogenous. (From Fogel CL, Woods NP:* Health Care of Women. *St. Louis: Mosby, 1981.)*

## POSTCOITAL TEST

The postcoital examination (**Sims/Huhner test**) is performed one or two days prior to the expected date of ovulation. This examination evaluates the cervical mucus and the number and motility of the sperm at the endocervix. The procedure assesses the sperm's ability to negotiate the cervical barrier and the interaction of sperm and mucus.

The couple is asked to have intercourse four to six hours before the examination. A small plastic catheter, attached to a 10-mL syringe, is placed in the cervix. Mucus is aspirated from the internal and external os, measured, and examined microscopically for signs of infection, number of active spermatozoa per high-powered field, number of spermatozoa with poor or no motility, and ability of sperm to penetrate the cervical mucus.

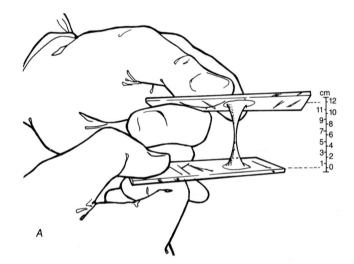

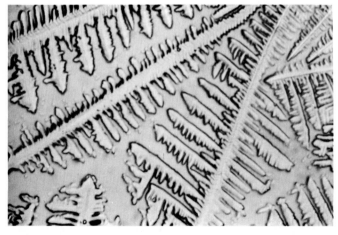

*Figure 4.4   (A) Spinnbarkeit (elasticity) (B) Ferning (Courtesy Lovena L Porter)*

glass slides (Figure 4.4, **A**) or by grasping some mucus at the external os and stretching it in the vagina toward the introitus. Studies are exploring the possibility of cervical mucus strand size and spacing as causes of infertility (Poon and McCoshen 1985).

The **ferning capacity** (Figure 4.4, **B**) of the cervical mucus also increases as ovulation approaches. *Ferning*, or crystallization, is caused by *decreased* levels of salt and water interacting with the glycoproteins in the mucus during the ovulatory period and is thus an indirect indication of estrogen production. To test for ferning, mucus is obtained from the cervical os, spread on a glass slide, allowed to air dry, and examined under the microscope.

***Assessment*** The nurse focuses on the woman's knowledge of her own body functions, mucus secretions, and menstrual cycle.

***Nursing Diagnosis*** The essential nursing diagnoses could include: Knowledge deficit related to normal body changes occurring with menstruation and ovulation, and ineffective individual coping related to self-care measures for determining fertile days.

***Nursing Plan and Implementation*** The teaching plan will include information on expected changes in cervical mucus and body temperature related to menstrual cycle, how to recognize that ovulation has occurred, and self-care methods for determining fertility days.

***Client Goals*** At the completion of the teaching session, the client will be able to:

1. Accurately identify cervical mucus changes.
2. Accurately take and record BBT temperature.
3. Identify the changes in BBT and cervical mucus that indicate ovulation has occurred.

---

## Teaching Plan

### Content

#### Basal Body Temperature (BBT)

Expected findings: The BBT can sometimes drop 12–24 hours before ovulation but a sustained rise *almost always* follows for several days, or a biphasic pattern with temperature elevation for 12–14 days prior to menstruation can be seen. At ovulation, temperature will rise 0.4–0.8°F above baseline preovulatory level. Some women notice a drop in temperature 24 hr prior to ovulation. Once a 0.4–0.8°F rise has occurred for three consecutive days a woman can safely have intercourse since her fertile days have passed. All three days should have higher temperature readings than any of the previous days in the cycle. A woman needs to take her BBT for three to four months to develop a consistent pattern.

Procedure: Instruct the woman to take her temperature for five min every morning before she gets out of bed (needs at least three hours of sleep) and before starting any activity (including smoking). Choose one site (oral, vaginal, rectal) and use same site each time. Use a BBT thermometer if possible. After five min she should record her temperature. Do this every day on special BBT chart (with 0.1 markings). Connect the dots for each day to see baseline temperature readings. (See Figure 3.2.)

Special considerations: Situations that can disturb body temperature: large alcohol intake, sleeplessness, GI or other illness, immunization, warm or hot climate, jet lag, or use of electric blanket.

### Teaching Method

*Discussion of BBT changes*
*Demonstration of BBT thermometer and chart*
*Pictures of anovulation cycle and biphasic cycle*

*(continues)*

## Teaching Plan (continued)

| Content | Teaching Method |
|---|---|

### Cervical Mucus Method

Expected findings: Pre- and postovulatory mucus is yellow, thick, and dry; or absent; or white and cloudy. Close to or during ovulation, mucus is clear, slippery (like egg whites), and elastic (can be stretched between two fingers–spinnbarkeit). Ovulation most likely occurs about 24 hr after the last day of abundant, slippery discharge (Hatcher et al 1988). Four days after peak mucus or when it is again dry, thick, and cloudy, the woman has passed her fertile days and may resume intercourse.

Mucus changes: During menstruation blood covers up sensation of wetness or mucus. For a few days after menstruation the vagina feels moist but is not distinctly wet (called "dry" days). The next mucus stage is thick, cloudy, whitish or yellowish, and sticky mucus. Vagina still doesn't feel wet and this lasts for several days. As ovulation nears, mucus usually becomes more abundant, accompanied by an increasingly wet sensation. Next the clear slippery mucus decreases until it is no longer detectable and either the thick, cloudy, sticky mucus returns or there is no mucus at all until the next menstrual period.

Procedure: Instruct woman to check her vagina each day when she uses the bathroom, either by dabbing the vaginal opening with toilet paper or by putting a finger inside the opening. Note the wetness (presence of mucus). Collect mucus; look at its color and consistency. Record findings on chart each day. Record several cycles of mucus changes to become familiar with the pattern before relying on this method.

Special considerations: Presence and consistency of mucus is altered by: vaginal infection, vaginal medications such as creams or suppositories, spermicides, lubricants, douching, sexual arousal, or semen.

Some advise complete abstinence throughout the *first* cycle a woman charts her mucus changes to help her avoid confusing mucus with semen and normal sexual lubrication.

*Show woman posters of mucus changes, spinnbarkeit of different elasticity.*
*Discuss feelings about actual procedure.*

---

***Evaluation*** The nurse discussed BBT and cervical mucus changes associated with ovulation, demonstrated BBT procedure and charting of BBT and cervical mucus changes. Woman feels comfortable with BBT and cervical mucus procedure and completion of charting. Woman learns about her body functions, how they change, and how they can be used to identify fertile periods and when ovulation may occur.

## SPERM ADEQUACY TESTS

A semen analysis is the most important initial diagnostic study of the male. It is one of the first steps in infertility testing because it is relatively simple and precludes unnecessary exposure of the female partner to high-risk painful procedures. Optimum results are obtained when a specimen is collected after two days of abstinence. If the male has difficulty producing sperm other than with intercourse, special sheaths are available to collect the sperm. Regular condoms should not be used because they contain spermicidal agents and sperm can be lost on the condom. The specimen should be placed in a glass container and brought to the laboratory within an hour of collection if possible (two to three hours maximum). It should be marked with the time of collection and date of previous ejaculation and maintained at body temperature. Repeated semen analysis may be required to identify the male's fertility potential adequately. Semen collections should be repeated at least 74 days apart to allow for new germ cell maturation (Speroff et al 1989).

Sperm analysis provides information about sperm motility and morphology as well as a determination of the absolute number of spermatozoa present (Table 4.5). Debate exists over the absolute number of sperm required for fertility. The chance for conception is remote if the semen analysis reveals fewer than ten million sperm per milliliter, less than 50% to 60% active sperm, or less than 70% normal sperm forms (Glass 1981).

Spermatozoa have been shown to possess intrinsic antigens that can provoke male immunologic infertility. This is especially apparent following vasectomy reversals where an autoimmunity (male produces antibodies to his sperm) to sperm develops (Bronson 1984). Research now indicates that it is the actual presence of antibodies on the spermatozoal surface (not just the presence of antibodies in the serum) that affects sperm function and thus leads to subfertility (Sogor 1986). Treatment for the presence of antibodies in the male ejaculate may include immunosuppression and sperm washing–dilution insemination techniques. The prostaglandin inhibitor effect of anti-inflammatory drugs has been shown to increase the sperm count, sperm motility, and fertilizing capacity (Barkay 1984).

## TUBAL PATENCY TESTS

Tubal patency tests are usually done after BBT evaluation, semen analysis, and the other less invasive tests have been done and results evaluated. Tubal patency is confirmed usually by hysterosalpingography. Other invasive tests of tubular function are laparoscopy and culdoscopy.

**Hysterosalpingography,** or **hysterogram,** involves an instillation of a radiopaque substance into the uterine cavity. As the substance fills the uterus and fallopian tubes and spills into the peritoneal cavity, it is viewed with x-ray techniques. This procedure can reveal tubal patency and any distortions of the endometrial cavity. Hysterosalpingography has also been known to have a therapeutic effect. Pregnancy is frequently achieved within the first three cycles following the test. This effect may be caused by the flushing of debris, breaking of adhesions, or induction of peristalsis by the instillation.

Hysterosalpingography causes moderate discomfort. The pain is referred from the peritoneum, which is irritated by the subdiaphragmatic collection of gas, to the shoulder. Some are now advocating hysteroscopy to detect peritubal disease, since the cervical canal and uterine cavity can be directly examined. Hysteroscopy is indicated for clients with iodine allergy and those with suspected uterine anomalies or polyps (Grimes and Richardson 1987).

*Laparoscopy* enables direct visualization of the pelvic organs and is usually done six to eight months after the hysterogram. The woman usually is given a general anesthetic for this procedure. Entry is generally made through an incision in the umbilical area, although it is occasionally done suprapubically. The peritoneal cavity is distended with carbon dioxide gas, and the pelvic organs can be directly visualized. Tubular function can be assessed by instillation of dye into the uterine cavity from below.

Visualization is best when the procedure is performed in the early follicular stage of the cycle (Valle 1984). The intraperitoneal gas is usually manually expressed at the end of the procedure. Routine preanesthesia instructions should be given. The woman should be told that she may have some discomfort from organ displacement, and shoulder and chest pain caused by gas in the abdomen lasting 24 to 48 hours after the procedure, but that she can resume normal activities after resting for about two days.

| Table 4.5 Normal Semen Analysis | |
|---|---|
| **Factor** | **Value** |
| Volume | 2–5 mL (range 1–7 mL) |
| pH | 7.2–8.9 |
| Total sperm count | ≥50 million/mL preferably |
| Liquification time | 5–20 minutes after collection |
| Motility | |
|    Immediate | >60% |
|    4 hours | >50% |
| Forward movement | >30% |
| Normal forms | >60% |
| No agglutination of sperm | |

Source: Ansbacher R: Male infertility. *Clin Obstet Gynecol* 1982; 25(3): 461.

*Culdoscopy* is sometimes used to assess fallopian tubular function. Culdoscopic examination of pelvic structures is accomplished by injecting indigo, carmine, or similar dyes through a cannula inserted into the cervix after local anesthetic infiltration.

# ● *Methods of Infertility Management*

## PHARMACOLOGIC METHODS

If an ovulation defect has been detected during the fertility testing, the treatment depends on the specific cause. In the presence of normal ovaries and intact pituitary gland, *clomiphene citrate* (Clomid) is often used. This medication induces ovulation in 80% of women by actions at both the hypothalamic and ovarian levels, and 40% of these women will become pregnant (Speroff et al 1989). Clomiphene works by increasing the secretion of follicle-stimulating hormone (FSH) and LH, which stimulates follicle growth (see Drug Guide—Clomid). The woman is instructed to take the medication daily for five days beginning on day 5 of the menstrual cycle. She is informed that if ovulation occurs, it will be during cycle days 14–16.

### Self-Care Measures

Women can assess the presence of ovulation and possible response to therapy by doing BBT and evaluating cervical mucus. The woman should be knowledgeable about side effects and call her health care provider if they occur. When visual disturbances (flashes, blurring, spots) occur, the woman should avoid brightly lit rooms. This side effect disappears within a few days or weeks after discontinuation of therapy (Kennedy and Adashi 1987). The occurrence of hot flashes may be due to the antiestrogenic properties of Clomid. Some relief can be obtained through increased intake of fluids and use of fans.

*Human menopausal gonadotropin (hMG),* also referred to as menotropin, is a combination of FSH and LH obtained from postmenopausal women's urine (Kennedy and Adashi 1987). The most common commercial preparation is Pergonal. Menotropins can be given during the first half of the cycle to stimulate follicular development and maturation (Smith 1985). To effect actual ovulation, hCG must also be given to stimulate the LH surge.

The couple is advised to have intercourse on the day of hMG administration and for the next two days. Multiple birth rate is reported to be about 20%, with 15% twins. Women who elect to have hMG medication usually have passed through all other forms of management without conceiving. Strong emotional support is needed because of the numerous office visits, injections, monthly ultrasounds, and stress in the woman's relationship.

Regimens combining clomiphene and hMG have been recommended for some women who respond poorly to clomiphene alone. This reduces the amount of hMG required per cycle.

When hyperprolactinemia accompanies anovulation, the infertility may be treated with *bromocriptine.* It inhibits the pituitary's secretion of prolactin, thus preventing suppression of the pulsatile secretion of FSH and LH. This restores normal menstrual cycles and induces ovulation by allowing FSH and LH production. If treatment is successful, the BBT record will show a normal biphasic pattern. The drug should be discontinued if pregnancy is suspected or at the anticipated time of ovulation because of its potential teratogenic effects (March 1987). Other side effects include nausea, diarrhea, dizziness, headache, and fatigue.

When endometriosis is determined to be the cause of the infertility, danazol (Danocrine) may be given to suppress ovulation and menstruation, and effect atrophy of the ectopic endometrial tissue. (For in-depth discussion of endometriosis see Chapter 3.) Temporary suppression has been shown to result in healing of the endometriosis. The treatment regimen may last for 6 to 12 months or longer, depending on the severity of the disease (Bultram et al 1982). The return of menstrual function and fertility is prompt after discontinuation of danazol, with the first menstrual period occurring within four to six weeks. (This same suppression can be achieved with the continuous use of oral contraceptives. However, troublesome side effects are much more frequent and symptomatic relief is less.) The woman is instructed to take danazol four times a day for 6 to 12 months.

Self-care measures to minimize the drug side effects  are as follows: Women should avoid foods containing excessive sodium, which may increase fluid retention, and add potassium foods to reduce muscle cramps. If mild hirsutism occurs they can use tweezers or a depilatory agent to remove the temporary hair. Conscientious skin care will minimize skin oiliness and acne. Another side effect, atrophic vaginitis, can be dealt with by using an iodine douche and using additional lubricants during intercourse.

*Gonadotropin-releasing hormone (GnRH)* is a new therapeutic tool being tested in the United States for ovulation stimulation. It is used for women who have insufficient endogenous release of GnRH, resulting in anovulation. Administration is by either subcutaneous injection or intravenous infusion. Subcutaneous injection is accomplished by a programmable portable infusion pump with a pulsatile mechanism worn on a belt around the waist (Loucopoulos et al 1984). The length of treatment varies from two to four weeks and hCG is also given to stimulate ovulation. Reports state that side effects such as multiple births and hyperstimulation syndrome are less than with combination hMG-hCG therapy (Hammond and Talbert 1985).

Progesterone therapy for luteal phase defects is also being done. Most authorities recommend the use of natural progesterone in conjunction with clomiphene or clomiphene and hCG for these problems (Wentz 1982).

## ✦ Drug Guide

# Clomid (Clomiphene Citrate)

### Overview of Action

Clomid stimulates follicular growth by increasing secretion of FSH and LH. Ovulation is expected to occur five to ten days after last dose. Used when anovulation is caused by hypothalamic suppression, luteal phase dysfunction, oligo-ovulation and in vitro fertilization (Kennedy and Adashi 1987).

### Route, Dosage, Frequency

Administered orally. Fifty mg/day to 250 mg/day from day 5 to day 9 (total of five days) of the menstrual cycle. Usually start with 50 mg/day and increase dose 50 mg each time (Kennedy and Adashi 1987). May need to give estrogen simultaneously if decrease in cervical mucus occurs.

### Contraindications

Presence of ovarian enlargement, ovarian cysts, hyperstimulation syndrome, liver disease, visual problems, pregnancy (Kennedy and Adashi 1987).

### Side Effects

Antiestrogenic effects may cause decrease in cervical mucus production.

Other side effects include: vasomotor flushes; abdominal distention and ovarian enlargement secondary to follicular growth and development and multiple corpus luteum formation; bloating, pain, soreness, breast discomfort; nausea and vomiting; visual symptoms (spots, flashes); headaches; dryness or loss of hair; multiple pregnancies.

### Nursing Considerations

Determine if couple has been advised to have sexual intercourse every other day for one week beginning five days after the last day of medications.

Instruct couple on use of BBT chart to assess if ovulation has occurred. Also inform couple that plasma progesterone, cervical mucus, and vaginal cytology may be done.

Remind couples that if the woman doesn't have a period she must be checked for the possibility of pregnancy before another trial of Clomid is started.

## ARTIFICIAL INSEMINATION

*Artificial insemination* is the depositing of semen at the cervical os by mechanical means. The semen may be the husband's (AIH) or that of a donor (AID). The conception rates are approximately 30% for AID and 15% for AIH. AIH is used in cases of too small or large a semen volume, too few or too many sperm, low levels of spermatozoal motility, anatomic defects accompanied by inadequate deposition or penetration of semen, or retrograde ejaculation.

AID is considered in cases of total lack of sperm motility or a combination of inadequate motility and viability of sperm, or inherited disorders affecting only males. AID is not appropriate therapy in cases of women with antibodies, since they have antibodies against antigens common to all human sperm cells, not just to their husband's sperm (Wallach et al 1984).

Numerous factors need to be evaluated before AID is performed. Has every possible effort been made to diagnose and treat the cause of the male infertility? Do tests indicate normal fertility and sperm/ovum transport in the woman? Is each member psychologically stable? Is this a voluntary decision on the part of the male partner? Are there any religious contraindications? Does the donor have

any diseases or genetic problems? If insemination by donor is being considered, screening for AIDS may need to be done (Quagliarello 1987).

Artificial insemination is accomplished by collecting semen from the male in a glass container. The semen then is drawn into a syringe and placed in a small plastic cervical cup. The cup is put in place at the cervical os, and the woman remains in the supine position with the hips elevated for about 30 minutes. An alternate method is to instill the semen directly into the uterus using a small plastic catheter on a syringe. The semen must first be chemically cleansed and centrifuged. This method enables the semen to bypass possible cervical or immunologic factors.

## IN VITRO FERTILIZATION

The first birth conceived by *in vitro fertilization* (IVF) was achieved in Great Britain in 1978. This procedure is selectively used in cases in which infertility has resulted from tubal factors, mucus abnormalities, and immunity to spermatozoa in either partner and when infertility is long-term and unexplained. IVF is felt to be the only hope for up to 25% of infertile couples (Phillips 1985).

Ovulation is induced using fertility drugs, and ovarian function is monitored daily with blood tests, cervical mucus tests, and ultrasound. Just before ovulation, the ripened ova are aspirated from the ovaries during a laparoscopy. The ova are fertilized with the prospective father's sperm and transferred to the mother's uterus when they reach the four- to eight-cell stage of development (Dodson et al 1986). A series of progesterone injections are given to assist the process of implantation. The procedure has had a success rate of up to 20%, with a spontaneous abortion rate of one in three.

In vitro fertilization is an invasive method of treating infertility. The risk to offspring can only be assessed with more experience. Controversy concerning IVF has elicited concern, criticism, opinions, and condemnation from a variety of church leaders and scientists. In spite of the ethical and legal issues, it has found fairly wide acceptance with childless couples. In the near future, it may be a routine treatment for many infertile couples (Creighton 1985).

## ADOPTION

The adoption of an infant is not as satisfactory an alternative to infertility today as it was in the past. In fact, there are 44 couples waiting to adopt each available white infant (Phillips 1985). A waiting period as long as seven years even to begin the adoption process is not uncommon. The decrease in number of available infants has occurred because many infants are reared by their single mothers instead of being relinquished for adoption as was customary in the past. In addition, many unwanted pregnancies are being terminated by elective abortion and many pregnancies are being prevented by more effective methods of birth control. Some couples seek international adoptions or consider adopting older children, children with handicaps, or children of mixed-race parentage. The adoption process is quicker and more children are available in these groups.

## THE NURSE'S ROLE

Approximately 15% of the childbearing population in the United States (one out of six couples) is unable to conceive or carry a pregnancy to term (Darland 1985). The couple may incur tremendous emotional and physical stress, as well as financial expense, for infertility testing. Treatment can cost an average of $20,000 a year. Years of effort and numerous evaluations and examinations may take place before a conception occurs, if one occurs at all. In a society that values children and considers them to be the natural result of marriage, infertile couples may face a myriad of tensions and discrimination.

The nurse must be constantly aware of the emotional needs and sometimes irrational thoughts and fears of the couple with a fertility problem. The emotional aspect of infertility is often more difficult for the couple than the testing and treatment. Constant attention to temperature charts and instructions about their sex life from a person outside the relationship naturally affect the spontaneity of a couple's interactions. Their relationship will be stressed by these and other intrusive but necessary measures. The tests may heighten feelings of frustration or anger between the partners. Correction of infertility may require surgery, administration of hormones, and other treatment measures. The need to share this intimate area of a relationship may cause feelings of guilt and shame. Throughout the evaluations and emotional-financial strains one or both partners may undergo at this time, the nurse plays a major role in teaching and offering emotional support. Extensive and repeated explanations may be necessary to help relieve anxiety.

Infertility may be perceived as a loss by one or both partners, and, as in the loss of a loved one who dies, this situation is attended by feelings of grief and mourning. Each couple passes through several stages of feelings, not unlike those identified by Kübler-Ross: surprise, denial, anger, isolation, guilt, grief, and resolution (Menning 1980). It is important to remember that each partner may progress through the stages at different rates. Nonjudgmental acceptance and a professional caring attitude on the nurse's part can go far to dissipate the negative emotions the couple may experience while going through this process. This is also a time when the nurse may assess the quality of the couple's relationship: Are they able and willing to communicate verbally and share feelings? Are they mutually supportive? The answers to such questions may help the nurse identify areas of strength and weakness and construct an appropriate plan of care. At times, individual

## Table 4.6 Tasks of the Infertile Couple

| Tasks | Nursing interventions |
|---|---|
| 1. Recognition of how infertility affects their lives and expression of feelings (may be negative toward self or mate) | 1. Supportive: help to understand and facilitate free expression of feelings |
| 2. Grieving the loss of potential offspring | 2. Help to recognize feelings |
| 3. Evaluation of reasons for wanting a child | 3. Help to understand motives |
| 4. Decision making about management | 4. Identify alternatives; facilitate partner communication |

Source: Sawatzky M: Tasks of the infertile couple. *J Obstet Gynecol Neonat Nurs* 1981; 10:132.

or group counseling with other infertile couples may facilitate the couple's resolution of feelings brought about by their own difficult situation. Support groups such as Resolve can be invaluable to these families. Sawatzky (1981) has identified the essential tasks of the infertile couple (Table 4.6).

# ● GENETIC DISORDERS

Even when conception has been achieved, families can have special reproductive concerns. The desired and expected outcome of any pregnancy is the birth of a healthy, "perfect" baby.

Unfortunately, a small but significant number of parents experience grief, fear, and anger when they discover that their baby has been born with a defect or a genetic disease. Such an abnormality may be evident at birth or may not appear for some time. The child may have inherited a disease from one parent, creating more guilt and strife within the family.

Regardless of the type or scope of the problem, parents will have many questions: "What did I do?" "What caused it?" "Will it happen again?" The nurse must anticipate the parents' questions and concerns and guide, direct, and support the family. To do so, the nurse must have a basic knowledge of genetics and genetic counseling. Many congenital malformations and diseases are genetic or have a strong genetic component. Others are not genetic at all. The genetic counselor attempts to categorize the problem and answer the family's questions. Professional nurses can help expedite this process if they already have an understanding of the principles involved and are able to direct the family to the appropriate resources.

# ● *Chromosomes and Chromosomal Abnormalities*

All hereditary material is carried on tightly coiled strands of DNA known as **chromosomes.** The chromosomes carry the genes, the smallest unit of inheritance, as discussed in Chapter 5.

All **somatic** (body) cells contain 46 chromosomes, which is the *diploid* number of chromosomes, while the sperm and egg contain 23 chromosomes, or the **haploid** number (see Chapter 5). There are 23 pairs of *homologous* chromosomes (a matched pair of chromosomes, one inherited from each parent). Twenty-two of the pairs are known as **autosomes** (nonsex chromosomes), and one pair are the **sex chromosomes,** X and Y. A normal male has a 46,XY chromosome constitution; the normal female, 46,XX (Figures 4.5 and 4.6).

The **karyotype,** or pictorial analysis of these chromosomes, is usually obtained from specially treated and stained peripheral blood lymphocytes. Although the use of

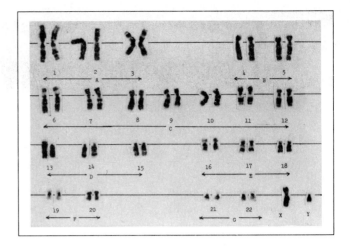

*Figure 4.5   Normal male karyotype (Courtesy Dr Arthur Robinson, National Jewish Hospital and Research Center)*

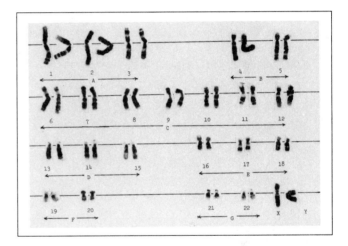

*Figure 4.6   Normal female karyotype (Courtesy Dr Arthur Robinson, National Jewish Hospital and Research Center)*

peripheral blood is an easy, convenient method of obtaining chromosomes, almost any tissue can be examined to get this information. In the case of a stillbirth or perinatal death in which there are multiple congenital abnormalities and there is a question of diagnosis or cause, karyotypes of cells in the child's thymus (if it has not been fixed in formalin) can be examined.

Chromosome abnormalities can occur in either the autosomes or the sex chromosomes and can be divided into two categories: abnormalities of number and abnormalities of structure. Even small alterations in chromosomes can cause problems, especially those associated with slow growth and development or with mental retardation. The child need not have obvious major malformations to be affected. In addition, some of these abnormalities can be passed on to other offspring. Thus, in some cases chro-

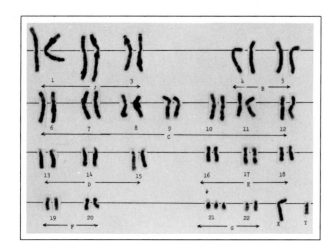

Figure 4.7 Karyotype of a male who has trisomy 21, Down syndrome. Note the extra 21 chromosome. (Courtesy Dr Arthur Robinson, National Jewish Hospital and Research Center)

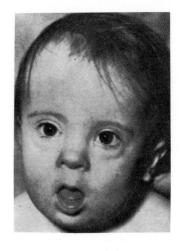

Figure 4.8 A child with Down syndrome (From Jones KL: Smith's Recognizable Patterns of Human Malformations, 4th ed. Philadelphia: Saunders, 1988.)

mosomal analysis is appropriate even if clinical manifestations are mild.

Indications for chromosomal analysis include:

- Chromosome syndrome suspected (or clients with a clinical diagnosis of Down syndrome)
- Mental retardation and congenital malformations
- Abnormal sexual development (primary amenorrhea and lack of secondary sex characteristics)
- Ambiguous genitals
- Multiple miscarriages
- Possible balanced translocation carrier (see "Abnormalities of Chromosome Structure," this chapter).

## AUTOSOMAL ABNORMALITIES

### Abnormalities of Chromosome Number

Abnormalities of chromosome number are most commonly seen as trisomies, monosomies, and mosaicism. In all three cases, the abnormality is most often caused by nondisjunction. *Nondisjunction* occurs when paired chromosomes fail to separate during cell division. If nondisjunction occurs in either the sperm or the egg before fertilization, the resulting zygote will have an abnormal chromosome makeup in all of the cells (trisomy or monosomy). If nondisjunction occurs after fertilization, the developing cell (zygote) will have cells with two or more different chromosome makeups, evolving into two or more different cell lines (mosaicism).

**Trisomies** are the product of the union of a normal gamete (egg or sperm) with a gamete that contains an extra chromosome. The individual will have 47 chromosomes and is trisomic (has three chromosomes the same) for

whichever chromosome is extra. Down syndrome (formerly called mongolism) is the most common trisomy abnormality seen in children (see Figure 4.7). The presence of the extra chromosome 21 produces distinctive clinical features (see Table 4.7 and Figure 4.8).

Trisomies can occur among other autosomes, the two most common being trisomy 18 and trisomy 13 (see Table 4.7 and Figures 4.9 and 4.10). The prognosis for both trisomy 13 and 18 is extremely poor. Most children (70%) die within the first three months of life secondary to complications related to respiratory and cardiac abnormalities. With the advent of modern surgical techniques and anti-

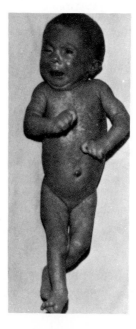

Figure 4.9 Infant with trisomy 18 (From Jones KL: Smith's Recognizable Patterns of Human Malformations, 4th ed. Philadelphia: Saunders, 1988.)

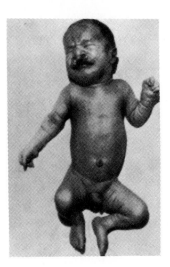

Figure 4.10  Infant with trisomy 13 (From Jones KL: Smith's Recognizable Patterns of Human Malformations, *4th ed. Philadelphia: Saunders, 1988.)*

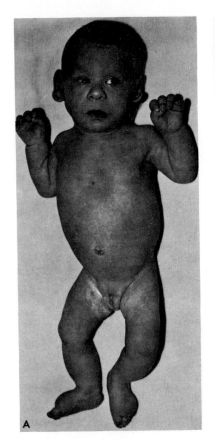

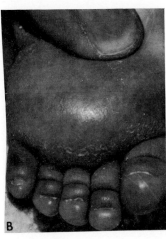

Figure 4.11  Infant with Turner syndrome at one month of age. Note: (A) Prominent ears (B) Lymphedema (From Lemli L, Smith DW: The XO syndrome: A study of the differentiated phenotype in 25 patients. J Pediatr 1963; 63:577.)

biotics, children with Down syndrome are now living into their fifth or sixth decade of life.

*Monosomies* occur when a normal gamete unites with a gamete that is missing a chromosome. In this case, the individual will have only 45 chromosomes and is said to be monosomic. Monosomy of an entire autosomal chromosome is incompatible with life. The only exception is in the sex chromosomes. A female can survive with only one X chromosome; this condition is known as *Turner syndrome* (Table 4.7 and Figure 4.11).

*Mosaicism* occurs after fertilization and results in an individual who has two different cell lines, each with a different chromosomal number. Mosaicism tends to be more common in the sex chromosomes, but when it does occur in the autosomes it is most common in Down syndrome.

Clinical signs and symptoms may vary if mosaicism is present. In Down syndrome, the clinical signs may be classic, minimal, or nonapparent, depending on the number and location of the abnormal cells. An individual with many classic signs of Down syndrome but with normal or near normal intelligence should be investigated for the possibility of mosaicism. In such a case, more than one tissue may have to be examined to make the diagnosis. The peripheral blood may contain 46 chromosomes while the skin fibroblasts contain 47, +21.

## Abnormalities of Chromosome Structure

Abnormalities of chromosome structure involving only parts of the chromosome generally occur in two forms: translocation, and deletions and/or additions. Over 100 such abnormalities have been described in the literature. Again, Down syndrome is one of the most common syndromes described.

Not all children born with Down syndrome have trisomy 21. Instead, they may have an abnormal rearrangement of chromosomal material known as a *translocation* (Figure 4.12). Clinically, the two types of Down syndrome are indistinguishable. What is of major importance to the family is that the two different types have significantly different risks of recurrence. The only way to distinguish the two is to do a chromosome analysis.

The translocation occurs when the carrier parent has 45 chromosomes, usually with one of the number 21 chromosomes fused to one of the number 14 chromosomes. The parent has one normal 14, one normal 21, and one 14/21 chromosome. Since all the chromosomal material is present and functioning normally, the parent is clinically normal. This individual is known as a *balanced translocation carrier*. When this person has a child with a person

### Table 4.7 Chromosomal Syndromes

| Altered chromosome | Genetic defect and incidence | Characteristics | |
|---|---|---|---|
| 21 | Trisomy 21 (Down syndrome) (secondary nondisjunction or 14/21 unbalanced translocation) 1 in 700 live births (Figure 4.8) | CNS: | Mental retardation<br>Hypotonia at birth |
| | | Head: | Flattened occiput<br>Depressed nasal bridge<br>Mongoloid slant of eyes<br>Epicanthal folds<br>White speckling of the iris (Brushfield spots)<br>Protrusion of the tongue<br>High, arched palate<br>Low-set ears<br>Broad, short fingers |
| | | Hands: | Short fingers<br>Abnormalities of finger and foot<br>Dermal ridge patterns (dermatoglyphics)<br>Transverse palmar crease (simian line) |
| | | Other: | Congenital heart disease |
| 21 | 2° mosaicism (Down syndrome) Incidence 1% | | Classic symptoms as described in trisomy 21 except that the child has normal intelligence |
| 18 | Trisomy 18 1 in 3000 live births (Figure 4.9) | CNS: | Mental retardation<br>Severe hypertonia |
| | | Head: | Prominent occiput<br>Low-set ears<br>Corneal opacities<br>Ptosis (drooping of eyelids) |
| | | Hands: | Third and fourth fingers overlapped by second and fifth fingers<br>Abnormal dermatoglyphics<br>Syndactyly (webbing of fingers) |
| | | Other: | Congenital heart defects<br>Renal abnormalities<br>Single umbilical artery<br>Gastrointestinal tract abnormalities<br>Rocker-bottom feet<br>Cryptorchidism<br>Various malformations of other organs |
| 18 | Deletion of long arm of chromosome 18 | CNS: | Severe psychomotor retardation |
| | | Head: | Microcephaly<br>Stenotic ear canals with conductive hearing loss |
| | | Other: | Various other organ malformations |

who has a structurally normal chromosome constitution, there are several possible outcomes. The offspring can receive the carrier parent's normal number 21 and normal number 14 chromosomes in combination with the noncarrier parent's normal chromosomes 21 and 14. In this case the offspring is chromosomally normal. Or the child may receive one of the balanced translocations, thus becoming a carrier like the carrier parent—chromosomally abnormal

but clinically normal. If, however, the offspring receives the carrier parent's normal number 21 chromosome and the 14/21 chromosome and the noncarrier parent's normal chromosomes, the offspring receives two functioning number 14 chromosomes and three functioning number 21 chromosomes. At first glance, the child seems to have 46 chromosomes but actually has an extra chromosome 21. Thus the child has an *unbalanced translocation* and has

## Table 4.7  Chromosomal Syndromes (continued)

| Altered chromosome | Genetic defect and incidence | Characteristics | |
|---|---|---|---|
| 13 | Trisomy 13 1 in 5000 live births (Figure 4.10) | CNS: | Mental retardation Severe hypertonia Seizures |
| | | Head: | Microcephaly Microphthalmia and/or coloboma Malformed ears Aplasia of external auditory canal Micrognathia Cleft lip and palate |
| | | Hands: | Polydactyly (extra digits) Abnormal posturing of fingers Abnormal dermatoglyphics |
| | | Other: | Congenital heart defects Hemangiomas Gastrointestinal tract defects Various malformations of other organs |
| 5 | Deletion of short arm of chromosome 5 (cri du chat—cat cry syndrome) 1 in 20,000 live births | CNS: | Severe mental retardation A catlike cry in infancy |
| | | Head: | Microcephaly Hypertelorism Epicanthal folds Low-set ears |
| | | Other: | Failure to thrive Various organ malformations |
| X (sex chromosome) | Only one X chromosome in female (Turner syndrome) 1 in 300 to 7000 live female births (Figure 4.11) | CNS: | No intellectual impairment Some perceptual difficulties |
| | | Head: | Low hairline Webbed neck |
| | | Trunk: | Short stature Cubitus valgus (increased carrying angle of arm) Excessive nevi Broad shieldlike chest with widely spaced nipples Puffy feet No toenails |
| | | Other: | Fibrous streaks in ovaries Underdeveloped secondary sex characteristics Primary amenorrhea Usually infertile Renal anomalies Coarctation of the aorta |
| X | Extra X in male (Klinefelter syndrome) 1 in 1000 live male births, approx. 1%–2% of institutionalized males | CNS: | Mild mental retardation |
| | | Trunk: | Occasional gynecomastia Eunuchoid body proportions |
| | | Other: | Small, soft testes Underdeveloped secondary sex characteristics Usually sterile |

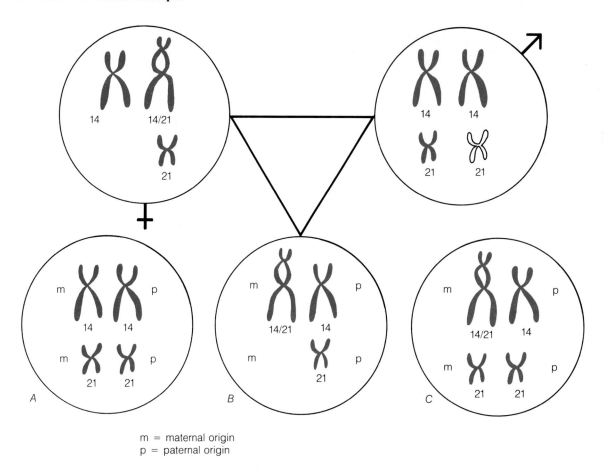

m = maternal origin
p = paternal origin

*Figure 4.12   Diagram of various types of offspring when mother has a balanced translocation between 14 and 21 and father has a normal arrangement of chromosomal material. (A) Normal offspring, (B) Balanced translocation carrier, (C) Unbalanced translocation: child has Down syndrome.*

Down syndrome. Other types of translocations can occur. But regardless of the chromosome involved, any person having a balanced chromosome rearrangement (translocation) has the potential of having a child with an unbalanced chromosome constitution. This usually means a substantial negative effect on normal growth and development.

The other type of structure abnormality seen is caused by *additions and/or deletions* of chromosomal material. Any portion of a chromosome may be lost or added, generally leading to some adverse effect. Depending on how much chromosomal material is involved, the clinical effects may be mild or severe. Many types of additions and deletions have been described, such as the deletion of the short arm of chromosome 5 (cri du chat syndrome) or the deletion of the long arm of chromosome 18 (see Table 4.7).

### Sex Chromosome Abnormalities

To better understand normal X chromosome function and thus abnormalities of the sex chromosomes, the nurse should know that in females, at an early embryonic stage,

one of the two normal X chromosomes becomes inactive. The inactive X chromosome forms a dark staining area known as the **Barr body,** or *sex chromatin body* (Figure 4.13).

The Barr body may be seen by examining the cells scraped from the inside of a woman's mouth. This procedure, the *buccal smear,* will show the number of inactivated X chromosomes of Barr bodies present. The normal female has one Barr body, since one of her two X chromosomes has been inactivated. The normal male has no Barr bodies, since he has only one X chromosome to begin with. The number of Barr bodies seen on the buccal smear *is always* one less than the number of X chromosomes present in the woman's cells.

When Y cells are stained and viewed, the Y chromosome appears as a bright body within the nucleus. The number of Y bodies present is equal to the number of Y chromosomes present. Males should have one Y body, and females should have none.

The most common sex chromosome abnormalities are **Turner syndrome** in females (45,XO with no Barr bodies

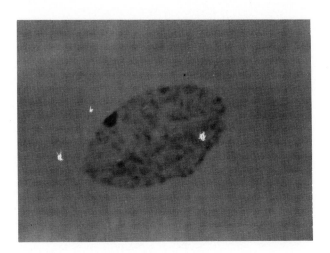

*Figure 4.13   Nucleus with one Barr body; the patient is sex chromatin positive. (Courtesy Dr Arthur Robinson, National Jewish Hospital and Research Center)*

present) and **Klinefelter syndrome** in males (47,XXY with one Barr body present). See Table 4.7 for clinical description of these abnormalities. During the newborn period, clinical signs and symptoms of Turner syndrome are lymphedema of the dorsum of the hands and feet and excessive skin in the neck.

## • *Patterns of Inheritance*

Many inherited diseases are produced by an abnormality in a single gene or pair of genes. In such instances, the chromosomes are grossly normal: The defect is at the gene level and cannot be detected by present laboratory techniques.

Therefore the pattern of inheritance for a particular disease or defect is determined by two methods: (a) close examination of the family in which the disease appears and (b) knowledge of how the disease has been previously inherited.

There are two major categories of inheritance: **Mendelian** or **single-gene inheritance,** and *non-Mendelian,* or *polygenic inheritance.* Each single-gene trait is determined by a pair of genes working together. These genes are responsible for the observable expression of the trait, referred to as the **phenotype** (ie, blue eyes, fair skin). The total genetic makeup of an individual is referred to as the **genotype** (ie, chromosomal structure). One of the genes for a trait is inherited from the mother, the other from the father. An individual who has two identical genes at a given locus is considered to be **homozygous** for that trait. An individual is considered to be **heterozygous** for a particular trait when he or she has two different **alleles** (alternate forms of the same gene) at a given locus on a pair of homologous chromosomes.

The well-known modes of single-gene inheritance are autosomal dominant, autosomal recessive, and X-linked (sex-linked) recessive. There is also an X-linked dominant mode of inheritance that is less common, and a newly identified mode of inheritance, the fragile-X syndrome.

## AUTOSOMAL DOMINANT INHERITANCE

An individual is said to have an autosomal dominantly inherited disorder if the disease trait is heterozygous. That is, the abnormal gene overshadows the normal gene of the pair. It is essential to remember that in autosomal dominant inheritance:

1.  An affected individual generally has an affected parent. Thus, the family pedigree (graphic representation of a family tree) usually shows multiple generations having the disorder.

2.  The affected individual has a 50% chance of passing on the abnormal gene to each of his or her offspring (Figure 4.14).

3.  Both males and females are equally affected, and a father can pass the abnormal gene on to his son. This is an important principle when distinguishing autosomal dominant disorders from X-linked disorders.

4.  An unaffected individual in most cases cannot transmit the disorder to his or her children.

5.  Autosomal dominant inherited disorders have varying degrees of presentation. This is an important factor when counseling families concerning autosomal dominant disorders. Although a parent may have a mild form of the disease, the child may have a more severe form. Unfortunately there is no method for predicting whether a child will be only mildly affected or more severely affected. The geneticist or health care provider must be thorough in the examination of family members to discern whether any of those individuals are indeed affected. They may express the disease in such a mild form that a cursory examination may miss clinical signs of the disease.

Some common autosomal dominantly inherited disorders are Huntington's chorea, polycystic kidney disease, neurofibromatosis (von Recklinghausen disease), and achondroplastic dwarfism.

## AUTOSOMAL RECESSIVE INHERITANCE

An individual has an autosomal recessively inherited disorder if the disease manifests itself only as a homozygous trait. That is, because the normal gene overshadows the abnormal one, the individual must have two abnormal genes to be affected. The notion of a *carrier state* is appropriate here. An individual who is heterozygous for the abnormal gene is clinically normal. It is not until two individu-

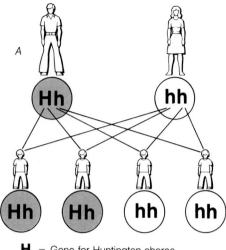

A

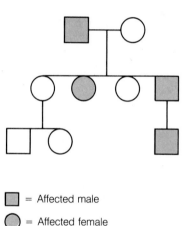

B

**H** = Gene for Huntington chorea
**h** = Normal allele
(**Hh**) = Affected individual
(**hh**) = Nonaffected individual

☐ = Affected male
◯ = Affected female

*Figure 4.14  (**A**) Autosomal dominant inheritance. One parent is affected. Statistically, 50% of offspring will be affected, regardless of sex. (**B**) Autosomal dominant pedigree.*

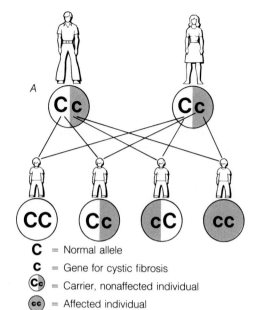

A

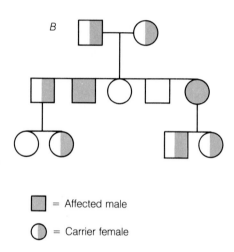

B

**C** = Normal allele
**c** = Gene for cystic fibrosis
(**Cc**) = Carrier, nonaffected individual
(**cc**) = Affected individual

☐ = Affected male
◯ = Carrier female

*Figure 4.15  (**A**) Autosomal recessive inheritance. Both parents are carriers. Statically, 25% of offspring are affected, regardless of sex. (**B**) Autosomal recessive pedigree.*

als mate and pass on the same abnormal gene that affected offspring may appear. It is essential to remember that in autosomal recessive inheritance:

1.  An affected individual has clinically normal parents, but they are both carriers of the abnormal gene (Figure 4.15).

2.  Parents who are both carriers of the same abnormal gene have a 25% chance of both passing the abnormal gene on to any of their offspring (Figure 4.15).

3.  If a child of two carrier parents is clinically normal,

there is a 50% chance that he or she is a carrier of the gene (Figure 4.15).

4.  Both males and females are equally affected.

5.  Parents who are closely related are more likely to have the same genes in common than two parents who are unrelated.

6.  The presence of the abnormal gene for some autosomal recessively inherited disorders can be detected in a normal carrier parent. For instance, Tay-Sachs disease is caused by an inborn error of metabolism, that is, a deficiency of the enzyme

hexosaminidase A. An affected individual has little or no enzyme activity present, whereas a carrier parent usually has 50% normal enzyme activity present. Biochemically the carrier is abnormal, and the heterozygous state can be detected, even though it is asymptomatic.

Some common autosomal recessive inherited disorders are cystic fibrosis, phenylketonuria (PKU), galactosemia, sickle cell anemia, Tay-Sachs disease, and most metabolic disorders.

## X-LINKED RECESSIVE INHERITANCE

X-linked or sex-linked disorders are those for which the abnormal gene is carried on the X chromosome. A female may be heterozygous or homozygous for a trait carried on the X chromosome, since she has two X chromosomes. A male, however, has only one X chromosome, and there are some traits for which no comparable genes are located on the Y chromosome. The male in this case is considered to be *hemizygous*, having only one alternate form of the gene, instead of a pair for a given trait or disorder. Thus an X-linked disorder is manifested in a male who carries the abnormal gene on his X chromosome. His mother is considered to be a carrier when the normal gene on one X chromosome overshadows the abnormal gene on the other X chromosome. It is essential to remember that in X-linked recessive inheritance:

1. There is no male-to-male transmission. Fathers pass only their Y chromosomes to their sons and their X chromosomes to their daughters. Daughters receive one X chromosome from the mother and one from the father.

2. Affected males are related through the female line.

3. There is a 50% chance that a carrier mother will pass the abnormal gene to each of her sons, who will thus be affected. There is a 50% chance that a carrier mother will pass the normal gene to each of her sons, who will thus be unaffected. Finally, there is a 50% chance that a carrier mother will pass the abnormal gene to each of her daughters, who become carriers like their mother (Figure 4.16).

4. Fathers affected with an X-linked disorder cannot pass the disorder to their sons, but *all* their daughters become carriers of the disorder.

5. Occasionally, a female carrier may show some symptoms of an X-linked disorder. This situation is probably due to random inactivation of the X chromosome carrying the normal allele. Thus, a heterozygous female may show some manifestation of an X-linked disorder.

Common X-linked recessive disorders are hemophilia, Duchenne muscular dystrophy, and color blindness.

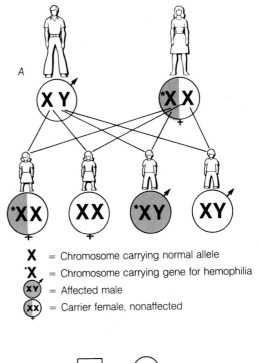

X = Chromosome carrying normal allele
*X = Chromosome carrying gene for hemophilia
(XY) = Affected male
(XX) = Carrier female, nonaffected

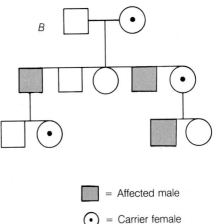

■ = Affected male
⊙ = Carrier female

*Figure 4.16   (A) X-linked recessive inheritance. The mother is the carrier. Statistically, 50% of male offspring are affected, and 50% of female offspring are carriers. (B) X-linked pedigree.*

## X-LINKED DOMINANT INHERITANCE

X-linked dominant disorders are extremely rare, the most common being vitamin-D–resistant rickets. When X-linked dominance does occur, the pattern is similar to X-linked recessive inheritance except that heterozygous females are affected. It is essential to remember that in X-linked dominant inheritance:

1. The abnormal gene is dominant and overshadows the normal gene.

2. There is no male-to-male transmission. An affected

father will have affected daughters, but no affected sons.

## FRAGILE-X SYNDROME

A newly identified chromosomal disorder is the *fragile-X syndrome*. It is a central nervous system disorder linked to a "fragile site" on the X chromosome. This fragile site is seen when cells are grown in a folic acid–deficient media and detectable in both affected males and heterozygous carrier females (Shapiro 1982). Fragile-X syndrome is characterized by moderate mental retardation, large protuberant ears, and large testes after puberty (Thompson and Thompson 1986).

## MULTIFACTORIAL (POLYGENIC) INHERITANCE

Many common congenital malformations, such as cleft palate, heart defects, spina bifida, dislocated hips, clubfoot, and pyloric stenosis, are caused by an interaction of many genes and environmental factors. They are, therefore, multifactorial in origin. It is essential to remember that in multifactorial inheritance:

1. The malformations may vary from mild to severe. For example, spina bifida may range in severity from mild, as spina bifida occulta, to more severe, as a myelomeningocele. It is believed that the more severe the defect, the greater the number of genes present for that defect.

2. There is often a sex bias. Pyloric stenosis is more common in males, whereas cleft palate is more common among females. When a member of the less commonly affected sex shows the condition, a greater number of genes must usually be present to cause the defect.

3. In the presence of environmental influence (such as seasonal changes, altitude, irradiation, chemicals in the environment, or exposure to toxic substances), it may take fewer genes to manifest the disease in the offspring.

4. In contrast to single-gene disorders, there is an additive effect in multifactorial inheritance. The more family members who have the defect, the greater the risk that the next pregnancy will also be affected.

Although most congenital malformations are polygenic traits, a careful family history should always be taken, since occasionally cleft lip and palate, certain congenital heart defects, and other malformations can be inherited as autosomal dominant or recessive traits. Other disorders thought to be within the polygenic inheritance group are diabetes, hypertension, some heart diseases, and mental illness.

## ● Nongenetic Conditions

Not all disorders or congenital malformations are inherited or have an inherited component. Malformations present at birth may represent an environmental insult during pregnancy, such as exposure to a drug or an infectious agent (see Chapter 12). Some malformations, however, cannot be explained by genetic mechanisms or teratogens. These disorders are considered to have a developmental cause. Thus, a couple who has a child with phocomelia (abnormality of the limbs), in the absence of any other problems or family history, may be reassured that the problem is developmental in etiology and the risk for future pregnancies is low. Such reassurance is also appropriate for families concerned about a child's seizures or developmental delays, if they can be attributed to an acquired problem.

## ● Prenatal Diagnosis

Parent-child and family planning counseling have become a major responsibility of professional nurses. To be effective counselors, nurses must have the most current knowledge available concerning prenatal diagnosis.

It is essential that the couple be completely informed as to the known and potential risks of each of the genetic diagnostic procedures. The nurse must recognize the emotional impact on the family of a decision to have or not to have a genetic diagnostic procedure.

The ability to diagnose certain genetic diseases by various diagnostic tools has enormous implications for the practice of preventive health care. Several methods are available for prenatal diagnosis, although some are still being used on an experimental basis.

### GENETIC ULTRASOUND

Ultrasound may be used to assess the fetus for genetic and/or congenital problems. With ultrasound, one can visualize the fetal head for abnormalities in size, shape, and structure. Craniospinal defects (anencephaly, microcephaly, hydrocephalus), gastrointestinal malformations (omphalocele, gastroschisis), renal malformations (dysplasias or obstruction), and skeletal malformations are only some of the disorders that have been diagnosed in utero by ultrasound. As ultrasound technology improves, the number of structural abnormalities being detected will increase. Screening for congenital anomalies is best done at 16 to 18 weeks when fetal structures have completed development (Lange 1985). Information about possible harmful effects to either the mother or the fetus from exposure to ultrasound is still limited (Kremkau 1984). The American College of Obstetricians and Gynecologists (ACOG) recommends that ultrasound be used only in medically indicated situations.

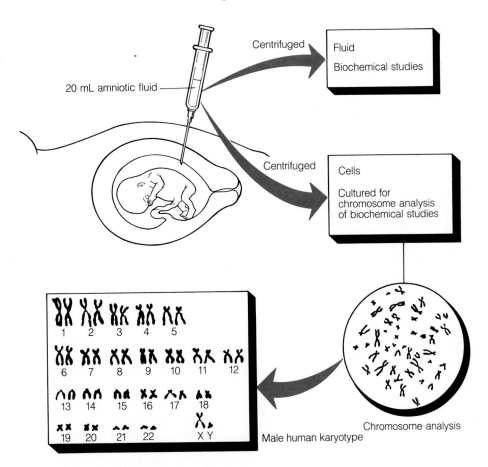

*Figure 4.17  Genetic amniocentesis for prenatal diagnosis is done at 14 to 16 weeks' gestation. (Modified from Richie DD, Carola R: Biology. Reading, MA: Addison-Wesley, 1979, p 302.)*

## GENETIC AMNIOCENTESIS

The major method of prenatal diagnosis is genetic amniocentesis (Figure 4.17). The procedure is described in Chapter 13. The indications for genetic amniocentesis include:

1. Advanced maternal age. Any woman 35 or older is at greater risk for having children with chromosome abnormalities. Approximately 85% of all amniocentesis is done because of advanced maternal age (Verp 1984). This maternal age effect is most pronounced for trisomy 21.

2. Previous child born with a chromosomal abnormality. Young couples who have had a child with trisomy 21 have approximately a 1% to 2% risk of a future child having a chromosome abnormality. Although no statistics of recurrence risks for other chromosome abnormalities have been established, genetic amniocentesis is made available to any couple who has already had a child with a chromosome abnormality.

3. Parent carrying a chromosomal abnormality

(balanced translocation). Any couple in which one of the partners is a carrier of a balanced translocation should be considered for prenatal diagnosis. Although the person with the chromosome rearrangement is clinically normal, he or she has the potential for conceiving a child with an unbalanced chromosome constitution, which usually has substantial adverse effects on normal development. For example, a woman who carries a balanced 14/21 translocation has a risk of approximately 10% to 15% that her offspring will be affected with the unbalanced translocation of Down syndrome; if the father is the carrier, there is a 2% to 5% risk (Henry and Robinson 1978).

4. Mother carrying an X-linked disease. In families in which the woman is a known or possible carrier of an X-linked disorder, such as hemophilia or Duchenne muscular dystrophy, genetic amniocentesis may be an appropriate option for the family. These disorders are becoming increasingly diagnosable in utero. Since they usually affect only males, the sex of the fetus can be determined and termination of pregnancy

## Essential Facts to Remember

### Couples to Be Offered Prenatal Diagnosis

Nurses should consider prenatal diagnosis for:

- Women 35 or over at time of conception and delivery
- Couples having a balanced translocation (chromosomal abnormality)
- Mother carrying X-linked disease, ie, hemophilia
- Couples having a previous child with chromosomal abnormality
- Couples in which either partner or a previous child is affected with a diagnosable metabolic disorder
- Couples in which both partners are carriers for a diagnosable metabolic or autosomal recessive disorder
- Family or personal history of neural tube defects
- Ethnic groups at increased risk for specific disorders
- Couples with history of two or more first trimester spontaneous abortions

considered when it is found to be male. For a known female carrier, the risk of an affected male fetus is 50%. The decision to abort a possibly normal male fetus must be discussed and made within each family. Similarly, couples in which the father is affected with an X-linked disorder may elect to have only male children so that the gene would not be continued in the family; all females (who would have to be carriers) could be aborted. Since many males with X-linked disorders, especially hemophilia, are surviving to reproduce as greater advances in medical treatment become available, genetic amniocentesis for these reasons may become more common.

5. Parents carrying an inborn error of metabolism that can be diagnosed in utero. The number of inherited metabolic disorders that can be diagnosed in utero is increasing at a rapid rate (Hogge and Golbus 1984). Some of the metabolic disorders that can be detected in utero include Tay-Sachs disease, galactosemia, maple syrup urine disease, and others.

6. Both parents carrying an autosomal recessive disease. When both parents are carriers of an autosomal recessive disease, there is a 25% risk for each pregnancy that the fetus will be affected. Diagnosis is made by testing the cultured amniotic fluid cells (either enzyme level, substrate level,

or product level) or the fluid itself. Autosomal recessive diseases identified by amniocentesis are hemoglobinopathies such as sickle cell anemia and β-thalassemia. Most research to date has been in the prenatal diagnosis of hemoglobinopathies. Both sickle cell anemia and β-thalassemia once were diagnosed using fetal blood samples obtained by amnioscopy, which has a 3% to 5% risk of fetal demise and spontaneous abortion. Now prenatal diagnosis of these conditions can be accomplished on uncultured amniotic fluid from an amniocentesis by a restriction endonuclease analysis of DNA test (Hogge and Golbus 1984).

Perhaps one of the most promising breakthroughs is the prenatal diagnosis of cystic fibrosis. Walsh and Nadler (1984) report reduced amounts of 4-methylumbelliferyl guanidinobenzoate (MUGB) reactive proteases in amniotic fluid samples from fetuses with cystic fibrosis. If these findings continue to be confirmed, the prenatal diagnosis of cystic fibrosis may become a reality (Brock et al 1985).

7. Family history of neural tube defects (anencephaly or spina bifida). Recently, genetic amniocentesis has been made available to those couples who have had a child with neural tube defects or who have a family history of these conditions, which include anencephaly, spina bifida, and myelomeningocele. Neural tube defects are usually polygenic traits.

Regardless of the statistical risk for a given family, whether for an isolated neural tube defect or a disorder in which a neural tube defect is a constant feature, the risk of recurrence can be reduced (possibly by as much as 90%) through α-fetoprotein (AFP) determination of the amniotic fluid (Main and Mennuti 1986). Normally α-fetoprotein is a substance found in high levels in a developing fetus and in low levels in maternal serum and in amniotic fluid. In pregnancies in which the fetus has an open neural tube defect, α-fetoprotein leaks into the amniotic fluid and levels are elevated (Davis et al 1985). Thus, genetic amniocentesis allows those families for whom the risk of a neural tube defect is increased the opportunity to choose whether to have a child affected with such a disorder.

See Essential Facts to Remember—Couples to Be Offered Prenatal Diagnosis.

## CHORIONIC VILLUS SAMPLING (CVS)

Chorionic villus sampling is a new technique that is used in selected regional centers. Its diagnostic capability is similar to amniocentesis. Its advantage is that diagnostic information is available before the completion of the first trimester of pregnancy.

## OTHER PRENATAL DIAGNOSTIC TECHNIQUES

*Amniography* (the instillation of dye into the amniotic cavity to outline the fetus) and *amnioscopy* (direct visualization of the fetus through a scope) are two methods of prenatal diagnosis that are not yet available for general clinical use. These methods are used primarily to observe the fetus for major structural abnormalities or to obtain fetal blood and tissue.

## IMPLICATIONS OF PRENATAL DIAGNOSTIC TESTING

It is imperative that counseling precede any procedure for prenatal diagnosis. Many questions and points must be considered if the family is to reach a satisfactory decision.

With the advent of diagnostic techniques such as amniocentesis and chorionic villus sampling, couples at risk, who would not otherwise have additional children, can decide to conceive. The percentage of therapeutic abortions after amniocentesis is small; most couples find peace of mind throughout the remainder of the pregnancy after prenatal diagnosis.

After prenatal diagnosis, a couple can decide not to have a child with a genetic disease. For many couples, prenatal diagnosis is not a solution, since the only method of preventing a genetic disease is preventing the birth by aborting the affected fetus. This decision can only be made by the family.

Prenatal diagnosis cannot guarantee the birth of a normal child. It can only determine the presence or absence of specific disorders (within the limits of laboratory error). Nonspecific mental retardation, cleft lip and palate, and PKU are a few of the disorders that cannot be determined by intrauterine diagnosis.

In the future, cure or treatment of diagnosable disorders may be possible. Prenatal diagnosis may allow for treatment to begin during the pregnancy, thus possibly preventing irreversible damage. For other disorders, effective postnatal treatment may make prenatal diagnosis unnecessary. The ability to diagnose many diseases in utero is improved every day. In light of the philosophy of preventive health care, this information should be made available to all couples who are expecting a child or who are contemplating pregnancy.

## ● Postnatal Diagnosis

Questions concerning genetic disorders, cause, treatment, and prognosis are most often first discussed in the newborn nursery or during the infant's first few months of life. When a child is born with anomalies, has a stormy neonatal period, or does not progress as expected, a genetic evaluation may well be warranted.

Accurate diagnosis and optimal treatment plan incorporate:

● Complete and detailed histories to determine if the problem is prenatal (congenital), postnatal, or familial in origin

● Thorough physical examination, including dermatoglyphic analysis (Figure 4.18)

● Laboratory analysis, which includes chromosome analysis; enzyme assay for inborn errors of metabolism (see Chapter 22 for further discussion on these specific tests); and antibody titers for infectious teratogens, such as toxoplasmosis, rubella, cytomegalovirus, and herpes virus (TORCH) (see Chapter 12).

To make an accurate diagnosis the geneticist consults with other specialists and reviews the current literature. This permits the geneticist to evaluate all the available information before arriving at a diagnosis and plan of action.

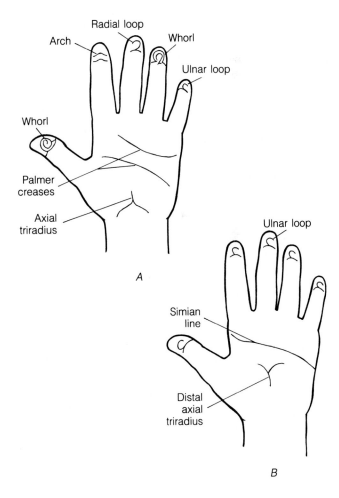

*Figure 4.18 Dermatoglyphic patterns of the hands in (A) a normal individual and (B) a child with Down syndrome. Note the simian line, distally placed axial triradius, and increased number of ulnar loops.*

## • The Family, the Nurse, and the Genetic Counseling Process

*Genetic counseling* is a communication process in which the family is provided with the most complete and accurate information on the occurrence or the risk of recurrence of a genetic disease in that family. The goals are threefold:

1. Genetic counseling allows families to make informed decisions about reproduction.

2. It helps families assess the available treatments, consider appropriate alternatives to decrease the risk, learn about the usual course and outcome of the genetic disease or abnormality, and deal with other psychologic and social implications that often accompany such problems.

3. Genetic counseling may help decrease the incidence and impact of genetic disease.

In retrospective genetic counseling, time is a crucial factor. One cannot expect a family who has just learned that their child has a birth defect or has Down syndrome to assimilate any information concerning future risks. However, the couple should never be "put off" from counseling for too long a period, only to find that they have borne another affected child. Here the nurse can be instrumental in directing the parents into counseling at the appropriate time. At the birth of an affected child, the nurse can inform the parents that genetic counseling is available before they attempt having another child. Asking one or two members of a genetics team to introduce themselves to the family is often enough to bring up the subject of genetic counseling. When the parents have begun to recover from the initial shock of bearing a child with an abnormality, or when they begin to contemplate having more children, the nurse can encourage the couple to seek counseling.

### THE NURSE'S ROLE

Nurses who are aware of families at an increased risk of having a child with a genetic disorder are in an ideal position to make referrals. Genetic counseling is an appropriate course of action for any family wondering, "Will it happen again?" The nursery nurse frequently has the first contact with the family and newborn with a congenital abnormality. The family nurse practitioner or family-planning nurse is in an excellent position to reach at-risk families before the birth of another baby with a congenital problem. Genetic counseling referral is advised for any of the following categories:

1. *Congenital abnormalities, including mental retardation.* Any couple who has a child or a relative with a congenital malformation may be at an increased risk and should be so informed. If mental retardation of unidentified cause has occurred in a family, there may be an increased risk of recurrence.

In many cases, the genetic counselor will identify the cause of a malformation as a teratogen (see Chapter 8). The family should be aware of teratogenic substances so they can avoid exposure during any subsequent pregnancy.

2. *Familial disorders.* Families should be told that certain diseases may have a genetic component and that the risk of their occurrence in a particular family may be higher than that for the general population. Such disorders as diabetes, heart disease, cancer, and mental illness fall into this category.

3. *Known inherited diseases.* Families may know that a disease is inherited but not know the mechanism or the specific risk for them. An important point to remember is that family members who are not at risk for passing on a disorder should be as well informed as those family members who are at an increased risk.

4. *Metabolic disorders.* Any families at risk for having a child with a metabolic disorder or biochemical defect should be referred. Because most inborn errors of metabolism are autosomal recessively inherited ones, a family may not be identified as at risk until the birth of an affected child.

Carriers of the sickle cell trait can be identified before pregnancy is begun, and the risk of having an affected child can be determined. Prenatal diagnosis of an affected fetus is available on an experimental basis only.

5. *Chromosomal abnormalities.* As discussed previously, any couple who has had a child with a chromosomal abnormality may be at an increased risk of having another child similarly affected. This group would include families in which there is concern for a possible translocation.

The process of genetic counseling usually begins after the birth of a child diagnosed as having a congenital abnormality or genetic disease. After the parents have been referred to the genetics clinic, they are sent a form requesting information on the health status of various family members. At this time, the nurse can help by discussing the form with the family or clarifying the information needed to complete it.

A pedigree and history facilitate identification of other family members who might also be at risk for the same disorder. The family being counseled may wish to notify those relatives at risk so that they, too, can be given genetic counseling. When done correctly, the family history and pedigree can be powerful and useful tools for determining a family risk.

The counselor gathers additional information about the pregnancy, the affected child's growth and development, and the family's understanding of the problem. Generally, the child is given a physical examination. Other family members may also be examined. If any laboratory tests, such as chromosomal analysis, metabolic studies, or viral titers, are indicated, they are performed at this time. The genetic counselor may then give the family some preliminary information based on the data at hand.

When all the data have been carefully examined and analyzed, the family returns for a follow-up visit. At this time, the parents are given all the information available, including the medical facts, diagnosis, probable course of the disorder, and any available management; the inheritance pattern for this particular family and the risk of recurrence; and the options or alternatives for dealing with the risk of recurrence. The remainder of the counseling session is spent discussing the course of action that seems appropriate to the family in view of their risk and family goals.

Among those options or alternatives are prenatal diagnosis and early detection and treatment, and, in some cases, adoption, artificial insemination, or delayed childbearing.

The family may consider *artificial insemination by donor (AID),* discussed earlier in this chapter. This alternative is appropriate in several instances; for example, if the male partner is affected with an autosomal dominant disease, AID would decrease the risk of having an affected child to zero, since the child would not inherit any genes from the affected parent. If the man is affected with an X-linked disorder and does not wish to continue the gene in the family (all his daughters will be carriers), AID would be an alternative to terminating all pregnancies with a female fetus. If the man is a carrier for a balanced translocation and if termination of pregnancy is against family ethics, AID is the most appropriate alternative. AID is also appropriate if both parents are carriers of an autosomal recessive disease. AID lowers the risk to a very low level or to zero if a carrier test is available. Finally, AID may be appropriate if the family is at high risk for a polygenic disorder.

Couples who are young and at risk may decide to delay childbearing for a few years. Medical science and medical genetics are continually making breakthroughs in early detection and treatment. These couples may find in a few years that prenatal diagnosis will be available or that a disease can be detected and treated early to prevent irreversible damage.

The family may return a number of times to air their questions and concerns. It is most desirable for the nurse working with the family to attend many or all of these counseling sessions. Since the nurse has already established a rapport with the family, the nurse can act as a liaison between the family and the genetic counselor. Hearing directly what the genetic counselor says helps the nurse clarify the issues for the family, which in turn helps them formulate questions.

## Essential Facts to Remember

### Nursing Responsibilities in Genetic Counseling

Identify families at risk for genetic problems.
Assist families in acquiring accurate information about the specific problem.
Act as liaison between family and genetic counselor.
Assist the family in understanding/dealing with information received.
Aid families in coping with this crisis.
Provide information about known genetic factors.
Assure continuity of nursing care to the family.

Perhaps one of the most important and crucial aspects of genetic counseling in which the nurse is involved is follow-up counseling. The nurse with the appropriate knowledge of genetics is in an ideal position to help families review what has been discussed during the counseling sessions and to answer any additional questions they might have. As the family returns to the daily aspects of living, the nurse can provide helpful information on the day-to-day aspects of caring for the child, answer questions as they arise, support parents in their decisions, and refer the family to other health and community agencies.

If the couple is considering having more children or if siblings want information concerning their affected brother or sister, the nurse should recommend that the family return for another follow-up visit with the genetic counselor. Appropriate options can again be defined and discussed, and any new information can again be given to the family. Many genetic centers have found the public health nurse to be the ideal health professional to provide such follow-up care.

When the parents have completed the counseling sessions, the counselor sends them and their physician a letter detailing the contents of the sessions. The family keeps this document for reference. See Essential Facts to Remember—Nursing Responsibilities in Genetic Counseling.

## ESSENTIAL CONCEPTS

● **A couple is considered infertile when they do not conceive after one year of unprotected coitus.**

● At least 2.8 million couples in the United States have undesired infertility.

● A thorough history and physical of both partners is essential as a basis for infertility investigation.

● General fertility investigations include: evaluation of ovarian function, cervical mucus adequacy and receptivity to sperm, sperm adequacy, tubal patency, general condition of the pelvic organs; and certain laboratory tests.

● Among cases of infertility, 40% involve male factors, 10% to 15% involve female hormonal defects, 20% to 30% involve female tubal disorders, 5% involve cervical factors, 10% to 20% have no identifiable cause, and 35% have multifactorial etiologies.

● Medications may be prescribed to induce ovulation, facilitate cervical mucus formation, reduce antibody concentration, increase sperm count and motility, and suppress endometriosis.

● The emotional aspect of infertility may be more difficult for the couple than the testing and therapy.

● With a sound knowledge base regarding common genetic problems, the nurse should initiate referrals, prepare the family for counseling, and act as a resource person during and after the counseling sessions.

● Those genetic conditions that can currently be diagnosed prenatally are craniospinal defects, renal malformations, hemophilia, fragile-X syndrome, thalassemia, cystic fibrosis, many inborn errors of metabolism such as Tay-Sachs disease or maple syrup urine disease, and neural tube defects.

● In autosomal dominant disorders an affected parent has a 50% chance of having an affected child. Such disorders equally affect both males and females. The characteristic presentation will vary in each individual with the gene. Some of the common autosomal dominant inherited disorders are Huntington chorea, polycystic kidney, and neurofibromatosis (von Recklinghausen disease).

● Autosomal recessive disorders are characterized by both parents being carriers; each offspring having a 25% chance of having the disease, a 25% chance of not being affected, and a 50% chance of being a carrier; and males and females being equally affected. Some common autosomal recessive inheritance disorders are cystic fibrosis, PKU, galactosemia, sickle cell anemia, Tay-Sachs disease, and most metabolic disorders.

● X-linked recessive disorders are characterized by no male-to-male transmission, effects limited to males, a 50% chance that a carrier mother will pass the abnormal gene to her son, a 50% chance that she will not transmit the abnormal gene to her son, a 50% chance that a daughter will be a carrier, and a 100% chance that daughters of affected fathers will be carriers. Common X-linked recessive disorders are hemophilia, color blindness, and Duchenne disease.

● Multifactorial inheritance disorders include cleft lip and palate, spina bifida, dislocated hips, clubfoot, and pyloric stenosis.

● The chief tools of prenatal diagnosis are ultrasound, amniocentesis, and chorionic villus sampling.

## References

Andrew LB: *New Conceptions: A Consumers Guide to the Newest Infertility Treatments.* New York: St. Martin's Press, 1984.

Ansbacher R: Male infertility. *Clin Obstet Gynecol* 1982; 25(3):461.

*Attending OB/GYN Patients.* Nursing 86 Books. Springhouse, PA: Springhouse, 1986.

Barkay J et al: The prostaglandin inhibitory effect of anti-inflammatory drugs in the therapy of male infertility. *Fertil Steril* 1984; 42(3):406.

Berg B: Early signs of infertility. *Ms* 1984; 6(8):72.

Brock DJH et al: Prospective prenatal diagnosis of cystic fibrosis. *Lancet* 1985; 1:1175.

Bronson R et al: Sperm antibodies: Their role in infertility. *Fertil Steril* 1984; 42(2):171.

Bultram VC, Belne JB, Reiter R: Interim report of a study of danazol for the treatment of endometriosis. *Fertil Steril* 1982; 37:478.

Coulam CB: The diagnosis and management of infertility. In: *Gynecology and Obstetrics.* Vol 5. Sciarra JL et al (editors). Hagerstown, MD: Harper and Row, 1982.

Creighton H: In vitro fertilization. *Nurs Manage* April 1985; 16:12.

Darland NW: Infertility associated with luteal phase defect. *J Obstet Gynecol Neonatal Nurs* May/June 1985; 14:212.

Davis RO et al: Decreased levels of amniotic fluid alphafetoprotein associated with Down syndrome, *Am J Obstet Gynecol* November 1985; 185:541.

Diamond MP: Surgical aspects of infertility. In: *Gynecology and Obstetrics.* Vol. 5. Sciarra JL et al (editors). Hagerstown, MD: Harper and Row, 1988.

Dodson MG: A detailed progam review of in vitro fertilization with a discussion and comparison of alternative approaches. *Surg Gynecol & Obstet* January 1986; 162:89.

Fogel CL, Woods NP: *Health Care of Women.* St. Louis: Mosby, 1981.

Glass RH: Infertility. In: *Office Gynecology,* 2nd ed. Glass RH (editor). Baltimore: Williams and Wilkins, 1981.

Grimes EM, Richardson MR: Management of the infertile couple.

In: *Gynecology and Obstetrics.* Vol. 5. Sciarra JL et al (editors). Hagerstown, MD: Harper and Row, 1987.

Hammond M, Talbert L: *Infertility.* Oradell, NJ: Medical Economics Books, 1985.

Hatcher RA et al: *Contraceptive Technology: 1988–1989,* 14th ed. New York: Irvington, 1988.

Henry GP, Robinson A: Prenatal diagnosis. *Clin Obstet Gynecol* 1978; 21:329.

Hogge WA, Golbus MS: Antenatal diagnosis of mendelian disorders. In: *Gynecology and Obstetrics.* Vol. 3. Sciarra JL et al (editors). Hagerstown, MD: Harper and Row, 1984.

Kennedy JL, Adashi EY: Ovulation induction. *Obstet Gynecol Clin North Am* December 1987; 14(4):831–864.

Kremkau F: Safety and long term effects of ultrasound. *Clin Obstet Gynecol* 1984; 27(2):269.

Lange IR: Congenital anomalies: Detection and strategies for management. *Semin Perinatol* October 1985; 151.

Loucopoulos A et al: Pulsatile administrations of gonadotropin-releasing hormone for induction of ovulation. *Am J Obstet Gynecol* 1984; 148:895.

Main DM, Mennuti MT: Neural tube defects: Issues in prenatal diagnosis and counseling. *Obstet Gynecol* January 1986; 67:1.

March CM: New methods for the induction of ovulation. In: *Gynecology and Obstetrics.* Vol. 5. Sciarra JL et al (editors). Hagerstown, MD: Harper and Row, 1987.

McShane PM, Schiff I, Trentham DE: Cellular immunity to sperm in infertile women. *JAMA* 1985; 253(24):3555.

Menning BE: The emotional needs of the infertile couple. *Fertil Steril* 1980; 34(4):313.

Moghissi K, Wallach E: Unexplained infertility. *Fertil Steril* 1983; 39:5.

Moghissi KS: How to document ovulation. In: *Gynecology and Obstetrics.* Vol. 5. Sciarra JL et al (editors). Hagerstown, MD: Harper and Row, 1987.

Phillips M: One woman's courage. *Am Heath* November 1985; 76.

Poon WW, McCoshen JA: Variances in mucus architecture as a cause of cervical factor infertility. *Fertil Steril* 1985; 44(3):361.

Quagliarello J: Artificial insemination. In: *Gynecology and Obstetrics.* Vol. 5. Sciarra JL et al (editors). Hagerstown, MD: Harper and Row, 1987.

Richie DD, Carola R: *Biology.* Reading, MA: Addison-Wesley, 1979.

Sawatzky M: Tasks of the infertile couple. *J Obstet Gynecol Neonatal Nurs* 1981; 10:132.

Shapiro LR et al: Prenatal diagnosis of fragile X chromosome. *Lancet* 1982; 1:99.

Smith P: Ovulation induction. *J Obstet Gynecol Neonatal Nurs* November/December 1985; 14:37s.

Sogor L: Immune aspects of infertility. In: *Gynecology and Obstetrics.* Vol. 5. Sciarra JL et al (editors). Hagerstown, MD: Harper and Row, 1986.

Speroff L, Glass RH, Kase NG: *Clinical Gynecologic Endocrinology and Infertility,* 4th ed. Baltimore: Williams and Wilkins, 1989.

Thompson JS, Thompson MW: *Genetics in Medicine,* 4th ed. Philadelphia: Saunders, 1986.

Valle RF: How endoscopy aids the infertility workup. *Contemp OB/GYN* 1984; 23:191.

Verp MS: Antenatal diagnosis of chromosome abnormalities. In: *Gynecology and Obstetrics.* Vol. 3. Sciarra JL et al (editors). Hagerstown, MD: Harper and Row, 1984.

Wallach EE, Beck WW, Eisenberg E, Hammond CB: Ethical considerations in treating infertility. *Contemp OB/GYN* 1984; 23:226.

Walsh MMJ, Nadler HL: Methylumbelliferyl quanidinobenzoate-reactive proteases in human amniotic fluid: Promising market for the intrauterine detection in cystic fibrosis. *Am J Obstet Gynecol* 1984; 137:978.

Wentz AC: Progesterone therapy of the inadequacy luteal phase. *Cur Prob Obstet Gynecol* 1982; 6:1.

Zacur H, Rock J: Diagnosis and treatment of infertility. *Female Patient* 1983; 8:52.

## Additional Readings

Berstein J, Mattox JH, Kellner R: Psychological status of previously infertile couples after a successful pregnancy. *J Obstet Gynecol Neonatal Nurs* 1988; 17(6):404–410.

Clapp D: Emotional responses to infertility: Nursing interventions. *J Obstet Gynecol Neonatal Nurs* November/December 1985; 14:32.

Christianson C: Support groups for infertile patients. *J Obstet Gynecol Neonatal Nurs* July/August 1986; 15:293.

Draye MA, Fugate-Woods N, Mitchell E: Coping with infertility in couples: Gender differences. *Health Care Women Inter* 1988; 9:163–175.

Embury SH et al: Rapid prenatal diagnosis of sickle cell anemia by a new method of DNA analysis. *N Engl J Med* March 12, 1987; 316:656.

Feichtinger W, Kemeter P (editors): *Future Aspects in Human In Vitro Fertilization.* New York: Springer-Verlag, 1987.

Fraser FC: Genetic counseling: Using the information wisely. *Hospital Practice* June 15, 1988; 245–266.

Hammon MG: Induction of ovulation with clomiphene citrate. In: *Gynecology and Obstetrics.* Vol. 5. Sciarra JL et al (editors). Hagerstown, MD: Harper and Row, 1987.

Haning RV: Induction of ovulation with pergonal. In: *Gynecology and Obstetrics.* Vol. 5. Sciarra JL et al (editors). Hagerstown, MD: Harper and Row, 1988.

Hearn MT et al: Psychological characteristics of in vitro fertilization participants. *Am J Obstet Gynecol* February 1987; 156:269.

Keating C: The impact of sexually transmitted diseases on human fertility. *Health Care Women Inter* 1987; 8(1):33.

Olshansky EF: Identity of self as infertile: An example of theory-generating research. *ANS* January 1987; 9:54.

Policy statement for maternal serum alpha-fetoprotein screening program. *Am J Human Genetics* February 1987; 40:75.

Sandelowski M: Without child: The world of infertile women. *Health Care Women Inter* 1988; 9:147–161.

Schlaff WD: New ways to prepare semen for IUI. *Contemp OB/GYN* April 1987; 29:79.

Shattuck JC: Pelvic inflammatory disease: Education for maintaining fertility. *Nurs Clin North Am* December 1988; 23(4):899–906.

Sokoloff BZ: Alternative methods of reproduction: Effects on the child. *Clin Pediatr* January 1987; 26:11.

Wallach EE et al: Ethical dilemmas of infertility. *Contemp OB/GYN* March 1987; 29:170.

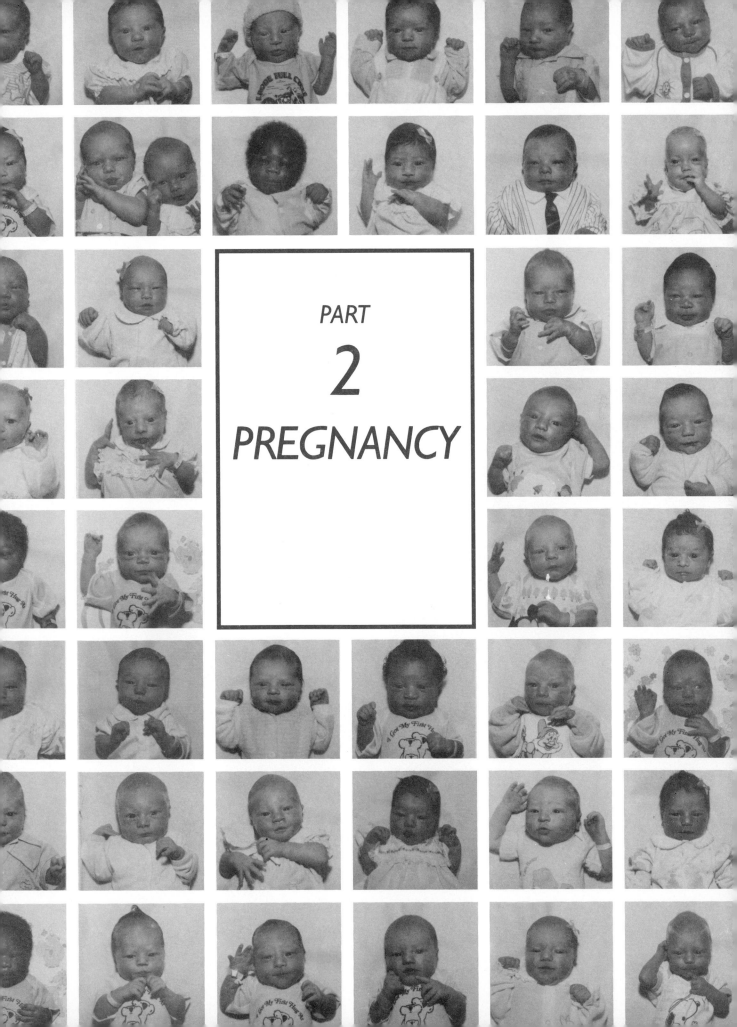

PART
2
PREGNANCY

# 5

# Conception and Fetal Development

*How amazing it is to realize that this little person is born so beautifully formed, whole and perfect, with all his fingers and toes. Now he is part of our family. One day perhaps he will look in amazement at a child of his own!*

## Objectives

- Explain the difference between meiotic cellular division and mitotic cellular division.

- Describe the components of the process of fertilization.

- Describe the development, structure, and functions of the placenta and umbilical cord during intrauterine life.

- Summarize the significant changes in growth and development of the fetus in utero at 4, 6, 12, 16, 20, 24, 28, 36, and 40 weeks' gestation.

- Identify the vulnerable periods during which malformations of the various organ systems may occur, and describe the resulting congenital malformations.

## Key Terms

amnion
amniotic fluid
bag of waters
blastocyst
chorion
cleavage
cotyledon
decidua basalis
decidua capsularis
decidua vera (parietalis)
diploid number of
    chromosomes
ductus arteriosus
ductus venosus
ectoderm
embryo
embryonic membrane
endoderm
fertilization

fetus
foramen ovale
gametogenesis
haploid number of
    chromosomes
lanugo
meiosis
mesoderm
mitosis
morula
placenta
postconceptual age
    periods
teratogen
trophoblast
umbilical cord
vernix caseosa
Wharton's jelly
zygote

Every person is unique. What is interesting about this uniqueness is that all of us have most if not all of the same "parts," and these parts usually function similarly. Even our chromosomes, those determiners of the structure and function of our organ systems and traits, are made of the same biochemical substances. How do we become unique, then? The answer lies in the physiologic mechanisms of heredity, the processes of cellular division, and the environmental factors that influence our development from the moment we are conceived. This chapter explores the processes involved in conception and fetal development—the basis of uniqueness.

## ● CELLULAR DIVISION

All humans begin life as a single cell (zygote). This single cell reproduces itself, and in turn each new cell also reproduces itself in a continuing process. The new cells must be basically similar to the cells from which they came.

Cells are reproduced either by **mitosis** or **meiosis**, two different but related processes. Mitosis results in the production of additional body (somatic) cells. Mitosis makes growth and development possible, and in mature individuals it is the process by which our body cells continue to divide and replace themselves. Meiosis, by contrast, leads to the development of a new organism.

## ● Mitosis

During mitosis, the cell undergoes several changes, ending in cell division. Before cell division occurs, the deoxyribonucleic acid (DNA) within the chromosomes replicates itself. The chromosomes then reproduce themselves, and the nuclear membrane and cell nucleus disappear. The duplicated chromosomes separate in pairs to opposite sides of the cell. A furrow develops in the cytoplasm at the midline of the cell, dividing it into two *daughter cells,* each with its own nucleus. Daughter cells have the same **diploid number of chromosomes** (46) and same genetic makeup as the cell from which they came. In other words, after a cell with 46 chromosomes undergoes mitosis, two identical (or daughter) cells, each with 46 chromosomes, result.

## ● Meiosis

Meiosis consists of two successive cell divisions. In the first division, the chromosomes replicate, making each of the 46 chromosomes double structured. Next, a pairing takes place between homologous chromosomes (Sadler 1985). Instead of separating immediately as in mitosis, the similar chromosomes become closely intertwined. An exchange of parts between chromatids (the arms of the chromosomes) often takes place. At each point of contact, there is also a physical exchange of genetic material between the chromatids. New combinations are provided by the newly formed chromosomes; these combinations account for the wide variation of traits in people. The chromosome pairs then separate, each member of a pair moving to opposite sides of the cell. (In contrast, during mitosis the chromatids of each chromosome separate and move to opposite poles.) The cell divides, forming two daughter cells, each with 23 double-structured chromosomes—the same amount of DNA as a normal somatic cell. In the second division, the chromatids of each chromosome separate and move to opposite poles of each of the daughter cells. Cell division occurs, resulting in the formation of four cells, each containing 23 single chromosomes (the **haploid number of chromosomes**). These daughter cells contain only half the DNA of a normal somatic cell (Sadler 1985).

Occasionally during the second meiotic division, two of the chromatids may not move apart rapidly enough when the cell divides. The still-paired chromatids are carried into one of the daughter cells and eventually form an extra chromosome. This condition is referred to as an autosomal nondisjunction (chromosomal mutation) and is harmful to the offspring that may result should fertilization occur. The implications of nondisjunction are discussed in Chapter 4.

Another type of chromosomal mutation can occur if chromosomes break during meiosis. If the broken segment is lost, the result is a shorter chromosome; this situation is known as deletion. If the broken segment becomes attached to another chromosome, it is called translocation, which often results in harmful structural mutations (Thompson and Thompson 1986). The effects of translocation are described in Chapter 4.

## ● GAMETOGENESIS

Meiosis occurs during **gametogenesis**, the process by which germ cells, or *gametes*, are produced. The gametes must have a haploid number (23) of chromosomes so that when the female gamete (ovum) and the male gamete (spermatozoon) unite to form the **zygote**, the normal human diploid number of chromosomes (46) is reestablished.

## ● Ovum

As discussed in Chapter 2, the ovaries begin to develop early in the fetal life of the female. All the ova that the female will produce are formed by the sixth month of fetal life. The ovary gives rise to oogonial cells, which develop into oocytes. Meiosis begins in all oocytes before the female infant is born but stops before the first division is complete and remains in this arrested phase until puberty. During puberty, the mature primary oocyte proceeds (by oogenesis) through the first meiotic division in the graafian follicle of the ovary.

The first meiotic division produces two cells of unequal size with unequal amounts of cytoplasm but with the same number of chromosomes. These two cells are the *secondary oocyte* and a minute *polar body*. Both the secondary oocyte and the first polar body contain 22 double-structured autosomal chromosomes and one double-structured sex chromosome (X). At the time of ovulation second meiotic division begins immediately and proceeds as the oocyte moves down the fallopian tube. Division is again not equal and the secondary oocyte proceeds to metaphase where its meiotic division is arrested.

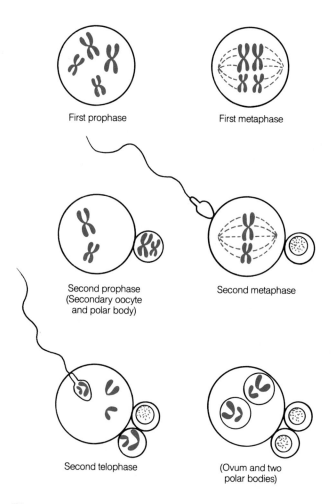

First prophase

First metaphase

Second prophase
(Secondary oocyte
and polar body)

Second metaphase

Second telophase

(Ovum and two
polar bodies)

*Figure 5.1   Human oogenesis and fertilization (From Thompson JS, Thompson MW:* Genetics in Medicine, *4th ed. Philadelphia: Saunders, 1986, p 23.)*

Only when fertilized by the sperm does the secondary oocyte complete the second meiotic division, becoming a mature ovum with the haploid number of chromosomes and having virtually all the cytoplasm. The second polar body is also formed at this time (Figure 5.1). The first polar body has now also divided, producing two additional polar bodies. Thus, when meiosis is completed, four haploid cells may have been produced: two or three small polar bodies, which eventually disintegrate, and one ovum (Sadler 1985) (Figure 5.2).

## ● *Sperm*

During puberty, the germinal epithelium in the seminiferous tubules of the testes begins the process of spermatogenesis, which produces the male gamete (sperm). The spermatogonium replicates before it enters the first meiotic division, during which it is called the *primary spermatocyte*. During this first meiotic division, the spermatogonium forms two cells termed *secondary spermatocytes*, each of which contains 22 double-structured autosomal

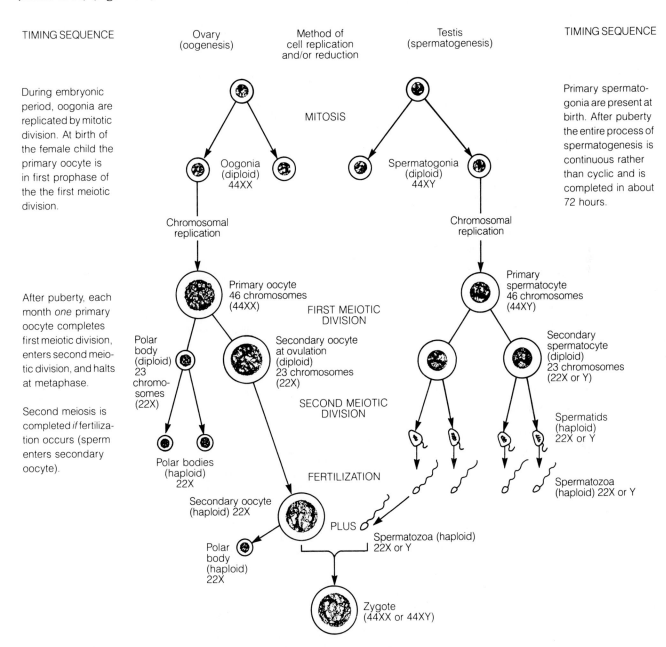

*Figure 5.2   Gametogenesis involves meiosis within the ovary and testis. Note that during meiosis, each oogonium produces a single haploid ovum, whereas each spermatogonium produces four haploid spermatozoa. (Modified from Spence AP, Mason EB:* Human Anatomy and Physiology, *3rd ed. Menlo Park, CA: Benjamin/Cummings, 1987, pp 822, 832.)*

chromosomes and either a double-structured X sex chromosome or a double-structured Y sex chromosome. During the second meiotic division, they divide to form four spermatids, each with the haploid number of chromosomes (Figure 5.2). The spermatids undergo a series of changes during which they lose most of their cytoplasm and become sperm (spermatozoa). The nucleus becomes compacted into the head of the sperm, which is covered by a cap called an acrosome (see Figure 5.2).

## ● SEX DETERMINATION

The two chromosomes of the twenty-third pair (either XX or XY) are called *sex chromosomes.* The larger of the sex chromosomes is designated X, and the smaller sex chromosome is called Y. Females have two X chromosomes, and males have an X and a Y chromosome. Because male cells contain both an X and a Y chromosome, meiosis in the male produces two gametes with an X chromosome and two gametes with a Y chromosome from each primary spermatocyte. The sex chromosomes in oocytes are both X, and thus the mature ovum can have only one type of sex chromosome. To produce a female child, each parent must contribute an X chromosome. To produce a male, the mother must contribute an X chromosome and the father a Y chromosome.

The Y chromosomes contain mainly genes for maleness. The X chromosomes carry several genes other than those for sexual traits. As discussed in Chapter 4, these other traits are termed *sex linked* because they are controlled by the genes on the X sex chromosome. Two examples of sex-linked traits are color blindness and hemophilia.

## ● FERTILIZATION

The process of **fertilization** takes place in the ampulla (or outer third) of the fallopian tube. High estrogen levels during ovulation increase the ability of the fallopian tubes to contract, which helps move the ovum down the tube. The high estrogen levels also cause a thinning of the cervical mucus, facilitating penetration by the sperm.

The ovum's cell membrane is surrounded by two layers of tissue. The layer closest to the cell membrane is called the *zona pellucida.* It is a clear, noncellular layer whose function is not known. Surrounding the zona pellucida is a ring of elongated cells, called the *corona radiata* because they radiate from the ovum like the gaseous corona around the sun. These cells are held together by hyaluronic acid.

The mature ovum and spermatozoa have only a brief time to unite. Ova are considered fertile for about a 24-hour period after ovulation (Glass 1987). Sperm can survive in the female reproductive tract for up to 72 hours but

are believed to be healthy and highly fertile for only about 24 hours (Silverstein 1980).

In a single ejaculation the male deposits approximately 200 to 400 million spermatozoa in the vagina, of which fewer than 200 actually reach the ampulla (Eddy and Pauerstein 1980). The spermatozoa propel themselves up the female tract by the flagellar movement of their tails. Transit time from the cervix into the fallopian tube can be as short as five minutes but usually takes an average of four to six hours after ejaculation (Pritchard et al 1985). Prostaglandins in the semen may increase uterine smooth muscle contractions, which help transport the sperm (Spence and Mason 1987). The fallopian tubes have a dual ciliary action that facilitates movement of the ovum toward the uterus and movement of the sperm from the uterus toward the ovary. The ovum has no inherent power of movement.

The sperm must undergo two processes before fertilization can happen; these are *capacitation and the acrosomal reaction* (Overstreet et al 1988). Capacitation is the removal of the plasma membrane overlying the spermatozoa's acrosomal area. Capacitation must occur in the female reproductive tract and is thought to take about seven hours.

The acrosomal reaction follows capacitation. The acrosomal covering of the head of the sperm is believed to contain the enzyme hyaluronidase. As millions of sperm surround the ovum, they deposit minute amounts of hyaluronidase in the *corona radiata,* the outer layer of the ovum. This activity is the acrosomal reaction. The hyaluronidase breaks down enough hyaluronic acid in the corona radiata layer of the ovum for one spermatozoon to penetrate the zona pellucida of the ovum. At the moment of penetration, a cellular change occurs in the ovum that renders it impenetrable by other spermatozoa, thus only one spermatozoon enters a single ovum (Wassarman 1988).

At the moment of penetration, the second meiotic division is completed in the nucleus of the oocyte, and the second polar body is produced. At the union of the gametes, each containing a haploid number of chromosomes (23), the diploid number (46) is restored. Also at this time, the sex of the new individual is established. Within the cell, the nuclei of the spermatozoon and oocyte unite, and their individual nuclear membranes disappear. Their chromosomes pair up, and a new cell, the zygote, is created. The zygote contains a new combination of genetic material, resulting in an individual different from either parent and from anyone else.

## ● INTRAUTERINE DEVELOPMENT

Intrauterine development after fertilization can be divided into three phases: cellular multiplication, cellular (embryonic membrane) differentiation, and development of organ systems. These phases and the process of implantation will be discussed next.

## ● Cellular Multiplication

Cellular multiplication begins as the zygote moves through the fallopian tube into the cavity of the uterus. This transport takes three days or more (Pritchard et al 1985).

The zygote now enters a period of rapid mitotic divisions called **cleavage**, in which it divides into two cells, four cells, eight cells, and so on. These cells, called *blastomeres,* are so small that the developing cell mass is only slightly larger than the original zygote. The blastomeres are held together by the zona pellucida, which is under the corona radiata. The blastomeres will eventually form a solid ball of cells called the **morula**. Upon reaching the uterus, the morula floats freely for a few days and then a cavity forms within the cell mass. The inner solid mass of cells is called the **blastocyst**. The outer layer of cells that surround the cavity and have replaced the zona pellucida is the **trophoblast**. Eventually, the trophoblast develops into one of the embryonic membranes, the chorion. The blastocyst develops into the embryo and the other embryonic membrane (the amnion.) The journey of the fertilized ovum to its destination in the uterus is illustrated in Figure 5.3.

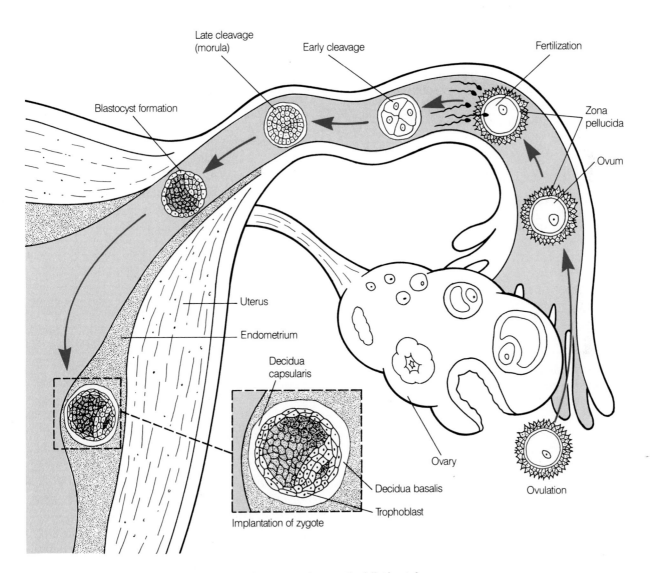

*Figure 5.3   During ovulation the ovum leaves the ovary and enters the fallopian tube. Fertilization generally occurs in the outer third of the fallopian tube. Subsequent changes in the fertilized ovum from conception to implantation are depicted.*

## ● *Implantation*

While floating in the uterine cavity, the blastocyst is nourished by the uterine glands, which secrete a mixture of lipids, mucopolysaccharides, and glycogen. The trophoblast attaches itself to the surface of the endometrium for further nourishment. The most frequent site of attachment is the upper part of the posterior uterine wall (Figure 5.3). Between days 7 and 9 after fertilization, the blastocyst implants itself by burrowing into the uterine lining until it is completely covered. The lining of the uterus thickens below the implanted blastocyst, and the cells of the trophoblast grow down into the thickened lining, forming processes called *villi*.

The endometrium, under the influence of progesterone, increases in thickness and vascularity in preparation for implantation and nutrition of the ovum. After implantation, the endometrium is called the *decidua*. The portion of the decidua that covers the blastocyst is called the **decidua capsularis**; the portion directly under the implanted blastocyst is the **decidua basalis**; and the portion that lines the rest of the uterine cavity is the **decidua vera (parietalis)**. The maternal part of the placenta develops from the decidua basalis, which contains large numbers of blood vessels.

## ● *Cellular Differentiation*
### EMBRYONIC MEMBRANES

The **embryonic membranes** begin to form at the time of implantation (Figure 5.4). These membranes protect and support the embryo as it grows and develops inside the uterus. The first membrane to form is the **chorion**, the outermost embryonic membrane that encloses the amnion, embryo, and yolk sac. The chorion is a thick membrane that develops from the trophoblast and has many fingerlike projections, called *chorionic villi,* on its surface. The villi begin to degenerate, except for those just under the embryo, which grow and branch into depressions in the uterine wall, forming the embryonic portion of the placenta. By the fourth month of pregnancy, the surface of the chorion is smooth except at the place of attachment to the uterine wall.

The second membrane, the **amnion**, originates from the ectoderm, a primary germ layer, during the early stages of embryonic development. The amnion is a thin protective membrane that contains amniotic fluid. The space between the membrane and the embryo is the *amniotic cavity*. This cavity surrounds the embryo and yolk sac, except where the developing embryo (germ layer disk) attaches to the trophoblast via the umbilical cord. As the embryo grows, the amnion expands until it comes in contact with the chorion. These two slightly adherent fetal membranes form the amniotic sac (amniotic fluid-filled) or **bag of waters** that protects the floating embryo.

### AMNIOTIC FLUID

**Amniotic fluid** functions as a cushion to protect against mechanical injury. It also helps control the embryo's temperature, permits symmetrical external growth of the embryo, prevents adherence of the amnion, and allows freedom of movement so that the embryo-fetus can change position. The amount of amniotic fluid at ten weeks is about 30 mL and increases to 350 mL at 20 weeks. After 20 weeks, the volume ranges from 500 to 1000 mL (Moore 1988). The amniotic fluid volume is constantly changing as the fluid moves back and forth across the placental membrane. As the pregnancy continues, the fetus contributes to the volume of amniotic fluid by excreting urine. The fetus also swallows up to 400 mL every 24 hours. Amniotic fluid is slightly alkaline and contains albumin, uric acid, creatinine, lecithin, sphingomyelin, bilirubin, vernix, leukocytes, epithelial cells, enzymes, and lanugo. Abnormal variations in amniotic fluid volume are oligohydramnios (less than normal amount of amniotic fluid) and hydramnios (over 2000 mL of amniotic fluid). See Chapter 18 for indepth discussion of alterations in amniotic fluid volume.

### YOLK SAC

In humans, the yolk sac is small and only functions early in embryonic life. It develops about the eighth or ninth day after conception and forms primitive red blood cells during the first six weeks of development until the embryo's liver takes over the process.

### PRIMARY GERM LAYERS

About the 10th to 14th day after conception, the homogenous mass of blastocyst cells differentiate into the primary germ layers. These layers, the **ectoderm, mesoderm**, and **endoderm** (Figure 5.5), are formed at the same time as the embryonic membranes. From these primary germ cell layers, all tissues, organs, and organ systems will develop (Table 5.1).

## ● *Intrauterine Organ Systems*
### PLACENTA

The **placenta** is the means of metabolic and nutrient exchange between the embryonic and maternal circulations. Placental development and circulation does not begin until the third week of development. The placenta develops at the site where the developing embryo attaches to the uterine wall. Expansion of the placenta continues until about the 20th week, when it covers about one-half of the internal surface of the uterus. After 20 weeks' gestation, the placenta becomes thicker but not wider. At 40 weeks' gestation, the placenta is about 15–20 cm (5.9–

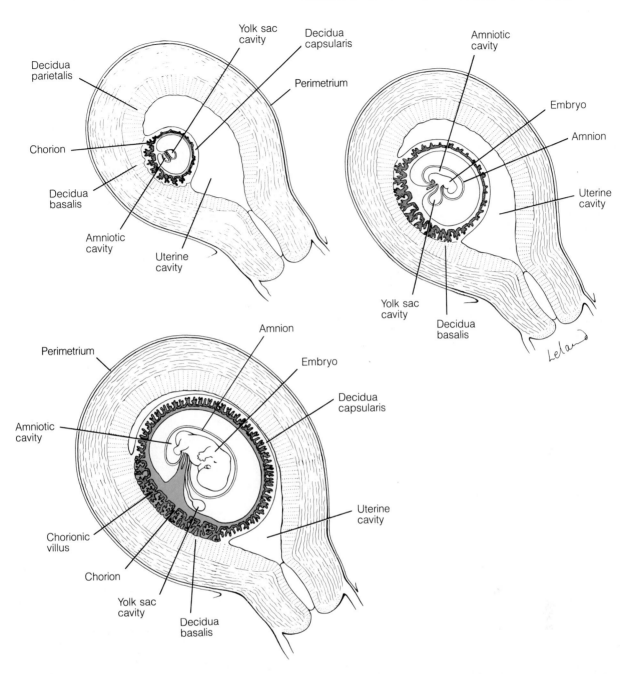

*Figure 5.4  Early development of the embryonic membranes. The early development of selected structures is depicted starting at the top left and moving clockwise. The time sequence is from day 10 to day 14 after conception to approximately eight weeks. (From Spence AP, Mason EB: Human Anatomy and Physiology, 3rd ed. Menlo Park, CA: Benjamin/Cummings, 1987, p 851.)*

7.9 in) in diameter and 2.5–3.0 cm (1.0–1.2 in) in thickness. At that time, it weighs about 400–600 g (14–21 oz).

The placenta has two parts: the maternal and fetal portions. The maternal portion consists of the decidua basalis and its circulation. Its surface is red and fleshlike. The fetal portion consists of the chorionic villi and their cir-

culation. The fetal surface of the placenta is covered by the amnion, which gives it a shiny, gray appearance.

Development of the placenta begins with the chorionic villi. The trophoblast cells of the chorionic villi form spaces in the tissue of the decidua basalis. These spaces fill with maternal blood, and the chorionic villi grow into these

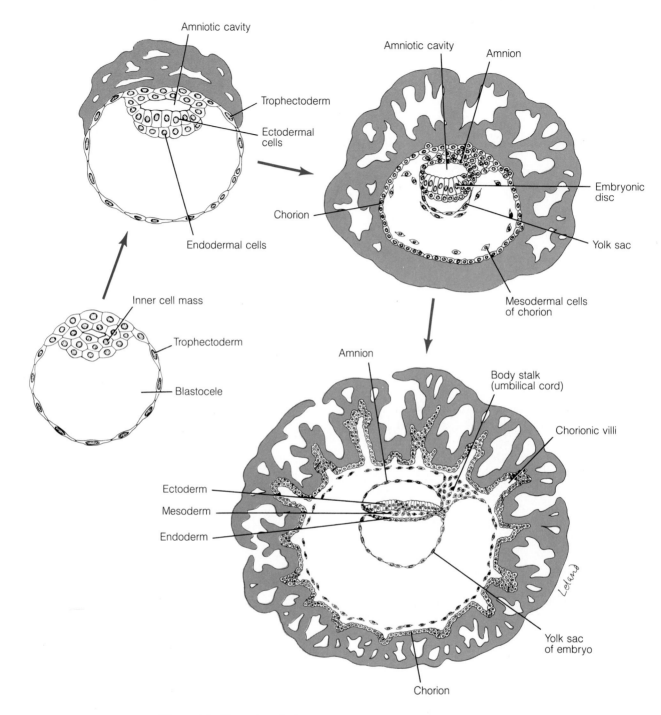

*Figure 5.5   Formation of primary germ layers (From Spence AP, Mason EB:* Human
Anatomy and Physiology, *3rd ed. Menlo Park, CA: Benjamin/Cummings, 1987, p 849.)*

spaces. As the chorionic villi differentiate, two trophoblastic layers appear: an outer layer, called the *syncytium*
(consisting of syncytiotrophoblasts) and an inner layer,
known as the *cytotrophoblast* (Chavez 1987). The cytotrophoblast thins out and disappears about the fifth month,
leaving only a single layer of syncytium covering the chorionic villi. The syncytium is in direct contact with the maternal blood in the intervillous spaces. It is the functional
layer of the placenta and secretes the placental hormones
of pregnancy.

A third, inner layer of connective mesoderm develops
in the chorionic villi, forming *anchoring villi*. These anchoring villi eventually form the *septa* (partitions) of the
placenta. These septa divide the mature placenta into
15–20 segments called **cotyledons**. In each cotyledon,
the *branching villi* form a highly complex vascular system

## Table 5.1  Derivation of Body Structures from Primary Cell Layers

| Ectoderm | Mesoderm | Endoderm |
|---|---|---|
| Epidermis | Dermis | Respiratory tract epithelium |
| Sweat glands | Wall of digestive tract | Epithelium (except nasal), including pharynx, tongue, tonsils, thyroid, parathyroid, thymus, tympanic cavity |
| Sebaceous glands | Kidneys and ureter (suprarenal cortex) | |
| Nails | Reproductive organs (gonads, genital ducts) | Lining of digestive tract |
| Hair follicles | | Primary tissue of liver and pancreas |
| Lens of eye | Connective tissue (cartilage, bone, joint cavities) | Urethra and associated glands |
| Sensory epithelium of internal and external ear, nasal cavity, sinuses, mouth, anal canal | Skeleton | Urinary bladder (except trigone) |
| | Muscles (all types) | Vagina (parts) |
| Central and peripheral nervous systems | Cardiovascular system (heart, arteries, veins, blood, bone marrow) | |
| Nasal cavity | Pleura | |
| Oral glands and tooth enamel | Lymphatic tissue and cells | |
| Pituitary glands | Spleen | |
| Mammary glands | | |

that allows compartmentalization of the uteroplacental circulation. The exchange of gases and nutrients takes place across these vascular systems.

In the fully developed placenta, fetal blood in the villi and maternal blood in the intervillous spaces are separated by three to four thin layers of tissue (Figure 5.6).

By the fourth week the placenta has begun to function as a means of metabolic exchange between embryo and mother. The completion of the maternal–placental–fetal circulation occurs about 17 days after conception when the embryonic heart begins functioning (Ahokas 1985). By 14 weeks, the placenta is a discrete organ. It has grown in thickness as a result of growth in the length and size of the chorionic villi and accompanying expansion of the intervillous space.

In the fully developed placenta, fetal blood flows through the two umbilical arteries to the capillaries of the villi and back through the umbilical vein into the fetus (Figure 5.6). Late in pregnancy, a soft blowing sound (*funic souffle*) can be heard over the area of the umbilical cord of the fetus. The sound is synchronous with the fetal heartbeat and the flow of fetal blood through the umbilical arteries.

Maternal blood, rich in oxygen and nutrients, spurts from the spiral uterine arteries into the intervillous spaces. These spurts are produced by the maternal blood pressure. The spurt of blood is directed toward the chorionic plate, and as the blood flow loses pressure, it becomes lateral (spreads out). Fresh blood continually enters and exerts pressure on the contents of the intervillous spaces, pushing blood toward the exits in the basal plate. The

blood is then drained through the uterine and other pelvic veins. A *uterine souffle*, timed precisely with the mother's pulse, is also heard just above the mother's symphysis pubis during the last months of pregnancy. This souffle is caused by the augmented blood flow entering the dilated uterine arteries.

Braxton Hicks contractions (Chapter 14) are believed to facilitate placental circulation by enhancing the movement of blood from the center of the cotyledon through the intervillous space.

### Functions

Placental exchange functions occur only in those fetal vessels in intimate contact with the covering syncytial membrane. The syncytium villi have brush borders containing many microvilli, which greatly increase the exchange rate between maternal and fetal circulation (Sadler 1985).

The placental functions, many of which begin soon after implantation, include fetal respiration, nutrition, and excretion. To carry out these functions, the placenta is involved in metabolic and transfer activities. It also has endocrine functions and special immunologic properties.

***Metabolic Activities***  The placenta produces glycogen, cholesterol, and fatty acids continuously for fetal use and hormone production. The placenta also produces numerous enzymes required for fetoplacental transfer, and it breaks down certain substances, such as epinephrine and histamine. In addition, it stores glycogen and iron.

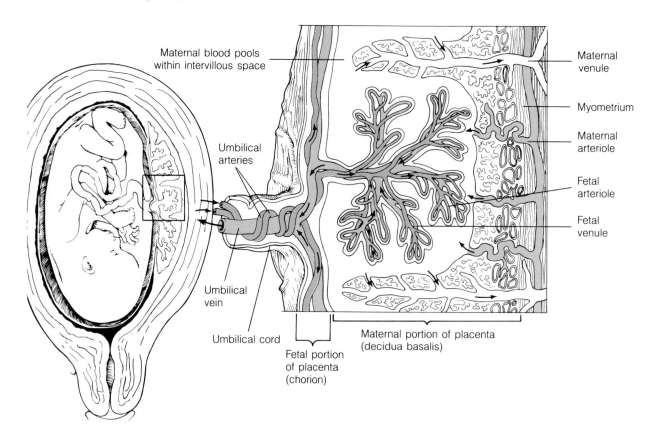

*Figure 5.6  Vascular arrangement of the placenta. Arrows indicate the direction of blood flow. Maternal blood flows through the uterine arteries to the intervillous spaces of the placenta and returns through the uterine veins to maternal circulation. Fetal blood flows through the umbilical arteries into the villous capillaries of the placenta and returns through the umbilical vein to the fetal circulation. (From Spence AP, Mason EB: Human Anatomy and Physiology, 3rd ed. Menlo Park, CA: Benjamin/Cummings, 1987, p 850.)*

**Transport Function**   The placental membranes actively control the transfer of a wide range of substances by five major mechanisms:

1. *Simple diffusion* moves substances such as water, oxygen, carbon dioxide, electrolytes (sodium and chloride), anesthetic gases, and drugs across the placenta from an area of higher concentration to an area of lower concentration.

2. *Facilitated transport* involves a carrier system to move molecules from an area of greater concentration to an area of lower concentration. Molecules such as glucose, galactose, and some oxygen are transported by this method. The glucose level in the fetal blood ordinarily is approximately 20% to 30% lower than the glucose level in the maternal blood because glucose is being metabolized rapidly by the fetus. This in turn causes rapid transport of additional glucose from the maternal blood into the fetal blood.

3. *Active transport* can work against a concentration gradient and allows molecules to move from areas of lower concentration to areas of higher concentration. Amino acids, calcium, iron, iodine, water-soluble vitamins, and glucose are transferred across the placenta this way.

4. *Pinocytosis* is important for transferring large molecules, such as albumin and gamma-globulin. Materials are engulfed by amebalike cells forming plasma droplets.

5. *Bulk flow of water* and some solutes result from hydrostatic and osmotic pressures. Most fetal water comes from the mother.

Other modes of transfer exist. For example, fetal red blood cells pass into the maternal circulation through breaks in the placental membrane, particularly during delivery. Certain cells, such as maternal leukocytes, and microorganisms, such as viruses and *Treponema pallidum* (which causes syphilis), also cross the placenta, but the exact transport mechanism is not known. Some bacteria and protozoa cause lesions in the placenta and then enter the fetal blood system.

Reduction of the placental surface area, as with abruptio placentae, lessens the area that is available for exchange. Placental diffusion distance also affects exchange. In conditions such as diabetes and placental infection, edema of the villi increases the diffusion distance, thus increasing the distance the substance has to be transferred. Blood flow alteration changes the transfer rate of substances. Decreased blood flow in the intervillous space is seen in labor and with certain maternal diseases such as hypertension. Mild fetal hypoxia increases the umbilical blood flow, and severe hypoxia results in decreased blood flow.

*Endocrine Functions*　The placenta produces hormones that are vital to the survival of the fetus. These include human chorionic gonadotropin (hCG); human placental lactogen (hPL); and two steroid hormones, estrogen and progesterone.

The hormone hCG is similar to LH and prevents the normal involution of the corpus luteum at the end of the menstrual cycle. If the corpus luteum stops functioning before the 11th week of pregnancy, spontaneous abortion occurs. The hCG also causes the corpus luteum to secrete increased amounts of estrogen and progesterone.

After the 11th week the placenta produces enough progesterone and estrogen to maintain pregnancy. In the male fetus hCG also exerts an interstitial cell-stimulating effect on the testes, resulting in the production of testosterone. This small secretion of testosterone during embryonic development is the factor that causes male sex organs to grow. Human chorionic gonadotropin may play a role in the trophoblasts' immunologic capabilities (ability to mask pregnancy) (Pritchard et al 1985). Human chorionic gonadotropin is present in maternal blood serum eight to ten days after fertilization, just as soon as implantation has occurred, and is detectable in maternal urine a few days after the missed menses. Chorionic gonadotropin reaches its maximum level at 50 to 70 days' gestation and then begins to decrease as placental hormone production increases.

Progesterone is a hormone essential for pregnancy. It increases the secretions of the fallopian tubes and uterus to provide appropriate nutritive matter for the developing morula and blastocyst. It also appears to aid in ovum transport through the fallopian tube (Ahokas 1985). Progesterone causes decidual cells to develop in the uterine endometrium, and it must be present in high levels for implantation to occur.

The hormone hPL (sometimes referred to as human chorionic somatomammotropin or hCS) is similar to human pituitary growth hormone; hPL stimulates certain changes in the mother's metabolic processes, which ensure that more protein, glucose, and minerals are available for the fetus. Secretion of hPL can be detected by about four weeks (Batzer 1980).

*Immunologic Properties*　The placenta and embryo are transplants of living tissue within the same species and are therefore considered *homografts*. Unlike other homografts, the placenta and embryo appear exempt from immunologic reaction by the host. Most recent data suggest that there is a suppression of cellular immunity by the placental hormones (progesterone and hCG) during pregnancy (Gudson and Sain 1981). One theory used to explain this phenomenon suggests that trophoblastic tissue is immunologically inert. It may contain a cell coating that masks transplantation antigens and that repels sensitized lymphocytes (Pritchard et al 1985).

As the placenta is developing, the **umbilical cord** is also being formed from the amnion. The *body stalk,* which attaches the embryo to the yolk sac, contains blood vessels that extend into the chorionic villi. The body stalk fuses with the embryonic portion of the placenta to provide a circulatory pathway from the chorionic villi to the embryo. As the body stalk elongates to become the umbilical cord, the vessels in the cord decrease to one large vein and two smaller arteries. About 1% of umbilical cords have only two vessels, an artery and a vein; this condition may be associated with congenital malformations. A specialized connective tissue known as **Wharton's jelly** surrounds the blood vessels. This tissue, plus the high blood volume pulsating through the vessels, prevents compression of the umbilical cord in utero. At term, the average cord is 2 cm (0.8 in) across and about 55 cm (22 in) long. The cord can attach itself to the placenta in various sites. Central insertion into the placenta is considered normal. (See Chapter 18 for a discussion of the various attachment sites.)

## FETAL CIRCULATORY SYSTEM

Because the fetus must maintain the blood flow to the placenta to obtain oxygen and nutrients and to remove carbon dioxide and other waste products, the circulatory system of the fetus has several unique features.

Most of the blood supply bypasses the fetal lungs since they do not carry out respiratory gas exchange. The placenta assumes the function of the fetal lungs by supplying oxygen and allowing the fetus to excrete carbon dioxide into the maternal bloodstream. The blood from the placenta flows through the umbilical vein, which penetrates the abdominal wall of the fetus. It divides into two branches, one of which circulates a small amount of blood through the fetal liver and empties into the inferior vena cava through the hepatic vein. The second and larger branch, called the **ductus venosus**, empties directly into the fetal vena cava. This blood then enters the right atrium, passes through

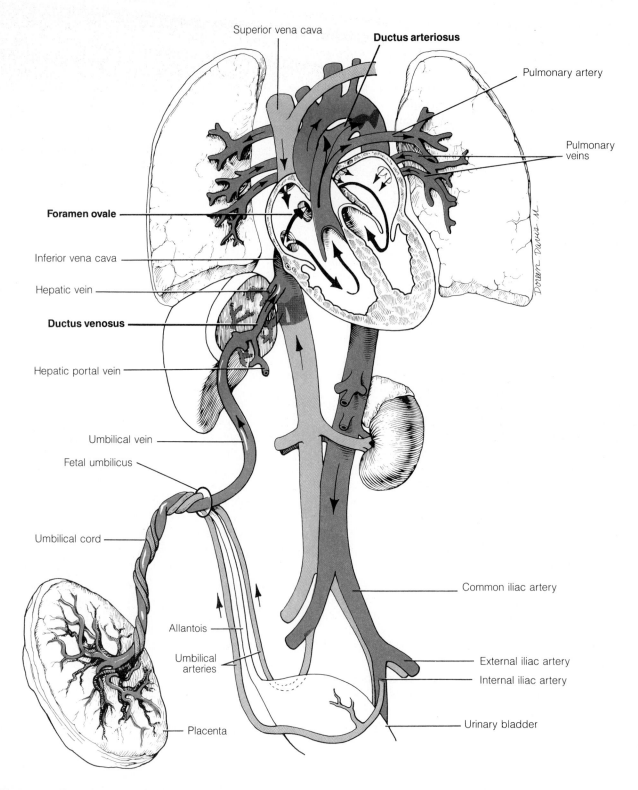

*Figure 5.7  Fetal circulation. Blood leaves the placenta and enters the fetus through the umbilical vein. After circulating through the fetus the blood returns to the placenta through the umbilical arteries. The ductus venosus, the foramen ovale, and the ductus arteriosus allow the blood to bypass the fetal liver and lungs. (From Spence AP, Mason EB:* Human Anatomy and Physiology, *3rd ed. Menlo Park, CA: Benjamin/Cummings, 1987, p 862.)*

the **foramen ovale** into the left atrium, and pours into the left ventricle, which pumps it into the aorta. Some blood returning from the head and upper extremities by way of the superior vena cava is emptied into the right atrium and passes through the tricuspid valve into the right ventricle. This blood is pumped into the pulmonary artery, and a small amount passes to the lungs, to provide nourishment only. The larger portion of blood passes from the pulmonary artery through the **ductus arteriosus** into the descending aorta, bypassing the lungs. Finally, blood returns to the placenta through the two umbilical arteries, and the process is repeated (Figure 5.7).

The fetus obtains oxygen via diffusion from the maternal circulation because of the gradient difference of $PO_2$ of 50 mm Hg in maternal blood in the placenta to a 30 mm Hg $PO_2$ in the fetus. At term the fetus receives oxygen from the mother's circulation at a rate of 20–30 mL/min (Sadler 1985). Fetal hemoglobin facilitates obtaining oxygen from the maternal circulation, since it carries as much as 20%–30% more oxygen than adult hemoglobin. For further discussion see Chapter 20.

Fetal circulation delivers the highest available oxygen concentration to the head, neck, brain, and heart (coronary circulation) and a lesser amount of oxygenated blood to the abdominal organs and the lower body. This circulatory pattern leads to *cephalocaudal* (head-to-tail) development.

## ● Embryo and Fetal Development and Organ Formation

Pregnancy is calculated to last an average of ten lunar months: 40 weeks, or 280 days. This period of 280 days is calculated from the beginning of the last menstrual period to the time of delivery. The fertilization age or postconception age of the fetus is calculated to be about two weeks less, or 266 days (38 weeks). The latter measurement is more accurate because it measures time from the fertilization of the ovum, or conception. The basic events of organ development in the embryo and fetus are outlined in Table 5.2. The time periods in the table are **postconception age periods.**

Development of the human being follows three stages. The preembryonic stage consists of the first 14 days of development after the ovum is fertilized; the embryonic stage covers the period from day 15 until approximately the eighth week and fetal stage extends from the end of the eighth week until delivery.

### PREEMBRYONIC STAGE

The first 14 days of human development, starting on the day the ovum is fertilized (conception), are referred to as the *preembryonic stage* or the *stage of the ovum.* This period is characterized by rapid cellular multiplication and differentiation and the establishment of the embryonic membranes and primary germ layers, discussed earlier.

### EMBRYONIC STAGE

The stage of the **embryo** starts on the fifteenth day (the beginning of the third week after conception) and continues until approximately the eighth week or until the embryo reaches a crown-to-rump (C–R) length of 3 cm or 1.2 in. This length is usually reached about 49 days after fertilization (the end of the eighth gestational week). During the embryonic stage, tissues differentiate into essential organs, and the main external features develop.

### Third Week

In the third week the embryonic disk becomes elongated and pear-shaped with a broad cephalic end and a narrow caudal end (Figure 5.8). The ectoderm has formed a long cylindrical tube for brain and spinal cord development. The gastrointestinal tract, created from the endoderm, appears as another tubelike structure communicating with the yolk sac. The most advanced organ is the heart. At three weeks, a single tubular heart forms just outside the body cavity of the embryo.

*(Text continues on page 152.)*

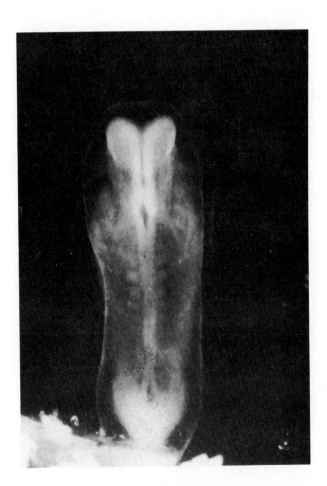

*Figure 5.8   The embryo at three weeks (Courtesy Drs Roberts Rugh and Landrum B Shettles)*

## Table 5.2 Classification of Organ System Development

| Postconception age* | Length† | Weight | Nervous system | Musculoskeletal system | Cardiovascular system |
|---|---|---|---|---|---|
| CONCEPTION | | | | | |
| 2–3 weeks | 2 mm C–R | | Groove is formed along middle of back as cells thicken; neural tube formed from closure of neural groove. | | Beginning of blood circulation; tubular heart begins to form during third week. |
| 4 weeks | 4–6 mm C–R | 0.4 g | Anterior portion of neural tube closes to form brain; closure of posterior end forms spinal cord. | Noticeable limb buds. | Tubular heart is beating at 28 days and primitive red blood cells are circulating through fetus and chorionic villi. |
| 5 weeks | 8 mm C–R | Only 0.5% of total body weight is fat (to 20 weeks). | Brain has differentiated and cranial nerves are present. | Developing muscles have innervation. | Atrial division has occurred. |
| 6 weeks | 12 mm C–R | | | Bone rudiments present; primitive skeletal shape forming; muscle mass begins to develop; ossification of skull and jaws begins. | Chambers present in heart; groups of blood cells can be identified. |
| 7 weeks | 18 mm C–R | | | | Fetal heartbeats can be detected. |

*Refers to gestational age of fetus/conceptus; fertilization age.
†C–R = crown–rump; C–H = crown–heel

Sources: Sadler TW: *Langman's Medical Embryology,* 5th ed. Baltimore: Williams and Wilkins, 1985; and Moore KL: *The Developing Human: Clinically Oriented Embryology,* 4th ed. Philadelphia: Saunders, 1988.

## Table 5.2  Classification of Organ System Development *(continued)*

| Gastrointestinal system | Genitourinary system | Respiratory system | Skin | Specific organ systems | Sexual development |
|---|---|---|---|---|---|
| | Formation of kidneys beginning. | Nasal pits forming. | | Endocrine system: thyroid tissue appears.<br>Eyes: optic cup and lens pit have formed; pigment in eyes.<br>Ear: auditory pit is now enclosed structure.<br>Liver function begins. | |
| Mouth: formation of oral cavity; primitive jaws present; esophagotracheal septum begins division of esophagus and trachea.<br>Digestive tract: stomach forms; esophagus and intestine become tubular; ducts of pancreas and liver forming. | | | | | |
| Oral and nasal cavities and upper lip formed. | | Trachea, bronchi, and lung buds present. | | Ear: formation of external, middle, and inner ear continues.<br>Liver begins to form red blood cells. | Embryonic sex glands appear. |
| Mouth: tongue separates; palate folds.<br>Digestive tract: stomach attains final form. | Separation of bladder and urethra from rectum. | Diaphragm separates abdominal and thoracic cavities. | | Eyes: optic nerve formed; eyelids appear, thickening of lens. | Differentiation of sex glands into ovaries and testes begins. |

## Table 5.2 Classification of Organ System Development *(continued)*

| Postconception age* | Length† | Weight | Nervous system | Musculoskeletal system | Cardiovascular system |
|---|---|---|---|---|---|
| 8 weeks | 2.5–3 cm C–R | 2 g | | Digits formed; further differentiation of cells in primitive skeleton; cartilaginous bones show first signs of ossification; development of muscles in trunk, limbs, and head; some movement of fetus is now possible. | Development of heart is essentially complete; fetal circulation follows two circuits—four extraembryonic and two intraembryonic. |
| 10 weeks | 5–6 cm C–H | 14 g | Neurons appear at caudal end of spinal cord; basic divisions of the brain present. | Fingers and toes begin nail growth. | |
| 12 weeks | 8 cm C–R, 11.5 cm C–H | 45 g | | Clear outlining of miniature bones (12–20 weeks); process of ossification is established throughout fetal body; appearance of involuntary muscles in viscera. | |
| 16 weeks | 13.5 cm C–R, 15 cm C–H | 200 g | | Teeth: beginning formation of hard tissue that will become central incisors. | |
| 18 weeks | | | | Teeth: beginning formation of hard tissue (enamel and dentine) that will become lateral incisors. | Fetal heart tones audible with fetoscope at 16–20 weeks. |
| 20 weeks | 19 cm C–R, 25 cm C–H | 435 g (6% of total body weight is fat) | Myelination of spinal cord begins. | Teeth: beginning formation of hard tissue that will become canine and first molar. Lower limbs are of final relative proportions. | |

## Table 5.2  Classification of Organ System Development *(continued)*

| Gastrointestinal system | Genitourinary system | Respiratory system | Skin | Specific organs systems | Sexual development |
|---|---|---|---|---|---|
| Mouth: completion of lip fusion. Digestive tract: rotation in midgut; anal membrane has perforated. | | | | Ear: external, middle, and inner ear assuming final structure forms. | Male and female external genitals appear similar until end of ninth week. |
| Mouth: separation of lips from jaw; fusion of palate folds. Digestive tract: developing intestines enclosed in abdomen. | Bladder sac formed. Urine formed. | | | Eyelids fused closed. Endocrine system: islets of Langerhans differentiated. Eyes: development of lacrimal duct. | |
| Mouth: completion of palate. Digestive tract: appearance of muscles in gut; bile secretion begins; liver is major producer of red blood cells. | | Lungs aquire definitive shape. | Skin pink, delicate. | Endocrine system: hormonal secretion from thyroid. Immunologic system: appearance of lymphoid tissue in fetal thymus gland. | |
| Mouth: differentiation of hard and soft palate. Digestive tract: development of gastric and intestinal glands; intestines begin to collect meconium. | Kidneys assume typical shape and organization. | | Appearance of scalp hair; lanugo present on body; transparent skin with visible blood vessels. | Eye, ear, and nose formed. Sweat glands developing. | Sex determination possible. |
| Fetus actively sucks and swallows amniotic fluid; peristaltic movements begin. | | | Lanugo covers entire body; brown fat begins to form; vernix caseosa begins to form. | Immunologic system: detectable levels of fetal antibodies (IgG type). Blood formation: iron is stored and bone marrow is increasingly important. | |

**Table 5.2   Classification of Organ System Development** *(continued)*

| Postconception age* | Length† | Weight | Nervous system | Musculoskeletal system | Cardiovascular system |
|---|---|---|---|---|---|
| 24 weeks | 23 cm C–R, 28 cm C–H | 780 g | Structure of brain: looks like mature brain. | Teeth: beginning formation of hard tissue that will become second molar. | |
| 28 weeks | 27 cm C–R, 35 cm C–H | 1200–1250 g | Nervous system begins regulation of some body functions. | | |
| 32 weeks | 31 cm C–R, 38–43 cm C–H | 2000 g | More reflexes present. | | |
| 36 weeks | 35 cm C–R, 42–48 cm C–H | 2500–2750 g | | Distal femoral ossification centers present. | |
| 40 weeks | 40 cm C–R, 48–52 cm C–H | 3200+ g (16% of total body weight is fat). | | | |

## Fourth to Fifth Weeks

During days 21 to 32, *somites,* a series of mesodermal blocks, form on either side of the embryo's midline. The vertebras that form the spinal column will develop from these somites. Prior to 28 days, arm and leg buds are not visible, but the tail bud is present. The pharyngeal arches—which will form the lower jaw, hyoid bone, and larynx—develop at this time. The pharyngeal pouches appear now; these pouches will form the eustachian tube and cavity of the middle ear, the tonsils, and the parathyroid and thymus glands. The primordia of the ear and eye are also present. By the end of 28 days, the tubular heart is beating at a regular rhythm and pushing its own primitive blood cells through the main blood vessels.

During the fifth week, the optic cups and lens vessels of the eye form and the nasal pits develop. Partitioning in the heart occurs with the dividing of the atrium. The embryo has a marked C-shaped body, accentuated by the rudimentary tail and the large head folded over a protuberant trunk. By day 35, the arm and leg buds are well developed, with paddle-shaped hand and foot plates. The

**Table 5.2   Classification of Organ System Development** *(continued)*

| Gastrointestinal system | Genitourinary system | Respiratory system | Skin | Specific organs systems | Sexual development |
|---|---|---|---|---|---|
| | | Respiratory movements may occur (24–40 weeks). Nostrils reopen. Alveoli appear in lungs and begin production of surfactant; gas exchange possible. | Skin reddish and wrinkled, vernix caseosa present. | Immunologic system: IgG levels reach maternal levels. Eyes structurally complete. | |
| | | | Adipose tissue accumulates rapidly; nails appear; eyebrows and eyelashes present. | Eyes: eyelids open (28–32 weeks). | Testes descend into inguinal canal and upper scrotum. |
| | | | Skin pale; body rounded; lanugo disappearing; hair fuzzy or woolly; few sole creases; sebaceous glands active and helping to produce vernix caseosa (36–40 weeks). | Ear lobes soft with little cartilage. | Scrotum small and few rugae present; descent of testes into upper scrotum to stay (36–40 weeks). |
| | | At 38 weeks, lecithin-sphingomyelin (L/S) ratio approaches 2:1. | Skin smooth and pink; vernix present in skinfolds; moderate to profuse silky hair; lanugo hair on shoulders and upper back; nails extend over tips of digits; creases cover sole. | Ear lobes stiffened by thick cartilage. | Males: rugous scrotum. Females: labia majora well developed. |

heart, circulatory system, and brain show the most advanced development. The brain has differentiated into five areas, and ten pairs of cranial nerves are recognizable.

## Sixth Week

At six weeks the head structures are more highly developed and the trunk is straighter than in earlier stages (Figure 5.9). The upper and lower jaws are recognizable, and the external nares are well formed. The trachea has developed, and its caudal end is bifurcated for beginning lung formation. The upper lip has formed, and the palate is developing. The ears are developing rapidly, as are the other postbranchial body parts. The arms have begun to extend ventrally across the chest, and both arms and legs have digits, although they may still be webbed. There is a slight elbow bend in the arm, and the arm is more advanced in development than the leg. Beginning at this stage the prominent tail will recede. The heart now has most of its definitive characteristics, and fetal circulation begins to be established. The liver begins to produce blood cells.

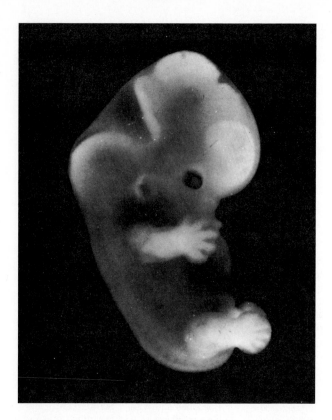

*Figure 5.9   The embryo at six weeks (Courtesy Drs Roberts Rugh and Landrum B Shettles)*

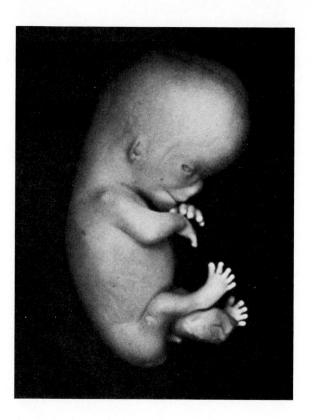

*Figure 5.10   The embryo at eight weeks (Courtesy Drs Roberts Rugh and Landrum B Shettles)*

### Eighth Week

At eight weeks the embryo is approximately 3 cm (1.2 in) long C–R and clearly resembles a human being (Figure 5.10). Facial features continue to develop. The eyelids begin to fuse. Auricles of the external ears begin to assume their final shape, but they are still set low (Moore 1988). External genitals appear but are not discernible, and the rectal passage opens with the perforation of the anal membrane. The circulatory system through the umbilical cord is well established. Long bones are beginning to form, and the large muscles are now capable of contracting.

### FETAL STAGE

By the end of the eighth week, the embryo is sufficiently developed to be called a **fetus**. Every organ system and external structure that will be found in the full-term newborn is present (Korones 1987). The remainder of gestation is devoted to refining structures and perfecting function.

### Twelfth Week

The fetus reaches an 8 cm (3.2 in) C–R length and weighs about 45 g (1.6 oz). The face is well formed, with the nose protruding, the chin small and receding, and the

ear acquiring a more adult shape. The eyelids close at about the tenth week and will not reopen until about 28 weeks. Some reflex movements of the lips suggestive of the sucking reflex have been observed at three months. Tooth buds now appear for all 20 of the child's first teeth (baby teeth). The limbs are long and slender, with well-formed digits. The fetus can curl the fingers toward the palm and make a tiny fist. The legs are still shorter and less developed than the arms. The urogenital tract completes its development, well-differentiated genitals appear, and the kidneys begin to produce urine. Red blood cells are produced primarily by the liver. Spontaneous movements of the fetus now occur.

### Twentieth Week

The fetus doubles it C–R length and now measures 19 cm or 8 in, and fetal weight is between 435 and 465 g. **Lanugo**, a fine, downy hair, covers the entire body and is especially prominent on the shoulders. Subcutaneous deposits of brown fat, which has a rich blood supply, make the skin less transparent. Nipples now appear over the mammary glands. The head is covered with fine, "wooly" hair, and the eyebrows and eyelashes are beginning to form. Nails are present on both fingers and toes. Muscles are well developed, and the fetus is active. The mother feels fetal movement, known as *quickening.* The fetal heartbeat is audible through a stethoscope. Quickening and fetal heartbeat can help confirm the estimated delivery date.

### Twenty-Fourth Week

The fetus reaches a crown-to-heel (C–H) length of 28 cm (11.2 in). It weighs about 780 g (1 lb 10 oz). The eyes are structurally complete and the eyelids will soon open. The fetus has a reflex hand grip (grasp reflex) and, by the end of the sixth month, a startle reflex. Skin covering the body is reddish and wrinkled, with little subcutaneous fat. Skin ridges on palms and soles form distinct footprints and fingerprints. The skin over the entire body is covered with a protective cheeselike fatty substance called **vernix caseosa**. The alveoli in the lungs are just beginning to form.

### Twenty-Eighth Week

The fetus looks like a little old man; the skin is still red, wrinkled, and covered with vernix. The brain develops rapidly, and the nervous system can regulate body functions to some degree. If the fetus is male, the testes begin to descend into the scrotal sac. Respiratory and circulatory systems have developed sufficiently to initiate extrauterine functioning. If born at this time, the fetus requires intensive specialized care to survive and to decrease the risk of major handicap. The fetus at 28 weeks (Figure 5.11) is about 35–38 cm (14–15 in) long (C–H) and weighs about 1200–1250 g (2 lb 10.5 oz–2 lb 12 oz).

### Thirty-Sixth Week

The fetus begins to get plump, with less wrinkled skin covering the deposits of subcutaneous fat. Lanugo hair begins to disappear, and the nails now reach the edge of the fingertips. By 36 weeks, the fetus weighs 2500–2750 g (5 lb 12 oz–6 lb 11.5 oz) and measures about 42–48 cm (16–19 in) C–H. If born at this time, the infant has a good chance of surviving but may require some special care.

### Thirty-Eighth to Fortieth Weeks

The fetus is considered full term 38 weeks after conception. Length varies from 48 to 52 cm C–H (19 to 21 in), with males usually longer than females. Males also generally weigh more than females. The weight at term is about 3000–3600 g (6 lb 10 oz–7 lb 15 oz). The skin is pink and has a smooth, polished look. The only lanugo left is on the upper arms and shoulders. The hair is now coarse and about an inch long. Vernix is more apparent in the creases and folds of the skin. The body and extremities are plump, and the fingernails extend beyond the fingertips. The chest is prominent but still a little smaller than the head and mammary glands protrude in both sexes. In males, the

*Figure 5.11   The fetus at twenty-eight weeks (Courtesy Drs Roberts Rugh and Landrum B Shettles)*

testes are in the scrotum or palpable in the inguinal canal. The amniotic fluid decreases to about 500 mL or less as the fetal body mass fills the uterine cavity. The fetus assumes what is called its *position of comfort* or *lie* and generally follows the shape of the uterus, with the head pointed downward. After the fifth month, feeding, sleeping, and activity patterns become established so that at term the fetus has its own body rhythms and individual style of response.

Essential Facts to Remember—Fetal Development—lists some important developmental milestones.

## ● TWINS

Twins may be either fraternal or identical. If they are fraternal, they are *dizygotic,* which means they arise from two separate ova fertilized by two separate spermatozoa (Figure 5.12). There are two placentas, two chorions, and two amnions; however, the placentas sometimes fuse together and look as if they are one. Despite their birth relationship, fraternal twins are no more similar to each other

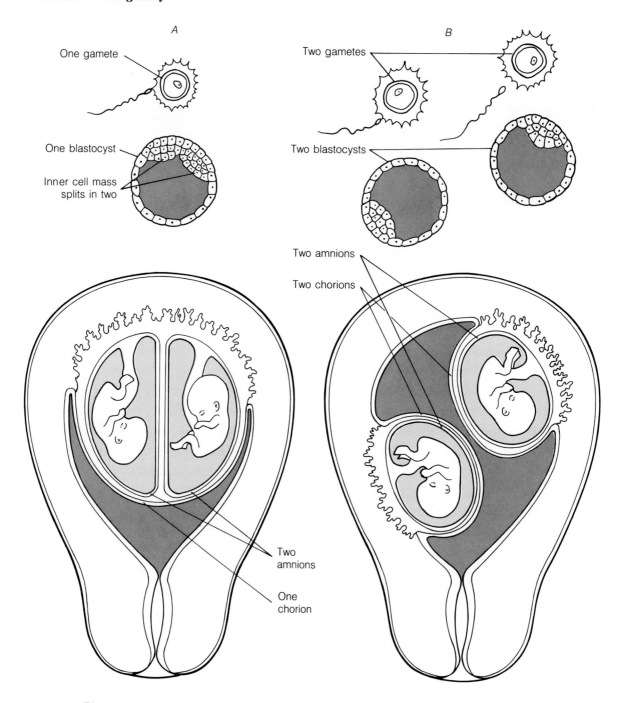

*Figure 5.12* (**A**) Formation of identical twins. (**B**) Formation of fraternal twins.

than they would be to siblings born singly. They may be the same or different sex.

Dizygotic twinning increases with maternal age up to about 35 years of age and then decreases abruptly. The chance of dizygotic twins increases with parity, decreases in periods of malnutrition, increases in conceptions that occur in the first three months of marriage, and increases with coital frequency (James 1981). Studies indicate dizygotic twins occur in certain families, perhaps because of genetic factors leading to double ovulation (Creasy and Resnik 1988).

Identical, or *monozygotic,* twins develop from a single fertilized ovum. They have the same sex and appearance. Division of the single fertilized ovum into two units occurs only after the embryo consists of thousands of cells. Complete separation of the cellular mass into two parts is necessary for twin formation. Identical twins have a common placenta and a single chorion but always two separate amnions (Figure 5.12).

# • FACTORS INFLUENCING EMBRYONIC AND FETAL DEVELOPMENT

Among factors that may affect embryonic development are the quality of the sperm or ovum from which the zygote was formed and the genetic code established at fertilization. In addition, the adequacy of the intrauterine environment is important for optimal growth. If the environment is unsuitable before cellular differentiation occurs, all the cells of the zygote are affected. The cells may die, which causes spontaneous abortion, or growth may be slowed, depending on the severity of the situation. When differentiation is complete and the fetal membranes have formed, an injurious agent has the greatest effect on those cells undergoing the most rapid growth. Thus the time of injury is critical in the development of anomalies.

## Table 5.3 Developmental Vulnerability Timetable

| Weeks since conception | Potential teratogen-induced malformation |
| --- | --- |
| 3 | Ectromelia (congenital absence of one or more limbs)<br>Ectopedia cordis (heart lies outside thoracic cavity) |
| 4 | Omphalocele<br>Tracheoesophageal fistula (4–5* weeks)<br>Hemivertebra (4–5* weeks) |
| 5 | Nuclear cataract<br>Microphthalmia (abnormally small eyeballs; 5–6* weeks)<br>Facial clefts<br>Carpal or pedal ablation (5–6* weeks) |
| 6 | Gross septal or aortic abnormalities<br>Cleft lip, agnathia (absence of the lower jaw) |
| 7 | Interventricular septal defects<br>Pulmonary stenosis<br>Cleft palate, micrognathia (smallness of the jaw)<br>Epicanthus<br>Brachycephalism (shortness of the head; 7–8* weeks)<br>Mixed sexual characteristics |
| 8 | Persistent ostium primum (persistent opening in atrial septum)<br>Digital stunting (shortening of fingers and toes) |

*May occur in several different time periods after conception.

Source: Modified from Danforth DN, Scott JR: *Obstetrics and Gynecology*, 5th ed. Philadelphia: Lippincott, 1986, p 319.

## Essential Facts to Remember

### Fetal Development: What Parents Want to Know

| | |
| --- | --- |
| 4 weeks: | The fetal heart begins to beat. |
| 16 weeks: | Baby's sex can be seen.<br>Although thin, looks like a baby. |
| 20 weeks: | Heartbeat can be heard with fetoscope.<br>Mother feels movement (quickening).<br>Baby develops a regular schedule of sleeping, sucking, and kicking.<br>Hands can grasp.<br>Assumes a favorite position in utero.<br>Vernix (lanolinlike covering) protects the body and lanugo (fine hair) keeps oil on skin.<br>Head hair, eyebrows, and eyelashes present. |
| 24 weeks: | Weighs 1 lb 10 oz.<br>Increasing activity.<br>Fetal respiratory movements begin. |
| 28 weeks: | Eyes begin to open and close.<br>Baby can breathe at this time.<br>Surfactant needed for breathing at birth is formed.<br>Baby is two-thirds its final size. |
| 32 weeks: | Has fingernails and toenails.<br>Subcutaneous fat being laid down.<br>Baby appears less red and wrinkled. |
| 38–40 weeks: | Fills total uterus.<br>Gets antibodies from mother.<br>Fingernails extend beyond fingertips. |

Because organs are formed primarily during embryonic development, the growing organism is considered most vulnerable to noxious agents during the first months of pregnancy (Paul and Himmelstein 1988). Table 5.3 lists potential malformations related to the time of insult. Any agent, such as a drug, virus, or radiation, that can cause development of abnormal structures in an embryo is referred to as a **teratogen**. Chapter 14 discusses the effects of specific teratogenic agents on the developing fetus.

Adequacy of the maternal environment is also important during the periods of rapid embryonic and fetal development. Maternal nutrition can affect brain development. The period of maximum brain growth and myelination begins with the fifth lunar month before birth and continues during the first six months after birth. During the first six months after birth there is a twofold increase in myelination; in the second six months to two years of age there is about a 50% further increase (Volpe 1987). Amino acids, glucose, and fatty acids are considered to be the primary dietary factors in brain growth. A subtle type of damage that affects the associative capacity of the brain, possibly leading to learning disabilities, may be caused by nutritional deficiency at this stage. (Maternal nutrition is discussed in depth in Chapter 10.)

Another prenatal influence on the intrauterine environment is maternal hyperthermia associated with sauna baths or hot tub use (Jones and Chernoff 1984). Studies of the effects of maternal hyperthermia during the first trimester have raised concern about possible central nervous system defects and failure of neural tube closure (Pleet et al 1980).

## ESSENTIAL CONCEPTS

● **Humans have 46 chromosomes, which are divided into 23 pairs—22 pairs of autosomes and one pair of sex chromosomes.**

● **Mitosis is the process by which additional somatic (body) cells are formed. It provides growth and development of the organisms and replacement of body cells.**

● **Meiosis is the process by which new organisms are formed. It occurs during gametogenesis and consists of two successive cell divisions (reduction division), which produce a gamete with 23 chromosomes (22 chromosomes and 1 sex chromosome)—the haploid number of chromosomes.**

● **Gametes must have a haploid number (23) of chromosomes so that when the female gamete (ovum) and the male gamete (spermatozoon) unite (fertilization) to form the zygote, the normal human diploid number of chromosomes (46) is reestablished.**

● **Sex chromosomes are referred to as X and Y. Females have two X chromosomes and males have an X and a Y chromosome. Y chromosomes are carried only by the sperm. To produce a male child the mother contributes an X chromosome and the father contributes a Y chromosome.**

● **Fertilization usually takes place in the ampulla (outer third) of the fallopian tube.**

● **An ovum is considered fertile for about a 24-hour period after ovulation, and the sperm is capable of fertilizing the ovum for only about 24 hours after it is deposited in the female reproductive system.**

● **Both capacitation and acrosomal reaction must occur for the sperm to fertilize the ovum. Capacitation is the removal of the plasma membrane, which exposes the acrosomal covering of the sperm head.**

**Acrosomal reaction is the deposit of hyaluronidase in the corona radiata, which allows the sperm head to penetrate the ovum.**

● **Intrauterine development first proceeds via cellular multiplication in which the zygote undergoes rapid mitotic division called cleavage. As a result of cleavage the zygote divides and multiplies into cell groupings called blastomeres, which are held together by the zona pellucida. The blastomeres will eventually become a solid ball of cells called the morula. When the cavity forms in the morula cell mass, the inner solid cell mass is called the blastocyst.**

● **Implantation usually occurs in the upper part of the posterior uterine wall when the blastocyst burrows into the uterine lining.**

● **After implantation the endometrium is called the decidua. Decidua capsularis is the portion that covers the blastocyst. Decidua basalis is the portion that is directly under the blastocyst. Decidua vera is the portion that lines the rest of the uterine cavity.**

● **Embryonic membranes are called the amnion and the chorion. The amnion is formed from the ectoderm and is a thin protective membrane that contains the amniotic fluid and the embryo. The chorion is a thick membrane that develops from the trophoblast and encloses the amnion, embryo, and yolk sac.**

● **Amniotic fluid cushions the fetus against mechanical injury, controls the embryo's temperature, allows symmetrical external growth, prevents adherence to the amnion, and permits freedom of movement.**

● **Amniotic fluid is made up of albumin, creatinine, lecithin, sphingomyelin, fat, bilirubin, proteins, epithelial cells, and lanugo. Normal volume produced is 500 to 1000 cc/day after about 20 weeks. The fetus contributes to the amniotic fluid via urination.**

● **Primary germ layers will give rise to all tissues, organs, and organ systems. The three primary germ cell layers are ectoderm, endoderm, and mesoderm.**

● **The placenta develops from the chorionic villi and has two parts: The maternal portion, consisting of the decidua basalis, is red and fresh looking. The fetal portion, consisting of chorionic villi, is covered by the amnion and appears shiny and gray. The placenta is made up of 15 to 20 segments called cotyledons.**

● The placenta serves endocrine (production of hPL, hCG, estrogen, and progesterone), metabolic, and immunologic functions; it acts as the fetus's respiratory organ, is an organ of excretion, and aids in the exchange of nutrients.

● The umbilical cord contains two umbilical arteries, which carry deoxygenated blood from the fetus to the placenta, and one umbilical vein, which carries oxygenated blood from the placenta to the fetus. The umbilical cord has a central insertion into the placenta. Wharton's jelly, a specialized connective tissue, prevents compression of the umbilical cord in utero.

● Fetal circulation is a specially designed circulatory system that provides for oxygenation of the fetus while bypassing the fetal lungs.

● Stages of fetal development include the preembryonic stage (the first 14 days of human development starting at the time of fertilization), the embryonic stage (from day 15 after fertilization, or the beginning of the third week, until approximately eight weeks after conception), and the fetal stage (from eight weeks until delivery at approximately 40 weeks postconception).

● Some significant events that occur during the embryonic stage are: at four weeks, the fetal heart begins to beat and at six weeks, fetal circulation is established.

● The fetal stage is devoted to refining structures and perfecting function. Some significant developments during the fetal stage are:

At 16 weeks sex can be determined visually.

At 20 weeks fetal heartbeat can be auscultated by a fetoscope, and the mother can feel movement (quickening).

At 24 weeks vernix caseosa covers the entire body.

At 26 to 28 weeks the eyes reopen.

At 36 weeks fingernails reach the ends of fingers.

At 40 weeks fingernails extend beyond fingertips, vernix is apparent only in creases and folds of skin, and lanugo remains on upper arms and shoulders only.

● Twins are either monozygotic (identical) or dizygotic (fraternal). Dizygotic twins arise from two separate ova fertilized by two separate spermatozoa. Monozygotic twins develop from a single fertilized ovum.

● ● ● ● ● ● ● ● ● ● ● ● ● ● ● ● ● ● ● ● ● ● ●

## References

Ahokas RA: Development and physiology of the placenta and membranes. In: *Gynecology and Obstetrics.* Vol. 2. Sciarra JL et al (editors). Hagerstown, MD: Harper and Row, 1985.

Batzer FR: Hormonal evaluation of early pregnancy. *Fertil Steril* July 1980; 34:1.

Chavez DJ: Implantation. In: *Gynecology and Obstetrics.* Vol. 5. Sciarra JL et al (editors). Hagerstown, MD: Harper and Row, 1987.

Creasy RK, Resnik JR: *Maternal Fetal Medicine Principles and Practice.* Philadelphia: Saunders, 1988.

Danforth DN, Scott JR: *Obstetrics and Gynecology,* 5th ed. Philadelphia: Lippincott, 1986.

Eddy CA, Pauerstein CJ: Anatomy and physiology of the fallopian tube. *Clin Obstet Gynecol* 1980; 23:1177.

Glass RH: Egg transport and fertilization. In: *Gynecology and Obstetrics.* Vol. 2. Sciarra JL et al (editors). Hagerstown, MD: Harper and Row, 1987.

Gudson JP, Sain LE: Uterine and peripheral blood concentrations and human chorionic gonadotropin and human placental lactogen. *Am J Obstet Gynecol* March 1981; 39(2):705.

James WH: Dizygotic twinning, marital stage and status and coital rates. *Ann Hum Biol* 1981; 8:371.

Jones KL, Chernoff GF: Effects of chemical and environmental agents. In: *Maternal-Fetal Medicine Principles and Practice.* Creasy RK, Resnik JR (editors). Philadelphia: Saunders, 1984; 190.

Korones SB: Anatomic and functional aspects of fetal development. In: *Gynecology and Obstetrics.* Vol. 2. Sciarra JL et al (editors). Hagerstown, MD: Harper and Row, 1987.

Moore KL: *The Developing Human: Clinically Oriented Embryology,* 4th ed. Philadelphia: Saunders, 1988.

Overstreet JW, Katz DF, Cross NL: Sperm transport and capacitation. In: *Gynecology and Obstetrics.* Vol. 5. Sciarra JL et al (editors). Hagerstown, MD: Harper and Row, 1988.

Paul M, Himmelstein J: Reproductive hazards in the workplace: What the practitioner needs to know about chemical exposures. *Obstet Gynecol* June 1988; 71(6):921.

Pleet HB et al: Patterns of malformations resulting from the teratogenic effects of first trimester hyperthermia. *Pediatr Res* 1980; 14:587.

Pritchard JA, MacDonald PC, Gant NF: *Williams Obstetrics,* 17th ed. New York: Appleton-Century-Crofts, 1985.

Sadler TW: *Langman's Medical Embryology,* 5th ed. Baltimore: Williams and Wilkins, 1985.

Silverstein A: *Human Anatomy and Physiology.* New York: John Wiley, 1980.

Spence AP, Mason EB: *Human Anatomy and Physiology,* 3rd ed. Menlo Park, CA: Benjamin/Cummings, 1987.

Thompson JS, Thompson MW: *Genetics in Medicine,* 4th ed. Philadelphia: Saunders, 1986.

Volpe JJ: *Neurology of the Newborn,* 2nd ed. Philadelphia: Saunders, 1987.

Wassarman PM: Fertilization in mammals. *Scientific American* December 1988; 259(6):78.

## Additional Readings

Agnorastos T et al: Features of vernix caseosa cells. *Am J Perinatol* July 1988; 5(3): 253–259.

Bernhardt J: Sensory capabilities of the fetus. *Am J Mat Child Nurs* January/February 1987; 12: 44.

Bingol N et al: Teratogenicity of cocaine in humans. *J Pediatr* January 1987; 110: 93.

Boylan P, Parisi V: An overview of hydramnios. *Semin Perinatol* April 1986; 10: 136.

Levine J et al: Help from the unborn: Fetal-cell surgery raises hopes—and issues. *Time* January 12, 1987; 62.

MacGregor SN et al: Underestimation of gestational age by conventional crown-rump length dating curves. *Obstetrics & Gynecology* September 1987; 70(3): 344–348.

Mulders LGM et al: The uterine artery blood flow velocity waveform: Reproducibility and results in normal pregnancy. *Early Human Development* 1988; 17: 55–70.

Nazir MA et al: Antibacterial activity on amniotic fluid in the early third trimester: Its association with preterm labor and delivery. *Am J Perinatol* January 1987; 4: 59.

O'Grady JP: Clinical management of twins. *Contemp OB/GYN* April 1987; 126.

Ramsay J: Prenatal influences on fetal development. *Nursing* December 1986; 3: 432.

Roger JC, Drake BL: The enigma of the fetal graft. *Am Sci* January/February 1987; 75: 51.

Stevens CA et al: Development of human palmar and digital flexion creases. *Pediatr* July 1988; 113(1): 128–132.

Whaley LF: *Understanding Inherited Disorders.* St. Louis: Mosby, 1974.

Winick M: Maternal nutrition and fetal growth. *Perinat Neonat* September/October 1986; 10: 28.

# 6

# Physical and Psychologic Changes of Pregnancy

*The atmosphere of approval in which I was bathed—even by strangers on the street, it seemed—was like an aura which I carried with me . . . this is what women have always done.* (Adrienne Rich, *Of Woman Born*)

## Objectives

● Identify the anatomic and physiologic changes that occur during pregnancy.

● Relate the physiologic and anatomic changes that occur in the body systems during pregnancy to the signs and symptoms that develop in the woman.

● Compare subjective (presumptive), objective (probable), and diagnostic (positive) changes of pregnancy.

● Contrast the various types of pregnancy tests.

● Discuss the emotional and psychologic changes that commonly occur in a woman, her partner, and her family during pregnancy.

● Summarize cultural factors that may influence a family's response to pregnancy.

## Key Terms

Braxton Hicks
    contractions
Chadwick's sign
chloasma
couvade
ethnocentrism
Goodell's sign
Hegar's sign
last menstrual period
    (LMP)
linea nigra
McDonald's sign
mitleiden
striae
vena caval syndrome

During pregnancy, a woman undergoes numerous physical and psychologic changes; her family, too, experiences change. Typically, a pregnancy is calculated as lasting about nine calendar months, ten lunar months, 40 weeks, or 280 days. However, ovulation actually occurs about two weeks before the *expected* date of the next menstrual period. Thus the real length of gestation is about 266 days, although considerable variation is possible.

Pregnancy is traditionally divided into three trimesters of three months each. Each trimester brings predictable changes for both the mother and the fetus. This chapter identifies the physical and psychologic changes that accompany each trimester. In subsequent chapters, the nurse will use this knowledge to plan and provide effective nursing care.

## ● ANATOMY AND PHYSIOLOGY OF PREGNANCY

### ● Reproductive System

#### UTERUS

The changes in the uterus during pregnancy are phenomenal. Before pregnancy, the uterus is a small, semisolid, pear-shaped organ measuring approximately $7.5 \times 5 \times 2.5$ cm and weighing about 60 g (2 oz). At the end of pregnancy it measures about $28 \times 24 \times 21$ cm and weighs approximately 1000 g; its capacity has also increased from about 10 mL to 5 L or more (Pritchard et al 1985).

The enlargement of the uterus is primarily due to enlargement of the preexisting myometrial cells. These cells increase greatly in size as a result of the stimulating influence of estrogen and the distention caused by the growing fetus. The fibrous tissue between the muscle bands increases markedly, which adds to the strength and elasticity of the muscle wall.

The enlarging uterus, developing placenta, and growing fetus require additional blood flow to the uterus. By the end of pregnancy, one sixth the total maternal blood volume is contained within the vascular system of the uterus.

**Braxton Hicks contractions**, which are irregular, painless contractions of the uterus, occur throughout pregnancy. They may be felt through the abdominal wall beginning about the fourth month of pregnancy. In later pregnancy, these contractions become uncomfortable and may be confused with true labor contractions.

## CERVIX

Estrogen stimulates the glandular tissue of the cervix, which increases in cell number and becomes hyperactive. The endocervical glands secrete a thick, sticky mucus that accumulates and forms a plug, which seals the endocervical canal and prevents the ascent of organisms into the uterus. This mucous plug is expelled when cervical dilatation begins. The hyperactivity of the glandular tissue also increases the normal physiologic mucorrhea, at times resulting in profuse discharge. Increased cervical vascularity also causes both the softening of the cervix and its bluish discoloration (Chadwick's sign).

## OVARIES

The ovaries stop producing ova during pregnancy. The corpus luteum continues to produce hormones until about weeks 10–12 of pregnancy. The progesterone it secretes maintains the endometrium until the placenta assumes this task. The corpus luteum begins to regress and is almost completely obliterated by the middle of pregnancy.

## VAGINA

Estrogen causes a thickening of the vaginal mucosa, a loosening of the connective tissue, and an increase in vaginal secretions. These secretions are thick, white, and acidic (pH 3.5–6.0). The acidity helps prevent bacterial infection but favors the growth of yeast organisms. Thus, the pregnant woman is more susceptible to monilial infection than usual.

The supportive connective tissue of the vagina loosens throughout pregnancy. By the time of delivery, the vagina and perineal body are sufficiently relaxed to permit passage of the infant. Because the blood flow to the vagina is increased, it may show the same blue-purple color (Chadwick's sign) seen in the cervix.

## ● Breasts

Estrogen and progesterone cause many changes in the mammary glands. The breasts enlarge and become more nodular as the glands increase in size and number in preparation for lactation. Superficial veins become more prominent, the nipples become more erectile, and the areolas darken. Montgomery's follicles enlarge, and striae may develop.

*Colostrum,* an antibody-rich yellow secretion, may leak or be expressed from the breasts during the last trimester. Colostrum gradually converts to mature milk during the first few days after delivery.

## ● Respiratory System

Many respiratory changes occur to meet the increased oxygen requirements of a pregnant woman. Progesterone decreases airway resistance, permitting a 15%–20% increase in oxygen consumption and a 30%–40% increase in the volume of air breathed each minute. The increased respiratory effort and accompanying decrease in $P_{CO_2}$ are also due primarily to the effects of progesterone.

As the uterus enlarges, it presses upward and the diaphragm is elevated. The substernal angle increases so that the rib cage flares. The anteroposterior diameter increases, and the chest circumference expands by as much as 6 cm; for this reason, there is no significant loss of intrathoracic volume. Breathing changes from abdominal to thoracic as pregnancy progresses, and descent of the diaphragm on inspiration becomes less possible. The respiratory rate may increase slightly, and some hyperventilation may occur.

## ● Cardiovascular System

During pregnancy, the blood flow increases to those organ systems with an increased work load. Thus, blood flow to the uterus and kidneys is increased, while hepatic and cerebral flow remains unchanged.

The pulse may increase by as many as 10–15 beats/min at term. The blood pressure decreases slightly during pregnancy, and reaches its lowest point during the second trimester. It gradually increases to near prepregnant levels during the third trimester.

The enlarged uterus may press on pelvic and femoral vessels, interfering with the returning blood flow and causing stagnation of blood in the lower extremities. This condition may lead to dependent edema and varicosity of the veins in the legs, vulva, and rectum (hemorrhoids) in late pregnancy. This increased blood volume in the lower legs may also make the pregnant woman more prone to postural hypotension.

The enlarging uterus may press on the vena cava when the pregnant woman lies supine, thus reducing blood flow to the right atrium, lowering blood pressure and causing dizziness, pallor, and clamminess. This is called the *supine hypotensive syndrome* (Figure 6.1) or the **vena caval syndrome**, and can be corrected by having the woman lie on her left side.

Blood volume progressively increases beginning in the first trimester, increasing rapidly in the second trimester, and slowing in the third. It peaks in the middle of the third trimester at 30%–50% above the prepregnant level.

The red blood cell count and hemoglobin levels increase during pregnancy. However, because the plasma volume increases more, the hematocrit decreases an average of 7%. This results in the *physiologic anemia of pregnancy (pseudoanemia).*

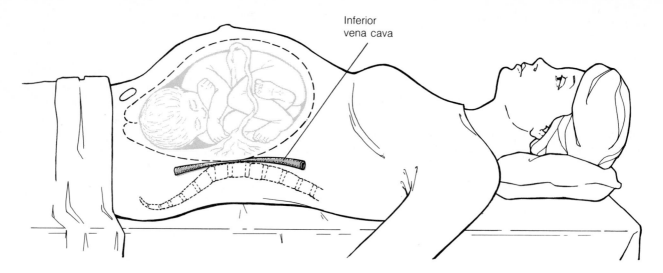

*Figure 6.1    Vena caval syndrome. The gravid uterus compresses the vena cava when the woman is supine. This reduces the blood flow returning to the heart and may cause maternal hypotension.*

Iron is necessary for hemoglobin formation, and hemoglobin is the oxygen-carrying component of erythrocytes. Thus the increase in erythrocyte levels results in an increased need for iron by the pregnant woman. Even though the gastrointestinal absorption of iron is moderately increased during pregnancy, it is usually necessary to add supplemental iron to the diet to meet the expanded red blood cell and fetal needs. This iron supplement, while necessary, may add to the tendency to develop constipation during pregnancy.

Leukocyte production increases slightly to an average of 10,000–11,000/mm³. During labor, these levels may reach 25,000/mm³.

Both the fibrin and plasma fibrinogen levels increase during pregnancy. Although the blood-clotting time of the pregnant woman does not differ significantly from that of the nonpregnant woman, clotting factors VII, IX, and X increase; thus, pregnancy is a somewhat hypercoagulable state. These changes, coupled with venous stasis in late pregnancy, increase the pregnant woman's risk of developing venous thrombosis.

● *Gastrointestinal System*

Nausea and vomiting are common during the first trimester because of elevated human chorionic gonadotropin (hCG) levels and changed carbohydrate metabolism. Gum tissue may soften and bleed easily. The secretion of saliva may increase and even become excessive (*ptyalism*). Gastric acidity also decreases.

Elevated progesterone levels cause smooth muscle relaxation, resulting in delayed gastric emptying and decreased peristalsis. As a result, the pregnant woman may complain of bloating and constipation. These symptoms

are aggravated as the enlarging uterus displaces the stomach superiorly and the intestines laterally and posteriorly. The cardiac sphincter also relaxes, and heartburn (*pyrosis*) may occur due to reflux of acidic secretions into the lower esophagus.

Hemorrhoids frequently develop in late pregnancy from constipation and from pressure on vessels below the level of the uterus.

Only minor liver changes occur with pregnancy. Plasma albumin concentrations and serum cholinesterase activity decrease with normal pregnancy as with certain liver diseases.

The emptying time of the gallbladder is prolonged during pregnancy as a result of smooth muscle relaxation from progesterone. This, coupled with the elevated levels of cholesterol in the bile, can predispose the woman to gallstone formation.

● *Urinary Tract*

During the first trimester, the enlarging uterus is still a pelvic organ and presses against the bladder, producing urinary frequency. This symptom decreases during the second trimester when the uterus is an abdominal organ. Frequency reappears during the third trimester, when the presenting part descends into the pelvis and again presses on the bladder, reducing bladder capacity, contributing to hyperemia, and irritating the bladder.

The ureters (especially the right ureter) elongate and dilate above the pelvic brim. The glomerular filtration rate (GFR) rises by as much as 50% beginning in the second trimester and remains elevated until delivery. To compensate for this, renal tubular reabsorption also increases. However, glycosuria is sometimes seen during pregnancy because of the kidneys' inability to reabsorb all the glucose filtered by the glomeruli. This may be normal or may indicate gestational diabetes, so glycosuria always warrants further testing.

## ● *Skin*

Changes in skin pigmentation commonly occur during pregnancy. They are thought to be stimulated by elevated levels of melanocyte-stimulating hormone, which may be caused by increased estrogen and progesterone levels. Pigmentation of the skin increases primarily in areas that are already hyperpigmented: the areola, the nipples, the vulva, and the perianal area. The skin in the middle of the abdomen may develop a pigmented line, the **linea nigra**. Facial **chloasma** (also known as the mask of pregnancy), a darkening of the skin over the forehead and around the eyes, may develop. Chloasma is more prominent in dark-haired women and is aggravated by exposure to the sun. Fortunately, chloasma fades or becomes less prominent soon after delivery when the hormonal influence of pregnancy subsides.

**Striae**, reddish, irregular streaks, may appear on the abdomen, thighs, buttocks, and breasts. Commonly called "stretch marks," they result from reduced connective tissue strength due to elevated adrenal steroid levels. In addition, the sweat and sebaceous glands are often hyperactive during pregnancy.

Vascular spider nevi, small, bright-red elevations of the skin radiating from a central body, may develop on the chest, neck, face, arms, and legs. They may be caused by increased subcutaneous blood flow in response to elevated estrogen levels.

The rate of hair growth may be decreased during pregnancy and the number of hair follicles in the resting or dormant phase is also decreased. After delivery the number of hair follicles in the resting phase increases sharply and the woman may notice increased hair shedding for three to four months. Practically all hair is replaced within six to nine months, however (Key and Resnik 1986).

## ● *Skeletal System*

No demonstrable changes occur in the teeth of pregnant women. The dental caries that sometimes accompany pregnancy are probably caused by the fact that saliva is slightly more acidic during pregnancy and by inadequate oral hygiene, especially if the woman has problems with bleeding gums.

The joints of the pelvis relax somewhat due to hormonal influences. The result is often a waddling gait. As the pregnant woman's center of gravity gradually changes, the lumbar spinal curve is accentuated, and the posture changes (see Figure 6.2). This posture change compensates for the increased weight of the uterus anteriorly and frequently results in low backache.

## ● *Metabolism*

Most metabolic functions increase during pregnancy because of the increased demands of the growing fetus and its support system. The expectant mother must meet her

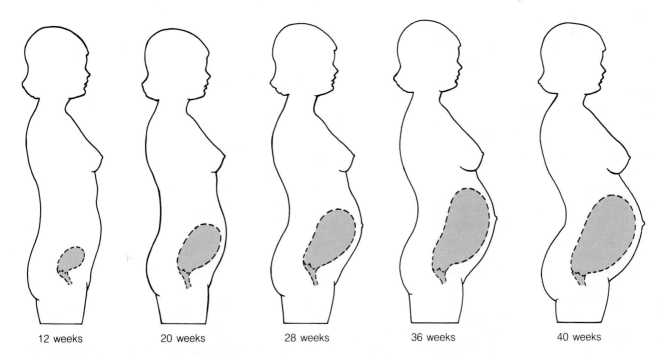

|                |          |          |          |          |
|----------------|----------|----------|----------|----------|
| 12 weeks       | 20 weeks | 28 weeks | 36 weeks | 40 weeks |

*Figure 6.2  Postural changes during pregnancy*

own tissue replacement needs and those of her unborn child. In addition, her body must anticipate the needs of labor and lactation.

For a detailed discussion of nutrient, vitamin, and mineral metabolism, see Chapter 10.

### WEIGHT GAIN

The average weight gain during a normal pregnancy is 25–30 lb (11–13.6 kg). An average increase of 3, 12, and 12 lb (1.4, 5.5, and 5.5 kg) occurs in the first, second, and third trimesters, respectively. The total weight gain may be accounted for as follows: fetus, 7.5 lb (3.4 kg); placenta and membranes, 1.5 lb (0.7 kg); amniotic fluid, 2 lb (0.9 kg); uterus, 2.5 lb (1.1 kg); breasts, 3 lb (1.4 kg); and increased blood volume, 2–4 lb (0.9–1.8 kg). The remaining 4–9 lb (1.8–4.1 kg) is extravascular fluid and fat reserves.

### WATER METABOLISM

Increased water retention is a basic alteration of pregnancy. Several interrelated factors cause this phenomenon. The increased level of steroid sex hormones affects sodium and fluid retention. The lowered serum protein also influences the fluid balance, as do the increased intracapillary pressure and permeability. The extra water is due to the products of conception—the fetus, placenta, and amniotic fluid—and the mother's increased blood volume, interstitial fluids, and enlarged organs.

### NUTRIENT METABOLISM

The fetus makes its greatest protein and fat demands during the second half of pregnancy, and doubles in weight during the last six to eight weeks. Protein must be stored during pregnancy to maintain a constant level within the breast milk and to avoid depletion of maternal tissues. Carbohydrate needs also increase, especially during the second and third trimesters.

Fats are more completely absorbed during pregnancy and the level of free fatty acids increases in response to human placental lactogen (hPL). The levels of lipoproteins and cholesterol also increase. Because of these changes increased levels of dietary fat or reduced carbohydrate production may lead to ketonuria in the pregnant woman.

The possibility of diabetes must not be overlooked during pregnancy. Plasma levels of insulin are increased during pregnancy, and rapid destruction of insulin takes place within the placenta. Insulin production must be increased by the mother, and any marginal pancreatic function quickly becomes apparent. The diabetic woman often experiences increased exogenous insulin demands during pregnancy.

## ● Endocrine System

### THYROID

The thyroid gland often enlarges slightly during pregnancy. Its capacity to bind thyroxine is greater, resulting in an increase in serum protein-bound iodine (PBI). These changes are due to higher blood levels of estrogen.

The basal metabolic rate increases by 25% in late pregnancy. However, within a few weeks after delivery, all thyroid function returns to normal limits.

### PITUITARY

Pregnancy is made possible by the hypothalamic stimulation of the anterior pituitary gland, which in turn produces the hormones follicle-stimulating hormone (FSH), which stimulates ova growth, and luteinizing hormone (LH), which brings about ovulation. Stimulation of the pituitary also prolongs the ovary's corpus luteal phase, which maintains the endometrium for development of the pregnancy. Prolactin, another anterior pituitary hormone, is responsible for initial lactation.

The posterior portion of the pituitary secretes oxytocin. Oxytocin promotes uterine contractility and stimulates ejection of milk from the breasts (the *let-down reflex*) in the postpartum period.

### ADRENALS

The adrenal cortex enlarges during pregnancy in response to high estrogen levels. Circulating cortisol, which regulates carbohydrate and protein metabolism, increases. Cortisol blood levels return to normal one to six weeks postpartum.

The adrenals secrete increased levels of aldosterone by the early part of the second trimester. This increase in aldosterone in a normal pregnancy may be the body's protective response to the increased sodium excretion associated with progesterone (Pritchard et al 1985).

### PANCREAS

The pregnant woman has increased insulin needs, and the islets of Langerhans, which secrete insulin, are stressed. Thus a latent deficiency state may become apparent, and the woman may show signs of gestational diabetes.

## ● Placental Hormones

### HUMAN CHORIONIC GONADOTROPIN (hCG)

The trophoblast secretes hCG in early pregnancy. hCG stimulates progesterone and estrogen production by the corpus luteum to maintain the pregnancy until the placenta is developed sufficiently to assume that function.

### HUMAN PLACENTAL LACTOGEN (hPL)

Also called human chorionic somatomammotropin, hPL is produced by the syncytiotrophoblast. Human placental lactogen is an antagonist of insulin; it increases the amount of circulating free fatty acids for maternal metabolic needs and decreases maternal metabolism of glucose to favor fetal growth.

### ESTROGEN

Estrogen, secreted originally by the corpus luteum, is produced primarily by the placenta as early as the seventh week of pregnancy. Estrogen stimulates uterine development to provide a suitable environment for the fetus. It also helps to develop the ductal system of the breasts in preparation for lactation.

### PROGESTERONE

Progesterone, also produced initially by the corpus luteum and then by the placenta, plays the greatest role in maintaining pregnancy. It maintains the endometrium and inhibits spontaneous uterine contractility, thus preventing early spontaneous abortion due to uterine activity. Progesterone also helps develop the acini and lobules of the breasts in preparation for lactation.

### RELAXIN

Relaxin is detectable in the serum of a pregnant woman by the time of the first missed menstrual period. Relaxin inhibits uterine activity, diminishes the strength of uterine contractions, aids in the softening of the cervix, and has the long-term effect of remodeling collagen. Its primary source is the corpus luteum, but small amounts are believed to be produced by the placenta and decidua.

## ● Prostaglandins in Pregnancy

Prostaglandins (PGs) are lipid substances that can arise from most body tissues but occur in high concentrations in the female reproductive tract and are present in the decidua during pregnancy. The exact functions of PGs during pregnancy are still unknown, but they play a role in the complex biochemistry that initiates labor.

## ● SUBJECTIVE (PRESUMPTIVE) CHANGES

Many of the changes the pregnant woman experiences during pregnancy are used to diagnose the preg-

## Essential Facts to Remember

### Differentiating the Signs of Pregnancy

These guidelines help differentiate among the presumptive, probable, and positive changes of pregnancy:

**Subjective (Presumptive) Changes**

- Symptoms the woman experiences and reports
- May have causes other than pregnancy

**Objective (Probable) Changes**

- Signs perceived by the examiner
- May have causes other than pregnancy

**Diagnostic (Positive) Changes**

- Signs perceived by the examiner
- Can be caused only by pregnancy

nancy itself. They are called the *subjective* or *presumptive* changes, the *objective* or *probable* changes, and the *diagnostic* or *positive* changes of pregnancy. The guidelines for differentiating among these three are identified in Essential Facts to Remember—Differentiating the Signs of Pregnancy.

The subjective changes of pregnancy are the symptoms the woman experiences and reports. Because they can be caused by other conditions, they cannot be considered proof of pregnancy (Table 6.1). The following subjective signs can be diagnostic clues when other signs and symptoms of pregnancy are also present.

*Amenorrhea,* or the absence of menses, is the earliest symptom of pregnancy. The missing of more than one menstrual period, especially in a woman whose cycle is ordinarily regular, is an especially useful diagnostic clue.

*Nausea and vomiting* occur frequently during the first three months of pregnancy. Because these symptoms often occur in the early part of the day, they are commonly referred to as *morning sickness.* In reality, the symptoms may occur at any time and can range from merely a distaste for food to severe vomiting. Recent research suggests that women who vomit in early pregnancy have a decreased incidence of spontaneous abortion, stillbirth, or premature labor (Klebanoff et al 1985).

*Excessive fatigue* may be noted within a few weeks after the first missed menstrual period and may persist throughout the first trimester.

*Urinary frequency* is experienced during the first trimester as the enlarging uterus presses on the bladder.

*Changes in the breasts* are frequently noted in early pregnancy. These changes include tenderness and tingling

## Table 6.1 Differential Diagnosis of Pregnancy—Subjective Changes

| Subjective changes | Possible causes |
|---|---|
| Amenorrhea | Endocrine factors: early menopause; lactation; thyroid, pituitary, adrenal, ovarian dysfunction<br>Metabolic factors: malnutrition, anemia, climatic changes, diabetes mellitus, degenerative disorders<br>Psychologic factors: emotional shock, fear of pregnancy or venereal disease, intense desire for pregnancy (pseudocyesis)<br>Obliteration of endometrial cavity by infection or curettage<br>Systemic disease (acute or chronic), such as tuberculosis or malignancy |
| Nausea and vomiting | Gastrointestinal disorders<br>Acute infections such as encephalitis<br>Emotional disorders such as pseudocyesis or anorexia nervosa |
| Urinary frequency | Urinary tract infection<br>Cystocele<br>Pelvic tumors<br>Urethral diverticula<br>Emotional tension |
| Breast tenderness | Premenstrual tension<br>Chronic cystic mastitis<br>Pseudocyesis<br>Elevated estrogen levels |
| Quickening | Increased peristalsis<br>Flatus ("gas")<br>Abdominal muscle contractions<br>Shifting of abdominal contents |

sensations, increased pigmentation of the areola and nipple, and changes in Montgomery's glands.

*Quickening,* or the mother's perception of fetal movement, occurs about 18–20 weeks after the **last menstrual period (LMP).** Quickening is a fluttering sensation in the abdomen that gradually increases in intensity and frequency.

## ● OBJECTIVE (PROBABLE) CHANGES

An examiner can perceive the objective changes that occur in pregnancy. However, since these changes also can have other causes, they do not confirm pregnancy (see Table 6.2).

Changes in the pelvic organs—the only physical changes detectable during the first three months of pregnancy—are caused by increased vascular congestion. These changes are noted on pelvic examination. There is a softening of the cervix called **Goodell's sign. Chadwick's sign** is a bluish or deep red discoloration of the mucous membranes of the cervix, vagina, and vulva (some sources consider this a presumptive sign). **Hegar's sign** is a softening of the isthmus of the uterus, the area between the cervix and the body of the uterus (Figure 6.3). **McDonald's sign** is an ease in flexing the body of the uterus against the cervix.

General enlargement and softening of the body of the uterus can be noted after the eighth week of pregnancy. The fundus of the uterus is palpable just above the symphysis pubis at about 10–12 weeks' gestation and at the level of the umbilicus at 20–22 weeks' gestation (Figure 6.4).

*Enlargement of the abdomen* during the childbearing years is usually regarded as evidence of pregnancy, especially if it is continuous and accompanied by amenorrhea.

*Braxton Hicks* contractions are painless uterine contractions that occur at irregular intervals throughout pregnancy but can be felt most commonly after the twenty-eighth week.

## Table 6.2 Differential Diagnosis of Pregnancy—Objective Changes

| Objective changes | Possible causes |
|---|---|
| Changes in pelvic organs<br>  Goodell's sign | Increased vascular congestion<br>Estrogen-progestin oral contraceptives |
|   Chadwick's sign | Vulvar, vaginal, cervical hyperemia |
|   Hegar's sign | Excessively soft walls of nonpregnant uterus |
|   Uterine enlargement | Uterine tumors |
| Enlargement of abdomen | Obesity, ascites, pelvic tumors |
| Braxton Hicks contractions | Hematometra; pedunculated, submucous, and soft myomas |
| Uterine souffle | Large uterine myomas, large ovarian tumors, or any condition with greatly increased uterine blood flow |
| Pigmentation of skin<br>  Chloasma<br>  Linea nigra<br>  Nipples/areola | Estrogen-progestin oral contraceptives<br>Melanocyte hormonal stimulation |
| Abdominal striae | Obesity, pelvic tumor |
| Ballottement | Uterine tumors/polyps, ascites |
| Pregnancy tests | Increased pituitary gonadotropins at menopause, choriocarcinoma, hydatidiform mole |
| Palpation for fetal outline | Uterine myomas |

*Uterine souffle* may be heard when the examiner auscultates the abdomen over the uterus. This souffle is a soft, blowing sound that occurs at the same rate as the maternal pulse and is due to the increased uterine blood flow and blood pulsating through the placenta.

*Changes in pigmentation of the skin* are common in pregnancy. The nipples and areola may darken, and the linea nigra may develop. Facial chloasma may become noticeable and striae may appear.

The *fetal outline* may be identified by palpation in many pregnant women after 24 weeks' gestation.

*Ballottement* is the fetal movement elicited when the examiner taps the cervix with two fingers. This pushes the fetal body up, and a rebound is felt as it falls back.

*Pregnancy tests* detect the presence of hCG in the maternal blood or urine. These are not considered a positive sign of pregnancy because other conditions can cause elevated hCG levels.

## ● Pregnancy Tests

Historically, most pregnancy tests were bioassays that used laboratory animals. These tests were time consuming and subject to error. Consequently, they are seldom used and have been replaced by immunoassays and radioreceptor assay tests.

*Immunoassay tests* are based on the antigenic properties of hCG. There are three types of tests. In the *hemagglutination-inhibition test (Pregnosticon R)* no clumping of cells occurs when the urine of a pregnant woman is added to the hCG-sensitized red blood cells of sheep. In the *latex agglutination tests (Gravidex and Pregnosticon Slide tests)*, latex particle agglutination is inhibited in the presence of urine containing hCG. Both these tests are done on the first early morning urine specimen of the woman because it is adequately concentrated. The tests become positive within 10 to 14 days after the first missed period.

The third test, the *β subunit radioimmunoassay or RIA,* uses an antiserum with specificity for the β subunit of hCG in maternal blood. This is the most accurate pregnancy test. It requires about one hour to complete and becomes positive a few days after presumed implantation, thereby permitting earlier diagnosis of pregnancy. This test is also used in the diagnosis of ectopic pregnancy or trophoblastic disease.

*Radioreceptor assay* (Biocept-G) uses radio-iodine-labeled hCG. It is a sensitive test and can be quickly performed in one hour, but because it fails to distinguish between hCG and LH, cross-reactions may occur.

### OVER-THE-COUNTER PREGNANCY TESTS

Over-the-counter pregnancy tests are available at a reasonable cost. These tests, performed on urine, use the hemagglutination-inhibition principle or the β subunit anti-

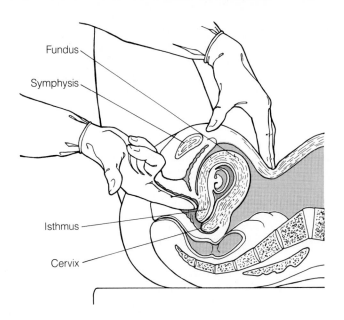

*Figure 6.3   Hegar's sign*

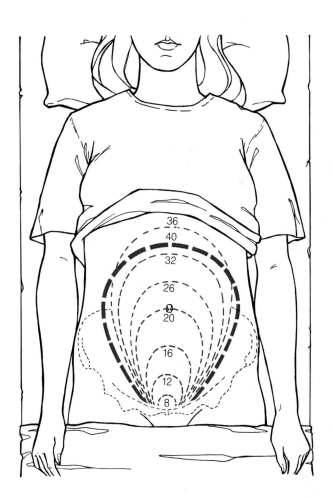

*Figure 6.4   Approximate height of the fundus at various weeks of pregnancy*

body principle. False results may occur if a test is performed too soon after a missed period or if the specimen used was not the first morning urine. Other factors that may contribute to a false reading include using a dirty kit or a kit containing traces of soap or detergent, exposing the sample to heat or sunlight, allowing the sample to stand longer than the specified time, or moving the test-tube sample during the timing period. The tests vary in the amount of time elapsing before they can detect a pregnancy, ranging from three to nine days after the missed expected menstrual period.

## ● *DIAGNOSTIC (POSITIVE) CHANGES*

A sign of pregnancy is positive if it proves conclusively that a woman is pregnant, but such signs are usually not present until after the fourth month of gestation.

The *fetal heartbeat* can be detected with a fetoscope by approximately weeks 17–20 of pregnancy. The electronic Doppler device allows the examiner to detect the fetal heartbeat as early as weeks 10–12 of pregnancy.

*Fetal movement* is actively palpable by a trained examiner after the eighteenth week of pregnancy.

*Visualization of the fetus by ultrasound or x-ray* examination confirms a pregnancy. Ultrasound may be used as early as the sixth week of pregnancy for a positive diagnosis. Fetal movement can be detected with real-time ultrasound methods by 12 weeks' gestation. Radiologic examination can show a fetal skeleton by week 16 of gestation but is not used to diagnose pregnancy because of the possibility of causing gonadal damage and genetic abnormalities. See Chapter 13 for further discussion of ultrasound.

## ● *PSYCHOLOGIC RESPONSE OF THE EXPECTANT FAMILY TO PREGNANCY*

Pregnancy is a developmental challenge, a turning point, in a family's life and therefore is accompanied by stress and anxiety whether the pregnancy is desired or not. Pregnancy confirms one's biologic capabilities to reproduce. It is evidence of one's participation in sexual activity and as such is an affirmation of one's sexuality. For beginning families pregnancy is the transition period from childlessness to parenthood. If the pregnancy results in the birth of a child, the couple enters a new stage of their life together, one that is irreversible and characterized by awesome responsibilities.

The expectant couple may be unaware of the physical, emotional, and cognitive changes of pregnancy and may anticipate no problems from such a normal event. Thus, they may be confused and distressed by feelings and behaviors that are essentially normal.

Parenthood brings significant role changes for the couple. Career goals and mobility may be affected, and the couple's relationship takes on new meanings to themselves and within their families and community. Routines and family dynamics are altered with each pregnancy, and require readjustment and realignment.

The couple must make decisions about financial matters—whether the woman will work during her pregnancy, and whether she will return to work after her child is born. They may also need to decide about the division of domestic tasks. Any differences of opinion must be discussed openly and resolved so that the family can meet the needs of its members.

The couple must face the anxieties of labor and delivery and must also deal with fears that the baby may be ill or disfigured. Classes in prepared childbirth can help the couple overcome concerns that are based on misinformation or lack of information.

Even if the pregnant woman has no stable partner or plans to place the infant for adoption, she must deal with the role changes, fears, and adjustments of pregnancy. She is no longer a separate individual; she must consider the needs of another being who depends on her totally, at least during pregnancy.

Pregnancy can be viewed as a developmental stage with its own distinct developmental tasks. Pregnancy can be a time of support or conflict for a couple, depending on the amount of adjustment each is willing to make to maintain the family's equilibrium.

During a first pregnancy the couple plans together for the child's arrival, collecting information on how to be parents. At the same time each continues to participate in some separate activities with friends or family members. The availability of social support is an important factor in psychosocial well-being during pregnancy. For example, Cronenwett (1985) found that availability of emotional and material support (financial assistance, gifts, help with housework, etc) is associated with positive postpartum outcomes for couples. During this time relatives tend to dominate a couple's social network. While men derive most emotional support from relatives, women derive somewhat less support from relatives and somewhat more support from friends (Cronenwett 1985).

Although individual activities are important, some conflict may arise if the couple's activities become too divergent. Thus they may find it necessary to limit their outside associations.

During pregnancy the expectant mother and father both face significant changes and must deal with major psychosocial adjustments (Table 6.3). Other family members, especially the couple's other children and the grandparents-to-be, must also adjust to the pregnancy.

For some couples pregnancy is more than a developmental stage; it is a crisis. *Crisis* can be defined as a disturbance or conflict in which the individual cannot maintain a state of equilibrium.

## Table 6.3  Parental Reactions to Pregnancy

| First trimester | | Second trimester (*continued*) | |
| --- | --- | --- | --- |
| MOTHER'S REACTIONS | FATHER'S REACTIONS | MOTHER'S REACTIONS | FATHER'S REACTIONS |
| Informs father secretively or openly. | Differ according to age, parity, desire for child, economic stability. | Remains regressive and introspective; all problems with authority figures projected onto partner; may become angry as if lack of interest is sign of weakness in him. | If he can cope, will give her extra attention she needs; if he cannot cope, will develop a new time-consuming interest outside of home. |
| Feels ambivalent toward pregnancy; anxious about labor and responsibility of child. | Acceptance of pregnant woman's attitude or complete rejection and lack of communication. | Continues to deal with feelings as a mother and looks for furniture as something concrete. | May develop a creative feeling and a "closeness to nature." |
| Is aware of physical changes; daydreams of possible miscarriage. | Is aware of his own sexual feelings; may develop more or less sexual arousal. | May have other extreme of anxiety and wait until ninth month to look for furniture and clothes for baby. | May become involved in pregnancy and buy or make furniture. |
| Develops special feelings for, renewed interest in mother, with formation of own mother identity. | Accepts, rejects, or resents mother-in-law. | | |
| | May develop new hobby outside of family as sign of stress. | | |
| **Second trimester** | | **Third trimester** | |
| MOTHER'S REACTIONS | FATHER'S REACTIONS | MOTHER'S REACTIONS | FATHER'S REACTIONS |
| Feels movement and is aware of fetus and incorporates it into herself. | Feels for movement of baby, listens to heartbeat, or remains aloof, with no physical contact. | Experiences more anxiety and tension, with physical awkwardness. | Adapts to alternative methods of sexual contact. |
| Dreams that partner will be killed, telephones him often for reassurance. | May have fears and fantasies about himself being pregnant; may become uneasy with this feminine aspect in himself. | Feels much discomfort and insomnia from physical condition. | Becomes concerned over financial responsibility |
| Experiences more distinct physical changes; sexual desires may increase or decrease. | May react negatively if partner is too demanding; may become jealous of physician and of his/her importance to partner and her pregnancy. | Prepares for delivery, assembles layette, picks out names. | May show new sense of tenderness and concern; treats partner like doll. |
| | | Dreams often about misplacing baby or not being able to deliver it; fears birth of deformed baby. | Daydreams about child as if older and not newborn; dreams of losing partner. |
| | | Feels ecstasy and excitement; has spurt of energy during last month. | Renewed sexual attraction to partner. |
| | | | Feels he is ultimately responsible for whatever happens. |

Pregnancy can be considered a *maturational crisis,* since it is a common event in the normal growth and development of the family. During such a crisis, the individual or family is in disequilibrium. Egos weaken, usual defense mechanisms are not effective, unresolved material from the past reappears, and relationships shift. The period of disequilibrium and disorganization is marked by unsuccessful attempts to solve the perceived problems. If the crisis is not resolved, it will result in maladaptive behaviors in one or more family members, and possible disintegration of the family. Families who are able to resolve a maturational crisis successfully will return to normal functioning and can even strengthen the bonds in the family relationship.

## ● The Mother

Pregnancy is a condition that alters body image and also necessitates a reordering of social relationships and changes in roles of family members. The way a particular woman meets the stresses of pregnancy is influenced by her emotional makeup, her sociologic and cultural background, and her acceptance or rejection of the pregnancy. Many women manifest similar psychologic and emotional responses during pregnancy, including ambivalence, acceptance, introversion, mood swings, and changes in body image.

Initially, even if the pregnancy is planned, there is an element of surprise. Many women commonly experience feelings of ambivalence during early pregnancy. This may be related to a feeling that the timing is somehow wrong, the need to modify existing relationships or career plans, fears about assuming a new role, unresolved emotional conflicts with one's own mother, and fears about pregnancy, labor, and delivery. These feelings may be more pronounced if the pregnancy is unplanned or unwanted. Indirect evidence of ambivalence includes complaints about depression, physical discomfort, and feeling "ugly" and unattractive (Lederman 1984).

Pregnancy produces marked changes in a woman's body within a relatively short period of time. Women perceive that they require more body space as pregnancy progresses (Fawcett el al 1986). They also experience changes in body image. The degree of this change is related to a certain extent to personality factors, social network responses, and attitudes toward pregnancy. However, research suggests that women tend to feel somewhat negative about their bodies by the third trimester of pregnancy (Strang and Sullivan 1985).

## FIRST TRIMESTER

During the first trimester, feelings of disbelief and ambivalence are paramount. The woman's baby does not seem real to her, and she focuses on herself and her pregnancy (Rubin 1984). She may experience early symptoms of pregnancy, such as breast tenderness or morning sickness, which are unsettling and at times unpleasant.

During the first trimester, the expectant mother begins to exhibit some characteristic behavioral changes. She becomes increasingly introspective and passive. She is also emotionally labile, with characteristic mood swings from joy to despair and tears. She may also fantasize about a miscarriage and feel guilt because of these fantasies.

## SECOND TRIMESTER

During the second trimester, quickening occurs. This perception of fetal movement helps the woman to think of her baby as a separate person, and she generally becomes excited about the pregnancy even if she was not earlier.

The woman becomes increasingly introspective as she evaluates her life, her plans, and her child's future. This introspection helps the woman prepare for her new mothering role. Emotional lability, which may be unsettling to her partner, persists. In some instances, he may react by withdrawing. This is especially distressing to the woman because she needs increased love and affection. Once the couple understands that these behaviors are characteristic of pregnancy, it is easier for the couple to deal with them

effectively, although they will be sources of stress to some extent throughout pregnancy.

As pregnancy becomes more noticeable, the woman's body image changes. She may feel great pride, she may feel embarrassed, she may feel concerned. Generally, women feel best during the second trimester, which is a relatively tranquil time.

## THIRD TRIMESTER

In the third trimester, the woman feels both pride about her pregnancy and anxiety about labor and delivery. Physical discomforts increase, and the woman is eager for the pregnancy to end. She experiences increased fatigue, her body movements are more awkward, and her interest in sexual activity may decrease. Toward the end of this period, there is often a surge of energy as the woman prepares a "nest" for the infant. Many women report bursts of energy during which they vigorously clean and organize their homes.

## • *Psychologic Tasks of the Mother*

Rubin (1984) has identified four major tasks that the pregnant woman undertakes to maintain her intactness and that of her family and at the same time incorporate her new child into the family system. These tasks form the foundation for a mutually gratifying relationship with her infant.

1. *Ensuring safe passage through pregnancy, labor, and birth.* The pregnant woman feels concern for both her unborn child and herself. She seeks competent maternity care to provide a sense of control. She may also seek information from literature, observation of other pregnant women and new mothers, and discussion with others. In the third trimester she becomes more aware of external threats in the environment—a toy on the stairs, the awkwardness of an escalator—that pose a threat to her well-being. She may worry if her partner is late or if she is home alone. Sleep becomes more difficult and she longs for delivery even though it, too, is frightening.

2. *Seeking acceptance of this child by others.* The birth of a child alters a woman's primary support group (her family) and her secondary affiliative groups. The woman slowly and subtly alters her network to meet the needs of her pregnancy. In this adjustment the woman's partner is the most important figure. His support and acceptance help her form a maternal identity. If there are other children in the home the mother also works to ensure their acceptance of the coming child. Acceptance of the anticipated change is sometimes stressful and the woman may work to maintain some special time with her partner or older child.

3. *Seeking commitment and acceptance of self as mother to the infant (binding-in).* During the first trimester the child remains a rather abstract concept. With quickening, however, the child begins to become a real person, and the mother begins to develop bonds of attachment. The mother experiences the movement of the child within her in an intimate exclusive way, and out of this experience bonds of love form. The mother develops a fantasy image of her ideal child. This possessive love increases her maternal commitment to protect her fetus now and her child after he or she is born.

4. *Learning to give of oneself on behalf of one's child.* Childbirth involves many acts of giving. The man "gives" a child to the woman; she in turn "gives" a child to the man. Life is given to an infant; a sibling is given to older children of the family. The woman begins to develop a capacity for self-denial and learns to delay immediate personal gratification to meet the needs of another. Baby showers and baby gifts are acts of giving that help the mother's self-esteem while also helping her acknowledge the separateness and needs of the coming baby.

Accomplishment of these tasks helps the expectant woman develop her self-concept as mother. Often the expectant mother turns to her own mother during pregnancy because her mother is a source of information and can serve as a role model (Lederman 1984). A woman's self-concept as mother expands with actual experience and continues to grow through subsequent childbearing and childrearing. Occasionally a woman never accepts the mother role but plays the role of babysitter or older sister.

## ● *The Father*

For the expectant father, pregnancy is a psychologically stressful time because he, too, must adjust to a new child. Initially, expectant fathers may feel pride in their virility, which pregnancy confirms, but may also have many of the same ambivalent feelings expectant mothers have. The extent of ambivalence depends on many factors, including the father's relationship with his partner, previous experience with pregnancy, and his age and economic stability. Another important factor is whether the pregnancy was planned.

The expectant father must establish a fatherhood role just as the woman develops a concept of herself as mother. Fathers who are most successful at this generally like children, are excited about the prospect of fatherhood, are eager to nurture a child, and have confidence in their ability to be a parent. They also share the experiences of pregnancy and delivery with their partners (Lederman 1984).

## FIRST TRIMESTER

After the initial excitement attending the announcement of the pregnancy, an expectant father may begin to feel left out. He may be confused by his partner's mood changes. He may resent the attention she receives and her need to modify their relationship as she experiences fatigue and possibly a decreased interest in sex. In addition, he is concerned about what kind of father he will be.

Some expectant fathers experience **mitleiden**, developing symptoms similar to those of the pregnant woman: weight gain, nausea, and various aches and pains. Strickland (1987) found that more symptoms were experienced by men who were black, who were working class, or who reported that the pregnancy was not planned. As pregnancy progressed white men tended to experience more symptoms, while black men experienced fewer. The exact cause of this phenomenon is not known.

## SECOND TRIMESTER

The father's role in the pregnancy is still vague in the second trimester, but his involvement may increase by watching and feeling fetal movement and by listening to the fetal heartbeat during a visit to the nurse or physician.

Like expectant mothers, expectant fathers need to confront and resolve some of their conflicts about the fathering they received. A father needs to sort out which behaviors of his own father he wants to imitate and which he does not.

Evidence suggests that anxiety in the father-to-be during pregnancy is lessened if both parents agree on the paternal role the man is to assume. For example, if both see his role as that of breadwinner, the man's stress is low. If the man views his role as that of breadwinner, however, and the woman expects him to be involved actively in child care, his stress increases (Fishbein 1984).

As the woman's appearance begins to change, her partner may have several reactions. Her changed appearance may decrease his sexual interest, or it may have the opposite effect. Because of the variety of emotions both partners may feel, continued communication and acceptance are important.

## THIRD TRIMESTER

If the couple's relationship has grown through effective communication of their concerns and feelings, the third trimester is a special and rewarding time. They may attend childbirth classes and make concrete preparations for the arrival of the baby. If the father has developed a detached attitude about the pregnancy prior to this time, it is unlikely he will become a willing participant, even though his role becomes more obvious.

Concerns and fears may recur. The father may worry about hurting the unborn baby during intercourse or become concerned about labor and delivery. Also, he may wonder what kind of parents he and his partner will be or may worry about financial stability.

## ● Couvade

The term **couvade** refers to the observance of certain rituals and taboos by the male to signify the transition to fatherhood. This affirms his psychosocial and biophysical relationship to the woman and child. Some taboos restrict his actions. For example, in some cultures or primitive groups he may be forbidden to eat certain foods, kill certain animals, or carry certain weapons prior to and immediately after the birth.

A father who observes couvade plays an active and vital role during labor. In one culture, the father writhes, cries out in agony, and is attended by others to draw the attention of evil spirits while his partner delivers quietly alone or with one attendant, safe from the harmful spirits.

## ● Siblings

Bringing a new baby home usually marks the beginning of sibling rivalry. The siblings view the baby as a threat to the security of their relationships with their parents. Parents who recognize this potential problem early in pregnancy and begin constructive actions can help minimize the problem of sibling rivalry.

Preparation of the young child begins several weeks prior to the anticipated birth. Because they do not have a clear concept of time, young children should not be told too early about the pregnancy. The mother may let the child feel the baby moving in her uterus, explaining that the uterus is "a special place where babies grow." The child can help the parents put the baby clothes in drawers or prepare the nursery.

The concept of consistency is important in dealing with young children. They need reassurance that certain people, special things, and familiar places will continue to exist after the new baby arrives. The crib is an important though transient object in a child's life. If it is to be given to the new baby the parents should thoughtfully help the child adjust to this change (Honig 1986). Any move from crib to bed or from one room to another should precede the baby's birth.

If the child is ready, toilet training is most effective several months before or after the baby's arrival. It is not unusual for the older, toilet-trained child to regress to wetting or soiling due to the attention the newborn gets for such behavior. The older, weaned child may want to nurse or drink from the bottle again after the baby comes. If the new mother anticipates these behaviors, they will be less frustrating during her early postpartum days.

Pregnant women may find it helpful to bring their children to a prenatal visit to the nurse or physician. The children may become involved in the prenatal care and are

*Figure 6.5   Children respond positively when they hear the heartbeat of their sibling-to-be.*

also given an opportunity to listen to the fetal heartbeat. These activities help make the baby more real to them (Figure 6.5).

If siblings are school-age children, pregnancy should be viewed as a family affair. Teaching should be appropriate to the child's level of understanding and may be supplemented with appropriate books. Taking part in family discussions, attending sibling preparation classes, feeling fetal movement, and listening to the fetal heartbeat help the school-age child take part in the experience of pregnancy and not feel like an outsider.

The older child or adolescent may appear to have sophisticated knowledge but in reality may have many misconceptions. Thus, opportunities should be provided for discussion and participation.

Even after birth, siblings need to feel that they are taking part. Permitting siblings to visit their mother and the new baby at the hospital helps this process. After the baby comes home, siblings can share in "showing off" the new baby.

Sibling preparation is essential, but other factors are equally important. These include how much parental attention the new arrival receives, how much attention the older child receives after the baby comes home, and how well the parents handle regressive or aggressive behavior.

For further information about sibling preparation, see Chapter 8.

## ● Grandparents

The first relatives told about a pregnancy are usually the grandparents. Often, the expectant grandparents become increasingly supportive of the couple, even if conflicts previously existed. But it can be difficult for even sensitive grandparents to know how deeply to become involved in the childrearing process.

Younger grandparents leading active lives may not demonstrate as much interest as the young couple would like. In other cases, expectant grandparents may give advice and gifts unsparingly. For grandparents, conflict may be related to the expectant couple's need to feel in control of their own lives, or it may stem from events signalling changing roles in their own lives (for example, retirement, financial concerns, menopause, death of a friend). Some parents of expectant couples may already be grandparents with a developed style of grandparenting. This fact influences their response to the pregnancy.

Because childbearing and childrearing practices have changed, family cohesiveness is promoted by frank discussion between young couples and interested grandparents about the changes and the reasons for them. Effective communication between new parents and grandparents is important. Clarifying the role of the helping grandparent ensures a comfortable situation for all.

In some areas classes are available to provide information for grandparents about changes in birth and parenting practices. These classes help familiarize grandparents with new parents' needs and may offer suggestions for ways in which the grandparents can support the childbearing couple (Horn and Manion 1985).

## ● *CULTURAL VALUES AND REPRODUCTIVE BEHAVIOR*

A universal tendency exists to create ceremonial rituals and rites around important life events. Thus pregnancy, childbirth, marriage, and death are often tied to ritual. Scott and Stern (1985) suggest that ritual is passed from one generation to another in three ways:

● *Formal teaching* such as childbirth preparation classes

● *Informal teaching* through role modeling or observation

● *Folktales or stories of advice or warning,* often passed on by the mother or grandmother of the family

The rituals, customs, and practices of a group are a reflection of the group's values. Thus the identification of cultural values is useful in predicting reactions to pregnancy. An understanding of male and female roles, family life-styles, or the meaning of children in a culture may explain reactions of joy or shame. Pregnancy is a joyful event in a culture that values children. In some cultures pregnancy is a shameful event if it occurs outside of marriage.

Health values and beliefs are also important in understanding reactions and behavior. Certain behaviors can be expected if a culture views pregnancy as a sickness, whereas other behaviors can be expected if pregnancy is viewed as a natural occurrence. Prenatal care may not be a priority for women who view pregnancy as a natural phenomenon.

Generalization about cultural characteristics or values is difficult because not every individual in a culture may display these characteristics. For example, a third-generation Chinese-American family might have very different values and beliefs because of their exposure to the American culture. For this reason, the nurse needs to supplement a general knowledge of cultural values and practices with a complete assessment of the individual's values and practices.

Blacks usually consider pregnancy as a state of wellness. Mexican Americans view pregnancy as a natural and desirable condition. Most Native American tribes consider pregnancy a normal process. For the Asian woman, pregnancy is a normal and natural process, but it is also a time of anticipation and anxiety (Char 1981).

In all these cultures, children are desired. In fact, children can improve the social standing of the traditional Chinese family. A woman who gives birth, especially to a son, achieves higher status. In Mexican-American society, having children proves the male's virility and is a sign of manliness or *machismo,* a desired trait among Mexican-American men.

## ● *Health Beliefs*

Although many cultures view pregnancy as a natural occurrence, it may also be seen as a time of increased vulnerability. Individuals belonging to groups who believe in evil spirits may take certain protective precautions. For example, pregnant Vietnamese women are warned to avoid funerals, places of worship, and streets at noon and five o'clock in the afternoon since spirits are present at these places and times (Stringfellow 1978). Many Vietnamese and Laotian women believe that overeating or inactivity during pregnancy leads to a difficult labor (Lee et al 1988). In the Mexican-American culture, the concept of *mal aire,* or bad air, is sometimes related to evil spirits. It is thought that air, especially night air, may enter the body and cause harm. For many Southeast Asians "wind" represents a bad external influence that may enter a person when the body is vulnerable, such as during and after childbirth or during surgery (Lee et al 1988).

Most of the taboos stemming from the belief in evil spirits are grounded in fear of injuring the unborn child. Taboos also arise from the belief that a pregnant woman has evil powers. For this reason, women are sometimes prohibited from taking part in certain activities.

The equilibrium model of health is based on the concept of balance between light and dark, heat and cold. Oriental belief focuses on the notion of *yin* and *yang.* Yin represents the female passive principle—darkness, cold, wetness—while yang is the masculine, active principle—light, heat, and dryness. When the two are combined, they are all that can be. The hot-cold classification is seen in cultures in Latin America, the Near East, and Asia. The dimensions and meanings of this classification vary, however, and require further investigation.

Mexican Americans often consider illness to be an excess of either hot or cold. To restore health, imbalances are often corrected by the proper use of foods, medications, or herbs. These substances are also classified as hot or cold. For example, an illness attributed to an excess of coldness will be treated only with hot foods or medications. The classification of foods is not always consistent but it does conform to a general structure of traditional knowledge. Certain foods, spices, herbs, and medications are perceived to cool or heat the body. These perceptions do not necessarily correspond to the actual temperature; some hot dishes are said to have a cooling quality.

The Vietnamese consider pregnancy a cold state because a great deal of body heat is lost. Therefore they avoid cold drinks and foods following birth (Calhoun 1985).

## ● Health Practices

Health care practices during pregnancy are influenced by numerous factors, such as the prevalence of traditional home remedies and folk beliefs, the importance of indigenous healers, and the influence of professional health care workers. In an urban setting the age, length of time in the city, marital status, and strength of the family may affect these patterns. Socioeconomic status is also important since modern medical services are more accessible to those who can afford it.

An awareness of alternative health sources is crucial for health professionals since these practices affect health outcomes. Many Mexican-American mothers are strongly influenced by familism and will seek and follow the advice of their mothers or older women in the childbearing period.

Indigenous healers are also important to specific cultures. In the Mexican-American culture the healer is called a *curandero*. In some Native American tribes the medicine man may fulfill the healing role. Herbalists are often found in Asian cultures, and faith healers, root doctors, and spiritualists are sometimes consulted in the black culture.

## ● Cultural Factors and Nursing Care

Health care providers are often unaware of the cultural characteristics they themselves demonstrate. Without cultural awareness care givers tend to project their own cultural responses onto foreign-born clients and assume that the clients are demonstrating a specific behavior for the same reason that they would. For example, health care providers sometimes label a pregnant or postpartum Filipino woman as "lazy" because of her rather sedentary life-style. In reality this style results from the cultural belief that inactivity is necessary to protect the mother and child (Stern et al 1985). Thiederman (1986) suggests that if health care providers fail to understand the reasons for a

person's behavior, it is impossible for them to intervene appropriately and assure cooperation.

To a certain extent most of us are guilty of ethnocentrism, at least some of the time. **Ethnocentrism** "involves the belief that the values and practices of one's own culture are the best ones, and, in some cases, the only ones of any worth" (Thiederman 1986, p 52). Thus the nurse who values stoicism during labor may be uncomfortable with the more vocal response of Hispanic women. Another nurse may be disconcerted by the Vietnamese woman who is so intent on maintaining self-control that she smiles throughout labor (Calhoun 1985).

Members of minority culture groups are often found living in a certain area of a community. The nurse can begin developing cultural sensitivity by becoming knowledgeable about the cultural practices of local groups.

Cultural assessment is an important aspect of prenatal care. The nurse should identify the main beliefs, values, and behaviors that relate to pregnancy and childbearing. This includes information about ethnic background, amount of affiliation with the ethnic group, patterns of decision making, religious preference, language, communication style, and common etiquette practices (Tripp-Reimer et al 1984). The nurse can also explore the woman's (or family's) expectations of the health care system.

In planning care the nurse considers the extent to which the woman's personal values, beliefs, and customs are in accord with the values, beliefs, and customs of the woman's identified cultural group, the nurse providing care, and the health care agency. If discrepancies exist, the nurse then considers whether the woman's system is supportive, neutral, or harmful in relation to possible interventions (Tripp-Reimer et al 1984). If the woman's system is supportive or neutral, it can be incorporated into the plan. For example, individual food practices or methods of pain expression may differ from those of the nurs or agency but would not necessarily interfere with the nursing plan. On the other hand, certain cultural practices might pose a threat to the health of the childbearing woman. For example, some Filipinas will not take any medication during pregnancy. The health care provider may consider a certain medication essential to the woman's well-being. In this case the woman's cultural belief may be detrimental to her own health. The nurse then faces two considerations: (1) identifying ways of persuading the woman to accept the proposed therapy; or (2) accepting the woman's rationale for refusing therapy if she is not willing to change her belief system (Tripp-Reimer et al 1984).

Essential Facts to Remember—Providing Effective Prenatal Care to Families of Different Cultures summarizes the key actions a nurse can take to become more culturally aware.

## Essential Facts to Remember

### Providing Effective Prenatal Care to Families of Different Cultures

Nurses who are interacting with expectant families from a different culture or ethnic group can provide more effective, culturally sensitive nursing care by:

- Identifying personal biases, attitudes, stereotypes, and prejudices
- Making a conscious commitment to respect the values and beliefs of others
- Learning the rituals, customs, and practices of the major cultural and ethnic groups with whom they have contact
- Including cultural assessment and assessment of the family's expectations of the health care system as a routine part of prenatal assessment
- Incorporating the family's cultural practices into prenatal care as much as possible
- Fostering an attitude of respect for and cooperation with alternative healers and care givers whenever possible
- Providing for the services of an interpreter if language barriers exist
- Learning the language (or at least several key phrases) of at least one of the cultural groups with whom they interact
- Recognizing that ultimately it is the woman's right to make her own health care choices

## ESSENTIAL CONCEPTS

- Virtually all systems of a woman's body are altered in some way during pregnancy.

- Blood pressure decreases slightly during pregnancy. It reaches its lowest point in the second trimester and gradually increases to near normal levels in the third trimester.

- The enlarging uterus may cause pressure on the vena cava when the woman lies supine. This is called the vena caval syndrome.

- Circulating blood volume increases by approximately 45%.

- A physiologic anemia may occur during pregnancy because the total plasma volume increases more than the total number of erythrocytes. This produces a drop in the hematocrit.

- The glomerular filtration rate increases somewhat during pregnancy. Glycosuria may be caused by the body's inability to reabsorb all the glucose filtered by the glomeruli.

- Changes in the skin include the development of chloasma; linea nigra; darkened nipples, areola, and vulva; striae; spider nevi; and palmar erythema.

- Insulin needs are increased during pregnancy. A woman with a latent deficiency state may respond to the increased stress on the islets of Langerhans by developing gestational diabetes.

- The placenta produces four hormones: estrogen, progesterone, human chorionic gonadotropin, and human placental lactogen.

- The presumptive signs of pregnancy are those symptoms experienced and reported by the woman, such as amenorrhea, nausea and vomiting, fatigue, urinary frequency, breast changes, and quickening.

- The probable signs of pregnancy can be perceived by the examiner but may be caused by conditions other than pregnancy.

- The positive signs of pregnancy can be perceived by the examiner and can only be caused by pregnancy.

- For many families pregnancy represents a developmental challenge; for some it is a maturational crisis.

- During pregnancy the expectant woman may experience ambivalence, acceptance, introversion, emotional lability, and changes in body image.

- Rubin (1984) has identified four developmental tasks for the pregnant woman: (1) ensuring safe passage through pregnancy, labor, and birth; (2) seeking acceptance of this child by others; (3) seeking commitment and acceptance of self as mother to the infant; and (4) learning to give of oneself on behalf of one's child.

- Fathers also face a series of adjustments as they accept their new role.

- Siblings of all ages require assistance in dealing with the birth of a new baby.

- Cultural values, beliefs, and behaviors influence a couple's response to childbearing and the health care system.

- The equilibrium model of health is based on a balance of yin and yang, cold and hot, dark and light.

● **Ethnocentrism is the belief that one's own cultural beliefs, values, and practices are the best ones, indeed the only ones worth considering.**

● **A cultural assessment does not have to be exhaustive, but it should focus on factors that will influence the practices of the childbearing family with regard to their health needs.**

● ● ● ● ● ● ● ● ● ● ● ● ● ● ● ● ● ● ● ● ● ● ● ● ● ● ● ● ● ● ● ● ●

## References

Brown MS: A cross-cultural look at pregnancy, labor, and delivery. *J Obstet Gynecol Neonatal Nurs* September/October 1976; 5:35.

Calhoun MA: The Vietnamese woman: Health/illness attitudes and behavior. *Health Care Women Int* 1985; 6:61.

Char EI: The Chinese American. In: *Culture and Childrearing.* Clark AL (editor). Philadelphia: Davis, 1981.

Cronenwett LR: Network structure, social support, and psychological outcomes of pregnancy. *Nurs Res* March/April 1985; 34:93.

Fawcett J et al: Spouses' body image changes during and after pregnancy: A replication and extension. *Nurs Res* July/August 1986; 35:220.

Fishbein EG: Expectant father's stress—Due to mother's expectations? *J Obstet Gynecol Neonatal Nurs* September/October 1984; 13:325.

Honig JC: Preparing preschool-aged children to be siblings. *MCN* January/February 1986; 11:37.

Horn M, Manion J: Creative grandparenting: Bonding the generations. *J Obstet Gynecol Neonatal Nurs* May/June 1985; 14:233.

Kay MA: The Mexican American. In: *Culture, Childbearing, Health Professionals.* Clark AL (editor). Philadelphia: Davis, 1978.

Key TC, Resnik R: Maternal changes in pregnancy. In: *Obstetrics and Gynecology,* 5th ed. Danforth DN, Scott JR (editors). Philadelphia: Lippincott, 1986.

Klebanoff R et al: Epidemiology of vomiting in early pregnancy. *Obstet Gynecol* November 1985; 66:612.

Lederman RP: *Psychosocial Adaptation in Pregnancy.* Englewood Cliffs, NJ: Prentice-Hall, 1984.

Lee RV et al: Southeast Asian folklore about pregnancy and parturition. *Obstet Gynecol* April 1988; 71:643.

Messer E: Hot-cold classification: Theoretical and practical applications of a Mexican study. *Soc Sci Med* 1981; 15B:133.

Pritchard JA, MacDonald PC, Gant NF: *Williams' Obstetrics,* 17th ed. New York: Appleton-Century-Crofts, 1985.

Rubin R: *Maternal Identity and the Maternal Experience.* New York: Springer, 1984.

Scott MDS, Stern PN: The ethno market theory: Factors influencing childbearing health practices of northern Louisiana black women. *Health Care Women Int* 1985; 6:45.

Stern PN et al: Culturally induced stress during childbearing: The Phillipine-American experience. *Health Care Women Int* 1985; 6:105.

Strang VR, Sullivan PL: Body image attitudes during pregnancy and the postpartum period. *J Obstet Gynecol Neonatal Nurs* July/August 1985; 14:332.

Strickland OL: The occurrence of symptoms in expectant fathers. *Nurs Res* May/June 1987; 36:184.

Stringfellow L: The Vietnamese. In: *Culture, Childbearing, Health Professionals.* Clark AL (editor). Philadelphia: Davis, 1978.

Tamez EG: Familism, machismo, and childbearing practices among Mexican Americans. *J Psychiatr Nurs* 1981; 19:21.

Thiederman SB: Ethnocentrism: A barrier to effective health care. *Nurse Practitioner* August 1986; 11:52.

Tripp-Reimer T et al: Cultural assessment: Content and process. *Nurs Outlook* March/April 1984; 32:78.

## Additional Readings

Anderson LL: Regulation of relaxin secretion and its role in pregnancy. *Adv Exp Med Biol* 1987; 219:421.

Avant KC: Stressors on the childbearing family. *J Obstet Gynecol Neonatal Nurs* May/June 1988; 17:179.

Brown MA: A comparison of health responses in expectant mothers and fathers. *West J Nurs Res* October 1988; 10:527.

Clinton JF: Expectant fathers at risk for couvade . . . physical and emotional symptoms. *Nurs Res* 1986; 35(5):290.

Daya S: Human chorionic gonadotropin increase in normal early pregnancy. *Am J Obstet Gynecol* 1987; 156(2):286.

Fawcett J et al: Pretty big . . . body attitudes during pregnancy. *Health* 1986; 18(6):6.

Mercer RT et al: Theoretical models for studying the effect of antepartum stress on the family. *Nurs Res* November/December 1986; 35:330.

Mercer RT et al: Effects of stress on family functioning during pregnancy. *Nurs Res* September/October 1988; 37:268.

Moore L et al: Self-assessment: A personalized approach to nursing during pregnancy. *J Obstet Gynecol Neonatal Nurs* September/October 1986; 15:375.

Sherwen LN: Third trimester fantasies of first-time expectant fathers. *MCN* 1986; 15(3):153.

# 7

# Antepartal Nursing Assessment

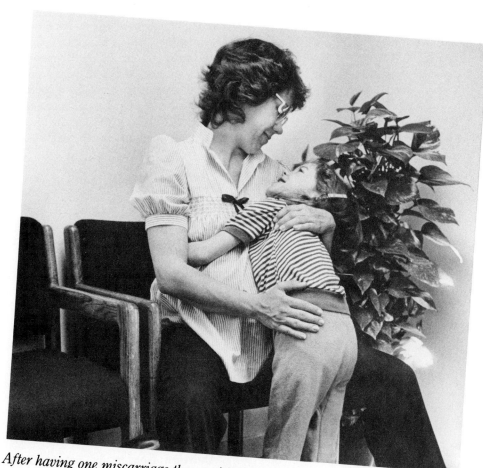

After having one miscarriage then waiting five years to get pregnant again, I found to my amazement after adopting a baby that I was pregnant. I was excited and petrified at the same time. After waiting for so long, what if I miscarried again? I still remember that Sunday afternoon in September when I first felt my baby move inside of me. I went to bed and cried because I knew that something had to be wrong. That week when I went to my doctor for my monthly checkup, the first thing he said was "Well, you must be feeling this little fellow moving by now." And I felt so foolish and relieved.

## Objectives

● Summarize the essential components of a prenatal history.

● Explain the common obstetric terminology found in the history of a maternity client.

● Identify factors related to the father's health that should be recorded on the prenatal record.

● Describe the normal physiologic changes one would expect to find when performing a physical assessment on a pregnant woman.

● Explain the use of Nägele's rule to determine estimated date of delivery.

● Describe areas that should be evaluated as part of the initial assessment of psychosocial factors related to a woman's pregnancy.

● Relate the danger signs of pregnancy to their possible causes.

## Key Terms

abortion
antepartum
diagonal conjugate
gestation
gravida
intrapartum
multigravida
multipara
Nägele's rule
nulligravida
nullipara
obstetric conjugate
para
postpartum
postterm labor
preterm or premature
  labor
primigravida
primipara
risk factors
stillbirth

Today nurses are assuming a more important role in prenatal care, particularly in the area of assessment. The certified nurse-midwife has the education and skill to perform in-depth prenatal assessments. The nurse practitioner may share the assessment responsibilities with a physician. An office nurse, whose primary role may be to counsel and meet the psychologic needs of the expectant family, performs assessments in those areas.

In the prenatal clinic or obstetrician's office, it is often the nurse who has the first contact with the pregnant woman, as the nurse performs initial assessments such as vital signs and weight. The nurse's attitude toward the woman during this early period can set the tone for the remainder of the visit.

An environment of comfort and open communication should be established with each antepartal visit. The nurse should convey concern for the woman as an individual and availability to listen and discuss the woman's concerns and desires. A supportive atmosphere coupled with the information found in the physical and psychosocial assessment guides in this chapter will enable the nurse to identify needed areas of education and counseling.

## ● CLIENT HISTORY

The course of a pregnancy depends on a number of factors, including the prepregnancy health of the woman, presence of disease states, emotional status, and past health care. Ideally health care before the advent of pregnancy has been adequate, and antenatal care will be a continuation of that established care. One important method of determining the adequacy of a woman's prepregnancy care is a thorough history.

## ● Definition of Terms

The following terms are used in the obstetric history of maternity clients:

**Gestation:** Time elapsed (measured in weeks) since the first day of the last menstrual period (LMP)

**Abortion:** Delivery that occurs prior to the end of 20 weeks' gestation

**Preterm or premature labor:** Labor that occurs after 20 weeks but before the completion of 37 weeks of gestation (pregnancy)

**Postterm labor:** Labor that occurs after 42 weeks of gestation

**Antepartum:** Time between conception and the onset of labor; usually used to describe the period during which a woman is pregnant

**Intrapartum:** Time from the onset of true labor until the delivery of the infant and placenta

**Postpartum:** Time from delivery until the woman's body returns to an essentially prepregnant condition

**Gravida:** Any pregnancy, regardless of duration, including present pregnancy

**Primigravida:** A woman who is pregnant for the first time

**Multigravida:** A woman who is in her second or any subsequent pregnancy

**Para:** Delivery after 20 weeks of gestation regardless of whether the infant is born alive or dead

**Nulligravida:** A woman who has never been pregnant

**Nullipara:** A woman who has not given birth at more than 20 weeks' gestation

**Primipara:** A woman who has had one birth at more than 20 weeks' gestation, regardless of whether the infant is born alive or dead

**Multipara:** A woman who has had two or more births at more than 20 weeks' gestation

**Stillbirth:** An infant born dead after 20 weeks of gestation

The terms *gravida* and *para* are used in relation to pregnancies, not to the number of fetuses.

The following examples illustrate how these terms are applied in clinical situations:

1.  Jean Smith has one child born at 38 weeks and is pregnant for the second time. At her initial prenatal visit, the nurse indicates her obstetric history as "gravida 2 para 1 ab 0." Jean Smith's present pregnancy terminates at 16 weeks' gestation. She is now "gravida 2 para 1 ab 1."

2.  Sue Sanchez is pregnant for the fourth time. She has a child born at 35 weeks at home. One pregnancy ended at ten weeks' gestation, and she delivered another infant stillborn at term. At her prenatal assessment the nurse records her obstetric history as "gravida 4 para 2 ab 1."

Because of the confusion that may result from this system when a multiple pregnancy occurs, a more detailed approach is used in some settings. Using the detailed system, *gravida* keeps the same meaning, while *para* changes to mean the number of infants born rather than the number of deliveries (Cunningham et al, 1989). A useful acronym for remembering the system is TPAL.

| Name | Gravida | Term | Preterm | Abort | Living Child |
|------|---------|------|---------|-------|--------------|
| Jean Smith | 2 | 1 | 0 | 0 | 1 |
| Sue Sanchez | 4 | 1 | 1 | 1 | 1 |

*Figure 7.1   The TPAL approach provides more detailed information about the woman's pregnancy history.*

First digit, T—number of *term* infants born; that is, the number of infants born after 37 weeks' gestation or more

Second digit, P—number of *preterm* infants born; that is, the number of infants born before 37 weeks' gestation

Third digit, A—number of pregnancies ending in either spontaneous or therapeutic *abortion*

Fourth digit, L—number of currently *living* children

Using this approach, the nurse would have described Jean Smith (see the first example above) initially as "gravida 2 para 1001." Following her abortion she would be "gravida 2 para 1011." Sue Sanchez would be described as "gravida 4 para 1111." (Figure 7.1 illustrates this method

## ● Client Profile

The history is essentially a screening tool that identifies factors that may negatively affect the course of a pregnancy. The following information should be obtained for each maternity client at the first prenatal assessment:

1.  Current pregnancy
    a.  First day of LMP
    b.  Presence of cramping, bleeding, or spotting since LMP
    c.  Woman's opinion about when conception occurred and when infant is due
    d.  Woman's attitude toward pregnancy (is this pregnancy planned? Wanted?)
    e.  Results of pregnancy tests, if completed
    f.  Any discomforts since LMP: nausea, vomiting, frequency, etc

2.  Past pregnancies
    a.  Number of pregnancies
    b.  Number of abortions, spontaneous or induced
    c.  Number of living children
    d.  History of previous pregnancies—length of pregnancy, complications (antepartal, intrapartal, postpartal), length of labor and delivery, type of

delivery (vaginal, forceps or silastic cup, cesarean, etc)

e. Perinatal status of previous children—birth weights, general development, complications, feeding patterns

f. Blood type and Rh factor (if negative—medication after delivery for immunization)

g. Prenatal education classes

3. Gynecologic history
   a. Date of last pap smear; any history of abnormal pap smear
   b. Previous infections—vaginal, cervical, sexually transmitted
   c. Previous surgery
   d. Age at menarche
   e. Regularity, frequency, and duration of menstrual flow
   f. History of dysmenorrhea
   g. Contraceptive history (if birth control pills were used, did pregnancy occur immediately following cessation of pills? If not, how long after?)
   h. Sexual history

4. Current medical history
   a. Weight
   b. Blood type and Rh factor, if known
   c. General health including nutrition, regular exercise program (type, frequency, duration)
   d. Any medications presently being taken (including nonprescription medications) or taken since the onset of pregnancy
   e. Alcohol and tobacco intake—ask specifically about the amounts of alcohol and cigarettes consumed each day
   f. Illicit drug use and/or abuse—ask about specific drugs such as cocaine, crack, marijuana
   g. Drug allergies and other allergies
   h. Potential teratogenic insults to this pregnancy (such as viral infections, medications, x-ray examinations, surgery)
   i. Presence of disease conditions such as diabetes, hypertension, cardiovascular disease, renal problems)
   j. Record of immunizations (especially rubella)
   k. Presence of any abnormal symptoms

5. Past medical history
   a. Childhood diseases
   b. Past treatment for any disease condition
   c. Surgical procedures
   d. Presence of bleeding disorders or tendencies (has she received blood transfusions?)

6. Family medical history
   a. Presence of diabetes, cardiovascular disease, hypertension, hematologic disorders, preeclampsia-eclampsia (pregnancy-induced hypertension [PIH])

b. Occurrence of multiple births
   c. History of congenital diseases or deformities
   d. Occurrence of cesarean births

7. Religious/cultural history
   a. Does the woman wish to specify a religious preference on her chart? Does she have any religious beliefs or practices that might influence her health care or that of her child, such as prohibition against receiving blood products, dietary considerations, circumcision rites, etc?
   b. Are there practices in her culture or that of her partner that might influence her care or that of her child?

8. Occupational history
   a. Occupation
   b. Does she stand all day, or are there opportunities to sit and elevate her legs? Any heavy lifting?
   c. Exposure to harmful substances
   d. Opportunity for regular lunch, breaks for nutritious snacks
   e. Provision for maternity leave

9. Partner's history
   a. Presence of genetic conditions or diseases
   b. Age
   c. Significant health problems
   d. Previous or present alcohol intake, drug use, tobacco use
   e. Blood type and Rh factor
   f. Occupation
   g. Educational level
   h. Attitude toward the pregnancy

10. Personal information
    a. Age
    b. Educational level
    c. Previous use of drugs, alcohol, and cigarettes
    d. Acceptance of pregnancy
    e. Race or ethnic group (to identify need for prenatal genetic screening or counseling)
    f. Stability of living conditions
    g. Economic level
    h. Housing
    i. Any history of emotional or physical deprivation (herself or children)
    j. History of emotional problems
    k. Support systems
    l. Plans regarding a support person to be present during labor and birth
    m. Plans for care of child following birth
    n. Overuse or underuse of health care system

## ● Obtaining Data

A questionnaire is used in many instances to obtain information. The woman should complete the questionnaire in a quiet place with a minimum of distractions.

The nurse can obtain further information in a direct interview, which allows the pregnant woman to expand or clarify her responses to questions, and gives the nurse and client the opportunity to begin developing a good relationship.

The expectant father should be encouraged to attend the prenatal examinations. He is often able to contribute information to the history and may use the opportunity to ask questions or express concerns.

The nurse can use the initial interview to observe the woman's nonverbal communications and any interactions between the woman and her support person, if present.

## ● *Prenatal High-Risk Screening*

**Risk factors** are any findings that suggest the pregnancy may have a negative outcome, either for the woman or her unborn child. Screening for risk factors is an important part of the prenatal assessment.

Many risks factors can be identified during the initial prenatal assessment; others may be detected during subsequent prenatal visits. It is important to identify high-risk pregnancies early so that appropriate interventions can be started immediately. Not all high-risk factors threaten the pregnancy equally; thus many agencies use a risk scoring sheet to determine the degree of risk. Information must

### Table 7.1   Prenatal High-Risk Factors

| Factor | Maternal implication | Fetal/neonatal implication |
|---|---|---|
| SOCIAL-PERSONAL | | |
| Low income level and/or low educational level | Poor antenatal care<br>Poor nutrition<br>↑ risk of preeclampsia | Low birth weight<br>Intrauterine growth retardation (IUGR) |
| Poor diet | Inadequate nutrition<br>↑ risk anemia<br>↑ risk preeclampsia | Fetal malnutrition<br>Prematurity |
| Living at high altitude | ↑ hemoglobin | Prematurity<br>IUGR |
| Multiparity > 3 | ↑ risk antepartum/postpartum hemorrhage | Anemia<br>Fetal death |
| Weight < 100 lb | Poor nutrition<br>Cephalopelvic disproportion<br>Prolonged labor | IUGR<br>Hypoxia associated with difficult labor and delivery |
| Weight > 200 lb | ↑ risk hypertension<br>↑ risk cephalopelvic disproportion | ↓ fetal nutrition |
| Age < 16 | Poor nutrition<br>Poor antenatal care<br>↑ risk preeclampsia<br>↑ risk cephalopelvic disproportion | Low birth weight<br>↑ fetal demise |
| Age > 35 | ↑ risk preeclampsia<br>↑ risk cesarean delivery | ↑ risk congenital anomalies<br>↑ chromosomal aberrations |
| Smoking one pack/day or more | ↑ risk hypertension<br>↑ risk cancer | ↓ placental perfusion → ↓ O$_2$ and nutrients available<br>Low birth weight<br>IUGR<br>Preterm birth |
| Use of addicting drugs | ↑ risk poor nutrition<br>↑ risk of infection with IV drugs | ↑ risk congenital anomalies<br>↑ risk low birth weight<br>Neonatal withdrawal<br>Lower serum bilirubin |
| Excessive alcohol consumption | ↑ risk poor nutrition<br>Possible hepatic effects with long-term consumption | ↑ risk fetal alcohol syndrome |

*(continues)*

## Table 7.1 Prenatal High-Risk Factors *(continued)*

| Factor | Maternal implication | Fetal/neonatal implication |
|---|---|---|
| **PREEXISTING MEDICAL DISORDERS** | | |
| Diabetes mellitus | ↑ risk preeclampsia, hypertension Episodes of hypoglycemia and hyperglycemia ↑ risk cesarean delivery | Low birth weight Macrosomia Neonatal hypoglycemia ↑ risk congenital anomalies ↑ risk respiratory distress syndrome |
| Cardiac disease | Cardiac decompensation Further strain on mother's body ↑ maternal death rate | ↑ risk fetal demise ↑ perinatal mortality |
| Anemia: * hemoglobin < 9 g/dL (white) < 29% hematocrit (white) < 8.2 g/dL hemoglobin (black) < 26% hematocrit (black) | Iron deficiency anemia Low energy level Decreased oxygen-carrying capacity | Fetal death Prematurity Low birth weight |
| Hypertension | ↑ vasospasm ↑ risk CNS irritability → convulsions ↑ risk CVA ↑ risk renal damage | ↓ placental perfusion → low birth weight Preterm birth |
| Thyroid disorder Hypothyroidism | ↑ infertility ↓ Basal metabolic rate (BMR), goiter, myxedema | ↑ spontaneous abortion ↑ risk congenital goiter Mental retardation → cretinism ↑ incidence congenital anomalies |
| Hyperthyroidism | ↑ risk postpartum hemorrhage ↑ risk preeclampsia Danger of thyroid storm | ↑ incidence preterm birth ↑ tendency to thyrotoxicosis |
| Renal disease (moderate to severe) | ↑ risk renal failure | ↑ risk IUGR ↑ risk preterm delivery |
| Diethylstilbestrol (DES) exposure | ↑ infertility, spontaneous abortion ↑ cervical incompetence | ↑ spontaneous abortion ↑ risk preterm delivery |
| **OBSTETRIC CONSIDERATIONS PREVIOUS PREGNANCY** | | |
| Stillborn | ↑ emotional/psychologic distress | ↑ risk IUGR ↑ risk preterm delivery |
| Habitual abortion | ↑ emotional/psychologic distress ↑ possibility diagnostic workup | ↑ risk abortion |
| Cesarean delivery | ↑ probability repeat cesarean delivery | ↑ risk preterm birth ↑ risk respiratory distress |

be updated throughout pregnancy as necessary. It is always possible that a pregnancy may begin as low risk and change to high risk because of complications.

Table 7.1 identifies the major risk factors currently recognized. The table also identifies maternal and fetal/neonatal implications if the risk is present in the pregnancy.

## • *INITIAL PHYSICAL ASSESSMENT*

After a complete history is obtained, the woman is prepared for a physical examination. The physical exami-

nation begins with assessment of vital signs, then the woman's body is examined. The pelvic examination is performed last. (See the Initial Prenatal Physical Assessment Guide starting on page 186.)

Before the examination, the woman should provide a clean urine specimen. When the bladder is empty, the woman is more comfortable during the pelvic examination, and the examiner can palpate the pelvic organs more easily. After emptying her bladder, she is asked to disrobe and is given a sheet or some other protective covering.

As a result of basic education programs or physical as-

## Table 7.1 Prenatal High-Risk Factors *(continued)*

| Factor | Maternal implication | Fetal/neonatal implication |
|---|---|---|
| **OBSTETRIC CONSIDERATIONS PREVIOUS PREGNANCY** *(continued)* | | |
| Rh or blood group sensitization | ↑ financial expenditure for testing | Hydrops fetalis<br>Icterus gravis<br>Neonatal anemia<br>Kernicterus<br>Hypoglycemia |
| Large baby | ↑ risk cesarean birth<br>↑ risk gestational diabetes | Birth injury<br>Hypoglycemia |
| **CURRENT PREGNANCY** | | |
| Rubella (first trimester) | | Congenital heart disease<br>Cataracts<br>Nerve deafness<br>Bone lesions<br>Prolonged virus shedding |
| Rubella (second trimester) | | Hepatitis<br>Thrombocytopenia |
| Cytomegalovirus | | IUGR<br>Encephalopathy |
| Herpesvirus type 2 | Severe discomfort<br>Concern about possibility of cesarean delivery, fetal infection | Neonatal herpesvirus type 2<br>2° hepatitis with jaundice<br>Neurologic abnormalities |
| Syphilis | ↑ incidence abortion | ↑ fetal demise<br>Congenital syphilis |
| Abruptio placenta and placenta previa | ↑ risk hemorrhage<br>Bed rest<br>Extended hospitalization | Fetal/neonatal anemia<br>Intrauterine hemorrhage<br>↑ fetal demise |
| Preeclampsia/eclampsia | See hypertension | ↓ placental perfusion → low birth weight |
| Multiple gestation | ↑ risk postpartum hemorrhage | ↑ risk preterm birth<br>↑ risk fetal demise |
| Elevated hematocrit*<br>> 41% (white)<br>> 38% (black) | Increased viscosity of blood | Fetal death rate five times normal rate |
| Spontaneous premature rupture of membranes | ↑ uterine infection | ↑ risk preterm birth<br>↑ fetal demise |

*Source: Garn SM et al: Maternal hematologic levels and pregnancy outcomes. *Semin Perinatol* April 1981; 5: 155.

sessment or practitioner courses, increasing numbers of nurses are prepared to perform physical examinations. The nurse who has not yet fully developed specific assessment skills assesses the woman's vital signs, explains the procedures to allay apprehension, positions her for examination, and assists the examiner as necessary.

Each nurse is responsible for operating at the expected standard for someone with that individual nurse's skill and knowledge base.

Thoroughness and a systematic procedure are the most important considerations when performing a physical exam. To promote completeness the assessment guide is organized into three columns: area to be assessed/normal findings, alterations and possible causes of the alterations, and nursing response to data. The nurse should be aware that certain organs and systems are assessed concurrently with other systems.

Nursing interventions based on assessment of the normal physiologic and psychologic changes associated with pregnancy and client teaching and counseling needs that have been mutually defined are discussed in more detail in Chapter 8.

# Initial Prenatal Physical Assessment Guide

| Assess/Normal Findings | Alterations and Possible Causes* | Nursing Responses to Data† |
|---|---|---|
| **Vital Signs** | | |
| Blood pressure (BP): 90–140/60–90 | High BP (essential hypertension; renal disease; pregestational hypertension; apprehension or anxiety associated with pregnancy diagnosis, exam, or other crises) | BP > 140/90 requires immediate consideration; establish woman's BP; refer to physician if necessary. Assess woman's knowledge about high BP; counsel on self-care and medical management. |
| Pulse: 60–90 beats/min. Rate may increase 10 beats/min during pregnancy | Increased pulse rate (excitement or anxiety, cardiac disorders) | Count for one full minute; note irregularities. |
| Respiration: 16–24 breaths/min (or pulse rate divided by four). Pregnancy may induce a degree of hyperventilation; thoracic breathing predominant | Marked tachypnea or abnormal patterns | Assess for respiratory disease. |
| Temperature: 36.2–37.6°C (98–99.6°F) | Elevated temperature (infection) | Assess for infection process or disease state if temperature is elevated; refer to physician. |
| **Weight** | | |
| Depends on body build | Weight <100 lb or >200 lb; rapid, sudden weight gain (preeclampsia-eclampsia [PIH]) | Evaluate need for nutritional counseling; obtain information on eating habits, cooking practices, foods regularly eaten, income limitations, need for food supplements, pica and other abnormal food habits. Note initial weight to establish baseline for weight gain throughout pregnancy. |
| **Skin** | | |
| Color: Consistent with racial background; pink nail beds | Pallor (anemia); bronze, yellow (hepatic disease, other causes of jaundice) | The following tests should be performed: complete blood count (CBC), bilirubin level, urinalysis, and blood urea nitrogen (BUN). |
| | Bluish, reddish, mottled; dusky appearance or pallor of palms and nail beds in dark-skinned women (anemia) | If abnormal, refer to physician. |
| Condition: Absence of edema (slight edema of lower extremities is normal during pregnancy) | Edema (preeclampsia); rashes, dermatitis (allergic response) | Counsel on relief measures for slight edema. Initiate preeclampsia assessment; refer to physician. |
| Lesions: Absence of lesions | Ulceration (varicose veins, decreased circulation) | Further assess circulatory status; refer to physician if lesion severe. |
| Spider névi common in pregnancy | Petechiae, multiple bruises, ecchymosis (hemorrhagic disorders) | Evaluate for bleeding or clotting disorder. |
| Moles | Change in size or color (carcinoma) | Refer to physician. |
| Pigmentation: Pigmentation changes of pregnancy include linea nigra, striae gravidarum, chloasma | | Assure woman that these are normal manifestations of pregnancy and explain the physiologic basis for the changes. |
| Café-au-lait spots | Six or more (Albright's syndrome or neurofibromatosis) | Consult with physician. |

*Possible causes of alterations are in parentheses.
†This column provides guidelines for further assessment and initial nursing intervention.

## Initial Prenatal Physical Assessment Guide *(continued)*

| Assess/Normal Findings | Alterations and Possible Causes* | Nursing Responses to Data† |
|---|---|---|
| **Nose**<br>Character of mucosa: Redder than oral mucosa; in pregnancy nasal mucosa is edematous in response to increased estrogen, resulting in nasal stuffiness and nosebleeds | Olfactory loss (first cranial nerve deficit) | Counsel woman about possible relief measures for nasal stuffiness and nose bleeds (epistaxis); refer to physician for olfactory loss. |
| **Mouth**<br>May note hypertrophy of gingival tissue because of estrogen | Edema, inflammation (infection); pale in color (anemia) | Assess hematocrit for anemia; counsel regarding dental hygiene habits.<br>Refer to physician or dentist if necessary. |
| **Neck**<br>Nodes: Small, mobile, nontender nodes | Tender, hard, fixed or prominent nodes (infection, carcinoma) | Examine for local infection; refer to physician. |
| Thyroid: Small, smooth lateral lobes palpable on either side of trachea; slight hyperplasia by third month of pregnancy | Enlargement or nodule tenderness (hyperthyroidism) | Listen over thyroid for bruits, which may indicate hyperthyroidism.<br>Question woman about dietary habits (iodine intake).<br>Ascertain history of thyroid problems; refer to physician. |
| **Chest and Lungs**<br>Chest: Symmetrical, elliptical, smaller anteroposterior (A–P) than transverse diameter | Increased A–P diameter, funnel chest, pigeon chest (emphysema, asthma, chronic obstructive pulmonary disease, COPD) | Evaluate for emphysema, asthma, pulmonary disease (COPD). |
| Ribs: Slope downward from nipple line | More horizontal (COPD)<br>Angular bumps<br>Rachitic rosary (vitamin C deficiency) | Evaluate for COPD. Evaluate for fractures. Consult physician.<br>Consult nutritionist. |
| Inspection and palpation: No retraction or bulging of intercostal spaces (ICS) during inspiration or expiration; symmetrical expansion<br>Tactile fremitus | ICS retractions with inspiration, bulging with expiration; unequal expansion (respiratory disease)<br><br>Tachypnea, hyperpnea, Cheyne-Stokes respirations (respiratory disease) | Do thorough initial assessment.<br>Refer to physician.<br><br>Refer to physician. |
| Percussion: Bilateral symmetry in tone | Flatness of percussion, which may be affected by chest wall thickness | Evaluate for pleural effusions, consolidations, or tumor. |
| Low-pitched resonance of moderate intensity | High diaphragm (atelectasis or paralysis), pleural effusion | Refer to physician. |
| Auscultation: Upper lobes: bronchovesicular sounds above sternum and scapulas; equal expiratory and inspiratory phases | Abnormal if heard over any other area of chest | Refer to physician. |
| Remainder of chest: vesicular breath sounds heard; inspiratory phase longer (3:1) | Rales, rhonchi, wheezes; pleural friction rub; absence of breath sounds; bronchophony, egophony; whispered pectoriloquy | Refer to physician. |

*Possible causes of alterations are in parentheses.
†This column provides guidelines for further assessment and initial nursing intervention.

*(continues)*

# Initial Prenatal Physical Assessment Guide (continued)

| Assess/Normal Findings | Alterations and Possible Causes* | Nursing Responses to Data† |
|---|---|---|
| **Breasts** | | |
| Supple; symmetrical in size and contour; darker pigmentation of nipple and areola; may have supernumerary nipples, usually 5–6 cm below normal nipple line | "Pigskin" or orange-peel appearance, nipple retractions, swelling, hardness (carcinoma); redness, heat, tenderness, cracked or fissured nipple (infection) | Encourage monthly breast checks; instruct woman how to examine own breasts. Refer to physician. |
| Axillary nodes unpalpable or pellet-sized | Tenderness, enlargement, hard node (carcinoma); may be visible bump (infection) | Refer to physician if evidence of inflammation. |
| Pregnancy changes:<br>1. Size increase noted primarily in first 20 weeks.<br>2. Become nodular.<br>3. Tingling sensation may be felt during first and third trimester; woman may report feeling of heaviness.<br>4. Pigmentation of nipples and areolas darkens.<br>5. Superficial veins dilate and become more prominent.<br>6. Striae seen in multiparas.<br>7. Tubercles of Montgomery enlarge.<br>8. Colostrum may be present after twelfth week.<br>9. Secondary areola appears at 20 weeks, characterized by series of washed-out spots surrounding primary areola.<br>10. Breasts less firm, old striae may be present in multiparas. | | Discuss normalcy of changes and their meaning with the woman. Teach and/or institute appropriate relief measures. Encourage use of supportive brassiere. |
| **Heart** | | |
| Normal rate, rhythm, and heart sounds<br>Pregnancy changes:<br>1. Palpitations may occur due to sympathetic nervous system disturbance.<br>2. Short systolic murmurs that ↑ in held expiration are normal due to increased volume. | Enlargement, thrills, thrusts, gross irregularity or skipped beats, gallop rhythm or extra sounds (cardiac disease) | Complete an initial assessment. Explain normalcy of pregnancy-induced changes. Refer to physician if indicated. |
| **Abdomen** | | |
| Normal appearance, skin texture, and hair distribution; liver nonpalpable; abdomen nontender<br>Pregnancy changes:<br>1. Purple striae may be present (or silver striae on a multipara).<br>2. Diastasis of the rectus muscles late in pregnancy. | Muscle guarding (anxiety, acute tenderness); tenderness, mass (ectopic pregnancy, inflammation, carcinoma) | Assure client of normalcy of diastasis. Provide initial information about appropriate postpartum exercises. Evaluate client anxiety level. Refer to physician if indicated. |
| 3. Size: Flat or rotund abdomen; progressive enlargement of uterus due to pregnancy.<br>10–12 weeks: Fundus slightly above symphysis pubis.<br>16 weeks: Fundus halfway between symphysis and umbilicus. | Size of uterus inconsistent with length of gestation (intrauterine growth retardation [IUGR] multiple pregnancy, fetal demise, hydatidiform mole) | Reassess menstrual history regarding pregnancy dating. Evaluate increase in size using McDonald's method. Use ultrasound to establish diagnosis. |

*Possible causes of alterations are in parentheses.
†This column provides guidelines for further assessment and initial nursing intervention.

# Initial Prenatal Physical Assessment Guide *(continued)*

| Assess/Normal Findings | Alterations and Possible Causes* | Nursing Responses to Data† |
|---|---|---|
| **Abdomen** *(continued)* | | |
| 20–22 weeks: Fundus at umbilicus. 28 weeks: Fundus three fingerbreadths above umbilicus. 36 weeks: Fundus just below ensiform cartilage. | | |
| 4. Fetal heartbeats: 120–160 beats/ min may be heard with Doppler at 10–12 weeks' gestation; may be heard with fetoscope at 17–20 weeks. | Failure to hear fetal heartbeat after 17–20 weeks (fetal demise, hydatidiform mole) | Refer to physician. Administer pregnancy tests. Use ultrasound to establish diagnosis. |
| 5. Fetal movement not felt prior to 20 weeks' gestation by examiner. | Failure to feel fetal movements after 20 weeks' gestation (fetal demise, hydatidiform mole) | Refer to physician for evaluation of fetal status. |
| 6. Ballottement: During fourth to fifth month, fetus rises and then re-bounds to original position when uterus is tapped sharply. | No ballottement (oligohydramnios) | Refer to physician for evaluation of fetal status. |
| **Extremities** | | |
| Skin warm, pulses palpable, full range of motion; may be some edema of hands and ankles in late pregnancy; varicose veins may become more pronounced | Unpalpable or diminished pulses (arterial insufficiency); marked edema (pre-eclampsia) | Evaluate for other symptoms of heart disease; initiate follow-up if woman mentions that her rings feel tight. Discuss prevention and self-treatment measures for varicose veins; refer to physician if indicated. |
| **Spine** | | |
| Normal spinal curves: Concave cervical, convex thoracic, concave lumbar | Abnormal spinal curves: flatness, kypho-sis, lordosis | Refer to physician for assessment of cephalopelvic disproportion (CPD). |
| In pregnancy, lumbar spinal curve may be accentuated | Backache | May have implications for administration of spinal anesthetics; see p 212 for relief measures. |
| Shoulders and iliac crests should be even | Uneven shoulders and iliac crests (scoliosis) | Refer very young women to a physician; discuss back-stretching exercises with older women. |
| **Reflexes** | | |
| Normal and symmetrical | Hyperactivity, clonus (PIH) | Evaluate for other symptoms of pre-eclampsia. |
| **Pelvic Area** | | |
| External female genitals: Normally formed with female hair distribution; in multiparas, labia majora loose and pig-mented; urinary and vaginal orifices visible and appropriately located | Lesions, hematomas, varicosities, in-flammation of Bartholin's glands; clitoral hypertrophy (masculinization) | Explain pelvic examination procedure (Procedure 7.1). Encourage woman to minimize her dis-comfort by relaxing her hips. Provide privacy (Figure 7.2). |

*Possible causes of alterations are in parentheses.
†This column provides guidelines for further assessment and initial nursing intervention.

*(continues)*

# Initial Prenatal Physical Assessment Guide (continued)

| Assess/Normal Findings | Alterations and Possible Causes* | Nursing Responses to Data† |
|---|---|---|
| **Pelvic Area** (continued) | | |
| Vagina: Pink or dark pink; vaginal discharge odorless, nonirritating; in multiparas, vaginal folds smooth and flattened; may have episiotomy scar | Abnormal discharge associated with vaginal infections | Obtain vaginal smear. Provide understandable verbal and written instructions about treatment for woman and partner, if indicated. |
| Cervix: Pink color; os closed except in multiparas, in whom os admits fingertip | Eversion, reddish erosion, Nabothian or retention cysts, cervical polyp; granular area that bleeds (carcinoma of cervix); lesions (herpes, human papilloma virus [HPV]) | Provide woman with a hand mirror and identify genital structures for her; encourage her to view her cervix if she wishes. Refer to physician if indicated. |
| | Presence of string or plastic tip from cervix (intrauterine device [IUD] in uterus) | Advise woman of potential serious risks of leaving an IUD in place during pregnancy; refer to physician for removal. |
| Pregnancy changes: 1–4 weeks' gestation: Enlargement in anteroposterior diameter 4–6 weeks' gestation: Softening of cervix (Goodell's sign), softening of isthmus of uterus (Hegar's sign); cervix takes on bluish coloring (Chadwick's sign) 8–12 weeks' gestation: Vagina and cervix appear bluish-violet in color (Chadwick's sign) | Absence of Goodell's sign (inflammatory conditions, carcinoma) | Refer to physician. |
| Uterus: Pear-shaped, mobile, smooth surface | Fixed (pelvic inflammatory disease—PID); nodular surface (fibromas) | Refer to physician. |
| Ovaries: Small, walnut-shaped, nontender (ovaries and fallopian tubes are located in the adnexal areas) | Pain on movement of cervix (PID); enlarged or nodular ovaries (cyst, tumor, tubal pregnancy, corpus luteum of pregnancy) | Evaluate adnexal areas; refer to physician. |
| **Pelvic Measurements** | | |
| Internal measurements: 1. Diagonal conjugate 12.5 cm (Figure 7.5A) | Measurement below normal | Vaginal delivery may not be possible if deviations are present. Consider possibility of cesarean delivery. Determine CPD by radiological examination and ultrasound. |
| 2. Obstetric conjugate estimated by subtracting 1.5–2 cm from diagonal conjugate | Disproportion of pubic arch | |
| 3. Inclination of sacrum | Abnormal curvature of sacrum | |
| 4. Motility of coccyx; external intertuberosity diameter > 8 cm | Fixed or malposition of coccyx | |
| **Anus and Rectum** | | |
| No lumps, rashes, excoriation, tenderness; cervix may be felt through rectal wall | Hemorrhoids, rectal prolapse; nodular lesion (carcinoma) | Counsel about appropriate prevention and relief measures; refer to physician for further evaluation. |
| **Laboratory Evaluation** | | |
| Hemoglobin: 12–16 g/dL; women residing in high altitudes may have higher levels of hemoglobin | < 12 g/dL (anemia) | Hemoglobin < 12 g/dL requires iron supplementation and nutritional counseling. |
| ABO and Rh typing: Normal distribution of blood types | Rh negative | If Rh negative, check for presence of anti-Rh antibodies. |

*Possible causes of alterations are in parentheses.
†This column provides guidelines for further assessment and initial nursing intervention.

# Initial Prenatal Physical Assessment Guide (continued)

| Assess/Normal Findings | Alterations and Possible Causes* | Nursing Responses to Data† |
|---|---|---|
| **Laboratory Evaluation** (continued) | | |
| | | Check partner's blood type; if partner is Rh positive, discuss with woman the need for antibody titers during pregnancy, management during the intrapartal period, and possible candidacy for RhoGAM. |
| Complete blood count (CBC) Hematocrit: 38%–47%; physiologic anemia (pseudoanemia) may occur Red blood cells (RBC): 4.2–5.4 million/μL | Marked anemia or blood dyscrasias | Perform CBC and Schilling differential cell count. |
| White blood cells (WBC): 4500–11,000/μL Differential Neutrophils 40%–60% Bands up to 5% Eosinophils 1%–3% Basophils up to 1% Lymphocytes 20%–40% Monocytes 4%–8% | Presence of infection; may be elevated in pregnancy and with labor | Evaluate for other signs of infection. |
| Syphilis tests—serologic test for syphilis (STS), complement fixation test, Venereal Disease Research Laboratory (VDRL) test—nonreactive | Positive reaction STS—tests may have 25%–45% incidence of biologic false positive results; false results may occur in individuals who have acute viral or bacterial infections, hypersensitivity reactions, recent vaccination, collagen disease, malaria, or tuberculosis | Positive results may be confirmed with the fluorescent treponemal antibody absorption (FTA-ABS) tests; all tests for syphilis give positive results in the secondary stage of the disease; antibiotic tests may cause negative test results. |
| Gonorrhea culture: Negative | Positive | Refer for treatment. |
| Urinalysis (u/a): Normal color, specific gravity; pH 4.6–8.0 | Abnormal color (porphyria, hemoglobinuria, bilirubinemia); alkaline urine (metabolic alkalemia, *Proteus* infection, old specimen) | Repeat u/a; refer to physician. |
| Negative for protein, red blood cells, white blood cells, casts | Positive findings (contaminated specimen, kidney disease) | Repeat u/a; refer to physician. |
| Glucose: Negative (small degree of glycosuria may occur in pregnancy) | Glycosuria (low renal threshold for glucose, diabetes mellitus) | Assess blood glucose; test urine for ketones. |
| Rubella titer: hemagglutination-inhibition test (HAI) > 1:10 indicates woman is immune | HAI titer < 1:10 | Immunization will be given on postpartum or within six weeks after delivery. Instruct woman whose titers are < 1:10 to avoid children who have rubella. |
| Antibody screen: Negative | Positive | If results are positive, further testing should be done to identify specific antibodies; in addition, antibody titers may be done during pregnancy. |
| Sickle cell screen for black clients: Negative | Positive; test results would include a description of cells | Refer to physician. |
| Papanicolaou (Pap) test: Negative | Test results that show atypical cells | Refer to physician. Discuss the meaning of the various classes with the woman and importance of follow-up. |

*Possible causes of alterations are in parentheses.
†This column provides guidelines for further assessment and initial nursing intervention.

## Procedure 7.1

## Assisting with Pelvic Examination

| Objective | Nursing action | Rationale |
|---|---|---|
| Prepare woman. | Explain procedure. | Explanation of procedure decreases anxiety. |
| | Provide privacy. | Many women find this procedure embarrassing. |
| | Give verbal support and encouragement. | |
| | Instruct woman to empty her bladder and to remove clothing below waist. She may be encouraged to keep her shoes on and may be given a disposable drape to hold in front of herself. | Comfort is promoted during internal examination. The woman may feel more comfortable with shoes on rather than supporting her weight with bare heels against cold stirrups. |
| | Position woman in lithotomy position with thighs flexed and adducted. Place her feet in stirrups. Buttocks should extend slightly beyond end of examining table (Figure 7.2). | |

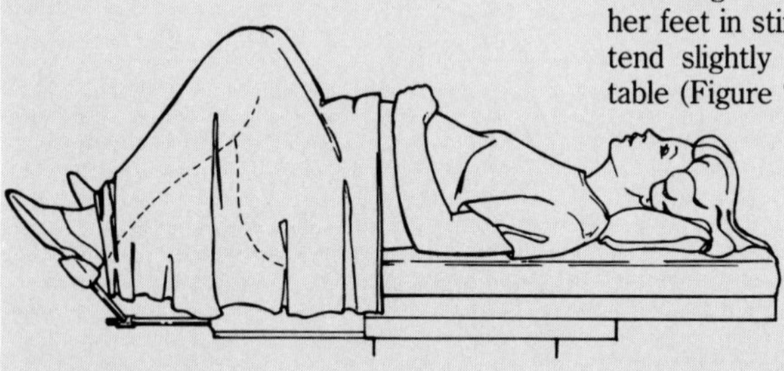

Figure 7.2  Woman in lithotomy position and draped for a pelvic examination

| Objective | Nursing action | Rationale |
|---|---|---|
| | Drape woman with a sheet, leaving flap so perineum can be exposed. | |
| Ensure smooth accomplishment of procedure. | Prepare and arrange following equipment so that they are easily accessible: | Examination is facilitated |
| | 1. Various-sized vaginal specula, warmed prior to insertion<br>2. Glove<br>3. Lubricant<br>4. Pelvimeter<br>5. Materials for Pap smear and gonorrhea culture<br>6. Good light source | Warmed speculum assists in lubrication and facilitates initial insertion when culture and smears are to be taken; many standard lubricants cannot be utilized |
| Provide support to woman as physician or nurse practitioner carries out examination. | Explain each part of examination as it is performed: inspection of external genitals, vagina, and cervix: bimanual examination of internal organs. Instruct woman to relax and breathe slowly. | Relaxation is promoted. |
| | Advise woman when speculum is to be inserted and ask her to bear down. | When speculum is inserted, woman may feel intravaginal pressure. Bearing down helps open vaginal orifice and relax perineal muscles. |
| | Lubricate examiner's finger well prior to bimanual examination. | |
| Provide for woman's comfort at end of examination. | Assist woman to sitting position. | Supine position may create postural hypotension. |
| | Provide tissues to wipe lubricant from perineum. | Upon assuming sitting position, vaginal secretions along with lubricant may be discharged. |
| | Provide privacy for woman to dress. | Comfort and sense of privacy is promoted. |

# DETERMINATION OF DELIVERY DATE

Childbearing families generally want to know the "due date," or the date around which delivery will occur. Historically the delivery date has been called the estimated date of confinement (EDC). The concept of confinement is, however, rather negative, and there is a trend in the literature to avoid it by referring to the delivery date as the EDD or *estimated date of delivery*.

To calculate the EDD it is helpful to know the LMP. However, some women have episodes of irregular bleeding or fail to keep track of menstrual cycles. Thus other techniques also help to determine how far along a woman is in her pregnancy, that is, at how many weeks' gestation she is. Other techniques that can be used include evaluating uterine size, determining when quickening occurs, and auscultating fetal heart rate with a fetoscope.

## Nägele's Rule

The most common method of determining the EDD is **Nägele's rule**. To use this method, one begins with the first day of the last menstrual period, subtracts three months, and adds seven days. For example:

| First day of LMP | November 21 |
| Subtract 3 months | − 3 months |
| | August 21 |
| Add 7 days | + 7 days |
| EDD | August 28 |

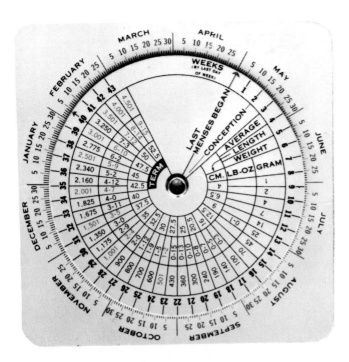

If a woman with a history of menses every 28 days remembers her LMP and was not taking oral contraceptives prior to becoming pregnant, Nägele's rule may be a fairly accurate determiner of her delivery date. However, if her cycle is irregular or 35–40 days long, the time of ovulation may be delayed by several days. If she has been using oral contraceptives, ovulation may be delayed several weeks following her last menses. *Ovulation usually occurs 14 days before the onset of the next menses, not 14 days after the previous menses.* Thus is it considered within normal range for birth to occur up to two weeks before or up to two weeks after the EDD.

A gestation calculator or "wheel" permits the care giver to calculate the EDD even more quickly (Figure 7.3).

## Uterine Assessment

### PHYSICAL EXAMINATION

When a woman is examined in the first 10–12 weeks of her pregnancy and her uterine size is compatible with her menstrual history, uterine size may be the single most important clinical method for dating her pregnancy. In many cases, however, women do not seek obstetric attention until well into their second trimester, when it becomes much more difficult to evaluate specific uterine size. In the obese woman, it is most difficult to determine uterine size early in a pregnancy.

### FUNDAL HEIGHT

Fundal height may be used as an indicator of uterine size, although this method of dating the pregnancy is at best accurate only within about four weeks and cannot be used late in pregnancy. A centimeter tape measure is used to measure the distance abdominally from the top of the symphysis pubis to the top of the uterine fundus (McDonald's method) (Figure 7.4). Fundal height usually correlates with gestational age until the third trimester, when fetal weights vary considerably. Thus, at 26 weeks' gestation, fundal height is probably about 26 cm. At 20 weeks' gestation, the fundus is about 20 cm and at the level of the umbilicus in an average female. If the woman is very tall or very short, fundal height will differ. To be most accurate, fundal height should be measured by the same examiner each time. The woman should have voided within one-half hour of the exam, and should lie in the same position (Engstrom 1988).

*Figure 7.3  The EDD wheel can be used to calculate delivery date.*

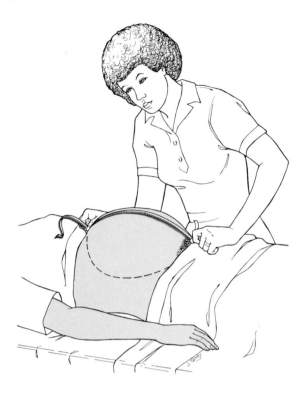

*Figure 7.4   Use of McDonald's method to measure fundal height*

Measurements of fundal height from month to month and week to week may signal intrauterine growth retardation (IUGR) if there is a lag in progression. A sudden increase in fundal height may indicate twins or hydramnios (excessive amount of amniotic fluid).

## Fetal Development

### QUICKENING

Fetal movements felt by the mother may indicate that the fetus is nearing 20 weeks' gestation. However, quickening may be experienced between 16 and 22 weeks' gestation, so this method is not completely accurate.

### FETAL HEARTBEAT

The fetal heartbeat can be detected with a fetoscope as early as week 16 and almost always by 19 or 20 weeks of gestation. Fetal heartbeat may be detected with the ultrasonic Doppler device (Figure 7.5) as early as eight weeks, but it is first heard, on average, at 10–12 weeks' gestation.

## ULTRASOUND FINDINGS

In the first trimester, ultrasound scanning can detect a gestational sac as early as five to six weeks after the LMP, fetal heart activity by nine to ten weeks, and fetal breathing movement by 11 weeks of pregnancy. Crown-to-rump (C–R) measurements can be used to assess fetal age until the fetal head can be visualized clearly. Biparietal diameter (BPD) can then be used. The BPD can be measured at approximately 12–13 weeks. This diameter is a more accurate determiner of age early in pregnancy, when less biologic variation occurs.

## ASSESSMENT OF PELVIC ADEQUACY

The pelvis is usually assessed during the prenatal course. Some agencies assess the pelvis as part of the initial physical assessment. Others wait until later in the pregnancy, when hormonal effects are greatest and it is possible to make some determination of fetal size.

The method of measurement is depicted in Figures 7.6, 7.7, and 7.8. The parts of the pelvis that are evaluated and their normal measurements include the following:

1. Pelvic inlet (Figure 7.6)
   a. **Diagonal conjugate**, 11.5 cm (the distance from the lower posterior border of the symphysis pubis to the sacral promontory)
   b. **Obstetric conjugate**, 10 cm (this measurement is approximately 1.5 cm smaller than the diagonal conjugate)
2. Pelvic cavity (midpelvis)
   a. Plane of greatest dimensions, 12.75 cm
   b. Plane of least dimension (midplane), 11.5–12.0 cm
3. Pelvic outlet (Figures 7.6, 7.7, 7.8)
   a. Anteroposterior diameter, 11.5 cm
   b. Transverse diameter, 10 cm

## INITIAL PSYCHOSOCIAL ASSESSMENT

At the initial visit the woman may be most concerned with the diagnosis of pregnancy. However, during this visit she (and her partner, if he is present) is also evaluating the health team that she has chosen. The establishment of the nurse-client relationship will help the woman evaluate the health team and also provides the nurse with a basis for an atmosphere that is conducive to interviewing, sup-

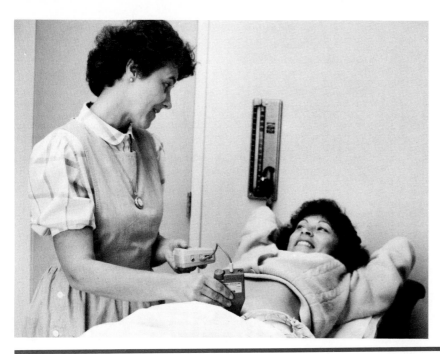

Figure 7.5 Listening to fetal heartbeat with Doppler device]

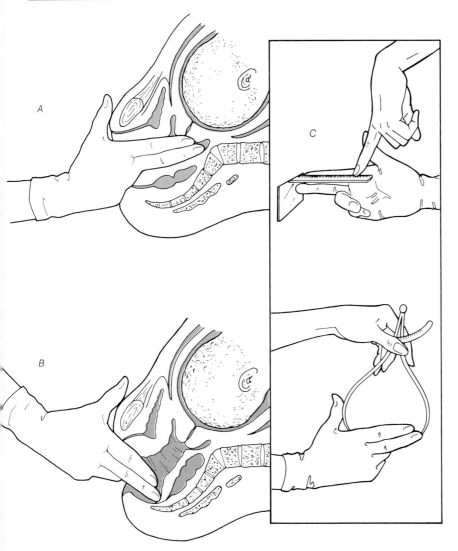

Figure 7.6 Manual measurement of inlet and outlet: (A) Estimation of diagonal conjugate, which extends from lower border of symphysis pubis to sacral promontory. (B) Estimation of anteroposterior diameter of the outlet, which extends from the lower border of the symphysis pubis to the tip of the sacrum. (C) Methods that may be used to check manual estimation of anteroposterior measurements

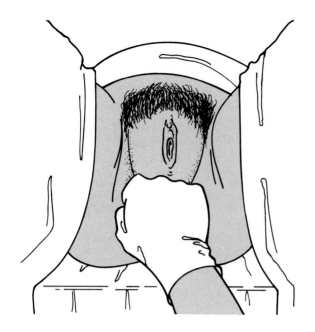

*Figure 7.7    Use of closed fist to measure outlet. Examiner should know distance between first and last proximal knuckles.*

port, and education. A psychosocial assessment is difficult to obtain if the woman does not feel free to talk.

Many women are excited and anxious on the initial visit. Because of this, the initial psychosocial assessment is general and the goal is to set the foundation for a trusting nurse-client relationship.

As part of the initial psychosocial assessment the nurse discusses with the woman any religious or cultural factors that influence the woman's expectations about the childbearing experience. It is especially helpful if the nurse is familiar with common practices of various religious and cultural groups that reside in the community. If the nurse gathers this data in a tactful, caring way it can help make the childbearing woman's experience a positive one.

The Initial Psychosocial Assessment Guide on the opposite page can be used as a basis for evaluating the woman's needs for education and support.

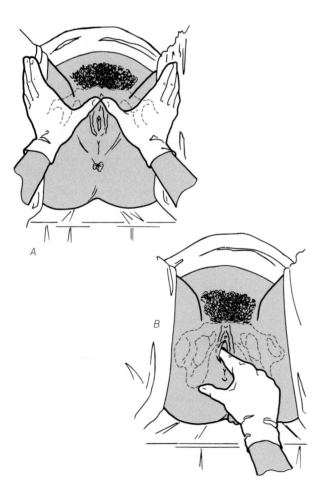

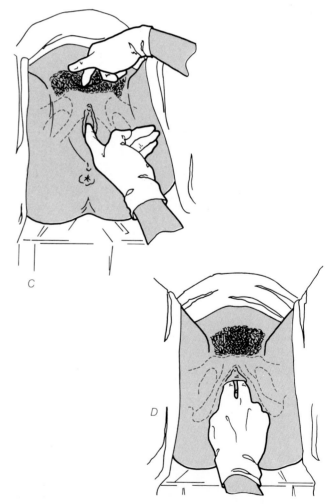

*Figure 7.8    Evaluation of outlet: (**A**) Estimation of subpubic angle. (**B**) Estimation of length of pubic ramus. (**C**) Estimation of depth and inclination of pubis. (**D**) Estimation of contour of subpubic angle.*

# Initial Psychosocial Assessment Guide

| Assess/Normal Findings | Alterations and Possible Causes* | Nursing Responses to Data† |
|---|---|---|
| **Psychologic Status** | | |
| Excitement and/or apprehension; ambivalence | Marked anxiety (fear of pregnancy diagnosis, fear of medical facility) | Establish lines of communication. Active listening is useful. Establish trusting relationship. Encourage woman to take active part in her care. |
| | Apathy<br>Display of anger with pregnancy diagnosis | Establish communication and begin counseling. Use active listening techniques. |
| **Educational Needs** | | |
| May have questions about pregnancy or may need time to adjust to reality of pregnancy | | Establish educational, supporting environment that can be expanded throughout pregnancy. |
| **Support Systems** | | |
| Can identify at least two or three individuals with whom woman is emotionally intimate (partner, parent, sibling, friend, etc) | Isolated (no telephone, unlisted number); cannot name a neighbor or friend whom she can call upon in an emergency; does not perceive parents as part of her support system | Institute support system through community groups. Develop trusting relationship with health care professionals. |
| **Cultural or Religious Considerations** | | |
| Any cultural or religious beliefs or practices that might influence pregnancy. Is able to express her personal preferences and beliefs about the childbearing experience. Identifies any people (mother, curendara, tribal healer, etc) that influence her | Language barriers that prevent effective communication<br>Cultural beliefs or practices that might endanger her health or that of fetus | Work with knowledgeable translator to provide information and answer questions.<br>Have information printed in the language of different cultural groups that live in the area.<br>Work with significant people to meet woman's health needs. |
| **Family Functioning** | | |
| Emotionally supportive<br>Communications adequate<br>Mutually satisfying<br>Cohesiveness in times of trouble | Long-term problems or specific problems related to this pregnancy, potential stressors within the family, pessimistic attitudes, unilateral decision making, unrealistic expectations of this pregnancy and/or child | Help identify the problems and stressors, encourage communication, discuss role changes and adaptations. |
| **Economic Status** | | |
| Source of income is stable and sufficient to meet basic needs of daily living and medical needs | Limited prenatal care<br>Poor physical health<br>Limited use of health care system<br>Unstable economic status | Discuss available resources for health maintenance and delivery. Institute appropriate referral for meeting expanding family's needs—food stamps, etc. |
| **Stability of Living Conditions** | | |
| Adequate, stable housing for expanding family's needs | Crowded living conditions<br>Questionable supportive environment for newborn | Refer to appropriate community agency. Work with family on self-help ways to improve situation. |

*Possible causes of alterations are placed in parentheses.
†This column provides guidelines for further assessment and initial nursing intervention.

# Essential Facts to Remember

## Danger Signs in Pregnancy

The woman should report the following danger signs in pregnancy immediately:

| Danger Sign | Possible Cause |
|---|---|
| 1. Sudden gush of fluid from vagina | Premature rupture of membranes |
| 2. Vaginal bleeding | Abruptio placentae, placenta previa<br>Lesions of cervix or vagina<br>"Bloody show" |
| 3. Abdominal pain | Premature labor, abruptio placentae |
| 4. Temperature above 38.3°C (101°F) and chills | Infection |
| 5. Dizziness, blurring of vision, double vision, spots before eyes | Hypertension, preeclampsia |
| 6. Persistent vomiting | Hyperemesis gravidarum |
| 7. Severe headache | Hypertension, preeclampsia |
| 8. Edema of hands, face, legs, and feet | Preeclampsia |
| 9. Muscular irritability, convulsions | Preeclampsia, eclampsia |
| 10. Epigastric pain | Preeclampsia–ischemia in major abdominal vessels |
| 11. Oliguria | Renal impairment, decreased fluid intake |
| 12. Dysuria | Urinary tract infection |
| 13. Absence of fetal movement | Maternal medication, obesity, fetal death |

## • SUBSEQUENT CLIENT HISTORY

At subsequent prenatal visits the nurse continues to gather data about the course of the pregnancy to date. The nurse asks specifically whether the woman has experienced any discomfort, especially the kinds of discomfort that are often seen at specific times during a pregnancy. The nurse inquires about physical changes that relate directly to the pregnancy, such as fetal movement. The nurse also asks about any of the danger signs of pregnancy (see Essential Facts to Remember—Danger Signs in Pregnancy.)

Other pertinent information includes: any exposure to contagious illnesses, medical treatment and therapy prescribed for nonpregnancy problems since the last visit, any prescription or over-the-counter medications that were not prescribed as part of the woman's prenatal care.

## • SUBSEQUENT PHYSICAL ASSESSMENT

The recommended frequency of prenatal visits in an uncomplicated pregnancy is as follows:

• Every four weeks for the first 28 weeks of gestation

• Every two weeks to week 36

• After week 36, every week until delivery

The Subsequent Physical Assessment Guide on the opposite page provides a systematic approach to the regular physical examinations that the pregnant woman should undergo for optimal prenatal care.

## • SUBSEQUENT PSYCHOSOCIAL ASSESSMENT

Periodic prenatal examinations offer the nurse an opportunity to assess the childbearing woman's psychologic needs and emotional status. If the woman's partner attends the prenatal visits, his needs and concerns can also be identified.

The interchange between the nurse and woman will be facilitated if it takes place in a friendly, trusting environment. The woman should be given sufficient time to ask questions and to air concerns. If the nurse provides the time and demonstrates genuine interest, the woman will feel more at ease bringing up questions that she may believe are silly or concerns that she has been afraid to verbalize. The nurse who has an accurate understanding of all the changes of pregnancy is most able to answer questions and provide information.

During the prenatal period, it is essential to begin assessing the ability of the woman, and her partner, if possible, to assume their responsibilities as parents successfully. Table 7.2 identifies areas for assessment and provides some sample questions the nurse might use to obtain necessary information. If the woman's responses are primarily negative, interventions can be planned for the prenatal and postpartal periods.

During the subsequent psychologic assessments, a woman may exhibit psychologic problems such as the following:

• Increasing anxiety

• Inability to establish communication

• Inappropriate responses or actions

• Denial of pregnancy

• Inability to cope with stress

• Failure to acknowledge quickening

# Subsequent Physical Assessment Guide

| Assess/Normal Findings | Alterations and Possible Causes* | Nursing Responses to Data† |
|---|---|---|
| **Vital Signs** | | |
| Temperature: 36.2–37.6°C (98–99.6°F) | Elevated temperature (infection) | Evaluate for signs of infection. Refer to physician. |
| Pulse: 60–90/min Rate may increase 10 beats/min during pregnancy | Increased pulse rate (anxiety, cardiac disorders) | Note irregularities. Evaluate anxiety and stress. |
| Respiration: 16–24/min | Marked tachypnea or abnormal patterns (respiratory disease) | Refer to physician. |
| Blood pressure: 90–140/60–90 (falls in second trimester) | > 140/90 or increase of 30 mm systolic and 15 mm diastolic (preeclampsia) | Assess for edema, proteinuria, hyperreflexia. Refer to physician. Schedule appointments more frequently. |
| **Weight Gain** | | |
| First trimester: 2–4 lb Second trimester: 12 lb Third trimester: 12 lb | Inadequate weight gain (poor nutrition, nausea, IUGR) Excessive weight gain (excessive caloric intake, edema, preeclampsia) | Discuss appropriate weight gain. Provide nutritional counseling. Assess for presence of edema or anemia. |
| **Edema** | | |
| Small amount of dependent edema, especially in last weeks of pregnancy | Edema in hands, face, legs, feet (preeclampsia) | Identify any correlation between edema and activities, blood pressure, or proteinuria. Refer to physician if indicated. |
| **Uterine Size** | | |
| See Initial Physical Assessment Guide for normal changes during pregnancy. | Unusually rapid growth (multiple gestation, hydatidiform mole, hydramnios, miscalculation of EDD) | Evaluate fetal status. Determine height of fundus (p 193). Use diagnostic ultrasound. |
| **Fetal Heartbeat** | | |
| 120–160/min Funic souffle | Absence of fetal heartbeat after 20 weeks' gestation (maternal obesity, fetal demise) | Evaluate fetal status. |
| **Laboratory Evaluation** | | |
| Hemoglobin: 12–16 g/dL Pseudoanemia of pregnancy | < 12 g/dL (anemia) | Provide nutritional counseling. Hemoglobin is repeated at seven months' gestation. Women of Mediterranean heritage need a close check on hemoglobin because of possibility of thalassemia. |
| Antibody screen: Negative | Positive | Refer to further testing to identify specific antibodies. Titers may be indicated. If negative repeat at seven months. |
| 50 g, one-hour glucose screen (done between 24 and 28 weeks' gestation) | Plasma glucose level > 140 mg/dL (gestational diabetes mellitus [GDM]) | Discuss implications of GDM. Refer for a diagnostic glucose tolerance test. |
| Urinalysis: See Initial Prenatal Physical Assessment Guide (p 191) for normal findings. | See Initial Prenatal Physical Assessment Guide (p 191) for deviations. | Repeat urinalysis at seven months' gestation. Dipstick test at each visit. |
| Protein: Negative | Proteinuria, albuminuria (contamination by vaginal discharge, urinary tract infection, preeclampsia) | Obtain dipstick urine sample. Refer to physician if deviations are present. |
| Glucose: Negative | Persistent glycosuria (diabetes mellitus) | Refer to physician. |

Note: Glycosuria may be present due to physiologic alterations in glomerular filtration rate and renal threshold.

*Possible causes of alterations are placed in parentheses.
† This column provides guidelines for further assessment and initial nursing intervention.

## Table 7.2   Prenatal Assessment of Parenting Guide*

| Areas assessed | Sample questions |
|---|---|

**I.  PERCEPTION OF COMPLEXITIES OF MOTHERING**

    A.  Baby is desired for itself
    Positive:
        1.  Feels positive about pregnancy
    Negative:
        1.  Wants baby to meet own needs such as someone to
        love her, someone to get her out of unhappy home

      1.  Did you plan on getting pregnant?
      2.  How do you feel about being pregnant?
      3.  Why do you want this baby?

    B.  Expresses concern about impact of mothering role on
    other roles (wife, career, school)
    Positive:
        1.  Realistic expectations of how baby will affect job, ca-
        reer, school, and personal goals
        2.  Interested in learning about child care
    Negative:
        1.  Feels pregnancy and baby will make no emotional,
        physical, or social demands on self
        2.  No insight that mothering role will affect other roles or
        life-style

      1.  What do you think it will be like to take care of a baby?
      2.  How do you think your life will be different after you
      have your baby?
      3.  How do you feel this baby will affect your job, career,
      school, and personal goals?
      4.  How will the baby affect your relationship with boy-
      friend or husband?
      5.  Have you done any reading, babysitting, or made any
      things for a baby?

    C.  Gives up routine habits because "not good for baby"; eg,
    quits smoking, adjusts time schedule, etc.†
    Positive:
        1.  Gives up routines not good for baby: quits smoking,
        adjusts eating habits, etc

**II.  ATTACHMENT**

    A.  Strong feelings regarding sex of baby
        Why?
    Positive:
        1.  Verbalizes positive thoughts about the baby
    Negative:
        1.  Baby will be like negative aspects of self and partner

      1.  Why do you prefer a certain sex? (Is reason inappropri-
      ate for a baby?)
      2.  Note comments woman makes about baby not being
      normal and why she feels this way

    B.  Interested in data regarding fetus, eg, growth and devel-
    opment, heart tones, etc
    Positive:
        1.  As above
    Negative:
        1.  Shows no interest in fetal growth and development,
        quickening, and fetal heart tones
        2.  Negative feelings about fetus expressed by rejection of
        counseling regarding nutrition, rest, hygiene

    C.  Fantasies about baby
    Positive:
        1.  Follows cultural norms regarding preparation
        2.  Time of attachment behaviors appropriate to her his-
        tory of pregnancy or pregnancy loss
    Negative:
        1.  Bonding is conditional depending on sex, age of baby,
        and/or labor and delivery experience
        2.  Patient only considers own needs when making plans
        for baby
        3.  Exhibits no attachment behaviors after critical period
        of previous pregnancy
        4.  Failure to follow cultural norms regarding preparation

      1.  What did you think or feel when you first felt the baby
      move?
      2.  Have you started preparing for the baby?
      3.  What do you think your baby will look like—what age
      do you see your baby at?
      4.  How would you like your new baby to look?

## Table 7.2 Prenatal Assessment of Parenting Guide* *(continued)*

| Areas assessed | Sample questions |
| --- | --- |
| III. ACCEPTANCE OF CHILD BY SIGNIFICANT OTHERS | |

### III. ACCEPTANCE OF CHILD BY SIGNIFICANT OTHERS

A. Acknowledges acceptance by significant other of the new responsibility inherent in child

Positive:

1. Acknowledges unconditional acceptance of pregnancy and baby by significant others
2. Partner accepts new responsibility inherent with child
3. Timely sharing of experience of pregnancy with significant others

Negative:

1. Significant others not supportively involved with pregnancy
2. Conditional acceptance of pregnancy depending on sex, race, age of baby
3. Decision making does not take in needs of fetus, eg, spends food money on new car
4. Takes no/little responsibility for needs of pregnancy, woman/fetus

*Sample questions:*

1. How does your partner feel about pregnancy?
2. How do your parents feel?
3. What do your friends think?
4. Does your partner have a preference regarding the baby's sex? Why?
5. How does your partner feel about being a father?
6. What do you think he'll be like as a father?
7. What do you think he'll do to help you with child care?
8. Have you and your partner talked about how the baby might change your lives?
9. Who have you told about your pregnancy?

B. Concrete demonstration of acceptance of pregnancy/baby by significant others, eg, baby shower, significant other involved in prenatal education[†]

Positive:

1. Baby shower
2. Significant other attends prenatal class with client

*Sample questions:*

1. Note if partner attends clinic with client (degree of interest), eg, listens to heart tones, etc. Significant other plans to be with client in labor and delivery.
2. Is your partner contributing financially?

### IV. ENSURES PHYSICAL WELL-BEING

A. Concerns about having normal pregnancy, labor and delivery, and baby

Positive:

1. Client preparing for labor and delivery, attends prenatal classes, interested in labor and delivery
2. Client aware of danger signs of pregnancy
3. Seeks and uses appropriate health care, eg, time of initial visit, keeps appointments, follows through on recommendations

Negative:

1. Denial of signs and symptoms that might suggest complications of pregnancy
2. Verbalizes extreme fear of labor and delivery—refuses to talk about labor and delivery
3. Fails appointments, failure to follow instructions, refuses to attend prenatal classes

*Sample questions:*

1. What have you heard about labor and delivery?
2. Note data about client's reaction to prenatal class

B. Family/client decision reflect concern for health of mother and baby, eg, use of finances, time[†]

Positive:

1. As above

*Source: Modified and used with permission of the Minneapolis Health Dept, Minneapolis, MN.

[†]When "Negative" is not listed in a section, the reader may assume that negative is the absence of positive responses.

## Subsequent Psychosocial Assessment Guide

| Assess/Normal Findings | Alterations and Possible Causes* | Nursing Responses to Data† |
|---|---|---|
| **Expectant Mother** | | |
| Psychologic status: First trimester: Incorporates idea of pregnancy; may feel ambivalent, especially if she must give up desired role; usually looks for signs of verification of pregnancy, such as increase in abdominal size, fetal movement, etc. Second trimester: Baby becomes more real to woman as abdominal size increases and she feels movement; she begins to turn inward, becoming more introspective. Third trimester: Begins to think of baby as separate being; may feel restless and may feel that time of labor will never come; remains self-centered and concentrates on preparing place for baby. | Increasing stress and anxiety Inability to establish communication; inability to accept pregnancy; inappropriate response or actions; denial of pregnancy; inability to cope | Encourage woman to take an active part in her care. Establish lines of communication. Establish a trusting relationship. Counsel as necessary. Refer to appropriate professional as needed. |
| Educational needs: Self-care measures and knowledge about following:   Breast care   Hygiene   Rest   Exercise   Nutrition   Relief measures for common discomforts of pregnancy   Danger signs of pregnancy (see Essential Facts to Remember, p 198) | Inadequate information | Teach and/or institute appropriate relief measures (see Chapter 8). |
| Sexual activity: Woman knows how pregnancy affects sexual activity | Lack of information about effects of pregnancy and/or alternative positions during sexual intercourse | Provide counseling. |
| Preparation for parenting: Appropriate preparation; see Table 7.2 | Lack of preparation (denial, failure to adjust to baby, unwanted child) See Table 7.2 | Counsel. If lack of preparation is due to inadequacy of information, provide information. |
| Preparation for childbirth: Client aware of following: 1. Prepared childbirth techniques 2. Normal processes and changes during childbirth | | If couple chooses particular technique, refer to classes (see Chapter 11 for description of childbirth preparation techniques). Encourage prenatal class attendance. Educate woman during visits based on current physical status. Provide reading list for more specific information. |

*Possible causes of alterations are in parentheses.
†This column provides guidelines for further assessment and initial nursing intervention.

*(continues)*

- Failure to plan and prepare for the baby (for example, living arrangements, clothing, feeding methods)

- Indications of substance abuse

If the woman appears to have these or other critical psychologic problems, the nurse should refer her to appropriate professionals.

The Subsequent Psychosocial Assessment Guide on this page provides a model for the evaluation of both the pregnant woman and the expectant father.

# *Subsequent Psychosocial Assessment Guide (continued)*

| Assess/Normal Findings | Alterations and Possible Causes* | Nursing Responses to Data† |
|---|---|---|
| **Expectant Mother** *(continued)* | | |
| 3. Problems that may occur as a result of drug and alcohol use and of smoking | Continued abuse of drugs and alcohol; denial of possible effect on self and baby. | Review danger signs that were presented on initial visit. |
| Woman has met other physician and/or nurse-midwife who may be attending her delivery in the absence of primary care giver | Introduction of new individual at delivery may increase stress and anxiety for woman and partner | Introduce woman to all members of group practice. |
| Impending labor: Client knows signs of impending labor: 1. Uterine contractions that increase in frequency, duration, intensity 2. Bloody show 3. Expulsion of mucous plug 4. Rupture of membranes | Lack of information | Provide appropriate teaching, stressing importance of seeking appropriate medical assistance. |
| **Expectant Father** | | |
| Psychologic status: First trimester: May express excitement over confirmation of pregnancy and of his virility; concerns move toward providing for financial needs; energetic; may identify with some discomforts of pregnancy and may even exhibit symptoms Second trimester: May feel more confident and be less concerned with financial matters; may have concerns about partner's changing size and shape, her increasing introspection Third trimester: May have feelings of rivalry with fetus, especially during sexual activity; may make changes in his physical appearance and exhibit more interest in himself; may become more energetic; fantasizes about child but usually imagines older child; fears of mutilation and death of woman and child arise. | Increasing stress and anxiety Inability to establish communication Inability to accept pregnancy diagnosis Withdrawal of support Abandonment of the mother | Encourage expectant father to come to prenatal visits. Establish lines of communication. Establish trusting relationship. Counsel. Let expectant father know that it is normal for him to experience these feelings. Include expectant father in pregnancy activities as he desires. Provide education, information, and support. Increasing number of expectant fathers are demonstrating desire to be involved in many or all aspects of prenatal care, education, and preparation. |

*Possible causes of alterations are in parentheses.
† This column provides guidelines for further assessment and initial nursing intervention.

# ESSENTIAL CONCEPTS

● A complete history forms the basis of prenatal care and is reevaluated and updated as necessary throughout the pregnancy.

● Screening for risk factors is an ongoing process beginning at the first prenatal visit.

● The initial prenatal physical assessment is a careful and thorough physical examination designed to identify physical variations and potential risk factors.

● Laboratory tests completed at the initial visit, such as a complete blood count, ABO and Rh typing, urinalysis, Pap smear, gonorrhea culture, rubella titer, and various blood screens, provide information about the woman's health during early pregnancy and also help detect potential problems.

● The estimated date of delivery (EDD) can be calculated using Nägele's rule. Using this approach, one begins with the first day of the last menstrual period (LMP), subtracts three months, and adds seven days. A "wheel" may also be used to calculate the EDD.

● Accuracy of the EDD may be evaluated by physical examination to assess uterine size, measurement of fundal height, and ultrasound. Perception of quickening and auscultation of fetal heartbeat are also useful tools in confirming the gestation of a pregnancy.

● The pelvis can be assessed vaginally to determine whether its size is adequate to permit vaginal delivery.

● The diagonal conjugate is the distance from the lower posterior border of the symphysis pubis to the sacral promontory. The obstetric conjugate is estimated by subtracting 1.5 cm from the length of the diagonal conjugate.

● The nurse begins evaluating the woman psychosocially during the initial prenatal assessment. This assessment continues and is modified throughout the pregnancy.

● Cultural and ethnic beliefs may strongly influence the woman's attitudes and apparent compliance with care during pregnancy.

## References

Cunningham FG et al: *Williams Obstetrics,* 18th ed. Appleton and Lange, Norwalk, CT 1989.

Engstrom JL: Measurement of fundal height. *J Obstet Gynecol Neonatal Nurs* May/June 1988; 17:172.

## Additional Readings

Engstrom JL: Quickening and auscultation of fetal heart tones as estimators of the gestational interval: A review. *J Nurse-Midwifery* 1985; 30(1):25.

Kemp VH et al: Health assessment in high risk pregnancies. *Fam Commun Health* 1986; 8(4):10.

Kemp VH, Page CK: Maternal prenatal attachment in normal and high-risk pregnancies. *J Obstet Gynecol Neonatal Nurs* May/June 1987; 16:179.

Lederman RP: Maternal anxiety in pregnancy: Relationship to fetal and newborn health status. *Ann Rev Nurs Res* 1986; 4:3.

Lester D, Beck A: Attempted suicide and pregnancy. *Am J Obstet Gynecol* 1988; 158(5):1084.

Marquette GP, Skoll MA: How should you screen for gestational diabetes? *Contemp OB/GYN* 1986; 27(4):67.

Mercer RT, Ferketich SL: Stress and social support as predictors of anxiety and depression during pregnancy. *Adv Nurs Science* 1988; 10(2):26.

Miller SJ: Prenatal assessment of the expectant family. *Nurse Pract* 1986; 11(5):40.

Wawrzyniak MN: The painless pelvic. *MCN* 1986; 11(3):178.

# 8

# The Expectant Family: Needs and Care

Talk about subtle messages from potential grandparents! My parents were really eager to become grandparents. Every once in a while, when they felt they couldn't stand it any longer, they would mention how much fun it would be to have grandchildren. But mostly they showed magnificent restraint.

One evening we got a call to come over to their house. When we got there we found packages piled up, all decorated with bright ribbons. Not being shy, we piled into them. First there was a delicate little yellow dress with ribbons and lace. Next came a tiny blue suit with knee pants and a striped handkerchief tucked in a pocket. These were followed by a blue and pink rattle and diaper pins and diapers and soft flannel blankets with kittens and ducks. My parents watched all this and then proudly proclaimed, "We're ready." Their timing was great because so were we. They made such proud grandparents!

## Objectives

● Summarize the areas of assessment that are important in establishing a comprehensive data base for the expectant woman and her family.

● Explain the causes of the common discomforts of pregnancy and appropriate measures to alleviate these discomforts.

● Discuss the basic information that the nurse should provide to the expectant family to allow them to carry out appropriate self-care.

● Identify some of the concerns that the expectant couple may have about sexual activity.

● Relate the significance of cultural considerations to the provision of effective prenatal care.

## Key Terms

fetal alcohol syndrome (FAS)
Kegel's exercises
leukorrhea
lightening
nipple preparation
pelvic tilt
ptyalism
teratogens

From the moment a woman finds out that she is pregnant, she faces a future marked by dramatic changes. Her appearance will be altered. Her relationships will change. She will experience a variety of unique physical changes throughout the pregnancy. Even her psychologic state will be affected.

Her family must also adjust to the pregnancy. Roles and responsibilities of family members will be altered as the woman's ability to perform certain activities changes. They too must adapt psychologically to the situation.

The expectant woman and her family will probably have many questions about the pregnancy and its impact on her and the other members of the family. The daily activities and health care practices of the woman are important for her well-being and the well-being of the unborn child.

The nurse often assumes the dual roles of teacher and counselor for expectant families who desire information about pregnancy and the adjustments they must make. In particular the nurse teaches the pregnant woman about the physical discomforts that may occur and the self-care measures that the woman can use to obtain relief.

This chapter provides the information necessary for nurses to teach and counsel pregnant women and their families. It describes the common discomforts of pregnancy, their causes, and self-care measures. The chapter also contains information and advice on general health practices and other activities that may affect or be affected by pregnancy.

## ● USING THE NURSING PROCESS DURING THE ANTEPARTAL PERIOD

Pregnancy is a healthy process for most women. Thus antepartal nursing care primarily involves anticipatory guidance and education. The nursing process provides a framework for the nurse to identify and meet the needs of the expectant woman and her family.

## ● Nursing Assessment

Because most pregnant women are healthy, the main purposes of ongoing prenatal assessment are to ensure that everything is progressing normally and to identify potential problems that may affect the well-being of the woman or her fetus. The nurse assesses the woman's physical health and any psychologic factors that affect her pregnancy experience. To be truly effective, the assessment must take into account the woman's age, religious and cultural beliefs, health practices, life experiences, family structure, attitudes, educational background, and interests.

The accuracy of the nurse's assessment often depends on the nurse's ability to develop rapport with the woman and use communication skills effectively. The nurse's comfort level in dealing with the concerns expressed by the pregnant woman and her family is also important. The concerns expressed during pregnancy are frequently very personal. Some nurses hesitate to assess the woman's needs in these areas due to their own discomfort or lack of clarity about the purpose of their data collection. For example, a nurse may feel uncomfortable assessing a woman's concerns about intercourse during pregnancy or use of alcohol or other drugs. A nonjudgmental approach and knowledge about health promotion behaviors during pregnancy are essential. The nurse must remember that promotion of maternal well-being and optimum fetal outcome is the purpose of care. With this thought in mind, personal concerns should not be as difficult to assess.

## ● Nursing Diagnosis

The nurse may see a specific woman only once every three to four weeks at the beginning of pregnancy. As a result, a written plan of care that incorporates the data base, nursing diagnoses, and goals is essential for continuity of care.

The American Nurses' Association's *Standards of Maternal and Child Health Nursing Practice* (ANA 1983) encourages the use of nursing diagnoses. Several existing nursing diagnoses may apply to a woman with a healthy pregnancy. Examples of applicable nursing diagnoses include:

- Knowledge deficit related to the use of medication during pregnancy
- Noncompliance with prenatal appointment schedule related to a lack of understanding about the importance of prenatal care
- Constipation related to the physiologic effects of pregnancy
- Altered sexuality patterns related to changed sexual activity during pregnancy

## ● Nursing Plan and Implementation

Once nursing diagnoses have been identified, the next step is to establish priorities of nursing care. Sometimes priorities of care are based on the most immediate needs or concerns perceived by the woman. For example, during the first trimester, when a woman is experiencing nausea or is concerned about sexual intimacy with her partner, she is not likely to be ready to hear about labor and birth.

The woman's priorities may not always be the same as the nurse's. If the safety of the woman or her fetus is at issue, however, that takes priority over other concerns of the woman or her family. It is the responsibility of the medical and nursing professions to help the woman and her family understand the significance of a problem and to plan appropriate interventions to deal with it.

The intervention methods most used by nurses in caring for the expectant woman and her family are communication techniques and teaching-learning strategies. These intervention methods are most obvious when used in groups, such as early pregnancy classes and childbirth education classes, but the nurse in the prenatal setting often applies these techniques on an individual basis.

The value of providing a primary care nurse to coordinate care for each childbearing family is beginning to be recognized (Mahan and McKay 1984). The nurse in a clinic or HMO may be the only source of continuity for the woman, who may see a different physician or nurse-midwife at each visit. The nurse can be extremely effective in working with the expectant family by providing them with necessary and complete information about pregnancy, self-care measures, and community resources or referral agencies that may be of help to them. Such education allows the family to assume equal responsibility with health care providers in working toward their common goal of a positive childbearing experience.

## ● Evaluation

Evaluation is an ongoing process. At each prenatal visit the nurse evaluates the effectiveness of previous teaching by using information obtained from the woman and from various assessment tools. For instance, the woman's pattern of weight gain, her vital signs, her degree of comfort, and her success in implementing previously discussed strategies provide information about the success of previous nursing interventions. When the woman has been unable to follow an established treatment plan, it may be due to factors in the woman's environment that were not previously known. Thus the cycle of the nursing process begins again with assessment as the nurse collects further data.

## ● NURSING ASSESSMENT OF THE EXPECTANT FAMILY

As described in Chapter 7, during the initial contact with the expectant mother or couple the nurse obtains a complete client profile that includes information about the following:

- The family's environment, life-style, habits, and relationships
- The family's sources and adequacy of income

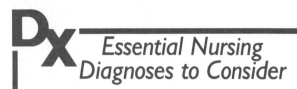

## Essential Nursing Diagnoses to Consider

### Pregnancy

| Early Pregnancy | Late Pregnancy |
|---|---|
| Impaired adjustment | Impaired adjustment |
| Anxiety | Anxiety |
| Ineffective family coping | Constipation |
| Ineffective individual coping | Ineffective family coping |
| Fear | Fear |
| Fluid volume deficit | Ineffective individual coping |
| Altered health maintenance | Altered family processes |
| Knowledge deficit | Knowledge deficit |
| Noncompliance | Noncompliance |
| Altered nutrition | Altered nutrition |
| Altered role performance | Altered role performance |
| Personal identity disturbance | Personal identity disturbance |
| Altered sexuality patterns | Altered sexuality patterns |
| Health seeking behaviors | Sleep pattern disturbance |
| Decisional conflict | Situational low self esteem |
| Fatigue | Fatigue |
| Sleep pattern disturbance | Health seeking behaviors |

- The family's race and/or culture
- The woman's temperament and usual way of coping with stressful situations
- An average day in the life of the family
- Impact of the pregnancy on the mother, the family, and significant others
- Personal habits relevant to pregnancy (patterns of diet, sleep, and sexual activity; exercise; hobbies; and use of alcohol, tobacco, caffeine, and other drugs)
- The woman's health history and significant factors in the family health history
- Family history to determine expected support of family members

The data base is completed after a description of body functioning, a complete physical examination, laboratory tests, and a psychologic evaluation (Chapter 7) are made.

During subsequent visits, the nurse may ask the woman what *mother* means to her, what she thinks an average day with the baby will be like, and what she expects from the father. The nurse can ask the father similar questions about his expectations of himself and his partner as parents.

Many nonparents are not prepared for the sleep and feeding patterns of newborns. They have not considered their feelings about the inevitable crying of the newborn and what they will do when the baby cries. Many couples are surprised to discover the sometimes extreme discrepancy between one partner's view of parenthood and the expectations of the other. Guided discussion of these topics allows parents-to-be to attack problems, to arrive at compromises, and to appreciate each other's uniqueness.

From the health assessment, the nurse develops an initial plan for interventions during the couple's preparation for childbearing and childrearing. The plan anticipates the need for information, guidance, and physical care. Interventions are timed to coincide with the woman's (couple's) readiness and needs.

## • NURSING DIAGNOSIS

The nurse can anticipate that for many women with a low-risk pregnancy, certain nursing diagnoses will be used more frequently than others. This will, of course, vary from woman to woman and according to the time in the pregnancy. Many of the more commonly used nursing diagnoses are identified in Essential Nursing Diagnoses to Consider—Pregnancy. After formulating an appropriate diagnosis the nurse would then establish goals to guide the nursing plan and interventions.

## • NURSING PLAN AND IMPLEMENTATION DURING PREGNANCY

Once the nurse has completed an initial assessment of the childbearing family and has identified pertinent nursing diagnoses, a plan for providing effective prenatal care is developed and implemented. See Essential Facts to Remember—Key Antepartal Nursing Interventions.

## • Promotion of Family Wellness
### ANTICIPATORY GUIDANCE

The problems and concerns of the pregnant woman, the relief of her discomforts, and the maintenance of her physical health receive much attention. However, her well-being also depends on the well-being of those she is closest to. Thus, the nurse must help meet the needs of the woman's family to maintain the integrity of the family unit.

### Father

Anticipatory guidance of the expectant father is a necessary part of any plan of care. He may need information about the anatomic, physiologic, and emotional changes that occur during pregnancy and postpartum, the couple's sexuality and sexual response, and the reactions that he may experience. He may wish to express his feelings about breast versus bottle-feeding, the sex of the child, and other topics. If it is culturally and personally acceptable to him, the nurse refers the couple to expectant parents' classes for further information and support from other couples. In some areas classes specially designed to meet the needs of expectant fathers are also available (Taubenheim and Silbernagel 1988).

The nurse assesses the father's intended degree of participation during labor and delivery and his knowledge of what to expect. If the couple prefers that his participation be minimal or restricted, the nurse supports their decision. With this type of consideration and collaboration, the father is less apt to develop feelings of alienation, helplessness, and guilt during the intrapartal period. Thus the relationship between the couple may be strengthened and his self-esteem raised. He is then better able to provide physical and emotional support to his partner during labor and birth.

### Siblings

The nurse incorporates in the plan for prenatal care a discussion about the negative feelings that older children may have. Parents may be distressed to see an older child become aggressive toward the newborn. Parents who are unprepared for the older child's feelings of anger, jealousy, and rejection may respond inappropriately in their confusion and surprise. The nurse emphasizes that open communication between parents and children (or acting out feelings with a doll if the child is too young to verbalize) helps children to master their feelings and may prevent them from hurting the baby when they are unsupervised. Children may feel less neglected and more secure if they know that their parents are willing to help with their anger and aggressiveness.

Parents may be encouraged to bring their children to antepartal visits. For siblings, seeing what is involved and listening to the fetal heartbeat may make the pregnancy more real. Many agencies also provide sibling classes geared to different ages and levels of understanding.

### PRENATAL EDUCATION

Throughout the prenatal period, the nurse provides informal and formal education to the childbearing family. This education is designed to help the family carry out self-care when appropriate and to report changes that may indicate a possible health problem. The nurse also provides anticipatory guidance to help the family plan for changes that will occur following childbirth. Issues that could be possible sources of postpartal stress should be discussed by the expectant couple. Some issues to be resolved beforehand may include the sharing of infant and household chores, help in the first few days, options for babysitting to allow the mother and couple some free time, the mother's return to work after the baby's birth, and sibling rivalry. Couples resolve these issues in different ways; however, postpartal adjustment is easier for a couple who

### Essential Facts to Remember

#### Key Antepartal Nursing Interventions

Antepartal nursing interventions focus on:

- Explaining the normal changes of pregnancy to the childbearing family
- Specifying those signs or symptoms that indicate a problem may be developing
- Providing appropriate information about self-care measures the pregnant woman may employ to relieve the common discomforts of pregnancy
- Answering questions about the common concerns that arise during pregnancy
- Referring the woman for additional or more specialized assistance when necessary

agree on the issues beforehand than for a couple who do not confront and resolve these issues.

### CULTURAL CONSIDERATIONS IN PREGNANCY

As discussed in Chapter 7, specific actions during pregnancy are often determined by cultural beliefs. Some beliefs, which are passed down from generation to generation, may be called "old wives' tales." At one time, these beliefs certainly had some meaning, but with the passing of time the meanings have often been lost. Other beliefs have definite meanings that are retained. Tables 8.1 and 8.2 present activities prescribed and proscribed by certain cultures. The tables are not meant to be all-inclusive; they offer a few examples of cultural activities important during the prenatal period.

In working with clients of another culture, the health professional is as open as possible to other beliefs. If certain activities are not harmful, there is no need to impose one's beliefs and practices upon a person of another culture. If the activities are harmful, the nurse can consult or work with someone within the culture or someone aware of cultural beliefs and values to help modify a client's behavior.

### • Relief of the Common Discomforts of Pregnancy

The common discomforts of pregnancy are a result of physical and anatomic changes and are fairly specific to each of the three trimesters. Health professionals often refer to these discomforts as minor, but they are not minor to the pregnant woman. They can make her quite uncomfortable and, if they are unexpected, anxious.

## Table 8.1 Activities or Rituals During Pregnancy

| Culture | Activity | Cultural meaning or belief | Nursing intervention |
|---|---|---|---|
| Mexican-American | Certain clothing is worn (muneco-cord worn beneath the breasts and knotted over the umbilicus) (Brown 1976). | Ensures a safe delivery. | If practice does not cause any danger, do not interfere with it. |
| | Use of spearmint or sassafras tea or Benedictine (Brown 1976). | Eases morning sickness. | Assess use of herbs and determine safety of their use. |
| | Use of cathartics during the last month of pregnancy (Brown 1976). | Ensures a good delivery of a healthy boy. | Assess use of cathartics. Provide teaching about dangers of the practice and explore other culturally acceptable means of resolving constipation (high fiber foods). |
| Black American | Use of self-medication for many discomforts of pregnancy is common (epsom salts, castor oil for constipation; herbs for nausea and vomiting; vinegar and baking soda for heartburn) (Carrington 1978). | Improves health and builds resistance. | Assess use of self-medication; discourage those practices that may present problems. |
| Native American (selected examples) | *Navajo* Meets with the medicine man two months prior to delivery (Farris 1976). | Prayers are said to ensure safe delivery and healthy baby. | Encourage the use of support systems. |
| | Exercise is important during pregnancy; woman is also taught to concentrate on good thoughts and to be joyful (Farris 1976). | "Body movement is said to produce efficiency and promote joy" (Sevcovic 1979, p 39). | |
| | *Muckeshoot Indians* Keep busy and walk a lot (Horn 1982). | The baby will be born earlier, and the labor and delivery will be easier. | |
| | *Tonawanda Seneca* Eat sparingly and exercise freely (Evaneshko 1982). | Delivery will be easier. | Assess nutritional patterns and provide teaching if needed. |
| Vietnamese | Consume ginseng tea. Woman is expected to carry on conversations with and counsel fetus (Hollingsworth et al 1980). | Gives strength. | Assess use and be certain it is not taken to the exclusion of necessary nutrients. |

Pregnancy aggravates some preexisting problems, such as hemorrhoids and varicose veins. For women who do not have these preexisting conditions, the second trimester may be a relatively comfortable time. The discomforts caused by the enlarging uterus do not affect women until the last trimester or even until the last month.

Table 8.3 identifies the common discomforts of pregnancy, their possible causes, and the self-care measures that might relieve the discomfort. The nurse caring for the pregnant woman continually assesses and anticipates the presence of discomforts. The nurse knows the appropriate interventions and evaluates the effectiveness of the relief measures used. If these methods are not effective, the nurse must determine why they are not helpful. Are they ineffective because the source of discomfort was incorrectly assessed or because the woman did not receive sufficient instruction? After the situation is reevaluated, nursing interventions can be changed as necessary to meet the woman's comfort and safety needs.

## Table 8.2 Proscribed Activities During Pregnancy

| Culture | Activity | Rationale |
|---|---|---|
| Mexican-American | Pregnant woman should not look at the full moon (Brown 1976). | It will cripple or deform the unborn child. |
| | She should not hang laundry or reach high. | This will cause knots in the umbilical cord. |
| | Baby showers should not be planned until delivery time (Kay 1978). | Earlier would invite bad luck or the "evil eye." |
| | The woman should not allow herself to quarrel or express anger (Kay 1978). | Consequences are spontaneous abortion, premature labor, or knots in the cord. |
| Black American | Avoid any emotional fright (Carrington 1978). | Baby will have a birthmark. |
| | Avoid reaching up. | The umbilical cord may wrap around the baby's neck. |
| Native American (selected examples) | *Navajo* Rug weaving is forbidden; carrying and lifting also avoided (Sevcovic 1979). | Puts unnatural strain on the body. |
| | Avoid funerals or looking at dead animals (Sevcovic 1979). | Exposes the baby to the realm of the dead and may cause later illness to the baby. |
| | *Laguna Pueblo* Do not sew with a bone or a needle (Farris 1978). | This will have an unkind effect on the baby. |
| Vietnamese | Do not attend weddings or funerals (Hollingsworth et al 1980). | Bad luck for the newlyweds; the baby may cry. |

## Table 8.3 Self-Care Measures for Common Discomforts of Pregnancy

| Discomfort | Influencing factors | Self-care measures |
|---|---|---|
| **FIRST TRIMESTER** | | |
| Nausea and vomiting | Increased levels of hCG Changes in carbohydrate metabolism Emotional factors Fatigue | Avoid odors or causative factors. Eat dry crackers or toast before arising in morning. Have small but frequent meals. Avoid greasy or highly seasoned foods. Take dry meals with fluids between meals. Drink carbonated beverages. |
| Urinary frequency | Pressure of uterus on bladder in both first and third trimester | Void when urge is felt. Increase fluid intake during the day. Decrease fluid intake *only* in the evening to decrease nocturia. |
| Breast tenderness | Increased levels of estrogen and progesterone | Wear well-fitting supportive bra. |
| Increased vaginal discharge | Hyperplasia of vaginal mucosa and increased production of mucus by the endocervical glands due to the increase in estrogen levels | Promote cleanliness by daily bathing. Avoid douching, nylon underpants, and pantyhose; cotton underpants are more absorbent; powder can be used to maintain dryness if not allowed to cake. |
| Nasal stuffiness and epistaxis | Elevated estrogen levels | May be unresponsive but cool air vaporizer may help; avoid use of nasal sprays and decongestants. |
| Ptyalism | Specific causative factors unknown | Use astringent mouthwashes, chew gum, or suck hard candy. |

*(continues)*

## Table 8.3  Self-Care Measures for Common Discomforts of Pregnancy (continued)

| Discomfort | Influencing factors | Self-care measures |
| --- | --- | --- |
| SECOND AND THIRD TRIMESTERS | | |
| Heartburn (pyrosis) | Increased production of progesterone; decreasing gastrointestinal motility and increasing relaxation of cardiac sphincter; displacement of stomach by enlarging uterus; thus regurgitation of acidic gastric contents into esophagus | Eat small and more frequent meals. Use low-sodium antacids. Avoid overeating, fatty and fried foods, lying down after eating, and sodium bicarbonate. |
| Ankle edema | Prolonged standing or sitting Increased levels of sodium due to hormonal influences Circulatory congestion of lower extremities Increased capillary permeability Varicose veins | Practice frequent dorsiflexion of feet when prolonged sitting or standing is necessary. Elevate legs when sitting or resting. Avoid tight garters or restrictive bands around the legs. |
| Varicose veins | Venous congestion in the lower veins that increases with pregnancy Hereditary factors (weakening of walls of veins, faulty valves) Increased age and weight gain | Elevate legs frequently (Figure 8.1). Wear supportive hose. Avoid crossing legs at the knees, standing for long periods, garters, and hosiery with constrictive bands |
| Hemorrhoids | Constipation (see following discussion) Increased pressure from gravid uterus on hemorrhoidal veins | Avoid constipation. Apply ice packs, topical ointments, anesthetic agents, warm soaks, or sitz baths; gently reinsert into rectum as necessary. |
| Constipation | Increased levels of progesterone, which cause general bowel sluggishness Pressure of enlarging uterus on intestine Iron supplements Diet, lack of exercise, and decreased fluids | Increase fluid intake, fiber in the diet, exercise. Develop regular bowel habits. Use stool softeners as recommended by physician. |
| Backache | Increased curvature of the lumbosacral vertebras as the uterus enlarges Increased levels of hormones, which cause softening of cartilage in body joints Fatigue Poor body mechanics | Use proper body mechanics. Practice the pelvic tilt exercise. Avoid uncomfortable working heights, high-heeled shoes, lifting heavy loads, and fatigue. |
| Leg cramps | Imbalance of calcium/phosphorus ratio Increased pressure of uterus on nerves Fatigue Poor circulation to lower extremities Pointing the toes | Practice dorsiflexion of feet in order to stretch affected muscle. Evaluate diet. Apply heat to affected muscles. |
| Faintness | Postural hypotension Sudden change of position causing venous pooling in dependent veins Standing for long periods in warm area Anemia | Arise slowly from resting position. Avoid prolonged standing in warm or stuffy environments. Evaluate hematocrit/hemoglobin. |
| Dyspnea | Decreased vital capacity from pressure of enlarging uterus on the diaphragm | Use proper posture when sitting and standing. Sleep propped up with pillows for relief if problem occurs at night. |

## FIRST TRIMESTER

### Nausea and Vomiting

Nausea and vomiting are early symptoms in pregnancy. These symptoms appear sometime after the first missed menstrual period and usually cease by the fourth missed menstrual period. Approximately 50% to 80% of pregnant women experience some degree of nausea (Di Iorio 1988). Some women develop an aversion only to specific foods, many experience nausea upon arising in the morning, and others experience nausea throughout the day. Vomiting does not occur in the majority of these women.

Nausea and vomiting in early pregnancy are believed to be caused by elevated human chorionic gonadotropin (hCG) levels and changes in carbohydrate metabolism, but fatigue and emotional factors may also play a part.

A woman should be advised to contact her health care provider if she vomits more than once a day or shows signs of dehydration such as dry mouth and concentrated urine. In such cases the physician may order antiemetics. However, antiemetics should be avoided if possible during this time because of possible harmful effects on embryo development.

### Urinary Frequency and Urgency

Two common discomforts of pregnancy are urinary frequency and urgency. They occur early in pregnancy and again during the last trimester due to pressure of the enlarging uterus on the bladder. If no other symptoms of urinary tract infection (such as dysuria or hematuria) exist, these are considered normal. The woman should be encouraged to maintain an adequate fluid intake—at least 2000 mL/day. If symptoms of urinary tract infection develop, she should contact her care giver.

### Breast Tenderness

Sensitivity of the breasts occurs early and continues throughout the pregnancy. Increased levels of estrogen and progesterone contribute to soreness and tingling of the breasts and increased sensitivity of the nipples.

### Increased Vaginal Discharge

Increased whitish vaginal discharge (**leukorrhea**) is common in pregnancy. It occurs as a result of hyperplasia of the vaginal mucosa and increased mucus production by the endocervical glands.

### Nasal Stuffiness and Epistaxis

Once pregnancy is well established, elevated estrogen levels may produce edema of the nasal mucosa. This results in nasal stuffiness, nasal discharge, and obstruction. Epistaxis (nosebleeds) may also result. Cool air vaporizers may help, but the problem is often unresponsive to treatment. Women experiencing these problems find it difficult to sleep and may resort to nasal sprays and decongestants. Such interventions can increase nasal stuffiness and create other discomforts. In addition, the use of any medications in pregnancy should be avoided unless approved by the woman's care giver.

### Ptyalism

**Ptyalism** is a rare discomfort of pregnancy in which excessive, often bitter saliva is produced. The cause is unknown, and effective treatments are limited.

## SECOND AND THIRD TRIMESTERS

It is more difficult to classify discomforts as specifically occurring in the second or third trimesters, since many problems are due to individual variations in women. The discomforts discussed in this section usually do not appear until the third trimester in primigravidas but occur earlier with each succeeding pregnancy.

### Heartburn (Pyrosis)

Heartburn is the regurgitation of acidic gastric contents into the esophagus. It creates a burning sensation in the esophagus and radiates upward, sometimes leaving a bad taste in the mouth. Heartburn appears to be primarily a result of the displacement of the stomach by the enlarging uterus. The increased production of progesterone in pregnancy, decreases in gastrointestinal motility, and relaxation of the cardiac (esophageal) sphincter also contribute to heartburn.

The care giver may recommend a low-sodium antacid, such as aluminum hydroxide (Amphojel) or a combination of aluminum hydroxide and magnesium hydroxide (Maalox). Since aluminum alone tends to cause constipation and magnesium alone is associated with diarrhea, the combined approach is more desirable. Although calcium-based antacids (Tums) neutralize well, they are sometimes associated with a rebound hyperacidity and are not the first choice during pregnancy (Brucker 1988). Common household remedies containing sodium bicarbonate (baking soda) should never be used for heartburn during pregnancy because they may lead to electrolyte imbalance.

### Ankle Edema

Most women experience ankle edema in the last part of pregnancy because of the increasing difficulty of venous return from the lower extremities. Prolonged standing or sitting and warm weather increase the edema. It is also associated with varicose veins.

### Varicose Veins

Varicose veins are a result of weakening of the walls of veins or faulty functioning of the valves. Poor circulation in

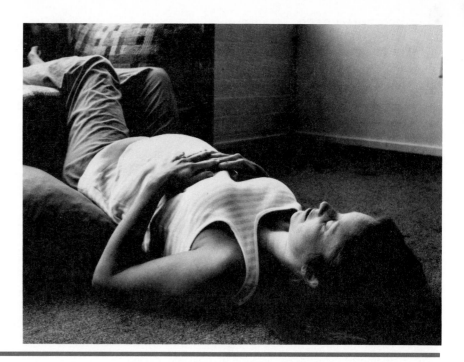

*Figure 8.1 Swelling and discomfort from varicosities can be decreased by lying down with the legs and one hip elevated (to avoid compression of the vena cava).*

the lower extremities predisposes to varicose veins in the legs and thighs, as does prolonged standing or sitting. Pressure of the gravid uterus on the pelvic veins prevents good venous return and may therefore aggravate existing problems or contribute to obvious changes in the veins of the legs.

Treatment of varicose veins by the injection method or by surgery is not recommended during pregnancy. The woman should be aware that treatment may be needed after pregnancy because the problem will be aggravated by a succeeding pregnancy.

Although they are less common, varicosities in the vulva and perineum may also develop. They produce aching and a sense of heaviness in these areas. The woman may relieve uterine pressure on the pelvic veins by resting on her side.

### Hemorrhoids

Hemorrhoids are varicosities of the veins in the lower rectum and the anus. During pregnancy, the gravid uterus presses on the veins and interferes with venous circulation. In addition, the straining that accompanies constipation frequently is a contributing cause of hemorrhoids.

Some women may not be bothered by hemorrhoids until the second stage of labor, when the hemorrhoids appear as they push. These usually become asymptomatic during the early postpartal period.

Symptoms of hemorrhoids include itching, swelling, pain, and bleeding. Women who had hemorrhoids prior to pregnancy will probably experience difficulties with them during pregnancy.

The woman can find relief by gently reinserting the  hemorrhoid. The woman lies on her side, places some lubricant on her finger, and presses against the hemorrhoids, pushing them inside. She holds them in place for one to two minutes and then gently withdraws her finger. The anal sphincter should then hold them inside the rectum. The woman will find it especially helpful if she can then maintain a side-lying (Sims') position for a time, so this method is best done before bed or prior to a daily rest period.

### Constipation

Conditions that predispose the pregnant woman to constipation include general bowel sluggishness caused by increased progesterone and steroid metabolism; displacement of the intestines, which increases with the growth of the fetus; and the oral iron supplements some women need.

In severe or preexisting cases of constipation, the physician may prescribe stool softeners, mild laxatives, or suppositories.

### Backache

Many pregnant women experience backache, due primarily to exaggeration of the lumbosacral curve that occurs as the uterus enlarges and becomes heavier.

The use of good posture and proper body mechanics throughout pregnancy is important in preventing backache. The woman should avoid bending over to pick up objects but should bend from the knees instead (Figure 8.2). She should place her feet 12–18 in apart to maintain body  balance. If the woman uses work surfaces that require her the foot during childbirth preparation exercises or during rest periods. The exact cause of leg cramps is not known but they may be caused by an imbalance of the calcium/phosphorus ratio of the body.

Leg cramps are more common in the third trimester because of increased weight of the uterus on the nerves supplying the lower extremities. Fatigue and poor circulation in the lower extremities contribute to this problem.

Immediate relief of the muscle spasm is achieved by stretching the muscle (Figure 8.3). The woman may also stand and put her foot flat on the floor. Massage and warm packs can alleviate the discomfort of leg cramps.

The physician may recommend that the woman drink no more than a pint of milk daily and take calcium carbonate or may suggest a quart of milk daily and prescribe aluminum hydroxide gel. This stops the action of phosphorus on calcium by absorbing the phosphorus and eliminating it directly through the intestinal tract. When planning a treatment regimen, care givers must be careful not to exclude milk from the woman's diet totally because it is an excellent source of other essential nutrients.

### Faintness

Many pregnant women feel faint, especially in warm, crowded areas. Faintness is caused by changes in the blood volume and postural hypotension due to pooling of blood in the dependent veins. Sudden change of position or standing for prolonged periods can cause the pregnant woman to feel faint or to faint.

If a woman begins to feel faint from prolonged standing or from being in a warm, crowded room, she should sit

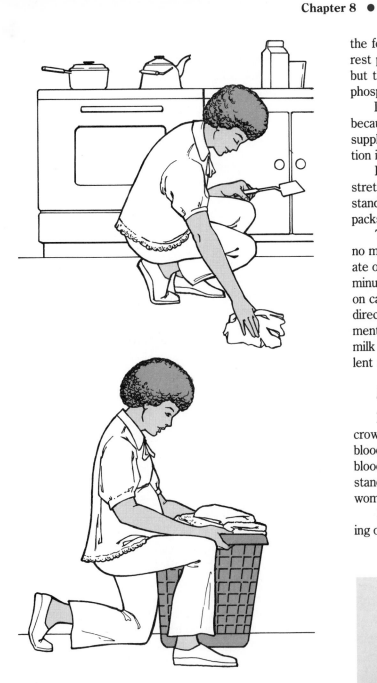

*Figure 8.2   Proper body mechanics must be used by the pregnant woman when picking up objects from floor level or when lifting objects.*

to bend, the nurse should advise the woman to adjust the height of the surfaces.

### Leg Cramps

Leg cramps are painful muscle spasms in the gastrocnemius muscles. They occur most frequently at night after the woman has gone to bed but may occur at other times. Extension of the foot can often cause leg cramps; the nurse should warn the pregnant woman not to extend

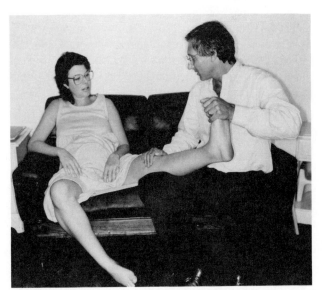

*Figure 8.3   The expectant father can help relieve the woman's painful leg cramps by dorsiflexing the foot while holding her knee flat.*

down and lower her head between her legs. If this procedure does not help, the woman should be assisted to an area where she can lie down and get fresh air. When arising from a resting position, she should move slowly. Women whose jobs require that they stand in one place for long periods should regularly "march in place" to increase venous return from the legs.

### Shortness of Breath

Shortness of breath occurs as the uterus rises into the abdomen and causes pressure on the diaphragm. This problem worsens in the last trimester as the enlarged uterus presses directly on the diaphragm, decreasing vital capacity. In the last few weeks of pregnancy in the primigravida, the fetus and uterus move down in the pelvis, and the woman experiences considerable relief. This feeling is called **lightening**. Because the multigravida does not usually experience lightening until labor, she feels short of breath throughout the later part of her pregnancy.

## ● Promotion of Self-Care During Pregnancy

### FETAL ACTIVITY MONITORING

Currently, many care givers are encouraging pregnant women to monitor their unborn child's well-being by regularly assessing fetal activity. Fetal activity is affected by drugs, cigarette smoking, fetal sleep status, blood glucose level, and time of day. There are times when minimal or no fetal activity occurs with a healthy fetus. Some clinicians have women keep fetal movement records (FMR) or a fetal activity diary (FAD) to monitor fetal activity. This practice helps a pregnant woman become more aware of her fetus's movements. Thus, she can be assured by her own assessment that no problem exists or, if overt decreased fetal activity does occur, she can contact her care giver with documentation of the need for further evaluation. (See Chapter 13 for further discussion.)

### BREAST CARE

Whether the pregnant woman plans to bottle- or breast-feed her infant, proper support of the breasts is important to promote comfort, retain breast shape, and prevent back strain, particularly if the breasts become large and pendulous. The sensitivity of the breasts in pregnancy is also relieved by good support.

A well-fitting, supportive brassiere has the following qualities:

● The straps are wide and do not stretch (elastic straps soon lose their tautness with the weight of the breasts and frequent washing).

● The cup holds all breast tissue comfortably.

● The brassiere has tucks or other devices that allow it to expand, thus accommodating the enlarging chest circumference.

● The brassiere supports the nipple line approximately midway between the elbow and shoulder. At the same time, the brassiere is not pulled up in the back by the weight of the breasts.

Cleanliness of the breasts is important, especially as the woman begins producing colostrum. Colostrum that crusts on the nipples should be removed with warm water. The woman planning to breast-feed should not use soap on her nipples because of its drying effect.

**Nipple preparation**, generally begun during the third trimester, helps prevent soreness during the first few days of breast-feeding. Nipple preparation promotes the distribution of natural lubricants produced by Montgomery's tubercles, stimulates blood flow to the breast, and helps develop the protective layer of skin over the nipple. Women who are planning to nurse can begin by occasionally going braless and by exposing their nipples to sunlight and air. Rubbing the nipples removes protective oils and should be avoided; but rolling the nipple—grasping it between thumb and forefinger and gently rolling it for a short time each day—helps prepare for breast-feeding. A woman with a history of preterm labor is advised not to do this because nipple stimulation triggers the release of oxytocin. (See Chapter 13 for further discussion of the effects of nipple stimulation on contractions.)

Nipple-rolling is more difficult for women with flat or inverted nipples but is still a useful preparation for breast-feeding. Breast shields designed to correct inverted nipples can be worn during pregnancy. The shields appear to be the only measure that really helps women with inverted nipples (Figure 8.4). For further discussion of inverted nipples, see Chapter 23.

Oral stimulation of the nipple by the woman's partner during sex play is also an excellent technique for toughening the nipple in preparation for breast-feeding. The couple who enjoys this stimulation should be encouraged to continue it throughout the pregnancy except in situations in which the woman has a history of preterm labor, as discussed earlier.

### CLOTHING

Clothing in pregnancy can be an important factor in  how the woman feels about herself and her appearance. Clothes affect her general comfort and should be loose and nonconstricting. Maternity clothes can be expensive, however, and are worn for a relatively short time. Women can economize by sharing clothes with friends, sewing their own garments, or buying used maternity clothes.

Maternity girdles are seldom worn today and are not necessary for most women. Some women athletes who

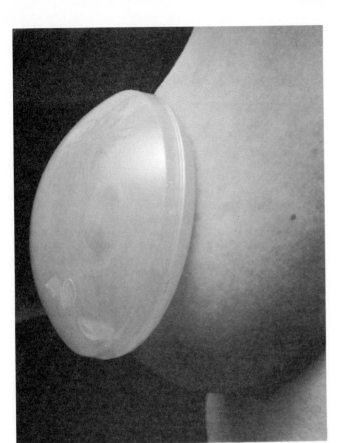

*Figure 8.4 This breast shield is designed to increase the protractility of inverted nipples. These shields, worn the last three to four months of pregnancy, exert gentle pulling pressure at the edge of the areola, gradually forcing the nipple through the center of the shield. They may be used after delivery if still necessary.*

maintain a light workout schedule during pregnancy use a girdle to provide support. Women who have large pendulous abdomens also benefit from a well-fitting, supportive girdle. Tight leg bands on girdles should be avoided.

High-heeled shoes aggravate back discomfort by increasing the curvature of the lower back. They should not be worn if the woman experiences backache or problems with balance. Shoes should fit properly and feel comfortable.

## BATHING

Daily bathing is important because perspiration and mucoid vaginal discharge increase during pregnancy. The woman may take showers or tub baths, but tub baths are contraindicated in the presence of vaginal bleeding or when the membranes are ruptured, because of the possibility of introducing infection.

Caution is needed because balance becomes a problem in pregnancy. Rubber mats in the tub and hand grips are important safety devices. Extremely warm bath water

causes vasodilation; after a hot bath, the woman may feel faint when she attempts to get out of the tub. Because of this possibility, she may need help getting out of the tub, especially during the last trimester.

## EMPLOYMENT

Most working women continue to work outside the home throughout pregnancy. Some women work because they need the money or because their work is personally satisfying and important to them. Others work to overcome boredom.

Fetotoxic hazards in the environment, overfatigue, excessive physical strain, and medical or obstetric complications are the major deterrents to employment during pregnancy. Employment involving balance may be terminated during the last half of pregnancy to protect the mother.

Fetotoxic hazards are always a concern to the expectant couple. The pregnant woman (or the woman contemplating pregnancy) who works in industry should contact her company physician or nurse about possible hazards in the work environment.

## TRAVEL

Pregnant women often have many questions about the  effects of travel on themselves and their unborn children. If there are no medical or obstetric complications, travel is not restricted.

Travel by automobile can be especially fatiguing, aggravating many of the discomforts of pregnancy. The pregnant woman needs frequent opportunities to get out of the car and walk. A good pattern for the woman to follow is to stop every two hours and walk around for approximately ten minutes. Seat belts, including both lap and shoulder belts, should be worn. The lap belt should fit snugly and be positioned under the abdomen. Although seat belts can cause internal damage during a collision, without them the woman could be fatally injured. To decrease the risk of bladder trauma in the event of an accident, the woman should be encouraged to void regularly while traveling.

As pregnancy progresses, long-distance trips are best taken by plane or train. The availability of medical care at the destination is an important factor for the near-term woman who travels.

## ACTIVITY AND REST

Normal participation in exercise can continue through-  out an uncomplicated pregnancy. The woman should check with her physician or nurse-midwife about taking part in strenuous sports, such as skiing, diving, and horseback riding. In general, however, the skilled sportswoman is no longer discouraged from participating in these activities if her pregnancy is uncomplicated. Pregnancy, however, is not the appropriate time to learn strenuous sports. Swimming and bicycling are safe, nonweight-bearing exercises for the pregnant woman. They eliminate the bouncing associated with other exercise and are well tolerated physically (Ketter and Shelton 1984).

Exercise helps prevent constipation, condition the body, and maintain a healthy mental state. It is, however, especially important during pregnancy not to overdo it.

The nurse may find the following guidelines useful in counseling pregnant women about exercise during pregnancy (Paolone and Worthington 1985):

● Exercise for shorter intervals. By exercising for 10 to 15 minutes, resting for a few minutes, and then exercising for an additional 10 to 15 minutes the woman decreases potential problems that may be associated with the shunting of blood to the musculoskeletal system and away from organs such as the uterus.

● As pregnancy progresses, decrease the intensity of the exercise. This helps compensate for the decreased cardiac reserve, increased respiratory effort, and increased weight of the pregnant woman.

● Avoid prolonged overheating. Strenuous exercise, especially in a humid environment, can raise the core body temperature. Prolonged maternal hyperthermia, especially in the first trimester, may increase the risk of teratogenesis. By the same token the woman should avoid hot tubs and saunas.

● As pregnancy progresses, avoid high-risk activities such as skydiving, mountain climbing, racquetball, and surfing. Such activities require balance and coordination but the woman's changed center of gravity and softened joints may decrease coordination.

● Warm up and stretch to help prepare the joints for activity, and cool down with a period of mild activity to help restore circulation while avoiding pooling of blood.

● After exercising, lie on the left side for ten minutes to rest. This improves return of circulation from the extremities and promotes placental perfusion.

● Wear supportive shoes and a supportive bra.

● Stop exercising and contact the care giver if dizziness, shortness of breath, tingling, numbness, vaginal bleeding, or abdominal pain occur.

● Reduce exercise significantly during the last four weeks of pregnancy. Some evidence suggests that strenuous exercise near term increases the risk of low birth weight, stillbirth, and infant death.

In addition, the American College of Obstetricians and Gynecologists (ACOG) guidelines on exercise during pregnancy (1985) recommend that the woman maintain her pulse rate at 140 beats/min or less, that she drink sufficient fluids before and after exercising, and that she avoid exercising while flat on her back after the fourth month of pregnancy.

Adequate rest in pregnancy is important for both physical and emotional health. Women need more sleep throughout pregnancy, particularly in the first and last trimesters, when they tire easily. Without adequate rest, pregnant women have less resilience.

Finding time to rest during the day may be difficult for women who work or have small children. The nurse can help the expectant mother examine her daily schedule to develop a realistic plan for short periods of rest and relaxation.

Sleeping becomes more difficult during the last trimester because of the enlarged abdomen, increased frequency of urination, and greater activity of the fetus. Finding a comfortable position becomes difficult for the pregnant woman. Figure 8.5 shows a position most pregnant women find comfortable. Progressive relaxation techniques similar to those taught in prepared childbirth classes can help prepare the woman for sleep.

*Figure 8.5 Position for relaxation and rest as pregnancy progresses*

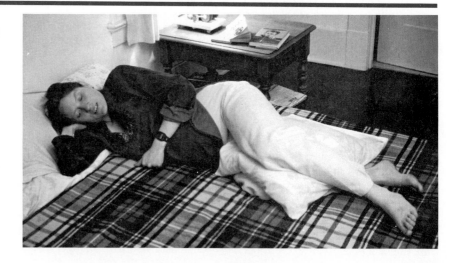

## EXERCISES

In pregnancy, exercises help strengthen muscle tone in preparation for delivery and promote more rapid restoration of muscle tone after delivery. Certain physical changes of pregnancy can be reduced considerably by faithfully practicing prescribed body conditioning exercises early in the prenatal period, as well as during the puerperium. A great variety of body conditioning exercises are taught, but only a few are discussed here.

The **pelvic tilt**, or pelvic rocking, helps prevent or reduce back strain and strengthens abdominal muscle tone. To do the pelvic tilt, the pregnant woman lies on her back and puts her feet flat on the floor. This bent position of the knees helps prevent strain and discomfort. She decreases the curvature in her back by pressing her spine toward the floor. With her back pressed to the floor, the woman tightens her abdominal muscles as she tightens and tucks in her buttocks. The pelvic tilt can also be performed on hands and knees (Figure 8.6), while sitting in a chair, or while standing with the back against a wall. The body alignment that results when the pelvic tilt is correctly done should be maintained as much as possible throughout the day.

### Abdominal Exercises

A basic exercise to increase abdominal muscle tone is tightening abdominal muscles in synchronization with respirations. It can be done in any position, but it is best learned while the woman lies supine. With knees flexed and feet flat on the floor, the woman expands her abdomen and slowly takes a deep breath. As she slowly exhales, she gradually pulls in her abdominal muscles until they are fully contracted. She relaxes for a few seconds, and then repeats the exercise.

Partial sit-ups strengthen abdominal muscle tone and are done according to individual comfort levels. When doing a partial sit-up, the woman lies on the floor as described above. This exercise must be done with the knees flexed and the feet flat on the floor to avoid undue strain on the lower back. The woman stretches her arms toward her knees as she slowly pulls her head and shoulders off the floor to a comfortable level (if she has poor abdominal muscle tone, she may not be able to pull up very far). She then slowly returns to the starting position, takes a deep breath, and repeats the exercise. To strengthen the oblique abdominal muscles, she repeats the process, but stretches the left arm to the side of her right knee, returns to the floor, takes a deep breath, and then reaches with the right arm to the left knee.

These exercises can be done approximately five times in a sequence, and the sequence can be repeated at other times during the day as desired. It is important to do the exercises slowly to prevent muscle strain and overtiring.

### Perineal Exercises

Perineal muscle tightening, also referred to as **Kegel's exercises**, strengthens the pubococcygeus muscle and increases its elasticity (Figure 8.7). The woman can feel the specific muscle group to be exercised by stopping urination midstream. Doing Kegel's exercises while urinating, however, is discouraged because this practice has been associated with urinary stasis and urinary tract infection. Childbirth educators sometimes use the following technique to teach Kegel's exercises. They tell the woman to think of her perineal muscles as an elevator. When she relaxes, the elevator is on the first floor. To do the exercises, she contracts, bringing the elevator to the second, third, and fourth floors. She keeps the elevator on the fourth floor for a few seconds, and then gradually relaxes the area (Fenlon et al 1986). If the exercise is properly done, the woman does not contract the muscles of the buttocks and thighs.

Kegel's exercises can be done at almost any time. Some women use ordinary events—for instance, stopping at a red light—as a cue to remember to do the exercise. Others do Kegel's exercises while waiting in a checkout line, talking on the telephone, or watching television.

### Inner Thigh Exercises

The pregnant woman should assume a cross-legged sitting position whenever possible. The *tailor sit* stretches the muscles of the inner thighs in preparation for labor and birth.

## SEXUAL ACTIVITY

As a result of the physiologic, anatomic, and emotional changes of pregnancy, the couple usually has many questions and concerns about sexual activity during pregnancy. Often, these questions are about possible injury to the baby or the woman during intercourse and about changes in the desire each partner feels for the other.

In the past, couples were frequently warned to avoid sexual intercourse during the last six to eight weeks of pregnancy to prevent complications such as infection or premature rupture of the membranes. However, these fears seem to be unfounded. In a healthy pregnancy, there is no valid reason to limit sexual activity (Reamy and White 1985). Intercourse is contraindicated only when bleeding is present, membranes are ruptured, or other complications that might lead to premature delivery exist.

The expectant mother may experience changes in sexual desire and response. Often, these are related to the various discomforts that occur throughout pregnancy. For instance, during the first trimester, fatigue or nausea and vomiting may decrease desire, while breast tenderness may make the woman less responsive to fondling of her breasts. During the second trimester, many of the discomforts have lessened, and, with the vascular congestion of

A

B

C

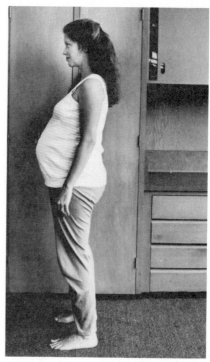

D

*Figure 8.6   (**A**) Starting position when the pelvic tilt is done on the hands and knees. The back is flat and parallel to the floor, the hands are under the head, and the knees are directly under the buttocks. (**B**) A prenatal yoga instructor offers pointers for proper positioning for the first part of the tilt: head up, neck long and separated from the shoulders, buttocks up and pelvis thrust back, allowing the back to drop and release on an inhaled breath. (**C**) The instructor assists the woman in assuming the correct position for the next part of the tilt. It is done on a long exhalation, allowing the pregnant woman to arch her back, drop her head loosely, push away from her hands, and draw in the muscles of her abdomen to strengthen them. Note that in this position the pelvis and buttocks are tucked under and the buttock muscles are tightened. (**D**) Proper posture. The knees are not locked but slightly bent, the pelvis and buttocks are tucked under, thereby lengthening the spine and helping to support the weighty abdomen. With her chin tucked in, this woman's neck, shoulders, hips, knees, and feet are all in a straight line perpendicular to the floor. Her feet are parallel. This is also the starting position for doing the pelvic tilt while standing.*

the pelvis, the woman may experience greater sexual satisfaction than she experienced prior to pregnancy.

During the third trimester, interest in coitus may again decrease as the woman becomes more uncomfortable and fatigued. In addition, shortness of breath, painful pelvic ligaments, urinary frequency, and decreased mobility may lessen sexual desire and activity. If they are not already being used, coital positions other than male superior, such as side-by-side, female superior, and rear-entry, should be considered.

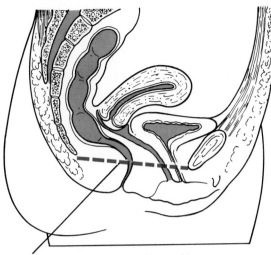

Pubococcygeus muscle with good tone

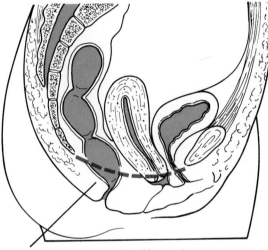

Pubococcygeus muscle with poor tone

*Figure 8.7 Kegel's exercises. The woman learns to tighten the pubococcygeus muscle, which improves support to the pelvic organs.*

Sexual activity does not have to include intercourse. Many of the nurturing and sexual needs of the pregnant woman can be satisfied by cuddling, kissing, and being held. The warm, sensual feelings that accompany these activities can be an end in themselves. Her partner, however, may need to masturbate more frequently than before. The sexual desires of men are also affected by many factors in pregnancy. These include the previous relationship with the partner, acceptance of the pregnancy, attitudes toward the partner's change of appearance, and concern about hurting the expectant mother or baby.

The expectant couple should be aware of their changing sexual desires, the normality of these changes, and the importance of communicating these changes to each other so that they can make nurturing adaptations. The nurse has an important role in helping the expectant couple adapt. It is essential that nurses feel comfortable about their own sexuality and be well informed about the subject. When nurses counsel expectant couples, an accepting and nonjudgmental attitude is important. The couple must feel free to express concerns about sexual activity, and the nurse must be able to respond and give anticipatory guidance in a comfortable manner. The Teaching Guide: Sexual Activity During Pregnancy provides further information and offers suggestions for covering this material.

## DENTAL CARE

Proper dental hygiene is important in pregnancy. In spite of such discomforts as nausea and vomiting, gum hypertrophy and tenderness, possible ptyalism, and heartburn, regular oral hygiene must not be neglected.

The pregnant woman is encouraged to have a dental checkup early in her pregnancy. General dental repair and extractions can be done during pregnancy, preferably under local anesthetic. The woman should inform her dentist of her pregnancy so that she is not exposed to teratogenic substances. Dental x-ray examinations and extensive dental work should be delayed until after childbirth when possible.

## IMMUNIZATIONS

All women of childbearing age should be aware of the risks of receiving certain immunizations if pregnancy is possible. Immunizations with attenuated live viruses should not be given in pregnancy because of the teratogenic effect of the live viruses on the developing embryo. Vaccinations using killed viruses can be used.

## TERATOGENIC SUBSTANCES

Substances that adversely affect the normal growth and development of the fetus are called **teratogens**. Many of these effects are readily apparent at birth, but others may not be identified for years. A well-known example is the development of cervical cancer in adolescent females whose mothers took diethylstilbestrol (DES) during pregnancy.

Many substances are known or suspected to be teratogens, including medications, cigarettes, psychotropic drugs, and alcohol. The harmful effects of others, such as some pesticides and exposure to x-rays in the first trimester of pregnancy, have been documented. During pregnancy, women need to have a realistic attitude about environmental hazards. Those factors that are suspected as hazards to the general population should obviously be avoided if possible.

## Medications

The use of medications during pregnancy, including both prescription and over-the-counter drugs, is of great concern. Even when a woman is highly motivated to avoid taking any medications, she may ingest potentially teratogenic medications before her pregnancy is diagnosed, especially if she has an irregular menstrual cycle.

The greatest potential for gross abnormalities in the fetus occurs during the first trimester of pregnancy, when initial organ development is taking place. Many factors influence teratogenic effects, including medication dosage and timing of ingestion as correlated with specific organ development. Individual metabolic and circulatory factors in the mother, placenta, and fetus are also important, as are other factors about the substance. Table 8.4 identifies the possible effects of selected drugs on the fetus and neonate.

Although the first trimester is the critical period for teratogenesis, some medications are known to have teratogenic effect when taken in the second and third trimesters. Two prescription drugs with teratogenic effects are tetracycline and sulfonamides. Tetracycline taken in late pregnancy is commonly associated with staining of teeth in children and has been shown to retard limb growth in premature infants. Sulfonamides in the last few weeks of pregnancy are known to compete with bilirubin attachment of protein-binding sites, resulting in the occurrence of jaundice in the newborn (Knothe and Dette 1985).

Although low doses of aspirin are being used in experimental trials to treat preeclampsia and to prevent fetal growth retardation, its use is associated with bleeding disorders in both the mother and the newborn. Thus, until evidence suggests otherwise, aspirin should be avoided during pregnancy and while breast-feeding (Sibai and Amon 1988).

Many pregnant women need medication for therapeutic purposes, such as the treatment of infections, allergies, or other pathologic processes. In these situations, the problem can be extremely complex. Known teratogenic agents are not prescribed and usually can be replaced by medications considered safe. Unfortunately, reliable data about how many medications affect a fetus are lacking.

All medication should be avoided if possible. If no alternative exists, the following guidelines should be followed when medication is prescribed (Whipkey et al 1984):

● Select well-known medications rather than newer drugs whose potential teratogenic effects may not be known.

● Reduce the effects of fetal exposure by using the lowest possible therapeutic dose for the shortest time possible.

● When possible, use the oral form of a medication.

● Carefully consider the multiple components of the medication.

Caution is the watchword for nurses caring for pregnant women who have been taking medications. It is essential that the pregnant woman check with her physician about medications that she was taking when pregnancy occurred and about any nonprescription drugs that she is contemplating using. A good rule to follow is that the advantage of using a particular medication must outweigh the risks. Any medication with possible teratogenic effects must be avoided.

## Smoking

Many studies in the last several years have shown that infants of mothers who smoke have a lower birth weight than infants of mothers who do not smoke. In addition, many studies have found that intrauterine growth retardation (IUGR) increases with the number of cigarettes smoked; IUGR was minimal or avoided when women stopped smoking early in the pregnancy (Naeye 1981).

The exact reason for this IUGR is not known. Many authorities believe that the passage of carbon monoxide through the placenta produces intrauterine hypoxia. Others suggest that the vasoconstrictive effect of nicotine influences the fetus directly or indirectly by decreasing placental perfusion (Mochizuki et al 1984).

Maternal smoking has also been implicated as a factor in preterm delivery, increased incidence of congenital anomalies, and infant developmental problems such as short attention span, low spelling and reading scores, and hyperactivity (Alexander 1987).

Fewer women smoke today than did 20 years ago. Women who do smoke tend to reduce their smoking significantly once pregnancy is diagnosed. Moreover, intervention programs designed to reduce smoking during pregnancy have been surprisingly successful and the results have been continued during the postpartum period (Kruse et al 1986).

Studies demonstrate that any decrease in smoking during pregnancy improves the fetal outcome. Pregnancy may be a difficult time for a woman to stop smoking, but the nurse should encourage her to reduce the number of cigarettes she smokes daily. The need to protect her unborn baby can increase her motivation.

## Marijuana and Cocaine

The use of marijuana in our society raises questions about its effect on a fetus. Research on marijuana use in pregnancy is difficult, however, because it is an illegal drug. A few studies have been done but their results are inconclusive. Some suggest that infants of mothers who use marijuana are small as a result either of IUGR or of decreased length of gestation. They may also have an increased risk of having features similar to those associated with fetal alcohol syndrome (FAS) (Fried et al 1984, Hingson et al 1982).

Cocaine does seem to have an impact on pregnancy

# Teaching Guide
## Sexual Activity During Pregnancy

**Assessment**  Occasionally a woman indicates her beliefs about sexual activity during pregnancy by asking a direct question. This is most likely to occur if the woman and the nurse have a good rapport. Often, however, the nurse must ask some general questions to determine the woman's level of understanding. A general statement may trigger a discussion and help the nurse in his or her determination. In many cases teaching about this topic is coupled with ongoing assessment of the woman's understanding of sexual activity during pregnancy.

**Nursing Diagnosis**  The essential nursing diagnosis will probably be: Knowledge deficit related to a lack of understanding about changes in sexuality and sexual activity during pregnancy.

**Nursing Plan and Implementation**  The teaching plan will generally focus on discussion or use a "question and answer" format. The presence of both partners may be beneficial in fostering communication between them and is acceptable unless personal or cultural factors indicate otherwise.

**Client Goals**  At the completion of the teaching the woman will:

1. Relate the changes in sexuality and sexual response that may occur during pregnancy to changes in technique, frequency, and response that may be indicated.

2. Explore personal attitudes, beliefs, and expectations about sexual activity during pregnancy.

3. Cite maternal factors that would contraindicate sexual intercourse.

## Teaching Plan

### Content

Begin by explaining that the pregnant woman may experience changes in desire during the course of pregnancy. During the first trimester discomforts such as nausea, fatigue, and breast tenderness may make intercourse less desirable for many women.

Other woman may have fewer discomforts and may find that their sexual desire is unchanged. In the second trimester as symptoms decrease desire may increase. In the third trimester discomfort and fatigue may lead to decreased desire in the woman.

Men may notice changes in their level of desire, too. Among other things, this may be related to feelings about their partner's changing appearance, their belief about the acceptability of sexual activity with a pregnant woman, or concern about hurting the woman or fetus. Some men find the changes of pregnancy erotic while others must adjust to the notion of their partner as a mother.

Explain that the woman may notice that orgasms are much more intense during the last weeks of pregnancy and may be followed by cramping. Because of the pressure of the enlarging uterus on the vena cava the woman should not lie flat on her back for intercourse after about the fourth month. If the couple prefer that position, a pillow should be placed under her right hip to displace the uterus. Alternate positions such as side-lying, female-superior or vaginal rear entry may become necessary as her uterus enlarges.

### Teaching Method

*Universal statements that give permission, such as "Many couples experience changes in sexual desire during pregnancy. What kind of changes have you experienced?" are often effective in starting discussion. Depending on the woman's (or couple's) level of knowledge and sophistication, part or all of this discussion may be necessary.*

*If the partner is present approach him in the same nonjudgmental way used above. If not, ask the woman if she has noticed any changes in her partner or if he has expressed any concerns.*

*Deal with any specific questions about the physical and psychologic changes that the couple may have.*

*(continues)*

## Teaching Plan (continued)

## Content

Stress that sexual activities that both partners enjoy are generally acceptable. It is not advisable for couples who favor anal sex to go from anal penetration to vaginal penetration because of the risk of introducing *E coli* into the vagina.

Alternate methods of expressing intimacy and affection such as cuddling, holding and stroking each other, and kissing may help maintain the couple's feelings of warmth and closeness.

If the man feels desire for further sexual release, his partner may help him masturbate to ejaculation or he may prefer to masturbate in private.

The woman who is interested in masturbation as a form of gratification should be advised that the orgasmic contractions may be especially intense in later pregnancy.

Stress that sexual intercourse is contraindicated once the membranes are ruptured or if bleeding is present. Women with a history of preterm labor may be advised to avoid intercourse because the oxytocin that is released with orgasm stimulates uterine contractions and may trigger preterm labor. Since oxytocin is also released with nipple stimulation, fondling the breasts may also be contraindicated in those cases.

A discussion of sexuality and sexual activity should stress the importance of open communication so that the couple feel comfortable expressing their feelings, preferences, and concerns.

## Teaching Method

*Discussion about various sexual activities requires that the nurse be comfortable with his/her sexuality and be tactful. Often the nurse may find it advisable to volunteer such information to show that discussion of sexual variations is acceptable.*

*The couple may be content with these approaches to meeting their sexual needs or they may require assurance that such approaches are indeed "normal."*

*An explanation of the contraindications accompanied by their rationale provides specific guidelines that most couples find helpful.*

*Some couples are skilled at expressing their feelings about sexual activity while others find it difficult and can benefit from specific suggestions.*

*The nurse should provide opportunities for discussion throughout the talk.*

*Specific handouts on sexual activity are also helpful for couples and may address topics that were not discussed.*

---

**Evaluation** The nurse determines the effectiveness of the teaching by evaluating the woman's (or couple's) response to information throughout the discussion. The nurse may also ask the woman to express information such as the contraindications to intercourse in her own words. Follow-up sessions and questions from the woman also provide information about teaching effectiveness.

and the status of the fetus/infant. Cocaine acts to block norepinephrine uptake in the peripheral nerves. This leads to increased norepinephrine levels, which cause vasoconstriction, tachycardia, and a rise in blood pressure. The pregnant woman who uses cocaine has decreased blood flow to the placenta because of the vasoconstriction. Uterine contractility also increases. Cocaine use in early pregnancy has been linked to an increased incidence of spontaneous abortion. Third trimester use of cocaine has been linked to preterm labor and an increased incidence of

### Table 8.4 Possible Effects of Selected Drugs on the Fetus and Neonate

| Maternal drug | Effects on fetus and neonate |
| --- | --- |
| RISK OUTWEIGHS BENEFITS IF THE FOLLOWING DRUGS ARE GIVEN IN THE FIRST TRIMESTER: | |
| Thalidomide | Limb, auricle, eye, and visceral malformations |
| Tolbutamide (Orinase) | Increase of anomalies |
| Streptomycin | Eighth nerve damage; multiple skeletal anomalies |
| Tetracycline | Inhibition of bone growth, syndactyly, discoloration of teeth |
| Iodide | Congenital goiter; hypothyroidism; mental retardation |
| Methotrexate | Multiple anomalies |
| Diethylstilbestrol | Clear-cell adenocarcinoma of the vagina and cervix; genital tract anomalies |
| Warfarin (Coumarin) | Skeletal and facial anomalies; mental retardation |
| RISK VS. BENEFITS UNCERTAIN IN THE FIRST TRIMESTER: | |
| Gentamicin | Eighth cranial nerve damage |
| Kanamycin | Eighth cranial nerve damage |
| Lithium | Goiter; eye anomalies; cleft palate |
| Barbiturates | Increase of anomalies |
| Quinine | Increase of anomalies |
| Septra or Bactrim | Cleft palate |
| Cytotoxic Drugs | Increase of anomalies |
| BENEFIT OUTWEIGHS RISK IN THE FIRST TRIMESTER: | |
| Clomiphene (Clomid) | Increase of anomalies; neural tube defects; Down syndrome |
| Glucocorticoids | Cleft palate; cardiac defects |
| General anesthesia | Increase of anomalies |
| Tricyclic antidepressants | CNS and limb malformations |
| Sulfonamides | Cleft palate; facial and skeletal defects |
| Antacids | Increase of anomalies |
| Salicylates | Central nervous system, visceral, and skeletal malformations |
| Acetominophen | None |
| Heparin | None |
| Terbutaline | None |
| Phenothiazines | None |
| Insulin | Skeletal malformations |
| Penicillins | None |
| Chloramphenicol | None |
| Isoniazide (INH) | Increase of anomalies |

Source: Adapted from Howard FM, Hill JM: *Obstet Gynecol Surv* 1979 34:643. Modified and used with permission from Danforth DN. *Obstetrics and Gynecology*, 4th ed. Philadelphia: Harper and Row, 1982, pp 496–497.

abruptio placentae, precipitous delivery, and meconium-stained amniotic fluid (Chasnoff 1987).

Alkaloidal cocaine ("crack"), an almost pure form of cocaine that is smoked, delivers large quantities of the drug to the blood vessels of the lungs, causing an effect similar to that which occurs with intravenous use. Women who used "crack" during pregnancy have a higher incidence of premature rupture of the membranes, while their infants tend to have IUGR and show neurologic signs such as irritability and tremulousness (Cherukuri 1988).

In general, infants born to cocaine users have an increased risk of IUGR (Chouteau 1988). They are less able to respond to environmental stimuli and show signs of depressed interactive behavior. These newborns have also been found to be poor feeders and to have increased respiratory and heart rates, irritability, irregular sleep patterns, and diarrhea (Newald 1986). In addition, they have an increased risk of dying from sudden infant death syndrome (SIDS) (Chasnoff 1987).

As cocaine becomes more widely used by women of childbearing age, health care providers must become alert to early signs of cocaine use. It is often difficult for a nurse or physician to face the fact that a woman with whom they have a relationship may be using cocaine, but ongoing alertness and an open, nonjudgmental approach are important in early detection. Urine screening for cocaine is not presently available in all agencies, but urine screening may become a useful tool in early detection.

### Alcohol

Alcohol was first recognized as a teratogenic substance during pregnancy in 1968 (Lemoine et al 1968). Newborns with a specific combination of characteristics were identified as having **fetal alcohol syndrome (FAS)**. Most of the research demonstrates that heavy alcohol consumption increases the risk of FAS, but the effect of moderate consumption of alcohol is still not clear. Some research has indicated increased association of alcohol use with spontaneous abortion, mental retardation, and behavioral problems (Kruse et al 1986). The general conclusion currently is that the risk of teratogenic effects increases proportionately with the consumption of alcohol. Pregnant women who have an occasional drink should not be unduly alarmed about the effect it will have on the fetus. However, the best advice to those planning a pregnancy or already pregnant is to avoid all alcohol.

In most cases, once a woman becomes aware of her pregnancy, she decreases her consumption of alcohol. However, the alcohol consumed immediately after conception and before pregnancy is diagnosed remains a cause for concern.

Assessment of alcohol intake should be a chief part of every woman's medical history; any questions should be asked in a direct and nonjudgmental manner. All women should be counseled about the role of alcohol in pregnancy.

If heavy consumption is involved, the woman should be referred immediately to an alcoholic treatment program. Counselors in these programs should be made aware of a woman's pregnancy before drug therapy is suggested, since certain drugs may be harmful to the developing fetus. For example, the drug disulfiram (Antabuse), often used in conjunction with alcohol treatment, is suspected as a teratogenic agent.

## One Family's Story

*Pamela Paulson is a 24-year-old gravida 2 para 0 whose first pregnancy ended in spontaneous abortion a year ago. Pam is a secretary for a construction firm and plans to continue working as long as possible. Her husband, Steve, is an electrician and has a fairly stable year-round income. Mrs Paulson was first seen in the clinic when she was nine weeks pregnant. Her first contact was Marie Carls, an RN. Ms Carls checked Mrs Paulson's vital signs, weight, and urine specimen; drew blood for laboratory tests; and completed the health history. She then asked Mrs Paulson if she had any questions or concerns. Mrs Paulson revealed that her pregnancy had been planned, and both she and her husband were eager to have a baby. However, she was constantly afraid that she would do something that might result in another miscarriage. Ms Carls reassured her that it was not unusual for a woman to have one miscarriage. She then asked Mrs Paulson if there was anything in her life-style or environment that might be a risk factor. Mrs Paulson stated she was an avid swimmer and generally stopped at the YWCA on her way home from work to swim. However, she had given that up once she suspected she was pregnant for fear of causing another miscarriage. Ms Carls reassured her that as long as she was not having any bleeding or other problems that might interfere, swimming was a wonderful exercise that she certainly could continue. She advised her to monitor her level of fatigue to avoid overdoing it. She and Mrs Paulson discussed her life-style further, and the nurse was able to reassure her that it was a healthy one. The remainder of the visit went well. Mrs Paulson's physician, Warren Lindsey, reported that her physical exam was normal and her pelvis appeared large enough for successful vaginal delivery. She was started on a vitamin and iron supplement; the warning signs of potential problems in pregnancy were reviewed; and she left with literature to read about all other aspects of pregnancy.*

*The early months of Mrs Paulson's pregnancy went smoothly. She did not suffer from nausea, and the urinary frequency she experienced eased in her fourth month. She continued prenatal visits every four weeks. As Mrs Paulson began wearing maternity clothes, her fear of miscarriage abated.*

*Mrs Paulson felt the first flutterings of fetal movement at 19 weeks, and the fetal heart tones (FHT) were auscultated a week later. She persuaded her husband to accompany her on a prenatal visit, and he obviously enjoyed hearing the FHT with the Doppler.*

*In her seventh month, Mrs Paulson began to develop varicose veins in her legs and had problems with hemorrhoids. Ms Carls and Mrs Paulson discussed her schedule and habits, identifying some changes she might make to ease her discomfort. Mrs*

*Paulson began wearing maternity support hose to work and walking around her office every hour. During breaks and at lunch, she lay on her side in the staff lounge with her feet elevated. She continued her evening swims. A review of Mrs Paulson's diet showed it had sufficient fiber, fresh fruit, and vegetables. She also drank several glasses of water every day. Nevertheless, constipation was still a problem. Ms Carls reported these findings to Dr Lindsey, and he prescribed a mild stool softener. Mrs Paulson continued to follow this regimen, and her symptoms eased.*

*At 37 weeks, Mrs Paulson began experiencing urinary frequency again, and physical assessment showed that lightening had occurred. Mrs Paulson reported to Ms Carls that the nursery was ready and her suitcase was packed. She and her husband had taken the childbirth preparation classes offered at the clinic, and she felt well prepared.*

*Mrs Paulson and Ms Carls spent some time talking about what being a parent meant, and Ms Carls gave Mrs Paulson some interesting articles on adjusting to a new baby. They also spoke about some of the sexual changes Mrs Paulson might experience. At the end of the conversation, Mrs Paulson said, "I'm so glad you brought this up. I wondered what sex would be like afterward but felt a little embarrassed about asking."*

*One day before her EDD, Mrs Paulson went into labor and, following a 12-hour labor, successfully delivered a 7 lb 2 oz son—Ryan Erik Paulson.*

## ● *EVALUATION*

Throughout the antepartal period evaluation is an essential part of effective nursing care. As nurses ask questions of the pregnant woman and her family or make observations of physical changes they are evaluating the results of previous interventions. In evaluating the effectiveness of the interventions the nurse should not be afraid to try creative solutions if they are logical and carefully thought out. This is especially important in dealing with families from other cultures. If a practice is important to a woman and not harmful, the culturally sensitive nurse will not discourage it.

In completing an evaluation the nurse must also recognize situations that require referral for further evaluation. For example, a woman who has gained four pounds in one week does not require counseling about nutrition, she needs further assessment for pregnancy-induced hypertension (PIH). The nurse who has a sound knowledge of theory will recognize this and act immediately.

The ongoing and cyclic nature of the nursing process is especially evident in the prenatal setting. However, throughout the course of pregnancy certain criteria can be used to determine the quality of care provided. In essence, nursing care has been effective if:

● The common discomforts of pregnancy are quickly identified and are relieved or lessened effectively.

● The woman is able to discuss the physiologic and psychologic changes of pregnancy.

● The woman implements appropriate self-care measures if they are indicated during pregnancy.

● The woman avoids substances and situations that pose a risk to her well-being or that of her child.

● The woman seeks regular prenatal care.

## ESSENTIAL CONCEPTS

● **The nursing process can be used effectively to plan and provide care to women during pregnancy.**

● **Provision of anticipatory guidance about childbirth, the puerperium, and childrearing is a primary responsibility of the nurse caring for women in an antepartal setting.**

● **The nurse assesses the expectant father's knowledge level and intended degree of participation and then works with the couple to help ensure a satisfying experience.**

● **Culturally based practices and proscribed activities may have a major impact on the childbearing family.**

● **The common discomforts of pregnancy occur as a result of physiologic and anatomic changes. The nurse provides the woman with information about self-care activities aimed at reducing or relieving discomfort.**

● **To make appropriate self-care choices and ensure healthful habits, a pregnant woman requires accurate information about a range of subjects from exercise to sexual activity, from bathing to immunizations.**

● **Teratogenic substances are substances that adversely affect the normal growth and development of the fetus.**

● **A pregnant woman should avoid taking medications or using over-the-counter preparations during pregnancy.**

● **Evidence exists that smoking, consuming alcohol, or using social drugs during pregnancy may be harmful to the fetus.**

● **Maternal assessment of fetal activity keeps the woman "in touch" with her fetus and provides ongoing assessment of fetal status.**

## References

Alexander LL: The pregnant smoker: Nursing implications. *J Obstet Gynecol Neonatal Nurs* May/June 1987; 16(3):167.

American College of Obstetrics and Gynecology: *Exercises During Pregnancy and the Postnatal Period.* (ACOG Home Exercise Programs.) Washington, DC: The College, 1985.

American Nurses' Association: *Standards of Maternal and Child Health Nursing Practice.* Pub. No. MCH-3. Kansas City, MO: The Association, 1983.

Brown MS: A cross-cultural look at pregnancy, labor, and delivery. *J Obstet Gynecol Neonatal Nurs* September/October 1976; 5:35.

Brucker MC: Management of common minor discomforts of pregnancy. Part III: Managing gastrointestinal problems in pregnancy. *J Nurse-Midwifery* March/April 1988; 33(2):67.

Carrington BW: The Afro American. In: *Culture, Childbearing, Health Professionals.* Clark AL (editor). Philadelphia: Davis, 1978.

Chasnoff IJ: Perinatal effects of cocaine. *Contemp OB/GYN* May 1987; 29(5):163.

Cherukuri R et al: A cohort study of alkaloidal cocaine ("crack") in pregnancy. *Obstet Gynecol* August 1988; 72:147.

Chouteau M et al: The effect of cocaine abuse on birth weight and gestational age. *Obstet Gynecol* September 1988; 72:351.

DiIorio C: The management of nausea and vomiting in pregnancy. *Nurse Pract* May 1988; 13(5):23.

Evaneshko V: Tonawanda Seneca childbearing culture. In: *Anthropology of Human Birth.* Kay MA (editor). Philadelphia: Davis, 1982.

Farris LS: Approaches to caring for the American Indian maternity patient. *MCN* March/April 1976; 1:81.

Fenlon A et al: *Getting Ready for Childbirth,* 2nd ed. Boston: Little, Brown, 1986.

Fried PA et al: Marijuana use during pregnancy and decreased length of gestation. *Am J Obstet Gynecol* September 1984; 150:23.

Hingson R et al: Effects of maternal drinking and marijuana use on fetal growth and development. *Pediatr* 1982; 70:539.

Hollingsworth AO et al: The refugees and childbearing: What to expect. *RN* November 1980; 43:45.

Horn BM: Northwest coast Indians: The Muckleshoot. In: *Anthropology of Human Birth.* Kay MA (editor). Philadelphia: Davis, 1982.

Kay MA: The Mexican American. In: *Culture, Childbearing, Health Professionals.* Clark AL (editor). Philadelphia: Davis, 1978.

Ketter DE, Sheldon BJ: Pregnant and physically fit, too. *MCN* March/April 1984; 9:120.

Knothe H, Dette GA: Antibiotics in pregnancy: Toxicity and teratogenicity. *Infection* 1985; 13:49.

Kruse J et al: Changes in smoking and alcohol consumption during pregnancy: A population-based study in a rural area. *Obstet Gynecol* 1986; 67(5):627.

Lemoine P et al: Children of alcoholic parents, observed anomalies (127 cases). *Quest Med* 1968; 21:476.

Mahan CS, McKay S: Let's reform our antenatal care methods. *Contemp OB/GYN* May 1984; 23:147.

Mochizuki M et al: Effects of smoking on fetoplacental-maternal systems during pregnancy. *Am J Obstet Gynecol* June 1984; 149:413.

Naeye RL: Influence of maternal cigarette smoking during pregnancy on fetal and childhood growth. *Obstet Gynecol* 1981; 57(1):18.

Newald J: Cocaine infants: A new arrival at hospitals' steps? *Hospitals* April 5, 1986, p 96.

Paolone AM, Worthington S: Cautions and advice on exercise during pregnancy. *Contemp OB/GYN* May 1985; 25:150.

Reamy K, White SE: Sexuality in pregnancy and the puerperium: A review. *Obstet Gynecol* 1985; 40(1):1.

Sevcovic L: Traditions of pregnancy which influence maternity care of the Navajo people. In: *Transcultural Nursing.* Leininger M (editor). New York: Masson Publishing, 1979.

Sibai BM, Amon EA: How safe is aspirin use during pregnancy? *Contemp OB/GYN* July 1988; 32(1):73.

Taubenheim AM, Silbernagel T: Meeting the needs of expectant fathers. *MCN* March/April 1988; 13:110.

Whipkey RR et al: Drug use in pregnancy. *Ann Emerg Med* 1984; 13:346.

## Additional Readings

Bliss-Holtz VJ: Primiparas' prenatal concern for learning infant care. *Nurs Res* January/February 1988; 37(1):20.

Brooten D et al: A survey of nutrition, caffeine, cigarette and alcohol intake in early pregnancy in an urban clinic population. *J Nurse-Midwifery* 1987; 32(2):85.

Brucker MC: Management of common minor discomforts in pregnancy. Part II: Managing pain in pregnancy. *J Nurse-Midwifery* January/February 1988; 33(1):25.

Davis L: Daily fetal movement counting: A valuable assessment tool. *J Nurse-Midwifery* 1987; 32(1):11.

deGrez SA: Bend and stretch. *MCN* September/October 1988; 13:357.

Drinville-Shank G: The pregnant OR employee: Ensuring maternal health, part I. *AORN J* 1987; 45(2):404.

MacDonald J: Prenatal review classes . . . expectant couples who already have children. *Can Nurse* October 1987; 83(9):26.

MacGregor SN, Keith L: Substance abuse in pregnancy. *Female Patient* January 1989; 14:49.

Maloni JA et al: Expectant grandparents class. *J Obstet Gynecol Neonatal Nurs* 1987; 16(1):26.

Poole CJ: Fatigue during the first trimester of pregnancy. *J Obstet Gynecol Neonatal Nurs* September/October 1986; 15:375.

Stevens KA: Nursing diagnoses in wellness childbearing settings. *J Obstet Gynecol Neonatal Nurs* September/October 1988; 17(5):329.

Swoiskin-Schwartz S et al: Parents' views about having a child after a SIDS death. *J Pediatr Nurs* February 1988; 3(1):24.

Wallace AM et al: Aerobic exercise, maternal self-esteem, and physical discomforts during pregnancy. *J Nurse-Midwifery* 1986; 31(6):255.

# 9

# The Expectant Family: Age-Related Considerations

*I know now how very young I am to have a child and how difficult it sometimes is to be a mother. I love my baby so much, but it scares me sometimes to think about how much I don't know.*

## Objectives

● Identify factors that have contributed to the increased incidence of adolescent pregnancy.

● Contrast the responses of the young adolescent, middle adolescent, and older adolescent to pregnancy.

● Compare the effects of pregnancy on the adolescent mother and the adolescent father.

● Relate the use of the nursing process to the provision of effective care for the pregnant adolescent.

● Describe factors that have contributed to the increased incidence of pregnancy in women over age 30.

● Discuss some of the special concerns felt by older expectant couples.

## Key Terms

young adolescent
middle adolescent
older adolescent
blended family

A woman's response to pregnancy is influenced by many things—the timing of the pregnancy, her previous experience with pregnancy or pregnant women, her partner's response, financial considerations, and a variety of other factors. One important factor to consider is the woman's age. In our society pregnancy, especially first pregnancy, most commonly occurs when a woman is in her twenties. Adolescent pregnancy is becoming more common, however, and is associated with increased risks. Recently the incidence of pregnancy for women over age 30 and even age 35 has also increased. Current research suggests that pregnancy at a later age is associated with far fewer risks than previously believed, but this is still being studied. This chapter considers the effects of pregnancy on the adolescent, her partner, and their parents. It also explores the effects of pregnancy on the older woman and her family.

## ● PREPARING THE ADOLESCENT FOR CHILDBIRTH AND CHILDREARING

Pregnancy is a developmental challenge no matter what the age of the individual involved. However, many factors make it more complicated for the adolescent. Physically, her development is incomplete. Psychologically, she has not yet completed the developmental tasks of adolescence, and her available support systems may be limited. In addition, her education is unfinished and plans for its completion may be jeopardized.

The teenage pregnancy rate has continued to increase, with at least one in ten young women becoming pregnant each year (Alan Guttmacher Institute 1981). Furthermore, in 1985 there were 1.2 live births per 1000 women aged 10–14 years, and 51.3 live births per 1000 women aged 15–19 years (National Center for Health Statistics 1988). Although contraceptive use has increased among adolescents, it has not kept pace with the increasing incidence of sexual activity.

Many factors contribute to the increase of adolescent pregnancy. Menarche is occurring at an earlier age, as is the age of first sexual intercourse. Marriage is being delayed until later years, and cohabitation is far more accepted than in the past.

Some pregnant adolescents are continuing school, usually with their classmates, thus increasing their visibility in the community. Twenty years ago, pregnant adolescents were expelled from school and generally not seen for several months. Fewer young women are choosing to "legitimize" their newborns by marriage, and more of them are choosing to keep their newborns rather than relinquishing them for adoption.

Even though the incidence of adolescent pregnancy has increased, the birth rate is declining, partially because of the availability of legal abortion services. Nevertheless, adolescents are becoming pregnant in greater numbers, and the consequences of this must be addressed by the health care profession.

## Psychosocial Effects of Adolescence

The adolescent years are often turbulent because of the effort required to deal with physical changes, changing relationships, and the increasing need for independence. Developmental tasks of the adolescent have been described by many writers. Mercer (1979) identified six of these tasks as follows:

● Acceptance and achievement of comfort with body image

● Determination and internalization of sexual identity and role

● Development of a personal value system

● Preparation for productive citizenship

● Achievement of independence from parents

● Development of an adult identity

These tasks may be overwhelming for many adolescents; the guidance, nurturing, and support offered by the family and community play a large part in determining successful achievement. Rebellion is one way for adolescents to accomplish developmental tasks, enhancing their ability to make the transition to adult social roles.

**The young adolescent** (under 15 years) still sees authority in parents; the middle adolescent (15–17 years) relies on the peer group for authority and decision making. **The middle adolescent** is in the critical time for challenging: experimenting with drugs, alcohol, and sex are avenues for rebellion. **Older adolescents** (17 years and older) are more at ease with their individuality and decision making.

Cognitive development is another crucial change of adolescence. Young people move from the concrete and egocentric thinking of childhood to abstract conceptualization. The ability of the young adolescent to see herself in the future or foresee the consequences of her behavior is minimal. She perceives her focus of control as external, that is, that her destiny is controlled by others, especially parents and other authority figures. As she matures, learns to solve problems, to conceptualize, and to make decisions, she gradually will see herself as having control. She will then be able to see the consequences of her behavior.

## The Adolescent Mother

Many possible explanations for adolescent pregnancy have been suggested. The conflicts of adolescence may serve as motivation: the adolescent girl uses pregnancy to maintain dependence on her own mother. Deficits in ego functioning also have been suggested as a cause for acting out sexually. The adolescent may have little sense of self-worth and some hopelessness regarding the future. Other psychologic rationales include unstable family relationships, needing someone to love, competition with her mother, punishment of her father and/or mother, emancipation from an undesirable home situation, and seeking attention. Pregnancy may be a young woman's form of delinquency. Cultural values may also cause a young woman to desire pregnancy. Many cultures equate evidence of fertility with adult status. Thus the young woman who sees being a mother as her primary adult role has little motivation to delay having a child (Moore et al 1984).

The research of Palmore and Shannan (1988) supported previous findings and showed that often pregnant adolescents have troubled family relationships, poor school achievement, exposure to drug abuse, and disturbed family relationships.

Another school of thought suggests that pregnancy is a result of unmotivated accidents. The adolescent has sex infrequently, often without planning it, and therefore does not consider contraception. She may have guilt feelings surrounding sex and may not be able to admit she is sexually active. She is incapable of understanding how pregnancy will affect her future. Rationale may include such comments as, "I don't have intercourse often enough," or "It was the safe time of the month." Many adolescent girls have no idea of when they ovulate and how they conceive.

### PHYSIOLOGIC RISKS

Adolescents over 15 years of age who receive early, thorough prenatal care are at no greater risk during pregnancy than women over 20 years (Brucker and Mueller 1985). The young adolescent (under 15 years of age) remains at high risk for premature births, low-birth-weight (LBW) infants, cephalopelvic disproportion (CPD), pregnancy-induced hypertension (PIH) and its sequelae, and iron deficiency anemia (Carey et al 1981). In this age group, prenatal care is the critical factor that most influences pregnancy outcome.

Teenagers between 15 and 19 years old have the second highest incidence of sexually transmitted diseases in the United States. The impact of herpesvirus, syphilis, and gonorrhea during a pregnancy increases the dangers greatly. In addition, the incidence of chlamydial infection increases (Osofsky 1985). Other problems seen in adolescents are cigarette smoking and alcohol and drug abuse. By the time pregnancy is confirmed in young women, the fetus already may be damaged by these substances.

## PSYCHOLOGIC RISKS

The major psychologic risk to the pregnant adolescent is the interruption in completing her developmental tasks. Add to this the tasks of pregnancy, and the young woman has an overwhelming amount of psychologic work to do, the completion of which will affect her own and her newborn's future.

Table 9.1 lists adolescent developmental tasks (as identified by Mercer), their impact on the pregnant adolescent, and nursing implications. Tasks of pregnancy are listed in Table 9.2.

Through the nursing process, the nurse should assist the adolescent in completing these tasks during prenatal visits. An interdisciplinary approach, with a social worker, nutritional counselor, and school counselor, will benefit the young woman.

## SOCIOLOGIC RISKS

The adolescent pregnancy not only affects the adolescent but society as well. The syndrome of failure (Waters 1969) describes the sequence of events for which the adolescent continues to be at risk, the brunt of which society must carry. This syndrome includes:

● Failure to fulfill the functions of adolescence

● Failure to remain in school

● Failure to limit family size

● Failure to establish stable families

● Failure to be self-supporting

● Failure to have healthy infants

The frustration of being forced into adult roles before completing adolescent developmental tasks causes a negative series of events that affects the adolescent's entire life.

Many adolescents who become pregnant drop out of school and never complete their education. Lack of education reduces the quality of jobs available to these individuals. Programs for pregnant adolescents and adolescent mothers may help decrease this problem.

Failure to limit family size is another element of the syndrome. The younger the adolescent at her first pregnancy, the more likely she is to become pregnant again while still an adolescent. These young women frequently fail to establish a stable family. Their family structure tends to be single parent and matriarchal, often the same family structure in which the adolescent was raised. If such women do marry, their divorce rate is the highest of any age group in the United States. Certainly situations of poverty aggravate this problem.

Failure to be self-supporting logically follows lack of education and lost career goals. Many adolescents with children end up on welfare.

Finally, adolescents are at risk for having unhealthy babies because of potential complications and lack of prenatal care.

## Table 9.1  Developmental Tasks of Adolescence and Their Implications During Pregnancy

| Developmental tasks of adolescence (Mercer 1979) | Impact on pregnant adolescent | Nursing implications |
| --- | --- | --- |
| Acceptance and comfort with body image | Must learn to deal with changing body: enlarging breasts and abdomen, striae, chloasma, weight gain; she may not yet have incorporated the changes of puberty. | Assist the adolescent in determining what the changes of puberty meant to her; how she feels about the changes of pregnancy. Help her think of ways she can feel good about herself. |
| | May be reticent about wearing maternity clothes. | Assess at what point in the pregnancy she begins to wear maternity clothes; ask why if she is not wearing them at the appropriate time. |
| | May try fad diets or eat junk food, due to peer pressure and the slender ideal society has of women; does not want to get fat. | Nutrition counseling will be in order for every adolescent. Emphasize that pregnant women do not diet, she can lose the weight later; give exercises for pregnant women. |
| | Must learn to cope with looking different from her peers. | Elicit feelings about how she is coping with this; does she have support from friends, family? |

**Table 9.1 Developmental Tasks of Adolescence and Their Implications During Pregnancy** *(continued)*

| Developmental tasks of adolescence (Mercer 1979) | Impact on pregnant adolescent | Nursing implications |
|---|---|---|
| Determination and internalization of sexual role and identity | May not be able to perceive herself as a sexual being (pregnancy confers overt sexuality). | Elicit feelings about sexuality. |
| | Must learn to incorporate the concept of becoming a mother. | What does motherhood mean to the adolescent? |
| | Must cope with possible changes in relationships with friends, boyfriend, and family. | How does she see relationships changing? How is she dealing with this? |
| | May see her role as solely procreator; other opportunities for development of other female roles may be temporarily abandoned. | What other roles does she see for herself now? In five years? |
| Development of a personal value system | Must cope with and adjust to the fact that she became pregnant; is this in conflict with her self ideal of chastity? | Discuss her feelings of conflict, if any: is she living up to her expectations and how can she do so? |
| | Adjust to premature motherhood and the inherent responsibilities. | Explore the value the adolescent places on becoming a mother and having children. How does she see her relationship with her newborn, now and five years from now? |
| | Incorporate problem-solving skills and decision-making skills. | Explore values regarding career, school, marriage. Reality test: "Tell me how you see a typical day with a 2-month-old infant?" |
| Preparation for productive citizenship | Adjust to interruption of school. May see school as unnecessary, or postpone indefinitely. | Explore provisions for school while pregnant: when can she return? Refer to Social Service; discuss importance of education regarding her career and future. |
| | Incorporate career goals with parenting; she may not consider working important. | Discuss future economic consolidation. Assist with problem solving in this area. |
| Achievement of independence from parents | Cope with realities of pregnancy and dependence on family (or someone) for financial help. | Elicit what changes she perceives and how she feels about them. Discuss the reality of her situation (reality testing is constructive). How can she adjust? How can she plan independence? Living at home may be out of the question; she may end up on welfare. Check her home and family situation often during the pregnancy. |
| | Adjust to need for financial assistance until she can earn her own living. | What role will the father of the child play? If she does not live at home, who will support her? |
| Development of an adult identity | Learn to accept the responsibilities of adulthood and parenthood. | Encourage prenatal classes, parenting classes. |
| | Learn to accept the responsibilities for her actions. | Discuss prenatal care and the effects on her pregnancy. |
| | Learn to plan for her future. | Explore options through all of the above. |

## Table 9.2  Tasks of Pregnancy and the Adolescent

| Task | Impact on adolescent | Nursing implications |
|------|---------------------|----------------------|
| Acceptance of pregnancy | May deny until well into pregnancy, thus having no alternative but to carry pregnancy.<br><br>May have difficulty bonding with fetus, which may carry over to unresponsiveness to newborn. | Counsel or refer for counseling regarding whether she will keep or relinquish her newborn.<br>Discuss importance of early prenatal care.<br>Elicit feelings about pregnancy (see Table 9.1, first developmental task). |
| Acceptance of termination of pregnancy | Toward end of pregnancy may focus on "wanting it to be over"; may have trouble individuating fetus. | Elicit why she has these feelings.<br>Assist with coping mechanisms.<br>Discuss preferred sex, names, showers, and readiness for newborn's arrival. |
| Acceptance of mother role | May not perceive newborn as being her own, especially if client's mother will be caring for the newborn; may think of newborn as a doll or sister. | Discuss plans for newborn; include adolescent's mother as indicated.<br>Elicit adolescent's perception of motherhood (see Table 9.1, second developmental task).<br>Discuss dreams, role playing, fantasies that she experiences.<br>Does she know any new mothers?<br>Encourage prenatal classes. |
| Resolution of fears about childbirth | May focus on labor and delivery as mutilating to her body.<br><br>May not see childbirth education as necessary for coping and learning.<br><br>May have fantasies, dreams or nightmares about childbirth. | Encourage attendance at prenatal classes, childbirth education.<br>Offer literature or references.<br>Elicit expectations, knowledge, and fears about childbirth.<br>Discuss analgesia, labor process; offer tour of facilities.<br>Reinforce that fantasies or dreams are normal.<br>Encourage support person to attend classes with adolescent. |
| Bonding | May feel ambivalent about pregnancy and motherhood. | Assess all parameters of feelings about pregnancy in other developmental tasks and tasks of pregnancy (Table 9.1). Refer for counseling if there is any sign of maladjustment to pregnancy. |

## ● The Adolescent Father

The unwed adolescent father historically has been met with less than supportive services. His stresses, concerns, and needs have been ignored by society.

Adolescent fathers are usually within three to four years of age of the adolescent mother. The mother and father are generally from similar socioeconomic backgrounds and have similar education. Many are involved in meaningful relationships. Frequently, the fathers are involved in the decision making regarding abortion or adoption. Many fathers are very involved in the pregnancy and in the childrearing.

Adolescent fathers do become sexually active at an earlier age than adolescent mothers, but, somewhat surprisingly, their knowledge of sexuality and reproduction is no greater than that of their nonfather peers (Barret and Robinson 1985).

Psychologic and sociologic risks to the adolescent father are in many ways similar to the adolescent mother's risks. Adolescent fathers tend to achieve less formal education than older fathers, and they enter the labor force earlier with less education. They tend to pursue less prestigious careers and have less job satisfaction. Adolescent fathers often marry at a younger age and have larger families than older fathers. In addition, the divorce rate of adolescent fathers is greater than that of couples who postpone childbearing and marriage (Teti et al 1987).

Psychologically the adolescent father's developmental tasks will be interrupted. Because he is not yet mature, his level of cognitive development and decision-making skills will influence whether he remains supportive or flees the situation. Certainly he will be more vulnerable to emotional stressors than will an adult man.

The stresses of pregnancy on the adolescent male come from many sources. He faces negative reactions from people in his own family and in the family of the young woman. Feelings of anger, shame, and disappointment will be aimed at him. He will feel isolated and alone, and if the young woman's parents refuse to allow him to see her, his sole emotional support may be gone.

Another source of stress arises from changes in his life. His educational and career goals may be threatened as he anticipates marriage or quitting school to support the young woman and his forthcoming child. His relationship with his peers may be altered as well.

A third stressor will be his concerns regarding the health of the young woman and the fetus. He may be protective, yet may not understand the physical and psychologic changes of pregnancy.

The adolescent father faces a serious situation that may be overwhelming for him. The unresolved stress may lead to a severe crisis, manifested by abnormal adaptive behavior, marked depression, somatic symptoms, sexually deviant behavior, or even acute psychosis.

The implications for the health care team are important. Even if the couple has severed their relationship, the father should be sought to assess how he is coping and to offer him counseling. He may not understand why he needs to come to the clinic and the nurse must let him know that the staff would like to help him, too.

Research indicates that input from the adolescent partner strongly influences the adolescent mother (Westney et al 1988). If the couple is still together, the father should be told that his participation is important, that he is an excellent support person for the young woman, and that he is welcome to attend clinic and classes. Many clinics interview the couple routinely on the first prenatal visit.

The young man will need education regarding pregnancy, childbirth, childcare, and parenting. Some clinics have couples attend classes together; others offer "father" classes. In becoming parents, men need to learn rates of growth and development so they understand their newborn's potential and do not become frustrated and dissatisfied with the child's behavior.

As part of his counseling, the nurse should assess the young man's stressors, his support systems, his plans for involvement in the pregnancy and childrearing, his future plans, and his health care needs. He should be referred to social services for an opportunity to be counseled regarding his educational and vocational future. When the father is involved in the pregnancy, the young mother feels less deserted, more confident in her decision making, and better able to discuss her future.

## ● Parents' Reactions to Adolescent Pregnancy

Telling her parents that she is pregnant often is very difficult for the adolescent, and she may avoid it until her pregnancy is obvious. Her mother is usually the first to find out and often attempts to prevent the young woman's father from discovering his daughter's pregnancy.

Parents' initial reactions to the news are usually shock, anger, shame, guilt, and sorrow. The angry mother may accompany her daughter to the clinic. The nurse should assess the disharmony that is occurring and explain the process of adaptation that follows.

The mother frequently feels guilty about her daughter's pregnancy and feels that she has been an inadequate parent. She may also be angry over having to help her daughter deal with a crisis just as her children are growing up and she is experiencing a new sense of freedom. The idea of being a grandmother may also be upsetting. Once these reactions are faced, normalcy returns to the mother-daughter relationship. The mother may become involved in decision making and in dealing with the father-to-be and his family. Family communication is important in the adolescent's decision making. The adolescent's decisions regarding abortion, relinquishing her newborn for adoption, or keeping the infant are influenced greatly by her family's reactions.

As the pregnancy progresses the adolescent's mother begins to take on the grandmother role. She may buy presents for the newborn and plan for the future. She may participate in prenatal care and classes and can be an excellent support for her daughter. She should be encouraged to participate if the mother-daughter relationship is positive. The mother should be updated on maternity care to clarify any misconceptions she might have. During labor and delivery, the mother will be a key figure for her daughter. She can offer reassurance and instill confidence in the adolescent.

The last stages of a mother's acceptance occur after her daughter's child is born. As the mother attempts to integrate her role of grandmother, an initial blurring of roles occurs. The grandmother now sees her daughter as a mother, and the daughter begins to identify herself as a mother. Role confusion may develop and sometimes continues for years—the grandmother may do essentially all the mothering and caretaking activities for the newborn, while the daughter remains only a daughter and becomes a sibling of her newborn. Until the daughter is able to internalize her role as mother, the grandmother will be unable to completely identify as a grandmother.

This new role development is clouded by the adolescent's struggle to complete her tasks of adolescence. The wise mother will gently encourage a balance between helping her daughter to be a parent and allowing her to complete the tasks of adolescence. As her daughter becomes more confident in the role of parent, the grandmother can gradually encourage her to be more independent.

# THE NURSING PROCESS AND ADOLESCENT PREGNANCY

## Nursing Assessment

The nurse must establish a data base to plan interventions for the adolescent mother-to-be. Areas of assessment include a history of personal and family physical health, developmental level and impact of pregnancy, and availability of emotional and financial support.

### PHYSICAL HEALTH

It is important to have general physical health information in the prenatal period. Often this is the first time an adolescent has ever provided a health history. Consequently the nurse may find it helpful to ask very specific questions and give examples when necessary.

The following areas should be assessed (see Chapter 7 for further discussion):

● Family and personal history
● Medical history
● Menstrual history
● Obstetric history

### DEVELOPMENTAL LEVEL AND THE IMPACT OF THE PREGNANCY

The developmental tasks common to adolescence and the implications of pregnancy are listed in Table 9.1. Within any age group personal maturity may vary widely, however, so it is important to consider maturational level individually. The mother's self-concept (including body image), her relationship with the significant adults in her life, her attitude toward her pregnancy, her degree of understanding of the realities of teenage pregnancy and parenting, and her coping methods in the situation are a few of the significant factors that need to be assessed.

### SUPPORT SYSTEMS

The socioeconomic status of the pregnant adolescent often places her baby at risk throughout life, beginning with conception. It is essential to assess emotional and financial support systems.

Adolescent life-styles and support systems vary tremendously. It is imperative that the interdisciplinary health team have information regarding expectant adolescents' feelings and perceptions about themselves, their

sexuality, and the coming baby; their knowledge of, attitude toward, and anticipated ability to care for and support the infant; and their maturational level and needs.

## Nursing Diagnosis

Nursing diagnoses that may apply to the pregnant adolescent are similar to those identified for any pregnancy and are listed in Chapter 8, p 208. Appropriate nursing diagnoses are influenced by the adolescent's age, support systems, health, and personal maturity. Certain diagnoses, however, may be especially applicable to the adolescent who is pregnant. These are identified in Essential Nursing Diagnoses to Consider—Adolescent Pregnancy.

## Nursing Plan and Implementation

Early, thorough, and consistent prenatal care is the strongest and most critical determinant for reducing risk for the adolescent mother and her newborn. This point cannot be overemphasized. In conjunction with prenatal care, prenatal education programs specifically designed for adolescents play an important role in helping adolescents

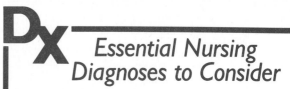

## **DX** Essential Nursing Diagnoses to Consider

### Adolescent Pregnancy

Altered family processes
Altered growth and development
Altered health maintenance
Altered nutrition: less than body requirements
Altered nutrition: more than body requirements
Body image disturbance
Chronic low self esteem
Decisional conflict
Defensive coping
Impaired adjustment
Impaired social interaction
Ineffective denial
Ineffective family coping
Ineffective individual coping
Knowledge deficit
Noncompliance
Parental role conflict
Potential altered parenting
Self esteem disturbance
Situational low self esteem
Social isolation

understand the changes that occur during pregnancy and labor and delivery. These classes also provide anticipatory guidance designed to help the adolescent make informed choices, establish lifelong health habits, and develop beginning knowledge about parenting. Moreover, research suggests that adolescents who have participated in such specialized education programs require less medication during labor and have fewer maternal and perinatal complications (Slager-Earnest et al 1987, Smoke and Grace 1988). See Essential Facts to Remember—The Pregnant Adolescent.

## DEVELOPMENT OF A TRUSTING RELATIONSHIP WITH THE PREGNANT ADOLESCENT

The first visit to the clinic or care giver's office for diagnosis of the pregnancy or beginning of prenatal care may cause the young woman to feel anxious and vulnerable. Making the experience as positive as possible will encourage the adolescent to return for follow-up care and to cooperate with her care givers, and will help ensure her recognition of the importance of health care for herself and her baby.

An overview of what the young woman will experience over the prenatal course, including thorough explanations and rationale for each procedure as it occurs, will help the client's understanding and give her a feeling of control. Actively involving the young woman in her care will give her a sense of participation and responsibility in her own health care (Figure 9.1).

Since this first office or clinic visit may include the young woman's first pelvic examination, a thorough explanation of the procedure is essential to lessen the inevitable anxiety provoked by this situation. Gentle and thoughtful examination technique will help put her at ease. A mirror is useful in allowing the client to see her cervix, educating her about her anatomy, and giving her an active role in the examination. Clinical pelvimetry is an important tool in predicting CPD, but it may be postponed until the next visit if the adolescent is extremely nervous and uncomfortable during the first pelvic exam.

Developing a trusting relationship with the pregnant adolescent is essential. Honesty and respect for the young woman and a caring attitude promote self-esteem. As a role model, the nurse's attitudes about self-care and responsibility affect the adolescent's maturation process.

## PROMOTION OF SELF-ESTEEM AND PROBLEM-SOLVING ABILITIES

The nurse assists the adolescent in her decision-making and problem-solving skills so that she can proceed with her developmental tasks and begin to assume responsibility for her life as well as her newborn's life. Adolescents tend to be egocentric and may not regard as impor-

## Essential Facts to Remember

### The Pregnant Adolescent

- The rate of adolescent pregnancy in the United States is among the highest of all the developed countries of the world.
- Early, regular, and excellent prenatal care can prevent many of the risks associated with adolescent pregnancy, especially for the young adolescent.
- Prenatal education especially designed for adolescents also plays a significant role in increasing an adolescent's knowledge and in decreasing maternal and perinatal complications.

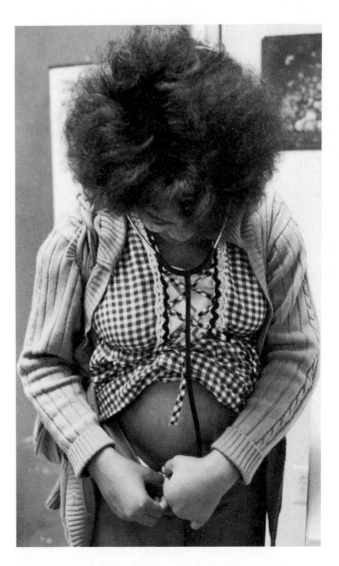

*Figure 9.1 The nurse provides this young mother with an opportunity to listen to her baby's heartbeat.*

tant the fact that their health and habits affect the fetus. It is often useful to emphasize the effects of these practices on the client herself. The young woman will also need help in problem solving and in visualizing the future so she can plan effectively. It is essential for the nurse to understand that the adolescent must meet the developmental tasks of pregnancy in addition to the developmental tasks of adolescence. Table 9.2 identifies the tasks of pregnancy and their impact on the adolescent.

## PROMOTION OF PHYSICAL WELL-BEING

Baseline weight and blood pressure measurements are valuable in assessing weight gain and predisposition to PIH. The adolescent may be encouraged to take part in her care by measuring and recording her weight. The nurse may use this time as an opportunity for assisting the young woman in problem solving: "Have I gained too much or too little weight?" "What influence does my diet have on my weight?" "How can I change my eating habits?"

Another way to introduce the subject of nutrition is during measurement of baseline and subsequent hemoglobin and hematocrit values. Since the adolescent is at risk for anemia, she will need education regarding the importance of iron in her diet. A nutritional consultation is indicated for all adolescents. Group classes are helpful because peer pressure is strong among this age group. For further discussion of adolescent nutrition during pregnancy, see Chapter 10.

Adolescents may fear laboratory tests, which can evoke early childhood memories of being "stuck" with needles or hurt. Explanations help relieve anxiety and coordination of services will avoid multiple venous punctures.

Pregnancy-induced hypertension represents the most prevalent medical complication of pregnant adolescents. The criteria of blood pressure readings of 140/90 mm Hg are not acceptable as the determinant of PIH in adolescents. Women aged 14 to 20 years without evidence of high blood pressure usually have diastolic readings between 50 and 66 mm Hg. Gradual increases from the prepregnant diastolic readings, along with excessive weight gain, must be evaluated as precursors to PIH. This is one reason why early prenatal care is vital to management of the adolescent.

As mentioned earlier, adolescents have an increased incidence of sexually transmitted diseases. The initial prenatal examination should include a gonococcal culture and wet prep for *Candida, Trichomonas,* and *Gardnerella.* Tests for syphilis should also be done. Education about sexually transmitted disease is important, as is careful observation of herpetic lesions or other symptoms throughout the young woman's pregnancy.

Substance abuse should be discussed with adolescents. It is important to review the risks associated with the use of cigarettes, caffeine, drugs, cocaine, marijuana, and alcohol with the young woman. She should be aware of the effects of these substances on her development as well as on the development of the fetus.

Ongoing care should include the same assessments that the older woman receives. Special attention should be paid to evaluating fetal growth by measurement of fundal height, fetal heart tones, quickening, and fetal movement. Corresponding dates of auscultating fetal heart tones with the date of last menstrual period and quickening can be helpful in determining correct estimations of delivery time. If there is a question of size—date discrepancy by 2 cm either way—an ultrasound is warranted to establish fetal age so that instances of intrauterine growth retardation (IUGR) may be diagnosed and treated early.

## PROMOTION OF FAMILY ADAPTATION

The nurse assesses the family situation during the first prenatal visit. The nurse determines what level of involvement the adolescent desires from each of her family members. A sensitive approach to the daughter-mother relationship helps motivate their communication. If the mother and daughter agree, the mother should participate in the client's care. Encouraging the mother to become part of the maternity team, grandmother crisis support groups, and counseling helps the mother adapt to her role and support her daughter.

The nurse should also help the mother assess and meet her daughter's needs. Some adolescents become more dependent during pregnancy, and some become more independent. The mother can ease and encourage her daughter's self-growth by understanding how to respond to and support the adolescent.

## FACILITATION OF PRENATAL EDUCATION

Ideally prenatal education programs should include both the clinic and the school system. Many adolescents cite the school as the preferred agency for education during pregnancy and early parenting. School systems are currently attempting to meet this need in a variety of ways. The most effective method appears to be mainstreaming the pregnant adolescent in academic classes with her peers and adding classes appropriate to her needs during pregnancy and early parenting. Classes about growth and development beginning with the newborn and early infancy can help teenage parents have more realistic expectations of their infants and may help decrease child abuse. Mainstreaming pregnant adolescents in school is also an ideal way to help them complete their education while learning the skills they need to cope with childbearing and parenting. Vocational guidance in this setting is also most beneficial to their future.

Regardless of the sponsorship or setting of prenatal classes for pregnant teenagers and adolescent fathers, the developmental tasks of the adolescent must be considered. For example, the methods of teaching this age group should be somewhat different from regular prenatal classes. The younger adolescent tends to be a more concrete thinker than the older and more mature pregnant adult. Increased use of audiovisuals appropriate to their social situation and age is helpful. More demonstrations may be required, and they need to be simple and direct.

Areas that might be included in prenatal classes are anatomy and physiology, sex education, exercises for pregnancy and postpartum, maternal and infant nutrition, growth and development of the fetus, labor and birth, family planning, and infant development. Adolescents may want to participate in the teaching of these classes and should be encouraged to do so. Peer support and friendships can blossom among these young women, helping them all to mature.

The clinic can offer rap sessions, pamphlets, or films in the waiting room. Giving the clients something to do while they wait for their appointments may encourage them to return and also may help them learn. Decorating the clinic with attractive educational posters and creating an informal atmosphere establishes an environment where adolescents feel free to interact with professionals.

Ideally, prenatal classes for the adolescent are oriented to more than just pregnancy, childbirth, and immediate newborn care (Figure 9.2). The goals of many of these classes are expanding to deal with more complex social issues that result from adolescent pregnancies. A multidisciplinary team approach is important in planning and implementing these classes. Goals for many of these classes now include promoting self-esteem; helping participants identify the problems and conflicts of teenage parenting and how to prepare for them; educating participants about sexuality, relationships, and contraception to deter unwanted pregnancies; teaching participants parenting skills, which include information about community resources and other resources available to teenage parents; and helping participants develop more adaptive coping skills.

## ● *Evaluation*

In working with the pregnant adolescent and her family, the nurse knows that care has been effective if:

● A trusting relationship is established with the pregnant adolescent.

● The adolescent is able to use her problem-solving abilities to make appropriate choices.

● The adolescent complies with the recommendations of the health care team and receives effective health care throughout her pregnancy and delivery and during the postpartum period.

● The adolescent, her partner (if he is involved), and their families are able to cope successfully with the effects of the pregnancy.

● The adolescent is knowledgeable about pregnancy and makes appropriate health care choices.

● The adolescent demonstrates developmental and pregnancy progression within established normal parameters.

● The adolescent develops skill in child care and parenting.

*Figure 9.2  Prenatal classes may be designed especially for adolescents.*

# CARE OF THE OLDER EXPECTANT COUPLE

Not too many years ago, women who were 30 years old or older and pregnant with their first baby were labeled *elderly primiparas* by the medical profession. Today an increasing number of women are choosing to have their first baby after age 30. Some are even waiting until after age 35. Many factors have contributed to this trend:

- Availability of effective birth control methods
- The women's liberation movement and its emphasis on expanded roles for women
- More women obtaining advanced education, pursuing careers, and delaying parenthood until they are established professionally
- Increased incidence of later marriage and second marriage
- High cost of living, causing some young couples to delay childbearing until they are more secure financially
- Increased growth in the population of women in this age group

There are advantages to having a first baby after the age of 30. Couples who delay childbearing until they are older tend to be well educated and financially secure. Usually their decision to have a baby was deliberately and thoughtfully made. Given their greater life experiences, they are much more aware of the realities of having a child and what it means to have a baby at their age. Many of the women have experienced fulfillment in their careers and feel secure enough to take on the added responsibility of a child. Some women are ready to make a change in their lives, desiring to stay home with a new baby. Those who plan to continue working are able to afford good child care (Figure 9.3).

## Medical Risks

Although older women are often considered by the medical profession to be at increased risk during pregnancy, their risk is not appreciably higher than the general population unless they have preexisting medical conditions such as hypertension or diabetes (Redwine 1988). Medical conditions associated with the reproductive organs such as uterine fibroids occur with greater frequency in women in their late thirties and fertility decreases in women as they grow older. The incidence of spontaneous abortion also increases with maternal age as does the incidence of cesarean birth (Symposium 1987).

The increased risk of fetal chromosomal abnormalities with advancing maternal age has long been recognized. Specifically, the incidence of Down syndrome increases after age 35 and rises dramatically after age 40. For women who are concerned that their age may adversely affect the well-being of their offspring, the use of chorionic villus sampling (CVS) or amniocentesis permits the early detection of several chromosomal abnormalities. Legalized abortion provides the opportunity to terminate the pregnancy if that option is acceptable to the couple.

The risk of having a baby who is small for gestational age is somewhat increased for women having a first child in their thirties, while infants born to multiparous women of similar age tend to be of normal birth weight. Multiparous women in their thirties are at increased risk for placenta previa, however (Symposium 1987).

## Special Concerns of the Older Expectant Couple

No matter what their age, most expectant couples have concerns regarding the well-being of the fetus and their ability to parent. The older couple has additional concerns related to their age, especially the closer they are to 40.

Some couples are concerned about whether they will have enough energy to care for a new baby. Of greater concern is their ability to deal with the needs of the child in ten years when they, too, are ten years older.

The financial concerns of the older couple are usually different from those of the younger couple. The older couple is generally more financially secure than the younger couple. However, when their "baby" is ready for college, the older couple may be close to retirement, when they might not have the means to provide for their child.

While considering their financial future and future retirement, the older couple may be forced to face their own mortality. Certainly this is not uncommon in midlife, but instead of confronting this issue at 40 to 45 years of age or later, the older expectant couple may confront the issue several years earlier as they consider what will happen as their child grows.

The older expectant couple faces a major life-style change and may find themselves somewhat isolated socially. They may feel "different" because they are often the only couple in their peer group expecting their first baby. In fact, many of their peers are parents of adolescents or young adults and may be grandparents as well. The 40-year-old woman holding a newborn is more often assumed to be the grandmother of the baby than the new mother.

The response of older couples who already have children to learning that the woman is pregnant may vary greatly depending on whether the pregnancy was planned or unexpected. Other factors influencing their response include the attitude of their children, family, and friends to the pregnancy; the impact on their life-style; and the financial implications of having another child. Sometimes couples who had previously been married to other mates will

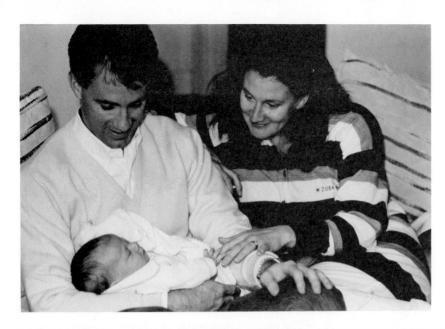

*Figure 9.3 For many older couples the decision to have a child can be satisfying and rewarding.*

choose to have a child together. The concept of **blended family** applies to situations in which "her" children, "his" children, and "their" children come together as a new family group and must work out the family dynamics of the situation.

Health care professionals may treat the older expectant couple differently than they would a younger couple, especially if the woman is having her first child. Older women may be asked to submit to more medical procedures, such as amniocentesis and ultrasound, than younger women. An older woman may be prevented from using a birthing room or birthing center even if she is healthy because her age is considered to put her at risk.

The woman who has delayed pregnancy may be concerned about the limited amount of time that she has to bear children. When pregnancy does not occur as quickly as she hoped, the older woman may become increasingly anxious as time slips away on her "biological clock." When an older woman becomes pregnant but experiences a spontaneous abortion, her grief for the loss of her unborn child is exacerbated by her anxiety about her ability to conceive again in her remaining time.

## ● THE NURSING PROCESS AND THE OLDER EXPECTANT COUPLE

### ● Nursing Assessment

In working with a woman in her thirties or forties who is pregnant the nurse makes the same assessments as are appropriate in caring for any woman who is pregnant. These include assessment of physical status, the woman's understanding of pregnancy and the changes that accom-

pany it, any health teaching needs that exist, the degree of support the woman has available to her, and her knowledge of infant care. In addition, the nurse explores the woman's and her partner's attitudes about the pregnancy and their expectations of the impact a baby will have on their lives.

### ● Nursing Diagnosis

The diagnoses that are applicable to any woman who is pregnant are identified in Chapter 8, p 208. In addition to those diagnoses, the older woman who is pregnant has specific needs that may lead the nurse to formulate additional diagnoses. Essential Nursing Diagnoses—The Older Expectant Couple identifies some of these.

### ● Nursing Plan and Implementation

Once an older couple has made the decision to have a child, it is the nurse's responsibility to respect and support the couple in this decision. As with any client, risks need to be discussed, concerns need to be identified, and strengths need to be promoted. The woman's age should not be made an issue.

To promote a sense of well-being, the nurse should treat the pregnancy as "normal" unless specific health risks are identified.

#### PROMOTION OF ADAPTATION TO PREGNANCY

As the pregnancy continues the nurse should identify and discuss concerns the woman may have related to her

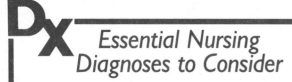

## Essential Nursing Diagnoses to Consider

### The Older Expectant Couple

Altered family processes
Decisional conflict
Family coping: potential for growth
Fatigue
Impaired adjustment
Impaired social interaction
Ineffective family coping
Knowledge deficit
Noncompliance
Ineffective individual coping
Parental role conflict
Potential altered parenting

age or to specific health problems. The older woman who has made a conscious decision to become pregnant often has carefully thought through potential problems and may actually have fewer concerns than a younger woman or one with an unplanned pregnancy.

Childbirth education classes are important in promoting adaptation to the event of childbirth for expectant couples of any age. However, older expectant couples, who are still in the minority, often feel uncomfortable in classes where the majority of participants are much younger. Because of the differences in age and life experiences, many of the needs of the older couple may not be met in the class. The nurse teaching a childbirth education class should try to anticipate the informational needs of the older couple. As the number of expectant older couples increases, the nurse may find it useful to offer an "over 30" childbirth education class to accommodate the specific needs of older couples.

Couples who are over 30 years of age are often better educated than other health care consumers. These clients frequently know the kind of care and services they want and are assertive in their interactions with the health care system. The nurse should neither be intimidated by these individuals nor assume that anticipatory guidance and support are not needed. Instead the nurse should support the couple's strengths and be sensitive to their individual needs.

### PROVISION OF SUPPORT IF AMNIOCENTESIS IS NECESSARY

In working with older expectant couples, the nurse must be sensitive to their special needs. A particularly difficult issue these couples face is the possibility of bearing an unhealthy child. Because of the risk of Down syndrome in these families, amniocentesis is often suggested. The decision to have amniocentesis can be difficult to make merely on the basis of its possible risks to the fetus. But that becomes almost a minor concern when the couple thinks of the implications of the possible finding of Down syndrome or other chromosomal abnormalities. The finding of abnormalities means that the couple may be faced with the even more difficult decision of whether or not to continue the pregnancy.

A couple's decision to have amniocentesis is usually related to their beliefs and attitudes about abortion. Amniocentesis is usually not even considered by couples who are strongly opposed to abortion for any reason. Health professionals must respect their decision and take a nonjudgmental approach to their continued care.

The nurse can support couples who decide to have amniocentesis in several ways:

1. The nurse should make sure that the couple is aware of the risks of amniocentesis and why it is being performed.

2. The nurse who is present during the amniocentesis procedure can offer comfort and emotional support to the expectant woman. The nurse can also provide information about the procedure as it is being performed.

3. The nurse can facilitate a support group for women during the difficult waiting period between the procedure and the results.

4. If the results indicate that the fetus has Down syndrome or another genetic abnormality, the nurse can ensure that the couple has complete information about the condition, its range of possible manifestations, and its developmental implications.

5. The nurse can support the couple in their decision to continue or terminate the pregnancy. It is essential that the nurse and other health professionals involved with the couple not impose their philosophical or political beliefs about abortion on the couple. The decision is the couple's, and it should be based on their belief system and a nonbiased presentation of risks and choices from care givers.

Essential Facts to Remember—Pregnancy in Women over Age 35 summarizes key points about pregnancy in this age group.

## • Evaluation

Nursing care for the older expectant couple has been effective if:

• The woman and her partner are knowledgeable about

## Essential Facts to Remember

### Pregnancy in Women over Age 35

- Couples who choose pregnancy at a later age are usually financially secure and have made a thoughtful, planned choice.

- If the woman has no existing health problems her risk during pregnancy is not appreciably higher than that of the general population.

- The decreased fertility of women over 35 may make conception more difficult.

- The incidence of Down syndrome does increase somewhat in women over age 35 and significantly in women over age 40.

- The couple may choose to have amniocentesis or CVS to gain information about the health of their unborn child.

the pregnancy and make appropriate health care choices.

- The expectant couple (and their other children) are able to cope successfully with the pregnancy and its implications for the future.

- The woman receives effective health care throughout her pregnancy and delivery and during the postpartum period.

- The woman and her partner develop skills in child care and parenting as necessary.

## ESSENTIAL CONCEPTS

- **Many factors contribute to the increase in the teenage pregnancy rate, including earlier onset of menarche, earlier age of first sexual intercourse, increased incidence of cohabitation and delay of marriage, and lessened stigma associated with adolescent pregnancy.**

- **Pregnancy poses physiologic, psychologic, and sociologic risks for an adolescent.**

- **The adolescent father is often overlooked but he, too, faces risks and decisions when his partner becomes pregnant.**

- **The parents of a pregnant adolescent may react in a variety of ways to the news of the pregnancy. Typically the mother is the first to learn of**

the pregnancy and must deal with her personal feelings so that she can be supportive of her partner and daughter.

- **The nursing process can help the nurse provide effective care to the pregnant adolescent.**

- **Often the adolescent has little understanding of pregnancy, delivery, or of parenting. Consequently, education for self-care is a primary responsibility of the nurse.**

- **Childbirth among women over 30 is becoming increasingly common. It poses fewer health risks than previously believed and offers definite advantages for the woman or couple who make the choice.**

- **A major risk for the older expectant woman who is pregnant relates to the increased incidence of Down syndrome in children born to women over age 35 or 40. Amniocentesis can provide information as to whether the fetus has Down syndrome. The couple can then decide whether they wish to continue the pregnancy.**

## References

The Alan Guttmacher Institute. *Teen Pregnancy: The Problem that Hasn't Gone Away.* New York: The Alan Guttmacher Institute, 1981.

Barrett RL, Robinson BE: The adolescent father. In: *Dimensions of Fatherhood.* Hanson S, Bozett F (editors). Beverly Hills, CA: Sage Publications, 1985.

Brucker MC, Mueller M: Nurse-midwifery care of adolescents. *J Nurse-Midwifery* 1985; 30:277.

Card JJ, Wise LL: Teenage mothers and teenage fathers: The impact of early childbearing on the parents' personal and professional lives. *Fam Plan Perspect* July/August 1978; 10:199.

Corey WB et al: Adolescent age and obstetric risk. *Semin Perinatol* 1981; 5(1):9.

Mercer R: *Perspectives on Adolescent Health Care.* New York: Lippincott, 1979.

Moore DS et al: Adolescent pregnancy and parenting: The role of the nurse. *Top Clin Nurs* October 1984; 6:72.

National Center for Health Statistics: *Vital Statistics of the United States: 1985.* Washington DC: U.S. Government Printing Office, 1988.

Osofsky HJ: Mitigating the adverse effects of early parenthood. *Contemp OB/GYN* January 1985; 25:57.

Palmore SU, Shannon MD: Risk factors for adolescent pregnancy in students. *Pediatr Nurs* May/June 1988; 14(3):241.

Redwine FO: Pregnancy in women over 35. *Female Patient* May 1988; 13(5):30.

Slager-Earnest SE et al: Effects of a specialized prenatal adolescent program on maternal and infant outcomes. *J Obstet Gynecol Neonatal Nurs* November/December 1987; 16(6):422.

Smoke J, Grace MC: Effectiveness of prenatal care and education for pregnant adolescents: Nurse-midwifery intervention and team approach. *J Nurse-Midwifery* July/August 1988; 33:178.

Symposium: Managing pregnancy in patients over 35. *Contemp OB/GYN* May 1987; 29(5):180.

Teti DM et al: Long-range socioeconomic and marital consequences of adolescent marriage in three cohorts of adult males. *J Marriage Family* 1987; 49:499.

Waters JL: Pregnancy in young adolescents: A syndrome of failure. *South Med J* June 1969; 62:655.

Westney OE et al: The effects of prenatal education intervention on unwed prospective adolescent fathers. *J Adolesc Health Care* 1988; 9:214.

## Additional Readings

Becerea RM et al: Pregnancy and motherhood among Mexican-American adolescents. *Health Soc Work* Spring 1984; 9:106.

Burt MR: Estimating the public costs of teenage childbearing. *Fam Plan Perspect* 1986; 18(5):221.

de la Luz Alvarez M et al: Sociocultural characteristics of pregnant and nonpregnant adolescents of low socioeconomic status: A comparative study. *Adolescence* Spring 1987; 22:149.

Friede A et al: Older maternal age and infant mortality in the United States. *Obstet Gynecol* August 1988; 72(2):152.

Fuller SA et al: A small group can go a long way. *MCN* November/December 1988; 16(6):414.

Goldberg BD et al: Teen pregnancy service: An interdisciplinary health care delivery system utilizing certified nurse-midwives. *J Nurse-Midwifery* 1986; 31(6):263.

Heller RG: School-based clinics: Impact on teenage pregnancy prevention. *Pediatr Nurs* March/April 1988; 14(2):103.

Pletsch PK: Substance use and health activities of pregnant adolescents. *J Adolesc Health Care* 1988; 38.

Proctor SE: A developmental approach to pregnancy prevention with early adolescent females. *J Sch Health* 1986; 56(8):313.

Robinson GE et al: Psychological adaptation to pregnancy in childless women more than 35 years of age. *Am J Obstet Gynecol* 1987; 156(2):328.

Young M: Parenting during mid-adolescence: A review of development theories and parenting behaviors. *Matern Child Nurs J* Spring 1988; 17(1):1.

Zdanuk JM et al: Adolescent pregnancy and incest: The nurse's role as counselor. *J Obstet Gynecol Neonatal Nurs* 1987; 16(2):99.

# 10

# Maternal Nutrition

*I'm trying to be very careful about what I eat. I've had more salads and fresh fruit than I can remember. Sometimes, though, I get a "cookie attack" and indulge myself. My husband said I should eat oatmeal cookies so I could feel that my cravings were nutritionally sound!*

## Objectives

● Identify the role of specific nutrients in the diet of the pregnant woman.

● Compare nutritional needs during pregnancy and lactation with nonpregnant requirements.

● Plan adequate prenatal vegetarian diets based on nutritional requirements of pregnancy.

● Describe ways in which various physical, psychosocial, and cultural factors can affect nutritional intake and status.

● Compare recommendations for weight gain and nutrient intakes in the pregnant adolescent with those for the mature pregnant adult.

● Describe basic factors a nurse should consider when offering nutritional counseling to a pregnant adolescent.

● Compare nutritional counseling issues for nursing and nonnursing mothers.

● Formulate a nutritional care plan for pregnant women based on a diagnosis of nutritional problems.

## Key Terms

calorie
folic acid
lacto-ovovegetarian
lactose intolerance
lactovegetarian
pica
recommended
　dietary allowances
　(RDA)
vegan

A woman's nutritional status prior to and during pregnancy can influence her health and that of her unborn child significantly. In most prenatal clinics and offices, nurses offer nutritional counseling directly or work closely with the nutritionist in providing necessary nutritional assessment and teaching.

This chapter focuses on the special nutritional needs of a normal pregnant woman. Special sections consider the nutritional needs of the pregnant adolescent and the woman after delivery.

Good prenatal nutrition is the result of proper eating for a lifetime, not just during pregnancy. Many factors influence the ability of a woman to achieve good prenatal nutrition:

● *General nutritional status prior to pregnancy.* Nutritional deficits present at the time of conception and continuing into the early prenatal period may influence the outcome of the pregnancy.

● *Maternal age.* An expectant adolescent must meet her own growth needs in addition to the nutritional needs of pregnancy. This may be especially difficult because teenagers often have nutritional deficiencies.

● *Maternal parity.* The mother's nutritional needs and the outcome of the pregnancy are influenced by the number of pregnancies she has had and the interval between them.

A mother's nutritional status does affect her fetus. Factors influencing fetal well-being are interrelated, but research suggests that nutrient deficiency can produce measurable effects on cell and organ growth.

Growth occurs in three overlapping stages: (a) growth by increase in cell number, (b) growth by increases in cell number and cell size, and (c) growth by increase in cell size alone. It is now thought that nutritional problems that interfere with cell division may have permanent consequences. If the nutritional insult occurs when cells are mainly enlarging, the changes are reversible when normal nutrition occurs.

Growth of fetal and maternal tissues requires increased quantities of essential dietary components. Table 10.1 compares the **recommended dietary allowances (RDA)** for nonpregnant females with those for pregnant and lactating teenage and adult women.

Most of the recommended nutrients can be obtained by eating a well-balanced diet each day. The basic food groups and recommended amounts during pregnancy and lactation are presented in Table 10.2.

## Table 10.1 Recommended Dietary Allowances for Women 11 to 40 Years of Age

| Nutrient | Nonpregnant | | | | Pregnant | Lactating |
|---|---|---|---|---|---|---|
| | (11–14 years) | (15–18 years) | (19–22 years) | (23–40 years) | | |
| Energy, calories | 2200 | 2100 | 2100 | 2000 | +300 | +500 |
| Protein (g) | 46 | 46 | 44 | 44 | +30 | +20 |
| Vitamin A ($\mu$g RE) | 800 | 800 | 800 | 800 | +200 | +400 |
| Vitamin D ($\mu$g) | 10 | 10 | 7.5 | 5 | +5 | +5 |
| Vitamin E (IU) | 8 | 8 | 8 | 8 | +2 | +3 |
| Ascorbic acid (mg) | 50 | 60 | 60 | 60 | +20 | +40 |
| Folacin ($\mu$g) | 400 | 400 | 400 | 400 | +400 | +100 |
| Niacin (mg) | 15 | 14 | 14 | 13 | +2 | +5 |
| Riboflavin (mg) | 1.3 | 1.3 | 1.3 | 1.2 | +0.3 | +0.5 |
| Thiamine (mg) | 1.1 | 1.1 | 1.1 | 1.0 | +0.4 | +0.5 |
| Vitamin $B_6$ (mg) | 1.8 | 2.0 | 2.0 | 2.0 | +0.6 | +0.5 |
| Vitamin $B_{12}$ ($\mu$g) | 3.0 | 3.0 | 3.0 | 3.0 | +1.0 | +1.0 |
| Calcium (mg) | 1200 | 1200 | 800 | 800 | +400 | +400 |
| Phosphorus (mg) | 1200 | 1200 | 800 | 800 | +400 | +400 |
| Iodine ($\mu$g) | 150 | 150 | 150 | 150 | +25 | +50 |
| Iron (mg) | 18 | 18 | 18 | 18 | * | * |
| Magnesium (mg) | 300 | 300 | 300 | 300 | +150 | +150 |
| Zinc (mg) | 15 | 15 | 15 | 15 | +5 | +10 |

*This iron requirement cannot be met by ordinary diets. Therefore, the use of 30–60 mg supplemental iron is recommended.

Source: Food and Nutrition Board: *Recommended Dietary Allowances.* Washington, DC: National Academy of Sciences, National Research Council, 1980.

## ● MATERNAL WEIGHT GAIN

Maternal weight gain and infant birth weight are related. A weight gain of 11–13.6 kg (25–30 lb) is generally recommended. A 25-pound weight gain would be distributed as follows: 11 lb—fetus, placenta, amniotic fluid; 2 lb—uterus and breasts; 4 lb—increased blood volume; 3 lb—tissue fluid; and 5 lb—maternal stores. The optimal weight gain depends on the woman's height, bone structure, and the prepregnant nutritional state. The ideal pattern of weight gain during pregnancy consists of a gain of 1–2 kg (2–4.4 lb) during the first trimester, followed by an average gain of 0.4 kg (slightly less than a pound) per week during the last two trimesters. The pattern of gain is important. Sharp increases may indicate excessive fluid retention and should be evaluated.

Sometimes a woman will gain excessively during the first two thirds of her pregnancy because of overeating. Dieting is not advised at this time, however, because the third trimester is the time of maximum fetal growth. Consequently nutritional counseling is directed toward helping the woman plan her diet to gain up to a pound per week. Calorie intake should focus on the RDA guidelines.

There are special concerns for weight gain in the obese woman (one who weighs 20% or more above her recommended prepregnant weight). Obese women (even if not diabetic) have an increased risk of having a large baby. They also have an increased risk of chronic hypertension and pregnancy-induced hypertension (PIH) (Wolfe and Gross 1988). Pregnancy is not a time for dieting, and severe weight restriction during pregnancy can result in maternal ketosis, a threat to fetal well-being.

Counseling for the obese pregnant woman usually focuses on encouraging her to eat according to the RDA for pregnancy. Less emphasis is placed on the amount of weight gain and more emphasis is placed on the quality of her intake (Anderson 1986).

Women who are 10% or more below their recom-

## Table 10.2 Daily Food Plan for Pregnancy and Lactation*

| Food group | Nutrients provided | Food source | Recommended daily amount during pregnancy | Recommended daily amount during lactation |
|---|---|---|---|---|
| Dairy products | Protein; riboflavin; vitamins A, D, and others; calcium; phosphorus; zinc; magnesium | Milk—whole, 2%, skim, dry, buttermilk Cheeses—hard, semisoft, cottage Yogurt—plain, low-fat Soybean milk—canned, dry | Four 8-oz cups (five for teenagers) used plain or with flavoring, in shakes, soups, puddings, custards, cocoa Calcium in 1 c milk equivalent to 1½ c cottage cheese, 1½ oz hard or semisoft cheese, 1 c yogurt, 1½ c ice cream (high in fat and sugar) | Four 8-oz cups (five for teenagers); equivalent amount of cheese; yogurt, etc |
| Meat group | Protein; iron; thiamine, niacin, and other vitamins; minerals | Beef, pork, veal, lamb, poultry, animal organ meats, fish, eggs; legumes; nuts, seeds, peanut butter, grains in proper vegetarian combination (vitamin $B_{12}$ supplement needed) | Three servings (one serving = 2 oz) Combination in amounts necessary for same nutrient equivalent (varies greatly) | Two servings |
| Grain products, whole grain or enriched | B vitamins; iron; whole grain also has zinc, magnesium, and other trace elements; provides fiber | Breads and bread products such as cornbread, muffins, waffles, hot cakes, biscuits, dumplings, cereals, pastas, rice | Four servings daily: one serving = one slice bread, ¾ c or 1 oz dry cereal, ½ c rice or pasta | Four servings |
| Fruits and fruit juices | Vitamins A and C; minerals; raw fruits for roughage | Citrus fruits and juices, melons, berries, all other fruits and juices | Two to three servings (one serving for vitamin C): one serving = one medium fruit, ½–1 c fruit, 4 oz orange or grapefruit juice | Same as for pregnancy |

*The pregnant woman should eat regularly, three meals a day, with nutritious snacks of fruits, cheese, milk, or other foods between meals if desired. (More frequent but smaller meals are also recommended.) Four to six glasses (8 oz) of water and a total of eight to ten cups (8 oz) total fluid should be consumed daily. Water is an essential nutrient.

mended weight prior to conception have an increased risk of delivering a low-birth-weight infant and may have an increased risk of developing preeclampsia as well (Pitkin 1986). Merely advocating the traditional weight gain is not adequate counseling for the underweight woman who is pregnant. The nurse first assesses why the woman is underweight. Once the cause is determined, intervention can be planned with the woman. The underweight woman is usually advised to increase her caloric intake by 500 kcal above the nonpregnant RDA (as opposed to the 300 kcal usual increase). She should also consume 20 g additional protein. Her ideal weight gain is a combination of the amount she is underweight plus a 25-lb gain (Anderson

1986). This is often difficult for the underweight woman, especially if she has a small appetite, and she will require support and encouragement.

## • NUTRITIONAL REQUIREMENTS

## • Calories

The term **calorie** (cal) designates the amount of heat required to raise the temperature of 1 g of water 1°C. The *kilocalorie* (kcal) is equivalent to 1000 cal and is the unit used to express the energy value of food.

## Table 10.2 Daily Food Plan for Pregnancy and Lactation (continued)

| Food group | Nutrients provided | Food source | Recommended daily amount during pregnancy | Recommended daily amount during lactation |
|---|---|---|---|---|
| Vegetables and vegetable juices | Vitamins A and C; minerals; provides roughage | Leafy green vegetables; deep yellow or orange vegetables such as carrots, sweet potatoes, squash, tomatoes; green vegetables such as peas, green beans, broccoli; other vegetables such as beets, cabbage, potatoes, corn, lima beans | Two to three servings (one serving of dark green or deep yellow vegetable for vitamin A): one serving = ½–1 c vegetable, two tomatoes, one medium potato | Same as for pregnancy |
| Fats | Vitamins A and D; linoleic acid | Butter, cream cheese, fortified table spreads; cream, whipped cream, whipped toppings; avocado, mayonnaise, oil, nuts | As desired in moderation (high in calories): one serving = 1 Tbsp butter or enriched margarine | Same as for pregnancy |
| Sugar and sweets | | Sugar, brown sugar, honey, molasses | Occasionally, if desired | Same as for pregnancy |
| Desserts | | Nutritious desserts such as puddings, custards, fruit whips, and crisps; other rich, sweet desserts and pastries | Occasionally, if desired (high in calories) | Same as for pregnancy |
| Beverages | | Coffee, decaffeinated beverages, tea, bouillon, carbonated drinks | As desired, in moderation | Same as for pregnancy |
| Miscellaneous | | Iodized salt, herbs, spices, condiments | As desired | Same as for pregnancy |

An extra daily caloric allowance of about 300 kcal above the individual requirement, or a total of 2300–2400 kilocalories per day, throughout pregnancy is considered adequate for most women. This allowance does not take into consideration such factors as physical activity. The Teaching Guide—Helping the Pregnant Woman Add 300 Kcal to Her Diet offers suggestions for providing basic nutritional information to pregnant women.

### ● Protein

Protein supplies the amino acids (nitrogen) required for the growth and maintenance of tissue and other physio-logic functions. Protein also contributes to the body's overall energy metabolism.

The body uses the increased protein that is retained, beginning in early pregnancy, for hyperplasia and hypertrophy of maternal tissues such as the uterus and breasts, and to meet fetal needs. The fetus makes its greatest demands during the last half of pregnancy, when fetal growth is greatest.

The protein requirement for the pregnant woman is at least 74–76 g/day, a 30 g increase. Approximately half this requirement can be met with milk. A quart of whole milk supplies 32 g of protein.

Milk can be incorporated into the diet in a variety of

dishes, including soups, puddings, custards, sauces, and yogurt. Beverages such as hot chocolate and milk-and-fruit drinks can also be included, but they are high in calories. Various kinds of hard and soft cheeses and cottage cheese are excellent protein sources, although cream cheese is categorized as a fat source only.

Women who have allergies to milk (lactose intolerance) or who practice vegetarianism may find dried or canned soybase milk acceptable. It can be used in cooked dishes or as a beverage. Tofu, or soybean curd, can replace cottage cheese. Those who are allergic to cow's milk can sometimes tolerate goat's milk and cheese. Frequently, cooked milk is readily tolerated.

Some women make a high-protein drink from a mixture of ingredients. They prepare a quart of this drink in the morning to drink between meals throughout the day as an easy way to increase protein intake. Ingredients may vary but generally include 3 cups of milk (cow, goat, or soy), ½ cup nonfat milk powder (cow or soy), 2 Tbsp wheat germ, 2 Tbsp brewer's yeast or protein powders, fruit, and vanilla (eggs are optional). These ingredients are mixed together and stored in a covered container in the refrigerator.

Meat, poultry, fish, eggs, and legumes are also good sources of protein. Small amounts of complete animal protein can be combined with partially complete plant protein for an excellent, easily utilized supply of protein. Several examples of complementary proteins are eggs and toast, tuna and rice, cereal and milk, spaghetti with meat sauce, macaroni and cheese, and peanut butter and bread. Except in unusual medical situations, dietary protein should be obtained through natural foods, and the use of protein supplements should be avoided (Johnstone 1984).

## ● Fat

Fats are valuable sources of energy for the body. Fats are more completely absorbed during pregnancy, resulting in a marked increase in serum lipids, lipoproteins, and cholesterol and decreased elimination of fat through the bowel. Fat deposits in the fetus increase from about 2% at midpregnancy to almost 12% at term.

## ● Carbohydrates

Carbohydrates provide protective substances, bulk, and energy. Carbohydrates contribute to the total caloric intake required. If the total caloric intake is not adequate, the body uses protein for energy. Protein then becomes unavailable for growth needs. In addition, protein breakdown leads to ketosis. Ketosis, which results from incomplete fatty acid metabolism, can be a problem, especially in diabetic women, due to glycosuria, reduced alkaline reserves, and lipidemia.

The carbohydrate and caloric needs of the pregnant woman increase, especially during the last two trimesters. Carbohydrate intake promotes weight gain and growth of the fetus, placenta, and other maternal tissues. Milk, fruits, vegetables, and whole-grain cereals and breads all contain carbohydrates and other important nutrients.

## ● Minerals

Increased minerals needed for the growth of new tissue during pregnancy are obtained by improved mineral absorption and an increase in mineral allowances.

### CALCIUM AND PHOSPHORUS

Calcium and phosphorus are involved in energy and cell production and in acid-base buffering. Calcium is absorbed and used more efficiently during pregnancy. Some calcium and phosphorus are required early in pregnancy, but most of the fetus's bone calcification occurs during the last two to three months. Teeth begin to form at about the eighth week of gestation and are formed by birth. The six-year molars begin to calcify just before birth.

The RDA of calcium for the adult woman is set at 800 mg/day, with an additional 400 mg/day during pregnancy. If calcium intakes are low, fetal needs will be met at the mother's expense by demineralization of maternal bone.

A diet that includes 4 cups of milk or an equivalent dairy alternate will provide sufficient calcium. Smaller amounts of calcium are supplied by legumes, nuts, dried fruits, and dark green leafy vegetables (such as kale, cabbage, collards, and turnip greens). It is important to remember that some of the calcium in beet greens, spinach, and chard is bound with oxalic acid, which makes it unavailable to the body.

The RDA for phosphorus is the same as the RDA for calcium: 800 mg/day with an extra 400 mg/day during pregnancy. As phosphorus is so widely available in foods, the dietary intake of phosphorus frequently exceeds calcium intake. An excess of phosphorus can result in a disturbance of the calcium-phosphorus ratio in the body, decreased calcium absorption, and increased excretion of calcium. Excess phosphorus can be reduced by avoiding the snack foods, processed meats, and cola drinks in which it abounds. However, if vitamin D and magnesium are adequate, most adults can tolerate relatively wide variations in dietary calcium-phosphorus ratios.

### IODINE

Inorganic iodine is excreted in the urine during pregnancy. Enlargement of the thyroid gland may occur if iodine is not replaced by adequate dietary intake or an additional supplement. Moreover, cretinism may occur in the infant if the mother has a severe iodine deficiency.

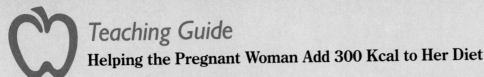

# Teaching Guide

## Helping the Pregnant Woman Add 300 Kcal to Her Diet

***Assessment*** The nurse recognizes that the notion of "eating for two" may cause a woman to overestimate the amount of food she should consume during pregnancy. The nurse assesses the pregnant woman's knowledge of basic nutrition, including the use of the basic four food groups, and assesses her awareness of the best way to increase the nutrients in her diet.

***Nursing Diagnosis*** The essential nursing diagnosis will probably be: Knowledge deficit related to nutritional needs during pregnancy.

***Nursing Plan and Implementation*** The teaching plan focuses on providing information about the basic four food groups and about the most effective way to use the additional 300 kcal that a woman needs daily during pregnancy.

***Client Goals*** At the completion of the teaching the woman will:

1. Identify the four basic food group categories and the foods included in each.
2. Cite the increase in kcal indicated during pregnancy.
3. Discuss the most nutritionally sound way to use the additional calories.
4. Use the information she has gained to plan a nutritionally sound sample menu.

## Teaching Plan

### Content

1. The four basic food groups include the following:

    Dairy: adult needs two servings (one serving = 1 c milk or yogurt, 1.5 oz hard cheese, 2 c cottage cheese, 1 c pudding made with milk)

    Grains: adult needs four servings (one serving = one slice bread, ½ hamburger roll, 1 oz dry cereal, 1 tortilla, ½ c pasta, rice, grits)

    Fruits/vegetables: adult needs four servings, one should be a good source of vitamin C (one serving = 1 medium sized piece of fruit, ½ c cooked vegetable, 1 c raw vegetables, ½ c juice, 1 c green leafy vegetable)

    Meats and alternates: adult needs at least two servings (one serving = 2 oz cooked lean meat, poultry, or fish; 2 eggs; ½ c cottage cheese; 1 c cooked legumes [kidney, lima, garbanzo, or soy beans, split peas, etc]; 6 oz tofu; 2 oz nuts or seeds; 4 Tbsp peanut butter)

2. Not all foods that are nutritionally equivalent have the same number of calories; it is important to consider that in making food choices.

### Teaching Method

*Ask woman if she has received nutritional information using this approach before. Discuss her understanding of it. Use that information to plan the amount of detail you will use.*

*Use a chart or colorful handout to explain the basic food groups and to give examples of equivalent foods.*

*Use a calorie counting guide to compare the calories in a variety of foods that are equivalent, such as 2 oz beef and 2 oz fish, or 1 c lowfat milk and 1 c whole milk.*

*(continues)*

## Teaching Plan (continued)

### Content

### Teaching Method

3. Limited extras are foods that have less nutrient value and should be eaten as limited supplements. Examples include sugary foods such as cake, doughnuts, candy; high-fat foods such as mayonnaise, potato chips, butter, etc.

*Use a similar approach to evaluate the calories in the limited extras, but also evaluate their nutrient content, especially levels of vitamin C, iron, etc.*

4. Emphasize that a woman only has to add 300 kcal/day during pregnancy. This can be achieved by adding two milk servings and one meat or alternate. Because of the varying caloric value a woman needs to consider the advisability of using lowfat milk, lean cuts of meat, or fish broiled or baked instead of fried, etc.

*In planning her diet to get optimum nutrition without too many additional calories it is often helpful to ask the woman to plan and evaluate a sample menu.*

Foods can be combined. For example, 1 c spaghetti with a 2 oz meatball would count as 1 serving meat, ¾ c spaghetti = 1 grain, and ¼ c tomato sauce = ½ serving vegetable.

*Provide handouts on which the woman can list the foods she has eaten and check off the nutrient categories they are in. Have her bring her completed handouts to a subsequent visit.*

---

**Evaluation** Teaching has been effective if all the identified goals are achieved and if the woman seems comfortable planning her diet to provide for the best nutrition possible.

## SODIUM

The sodium ion is essential for proper metabolism. Sodium intake in the form of salt is never entirely curtailed during pregnancy, even when hypertension or PIH is present. Food may be seasoned to taste during cooking. Salty foods such as potato chips, ham, sausages, and sodium-based seasonings can be eliminated to avoid excessive intake.

## ZINC

Zinc was recognized as a nutrient factor affecting growth in 1974. The RDA in pregnancy is 20 mg. Sources include milk, liver, shellfish, and wheat bran.

## MAGNESIUM

Magnesium is essential for cellular metabolism and structural growth. The RDA for pregnancy is 450 mg. Sources include milk, whole grains, beet greens, nuts, legumes, and tea.

## IRON

Anemia in pregnancy is mainly caused by low iron stores, although it may also be caused by inadequate intake of other nutrients, such as vitamins $B_6$ and $B_{12}$, folic acid, ascorbic acid, copper, and zinc. Anemia is generally defined as a decrease in the oxygen-carrying capacity of the blood. Anemia leads to a significant reduction in hemoglobin in the volume of packed red cells per decaliter of blood (hematocrit), or in the number of erythrocytes.

The normal hematocrit in the nonpregnant woman is 38%–47%. In the pregnant woman, the level may drop as low as 34%, even when nutrition is adequate. This condition is called the *physiologic anemia of pregnancy*. It is a result of increased plasma volume, which dilutes the blood and causes a drop in hematocrit level between 24 and 32 weeks' gestation.

Fetal demands for iron further contribute to symptoms of anemia in the pregnant woman. The fetal liver stores iron, especially during the third trimester. The infant needs this stored iron during the first four months of life to compensate for the normally inadequate levels of iron in breast milk and non–iron-fortified formulas.

To prevent anemia, the woman must balance iron requirements and intake. This is a problem for nonpregnant women and a greater one for pregnant women. By carefully selecting foods high in iron, the woman can increase her daily iron intake considerably. Lean meats, dark green leafy vegetables, eggs, and whole-grain and enriched breads and cereals are the foods usually depended on for their iron content. Other iron sources include dried fruits, legumes, shellfish, and molasses.

Iron absorption is generally higher for animal products than for vegetable products. However, absorption of iron from nonmeat sources may be enhanced by combining them with meat or a good vitamin C source. A supplement of simple iron salt, such as ferrous gluconate, ferrous fumarate, or ferrous sulfate (30–60 mg daily) should be taken during the second and third trimesters of pregnancy when fetal demand is the greatest. Supplements are not usually given during the first trimester because the increased demand is still minimal, and iron may increase the woman's nausea.

## ● Vitamins

Vitamins are organic substances necessary for life and growth. They are found in small amounts in specific foods and generally cannot be synthesized by the body.

Vitamins are grouped according to solubility. Those vitamins that dissolve in fat are A, D, E, and K; those soluble in water include vitamin C and the B complex. An adequate intake of all vitamins is essential during pregnancy; however, several are required in larger amounts to fulfill specific needs.

### FAT-SOLUBLE VITAMINS

The fat-soluble vitamins A, D, E, and K are stored in the liver and thus are available should the dietary intake become inadequate. The major complication related to these vitamins is not deficiency but toxicity due to overdose. Unlike water-soluble vitamins, excess amounts of A, D, E, and K are not excreted in the urine. Symptoms of vitamin toxicity include nausea, gastrointestinal upset, dryness and cracking of the skin, and loss of hair.

*Vitamin A* is involved in the growth of epithelial cells, which line the entire gastrointestinal tract and compose the skin. Vitamin A plays a role in the metabolism of carbohydrates and fats. In the absence of A, the body cannot synthesize glycogen, and the body's ability to handle cholesterol is also affected. The protective layer of tissue surrounding nerve fibers does not form properly if vitamin A is lacking.

Probably the best-known function of vitamin A is its effect on vision in dim light. A person's ability to see in the dark depends on the eye's supply of retinol, a form of vitamin A. In this manner, vitamin A prevents night blindness. Vitamin A is associated with the formation and development of healthy eyes in the fetus.

If maternal stores of vitamin A are adequate, the overall effects of pregnancy on the woman's vitamin A requirements are not remarkable. The blood serum level of vitamin A decreases slightly in early pregnancy, rises in late pregnancy, and falls before the onset of labor.

Excessive intake of preformed vitamin A is toxic to both children and adults. There are indications that excessive intake of vitamin A in the fetus can cause eye, ear, and bone malformation, cleft palate, possible renal anomalies, and central nervous system damage (Luke 1985).

Rich plant sources of vitamin A include deep green and yellow vegetables; animal sources include liver, liver oil, kidney, egg yolk, cream, butter, and fortified margarine.

*Vitamin D* is best known for its role in the absorption and utilization of calcium and phosphorus in skeletal development. To supply the needs of the developing fetus, the woman should increase vitamin D intake by 5 µg/day.

A deficiency of vitamin D results in rickets, a condition caused by improper calcification of the bones. It is treated with relatively large doses of vitamin D under a physician's direction.

Main food sources of vitamin D include fortified milk, margarine, butter, liver, and egg yolks. Drinking a quart of milk daily provides the vitamin D needed during pregnancy.

Excessive intake of vitamin D is not usually a result of eating but of taking high-potency vitamin preparations. Overdoses during pregnancy can cause hypercalcemia or high blood calcium levels due to withdrawal of calcium from the skeletal tissue. In the fetus, cardiac defects, especially aortic stenosis, may occur (Luke 1985). Continued overdose can also cause hypercalcemia and eventually death, especially in young children. Symptoms of toxicity are excessive thirst, loss of appetite, vomiting, weight loss, irritability, and high blood calcium levels.

The major function of *vitamin E,* or tocopherol, is antioxidation. Vitamin E takes on oxygen, thus preventing another substance from undergoing chemical change. For example, vitamin E helps spare vitamin A by preventing its oxidation in the intestinal tract and in the tissues. It decreases the oxidation of polyunsaturated fats, thus helping to retain the flexibility and health of the cell membrane. In protecting the cell membrane, vitamin E affects the health of all cells in the body. Its role during pregnancy is not known.

Vitamin E is also involved in certain enzymatic and metabolic reactions. It is an essential nutrient for the synthesis of nucleic acids required in the formation of red blood cells in the bone marrow. Vitamin E is beneficial in treating certain types of muscular pain and intermittent claudication, in surface healing of wounds and burns, and in protecting lung tissue from the damaging effects of smog. These functions may help explain the abundant claims and cures attributed to vitamin E, many of which have not been scientifically proved.

The newborn's need for vitamin E has been widely recognized. Human milk provides adequate vitamin E, whereas cow's milk is lower in E content. Deficiency symptoms of vitamin E are related to long-term inability to absorb fats. In humans, malabsorption problems exist in cases of cystic fibrosis, liver cirrhosis, postgastrectomy, obstructive jaundice, pancreatic problems, and sprue.

The recommended intake of vitamin E increases from 8 IU for nonpregnant females to 10 IU for pregnant women. The vitamin E requirement varies with the polyunsaturated fat content of the diet. Vitamin E is widely distributed in foodstuffs, especially vegetable fats and oils, whole grains, greens, and eggs.

Some pregnant women use vitamin E oil on the abdominal skin to make it supple and possibly prevent permanent stretch marks. It is questionable whether taking high doses internally will accomplish this goal or satisfy any other claims related to vitamin E's role in reproduction or virility. Excessive intake of vitamin E has been associated with abnormal coagulation in the newborn.

*Vitamin K,* or menadione as used synthetically in medicine, is an essential factor for the synthesis of prothrombin; its function is thus related to normal blood clotting. Synthesis occurs in the intestinal tract by the *Escherichia coli* bacteria normally inhabiting the large intestine. These organisms generally provide adequate vitamin K. Newborn infants, having a sterile intestinal tract and receiving sterile feeding, lack vitamin K. Thus newborns often receive a dose of menadione as a protective measure.

Intake of vitamin K is usually adequate in a well-balanced prenatal diet; an increased requirement has not been identified. Secondary problems may arise if an illness is present that results in malabsorption of fats or if antibiotics are used for an extended period, which would inhibit vitamin K synthesis.

## WATER-SOLUBLE VITAMINS

Water-soluble vitamins are excreted in the urine. Only small amounts are stored, so there is little protection from dietary inadequacies. Thus, adequate amounts must be ingested daily. During pregnancy, the concentration of water-soluble vitamins in the maternal serum falls, whereas high concentrations are found in the fetus.

The requirement for *vitamin C* (ascorbic acid) increases in pregnancy. The major function of vitamin C is to aid the formation and development of connective tissue and the vascular system. Ascorbic acid is essential to the formation of collagen. Collagen is like a cement that binds cells together, just as mortar holds bricks together. If the collagen begins to disintegrate due to a lack of ascorbic acid, cell functioning is disturbed and cell structure breaks down, resulting in muscular weakness, capillary hemorrhage, and eventual death. These are symptoms of scurvy, the disease caused by vitamin C deficiency. Infants fed mainly cow's milk become deficient in vitamin C, and they constitute the main population group that develops these symptoms (Food and Nutrition Board 1980). Surprisingly, newborns of women who have taken megadoses of vitamin C may experience a rebound form of scurvy (Anderson 1986).

Maternal plasma levels of vitamin C progressively decline throughout pregnancy, with values at term being about half those at midpregnancy. It appears that ascorbic acid concentrates in the placenta; thus levels in the fetus are 50% or more above maternal levels.

A nutritious diet should meet the pregnant woman's needs for vitamin C without additional supplementation. Common food sources of vitamin C include citrus fruit, tomatoes, cantaloupe, strawberries, potatoes, broccoli, and other leafy greens. Ascorbic acid is readily destroyed by oxidation. Therefore, foods containing vitamin C must be stored and cooked properly.

The *B vitamins* include thiamine ($B_1$), riboflavin ($B_2$), niacin, folic acid, pantothenic acid, vitamin $B_6$, and vitamin $B_{12}$. These vitamins serve as vital coenzyme factors in many reactions such as cell respiration, glucose oxidation, and energy metabolism. The quantities needed, therefore, invariably increase as caloric intake increases to meet the metabolic and growth needs of the pregnant woman.

The *thiamine* requirement increases from the prepregnant level of 1.1 mg/day to 1.5 mg/day. Sources include pork, liver, milk, potatoes, enriched breads, and cereals.

*Riboflavin* deficiency is manifested by cheilosis and other skin lesions. During pregnancy, women may excrete less riboflavin and still require more, because of increased energy and protein needs. An additional 0.3 mg/day is recommended. Sources include milk, liver, eggs, enriched breads, and cereals.

An increase of 2 mg daily in *niacin* intake is recommended during pregnancy and 5 mg during lactation, although no information on the niacin requirements of pregnant and nursing women is available. Sources of niacin include meat, fish, poultry, liver, whole grains, enriched breads, cereals, and peanuts.

**Folic acid** is directly related to the outcome of pregnancy and to maternal and fetal health. Folate deficiency has been associated with abortion, fetal malformation, abruptio placentae, and other late bleeding conditions. Severe maternal folate deficiency may have other unrecognized effects on the fetus and newborn. Hemorrhagic anemia in the newborn is attributed to this deficiency.

Megaloblastic anemia due to folate deficiency is rarely found in the United States, but those caring for pregnant women must be aware that it does occur. Folate deficiency can also be present in the absence of overt anemia. Because of the risks associated with deficiency during pregnancy, folic acid supplementation often begins with the onset of pregnancy or even before.

The RDA for folic acid increases by 100%—from 400 μg to 800 μg—during pregnancy. Many women have problems ingesting this amount since good dietary sources of folic acid are limited (see Table 10.3). For this reason, a supplement of 0.4 mg (400 μg) of folic acid daily is recommended.

Normal serum folic acid levels in pregnancy range from 3 to 15 mg/mL; less than 3 mg/mL constitutes acute deficiency. If no other complications are present, this deficiency can be easily remedied with folic acid therapy. After the baby is born, a routine nutritious diet generally provides adequate folic acid to alleviate the woman's symptoms; however, it is wise to give additional folate therapy to build up stores and promote rapid hematologic changes.

Women on phenytoin (Dilantin) for the control of seizures and women carrying twins are also especially susceptible to folic acid deficiency. Daily supplements of 0.8 to 1.0 mg folic acid are indicated for these women (Cruikshank 1986).

The best food sources of folates are fresh green leafy vegetables, kidney, liver, food yeasts, and peanuts. As indicated by the list of food sources in Table 10.3, many foods contain small amounts of folic acid. Cow's milk contains a small amount of folic acid, but goat's milk contains none. Therefore, infants and children who are given goat's milk must receive a folate supplement to prevent a deficiency. Adults can generally receive adequate folate from other food sources.

Folic acid content of foods can be altered by preparation methods. Since folic acid is a water-soluble nutrient, care must be taken in cooking. Loss of the vitamin from vegetables and meats can be considerable when they are cooked in large amounts of water.

No allowance has been set for *pantothenic acid* in pregnancy. Some studies suggest that it is advisable to supplement the diet with 5–10 mg of pantothenic acid daily. Sources include liver, egg yolk, yeast, and whole-grain cereals and breads.

*Vitamin $B_6$* (pyridoxine) has long been associated biochemically with pregnancy. The RDA for vitamin $B_6$ during pregnancy is 2.6 mg, an increase of 0.6 mg over the allowance for nonpregnant women. Since pyridoxine is associated with amino acid metabolism, a higher-than-average protein intake requires increased pyridoxine intake. Generally, the slightly increased need can be supplied by dietary sources, which include wheat germ, yeast, fish, liver, pork, potatoes, and lentils.

*Vitamin $B_{12}$*, or cobalamin, is the cobalt-containing vitamin found only in animal sources. Rarely is $B_{12}$ deficiency found in women of reproductive age. Vegetarians can develop a deficiency, however, so it is essential that their dietary intake be supplemented with this vitamin. Occasionally vitamin $B_{12}$ levels decrease during pregnancy but increase again after delivery. The RDA during pregnancy is 4 μg/day.

A deficiency may be due to inability to absorb vitamin $B_{12}$. Pernicious anemia results; infertility is a complication of this type of anemia.

● *Fluid*

Water is essential for life and is found in all body tissues. It is necessary for many biochemical reactions. It

## Table 10.3 Folic Acid Content of Selected Foods

| Food | Amount | Folic acid ($\mu$g) | Food | Amount | Folic acid ($\mu$g) |
|------|--------|---------|------|--------|---------|
| Yeast, torula | 1 Tbsp | 240.0 | Chocolate | 1 oz | 28.1 |
| Beef liver, cooked | 2 oz | 167.6 | Corn, fresh | 3½ oz | 28.0 |
| Yeast, brewer's | 1 Tbsp | 161.8 | Snap beans, green, fresh | 3½ oz | 27.5 |
| Cowpeas, cooked | ½ c | 140.5 | Peas, green, fresh | 3½ oz | 25.0 |
| Pork liver, cooked | 2 oz | 126.0 | Shredded wheat cereal | 1 biscuit | 16.5 |
| Asparagus, white, fresh | 3½ oz | 109.0 | Figs, fresh | 3 small | 16.0 |
| Wheat germ | 1 oz | 91.5 | Sweet potatoes, fresh | ½ medium | 12.0 |
| Spinach | 3½ oz | 75.0 | Walnut halves, raw | 8–15 | 11.5 |
| Soybeans, cooked | ½ c | 71.7 | Oysters, canned | 3½ oz | 11.3 |
| Wheat bran | 1 oz | 58.5 | Pork (ham) | 3½ oz | 10.6 |
| Kidney beans, cooked | ½ c | 57.6 | Banana, fresh | 1 medium | 9.7 |
| Broccoli, fresh | ⅔ c | 53.5 | Cantaloupe, diced, fresh | ⅔ c | 9.0 |
| Brussels sprouts, fresh | 3½ oz | 49.0 | Cottage cheese | 1 oz | 8.8 |
| Whole-wheat flour | 1 c | 45.6 | White flour | 1 c | 8.8 |
| Garbanzos, cooked | ½ c | 40.0 | Peanut butter | 1 Tbsp | 8.5 |
| Wheat bran cereal | 1 c | 35.0 | Blueberries, fresh | ⅔ c | 8.0 |
| Beans, lima, fresh | 3½ oz | 34.0 | Turkey | 3½ oz | 7.5 |
| Asparagus, green, fresh | 3½ oz | 32.4 | Celery, diced, fresh | 1 c | 7.0 |

Source: Modified from Hardinga MG and Crooks HN: Lesser known vitamins in food. © The American Dietetic Association. Reprinted by permission from *J Am Diet Assoc*, 1961, 38:240.

also serves as a lubricant, as a medium of transport for carrying substances in and out of the body, and aids in temperature control. A pregnant woman should consume at least eight to ten (8-oz) glasses of fluid each day, of which four to six glasses are water.

## ● VEGETARIANISM

Vegetarianism is the dietary choice of many persons. Some are vegetarians for religious reasons (Seventh-Day Adventists); others believe that this practice leads to a healthier body and mind.

There are several types of vegetarians. **Lacto-ovovegetarians** include milk, dairy products, and eggs in their diet. Occasionally fish, poultry, and liver are allowed. **Lactovegetarians** include dairy products but no eggs in their diets. **Vegans** are "pure" vegetarians; these individuals will not eat any food from animal sources.

Whether the family is currently practicing vegetarianism or is considering it as an alternative, it is vital that the expectant woman eat the proper combination of foods to obtain adequate nutrients. If her diet allows, a woman can obtain ample and complete proteins from dairy products and eggs. An adequate pure vegetarian diet contains protein from unrefined grains (brown rice and whole wheat), legumes (beans, split peas, lentils), nuts in large quantities, and a variety of cooked and fresh vegetables and fruits. Complete protein may be obtained by eating any of the following food combinations at the same meal: legumes and whole-grain cereals, nuts and whole-grain cereals, or nuts and legumes. Seeds may be used in the vegetarian diet if the quantity is large enough. Because proteins are less concentrated in plant tissue than in animal tissue, vegetarians must eat larger quantities of food to meet body needs and obtaining sufficient calories to achieve adequate weight gain can be difficult.

Because vegans use no animal products, a daily supplement of 4 $\mu$g of vitamin $B_{12}$ is necessary. If soy milk is used, only partial supplementation may be needed. If no soy milk is taken, daily supplements of 1200 mg of calcium and 10 $\mu$g of vitamin D are needed.

As the best sources of iron and zinc are found in animal products, strict vegetarian diets are also low in these minerals. In addition, a high fiber intake may reduce mineral (calcium, iron, and zinc) bioavailability. Emphasis should be placed on use of foods containing these nutrients.

Sample vegetarian menus that meet the requirements of good prenatal nutrition are given in Table 10.4.

## ● FACTORS INFLUENCING NUTRITION

Besides having knowledge of nutritional needs and food sources, the nurse must be aware of other factors that affect a client's nutrition. What is the age, life-style, and culture of the pregnant woman? What food beliefs and habits does she have? What a person eats is determined by availability, economics, and symbolism. These factors and others influence the expectant mother's acceptance of the nurse's intervention.

## ● Lactose Intolerance

Some individuals have difficulty digesting milk and milk products. This condition, known as **lactose intolerance**, results from an inadequate amount of the enzyme lactase, which breaks down the milk sugar lactose into smaller digestible substances.

Lactose intolerance is found in many blacks, Mexican Americans, Native Americans, Ashkenazic Jews, and Asians. Symptoms include abdominal distention, discomfort, nausea, vomiting, loose stools, and cramps.

| Table 10.4 Suggested Menus for Prenatal Vegetarian Diets to Meet RDA | | | | | |
|---|---|---|---|---|---|
| **Meal pattern** | **Mixed diet** | **Lacto-ovovegetarian** | **Lacto-vegetarian** | **Seventh-Day Adventist** | **Vegan** |
| BREAKFAST | | | | | |
| Fruit | ¾ c orange juice | Same as mixed diet | Same as mixed diet | Same as mixed diet | Same as mixed diet |
| Grains | ½ c granola, 1 slice whole-wheat toast | | | | 1 c granola, 1 slice whole-grain toast |
| Meat group | 1 scrambled egg with cheese | | 1 oz cheese melted over toast (no egg) | | |
| Fat | 1 tsp butter | | Same as mixed diet | | 1 tsp sesame butter |
| Milk | ½ c milk | | | | 1 c soy milk |
| MIDMORNING | | | | | |
| Milk | 1 c hot chocolate | | | | 1 c protein drink* |
| LUNCH | | | | | |
| Meat group/ vegetable | 1 c lentil chowder† (made with ground beef) | 1 c lentil chowder† (no ground beef) | 1 c lentil chowder† (no ground beef) | 1 c lentil chowder† (made with vegeburger)‡ | 1½ c lentil chowder† (1 Tbsp torula yeast, wheat germ added) |
| Grains | 1 corn muffin | Same as mixed diet | Same as mixed diet | Same as mixed diet | 2 corn muffins§ |
| Fat | 1 tsp butter, honey | | | | 2 tsp margarine, honey |

*Protein drink recipe is given on p 250. Use soy milk instead of cow's or goat's milk. Do not use eggs.

†Lentil chowder is made from lentils, celery, carrots, potatoes, onion, and tomatoes.

‡Vegeburger is made from meat analogs.

§Wheat germ and soy flour are added to corn muffin mixture.

*(continues)*

## Table 10.4 Suggested Menus for Prenatal Vegetarian Diets to Meet RDA (continued)

| Meal pattern | Mixed diet | Lacto-ovovegetarian | Lacto-vegetarian | Seventh-Day Adventist | Vegan |
|---|---|---|---|---|---|
| Fruit/dessert | ½ peach, ½ c cottage cheese salad | | | ↓ | ½ peach, ½ c tofu salad |
| Tea | 1 c tea | | | Decaffeinated or herbal tea | Same as Seventh-Day Adventist |
| **MIDAFTERNOON** | | | | | |
| Milk | ¾ c vanilla pudding | | | Same as mixed diet | 1 c pudding (soy milk) |
| Fruit | ¼ c sliced banana | | | | ½ banana |
| Grain | 1 graham cracker | | | | 1 graham cracker with peanut butter |
| **DINNER** | | ↓ | ↓ | ↓ | |
| Meat group/ vegetable | ¾ c meat sauce (onion, celery, carrot, tomato, mushroom in sauce) parmesan cheese | ¾ c tomato sauce (same vegetables as in mixed diet), ¼ c cheese | Same as lacto-ovovegetarian | Same as lacto-ovovegetarian (add vege-burger‡ to tomato sauce) | Same as lacto-ovovegetarian (use tofu instead of cheese) |
| Grains | ¾ c spaghetti, bread | 1 c whole-wheat spaghetti, 1 slice French bread | ↓ | | ↓ |
| Vegetable | Mixed vegetable salad | Mixed vegetable salad with ¼ c sprouts, ½ egg, ½ oz cheese, ¼ c kidney beans added | (No egg in salad) | | (Add tofu; no egg in salad) |
| Fat | Oil-vinegar dressing, ½ tsp butter | Same as mixed diet | Same as mixed diet | | 1 tsp margarine, oil-vinegar dressing |
| Fruit | Fresh pear or baked pear half | | | ↓ | Same as mixed diet |
| Tea | 1 c tea | | | Decaffeinated or herbal tea | Same as Seventh-Day Adventist |
| **BEDTIME** | | | | | |
| Milk | 1 c milk | | | Same as mixed diet | 1 c protein drink* |
| Meat group/ vegetable | 2 tsp peanut butter on celery or on wheat crackers | | | | |
| Grain | | ↓ | ↓ | ↓ | Corn muffins§ |

*Protein drink recipe is given on p 250. Use soy milk instead of cow's or goat's milk. Do not use eggs.

†Lentil chowder is made from lentils, celery, carrots, potatoes, onion, and tomatoes.

‡Vegeburger is made from meat analogs.

§Wheat germ and soy flour are added to corn muffin mixture.

In counseling pregnant women who might be intolerant of milk and milk products, the nurse should be aware that even one glass of milk can produce symptoms. Milk in cooked form, such as in custards, or mixed with Ovaltine, is sometimes tolerated. Green leafy vegetables are a non-dairy source of calcium. In some instances, the enzyme lactase may be taken to alleviate this problem. Lactase-treated milk is also available commercially in some grocery stores.

## ● Pica

**Pica** is the eating of substances that are not ordinarily considered edible or to have nutritive value. Most women who practice pica in pregnancy eat such substances only during that time. Women usually explain this practice by saying it relieves various discomforts of pregnancy or that it ensures a beautiful baby (Curda 1977).

Pica is most commonly practiced in poverty-stricken areas, where diets tend to be inadequate, but may also be found in other socioeconomic levels. The substances most commonly ingested in this country are dirt, clay, starch, and freezer frost. Iron-deficiency anemia is the most common concern in pica. Studies indicate that ingestion of laundry starch contributes to iron deficiency because it interferes with iron absorption. The ingestion of large quantities of clay could fill the intestine and cause fecal impaction, while the ingestion of starch may be associated with excessive weight gain (Pritchard et al 1985).

Nurses should be aware of pica and its implications for the woman and fetus. Assessment for the practice of pica is an important part of a nutritional history. Nurses may detect this practice as they help determine appropriate and effective relief measures for discomforts the woman is experiencing. Reeducation of the expectant woman is important in helping her to decrease or eliminate this practice.

## ● Food Myths

The relationship of food to pregnancy is reflected in some common beliefs or sayings. Nurses frequently hear that the pregnant woman must eat for two or that the fetus takes from the mother all the nutrients it needs. The practice of pica, for example, has roots in myth. Common beliefs regarding pica include (a) that laundry starch will make the newborn lighter in color, and (b) that the baby will "slide out" more easily during delivery (Curda 1977).

## ● Cultural, Ethnic, and Religious Influences

Cultural, ethnic, and occasionally religious background determines one's experiences with food and influences food preferences and habits (Figure 10.1). People of different nationalities are accustomed to eating different foods because of the kinds of foodstuffs available in their countries of origin. The way food is prepared varies, depending

*Figure 10.1  Food preferences and habits are affected by cultural factors.*

on the customs and traditions of the ethnic and cultural group. In addition, the laws of certain religions sanction particular foods, prohibit others, and direct the preparation and serving of meals.

In each culture, certain foods have symbolic significance. Generally, these symbolic foods are related to major life experiences such as birth, death, or developmental milestones. (General food practices of different cultural and ethnic groups are presented in Table 10.5. Sample daily menus for differing cultural groups that meet minimal nutritional requirements during pregnancy are presented in Table 10.6.)

For example, Navajo Indian women believe that eating raisins will cause brown spots on the mother or baby. Many black Americans believe that craving one food ex-cessively can cause the baby to be "marked"; some say the shape of the birthmark echoes the shape of the food the mother craved during pregnancy. This belief is also held by some Mexican-American women. Also, some Mexican Americans believe drinking milk makes their babies too big, thereby creating difficult deliveries.

The traditional Chinese classify food as either hot or cold, and these classifications are related to the balance of forces for good health. Since childbirth is considered a cold condition, it must be treated with hot foods, such as chicken, squash, and broccoli. Vietnamese women believe that eating "unclean foods," such as beef, dog, and snake, during pregnancy will cause the baby to be born an imbecile. Cabbage is also avoided because it is believed to produce flatulence that might bring on false labor (Clark 1978).

## Table 10.5 Food Practices of Various Ethnic and Religious Groups

| Cultural group | Staple foods | Prohibitions (foods not used) | Food preparation |
|---|---|---|---|
| Jewish Orthodox | Meat: Forequarter of cattle, sheep, goat, deer. Poultry: chicken, pheasant, turkey, goose, duck. Dairy products. | No blood may be eaten in any form; pork prohibited. Combining milk and meat at meal not allowed; milk and cheese may be eaten before meal, but must not be eaten for six hours after meal containing meat. | Animal slaughter must follow certain rules, including minimal pain to animal and maximal blood drainage. Two sets of dishes are used: one for meat, one for milk meals. |
| | Fish with fins and scales. No restrictions on cereals, fruits, or vegetables. | No shellfish or eels. | |
| Mexican American | Main vegetables: corn (source of calcium) and chili peppers (source of vitamin C); pinto beans or calice beans; potatoes. Coffee and eggs. Grain products: corn is basic grain; tortillas from enriched flour made daily. | Milk rarely used. | Chief cooking fat is lard. Usually beans are served with every meal. |
| Chinese | Rice is staple grain and used at most meals. Traditional beverage is green tea. Most meats are used, but in limited amounts. Fruits are usually eaten fresh. | Milk and cheese rarely used. Meat considered difficult to chew, so may be eliminated from child's diet. | Foods are kept short time and are cooked quickly at high temperature so that natural flavors are enhanced and texture and color are maintained. Chief cooking fat is lard or peanut oil. |
| Japanese | Seafood (raw fish) eaten frequently. Most meats; large variety of vegetables and fresh fruits. Rice is staple grain, but corn and oats also used. | Milk and cheese rarely used. | Chief cooking fat is soybean oil. |

## Table 10.6 Sample Menus for Adequate Prenatal Diet for Various Cultural Groups

| Caucasian | Mexican American | Southern U.S. | Asian | Jewish | Italian |
|---|---|---|---|---|---|
| **BREAKFAST** | | | | | |
| Peaches | Peaches | Peaches | Peaches | Peaches | Peaches |
| Oatmeal/milk | Oatmeal/milk | Oatmeal/milk | Steamed rice/ | Oatmeal/milk | Oatmeal/milk |
| Toast with peanut | Corn tortilla | Cornbread with | milk (soy) | Bagel with | Bread with |
| butter | Refried beans | molasses | Rice cracker | unsalted butter | butter |
| Milk | Milk | Milk | Tea | Milk | Cheese |
| | | | | | Coffee/milk |
| **MIDMORNING** | | | | | |
| Fruit/juice | Fruit/juice | Fruit | Fruit | Fruit | Fruit/juice |
| **LUNCH** | | | | | |
| Cheese omelet and | 1 fried egg | 1 fried egg | Miso soup | Cheese omelet | Cheese omelet |
| vegetables | Refried beans | Black-eyed peas | Chinese omelet | Brown rice | Zucchini, green |
| Whole-grain muffin | with cheese | and salt pork | (with bean | Lettuce and | salad |
| with butter | Corn tortilla | Cornbread with | sprouts, pepper, | tomato salad | Grapes/cheese |
| Lettuce and tomato | Fresh tomato and | molasses | green onion, | Honey cookie | Milk |
| salad | chilies | Turnip greens | mushroom) and | Milk | |
| Raw apple | Banana | Ice cream | fried rice | | |
| Milk | Milk | | Spinach | | |
| | | | Tea | | |
| **MIDAFTERNOON** | | | | | |
| Fruit | Fruit | Fruit | Fruit | Fruit | Fruit |
| Cottage cheese | Cottage cheese | | Tofu | | Cheese |
| **DINNER** | | | | | |
| Roast beef and | Refried beans | Beef stew with | Beef strips with | Beef stew with | Spaghetti and |
| gravy | with cheese | vegetables | pan-fried | vegetables | meatballs with |
| Whole-grain roll | Fried macaroni | (carrots, | vegetables | Barley pilaf | tomato sauce |
| with butter | Tortilla | greens) | Brown rice, | Cooked cabbage | Italian bread |
| Parsley, carrots, | Carrots, steamed | Dumplings | steamed | Unsalted butter | with butter |
| cabbage slaw | tomato, chilies | Steamed | Milk custard | Coffee cake | Sauteed |
| Banana cream pie | Corn pudding | potato, | | Fruit/juice | eggplant, |
| Tea | Milk | cabbage slaw | | | cabbage, salad |
| | | Corn pudding | | | Fruit |
| | | | | | Coffee/milk |
| **BEDTIME** | | | | | |
| Milk | Milk | Milk | Ice cream | Ice cream | Ice cream |
| Wheat crackers | Tortilla with | Corn pudding | | | |
| 1 oz cheese | beans | | | | |
| | Cheese | | | | |

Source: Modified from American Dietetic Association: *Cultural Food Patterns in the USA.*

## ● *Psychosocial Factors*

Sharing food has long been a symbol of friendliness, warmth, and social acceptance in many cultures. Food is also symbolic of motherliness; that is, taking care of the family and feeding them well is a part of the traditional mothering role. The mother influences her children's likes and dislikes by what she prepares and by her attitude about foods. Certain foods are assigned positive or negative values, as reflected in the statements "Milk helps you grow" and "Coffee stunts your growth."

Some foods and food-related practices are associated with status. Some foods are prepared "just for company." Other foods are served only on special occasions—for example, holidays such as Thanksgiving.

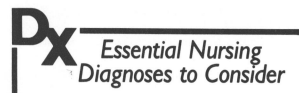

## DX Essential Nursing Diagnoses to Consider

### Nutrition for the Pregnant Woman

Constipation

Diarrhea

Fluid volume excess

Fluid volume deficit

Potential fluid volume deficit

Altered health maintenance

Knowledge deficit

Noncompliance

Altered nutrition: Less than body requirements

Altered nutrition: More than body requirements

Altered nutrition: Potential for more than body requirements

Body image disturbance

### SOCIOECONOMIC FACTORS

Socioeconomic level may be a determinant of nutritional status. Poverty-level families are unable to afford the same foods that higher-income families can. Thus, pregnant women with low incomes frequently are at risk for poor nutrition. Federal and state programs such as Women, Infants, and Children (WIC), food stamps, and others do enable low-income pregnant women to eat nutritionally sound meals. The nursing challenge is to aid the woman in identifying alternate foods that are nutritious, inexpensive, accessible, and acceptable.

### EDUCATION

Knowledge about the basic components of a balanced diet is essential. Often educational level is related to economic status, but even people on very limited incomes can prepare well-balanced meals if their knowledge of nutrition is adequate.

### PSYCHOLOGIC FACTORS

Emotions affect nutritional well-being directly. For example, anorexia nervosa, a psychologic disorder that occurs primarily in adolescent girls, is due chiefly to self-inflicted starvation, resulting in malnutrition and ultimately death if not treated. Loss of appetite is also a common symptom of serious depression.

The expectant woman's attitudes and feelings about her pregnancy influence her nutritional status. The woman who is depressed or who does not wish to be pregnant may manifest these feelings by loss of appetite or by improper food practices, such as overindulgence in sweets or alcohol.

## • THE PREGNANT ADOLESCENT

Nutritional care of the pregnant adolescent is of particular concern to health professionals. Many adolescents are nutritionally at risk due to a variety of complex and interrelated emotional, social, and economic factors that may adversely affect dietary intake.

## • Nutritional Concerns

Very little information is currently available on the nutritional needs of adolescents. Estimates are usually obtained by using the RDA for nonpregnant teenagers (ages 11 to 14 or 15 to 18) and adding nutrient amounts recommended for all pregnant women (see Table 10.1). Although the RDA are based on chronological age, they are probably the best available figures to use if the pregnant female is still growing. However, if mature, the pregnant adolescent's nutritional needs would approach those reported for pregnant adults.

### WEIGHT GAIN

Preliminary studies have confirmed that adolescents tend to gain a greater amount of weight during pregnancy than adults (Meserole 1984). In addition, it has been shown that young adolescents (13 to 15 years) need to gain more weight than older adolescents (16 years or older) to produce babies of equal size (Frisancho et al 1983). In determining the optimum weight gain for the pregnant adolescent, it is important to consider the following factors:

● Recommended weight gain for a normal pregnancy

● Amount of weight gain expected during the postmenarcheal year during which the pregnancy occurs

The weight gain for a normal pregnancy and the expected weight gain due to growth would be added together to obtain a recommended weight gain for the pregnant adolescent. If the teenager is underweight, additional weight gain is recommended to bring her to a normal weight for her height.

### SPECIFIC NUTRIENT CONCERNS

Caloric needs of pregnant adolescents will vary widely. Major factors in determining calorie needs include whether growth has been completed and the amount of physical activity. Figures as high as 50 kcal per kg have been suggested for young, growing teens who are very active physically. A satisfactory weight gain will confirm adequacy of caloric intake in most cases.

In order to promote optimal physical development of the pregnant adolescent, the Food and Nutrition Board recommends a higher protein intake for the younger pregnant female. Girls 15 to 18 years of age should consume about 1.5 g/kg of body weight. Those who are 11 to 14 years old should consume about 1.7 g/kg of body weight. As mentioned earlier, if growth has been completed, nutritional needs approach those of the pregnant adult female (1.3 g/kg).

Inadequate iron intake is a main concern with the adolescent diet. Estimates suggest that 20% of the adolescent population is at risk of iron deficiency anemia (Mellendick 1983). Iron needs are high for the pregnant teen due to the requirement for iron by the enlarging muscle mass and blood volume. Iron supplements—providing between 30 to 60 mg of elemental iron—are definitely indicated.

Calcium is another nutrient that demands special attention from pregnant adolescents. Inadequate intake of calcium is frequently a problem in this age group. To provide for these needs, an intake of 1600 mg/day of calcium is recommended (see Table 10.1). This is 400 mg/day more than the recommended amount for pregnant adults. An extra serving of dairy products is usually suggested for teenagers (see Table 10.2). Calcium supplementation is indicated for teens with an aversion to milk, unless other dairy products or significant calcium sources are consumed in sufficient quantities.

As folic acid plays a role in cell reproduction, it is also an important nutrient for pregnant teens. As previously indicated, a supplement is usually suggested for all pregnant females, whether adult or teenager.

Other nutrients and vitamins must be considered when evaluating the overall nutritional quality of the teenager's diet. Nutrients that have frequently been found to be deficient in this age group include zinc and vitamins A, D, and $B_6$. Inclusion of a wide variety of foods—especially fresh and lightly processed foods—is helpful in obtaining adequate amounts of trace minerals, fiber, and other vitamins.

## DIETARY PATTERNS

Healthy adolescents often have irregular eating patterns. Many skip breakfast, and most tend to be frequent snackers. Teens rarely follow the traditional three-meals-a-day pattern. Their day-to-day intake often varies drastically, and they eat food combinations that may seem bizarre to adults. Despite this, adolescents usually achieve a better nutritional balance than most adults would expect.

In assessing the diet of the pregnant adolescent, the nurse should consider the eating pattern over time, not simply a single day's intake. This pattern is critical because of the irregularity of most adolescent eating patterns. Once the pattern is identified, counseling can be directed toward correcting deficiencies.

## ● Counseling Issues

The pregnant teenager will soon become a parent, and her understanding of nutrition will influence not only her well-being but also that of her child. However, teens tend to live in the present, and counseling that stresses long-term changes may be less effective than more concrete approaches. In many cases, group classes are effective, especially those with other teens. In a group atmosphere, adolescents often work together to plan adequate meals including foods that are special favorites.

## ● POSTPARTUM NUTRITION

Nutritional needs will change following childbirth. Nutrient requirements will vary depending on whether the mother decides to breast-feed. An assessment of postpartal nutritional status is necessary before nutritional guidance is given.

## ● Postpartal Nutritional Status

Determination of postpartal nutritional status is based primarily on the new mother's weight, hemoglobin and hematocrit levels, clinical signs, and dietary history. As mentioned previously, an ideal weight gain is 25 to 30 pounds. Upon delivery there is a weight loss of approximately 10 to 12 pounds. Additional weight loss is most rapid during the next few weeks as the body adjusts to the completion of pregnancy. The mother's weight will then begin to stabilize. This may take several weeks or longer. It is important to consider the mother's weight in terms of ideal weight, prepregnancy weight, and weight gain during pregnancy. Women who desire information about weight reduction can be referred to a dietitian.

Hemoglobin and erythrocyte levels should return to normal within two to six weeks. Hematocrit levels gradually rise due to hemoconcentration as extracellular fluid is excreted. Iron supplements are generally continued for two to three months following delivery to replenish depleted stores.

Clinical symptoms the new mother may be experiencing are assessed. Constipation, in particular, is a common problem following delivery. The nurse can encourage the woman to maintain a high fluid intake to keep the stool soft. Dietary sources of fiber, such as whole grains, fruits, and vegetables, are also helpful in preventing constipation.

Specific information on dietary intake and eating habits is obtained directly from the woman. Visiting the mother during mealtimes provides an opportunity for unobtrusive nutritional assessment. Which foods has the woman selected? Is her diet nutritionally sound? A comment focusing on a positive aspect of her meal selection may initiate a discussion of nutrition.

The dietitian should be informed of any woman whose cultural or religious beliefs require specific foods. Appropriate meals can then be prepared for her. The nurse may also refer women with unusual eating habits or numerous questions about good nutrition to the dietitian. In all cases, the nurse should provide literature on nutrition so that the woman will have a source of appropriate information at home.

## • Nutritional Care of Nonnursing Mothers

After delivery, the nonnursing mother's dietary requirements return to prepregnancy levels (see Table 10.1). If the mother has a good understanding of nutritional principles, it is sufficient to advise her to reduce her daily caloric intake by about 300 kcal and to return to prepregnancy levels for other nutrients.

If the mother has a poor understanding of nutrition, now is the time to teach her the basic principles and the importance of a well-balanced diet. Her eating habits and dietary practices will eventually be reflected in the diet of her child.

If the mother has gained excessive weight during pregnancy (or perhaps was overweight before pregnancy), a referral to the dietitian is appropriate. The dietitian can design weight-reduction diets to meet nutritional needs and food preferences. Weight loss goals of 1 to 2 lb/week are usually suggested.

In addition to meeting her own nutritional needs, the new mother will be interested in learning how to provide for her infant's nutritional needs. A discussion on infant feeding, which includes topics such as selecting infant formulas, formula preparation, and vitamin/mineral supplementation, is appropriate and generally well accepted.

## • Nutritional Care of Nursing Mothers
### NUTRIENT NEEDS

Nutrient needs are increased during breast-feeding. Table 10.1 lists the RDA during breast-feeding for specific nutrients. Table 10.2 provides a sample daily food guide for lactating women.

It is especially important for the nursing mother to consume sufficient calories because inadequate caloric intake can reduce milk volume. However, milk quality generally remains unaffected. The nursing mother should increase her calories by about 200 kcal over her pregnancy requirement, or 500 kcal over her prepregnancy requirement.

The mother still requires increased protein, although her need is somewhat less for lactation than during pregnancy. Thus the breast-feeding mother should increase her protein intake by 20 g to a total of 64 to 66 g/day. (This is 10 g/day less than is needed during pregnancy.)

Calcium requirements during breast-feeding remain the same as during pregnancy—an increase of 400 mg/day. If the intake of calcium from food sources is not adequate, calcium supplements are recommended.

Liquids are especially important during lactation, since inadequate fluid intake may decrease milk volume. Fluid recommendations while breast-feeding are eight to ten glasses daily, including water, juice, milk, soups, etc.

In addition to counseling nursing mothers on how to meet their increased nutrient needs during breast-feeding, it is important to discuss a few issues related to infant feeding.

For example, many mothers are concerned about how specific foods they eat will affect their babies during breast-feeding. Generally there are no foods the nursing mother must avoid except those to which she might be allergic. Occasionally, however, some nursing mothers find that their babies are affected by certain foods. Onions, turnips, cabbage, chocolate, spices, and seasonings are commonly listed as offenders. The best advice to give the nursing mother is to avoid those foods she suspects cause distress in her infant. For the most part, however, she should be able to eat any nourishing food she wants without fear that her baby will be affected. For further discussion of successful infant feeding see Chapter 23.

## • USING THE NURSING PROCESS
## • Assessment

Assessment of nutritional status should be made to facilitate planning an optimal diet with each woman. Data may be gathered from the woman's chart and by interviewing her. Information is obtained about: (1) the woman's height and weight, as well as her weight gain during pregnancy, (2) pertinent laboratory values, especially hemoglobin and hematocrit, (3) clinical signs that have possible nutritional implications, such as constipation, anorexia, or heartburn, and (4) dietary history to evaluate the woman's views on nutrition as well as her specific nutrient intake.

During the data-gathering process the nurse has an opportunity to discuss important aspects of nutrition within the context of the family's needs and life-style. The nurse also seeks information about psychologic, cultural, and socioeconomic factors that may influence food intake.

The nurse can use a nutritional questionnaire such as the one shown in Figure 10.2 to gather and record important facts. This information provides a data base the nurse can use to develop an intervention plan to fit the woman's individual needs. The sample questionnaire has been filled in to demonstrate this process.

## • Nursing Diagnosis

Once the data are obtained, the nurse begins to analyze the information, formulate appropriate nursing diagnoses, and develop client goals. For a woman during the

## NUTRITIONAL QUESTIONNAIRE

**Name** Susan Longmont      **Date** 12-16-87

**Age** 20

**Ethnic group** white middle class

**Religion** Protestant

**Gravida** $\overset{\bullet}{1}$      **Para** $\overset{\bullet}{0}$      **EDC** 7-7-88

**Age of youngest child?** NA

**Birth weights of previous children?** NA

**Usual nonpregnant weight** 115      **Present weight** 125

**Weight gain during last pregnancy?** NA

**Vitamin supplements?** none

**Current medications?** aspirin for headache

**Do you smoke?** yes      **How much per day?** 1-1½ packs

**Eating patterns:**

1. How many meals per day?   2   when   12:30 pm   6:30 pm
2. How many snacks per day?   3   when   10:30 am   4:00 pm   10:00 pm
3. What other foods are important to your usual diet? chocolate and candy bars
4. Amount per day   4 bars/week
5. Do you have any different food preferences now?   no
6. Do you eat nonfoods such as:

                       **Amount**

   laundry starch    no    NA

   ice    yes    10 cubes/day

   other (name)    no    NA

7. What foods do you dislike or do not eat?   spinach and dried beans
8. For added information complete a typical daily intake (24 hour recall is suggested).

---

**Do you have special problems in food preparation such as:**

1. Physical disability     yes _____ no __✓__ Explain _____
2. Cooking appliances     yes _____ no __✓__ Explain _____
3. Refrigeration of food     yes _____ no __✓__ Explain _____

**Who does the meal planning?** I do.     **shopping?** We both do.

**cooking?** I do most of the time but my husband likes to help.

**Are there transportation problems?** We have only one car but we go in the evening.

**Financial situation:** My husband is working and going to school.

I am not working.     **Foodstamps** yes _____ w/c _____ no

**Do you have any previous nutritional problems?** No. I have never paid much attention to food before, but now I have a lot of questions.

**Are there any problems with this pregnancy?** Nausea   Yes, in the morning.

    Constipation   No     Other   NA

**Assessment by the nurse following the completion of the questionnaire.**

Basic estimated nutrient and caloric value of typical daily intake.

Please circle one of the following:

| | | | |
|---|---|---|---|
| Protein intake was | low | (adequate) | high |
| Caloric intake was | low | adequate | (high) |
| Calcium intake was | (low) | adequate | high |
| Iron intake was | (low) | adequate | high |
| Vitamin C intake was | low | (adequate) | high |

*Figure 10.2   Sample nutritional questionnaire used in nursing management of a pregnant woman*

first trimester, for example, the diagnosis may be "Altered nutrition: less than body requirements related to nausea and vomiting." In many cases the diagnosis may be related to excessive weight gain. In such cases the diagnosis might be "Altered nutrition: more than body requirements related to excessive intake of calories." Although these diagnoses are broad, the nurse must be specific in addressing issues such as inadequate intake of nutrients such as iron, calcium, or folic acid; problems with nutrition due to a limited food budget; problems related to physiologic alterations such as anorexia, heartburn, or nausea; and behavioral problems related to excessive dieting, anorexia nervosa, etc. In some instances the category "Knowledge deficit" may seem most appropriate. For additional examples of possible diagnoses, see Essential Nursing Diagnoses to Consider—Nutrition for the Pregnant Woman.

### • Nursing Plan and Implementation

After the nursing diagnosis is made, the nurse can plan an approach to correct any nutritional deficiencies or improve the overall quality of the diet. To be truly effective, this plan must be made in cooperation with the woman. The following example demonstrates ways in which the nurse can plan with the woman based on the nursing diagnosis.

Diagnosis: Altered nutrition: less than body requirements related to low intake of calcium

Goal: The woman will increase her daily intake of calcium to the minimum RDA levels.

Implementation:

1. Plan with the woman additional milk or dairy products that can reasonably be added to the diet (specify amounts).

2. Encourage the use of other calcium sources such as leafy greens and legumes.

3. Plan for the addition of powdered milk in cooking and baking.

4. If none of the above are realistic or acceptable, consider the use of calcium supplements.

### • Evaluation

Once a plan has been developed and implemented, the nurse and client may wish to identify ways of evaluating its effectiveness. Evaluation techniques may involve keeping a food journal, writing out weekly menus, returning for weekly weigh-ins, and the like. If anemia is a special problem, periodic hematocrit assessments are also indicated. Essential Facts to Remember—Prenatal Nutrition summarizes key points that the pregnant woman should thoroughly understand.

Women with serious nutritional deficiencies are re-

## Essential Facts to Remember

### Prenatal Nutrition

- The pregnant woman should eat regularly, three meals a day, and snack on fruits, cheese, milk, or other nutritious foods between meals if desired.

- More frequent but smaller meals are also recommended.

- The woman should diet *only* under the guidance of her primary health care provider.

- Water is an essential nutrient. The woman should drink four to six (8-ounce) glasses of water and a total of eight to ten glasses of fluid daily.

- If the diet is adequate, folic acid and iron are the only supplements generally recommended during pregnancy.

- To avoid possible deficiencies, many care givers also recommend a daily vitamin supplement.

- Taking megadoses of vitamins during pregnancy is unnecessary and potentially dangerous.

ferred to a nutritionist. The nurse can then work closely with the nutritionist and the client to improve the pregnant woman's health by modification of her diet.

## One Family's Story

*Mrs Jennifer Snow, age 26, is a slender and well-groomed woman. The Snows have been married for eight months. Mrs Snow is employed as a postal clerk in her hometown.*

*Mrs Snow is weight conscious and has attempted many fad diets to lose weight. She describes herself as having a small appetite at mealtime. She does not drink milk. Breakfast usually consists of a glass of orange juice and a piece of toast. At noon she eats a slice of cheese or hard-cooked egg plus a piece of fresh fruit. However, after work she is famished and snacks on soda pop and cookies. Mrs Snow eats a late dinner of meat, potatoes, vegetable, and a green salad. Portions are small. Before retiring for the evening, the Snows snack on potato chips, pretzels, and soda pop.*

*Recently, Mrs Snow has felt queasy in the morning before breakfast. After she missed her menstrual period, a pregnancy test confirmed she was pregnant.*

*The medical history and physical examination were unremarkable. A year ago, she weighed 50 kg (110 lb). Currently she is 46 kg (101 lb) and 164 cm (65 in) tall. Laboratory test results were: hemoglobin, 12 g/100 mL; hematocrit, 36%; and albumin 3.1 g/100 mL. There was no evidence of glucose, protein, or ketones in her urine.*

The nurse noted a concern about Mrs Snow's weight and history of weight loss attempts. She talked with Mrs Snow about the importance of a well-balanced diet during pregnancy. Mrs Snow was given a prescription for a vitamin and iron supplement and a pamphlet on nutrition and pregnancy. An appointment was scheduled for one month later. Mrs Snow was instructed to bring the nurse a three-day food record.

During the consultation one month later, the nurse learned that Mrs Snow had not followed the diet described in the pamphlet. Her intake was approximately 1200 calories. Mrs Snow feared she would gain too much weight and lose her figure. She had gained ½ lb and reported continued nausea.

The nurse recognized that her client's concerns about weight gain were interfering with her ability to make appropriate nutritional choices. The nurse consulted with the staff dietitian who had had some experience working with this type of client. Together they met with Mrs Snow to express their concerns and to plan a nutritional approach that would accomplish the following:

1. Develop a diet that was higher in calories, protein, and essential nutrients such as calcium, while limiting fat.

2. Arrange for ongoing nutrition education and counseling for Mrs Snow, especially involving topics of interest to her.

To accomplish these goals, the nutritionist agreed to work closely with Mrs Snow following delivery to assist her in losing any remaining weight. Mrs Snow agreed to keep a food diary and to practice evaluating the nutritional content of the food she consumed. In addition to her prenatal vitamin and iron supplements, Mrs Snow began taking a calcium supplement. The nurse and dietitian discussed with Mrs Snow several approaches to relieve her nausea.

It was very difficult for Mrs Snow to change her eating habits, but she was eager to do what she could for her unborn child. She made a conscious effort to improve the nutritional quality of the foods she chose and to avoid an excessive intake of fatty convenience snack foods.

The nurse did not want Mrs Snow to begin feeling that her eating was the entire focus of each visit, so she made certain that all aspects of good prenatal care were discussed. She encouraged Mrs Snow to attend childbirth preparation classes with her husband. At one of the classes a nursing mother spoke about breast-feeding. This mother was fit and slender. Mrs Snow was able to relate to the woman and accept her advice about the importance of an adequate diet and sufficient fluid intake for successful breast-feeding.

Although it was difficult at times, Mrs Snow did improve her eating habits. She rode her bicycle several times a week and did prenatal exercises to keep toned. At term she had gained 26¼ lb. Her baby, a son, weighed 6 lb 14 oz and did well after birth. In the weeks following her delivery, Mrs Snow followed the guidelines for intake for a nursing mother. To help with weight loss she also attended postpartum exercise classes. With the advice of the nurse and dietitian and the support of her husband, Mrs Snow stabilized her weight at 112 lb. Both the Snows agreed that although they occasionally "splurged on junk food," they were far more conscious about nutrition and planned to remain so to set a good example for their young son.

## ESSENTIAL CONCEPTS

● Maternal weight gains, averaging 25 to 30 lb are generally recommended.

● If the diet is adequate, folic acid and iron are the only supplements generally recommended during pregnancy.

● Caloric restriction to reduce weight should not be undertaken during pregnancy.

● Pregnant women should be encouraged to eat regularly and to eat a wide variety of foods, especially fresh and lightly processed foods.

● Taking megadoses of vitamins during pregnancy is unnecessary and potentially dangerous.

● In vegetarian diets, special emphasis should be placed on obtaining ample complete proteins, calories, calcium, iron, vitamin D, vitamin $B_{12}$, and zinc through food sources or supplementation if necessary.

● Evaluation of physical, psychosocial, and cultural factors that affect food intake is essential before nutritional status can be determined and nutritional counseling planned.

● Weight gains during adolescent pregnancy must accommodate recommended gains for a normal pregnancy plus necessary gains due to growth.

● After giving birth the nonnursing mother's dietary requirements return to prepregnancy levels.

● Nursing mothers require an adequate calorie and fluid intake to maintain ample milk volume.

### References

Anderson GD: Nutrition in pregnancy. In: *Gynecology and Obstetrics.* Vol. 2. Sciarra JL (editor). Philadelphia: Harper and Row, 1986.

Clark AL (editor): *Culture, Childbearing, Health Professionals.* Philadelphia: Davis, 1978.

Cruikshank DP: Don't overdo nutritional supplements during pregnancy. *Contemp OB/GYN* February 1986; 27:101.

Curda LR: What about pica? *J Nurse-Midwifery* Spring 1977; 23:8.

Food and Nutrition Board: *Recommended Dietary Allowances.* Washington, DC: National Academy of Sciences, National Research Council, 1980.

Frisancho AR et al: Maternal nutritional status and adolescent pregnancy outcome. *Am J Clin Nutr* 1983; 38:739.

Johnstone FD: Nutrition intervention and pregnancy: What are clinicians' choices? *Contemp OB/GYN* January 1984; 23:211.

Karls L: *Nutrition for Pregnancy.* Madison, WI: Jackson Clinic, 1983.

Luke B: Megavitamins and pregnancy: A dangerous combination. *MCN* January/February 1985; 10:18.

Mellendick GJ: Nutritional issues in adolescence. In: *Adolescent Medicine.* Hofmann AD (editor). Menlo Park, CA: Addison-Wesley, 1983.

Meserole LP et al: Prenatal weight gain and postpartum weight loss patterns in adolescents. *J Adolescent Health* 1984; 5:21.

Pitkin RL: Nutrition in obstetrics and gynecology. In: *Obstetrics and Gynecology,* 5th ed. Danforth DN, Scott JR (editors). Philadelphia: Lippincott, 1986.

Pritchard JA, MacDonald PC, Gant NF: *Williams' Obstetrics,* 17th ed. New York: Appleton-Century-Crofts, 1985.

Wolfe, HM, Gross TL: Obesity: Counseling before and during pregnancy. *Contemp OB/GYN* January 1988; 31:45.

## Additional Readings

Allard JP: Maternal nutrition for clients in the private sector. *J Am Diet Assoc* 1986; 86(8):1069.

Cann B et al: Benefits associated with WIC supplemental feeding during the interpregnancy interval. *Am J Clin Nutr* 1987; 45(1):29.

Cerrat PL: When your patient is eating for two. *RN* 1986; 49(6):67.

Franz MJ et al: Exchange lists: Revised 1986. *J Am Diet Assoc* 1987; 87(1):28.

Greene GW et al: Postpartum weight change: How much of the weight gained in pregnancy will be lost after delivery? *Obstet Gynecol* May 1988; 71:701.

Johnston PK: Counseling the pregnant vegetarian. *Am J Clin Nutr* 1988; 48:901.

Roberts SB et al: Energy expenditure and intake in infants born to lean and overweight mothers. *New Engl J Med* February 25, 1988; 318(8):461.

Scholl TO et al: Weight gain during adolescent pregnancy: Associated maternal characteristics and effects on birth weight. *J Adolesc Health Care* July 1988; 9(4):286.

Viegas OA et al: Impaired fat deposition in pregnancy: An indicator for nutritional intervention. *Am J Clin Nutr* 1987; 45(1):23.

Winick M: Maternal nutrition and fetal growth. *Perinat Neonat* 1986; 10(5):28.

# Preparation for Parenthood

*Birth is something that you go through . . . into parenting. Although signifi-cant and intense, it usually lasts only a short time in comparison with the nine months of pregnancy and the decades of parenting. It is not to be focused on primarily for itself, but as a means through which your baby enters the world. (Pregnant Feelings)*

## Objectives

● Identify the various issues related to pregnancy, labor, and birth that require decision making by the parents.

● Discuss the basic goals of childbirth education.

● Describe the types of antepartal education programs available to expectant couples and their families.

● Discuss ways of making group teaching effective for maternity clients.

● Compare methods of childbirth preparation.

## Key Terms

abdominal effleurage
antepartal education
La Leche League
psychoprophylactic (Lamaze) method

A person's preparation for parenthood begins with his or her own birth into a family. An individual's attitudes, feelings, and fears about parenthood are molded by the relationship that he or she had with his or her parents as well as observations of and encounters with other children and parents.

A person's experiences with parenting or children may have been pleasant or uncomfortable. The information an individual has about parenthood and related areas may or may not be accurate. Since people bring their beliefs and fears with them to the childbearing period, the nurse can do much to correct misconceptions and calm fears regarding pregnancy, childbirth, and parenthood in general.

One way that a couple can cope with feelings about impending parenthood is to assume an active, participatory role during the antepartal, intrapartal, and postpartal periods. An active role involves the parents-to-be. It enables them to be involved in many of the decisions regarding the conduct of the birth. It offers them a degree of control over what could be an overwhelming experience.

Some of the decisions that the childbearing family must consider are presented in this chapter. The chapter addresses issues such as the choice of care provider, type of childbirth preparation, place of birth, activities during the birth, method of infant feeding, and choices surrounding treatment of the newborn. It also considers the role of the nurse, who provides information that enables the couple to make informed decisions.

## ● USING THE NURSING PROCESS WITH COUPLES PREPARING FOR PARENTHOOD

## ● Nursing Assessment

The nurse assesses the couple's information base and need for additional information. Cultural factors and developmental needs are also assessed so that the nursing plan of care can deal with the couple holistically. In preparing for childbirth parents have many decisions to make. The nurse needs to assess the parents' knowledge about selecting a health care provider, where the baby is to be born, who will be at the birth, and which classes would benefit them the most. The nurse should also ascertain the mother's preferences regarding use of analgesia, enema, perineal preparation, stirrups, position for birth, and method of feeding her newborn.

## ● *Nursing Diagnosis*

After analysis of the learning needs of the couple or family, the nurse establishes appropriate nursing diagnoses. The nurse knows that the childbearing couple's knowledge base will affect the many decisions that they face. Nursing diagnoses that may apply to couples preparing for childbirth and parenthood are as follows:

● Knowledge deficit related to information needs during pregnancy and childbirth

● Knowledge deficit related to self-care measures during childbirth

● Ineffective individual coping related to unknown childbirth environment

## ● *Nursing Plan and Implementation*

The nurse devises a plan to clarify learning needs and factors that may affect the learning process. The nurse assists the couple in identifying learning goals and helps the family gather information so that the decisions they make during this time are based on thorough, accurate information.

Another important nursing action is to be an advocate for the childbearing couple. As parent advocates and supporters, nurses need to provide information that reflects respect for the dignity and rights of the couple and promotes the safety of the mother and fetus. The health care information given should focus on:

● The right of the woman to know her own personal health status and the health status of her baby

● The parents' options

● Their participation in decision making

● Responsibilities for self-care

● Treatments and their rationale

● Maintenance of family support systems

● Consideration and respect for each individual's needs

Finally, the nurse needs to operate from a sound knowledge base in order to be able to assist the parents in gaining desired information. Parent education literature and conversations with parents help the nurse stay abreast of parental concerns and trends in childbearing.

## ● *Evaluation*

In the evaluation process the nurse assesses not only the success of specific teaching situations but also the adequacy of the overall nursing diagnosis. Does the couple have the knowledge base that they need? Have unknown factors interfered with the learning process? Does the couple feel confident in making the needed decisions during pregnancy, childbirth, and newborn care?

## ● *CHILDBEARING DECISIONS*

When a man and woman decide to have a child or learn that they are pregnant, they are faced with many decisions. For instance, they must make decisions about who will provide health care, where their child will be born, who will attend the birth, and whether to attend prepregnancy or prenatal classes (Figure 11.1). The woman must also make decisions about whether to allow analgesia, perineal preparation, an enema, or the use of stirrups; what position to use during labor and birth; and whether to breastfeed her child.

Some parents deal with the numerous decisions regarding childbirth by devising a birth plan. In this plan they identify aspects of the childbearing experience that are most important to them. The birth plan helps identify options that may be available, and it becomes a tool for communication between the couple, the health care providers, and the birth setting. The plan helps the couple set priorities for activities that they want. A sample birth plan is presented in Figure 11.2. Once the couple has used the plan to identify their priorities, the birth plan can be shared with health care providers and can also be taken to the birth setting.

The birth plan identifies many factors associated with childbirth. One of the first decisions that the woman or couple needs to make is the type of care provider to use and how to choose that health care provider. The choice of care provider and place of birth frequently go hand in hand.

As the couple seeks information, nurses can assist in the decision-making process. The nurse can discuss various types of care providers so that the couple knows what to expect from each type. The couple needs to know the differences between the educational preparation, skill level, and general philosophy of certified nurse-midwives, obstetricians, family practice physicians, and lay midwives. The nurse also provides information about different types of birth settings and assists the couple in obtaining further information through tours of facilities and reading. Questions regarding the care provider's credentials, basic and special education and training, fee schedule, and availability for new clients can be answered by telephoning a receptionist in the office. As the couple prepares to interview different care providers, they may want to develop a list of questions so that they will learn the desired information during the interview process. Sample questions may include:

● Who is in practice with you, or who covers for you when you are off?

● How do your partners' philosophies compare to yours?

● What are your feelings about my partner (or other children) coming to the prenatal visits?

● What weight gain do you recommend and why?

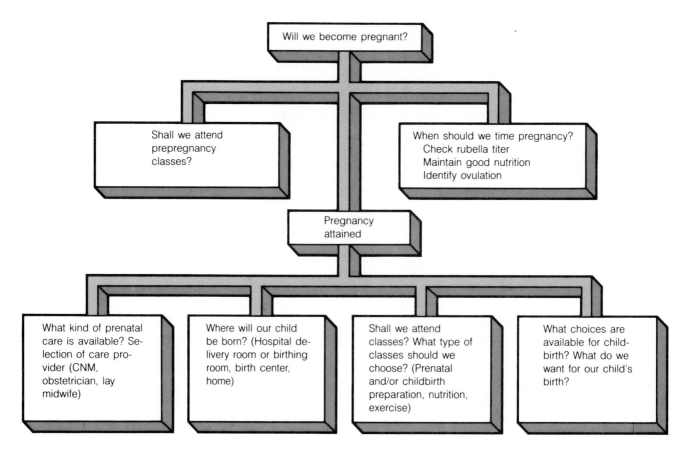

**Figure 11.1** *Pregnancy decision tree*

- How many of your parents attend prenatal and/or childbirth preparation classes, and what type do they choose?

- What are your feelings about (add in special desires for the birth event, such as different positions during labor, episiotomy, induction of labor, other people being present during birth, breast-feeding immediately after delivery, no separation of infant and parents following birth, and so on)?

- If a cesarean is necessary could my partner be present?

The couple will also need to discuss the qualities that they want in a care provider for their newborn. They will probably want to visit with care providers prior to birth in order to select one who meets their needs.

Choosing a care provider is just one of the myriad of choices and decisions with which the couple is faced (see Table 11.1). Another area of decision making is demonstrated in the following situation.

## One Couple's Story: Preparation for Parenthood

*Mr and Mrs Cline were discussing newborn care with Ms Gayle, the clinic nurse during one of their prenatal appointments. The Clines had been gathering information about the clothes needed for a newborn and about infant feeding but had not yet considered whether to use cloth or disposable diapers. They wanted some help in getting information. Ms Gayle suggested that they collect information from a variety of sources. Together they devised a plan to obtain information regarding cost, convenience, and any implications for their baby. They called a number of stores to determine the prices for cloth and disposable diapers. They investigated the cost of diaper service, as well as the cost of laundering their own diapers. They found that laundering their own diapers was the least expensive, but having a diaper service was only about a dollar more a week, and the convenience was important because of the work schedule that both the Clines would have to keep even after the baby was born. Disposables were the most expensive and were almost double the cost of laundering their own diapers (Martin 1985). They had seen coupons for disposables and knew that that would affect the price, but they anticipated having a storage problem with the boxes if they purchased many at once. They reviewed current literature regarding implications for their baby and found* comments regarding health care concerns (Solomon 1986) and the possibility of foreign body hazards (Johnson 1985) with disposables.

The Clines were surprised at the amount of information they were gathering. One other concern began to surface due to their beliefs in ecology. They noted that they needed to consider the implications of a natural product (cotton cloth diapers) vs. the use of natural resources (trees) to create disposable diapers. They were also concerned when they learned that one million plastic diapers are discarded every day and do not decompose (National Association of Diaper Services 1987). The Clines studied all the information and—based on cost, convenience, identified concerns for their baby, and ecological concerns—decided to have a diaper service. They shared their information with Ms Gayle and put together a packet for other parents to review if they wanted to.

The Clines felt they had investigated the questions thoroughly and were able to make an informed decision.

Although most birth experiences are very close to the desired experience, at times the expectations cannot be met. This may be due to unavailability of some choices in the couple's community or the presence of unexpected problems during pregnancy or birth. It is important for nurses to help expectant parents keep sight of what is realistic and possible and to help them understand that when choices are made alternatives may be needed (Sandelowski 1984).

## ● Choosing the Birth Setting

Information regarding the birth setting can be obtained from tours of facilities and from talking with nurses and recent parents. Expectant couples may ask new parents the following questions:

● What kind of support did you receive during labor? Was it what you wanted?

● If the setting has both labor and delivery rooms and birthing rooms, was a birthing room available when you wanted it?

● Were you encouraged to be mobile during labor or to do what you wanted to do (walking, sitting in a rocking chair, remaining in bed, sitting in a hot tub, standing in a shower, and so on)?

● Was your labor partner or coach treated well?

● Was your birth plan respected? Did you share it with the facility before the birth? If something didn't work, why do you think there were problems?

● How were medications handled during labor? Were you comfortable with it?

● Were siblings welcomed in the birth setting? After the birth?

| Choice | I would like to have Yes | No | Available Yes | No |
|---|---|---|---|---|
| Care provider | | | | |
| Certified nurse-midwife | | | | |
| Obstetrician | | | | |
| Lay midwife | | | | |
| Birth setting | | | | |
| Hospital: | | | | |
| Birthing room | | | | |
| Delivery room | | | | |
| Birth center | | | | |
| Home | | | | |
| Partner present | | | | |
| During labor | | | | |
| During birth | | | | |
| During cesarean | | | | |
| During whole postpartum period | | | | |
| During labor | | | | |
| Ambulate as desired | | | | |
| Shower if desired | | | | |
| Wear own clothes | | | | |
| Use hot tub | | | | |
| Use own rocking chair | | | | |
| Have perineal prep | | | | |
| Have enema | | | | |
| Electronic fetal monitor | | | | |
| Membranes: | | | | |
| Rupture naturally | | | | |
| Amniotomy if needed | | | | |
| Labor stimulation if needed | | | | |
| Medication: | | | | |
| Identify type desired | | | | |
| Fluids or ice as desired | | | | |
| Music during labor and birth | | | | |
| During birth | | | | |
| Position: | | | | |
| On side | | | | |
| Hands and knees | | | | |
| Kneeling | | | | |
| Squatting | | | | |
| Birthing chair | | | | |
| Birthing bed | | | | |
| Other: | | | | |
| Family present (sibs) | | | | |
| Filming of birth | | | | |
| Leboyer | | | | |
| Episiotomy | | | | |
| No sterile drapes | | | | |
| Partner to cut umbilical cord | | | | |
| Hold baby immediately after birth | | | | |
| Breast-feed immediately after birth | | | | |
| No separation after birth | | | | |
| Save the placenta | | | | |
| Newborn care: | | | | |
| Eye treatment for the baby | | | | |
| Vitamin K injection | | | | |
| Breast-feeding | | | | |
| Formula feeding | | | | |
| Glucose water | | | | |
| Circumcision | | | | |
| Feeding on demand | | | | |
| Postpartum care: | | | | |
| Rooming-in | | | | |
| Short stay | | | | |
| Sibling visitation | | | | |
| Infant care classes | | | | |
| Self-care classes | | | | |
| Other: | | | | |

*Figure 11.2   Birth plan for childbirth choices*

## Table 11.1  Some Consumer Decisions During Pregnancy and Labor and Delivery

| Issue | Benefits | Risks |
|---|---|---|
| Breast-feeding | No additional expense<br>Contains maternal antibodies<br>Decreases incidence of infant otitis media, vomiting, and diarrhea<br>Easier to digest than formula<br>Immediately after birth, promotes uterine contractions and decreases incidence of postpartum hemorrhage | Transmission of pollutants to newborn<br>Irregular ovulation and menses can cause false sense of security and nonuse of contraceptives<br>Increased nutritional requirement in mother |
| Perineal prep | May decrease risk of infection<br>Facilitates episiotomy repair | Nicks can be portal for bacteria<br>Discomfort as hair grows back |
| Enema | May facilitate labor<br>Increases space for infant in pelvis<br>May increase strength of contractions<br>May prevent contamination of sterile field | Increases discomfort and anxiety |
| Ambulation during labor | Comfort for laboring woman<br>May assist in labor progression by:<br>a. Stimulating contractions<br>b. Allowing gravity to help descent of fetus<br>c. Giving sense of independence and control | Cord prolapse with ruptured membranes unless engagement has occurred<br>Birth of infant in undesirable situations |
| Electronic fetal monitoring | Helps evaluate fetal well-being<br>Helps diagnose fetal distress<br>Useful in diagnostic testing<br>Helps evaluate labor progress | Supine postural hypotension<br>Intrauterine perforation (with internal monitoring)<br>Infection (with internal monitoring)<br>Decreases personal interaction with mother because of attention paid to the machine<br>Mother is unable to ambulate or change her position freely |
| Oxytocin | Decreases incidence of cesarean birth with augmentation of labor<br>Restimulates labor in cases of slowing contractions resulting from epidural blocks or uterine atony | Hyperstimulated contractions interfere with oxygenation of fetus<br>Uterine rupture<br>Early placental separation |
| Analgesia | Maternal relaxation facilitates labor | All drugs reach the fetus in varying degrees and with varying effects |
| Delivery position (lithotomy) (see Chapter 16 for further discussion of positions) | Ease of visualization of perineum by birth attendant<br>Facilitates elective operative intervention, if necessary | Increases need for episiotomy<br>May decrease normal intensity of contractions |
| Stirrups | Assist in positioning for pushing (can be used in side-lying position)<br>Comfortable for some women<br>Convenient for the person delivering the baby | Supine postural hypotension<br>Uncomfortable for some women<br>Leg cramping and/or palsy<br>Increased chance of tearing the perineum<br>Thrombophlebitis<br>Prolonged 2nd stage due to ineffective positioning for pushing |
| Episiotomy | Decreases irregular tearing of perineum<br>May decrease stretch and loss of sexual pleasure after pregnancy | Painful healing<br>May spasm during sexual intercourse due to poor repair<br>Permanent scarring with certain episiotomies<br>Infection<br>May still tear through rectum |

Sources: Burst H: The influence of consumers on the birthing movement. *Topics Clin Nurs* October 1983; 5:42. Hotchner T: *Pregnancy and Childbirth: A Complete Guide for a New Life.* New York: Avon Books, 1984.

● Was the nursing staff helpful after the baby was born? Did you receive self-care and infant-care information? Was it in a usable form? Did you have a choice about what information you got? Did they let you decide what information you needed?

The prospective parents have many choices of birth settings available to them. It is important to ascertain the care providers' philosophy early in the pregnancy as it may affect the possibility of using some birth settings.

# ● CLASSES FOR FAMILY MEMBERS DURING PREGNANCY

## ● Prenatal Education

**Antepartal educational** programs vary in their goals, content, leadership techniques, and method of teaching. The content of a class is generally dictated by its goals. For example, the goal of some classes is to prepare the couple for childbirth; therefore, they do not address the discomforts of pregnancy and the care of the newborn. Other classes may focus only on pregnancy, not labor and delivery. Special classes are also available for couples who know that the woman will be having a cesarean birth. Nurses should be aware of the couple's goals before directing them to specific classes.

### ONE-TO-ONE TEACHING

Teaching on an individual basis occurs when the woman needs it. Anticipatory guidance is also a positive part of teaching and is useful for discussing such topics as care of the breasts in pregnancy, sexual activity, and preparation for labor and delivery. DiFloria and Duncan (1986) identified several components of the teaching process that make the nurse a more effective teacher. Some of these are:

1. Identification of an instructional goal: What does the educator want the couple to know, or what does the learner want to know?

2. Analysis of the characteristics of the learner and the information that needs to be learned

3. Identification of behavioral objectives: What will the learner learn, or what behavior will be demonstrated?

4. Selection of teaching strategies: What method will be most appropriate for the situation?

5. The actual teaching situation with presentation of information

6. Evaluation of the teaching session: Does the couple have the information they needed? Do they feel they

can make informed decisions? Do they know where to seek further information?

7. Revision of the teaching plan to address components identified in the evaluation process

Incorporating these components helps the nurse be more successful in teaching situations.

Nurses' teaching skills improve as they broaden their base of knowledge and become more aware of the needs of expectant families. A continuous evaluation of the effectiveness of one's teaching is essential in developing these skills.

### GROUP TEACHING

Group discussion is a useful teaching method. In group teaching, the nurse assesses the needs of the group instead of the needs of an individual. Skill in dealing with groups is essential. Skill in teaching groups can be developed in several ways, including professional reading on the subject, attendance at workshops or courses, and ongoing practice. The following guidelines identify some basic principles of effective group teaching:

● Groups of couples should contain no more than 20 individuals

● Groups of mothers only should be smaller.

● The environment should be informal and friendly.

● Members should be encouraged to attend consistently, and other activities should be encouraged to increase group cohesiveness.

Helping the group to set an agenda at the initial session is one way of assessing members' needs. The individuals in the group must first become comfortable with each other so that they feel free to share concerns, questions, and information.

Nursing intervention during group discussion takes many forms and frequently overlaps with assessment and evaluation as specific interests and concerns are clarified. The nurse may need to draw other members into the discussion or clarify information. However, most prenatal classes are not purely discussion groups but include films, tours of maternity wards, demonstrations, and lengthy explanations. In classes concerned with selected methods of childbirth preparation, many group members may have read extensively on the subject and can contribute considerably to the discussion. Other members may know nothing about it and thus require more explanations and demonstrations by the nurse. In situations where group members know little about the method, a more structured approach to discussion and exercises may be useful.

Evaluation of the effectiveness of the teaching-learning process is continuous and difficult. Checking each individual's performance after demonstration of an exercise is

## Essential Facts to Remember

### Possible Content for Preparation for Childbirth Classes

**Early Classes (First Trimester)**

- Early gestational changes
- Self-care during pregnancy
- Fetal development, environmental dangers for the fetus
- Sexuality in pregnancy
- Birth settings and types of care providers
- Nutrition, rest, and exercise suggestions
- Relief measures for common discomforts of pregnancy
- Psychologic changes in pregnancy
- Information for getting pregnancy off to a good start

**Later Classes (Second and Third Trimesters)**

- Preparation for birth process
- Postpartum self-care
- Birth choices (episiotomy, medications, fetal monitoring, perineal prep, enema, etc)
- Newborn safety issues, ie, car seats

**Adolescent Preparation Classes**

- How to be a good parent
- Newborn care
- Health dangers for the baby
- Healthy diet during pregnancy
- How to recognize when baby is ill
- Baby care: physical and emotional

**Breast-Feeding Programs**

- Advantages and disadvantages
- Techniques of breast-feeding
- Methods of breast preparation
- Involvement of fathers in feeding process

**Sibling Preparation**

**Grandparents' Classes**

**Preparation for Cesarean Birth**

**Preparation for Vaginal Birth After Cesarean Birth (VBAC)**

ducted in the last class, or the nurse can give group members evaluation forms to return by mail (Whitley 1985).

## CLASS CONTENT

Childbirth preparation classes usually contain information regarding changes in the woman and the developing baby. (See Essential Facts to Remember—Possible Content for Preparation for Childbirth Classes.)

From the expectant parents' point of view, class content is best presented in chronology with the pregnancy. While both parents expect to learn breathing and relaxation techniques and infant care, fathers usually expect facts and mothers expect coping strategies (Maloney 1985).

At times prenatal classes are divided into early and late classes.

## EARLY CLASSES: FIRST TRIMESTER

Early prenatal classes should include couples in early pregnancy as well as prepregnant couples. The classes contain information regarding early gestational changes; self-care during pregnancy; fetal development and environmental dangers for the fetus; sexuality in pregnancy; birth settings and types of care providers; nutrition, rest, and exercise suggestions; common discomforts of pregnancy and relief measures; psychologic changes in pregnancy for the woman and man; and information needed to get the pregnancy off to a good start. Early classes should provide information about factors that place the woman at risk for preterm labor and recognition of possible signs and symptoms of preterm labor. Early classes should also include information on advantages and disadvantages of breast- and bottle-feeding. The majority of women (50% to 80%) have made their infant feeding decision before the sixth month of pregnancy, so early prenatal class information would be helpful (Aberman and Kirchoff 1985).

## LATER CLASSES: SECOND AND THIRD TRIMESTERS

The later classes focus on preparation for the birth, infant care and feeding, postpartum self-care, birth choices (episiotomy, medications, fetal monitoring, perineal prep, enema, and so forth), and newborn safety issues. Since many parents purchase the car seat prior to birth, later classes should include information regarding how car seats work, the importance of car seats, and how to select an approved car seat (Davis 1985).

## ADOLESCENT PARENTING CLASSES

Adolescents have special content learning needs during pregnancy. In a survey by Levenson, Smith, and Mor-

the most concrete way to evaluate learning. Evaluating members' changes in attitude or misconceptions is more difficult. A general evaluation of the series may be conrow (1986), teens identified informational needs according to priority. The most important areas of concern were: how to be a good parent, how to care for the new baby, health dangers to the baby, and healthy foods to eat during pregnancy. The teens stated that the need for information about these areas continues after the birth of the baby. Howard and Sater (1985) found that teens identified the highest priority information needs as: how to recognize when the baby is sick, take care of the baby, protect the baby from accidents, and make the baby feel happy and loved.

## BREAST-FEEDING PROGRAMS

Programs offering prenatal and postpartal information on breast-feeding are increasing. For many years, the primary source of information has been **La Leche League**. Information can also be obtained from birthing centers, hospitals, health clinics, and individuals such as lactation consultants (Edwards 1985). Content includes advantages-disadvantages, techniques of breast-feeding, and methods of breast preparation. The father is being included in the educational programs more frequently as his support and encouragement is vital and it is important to include him in decision making. Some fathers may feel negative and resentful about breast-feeding and need opportunities in the prenatal period for discussion and sharing of information (Jordan 1986).

## PREPARED SIBLING PROGRAMS

The birth of a new sibling is a significant event in a child's life. It may be associated with negative behavior toward the newborn, withdrawal, and sleep problems. More positively, the child seems to increase in developmental maturity after the birth of a sibling (Marecki et al 1985). With increased emphasis on family-centered birth, siblings are now being included in the birthing process. Their involvement may include visiting during labor, being present at birth, and/or visiting in the postpartal period.

The decision to have children present at birth is a personal and individual one. Children who will attend a birth can be prepared through books, audiovisual materials, models, and discussion. Nurses can assist parents with sibling preparation by helping them understand the stresses a child may experience. For example, the child may feel left out when there is a new child to love, or a brother may come when a sister was expected (Neifert 1986).

It is highly recommended that the child have his or her own support person or coach whose sole responsibility is tending to the needs of the child. The support person should be well known to the child, warm, sensitive, flexible, knowledgeable about the birth process, and comfortable with sexuality and birth. This person must be pre-

pared to interpret what is happening to the child and intervene when necessary (Feinbloom and Forman 1985). The support person should not be one who would be hesitant to leave (such as a maternal grandmother). Instead, the person responsible for the child must be amenable to the child's desire to leave the birthing room.

The child should be given the option of relating to the birth in whatever manner he or she chooses as long as it is not disruptive. Children should understand that it is their own choice to be there and that they may stay or leave the room as they choose. To help the child meet his or her goal, the nurse may wish to elicit from the child exactly what he or she expects from the experience. The child needs to feel free to ask questions and express feelings.

Many agencies are concerned about neonatal infection when siblings are present. However, it has been demonstrated that sibling contact with newborns does not increase bacterial colonization rates in the newborn (Kowba and Schwirian 1985). Parents are requested not to bring children who are obviously ill. Children are requested to perform an antiseptic scrub and put on a cover gown. In agencies that allow siblings to visit only after the birth, infection has not been an issue.

In general, the presence of siblings at birth engenders feelings of interest and the desire to nurture "our" baby, as opposed to jealousy and rivalry directed at "Mom's" baby. The mother does not disappear mysteriously to the hospital and return with a demanding outsider. Instead, the family attending delivery together finds a new opportunity for closeness and growth by sharing in the birth of a new member. Parents view the children's presence as positive, feel it added to family unity, and would have the children present again (Krutsky 1985). Another group of parents who had siblings present at birth felt that sharing the birth experience brought the family closer together. In addition, the parents thought that the event was a good learning experience and taught the child that birth was normal. Finally, the parents felt that the presence of siblings made the baby feel welcome and provided memories that the family could share for many years (Clark 1986).

The classes usually involve a tour of the maternity ward where the children will visit their mothers. Children generally show interest in such items as television sets, electric beds, and telephones the mothers will use to call them. The youngsters can climb on footstools at the nursery window to see the new babies. Most tours involve a visit to a birthing room, but not to delivery rooms. After the tour, the children have an opportunity to see and hear more about what happens to the parents and newborn in the hospital, how babies are born, and what babies are like. This teaching usually involves a combination of books, audiovisual materials, models, parental discussion, formal classes, and play experiences. They also have the opportunity to discuss their feelings about having a new baby in the family (Honig 1986). Discussion sessions may be di-

*Figure 11.3 It is especially important that siblings be well-prepared when they are going to be present for the birth. But all siblings can benefit from information about birth and the new baby ahead of time.*

vided into two age groups if the ages of the children attending vary greatly (see Figure 11.3).

After the class, parents usually receive additional resources that tell how to prepare children for a baby in the family. Some programs award certificates to the children who attend, offer refreshments to the children and their parents, and give gift packets with articles similar to those new mothers receive (lotion, diapers for the new baby).

Classes that prepare children for attendance at birth vary. It is important that the children be at least familiar with what to expect during the labor and delivery: how the parents will act, especially the sounds and faces the mother may make; what they will see, including the messiness, blood, and equipment; and how the baby will look and act at birth. In addition, parents are encouraged to involve the child early in the pregnancy, including taking the child on a prenatal visit to see the CNM/physician and listen to the fetal heart beat. Most advocates feel the child also needs to be comfortable with seeing the mother without clothes prior to seeing her during labor and birth.

### CLASSES FOR GRANDPARENTS

Grandparents are an important source of support and information for prospective and new parents. They are now being included in the birthing process more frequently. Prenatal programs for grandparents can be an important source of information regarding current beliefs and practices in childbearing. The most useful content may include changes in birthing and parenting practices and helpful tips for being a supportive grandparent. Some grandparents are integral members of the labor and birth experience and also need information on being a coach (Horn and Manion 1985).

## ● EDUCATION OF THE FAMILY HAVING CESAREAN BIRTH

## ● *Preparation for Cesarean Birth*

Cesarean birth is an alternative method of delivery. Since one out of every five or six deliveries is a cesarean, preparation for this possibility should be an integral part of every childbirth education curriculum. The instructor should treat cesarean birth as a normal event and present factual information that will allow a couple to make choices and participate in their birth experience. The instructor can emphasize the similarities between cesarean and vaginal births to minimize undertones of "normal" versus "abnormal" birth (Affonso 1981). This will diminish feelings of anger, loss, and grief that often accompany cesarean births.

Cesarean birth classes should cover what happens during a cesarean birth, what the parents will feel, and what the parents can do. Fawcett and Burritt (1985) used a pamphlet to give this information. The pamphlet was followed by a home visit or telephone call to emphasize the information and provide time for questions. Their findings indicated that parents found the program very helpful and useful.

*All* couples should be encouraged to discuss with their physician or nurse-midwife what the approach would be in the event of a cesarean. They can also discuss their needs and desires. Their preferences may include the following:

● Participating in the choice of anesthetic
● Father (or significant other) being present during the procedures and/or birth

## Preparation for Repeat Cesarean Birth

When a couple is anticipating a repeat cesarean birth, they have time to analyze the experience, synthesize information, and prepare for some of the specifics. Many hospitals or local groups (such as C-Sec, Inc.) provide preparation classes for cesarean birth. Couples who have had previous negative experiences need an opportunity to describe what they felt contributed to their feelings. They should be encouraged to identify what they would like to change and to list interventions that would make the experience more positive. Those who have had positive experiences need reassurance that their needs and desires will be met in the same manner. In addition, an opportunity should be given to discuss any fears or anxieties.

A specific concern of the woman facing a repeat cesarean is anticipation of the pain. She needs reassurance that subsequent cesareans are often less painful than the first. If her first cesarean was preceded by a long or strenuous labor, she will not experience the same fatigue. Giving this information will help her cope more effectively with stressful stimuli, including pain. The nurse can remind the client that she has already had experience with how to prevent, cope with, and alleviate painful stimuli.

## Preparation for Couples Desiring Vaginal Birth After Cesarean Birth (VBAC)

Couples who have had a cesarean birth and are now anticipating a vaginal birth have different needs from other couples. Because they may have unresolved questions and concerns about the last birth, it is helpful to begin the series of classes with an informational session. During this session, couples can ask questions, share experiences, and begin to form bonds with each other. The nurse can supply information regarding the criteria necessary to attempt a trial of labor and identify decisions regarding the birth experience. Some childbirth educators find it is helpful to have the couples prepare two birth plans: one for vaginal birth and one for cesarean birth. The preparation of the birth plans seems to assist the couple in taking more control of the birth experience and tends to increase the positive aspects of the experience (Austin 1986).

After an informational session, the classes may be divided depending on the needs of the couple. Those with recent coached childbirth experiences may only need refresher classes, while other couples may need complete training. Some couples may choose to attend regular classes after obtaining the beginning information in the informational session.

## SELECTED METHODS OF CHILDBIRTH PREPARATION

Various methods of childbirth preparation are taught in North America. Some antepartal classes are more specifically oriented to preparation for labor and delivery, have a name indicating a theory of pain reduction in childbirth, and teach specific exercises to reduce pain. The most common methods of this type are the Read (natural childbirth), the Lamaze (psychoprophylactic), the Kitzinger (sensory-memory method), and the Bradley (partner-coached childbirth) methods. Hypnosis is also discussed here because it is sometimes used to help the expectant mother reduce or even eliminate pain in labor and delivery. See Table 11.2 for differentiating characteristics of each method.

Each of these methods is designed to provide the woman with self-help measures so that her pregnancy and birth are healthy and happy events in which she participates.

Expectant parents are taught that childbirth exercises and preparation for childbirth do not exclude the use of analgesics but that they often reduce the amount necessary. Some women will not require medication. Unfortunately, some groups teach that painless childbirth is the desired goal, causing those women who experience discomfort and accept pain medication to feel as failures. This feeling can be extremely destructive to the woman's self-concept at a time when she needs positive reinforcement in her abilities to achieve and perform competently. Fortunately, current thinking recognizes that individuals vary in their responses to stress, that the character of individual labors differs, and that pain medication used judiciously may enhance the woman's ability to use relaxation techniques.

The programs in prepared childbirth have some similarities. All have an educational component to help eliminate fear. The classes vary in the amount of coverage of various subjects related to the maternity cycle, but they all teach relaxation techniques and all prepare the participants for what to expect during labor and delivery. Except for hypnosis, these methods also feature exercises to condition muscles and breathing patterns used in labor. The greatest differences among the methods lie in the theories of why they work and in the relaxation techniques and breathing patterns they teach (see Table 11.2).

The advantages of these methods of childbirth preparation are several. The most important is that the baby may be healthier because of the reduced need for analgesics and anesthetics. Another advantage is the satisfaction of the couples for whom childbirth becomes a shared and profound emotional experience. In addition, proponents of each method claim that they shorten the labor process, a claim that has been clinically validated.

All maternity nurses must know how these methods differ so that they can support each couple in their chosen

**Table 11.2 Summary of Selected Childbirth Preparation Methods**

| Method | Characteristics | Breathing technique |
|---|---|---|
| Lamaze | See narrative discussion. | |
| Read | First of the "natural" childbirth methods. Method utilizes information on progressive relaxation techniques and on abdominal breathing. | Primarily abdominal. Woman concentrates on forcing the abdominal muscles to rise. Works on slowing number of respirations per minute so that she can take one breath/minute (30 sec inhalation and 30 sec exhalation). Slow abdominal breathing used during first stage. Rapid chest breathing used toward end of labor if abdominal breathing not sufficient; panting is used to prevent pushing until needed. |
| Bradley | Frequently referred to as partner- or husband-coached natural childbirth. The exercises used to accomplish relaxation and slow controlled breathing are basically those used in the Read method. | Primarily abdominal as in Read method. |
| Kitzinger | Uses sensory memory to help the woman understand and work with her body in preparation for birth. Incorporates the Stanislavsky method of acting as a way to teach relaxation. | Uses chest breathing in conjunction with abdominal relaxation. |
| Hypnosis | Basic technique of hypnosis used in obstetrics is called hypnoreflexogenous method and is a combination of hypnosis and conditioned reflexes. Specific techniques of producing anesthesia and analgesia are not taught, but they are believed to be by-products of the method. | Normal breathing pattern. |

method. It is important for the nurse to assess the couple's emotional resources and their expectations so that she or he can help them achieve their goals more effectively.

## • *Psychoprophylactic (Lamaze) Method*

The terms **psychoprophylactic** and *Lamaze* are used interchangeably. Psychoprophylactic means "mind prevention," and Dr. Fernand Lamaze, a French obstetrician, was the first person to introduce this method of childbirth preparation to the Western world. Psychoprophylaxis actually originated in Russia and is based on Pavlov's research with conditioned reflexes. Pavlov found that the cortical centers of the brain can respond to only one set of signals at a time and that they accept only the strongest signal; the weaker signals are inhibited. Pavlov's research also demonstrated that verbal representation of a stimulus can create a response. When the real stimulus is substituted, the conditioned response continues to be produced.

Lamaze was popularized in this country through Marjorie Karmel's book *Thank You, Dr. Lamaze* (1965). The method was called "painless childbirth" and thus received much resistance from the medical profession in this country because many believed that pain in childbirth is inevitable. Also, with the development of many analgesics and anesthetics, it did not seem necessary to condition women for childbirth.

Proponents of the method gradually organized and in 1960 formed a nonprofit group called the American Society for Psychoprophylaxis in Obstetrics (ASPO). Two of the founders were Marjorie Karmel and Elizabeth Bing, a physical therapist who had also written about childbirth preparation using this method (Bing 1967). This organization helped establish many programs throughout the country, and Lamaze has become one of the most popular methods of childbirth education.

The two components of Lamaze classes are education and training. Class content originally was confined to exercises, relaxation, breathing techniques, and the normal labor and delivery experience. Childbirth educators have added information on prenatal nutrition, infant feeding, cesarean birth, and other variations from usual labor as well as discussions concerning sexuality, early parenting, and coping skills for the postpartum period.

Instructors teaching the method in this country have modified many of the original exercises, but the basic theory of conditioned reflex remains the same. Women are taught to substitute favorable conditioned responses for unfavorable ones. Rather than restlessness and loss of control in labor, the woman learns to respond to contractions with conditioned relaxation of the uninvolved muscles and a learned respiratory pattern. Exercises taught in these classes include proper body mechanics and body conditioning, breathing techniques for labor, and relaxation.

Another major modification in the Lamaze method involves the goals of expectant couples. Lamaze and his supporters implied that, if the childbirth experience was to be successful (painless with no anesthetic), specific criteria must be adhered to. Couples using this method are now encouraged to set their own goals for success. Lamaze childbirth education in this country supplies them with the tools to accomplish these goals. The couple is encouraged to discuss their goals with the obstetrician and maternity nursing personnel in labor and birth. The nursing staff who knows the couple's goals and resources is able to offer effective support.

## TONING EXERCISES

Some of the body conditioning exercises, such as the pelvic tilt, pelvic rock, and Kegel's exercises, are taught in childbirth preparation classes. Other exercises strengthen the abdominal muscles for the expulsive phase of labor. (See Chapter 8 for a description of recommended exercises.)

## RELAXATION EXERCISES

Relaxation during labor allows the woman to conserve energy and allow the uterine muscles to work more efficiently. Without practice it is very difficult to relax the whole body in the midst of intense uterine contractions. Many people are familiar with progressive relaxation exercises such as those taught to aid relaxation and induce sleep. One example follows:

> Lie down on your back or side. (The left side position is best for pregnant women.) Tighten your muscles in both feet. Hold the tightness for a few seconds and then relax the muscles completely, letting all the tension drain out. Tighten your lower legs, hold for a few seconds, and then relax the muscles letting all the tension drain out. Continue tensing and relaxing parts of your body, moving up the body as you do so.

Another type of relaxation exercise requires cooperation between the woman and her coach. It is particularly useful in learning how to work together during labor. (See Table 11.3.)

An additional exercise specific to Lamaze is disassociation relaxation. This pattern of active relaxation is in contrast to the Read method of passive relaxation (where the woman is taught progressive contraction and relaxation of muscle groups moving from head to toe to promote sleep). The woman is taught to become familiar with the sensation of contracting and relaxing the voluntary muscle groups throughout her body. She then learns to contract a specific muscle group and relax the rest of her body. This process of isolating the action of one group of voluntary muscles from the rest of the body is called *neuromuscular disassociation* and is basic to the psychoprophylaxis method of prepared childbirth. The exercise conditions the woman to relax uninvolved muscles while the uterus contracts, creating an active relaxation pattern. (See Table 11.4.)

While practicing, the coach checks the woman's neck, shoulders, arms, and legs for relaxation. As tense areas are found, the coach encourages the woman to relax those particular body parts. The woman learns to respond to her own perceptions of tense muscles and also to the suggestion from others. The suggestion can come verbally or from touch. The exercises are usually practiced each day so that they become comfortable and easy to do.

A specific type of cutaneous stimulation used prior to the transitional phase of labor is known as **abdominal effleurage** (Figure 11.4). This light abdominal stroking is used in the Lamaze method of childbirth preparation. It effectively relieves mild to moderate pain, but not intense pain. Deep pressure over the sacrum is more effective for relieving back pain. In addition to the measures just described, the nurse can promote relaxation by encouraging and supporting the client's controlled breathing.

## BREATHING TECHNIQUES

The breathing techniques use three levels of chest breathing. Proponents of the Lamaze method believe that this variety of breathing patterns helps keep the pressure of the diaphragm off the contracting uterus. The patterns

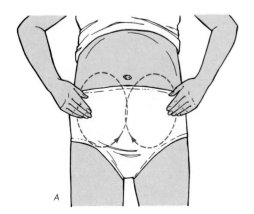

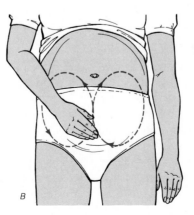

A

B

*Figure 11.4 Effleurage is light stroking of the abdomen with the fingertips. (**A**) Starting at the symphysis, the woman lightly moves her fingertips up and around in a circular pattern. (**B**) An alternative approach involves the use of one hand in a figure-eight pattern. This light stroking can also be done by the support person.*

## Table 11.3  Touch Relaxation

Practice is vital to the following exercises, which require that the pregnant woman and her partner work very closely together. Tell the woman, "With practice you will train yourself to release not only in response to your partner's touch but also to the touch of doctors or nurses as they examine you. This technique will also help you to be more comfortable with your own body.

GOALS:

(For her) To recognize and release tension in response to partner's touch; to be able to do this automatically and spontaneously.
(For partner) To recognize her tension in its very early stages; to learn how to touch in a firm yet sensitive way; to concentrate on her problem areas.

TOOLS:

(For her) Conscious relaxation, comfortable positioning, and trust.
(For him) Sensitivity, patience, and warm hands!

PROCEDURE:

She tenses.
Partner touches.
She immediately releases towards touch.
Partner strokes, "drawing" tension from her.
She releases all residual tension.

SEQUENCE:

- Contract muscles of the scalp and raise eyebrows. Partner cups hands on either side of the scalp. Immediately release tension in response to the pressure of your partner's touch. Then release any residual tension as your partner strokes your head.
- Frown, wrinkle nose, and squeeze eyes shut. Partner rests hands on brow and then strokes down over temples. Release.
- Grit teeth and clench jaw. Partner rests hands on either side of jaw. Release.

- Press shoulder blades back. Partner rests hands on front of shoulders. Release.
- Pull abdominal wall towards spine. Partner rests hands on sides of abdomen and then strokes down over her hips. Partner might also stroke the lower curve of abdomen across pubic symphysis. Release.
- Press thighs together. Partner touches outside of each leg. Relax and let legs move apart. Partner strokes firmly down outside of leg with light strokes up on inner thigh.
- Press legs outward, still flexed but forcing thighs apart. Partner rests hands with fingers pointing downward, on inner thighs. Firmly stroke down to knees, then lightly stroke upward on outside of leg. Release.
- Tense arm muscles. Partner places hands on the upper arm and shoulder area, one on the inside and one on the outside of the arm. Stroke down to the elbow and then down forearm to wrist, and over fingertips. Release. Repeat with other arm.
- Tighten leg muscles, being careful not to cramp them. Partner touches foot around the instep, firmly without tickling. Release whole leg. Partner moves hands up, placing one on either side of the thigh, stroking down to the knee then down the calf to the foot and over the toes. Release. Repeat with other leg.
- Change to the Sims lateral or side-lying position. Raise chin, contracting the muscles at the back of the neck. Partner rests hand on nape of neck and massages. Release.
- Curl into fetal position, drawing shoulders forward. Partner applies pressure to back of shoulders. Stroke upper back. Release.
- Hollow the small of back by arching back. Partner rests hands against either side of spine and follows with stroking down over buttocks. Release.
- Press buttocks together. Partner rests one hand on each buttock. After initial release, stroke down toward thighs.

Source: O'Halloran S: *Pregnant and Prepared: A Guide to Preparing for Childbirth.* Wayne, NJ: Avery, 1984, pp 43–44.

of breathing taught in different classes vary. The woman is taught to use one pattern until it is no longer effective rather than in conjunction with the phases of labor.

Regardless of the level of breathing used, a cleansing breath begins and ends each pattern. A cleansing breath involves only the chest. It consists of inhaling through the nose and exhaling through pursed lips. To enhance oxygenation, the cleansing breath should be a deep relaxed breath and should serve as a signal for relaxation (Nichols and Humenick 1988).

### First Level

This pattern may also be called slow, deep breathing or slow-paced breathing. During the breathing movements only the chest is moved. The woman inhales slowly through her nose. She lifts her chest up and out during the inhalation. She exhales through pursed lips. The breathing rate is six to nine breaths a minute (or two breaths every 15 seconds). When the first level is no longer effective, the second level is used (see Figure 11.5).

## Second Level

This pattern may also be called shallow breathing or modified paced breathing. The woman begins with a cleansing breath and at the end of the cleansing breath she pushes out a short breath. She then inhales and exhales through the mouth at a rate of about four breaths every five seconds. She keeps her jaw relaxed and her mouth slightly open. The air should move in and out smoothly and silently, and the breathing should be mouth centered.

This pattern can be altered into a more rapid rate that does not exceed two to two and one-half breaths every second. During the second level it is important for the whole body to be relaxed. It may help for the woman to count silently to pace the breathing (eg, count "one and two and three and. . . ." Inhalations occur on the *number* and exhalations on the *and*). Slow and rapid shallow breathing may be combined during the contraction. The more rapid rate is usually used at the height of the contraction.

## Third Level

This is also called pant-blow or pattern-paced breathing. This pattern is very similar to the modified paced breathing except the breathing is punctuated every few breaths by a forceful exhalation through pursed lips. A variation of this pattern consists of drawing the lips back

to the teeth and making a "hee" sound with the exhalations. The forceful exhalation is through more pursed lips, making a "hoo" sound (Green and Naab 1985). Some suggest that this variation should be avoided because it forces tightening of the vocal cords and contraction of the intercostal muscles (Nichols and Humenick 1988).

A pattern of four breaths may be used to begin. All breaths are kept equal and rhythmical. As the contraction becomes more intense, the pattern may be changed to 3:1, 2:1, and finally 1:1, as it is important for the woman to adjust the pattern as needed. Thus the pattern evolves as hee-hee-hee-hoo (3:1), hee-hee-hoo (2:1), or hee-hoo, depending on the count used.

Slow-paced breathing is the basic breathing skill that provides the most effective way of enhancing relaxation. Modified and pattern-paced breathing are used to assist the women to concentrate and work with the contractions. Once the desired effect is obtained, a return to slow-paced breathing is desirable. All three breathing patterns are valuable without reference to any specific phase of labor. The decision of how best to use the breathing pattern is in the hands of the expectant parents. See Essential Facts to Remember—Breathing Techniques Goals.

In the second stage of labor, the woman may assume any comfortable physiologic position (a 35° semisitting, squatting, or side-lying position), take several deep breaths, then hold her breath, bulge abdominal muscles,

---

**Table 11.4 Disassociation Relaxation**

The uterus, an involuntary muscle over which you have no control, will work most efficiently and effectively when the rest of your body is free from tension. The following exercises will give you further practice in conscious release. They will also give you and your partner a way to evaluate your progress.

GOALS:

During pregnancy, disassociation relaxation will teach you consciously to release certain sets of muscles, while contracting others, and to disassociate yourself from voluntary tension.
During labor, this technique will release all voluntary muscles of your body at will, while the uterus contracts. This conserves energy and fights fatigue.

TOOLS:

Body awareness, touch release, and concentration.

PROCEDURE:

Partner gives consistent suggestions.
Partner checks relaxation using touching.

EXAMPLE:

Partner: "Contraction begins."
Mother: Relaxation breath (following with a comfortable rate of breathing).
Partner: See suggested patterns below.
Mother: Relaxation breath.

SEQUENCE:

"Contract right arm. Hold. Release."
"Contract left arm. Hold. Release."
"Contract right leg. Hold. Release."
"Contract left leg. Hold. Release."
"Contract both arms. Hold. Release."
"Contract both legs. Hold. Release."
"Contract right side (arm and leg). Hold. Release."
"Contract left side (arm and leg). Hold. Release."
"Contract right arm and left leg. Hold. Release."
"Contract left arm and right leg. Hold. Release."

FOR VARIETY:

● Contract right arm and left leg.
● Release left leg. Contract right leg. Release right arm. Contract left arm.
● Release.

Source: O'Halloran S: *Pregnant and Prepared: A Guide to Preparing for Childbirth.* Wayne, NJ: Avery, 1984, pp. 45–46.

relax the perineum, and push out through the vagina. This pushing effort is repeated throughout the contraction, timed and coached by the partner (Green and Naab 1985).

A variation to the Lamaze breathing method is for the woman to take a cleansing breath then hold her breath for no longer than five to six seconds. She then exhales forcefully with pushing. The woman vocalizes during her pushing efforts, grunting with an open glottis at will. Between contractions she rests and uses chest breathing.

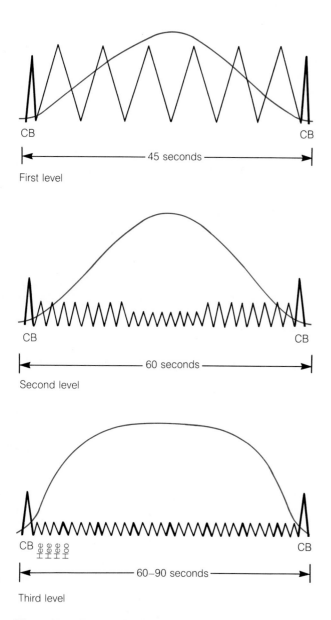

First level

Second level

Third level

*Figure 11.5  Lamaze breathing patterns: Each diagram represents a different breathing pattern. The curved line represents the uterine contraction. The peaked lines represent the breaths taken during the contraction. Each pattern begins and ends with a cleansing breath.*

## Essential Facts to Remember

### Breathing Techniques Goals

● Provide adequate oxygenation of mother and baby, open maternal airways, and avoid inefficient use of muscles

● Increase physical and mental relaxation

● Decrease pain and anxiety

● Provide a means of focusing attention

● Control inadequate ventilation patterns that are related to pain and stress

### Nursing Care

During breathing patterns the woman's mouth may become dry. To help correct this she may put her tongue up behind the front top teeth during breathing. She may suck on ice chips or a sucker at intervals. Small sips of water can be swished around the mouth to moisten mucous membranes. The woman may begin to feel tingling in her fingers and toes, which proceeds to numbness and a feeling of dizziness. These feelings are caused by hyperventilation (breathing at a rate that is too rapid or deep), which brings in more oxygen than is needed. The woman may cup her hands over her mouth, breathe through a washcloth, or breathe into a paper bag. These interventions increase the carbon dioxide content of the inhaled air and usually relieve the symptoms of hyperventilation very efficiently. At times it is also necessary to talk the woman through her breathing and to count out loud so that she can slow the rate. As the nurse or coach does this, it is important to maintain eye contact. If it is during the early stages of labor, touching her hand or shoulder may also be comforting. Even though she is hyperventilating, the woman often feels that she cannot get enough air and must breathe faster and deeper. It is important for the nurse to reiterate that she or he understands what is happening and how the woman feels. The nurse provides reassurance that as the woman slows her breathing, she will feel better, and the feeling that she cannot get her breath will lessen and then go away.

Nurses involved in childbirth education need to include the concept of individuality when providing information to expectant parents about the process of childbirth and their own pattern of coping. Controversy exists over the use of ritualistic breathing techniques in childbirth. The wave of the future in childbirth education is to encourage women to incorporate their natural responses into coping with the pain of labor and birth. Self-care activities that may be used include:

- Vocalization or "sounding" to relieve tension in pregnancy and labor
- Massage (light touch) to facilitate relaxation
- Use of warm water for showers or bathing during labor
- Visualization (imagery)
- Relaxing music and subdued lighting

## ESSENTIAL CONCEPTS

● **Antepartal education programs vary in their goals, content, leadership techniques, and method of teaching.**

● **Antepartal classes may be offered early and/or late in the gestational period. The class content varies depending on the type of class and the individual offering it. Expectant parents tend to want information in chronological sequence with the pregnancy. Adolescents have special content learning needs.**

● **Breast-feeding programs are offered in the prenatal period. Siblings are now being included in the whole birthing process, and classes for them are available from many sources.**

● **Grandparents have unique needs for information in grandparents' classes.**

● **Information regarding cesarean birth is included in antepartal classes to help prepare parents.**

● **The major types of childbirth preparation methods are Bradley, Read, Kitzinger, hypnosis, and Lamaze.**

● **Lamaze is a type of psychoprophylactic method. The classes include information on toning exercises, relaxation exercises and techniques, and breathing methods for labor.**

### References

Aberman S, Kirchoff KT: Infant-feeding practices: Mothers' decision making. *J Obstet Gynecol Neonatal Nurs* September/October 1985; 14:394.

Affonso DD: *Impact of Cesarean Childbirth,* Philadelphia: Davis, 1981.

Austin SEJ: Childbirth classes for couples desiring VBAC. *Am J Mat Child Nurs* 1986; 11:250.

Bing E: *Six Practical Lessons for an Easier Childbirth.* New York: Bantam Books, 1967.

Clark L: When children watch their mothers deliver. *Contemp OB/GYN* August 1986; 28:69.

Davis DJ: Infant care safety: The role of perinatal caregivers. *Birth Suppl* Fall 1985; 12:21.

DiFloria IA, Duncan PA: Design for successful patient teaching. *Am J Mat Child Nurs* 1986; 11:246.

Edwards M: The lactation consultant: A new profession. *Birth Suppl* Fall 1985; 12:9.

Fawcett J, Burritt J: An exploratory study of antenatal preparation for cesarean birth. *J Obstet Gynecol Neonatal Nurs* May/June 1985; 14:224.

Feinbloom RI, Forman BY: *Pregnancy, Birth, and the Early Months.* Reading MA: Addison-Wesley, 1985.

Green M, Naab M: *Lamaze Is for Chickens: A Guide for Prepared Childbirth.* Wayne, NJ: Avery, 1985.

Honig JC: Preparing preschool-aged children to be siblings. *Am J Mat Child Nurs* January/February 1986; 11:37.

Horn M, Manion J: Creative grandparenting: Bonding the generations. *J Obstet Gynecol Neonatal Nurs* May/June 1985; 14:233.

Howard JS, Sater J: Adolescent mothers: Self-perceived health education needs. *J Obstet Gynecol Neonatal Nurs* September/October 1985; 14:399.

Johnson CM: Disposable diapers: A foreign body hazard. Department of Otolaryngology/Head and Neck Surgery, The University of Virginia Medical Center, Charlottesville, Virginia, 1985.

Jordan PL: Breast-feeding as a risk factor for fathers, the marital relationship, breast-feeding success and father-infant attachment. *J Obstet Gynecol Neonatal Nurs* March/April 1986; 15:94.

Karmel M: *Thank You, Dr. Lamaze.* New York: Doubleday, 1965.

Kowba MD, Schwirian PM: Direct sibling contact and bacterial colonization in newborns. *J Obstet Gynecol Neonatal Nurs* September/October 1985; 14:412.

Krutsky CD: Siblings at birth: Impact on parents. *J Nurs-Midwifery* September/October 1985; 30:269.

Levenson PM, Smith PB, Morrow JR: A comparison of physician-patient views of teen prenatal information needs. *J Adolesc Health Care* 1986; 7:6.

Maloney R: Childbirth education classes: Expectant parents' expectations. *J Obstet Gynecol Neonatal Nurs* May/June 1985; 14:245.

Marecki M et al: Early sibling attachment period. *J Obstet Gynecol Neonatal Nurs* September/October 1985; 14:418.

Martin D: Diapering alternatives. *Baby Talk* April 1985; 22:18.

Neifert M: *Dr. Mom: A Guide to Baby and Child Care.* New York: Signet Books, 1986.

Nichols FH, Humenick SS: *Childbirth Education: Practice, Research and Theory.* Philadelphia: Saunders, 1988.

Sandelowski M: Expectations for childbirth versus actual experiences: The gap widens. *Am J Mat Child Nurs* 1984; 9:237.

Solomon J: Superabsorbent diapers: Marketers seek doctors' support amid health concerns. *Wall Street Journal* September 5, 1986.

Whitley N: *Clinical Obstetrics.* Philadelphia: Lippincott, 1985.

## Additional Readings

Austin SEJ: Childbirth classes for couples desiring VBAC . . . vaginal birth after cesarean. *Am J Mat Child Nurs* July/August 1986; 11:250.

Brucker MC et al: Delivery scripts: Fantasy vs. reality. *Point View* January 1987; 24:20.

Crafter HR: Study of a couple's planned labour. *Midwives Chron* October 1987; 100(1197):302–3.

Davis B et al: Implementation and preliminary evaluation of a community-based prenatal health education program. *Fam Community Health* May 1988; 11(1):8.

Dick-Read G: *Childbirth Without Fear,* 2nd ed. New York: Harper and Row, 1959.

Does my life-style have to change just because I'm pregnant? *Patient Care* December 15, 1987; 2(20):139, 143.

Fawcett J et al: Antenatal education for cesarean birth: Extension of a field test. *J Obstet Gynecol Neonatal Nurs* January/February 1987; 16:61.

Flanagan JA: Childbirth in the 80's: What next? When alternatives become mainstream. *J Nurs-Midwifery* July/August 1986; 31:194.

Geden E et al: Self report and psychophysiological effects of Lamaze preparation: An analogue of labor pain. *Res Nurs Health* June 1985; 155.

Giblin PT et al: Pregnant adolescents' health-information needs: Implications for health education and health seeking. *J Adolesc Health Care* May 1986; 7:168.

Lesko W: The birth chart . . . 21 ways to have a baby. *Good Housekeep* June 1986; 202:123.

Lindell SG: Education for childbirth: A time for change. *J Obstet Gynecol Neonatal Nurs* March/April 1988; 17(2)108.

MacDonald J: Prenatal review classes . . . expectant couples who already have children. *Can Nurse* October 1987; 83(9):26–29.

Maloni JA et al: Expectant grandparents class. *J Obstet Gynecol Neonatal Nurs* January/February 1987; 16:26.

Mansfield PK: Teenage and midlife childbearing update: Implications for health educators. *Health Educ* August/September 1987; 18(4):18.

McIntosh J: A consumer view of birth preparation classes: Attitudes of a sample of working class primiparae. *Midwives Chron* January 1988; 101(1200):8.

O'Brien A et al: Evaluation of the effectiveness of a community-based prenatal health education program. *Fam Community Health* August 1987; 10(2):30.

Romito P: The humanizing of childbirth: The response of medical institutions to women's demands for change. *Midwifery* September 1986; 2:135.

Slager-Earnest SE et al: Effects of a specialized prenatal adolescent program on maternal and infant outcomes. *J Obstet Gynecol Neonatal Nurs* November/December 1987; 16(6):422–29.

Zander LI: Maternity care: An international perspective. *J Nurs-Midwifery* September/October 1986; 31:227.

# 12 /\/\/\/\/\/\/\/\/\/\/\/\/\/\/\/\/\/\/\/\/\/\

# Pregnancy at Risk

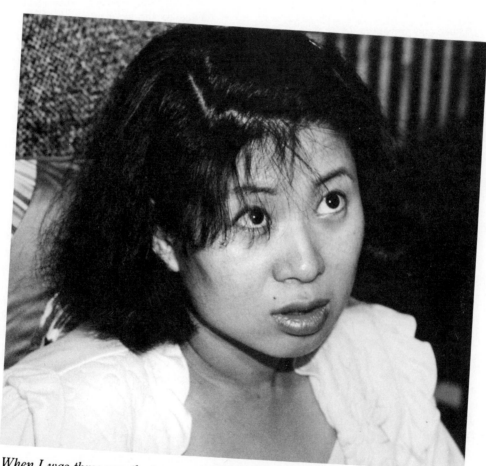

*When I was three months pregnant I began to bleed heavily and my husband rushed me to the hospital. I was in the bathroom when I passed my baby into a johnny cap. The poor thing was so small—only 3 or 4 inches long. I began to sob uncontrollably and my husband helped me to bed while the nurse took my baby out. A short time later she returned and said, "I saw on your record that you are Catholic. Would you like me to baptize your baby?" I said "Oh, yes, please," and she left. I've never forgotten how that made me feel. She saw me as a total person.*

## Objectives

- Compare the effects of different preexisting medical conditions on pregnancy.

- Discriminate among the bleeding problems associated with pregnancy.

- Describe the development and course of hypertensive disorders associated with pregnancy.

- Explain the cause and prevention of Rh hemolytic disease of the newborn.

- Describe the effects of surgical procedures on pregnancy, and how pregnancy may complicate diagnosis.

- Discuss selected common infections that may be contracted during pregnancy or may coexist with pregnancy.

- Discuss possible teratogenic effects of infections and drugs.

- Discuss drug use and abuse during pregnancy.

## Key Terms

abortion
acquired
   immunodeficiency
   syndrome (AIDS)
eclampsia
ectopic pregnancy
erythroblastosis fetalis
gestational trophoblastic
   disease (GTD)
hydatidiform mole
hydrops fetalis
hyperemesis gravidarum
macrosomia
miscarriage
preeclampsia
pregnancy-induced
   hypertension (PIH)
RhoGAM
TORCH

Pregnancy puts stress on the healthy female biologically, physiologically, and psychologically. In the presence of certain factors, pregnancy can become a life-threatening event. Thus, for women whose pregnancies are at risk because of potential or existing complications, prenatal care provides necessary health teaching and is also aimed toward specific identification, assessment, and management of problems that arise.

In this chapter, the discussion focuses on pregestational medical disorders and specific disorders that are unique to the pregnant woman. The possible effects of these disorders on the outcome of pregnancy are examined. In addition, surgical procedures, accidents and trauma, and infectious processes that may influence maternal and fetal well-being are described.

## • USING THE NURSING PROCESS WITH PREGNANT WOMEN AT RISK

### • Nursing Assessment

Often the initial prenatal nursing assessment enables the nurse to identify factors in a woman's history that place her at risk during a pregnancy. Once these risk factors are identified, the nurse can plan appropriate care with the woman and her family. In other cases a woman enters a pregnancy with a preexisting condition such as heart disease or diabetes. In these cases the nurse assesses the course of the pregnancy, the impact of the condition on the pregnancy, and the effects of pregnancy on the existing condition. In all cases the nurse assesses the woman's physical condition and her psychosocial response, taking a holistic view of the woman and her family.

### • Nursing Diagnosis

Once the nurse has assessed the woman, it is necessary to analyze the data, draw some conclusions, and formulate nursing diagnoses. For example, for a woman with herpesvirus type 2, a possible nursing diagnosis might be "Knowledge deficit related to the impact of the presence of herpes lesions on the method of birth."

For a woman with preexisting heart disease who has had no limitation of activity prior to pregnancy, and feels there is no need to restrict her activity during pregnancy, a possible nursing diagnosis might be "Noncompliance with rest schedule related to lack of understanding of the strain pregnancy places on the heart."

The nursing diagnosis helps focus and guide the development of the plan of care. Once suitable, validated diagnoses are formulated, the nurse can apply the remaining steps of the nursing process.

## • Nursing Plan and Implementation

The nursing plan and its implementation should follow logically from assessment and nursing diagnoses. The plan reflects the nurse's understanding of the woman's pregnancy and the risk factors that affect it. In some instances the plan will include provisions for ongoing assessment of the woman's health status. Implementation of the plan is best accomplished when the nurse has established an effective relationship with the woman and her family. The plan should reflect the nurse's awareness of the woman's needs, personal preferences, cultural focus, and beliefs. For example, dietary counseling for a woman who develops gestational diabetes will not be very effective if the food choices identified as appropriate do not reflect cultural food preferences. Thus, implementation of the plan is a joint effort by the nurse and the pregnant woman.

## • Evaluation

Evaluation requires that the nurse critically review the plan and its implementation to determine whether it was effective. If the plan was effective, the nurse determines whether it can continue or if changes in the woman's situation require modifications. If it was not effective, the nurse must try to determine why. Were the data inadequate? Did the situation change? Did the nurse fail to consider certain aspects of the available information? The nurse then makes necessary additional assessments and modifies the plan accordingly. The goal in all cases is to provide effective nursing care.

## • CARE OF THE WOMAN WITH HEART DISEASE

Pregnancy results in increased cardiac output, heart rate, and blood volume. The normal heart is able to adapt to these changes without undue difficulty. These changes, however, may strain the cardiac reserve of a woman with heart disease. Initially her heart compensates by ventricular dilation, ventricular hypertrophy, and tachycardia. When these mechanisms provide adequate blood flow to the tissues in the presence of pathologic changes, the heart is in a state of compensation. Decompensation occurs when these mechanisms fail and the heart is no longer able to cope with the demands placed on it. Symptoms develop when the woman increases her activity because her cardiac reserve is reduced.

Approximately 0.5% to 1% of pregnant women are at risk because of preexisting heart disease. Rheumatic heart disease formerly accounted for the great majority of cases but is now responsible for only about half the cases. Congenital heart defects are responsible for most of the remaining half (Cruikshank 1986). Other, less common causes of heart disease in pregnancy include syphilis; arteriosclerosis; coronary occlusion; and renal, pulmonary, and thyroid disorders.

The pathophysiology found in a pregnant woman with heart disease varies with the type of disorder. More common conditions are discussed briefly here.

*Rheumatic heart disease* is far less common today because of the prompt diagnosis and treatment of pharyngeal streptococcal infections. Recurrent inflammation from bouts of rheumatic fever causes scar tissue formation on the valves. The scarring results in stenosis (failure of the valve to open completely), regurgitation due to failure of the valve to close completely, or a combination of both, thereby increasing the workload of the heart. Although mitral valve stenosis is the most commonly seen lesion, the aortic or tricuspid valves may also be affected.

The increased blood volume of pregnancy, coupled with the pregnant woman's need for increased cardiac output, stresses the heart of a woman with mitral stenosis and increases her risk of developing congestive heart failure. Even the woman who has no symptoms at the onset of her pregnancy is at risk.

*Congenital heart defects* commonly seen in pregnant women include atrial septal defect, ventricular septal defect, patent ductus arteriosus, pulmonary stenosis, coarctation of the aorta, and tetralogy of Fallot.

For women with congenital heart disease, the implications of pregnancy depend on the specific defect. If the heart defect has been surgically repaired and no evidence of organic heart disease remains, pregnancy may be undertaken with confidence. In such cases, antibiotic prophylaxis is recommended to prevent subacute bacterial endocarditis at the time of birth. Women with congenital heart disease who experience cyanosis should be counseled to avoid pregnancy because the risk to mother and fetus is high.

*Mitral valve prolapse* (MVP) is a usually asymptomatic condition that is found in about 6% to 10% of women of childbearing age (Cruikshank 1986). The condition is more common in women than in men and seems to run in families. In MVP the mitral valve leaflets tend to prolapse into the left atrium during ventricular systole because the chordae tendineae that support them are long, stretched, and thin. As a result, some mitral regurgitation may occur.

Women with MVP usually tolerate pregnancy well. In fact, many women notice that symptoms decrease because the increased blood volume allows less prolapse (Arias 1988). Most women require assurance that they can continue with normal activities. A few women experience symptoms—primarily palpitations, chest pain, and dyspnea—which are often due to arrhythmias. They are usually treated with propranolol hydrochloride (Inderal), which is well tolerated by both the pregnant woman and her fetus (Campbell and Vintzileos 1988). Limiting caffeine intake also helps decrease palpitations. Antibiotics are given prophylactically at the time of birth to prevent bacterial endocarditis.

*Peripartum cardiomyopathy* is a dysfunction of the left ventricle that occurs in the last month of pregnancy or the first five months postpartum in a woman with no previous history of heart disease. The symptoms are similar to those in congestive heart failure: dyspnea, orthopnea, chest pain, palpitations, weakness, and edema. The cause is unknown. Treatment includes digitalis, diuretics, anticoagulants, and bed rest. The condition may resolve with bed rest as the heart gradually returns to normal size. Subsequent pregnancy is strongly discouraged because the disease tends to recur during pregnancy.

## ● Medical Therapy

The primary goal of medical therapy is early diagnosis and ongoing management of the woman with cardiac disease. Echocardiogram, chest x-ray, and auscultation of heart sounds are essential for establishing the type and severity of the heart disease. The severity of heart disease can also be determined by the individual's ability to perform ordinary physical activity. The following classification of functional capacity has been standardized by the Criteria Committee of the New York Heart Association (1955):

● Class I. No limitation of physical activity. Ordinary physical activity causes no discomfort; anginal pain is not present.

● Class II. Slight limitation of physical activity. Ordinary physical activity causes fatigue, dyspnea, palpitation, or anginal pain.

● Class III. Moderate to marked limitation of physical activity. During less than ordinary physical activity, the person experiences excessive fatigue, dyspnea, palpitation, or anginal pain.

● Class IV. Inability to carry on any physical activity without experiencing discomfort. Even at rest, the person experiences symptoms of cardiac insufficiency or anginal pain.

Women in classes I and II usually experience a normal pregnancy and have few complications, whereas those in classes III and IV are at risk for more severe complications.

### DRUG THERAPY

The pregnant woman with heart disease may need drug therapy in addition to the normal iron and vitamin supplements prescribed in order to maintain health during pregnancy. If the woman develops coagulation problems,

the anticoagulant heparin may be used. Heparin offers the greatest safety to the fetus because it does not cross the placenta. The thiazide diuretics and furosemide (Lasix) may be used to treat congestive heart failure if it develops. Digitalis glycosides and common antiarrhythmic drugs may be used to treat cardiac failure and arrhythmias. These agents do cross the placenta but have no reported teratogenic effect. Penicillin is used to protect against infection if not contraindicated by allergy.

### BIRTH

Use of low forceps provides the safest method of birth, with a regional anesthetic to reduce the stress of pushing. Cesarean birth is used only if fetal or maternal indications exist, not on the basis of heart disease alone.

## ● Nursing Assessment

The stress of pregnancy on the functional capacity of the heart is assessed during every antepartal visit. The nurse notes the category of functional capacity assigned to the woman, takes the woman's pulse, respirations, and blood pressure, and compares them to the normal values expected during pregnancy. The nurse then determines the woman's activity level, including rest, and any changes in the pulse and respirations that have occurred since previous visits. Fatigue with activity is a characteristic of classes II, III, and IV. Because it is also an early sign of decompensation, the nurse should ask the woman about any increased fatigue with activity. The nurse also identifies and evaluates other factors that would increase strain on the heart. These might include anemia, infection, anxiety, lack of a support system, and insufficient household help.

The following symptoms, if they are progressive, are indicative of congestive heart failure, the heart's signal of its decreased ability to meet the demands of pregnancy.

● Cough (frequent, with or without blood-stained sputum [*hemoptysis*])

● Dyspnea (progressive, upon exertion)

● Edema (progressive, generalized, including extremities, face, eyelids)

● Diastolic heart murmurs (heard on auscultation)

● Palpitations

● Moist rales (auscultated in lung bases)

It should be noted that this cycle is *progressive*, because some of these same behaviors are seen to a minor degree in a pregnancy without cardiac problems.

## ● Nursing Diagnosis

Nursing diagnoses that might apply to the pregnant woman with heart disease include:

- Decreased cardiac output: easy fatigability
- Potential impaired gas exchange related to pulmonary edema secondary to cardiac decompensation
- Knowledge deficit related to the cardiac condition and requirement to alter self-care activities
- Fear related to the effects of the maternal cardiac condition on fetal well-being

### • *Nursing Plan and Implementation*

Nursing care is directed toward maintaining a balance between cardiac reserve and cardiac workload. As a result, nursing actions vary in the antepartal, intrapartal, and postpartal periods.

### ANTEPARTAL NURSING CARE

Nursing actions are designed to meet the physiologic and psychosocial needs of the pregnant woman with heart disease. The priority of nursing action varies based on the severity of the disease process and the individual needs of the woman as determined by the nursing assessment.

The woman and her family should thoroughly understand her condition and its management and should recognize signs of potential complications. This will increase their understanding and decrease anxiety. When the nurse provides thorough explanations, uses printed material, and provides frequent opportunities to ask questions and discuss concerns, the woman is better able to meet her own health care needs and seek assistance appropriately.

As part of health teaching, the nurse explains the purposes of the dietary and activity changes that are required. A diet is instituted that is high in iron, protein, and essential nutrients but low in sodium, with adequate calories to ensure normal weight gain. Such a diet best meets the nutrition needs of the client with cardiac disease. To help preserve her cardiac reserves, the woman may need to restrict her activities. In addition, 8–10 hours of sleep, with frequent daily rest periods, is essential. Because upper respiratory infections may tax the heart and lead to decompensation, the woman must avoid contact with sources of infection.

During the first half of pregnancy the woman is seen approximately every two weeks to assess cardiac status. During the second half of pregnancy the woman is seen weekly. These assessments are especially important between weeks 28 and 30 when the blood volume reaches maximum amounts. If symptoms of cardiac decompensation occur, prompt medical intervention is indicated to correct the cardiac problem.

### INTRAPARTAL NURSING CARE

Labor and birth exert tremendous stress on the woman and her fetus. This stress could be fatal to the fetus of a woman with cardiac disease because it may be receiving a decreased oxygen and blood supply. Thus, the intrapartal care of a woman with cardiac disease is aimed at reducing the amount of physical exertion and accompanying fatigue.

The nurse evaluates maternal vital signs frequently to determine the woman's response to labor. A pulse rate greater than 100 beats/min or respirations greater than 25/min may indicate beginning cardiac decompensation and require further evaluation. The nurse also auscultates the woman's lungs frequently for evidence of rales and carefully observes for other signs of developing decompensation.

To ensure cardiac emptying and adequate oxygenation, the nurse encourages the laboring woman to assume either a semi-Fowler's or side-lying position with her head and shoulders elevated. Oxygen by mask, diuretics to reduce fluid retention, sedatives and analgesics, prophylactic antibiotics, and digitalis may also be used as indicated by the woman's status.

The nurse remains with the woman to support her. It is essential that the nurse keep the woman and her family informed of labor progress and management plans, collaborating with them to fulfill their wishes for the birth experience as much as possible. The nurse needs to maintain an atmosphere of calm to lessen the anxiety of the woman and her family.

Continuous electronic fetal monitoring is used to provide ongoing assessment of the fetus's response to labor. To prevent overexertion and the accompanying fatigue, the nurse encourages the woman to sleep and relax between contractions and provides her with emotional support and encouragement. During pushing the nurse encourages the woman to use shorter, more moderate open glottis pushing, with complete relaxation between pushes. Vital signs are monitored closely during the second stage.

### POSTPARTAL NURSING CARE

The postpartal period is a most significant time for the woman with cardiac disease. As extravascular fluid returns to the bloodstream for excretion, cardiac output and blood volume increase. This physiologic adaptation places great strain on the heart and may lead to decompensation, especially in the first 48 hours postpartum.

So that the health team can detect any possible problems, the woman remains in the hospital for approximately one week to rest and recover. Her vital signs are monitored frequently and she is assessed for signs of decompensation. She stays in the semi-Fowler's or side-lying position, with her head and shoulders elevated, and begins a gradual, progressive activity program. Appropriate diet and stool softeners facilitate bowel movement without undue strain.

The postpartum nurse gives the woman opportunities to discuss her birth experience and helps her deal with any feelings or concerns that cause her distress. The nurse also encourages maternal-infant attachment by providing frequent opportunities for the mother to interact with her child.

For the first few days, as determined by the mother's cardiac status, the nurse will provide care for the newborn. This is best done at the mother's bedside to increase her contact with her newborn and to provide teaching opportunities. If the mother's cardiac condition is class I or class II, she may breast-feed her baby in bed. The nurse can assist her to a comfortable side-lying position with her head moderately elevated or to a semi-Fowler's position. The nurse should position the newborn at the breast and be available to burp the baby and reposition him or her at the other breast.

The advisability of breast-feeding for the woman with class III or class IV cardiac disease must be evaluated carefully. In many cases, because of the excessive fatigue factor and because the mother may be taking several medications that pass into the breast milk, breast-feeding may not be advisable. The care giver should give the woman accurate, understandable information about the associated risk so that she can make an informed decision.

In addition to providing the normal postpartum discharge teaching, the nurse should ensure that the woman and her family understand the signs of possible problems from her heart disease or other postpartal complications. The nurse also plans an activity schedule with the woman and her family. Visiting nurse referrals may be necessary, depending on the woman's status.

## • Evaluation

Anticipated outcomes of nursing care include the following:

- The woman clearly understands her condition and its possible impact on pregnancy, labor and birth, and the postpartal period.
- The woman participates in developing an appropriate health care regimen and follows it throughout her pregnancy.
- The woman successfully delivers a healthy infant.
- The woman avoids congestive heart failure.
- The woman is able to identify signs and symptoms of possible complications postpartally.
- The woman is comfortable caring for her newborn infant.

## • CARE OF THE WOMAN WITH DIABETES MELLITUS

Diabetes mellitus, an endocrine disorder of carbohydrate metabolism, complicates 2% to 3% of pregnancies (Gabbe 1986). It results from inadequate production or uti-

lization of insulin. Insulin, produced by the $\beta$ cells of the islets of Langerhans in the pancreas, enables glucose to move from the blood into muscle and adipose tissue cells.

## • Carbohydrate Metabolism in Normal Pregnancy

In early pregnancy the rise in serum levels of estrogen and progesterone stimulates increased insulin production by the maternal pancreas, and increased tissue response to insulin. Thus an anabolic state exists during the first half of pregnancy with storage of glycogen in the liver and other tissues.

In the second half of pregnancy, placental secretion of human placental lactogen (hPL), and elevated levels of estrogen, progesterone, and other hormones cause increased resistance to insulin (Hollingsworth 1985). This decreased effectiveness of insulin results in a catabolic state during fasting periods such as during the night or after meal absorption. Fat is metabolized more readily at these times and ketones may be present in the urine.

The delicate system of checks and balances that exists between glucose production and glucose utilization is stressed by the growing fetus, who derives energy from glucose taken solely from maternal stores. This stress is referred to as the *diabetogenic effect* of pregnancy. Thus any preexisting disruption in carbohydrate metabolism is augmented by pregnancy, and any diabetic potential may precipitate *gestational diabetes mellitus*.

## • Pathophysiology of Diabetes Mellitus

In diabetes mellitus the pancreas does not produce enough insulin to allow necessary carbohydrate metabolism. Without adequate insulin, glucose does not enter the cells and they become energy depleted. Blood glucose levels remain high (hyperglycemia), and the cells then break down their stores of fats and protein for energy. Protein breakdown results in a negative nitrogen balance; fat metabolism causes ketosis.

These are the four cardinal signs and symptoms of diabetes mellitus:

- Polyuria (frequent urination), because water is not reabsorbed by the renal tubules due to the osmotic activity of glucose
- Polydipsia (excessive thirst), caused by dehydration from polyuria
- Polyphagia (excessive hunger), caused by tissue loss and a state of starvation, which results from the inability of the cells to utilize the blood glucose
- Weight loss (seen in insulin-dependent diabetes mellitus [IDDM], also called type I diabetes), due to the use of fat and muscle tissue for energy

## Table 12.1 Classification of Diabetes Mellitus (DM) and Other Categories of Glucose Intolerance

1. Diabetes mellitus
   a. Type I, insulin dependent (IDDM)
   b. Type II, noninsulin dependent (NIDDM)
      (1) Nonobese NIDDM
      (2) Obese NIDDM
   c. Secondary diabetes
2. Impaired glucose tolerance (IGT)
3. Gestational diabetes (GDM)

Source: National Diabetes Data Group of National Institutes of Health: *Diabetes* 1979; 28:1039.

## CLASSIFICATION

States of altered carbohydrate metabolism have been classified in several ways. Table 12.1 shows the current accepted classification, a result of the 1979 report of a special committee of the National Institutes of Health (National Diabetes Data Group 1979). This classification contains three main categories: diabetes mellitus (DM), impaired glucose tolerance (IGT), and gestational diabetes mellitus (GDM).

*GDM* is diabetes mellitus that has its onset or is first diagnosed during pregnancy. Except for showing an impaired tolerance to glucose, the woman may remain asymptomatic or may have a mild form of the disease. Diagnosis of GDM is very important, however, because even mild diabetes causes increased risk for perinatal morbidity and mortality.

Table 12.2 shows White's (1978) classification of diabetes in pregnancy. This classification is still used in many agencies.

## INFLUENCE OF PREGNANCY ON DIABETES

Pregnancy can affect diabetes significantly because the physiologic changes of pregnancy can drastically alter insulin requirements. In addition, pregnancy may alter the progress of vascular disease secondary to pregnancy.

Pregnancy can affect diabetes in the following ways:

1. Diabetic control
   a. Change in insulin requirements
      (1) Frequently, the need for insulin decreases during the first trimester. Levels of hPL, an insulin antagonist, are low, and the woman and developing fetus use more glycogen and glucose.
      (2) Nausea and vomiting may cause dietary fluctuations and increase the risk of hypoglycemia or insulin shock.
      (3) Insulin requirements begin to rise in the second trimester and may double or quadruple by the end of pregnancy as a result of placental maturation and hPL production.
      (4) Increased energy needs during labor may require increased insulin to balance intravenous glucose.
      (5) Usually an abrupt decrease in insulin requirement occurs after the passage of the placenta and the resulting loss of hPL in maternal circulation.
   b. Decreased renal threshold for glucose
   c. Increased risk of ketoacidosis, insulin shock, and coma
2. Possible accelerations of vascular disease
   a. Hypertension: increase in blood pressure of greater than 30 mm Hg systolic and 15 mm Hg diastolic
   b. Nephropathy: renal impairment
   c. Retinopathy

## Table 12.2 White's Classification of Diabetes in Pregnancy

| Class | Criterion |
|---|---|
| A | Chemical diabetes |
| B | Maturity onset (age over 20 years), duration under 10 years, no vascular lesions |
| $C_1$ | Age 10 to 19 years at onset |
| $C_2$ | 10 to 19 years' duration |
| $D_1$ | Under 10 years at onset |
| $D_2$ | Over 20 years' duration |
| $D_3$ | Benign retinopathy |
| $D_4$ | Calcified vessels of legs |
| $D_5$ | Hypertension |
| E | No longer sought |
| F | Nephropathy |
| G | Many failures |
| H | Cardiopathy |
| R | Proliferating retinopathy |
| T | Renal transplant (added by Tagatz and colleagues of the University of Minnesota) |

Source: From White P: Classification of obstetric diabetes. *Am J Obstet Gynecol* 1978; 130:228.

## INFLUENCE OF DIABETES ON PREGNANCY OUTCOME

The pregnancy of a woman who has diabetes carries a higher risk of complications, especially perinatal mortality. This risk has been reduced by the recent recognition of the importance of tight metabolic control (glucose between 70 mg/dL and 120 mg/dL). New techniques for monitoring blood glucose, delivering insulin, and monitoring the fetus have also reduced perinatal mortality in major medical centers to between 2% and 4% (Hollander and Maeder 1985) or less.

### MATERNAL RISKS

The prognosis for the pregnant woman with gestational, type I, or type II diabetes (see Table 12.1) without significant vascular damage is positive. However, diabetic pregnancy still carries a higher risk of complications than normal pregnancy.

Hydramnios, or an increase in the volume of amniotic fluid, occurs in 10% of pregnant diabetics (Gilbert and Harmon 1986). The exact mechanism causing the increase is unknown, although osmotic pressure, hypersecretion of amniotic fluid, and diuresis due to fetal hyperglycemia are suspected. Premature rupture of membranes and onset of labor may occasionally be a problem with hydramnios.

Pregnancy-induced hypertension (PIH) occurs more often in diabetic pregnancies, especially when diabetes-related vascular changes already exist.

Hyperglycemia can lead to ketoacidosis as a result of the increase in ketone bodies (which are acidic) released in the blood from the metabolism of fatty acids. Ketoacidosis usually develops slowly, but if untreated it can lead to coma and death for mother and fetus.

### FETAL-NEONATAL RISKS

Characteristically, infants of type I diabetic mothers (or classes A, B, and C, see Table 12.2) are large for gestational age (LGA) as a result of the high maternal levels of blood glucose, from which the fetus derives its glucose. These elevated levels continually stimulate the fetal islets of Langerhans to produce insulin. This hyperinsulin state causes the fetus to utilize the available glucose. This leads to excessive growth (known as **macrosomia**) and fat deposits.

After birth the umbilical cord is severed, and thus the generous maternal blood glucose supply is eliminated. However, continued islet cell hyperactivity leads to excessive insulin levels and depleted blood glucose (hypoglycemia) in two to four hours. Macrosomia can be significantly reduced by tight maternal blood glucose control before 32 weeks' gestation (Lin et al 1986).

Infants of mothers with advanced diabetes may demonstrate intrauterine growth retardation (IUGR). This occurs because vascular changes in the diabetic woman decrease the efficiency of placental perfusion and the infant is not as well sustained in utero.

*Respiratory distress syndrome* appears to result from inhibition, by high levels of fetal insulin, of some fetal enzymes necessary for surfactant production. *Polycythemia* in the neonate is due primarily to the diminished ability of glycosylated hemoglobin in the mother's blood to release oxygen. *Hyperbilirubinemia* is a direct result of the inability of immature liver enzymes to metabolize the increased bilirubin resulting from the polycythemia.

In the presence of untreated maternal ketoacidosis, the risk of fetal death increases to between 50% and 90% (Brumfield and Huddleson 1984). The fetal enzymes systems cease functioning in an acidic environment.

Despite the reduction in perinatal mortality and morbidity, the incidence of *congenital anomalies* in diabetic pregnancies remains at least four times the rate in nondiabetic pregnancies (Steel 1985). Most of the anomalies involve the heart, central nervous system, and skeletal system and occur in the presence of poor glucose control (as indicated by an elevated hemoglobin $A_{1c}$ level, discussed on p 295) in the first several weeks of pregnancy. Women with diabetic vascular changes (retinopathy and nephropathy) also have an increased risk of having an infant with congenital anomalies. To reduce the incidence of congenital anomalies there is a clear need for preconception counseling and strict diabetes control prior to conception (Miodovnik 1988).

## • Medical Therapy

Screening for the detection of diabetes is a standard part of prenatal care. If the possibility of diabetes is suspected, further testing is undertaken for diagnosis.

### DETECTION AND DIAGNOSIS

Two screening tests are commonly administered to pregnant women:

1. *Urine testing.* Tes-Tape and Diastix are generally used to test urine at the first prenatal visit and again on subsequent visits. Because the renal threshold is lower during pregnancy, glucose may spill into the urine when blood glucose levels are 130 mg/dL. Thus glycosuria is not considered diagnostic of diabetes but does indicate the need for further testing.

2. *50 g, 1-hour diabetes screening test.* It has become common practice to screen all pregnant women for gestational diabetes between 24 and 28 weeks' gestation. To do this test, the woman ingests a 50 g oral glucose solution. One hour later a blood sample

is obtained. If the plasma glucose level exceeds 140 mg/dL, a diagnostic glucose tolerance test (GTT) is necessary. The 50 g screen test is convenient because the woman does not need to be fasting, and the test does not need to be done following a meal (Coustan and Carpenter 1985). Some researchers suggest that greater accuracy in predicting gestational diabetes is possible when the 50 g screen is administered after a meal and a cut-off level for doing a GTT is set at 130 mg/dL (Kitzmiller et al 1988).

During pregnancy gestational diabetes mellitus is diagnosed using a 100 g oral glucose tolerance test. To do this test the woman eats a high-carbohydrate (greater than 200 g carbohydrate daily) diet for two days prior to her scheduled test. She then fasts from midnight on the day of the test. A fasting plasma glucose level is obtained, and the woman ingests 100 g oral glucose solution. Plasma glucose levels are determined at one, two, and three hours. Gestational diabetes is diagnosed if two or more of the following values are equaled or exceeded (Gabbe 1986):

| Fasting | 105 mg/dL |
| 1 hr | 190 mg/dL |
| 2 hr | 165 mg/dL |
| 3 hr | 145 mg/dL |

If the woman presents with any of the following, the screen is omitted and she is given a three-hour glucose tolerance test:

- The cardinal signs of DM (polyuria, polydipsia, polyphagia, weight loss)
- Obesity
- Family history of DM
- Obstetric history that includes a large-for-gestational-age (LGA) neonate, hydramnios, unexplained stillbirth, or congenital anomalies

## LABORATORY ASSESSMENT OF LONG-TERM GLUCOSE CONTROL

Measurement of glycosylated hemoglobin levels reflects glucose control over the previous 4 to 12 weeks (Cousins et al 1985). It measures the percentage in the blood of glycohemoglobin ($HbA_{1c}$, hemoglobin to which a glucose molecule is attached). Because glycosylation is a rather slow and essentially irreversible process, the level of $HbA_{1c}$ gives an indication of previous average serum glucose concentrations. For a woman who is a known diabetic, this test should be done at preconception counseling, again at the first prenatal visit, and once each succeeding trimester.

## MANAGEMENT OF PREGESTATIONAL DIABETES MELLITUS

The major goals of medical care for a pregnant woman with diabetes are: (a) to maintain a physiologic equilibrium of insulin availability and glucose utilization during pregnancy, and (b) to deliver an optimally healthy mother and newborn. To achieve these goals, good prenatal care using a team approach must be a top priority.

### Antepartal Period

During the antepartal period, medical therapy focuses on several aspects including the following:

- *Dietary regulation.* In early pregnancy the recommended daily calorie intake remains at 25 to 30 kcal/kg body weight. During the second and third trimesters daily intake increases by about 200 kcal or to about 30–35 kcal/kg. Approximately 45%–50% of the calories should come from complex carbohydrates, 20%–25% should be protein, and 30%–35% should be fat (Kitzmiller 1988). The food is divided among three meals and three snacks. The bedtime snack is the most important and should include both protein and complex carbohydrates to prevent nighttime hypoglycemia. A nutritionist should work out meal plans with the woman based on the woman's life-style, culture, and food preferences. The woman should also be familiar with the use of food exchanges so she can plan her own meals.

- *Glucose monitoring.* Home monitoring of blood glucose levels is the most accurate and convenient method for determining insulin dose and assessing control. Women are taught self-monitoring techniques that they perform several times a day according to a specified schedule. They then regulate their insulin dosage based on blood glucose values and anticipated activity level.

- *Insulin administration.* Insulin is given either in multiple injections or by continuous subcutaneous infusion. Multiple injections are used more commonly, and with excellent results. A mixture of intermediate-acting (NPH) and short-acting (regular) insulin is taken twice a day. Usually two thirds of the total insulin dose is taken with breakfast in a ratio of NPH to regular of 2 : 1. The remaining third is taken with supper in a 1 : 1 ratio (Kitzmiller 1988).

- *Evaluation of fetal status.* Information regarding the well-being and maturation of the fetus is important for planning the course of pregnancy and the timing of delivery. Biophysical methods of fetal surveillance, such as the nonstress test (NST), serial ultrasounds, fetal movement counts, and contraction stress tests (CST), have proved more valuable than biochemical tests (Gabbe 1985).

## Intrapartal Period

During the intrapartal period medical therapy includes:

**Timing of Delivery**   In most diabetic pregnancies, pregnancy is allowed to go to term, with spontaneous labor, thereby decreasing the risk of respiratory distress in the neonate. In pregnancies in which there is evidence of fetal macrosomia, fetal compromise, or elevated maternal HbA$_{1c}$, amniocentesis is done for lecithin/sphingomyelin ratio and the presence of the phospholipid phosphatidylglycerol (PG). If the L/S ratio is ≥2.0 (some agencies prefer ≥3.0) and PG is present, the fetal lungs are considered mature and birth can be undertaken by induction or cesarean.

**Labor Management**   To maintain normal maternal glucose levels (euglycemia) during labor, a 5% dextrose solution is given by intravenous infusion covered by subcutaneous or IV insulin. Maternal glucose levels are measured every one to two hours to determine insulin dosage. Because insulin clings to plastic IV bags and tubing, the tubing should be flushed with insulin before the prescribed amount is added to the intravenous bag of dextrose and water. During the second stage of labor and the immediate postdelivery period, the woman may not need additional insulin. The intravenous insulin is discontinued with the completion of the third stage of labor.

## Postpartal Period

Postpartally maternal insulin requirements fall significantly. This occurs because with placental separation hormone levels fall and the anti-insulin effect ceases. For the first 24 hours the diabetic mother may require no insulin or only ¼ to ½ her normal dose. Then insulin needs are reestablished based on blood glucose testing.

The establishment of parent-child relationships is a high priority. If the newborn requires care in a special care nursery, the parents need ongoing information, support, and encouragement to visit their child and be involved in the newborn's care.

Breast-feeding is encouraged as beneficial to both mother and baby. Calorie needs increase during lactation, and insulin must be adjusted accordingly. Home blood glucose monitoring should continue for the insulin-dependent diabetic.

The couple should also receive information on family planning. Combined estrogen/progesterone oral contraceptives are not recommended for insulin-dependent diabetic women because of the increased risk of thromboembolic disease and vasculopathy (Gabbe 1985). The progesterone-only pill carries a higher failure rate but is otherwise safer. The IUD remains controversial. Barrier methods are safe but have a slightly higher failure rate. Elective sterilization is often discussed with the couple who have completed their family.

## MANAGEMENT OF GESTATIONAL DIABETES MELLITUS

Gestational diabetes most often develops in the third trimester. Therefore women should be screened for diabetes at approximately 24 to 28 weeks' gestation with the 50 g oral glucose test. Most gestational diabetics can be controlled by diet, but about 10% to 15% will need supplemental insulin, as evidenced by a fasting plasma glucose level >105 mg/dL or a postprandial (two hours after breakfast) plasma glucose level >120 mg/dL (Gabbe 1985). Oral hypoglycemics are never used during pregnancy as they are considered teratogenic. Fetal surveillance, usually by NST, is important during the last two months of pregnancy to ensure optimal timing of birth. The mother may also be asked to keep a fetal activity diary to monitor fetal movement (see discussion in Chapter 13).

## ● Nursing Assessment

Whether diabetes (usually type I) has been diagnosed before pregnancy occurs or the diagnosis is made during pregnancy (GDM), careful assessment of the disease process and the woman's understanding of diabetes is important. Thorough physical examination, including assessment for vascular complications of the disease, any signs of infectious conditions, and urine and blood testing for glucose, is essential on the first antenatal visit. Follow-up visits are usually scheduled twice a month during the first two trimesters and once a week during the last trimester.

Assessment is also needed to yield information about the woman's ability to cope with the combined stress of pregnancy and diabetes, and her ability to follow a recommended regimen of care. Determination of the woman's knowledge about diabetes and self-care is needed before formulating a teaching plan.

## ● Nursing Diagnosis

Examples of nursing diagnoses that may apply are identified in Essential Nursing Diagnoses to Consider—Diabetes Mellitus and in the Nursing Care Plan beginning on page 298.

## ● Nursing Plan and Implementation

Once a nursing assessment has been made and nursing diagnoses have been developed, the plan of care for the pregnant woman with diabetes can be developed and implemented.

### PROVISION OF PREPREGNANCY COUNSELING

Counseling may be provided by a nurse and a physician using a team approach. Ideally the couple is seen prior

## Essential Nursing Diagnoses to Consider

### Diabetes Mellitus

Potential activity intolerance
Ineffective family coping
Ineffective individual coping
Altered family processes
Potential for injury
Knowledge deficit
Noncompliance
Altered nutrition: Less than body requirements
Altered nutrition: More than body requirements
Potential altered parenting
Body image disturbance
Self esteem disturbance
Altered tissue perfusion
Defensive coping
Ineffective denial
Potential impaired skin integrity

the purpose of insulin, the types of insulin to be used, and the correct procedure for administering it. The woman's partner is also instructed about insulin administration in case it should be necessary for him to administer it. For some highly motivated women whose glucose levels are not well controlled with multiple injections, the continuous infusion pump offers the best control (Granados 1984).

As part of the ongoing care of the pregnant woman with diabetes, she is taught to monitor her blood glucose levels at home. The information this monitoring provides is used to regulate insulin dosage. The nurse works with the woman to teach her the correct method for home glucose monitoring (Figure 12.1). Spring devices are available for sticking the finger to obtain blood samples. These devices make the procedure easier and less painful. The woman should be taught to use the sides of her fingertips rather than the more sensitive tips themselves. She should be taught to cleanse the area before sticking to avoid infection. The reagent strip container should be kept tightly closed when not being used. Once the specimen of blood has been obtained and is placed on the reagent strip, directions for timing and for washing or wiping the blood off should be followed exactly to ensure accurate readings.

to pregnancy so that the diabetes can be evaluated. The outlook for pregnancy is good if the diabetes is of recent onset without vascular complications and if glucose levels can be controlled.

### PROMOTION OF EFFECTIVE INSULIN USE

Based on the assessment of the couple's level of knowledge, the nurse ensures that the couple understands

### PROMOTION OF A PLANNED EXERCISE PROGRAM

Exercise is encouraged for the woman's overall well-being. If she is used to a regular exercise program she is encouraged to continue. She is advised to exercise after meals when blood sugar levels are high, to wear diabetic identification, to carry a simple sugar such as hard candy, to monitor her blood glucose levels regularly, and to avoid

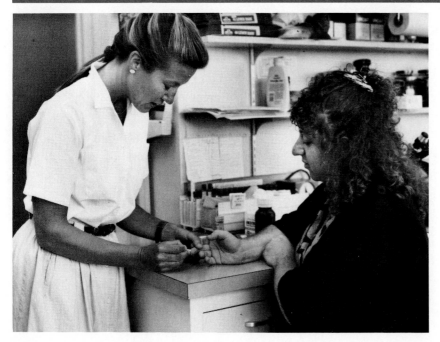

*Figure 12.1   The nurse teaches the mother how to do home glucose monitoring.*

# Nursing Care Plan

## Diabetes Mellitus

### Client Assessment

#### Nursing History

1. Complete assessment: client and family

2. Identification of client's predisposition to diabetes
   a. Recurrent preeclampsia-eclampsia
   b. Previous LGA infants (≥ 4000 g)
   c. Hydramnios
   d. Unexplained fetal death
   e. Obesity
   f. Family history of diabetes

#### Physical Examination

1. Length of gestation

2. Complaints of thirst and hunger

3. Recurrent monilial vaginitis

4. Frequent urination beyond first trimester and prior to third trimester

5. Fundal height greater than expected for gestation

6. Obesity

#### Diagnostic Studies

1. Fasting plasma glucose (FPG)

2. 3-hour GTT

3. Urine test for glucose

4. Ultrasound to evaluate fetal growth and detect hydramnios

5. If woman has IDDM, glycosylated hemoglobin level ($HbA_{1c}$) determined

#### Third Trimester—Fetal Assessment

1. Serial NSTs

2. CST as necessary

3. Serial ultrasound

4. Biophysical profile to determine fetal maturity

| Nursing Diagnosis/Goal | Nursing Interventions | Rationale/Evaluation |
| --- | --- | --- |
| **Nursing Diagnosis:**<br><br>Pattern 1: Exchanging<br>Altered nutrition: potential for more than body requirements related to imbalance between intake and available insulin.<br><br>**Client Goal:**<br><br>The woman will understand and follow her prescribed diet as evidenced by weight gain within desired range, ability to discuss diet and plan menus, glycosylated hemoglobin ($HbA_{1c}$) levels in normal range. | 1. Discuss importance of strict dietary control.<br>2. Work with nutritionist and client to plan an individualized diet.<br><br>3. Recommended intake<br>30–35% kcal/kg body wt<br>20–25% protein<br>45–50% carbohydrate<br>30–35% fat<br>Sodium intake may be restricted somewhat. | **Rationale:**<br><br>Dietary management is designed to ensure optimum fetal growth and normalize blood glucose levels. The greatest success occurs when a dietary plan is individualized to meet client needs and preferences.<br><br>Recommended intake is designed to permit the following weight gain (Kitzmiller 1988):<br>underweight 30+ lb<br>desirable wt 24–30 lb<br>overweight 20–24 lb<br>very overweight 15–20 lb<br><br>**Evaluation:**<br><br>Woman understands her prescribed diet, follows it carefully, and gains the optimum amount of weight for her prepregnant size. |
| **Nursing Diagnosis:**<br><br>Pattern 1: Exchanging<br>Potential for injury related to possible complications secondary to hypoglycemia or hyperglycemia | Determine insulin needs:<br>1. Check lab results of FPG and 2-hour postprandial.<br>2. Test blood four times daily using Dextrostix. | **Rationale:**<br><br>Sufficient insulin must be present to enable proper carbohydrate metabolism to take place; pregnancy requires a marked increase in circulating insulin to maintain normal blood glucose. |

# Nursing Care Plan

## Diabetes Mellitus *(continued)*

| Nursing Diagnosis/Goal | Nursing Interventions | Rationale/Evaluation |
|---|---|---|
| | 3. Teach use of home blood glucose monitoring device; determine amount of insulin based on sliding scale.<br>4. Administer regular or NPH insulin, or combination, as ordered. | Fasting glucose level tends to be lower than nonpregnant value<br>Effectiveness of insulin may be reduced by presence of hPL |
| **Client Goal:**<br>Woman will avoid injury associated with hypoglycemia or hyperglycemia as evidenced by absence of signs or symptoms, blood glucose readings in normal range, and stabilization of insulin requirements. | 1. Teach early signs of hypoglycemia, including sweating, periodic tingling, disorientation, shakiness, pallor, clammy skin, irritability, hunger, headache, blurred vision, and, if untreated, coma or convulsions. | Insulin requirements fluctuate widely during pregnancy because of factors mentioned in text and because of lowered glucose tolerance, especially in second half of pregnancy, and fluctuate during intrapartal period because of depletion of glycogen stores during labor; fluctuations during puerperium are a result of involuntary process; in addition, conversion of blood glucose into lactose during lactation may cause marked changes in glucose tolerance and/or hypoglycemia.<br><br>Client needs to understand appropriate interventions because self-care at home in the event of hypoglycemia may save her life.<br><br>Rapid treatment of hypoglycemia is essential to prevent brain damage because the brain requires glucose to function (skeletal and heart muscles can derive energy from ketones and free fatty acids). |
| | 2. Treat within minutes of onset<br><br>  a. Obtain immediate blood glucose level. If < 60 mg/dL have client drink 8 oz milk (some agencies prefer to use ½ glass orange juice) and notify physician.<br>  b. If woman is not alert enough to swallow give 1 mg glucagon subcutaneously or intramuscularly; notify physician.<br>  c. If woman is in labor with intravenous lines in place, 10–20 mL of 50% dextrose may be given IV.<br>Standing order should be available; notify physician.<br>1. Teach woman early signs of hyperglycemia and treatment.<br><br>2. Observe for signs of hyperglycemia such as polyuria, polydipsia, dry mouth, increased appetite, fatigue, nausea, hot flushed skin, rapid deep | Provides baseline information on glucose levels.<br>Liquids are absorbed from the GI tract faster than solids.<br><br>Glucagon triggers the conversion of glycogen stored in the liver to glucose.<br><br><br><br>Woman can recognize signs and administer self-treatment.<br>Woman can also report any symptoms that may occur. |

*(continues)*

# Nursing Care Plan

## Diabetes Mellitus (continued)

| Nursing Diagnosis/Goal | Nursing Interventions | Rationale/Evaluation |
|---|---|---|
| | breathing, abdominal cramps, acetone breath, headache, drowsiness, depressed reflexes, oliguria or anuria, stupor, coma.<br>3. Administer treatment; notify physician. | Administer insulin to restore body's normal metabolism of carbohydrate, protein, and fat. |
| | a. Obtain frequent measurement of blood and urine glucose; measure urine acetone. | Need to establish a baseline and to determine additional insulin dosage and prevent overtreatment; urine acetone indicates development of ketoacidosis. |
| | b. Administer prescribed amount regular insulin subcutaneously or intravenously, or combination of routes. | Regular insulin is used because it acts immediately and is of short duration. |
| | c. Replace fluids IV, orally, or both. | Fluids are depleted in the process of ketoacidosis; hypotension can result from decreased blood volume due to dehydration. |
| | d. Measure intake and output. | Polyuria is an early sign of hyperglycemia; oliguria develops with hypotension and decreased bloodflow to kidneys. |
| | e. Observe for symptoms of circulatory collapse; monitor BP and pulse. | Circulatory collapse can result from hypotension.<br><br>**Evaluation:**<br>Woman avoids episodes of hyperglycemia or hypoglycemia, or, if they occur, they are detected early and treated successfully. Insulin requirements become stabilized. |
| **Nursing Diagnosis:**<br>Pattern 1: Exchanging<br>Potential for injury related to signs of urinary tract infection (UTI) secondary to glycosuria | Review preventive measures such as voiding frequently, voiding following intercourse, wiping from front to back, wearing cotton crotch underpants, drinking cranberry juice. | **Rationale:**<br>Preventive measures are designed to remove bacteria from the bladder, avoid contamination from the rectal area or outside sources, facilitate air flow in the perineal area, and acidify the urine. |
| **Client Goal:**<br>Woman will be able to identify signs of developing UTI and appropriate self-care measures to help prevent UTI. If signs of UTI do develop, therapy will be effective in preventing injury from complications. | 1. Teach signs of developing UTI, including urgency, frequency, dysuria, and hematuria; low back pain with kidney involvement. Obtain clean catch urine for culture and sensitivity.<br>2. Administer prescribed antibiotics.<br><br>3. Encourage fluids to 2000–3000 mL/day.<br>4. Measure intake and output. | Incidence of UTI is increased in diabetes, possibly because the existence of glycosuria provides rich medium for bacterial growth.<br><br>Antibiotic prescribed is specific to causative organism.<br>Increased fluid intake promotes urinary removal of organisms.<br>**Evaluation:**<br>Woman implements self-care measures to avoid UTI. If UTI develops, treatment is effective and complications are avoided. |

## Nursing Care Plan

### Diabetes Mellitus *(continued)*

| Nursing Diagnosis/Goal | Nursing Interventions | Rationale/Evaluation |
|---|---|---|
| **Nursing Diagnosis:**<br><br>Pattern 8: Knowing<br>Knowledge deficit related to the disease, its treatment, its implications for the woman, her unborn child, and the birth process | Provide teaching as indicated based on individualized assessment of couple's knowledge level:<br>1. Explain procedures.<br>2. Allow them to ask questions.<br>3. Develop a teaching plan to discuss and provide opportunities to practice administering insulin. Provide written information. Include partner so he can administer insulin if necessary.<br>4. Assess their level of knowledge of childbirth and use this to teach about what is happening.<br>5. Provide information about possible changes to expect during labor and birth due to DM. Explain about IV insulin, continuous monitoring of fetal status. Stress unchanged aspects of the experience. | **Rationale:**<br><br>Decreasing fear and increasing knowledge will make the client a more effective member of the antepartal-intrapartal health team.<br>Anticipatory guidance helps the couple prepare for the upcoming experience. |
| **Client Goal:**<br><br>Woman and her partner will understand the diabetes and its possible implications for her pregnancy as evidenced by their ability to administer insulin, to identify signs of hypo- or hyperglycemia, to discuss basic information about birth and anticipated therapy measures. | | **Evaluation:**<br><br>Woman is able to discuss her condition and its implications, follows the recommendations of her care givers, and correctly carries out self-care activities related to her diabetes. |
| **Nursing Diagnosis:**<br><br>Pattern 1: Exchanging<br>Potential for injury to fetus related to the effects of diabetes on uteroplacental functioning and fetal growth | Explain purpose of all scheduled tests and procedures:<br>1. Ultrasound as ordered to provide periodic assessment of fetal size.<br>2. Fetal activity diary<br>3. Serial NSTs<br>4. CST if indicated.<br>5. Measurement of L/S ratio and PG levels to determine fetal lung maturity.<br>6. Biophysical profile | **Rationale:**<br><br>Compliance is increased when client understands purpose of tests. Information about fetal growth and activity helps care givers evaluate placental functioning, anticipate the need for cesarean birth, determine fetal maturity, and decide on best time for birth. |
| **Client Goal:**<br><br>Woman will be able to discuss rationale for fetal monitoring and testing, and will cooperate with fetal testing and assessment schedule. | | **Evaluation:**<br><br>Woman cooperates with fetal testing schedule. Fetus responds well to tests and shows evidence of normal growth and placental functioning. |

*(continues)*

## Nursing Care Plan

### Diabetes Mellitus *(continued)*

| Nursing Diagnosis/Goal | Nursing Interventions | Rationale/Evaluation |
|---|---|---|
| **Nursing Diagnosis:**<br><br>Pattern 3: Relating<br>Altered family processes related to client's DM and the need for hospitalization. | 1. Encourage visits from family members and older siblings.<br>2. Discuss with client and family changes that are necessary following discharge with regard to insulin, diet, exercise, and so forth.<br>3. Assist family to make specific plans.<br>4. Arrange for social services to visit or for homemaker assistance if necessary following discharge.<br>5. Give the family members information about the frustration that can occur when a family member is ill. Provide opportunities for them to discuss their feelings. Offer suggestions for coping. | **Rationale:**<br><br>Illness in one family member impacts the entire family. Sometimes outside support is necessary to help the family deal with feelings and identify ways of dealing with the illness of a member. |
| **Client Goal:**<br><br>Family will deal successfully with the woman's illness, plan for changes necessary following discharge, and share their thoughts, feelings, and concerns with each other. | | **Evaluation:**<br><br>Woman and family cope successfully with illness, make necessary plans for managing following discharge, and discuss their feelings in an open caring way. |

injecting insulin into an extremity that will soon be used during exercise (McCoy and Oswald 1983).

If she has not been following a regular exercise plan she is encouraged to begin gradually. Due to alterations in metabolism with exercise, the woman's blood glucose should be well controlled before she begins an exercise program.

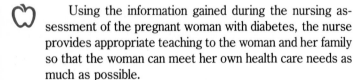

### EDUCATION FOR SELF-CARE

Using the information gained during the nursing assessment of the pregnant woman with diabetes, the nurse provides appropriate teaching to the woman and her family so that the woman can meet her own health care needs as much as possible.

● *Symptoms of hypoglycemia and ketoacidosis.* The pregnant diabetic woman must recognize symptoms of changing glucose levels and take appropriate action by immediately checking her capillary blood glucose level. If it is less than 60 mg/dL she is advised to drink 8 oz of milk and recheck in 15 minutes. Milk is used when possible to avoid a rebound hyperglycemia (Kitzmiller 1988). The woman should carry a snack at all times

and should have other fast sources of glucose (simple carbohydrates) at hand so that she can treat an insulin reaction when milk is not available. Family members are also taught how to inject glucagon in the event that food does not work or is not feasible, for instance, in the presence of severe morning sickness.

● *Smoking.* Smoking has harmful effects on both the maternal vascular system and the developing fetus and is contraindicated for both pregnancy and diabetes.

● *Travel.* Insulin can be kept at room temperature while traveling. Insulin supplies should be kept with the traveler and not packed in the baggage. Special meals can be arranged by notifying most airlines a few days before departure. A diabetic identification bracelet or necklace should be worn. In addition, the woman should check with her physician for any instructions or advice before leaving.

● *Hospitalization.* Hospitalization may become necessary during the pregnancy to evaluate blood glucose levels and adjust insulin dosages.

● *Support groups.* Many communities have diabetes support groups or education classes, which can be most helpful to women with newly diagnosed diabetes.

• *Cesarean birth.* Chances for a cesarean birth are increased if the pregnant woman is diabetic. This possibility should be anticipated—enrollment in cesarean birth preparation classes may be suggested. Many hospitals offer classes, and information is available through organizations such as Cesarean/Support Education and Concern (C/Sec, Inc); Cesarean Birth Council; or the Cesarean Association for Research, Education, Support and Satisfaction in Birthing (CARESS). The couple may prefer simply to discuss cesarean birth with the nurse and their obstetrician and read some books on the topic.

## • Evaluation

Anticipated outcomes of nursing care include the following:

• The woman clearly understands her condition and its possible impact on her pregnancy, labor and birth, and postpartal period.

• The woman cooperates and participates in developing a health care regimen to meet her needs and follows it throughout her pregnancy.

• The woman successfully delivers a healthy newborn.

• The woman avoids developing hypoglycemia or hyperglycemia.

• The woman is able to care for her newborn.

## • CARE OF THE WOMAN WITH ANEMIA

Anemia is a common problem in pregnancy. Anemia may be due specifically to pregnancy, or it may exist coincidently with pregnancy. For example, iron deficiency anemia and folic acid deficiency anemia may be caused by pregnancy. Anemias that are acquired or hereditary, such as sickle cell anemia, may be exacerbated by pregnancy. Table 12.3 describes these three common anemias.

## • CARE OF THE WOMAN WITH HYPEREMESIS GRAVIDARUM

**Hyperemesis gravidarum** is pernicious vomiting during pregnancy. It may be mild at first, but true hyperemesis progresses to a point at which the woman not only vomits everything she swallows, but retches between meals.

Although the exact cause of hyperemesis is unclear, it is probably related to trophoblastic activity and gonadotropin production, and may sometimes be stimulated or exaggerated by psychologic factors.

In severe cases the pathology begins with dehydration, which leads to fluid-electrolyte imbalance. Hypo-

volemia, hypotension, tachycardia, increased hematocrit and blood urea nitrogen (BUN), and decreased urine output can also occur. If untreated, metabolic acidosis may develop.

Severe potassium loss may disrupt cardiac functioning. Starvation may also cause severe protein and vitamin deficiencies. Fetal or embryonic death may result, and the woman may suffer irreversible metabolic changes or death.

## • Medical Therapy

The goals of treatment include control of vomiting, correction of dehydration, restoration of electrolyte balance, and maintenance of adequate nutrition. Initially the woman is given nothing by mouth. Intravenous fluids containing glucose, vitamins (B-complex, C, A, and D) and electrolytes are administered. Promethazine (Phenergan) given parenterally in a continuous low dose may help control nausea and vomiting (Cruikshank 1986). In 48 hours the woman's condition usually improves sufficiently to try controlled oral feedings.

## • Nursing Assessment

When a woman is hospitalized for control of vomiting, the nurse regularly assesses the amount and character of further emesis, intake and output, fetal heart rate, evidence of jaundice or bleeding, and the woman's emotional state.

## • Nursing Diagnosis

Nursing diagnoses that may apply to a woman with hyperemesis gravidarum include:

• Altered nutrition: less than body requirements related to persistent vomiting secondary to hyperemesis

• Fear related to the effects of hyperemesis on fetal well-being

• Fluid volume deficit related to severe dehydration secondary to persistent vomiting

## • Nursing Plan and Implementation

Nursing care is directed at monitoring the woman's status. Intake and output are measured and oral care is provided. Changes in fetal status are reported promptly. In addition, the nurse maintains a quiet, supportive environment away from food odors or offensive smells. Once the woman begins tolerating oral feedings, the food should be attractively served. Bedpans and emesis basins should be kept out of sight during meals and dirty dishes should be removed promptly. Because emotional factors may play a role in this condition, psychotherapy may be recommended. With proper treatment, prognosis is favorable.

## Table 12.3   Anemia and Pregnancy

| Condition | Brief description | Maternal implications | Fetal-neonatal implications |
|---|---|---|---|
| Iron deficiency anemia | Condition caused by inadequate iron intake resulting in hemoglobin levels below 11 g/dL. To prevent this, most women are advised to take supplemental iron during pregnancy. | Pregnant woman with this anemia tires easily, is more susceptible to infection, has increased chance of postpartal hemorrhage, and cannot tolerate even minimal blood loss during delivery. | Abortion and prematurity rates are increased, and the neonate may be SGA. Fetus may be hypoxic during labor due to impaired uteroplacental oxygenation. |
| Sickle cell anemia | Recessive autosomal disease present in about 1 in 600 of the blacks in the U.S. The sickle cell trait is carried by 8% of American blacks. The disease is characterized by sickling of the RBCs in the presence of decreased oxygenation. Condition may be marked by crisis with profound anemia, jaundice, high temperature, infarction, and acute pain. Crisis is treated by partial exchange transfusion, rehydration with IV fluids, antibiotics and analgesics. The fetus is monitored throughout. | Pregnancy may aggravate anemia and bring on more crises. Increased risk of developing preeclampsia exists. There is also increased risk of urinary tract infection, pneumonia, congestive heart failure, and pulmonary infarction. The goal of treatment is to reduce the anemia and maintain good health. Oxygen supplementation should be used continuously during labor. Additional blood should be available if transfusion is necessary following birth. | Abortion, fetal death, and prematurity may occur. IUGR is also a characteristic finding in neonates of women with sickle cell anemia. |
| Megaloblastic anemia | Folic acid deficiency is most common cause of megaloblastic anemia. In the absence of folic acid, immature RBCs fail to divide, become enlarged (megaloblastic) and are fewer in number. Increased folic acid metabolism during pregnancy and lactation can result in deficiency. Because the condition is difficult to diagnose, the best approach is prevention by supplementing with 0.4 mg folate daily (generally found in prenatal vitamin supplements). The condition is treated with 1 mg folate daily. | Folate deficiency is the second most common cause of anemia in pregnancy. Severe deficiency increases the risk that the mother may need a blood transfusion following birth due to anemia. She also has an increased risk of hemorrhage due to thrombocytopenia, and is more susceptible to infection. Folic acid is readily available in foods such as fresh leafy green vegetables, red meat, fish, poultry, and legumes, but it is easily destroyed by overcooking or cooking with large quantities of water. | Early studies suggested a link between folate deficiency and complications such as spontaneous abortion or abruptio placentae with resultant fetal death, but newer studies have not replicated these findings. Generally the fetus is not anemic at birth even in the presence of severe maternal anemia. |

● *Evaluation*

Anticipated outcomes of nursing care include the following:

● The woman's vomiting ceases, electrolyte balance is restored, oral intake of food and fluid is well tolerated, and complications are avoided.

● The woman is able to explain hyperemesis gravidarum, its therapy, and the possible effects on her pregnancy.

● *CARE OF THE WOMAN WITH A BLEEDING DISORDER*

During the first and second trimesters of pregnancy, the major cause of bleeding is **abortion**. This is defined as the termination of pregnancy prior to viability of the fetus, which now occurs at about 26 weeks' gestation. Abortions are either *spontaneous*, that is, occurring naturally; or *induced*, occurring as the result of artificial or mechanical interruption. **Miscarriage** is a lay term used to describe a spontaneous abortion. Induced abortion is also referred to as therapeutic abortion or planned abortion.

Other complications that can cause bleeding in the first half of pregnancy are ectopic pregnancy and gestational trophoblastic disease. In the second half of pregnancy, particularly in the third trimester, the two major causes of bleeding are placenta previa and abruptio placentae.

## ● General Principles of Nursing Intervention

Spotting is relatively common during pregnancy and usually occurs following sexual intercourse or exercise due to trauma to the highly vascular cervix. However, the woman is advised to report any spotting or bleeding that occurs during pregnancy so that it can be evaluated.

It is often the nurse's responsibility to make the initial assessment of bleeding. In general, the following nursing measures should be implemented for pregnant women being treated for bleeding disorders:

- Monitor vital signs of blood pressure and pulse constantly.
- Observe woman for behaviors indicative of shock, such as pallor, clammy skin, perspiration, dyspnea, or restlessness.
- Count pads to assess amount of bleeding over a given time period; save any tissue or clots expelled.
- If pregnancy is of 12 weeks' gestation or beyond, assess fetal heart tones with a Doppler.
- Prepare for intravenous therapy.
- Prepare equipment for examination.
- Have oxygen therapy available.
- Collect and organize all data, including antepartal history, onset of bleeding episode, laboratory studies (hemoglobin, hematocrit, and hormonal assays).
- Assess coping mechanisms of woman in crisis. Give emotional support to enhance her coping abilities by continuous, sustained presence; by clear explanation of procedures; and by communicating her status to her family. Most important, prepare the woman for possible fetal loss. Assess her expressions of anger, denial, silence, guilt, depression, or self-blame.

## ● Spontaneous Abortion

Many pregnancies end in the first trimester because of spontaneous abortion. Often the woman assumes she is having a heavy menstrual period when in reality she is having an early abortion. Statistics are inaccurate but estimates suggest that 15% of all pregnancies end in spontaneous abortion (Scott 1986b).

About 60% of early spontaneous abortions are related to chromosomal abnormalities. Other causes include teratogenic drugs, faulty implantation due to abnormalities of the female reproductive tract, a weakened cervix, placental abnormalities, chronic maternal diseases, endocrine imbalances, and maternal infections from the TORCH group. It is believed by some that psychic trauma and accidents are a primary cause of abortion, but statistics do not support this belief.

Abortion can be extremely distressing to the couple desiring a child. Chances for carrying the next pregnancy to term after one spontaneous abortion are as good as they are for the general population. Thereafter, however, chances of successful pregnancy decrease with each succeeding abortion.

### CLASSIFICATION

Spontaneous abortions are subdivided into the following categories so that they can be differentiated clinically:

1. *Threatened abortion.* The fetus is jeopardized by unexplained bleeding, cramping, and backache. The cervix is closed. Bleeding may persist for days. It may be followed by partial or complete expulsion of the products of pregnancy (Figure 12.2).

2. *Imminent abortion.* Bleeding and cramping increase. The internal cervical os dilates. Membranes may rupture. The term *inevitable abortion* applies.

3. *Complete abortion.* All the products of conception are expelled.

4. *Incomplete abortion.* Part of the products of conception are retained, most often the placenta. The internal cervical os is dilated slightly.

5. *Missed abortion.* The fetus dies in utero but is not expelled. Uterine growth ceases, breast changes regress, and the woman may report a brownish vaginal discharge. The cervix is closed. Diagnosis is made based on history, pelvic examination, and a negative pregnancy test and may be confirmed by ultrasound if necessary. If the fetus is retained beyond six weeks, the breakdown of fetal tissues results in the release of thromboplastin, and disseminated intravascular coagulation (DIC) may develop.

6. *Habitual abortion.* Abortion occurs consecutively in three or more pregnancies.

### MEDICAL THERAPY

Because 20% to 25% of pregnant women have episodes of spotting or bleeding during early pregnancy, it is important to determine whether vaginal bleeding is related to spontaneous abortion or other factors (Scott 1986b). One of the more reliable indicators is the presence of pel-

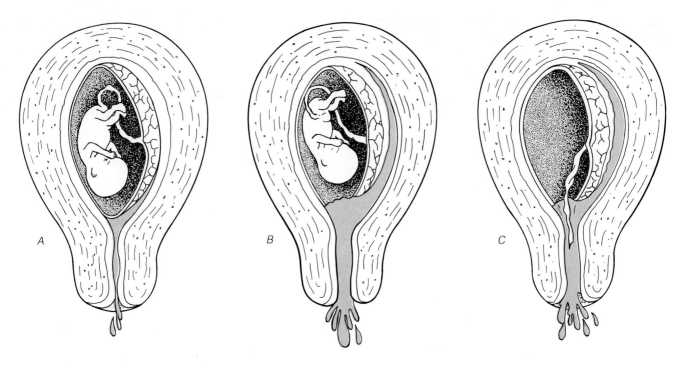

*Figure 12.2   Types of spontaneous abortion: (**A**) Threatened abortion, (**B**) Imminent abortion, (**C**) Incomplete abortion*

vic cramping and backache. These symptoms are usually absent in bleeding caused by polyps, ruptured cervical blood vessels, or cervical erosion. Ultrasound scanning may be used to detect the presence of a gestational sac if the cause of bleeding is unclear. Results of human chorionic gonadotropin (hCG) levels are not particularly helpful because hCG levels fall slowly after fetal death and therefore cannot confirm a live embryo/fetus.

The therapy prescribed for the pregnant woman with bleeding is abstinence from coitus, and perhaps sedation. If bleeding persists and abortion is imminent or incomplete, the woman is hospitalized, intravenous therapy or blood transfusions may be started to replace fluid, and dilatation and curettage or suction evacuation is performed to remove the remainder of the products of conception. If the woman is Rh negative and not sensitized, $Rh_0$ (D) immune globulin (RhoGAM) is given within 72 hours (see discussion on p 323).

In missed abortions, the products of conception eventually are expelled spontaneously. If this does not occur within four to six weeks, hospitalization is necessary. Suction evacuation or dilatation and curettage is done if the pregnancy is in the first trimester. Beyond 12 weeks' gestation, induction of labor by intravenous oxytocin and prostaglandins may be used to expel the dead fetus.

## NURSING ASSESSMENT

The nurse assesses the woman's vital signs, amount of bleeding, level of comfort, and physical health. The nurse also assesses the responses of the woman and her family to this crisis and evaluates their coping mechanisms and ability to comfort each other.

## NURSING DIAGNOSIS

Examples of nursing diagnoses that may apply include:

● Fear related to possible pregnancy loss

● Pain related to abdominal cramping secondary to threatened abortion

● Anticipatory grieving related to expected loss of unborn child

## NURSING PLAN AND IMPLEMENTATION

The physical pain of the cramps and the amount of bleeding may be more severe than a couple anticipates, even when they are prepared for the possibility of an abortion. Nurses can provide support by explaining why the discomfort is occurring and by providing analgesics for pain relief.

Providing emotional support is an important task for nurses caring for women who have aborted because the attachment process already begun is disrupted (Wall-Haas 1985). Feelings of shock or disbelief are normal at first. Couples who approached the pregnancy with feelings of joy and a sense of expectancy now feel grief, sadness, and possibly anger.

Since many women, even with planned pregnancies, feel some ambivalence initially, guilt is a common emotion. These feelings may be even stronger for women who were negative about their pregnancies. The woman may harbor negative feelings about herself or even believe that the abortion may be a punishment for some wrongdoing.

The nurse can offer invaluable psychologic support to the woman and her family by encouraging them to talk about their feelings, by allowing them the privacy to grieve, and by sympathetically listening to their concerns about this pregnancy and future ones. Feelings of guilt or blame may be decreased by informing the woman and her family about the causes of spontaneous abortion. The nurse can also refer them to other health care professionals for additional help as necessary.

The grieving period following a spontaneous abortion usually lasts 6 to 24 months (Borg and Lasker 1981). Many couples can be helped during this period by an organization or support group established for parents who have lost a fetus or newborn.

## EVALUATION

Anticipated outcomes of nursing care include the following:

● The woman is able to explain spontaneous abortion, the treatment measures employed in her care, and long-term implications for future pregnancies.

● The woman suffers no complications.

● The woman and her partner are able to begin verbalizing their grief and recognize that the grieving process usually lasts several months.

## ● *Ectopic Pregnancy*

**Ectopic pregnancy** is an implantation of the blastocyst in a site other than the endometrial lining of the uterus. It may result from many causes, including tubal damage caused by pelvic inflammatory disease (PID), previous pelvic or tubal surgery, hormonal factors that may interfere with forward motion of the egg in the fallopian tube, tubal atony or spasms, and blighted ovum.

The incidence of ectopic pregnancy has increased dramatically in the past several years, and by 1983 it was 14 per 1000 reported pregnancies. This increased incidence may be related to improved diagnostic technology and to the increase in pelvic inflammatory disease (Dorfman 1987). Although ectopic pregnancy is second only to PIH as a cause of maternal mortality, the actual death rate has decreased dramatically because of earlier detection and treatment (Queenan 1987).

Ectopic pregnancy occurs when the fertilized ovum is prevented or slowed in its passage through the tube. The fertilized ovum then implants elsewhere. The most common location for implantation is the ampulla of the fallopian tube. Other implantation sites are identified in Figure 12.3.

Initially the normal symptoms of pregnancy may be present, specifically amenorrhea, breast tenderness, and nausea. The hormone hCG is present in the blood and urine. As the pregnancy progresses the chorionic villi grow into the wall of the tube or site of implantation and a blood supply is established. When the embryo outgrows this space, the tube ruptures and there is bleeding into the abdominal cavity. This bleeding causes the characteristic symptoms of sharp, one-sided pain, syncope, and referred shoulder pain. The woman may also experience lower ab-

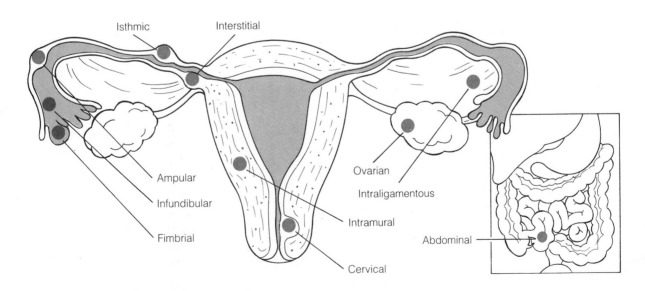

*Figure 12.3  Implantation sites in ectopic pregnancy. Implantation may also occur within the abdominal cavity.*

dominal pain. Vaginal bleeding, a common finding, occurs when the embryo dies and the decidua begins to slough.

Physical examination usually reveals adnexal tenderness. (The adnexae are the areas of the lower abdomen located over each ovary and fallopian tube.) An adnexal mass is palpable about half the time. Bleeding tends to be slow and chronic, and the abdomen gradually becomes rigid and very tender. With extensive bleeding into the abdominal cavity, pelvic examination causes extreme pain.

Laboratory tests may reveal low hemoglobin and hematocrit levels and rising leukocyte levels. The hCG titers are lower than in intrauterine pregnancy.

## MEDICAL THERAPY

The following procedures are used to establish the diagnosis of ectopic pregnancy:

- A careful assessment of menstrual history, particularly the last menstrual period (LMP).

- Careful pelvic exam to identify any abnormal pelvic masses and tenderness.

- Culdocentesis. The woman is positioned with her legs in stirrups, and a needle is inserted through the posterior vaginal vault into the cul-de-sac of Douglas. If nonclotting blood (blood that was clotted and then fibrinolysed) is aspirated, it is indicative of ectopic pregnancy.

- Laparoscopy, which may reveal an extrauterine pregnancy and detect an unruptured tubal pregnancy. If culdocentesis reveals free abdominal blood, laparoscopy is not necessary.

- Ultrasound, which may be useful in identifying a gestational sac in an unruptured tubal pregnancy or in confirming an intrauterine pregnancy, which usually rules out an ectopic one.

- Laparotomy, which will give a confirmed diagnosis and allow opportunity for immediate treatment.

Once the diagnosis of ectopic pregnancy has been made, surgery is necessary. Conservative management by linear salpingotomy is the treatment of choice when this is possible (Weckstein 1985). Using this method, a linear incision is made in the tube and the products of conception are gently removed with a forceps or by washing. The surgical incision in the tube is left open and allowed to close by secondary intention (Droegemueller 1986). In a woman whose condition is stable and who has no contraindications, this procedure is sometimes done using a laparoscope and two to three incisions, thereby avoiding an abdominal incision (Shapiro et al 1988). If the tube is badly damaged, a total salpingectomy is performed, leaving the ovary in place unless it is damaged. If massive infection is found, a complete removal of uterus, tubes, and ovaries may be necessary.

Intravenous therapy and blood transfusion are used to replace fluid loss. During surgery the most important risk to be considered is potential hemorrhage. Bleeding must be controlled and replacement therapy should be on hand. The Rh negative nonsensitized woman is given $Rh_0(D)$ immune globulin (RhoGAM) to prevent sensitization.

## NURSING ASSESSMENT

When the woman with a suspected ectopic pregnancy is admitted to the hospital, the nurse assesses the appearance and amount of vaginal bleeding, and monitors vital signs for evidence of developing shock. The woman's orthostatic blood pressure is checked if her condition permits. A drop of 10 mm Hg accompanied by an increase in pulse rate of 15 to 20 beats/min suggests possible hypovolemic shock (Donner and Cooper 1988).

The nurse assesses the woman's emotional state and coping abilities, and determines the couple's informational needs. The woman may experience marked abdominal discomfort, so the nurse also determines the woman's level of pain. If surgery is necessary the nurse performs the ongoing assessments appropriate postoperatively.

## NURSING DIAGNOSIS

Nursing diagnoses that may apply for a woman with an ectopic pregnancy include:

- Anticipatory grieving related to the loss of the pregnancy

- Pain related to abdominal bleeding secondary to tubal rupture

- Knowledge deficit related to treatment of ectopic pregnancy and its long-term implications

## NURSING PLAN AND IMPLEMENTATION

Once a diagnosis of ectopic pregnancy is made and surgery is scheduled, the nurse starts an IV as ordered and begins preoperative teaching. Signs of developing shock should be reported immediately. If the woman is experiencing severe abdominal pain, the nurse can administer appropriate analgesics and evaluate their effectiveness.

Teaching is an important part of the nursing care. The woman may want her condition and various procedures explained. She may need instruction regarding measures to prevent infection, symptoms to report (pain, bleeding, fever), and her follow-up visit.

The woman and her family will need emotional support during this difficult time. Their feelings and responses to this crisis will probably be similar to those that occur in cases of spontaneous abortion. As a result, similar nursing actions are required for these women.

## EVALUATION

Anticipated outcomes of nursing care include the following:

● The woman is able to explain ectopic pregnancy, treatment alternatives, and implications for future childbearing.

● The woman and her care givers detect possible complications of therapy early and manage them successfully.

● The woman and her partner are able to begin verbalizing their loss and recognize that the grieving process usually lasts several months.

## ● Gestational Trophoblastic Disease

**Gestational trophoblastic disease (GTD)** has been categorized into benign (hydatidiform mole) and malignant (nonmetastatic and metastatic) components (Runowicz 1985).

**Hydatidiform mole** (molar pregnancy) is a disease in which (1) the chorionic villi of the placenta become swollen, fluid-filled (hydropic) grapelike clusters, while a central fluid-filled space forms in the placenta (central cistern formation); and (2) the trophoblastic tissue proliferates. The significance of this disease for the woman who has it is the loss of the pregnancy and the possibility, though remote, of developing choriocarcinoma from the trophoblastic tissue.

Molar pregnancies are classified into two types, complete and partial, both of which meet the above criteria. A complete mole develops from an ovum that contains no maternal genetic material but that is fertilized by a normal sperm. The embryo dies very early, no circulation is established, the hydropic vesicles are avascular, and no embryonic tissue or membranes are found. Choriocarcinoma seems to be associated exclusively with the complete mole.

The partial mole usually has a triploid karyotype (69 chromosomes) because of failure of either the ovum or sperm to undergo the first meiotic division. There may be a fetal sac or even a fetus with heart tones. The fetus has multiple anomalies because of the triploidy and little chance for survival. The villi are often vascularized and may be hydropic in only portions of the placenta. Partial moles are twice as common as complete moles (Buckley 1984). Women with partial molar pregnancies have an increased risk of molar disease in subsequent pregnancies. They are advised to have an ultrasound done in the first trimester to confirm that the pregnancy is normal (Berkowitz et al 1988).

### MEDICAL THERAPY

Initially the clinical picture is similar to that of pregnancy. However, classic signs soon appear. Vaginal bleed-

ing almost universally occurs. It is often brownish (called prune juice) due to liquefaction of the uterine clot, but may be bright red. Because of the rapid proliferation of the trophoblastic cells that occurs with complete moles uterine enlargement is often greater than expected for gestational age. Hydropic vesicles may be passed, and, if so, are diagnostic. With a partial mole the vesicles are often smaller and may not be noticed. In addition, because serum hCG levels are higher than with normal pregnancy, the woman may experience hyperemesis gravidarum. Symptoms of PIH prior to 24 weeks' gestation strongly suggest a molar pregnancy. No fetal heart tones are heard and no fetal movement is palpated. Ultrasound may reveal a characteristic molar pattern.

Therapy begins with evacuation of the mole and curettage of the uterus to remove all fragments of the placenta. Early evacuation decreases the possibility of other complications (Runowicz 1985). If the woman is older and therefore at increased risk of malignant sequelae, or if there is excessive bleeding, hysterectomy may be the treatment of choice.

The woman treated for hydatidiform mole should receive follow-up therapy for a year. Pregnancy is avoided during that time because the elevated hCG levels associated with pregnancy would cause confusion as to whether choriocarcinoma had developed.

Continued high or rising hCG titers are abnormal. If they occur, dilatation and curettage are performed, and tissue is examined. If malignant cells are found, chemotherapy for choriocarcinoma is started. If therapy is ineffective, the choriocarcinoma has a tendency to metastasize rapidly.

If, after a year of monitoring, the hCG serum titers are within normal limits, a couple may be assured that subsequent normal pregnancy can be anticipated with low probability of recurrent hydatidiform mole.

### NURSING ASSESSMENT

It is important for nurses involved in antepartal care to be aware of symptoms of hydatidiform mole and observe for these at each antepartal visit. The classic symptoms used to diagnose molar pregnancy are found more frequently with the complete than with the partial mole. The partial mole may be difficult to distinguish from a missed abortion prior to evacuation. If a molar pregnancy is diagnosed the nurse should assess the couple's understanding of the condition and its implications.

### NURSING DIAGNOSIS

Nursing diagnoses that may apply to a woman with a hydatidiform mole include:

● Fear related to the possible development of choriocarcinoma

- Knowledge deficit related to a lack of understanding of the need for regular monitoring of hCG levels
- Anticipatory grieving related to loss of pregnancy

### NURSING PLAN AND IMPLEMENTATION

When a molar pregnancy is suspected, the woman needs support. The nurse can relieve some of the woman's anxiety by answering questions about the condition and explaining what ultrasound and other diagnostic procedures will entail. If a molar pregnancy is diagnosed, the nurse supports the childbearing family as they deal with their grief about the lost pregnancy. The hospital chaplain or their own clergy may be of assistance in helping them deal with this loss.

When the woman is hospitalized for evacuation of the mole, the nurse must monitor vital signs and vaginal bleeding for evidence of hemorrhage. In addition, the nurse determines whether abdominal pain is present and evaluates the woman's emotional state and coping ability.

If the woman is Rh negative and not sensitized, she is given $Rh_0(D)$ immune globulin (RhoGAM) to prevent antibody formation.

The woman needs to know the importance of the follow-up visits. She is advised to delay becoming pregnant again until after the follow-up program is completed. She should be advised against using an intrauterine contraceptive device because of bleeding irregularities associated with it. Oral contraceptives are considered ideal as they are highly effective and suppress the midcycle LH surge (Runowicz 1985).

### EVALUATION

Anticipated outcomes of nursing care include the following:

- The woman has a smooth recovery following successful evacuation of the mole.
- The woman is able to explain GTD, its treatment, follow-up, and long-term implications for pregnancy.
- The woman and her partner are able to begin verbalizing their grief at the loss of their anticipated child.
- The woman understands the importance of follow-up assessment and indicates her willingness to cooperate with the regimen.

● *Placenta Previa*

In *placenta previa* the placenta is improperly implanted in the lower uterine segment, perhaps on a portion of the lower segment or over the internal os. As the lower uterine segment contracts and the cervix dilates in the later weeks of pregnancy, the placental villi are torn from the uterine wall, thus exposing the uterine sinuses at the placental site. Bleeding begins, but because its amount depends on the number of sinuses exposed, it may initially be either scanty or profuse. The classic symptom is painless vaginal bleeding usually occurring after 20 weeks' gestation. See Chapter 18 for an in-depth discussion of placenta previa.

● *Abruptio Placentae*

*Abruptio placentae* is the premature separation of the placenta from the uterine wall. It occurs prior to birth, usually during the labor process. See Chapter 18 for an in-depth description of abruptio placentae.

● CARE OF THE WOMAN WITH AN INCOMPETENT CERVIX

Cervical incompetence is the premature dilatation of the cervix, usually about the fourth or fifth month of pregnancy. It is associated with repeated second trimester abortions. Possible causes are cervical trauma associated with previous surgery or birth, or congenital cervical structural defects.

Diagnosis is established by eliciting a positive history of repeated, relatively painless and bloodless second trimester abortions. Serial pelvic exams early in the second trimester reveal progressive effacement and dilatation of the cervix and bulging of the membranes through the cervical os.

Incompetent cervix is managed surgically with a Shirodkar-Barter operation (cerclage), or a modification of it by McDonald, which reinforces the weakened cervix by encircling it at the level of the internal os with suture material. A purse-string suture is placed in the cervix between 14 and 18 weeks of gestation. Once the suture is in place, a cesarean birth may be planned (to prevent repeating the procedure in subsequent pregnancies), or the suture may be released at term and vaginal birth permitted. The woman must understand the importance of contacting her physician immediately if her membranes rupture or labor begins. The physician can remove the suture to prevent possible complications. The success rate for carrying the pregnancy to term is 80% to 90%.

● CARE OF THE WOMAN WITH A HYPERTENSIVE DISORDER

In the past several years Gant and Worley (1980) and then Worley alone (1984) have attempted to develop a classification for related yet distinct conditions characterized by hypertension that can occur in pregnancy. The following is the current classification of the hypertensive disorders of pregnancy:

1. Pregnancy-induced hypertension (PIH)
   a. Preeclampsia
   b. Eclampsia
2. Chronic hypertension preceding pregnancy
3. Chronic hypertension with superimposed pregnancy-induced hypertension
   a. Superimposed preeclampsia
   b. Superimposed eclampsia
4. Transient hypertension

## ● *Pregnancy-Induced Hypertension*

**Pregnancy-induced hypertension** (PIH) is the most common hypertensive disorder in pregnancy. It is characterized by the development of hypertension, proteinuria, and edema. Because only hypertension may be present early in the disease process, that finding is therefore the basis for diagnosis.

The definition of PIH is a blood pressure of 140/90 mm Hg during the second half of pregnancy in a previously normotensive woman. An increase in systolic blood pressure of 30 mm Hg and/or of diastolic of 15 mm Hg over baseline also defines PIH. These blood pressure changes must be noted on at least two occasions six hours or more apart for the diagnosis to be made (Sibai 1988b, Worley 1984).

Preeclampsia and eclampsia are types of PIH. **Preeclampsia** indicates that this is a progressive disease unless there is intervention to control it. Preeclampsia is characterized by hypertension with proteinuria and/or edema after 20 weeks' gestation (Poole 1988). **Eclampsia** means "convulsion." If a woman has a convulsion she is considered "eclamptic." Most often PIH is seen in the last ten weeks of gestation, during labor, or in the first 48 hours after birth. Although birth of the fetus is the only known cure for PIH, it can be controlled with early diagnosis and careful management.

PIH occurs in 7% of all pregnancies; however, the incidence of superimposed PIH among women with chronic hypertension is 15% to 30% (DeVoe and O'Shaughnessy 1984). PIH is seen more often in primigravidas, teenagers of lower socioeconomic class, and women over 35, especially if they are primigravidas. Women with a family history of PIH are at higher risk for it, as are women with a large placental mass associated with multiple gestation, hydatidiform mole, Rh incompatibility, and diabetes mellitus.

Today PIH seldom progresses to the eclamptic state due to early diagnosis and careful management. Eclampsia is, however, the leading cause of maternal death in the United States.

### PATHOPHYSIOLOGY OF PIH

The cause of PIH remains unknown despite much research over many decades. The condition was previously called "toxemia" because of a theory that a toxin produced in a pregnant woman's body caused the disease. This term is no longer used because the theory has not been substantiated.

PIH affects all the major systems of the body. The following pathophysiologic changes are associated with the disease:

● In normal pregnancy the lowered peripheral vascular resistance and the increased maternal resistance to the pressor effects of angiotensin II result in lowered blood pressure. In PIH blood pressure begins to rise after 20 weeks' gestation, probably due to a gradual loss of resistance to angiotensin II. In addition, the synthesis of the prostaglandin $PGE_2$ and prostacyclin ($PGI_2$) is decreased in women with PIH. Both are potent vasodilators. It may be that their decrease is responsible for the increased sensitivity to angiotensin II.

● The loss of normal vasodilation of uterine arterioles results in decreased placental perfusion. The effect on the fetus may be growth retardation, decrease in fetal movement, and chronic hypoxia or fetal distress.

● In PIH normal renal perfusion is decreased. With a reduction of glomerular filtration rate (GFR), serum levels of creatinine, BUN, and uric acid begin to rise from normal pregnant levels, while urine output decreases. Sodium is retained in increased amounts, which results in increased extracellular volume and edema. Stretching of the capillary walls of the glomerular endothelial cells allows the large protein molecules, primarily albumin, to escape in the urine, decreasing serum albumin. The decreased serum albumin causes decreased plasma colloid osmotic pressure. This results in a further movement of fluid to the extracellular spaces, which also contributes to the development of edema.

● The decreased intravascular volume causes increased viscosity of the blood and a corresponding rise in hematocrit.

### MATERNAL RISKS

Central nervous system changes associated with PIH are hyperreflexia, headache, and convulsions. Hyperreflexia may be due to increased intracellular sodium and decreased intracellular potassium levels. Headaches are caused by cerebral vasospasm, and cerebral edema and vasoconstriction are responsible for convulsions.

Women with severe preeclampsia/eclampsia are at increased risk for renal failure, abruptio placentae, disseminated intravascular coagulation (DIC), ruptured liver, and pulmonary embolism. If pulmonary edema develops the maternal mortality rate is about 10% (Sibai 1988c).

A syndrome called HELLP, an acronym for *h*emolysis, *e*levated *l*iver function tests, and *l*ow *p*latelet count, has been described (Weinstein 1982, 1985). Currently it is viewed as a variant form of PIH. The maternal mortality rate for women who develop HELLP is about 2% to 4% (Sibai 1988c).

## FETAL-NEONATAL RISKS

Infants of women with hypertension during pregnancy tend to be small for gestational age (SGA). The cause is related specifically to maternal vasospasm and hypovolemia, which result in fetal hypoxia and malnutrition. In addition, the neonate may be premature because of the necessity for early delivery. Perinatal mortality associated with preeclampsia is approximately 10%, and that associated with eclampsia is 24% (Zuspan 1984).

At the time of birth, the neonate may be oversedated because of medications administered to the woman. The neonate may also have hypermagnesemia due to treatment of the woman with large doses of magnesium sulfate.

## MEDICAL THERAPY

The goals of medical management are prompt diagnosis of the disease; prevention of convulsion, hematologic complications, and renal and hepatic diseases; and birth of an uncompromised newborn as close to term as possible. Reduction of elevated blood pressure is essential in accomplishing these goals.

### Clinical Manifestations and Diagnosis

*Mild Preeclampsia* Women with mild preeclampsia may exhibit few if any symptoms. The blood pressure is elevated to 140/90 or more, or increases 30 mm Hg systolic and 15 mm Hg diastolic. Thus, a young woman who normally has a blood pressure of 90/60 would be hypertensive at 120/76. Therefore, a baseline blood pressure obtained early in the pregnancy is essential.

Generalized edema, seen as puffy face, hands, and dependent areas such as the ankles, may be present. Edema is identified by a weight gain of more than 1.5 kg/month in the second trimester or more than 0.5 kg/week in the third trimester. Edema is assessed on a 1+ to 4+ scale.

Urine testing may show a 1+ to 2+ albumin, although proteinuria is the last of the three cardinal signs to appear.

*Severe Preeclampsia* Severe preeclampsia may develop suddenly. Edema becomes generalized and readily apparent in face, hands, sacral area, lower extremities, and the abdominal wall. Edema is also characterized by an excessive weight gain of more than 0.9 kg (2 lb) over a couple of days to a week. Blood pressure is 160/100 or higher, a dipstick albumin measurement is 3+ to 4+, and the 24-hour urine protein is greater than 5 g. Hematocrit,

serum creatinine, and uric acid levels are elevated. Other characteristic symptoms are frontal headaches, blurred vision, scotomata, nausea, vomiting, irritability, hyperreflexia, cerebral disturbances, oliguria (less than 400 mL of urine in 24 hours), pulmonary edema or cyanosis, and finally, epigastric pain. The epigastric pain is often the sign of impending convulsion and is thought to be caused by increased vascular engorgement of the liver.

*Eclampsia* Eclampsia is characterized by a grand mal seizure. An elevated temperature may accompany the seizure. The seizure usually has a tonic phase, then a clonic phase. As the convulsive movements gradually cease, the woman often slips into a coma that may last for an hour or more. In other cases, the coma may be quite brief and, if the woman is not treated, convulsions may recur in a few minutes. Some women experience only one convulsion. Others may have several. Unless they occur quite frequently, the woman often regains consciousness between convulsions.

### Antepartal Management

The medical therapy for PIH depends on the severity of the disease.

*Mild Preeclampsia* The woman is placed on bed rest, primarily in the left lateral recumbent position, to decrease pressure on the vena cava, thereby increasing venous return, circulatory volume, and placental and renal perfusion. Improved renal blood flow helps decrease angiotensin II levels, promotes diuresis, and lowers blood pressure.

Diet should be well balanced and moderate to high in protein (80 to 100 g/day, or 1.5 g/kg/day) to replace protein lost in the urine. Sodium intake should be moderate, not to exceed 6 g/day. Excessively salty foods should be avoided, but sodium restriction and diuretics are no longer used in treating PIH.

Physicians are often wary about managing even mild preeclampsia on an outpatient basis because it can rapidly progress to severe preeclampsia. The woman whose blood pressure is at the lower end of the range for mild preeclampsia and who has no proteinuria may try home management. The woman and her family must understand the importance of bed rest. In such cases the woman is generally seen every one to two weeks and is carefully instructed about signs that her condition is worsening.

Tests to evaluate fetal status are done more frequently as PIH progresses. Monitoring fetal well-being is essential to achieving a safe outcome for the fetus. The following tests are used:

- Fetal movement record
- Nonstress test (NST)
- Ultrasonography for serial determination of growth

- Contraction stress test (CST)
- Estriol and creatinine determinations. Estriol (serum or urine) is being used less as a test for fetal well-being than formerly because of the lag time between fetal problem and test result, difficulty in interpretation, and expense.
- Amniocentesis to determine fetal lung maturity

These tests are described in detail in Chapter 13.

***Severe Preeclampsia*** The woman should be hospitalized. If the uterine environment is considered detrimental to fetal well-being, delivery may be the treatment of choice for both mother and fetus even if the fetus is immature (Sibai 1988a).

Other medical therapies for severe preeclampsia include the following:

- *Bed rest.* Bed rest must be complete. Stimuli that may bring on a convulsion should be reduced.
- *Diet.* A high-protein, moderate-sodium diet is given as long as the woman is alert and has no nausea or indication of impending convulsion.
- *Anticonvulsants.* Magnesium sulfate ($MgSO_4$) is the treatment of choice for convulsions. Its CNS-depressant action reduces possibility of convulsion. (See the Drug Guide for Magnesium Sulfate.)
- *Fluid and electrolyte replacement.* The goal of fluid intake is to achieve a balance between correcting hypovolemia and preventing circulatory overload. Fluid intake may be oral or supplemented with intravenous therapy. Intravenous fluids may be started "to keep lines open" in case they are needed for drug therapy even when oral intake is adequate. Electrolytes are replaced as indicated by daily serum electrolyte levels.
- *Medication.* A sedative, such as diazepam (Valium) or phenobarbital is sometimes given to encourage quiet bed rest.
- *Antihypertensives.* The drug of choice is the vasodilator hydralazine (Apresoline) (Worley 1986). It effectively lowers the blood pressure without adverse fetal effects. Hydralazine, administered by slow intravenous push or continuous infusion, is used if the diastolic pressure is higher than 110 mm Hg.

***Eclampsia*** An eclamptic seizure requires immediate effective treatment. Magnesium sulfate is given intravenously to control convulsions. Sedatives such as diazepam or amobarbitol are used only if the convulsions are not controlled by magnesium sulfate. The lungs are auscultated for pulmonary edema. The woman is observed for circulatory and renal failure and signs of cerebral hemorrhage. Furosemide (Lasix) may be given for pulmonary edema, digitalis for circulatory failure. Urinary output is monitored.

The woman is observed for signs of labor. She is also checked every 15 minutes for evidence of vaginal bleeding and abdominal rigidity, which might indicate abruptio placentae. While she is comatose she is positioned on her side with the side rails up.

Because of the severity of her condition the woman is often cared for in an intensive care unit. When the condition of the woman and the fetus are stabilized induction of labor is considered because birth is the only known cure for PIH. The woman and her partner should be given a careful explanation about her status and that of her unborn child, and the treatment they are receiving. Plans for further treatment and for delivery must be discussed with them.

## Intrapartal Management

If PIH is diagnosed, labor may be induced by intravenous oxytocin when there is evidence of fetal maturity and cervical readiness. In very severe cases, cesarean birth may be necessary even if the fetus is immature.

The woman may receive both intravenous oxytocin and magnesium sulfate simultaneously. Infusion pumps should be used and bags and tubing should be carefully labeled.

Meperidine (Demerol) or fentanyl may be given intravenously for labor. A pudendal block is often used for vaginal birth. An epidural block may be used if it is administered by a skilled anesthesiologist who is knowledgeable about PIH (Worley 1986).

Birth in the Sims' or semi-sitting position should be considered. If the lithotomy position is used, a wedge should be placed under the right buttock to displace the uterus. The wedge should also be used if birth is by cesarean. Oxygen is administered to the woman during labor if need is indicated by fetal response to the contractions.

A pediatrician or neonatal nurse practitioner must be available to care for the newborn at birth. This care giver must be aware of all amounts and times of medication the woman has received during labor.

## Postpartum Management

The woman with PIH usually improves rapidly after giving birth, although seizures can still occur during the first 48 hours postpartum. For this reason, when the hypertension is severe the woman may continue to receive hydralazine or magnesium sulfate postpartally.

## NURSING ASSESSMENT

Blood pressure is taken and recorded each antepartal visit. If the blood pressure rises or even if the normal slight decrease in blood pressure expected between 8 and 28 weeks of pregnancy does not occur, the woman should be followed closely. The woman's urine is checked for proteinuria at each visit.

# 🔬 Drug Guide

## Magnesium Sulfate (MgSO₄)

### Overview of Obstetric Action

$MgSO_4$ acts as a CNS depressant by decreasing the quantity of acetylcholine released by motor nerve impulses and thereby blocking neuromuscular transmission. This action reduces the possibility of convulsion, which is why $MgSO_4$ is used in the treatment of preeclampsia. Because magnesium sulfate secondarily relaxes smooth muscle, it may decrease the blood pressure, although it is not considered an antihypertensive, and may also decrease the frequency and intensity of uterine contractions.

### Route, Dosage, Frequency

$MgSO_4$ is generally given intravenously to control dosage more accurately and prevent overdosage. An occasional physician still prescribes intramuscular administration. However, it is painful and irritating to the tissues and does not permit the close control that IV administration does.

IV: The intravenous route allows for immediate onset of action and avoids the discomfort associated with IM administration. It must be given by infusion pump for accurate dosage.

**Loading Dose:** 3–4 g $MgSO_4$ in $D_5W$ (5% dextrose in water) is administered over a 15- to 20-minute period. (One authority recommends a loading dose of 6 g $MgSO_4$ in 100 mL $D_5W$ infused over a 15-minute period [Sibai 1987]).

**Maintenance Dose:** Based on serum magnesium levels and deep tendon reflexes, 1–2 g/hr is administered.

### Maternal Contraindications

Extreme care is necessary in administration to women with impaired renal function because the drug is eliminated by the kidneys and toxic magnesium levels may develop quickly.

### Maternal Side Effects

Most maternal side effects are related to magnesium toxicity. Sweating, a feeling of warmth, flushing, nausea, slurred speech, depression or absence of reflexes, muscular weakness, hypothermia, oliguria, confusion, circulatory collapse, and respiratory paralysis are all possible side effects. Rapid administration of large doses may cause cardiac arrest.

### Effects on Fetus/Neonate

The drug readily crosses the placenta. Some authorities suggest that transient decrease in fetal heart rate (FHR) variability may occur, while others report that no change occurred. Similarly some report low Apgar scores, hypotonia, and respiratory depression in the newborn, while others report no ill effects. Sibai (1987) suggests that the majority of ill effects observed in the newborn may actually be related to fetal growth retardation, prematurity, or perinatal asphyxia.

### Nursing Considerations

1. Monitor the blood pressure closely during administration.

2. Monitor respirations closely. If the rate is less than 14–16/min, magnesium toxicity may be developing, and further assessments are indicated. Many protocols require stopping the medication if the respiratory rate falls below 12/min.

3. Assess knee jerk (patellar tendon reflex) for evidence of diminished or absent reflexes. Loss of reflexes is often the first sign of developing toxicity.

4. Determine urinary output. Output less than 100 mL during the preceding 4-hour period may result in the accumulation of toxic levels of magnesium.

5. If the respirations or urinary output fall below specified levels or if the reflexes are diminished or absent, no further magnesium should be administered until these factors return to normal.

6. The antagonist of magnesium sulfate is calcium. Consequently an ampule of calcium gluconate should be available at the bedside. The usual dose is 1 g given IV by a physician over a period of about 3 minutes.

7. Monitor fetal heart tones continuously with IV administration.

8. Continue $MgSO_4$ infusion for approximately 24 hours after birth as prophylaxis against postpartum seizures.

Note: Protocols for magnesium sulfate administration may vary somewhat according to agency policy. Consequently individuals are referred to their own agency protocols for specific guidelines.

---

If hospitalization becomes necessary the nurse then assesses the following:

- *Blood pressure.* Blood pressure should be determined every two to four hours, more frequently if indicated by medication or other changes in the woman's status.

- *Temperature.* Temperature should be determined every four hours; every two hours if elevated.

- *Pulse and respirations.* Pulse rate and respiration should be determined along with blood pressure.

- *Fetal heart rate.* The fetal heart rate should be determined with the blood pressure or monitored continuously with the electronic fetal monitor if the situation indicates.

- *Urinary output.* Every voiding should be measured. Frequently, the woman will have an in-dwelling catheter. In this case, hourly urine output can be assessed. Output should be 700 mL or greater in 24 hours or at least 30 mL per hour.

- *Urine protein.* Urinary protein is determined hourly if an in-dwelling catheter is in place or with each voiding. Readings of 3+ or 4+ indicate loss of 5 g or more of protein in 24 hours.

- *Urine specific gravity.* Specific gravity of the urine should be determined hourly or with each voiding. Readings over 1.040 correlate with oliguria and proteinuria.

- *Edema.* The face (especially eyelids and cheekbone area), fingers, hands, arms (ulnar surface and wrist), legs (tibial surface), ankles, feet, and sacral area are inspected and palpated for edema. The degree of pitting is determined by pressing over bony areas.

- *Weight.* The woman is weighed daily at the same time, wearing the same robe or gown and slippers. Weighing may be omitted if the woman is to maintain strict bed rest.

- *Pulmonary edema.* The woman is observed for coughing. The lungs are auscultated for moist respirations.

- *Deep tendon reflexes.* The woman is assessed for evidence of hyperreflexia in the brachial, wrist, patellar, or Achilles tendons (Table 12.4). The patellar reflex is the easiest to assess. Clonus should also be assessed by vigorously dorsiflexing the foot while the knee is held in a fixed position. Normally no clonus is present. If it is present it is measured as one to four beats and is recorded as such.

- *Placental separation.* The woman should be assessed hourly for vaginal bleeding and/or uterine rigidity.

- *Headache.* The woman should be questioned about the existence and location of any headache.

- *Visual disturbance.* The woman should be questioned about any visual blurring or changes, or scotomata.

- *Epigastric pain.* The woman should be asked about any epigastric pain. It is important to differentiate it

## Essential Nursing Diagnoses to Consider

### Pregnancy-Induced Hypertension (PIH)

Potential activity intolerance
Anxiety
Ineffective family coping
Ineffective individual coping
Diversional activity deficit
Altered family processes
Fear
Fluid volume excess: (actual or potential)
Potential for injury
Knowledge deficit
Impaired physical mobility
Noncompliance
Sexual dysfunction
Altered tissue perfusion
Self esteem disturbance
Defensive coping
Ineffective denial
Altered role performance

from simple heartburn, which tends to be familiar and less intense.

- *Laboratory blood tests.* Daily tests of hematocrit to measure hemoconcentration; blood urea nitrogen, creatinine, and uric acid levels to assess kidney function; serum estriol determinations to assess fetal status; clotting studies for any indication of thrombocytopenia or DIC; and electrolyte levels for deficiencies are all indicated.

- *Level of consciousness.* The woman is observed for alertness, mood changes, and any signs of impending convulsion or coma.

- *Emotional response and level of understanding.* The woman's emotional response should be carefully assessed, so that support and teaching can be planned accordingly.

In addition, the nurse continues to assess the effects of any medications administered. Since the administration of prescribed medications is an important aspect of care, the nurse is, of course, familiar with the more commonly used medications, their purpose, implications, and associated untoward or toxic effects.

### NURSING DIAGNOSIS

Examples of nursing diagnoses that might apply are listed in Essential Nursing Diagnoses to Consider— Pregnancy-Induced Hypertension. See also the Nursing Care Plan for Pregnancy-Induced Hypertension.

## Table 12.4 Deep Tendon Reflex Rating Scale

| Rating | Assessment |
| --- | --- |
| 4+ | Hyperactive; very brisk, jerky, or clonic response; abnormal |
| 3+ | Brisker than average; may not be abnormal |
| 2+ | Average response; normal |
| 1+ | Diminished response; low normal |
| 0 | No response; abnormal |

## Nursing Care Plan

## Pregnancy-Induced Hypertension (PIH) (Preeclampsia/Eclampsia)

### Client Assessment

#### Nursing History

1. Identification of predisposing factors in client history:
   a. Primigravida
   b. Presence of diabetes mellitus
   c. Multiple pregnancy
   d. Hydramnios
   e. Gestational trophoblastic disease
   f. Preexisting vascular or renal disease
   g. Adolescent or older maternal age

#### Physical Examination

1. Blood pressure elevated (compare with baseline if possible)

2. Presence of edema as indicated by weight gain, puffy hands and feet; requires ongoing assessment for development of periorbital or facial edema

3. Presence of hyperreflexia and clonus

4. Presence of headache, visual disturbances, drowsiness, epigastric pain

5. Observe any vaginal bleeding, abdominal tenderness, or signs of labor

#### Diagnostic Studies

1. Evaluate urinary output for quantity and specific gravity.

2. Urine for urinary protein: 1 g protein/24 hr = 1–2+; 5 g protein/24 hr = 3–4+.

3. Hematocrit: Elevation of hematocrit implies hemoconcentration, which occurs as fluid leaves the intravascular space and enters the extravascular space.

4. BUN: Not usually elevated except in women with cardiovascular or renal disease.

5. Blood uric acid appears to correlate well with the severity of the preeclampsia-eclampsia (Note: thiazide diuretics can cause significant increases in uric acid levels).

| Nursing Diagnosis/Goal | Nursing Interventions | Rationale/Evaluation |
| --- | --- | --- |

#### Nursing Diagnosis:

**Pattern 1: Exchanging**
Fluid volume deficit related to fluid shift from intravascular to extravascular space secondary to vasospasm

Assess BP every 1–4 hr, using same arm, with woman in same position.

Weigh daily; gain of 1 kg/wk or more in second trimester or ½ kg/wk or more in third trimester is suggestive of PIH.

Assess edema:
+(1+) Minimal; slight edema of pedal and pretibial areas
++(2+) Marked edema of lower extremities
+++(3+) Edema of hands, face, lower abdominal wall, and sacrum
++++(4+) Anasarca with ascites

Maintain on bed rest. Encourage left lateral recumbent position.

Maintain normal salt intake (4–6 g/24 hr).

#### Rationale:

Blood pressure can fluctuate hourly; BP increases as a result of increased peripheral resistance due to peripheral vasoconstriction and arteriolar spasm.

Weight gain and edema are due to sodium and water retention.

Decreased plasma colloid osmotic pressure causes movement of fluid from the intravascular to extravascular space.

Bed rest produces an increase in GFR.

Normal salt intake is now advised, but excessive salt intake may make the condition worse.

## Nursing Care Plan

## Pregnancy-Induced Hypertension (PIH) (Preeclampsia/Eclampsia) *(continued)*

| Nursing Diagnosis/Goal | Nursing Interventions | Rationale/Evaluation |
|---|---|---|
| **Client Goal:**<br><br>Fluid volume deficit will be controlled and intravascular volume will be maintained as evidenced by decreased edema, adequate urine output, normal specific gravity, decreased proteinuria, and improved hematocrit. | Report urine output < 30 mL/hr or urine specific gravity > 1.040.<br><br>Test urine for protein hourly or as ordered. Maintain in-dwelling catheter.<br><br>Evaluate hematocrit levels regularly.<br><br><br><br>Provide adequate protein: 1.5 g/kg/24 hr for incipient and mild preeclampsia. | Renal plasma flow and glomerular filtration are decreased in PIH. Increasing oliguria indicates a worsening condition.<br><br>Proteinuria results from swelling of the endothelium of the glomerular capillaries.<br><br>Decreased intravascular fluid volume leads to increased hematocrit level because of change in proportion of RBCs to volume of fluid.<br><br>Plasma proteins affect movement of intravascular and extravascular fluids.<br><br>**Evaluation:**<br><br>Woman's edema decreases, urine output remains normal, proteinuria decreases, and hematocrit is within normal limits. |
| **Nursing Diagnosis:**<br><br>Pattern 8: Knowing<br>Knowledge deficit related to PIH, its treatment, and the implications for the woman and her unborn child | 1. Discuss PIH, its implications for client and fetus/neonate.<br><br>2. Explain purpose and importance of treatment measures.<br><br>3. Work with woman and support person to plan ways for the family to deal with the woman's hospitalization. | **Rationale:**<br><br>Illness and hospitalization during pregnancy is usually unanticipated and may cause a major disruption in a couple's life. With thorough information they are better able to understand the condition and its implications. |
| **Client Goal:**<br><br>Woman will clearly understand her condition and its implications as evidenced by her ability to discuss PIH and its therapy and her cooperation with the treatment regimen. | | **Evaluation:**<br><br>Woman is able to discuss PIH, its therapy and implications, and cooperates with the care regimen. |
| **Nursing Diagnosis:**<br><br>Pattern 1: Exchanging<br>Potential for injury related to possibility of convulsion secondary to cerebral vasospasm or edema | Monitor knee, ankle, and biceps reflexes and beats of clonus.<br><br>Promote bed rest. Encourage woman to rest quietly in a darkened, quiet room.<br><br>Limit visitors.<br><br>Administer magnesium sulfate per physician order:<br>1. IV dose: 3–4 g loading dose MgSO$_4$ followed by continuous infusion at a rate of 1–2 g/hr. | **Rationale:**<br><br>Hyperreflexia indicates central nervous system (CNS) irritability.<br><br><br><br>Magnesium sulfate is a cerebral depressant; it also reduces neuromuscular irritability and causes vasodilation and drop in BP.<br><br>Therapeutic blood level is 4–7 mEq/L. |

*(continues)*

# Nursing Care Plan

## Pregnancy-Induced Hypertension (PIH) (Preeclampsia/Eclampsia) *(continued)*

| Nursing Diagnosis/Goal | Nursing Interventions | Rationale/Evaluation |
|---|---|---|
| | 2. IM dose: 10 g of 50% $MgSO_4$ injected deep IM (½ in the upper outer quadrants of each buttock) using a 20-gauge, 3-inch needle. (1.0 mL of 2% lidocaine may be added to the syringe to decrease the discomfort.) | |
| | Monitor magnesium levels frequently to prevent overdose (either 2 hours after beginning infusion or prior to next IM dose). | |
| | Before administering subsequent doses of magnesium sulfate, check reflexes (knee, ankle, biceps), respirations and urine output. | Knee jerk disappears when magnesium sulfate blood levels are 7 to 10 mEq/L. Toxic signs and symptoms develop with increased blood levels; respiratory arrest can be associated with blood levels of 10 to 15 mEq/L. |
| | Do not give magnesium sulfate if: 1. Reflexes are absent. 2. Respirations are <12/min 3. <100 mL urine output in past four hours | Cardiac arrest can occur if blood levels are 30 mEq/L (Worley 1986). Kidneys are only route for excretion of magnesium sulfate. |
| | Have calcium gluconate available. | Calcium gluconate is antidote for magnesium sulfate. |
| | Maintain seizure precautions: 1. Keep room quiet, darkened. 2. Have emergency equipment available—$O_2$, suction, padded tongue blade. 3. Pad side rails. 4. Educate other care givers regarding the possibility of convulsions and appropriate actions. | Quiet reduces stimuli.  Padding protects client. |
| | Provide supportive care during convulsion: 1. Place tongue blade or airway in patient's mouth, if can be done without force. 2. Suction nasopharynx as necessary. 3. Administer oxygen. 4. Note type of seizure and length of time it lasts. After seizure, assess for uterine contractions. Assess fetal status. | Acts to maintain airway and to prevent patient from biting tongue  Removes mucus and secretions Promotes oxygenation Precipitous labor may start during seizures.  Continuous fetal monitoring is necessary to identify fetal stress. |
| **Client Goal:** Woman will not develop seizures, and signs that her condition is worsening will not develop. | | **Evaluation:** No seizures develop; client's condition improves. |

## Nursing Care Plan

### Pregnancy-Induced Hypertension (PIH) (Preeclampsia/Eclampsia) (*continued*)

| Nursing Diagnosis/Goal | Nursing Interventions | Rationale/Evaluation |
|---|---|---|
| **Nursing Diagnosis:**<br><br>Pattern 1: Exchanging<br>Potential for injury to fetus related to inadequate placental perfusion secondary to vasospasm or possible abruptio placentae. | Encourage mother to assume a side-lying position.<br><br>Evaluate results of serial fetal assessments such as NST, CST, ultrasound, biophysical profile.<br>Report any signs of abruptio placentae such as uterine tenderness, vaginal bleeding, change in fetal activity, change in fetal heart rate, sustained abdominal pain.<br>If labor begins, monitor fetus closely with electronic fetal monitor. Report evidence of late decelerations. | **Rationale:**<br><br>Side-lying position avoids pressure on vena cava and promotes optimum placental perfusion.<br><br>Fetal assessment determines fetal status and ability to withstand stress of labor, as well as fetal maturity.<br>Vasospasm and high blood pressure of PIH increase the risk of abruptio placentae.<br><br>Because of decreased placental perfusion due to vasospasm, fetus may have difficulty tolerating the stress of labor and cesarean birth may be necessary. |
| **Client Goal:**<br><br>Fetus will tolerate the stress of maternal condition without injury as evidenced by normal intrauterine growth, reactive NST, and/or negative CST. | | **Evaluation:**<br><br>Fetus develops normally and IUGR is avoided. Fetus tolerates stress of labor well. |
| **Nursing Diagnosis:**<br><br>Pattern 1: Exchanging<br>Potential for injury related to development of hematologic and hepatic abnormalities secondary to the HELLP syndrome | 1. Obtain blood samples as ordered to evaluate hemoglobin and hematocrit, SGOT, SGPT, and platelet count.<br>2. Monitor test results and report abnormal findings.<br>3. Report signs of hemolytic anemia including pallor, fatigue, anorexia, and dyspnea.<br>4. Report signs of liver dysfunction including nausea and vomiting, right upper quadrant pain, jaundice, and malaise.<br>5. Report signs of developing DIC immediately. Signs include epistaxis, hematuria, petechiae, bleeding gums, GI tract bleeding, and retinal or conjunctival hemorrhages. | **Rationale:**<br><br>HELLP syndrome refers to hemolysis of RBCs (causing signs of anemia), elevated liver enzymes because of liver damage (causing jaundice, etc) and low platelet count related to severe vasospasm and developing DIC. |
| **Client Goal:**<br><br>Woman will not develop injury from the development of complications, as evidenced by normal hemoglobin levels, absence of signs of anemia, normal liver function tests, and adequate platelet count. | | **Evaluation:**<br><br>Woman does not develop signs of hematologic and hepatic complications. |

## NURSING PLAN AND IMPLEMENTATION
### Provision of Support and Teaching

A woman with PIH has several major concerns. She may fear losing her fetus; she may worry about her personal relationship with her other children and her personal and sexual relationship with her partner; she may be concerned about finances; she may also feel bored and a little resentful if she faces prolonged bed rest. The nurse should help the couple identify and discuss their concerns. The nurse can offer information and explanations if certain aspects of therapy are creating difficulty. The nurse can also refer the couple to community resources such as homemaking services, a support group for the partner, or a hot-line.

The woman should know which symptoms are significant and should be reported at once. Usually the woman with mild preeclampsia is seen every one to two weeks, but she may need to come in earlier if symptoms indicate that her condition is worsening.

The development of severe preeclampsia is a cause for increased concern for the woman and her family. The most immediate concerns usually are about the prognosis for the woman and for her fetus. The nurse can explain medical therapy and its purpose and offer honest, hopeful information. The nurse should keep the couple informed of fetal status and should also take the time to discuss other concerns the couple may express. The nurse provides as much information as possible and seeks other sources of information or aid for the family as needed. The nurse can offer to contact a minister or hospital chaplain for additional support if the couple so chooses.

### Prevention of Convulsion

The nurse maintains a quiet, low-stimulus environment for the woman. The woman should be placed in a private room and where visitors are limited. The woman should maintain the left lateral recumbent position most of the time, with side rails up for her protection. She should not receive phone calls because the phone ringing may be too jarring. Bright lights and sudden loud noises may precipitate seizures in the woman with severe preeclampsia.

### Provision of Effective Care and Support If Convulsions Develop

The occurrence of a convulsion is frightening to any family members who may be present, although the woman will not be able to recall it when she becomes conscious. Therefore, offering explanations to the family member, and to the woman herself later, is essential.

When the tonic phase of the contraction begins, the woman should be turned to her side (if she is not already in that position) to aid circulation to the placenta. Her head should be turned face down to allow saliva to drain from her mouth. Attempting to insert a padded tongue blade has been questioned, but if it can be done without force, injury may be prevented to the woman's mouth. The side rails should be padded, or a pillow put between the woman and each side rail.

After 15 to 20 seconds the clonic phase starts. When the thrashing subsides, intensive monitoring and therapy begin. An oral airway is inserted, the woman's nasopharynx is suctioned, and oxygen administration is begun by nasal catheter. Fetal heart tones are monitored continuously. Maternal vital signs are monitored every five minutes until they are stable, then every 15 minutes.

### Promotion of Maternal and Fetal Well-Being During Labor and Delivery

The laboring woman with PIH must receive all the care and precautions necessary for normal labor as well as those required for managing PIH. The woman is kept positioned on her left side as much as possible. Both the woman and the fetus are monitored carefully throughout labor. The nurse notes the progress of labor and is alert to detect signs of worsening PIH or its complications.

During the second stage the woman is encouraged to push in the side-lying position if possible. Birth is in the side-lying position, or if the lithotomy position is used, a wedge is placed under the woman's hip.

A family member is encouraged to stay with the woman as much as possible. The woman in labor and the family member or support person should be kept informed of the progress and plan of care. Their wishes concerning the birth experience should be respected whenever possible. The woman should be cared for by the same nurses throughout her hospital stay.

### Promotion of Maternal Well-Being During the Postpartal Period

Because the woman with PIH is hypovolemic, even normal blood loss can be serious. The amount of vaginal bleeding should be assessed and the woman should be observed for signs of shock. Blood pressure and pulse are monitored every four hours for 48 hours. Hematocrit is checked daily. The woman is assessed for any further signs of PIH. Intake and output are measured. Normal postpartum diuresis helps eliminate edema and is a favorable sign.

Postpartal depression may develop after such a difficult pregnancy. To help prevent it, opportunities for frequent maternal-infant contact are provided and family members are encouraged to visit. The couple may have many questions and the nurse should be available for discussion. The couple should be given family planning information. Oral contraceptives may be used if the woman's blood pressure has returned to normal by the time they are prescribed (usually four to six weeks postpartum) (Worley 1986).

For a brief summary of PIH, see Essential Facts to Remember—Pregnancy-Induced Hypertension.

## EVALUATION

Anticipated outcomes of nursing care include the following:

- The woman is able to explain PIH, its implications for her pregnancy, the treatment regimen, and possible complications.
- The woman suffers no eclamptic convulsions.
- The woman and her care givers detect evidence of increasing severity of the PIH or possible complications early so that appropriate treatment measures can be instituted.
- The woman successfully delivers a healthy newborn.

## ● Chronic Hypertensive Disease

Chronic hypertension exists when the blood pressure is 140/90 or higher before pregnancy or before the twentieth week of gestation and persists indefinitely following delivery. If the diastolic blood pressure is greater than 80 mm Hg during the second trimester, chronic hypertension should be suspected (Zuspan 1984). The cause of chronic hypertension has not been determined. For the majority of chronic hypertensive women the disease is mild.

The goal of care is to prevent the development of preeclampsia and to ensure normal growth of the fetus. The woman is seen regularly for prenatal care (at least every two weeks). Ultrasound is done early to date the pregnancy, and then at 20 to 26 weeks and at 32 weeks to detect IUGR.

The woman is taught the importance of daily rest periods in the left lateral recumbent position and also learns to monitor her blood pressure at home. A diet that provides a protein intake of 1.5 g/kg body weight/day with sodium restricted to ≤ 5 g/day is prescribed. Antihypertensive medication is continued throughout pregnancy. The drug of choice is methyldopa (Aldomet) (Repke 1987).

Nursing care is directed at providing sufficient information so that the woman can meet her health care needs. She is given information about her diet, the importance of regular rest, her medications, the need for blood pressure control, and any procedures used to monitor the well-being of her fetus.

## ● Chronic Hypertension with Superimposed PIH

Preeclampsia may develop in a woman previously found to have chronic hypertension. When elevations of systolic blood pressure 30 mm Hg above the baseline or of diastolic blood pressure 15 to 20 mm Hg above the baseline are discovered on two occasions at least six hours apart, proteinuria develops, or edema occurs in the upper half of the body (Gant and Worley 1980), the woman needs

## Essential Facts to Remember

### Pregnancy-Induced Hypertension (PIH)

- PIH is characterized by elevated blood pressure after the 20th week of pregnancy.
- Preeclampsia, a form of PIH, involves elevated BP, edema, and proteinuria. It may be mild or severe.
- A woman with preeclampsia who has a seizure is said to have eclampsia.
- The exact cause of PIH is unknown.
- Vasospasm is responsible for most of the clinical manifestations including the CNS signs of headache, hyperreflexia, and convulsion. Vasospasm also causes poor placental perfusion, which leads to IUGR.
- The only known cure for PIH is birth of the infant.
- Management is supportive and includes anticonvulsant therapy, generally with MgSO$_4$; prevention of renal, hepatic, and hematologic complications; and careful assessment of fetal well-being.
- Nursing care focuses on implementing appropriate interventions based on the data gathered from regular assessment of vital signs, reflexes, degree of edema and proteinuria, response to therapy, fetal status, detection of developing complications, knowledge level and psychologic state of the woman and her family.

close monitoring and careful management. Her condition often progresses quickly to eclampsia, sometimes before 30 weeks of pregnancy.

## ● Late or Transient Hypertension

Late hypertension exists when transient elevation of blood pressure occurs during labor or in the early postpartal period, returning to normal within 10 days postpartum (Gant and Worley 1980).

## ● CARE OF THE WOMAN AT RISK FOR RH SENSITIZATION

Rh sensitization results from an antigen-antibody immunologic reaction within the body. Sensitization most commonly occurs when an Rh-negative woman carries an Rh-positive fetus, either to term or terminated by spontaneous or induced abortion. It can also occur if an Rh-negative nonpregnant woman receives an Rh-positive blood transfusion.

The red blood cells from the fetus invade the maternal circulation, thereby stimulating the production of Rh antibodies. Because this usually occurs at birth, the first offspring is not affected. However, in a subsequent pregnancy Rh antibodies cross the placenta and enter the fetal circulation, causing severe hemolysis. The destruction of fetal red blood cells causing anemia in the fetus is proportional to the extent of maternal sensitization (Figure 12.4).

## ● Fetal-Neonatal Risks

Although maternal sensitization can now be prevented by appropriate administration of RhoGAM, infants still die of Rh hemolytic disease. If treatment is not initiated, the anemia resulting from this disorder can cause marked fetal edema, called **hydrops fetalis.** Congestive heart failure may result, as well as marked jaundice (called *icterus gravis*), which can lead to neurologic damage (kernicterus). This severe hemolytic syndrome is known as **erythroblastosis fetalis.**

## ● Screening for Rh Incompatibility and Sensitization

At the first prenatal visit (1) a history is taken of previous sensitization, abortions, blood transfusions, or children who developed jaundice or anemia during the neonatal period; (2) maternal blood type (ABO) and Rh factor are determined and a routine Rh antibody screen is done; and (3) presence of other medical complications such as diabetes, infections, or hypertension is identified.

When assessment has identified the Rh-negative woman who may be pregnant with an Rh-positive fetus, an antibody screen (indirect Coombs' test) is done to determine if the woman is sensitized (has developed isoimmunity) to the Rh antigen. The indirect Coombs' test measures the number of antibodies in the maternal blood.

Negative antibody titers and a negative indirect Coombs' test can consistently identify the fetus *not* at risk. However, the titers cannot reliably point out the fetus in danger, since titer level does not correlate with the severity of the disease. Antibody titers are determined periodically throughout the pregnancy. If the maternal antibody titer is 1:16 or greater, an optical density (ΔOD) analysis of the amniotic fluid is performed. This optical density analysis measures the amount of pigment from the breakdown of red blood cells and can determine the severity of the hemolytic process.

Ultrasound scanning can help determine the fetal condition. It would demonstrate an increase in fetal heart size, ascites, hydramnios, and subcutaneous edema. Placental size and texture are also indicators of fetal condition (Scott 1986a).

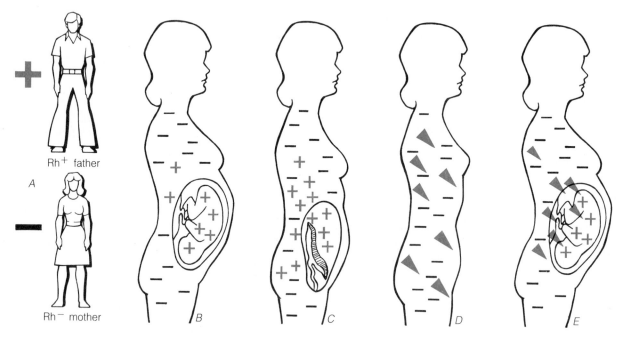

*Figure 12.4  Rh isoimmunization sequence. (A) Rh-positive father and Rh-negative mother. (B) Pregnancy with Rh-positive fetus. Some Rh-positive blood enters the mother's blood. (C) As the placenta separates, the mother is further exposed to Rh-positive blood. (D) The mother is sensitized to Rh-positive blood; anti–Rh-positive antibodies are formed. (E) In subsequent pregnancies with an Rh-positive fetus, Rh-positive red blood cells are attacked by the anti–Rh-positive maternal antibodies, causing hemolysis of red blood cells in the fetus.*

## • *Medical Therapy*

The goal of medical management is the birth of a mature fetus who has not developed severe hemolysis in utero. This requires early identification and treatment of maternal conditions that predispose to hemolytic disease, identification and evaluation of the Rh-sensitized woman, coordinated obstetric-pediatric treatment for the seriously affected neonate, and prevention of Rh sensitization if none is present.

### ANTEPARTAL MANAGEMENT

Two primary interventions can help the fetus whose blood cells are being destroyed by maternal antibodies: early birth and intrauterine transfusion, both of which carry risks. Ideally, birth should be delayed until fetal maturity is confirmed at about 36–37 weeks. Only fetuses with a prognosis of death before 32 weeks as indicated by the $\Delta OD$ should be given intrauterine transfusion (Pritchard et al 1985).

### POSTPARTAL MANAGEMENT

The Rh-negative mother who has no antibody titer (indirect Coombs' negative, nonsensitized) and who has delivered an Rh-positive fetus (direct Coombs' negative) is given an intramuscular injection of RhIgG (**RhoGAM**), an anti-$Rh_0$(D) gamma globulin. She must receive RhoGAM within 72 hours of childbirth so that she does not have time to produce antibodies to fetal cells that entered her bloodstream when the placenta separated. Administration of RhIgG in a dose of 300 μg generally provides temporary passive immunity to the mother, which prevents the development of permanent active immunity (antibody formation).

When the woman is Rh negative and not sensitized and the father is Rh positive or unknown, RhoGAM is also given after each abortion, ectopic pregnancy, or amniocentesis. If abortion or ectopic pregnancy occurs in the first trimester, a smaller (50 μg) dose of RhIgG (MICRhoGAM® or Mini-Gamulin Rh®) is used. A full dose is used following second trimester amniocentesis. Since transplacental hemorrhage is possible during pregnancy, RhoGAM is generally administered prophylactically at 28 weeks' gestation to prevent sensitization. RhoGAM is not given to the neonate or the father. It is not effective for and should not be given to a previously sensitized woman. However, sometimes after birth or an abortion, the results of the blood test do not clearly show whether the mother is already sensitized to the Rh antigen or not. In such cases, the anti-$Rh_0$(D) immunoglobulin should be given as it will cause no harm. For the major considerations in caring for an Rh-negative woman see Essential Facts to Remember—Rh Sensitization. The treatment of

## Essential Facts to Remember

### Rh Sensitization

When trying to work through Rh problems, the nurse should remember the following:

- A potential problem exists when an Rh− mother and an Rh+ father conceive a child that is Rh+.
- In this situation, the mother may become sensitized or produce antibodies to her fetus's Rh+ blood.

The following tests are used to detect sensitization:

- Indirect Coombs' tests—done on the mother's blood to measure the number of Rh+ antibodies.
- Direct Coombs' test—done on the infant's blood to detect antibody-coated Rh+ RBCs.

Based on the results of these tests, the following may be done:

- If the mother's indirect Coombs' test is negative and the infant's direct Coombs' test is negative, the mother is given RhoGAM within 72 hours of birth.
- If the mother's indirect Coombs' test is positive and her Rh+ infant has a positive direct Coombs' test, RhoGAM is *not* given; in this case the infant is carefully monitored for hemolytic disease.
- It is recommended that RhoGAM be given at 28 weeks antenatally to decrease possible transplacental bleeding concerns.
- RhoGAM is also administered after each abortion (spontaneous or therapeutic), ectopic pregnancy, or amniocentesis.

the newborn with isoimmune hemolytic disease is discussed in Chapter 24.

## • *Nursing Assessment*

As part of the initial prenatal history the nurse asks the mother if she knows her blood type and Rh factor. Many woman are aware that they are Rh negative and that this status has implications for pregnancy. If the woman knows she is Rh negative, the nurse can assess the woman's knowledge of what that means. The nurse can also ask the woman if she has ever received RhoGAM, if she has had any previous pregnancies and what their outcome was, and if she knows her partner's Rh factor. Should the partner be Rh negative, there is no risk to the fetus, who will also be Rh negative.

If the woman does not know what Rh type she is, intervention cannot begin until the initial laboratory data are obtained. Once that is done, the nurse plans interventions based on the findings.

If the woman becomes sensitized during her pregnancy, nursing assessment focuses on the knowledge level and coping skills of the woman and her family. The nurse also provides ongoing assessment during procedures to evaluate fetal well-being, such as ultrasound and amniocentesis.

Postpartally, the nurse reviews data about the Rh type of the fetus. If the fetus is Rh positive, the mother is Rh negative, and no sensitization has occurred, nursing assessment reveals the need to administer RhoGAM.

## ● Nursing Diagnosis

Nursing diagnoses that might apply include:

● Knowledge deficit related to a lack of understanding of the need to receive RhoGAM and when it should be administered

● Ineffective individual coping related to depression secondary to the development of indications of the need for fetal exchange transfusion

## ● Nursing Plan and Implementation

During the antepartal period the nurse explains the mechanisms involved in isoimmunization and answers any questions the woman and her partner may have. It is imperative that the woman understand the importance of receiving RhoGAM after every spontaneous or therapeutic abortion or ectopic pregnancy. The nurse also explains the purpose of the RhoGAM administered at 28 weeks' gestation if the woman is not sensitized.

If the woman is sensitized to the Rh factor, it poses a threat to any Rh-positive fetus she carries. The nurse provides emotional support to the family to help them deal with their grief and any feelings of guilt about the infant's condition. Should an intrauterine transfusion become necessary, the nurse continues to provide emotional support while also assuming his or her responsibilities as part of the health care team.

During labor the nurse caring for an Rh-negative woman who has not been sensitized ensures that the woman's blood is assessed for any antibodies and also has been cross-matched for RhoGAM. On the postpartum unit the nurse generally is responsible for administering the RhoGAM intramuscularly if the newborn is Rh-positive.

## ● Evaluation

Anticipated outcomes of nursing care include the following:

● The woman is able to explain the process of Rh sen-

sitization and its implications for her unborn child and for subsequent pregnancies.

● If the woman has not been sensitized, she is able to explain the importance of receiving RhoGAM when necessary and cooperates with the recommended dosage schedule.

● The woman successfully delivers a healthy newborn.

● If complications develop for the fetus (or newborn) they are detected quickly and therapy is instituted.

## ● CARE OF THE WOMAN AT RISK DUE TO ABO INCOMPATIBILITY

ABO incompatibility is rather common (occurring in 12% of pregnancies) but rarely causes significant hemolysis. In most cases ABO incompatibility is limited to type O mothers with a type A or B fetus. Group O infants, because they have no antigenic sites on the red blood cells, are never affected regardless of the mother's blood type. The incompatibility occurs as a result of the interaction of antibodies present in maternal serum and the antigen sites on the fetal red blood cells.

Anti-A and anti-B antibodies are naturally occurring; that is, women are naturally exposed to the A and B antigens through the foods they eat and through exposure to infection by gram negative bacteria. As a result, some women have high serum anti-A and anti-B titers before they become pregnant. Once the woman becomes pregnant, the maternal serum anti-A and anti-B antibodies cross the placenta and produce hemolysis of the fetal red blood cells. With ABO incompatibility the first infant is frequently involved, and no relationship exists between the appearance of the disease and repeated sensitization from one pregnancy to the next.

Unlike Rh incompatibility, treatment is never warranted antepartally. As part of the initial assessment, however, the nurse should note whether the potential for an ABO incompatibility exists. This alerts care givers so that following birth the newborn can be assessed carefully for the development of hyperbilirubinemia (see Chapter 24).

## ● CARE OF THE WOMAN REQUIRING SURGERY DURING PREGNANCY

While elective surgery should be delayed until the postpartal period, essential surgery can generally be undertaken during pregnancy. Surgery does pose some risks. The incidence of spontaneous abortion is increased for women who have surgery in the first trimester. There is also an increased incidence of fetal mortality and of low-birth-weight (less than 2500 g) infants. Finally, when pelvic surgery is necessary the incidence of premature labor increases (Triolo 1985).

Although general preoperative and postoperative care is similar for gravid and nongravid women, special considerations must be kept in mind whenever the surgical client is pregnant. The early second trimester is the best time to operate because there is less risk of causing spontaneous abortion or early labor, and the uterus is not so large as to impinge on the abdominal field.

To prevent uterine compression of major blood vessels while the woman is supine, the care giver must place a wedge under her right hip to tilt the uterus during both surgery and recovery. Because of the decreased intestinal motility and delayed gastric emptying that occurs in pregnancy, the risk of vomiting when anesthetics are given and during the postoperative period is increased. Thus, inserting a nasogastric tube is recommended before a pregnant woman has major surgery.

Pregnancy causes increased secretions of the respiratory tract and engorgement of the nasal mucous membrane, often making breathing through the nose difficult. Because of this, pregnant women often need an endotracheal tube for respiratory support during surgery.

Care givers must guard against maternal hypoxia. During surgery, uterine circulation is decreased, and fetal oxygenation may be reduced quickly. Fetal heart tones must be monitored electronically before, during, and after surgery. Blood loss is also closely monitored throughout the procedure and following it.

## ● CARE OF THE WOMAN SUFFERING TRAUMA FROM AN ACCIDENT

Accidents and injury are not uncommon during pregnancy. Accidental injury may complicate 6% to 7% of all pregnancies (Patterson 1984).

Fortunately, most accidents produce minor injuries, and the outcome of the pregnancy is seldom affected. Late in pregnancy, when balance and coordination are adversely affected, the woman may fall. Her protruding abdomen is vulnerable to a variety of minor injuries. The fetus is usually well protected by the amniotic fluid, which distributes the force of a blow equally in all directions, and by the muscle layers of the uterus and abdominal wall. In early pregnancy, while the uterus is still in the pelvis, it is shielded from blows by the surrounding pelvic organs, muscles, and bony structures.

Trauma that causes concern includes blunt trauma, from an automobile accident, for example; penetrating abdominal injuries, such as knife and gunshot wounds; and the complications of maternal shock, premature labor, and spontaneous abortion.

Maternal mortality most often occurs from head

trauma or hemorrhage. Uterine rupture may result from strong deceleration forces in an automobile accident with or without seat belts. Traumatic separation of the placenta can occur; it results in a high rate of fetal mortality. Premature labor is another serious hazard to the fetus, often following rupture of membranes during an accident. Premature labor can ensue even if the woman is not injured.

Treatment of major injuries during pregnancy focuses initially on life-saving measures for the woman. Specifically, such measures include establishing an airway, controlling external bleeding, and administering intravenous fluid to alleviate shock. The woman must be kept on her left side to avoid further hypotension. Fetal heart tones are monitored. Exploratory surgery is necessary following abdominal trauma to determine the extent of injuries. If the fetus is near term and the uterus has been damaged, cesarean delivery is performed. If the fetus is still immature, the uterus can often be repaired, and the pregnancy continues until term.

## ● CARE OF THE BATTERED PREGNANT WOMAN

There are conflicting opinions about whether family violence increases or decreases during pregnancy. However, women who have been abused are usually at risk for abuse during pregnancy (Hillard 1985). The first step toward helping the battered woman is to identify her. She needs support, confidence in her decision making, and the recognition that she can help herself.

Chronic psychosomatic symptoms can be an indicator of abuse. The woman may have nonspecific or vague complaints. It is important to assess old scars around the head, chest, arms, abdomen, and genitalia. Any bruising or evidence of pain is also evaluated. Some reports suggest that an abusive partner's tendency to concentrate abuse on the woman's breasts and abdomen is increased during pregnancy (Symposium 1987), so evidence of trauma in these areas is significant. Other indicators include a decrease in eye contact, silence when the partner is in the room, and a history of nervousness, insomnia, drug overdose, or alcohol problems. Frequent visits to the emergency room and a history of accidents without understandable causes are possible indicators of abuse.

The goals of treatment are to identify the woman at risk, increase her decision-making abilities to decrease the potential for further abuse, and provide a safe environment for the pregnant woman and her unborn child.

It is important to provide an environment that is private, accepting, and nonjudgmental so the woman can express her concerns. She needs to be aware of community resources available to her, such as emergency shelters; police, legal, and social services; and counseling (Hillard 1985).

## ● CARE OF THE WOMAN WITH AN INFECTION

A major factor contributing to risk during pregnancy is the presence of maternal infection, whether contracted prior to conception or during the pregnancy. Spontaneous abortion is frequently the result of a severe maternal infection.

Evidence exists that links infection to prematurity. In addition, if the pregnancy is carried to term in the presence of infection, the risk of maternal and fetal morbidity and mortality increases. In many instances of fetal risk due to infection, the woman presents few or no signs or symptoms. It is essential to maternal and fetal health that diagnosis and treatment be prompt.

Urinary tract, vaginal, and sexually transmitted infections are discussed in detail in Chapter 3. Table 12.5 provides a summary of these infections and their implications for pregnancy.

## ● TORCH

The **TORCH** group of infectious diseases may cause serious harm to the embryo-fetus. These are **t**oxoplasmosis, **r**ubella, **c**ytomegalovirus, and **h**erpesvirus type 2. Some sources consider the O in TORCH to represent other infections.

Use of the TORCH label assists health team members to assess quickly the potential risk to each pregnant woman. Exposure of the woman during the first 12 weeks of gestation may cause developmental anomalies.

### TOXOPLASMOSIS

Toxoplasmosis is caused by the protozoan *Toxoplasma gondii*. It is innocuous in adults, but when contracted in pregnancy, it can profoundly affect the fetus. The pregnant woman may contract the organism by eating raw or poorly cooked meat or by contact with the feces of infected cats, either through the cat litter box or by gardening in areas frequented by cats.

The incubation period for the disease is ten days. The woman with acute toxoplasmosis may be asymptomatic, or she may develop myalgia, malaise, rash, splenomegaly, and enlarged posterior cervical nodes. Symptoms usually disappear in a few days or weeks.

Diagnosis of toxoplasmosis can be made by serologic testing, including the IgM fluorescent antibody test. If the diagnosis can be established by physical findings, history, and positive serological results, the woman may be treated with sulfadiazine and pyrimethamine. If toxoplasmosis is diagnosed before 20 weeks' gestation, therapeutic abortion should be considered if acceptable to the couple, because damage to the fetus is generally more severe than if the disease is acquired later in the pregnancy.

The nurse caring for the woman antepartally should  discuss methods of preventing toxoplasmosis. The woman must understand the importance of avoiding poorly cooked meat, especially pork, beef, and lamb. The cat litter box should be cleaned regularly by someone other than the woman so that she can avoid contact with infected cat feces. The nurse should stress the importance of wearing gloves when gardening and of avoiding garden areas frequented by cats.

### Fetal-Neonatal Risks

The incidence of abortion, prematurity, stillbirths, neonatal deaths, and severe congenital anomalies is increased in the fetus and neonate infected with toxoplasmosis. In very mild cases, retinochoroiditis may be the only recognizable damage, and it and other manifestations may not appear until adolescence or young adulthood. Severe neonatal disorders associated with congenital infection include convulsions, coma, microcephaly, and hydrocephalus. The infant with a severe infection may die soon after birth. Survivors are often blind, deaf, and severely retarded.

### RUBELLA

The effects of rubella (German measles) are no more severe, nor are there greater complications for pregnant women than for nonpregnant women of comparable age. But the effects of this infection on the fetus and neonate are profound.

The best therapy for rubella is prevention. Live attenuated vaccine is available and should be given to all children. It is recommended that women of childbearing age be tested for immunity and vaccinated if they are susceptible and *not pregnant*.

As part of the prenatal laboratory screen the woman is evaluated for rubella using hemagglutination inhibition (HAI), a serology test. The presence of a 1:16 titer or greater is evidence of immunity. A titer less than 1:8 indicates susceptibility to rubella.

A woman who develops rubella during pregnancy may be asymptomatic or may show signs of a mild infection including a maculopapular rash, lymphadenopathy, muscular achiness, and joint pain. The presence of IgM antirubella antibody is diagnostic of a recent infection. These titers remain elevated for approximately one month following infection.

If a woman becomes infected during the first trimester, therapeutic abortion, if acceptable to the couple, is an alternative. Nursing support and understanding are vital at this time because such a decision may initiate a crisis for a couple who has planned the pregnancy. They need objective data to understand the possible effects on the fetus and the prognosis for the child.

## Table 12.5 Infections That Put Pregnancy at Risk

| Condition and causative organism | Signs and symptoms | Treatment | Implications for pregnancy |
|---|---|---|---|
| **URINARY TRACT INFECTIONS** | | | |
| Asymptomatic bacteriuria (ASB): *E coli, Klebsiella, Proteus* most common. | Bacteria present in urine on culture with no accompanying symptoms. | Oral sulfonamides early in pregnancy, ampicillin and nitrofurantoin (Furadantin) in late pregnancy. | Women with ASB in early pregnancy may go on to develop cystitis or acute pyelonephritis by third trimester if not treated. Oral sulfonamides taken in the last few weeks of pregnancy may lead to neonatal hyperbilirubinemia and kernicterus. |
| Cystitis (lower UTI): Causative organisms same as ASB. | Dysuria, urgency, frequency; low-grade fever and hematuria may occur. Urine culture (clean catch) show ↑ leukocytes. Presence of $10^5$ (100,000) or more colonies bacteria per mL urine. | Same. | If not treated, infection may ascend and lead to acute pyelonephritis. |
| Acute pyelonephritis: Causative organisms same as ASB. | Sudden onset. Chills, high fever, flank pain. Nausea, vomiting, malaise. May have decreased urine output, severe colicky pain, dehydration. Increased diastolic BP, positive FA test, low creatinine clearance. Marked bacteremia in urine culture, pyuria, WBC casts. | Hospitalization; IV antibiotic therapy. Other antibiotics safe during pregnancy include carbenicillin, methenamine, cephalosporins. Catheterization if output is ↓. Supportive therapy for comfort. Follow-up urine cultures are necessary. | Increased risk of premature delivery and IUGR. These antibiotics interfere with urinary estriol levels and can cause false interpretations of estriol levels during pregnancy. |
| **VAGINAL INFECTIONS** | | | |
| Monilial (yeast infection): *Candida albicans* | Often thick, white, curdy discharge, severe itching, dysuria, dyspareunia. Diagnosis based on presence of hyphae and spores in a wet mount preparation of vaginal secretions. | Intravaginal insertion of miconazole or clotrimazole suppositories at bedtime for 1 week. Cream may be prescribed for topical application to the vulva if necessary. | If the infection is present at birth and the fetus is born vaginally, the fetus may contract thrush. |
| Bacterial vaginosis: *Gardnerella vaginalis* | Thin, watery, yellow-grey discharge with foul odor often described as "fishy." Wet mount preparation reveals "clue cells." Application of KOH (potassium hydroxide) to a specimen of vaginal secretions produces a pronounced fishy odor. | Nonpregnant women treated with metronidazole (Flagyl). Pregnant women treated with ampicillin, at least during first half of pregnancy. | Metronidazole has potential teratogenic effects. |
| Trichomoniasis: *Trichomonas vaginalis* | Occasionally asymptomatic. May have frothy greenish gray vaginal discharge, pruritus, urinary symptoms. Strawberry patches may be visible on vaginal walls or cervix. Wet mount preparation of vaginal secretions shows motile flagellated trichomonads. | During early pregnancy symptoms may be controlled with clotrimazole vaginal suppositories. Both partners are treated. | Clotrimazole has potential teratogenic effects. |

*(continues)*

## Table 12.5  Infections That Put Pregnancy at Risk *(continued)*

| Condition and causative organism | Signs and symptoms | Treatment | Implications for pregnancy |
|---|---|---|---|
| **SEXUALLY TRANSMITTED INFECTIONS** | | | |
| Chlamydial infection: *Chlamydia trachomatis* | Women are often asymptomatic. Symptoms may include thin or purulent discharge, burning and frequency with urination, or lower abdominal pain. Lab test available to detect monoclonal antibodies specific for *Chlamydia*. | Although nonpregnant women are treated with tetracycline, it may permanently discolor fetal teeth. Thus, pregnant women are treated with erythromycin ethyl succinate. | Infant of woman with untreated chlamydial infection may develop newborn conjunctivitis, which can be treated with erythromycin eye ointment (but not silver nitrate). Infant may also develop chlamydial pneumonia. May be responsible for premature labor and fetal death. |
| Syphilis: *Treponema pallidum,* a spirochete | Primary stage: chancre, slight fever, malaise. Chancre lasts about four weeks, then disappears. Secondary stage: occurs six weeks to six months after infection. Skin eruptions (condyloma lata); also symptoms of acute arthritis, liver enlargement, iritis, chronic sore throat with hoarseness. Diagnosed by blood tests such as VDRL, RPR, FTA-ABS. Dark field examination for spirochetes may also be done. | For syphilis less than one year in duration: 2.4 million U benzathine penicillin G IM. For syphilis of more than 1 year's duration: 2.4 million U benzathine penicillin G once a week for three weeks. | Syphilis can be passed transplacentally to the fetus. If untreated, one of the following can occur: second trimester abortion, stillborn infant at term, congenitally infected infant, uninfected live infant. |
| Gonorrhea: *Neisseria gonorrhoeae* | Majority of women asymptomatic; disease often diagnosed during routine prenatal cervical culture. If symptoms are present they may include purulent vaginal discharge, dysuria, urinary frequency, inflammation and swelling of the vulva. Cervix may appear eroded. | Nonpregnant women are treated with tetracycline. Pregnant women are treated with aqueous procaine penicillin G 4.8 million U IM with 1.0 g probenicid by mouth. If the woman is allergic to penicillin, spectinomycin is used. The sexual partner is also treated. | Infection at time of birth may cause ophthalmia neonatorum in the newborn. |
| Condyloma accuminata: caused by human papilloma virus (HPV) | Soft, grayish-pink lesions on the vulva, vagina, cervix, or anus. | Podophyllin not used during pregnancy. Trichloroacetic acid, liquid nitrogen, or cryocautery; $CO_2$ laser therapy done under colposcopy is also successful (Eschenbach 1986). | Possible teratogenic effect of podophyllin. Large doses have been associated with fetal death. |

### Fetal-Neonatal Risks

The period of greatest risk for the teratogenic effects of rubella on the fetus is during the first trimester.

Clinical signs of congenital infection are congenital heart disease, IUGR, and cataracts. Cardiac involvements most often seen are patent ductus arteriosis and narrowing of peripheral pulmonary arteries. Other abnormalities may become evident in infancy, such as mental retardation or cerebral palsy. Conclusive diagnosis in the neonate can be made in the presence of these conditions and with an elevated rubella antibody titer at birth.

Infants born with congenital rubella syndrome are infectious and should be isolated. These infants may continue to shed the virus for months.

The expanded rubella syndrome relates to effects that may develop for years after the infection. These include an increased incidence of insulin-dependent diabetes mellitus; sudden hearing loss; glaucoma; and a slow, progressive form of encephalitis.

## CYTOMEGALOVIRUS

Cytomegalovirus (CMV) belongs to the herpesvirus group and causes both congenital and acquired infections referred to as *cytomegalic inclusion disease* (CID). The significance of this virus in pregnancy is related to its ability to be transmitted by asymptomatic women across the placenta to the fetus or by the cervical route during birth.

CID is probably the most prevalent infection in the TORCH group. Nearly half of adults have antibodies for the virus. The virus can be found in urine, saliva, cervical mucus, semen, and breast milk. It can be passed between humans by any close contact such as kissing, breast-feeding, and sexual intercourse. Asymptomatic CMV infection is particularly common in children and gravid women. It is a chronic, persistent infection in that the individual may shed the virus continually over many years. The cervix can harbor the virus, and an ascending infection can develop after birth. While the virus is usually innocuous in adults and children, it may be fatal to the fetus.

Accurate diagnosis in the pregnant woman depends on the presence of CMV in the urine, a rise in IgM levels, and identification of the CMV antibodies within the serum IgM fraction. At present, no treatment exists for maternal CMV or for the congenital disease in the neonate.

### Fetal-Neonatal Risks

The cytomegalovirus is the most frequent agent of viral infection in the human fetus. It infects 0.5% to 2% of neonates, and of these about 10% develop serious manifestations (Pritchard et al 1985). Subclinical infections in the newborn are capable of producing mental retardation and auditory deficits, sometimes not recognized for several months, or learning disabilities not seen until childhood. CMV may be the most common cause of mental retardation.

For the fetus, this infection can result in extensive intrauterine tissue damage that is incompatible with life; in survival with microcephaly, hydrocephaly, cerebral palsy, or mental retardation; or in survival with no damage at all.

## HERPES GENITALIS (HERPESVIRUS TYPE 2)

Herpesvirus type 2 is a viral infection that can cause painful lesions in the genital area. Lesions may also develop on the cervix. This condition and its implications for nonpregnant women are discussed in Chapter 3. However, because the presence of herpes lesions in the genital tract may profoundly affect the fetus, herpes infection as it relates to a pregnant woman is discussed here as part of the TORCH complex of infections.

### Fetal-Neonatal Risks

Transmission of herpesvirus type 2 to the fetus almost always occurs after the membranes rupture, as the virus ascends from active lesions. It also occurs during vaginal birth, when the fetus comes in contact with genital lesions. Transplacental infection is rare.

If active herpesvirus type 2 infection occurs during the first trimester there is a 20% to 50% rate of spontaneous abortion or stillbirth (Stagno and Whitley 1985). Infection after 20 weeks of gestation is associated with an increased risk of preterm labor.

Approximately 54% of all infants who are born vaginally when the mother is shedding herpesvirus type 2 in her vagina or cervix develop some form of herpes infection. Of these infants, approximately 70% will die if untreated, while 83% of the survivors will have permanent brain damage (Harger 1985).

The infected infant is often asymptomatic at birth but after an incubation period of 2 to 12 days develops symptoms of fever (or hypothermia), jaundice, seizures, and poor feeding. Approximately one half of infected infants develop the characteristic vesicular skin lesions. Vidarabine has been useful in decreasing serious effects from neonatal herpes, but no definitive treatment exists as yet (Corey and Spear 1986).

### Medical Therapy

Although the vesicular lesions of herpes have a characteristic appearance, they are not always present for inspection because they rupture easily. Thus diagnosis is made by culturing the lesions. As an alternative, a sample of discharge from the lesion may be obtained. A slide is prepared as for a Pap test. The presence of multinucleated giant cells indicates herpes.

Treatment is directed first toward relieving the woman's vulvar pain. If the attack is severe, walking, sitting, and even wearing clothing may be painful. The woman may be most comfortable in bed during the peak of the infection. Sitz baths three to four times daily, followed by drying of the vulva with a hair dryer or light bulb, may promote healing and help prevent secondary infection. Cotton underwear helps keep the genital area dry.

Although acyclovir (Zovirax) does not cure the infection or prevent recurrence, it does reduce healing time of the initial attack and shortens the time that the live virus is in the lesions, thereby reducing the infectious period. Its effects during pregnancy are not yet known.

Herpesvirus type 2 has not been found in breast milk. Present experience shows that breast-feeding is acceptable if the mother washes her hands well to prevent any direct transfer of the virus.

Because most infants become infected when they pass through a birth canal containing herpesvirus it is necessary to determine whether the woman with a history of herpes is shedding virus at the time of birth. This is done by obtaining viral cultures. If virus is present, the woman is delivered by cesarean; if no virus is present, a vaginal birth is possible.

Recent evidence suggests that many of the women who give birth to infants infected with herpes are young, white primiparas without a history of genital herpes. Because of this, some care givers are recommending that all women beginning labor have a physical and speculum examination. Women with lesions or suspicious symptoms would be offered the opportunity to have a cesarean birth (Wilson 1988).

If the woman has a genital herpes lesion but her membranes rupture, she is at risk for an ascending herpes infection. Then the most appropriate birth method is less clear. Many physicians recommend a cesarean birth if the membranes have been ruptured less than four hours.

### Nursing Assessment

During the initial prenatal visit it is important to learn whether the woman or her partner have had previous herpes infections. If so, ongoing assessment by means of cervical cultures is indicated as pregnancy progresses. In dealing with women with newly diagnosed herpes or an existing history, the nurse needs to assess their knowledge of the disorder and its implications.

### Nursing Diagnosis

Nursing diagnoses that may apply to the pregnant woman with herpesvirus type 2 include:

- Sexual dysfunction related to unwillingness to engage in sexual intercourse secondary to the presence of active herpes lesions

- Ineffective individual coping related to depression sec-

ondary to the risk to the fetus if herpes lesions are present at birth

- Knowledge deficit related to the possible effects of herpes on the infant

### Nursing Plan and Implementation

Nurses must be especially concerned about client education about herpes. Women should be informed about the possible effects of herpes on the fetus and about the possibility of cesarean birth. The woman should be informed of the possible association of genital herpes with cervical cancer and the importance of a yearly Pap smear.

Because, once acquired, there is currently no cure for herpes, it can have a profound effect on those who contract it. People need realistic information about effective ways of dealing with herpes, both physically and emotionally. Clients may be helped by counseling that allows expression of the anger, shame, and depression often experienced by the herpes victim. Literature is available from many public agencies. In addition, The American Social Health Association has established the HELP program to provide information and the latest research results on genital herpes. The Association has a quarterly journal, *The Helper,* for nurses and herpes clients.

### Evaluation

Anticipated outcomes of nursing care include the following:

- The woman is able to describe her infection with regard to its method of spread, therapy and comfort measures, implications for her pregnancy, and long-term implications.

- The woman has appropriate cultures done as recommended throughout her pregnancy.

- The woman successfully delivers a healthy infant.

## • Acquired Immunodeficiency Syndrome

**Acquired immunodeficiency syndrome (AIDS)** is one of today's major health concerns. Approximately 79,823 cases have been diagnosed in the United States, although that figure changes daily; of these, 1278 are children (AWSR 1988).

The persons at risk for AIDS are homosexual or bisexual men, heterosexual partners of persons with AIDS, drug users, recipients of blood transfusions, hemophiliacs, Haitians, Africans in Zaire, and fetuses of mothers at risk (perinatal transmission).

Acquired immune deficiency is caused by a virus, the human immunodeficiency virus (HIV). It enters the body through blood, blood products, or sexual contact (semen) and affects specific T-cells, which decrease the body's immune responses. This makes the affected person susceptible to opportunistic organisms such as cytomegalovirus, herpes simplex and zoster, candidas, *Pneumocystis carinii,* and *Toxoplasma gondii.*

Opportunistic infections are the cause of most fatalities from AIDS; Kaposi's sarcoma is rarely the direct cause. *Pneumocystis carinii* pneumonia is the most common opportunistic infection. The pneumonia creates dyspnea with progressive hypoxemia.

The incubation period for AIDS can be five to seven years or longer. Thus an infant born to a woman with AIDS is not necessarily free of the disease even if he or she shows no symptoms at birth.

## FETAL-NEONATAL RISKS

AIDS may develop in infants whose mothers are seropositive. Research suggests that the risk of perinatal transmission is 20% to 50%. Although initially the infant may appear healthy, the child diagnosed with AIDS has a very poor prognosis—most die within the first few years of life (Minkoff 1988).

The signs of AIDS in infants include: failure to thrive, enlarged liver and spleen (hepatosplenomegaly), interstitial pneumonia, recurrent infections, cell-mediated immunodeficiency, evidence of Epstein-Barr virus, and neurologic abnormalities (Cowen et al 1984).

Apparently infection can occur early in fetal development. Facial characteristics that may indicate that the infant has been infected with the AIDS virus include: microcephaly; patulous lips; prominent, boxlike forehead; increased distance between the inner canthus of the eyes; a flattened nasal bridge; and a mild obliquity of the eyes. The mortality rate for these infants is especially high (Klug 1986).

## MEDICAL THERAPY

Currently there is no definitive treatment for AIDS. The goal for antenatal care is identification of the pregnant woman at risk and education of the public about the transmission of AIDS to decrease its potential spread. Following recommended techniques to decrease nosocomial transmission of AIDS in a hospital setting can decrease the potential risk to health workers. It is very important to decrease exposure to contaminated blood and body fluids, which may harbor potential infectious agents, especially during labor and delivery.

Routine laboratory tests appear to be of little value in diagnosing AIDS. Findings include leukopenia, anemia, elevated transaminase and alkaline phosphate, and low serum albumin (LaCamera 1985).

The following women should be screened for a positive HIV: women who use intravenous drugs; prostitutes; women whose current or previous sexual partners have been bisexual, abused IV drugs, have hemophilia, or test positive for HIV; and women from countries where heterosexual transmission is common. In addition, clinical facilities that are located in areas with a large population of people who test HIV positive may require routine HIV screening of all prenatal clients.

## NURSING ASSESSMENT

A woman who tests positive for HIV may present with any of the following signs or symptoms: fatigue, anemia, malaise, progressive weight loss, lymphadenopathy, diarrhea, fever, neurologic dysfunction, cell-mediated immunodeficiency, or evidence of Kaposi's sarcoma (purplish, reddish-brown lesions either externally or internally).

If a woman tests HIV positive or is involved in a relationship that places her at high risk, the nurse should assess the woman's knowledge level about the disease, its implications for her and her unborn child, and self-care measures the woman can take.

## NURSING DIAGNOSIS

Examples of nursing diagnoses that might apply for a pregnant woman who tests HIV positive include:

● Knowledge deficit related to AIDS and its long-term implications for the woman and her unborn child

● Potential for infection related to altered immunity secondary to AIDS

● Ineffective family coping related to the implications of a positive HIV test in one of the family members

## NURSING PLAN AND IMPLEMENTATION

Women at high risk for AIDS should have premarital and prenatal screening for HIV before considering a pregnancy. In many instances the nurse will be responsible for counseling the woman about the test and its implications for her, for her partner, and for a child should she become pregnant.

Because two early signs of AIDS—anemia and fatigue—are common to pregnancy, the nurse must be alert for their development. The woman should be advised to contact her care giver immediately if she notices increased fatigue or if she develops other symptoms such as fever, cough, diarrhea, or sweats (Minkoff 1988). See Nursing Care Plan: Care of the Woman with AIDS.

### Reduction of Risk of Transmission

The nurse is faced with the important task of taking the precautions necessary to protect staff, other clients, and families, while at the same time meeting the needs of the childbearing woman with AIDS.

## *Nursing Care Plan*

## Care of the Woman with AIDS

### Client Assessment

#### Nursing History

1. Present pregnancy course
2. Estimated gestational age
3. Sensitivity to medications
4. History of infections

#### Physical Examination

1. Fetal size, fetal status (FHR), and fetal maturity
2. Observe for signs of fatigue and weakness, recurrent diarrhea, pallor, night sweats
3. Lymphadenopathy
4. Present weight and amount of weight gain or weight loss
5. Presence of nonproductive cough, fever, sore throat, chills, shortness of breath (*Pneumocystis carinii* pneumonia)
6. Dark purplish marks or lesions, especially on the lower extremities (Kaposi's sarcoma)

#### Diagnostic Studies

1. Ultrasound
2. Fetal maturity studies (L/S ratio, PG, creatinine)
3. Hemoglobin and hematocrit
4. WBC
5. Testing for HIV-1 virus

| Nursing Diagnosis/Client Goal | Nursing Interventions | Rationale/Evaluation |
|---|---|---|
| **Nursing Diagnosis:**<br><br>Pattern 1: Exchanging<br>Altered nutrition: less than body requirements | Weigh woman.<br>Obtain food history.<br><br>Plan high-protein, high-calorie diet.<br><br>Provide teaching regarding nutritional needs. | **Rationale:**<br><br>Establishes baseline weight. Identifying food likes and dislikes will assist in meal planning.<br>Diet must take woman's needs and pregnancy needs into account.<br>Nutritional education and support may assist the woman in planning her daily diet. |
| **Client Goal:**<br><br>The woman will maintain current body weight or gain weight. | | **Evaluation:**<br><br>The woman maintains current weight or gains weight. |

In 1987 the Centers for Disease Control (CDC) stated that the increasing prevalence of AIDS and the risk of exposure faced by health care workers is significant enough that precautions should be taken with *all* patients (not only those with known HIV infection), especially in dealing with blood and body fluids (MMWR Supplement 1987). These precautions are now called *universal precautions*.

Nurses who deal with childbearing families are exposed frequently to blood and body fluids, and should pay careful attention to the CDC guidelines, including the following (Wiley and Grohar 1988):

1. Care givers should wear disposable latex gloves when having contact with a client's mucous

*Nursing Care Plan*

## *Nursing Care Plan*

## Care of the Woman with AIDS *(continued)*

| Nursing Diagnosis/Client Goal | Nursing Interventions | Rationale/Evaluation |
|---|---|---|
| **Nursing Diagnosis:**<br><br>Pattern 9: Feeling<br>Fear related to outcome of disease | Establish rapport.<br><br>Provide opportunities to talk without interruption.<br><br>Provide support and counseling.<br><br>Refer to community resources. | **Rationale:**<br><br>Establishment of rapport helps create a therapeutic relationship. |
| **Client Goal:**<br><br>The woman will have opportunities to talk with nursing staff and other persons she identifies as supportive. | | **Evaluation:**<br><br>The woman has opportunities to talk with staff and contacts other sources of support. |
| **Nursing Diagnosis:**<br><br>Pattern 1: Exchanging<br>Potential for infection related to suppressed immune status | Monitor for signs of infection (fever, cough, sore throat, night sweats, etc). | **Rationale:**<br><br>Any pathogen may be able to establish itself in an immunosuppressed body. *Pneumocystis carinii* pneumonia is an infection frequently associated with AIDS. |
| | Maintain body secretion isolation. | Universal precautions with body secretions are advised for all clients who are hospitalized. In this case, the nurse and others will be protected from exposure to the woman's body secretions. In addition, the woman needs to be protected from other infectious agents. |
| | Provide education regarding infection control and measures to prevent infection.<br>Provide contraceptive information if the woman desires. | Information regarding how the AIDS virus is spread is an important basis of medical asepsis. As the woman understands more about the disease, she will be able to take precautions against other infections and to protect against the spread of the AIDS virus. Use of barrier contraceptives will protect others from the AIDS virus and will protect the woman from other infections. |
| | Discuss the implications of breast-feeding her infant. | Current information suggests that the virus may be spread in breast milk. |
| **Client Goal:**<br><br>The woman will not develop infections during the hospital stay. | | **Evaluation:**<br><br>The woman does not develop a superimposed infectious disease. |

membranes, nonintact skin, body fluids, or blood. Contact includes, for example, changing chux pads, peripads, diapers, or dressings; starting or discontinuing intravenous fluids, and drawing blood.

2. After giving care to a client, gloves should be removed and hands should be washed before caring for another client.

3. In addition to gloves, protective coverings such as a plastic apron, gown, mask, and eye or face shield should be worn during any procedures that frequently result in contamination from splashing of body fluids. These include amniotomy, vaginal examination, vaginal or cesarean birth, suctioning, and care of the newborn until after the initial bath has

been done. (Note: full-size glasses are considered sufficient eye protection. While agencies are required to provide eye shields, nurses may choose to purchase their own eye goggles and clean them with soap and water.)

4. At birth, the newborn should be suctioned with a disposable bulb syringe or mucus extractor attached to wall suction at a low setting. DeLee mucus traps with mouth suction are not used because of the risk of inadvertently ingesting secretions.

5. Similar care should be taken during any resuscitation procedures. To avoid the need for mouth-to-mouth resuscitation, sufficient mouthpieces and ventilation equipment should be available. Disposable resuscitation masks are recommended.

6. Care should be taken when handling syringes and needles. They are disposed of in a special container. Needles are not broken, bent, or even returned to their protective cap because of the risk of an inadvertent puncture.

7. In the event that a glove is torn, it should be removed, the hands should be cleansed, and new gloves should be applied.

8. Gloves and protective coverings should also be worn during any cleaning procedures.

### Provision of Emotional Support

The psychologic implications of AIDS for the childbearing family are staggering. The woman is faced with the knowledge that she and her newborn have decreased chances for survival. The couple must deal with the impact of the illness on the partner, who may or may not be infected, and on other children. Dealing with the tasks and responsibilities of a newborn may be especially difficult if the woman is physically depleted or if she is trying to come to grips with the long-term implications of her condition.

Nurses can help ensure that the woman receives complete, accurate information about her condition and ways she might cope. This usually involves a referral to social services for follow-up care. The hospitalized woman will often welcome the opportunity to talk with someone about her fears and desires.

### EVALUATION

Anticipated outcomes of nursing care include the following:

● The woman is able to discuss the implications of her positive HIV results for herself and her unborn child, the method of spread, and treatment options.

● The woman agrees to follow-up referral and assistance.

● Contamination of others is avoided.

## ● CARE OF THE WOMAN PRACTICING SUBSTANCE ABUSE

As discussed in Chapter 8, drugs that adversely affect fetal growth and development are called teratogens. Table 12.6 identifies common addictive drugs and their effects on the fetus or neonate.

Drugs that are commonly misused include alcohol, amphetamines, barbiturates, hallucinogens, cocaine, crack, and heroin and other narcotics. Abuse of these drugs constitutes a major threat to the successful completion of pregnancy.

## ● Drug Addiction

Indiscriminate drug use during pregnancy, particularly in the first trimester, may adversely affect the health of the woman and the growth and development of the fetus. Originally it was thought that the placenta acted as a protective barrier to keep the drugs ingested by the woman from reaching the fetal system. This is not true. The degree to which a drug is passed to the fetus depends on the drug's chemical properties, including molecular weight, and on whether it is administered alone or in combination with other drugs.

### MATERNAL RISKS

Drug addiction has an adverse effect on the expectant woman. It affects her state of health, nutritional status, susceptibility to infection, and psychosocial condition. A majority of drug-abusing pregnant women are malnourished and receive little or no antepartal care. Heroin-addicted pregnant women have two to six times the risk of PIH, malpresentation, third trimester bleeding, and puerperal morbidity. In addition, the risk of drug toxicity is present. In general, the woman's psychologic and physiologic ability to handle the stress of pregnancy is severely reduced.

Cocaine use in pregnancy has sharply increased in recent years. Cocaine causes vasoconstriction, tachycardia, and increased blood pressure. This increases a woman's risk of spontaneous abortion in the first or second trimester. In the third trimester it leads to increased uterine contractility, placental vasoconstriction, increased incidence of meconium staining, fetal tachycardia, and the potential for abruptio placentae (Chasnoff et al 1986). For further discussion, see Chapter 8.

### FETAL-NEONATAL RISKS

The fetus of a pregnant addict is at increased risk for congenital malformations, IUGR, and premature birth. The newborn may also experience symptoms of withdrawal during the first days of life. (For a discussion of the effects of drug addiction on the newborn, see Chapter 24.)

## Table 12.6 Possible Effects of Selected Drugs of Abuse/Addiction on Fetus and Neonate

| Maternal drug | Effect on fetus/neonate |
|---|---|
| I. Depressants | |
|   A. Alcohol | Cardiac anomalies, IUGR, potential teratogenic effects, FAS |
|   B. Narcotics | |
|     1. Heroin | Withdrawal symptoms, convulsions, death, IUGR, respiratory alkalosis, hyperbilirubinemia |
|     2. Methadone | Fetal distress, meconium aspiration; with abrupt termination of the drug, severe withdrawal symptoms, neonatal death |
|   C. Barbiturates | Neonatal depression, increased anomalies; teratogenic effect (?); withdrawal symptoms, convulsions, hyperactivity, hyperreflexia, vasomotor instability |
|     1. Phenobarbital | Bleeding (with excessive doses) |
|   D. "T's and Blues" (combination of the following) | |
|     1. Talwin (narcotic) | Safe for use in pregnancy; depresses respiration if taken close to time of birth |
|     2. Amytal (barbiturate) | See barbiturates |
|   E. Tranquilizers | |
|     1. Phenothiazine derivatives | Withdrawal, extrapyramidal dysfunction, delayed respiratory onset, hyperbilirubinemia, hypotonia or hyperactivity, decreased platelet count |
|     2. Diazepam (Valium) | Hypotonia, hypothermia, low Apgar score, respiratory depression, poor sucking reflex, possible cleft lip |
|   F. Antianxiety drugs | |
|     1. Lithium | Congenital anomalies; lethargy and cyanosis in the newborn |
| II. Stimulants | |
|   A. Amphetamines | |
|     1. Amphetamine sulfate (Benzedrine) | Generalized arthritis, learning disabilities, poor motor coordination, transposition of the great vessels, cleft palate |
|     2. Dextroamphetamine sulfate (dexedrine sulfate) | Congenital heart defects, hyperbilirubinemia |
|   B. Cocaine | Learning disabilities, poor state organization, decreased interactive behavior, IUGR, irregular sleep patterns, diarrhea (Newald 1986); increased risk SIDS (Chasnoff 1987) |
|   C. Caffeine (more than 600 mg/day) | Spontaneous abortion, IUGR, increased incidence of cleft palate; other anomalies suspected |
|   D. Nicotine (half to one pack cigarettes/day) | Increased rate of spontaneous abortion, increased incidence abruptio placentae, SGA, small head circumference, decreased length |
| III. Psychotropics | |
|   A. PCP ("angel dust") | Flaccid appearance, poor head control, impaired neurologic development |
|   B. LSD | Chromosomal breakage? |
|   C. Marijuana | IUGR, potential impaired immunologic mechanisms |

## MEDICAL THERAPY

Antepartal care of the pregnant addict involves medical, socioeconomic, and legal considerations. A team approach allows the comprehensive management necessary to provide safe labor and delivery for woman and fetus. Care should be taken to maintain and improve the woman's general health and nutritional status. Urine screening should be done regularly throughout pregnancy. This testing helps identify the type and amount of substance being abused. The woman should receive regular prenatal care and, if she is willing, support and counseling. "Cold turkey" withdrawal should be avoided because of the potential risk to the fetus. Immediate intensive care should be available for the newborn, who will probably be depressed, small for gestational age (SGA), and premature.

## NURSING ASSESSMENT

Nursing assessment of a substance abuser who is pregnant focuses on the woman's general health status, with specific attention to skin abscesses and infections, as well as evaluation of other body systems.

The nurse also assesses the woman with regard to her drug addiction. Some women are reluctant to discuss their drug habit, while others are quite open about it. Once the nurse establishes a relationship of trust, he or she can gain information that can be used to plan the woman's ongoing care.

## NURSING DIAGNOSIS

Nursing diagnoses that may apply to the pregnant woman who is addicted to drugs include:

## Table 12.7  Less Common Medical Conditions and Pregnancy

| Condition | Brief description | Maternal implications | Fetal-neonatal implications |
|---|---|---|---|
| Arthritis | Chronic inflammatory disease believed to be caused by a genetically influenced antigen-antibody reaction (Harris 1985). Symptoms include fatigue, low-grade fever, pain and swelling of joints, morning stiffness, pain on movement. Treated with salicylates, physical therapy, and rest. Corticosteroids used cautiously if not responsive to above. | Usually there is remission of rheumatoid arthritis symptoms during pregnancy, often with a relapse postpartum. Anemia may be present due to blood loss from salicylate therapy. Mother needs extra rest, particularly to relieve weight-bearing joints, but needs to continue range-of-motion exercises. If in remission, may stop medication during pregnancy. Oral contraception acceptable. | Possibility of prolonged gestation and longer labor with heavy salicylate use due to interference with prostaglandin synthesis (Mor-Yosef et al 1984). Possible teratogenic effects of salicylates. |
| Epilepsy | Chronic disorder characterized by seizures; may be idiopathic or secondary to other conditions, such as head injury, metabolic and nutritional disorders such as PKU or vitamin $B_6$ deficiency, encephalitis, neoplasms, or circulatory interferences. Treated with anticonvulsants. | Seizure frequency often increases during pregnancy, with slightly higher incidence of hyperemesis gravidarum, preeclampsia, and vaginal hemorrhage. A woman who has been seizure free for a year should be withdrawn from medication prior to conception; a woman who requires medication has a 90% chance of having a normal child; women who seek advice after the first trimester should be maintained on their medication. | Higher incidence of major congenital anomalies and perinatal mortality. Certain anticonvulsant medications have teratogenic effects. Some anticonvulsants cause a decrease in clotting factors. To prevent neonatal hemorrhage, prophylactic vitamin K (10 mg/day) should be given to the mother during the last month of pregnancy. |

- Noncompliance with treatment related to an inability to give up drugs
- Potential alteration in parenting: neglect related to maternal substance abuse

### NURSING PLAN AND IMPLEMENTATION

Preparation for labor and birth should be part of the prenatal planning. Analgesic agents may be used if needed. Relief of fear, tension, or discomfort may be achieved through nonnarcotic psychologic support and careful explanation of the labor process. Preferred methods of pain relief include the use of psychoprophylaxis and regional or local anesthetics such as pudendal block and local infiltration.

### EVALUATION

Anticipated outcomes of nursing care include the following:

- The woman is able to describe the impact of substance abuse on herself and her fetus/neonate.
- The woman participates in a drug therapy or counseling program.
- The woman successfully delivers a healthy infant. If potential problems develop they are quickly detected and appropriate therapy is instituted.

### • Alcoholism

Alcoholism has increased dramatically among women in the United States. The incidence is highest among women 20–40 years old; alcoholism is also seen in teenagers. Chronic abuse of alcohol can undermine maternal health by causing malnutrition (especially folic acid and thiamine deficiencies), bone marrow suppression, increased incidence of infections, and liver disease. As a result of alcohol dependence, the woman may have withdrawal seizures in the intrapartal period as early 12–48 hours after she stops drinking. Delirium tremens may occur in the

## Table 12.7  Less Common Medical Conditions and Pregnancy *(continued)*

| Condition | Brief description | Maternal implications | Fetal-neonatal implications |
|---|---|---|---|
| Hepatitis B | Hepatitis B is caused by the hepatitis B virus (HBV). Although HBV can theoretically be transmitted by all body fluids, it is primarily blood borne or sexually transmitted. Groups at risk include women from areas with a high incidence (primarily developing countries), illegal IV drug users, prostitutes, and women with multiple sexual partners. Symptoms range from none to mild flulike symptoms to fulminating illness. No specific treatment is available. Supportive care is indicated. A vaccine is available for women in high-risk groups and for health care workers. | Hepatitis B does not usually affect the course of pregnancy. Pregnant women have no higher incidence of complications than the general population (Shaw and Maynard 1986). The CDC has recommended that all pregnant women be screened for hepatitis B surface antigen early in pregnancy (MMWR 1988). Special attention should be given to screening women in high-risk groups. A woman in a high-risk group who is negative may be given hepatitis vaccine. If she is positive the infant should receive prophylactic treatment. | The incidence of fetal malformation is not influenced by maternal infection with hepatitis. Infected newborns have 80% to 90% risk of becoming carriers and may remain infected indefinitely. The newborn who becomes a carrier faces a one in four risk of dying from liver-related disease (Shaw and Maynard 1986). The infant born to a woman with hepatitis can be treated prophylactically with a dose of hepatitis B immunoglobulin given within the first 12 hours after birth, followed by a series of injections of vaccine, the first during the first week of life, the second at one month, and the third at six months. |
| Hyperthyroidism (thyrotoxicosis) | Enlarged, overactive thyroid gland; increased T4:TBG ratio and increased BMR. Symptoms include muscle wasting, tachycardia, excessive sweating, and exophthalmos. | Mild hyperthyroidism is not dangerous (Davies and Cobin 1985). Increased incidence of PIH and postpartum hemorrhage if not well controlled. | Neonatal thyrotoxicosis is rare. Even low doses of antithyroid drug in mother may produce a mild fetal-neonatal hypothyroidism; higher dose may produce a goiter or mental deficiencies. |

*(continues)*

postpartal period, and the neonate may suffer a withdrawal syndrome.

The effects of alcohol on the fetus may result in a group of signs referred to as *fetal alcohol syndrome (FAS)*. The syndrome has characteristic physical and mental abnormalities that vary in severity and combination. (The abnormalities and care of these infants are discussed in Chapter 24.)

There is no definitive answer to how much alcohol a woman can safely consume during pregnancy. The expectant woman should "play it safe" by avoiding alcohol completely during the early weeks of pregnancy when organogenesis is occurring. During the remainder of pregnancy, she may have an occasional drink, although none at all is safest.

The nursing staff in the maternity unit must be aware of the manifestations of alcohol abuse so that they can prepare for the client's special needs. The care regimen includes sedation to decrease irritability and tremors, seizure precautions, intravenous fluid therapy for hydration,

and preparation for an addicted neonate. Although high doses of sedatives and analgesics may be necessary for the woman, caution is advised because these can cause fetal depression.

Breast-feeding generally is not contraindicated, although alcohol is excreted in breast milk. Excessive alcohol consumption may intoxicate the infant and inhibit maternal let-down reflex. Discharge planning for the alcohol-addicted mother and newborn should be correlated with the social service department of the hospital.

## ● OTHER MEDICAL CONDITIONS AND PREGNANCY

A woman with a preexisting medical condition should be aware of the possible impact of pregnancy on her condition, as well as the impact of her condition on the successful outcome of her pregnancy. Table 12.7 discusses some of the less common medical conditions and pregnancy.

## Table 12.7 Less Common Medical Conditions and Pregnancy (*continued*)

| Condition | Brief description | Maternal implications | Fetal-neonatal implications |
|---|---|---|---|
| Hyperthyroidism (thyrotoxicosis) (*continued*) | Treatment by antithyroid drug propylthiouracil (PTU) while monitoring free T4 levels (Davies and Cobin 1985). Surgery used only if drug intolerance exists. | Serious risk related to thyroid storm characterized by high fever, tachycardia, sweating, and congestive heart failure. Now occurs rarely. When diagnosed during pregnancy may be transient or permanent. | Fetal loss not increased in euthyroid women. If untreated, rates of abortion, intrauterine death, and stillbirth increase. Breast-feeding contraindicated for women on antithyroid medication because it is excreted in the milk (may be tried by women on low dose if neonatal T4 levels are monitored). |
| Hypothyroidism | Characterized by inadequate thyroid secretions (decreased T4 : TGB ratio), elevated TSH, lowered BMR, and enlarged thyroid gland (goiter). Symptoms include lack of energy, excessive weight gain, cold intolerance, dry skin, and constipation. Treated by thyroxine replacement therapy. | Long-term replacement therapy usually continues at same dosage during pregnancy as before. Weekly NST after 35 weeks' gestation. | If mother untreated, fetal loss 50%; high risk of congenital goiter or true cretinism. Therefore, newborns are screened for T4 level. Mild TSH elevation presents little risk since it does not cross the placenta. |
| Maternal phenyl-ketonuria (PKU) (hyperphenyl-alaninemia) | Inherited recessive single gene anomaly causing a deficiency of the liver enzyme needed to convert the amino acid phenylalanine to tyrosine, resulting in high serum levels of phenylalanine. Brain damage and mental retardation occur if not treated early. | Low phenylalanine diet is mandatory prior to conception and during pregnancy. The woman should be counseled that her children will either inherit the disease or be carriers depending on the zygosity of the father for the disease. Treatment at a PKU center is recommended. | Risk to fetus if maternal treatment not begun preconception. In untreated women, increased incidence of mental retardation, microcephaly, congenital heart defects, and growth retardation. Fetal phenylalanine levels are approximately 50% higher than maternal levels (Lenke 1985). |

## ESSENTIAL CONCEPTS

● The diagnosis of high-risk pregnancy can shock an expectant couple. Providing emotional support, teaching about the condition and prognosis, and educating for self-care are important nursing measures that help the client cope.

● Cardiac disease during pregnancy requires careful assessment, limitation of activity, and knowing and reporting signs of impending cardiac decompensation by both client and nurse.

● The key point in the care of the pregnant diabetic is scrupulous maternal plasma glucose control. This is best achieved by home blood glucose monitoring, multiple daily insulin injections, and a careful diet. To reduce incidence of congenital anomalies and other problems in the neonate, the woman should be euglycemic prior to conception and throughout the pregnancy. Diabetics more than most other clients need to be educated about their condition and involved with their own care.

● Almost any health problem that a person can have when not pregnant can coexist with pregnancy. Some problems, such as anemias, may be exacerbated by pregnancy. Others, such as collagen disease, may go into temporary remission with pregnancy. Regardless of the health problem, careful health care is needed throughout pregnancy to improve the outcome for mother and fetus.

## Table 12.7   Less Common Medical Conditions and Pregnancy *(continued)*

| Condition | Brief description | Maternal implications | Fetal-neonatal implications |
|---|---|---|---|
| Multiple sclerosis | Neurologic disorder characterized by destruction of the myelin sheath of nerve fibers.<br>The condition occurs primarily in young adults, is marked by periods of remission, progresses to marked physical disability in 10 to 20 years. | Associated with remission during pregnancy, but with increased rate of exacerbation postpartum (Korn-Lubetzki et al 1984). Rest is important; help with child care should be planned.<br>Uterine contraction strength is not diminished, but because sensation is frequently lessened labor may be almost painless. | Increased evidence of a genetic causal effect (Sadovnik and Baird 1985). Therefore reproductive counseling is recommended. |
| Systemic lupus erythematosus (SLE) | Chronic autoimmune collagen disease, characterized by exacerbations and remissions; symptoms range from characteristic rash to inflammation and pain in joints, fever, nephritis, depression, cranial nerve disorders, and peripheral neuropathies | Mild cases—little risk to mother or fetus.<br>Severe cases—because of extra burden on the kidneys, therapeutic abortion may be indicated. Woman must be careful to avoid fatigue, infection, strong sunlight, and so on. Acute postpartum exacerbation is common and often severe. | Increased incidence of spontaneous abortion, stillbirth, prematurity, and SGA neonates.<br>Rarely, the neonate shows manifestations of the disease that respond to steroids and disappear within three months. |
| Tuberculosis (TB) | Infection caused by *Mycobacterium tuberculosis;* inflammatory process causes destruction of lung tissue, increased sputum, and coughing. Associated primarily with poverty and malnutrition and may be found among refugees from countries where TB is prevalent. Treated with isoniazid and either ethambutol or rifampin or both. | If TB inactive due to prior treatment, relapse rate no greater than for nonpregnant women.<br>When isoniazid is used during pregnancy, the woman should take supplemental pyridoxine (vitamin $B_6$).<br>Extra rest and limited contact with others is required until disease becomes inactive. | If maternal TB is inactive, mother may breast-feed and care for her infant. If TB is active, neonate should not have direct contact with mother until she is noninfectious.<br>Isoniazid crosses the placenta, but most studies show no teratogenic effects. Rifampin crosses the placenta. Possibility of harmful effects still being studied. |

● Several health problems associated with bleeding arise from the pregnancy itself, such as spontaneous abortion, ectopic pregnancy, and gestational trophoblastic disease. The nurse needs to be alert to early signs of these situations, to guard the woman against heavy bleeding and shock, to facilitate the medical treatment, and to provide educational and emotional support.

● Hypertension may exist prior to pregnancy or, more often, may develop during pregnancy. Pregnancy-induced hypertension can lead to growth retardation for the fetus, and if untreated may lead to convulsions (eclampsia) and even death for the mother and fetus. A woman's understanding of the disease process helps motivate her to maintain the required rest periods in the left lateral position. Antihypertensive or anticonvulsive drugs may be part of the therapy.

● Rh incompatibility can exist when an Rh− woman and an Rh+ partner conceive a child that is Rh+. The use of RhoGAM has greatly decreased the incidence of severe sequelae due to Rh because the drug "tricks" the body into thinking antibodies have been produced in response to the Rh antigen.

● The impact of surgery, trauma, or battering on the pregnant woman and her fetus is related to timing in the pregnancy, seriousness of the situation, and other factors influencing the situation.

● Urinary tract infections are a common problem in pregnancy. If untreated, the infection may ascend, causing more serious illness for the mother. Urinary tract infections are also associated with an increased risk of premature labor.

● **TORCH is an acronym standing for toxoplasmosis, rubella, cytomegalovirus, and herpes, all of which pose a grave threat to the fetus.**

● **Sexually transmitted diseases pose less threat to the fetus if detected and treated as soon as possible.**

● **Substance abuse (either drugs or alcohol) not only is detrimental to the mother's health but also may have profound lasting effects on the fetus.**

● ● ● ● ● ● ● ● ● ● ● ● ● ● ● ● ● ● ● ● ● ● ● ● ● ● ● ● ●

## REFERENCES

AIDS Weekly Surveillance Report: United States cases reported to CDC. December 5, 1988.

Arias F: When the pregnant patient has mitral valve prolapse. *Contemp OB/GYN* November 1988; 32(5): 84.

Berkowitz RS et al: Partial molar pregnancy: A separate entity. *Contemp OB/GYN* June 1988; 31: 99.

Borg S, Lasker J: *When Pregnancy Fails.* Boston: Beacon Press, 1981.

Brumfield C, Huddleson J: The management of ketoacidosis in pregnancy. *Clin Obstet Gynecol* March 1984; 27: 50.

Buckley J: The epidemiology of molar pregnancy and choriocarcinoma. *Clin Obstet Gynecol* March 1984; 27: 153.

Campbell WA, Vintzileos AV: Are β-blockers safe for hypertension during pregnancy? *Contemp OB/GYN* January 1988; 31: 178.

Chasnoff IJ et al: Perinatal cerebral infarction and maternal cocaine use. *J Pediatr* 1986; 109: 456.

Corey L, Spear PG: Infections with herpes simplex. *New Engl J Med* 1986; 314(11): 686.

Cousins L et al: Screening for carbohydrate intolerance in pregnancy: A comparison of two tests and reassessment of a common approach. *Am J Obstet Gynecol* October 1985; 153: 381.

Coustan D, Carpenter M: Detection and treatment of gestational diabetes. *Clin Obstet Gynecol* September 1985; 28: 507.

Cowen MJ et al: Maternal transmission of acquired immune deficiency syndrome. *Pediatr* 1984; 73: 382.

Criteria Committee of the New York Heart Association, Inc: *Nomenclature and Criteria for Diagnosis of Diseases of the Heart and Blood Vessels,* 5th ed. New York: The New York Heart Association, 1955.

Cruikshank DP: Diseases of the alimentary tract. In: *Obstetrics and Gynecology,* 5th ed. Danforth DN, Scott JR (editors). Philadelphia: Lippincott, 1986.

Davies T, Cobin R: Thyroid disease in pregnancy and the postpartum period. *Mt Sinai J Med* January 1985; 52: 59.

DeVoe S, O'Shaughnessy R: Clinical manifestations and diagnosis of pregnancy-induced hypertension. *Clin Obstet Gynecol* December 1984; 27: 836.

Donner C, Cooper K: The critical difference: Ectopic pregnancy. *Am J Nurs* June 1988; 88: 843.

Dorfman SF: Epidemiology of ectopic pregnancy. *Clin Obstet Gynecol* March 1987; 30: 173.

Droegemueller W: Ectopic pregnancy. In: *Obstetrics and Gynecology,* 5th ed. Danforth DN, Scott JR (editors). Philadelphia: Lippincott, 1986.

Eschenbach DA: Pelvic infections. In: *Obstetrics and Gynecology,* 5th ed. Danforth DN, Scott JR (editors). Philadelphia: Lippincott, 1986.

Gabbe SG: Management of diabetes mellitus in pregnancy. *Am J Obstet Gynecol* December 1985; 153: 824.

Gabbe SG: Diabetes mellitus. In: *Obstetrics and Gynecology,* 5th ed. Danforth DN, Scott JR (editors). Philadelphia: Lippincott, 1986.

Gant N, Worley R: *Hypertension in Pregnancy: Concepts and Management.* New York: Appleton-Century-Crofts, 1980.

Gilbert ES, Harmon JS: *High Risk Pregnancy and Delivery: Nursing Perspectives.* St Louis: Mosby, 1986.

Granados JL: Recent developments in the outpatient management of insulin-dependent diabetes mellitus during pregnancy. *Obstet Gynecol Annal* 1984; 13: 83.

Harger JH: Improving the care of pregnant women with genital herpes. *Contemp OB/GYN* 1985; 26(4): 85.

Harris C: Pregnancy can offer a welcome relief from the chronic inflammation of arthritis. *Am J Nurs* April 1985; 85: 415.

Hillard PJA: Physical abuse in pregnancy. *Obstet Gynecol* 1985; 66: 185.

Hollander P, Maeder E: Diabetes in pregnancy: No longer a barrier to successful outcome. *Postgrad Med* February 1985; 77: 137.

Hollingsworth DR: Maternal metabolism in normal pregnancy and pregnancy complicated by diabetes mellitus. *Clin Obstet Gynecol* September 1985; 28: 457.

Kitzmiller JL et al: Managing diabetes and pregnancy. *Current Prob Obstet Gynecol Fertil* July/August 1988; 11: 125.

Klug RM: Children with AIDS. *Am J Nurs* October 1986; 88: 1127.

Korn-Lubetzki I et al: Activity of multiple sclerosis during pregnancy and puerperium. *Ann Neurol* 1984; 16: 229.

LaCamera D: The acquired immunodeficiency syndrome. *Nurs Clin North Am* 1985; 20(1): 241.

Lenke RR: Maternal hyperphenylalaninemia. In: *Principles of Medical Therapy in Pregnancy.* Gleicher N (editor). New York: Plenum, 1985.

Lin C et al: Good diabetic control early in pregnancy and favorable fetal outcome. *Obstet Gynecol* January 1986; 67: 51.

McCoy D, Oswald J: An interactive model program of care for diabetic women before and during pregnancy. *Diabetes Educator* Summer 1983; 9: 11s.

Minkoff HL: Managing AIDS in pregnant patients. *Contemp OB/GYN* September 1988; 32(3): 106.

Miodovnik M: Major malformations in infants of IDDM women. *Diabetes Care* October 1988; 11: 713.

MMWR: Prevention of perinatal transmission of hepatitis B virus: Prenatal screening of all pregnant women for hepatitis B surface antigen. 1988; 37(22): 341.

MMWR Supplement. Recommendations for prevention of HIV transmission in health-care settings. August 21, 1987; 36(2S): 2.

Mor-Yosef S et al: Collagen diseases in pregnancy. *Obstet Gynecol Surv* February 1984; 39: 67.

Patterson RM: Trauma in pregnancy. *Clin Obstet Gynecol* 1984; 27: 1.

Poole JH: Getting perspective on HELLP syndrome. *MCN* November/December 1988; 13:432.

Pritchard JA, MacDonald P, Gant NF: *Williams' Obstetrics,* 17th ed. New York: Appleton-Century-Crofts, 1985.

Queenan JT: Losing the battle and winning the war on ectopics. *Contemp OB/GYN* January 1987; 29:9.

Repke JT: Approaches to chronic hypertension during pregnancy. *Contemp OB/GYN* June 1987; 29:69.

Runowicz CD: Clinical aspects of gestational trophoblastic disease. *Mt Sinai J Med* January 1985; 52:35.

Sadovnik A, Baird P: Reproductive counseling for multiple sclerosis patients. *Am J Med Genetics* 1985; 20:349.

Scott JR: Isoimmunization in pregnancy. In: *Obstetrics and Gynecology,* 5th ed. Danforth DN, Scott JR (editors). Philadelphia: Lippincott, 1986a.

Scott JR: Spontaneous abortion. In: *Obstetrics and Gynecology,* 5th ed. Danforth DN, Scott JR (editors). Philadelphia: Lippincott, 1986b.

Shapiro BS et al: A conservative approach to ectopic pregnancy. *Contemp OB/GYN* June 15, 1988; 32S:58.

Shaw FE, Maynard JE: Hepatitis B: Still a concern for you and your patients. *Contemp OB/GYN* March 1986; 27:27.

Sibai BM: Seeking the best use for magnesium sulfate in preeclampsia-eclampsia. *Contemp OB/GYN* January 1987; 29:155.

Sibai BM: Definitive therapy for pregnancy-induced hypertension. *Contemp OB/GYN* May 1988a; 31:51.

Sibai BM: Pitfalls in diagnosis and management of preeclampsia. *Am J Obstet Gynecol* July 1988b; 159:1.

Sibai BM: Preeclampsia-eclampsia: Maternal and perinatal outcomes. *Contemp OB/GYN* December 1988c; 32:109.

Stagno S, Whitley RJ: Herpesvirus infections of pregnancy. Part II: Herpes simplex virus and varicella-zoster virus infections. *New Engl J Med* 1985; 313(21):1327.

Steel JM: Pre-pregnancy counseling and contraception in the insulin-dependent diabetic patient. *Clin Obstet Gynecol* September 1985; 28:553.

Symposium: If you suspect a patient is a victim of abuse. *Contemp OB/GYN* June 1987; 29:132.

Triolo PK: Nonobstetric surgery during pregnancy. *J Obstet Gynecol Neonatal Nurs* 1985; 14(3):179.

Wall-Haas C: Women's perceptions of first trimester spontaneous abortion. *J Obstet Gynecol Neonatal Nurs* January/February 1985; 14:50.

Weckstein L: Current perspectives on ectopic pregnancy. *Obstet Gynecol Surv* 1985; 40(5):259.

Weinstein L: Syndrome of hemolysis, elevated liver enzymes, and low platelet count: A severe consequence of hypertension in pregnancy. *Am J Obstet Gynecol* January 15, 1982; 142:159.

Weinstein L: Preeclampsia-eclampsia with hemolysis, elevated liver enzymes, and thrombocytopenia. *Obstet Gynecol* November 1985; 66:657.

White P: Classification of obstetric diabetes. *Am J Obstet Gynecol* 1978; 130:228.

Wiley K, Grohar J: Human immunodeficiency virus and precautions for obstetric, gynecologic, and neonatal nurses. *J Obstet Gynecol Neonatal Nurs* May/June 1988; 17:165.

Wilson D: An overview of sexually transmissible diseases in the perinatal period. *J Nurse-Midwifery* May/June 1988; 33(3):115.

Worley RJ: Pathophysiology of pregnancy-induced hypertension. *Clin Obstet Gynecol* December 1984; 27:821.

Worley RJ: Pregnancy-induced hypertension. In: *Obstetrics and Gynecology,* 5th ed. Danforth DN, Scott JR (editors). Philadelphia: Lippincott, 1986.

Zuspan FP: Chronic hypertension in pregnancy. *Clin Obstet Gynecol* December 1984; 27:854.

## Additional Readings

Anderson GD: A systematic approach to eclamptic convulsion. *Contemp OB/GYN* March 1987; 29:65.

Bremer C et al: Trauma in pregnancy. *Nurs Clin North Am* December 1986; 21:705.

Chez R: Woman battering. *Am J Obstet Gynecol* 1988; 158(1):1.

Chow W et al: Maternal cigarette smoking and tubal pregnancy. *Obstet Gynecol* 1988; 71(2):167.

DeVore N et al: Ectopic pregnancy on the rise. *Am J Nurs* June 1986; 86:672.

Fayez JA: Evaluation and management of recurrent early pregnancy losses. *Female Patient* September 1988; 13:13.

Lia-Hoagberg B et al: Relationship of street drug use, hospitalization, and psychosocial factors to low birth weight among low income women. *Birth: Issues in Perinatal Care and Education* 1988; 15(1):8.

Marchbanks P et al: Risk factors for ectopic pregnancy. *JAMA* 1988; 259(12):1823.

Mason J et al: Current CDC efforts to prevent and control human immunodeficiency virus infection and AIDS in the United States through information and education. *Public Health Rep* 1988; 103(3):255.

O'Brien ME, Gibson G: Detection and management of gestational diabetes in an out-of-hospital birth center. *J Nurse-Midwifery* March/April 1987; 32:79.

Petri M: Outcomes encouraging in mothers with lupus. *Contemp OB/GYN* March 1988; 31:103.

Ronkin S et al: Protecting mother and fetus from narcotic abuse. *Contemp OB/GYN* March 1988; 31:178.

Tilden V, Shepherd P: Increasing the rate of identification of battered women in an emergency department: Use of a nursing protocol. *Res Nurs Health* 1987; 10(4):209.

Zigrossi ST et al: The stress of medical management on pregnant diabetics. *MCN* September/October 1986; 11:320.

# 13

# Assessment of Fetal Well-Being

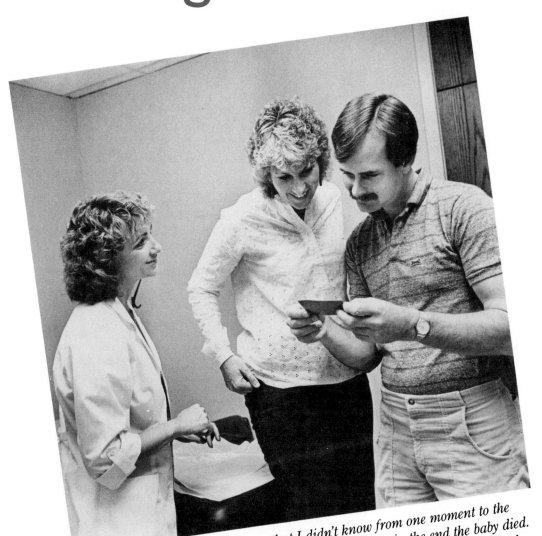

My first pregnancy was so tenuous that I didn't know from one moment to the next how it would end. I hoped for our baby's safety, but in the end the baby died. When I became pregnant the next time I was very nervous. Being able to see the baby on ultrasound helped me so much. I knew then that our baby was alive and growing.

## Objectives

● List indications for ultrasonic examination and the information that can be obtained from this procedure.

● Outline pertinent information to be discussed with the woman regarding her assessment of fetal activity and methods of recording fetal activity.

● Compare the nonstress test (NST) and the contraction stress test (CST), giving indications, contraindications, and predictive value of each.

● Discuss the value of estriols as a measure of fetal well-being.

● Discuss the use of amniocentesis as a diagnostic tool.

● Describe the tests that may be done on amniotic fluid.

## Key Terms

amniocentesis
amnioscopy
contraction stress test (CST)
fetal biophysical profile
fetoscopy
lecithin/sphingomyelin (L/S) ratio
nonstress test (NST)
phosphatidylglycerol (PG)
surfactant
ultrasound

During the past 15–20 years, the problems of the high-risk pregnant woman and her baby have received increasing attention. This attention has been stimulated by the observation that conditions such as prematurity, congenital anomalies, mental retardation, and cerebral palsy seem to be associated with the presence of certain factors, such as maternal infections or diabetes mellitus, during pregnancy and delivery. In addition, it has been demonstrated that perinatal morbidity (sickness) and mortality (death) can be significantly reduced when there is early diagnosis of pregnancy and of high-risk factors and ongoing prenatal care of the pregnant woman.

A variety of tests can be used to assess fetal well-being during the pregnancy. These tests include diagnostic ultrasound, measurements of specific hormones and enzymes in the maternal plasma and urine, amniocentesis for lung maturity studies, amnioscopy, and fetal stress tests. The tests provide information regarding fetal well-being, normal growth of the fetus, the presence of congenital anomalies, the location of the placenta, and fetal lung maturity (see Table 13.1). New diagnostic tests that are being developed are summarized in Table 13.2.

Many of these tests pose risks to the fetus and possibly to the pregnant woman, and these risks should be considered before a particular test is done. One must be certain that the advantages outweigh the potential risks and the added expense. In addition, the diagnostic accuracy and applicability of these tests may vary. Certainly, not all high-risk pregnancies require the same tests. Conditions that indicate a high-risk pregnancy include:

● Maternal age less than 16 years or more than 35 years

● Chronic maternal hypertension, preeclampsia, diabetes mellitus, or heart disease

● Presence of Rh isoimmunization

● A maternal history of unexplained stillbirth

● Suspected intrauterine growth retardation (IUGR)

● Pregnancy prolonged past 42 weeks' gestation

See Chapter 7 for further discussion of prenatal high-risk factors and Chapter 12 for descriptions of various conditions that may threaten the successful completion of pregnancy.

## ● USING THE NURSING PROCESS DURING DIAGNOSTIC TESTING

Because many of the diagnostic tests are completed on an outpatient basis, the nurse has only brief contact with the woman and her support person. The nurse uses the nursing process to guide nursing care during these interactions.

## ● Nursing Assessment

The nursing assessment begins with a history of the prenatal course and identification of possible indications for the particular diagnostic testing. The nurse assesses the woman's and her support person's knowledge about the test and the presence of any particular factors that may influence the teaching process. During the test, the nurse completes assessments needed to monitor the status of the mother and her unborn child.

## ● Nursing Diagnosis

The primary nursing diagnoses are directed toward the woman's knowledge about the diagnostic test and any risks to herself and her unborn child. The woman may also be fearful of the outcome of the tests, and nurses can play

an important role in providing support and counseling. Examples of nursing diagnoses that may be applicable include:

● Knowledge deficit related to insufficient information about the fetal assessment test, purpose, benefits, risks, and alternatives

● Fear related to possible unfavorable test results

## ● Nursing Plan and Implementation

The nursing plan of care will be directed toward each specific nursing diagnosis. The nurse generally plays a vital role in providing information about the diagnostic test. The nurse assesses the woman's knowledge of the test and then provides information as needed. Some of the tests require written informed consent; in these cases the physician is responsible for informing the woman about all aspects of the test. The nurse can reinforce information and clarify information that is not fully understood (see Table 13.3).

Contact with the expectant woman may be very brief.

## Table 13.1  Summary of Screening and Diagnostic Tests

| Goal | Test | When test may be done |
|---|---|---|
| To validate the pregnancy | Ultrasound for gestational sac volume | Five and six weeks after LMP |
| To determine how advanced the pregnancy is | Ultrasound: Crown–rump length<br>Ultrasound: Biparietal diameter and femur length | 7 to 10 weeks' gestation<br>13 to 40 weeks' gestation |
| To identify normal growth of the fetus | Ultrasound: Biparietal diameter<br><br>Ultrasound: Head–abdomen ratio<br>Ultrasound: Estimated fetal weight | Most useful from 20 to 30 weeks' gestation<br>13 to 40 weeks' gestation<br>About 28 to 40 weeks' gestation |
| To detect congenital anomalies and problems | Ultrasound<br>Chorionic villus sampling<br>Fetoscopy<br>Percutaneous blood sampling | 18 to 40 weeks' gestation<br>8 to 12 weeks' gestation<br>18 weeks' gestation<br>Second and third trimesters |
| To localize the placenta | Ultrasound | Usually in third trimester or before amniocentesis |
| To assess fetal status | Fetal biophysical profile<br>Maternal assessment of fetal activity<br>Estriols<br>Magnetic resonance imaging<br>Nonstress test<br>Contraction stress test | Approximately 28 weeks to delivery<br>About 27 weeks to delivery<br>During the second and third trimesters<br>During the second and third trimesters<br>Approximately 30 weeks to delivery<br>Last few weeks of gestation |
| To diagnose cardiac problems | Fetal echocardiography | Second and third trimesters |
| To assess fetal lung maturity | Amniocentesis<br>  L/S ratio<br>  Phosphatidylglycerol<br>  Phosphatidylcholine<br>  Shake test | 33 to 40 weeks<br>33 weeks to delivery<br>33 weeks to delivery<br>33 weeks to delivery<br>33 weeks to delivery |
| To obtain more information about breech presentation | Computerized tomography<br>X-ray | Just before labor is anticipated or during labor |

## Table 13.2 Diagnostic Techniques Under Development

| Diagnostic technique | Purpose of the test | When the test may be done |
|---|---|---|
| **CHORIONIC VILLUS SAMPLING (CVS)** | | |
| A sample of chorionic villi from the placenta is obtained by introducing an aspiration catheter or biopsy forcep through the cervix (Brambati and Oldrini 1985). The whole procedure is guided and monitored by ultrasound. | To obtain tissue for genetic studies, sex determination<br>When a genetic problem may be anticipated | Between 8 and 12 weeks |
| **PERCUTANEOUS UMBILICAL BLOOD SAMPLING** | | |
| An ultrasound scan is used to locate the fetal umbilical cord. A needle is introduced through the maternal abdomen into the umbilical cord and blood is aspirated. | To obtain a fetal blood sample for use in diagnosis of hemophilias, hemoglobinopathies, congenital rubella and toxoplasmosis, and in fetal karyotyping | In the second and third trimesters |
| **COMPUTED TOMOGRAPHY (CT SCANNING)** | | |
| A CT machine is used to scan the expectant woman's lower abdomen and pelvis. | To obtain accurate maternal pelvic and fetal diameters, especially in a breech presentation | At term or during labor<br>When the fetus is in a breech presentation |
| **MAGNETIC RESONANCE IMAGING (MRI)** | | |
| The MRI provides imaging similar to CT and ultrasound scanning; however, the image is more precise and detailed and the entire fetus can be imaged in one scan. | To obtain confirmation of fetal abnormalities suggested by ultrasound, for pelvimetry, and for assessment of placental localization and size | During second or third trimesters |

The nurse uses basic knowledge of communication, developmental psychology, cultural factors, and so forth to quickly establish a trusting relationship with the woman and her support person.

The nurse also functions as an advocate for the expectant woman by helping her clarify question areas and obtain needed information. The nurse frequently knows the areas about which most women have questions and can anticipate many of their fears. When the woman is not able to verbalize questions, the nurse can assist by bringing up questions that other women have had.

During the testing sessions, the nurse addresses the woman's fear by providing support and comfort measures. The presence of the nurse reassures the woman and helps her cope with the tests.

## ● Evaluation

The expected outcomes for the woman who is having diagnostic testing are that she understands the reasons for the test and the test results and has had support during the test. In addition, the tests have been done without complication and the safety of the mother and her unborn child has been maintained.

## Table 13.3 Sample Nursing Approaches to Pretest Teaching

- Assess whether the woman knows the reason the screening or diagnostic test is being recommended.
  Example:
  "Has your doctor/nurse-midwife told you why this test is necessary?"
  "Sometimes tests are done for many different reasons. Can you tell me why you are having this test?"
  "What is your understanding about what the test will show?"

- Provide an opportunity for questions.
  Example:
  "Do you have any questions about the test?"
  "Is there anything that is not clear to you?"

- Explain the test procedure, paying particular attention to any preparation the woman needs to do prior to the test.
  Example:
  "The test that has been ordered for you is designed to . . ." (add specific information about the particular test. Give the explanation in simple language).

- Validate the woman's understanding of the preparation.
  Example:
  "Tell me what you will have to do to get ready for this test."

- Give permission for woman to continue to ask questions if needed.
  Example:
  "I'll be with you during the test. If you have any questions at any time, please don't hesitate to ask."

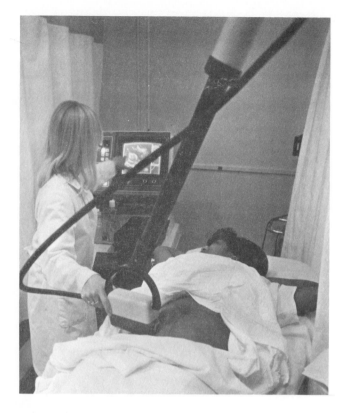

*Figure 13.1    Ultrasound scanning permits visualization of the fetus in utero.*

## ● ULTRASOUND

Valuable information about the fetus may be obtained from pulsed echo **ultrasound** testing. Intermittent ultrasonic waves (high-frequency sound waves) are transmitted by an alternating current to a transducer, which is applied to the woman's abdomen. The ultrasonic waves deflect off tissues within the woman's abdomen, showing structures of varying densities (Figure 13.1).

The most common types of obstetric ultrasound are gray-scale and real-time scanning. *Gray-scale ultrasound* provides a static or fixed image. Various internal structures can be visualized in many shades of gray (Figure 13.2). This type of ultrasound is done in an x-ray or ultrasound department. In *real-time scanning,* a transducer produces a rapid sequence of fixed images, which are displayed on a small screen similar to a television screen. Real-time scanning allows the observer to detect movement, such as that of the beating fetal heart. The operator may "freeze" an image on the screen and photograph the image for a permanent record. Real-time ultrasound is particularly helpful in late pregnancy for assessing functions that can be detected through movement, such as fetal breathing, cardiac activity, and bladder function. Real-time ultrasound equipment is small and easily moved and need not be used in the x-ray department. Thus, it is frequently kept in birthing areas so a pregnant woman can have the procedure done without the inconvenience of a trip to a different department.

In addition to the transabdominal approach, a new endovaginal technique has been developed. With this method, a probe is inserted into the vagina. Pennell et al (1987) report that the endovaginal technique is particularly useful when the woman is obese, when adequate bladder filling is not possible, when there is shadowing from the symphysis pubis, or when there is poor visualization of the gestational sac or its contents.

Although ultrasound testing can be beneficial, the National Institutes of Health (NIH) Consensus Development Conference on Ultrasound Imaging in Pregnancy recommends that it not be routinely used on all pregnant women because its long-term effects are not fully known (Carson et al 1988).

Diagnostic ultrasound has several advantages. It is noninvasive, painless, nonradiating to both the woman and the fetus, and has no known harmful effects to either. Serial studies (several ultrasound tests done over a span of time) may be done for assessment and comparison. Soft tissue masses can be differentiated. The practitioner obtains results immediately. Finally, ultrasound does not pose the same risk as other diagnostic or medical procedures, such as amniocentesis or intrauterine surgery, yet allows the clinician to "see" the fetus.

## ● Procedure for Transabdominal Technique

The woman is usually scanned with a full bladder except when ultrasound is used to localize the placenta prior

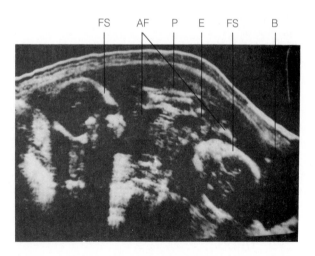

*Figure 13.2    Gray scale. Longitudinal scan demonstrating twin gestation, anterior placenta, fetal extremity. Both biparietal diameters (BPDs) correlate with approximately 25–26 weeks' gestation. (AF = amniotic fluid, FS = fetal skull, E = extremity, B = woman's urinary bladder, P = placenta.) (Courtesy Section of Diagnostic Ultrasound, Department of Diagnostic Radiology, Kansas University Medical Center.)*

to amniocentesis. When the bladder is full, the examiner can assess other structures, especially the vagina and cervix, in relation to the bladder. This is particularly important when vaginal bleeding is noted and placenta previa is the suspected cause. The woman is advised to drink one quart of water approximately two hours before the examination, and she is asked to refrain from emptying her bladder. If the bladder is not sufficiently filled, she is asked to drink three to four 8-oz glasses of water and is rescanned 30–45 minutes later.

Mineral oil or a transmission gel is generously spread over the woman's abdomen, and the sonographer slowly moves a transducer over the abdomen to obtain a picture of the contents of the uterus. Ultrasound testing takes 20–30 minutes. The woman may feel discomfort due to pressure applied over a full bladder. In addition, the woman lies on her back during the test, which may cause shortness of breath. This may be relieved by elevating her upper body during the test.

Some clinicians have questioned whether the actual ultrasound examination creates anxiety for the pregnant woman. Cox et al (1987) found that the ultrasound examination relieved anxiety and stress. The emotional impact of the examination was influenced by the level of feedback provided to the woman and her partner. Couples who stated they felt the most relief of anxiety during the testing were able to view the screen during the ultrasound exam and received ample verbal explanation and support from the health care providers.

## Clinical Application

Ultrasound testing can be of benefit in the following ways:

- Early identification of pregnancy. (Pregnancy may be detected as early as the fifth or sixth week following the last menstrual period [LMP].)
- Identification of more than one fetus (see Figure 13.2).
- Measurement of the biparietal diameter of the fetal head or the fetal femur length. These measurements help to determine the gestational age of the fetus and also to identify IUGR (Figure 13.3).
- Detection of fetal anomalies. Two major abnormalities that may be detected are anencephaly and hydrocephalus.
- Detection of hydramnios (or polyhydramnios) or oligohydramnios. The presence of more or less than normal amounts of amniotic fluid is frequently associated with fetal anomalies.
- Identification of amniotic fluid pockets. The presence of a pocket of amniotic fluid measuring at least 1 cm is associated with normal fetal status. The presence of one pocket measuring less than 1 cm or the absence

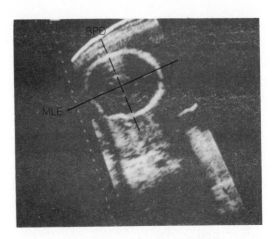

*Figure 13.3  Transverse scan of the skull of a fetus of 25–26 weeks. BPD is measured perpendicular to midline echo (MLE). (Courtesy Section of Diagnostic Ultrasound, Department of Diagnostic Radiology, Kansas University Medical Center.)*

of a pocket is abnormal. It is associated with increased risk of perinatal death (Manning 1985).

- Location of the placenta. This is done prior to amniocentesis to avoid puncturing the placenta. Ultrasound is also used to determine the presence of placenta previa.
- Observation of fetal heart beat and respiration by real-time scanning. Respirations (fetal breathing movements, or FBM) have been observed as early as the eleventh week of gestation. Some researchers suggest that evaluation of fetal breathing movements may give information about the health of the fetus.
- Placental grading. As the fetus matures, the placenta calcifies. These changes can be visualized by ultrasound and graded according to the degree of calcification (grades 0 to 3). Grade 3 placentas appear to be correlated with fetal lung maturity as determined by amniotic fluid analysis (Golde and Platt 1984). Placental grading may be a way of determining fetal maturity when amniocentesis cannot be done.
- Detection of fetal death. Inability to visualize the fetal heart beating and the separation of the bones in the fetal head are signs of fetal death.
- Determination of fetal position and presentation. Ultrasound images give information about position and presentation.

## Risks of Ultrasound

Ultrasound has been used clinically for over 25 years, and to date no clinical studies verify harmful effects to the mother, fetus, or child. Several studies with animals suggest that ultrasound may retard fetal growth, cause cell damage, and impair the immune response, but the ultrasound levels used in these studies were higher than those levels used in medical diagnosis in pregnancy (Carson et al 1988).

## ● Role of the Nurse

It is important for the nurse to ascertain whether the woman understands the reason the ultrasound is being suggested. The nurse can provide an opportunity for the woman to ask questions and can act as an advocate if there are questions or concerns that need to be addressed prior to the ultrasound examination.

### CLIENT EDUCATION

The nurse explains the preparation needed and assures that adequate preparation is done. After the test is completed, the nurse can assist with clarifying or interpreting test results to the woman.

## ● MATERNAL ASSESSMENT OF FETAL ACTIVITY

Assessment of fetal movement patterns has been used as a screening procedure in the evaluation of fetal status since 1971 when the clinical significance of various types of fetal activity was first described (Sadovsky 1985b). Clinicians now generally agree that vigorous fetal activity provides reassurance of fetal well-being and that marked decrease in activity or cessation of movement may indicate possible fetal compromise requiring immediate follow-up evaluation. The woman can conduct daily fetal movement recording (DFMR) at her convenience and without any expense.

Sadovsky (1985a) noted that, although there is considerable variation among individuals, the average number of daily movements rises from about 200 at 20 weeks to a maximum of 575 at 32 weeks and gradually decreases to an average of 282 at term. In women with a multiple gestation, daily fetal movements are significantly higher. Connors et al (1988) found that the fetus has 90-minute rest and activity cycles during the last ten weeks of gestation.

Fetal activity is affected by many factors, including sound, drugs, cigarette smoking, sleep states of the fetus, blood glucose levels, and time of day. The expectant mother's perception of fetal movements and her commitment to completing the movement record may vary. When the woman understands the purpose of the assessment, how to complete the form, whom to call with questions, and what to report, and has the opportunity for follow-up during each visit, she will also see this as an important activity. (See Teaching Guide—What to Tell the Pregnant Woman About Assessing Fetal Activity.)

## ● Role of the Nurse

### CLIENT EDUCATION

The nurse assists in teaching the technique for DFMR. The nurse can also help the woman devise a daily record in which she can report fetal movements. The nurse is available for questions and to clarify areas of concern (see Teaching Guide).

## ● NONSTRESS TEST

The **nonstress test (NST)** has become a widely accepted method of evaluating fetal status. The test involves using an electronic fetal monitor in order to observe baseline variability and acceleration of the fetal heart rate (FHR) with fetal movement. FHR accelerations indicate central and autonomic nervous systems that are not being affected by a decrease of oxygen to the fetus, or *intrauterine hypoxia* (see the discussion of baseline variability and acceleration in Chapter 15).

The advantages of the NST are as follows:

- It is quick to perform.
- It permits easy interpretation.
- It is inexpensive.
- It can be done in an office or clinic setting.
- There are no known side effects.

The disadvantages of the NST include:

- It is sometimes difficult to obtain a suitable tracing.
- The woman has to lie relatively still for at least 20 minutes.

## ● Procedure for NST

The test may be done with the woman in a reclining chair or in bed in a semi-Fowler's or side-lying position. An electronic fetal monitor is used to obtain a tracing of FHR and fetal movement (FM). The examiner puts two belts on the woman's abdomen. One belt holds a device that detects uterine or fetal movement. The other belt holds a device that detects the FHR. As the NST is done, each fetal movement is documented so that associated or simultaneous FHR changes may be evaluated.

## ● Interpretation of NST Results

The results of the NST are interpreted as follows:

- *Reactive test.* A reactive NST shows at least two accelerations of FHR with fetal movements, of 15 beats per minute, lasting 15 seconds or more, over 20 minutes (Figure 13.5).

*(Text continues on page 352.)*

**Assessment** The nurse focuses on the woman's prior knowledge and former use of fetal movement assessment methods, the week of gestation, and her communication and ability to understand and process information.

**Nursing Diagnosis** The essential nursing diagnosis will probably be: knowledge deficit related to fetal movement assessment methods.

**Nursing Plan and Implementation**

**Client Goals** At the completion of the teaching session:

- The woman will gain knowledge regarding the types of fetal assessment methods, reasons for assessment, how to accomplish the assessment, and methods of record keeping.
- The woman will demonstrate the use of a movement record.
- The woman will have resources to call if questions arise.
- The woman will agree to bring movement record to each prenatal visit.

The teaching plan will consist of presenting the two most commonly used fetal movement assessment methods. The nurse may want to present the information verbally and then demonstrate how to mark the movement record. The nurse may prepare a written teaching sheet for the woman's use at home to further assure that the information is understood. Before the woman leaves the care setting it is important to evaluate her understanding of the method and how to complete the chart, and ensure that she has a name and phone number in case she has further questions.

**Teaching Content** The goal of the teaching sessions is to provide general information regarding fetal movement and assessment methods. The expectant woman needs to know that fetal movements are first felt around 18 weeks' gestation. From that time the fetal movements get stronger and easier to detect. A slowing or stopping of fetal movement may be an indication that the baby needs some attention and evaluation. The normal amount of movement varies considerably; however, most healthy babies move at least 10 times in 12 hours. The nurse teaches the woman a fetal assessment method and encourages her to complete the record each day. The record will be discussed at each prenatal visit and questions may be addressed at that time if desired.

## Teaching Plan

### Daily Fetal Movement Record (DFMR) (Figure 13.4, A)

| Content | When to Contact the Care Provider | What Happens Next | Teaching Method |
|---|---|---|---|
| The low-risk woman begins at 27 weeks' gestation. The fetal movements are counted twice a day for 20–30 minutes each session. Five or six movements during each period of counting is looked on as reassuring. | If the woman has questions or concerns. If there are fewer than 10 fetal movements in a 12-hour period OR no movements in the morning OR less than three fetal movements in eight hours. | The care provider will probably suggest a NST to further evaluate the baby. Additional testing may include a CST, tests for pulmonary maturity, and ultrasound (Gantes et al 1985, Chez and Sadovsky 1984). | Verbal presentation |
| The high-risk woman begins at 27 weeks of gestation. The fetal movements are counted three times a day for 30 minutes. Five or six movements during each period is desired. If there are less than three movements in a counting period the woman should continue counting for an hour or more. | Same as above | | Verbal presentation Demonstrate how to palpate abdomen. Demonstrate how to record movements on DMFR scoring card. |

(continues)

## Teaching Plan (continued)

| Content | When to Contact the Care Provider | What Happens Next | Teaching Method |
|---|---|---|---|
| **Daily Fetal Movement Record (DFMR) (Figure 13.4, *A*)** | | | |
| Regardless of risk category, it will be advantageous for the woman to schedule the counting periods about one hour past eating and to combine the counting period with rest. A side-lying position provides optimal circulation to the uterus-placenta-fetus unit. In addition, the baby's movements are felt more readily while lying on the side. Later in the pregnancy, some women may be bothered by indigestion after eating. In this case they can prop up the upper body but still maintain a side-lying position. | | | |
| **Cardiff-Count-to-Ten (Figure 13.4, *B*)** | | | |
| The woman begins these assessments in the 27th week of gestation. At 9:00 each morning, the woman begins counting the baby's movements. When there have been ten movements, an X is placed at the appropriate time on the card (Clark and Britton 1985; Eggertsen and Benedetti 1987). | When there are questions or concerns.<br><br>If there are fewer than ten movements by 9:00 PM (12 hours).<br><br>If overall the baby's movements are slowing and it takes much longer each day to note ten movements. | Same as above | *Verbal presentation*<br>*Demonstrate how to record movements on Cardiff-count-to-ten scoring card.*<br>*Watch woman fill out record as examples are provided.* |

*Evaluation*    The nurse may evaluate learning by having the woman explain the method to the nurse and by asking the woman to fill the card in using a fictitious situation. At each prenatal visit, the expectant woman's record is reviewed and this provides another opportunity for evaluation of learning.

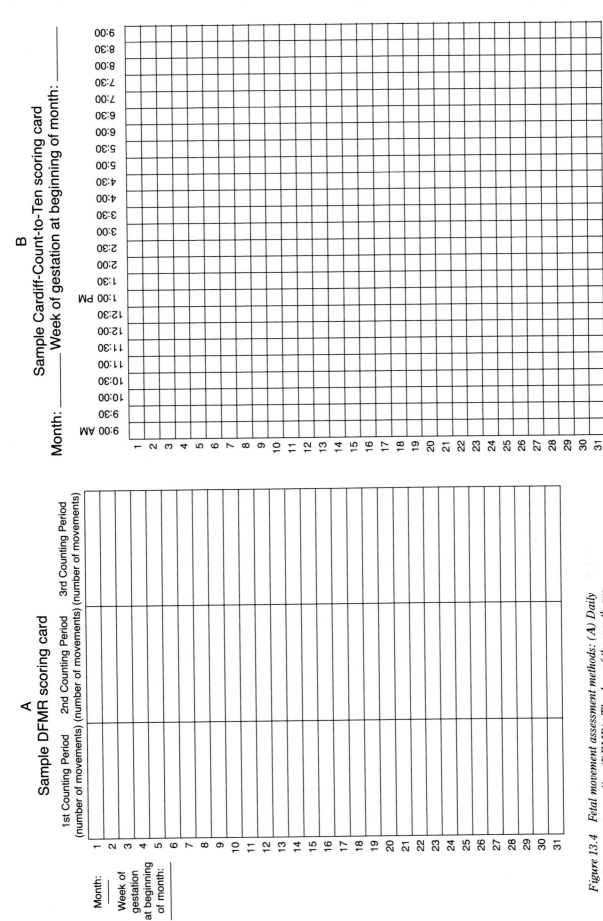

*Figure 13.4 Fetal movement assessment methods: (A) Daily fetal movement recording (DFMR). The days of the month are located from top to bottom on the left side. The chart is started on the correct day of the month. Three counting periods are recorded for each day. (B) The Cardiff-Count-to-Ten scoring card (adaptation).*

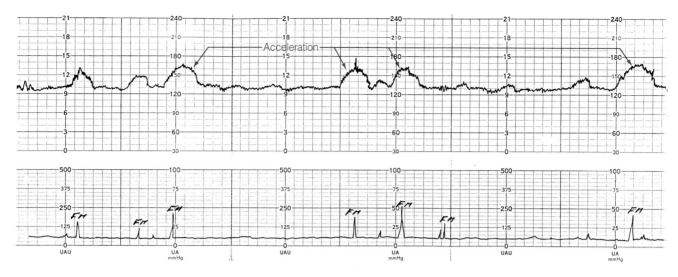

*Figure 13.5  Example of a reactive nonstress test (NST). The top portion of the strip is a recording of the FHR. Note that most of the FHR tracing is relatively straight with some areas that rise from this relatively straight line. These are accelerations. Each small square of the graph paper equals 10 seconds, so each of the indicated accelerations is more than 15 seconds in length. Each of the identified accelerations occurs with a fetal movement (FM), which is recorded on the bottom portion of the strip. The criteria for a reactive nonstress test have been met on this tracing.*

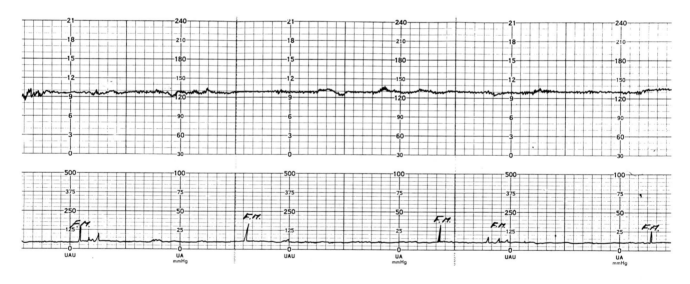

*Figure 13.6  Example of a nonreactive NST. There are no accelerations of FHR with the five episodes of fetal movement indicated on the bottom portion of the strip.*

- *Nonreactive test.* In a nonreactive test, the reactive criteria are not met. For example, the accelerations are not as much as 15 beats per minute, or do not last 15 seconds, and so on (Figure 13.6).

- *Unsatisfactory test.* An unsatisfactory NST has data that cannot be interpreted, or inadequate fetal activity.

Criteria for the NST appear to vary somewhat from one author to another. Some require two accelerations of FHR in 20 minutes; others require two in 10 minutes.

It is particularly important that anyone who performs the NST also understand the significance of any decelerations of the FHR during testing. If decelerations are noted, the physician/nurse-midwife should be notified for further evaluation of fetal status. (See Chapter 15 for further discussion of FHR decelerations.)

## ● Prognostic Value

A reactive NST appears to be indicative of fetal well-being, and the test usually does not need to be repeated for one week. Any change in maternal or fetal status—such as decreased fetal movement, decreasing estriol levels, vaginal bleeding, or deterioration of maternal condition—warrants more frequent testing.

A nonreactive NST indicates the need for further testing. Some authorities recommend rescheduling the NST again within 24 hours, while others believe a contraction stress test should be done immediately. (See Essential Facts to Remember—Nonstress Test.)

A new method of conducting an NST is currently being investigated. The new method is called an *acoustic stimulation test* and uses sound to stimulate the fetus. The test is evaluated in the same way as other NSTs (Ingemarsson et al 1988, Richards et al 1988).

## ● Role of the Nurse

The nurse ascertains the woman's understanding of the NST and the possible results. The reasons for the NST and the procedure are reviewed prior to beginning the test. The nurse administers the NST, interprets the results, and reports the findings to the physician/nurse-midwife and the expectant woman.

## ● FETAL BIOPHYSICAL PROFILE

The **fetal biophysical profile** is a collection of information regarding selected fetal measurements and assess-

## Essential Facts to Remember

### Nonstress Test

Diagnostic value: Demonstrates fetus's ability to respond to its environment by acceleration of FHR with movement
Results:

- Reactive test: Accelerations are present, indicating fetal well-being.
- Nonreactive test: Accelerations are not present, indicating that the fetus is sick or asleep.

ments of the fetus and amniotic fluid. It includes five variables: fetal breathing movements, body movement, tone, amniotic fluid volume, and FHR reactivity. While information is obtained regarding the variables, the examiner also uses ultrasound to determine fetal biparietal diameter, femur length, and abdominal circumference (Table 13.4).

The fetal biophysical profile can be used to monitor fetal well-being. Some researchers suggest that it can be used to identify a fetus at risk for asphyxia (Manning et al 1987).

A management protocol regarding the fetal biophysical profile is outlined in Table 13.5. A detailed explanation of the fetal biophysical profile is beyond the scope of this book. (For further information, see Manning et al 1987, Baskett 1988.)

### Table 13.4 Biophysical Profile Scoring: Technique and Interpretation

| Biophysical variable | Normal (score = 2) | Abnormal (score = 0) |
|---|---|---|
| 1. Fetal breathing movements | ≥1 episode of ≥30 sec in 30 min | Absent or no episode of ≥30 sec in 30 min |
| 2. Gross body movements | ≥3 discrete body/limb movements in 30 min (episodes of active continuous movement considered as single movement) | ≤2 episodes of body/limb movements in 30 min |
| 3. Fetal tone | ≥1 episode of active extension with return to flexion of fetal limb(s) or trunk. Opening and closing of hand considered normal tone | Either slow extension with return to partial flexion or movement of limb in full extension or absent fetal movement |
| 4. Reactive fetal heart rate | ≥2 episodes of acceleration of ≥15 bpm and of ≥15 sec associated with fetal movement in 20 min | <2 episodes of acceleration of fetal heart rate or acceleration of <15 bpm in 20 min |
| 5. Qualitative amniotic fluid volume | ≥1 pocket of fluid measuring ≥1 cm in two perpendicular planes | Either no pockets or a pocket <1 cm in two perpendicular planes |

Source: Manning FA et al: Fetal assessment based on fetal biophysical profile scoring: Experience in 12,620 referred high-risk pregnancies. *Am J Obstet Gynecol* 1985; 151(3): 344.

## Table 13.5  Biophysical Profile Scoring: Management Protocol

| Score | Interpretation | Recommended management |
|---|---|---|
| 10 | Normal infant, low risk for chronic asphyxia | Repeat testing at weekly intervals. Repeat twice weekly in diabetic patients and patients ≥42 wk |
| 8 | Normal infant, low risk for chronic asphyxia | Repeat testing at weekly intervals. Repeat twice weekly in diabetic patients and patients ≥42 wk. Indication for delivery = oligohydramnios |
| 6 | Suspected chronic asphyxia | Repeat testing within 24 hr. Indication for delivery = oligohydramnios or persisting ≤6 |
| 4 | Suspected chronic asphyxia | ≥36 score and favorable cervix. If <36 wk and lecithin/sphingomyelin ratio <2.0, repeat test in 24 hr. Indication for delivery = repeat score ≤6 or oligohydramnios |
| 0–2 | Strong suspicion of chronic asphyxia | Extend testing time to 120 min. Indication for delivery = persistent score ≤4, regardless of gestational age |

Source: Manning FA et al: Fetal assessment based on fetal biophysical profile scoring: Experience in 12,620 referred high-risk pregnancies. *Am J Obstet Gynecol* 1985; 151(3): 344.

# CONTRACTION STRESS TEST

The **contraction stress test (CST)** is a means of evaluating the respiratory function (oxygen and carbon dioxide exchange) of the placenta. It enables the health care team to identify the fetus at risk for intrauterine asphyxia by observing the response of the FHR to the stress of uterine contractions (spontaneous or induced). During contractions, intrauterine pressure increases. Blood flow to the intervillous space of the placenta is reduced momentarily, thereby decreasing oxygen transport to the fetus. A healthy fetus usually tolerates this reduction well. If the placental reserve is insufficient, fetal hypoxia, depression of the myocardium, and a decrease in FHR occur. (See Figure 15.15, *B*.)

The CST is indicated when there is risk of placental insufficiency or fetal compromise because of the following:

- IUGR
- Diabetes mellitus
- Heart disease
- Chronic hypertension
- Preeclampsia-eclampsia (pregnancy-induced hypertension, or PIH)
- Sickle cell anemia
- Suspected postmaturity (more than 42 weeks' gestation)
- History of previous stillbirths
- Rh sensitization
- Abnormal estriol excretion
- Hyperthyroidism
- Renal disease
- Nonreactive NST

The CST is contraindicated if there is third trimester bleeding from placenta previa or marginal abruptio placenta, previous cesarean with classical uterine incision, risk of precipitating premature labor outweighing the advantage of the CST, premature rupture of the membranes, incompetent cervix, or multiple gestation.

The advantages of the CST are:

- The test provides information about how the fetus will react to the stress of uterine contractions.
- It can show that the fetal environment is deteriorating.

The disadvantages include:

- The test needs to be administered in a birthing setting.
- It is an invasive procedure if an intravenous line is used.
- It may initiate uterine contractions that precipitate labor.

## Procedure

A necessary component of the CST is the presence of uterine contractions. They may occur spontaneously (which is unusual), or they may be induced (stimulated) with oxytocin. The most common method of stimulating uterine contractions for a CST is through intravenous administration of oxytocin (Pitocin). Consequently, the CST has been called the *oxytocin challenge test (OCT)*. Another method of obtaining oxytocin is through the use of breast stimulation during a breast self-stimulation test (also called nipple stimulation). This method is based on the knowledge that the body produces oxytocin in response to stimulation of the breasts or nipples.

The procedure for CST, reasons for administering the test, equipment used, and normal variations in monitoring that occur during the test should be clearly explained to the woman prior to the test. A consent form is signed. The woman should empty her bladder before the CST is begun because she may be confined to bed for 1.5–2 hours.

The woman is positioned in a sitting or side-lying position to maintain optimum uteroplacental circulation and to enhance the quality of the uterine contractions as they occur. When the woman lies on her side, uterine contractions seem to be less frequent but more intense than when she is in a semi-Fowler's position (Marshall 1986). The semi-Fowler's position is also more often associated with hyperstimulation (Marshall 1986).

An electronic fetal monitor is used to provide continuous data regarding the fetal heart rate and uterine contractions. Maternal blood pressure and pulse are assessed as the recording is begun. After a 15-minute baseline recording of uterine activity and FHR, the tracing is evaluated for evidence of spontaneous contractions. If three spontaneous contractions of good quality and lasting 40–60 seconds occur in a ten-minute period, the results are evaluated, and the test is concluded. If no contractions occur or if they are insufficient for interpretation, oxytocin is administered intravenously or breast stimulation is done to produce contractions of good quality.

## CST WITH INTRAVENOUS OXYTOCIN

An electrolyte solution such as lactated Ringer's solution is started as a primary infusion. A piggyback infusion of oxytocin in a similar solution is attached. An infusion pump is used so that the amount of oxytocin being infused can be measured accurately. The administration procedure is the same for inducing labor through oxytocin administration. See Chapter 19 for further discussion. Oxytocin is administered until three uterine contractions lasting 40–60 seconds occur in a ten-minute period. If late decelerations are repetitive or occur more than three times, the oxytocin infusion should be discontinued.

## CST WITH BREAST SELF-STIMULATION TEST (BSST)

In BSST, the breasts are stimulated by applying warm washcloths and/or manually rolling one nipple. When the contractions are sufficient to allow interpretation, the test is concluded. Continued assessment is maintained until contractions subside. The results are reviewed, recorded, and explained to the woman.

If a decrease in the fetal heart rate occurs with a uterine contraction, nipple stimulation is discontinued, the left lateral position is maintained, oxygen is begun per mask at 6 to 8 L/min, and the physician/nurse-midwife is notified (Marshall 1986). If a hyperstimulation pattern occurs (contractions occur more frequently than every two minutes, and/or last more than 90 seconds), the nipple stimulation should be discontinued, the side-lying position maintained, the FHR carefully observed, and the physician/nurse-

midwife notified (Marshall 1986). Oxygen may be administered. The woman's blood pressure and pulse should be assessed. In the presence of a hyperstimulation pattern the nurse should also be prepared to administer tocolytics or prepare for emergency delivery in the event of unresolved fetal distress.

## • Interpretation of CST Results

The CST is classified as follows:

- *Negative.* A negative CST shows three contractions of good quality lasting 40 or more seconds in ten minutes without evidence of late decelerations.

- *Positive.* A positive CST shows repetitive persistent late decelerations with more than 50% of the contractions (Figure 13.7).

- *Hyperstimulation.* A hyperstimulation test is signalled by contractions occurring more frequently than every two minutes or lasting more than 90 seconds.

- *Suspicious.* A suspicious CST occurs when the tracing cannot be interpreted or when contractions are inadequate.

## • Clinical Application

CSTs are usually begun at approximately 32–34 weeks' gestation and are repeated at weekly intervals until intervention is necessary or the woman delivers.

A negative CST implies that placental support is adequate. In that case, the physician can avoid premature intervention and gain approximately one additional week of intrauterine life for the fetus. A negative test also suggests that the fetus is probably able to tolerate the stress of labor should it ensue within the week (Collea and Holls 1982).

A positive CST may indicate a fetus who has compromised placental reserves. A positive CST, however, does not appear to be as reliable an indicator of fetal status as a negative one (Collea and Holls 1982). Because false-positive results are not uncommon, a positive test requires further evaluation, as follows:

1. Does the monitor tracing show variability of the fetal heartbeat? Good variability is usually associated with a healthy fetus. In addition, are FHR accelerations present? Accelerations with fetal movement are also a good sign. The absence of variability and accelerations is usually not seen with a healthy fetus and therefore is another sign of fetal problems.

2. Was the woman's blood pressure maintained at baseline levels during the testing? If she lay flat on her back and became hypotensive, the test results may be misleading.

3. If intravenous oxytocin was used, were the contractions more intense than normally occurring contractions?

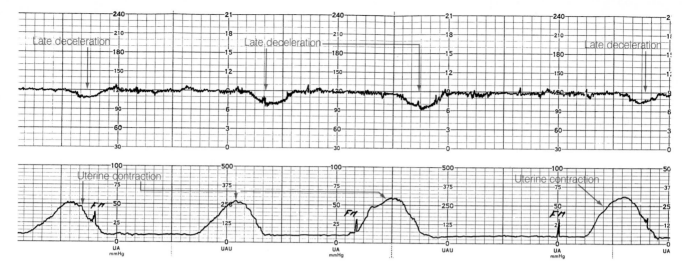

*Figure 13.7 Example of a positive contraction stress test (CST). Repetitive late decelerations occur with each contraction.* Note: *Additional information may be obtained from reviewing the strip. There are no accelerations of FHR with the three fetal movements (FM), which indicates a nonreactive pattern. Baseline FHR = 120 beats/minute. Uterine contractions (bottom half of strip) occurred three times in eight minutes.*

If the CST is positive, FHR variability is minimal, FHR accelerations do not occur with fetal movement, and the fetal lungs are mature (as demonstrated by lecithin/sphingomyelin [L/S] ratio or phosphatidylglycerol [PG]), the fetus must be delivered immediately. Whether the woman with a positive CST should have a cesarean birth instead of a vaginal birth depends on the speed with which the fetus must be delivered to avoid severe fetal distress, the adequacy of cervical dilatation and effacement at the time the decision is being made, and the woman's condition (see Essential Facts to Remember—Contraction Stress Test).

### ● Role of the Nurse

The nurse ascertains the woman's understanding of the CST and the possible results. The reasons for the CST and the procedure are reviewed before beginning the test. Written consent is required in some settings. In this case, the physician/nurse-midwife is responsible for fully informing the woman about the test. The nurse administers the CST, interprets the results, and reports the findings to the physician/nurse-midwife and the expectant woman. The nurse is available to clarify any further treatment ordered by the physician/nurse-midwife.

### ● ESTRIOL DETERMINATIONS

*Estriol* is a form of estrogen produced by the placenta. Its production depends on precursors from both the woman and the fetus. For estrogen levels to be within nor-

mal limits, the mother, fetus, and placenta must be healthy, and all three must be functioning in harmony.

The amount of estriol in the maternal plasma or urine is an indication of the well-being of the maternal-fetal-placental unit. Estriol levels in both plasma and urine should increase as pregnancy advances, with significant amounts being produced in the third trimester. At term (40 weeks' gestation) the normal mean values of urine estriol are approximately 28 mg/24 hr and 14 ng/mL for plasma estriol (Kochenour 1982). Conditions that affect one of the parts of the maternal-fetal-placental unit can cause a decrease in the amount of estriol produced.

### ● Procedure

Determinations of estriol levels may be obtained by either a plasma (serum) test or urine. Plasma tests are gradually replacing urine estriols because they are easily obtained and accurate. Urinary estriols require a 24-hour, accurate collection, which is often inconvenient for the pregnant woman. Estriol level determinations are done serially (over time) in the management of high-risk maternity clients with hypertension, PIH, diabetes, renal disease, suspected placental insufficiency, IUGR, and postmaturity. Currently the role of estriol determinations is being questioned in light of other fetal assessment methods that are now available (Ray et al 1986).

### ● Interpretation of Results

The range of normal values is broad, and various patterns are seen in both plasma and urinary estriol levels. A

## Essential Facts to Remember

**Contraction Stress Test**

Diagnostic value: Demonstrates reaction of FHR to stress of uterine contraction
  Results:

- Negative test: Stress of uterine contraction does not cause a late deceleration of the FHR.
- Positive test: Stress of uterine contraction is associated with a late deceleration in the FHR.

## Essential Facts to Remember

**Estriol Determinations**

Diagnostic value: Indicates metabolic placental function and fetal jeopardy
  Results: Plasma estriol of at least 12 ng/mL, urinary estriol of at least 12 mg/24 hr are suggestive of fetal well-being.
  If estriol levels are lower than expected, one of the following may be indicated:

- Normal fluctuation
- Gestation less advanced than expected
- Problem with placenta, or fetus, or maternal production
- Fetal anomalies; eg, anencephaly, hydrocephalus
- Use of drugs; eg, penicillin
- Laboratory error

If estriol levels are higher than expected, one of the following may be indicated:

- Gestation more advanced than expected
- More than one fetus
- Laboratory error

single estriol measurement in the normal range does not necessarily indicate fetal well-being. Of more significance than any specific single value is the general trend in day-to-day or week-to-week values. Similar or gradually increasing estriol values are a sign of fetal well-being as long as the value stays above the critical level—12 ng/mL for plasma estriol and 12 mg/24 hr for urinary estriol. A drop of 40% from the mean of the three previous highest consecutive values generally signifies fetal distress (Ray et al 1986). (See Essential Facts to Remember—Estriol Determinations.)

## ● AMNIOTIC FLUID ANALYSIS
### ● Amniocentesis

The analysis of amniotic fluid (**amniocentesis**) provides valuable information about fetal status. The amniotic fluid is withdrawn through a needle inserted through the abdominal wall into the uterus (Figure 13.8). Amniocentesis is a fairly simple procedure, although complications do occur rarely (less than 1% of cases). Procedure 13.1 describes the nursing interventions during amniocentesis.

### ● Role of the Nurse

The nurse assists the physician during the amniocentesis. Nursing responsibilities are listed in Procedure 13.1. In addition, the nurse supports the woman undergoing amniocentesis. Women are usually apprehensive about what is about to happen as well as about the information that will be obtained by amniocentesis. The physician explains the procedure before the woman signs the consent form. As it is being performed, the woman may need additional emotional support. She may become anxious during the procedure. She may also become lightheaded, nauseated, and diaphoretic from lying on her back with a gravid uterus compressing the abdominal vessels. The nurse can provide sup-

port to the woman by further clarifying the physician's instructions or explanations, by relieving the woman's physical discomfort when possible, and by responding verbally and physically to the woman's need for reassurance.

### CLIENT EDUCATION

The nurse reiterates explanations given by the physician and provides opportunities for questions. The procedure is reviewed and self-care measures following the amniocentesis are discussed.

A number of studies can be performed on amniotic fluid. These tests can provide genetic information about the fetus (see Chapter 4) as well as information about the health and maturity of the fetus. The remainder of the section describes the amniotic fluid studies.

### ● Evaluation of Fetal Maturity

When managing a high-risk pregnancy, the care giver is faced with the possibility of naturally occurring preterm labor or the need to terminate the pregnancy by induction of labor or cesarean birth. Indications for early termination of pregnancy include premature rupture of membranes and developing amnionitis, severe preeclampsia or eclampsia,

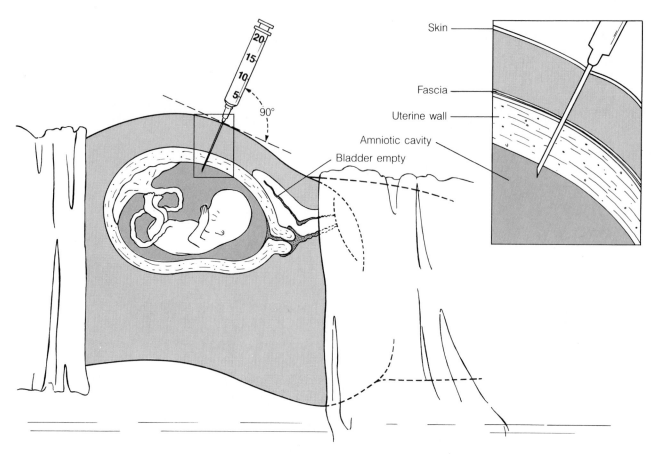

*Figure 13.8  Amniocentesis. The woman is scanned by ultrasound to determine the placental site and to locate a pocket of amniotic fluid. When the needle is placed within the uterine cavity, amniotic fluid is withdrawn.*

bleeding problems, and placental insufficiency. When an infant is delivered before the lungs are mature, the risk of such complications as respiratory distress syndrome is high.

Concentrations of certain substances in amniotic fluid reflect the pulmonary condition of the fetus. Because gestational age, birth weight, and the rate of development of organ systems do not necessarily correspond, amniotic fluid may be analyzed to determine the maturity of the fetal lungs.

## LECITHIN/SPHINGOMYELIN RATIO

The alveoli of the lungs are lined with a substance called **surfactant,** which is composed of phospholipids. Surfactant lowers the surface tension of the alveoli when the newborn exhales. When a newborn with mature pulmonary function takes its first breath, a tremendously high pressure is needed to open the lungs. By lowering the alveolar surface tension, surfactant stabilizes the alveoli, and a certain amount of air always remains in the alveoli during expiration. Thus, when the infant exhales, the lungs do not collapse. An infant born before synthesis of

surfactant is complete is unable to maintain lung stability. Each breath requires an effort similar to that of the first breath. This results in underinflation of the lungs and development of respiratory distress syndrome (RDS).

Fetal lung maturity can be ascertained by determining the ratio of two components of surfactant—lecithin and sphingomyelin. Early in pregnancy, the sphingomyelin concentration in amniotic fluid is greater than the concentration of lecithin, and so the **lecithin/sphingomyelin (L/S)** ratio is low. At about 30–32 weeks' gestation, the amounts of the two substances become equal. The concentration of lecithin begins to exceed that of sphingomyelin, rising abruptly at about 35 weeks' gestation (Gomella 1988). At the same time, the sphingomyelin concentration begins to decrease. Fetal maturity is attained when the L/S ratio is 2:1 or greater; that is, when the amniotic fluid contains at least twice as much lecithin as sphingomyelin.

Under certain conditions of stress, the fetal lungs mature more rapidly. Prolonged rupture of membranes (over 24 hours) results in acceleration of lung maturation by approximately one week and therefore exerts a protective effect. Amnionitis and vaginal bleeding more than 24 hours before delivery also have a protective effect for the fetus (White et al 1986).

## Procedure 13.1

# Nursing Responsibilities During Amniocentesis

| Objective | Nursing Action | Rationale |
|---|---|---|
| Prepare woman. | Explain procedure. | Information will decrease anxiety. |
| | Reassure woman. | |
| | Have woman sign consent form. | Signing indicates woman's awareness of risks and consent to procedure. |
| | Have woman empty bladder. | Emptying bladder decreases risk of bladder perforation. |
| Prepare equipment. | Collect supplies:<br>22-gauge spinal needle with stylet<br>10-mL syringe<br>20-mL syringe<br>Three 10-mL test tubes with tops (amber-colored or covered with tape) | Amniotic fluid must be shielded from light to prevent breakdown of bilirubin. |
| Monitor vital signs. | Obtain baseline data on maternal BP, pulse, respiration, and FHR. | Status of woman and fetus is assessed. |
| | Monitor every 15 minutes. | |
| Locate fetus and placenta. | Provide assistance as physician palpates for fetal position. | |
| | Assist with real-time ultrasound. | Real-time ultrasound is used to identify fetal parts and placenta and locate pockets of amniotic fluid. Amniocentesis is usually performed laterally in the area of fetal small parts where pockets of amniotic fluid are usually seen. |
| Cleanse abdomen. | Prep abdomen with Betadine or other cleansing agent. | Incidence of infection is decreased. |
| Collect specimen of amniotic fluid. | Obtain test tubes from physician; provide correct identification; send to lab with appropriate lab slips. | |
| Reassess vital signs. | Determine woman's BP, pulse, respirations, and FHR; palpate fundus to assess fetal and uterine activity; monitor woman with external fetal monitor for 20–30 minutes after amniocentesis. | Fetus may have been inadvertently punctured.<br><br>Uterine contractions may ensue following procedure; treatment course should be determined to counteract any supine hypotension and to increase venous return and cardiac output. |
| | Have woman rest on left side. | |
| Complete client record. | Record type of procedure done, date, time, name of physician performing test, maternal-fetal response, and disposition of specimen. | Client records will be complete and current. |
| Educate woman. | Reassure woman; instruct her to report any of the following side effects:<br>1. Unusual fetal hyperactivity or lack of movement<br>2. Vaginal discharge—clear drainage or bleeding<br>3. Uterine contractions or abdominal pain<br>4. Fever or chills | Client will know how to recognize side effects or conditions that warrant further treatment. |

Delayed maturation is often seen in infants born to mothers with class A, B, and C diabetes, and in those born to mothers with nonhypertensive glomerulonephritis or hydrops fetalis (Gomella 1988). In these instances, a higher L/S ratio (3:1) may be necessary to ensure adequate lung maturity.

Although the L/S ratio has been one of the most universally used assays in evaluating pulmonary maturity, there are some associated limitations, including the following (Garite and Freeman 1986):

● It is time-consuming and expensive; results take four to five hours to obtain if testing is done in the same facility and more than 24 hours if fluid has to be sent away to a laboratory.

● Extensive training is required to perform the test.

● The presence of blood or other contaminants alters the results.

● There is a high rate of inaccuracy—that is, of predicting immaturity when the fetus is really mature.

Because of these problems, other tests have been developed and used to aid in assessing fetal lung maturity.

### LUNG PROFILE

Some of the difficulties with the L/S ratio have been overcome by utilizing a lung profile of amniotic fluid to evaluate fetal lung maturity. The lung profile determines the presence of lecithin (phosphatidylcholine) and **phosphatidylglycerol (PG),** which are reported to be the major phospholipids of surfactant (Kogon et al 1986).

Lecithin accounts for approximately 80% of the total phospholipids in surfactant. Phosphatidylglycerol is the second most abundant phospholipid. Phosphatidylglycerol appears in amniotic fluid after 35 weeks of gestation and the amount continues to increase until term (Fletcher 1984).

In recent years, lung maturity has been most frequently assessed by a combination of L/S ratio and PG. It appears that lung maturity can be confirmed in most pregnancies if PG is present in conjunction with an L/S ratio of 2:1.

Phosphatidylglycerol determination is also useful in blood-contaminated specimens. Since PG is not present in blood or vaginal fluids, its presence is reliable in predicting lung maturity (Creasy and Resnik 1989).

### SHAKE TEST AND FOAM STABILITY INDEX

The shake test is a quick and inexpensive test for prediction of fetal lung maturity. It is based on the ability of surfactant in the amniotic fluid to form bubbles or foam in the presence of ethanol. The test requires 15 to 30 min-

## Essential Facts to Remember

### Creatinine Level

Diagnostic value: provides information to help determine fetal age

Results: 2 mg/dL correlates with 37 weeks' gestation

If creatinine values are lower than expected, one of the following may be indicated:

● Gestation less advanced than expected

● Fetus smaller than normal

● Fetal kidney abnormalities

If creatinine levels are higher than expected, one of the following may be indicated:

● Gestation more advanced than expected

● Fetus larger than normal

● Elevated maternal creatinine levels

utes. Exact amounts of 95% ethanol, isotonic saline, and amniotic fluid are shaken together for 15 seconds. The persistence of a complete ring of bubbles on the surface of the liquid after 15 minutes indicates a positive shake test, indicating lung maturity. There is a high false negative rate but a low false positive rate (Cruikshank 1982).

### CREATININE LEVEL

Amniotic creatinine progressively increases as pregnancy advances, apparently because of increasing fetal muscle mass and maturing fetal renal function. Creatinine levels of 2 mg/dL of amniotic fluid seem to correlate closely with a pregnancy of 37 weeks or more (Creasy and Resnik 1989). (See Essential Facts to Remember—Creatinine Level.)

### ● Identification of Meconium Staining

Amniotic fluid is normally clear, but the presence of meconium makes the fluid greenish. Once meconium staining is identified, more assessments must be made to determine if the fetus is suffering ongoing episodes of hypoxia.

### ● AMNIOSCOPY

The amniotic membranes can be seen by inserting an amnioscope in the vagina and placing the amnioscope against the fetal presenting part (**amnioscopy**). The purpose of this procedure is usually to evaluate if the fluid is stained with meconium.

# FETOSCOPY

**Fetoscopy**, a technique for directly observing the fetus and obtaining a sample of fetal blood or skin, was developed in 1972. Real-time ultrasound is used to locate an area through which to insert a cannula and trocar into the uterus. Following insertion, an endoscope is inserted to the desired part of the fetus for viewing and sampling. Skin biopsies may be obtained as well as blood samples. These samples can be tested for the presence of different congenital diseases or disorders. At this time, only a few perinatal centers are equipped to do fetoscopy (Hobbins 1982).

# ESSENTIAL CONCEPTS

● **Diagnostic ultrasound is advantageous because it is noninvasive and painless, allows the physician to study the gestation serially, is nonradiating to both the woman and her fetus, and to date has no known harmful effects.**

● **Ultrasound offers a valuable means of assessing intrauterine fetal growth because the growth can be followed over a period of time.**

● **Maternal assessment of fetal activity can be used as a screening procedure in evaluation of fetal status.**

● **A nonstress test (NST) is based on the knowledge that the heart rate normally increases in response to fetal activity. The desired result is a reactive test.**

● **A fetal biophysical profile includes five variables (fetal breathing movement, body movement, tone, amniotic fluid volume, and FHR reactivity) to assess the fetus at risk for intrauterine compromise.**

● **A contraction stress test (CST) provides a method for observing the response of the fetal heart rate to the stress of uterine contractions. The desired result is a negative test.**

● **Estriol is a form of estrogen produced by the placenta. The amount of estriol in the maternal plasma or urine is an indication of the well-being of the maternal-fetal-placental unit.**

● **Amniocentesis can be used to obtain amniotic fluid for testing.**

● **The L/S ratio can be used to assess fetal lung maturity. The presence of PG may also provide information about fetal lung maturity.**

● **Fetoscopy is a procedure for observing the fetus directly and obtaining a sample of blood or skin.**

## References

Baskett TF: Gestational age and fetal biophysical assessment. *Am J Obstet Gynecol* February 1988; 158(2):332.

Brambati B, Oldrini A: CVS for first-trimester fetal diagnosis. *Contemp OB/GYN* 1985; 25:94.

Carson PL, Wagner LK, Chenevert TL: Risk assessment for the conceptus from diagnostic ultrasound. Chapter 102 in: Sciarra JL (editor): *Gynecology and Obstetrics*. Vol 2. Philadelphia: Harper and Row, 1988.

Chez RA, Sadovsky E: Teaching patients how to record fetal movements. *Contemp OB/GYN* October 1984; 24(4):85.

Clark J, Britton K: Factors contributing to client nonuse of the Cardiff count-to-ten fetal activity chart. *J Nurse-Midwifery* November/December 1985; 30(6):320.

Connors G, Natale R, Nasello-Paterson C: Maternally perceived fetal activity from twenty-four weeks' gestation to term in normal and at-risk pregnancies. *Am J Obstet Gynecol* February 1988; 158(2):294.

Cox DN et al: The psychological impact of diagnostic ultrasound. *Obstet Gynecol* November 1987; 70(5):673.

Creasy RK, Resnik R: *Maternal Fetal Medicine*. Philadelphia: Saunders, 1989.

Eggertson SC, Benedetti TJ: Maternal response to daily fetal movement counting in primary care settings. *Am J Perinatol* October 1987; 4(4):337.

Fletcher MA: Prematurity. Chapter 70 in: *Gynecology and Obstetrics*. Vol 3. Sciarra JL (editor). Philadelphia: Harper and Row, 1984.

Gantes M et al: The use of daily fetal movement records in a clinical setting. *J Obstet Gynecol Neonatal Nurs* September/October 1986; 16:390.

Garite TJ, Freeman RK: Fetal maturity cascade: A rapid and cost effective method for fetal lung maturity testing. *Obstet Gynecol* 1986; 67:619.

Golde SH, Platt LD: The use of ultrasound in the diagnosis of fetal lung maturity. *Clin Obstet Gynecol* June 1984; 27(2):391.

Gomella T: *Neonatology 88/89*. Norwalk, CT: Appleton and Lange, 1988.

Hobbins JC: Fetoscopy. In: *Protocols for High-Risk Pregnancies*. Queenan JT, Hobbins JE (editors). Oradell, NJ: Medical Economics, 1982.

Ingemarsson et al: Fetal acoustic stimulation in early labor in patients screened with the admission test. *Am J Obstet Gynecol* January 1988; 158(1):70.

Kochenour NK: Estrogen assay during pregnancy. *Clin Obstet Gynecol* December 1982; 25(4):659.

Kogon DP et al: Amniotic fluid phosphatidylglycerol and phosphatidylcholine phosphorus as predictors of fetal lung maturity. *Am J Obstet Gynecol* 1986; 154(2):226.

Manning FA: Fetal biophysical profile scoring predicts trouble—when it counts. *Contemp OB/GYN* January 1985; 25(1):126.

Manning FA et al: Fetal biophysical profile scoring: selective use of the nonstress test. *Am J Obstet Gynecol* March 1987; 59(3): 709.

Marshall C et al: The nipple stimulation contraction stress test. *J Obstet Gynecol Neonatal Nurs* 1986; 15: 459.

Pennell JS et al: Complicated first-trimester pregnancies: Evaluation with endovaginal US versus transabdominal techniques. *Radiology* October 1987; 165(1): 79.

Ray DA, Yeast JD, Freeman RK: The current role of daily serum estriol monitoring in the insulin-dependent pregnant diabetic woman. *Am J Obstet Gynecol* 1986; 154: 1257.

Richards DS et al: Determinants of fetal heart rate response to vibroacoustic stimulation in labor. *Obstet Gynecol* April 1988; 71(4): 535.

Sadovsky E: Fetal movement. In: *Management of High-Risk Pregnancy,* 2nd ed. Queenan JT (editor). Oradell, NJ: Medical Economics Books, 1985a.

Sadovsky E: Monitoring fetal movement: A useful screening test. *Contemp OB/GYN* April 1985b; 25: 123.

White E, Shy KK, Benedetti TJ: Chronic fetal stress and the risk of infant respiratory distress syndrome. *Obstet Gynecol* 1986; 67: 57.

## Additional Readings

Borgatta L, Shrout PE, Divon MY: Reliability and reproducibility of nonstress test readings. *Am J Obstet Gynecol* September 1988; 159(3): 554.

Delke I et al: Avoidable causes of perinatal death at or after term pregnancy in an inner-city hospital: Medical versus social. *Am J Obstet Gynecol* September 1988; 159(5): 562.

Deutinger J, Rudelstorfer R, Bernaschek G: Vaginosonographic velocimetry of both main uterine arteries by visual vessel recognition and pulsed Doppler method during pregnancy. *Am J Obstet Gynecol* November 1988; 159(5): 1072.

Devoe LD, Ruedrich DA, Searle N: Does the onset of spontaneous labor at term influence fetal biophysical test parameters? *Obstet Gynecol* December 1988; 72(6): 838.

Dicker D et al: Fetal surveillance in insulin-dependent diabetic pregnancy: Predictive value of the biophysical profile. *Am J Obstet Gynecol* October 1988; 159(4): 800.

Drugan A et al: A normal ultrasound does not obviate the need for amniocentesis in patients with elevated serum alpha-fetoprotein. *Obstet Gynecol* October 1988; 72(4): 627.

Johnson JM et al: Biophysical profile scoring in the management of the diabetic pregnancy. *Obstet Gynecol* December 1988; 72(6): 841.

Kemp VH, Page CK: The psychosocial impact of a high risk pregnancy on the family. *J Obstet Gynecol Neonatal Nurs* 1987; 15: 232.

Mercer RT et al: Effect of stress on family functioning during pregnancy. *Nurs Research* September/October 1988; 37(5): 268.

Milunsky A et al: First-trimester maternal serum fetoprotein screening for chromosome defects. *Am J Obstet Gynecol* November 1988; 159(5): 1209.

Perry SE, Parer JT, Inturrisi M: Intrauterine transfusion for severe isoimmunization. *Am J Mat Child Nurs* 1986; 11: 182.

Polzin GB et al: Fetal vibro-acoustic stimulation: Magnitude and duration of fetal heart rate accelerations as a marker of fetal health. *Obstet Gynecol* October 1988; 72(4): 621.

Reece EA et al: Diagnostic fetal umbilical blood sampling in the management of isoimmunization. *Am J Obstet Gynecol* November 1988; 159(5): 693.

Robinson GE et al: Anxiety reduction after chorionic villus sampling and genetic amniocentesis. *Am J Obstet Gynecol* October 1988; 159(4): 953.

Siddiqi TA et al: Ultrasound effects on fetal auditory brain stem responses. *Obstet Gynecol* November 1988; 72(5): 752.

Spencer JW, Cox DN: A comparison of chorionic villi sampling and amniocentesis: Acceptability of procedure and maternal attachment to pregnancy. *Obstet Gynecol* November 1988; 72(5): 714.

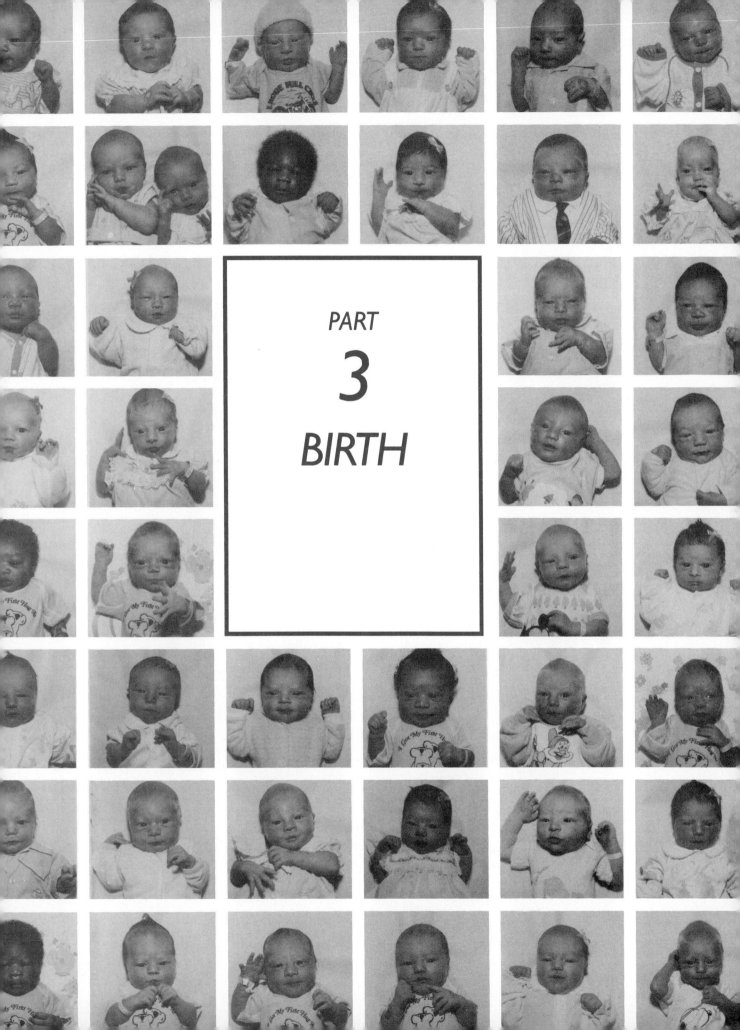

PART

# 3

*BIRTH*

# 14

# Processes and Stages of Birth

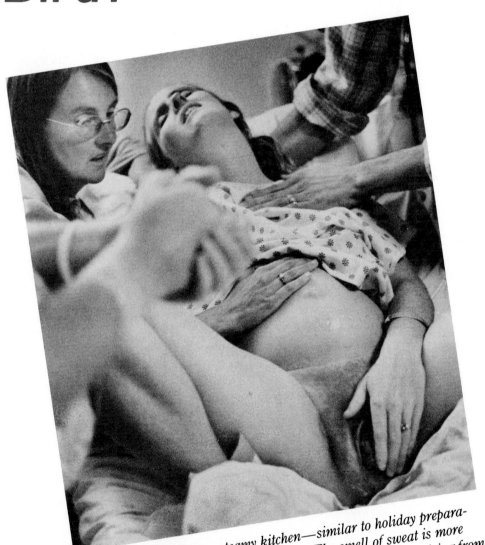

*Birth usually feels like a steamy kitchen—similar to holiday preparations, except that the smells are different. The smell of sweat is more acrid, there are some fetid odors, there is the smell and steam rising from blood. The air is thick, pungent, fertile. It is hard not to be reminded of fresh straw and night stars. There is near and heady promise. (A Midwife's Story)*

## Objectives

● Discuss the significance of each type of pelvis to the birth process.

● Examine the factors that influence labor and the physiology of the mechanisms of labor.

● Describe the fetal positional changes that constitute the mechanisms of labor

● Discuss the probable causes of labor onset and the premonitory signs of labor.

● Differentiate between false and true labor.

● Describe the physiologic and psychologic changes occurring in each of the stages of labor.

## Key Terms

bloody show
cardinal movements
cervical dilatation
crowning
duration
effacement
engagement
fetal attitude
fetal lie
fetal position
fetal presentation
fontanelles
frequency
intensity
lightening
malposition
malpresentation
molding
presenting part
rupture of membranes (ROM)
station
sutures

**D**uring the weeks of gestation, the fetus and the expectant woman prepare themselves for birth. The fetus progresses through various stages of growth and development in readiness for the independence of extrauterine life. The expectant woman undergoes various physiologic and psychologic adaptations during pregnancy that gradually prepare her for childbirth and the role of mother. The onset of labor marks a significant change in the relationship between the woman and the fetus.

## ● CRITICAL FACTORS IN LABOR

Four factors are important in the process of labor and delivery: the passage, the passenger, the powers, and the psyche. The "four Ps," as they are commonly known, are defined as follows:

1. Passage
   a. Size of the pelvis (diameters of the pelvic inlet, midpelvis, and outlet)
   b. Type of pelvis (gynecoid, android, anthropoid, platypelloid, or a combination)
   c. Ability of the cervix to dilate and efface, and ability of the vaginal canal and the external opening of the vagina (the *introitus*) to distend

2. Passenger
   a. Fetal head (size and presence of molding)
   b. Fetal attitude (flexion or extension of the fetal body and extremities)
   c. Fetal lie
   d. Fetal presentation (the part of the fetal body entering the pelvis in a single or multiple pregnancy)
   e. Fetal position (relationship of the presenting part to one of the four quadrants of the maternal pelvis)
   f. Placenta (implantation site)

3. Powers
   a. The frequency, duration, and intensity of uterine contractions as the passenger moves through the passage
   b. The effectiveness of pushing effort
   c. The duration of labor

4. Psyche
   a. Physical preparation for childbirth
   b. Sociocultural heritage
   c. Previous childbirth experience
   d. Support from significant others
   e. Emotional integrity

The progress of labor is critically dependent on the complementary relationship of these four factors. Abnormalities of the passage, the passenger, the powers, or the psyche can alter the outcome of labor and jeopardize both the expectant woman and her baby. Complications involving the four Ps are discussed in Chapter 18.

# ● THE PASSAGE

The true pelvis, which forms the bony canal through which the baby must pass, is divided into three sections: the inlet, the pelvic cavity (midpelvis), and the outlet. (*Note:* See Chapter 3 for discussion of each part of the pelvis and Chapter 7 for assessment techniques of the pelvis.)

## ● Pelvic Types

The Caldwell-Moloy classification of pelvic types is based on pertinent characteristics of both male and female pelves (Caldwell and Moloy 1933). Although it is common for a particular pelvis to have characteristics of more than one type of pelvis, the four classic types are gynecoid, android, anthropoid, and platypelloid.

The *gynecoid* pelvis is often referred to as the "female" pelvis. Approximately 50% of women have this type of pelvis. All diameters of the gynecoid are adequate for childbirth.

The *android* pelvis is often referred to as the "male" pelvis. Approximately 20% of women have this type of pelvis. The diameters of the android pelvis are usually not adequate for vaginal birth.

The *anthropoid* pelvis is narrowed from side to side and widened from front to back. The diameters are usually adequate for vaginal birth.

The *platypelloid* pelvis is flattened (narrowed) from front to back and widened from side to side. Diameters are usually not adequate for vaginal birth.

# ● THE PASSENGER
## ● Fetal Head

The fetal head is composed of bony parts that can either hinder childbirth or make it easier. Once the head (the least compressible and largest part of the fetus) has been delivered, the birth of the rest of the body is rarely delayed.

The fetal skull has three major parts: the face, the base of the skull (cranium), and the vault of the cranium (roof). The bones of the face and cranial base are well fused and are basically fixed. The base of the cranium is composed of the two temporal bones, each with a sphenoid and ethmoid bone. The bones composing the vault are the two frontal bones, the two parietal bones, and the occipital

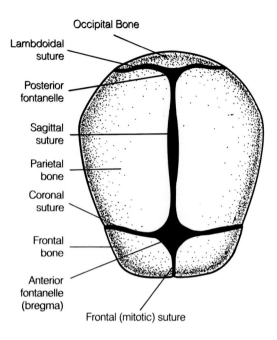

*Figure 14.1   Superior view of the fetal skull*

bone (Figure 14.1). These bones are not fused, allowing this portion of the head to adjust in shape as the presenting part of the passenger passes through the narrow portions of the pelvis. The cranial bones overlap under pressure of the powers of labor and the demands of the unyielding pelvis. This overlapping is called **molding**.

The **sutures** of the fetal skull are membranous spaces between the cranial bones. The intersections of the cranial sutures are called **fontanelles**. These sutures allow for molding of the fetal head and help the examiner to identify the position of the fetal head during vaginal examination. The important sutures of the cranial vault are as follows (see Figure 14.1):

● *Mitotic suture:* Located between the two frontal bones; becomes the anterior continuation of the sagittal suture

● *Sagittal suture:* Located between the parietal bones; divides the skull into left and right halves; runs anteroposteriorly, connecting the two fontanelles

● *Coronal sutures:* Located between the frontal and parietal bones; extend transversely left and right from the anterior fontanelle

● *Lambdoidal suture:* Located between the two parietal bones and the occipital bone; extends transversely left and right from the posterior fontanelle

The anterior and posterior fontanelles are clinically useful in identifying the position of the fetal head in the pelvis and in assessing the status of the newborn after birth. The anterior fontanelle is diamond-shaped and measures 2 × 3 cm. It permits growth of the brain by remaining unossified for as long as 18 months. The posterior fontanelle is much smaller and closes within 8–12 weeks after birth. It is shaped like a small triangle and marks the meeting point of the sagittal suture and the lambdoidal suture (Oxorn 1986).

Following are several important landmarks of the fetal skull (Figure 14.2):

- *Sinciput:* The anterior area known as the brow
- *Bregma:* The large diamond-shaped anterior fontanelle
- *Vertex:* The area between the anterior and posterior fontanelles
- *Posterior fontanelle:* The intersection between posterior cranial sutures
- *Occiput:* The area of the fetal skull occupied by the occipital bone, beneath the posterior fontanelle
- *Mentum:* The fetal chin

The diameters of the fetal skull vary considerably within normal limits. Some diameters shorten and others lengthen as the head is molded during labor. Fetal head diameters are measured between the various landmarks on the skull (Figure 14.3). The compound words used to designate the various diameters allow one to identify which measurement is actually being reported. For example, the suboccipitobregmatic diameter is the distance from the undersurface of the occiput to the center of the bregma, or anterior fontanelle. Fetal skull measurements are given in Figure 14.3.

Much can be learned about the degree of extension or flexion of the fetal head from these diameters. Extension of the head results in a larger diameter presenting to the maternal pelvis than if the head is strongly flexed. Alterations in flexion of the fetal head can cause problems during the process of labor. The fetus tries to accommodate its most favorable head diameters to the limited measurements of the bony pelvis.

## • Fetal Attitude

**Fetal attitude** refers to the relation of the fetal parts to one another. The normal attitude of the fetus is one of moderate flexion of the head, flexion of the arms onto the chest, and flexion of the legs onto the abdomen.

Changes in fetal attitude, particularly in the position of the head, cause the fetus to present larger diameters of the fetal head to the maternal pelvis. These deviations from a normal fetal attitude often contribute to difficult labor.

## • Fetal Lie

**Fetal lie** refers to the relationship of the cephalocaudal axis of the fetus to the cephalocaudal axis of the woman. The fetus may assume either a longitudinal or a transverse lie. A *longitudinal lie* occurs when the cephalocaudal axis of the fetus is parallel to the woman's spine. A *transverse lie* occurs when the cephalocaudal axis of the fetus is at right angles to the woman's spine.

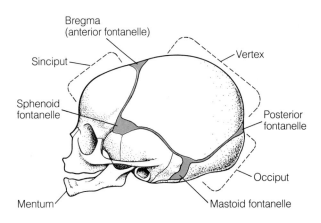

*Figure 14.2   Lateral view of the fetal skull identifying the landmarks that have significance during birth*

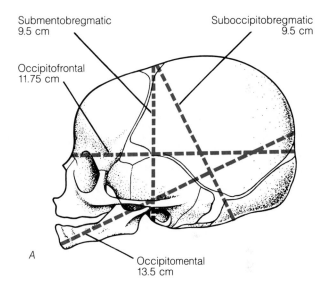

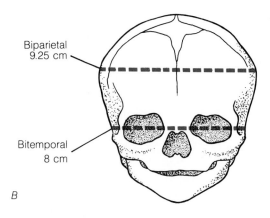

*Figure 14.3   (A) Anteroposterior diameters of the fetal skull. When the vertex of the fetus presents and the fetal head is flexed with the chin on the chest, the smallest anteroposterior diameter (suboccipitobregmatic) enters the birth canal. (B) Transverse diameters of the fetal skull.*

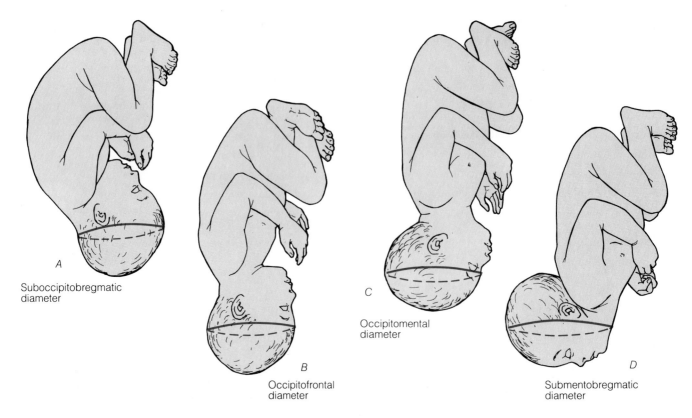

*A* Suboccipitobregmatic diameter

*B* Occipitofrontal diameter

*C* Occipitomental diameter

*D* Submentobregmatic diameter

*Figure 14.4   Cephalic presentations: (A) Vertex presentation. Complete flexion of the head allows the suboccipitobregmatic diameter to present to the pelvis. (B) Military (median vertex) presentation, with no flexion or extension. The occipitofrontal diameter presents to the pelvis. (C) Brow presentation. The fetal head is in partial (halfway) extension. The occipitomental diameter, which is the largest diameter of the fetal head, presents to the pelvis. (D) Face presentation. The fetal head is in complete extension and the submentobregmatic diameter presents to the pelvis.*

## ● *Fetal Presentation*

**Fetal presentation** is determined by fetal lie and by the body part of the fetus that enters the pelvic passageway first. This portion of the fetus is referred to as the **presenting part**. Fetal presentation may be either cephalic, breech, or shoulder.

### CEPHALIC PRESENTATION

The fetal head presents itself to the passage in approximately 97% of term deliveries. The cephalic presentation can be further classified according to the degree of flexion or extension of the fetal head (attitude).

### *Vertex Presentation*

- The fetal head is completely flexed on the chest.
- The smallest diameter of fetal head (suboccipitobregmatic) presents to the maternal pelvis (Figure 14.4, **A**).
- The occiput is the presenting part.
- The vertex is the most common type of presentation.

### *Military Presentation*

- The fetal head is neither flexed nor extended.
- The occipitofrontal diameter presents to the maternal pelvis (Figure 14.4, **B**).
- The top of the head is the presenting part.

### *Brow Presentation*

- The fetal head is partially extended.
- The occipitomental diameter, the largest anteroposterior diameter, is presented to the maternal pelvis (Figure 14.4, **C**).
- The sinciput (see Figure 14.2) is the presenting part.

### *Face Presentation*

- The fetal head is hyperextended (complete extension).
- The submentobregmatic diameter presents to the maternal pelvis (Figure 14.4, **D**).
- The face is the presenting part.

## BREECH PRESENTATION

Breech presentations occur in 3% of term births. These presentations are classified according to the attitude of the fetus's hips and knees. In all variations of the breech presentation, the sacrum is the landmark to be noted (see Figure 18.7).

### Complete Breech

- The fetal knees and hips are both flexed; the thighs are on the abdomen, and the calves are on the posterior aspect of the thighs.
- The buttocks and feet of the fetus present to the maternal pelvis.

### Frank Breech

- The fetal hips are flexed, and the knees are extended.
- The buttocks of the fetus present to the maternal pelvis.

### Footling Breech

- The fetal hips and legs are extended.
- The feet of the fetus present to the maternal pelvis.
- In a single footling, one foot presents; in a double footling, both feet present.

## SHOULDER PRESENTATION

A shoulder presentation is also called a *transverse lie*. Most frequently, the shoulder is the presenting part, and the acromion process of the scapula is the landmark to be noted. However, the fetal arm, back, abdomen, or side may present in a transverse lie.

## PRESENTATION

The most common presentation is cephalic. When this presentation occurs, labor and birth are more likely to proceed normally. Breech and shoulder presentations are associated with difficulties during labor and do not proceed as normal; therefore, they are called **malpresentations**. (See Chapter 18 for discussion of malpresentations.)

## • Functional Relationships of Presenting Part and Passage

### ENGAGEMENT

**Engagement** of the presenting part occurs when the largest diameter of the presenting part reaches or passes through the pelvic inlet (Figure 14.5).

Engagement can be determined by vaginal examination. In primigravidas, engagement usually occurs two weeks before term. Multiparas, however, may experience

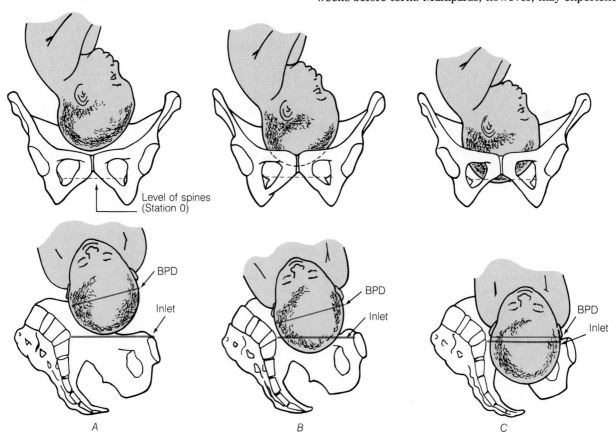

*Figure 14.5   Process of engagement: (A) floating, (B) dipping, (C) engaged*

engagement several weeks before the onset of labor or during the process of labor. Engagement confirms the adequacy of the pelvic inlet. Engagement does not indicate that the midpelvis and outlet are also adequate.

## STATION

**Station** refers to the relationship of the presenting part to an imaginary line drawn between the ischial spines of the maternal pelvis. In a normal pelvis, the ischial spines mark the narrowest diameter through which the fetus must pass. These spines are not sharp protrusions that harm the fetus but rather blunted prominences at the midpelvis. The ischial spines as a landmark have been designated as zero station (Figure 14.6). If the presenting part is higher than the ischial spines, a negative number is assigned, noting centimeters above zero station. Station −5 is at the inlet, and station +4 is at the outlet. If the presenting part can be seen at the woman's perineum, birth is imminent. During labor, the presenting part should move progressively from the negative stations to the midpelvis at zero station and into the positive stations. Failure of the presenting part to descend in the presence of strong contractions may be due to disproportion between the mater-

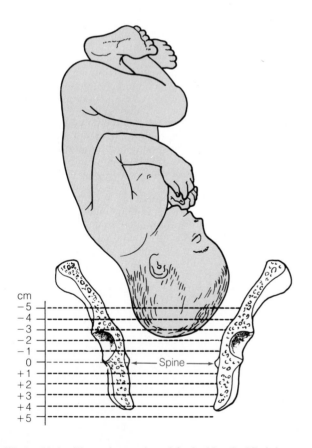

*Figure 14.6  Measuring station of the fetal head while it is descending*

nal pelvis and fetal presenting part, or to a short and/or entangled umbilical cord.

## FETAL POSITION

**Fetal position** refers to the relationship of the landmark on the presenting fetal part to the front, sides, or back of the maternal pelvis. The landmark on the fetal presenting part is related to four imaginary quadrants of the pelvis: left anterior, right anterior, left posterior, and right posterior. These quadrants designate whether the presenting part is directed toward the front, back, left, or right of the passage. The landmark chosen for vertex presentations is the occiput, and the landmark for face presentations is the mentum. In breech presentations, the sacrum is the designated landmark, and the acromion process on the scapula is the landmark in shoulder presentations. If the landmark is directed toward the center of the side of the pelvis, fetal position is designated as *transverse,* rather than anterior or posterior.

Three notations are used to describe the fetal position:

1. Right (R) or left (L) side of the maternal pelvis
2. The landmark of the fetal presenting part: occiput (O), mentum (M), sacrum (S), or acromion process (A)
3. Anterior (A), posterior (P), or transverse (T), depending on whether the landmark is in the front, back, or side of the pelvis.

The abbreviations of these notations help the health care team communicate the fetal position. Thus, when the fetal occiput is directed toward the back and to the left of the passage, the abbreviation used is LOP (left-occiput-posterior). The term *dorsal* (D) is used when denoting the fetal position in a transverse lie; it refers to the fetal back. Thus the abbreviation RADA indicates that the acromion process of the scapula is directed toward the woman's right and the fetus's back is anterior.

Following is a list of the positions for various fetal presentations, some of which are illustrated in Figure 14.7.

Positions in vertex presentation:

ROA  Right-occiput-anterior
ROT  Right-occiput-transverse
ROP  Right-occiput-posterior
LOA  Left-occiput-anterior
LOT  Left-occiput-transverse
LOP  Left-occiput-posterior

Positions in face presentation:

RMA  Right-mentum-anterior
RMT  Right-mentum-transverse
RMP  Right-mentum-posterior
LMA  Left-mentum-anterior

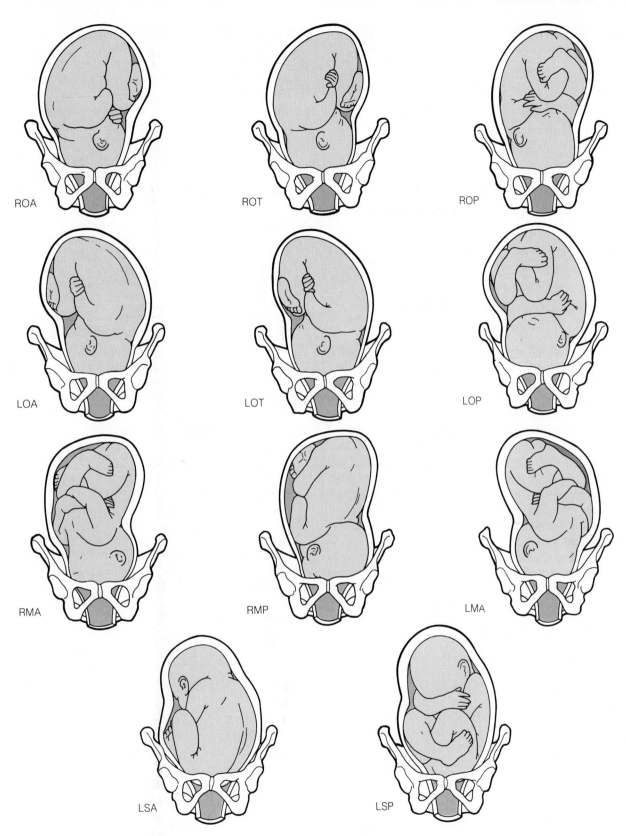

*Figure 14.7   Categories of presentation (Reprinted with permission of Ross Laboratories, Columbus, OH 43216. From Clinical Education Aid.)*

LMT    Left-mentum-transverse

LMP    Left-mentum-posterior

Positions in breech presentation:

RSA    Right-sacrum-anterior

RST    Right-sacrum-transverse

RSP    Right-sacrum-posterior

LSA    Left-sacrum-anterior

LST    Left-sacrum-transverse

LSP    Left-sacrum-posterior

Positions in shoulder presentation:

RADA    Right-acromion-dorsal-anterior

RADP    Right-acromion-dorsal-posterior

LADA    Left-acromion-dorsal-anterior

LADP    Left-acromion-dorsal-posterior

The fetal position influences labor and birth. For example, in a posterior position the fetal head presents a larger diameter than in an anterior position. A posterior position increases the pressure on the maternal sacral nerves, causing the laboring woman backache and pelvic pressure and perhaps encouraging her to bear down or push earlier than normal. The most common fetal position is occiput anterior. When this position occurs the labor and birth is more likely to proceed normally. Positions other than occiput anterior are more frequently associated with problems during labor; therefore they are called **malpositions**. (See Chapter 18 for discussion of malpositions and their management.)

Assessment techniques to determine fetal position include inspection and palpation of the maternal abdomen, and vaginal examination (see Chapter 15 for further discussion of assessment of fetal position).

## • THE POWERS

Primary and secondary powers work together to deliver the fetus, the fetal membranes, and the placenta from the uterus into the external environment. The *primary power* is uterine muscular contractions, which cause the changes of the first stage of labor—complete effacement and dilatation of the cervix. The *secondary power* is the use of abdominal muscles to push during the second stage of labor. The pushing adds to the primary power after full dilatation has occurred.

In labor, uterine contractions are rhythmic but intermittent. Between contractions is a period of relaxation. This period of relaxation allows uterine muscles to rest and provides respite for the laboring woman. It also restores uteroplacental circulation, which is important to fetal oxygenation and adequate circulation in the uterine blood vessels.

Each contraction has three phases: (a) *increment,* the "building up" of the contraction (the longest phase); (b) *acme,* or the peak of the contraction; and (c) *decrement,* or the "letting up" of the contraction. When describing uterine contractions during labor, care givers use the terms *frequency, duration,* and *intensity.* **Frequency** refers to the time between the beginning of one contraction and the beginning of the next contraction.

The **duration** of each contraction is measured from the beginning of the increment to the completion of decrement (Figure 14.8). In beginning labor, the duration is about 30 seconds. As labor continues, duration increases to an average of 60 seconds with a range of 45–90 seconds (Varney 1987).

**Intensity** refers to the strength of the uterine contraction during acme. In most instances, the intensity is estimated by palpating the contraction but it may be measured directly with an intrauterine catheter. When estimating intensity by palpation, the nurse determines whether

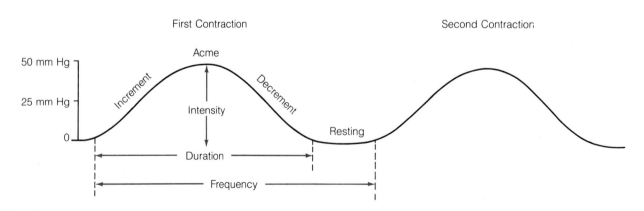

*Figure 14.8   Characteristics of uterine contractions*

it is mild, moderate, or strong by judging the amount of indentability of the uterine wall during the acme of a contraction. If the uterine wall can be indented easily, the contraction is considered mild. Strong intensity exists when the uterine wall cannot be indented. Moderate intensity falls between these two ranges. When intensity is measured with an intrauterine catheter, the normal resting tonus (between contractions) averages 10 mm Hg of pressure. During acme, the intensity ranges from 30 to 55 mm Hg of pressure (Cibils 1981). (See Chapter 15 for further discussions of assessment techniques.)

At the beginning of labor, the contractions are usually mild, of short duration, and relatively infrequent. As labor progresses, duration of contractions lengthens, the intensity increases, and the frequency is every two to three minutes. Because the contractions are involuntary, the laboring woman cannot control their duration, frequency, or intensity.

## ● THE PSYCHE

Rubin (1984, p 52) notes that childbearing "requires an exchange of a known self in a known world for an unknown self in an unknown world. This is an act of courage." And no part of the childbearing period brings this more to light than labor. Every woman is uncertain about what her labor will be like: A woman anticipating her first labor faces a totally new experience, and even multiparas cannot be certain what each new labor will bring. The woman does not know whether she will live up to her expectations for herself in relation to her friends and relatives, whether she will be physically injured through laceration, episiotomy, or cesarean incision, or whether significant others will be as supportive as she hopes (Mercer 1981, Mercer 1985). The woman faces an irrevocable event—the birth of a new family member—and, consequently, disruption of life-style, relationships, and self-image. Finally, the woman must deal with concerns about her loss of control of bodily functions, emotional responses to an unfamiliar situation, and reactions to the pain associated with labor.

Various factors influence a woman's reaction to the physical and emotional crisis of labor (Table 14.1). Her accomplishment of the tasks of pregnancy, usual coping mechanisms in response to stressful life events, support system, preparation for childbirth, and cultural influences are all significant factors.

## ● Preparation for Labor

In her study of the psychosocial adaptations of pregnancy Lederman (1984) found that certain psychosocial factors of pregnancy were predictive of progress in labor. One such factor was related to a woman's psychologic prepara-

### Table 14.1 Factors Associated with a Positive Birth Experience

Motivation for the pregnancy

Attendance at childbirth education classes

A sense of competence or mastery

Self-confidence and self-esteem

Positive relationship with mate

Maintaining control during labor

Support from mate or other person during labor

Not being left alone in labor

Trust in the medical/nursing staff

tion for labor. Lederman found that expectant women prepared for labor through actions and through imaginary rehearsal. The actions frequently consisted of "nesting behavior" and a "psyching up" for the labor, which seemed to vary depending on the woman's sense of self-confidence, self-esteem, and previous experiences with stress. Specific actions to prepare for labor are usually focused on becoming better informed and prepared. Many women attended prenatal classes to learn about labor and to share the birth experience with their husbands. Others hoped that learning specific techniques of relaxation and breathing would allow them more control during labor so they could take a more active part. Additional information was gained through viewing films, reading books, and talking to other women.

An important developmental step for expectant women is to anticipate the labor in fantasy. Just as a woman "tries on" the maternal role during pregnancy, fantasizing about labor seems to help the woman understand and become more prepared for labor. Her fantasies about the excitement of the baby's birth and the sharing of the experience involve her in constructive preparation even though she may still have some fears of labor. Women who have a great deal of apprehension about becoming a mother or a high fear of pain during labor are not able to fantasize the labor in positive ways and instead have many disturbing thoughts (Lederman 1984).

Positive fantasies seem to involve many areas. The woman thinks about the contractions and the work and pain that will be involved, and this seems to provide a stimulus to becoming more prepared for labor. Lederman (1984) found that women who were able to visualize themselves as active participants in labor were usually well prepared and had positive self-images. Fantasy and thoughts about labor help the woman to have realistic ideas about the work, pain, and risks involved and to develop a sense of confidence in her ability to cope.

Many women fear the pain of contractions. They not only see the pain as threatening but also associate it with a loss of control over their bodies and emotions. Our society seems to value control and cooperation with established routines in health care settings. When a woman is facing labor, especially for the first time, she may worry about her ability to withstand the pain of labor and maintain control over herself. Women are afraid of becoming fatigued and unable to relax because they may then act in a way that is undesirable or may induce bodily injury. In Lederman's study the women who were confident of their abilities usually had less fear than women who doubted their ability to maintain control of themselves.

The laboring woman's support system may also influence the course of labor and birth. For some women the presence of the father and other significant persons, including the nurse, tends to have a positive effect. Other women may prefer not to have a support person or family with them.

Preparation for childbirth is another factor that influences a woman's reaction to childbirth. Much attention has been focused on preparation during pregnancy as a way of increasing the woman's ability to cope during childbirth, decreasing her stress, anxiety, and pain, and imparting satisfaction with the childbearing experience. Although opinions vary concerning whether the amount of pain or discomfort is actually decreased, there is agreement that preparation tends to increase perceived satisfaction. Nichols and Humenick (1987) suggest that *mastery,* or control, of the childbearing experience is the key factor in perceived satisfaction. Childbirth education helps to increase positive reactions to the birth experience because education gives the laboring woman and her support persons greater opportunities to control the experience of labor.

How the woman views the birth experience after the delivery may have implications for mothering behaviors. Mercer (1985) found a significant relationship between the birth experience and mothering behaviors. It appears that any activities—by the expectant woman or by maternal–child health care providers—that enhance the birth experience will be beneficial as the woman prepares for labor, experiences labor, and begins her new role as a mother.

## ● PHYSIOLOGY OF LABOR

### ● Possible Causes of Labor Onset

For some reason, usually at the appropriate time for the uterus and the fetus, the process of labor begins. Although medical researchers have been conducting numerous studies to determine the exact cause, it still is not clearly understood. The relationship of some factors is presented in Figure 14.9. Some of the more widely accepted theories are discussed in the following sections.

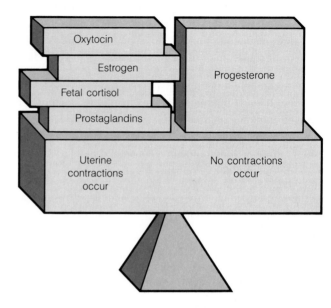

Factors that stimulate uterine muscle contractions

Factors that act to quiet the uterine muscles

*Figure 14.9   Factors affecting initiation of labor: The factors listed on the left have all been identified as providing stimulus to the beginning of labor. Progesterone exerts a relaxing effect, and a balance between all of the factors keeps the uterus quiet without contraction. When the relationship of factors changes, the balance is tipped and uterine labor begins.*

### OXYTOCIN STIMULATION THEORY

Oxytocin is produced by the maternal posterior pituitary. One of the effects of oxytocin is to stimulate contractions of the smooth muscle of the uterus. The uterus becomes increasingly sensitive (or responsive) to the effects of oxytocin as the pregnancy nears term (40 weeks). This increased responsiveness may be the result of increased production of oxytocin, and/or a change in the threshold of response.

### ESTROGEN STIMULATION THEORY

Estrogen stimulates the smooth muscle of the uterus to contract. During pregnancy, the stimulatory effects of estrogen are counterbalanced by the relaxant effects of progesterone. The balance between these two hormones keeps the uterine muscles from contracting in a regular pattern during pregnancy. Some researchers support the theory that as term approaches the balance changes because estrogen levels increase and progesterone levels decrease (Hariharan et al 1986). This leads to increased irritability (a readiness to contract) of the uterine smooth muscle and the promotion of uterine contractions.

The stimulatory effect is increased further because estrogen promotes the synthesis of prostaglandin in the decidua and the fetal membranes (amnion and chorion). Prostaglandins also stimulate the smooth muscle of the uterus (Hariharan et al 1986).

### PROGESTERONE WITHDRAWAL THEORY

Progesterone exerts a relaxant effect on the uterine smooth muscle by interfering with conduction of impulses from one cell to the next. The placenta produces progesterone, and toward the end of gestation, the amount or effectiveness of progesterone may decrease, contributing to increased uterine contractility.

### FETAL CORTISOL THEORY

As the woman approaches term, the fetus produces more cortisol. Cortisol is thought to exert two effects: (a) It slows the production of progesterone by the placenta, and (b) it stimulates the precursors to prostaglandins. These two effects decrease the relaxant effect of progesterone on the uterus and increase the stimulatory effect of prostaglandins.

### UTERINE DISTENTION THEORY

The uterus slowly increases in size during the gestation, and its smooth muscle is stretched. Most smooth muscle contracts when stretched, but the uterine smooth muscle does not because of the effect of progesterone. As the woman approaches term, the decreased amount or effectiveness of progesterone increases uterine irritability and contractions. The irritability of the smooth muscle is enhanced by uterine distention, which stimulates the production of prostaglandins.

### PROSTAGLANDIN THEORY

Although the exact relationship between prostaglandins and the onset of labor is not yet established, there is growing evidence that prostaglandin involvement is significant. Prostaglandin is known to stimulate smooth muscle contractions. It may also stimulate the production and release of oxytocin and lower the uterine threshold to oxytocin. The production of prostaglandins increases just before labor begins, most likely as a result of the interaction of such factors as increased estrogen and decreased progesterone, increased fetal cortisol, and increased distention of the uterus.

## ● Myometrial Activity

Stretching of the cervix causes an increase in endogenous oxytocin, which increases myometrial activity. Pressures exerted by the contracting uterus vary from 30 to 55 mm Hg, with an average of 40 mm Hg.

In true labor, the uterus divides into two portions. This division is known as the *physiologic retraction ring.* The upper portion, which is the contractile segment, becomes progressively thicker as labor advances. The lower portion, which includes the lower uterine segment and cervix, is passive. As labor continues, the lower uterine segment expands and thins out.

With each contraction the muscles of the upper uterine segment shorten and exert a longitudinal traction on the cervix, causing effacement. **Effacement** is the taking up of the internal os and the cervical canal into the uterine side walls. The cervix changes progressively from a long, thick structure to a structure that is tissue-paper thin (Figure 14.10). In primigravidas, effacement usually precedes dilatation.

The uterus elongates with each contraction, decreasing the horizontal diameter. This elongation causes a straightening of the fetal body, pressing the upper portion against the fundus and thrusting the presenting part down toward the lower uterine segment and the cervix. The pressure exerted by the fetus is called the fetal axis pressure. As the uterus elongates, the longitudinal muscle fibers are pulled upward over the presenting part. This action, plus the hydrostatic pressure of the fetal membranes, causes **cervical dilatation**. The cervical os and cervical canal widen from less than a centimeter to approximately 10 cm, allowing delivery of the fetus. When the cervix is completely dilated and retracted up into the lower uterine segment, it can no longer be palpated.

The round ligament pulls the fundus forward, thus aligning the fetus with the bony pelvis.

## ● Intraabdominal Pressure

After the cervix is completely dilated, the maternal abdominal muscles contract as the woman pushes. The pushing aids in expulsion of the fetus and placenta. If the cervix is not completely dilated, bearing down can cause cervical edema (which retards dilatation), possible tearing and bruising of the cervix, and maternal exhaustion.

## ● Musculature Changes in the Pelvic Floor

The levator ani muscle and fascia of the pelvic floor draw the rectum and vagina upward and forward with each contraction, along the curve of the pelvic floor. As the fetal head descends to the pelvic floor, the pressure of the presenting part causes the perineal structure, which was once 5 cm in thickness, to change to a structure of less than a centimeter. A normal physiologic anesthesia is produced as a result of the decreased blood supply to the area. The anus everts, exposing the interior rectal wall as the fetal head descends forward (Pritchard et al 1985).

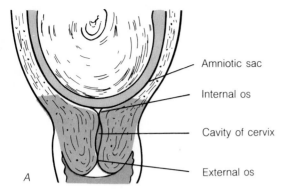

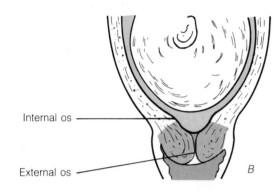

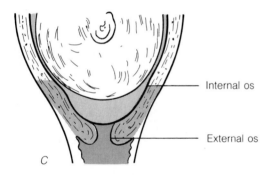

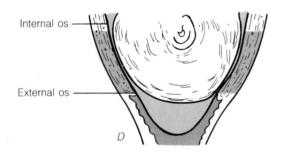

*Figure 14.10  Effacement of the cervix in the primigravida: (A) At the beginning of labor, there is no cervical effacement or dilatation. (B) Beginning cervical effacement. (C) Cervix is about one-half effaced and slightly dilated. (D) Complete effacement and dilatation.*

## ● PREMONITORY SIGNS OF LABOR

Most primigravidas and many multiparas experience the following signs and symptoms of impending labor.

## ● Lightening

**Lightening** occurs because the fetus begins to settle into the pelvic inlet (engagement). With its descent, the uterus moves downward, and the fundus no longer presses on the diaphragm.

The woman can breathe more easily after lightening. With increased downward pressure of the presenting part, however, the woman may notice the following:

- Leg cramps or pains due to pressure on the nerves that course through the obturator foramen in the pelvis
- Increased pelvic pressure
- Increased venous stasis leading to dependent edema
- Increased vaginal secretions resulting from congestion of the vaginal mucous membranes

## ● Braxton Hicks Contractions

Prior to the onset of labor, Braxton Hicks contractions, the irregular, intermittent contractions that have been occurring throughout the pregnancy, may become uncomfortable. The pain seems to be in the abdomen and groin but may feel like the "drawing" sensations experienced by some with dysmenorrhea. When these contractions are strong enough for the woman to believe she is in labor, she is said to be in false labor. *False labor* is uncomfortable and may be exhausting as the woman wonders if "this is it." Since the contractions can be fairly regular, she has no way of knowing if they are the beginning of true labor. She may come to the hospital for a vaginal examination to determine if cervical dilatation is occurring. Frequent episodes of false labor and trips back and forth to the physician's or nurse-midwife's office or hospital may frustrate or embarrass the woman, who feels that she should know when she is really in labor. Reassurance by nursing staff can ease embarrassment.

## ● Cervical Changes

For some time, the softening (also called *ripening*) of the cervix was thought to be caused by increasing intensity of Braxton Hicks contractions. A few days before the onset of labor, the cervix becomes even more soft and begins to efface and dilate slightly. The mechanism for this ripening is biochemical and is the result of changes in the connective tissue of the cervix.

## Bloody Show

The mucous plug is accumulated cervical secretions that have closed off the opening of the uterine cavity. With softening and effacement of the cervix, the mucous plug is often expelled, resulting in a small amount of blood loss from the exposed cervical capillaries. The resulting pink-tinged secretions are called **bloody show**.

Bloody show is considered a sign of imminent labor, which usually begins within 24–48 hours. Vaginal examination with manipulation of the cervix may also result in a blood-tinged discharge, which may be confused with bloody show.

## Rupture of Membranes

In approximately 12% of women, the amniotic membranes rupture before the onset of labor. This is called **rupture of membranes (ROM)**. After membranes rupture, 80% of women will experience spontaneous labor within 24 hours. If membranes rupture and labor does not begin spontaneously within 12–24 hours, labor may be induced to avoid infection. An induction of labor is done only if the pregnancy is near term.

When the membranes rupture, the amniotic fluid may be expelled in large amounts. If engagement has not occurred, the danger of the umbilical cord washing out with the fluid (called *prolapsed cord*) exists. In addition, the open pathway into the uterus causes danger of infection. Because of these threats, the woman is advised to notify her physician or nurse-midwife and proceed to the hospital/birthing center. In some instances, the fluid is expelled in small amounts and may be confused with episodes of urinary incontinence associated with urinary urgency, coughing, or sneezing. The discharge should be checked to ascertain its source and to determine further action. (See Chapter 15 for assessment techniques.)

## Sudden Burst of Energy

Some women report a sudden burst of energy approximately 24–48 hours before labor. They may do their spring housecleaning or rearrange all the furniture; these activities are often referred to as the *nesting instinct*. The cause of the energy spurt is unknown. The nurse in prenatal teaching should warn prospective mothers not to overexert themselves at this time so that they will not be excessively tired when labor begins.

## Other Signs

Other premonitory signs include:

● Weight loss of 1–3 pounds resulting from fluid loss and electrolyte shifts produced by changes in estrogen and progesterone levels

● Increased backache and sacroiliac pressure from the influence of relaxin hormone on the pelvic joints

● Diarrhea, indigestion, or nausea and vomiting just prior to the onset of labor

The causes of these signs are unknown.

## Differences Between True and False Labor

The contractions of true labor produce progressive dilatation and effacement of the cervix. They occur regularly and increase in frequency, duration, and intensity. The discomfort of true labor contractions usually starts in the back and radiates around to the abdomen. The pain is not relieved by ambulation (in fact, walking may intensify the pain).

The contractions of false labor do not produce progressive cervical effacement and dilatation. Classically, they are irregular and do not increase in frequency, duration, and intensity. The contractions may be perceived as a hardening or "balling up" without discomfort, or discomfort may occur mainly in the lower abdomen and groin. The discomfort may be relieved by ambulation.

The woman will find it helpful to know the characteristics of true labor contractions as well as the premonitory signs of ensuing labor. However, many times the only way to differentiate accurately between true and false labor is to assess dilatation. The woman must feel free to come in for accurate assessment of labor and should never be allowed to feel foolish if the labor is false. The nurse must reassure the woman that false labor is common and that it often cannot be distinguished from true labor except by vaginal examination. (See Essential Facts to Remember—Comparison of True and False Labor.)

## STAGES OF LABOR AND BIRTH

There are three stages of labor. The *first stage* begins with the beginning of true labor and ends when the cervix is completely dilated at 10 cm. The *second stage* begins with complete dilatation and ends with the birth of the infant. The *third stage* begins with the birth of the infant and ends with the delivery of the placenta.

Some clinicians identify a *fourth stage* of labor. During this stage, which lasts one to four hours after delivery of the placenta, the uterus effectively contracts to control bleeding at the placental site (Pritchard et al 1985).

The care of the laboring woman is discussed in Chapter 16.

## Essential Facts to Remember

### Comparison of True and False Labor

| True Labor | False Labor |
|---|---|
| Contractions are at regular intervals. | Contractions are irregular. |
| Intervals between contractions gradually shorten. | Usually no change. |
| Contractions increase in duration and intensity. | Usually no change. |
| Discomfort begins in back and radiates around to abdomen. | Discomfort is usually in abdomen. |
| Intensity usually increases with walking. | Walking has no effect or lessens contractions. |
| Cervical dilatation and effacement are progressive. | No change. |

## • First Stage

The first stage of labor is divided into the *latent, active,* and *transition* phases. Each phase of labor is characterized by physical and psychologic changes.

### LATENT PHASE

The *latent phase* begins with the onset of regular contractions. As the cervix begins to dilate, it also effaces, although little or no fetal descent is evident. For a woman in her first labor (nullipara), the latent phase averages 8.6 hours but should not exceed 20 hours. The latent phase in multiparas averages 5.3 hours but should not exceed 14 hours.

Uterine contractions become established during the latent phase and increase in frequency, duration, and intensity. They may start as mild contractions lasting 15–20 seconds with a frequency of 10–20 minutes and progress to moderate ones lasting 30–40 seconds with a frequency of five to seven minutes. They average 40 mm Hg during acme from a baseline tonus of 10 mm Hg (Varney 1987).

In the early or latent phase of the first stage of labor, contractions are usually mild. The woman feels able to cope with the discomfort. She may be relieved that labor has finally started. Although she may be anxious, she is able to recognize and express those feelings of anxiety. The woman is often talkative and smiling and is eager to talk about herself and answer questions. Excitement is high, and her partner or other support person is often as elated as she is.

### ACTIVE PHASE

During the *active phase,* the cervix dilates from about 3–4 cm to 8 cm. Fetal descent is progressive. The cervical dilatation should be at least 1.2 cm/hr in nulliparas, and 1.5 cm/hr in multiparas (Pritchard et al 1985).

### TRANSITION PHASE

The *transition phase* is the last part of the first stage. Cervical dilatation slows as it progresses from 8 to 10 cm and the rate of fetal descent increases. The average rate of descent is at least 1 cm/hr in nulliparas, and 2 cm/hr in multiparas. The transition phase should not be longer than three hours for nulliparas and one hour for multiparas (Pritchard and MacDonald 1985).

During the active and transition phases, contractions become more frequent, are longer in duration, and increase in intensity. At the beginning of the active phase the contractions have a frequency of two to three minutes, a duration of 60 seconds, and are strong in intensity. During transition, contractions have a frequency of 1½–2 minutes, a duration of 60–90 seconds, and are strong in intensity (Varney 1987).

When the woman enters the early active phase, her anxiety tends to increase as she senses the fairly constant intensification of contractions and pain. She begins to fear a loss of control and may use coping mechanisms to maintain control. Some women exhibit decreased ability to cope and a sense of helplessness. Women who have support persons available, particularly fathers, experience greater satisfaction and less anxiety throughout the birth process than those without these supports (Doering et al 1980).

When the woman enters the transition phase, she may demonstrate significant anxiety. She becomes acutely aware of the increasing force and intensity of the contractions. She may become restless, frequently changing position. Because the most commonly expressed fear at this time is that of abandonment, it is crucial that the nurse be available as backup and relief for the support person. By the time the woman enters the transition phase, she is inner-directed and, often, tired. At the same time, the support person may be feeling the need for a break. The woman should be reassured that she will not be left alone and should always be told where her support people are if they leave the room and how to reach the nurse.

The woman may also fear that she will be "torn open" or "split apart" by the force of the contractions. Many clients experience a sensation of pressure so great with the peak of a contraction that it seems to them that their abdomens will burst open with the force. The woman should be informed that this is a normal sensation and reassured that such bursting will not happen.

During transition the woman will most likely be withdrawn and inner-focused. Increasingly, she may doubt her ability to cope with her labor. The woman may become apprehensive and irritable. She is often terrified of being left alone but also does not want anyone to talk to or touch her. However, with the next contraction, she may ask for verbal and physical support. Other characteristics may accompany this phase:

● Hyperventilation as the woman increases her breathing rate

● Restlessness

● Difficulty understanding directions

● A sense of bewilderment and anger at the contractions

● Statements that she "can't take it anymore"

● Requests for medication

● Hiccupping, belching, nausea, or vomiting

● Beads of perspiration on the upper lip

● Increasing rectal pressure

The woman in this phase is anxious to "get it over with." She may be amnesic and sleep between her now-frequent contractions. Her support persons may start to feel helpless and may turn to the nurse for increased participation as their efforts to alleviate her discomfort seem less effective.

As dilatation approaches 10 centimeters, increased rectal pressure and uncontrollable desire to bear down, increased amount of bloody show, and rupture of membranes may occur.

### Amniotic Membranes

At the beginning of labor, the amniotic membranes bulge through the cervix in the shape of a cone. ROM generally occurs at the height of an intense contraction with a gush of the fluid out the introitus.

## ● Second Stage

The second stage of labor begins when the cervix is completely dilated (10 cm) and ends with birth of the infant. The second stage should be completed within an hour after the cervix becomes fully dilated for primigravidas (multiparas average 15 minutes). Contractions continue with a frequency of 1½–2 minutes, a duration of 60–90 seconds, and strong intensity (Varney 1987). Descent of the fetal presenting part continues until it reaches the perineal floor.

As the fetal head descends, the woman has the urge to push because of pressure of the fetal head on the sacral and obturator nerves. As she pushes, intraabdominal pressure is exerted from contraction of the maternal abdominal muscles. As the fetal head continues its descent, the perineum begins to bulge, flatten, and move anteriorly. The amount of bloody show may increase. The labia begin to part with each contraction. Between contractions the fetal head appears to recede. With succeeding contractions and maternal pushing effort, the fetal head descends farther. **Crowning** occurs when the fetal head is encircled by the external opening of the vagina (introitus) and means birth is imminent.

Usually, a childbirth-prepared woman feels relieved that the acute pain she felt during the transition phase is over (see Essential Facts to Remember—Characteristics of Labor). She also may be relieved that the birth is near and she can now push. Some women feel a sense of control now that they can be actively involved. Others, particularly those without childbirth preparation, may become frightened. They tend to fight each contraction and any attempt of others to persuade them to push with contractions. Such behavior may be frightening and disconcerting to her support persons. The woman may feel she has lost control and become embarrassed and apologetic or she may demonstrate extreme irritability toward the staff or her supporters in an attempt to regain control over external forces against which she feels helpless. Some women feel acute, increasingly severe pain and a burning sensation as the perineum distends.

### SPONTANEOUS BIRTH (VERTEX PRESENTATION)

As the head distends the vulva with each contraction, the perineum becomes extremely thin and the anus stretches and protrudes.

As extension occurs under the symphysis pubis, the head is born. When the anterior shoulder meets the underside of the symphysis pubis, a gentle push by the mother aids in birth of the shoulders. The body then follows.

Birth of infants in other than vertex presentations is discussed in Chapter 18.

## ● Third Stage

### PLACENTAL SEPARATION

After the infant is born, the uterus contracts firmly, diminishing its capacity and the surface area of placental attachment. The placenta begins to separate because of this decrease in surface area. As this separation occurs, bleeding results in the formation of a hematoma between the placental tissue and the remaining decidua. This hematoma accelerates the separation process. The membranes are the last to separate. They are peeled off the uterine wall as the placenta descends into the vagina.

Signs of placental separation usually appear around

## Essential Facts to Remember

### Characteristics of Labor

| | First Stage | | | Second Stage |
|---|---|---|---|---|
| | *Latent Phase* | *Active Phase* | *Transition Phase* | |
| Nullipara | 8½ hours | 6 hours | | 1 hour |
| Multipara | 5 hours | 4½ hours | | 15 minutes |
| Cervical Dilatation | 0 to 3–4 cm | 4 to 8 cm | 8–10 cm | |
| Contractions | | | | |
| Frequency | Every 10–20 minutes at the beginning and progressing to every 5–7 minutes | Every 2–3 minutes | Every 1½–2 minutes | Every 1½–2 minutes |
| Duration | 15–20 seconds progressing to 30–40 seconds | 60 seconds | 60–90 seconds | 60–90 seconds |
| Intensity | Begin as mild and progress to moderate | Begin as moderate and progress to strong | Strong | Strong |

five minutes after birth of the infant. These signs are (a) a globular-shaped uterus, (b) a rise of the fundus in the abdomen, (c) a sudden gush or trickle of blood, and (d) further protrusion of the umbilical cord out of the vagina.

### PLACENTAL DELIVERY

When the signs of placental separation appear, the woman may bear down to aid in placental expulsion. If this fails and the clinician has ascertained that the fundus is firm, gentle traction may be applied to the cord while pressure is exerted on the fundus. The weight of the placenta as it is guided into the placental pan aids in the removal of the membranes from the uterine wall. A placenta is considered to be *retained* if 30 minutes have elapsed from completion of the second stage of labor.

If the placenta separates from the inside to the outer margins, it is delivered with the fetal or shiny side presenting (Figure 14.11). This is known as the *Schultze mechanism* of placental delivery, or more commonly *shiny Schultze*. If the placenta separates from the outer margins inward, it will roll up and present sideways with the maternal surface delivering first. This is known as the *Duncan mechanism* of placental delivery and is commonly called *dirty Duncan* because the placental surface is rough.

Nursing and medical interventions during the third stage of labor are discussed in detail in Chapter 16.

## • Fourth Stage

The fourth stage of labor is the time from one to four hours after birth, in which physiologic readjustment of the mother's body begins. With the birth, hemodynamic changes occur. Blood loss at birth ranges from 250 to 500 mL. With this blood loss and the weight of the pregnant uterus off of the surrounding vessels, blood is redistributed into venous beds. This results in a moderate drop in both systolic and diastolic blood pressure, increased pulse pressure, and moderate tachycardia (Albright et al 1986).

The cerebrospinal fluid pressure, which increased during labor, now drops and rapidly returns to normal values (Albright et al 1986).

The uterus remains contracted and is in the midline of the abdomen. The fundus is usually midway between the symphysis pubis and umbilicus. Its contracted state constricts the vessels at the site of placental implantation. Immediately after birth of the placenta, the cervix is widely spread and thick.

Nausea and vomiting usually cease. The woman may be thirsty and hungry. She may experience a shaking chill, which is thought to be associated with the ending of the physical exertion of labor. The bladder is often hypotonic due to trauma during the second stage and/or the administration of anesthetics that may decrease sensations. Hypotonic bladder leads to urinary retention. Nursing care of this stage is discussed in Chapter 16.

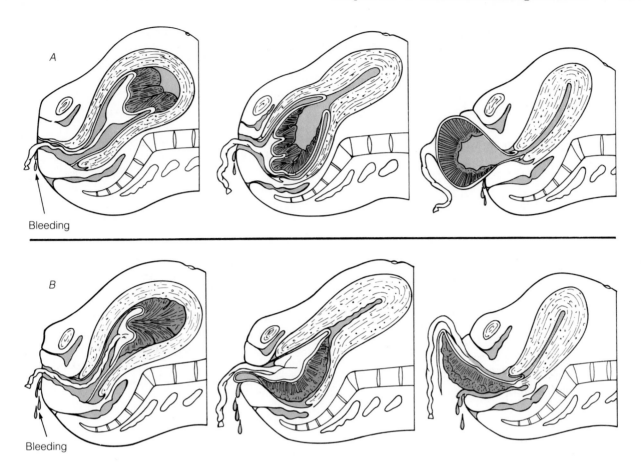

*Figure 14.11     Placental separation and birth: (A) Schultze mechanism, (B) Duncan mechanism*

# MATERNAL SYSTEMIC RESPONSE TO LABOR

## Cardiovascular System

A strong contraction greatly diminishes or completely stops the blood flow in the branches of the uterine artery, which supplies the intervillous space. This leads to a redistribution of the blood flow to the peripheral circulation and an increase in peripheral resistance. Increase of the systolic and diastolic blood pressure and a slowing of the pulse rate result. Changes in maternal blood pressure and pulse also depend on the woman's position.

Cardiac output is increased by 10%–15% during rest periods between contractions in early labor and by 30%–50% in the second stage (Albright et al 1986). Additional increases and decreases in cardiac output mirror the changes in uterine pressure; that is, cardiac output increases as the contraction builds and peaks and slowly returns to precontraction levels as the contraction diminishes.

Immediately after birth, cardiac output peaks with an 80% increase over prelabor values, and then in the first ten minutes decreases by 20%–25%. Cardiac output further decreases by 20%–25% in the first hour after birth (Albright et al 1986).

## Blood Pressure

As a result of increased cardiac output, systolic blood pressure rises during uterine contractions. Between contractions, the blood pressure returns to its prelabor level. In the immediate postpartal period, the arterial pressure remains essentially normal even though the cardiac output increases due to peripheral vasodilatation.

Approximately 10%–15% of women demonstrate clinical symptoms (hypotension, tachycardia) of vena cava syndrome. Some women with this syndrome are asymptomatic due to compensatory mechanisms. Women who are asymptomatic are still at risk because blood flow to the placenta is slowly compromised by vasoconstriction of the peripheral arteries (Albright el at 1986).

Women with the highest risk of developing supine hypertensive syndrome are nulliparas with strong abdominal muscles and tightly drawn abdominal skin, gravidas with hydramnios and/or multiple pregnancy, and obese women. Other predisposing factors include hypovolemia, dehydration, hemorrhage, metabolic acidosis, administration of narcotics (which results in vasodilatation and inhibits compensatory mechanisms), and administration of regional anesthetics that results in *sympathetic blockade* (blocking of the sympathetic nervous system, which results in vasodilatation and hypotension). A sympathetic blockade may occur with an epidural or a spinal block.

## • Fluid and Electrolyte Balance

Profuse perspiration (diaphoresis) occurs during labor. Hyperventilation also occurs, altering electrolyte and fluid balance from insensible water loss. The muscle activity elevates the body temperature, which increases sweating and evaporation from the skin. As the woman responds to the work of labor the rise in the respiratory rate increases the evaporative water volume, since each breath of air must be warmed to the body temperature and humidified. With the increased evaporative water volume, giving parenteral fluids during labor to ensure adequate hydration becomes increasingly important.

## • Gastrointestinal System

During labor, gastric motility and absorption of solid food are reduced. Gastric emptying time is prolonged. It is not uncommon for a laboring woman to vomit food she ate up to 12 hours earlier.

## • Respiratory System

Oxygen consumption, which increased approximately 20% during pregnancy, is further increased during labor. During the early first stage of labor, oxygen consumption increases 40%, with a further increase to 100% during the second stage.

Minute ventilation increases to 20–25 L/min (normal 10 L/min), and in the unprepared and unmedicated woman it may reach 35 L/min or more. This hyperventilation results in a rise in the maternal pH in early labor, followed by a return to normal toward the end of the first stage. If the first stage is prolonged, the woman may develop acidosis (Albright et al 1986).

## • Hemopoietic System

Leukocyte levels may reach 25,000/mm³ or more during labor. Although the precise cause of the leukocytosis is unknown, it may be due to the strenuous exercise and stress response of labor (Pritchard et al 1985). Blood glucose levels may decrease as a result of increased activity of uterine and skeletal muscles (Varney 1987).

## • Renal System

The base of the bladder is pushed forward and upward when engagement occurs. The pressure from the presenting part may impair blood and lymph drainage from the base of the bladder, leading to edema of the tissues (Pritchard et al 1985).

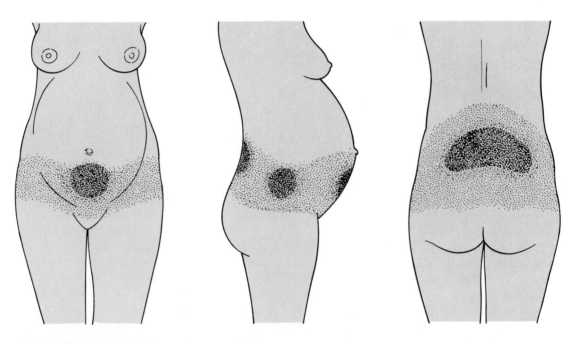

*Figure 14.12   Area of reference of labor pain during the first stage. Density of stippling indicates intensity of pain. (From Bonica JJ:* Principles and Practice of Obstetric Analgesia and Anesthesia. *Philadelphia: Davis, 1972, p 108.)*

Approximately one-third to one-half of all laboring women have slight proteinuria of 1+ as a result of muscle breakdown from exercise. An increase to 2+ or above is indicative of PIH (Varney 1987).

## ● *Pain*

### THEORIES OF PAIN

According to the *gate-control theory* pain results from activity in several interacting specialized neural systems. The gate-control theory proposes that a mechanism in the dorsal horn of the spinal column serves as a valve or gate that increases or decreases the flow of nerve impulses from the periphery to the central nervous system. The gate mechanism is influenced by the size of the transmitting fibers and by the nerve impulses that descend from the brain. Psychologic processes such as past experiences, attention, and emotion may influence pain perception and response by activating the gate mechanism. The gates may be opened or closed by central nervous system activities, such as anxiety or excitement, or through selective localized activity.

The gate-control theory has two important implications for obstetrics: Pain may be controlled by tactile stimulation and can be modified by activities controlled by the central nervous system. These include back rub, sacral pressure, effleurage, suggestion, distraction, and conditioning.

### CAUSES OF PAIN DURING LABOR

The pain associated with the first stage of labor is unique in that it accompanies a normal physiologic process. Even though perception of the pain of childbirth may vary among women, there is a physiologic basis for discomfort during labor. Pain during the first stage of labor arises from (a) dilatation of the cervix, which is the primary source of pain; (b) hypoxia of the uterine muscle cells during contraction; (c) stretching of the lower uterine segment; and (d) pressure on adjacent structures. The areas of pain include the lower abdominal wall and the areas over the lower lumbar region and the upper sacrum (Figure 14.12).

During the second stage of labor, discomfort is due to (a) hypoxia of the contracting uterine muscle cells, (b) distention of the vagina and perineum, and (c) pressure on adjacent structures. The area of pain increases as shown in Figures 14.13 and 14.14.

Pain during the third stage results from uterine con-

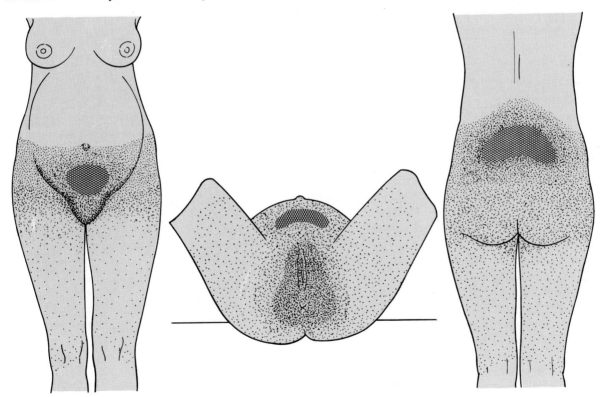

*Figure 14.13    Distribution of labor pain during the later phase of the first stage and early phase of the second stage. Cross-hatched areas indicate location of the most intense pain; dense stippling, moderate pain; and light stippling, mild pain. Note that the uterine contractions, which at this stage are very strong, produce intense pain. (From Bonica JJ: Principles and Practice of Obstetric Analgesia and Anesthesia. Philadelphia: Davis, 1972, p 109.)*

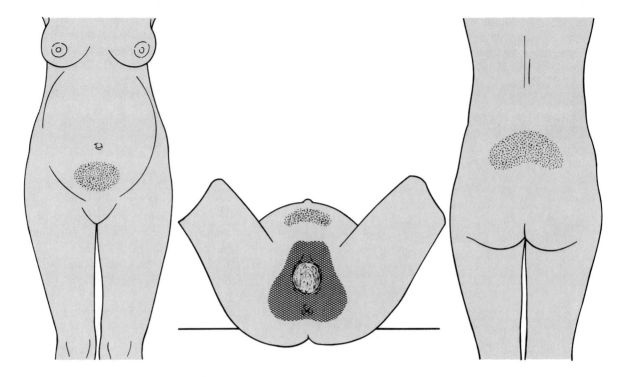

*Figure 14.14    Distribution of labor pain during the later phase of the second stage and actual birth. The perineal component is the main cause of discomfort. Uterine contractions contribute much less. (From Bonica JJ:* Principles of Obstetric Analgesia and Anesthesia. *Philadelphia: Davis, 1972, p 109.)*

tractions and cervical dilatation as the placenta is expelled. This stage of labor is short, and after this phase of labor, anesthesia is needed primarily for episiotomy repair.

### FACTORS AFFECTING RESPONSE TO PAIN

Many factors affect the individual's perception of pain impulses. Individuals tend to respond to painful stimuli in the way that is acceptable in their culture. When assessing a woman's need for assistance, the nurse must remember that there are many ways to respond to pain. The absence of crying and moaning does not necessarily mean that pain is absent, nor does the presence of crying and moaning necessarily mean that pain relief is desired at that moment. In some cultures, it is natural to communicate pain, no matter how mild, while members of other cultures stoically accept pain out of fear or because it is expected.

Another factor that may influence response to pain is *fatigue and sleep deprivation.* The fatigued woman has less energy and ability to use such strategies as distraction or imagination to deal with pain. As a result, the fatigued woman may choose analgesics or other medications to relieve the discomfort.

The woman's *previous experience* with pain also affects her ability to manage current and future pain. Those who have had experience with pain seem more sensitive to painful stimuli than those who have not.

*Anxiety* can affect a woman's response to pain. Unfamiliar surroundings and events can increase anxiety as does separation from family and loved ones. Anticipation of discomfort and questions about whether she can cope with the contractions can also increase anxiety.

### ● FETAL RESPONSE TO LABOR

When the fetus is normal, the mechanical and hemodynamic changes of normal labor have no adverse effects.

### ● Biochemical Changes

High pressures are exerted on the fetal head during contractions and to an even greater extent after ROM.

### ● Heart Rate Changes

Fetal heart rate decelerations can occur with intracranial pressures of 40–55 mm Hg. The currently accepted explanation of this early deceleration is hypoxic depression of the central nervous system, which is under vagal control. The absence of these head compression decelerations (early decelerations) in some fetuses during labor is explained by the existence of a threshold that is reached more gradually in the presence of intact membranes and lack of maternal resistance. Early decelerations are harmless in the normal fetus.

## ● Hemodynamic Changes

The adequate exchange of nutrients and gases in the fetal capillaries and intervillous spaces depends in part on the fetal blood pressure. Fetal blood pressure is a protective mechanism for the normal fetus during the anoxic periods caused by the contracting uterus during labor. The fetal and placental reserve is enough to see the fetus through these anoxic periods unharmed (Creasy and Resnik 1989).

## ● Positional Changes

For the fetus to pass through the birth canal, the fetal head and body must adjust to the passage by certain positional changes. These changes, called **cardinal movements** or *mechanisms of labor,* are described in the order in which they occur (Figure 14.15).

### DESCENT

Descent is thought to occur because of four forces: (a) pressure of the amniotic fluid, (b) direct pressure of the fundus on the breech, (c) contraction of the abdominal

muscles, and (d) extension and straightening of the fetal body. The head enters the inlet in the occiput transverse or oblique position because the pelvic inlet is widest from side to side. The sagittal suture is an equal distance from the maternal symphysis pubis and sacral promontory.

### FLEXION

Flexion occurs as the fetal head descends and meets resistance from the soft tissues of the pelvis, the muscles of the pelvic floor, and the cervix.

### INTERNAL ROTATION

The fetal head must rotate to fit the diameter of the pelvic cavity, which is widest in the anteroposterior diameter. As the occiput of the fetal head meets resistance from the levator ani muscles and their fascia, the occiput rotates usually from left to right and the sagittal suture aligns in the anteroposterior pelvic diameter.

### EXTENSION

The resistance of the pelvic floor and the mechanical movement of the vulva opening anteriorly and forward assist with extension of the fetal head as it passes under the symphysis pubis. With this positional change, the occiput, then brow and face, emerge from the vagina.

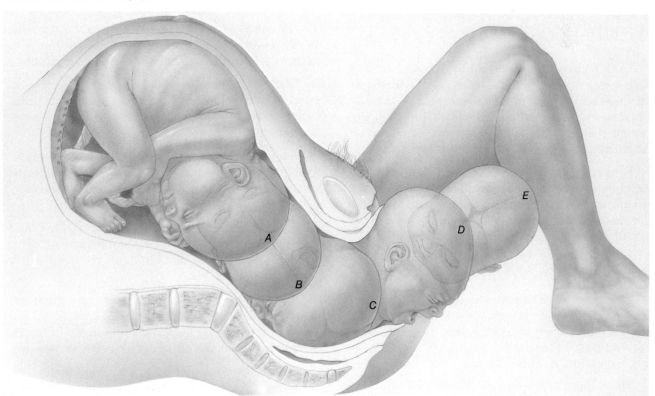

*Figure 14.15   Mechanisms of labor: (**A**), (**B**) descent, (**C**) internal rotation,
(**D**) extension, (**E**) external rotation*

## RESTITUTION

The shoulders of the infant enter the pelvis obliquely and remain oblique when the head rotates to the anteroposterior diameter through internal rotation. Because of this rotation, the neck becomes twisted. Once the head is born and is free of pelvic resistance, the neck untwists, turning the head to one side (restitution), and aligns with the position of the back in the birth canal.

## EXTERNAL ROTATION

As the shoulders rotate to the anteroposterior position in the pelvis, the head is turned farther to one side (external rotation).

## EXPULSION

After the external rotation and through the pushing efforts of the laboring woman, the anterior shoulder meets the undersurface of the symphysis pubis and slips under it. As lateral flexion of the shoulder and head occurs, the anterior shoulder is born before the posterior shoulder. The body follows quickly (Oxorn 1986).

The adaptations of the newborn to extrauterine life are discussed in Chapter 20.

## ESSENTIAL CONCEPTS

● Four factors that continually interact during the process of labor and delivery are the birth canal (passage), the fetus (passenger), the uterine contractions and pushing efforts of the laboring woman (powers), and the emotional components the woman brings to the birth setting (psyche).

● Four types of pelvises have been identified and each has a different effect on labor. The gynecoid and anthropoid are favorable to labor and delivery. The android and platypelloid are associated with difficult labor because of diminished diameters.

● Important parts of the maternal pelvis include the pelvic inlet, pelvic cavity, and pelvic outlet.

● The fetus accommodates itself to the maternal pelvis in a series of movements called the cardinal movements of labor, which include descent, flexion, internal rotation, extension, external rotation, expulsion, and restitution.

● The fetal head contains bones that are not fused. This allows for some overlapping and molding to facilitate birth.

● Fetal *attitude* refers to the relation of the fetal parts to one another.

● Fetal *lie* refers to the relationship of the cephalocaudal axis of the fetus to the maternal spine. The fetal lie is either longitudinal or transverse.

● Fetal *presentation* is determined by the body part lying closest to the maternal pelvis. Fetal presentations are cephalic, breech, or shoulder.

● Fetal *position* is the relationship of the landmark on the presenting fetal part to the front, sides, or back of the maternal pelvis.

● *Engagement* of the presenting part takes place when the largest diameter of the presenting part reaches or passes through the pelvic inlet.

● *Station* refers to the relationship of the presenting part to an imaginary line drawn between the ischial spines of the maternal pelvis.

● Each uterine contraction has an increment, acme, and decrement. Contraction frequency is the time from the beginning of one contraction to the beginning of the next contraction.

● Duration of contractions refers to the period of time from the beginning to the end of one contraction.

● Intensity of contractions refers to the strength of the contraction during acme. Intensity of contractions is termed as mild, moderate, or strong.

● Possible causes of labor include oxytocin stimulation, progesterone withdrawal, estrogen stimulation, fetal cortisol, uterine distention, and prostaglandin theory.

● Labor stresses the coping skills of women. Women with prenatal education about childbirth usually report more positive responses to labor.

● Factors that affect the response to labor pain include education, cultural beliefs, fatigue and sleep deprivation, personal significance of pain, previous experience, anxiety, and the availability of coping techniques.

● Premonitory signs of labor include lightening, Braxton Hicks contractions, cervical softening and effacement, bloody show, sudden burst of energy, weight loss, and sometimes rupture of membranes.

● There are four stages of labor and birth. The first stage is from beginning of true labor to complete dilatation of the cervix. Second stage is from complete dilatation of the cervix to birth. Third stage is from birth to expulsion of the placenta. Fourth stage is from expulsion of the placenta to a period of one to four hours after.

● Placental separation is indicated by lengthening of the umbilical cord, a small spurt of blood, change in uterine shape, and a rise of the fundus in the abdomen.

● The placenta is delivered by Schultze or Duncan mechanism. This is determined by the way it separates from the uterine wall.

• • • • • • • • • • • • • • • • • • • • • • • • • • • •

## References

Albright GA et al: *Anesthesia in Obstetrics: Maternal, Fetal and Neonatal Aspects,* 2nd ed. Boston: Butterworths, 1986.

Caldwell WE, Moloy HC: Anatomical variations in the female pelvis and their effect on labor with a suggested classification. *Am J Obstet Gynecol* 1933; 26:479.

Cibils, LA: *Electronic Fetal-Neonatal Monitoring.* Boston: PSG, 1981.

Creasy RK, Resnik R: *Maternal-Fetal Medicine, Principles and Practice.* Philadelphia: Saunders, 1989.

Doering SG et al: Modeling the quality of women's birth experience. *J Health Social Behavior* March 1980; 21:12.

Hariharan S et al: Initiation of labor. Chapter 86 in: *Gynecology and Obstetrics.* Sciarra JL (editor). Philadelphia: Saunders, 1986.

Lederman RP: *Psychosocial Adaptation in Pregnancy: Assessment of Seven Dimensions of Maternal Development.* Englewood Cliffs, NJ: Prentice-Hall, 1984.

Mercer RT: A theoretical framework for studying factors that impact on the maternal role. *Nurs Res* March/April 1981; 30:73.

Mercer RT: Relationship of the birth experience to later mothering behaviors. *J Nurse-Midwifery* July/August 1985; 30:204.

Nichols F, Humenick SS: *Childbirth Education: Practice, Research, and Theory.* Philadelphia: Saunders, 1988.

Oxorn H: *Human Labor and Birth.* New York: Appleton-Century-Crofts, 1986.

Pritchard J et al: *Williams Obstetrics,* 17th ed. New York: Appleton-Century-Crofts, 1985.

Rubin R: *Maternal Identity and the Maternal Experience.* New York: Springer, 1984.

Varney H: *Nurse-Midwifery,* 2nd ed. Boston: Blackwell Scientific Publications, 1987.

## Additional Readings

Flagler S: Maternal role competence. *West J Nurs Res* 1988; 10(3):274.

Gilson GJ et al: Expectant management of premature rupture of membranes at term in a birthing center setting. *J Nurse-Midwifery* May/June 1988; 33(3):134.

Herbert WN, Owen HG, Collins ML: Autologous blood storage in obstetrics. *Obstet Gynecol* August 1988; 72(2):166.

Joseph J: The joints of the pelvis and their relation to posture in labour. *Midwives Chronicle and Nurs Notes* March 1988; 63.

Lomas J et al: The labor and delivery satisfaction index: The development and evaluation of a soft outcome measure. *Birth* September 1987; 14(3):125.

McKay S, Mahan C: Modifying the stomach contents of laboring women: Why and how; success and risks. *Birth* December 1988; 15(4):213.

Nesheim BI: Duration of labor. An analysis of influencing factors. *Acta Obstet Gynecol Scand* 1988; 67(2):121.

Nodine PM, Robert J: Factors associated with perineal outcome during childbirth. *J Nurse-Midwifery* May/June 1987; 32(3):123.

Poma PA: Pregnancy in Hispanic women. *J Nat Med Assoc* 1987; 79:929.

Roberts J et al: A descriptive analysis of involuntary bearing down efforts during the expulsive phase of labor. *J Obstet Gynecol Neonatal Nurs* January/February 1987; 16(1):48.

Shearer M: Commentary: How well does the LADSI measure satisfaction with labor and delivery? *Birth* September 1987; 14(3):130.

Thomson M: Different rates of prolonged first stage labor in primiparas at two hospitals. *Birth* December 1988; 15(4):209.

Weller RH, Eberstein IW, Bailey M: Pregnancy wantedness and maternal behavior during pregnancy. *Demography* 1987; 24(3):407.

# 15

# Intrapartal Nursing Assessment

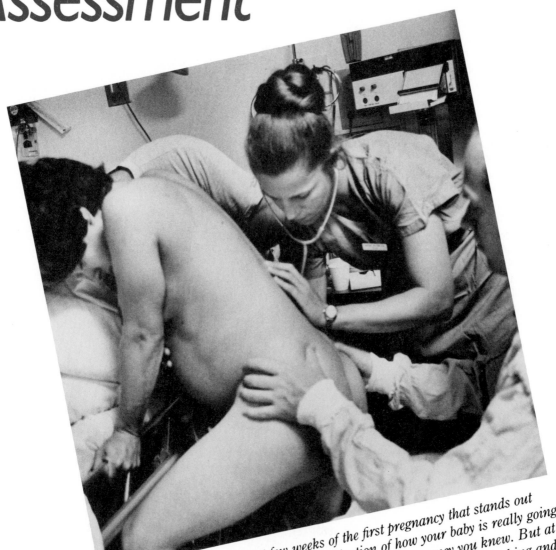

There is a moment in the last few weeks of the first pregnancy that stands out beyond all others. At that moment the realization of how your baby is really going to be born hits you like a brick. Yes, all through the pregnancy you knew. But at this moment you know, without any way out, that this baby you feel kicking and turning—and surely weighing more than anyone expects—is going to come out your vagina. Let me tell you, that's quite a moment!

## Objectives

● Discuss intrapartal physical and psychologic assessment.

● Identify methods used to evaluate the progress of labor.

● Describe the procedure for performing Leopold's maneuvers and the information that may be obtained.

● Differentiate between baseline and periodic changes in fetal monitoring and describe the appearance of each and their significance.

● Outline steps to be performed in the systematic evaluation of fetal heart rate tracings.

● Identify nonreassuring fetal heart rate patterns and nursing interventions that should be carried out in the management of fetal distress.

● Discuss the indications for fetal blood sampling and state related pH values.

● Discuss psychologic reactions to electronic fetal monitoring.

## Key Terms

accelerations
baseline rate
baseline variability
early deceleration
fetal blood sampling
fetal bradycardia
fetal tachycardia
late deceleration
Leopold's maneuvers
sinusoidal pattern
variable deceleration

The physiologic events that occur during labor call for many adaptations by the mother and fetus. Accurate and frequent assessment is crucial because the changes are rapid and involve two individuals, mother and child.

The number and effectiveness of intrapartal assessment techniques have increased over the years. In the past, observation, palpation, and auscultation were the only assessment techniques available. In current practice, these techniques are enhanced by the use of ultrasound and electronic monitoring. These tools can provide more detailed information and assessment.

## ● MATERNAL ASSESSMENT
## ● History

A brief history is obtained when the woman is admitted to the birthing area. Each agency has its own admission form but the following information is usually obtained:

● Woman's name and age

● Attending physician or certified nurse-midwife (CNM)

● Personal data: blood type; Rh factor; results of serology testing; prepregnant and present weight; allergies to medications, foods, or substances; and medications taken during pregnancy

● History of previous illness, such as tuberculosis, heart disease, diabetes, convulsive disorders, thyroid disorders

● Problems in the prenatal period, such as elevated blood pressure, bleeding problems, recurrent urinary tract infection

● Pregnancy data: gravida, para, abortions, neo-natal deaths

● The method the woman has chosen for infant feeding

● Type of prenatal education classes

● Woman's requests regarding labor and birth, such as no enema, no analgesics or anesthetics, or the presence of the father in the delivery room

## ● Intrapartal High-Risk Screening

Screening for intrapartal high-risk factors is an integral part of assessing the normal laboring woman. As the history is obtained, the nurse notes the presence of any factors that may be associated with a high-risk condition. For example, the woman who reports a physical symptom

## Table 15.1 Intrapartal High-Risk Factors

| Factor | Maternal implication | Fetal/neonatal implication |
|---|---|---|
| **PHYSICAL FACTORS** | | |
| Abnormal presentation (mal presentation) | ↑ Risk cesarean delivery<br>↑ Risk prolonged labor | Cesarean delivery<br>Prematurity<br>↑ Risk congenital abnormality<br>Neonatal physical trauma |
| Multiple gestation (twins, triplets, etc) | ↑ Uterine distention → ↑ risk postpartum hemorrhage<br>↑ Risk premature labor | Low birth weight<br>Prematurity<br>Fetus to fetus transfusion |
| Hydramnios (more fluid than normal) | ↑ Discomfort<br>↑ Distention | ↑ Risk esophageal or other high alimentary tract atresias<br>↑ Risk CNS anomalies (myelocelé) |
| Oligohydramnios (less fluid than normal) | Maternal fear of "dry birth" | ↑ Risk congenital anomalies<br>↑ Risk renal lesions<br>Postmaturity |
| Meconium staining of amniotic fluid (release of meconium in amniotic fluid) | ↑ Psychologic stress due to fear for fetus | Fetal asphyxia<br>↑ Risk meconium aspiration<br>↑ Risk pneumonia due to aspiration of meconium |
| Rupture of membranes (>48 hours) | ↑ Risk infection (amnionitis) | ↑ Risk infection<br>Prematurity |
| Premature labor (before 37 weeks of gestation) | Fear for baby | Prematurity<br>Respiratory distress syndrome<br>Prolonged hospitalization |
| Induction-tetanic contractions (contractions with frequency of < two minutes) | ↑ Risk hypercontractility of uterus<br>↑ Risk uterine rupture | Prematurity if gestational age not assessed correctly<br>Hypoxia |
| Abruptio placentae-placenta previa | Hemorrhage<br>↓ Uterine contractions after delivery | Fetal asphyxia<br>Fetal exsanguination<br>↑ Perinatal mortality |
| Prolonged labor (>24 hr) | Maternal exhaustion | Fetal asphyxia<br>Intracranial birth injury |
| Precipitous labor (< three hr) | Perineal lacerations | Tentorial tears<br>Neonatal asphyxia |
| Prolapse of umbilical cord | ↑ Fear for fetus | Fetal asphyxia |
| Fetal heart aberrations (tachycardia, bradycardia, late or variable decelerations, loss of variability) | ↑ Fear for fetus | Tachycardia, acute asphyxic insult, bradycardia<br>Chronic asphyxia<br>Congenital heart disease |
| Uterine rupture | Hemorrhage<br>Death | Fetal asphyxia<br>Fetal hemorrhage<br>Fetal death |

such as intermittent bleeding needs further assessment to rule out abruptio placentae or placenta previa before the admission process continues. In addition to identifying the presence of a high-risk condition, the nurse must recognize the implications of the condition for the laboring woman and her fetus. For example, if an abnormal fetal presentation is present, the nurse understands that the labor may be prolonged, prolapse of the umbilical cord may be more likely, and the possibility of a cesarean birth is increased.

Although physical conditions are frequently listed as the major factors that increase risk in the intrapartal period, sociocultural aspects such as poverty, nutrition, the amount of prenatal care, cultural beliefs regarding pregnancy, and communication patterns may also precipitate a high-risk situation in the intrapartal period. The nurse can began gathering data regarding sociocultural factors as the woman enters the birthing area. The nurse observes the communication pattern between the woman and her sup-

## Table 15.1 Intrapartal High-Risk Factors *(continued)*

| Factor | Maternal implication | Fetal/neonatal implication |
|---|---|---|
| SOCIOCULTURAL FACTORS | | |
| Poverty | ↑ Risk of maternal exhaustion<br>↑ Risk of anemia, hemorrhage<br>↑ Risk of depleting energy stores during labor | IUGR<br>Prematurity<br>Fetal asphyxia |
| Malnutrition | ↓ Nutritional stores for the physical activity of labor<br>Anemia<br>↑ Risk of infection | Prematurity<br>Low birth weight<br>IUGR<br>Risk of infection |
| Difficulty in communication | ↑ Risk of misunderstanding<br>↑ Difficulty in communicating needs | Specific implication depends on specific problem |
| Cultural practices | ↑ Risk of misunderstanding<br>↑ Difficulty in communicating needs | Same as above |
| Anxiety | ↑ Discomfort | Risk fetal distress |

port person(s) and their responses to admission questions and initial teaching. If the woman and her support person(s) do not speak English and translators are not available within the birthing room staff, the course of labor and the nurse's ability to interact and provide support and education is affected. The ability of the couple to make informed decisions is severely affected; therefore, information in their primary language needs to be provided. Communication may also be affected by cultural practices such as beliefs regarding when to speak, who should ask questions, or whether it is acceptable to let others know if discomfort is occurring. The prenatal record may be quickly reviewed for number of prenatal visits, weight gain during pregnancy, progression of fundal height, assistance such as Medicaid and Women, Infants, and Children (WIC), and exposure to environmental agents.

A partial list of intrapartal risk factors is presented in Table 15.1. The factors precede the Intrapartal Assessment Guide because they must be kept in mind during the assessment.

## ● *Intrapartal Assessment*
### PHYSICAL ASSESSMENT

A physical examination is part of the admission procedure and part of the ongoing care of the client. Although the intrapartal physical assessment is not as complete and thorough as the initial prenatal physical examination (Chapter 7), the former involves assessment of some body systems and the actual labor process. The accompanying Intrapartal Assessment Guide provides a framework the maternity nurse can use when examining the laboring woman.

The guide includes assessments performed immediately on admission and on an ongoing basis. Critical as-

sessments include vital signs, labor status, fetal status, laboratory findings, and psychologic status. These assessments are continued throughout the labor process (see the Intrapartal Assessment Guide).

## PSYCHOLOGIC/SOCIOCULTURAL ASSESSMENT

Assessing the laboring woman's psychologic status is an important part of the total assessment. The woman has previous ideas, knowledge, and fears about childbearing. By assessing her psychologic status, the nurse can meet the woman's needs for information and support. The nurse can support the woman and her partner or, in the absence of a partner, the nurse may become the support person.

## ● *Methods of Evaluating Labor Progress*
### CONTRACTION ASSESSMENT

Uterine contractions may be assessed by palpation and/or continuous electronic monitoring.

### Palpation

Contractions are assessed for frequency, duration, and intensity by placing one hand on the uterine fundus. The hand is kept relatively still because excessive movement may stimulate contractions or cause discomfort. Frequency of the contractions is determined by noting the time from the beginning of one contraction to the beginning of the next. Thus, if contractions begin at 7:00, 7:04, and 7:08, their frequency is every four minutes. To determine contraction duration, the nurse notes the time when tensing of the fundus is first felt (beginning of contraction)

*(Text continues on page 398.)*

## First Stage of Labor

| Assess/Normal Findings | Alterations and Possible Causes of Alterations* | Nursing Responses to Data Base[†] |
|---|---|---|
| **PHYSICAL ASSESSMENT** | | |
| **Vital Signs** | | |
| Blood pressure (BP): 90–140/60–90 or no more than 15–20 mm Hg rise over baseline BP during early pregnancy | High blood pressure (essential hypertension, preeclampsia, renal disease, apprehension or anxiety)<br>Low blood pressure (supine hypotension) | Evaluate history of preexisting disorders and check for presence of other signs of preeclampsia.<br>Do not assess during contractions; implement measures to decrease anxiety and then reassess.<br>Turn woman on her side and recheck blood pressure. |
| Pulse: 60–90 beats/min | Increased pulse rate (excitement or anxiety, cardiac disorders) | Evaluate cause, reassess to see if rate continues; report to physician. |
| Respirations: 6–24/min (or pulse rate divided by four) | Marked tachypnea (respiratory disease) | Assess between contractions; if marked tachypnea continues, assess for signs of respiratory disease. |
| | Hyperventilation (anxiety) | Encourage slow breaths if woman is hyperventilating. |
| Temperature: 36.2–37.6°C (98–99.6°F) | Elevated temperature (infection, dehydration) | Assess for other signs of infection or dehydration. |
| **Weight** | | |
| 15–30 lb greater than prepregnant weight | Weight gain > 30 lb (fluid retention, obesity, large infant, PIH) | Assess for signs of edema. |
| **Fundus** | | |
| At 40 weeks' gestation, located just below xyphoid process | Uterine size not compatible with estimated delivery time (small for gestational age [SGA], hydramnios, multiple pregnancy) | Reevaluate history regarding pregnancy dating. Refer to physician for additional assessment. |
| **Edema** | | |
| Slight amount of dependent edema | Pitting edema of face, legs, abdomen (preeclampsia) | Check deep tendon reflexes for hyperactivity, check for clonus; refer to physician. |
| **Hydration** | | |
| Normal skin turgor | Poor skin turgor (dehydration) | Assess skin turgor; refer to physician for deviations. |
| **Perineum** | | |
| Tissues smooth, pink color (see Prenatal Initial Physical Assessment Guide, Chapter 7) | Varicose veins of vulva | Exercise care while doing a perineal prep; note on client record need for follow-up in postpartal period; reassess after birth. |
| Clear mucus | Profuse, purulent drainage | Suspect gonorrhea; report to physician; initiate care to newborn's eyes; notify neonatal nursing staff and pediatrician. |
| Presence of small amount of bloody show that gradually increases with further cervical dilatation | Hemorrhage | Assess BP and pulse, pallor, diaphoresis; report any marked changes.<br>(Note: Gaping of vagina and/or anus and bulging of perineum are suggestive signs of second stage of labor.) |

*Possible causes of alterations are placed in parentheses.
[†]This column provides guidelines for further assessment and initial nursing interventions.

## First Stage of Labor *(continued)*

| Assess/Normal Findings | Alterations and Possible Causes of Alterations* | Nursing Responses to Data Base† |
|---|---|---|
| **PHYSICAL ASSESSMENT** *(continued)* **Labor Status** | | |
| Uterine contractions: Regular pattern | Failure to establish a regular pattern, prolonged latent phase Hypertonicity Hypotonicity | Evaluate whether woman is in true labor; ambulate if in early labor. Evaluate client status and contractile pattern. |
| Cervical dilatation: Progressive cervical dilatation from size of fingertip to 10 cm (Procedure 15.1) | Rigidity of cervix (frequent cervical infections, scar tissue, failure of presenting part to descend) | Evaluate contractions, fetal engagement, position, and cervical dilatation. Inform client of progress. |
| Cervical effacement: Progressive thinning of cervix (Procedure 15.1) | Failure to efface (rigidity of cervix, failure of presenting part to engage); cervical edema (pushing effort by woman before cervix is fully dilated and effaced, trapped cervix) | Evaluate contractions, fetal engagement, and position. Notify physician/nurse-midwife if cervix is becoming edematous; work with client to prevent pushing until cervix is completely dilated. |
| Fetal descent: Progressive descent of fetal presenting part from station −5 to +4 (see Figure 14.6) | Failure of descent (abnormal fetal position or presentation, macrosomic fetus, inadequate pelvic measurement) | Evaluate fetal position, presentation, and size. Evaluate maternal pelvic measurements. |
| Membranes: May rupture before or during labor | Rupture of membranes more than 12–24 hours before initiation of labor | Assess for ruptured membranes using Nitrazine test tape before doing vaginal exam. Instruct women with ruptured membranes to remain on bed rest if presenting part is not engaged and presenting part is not firmly down against the cervix. Keep vaginal exams to a minimum to prevent infection. When membranes rupture in the birth setting, **the nurse immediately assesses FHR** to detect changes associated with prolapse of umbilical cord (FHR slows). |
| Findings on Nitrazine test tape: Membranes probably intact   yellow     pH 5.0   olive     pH 5.5   olive green     pH 6.0 Membranes probably ruptured   blue-green     pH 6.5   blue-gray     pH 7.0   deep blue     pH 7.5 | False-positive results may be obtained if large amount of bloody show is present or if previous vaginal examination has been done using lubricant | Assess fluid for consistency, amount, odor; assess FHR frequently. Assess fluid at regular intervals for presence of meconium staining. |
| Amniotic fluid clear, no odor | Greenish amniotic fluid (fetal distress) | Assess FHR; do vaginal exam to evaluate for prolapsed cord; apply fetal monitor for continuous data; report to physician. |
| | Strong odor (amnionitis) | Take woman's temperature and report to physician. |

*Possible causes of alterations are placed in parentheses.
†This column provides guidelines for further assessment and initial nursing interventions.

*(continues)*

| Assess/Normal Findings | Alterations and Possible Causes of Alterations* | Nursing Responses to Data Base† |
|---|---|---|
| **PHYSICAL ASSESSMENT** (continued) | | |
| **Fetal Status** | | |
| Fetal heart rate (FHR): 120–160 beats/min | <120 or >160 beats/min (fetal distress); abnormal patterns on fetal monitor: decreased variability, late decelerations, variable decelerations (p 407) | Initiate interventions based on particular FHR pattern. |
| Presentation: Cephalic, 97% Breech, 3% | Face, brow, or shoulder presentation | Report to physician; after presentation is confirmed as face, brow, or shoulder, woman may be prepared for cesarean birth. |
| Position: LOA most common | Persistent occipital-posterior position; transverse arrest | Carefully monitor maternal and fetal status. |
| Activity: Fetal movement | Hyperactivity (may precede fetal hypoxia) | Carefully evaluate FHR; may apply fetal monitor. |
| | Complete lack of movement (fetal distress or fetal demise) | Carefully evaluate FHR; may apply fetal monitor. |
| **Laboratory Evaluation** | | |
| Hematologic tests Hemoglobin: 12–16 g/dL | <12 g (anemia, hemorrhage) | Evaluate woman for problems due to decreased oxygen-carrying capacity caused by lowered hemoglobin. |
| CBC Hematocrit: 38%–47% RBC: 4.2–5.4 million/μL WBC: 4,500–11,000/μL although leukocytosis to 20,000/μL is not unusual | Presence of infection or blood dyscrasias | Evaluate for other signs of infection or for petechia, bruising, or unusual bleeding. |
| Serologic testing STS or VDRL test: Nonreactive | Positive reaction (see Chapter 7, Initial Prenatal Physical Assessment Guide) | For reactive test, notify newborn nursery and pediatrician. |
| Urinalysis Glucose: Negative | Glycosuria (low renal threshold for glucose, diabetes mellitus) | Assess blood glucose; test urine for ketones; ketonuria and glycosuria require further assessment of blood sugars.‡ |
| Ketones: Negative | Kentonuria (starvation ketosis) | |
| Proteins: Negative | Proteinuria (urine specimen contaminated with vaginal secretions, fever, kidney disease); proteinuria of 2+ or greater found in uncontaminated urine may be a sign of ensuing preeclampsia | Instruct woman in collection technique; incidence of contamination from vaginal discharge is common. |
| Red blood cells: Negative | Blood in urine (calculi, cystitis, glomerulonephritis, neoplasm) | Assess collection technique. |
| White blood cells: Negative | Presence of white blood cells (infection in genitourinary tract) | Assess for signs of urinary tract infection. |
| Casts: None | Presence of casts (nephrotic syndrome) | |

*Possible causes of alterations are placed in parentheses.
†This column provides guidelines for further assessment and initial nursing interventions.
‡Glycosuria should not be discounted. The presence of glycosuria necessitates follow-up.

*(continues)*

## First Stage of Labor (continued)

| Assess/Normal Findings | Alterations and Possible Causes of Alterations* | Nursing Responses to Data Base† |
|---|---|---|
| **PSYCHOLOGIC/SOCIOCULTURAL ASSESSMENT** | | |
| **Response to Labor** | | |
| Latent phase: relaxed, excited, anxious for labor to be well established | Inability to cope with contractions (fear, anxiety, lack of education) | Provide support and encouragement; establish trusting relationship. |
| Active phase: becomes more intense, begins to tire | | |
| Transitional phase: feels tired, may feel unable to cope, needs frequent coaching to maintain breathing patterns | | Provide support and coaching if needed. |
| Coping mechanisms: Ability to cope with labor through utilization of support system, breathing, relaxation techniques | Marked anxiety, apprehension (insufficient coping mechanisms) | Support coping mechanisms if they are working for the woman; provide information and support if woman is exhibiting anxiety or needs additional alternatives to present coping methods. |
| **Anxiety** | | |
| Some anxiety and apprehension is within normal limits | Rapid breathing, nervous tremors, frowning, grimacing or clenching of teeth, thrashing movements, crying, increased pulse and blood pressure (anxiety, apprehension) | Provide support, encouragement, and information. Teach relaxation techniques; support controlled breathing efforts. |
| **Preparation for Childbirth** | | |
| Woman has some information regarding process of normal labor and birth | Insufficient information | Add to present information base. |
| Woman has breathing and/or relaxation techniques to use during labor | No breathing or relaxation techniques (insufficient information) | Support breathing and relaxation techniques that client is using; provide information if needed. |
| **Support System** | | |
| Physical intimacy of mother-father (or mother-support relationship): Care-taking activities such as soothing conversation, touching | Limited physical contact or continual clinging together (may reflect normal pattern for this couple or their attempt to cope with this situation) | Encourage care-taking activities that appear to comfort the woman; encourage support to the woman; if support is limited, the nurse may take a more active role. |
| Support person stays in close proximity | Maintaining a distance from woman for prolonged periods (may be normal pattern for this couple or may indicate strained relationship or anxiety due to labor) | Encourage support person to stay close (if this seems appropriate). |
| Relationship of mother-father (or support person): Involved interaction | Limited interaction (may reflect normal interaction pattern or strained relationship) | Support interactions; if interaction is limited, the nurse may provide more information and support. |
| **Cultural Practices** | | |
| | Limited communication (does not speak English, communication method emphasizes little verbal communication, designated person speaks for the mother) | Assess communication pattern; assess understanding of language and ability to understand; provide translator for interpretation during labor and birth; direct communication to designated person; use nonverbal communication techniques. Determine cultural needs and provide for belief system. Interpret and communicate beliefs and needs to others as needed. |

*Possible causes of alterations are placed in parentheses.
†This column provides guidelines for further assessment and initial nursing interventions.

## Procedure 15.1

## Intrapartal Vaginal Examination

| Objective | Nursing Action | Rationale |
|---|---|---|
| Prepare woman. | Explain procedure, indications for carrying out procedure, and information being obtained. | Explanation of procedure decreases anxiety and increases relaxation. |
| | Position woman with thighs flexed and abducted; instruct her to put heels of feet together. | Prevents contamination of area during examination and allows for visualization of external signs of labor progress. |
| | Drape so that only the perineum is exposed. | Provides as much privacy as possible. |
| | Encourage her to relax her muscles and legs during procedure. | |
| Assemble and prepare equipment. | Have following equipment easily accessible: <br> ● Sterile disposable gloves <br> ● Lubricant <br> ● Nitrazine test tape | Examination is facilitated and can be done quickly. |
| Use aseptic technique during examination. | If leakage of fluid has been noted or if woman reports leakage of fluid, use Nitrazine test tape before doing vaginal exam. | Nitrazine test tape registers a change in pH if amniotic fluid is present (unless a lubricant has already been used). |
| | Put on both gloves; using thumb and forefinger of left hand, spread labia widely, insert well-lubricated second and index fingers of right hand into vagina until they touch the cervix. | Avoid contaminating hand by contact with anus; positioning of hand with wrist straight and elbow tilted downward allows fingertips to point toward umbilicus and find cervix. |
| Determine status of fetal membranes. | Palpate for movable bulging sac through the cervix; observe for expression of amniotic fluid during exam. | If intact, bag of waters feels like a bulge. |
| Determine status of labor progress during and after contractions. | Carry out vaginal examination during and between contractions. | Examination varies. |
| Identify degree of: <br> 1. Cervical dilatation | Palpate for opening or what appears as a depression in the cervix (Figure 15.1). Estimate diameter of cervical opening in centimeters (0–10 cm). | Estimation of the diameter of the depression identifies degree of dilatation. One finger represents approximately 1.5–2 cm cervical dilatation. |

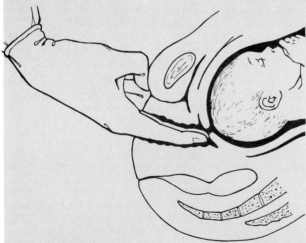

*Figure 15.1   Determination of cervical dilatation*

# Procedure 15.1

## Intrapartal Vaginal Examination *(continued)*

| Objective | Nursing Action | Rationale |
|---|---|---|
| 2. Cervical effacement | Palpate the thickness of the surrounding circular ridge of tissue; estimate degree of thinning in percentages. | Degree of thinning determines the amount of lower uterine segment that has been taken up into the fundal area. |
| Determine presentation and position of presenting part. | As cervix opens, palpate for presenting part and identify its relationship to the maternal pelvis (Figures 15.2 and 15.3). | Presenting part is easier to palpate through a dilated cervix and differentiation of landmarks is easier. |

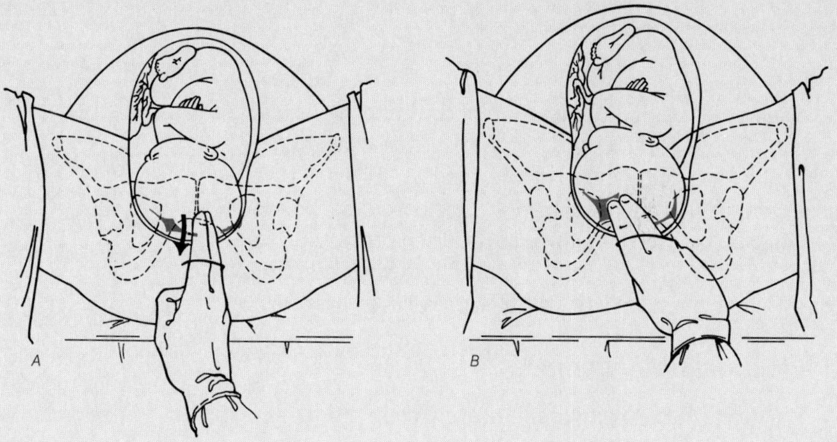

*Figure 15.2   Assessment of fetal position and station:* (A) *Palpate sagittal suture and assess station.* (B) *Identify anterior fontanelle.*

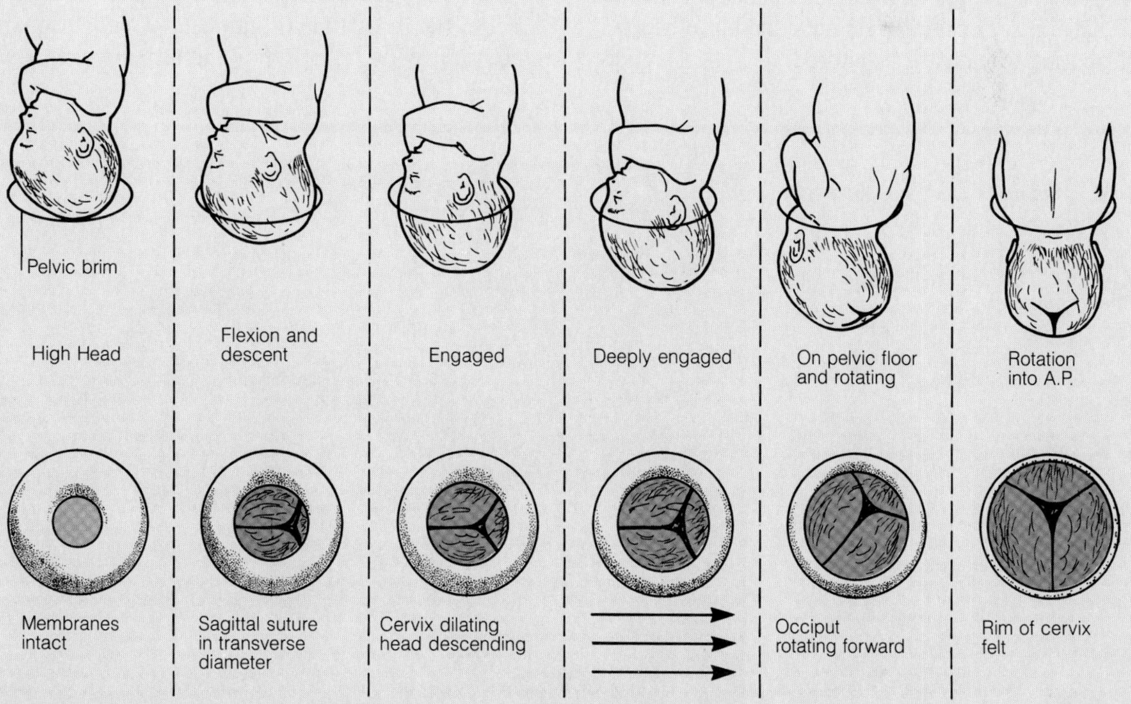

Pelvic brim

| High Head | Flexion and descent | Engaged | Deeply engaged | On pelvic floor and rotating | Rotation into A.P. |

| Membranes intact | Sagittal suture in transverse diameter | Cervix dilating head descending | | Occiput rotating forward | Rim of cervix felt |

*Figure 15.3   **Top:** The fetal head progressing through the pelvis. **Bottom:** The changes that the nurse will detect on palpation of the occiput through the cervix while doing a vaginal examination. (From Myles MF:* Textbook for Midwives. *Edinburgh, Scotland: Churchill Livingstone, 1975, p 246.)*

*(continues)*

## Procedure 15.1

### Intrapartal Vaginal Examination (continued)

| Objective | Nursing Action | Rationale |
|---|---|---|
| Determine station. | Locate lowest portion of presenting part. | Identification of station provides information as to degree of descent. |
| Inform woman about progress in labor. | Discuss with woman findings of the vaginal examination and correlate them to her progress in labor. | Assists the woman in identifying progress and reinforces need for frequency of procedure. Information is reassuring and supportive for woman and family. |

and again as relaxation occurs (end of contraction). During the acme of the contraction, intensity can be evaluated by estimating the indentability of the fundus. At least three successive contractions should be assessed to provide enough data to determine the contraction pattern. See Essential Facts to Remember—Contraction Characteristics for review of characteristics in different phases of labor.

### Electronic Monitoring

Electronic monitoring of the uterine contractions provides continuous data. In many birth settings, electronic monitoring is routine for all high-risk clients and women who are having oxytocin-induced labor, and in other settings all laboring women are monitored.

### External Monitoring with Tocodynamometer

The tocodynamometer provides an external or indirect method of monitoring uterine activity. This instrument contains a flexible disk that responds to pressure. This disk is strapped to the woman's abdomen directly over the fundus, which is the area of greatest contractility. The disk records the external tension exerted by contractions (Figure 15.4). The pressure is amplified and recorded on graph paper.

The advantage of this method is that it provides a continuous recording of the duration and frequency of contractions. The disadvantages are: (a) this method does not record the magnitude or intensity of a contraction, (b) the woman may be bothered by the strap, which requires fre-

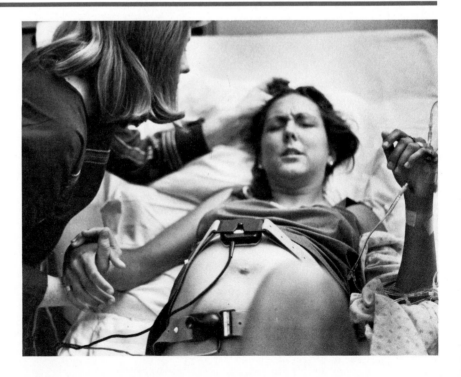

Figure 15.4  Woman in labor with external monitor applied

quent readjustment when she changes position, and (c) it is difficult to obtain an accurate fetal heart rate in some women, such as those who are very obese or who have hydramnios.

Internal monitoring of uterine pressure during labor is discussed on page 405.

## RECORDING ASSESSMENTS

Once labor contractions are assessed they are recorded in the woman's record using an abbreviated method. For example, if assessed contractions have a frequency of two to three minutes, a duration of 60 seconds, and are moderate in intensity, they are recorded as: "every 2–3 × 60 moderate." See Essential Facts to Remember—Charting Assessment Findings for another example.

## CERVICAL ASSESSMENT

Cervical dilatation and effacement are evaluated directly by sterile vaginal examination (see Procedure 15.1, Intrapartal Vaginal Examination). The vaginal examination can also provide information about membrane status, fetal position, and station of the presenting part.

## USING THE FRIEDMAN GRAPH

Evaluation of the intensity, frequency, and duration of contractions does not present the entire labor picture. Nurses can document labor progress objectively by using the Friedman graph, which evaluates uterine activity, cervical dilatation, and fetal descent.

To use the Friedman graph, one needs special graph paper and skill in determining cervical dilatation and fetal

## *Essential Facts to Remember*

### Contraction Characteristics

| | |
|---|---|
| Latent phase: | Every 10–20 min × 15–20 seconds; mild, progressing to Every 5–7 min × 30–40 seconds; moderate |
| Active phase: | Every 2–3 min × 60 seconds; moderate to strong |
| Transition phase: | Every 2 min × 60–90 seconds; strong |

*Source: Varney H: Nurse Midwifery, 2nd ed. Boston: Blackwell Scientific, 1987.*

descent. The numbers at the bottom of the graph in Figure 15.5 are hours of labor from 1 to 16. Vertically, at the left, cervical dilatation is measured from 0 to 10 cm. The vertical line on the right indicates fetal station in centimeters, from −5 to +5 (Friedman 1970). When one plots cervical dilatation and descent on the basic graph, a characteristic pattern emerges: An S curve represents dilation and an inverse S curve represents descent.

To determine the appropriate point to begin plotting data, the nurse must know how many hours the woman has been having regular contractions. When the laboring woman enters the birthing center, she is asked at what time her contractions became regular and five minutes apart. A sterile vaginal examination determines cervical dilatation and the station of the presenting part of the

## *Essential Facts to Remember*

### Charting Assessment Findings

Assessments are recorded on a labor record. An example of information that may be contained on a labor record follows.

| Time | B/P | TPR | Contractions | Cervical dilatation | Effacement | Membranes | Station | FHR | NOTES: |
|---|---|---|---|---|---|---|---|---|---|
| 0800 | 122/80 | 98⁶ 88 18 | q̄ 3 × 45 mod | 4 cm | 50% | SROM Nitrazine positive | − 1 fetal head firmly against cervix | aus 140 x | |
| 0810 | | | q̄ 3 × 45 mod | | | | | BL 140–148 | |

Graphic Labor Record

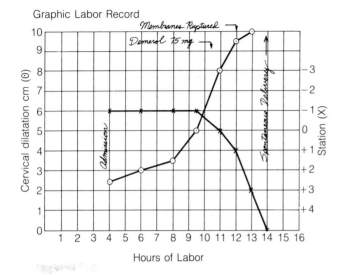

*Figure 15.5   Example of charting labor progress on a Friedman graph (Modified with permission from Friedman EA: An objective method of evaluating labor. Hospital Practice 1970; 5:7. Chart by Albert Miller.)*

fetus. This information is plotted on the graph. In the example shown in Figure 15.5, on admission the cervix was dilated 2–3 cm after four hours of labor, and the station was −1. Later examinations are noted on the graph. When the client was in the eleventh hour of labor, the graph indicates that cervical dilatation was 8 cm and the station was zero. At 14 hours of labor, she delivered spontaneously, as the graph shows.

The progress of cervical dilatation (in centimeters) per hour can be calculated as follows: Divide the difference between two consecutive observations by the intervening time interval to obtain centimeters per hour. For example, in the case illustrated in Figure 15.5, at 9½ hours of labor, the cervix dilated to 5 cm. At 11 hours of labor, the cervix dilated to 8 cm. The difference is 3 cm. Divide the difference by the intervening time interval, which is 1½ hours: 3 cm ÷ 1½ = 2 cm/hr.

Evaluating labor progress by using the Friedman graph helps the health care team identify normal and abnormal labor patterns.

## ● FETAL ASSESSMENT
### ● Fetal Position

Fetal position is determined in several ways. The woman's abdomen is inspected and palpated to determine fetal position; also, auscultation of fetal heart tones helps determine fetal position. A vaginal examination may be done to determine the presenting part, and ultrasound examination may be used.

### INSPECTION

The nurse should observe the woman's abdomen for size and shape. The lie of the fetus should be assessed by noting whether the uterus projects up and down (longitudinal lie) or left to right (transverse lie).

### PALPATION

**Leopold's maneuvers** are a systematic way to evaluate the maternal abdomen. Frequent practice increases the examiner's skill in determining fetal position by palpation. Leopold's maneuvers may be difficult to perform on an obese woman or on a woman who has excessive amniotic fluid (hydramnios).

Before performing Leopold's maneuvers:

1. Have the woman empty her bladder.
2. Have the woman lie on her back with her feet on the bed and her knees bent.

#### First Maneuver

Face the woman. Palpate the upper abdomen with both hands. Note the shape, consistency, and mobility of the palpated part. The fetal head is firm, hard, and round and moves independently of the trunk. The breech (buttocks) feels softer and it moves with the trunk.

#### Second Maneuver

Moving the hands down toward the pelvis, palpate the abdomen with gentle but deep pressure. The fetal back, on one side of the abdomen, feels smooth, and the fetal arms, legs, and feet, on the other side, feel knobby and bumpy.

#### Third Maneuver

Place one hand just above the symphysis. Note whether the part palpated feels like the fetal head or the breech and whether the presenting part is engaged.

#### Fourth Maneuver

Face the woman's feet. Place both hands on the lower abdomen, and move the fingers of both hands gently down the sides of the uterus toward the pubis. Note the cephalic prominence or brow (Figure 15.6).

### VAGINAL EXAMINATION AND ULTRASOUND

Other assessment techniques to determine fetal position and presentation include vaginal examination and the use of ultrasound. During the vaginal examination, the examiner can palpate the presenting part if the cervix is di-

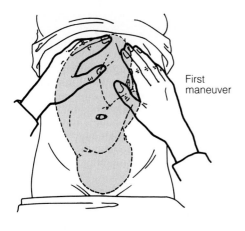
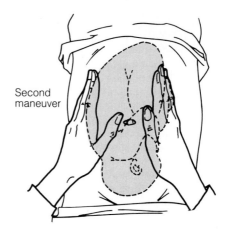
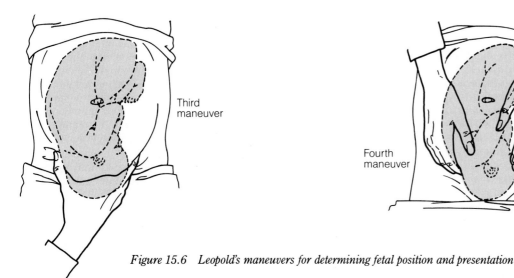
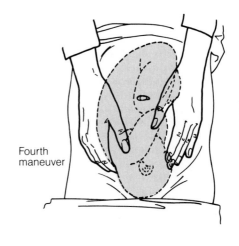

*Figure 15.6   Leopold's maneuvers for determining fetal position and presentation*

lated. Information about the position of the fetus and the degree of flexion of its head (in cephalic presentations) also can be obtained.

Ultrasound is used when the fetus's position cannot be determined by abdominal palpation (see Chapter 13 for an in-depth discussion of ultrasound).

## ● Evaluation of Fetal Status During Labor

### AUSCULTATION OF FETAL HEART RATE (FHR)

The fetoscope is used to auscultate the fetal heart rate between, during, and immediately after uterine contractions (see Procedure 15.2).

Instead of listening haphazardly over the client's abdomen for FHR, the nurse may choose to perform Leopold's maneuvers first. Leopold's maneuvers not only indicate the probable location of FHR but also help to determine the presence of multiple fetuses, fetal lie, and fetal presen-

tation. FHR is heard most clearly at the fetal back (Figure 15.7). Thus, in a cephalic presentation, FHR is best heard in the lower quadrant of the maternal abdomen. In a breech presentation, it is heard at or above the level of the maternal umbilicus. In a transverse lie, FHR may be heard best just above or just below the umbilicus. As the presenting part descends and rotates through the pelvic structure during labor, the location of the FHR tends to descend and move toward the midline.

After FHR is located, it is counted for at least 30 seconds and multiplied by two to obtain the number of beats per minute. The nurse should occasionally listen for one full minute through a contraction to detect any abnormal heart rate, especially if tachycardia, bradycardia, or irregular beats are heard. If the FHR is irregular or has changed markedly from the last assessment, the nurse should listen for one full minute through and immediately after a contraction. See Essential Facts to Remember— Frequency of FHR Assessment, Evaluation, and Documentation for guidelines regarding how often to auscultate FHR. The American College of Obstetricians and Gyne-

## Procedure 15.2

## Auscultation of Fetal Heart Rate

| Objective | Nursing Action | Rationale |
|---|---|---|
| Assemble equipment. | Obtain a fetoscope or Doppler. | Fetoscope is a special type of stethoscope that amplifies sound. Doppler uses ultrasound. |
| Prepare woman. | Explain the procedure, indications for the procedure, and the information that will be obtained. Uncover woman's abdomen. *To use the fetoscope:* | Explanation of the procedure decreases anxiety and increases relaxation. The fetoscope is an older assessment tool; however, some clinicians prefer it because it is "natural" and does not rely on ultrasound. |
| | Place the metal band of the fetoscope on your head; the diaphragm should extend out from your forehead. | The metal band conducts sound. |
| | Place the diaphragm on the woman's abdomen halfway between the umbilicus and symphysis and in the midline. | The FHR is most likely to be heard in this area. |
| | Without touching the fetoscope, listen carefully for the FHR (Figure 15.8, *A*). *To use the Doppler:* Place "ultrasonic gel" on the diaphragm of the Doppler. | Gel is used to maintain contact with maternal abdomen and to enhance conduction of ultrasound. |
| | Place diaphragm on the woman's abdomen halfway between the umbilicus and symphysis and in the midline. | The FHR is most likely to be heard in this area. |
| | Listen carefully for the FHR (Figure 15.8, *B*). *For both methods:* | Sound level may be controlled with a volume knob. |
| | Check the woman's pulse against the sounds heard; if rates are not similar, count FHR. | Ensures the FHR, not the woman's pulse, is being heard. |
| | If FHR not found, move fetoscope out from this area in a circle. | |
| Report and record findings. | Tell parents what the FHR is; offer to help them listen if they would like. Record the FHR on the client's chart. | Provides permanent record. |

cologists (NAACOG 1988) has indicated that auscultation as outlined is equivalent to electronic fetal monitoring.

Auscultation is effective in evaluating fetal heart rate and changes in the rate associated with contractions; however, in some instances complete information on all characteristics of the FHR (such as acceleration and beat-to-beat variability) will not be available through auscultation.

## ELECTRONIC MONITORING

Electronic fetal monitoring (EFM) provides an auditory and visual assessment of fetal heart rate. There are two methods of assessing FHR during labor: indirect (external) and direct (internal) (Figure 15.8, Procedure 15.2).

The indirect method may be accomplished using a fetoscope, fetal electrocardiography, and Doppler ultrasound (intermittent or continuous). Direct monitoring provides continuous information about the FHR from a scalp electrode. Uterine contractions may be monitored externally with a tocodynamometer or internally with an intrauterine pressure catheter.

When the FHR is monitored electronically, the interval between two successive fetal heart beats is measured and the rate is displayed as if the beats occurred at the same interval for 60 seconds. For example, if the interval between two beats is 0.5 seconds, the rate for one full minute would be 120 beats per minute. This measurement is called the instantaneous rate. The instantaneous rate provides documentation that the normal FHR varies from one moment to the next. Figure 15.9 compares instantaneous rates with those averaged by auscultation.

Electronic monitoring is thought to have an advantage over auscultation in that EFM provides a continuous tracing of the FHR, and accelerations and beat-to-beat variability can be evaluated.

### Indications for Electronic Monitoring

If one or more of the following factors are present, the woman should be monitored electronically:

1. Previous history of a stillborn at 38 or more weeks of gestation
2. Complication of pregnancy (for example, pregnancy-induced hypertension [PIH], placenta previa)
3. Induction of labor
4. Preterm labor
5. Fetal distress
6. Meconium staining of amniotic fluid

## Essential Facts to Remember

### Frequency of FHR Assessment, Evaluation, and Documentation

**For Low-Risk Women:**

● Auscultate every 30 minutes in active first stage labor.

● Auscultate every 15 minutes in second stage of labor.

**For High-Risk Women:**

● Auscultate every 15 minutes during active first stage.

● Auscultate every 5 minutes during second stage of labor.

*Source: American Academy of Pediatrics and the American College of Obstetricians and Gynecologists 1988, NAACOG 1988.*

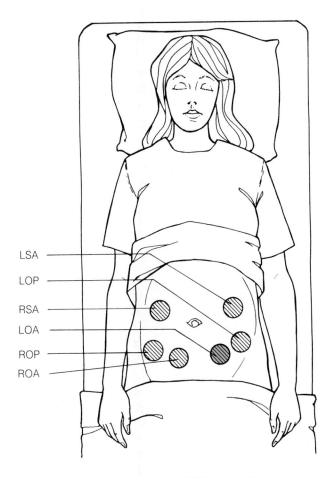

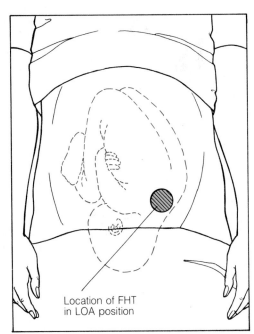

Location of FHT in LOA position

LSA
LOP
RSA
LOA
ROP
ROA

*Figure 15.7   Location of FHR in relation to the more commonly seen fetal positions*

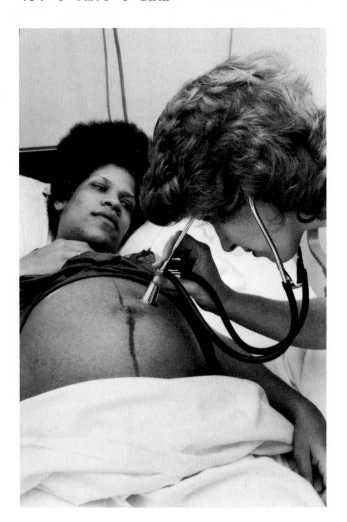
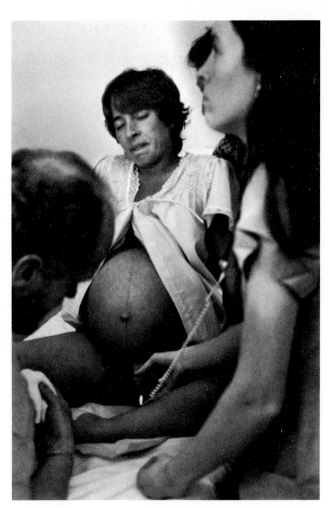

*Figure 15.8   Two methods of assessing fetal heart rate: (A) fetoscope, (B) Doppler*

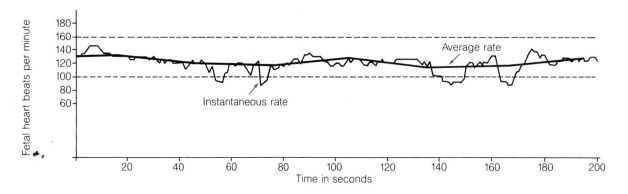

*Figure 15.9   Comparison of instantaneous and average FHRs. The average FHR illustrates a more constant rate, while the instantaneous rate illustrates the normal variation of the FHR. (From Hon E:* An Introduction to Fetal Heart Rate Monitoring, *2nd ed. Los Angeles: University of Southern California School of Medicine, 1976, p 9.)*

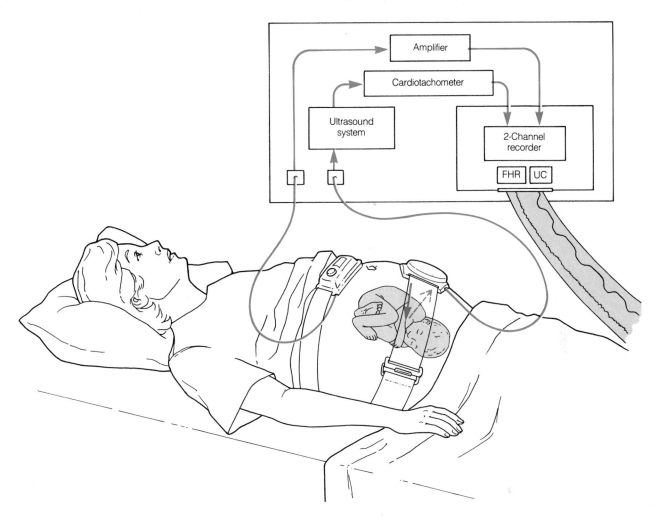

*Figure 15.10    Tocodynamometer and ultrasonic technique to monitor maternal and fetal status during labor (From Hon E:* An Introduction to Fetal Heart Monitoring, *2nd ed. Los Angeles: University of California School of Medicine, 1972, p 65.)*

## Methods of Electronic Monitoring

*External monitoring* of the fetus is usually accomplished by the use of ultrasound. A transducer, which emits continuous sound waves, is placed on the maternal abdomen. When placed correctly, the sound waves bounce off the fetal heart and are picked up by the electronic monitor. The actual moment-by-moment FHR is displayed graphically on a screen (Figure 15.10).

*Internal monitoring* requires an internal spiral electrode and intrauterine pressure catheter. These conditions must be present for internal monitoring to be possible: The cervix must be dilated at least 2 cm, the fetal position and presenting part must be known, the presenting fetal part must be accessible by vaginal examination, and the amniotic membranes must have ruptured. After cleansing the perineum, the care giver inserts a sterile internal electrode into the vagina and places it against the fetal presenting part. The electrode is rotated clockwise until it is attached

to the presenting part. Wires that extend from the electrode are attached to a leg plate (which is placed on the woman's thigh) and then attached to the monitor. This method of monitoring the FHR provides more accurate continuous data than external monitoring provides (Figure 15.11).

Uterine contractions can be monitored with an internal pressure catheter. The sterile catheter is introduced into the uterus, connected to a strain gauge (a transducer that interprets pressure changes), and then attached to the monitor. The uterine contractions can be evaluated by the intrauterine pressure that is present both during contractions and between contractions.

The FHR tracing at the top of Figure 15.12 was obtained by internal monitoring, and the uterine contraction tracing at the bottom of the figure by external monitoring. Note the FHR is variable (the tracing moves up and down instead of in a straight line), and the tracing stays close to the line numbered 150. If the graph paper moves through

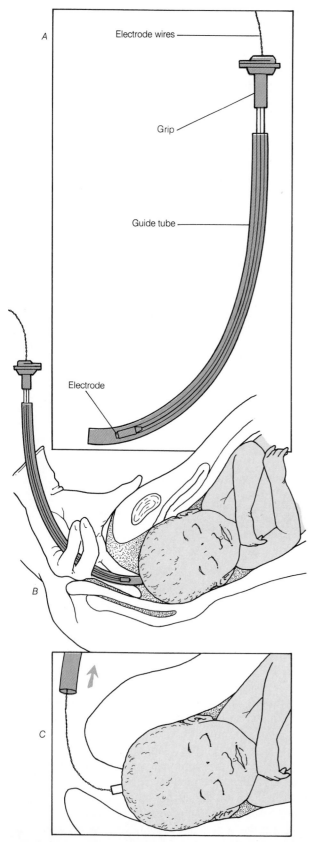

*Figure 15.11  Technique for internal, direct fetal monitoring: (A) Spiral electrode. (B) Attaching the spiral electrode to the scalp. (C) Attached spiral electrode with the guide tube removed.*

the monitor at 3 cm/min, each vertical dark line represents one minute. The frequency of the uterine contractions is every 2½–3 minutes. The duration of the contractions is 50–60 seconds.

### FHR

FHR is evaluated by assessing an electronic monitor tracing for baseline and periodic changes. These changes are described in this section. Normal FHR ranges from 120–160 beats/min. The **baseline rate** refers to the average FHR observed during a ten-minute period of monitoring. *Baseline changes* in FHR are defined in terms of ten-minute periods. These changes are tachycardia, bradycardia, and beat-to-beat variability of the FHR.

**Fetal tachycardia** is defined as a rate of 160 beats/min or more during a ten-minute period. Moderate tachycardia is 160–179 beats/min, and severe tachycardia is 180 beats/min or more. Causes of fetal tachycardia include:

● Prematurity of the fetus

● Insufficient oxygenation of the fetus

● Fetal infection

● Fetal anemia

● Maternal fever or anxiety

**Fetal bradycardia** is defined as a rate less than 120 beats/min during a ten-minute period. Mild bradycardia ranges from 100 to 119 beats/min and is considered benign. Moderate bradycardia is a FHR less than 100 beats/min, and severe bradycardia is a FHR rate of less than 70 beats/min. Causes of fetal bradycardia include:

● Fetal hypoxia

● Prolapse or prolonged compression of the umbilical cord

● Fetal arrhythmias as seen with congenital heart block

● Prolonged maternal hypotension

**Baseline variability** is a measure of the interplay (the "push-pull" effect) between the sympathetic and parasympathetic nervous systems. There are two types of fetal heart variability—short term and long term. *Short-term variability* is the beat-to-beat irregularity. It represents fluctuations that average 2–3 beats/min. Short-term variability is classified as either present or absent. *Long-term variability* is the waviness or rhythmic fluctuations of the FHR tracing, which occur from two to six times per minute. Variability can be classified as none, minimal, average, moderate, or marked (Figure 15.13). The most important aspect of variability is that even in the presence of abnormal or questionable FHR patterns, if the variability is normal, the fetus is not suffering from cerebral asphyxia (Parer 1989).

Causes of decreased variability include:

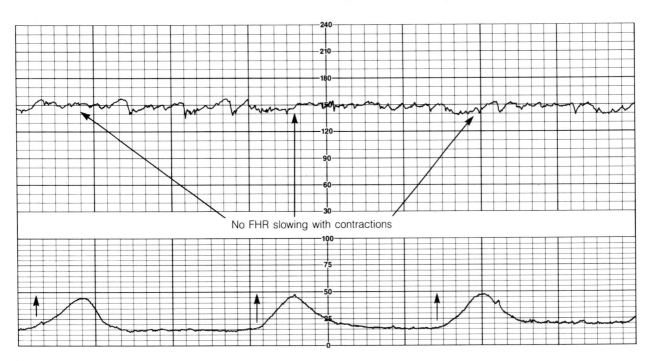

No FHR slowing with contractions

*Figure 15.12  Normal fetal heart rate pattern utilizing internal monitoring. Note normal FHR, 140–158 beats/min, presence of long- and short-term variability, and absence of deceleration with adequate contractions. Arrows on bottom of tracing indicate beginning of uterine contraction.*

- Deep fetal sleep
- Fetal congenital anomalies
- Fetal hypoxia and acidosis
- Fetus of less than 32 weeks' gestation
- Administration of certain drugs (hypnotics, analgesics, magnesium sulfate, atropine) to the woman

  Causes of increased variability include:

- Maternal activity
- Abdominal palpation
- Strong uterine contractions

It is difficult to assess variability accurately on an external monitor. When questions about FHR variability occur, an internal fetal scalp electrode is frequently used to provide more precise data for evaluation.

### Periodic Changes

Periodic changes are transient decelerations or accelerations of the FHR from the baseline. They usually occur in response to uterine contractions and fetal movement.

**Accelerations** are transient increases in the FHR normally caused by fetal movement. When the fetus moves, its heart rate increases, just as the heart rates of adults increase during exercise. Often, accelerations accompany uterine contractions, usually due to fetal movement in response to the pressure of the contractions. Accelerations of this type are thought to be a sign of fetal well-being and adequate oxygen reserve. The accelerations with fetal movement are the basis for nonstress tests (see Chapter 13).

**Decelerations** are periodic decreases in FHR from the normal baseline that are categorized into three types—early, late, and variable—according to the time of their occurrence in the contraction cycle and their waveform (Figure 15.14).

When the fetal head is compressed, cerebral blood flow is decreased, which leads to central vagal stimulation and results in **early deceleration.** The onset of early deceleration occurs before the onset of the uterine contraction. This type of deceleration is of uniform shape, is usually considered benign, and does not require intervention (see Figure 15.15, *A*).

**Late deceleration** is due to uteroplacental insufficiency resulting from decreased blood flow and oxygen transfer to the fetus through the intervillous spaces during uterine contractions. The onset of the deceleration occurs after the onset of the uterine contraction and is of uniform shape that tends to reflect associated uterine contractions. The late deceleration pattern is considered an ominous sign but does not necessarily require immediate delivery (Figure 15.15, *B*).

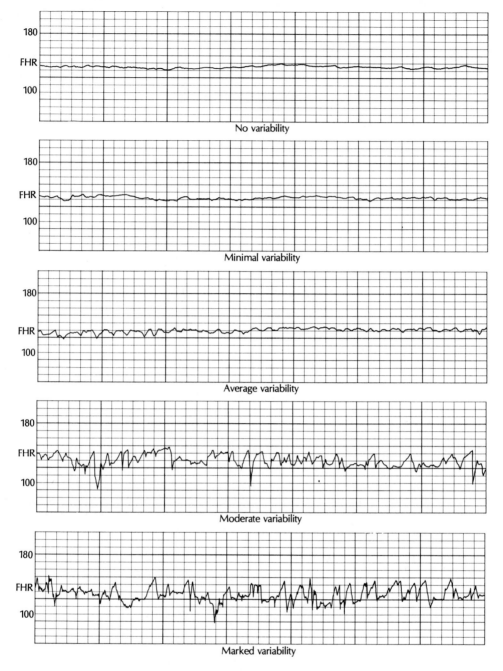

*Figure 15.13    Types of variability: No variability = 0–2 beats/min; minimal variability = 3–5 beats/min; average variability = 6–10 beats/min; moderate variability = 11–25 beats/ min; marked variability = more than 25 beats/min. (From Hon E:* An Introduction to Fetal Heart Monitoring, *2nd ed. Los Angeles: University of Southern California School of Medicine, 1976, p 41.)*

**Variable decelerations** occur if the umbilical cord becomes compressed, thus reducing blood flow between the placenta and fetus. The resulting increase in peripheral resistance in the fetal circulation causes fetal hypertension. The fetal hypertension stimulates the baroreceptors in the aortic arch and carotid sinuses, which slow the FHR. The onset of variable decelerations varies in timing with the onset of the contraction and they are variable in shape. This pattern requires further assessment (Figure 15.15, **C**).

Nursing interventions for periodic changes in FHR are presented in Table 15.2

**Sinusoidal pattern** appears similar to a wave form. Long-term variability is present, but there is no short-term variability. The baseline FHR usually ranges from

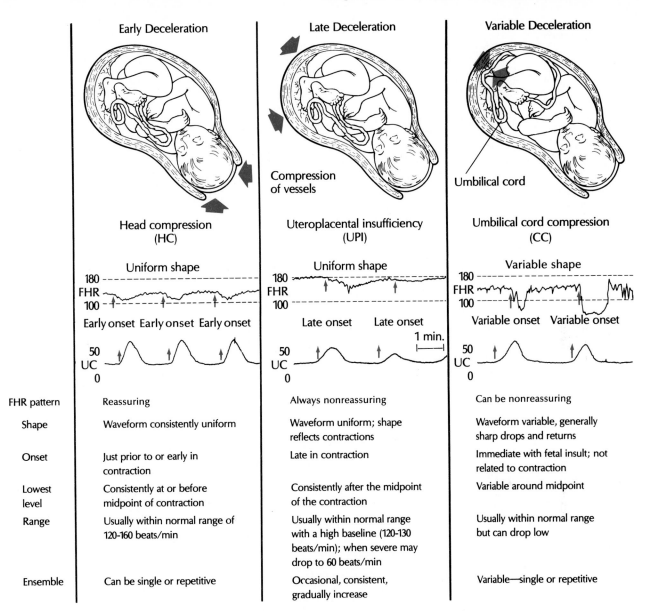

| FHR pattern | **Early Deceleration**<br>Head compression<br>(HC) | **Late Deceleration**<br>Uteroplacental insufficiency<br>(UPI) | **Variable Deceleration**<br>Umbilical cord compression<br>(CC) |
|---|---|---|---|
| FHR pattern | Reassuring | Always nonreassuring | Can be nonreassuring |
| Shape | Waveform consistently uniform | Waveform uniform; shape reflects contractions | Waveform variable, generally sharp drops and returns |
| Onset | Just prior to or early in contraction | Late in contraction | Immediate with fetal insult; not related to contraction |
| Lowest level | Consistently at or before midpoint of contraction | Consistently after the midpoint of the contraction | Variable around midpoint |
| Range | Usually within normal range of 120-160 beats/min | Usually within normal range with a high baseline (120-130 beats/min); when severe may drop to 60 beats/min | Usually within normal range but can drop low |
| Ensemble | Can be single or repetitive | Occasional, consistent, gradually increase | Variable—single or repetitive |

*Figure 15.14 Types and characteristics of early, late, and variable decelerations (From Hon E:* An Introduction to Fetal Heart Rate Monitoring, *2nd ed. Los Angeles: University of California School of Medicine, 1976, p 29.)*

110 to 115 beats/min. Fetal activity may be minimal or absent, and accelerations of FHR are not seen. The cause of the pattern is not clearly known, although it seems to "imply severe fetal jeopardy and impending death" (Mondanlou and Freeman 1982) (Figure 15.15, **D**). Some researchers report that the administration of nalbuphine hydrochloride (Nubain) has been associated with sinusoidal patterns (Feinstein et al 1986).

### Reassuring and Nonreassuring FHR Patterns

FHR patterns must be assessed for evidence that shows whether they are reassuring or nonreassuring. Re-

assuring patterns indicate that the fetus is tolerating the contractions and labor can continue. Nonreassuring patterns indicate that the fetus may be at risk and intervention is required. The charactistics of both types of patterns are presented in Table 15.3.

### Psychologic Reactions to Electronic Monitoring

Women have many different reactions to electronic monitoring. Many women have little knowledge of monitoring unless they have attended a prenatal class that dealt

*(Text continues on page 412.)*

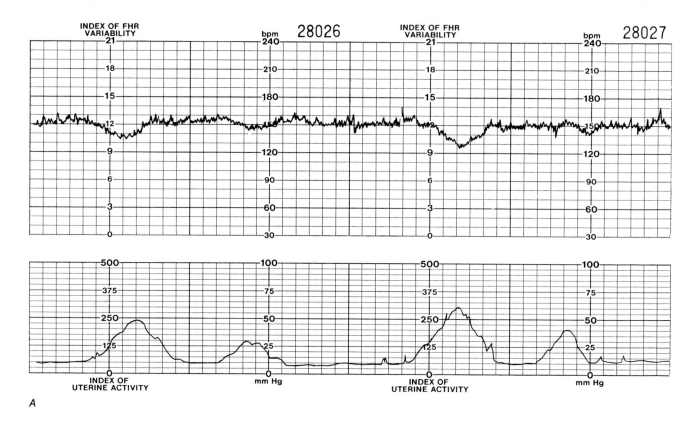

A

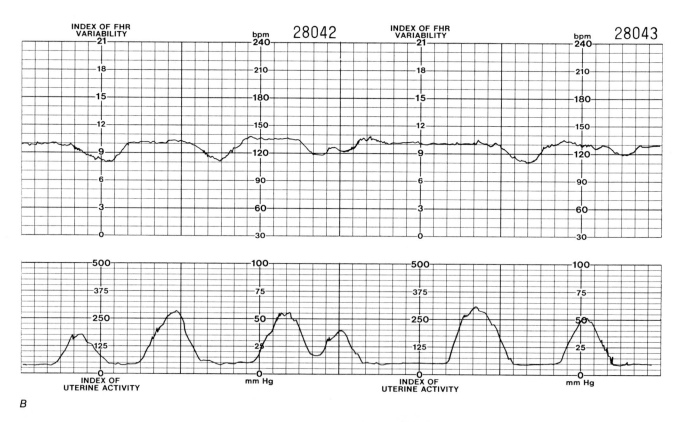

B

Figure 15.15   Types of decelerations: (A) Early decelerations. (B) Late decelerations.
(C) Variable decelerations with overshoot. The timing of the decelerations is variable and
most have a sharp decline. An acceleration (overshoot) occurs after most of the decelerations.
(D) Sinusoidal pattern.

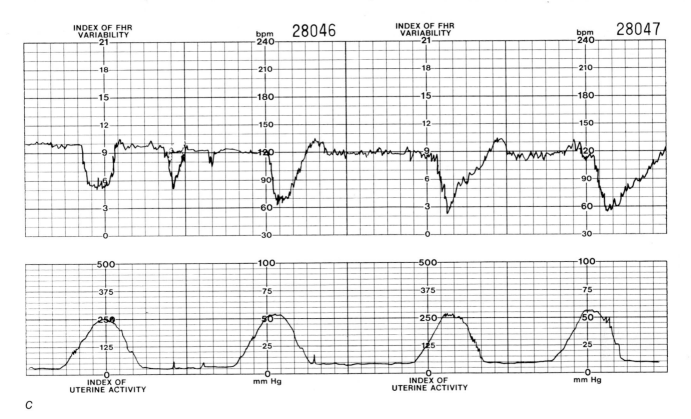

C

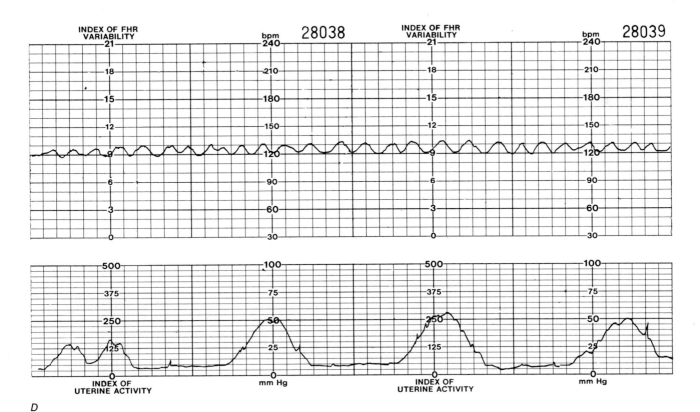

D

## Table 15.2  General Principles of Management of FHR Patterns

| Pattern | Therapeutic intervention |
|---|---|
| Normal | Evaluate maternal vital signs. Follow labor by means of vaginal examination at appropriate intervals. Observe and assess quality of labor and FHR patterns. Document data and assessment of findings. Ensure adequate hydration. Change maternal position when indicated. Decrease or discontinue oxytocin when indicated. Administer oxygen when needed. Maintain communication. |
| Tachycardia | Assess maternal temperature. Reconfirm EDD. Monitor for changes in FHR pattern. |
| Bradycardia | Monitor for changes in FHR pattern. |
| Early decelerations | Monitor for changes in FHR pattern. |
| Variable decelerations<br>  Isolated or occasional<br>  Severe | Monitor for changes in FHR pattern. Change maternal position to one in which FHR pattern is most improved. Discontinue oxytocin if it is being administered. Perform vaginal examination to assess for prolapsed cord or imminent delivery. Administer 100% oxygen by tight face mask. Monitor FHR continuously to assess current status and further changes in FHR pattern. |
| If variable decelerations are severe and uncorrectable and woman is in:<br>  Early labor<br>  Second stage labor | Cesarean birth should be performed. Vaginal birth should be permitted unless baseline variability is decreasing or FHR is progressively rising, then cesarean delivery. |
| Late decelerations occasional with good or increased variability | Monitor for further FHR changes. Maintain woman in side-lying position. Maintain good hydration. Discontinue oxytocin if it is being administered. Administer oxygen. Monitor maternal blood pressure and pulse for signs of hypotension. Treat hypotension. |
| Late decelerations persistent with good variability | Maintain side-lying position. Administer oxygen. Discontinue oxytocin if it is being administered. Assess maternal blood pressure and pulse. Begin intravenous fluids to maintain volume and hydration or increase rate of current IV fluids if maternal hypotension occurs. Assess labor progress. Perform fetal blood sampling; if pH stays above 7.25, continue monitoring and resample as needed; if pH shows downward trend (between 7.25 and 7.20) resample in 10–15 minutes; if pH is below 7.20, deliver the infant immediately. |
| Ominous patterns | Delivery should occur without delay. If delivery is not in progress, cesarean delivery is performed. Supportive care while waiting for delivery includes: administer $O_2$; maintain side-lying or any position in which FHR is most improved; assess FHR continuously; assess maternal blood pressure and pulse; correct maternal hypotension. |

with this subject. Some women react to electronic monitoring positively, viewing it as a reassurance that "the baby is OK." They may also feel that the monitor will help identify problems that develop in labor. Other women may feel negatively about the monitor. They may think that the monitor is interfering with a natural process, and they do not want the intrusion. They may resent the time and attention that the monitor requires, time that could otherwise be spent providing nursing care. Some women may find that the equipment, wires, and sounds increase their anxiety. The discomfort of lying in one position and fear of injury to the baby are other objections (Molfese et al 1982).

### Nursing Responsibilities

Before applying the monitor, the nurse should fully explain the reason for its use and the information that it can provide. After the monitor is applied, basic information should be recorded on a label attached to the monitor strip. The data included are the date, client's name, physician/nurse-midwife, hospital number, age, gravida, para, EDD, membrane status, and maternal vital signs. As the monitor strip continues to run and care is provided, occurrences during labor should be recorded not only in the medical record but also on the fetal monitoring tracing. This information helps the health care team assess current status and evaluate the tracing (Chez and Verklan 1987).

The following information should be included on the tracing:

1. Vaginal examination (dilatation, effacement, station, and position)
2. Amniotomy or spontaneous rupture of membranes
3. Maternal vital signs
4. Maternal position changes
5. Application of internal monitor
6. Medications
7. Oxygen administration
8. Maternal behaviors (emesis, coughing, hiccups)
9. Fetal blood sampling
10. Vomiting
11. Pushing
12. Anesthesia

The tracing is considered a legal part of the woman's medical record and is submissible as evidence in court.

### Interpretation of FHR Tracings

The nurse needs to use a systematic approach in evaluating FHR tracings to avoid interpreting findings on the basis of inadequate or erroneous data. With a systematic approach, the nurse can make a more accurate and rapid assessment, communicate data to the woman, physician/nurse-midwife, and staff easily, and have a systematic, universal language for documenting the woman's record.

In assessing tracings, the nurse should first identify the uterine contractions. The contractions should be in evidence on the tracing at or even before the time the woman actually feels them. If not, adjustments are needed. The contraction pattern (frequency, duration, intensity, and baseline resting tone between contractions) is assessed. The nurse needs to remember that contraction intensity cannot be assessed with an external monitor. Next,

the fetal response to the uterine contractions is assessed. Baseline FHR and changes are evaluated. What is the FHR? Is it increasing? Is it decreasing? Is the variability increasing or decreasing? Finally, the nurse looks at periodic changes. Are there accelerations with fetal movement? Are there decelerations? What are the characteristics of decelerations? See Essential Facts to Remember—Characteristics of Normal Fetal Heart Rate.

---

### Table 15.3   Reassuring and Nonreassuring FHR Patterns

FHR patterns need to be assessed for evidence that shows whether they are reassuring or nonreassuring.

*Reassuring* patterns include (Freeman 1982):

1. No periodic changes
2. Early decelerations
3. Variable decelerations that do not exceed the following limits:
   a. Accelerations lasting less than 45 seconds
   b. Return to baseline is abrupt
   c. Baseline rate is not increasing
   d. Baseline variability is not decreasing
4. FHR accelerations
   a. With contractions
   b. With fetal movement

*Nonreassuring* patterns include (Freeman 1982):

1. Intermittent late deceleration with good FHR variability
2. Variable deceleration that exceeds the criteria (in reassuring patterns) with respect to duration and/or rate of return but still has good FHR variability and no rising baseline
3. Total loss of FHR variability with deceleration
4. Prolonged deceleration due to:
   a. Paracervical block
   b. Epidural block
   c. Supine hypotension
   d. Vaginal examination or manipulation

*Ominous* FHR patterns include (Freeman 1982):

1. Persistent, uncorrectable late decelerations with loss of FHR variability with or without fetal tachycardia
2. Variable decelerations accompanied by:
   a. Loss of FHR variability
   b. Fetal tachycardia
   c. Prolonged "overshoot"
   d. Blunted shapes
3. Sinusoidal FHR patterns

## Essential Facts to Remember

### Characteristics of Normal Fetal Heart Rate

| | |
|---|---|
| Baseline rate: | 120–160 beats/min |
| Baseline variability: | Long-term variability (LTV) greater than 6 beats/min |
| | Short-term variability (STV) present |
| Periodic changes: | |
| Accelerations: | With fetal movement |
| Decelerations: | Early decelerations may be present |

Under current standards of practice the nurse must be able to recognize FHR patterns and to communicate an accurate assessment of fetal status so that appropriate intervention can be made. Unless nurses are able to distinguish between nonreassuring and reassuring patterns and can take responsibility for evaluating the status of labor, they cannot detect impending problems.

### FETAL BLOOD SAMPLING

When nonreassuring or confusing FHR patterns are noted, additional information regarding the acid-base status of the fetus must be sought. This may be accomplished by the physician obtaining a **fetal blood sample**. The blood sample is usually drawn from the fetal scalp, but may be obtained from the fetus in the breech position.

Indications for fetal blood sampling are as follows (Freeman 1982):

1. Persistent uncorrectable late decelerations with good variability in a woman who is expected to deliver in less than two hours

2. Confusing FHR patterns with possibly ominous elements

3. Total loss of FHR variability but no deceleration pattern

Before fetal blood can be sampled, the membranes must be ruptured, the cervix must be dilated at least 2–3 cm, and the presenting part must not be above −2 station. Sampling is not done when FHR patterns are ominous. It is contraindicated in acute emergencies and in cases of vaginal bleeding. In these instances, delivery by the most expeditious means is indicated.

Normal fetal pH values during labor are at or above 7.25, with 7.20–7.24 considered preacidotic. Values below 7.20 indicate serious acidosis.

Intervention based on fetal pH is recommended as follows:

1. If pH is greater than 7.25, allow labor to continue and resample as needed.

2. If pH is between 7.20 and 7.25, resample in 10–15 minutes.

3. If pH is less than 7.20, resample immediately. If low pH is confirmed, deliver the infant immediately (Monheit and Cousins 1981).

The more information available about FHR monitoring, the less need for taking a fetal blood sample. Only when FHR patterns are uninterpretable, worsening, or suggestive of high risk is this adjunctive procedure indicated. Fetal blood sampling may prevent unnecessary cesarean delivery. Fetal blood sampling and electronic fetal monitoring are complementary tools. They give the physician the knowledge to make appropriate decisions about intervention or nonintervention.

## ESSENTIAL CONCEPTS

● **Intrapartal assessment includes attention to both physical and psychologic parameters of the laboring woman, assessment of the fetus, and ongoing assessment for conditions that place the woman and her fetus at increased risk.**

● **A sterile vaginal examination determines status of fetal membranes, cervical dilatation and effacement, and fetal presentation, position, and station.**

● **Uterine contractions may be assessed by palpation or by an electronic monitor. The electronic monitor may be used for external or internal monitoring.**

● **Labor progress may be objectively evaluated using a Friedman graph, which plots cervical dilatation and fetal descent.**

● **Leopold's maneuvers provide a systematic evaluation of fetal presentation and position.**

● **Fetal presentation and position may also be assessed by vaginal examination, ultrasound.**

● **The fetal heart rate may be assessed by auscultation (with a fetoscope) or electronic monitoring.**

● **Electronic fetal monitoring is accomplished by indirect ultrasound or by direct methods that require the placement of a spiral electrode on the fetal presenting part.**

● **Indications for electronic monitoring include fetal, maternal, and uterine factors; presence of** pregnancy complications; regional anesthesia; and elective monitoring.

● True variability of the FHR can only be assessed by direct electronic monitoring.

● Baseline FHR refers to the range of FHR observed between contractions, during a ten-minute period of monitoring.

● The normal range of FHR is 120 to 160 beats per minute.

● Baseline changes of the FHR include tachycardia, bradycardia, and variability.

● Tachycardia is defined as a rate of 160 beats per minute or more for a ten-minute segment of time.

● Bradycardia is defined as a rate of less than 120 beats per minute for a ten-minute segment of time.

● Baseline variability is an important parameter of fetal well-being. It includes both long- and short-term variability.

● Periodic changes are transient decelerations or accelerations of the FHR from the baseline. Accelerations are normally caused by fetal movement; decelerations may be termed early, late, variable, or sinusoidal.

● Early decelerations are due to compression of the fetal head during contractions and are considered reassuring.

● Late decelerations are associated with uteroplacental insufficiency and are considered ominous.

● Variable decelerations are associated with compression of the umbilical cord.

● Sinusoidal patterns are characterized by an undulant sinewave.

● Psychologic reactions to monitoring vary between feelings of relief and feelings of being tied down.

● Birthing room nurses have responsibilities in recognizing and interpreting fetal monitoring patterns, notifying the physician/CNM of problems, and initiating corrective and supportive measures when needed.

● Fetal acid-base status may be assessed by fetal scalp sampling.

● ● ● ● ● ● ● ● ● ● ● ● ● ● ● ● ● ● ● ● ● ● ● ● ● ● ● ● ●

## References

American Academy of Pediatrics and The American College of Obstetricians and Gynecologists: *Guidelines for Perinatal Care*, 2nd ed. Washington, DC, 1988.

Chez BF, Verklan MT: Documentation and electronic fetal monitoring: How, where, and what? *J Perinat Neonatol Nurs* July 1987; 1(1): 22.

Feinstein SJ et al: Sinusoidal fetal heart rate pattern after administration of nalbuphine hydrochloride: A case report. *Am J Obstet Gynecol* 1986; 154(1): 159.

Freeman RK: Fetal distress: Diagnosis and management. Presented at the Sixth International Symposium on Perinatal Medicine, April 1982, Las Vegas, Nevada.

Friedman EA: An objective method of evaluating labor. *Hosp Pract* 1970; 5: 82.

Molfese V, Sunshine P, Bennett A: Reactions of women to intrapartum fetal monitoring. *Obstet Gynecol* 1982; 59(6): 705.

Mondanlou HD, Freeman RK: Sinusoidal fetal heart rate pattern: Its definition and clinical significance. *Am J Obstet Gynecol* 1982; 142(8): 1033.

Monheit A, Cousins L: When do you measure scalp and blood pH? *Contemp OB/GYN* August 1981: 55.

NAACOG statement: Nursing responsibilities in implementing intrapartum fetal heart rate monitoring. October 1988.

Parer JT: Fetal heart rate. In: *Maternal-Fetal Medicine*. Creasy RK, Resnik R (editors). Philadelphia: Saunders, 1989.

Varney H: *Nurse-Midwifery*, 2nd ed. Boston: Blackwell Scientific, 1987.

## Additional Readings

Brubaker K, Garite TJ: The Lambda fetal heart rate pattern: An assessment of its significance in the intrapartum period. *Obstet Gynecol* December 1988; 72(6): 881.

Gagnon R, Hunse C, Patrick J: Fetal responses to vibratory acoustic stimulation: Influence of basal heart rate. *Am J Obstet Gynecol* October 1988; 159(4): 835.

Low JA: The role of blood gas and acid-base assessment in the diagnosis of intrapartum fetal asphyxia. *Am J Obstet Gynecol* November 1988; 159(5): 1235.

NAACOG: *Electronic Fetal Monitoring: Nursing Practice Competencies and Educational Guidelines*. Washington, DC, 1986.

NAACOG: Competency validation. Resource book from essentials of electronic fetal monitoring. Videotape, 1988.

NAACOG: Considerations for professional nurse staffing in perinatal units. OGN nursing practice resource. Washington, DC, 1988.

Paine LL, Johnson TR, Alexander GR: Auscultated fetal heart rate accelerations. III. Use of vibratory acoustic stimulation. *Am J Obstet Gynecol* November 1988; 159(5): 1163.

Paine LL et al: Auscultated FHR accelerations. Part 2. An alternative to the nonstress test. *J Nurse-Midwifery* 1986; 31: 73.

Piquard F et al: The validity of fetal heart rate monitoring during the second stage of labor. *Obstet Gynecol* November 1988; 72(5): 746.

Shaw K, Clark SL: Reliability of intrapartum fetal heart rate monitoring in the postterm fetus with meconium passage. *Obstet Gynecol* December 1988; 72(6): 886.

Shy KK, Lawson EB, Luthy DA: Evaluating a new technology: The effectiveness of electronic fetal heart rate monitoring. *Am Rev Public Health* 1987; 8: 165.

# 16

# The Family in Childbirth: Needs and Care

*The sheer pleasure of the feeling of a born baby on one's thighs is like nothing on earth.* (Margaret Drabble, in *Ever Since Eve*)

## Objectives

Identify the data base to be obtained when a woman is admitted to the birthing area and the nursing care that is given at that time.

● Discuss nursing interventions to meet the psychologic and physiologic needs of the woman during each stage of labor.

● Identify the immediate needs of the newborn following birth.

● Discuss management of a birth in less-than-ideal situations.

## Key Terms

Apgar score
attachment
birthing room
hyperventilation
Leboyer method
lochia rubra
nuchal cord
precipitous birth
prep

It is time for a child to be born. The waiting is over; labor has begun. The dreams and wishes of the past months fade as the expectant parents face the reality of the tasks of childbearing and childrearing that are ahead.

The couple is about to undergo one of the most meaningful and stressful events in their life together. The adequacy of their preparation for childbirth will now be tested. The coping mechanisms, communication, and support systems that they have established as a couple will be put to the test. In particular, the childbearing woman may feel that her psychologic and physical limits are about to be challenged.

The couple has also been involved in collecting information and making decisions regarding the setting for childbirth. Not many years ago, the only choice was an in-hospital labor unit with separate labor room, delivery room, and recovery area. This type of unit is still available in some hospitals. However, many hospitals have changed their labor and delivery units to more closely reflect changing philosophies of family-centered childbirth. Many have single purpose units, which means that the woman stays in the same room for labor, delivery, recovery, and possibly the postpartal period. These rooms may be called LDR (meaning labor, delivery, and recovery) or LDRPP (meaning labor, delivery, recovery, and postpartum). Some labor and delivery units use the term "alternative birthing room" or "birthing room" instead of LDR or LDRPP.

Maternity nursing has also kept pace with the changing philosophy of childbirth. In the past, a major portion of maternity nurses' roles involved doing what they were told to do by the physician and then informing parents of what would happen to them. However, the maternity nursing role has developed its own identity. Today's maternity nurse in the labor and delivery setting uses the full spectrum of nursing skills in working with childbearing families. Maternity nurses assess clients, gather information, provide information and teaching so that couples can make informed choices, function as a client advocate, collaborate with other health care professionals, ensure that they function within current nursing standards of care, and communicate with physicians and certified nurse-midwives. Maternity nurses have become an integral part of family-centered care as they provide support, encouragement, and safe, caring nursing care.

# ● USING THE NURSING PROCESS DURING THE INTRAPARTAL PERIOD

Maternity nurses will find that using the nursing process enhances their ability to provide individualized family-centered care during the intrapartal period. By applying the nursing process, nursing skills and theory, and their knowledge about childbirth, maternity nurses can function in a variety of birthing settings.

## ● Nursing Assessment

When the laboring woman is admitted to the birthing unit, the first member of the health care team that she and her partner encounter is usually the nurse. The accuracy of the nurse's admission assessment of the woman's physical and psychologic status is significant in determining the quality of the childbearing experience the couple will have. The nursing assessment is the basis for determining initial management of care by other members of the health care team.

The initial nursing assessment usually focuses on the imminence of delivery. Careful assessment of labor progress will help the nurse determine the priorities of care that must follow. After safety of the mother and fetus have been assured, the nursing assessment focuses on the woman's coping mechanisms and her support system. The nurse also determines the goals the couple have established for their birth experience.

During labor, the nurse continually reassesses maternal and fetal physical status and the couple's coping mechanisms in order to intervene appropriately.

## ● Nursing Diagnosis

Nursing diagnoses are based on physical and psychosocial assessments of the childbearing woman. Examples of nursing diagnoses are:

● Pain related to uterine contractions and cervical dilatation
● Anxiety related to unknown labor outcome

## ● Nursing Plan and Implementation

Once nursing diagnoses are formulated, the nurse must determine which are most significant to the woman's well-being. Priorities of care differ for every woman admitted to the birthing unit. While physiologic alterations usually form the basis for priorities of care when labor is progressing rapidly or high-risk factors are identified, this may not be the situation with a healthy woman admitted in early labor. After safety of the mother and fetus have been assured, important factors that must be considered in developing the nursing plan of care include the woman's goals

for her birth experience, her coping mechanisms, and the strength of her support systems. For example, the 16-year-old single nullipara who has had no prenatal care and comes to the hospital alone has different needs from the couple who planned the pregnancy and attended prepared childbirth classes. Nursing diagnoses and priorities for the plan of care will be quite different in these two situations. The nurse may be the 16-year-old girl's only support, but the couple may have only minimal need for the nurse's support.

A major challenge for the nurse is helping laboring women to achieve realistic goals for their birthing experience. Each woman is admitted to the birthing unit at a different phase in the laboring process and with a different level of wellness. The nurse may not have time to assess the choice of birthing options of a multipara whose delivery is imminent on admission or to support the goal of unmedicated labor in a primigravida who develops severe pre-eclampsia during her labor. Regardless of the individual factors each woman or couple brings to the labor, the nurse and the woman or couple work together to achieve a safe labor and birth.

To be effective, the nurse must use many types of interventions during labor and delivery. These include technical interventions; interventions that ensure that the birth setting is safe and comfortable for the woman and her baby; communication techniques for use with the laboring woman, her support person(s), and other members of the health team; and teaching techniques.

## ● Evaluation

Evaluation of the effectiveness of nursing interventions and achievement of client goals is ongoing as the nurse continually reassesses the woman. Evaluation results in a constant cycle of nursing process application.

# ● NURSING ASSESSMENT DURING ADMISSION

The woman is instructed during her prenatal visits to come to the hospital or birth center if any of the following occurs:

● Rupture of membranes (ROM)
● Uterine contractions (nullipara, 8–12 minutes apart; multiparas, 10–15 minutes apart)
● Vaginal bleeding

Early admission means less discomfort for the laboring woman when traveling to the hospital and more time to prepare for the delivery. Sometimes the labor is advanced and delivery is imminent, but usually the woman is in early labor at admission. If time permits, the woman can be instructed on what she may expect during labor. See Teaching Guide—What to Expect During Your Labor.

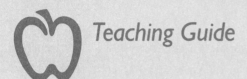

# Teaching Guide

*Assessment*  As each woman is admitted into the birthing area, the nurse assesses the woman's knowledge regarding the childbirth experience. The woman's knowledge base will be affected by previous births, attendance at childbirth education classes, and the amount of information she has been able to gather during her pregnancy by asking questions or reading. The nurse also assesses the factors that affect communication and anxiety level. Labor process is assessed so that decisions regarding what to teach and the time available for teaching can be ascertained. If the woman is in early labor and she needs additional information, the nurse proceeds as follows:

*Nursing Diagnosis*  The essential nursing diagnosis probably will be: knowledge deficit related to nursing care during labor.

*Nursing Plan and Implementation*  The teaching guide will consist of providing information regarding the assessments and support the woman will receive during labor.

*Client Goals*  At the completion of the teaching the woman will be able to:

1. Verbalize the assessments the nurse will complete during labor.
2. Discuss the support/comfort measures that are available.

## Teaching Plan

### Content

Discuss aspects of the admission process:

- Abbreviated history
- Physical assessment (maternal vital signs [VS], fetal heart rate [FHR], contraction status, status of membranes)
- Assessment of uterine contractions (frequency, duration, intensity)
- Orientation to surroundings
- Introductions to other staff that will be assisting her

Present aspects of ongoing physical care, such as when to expect assessment of maternal VS, FHR, and contractions.

If electronic fetal monitor is used, orient the woman to how it works and the information that it provides. Orient woman to the sights and sounds of the monitor. Explain what the "normal" data will look like and what characteristics are being watched for.

Be sure to note that the assessments will increase as the labor progresses; about the time that the woman would like to be left alone (transition phase), the assessments increase in order to help keep the mother and baby safe by noting any changes from the normal course.

### Teaching Method

*Discussion*

*Bring a fetal monitor into the birthing room and demonstrate how it works.*

*(continues)*

## Teaching Plan (continued)

### Content

Explain the vaginal examination and what information can be obtained.

Review comfort techniques that may be used in labor. First ascertain what the woman thinks will be effective in promoting comfort.

Review the breathing techniques that the woman has learned so the nurse will be able to support her technique.

Review comfort/support measures such as: positioning, back rub, effleurage, touch, distraction techniques, ambulation, etc.

If the woman is in early labor, offer to give her a tour of the birthing area.

### Teaching Method

*Use a cervical dilatation chart to illustrate the amount of dilatation.*

*Discussion*

*Ask woman to demonstrate technique.*

*Discussion*

*Tour area.*

---

**Evaluation**   At the end of this teaching session the woman will be able to verbalize the assessments that will occur during her labor and will be able to discuss comfort/support measures that may be used.

The woman may be facing a number of unfamiliar procedures that are routine for health care providers. It is important to remember that all women have the right to determine what happens to their bodies. *The woman's informed consent should be obtained prior to any procedure that involves touching her body.*

The manner in which the woman and her partner are greeted by the maternity nurse influences the course of her hospital stay. The sudden environmental change and the sometimes impersonal and technical aspects of admission can produce additional stress. If women are greeted in a brusque, harried manner, they are less likely to look to the nurse for support. A calm, pleasant manner indicates to the woman that she is an important person. It helps instill in the couple a sense of confidence in the staff's ability to provide quality care during this critical time.

Following the initial greeting, the woman is taken into the labor or birthing room. Some couples prefer to remain together during the admission process, and others prefer to have the partner wait outside. As the nurse helps the woman undress and get into a hospital gown, the nurse can begin conversing with her to develop rapport and establish the nursing data base. The experienced labor and delivery nurse can obtain essential information regarding the woman and her pregnancy within a few minutes after admission, initiate any immediate interventions needed, and establish individualized priorities. The nurse is then able to make effective nursing decisions regarding intrapartal care:

- Will a "prep" and/or enema be given?
- Should ambulation or bed rest be encouraged?
- Is more frequent monitoring needed?
- What does the woman want during her labor and delivery?
- Is a support person available?

A major challenge for nurses is the formulation of realistic objectives for laboring women. Each woman has different coping mechanisms and support systems.

If indicated, the woman is assisted into bed. A side-lying or semi-Fowler's position rather than a supine position is most comfortable and avoids supine hypotensive syndrome (vena caval syndrome).

After obtaining the essential information from the woman and her records, the nurse begins the intrapartal assessment. (Chapter 15 considers intrapartal maternal assessment in depth.)

The nurse auscultates the fetal heart rate (FHR). (Detailed information on monitoring FHR is presented in Chapter 15.) The woman's blood pressure, pulse, respiration, and oral temperature are determined. Contraction frequency, duration, and intensity are assessed; this may be done as other data are gathered. Before the sterile vaginal examination, the woman should be informed about the procedure and its purpose. Afterward the nurse tells the woman about the findings. If there are signs of advanced labor (frequent contractions, an urge to bear down, and so on), a vaginal examination must be done quickly. If there are signs of excessive bleeding or if the woman reports episodes of bleeding in the last trimester, a vaginal examination should *not* be done.

Results of FHR assessment, uterine contraction evaluation, and the vaginal examination help determine whether the rest of the admission process can proceed at a more leisurely pace or whether additional interventions have higher priority. For example, a FHR of 110 beats/min on auscultation indicates that a fetal monitor should be applied immediately to obtain additional data. The woman's vital signs can be assessed after this is done.

## ● NURSING DIAGNOSIS

The nurse can anticipate that for many women with a low-risk pregnancy, certain nursing diagnoses will be used more frequently than others. This will of course vary from woman to woman according to the individual labor experience. Many of the more commonly used nursing diagnoses are identified in Essential Nursing Diagnoses to Consider—The Birth Process.

## ● NURSING PLAN AND IMPLEMENTATION DURING ADMISSION

After admission data are obtained, a clean-voided midstream urine specimen is collected. The woman with intact membranes may walk to the bathroom. If the membranes are ruptured and the presenting part is not engaged, the woman is generally asked to remain in bed to avoid prolapse of the umbilical cord. The advisability of ambulation when membranes are ruptured depends on the woman's desires, clinician requests, or agency policy.

The nurse can test the woman's urine for the presence of protein, ketones, and glucose by using a dipstick before sending the sample to the laboratory. This procedure is especially important if edema or elevated blood pressure is noted on admission. Proteinuria of 2+ or more may be a sign of impending preeclampsia. Ketonuria is an index of starvation ketosis. Glycosuria is found frequently in pregnant women because of the increased glomerular filtration rate in the proximal tubules and the inability of these tubules to increase reabsorption of glucose. However, it may also be associated with latent diabetes and should not be discounted.

While the woman is collecting the urine specimen, the nurse can prepare the equipment for shaving the pubic area (the shaving is referred to as the **prep**) and for the enema if one is to be given. Prep orders vary, but many clinicians leave standing orders for prep measures. The use of preps is a controversial issue. Some clinicians believe that this form of skin preparation facilitates their work during the delivery, makes perineal repair easier, and prevents infection (Mahan and McKay 1983). Many women question the need for a prep and request that it be omitted. The nurse needs to ascertain the woman's wishes in this matter. Women who do not want a prep probably have discussed this with the physician/nurse-midwife during the prenatal period.

If a prep is to be done, the perineal hair below the vaginal opening is either shaved or clipped with a pair of sterile scissors.

The administration of an enema is also controversial. Proponents say the purposes of an enema are to (a) evacuate the lower bowel so that labor will not be impeded, (b) stimulate uterine contractions, (c) avoid embarrassment if bowel contents are expelled during pushing efforts, and (d) prevent contamination of the sterile field during delivery. Those who question the routine use of an enema on admission suggest that labor is impeded only by a severe bowel impaction, question whether labor is stimulated, and find that feces still may be expelled during pushing efforts. They also note that the enema may be uncomfortable.

After determining the woman's wishes regarding an enema, the nurse notifies the clinician. Some factors contraindicate the enema. They are vaginal bleeding, unengaged presenting part, mal presentation, rapid labor progress, and imminent delivery. These factors need to be identified. If an enema is to be given, the reasons and the procedure are explained to the woman. Then the enema is administered while she is on her left side.

If the membranes are intact and labor is not far advanced, the woman may expel the enema in the bathroom. Otherwise she is positioned on a bedpan in bed. The side rails of the bed should be raised for safety. They also support the woman as she positions herself over the bedpan.

Before leaving the labor area, the nurse must be sure that the woman knows how to operate the call system so that she can obtain help if she needs it. After the enema is expelled, the nurse monitors the FHR again to assess any changes. The contraction pattern is reevaluated because the enema may act to stimulate labor. If the woman's partner has been out of the labor room, the couple is reunited as soon as possible.

Laboratory tests are also carried out during admission. Hemoglobin and hematocrit values help determine the oxygen-carrying capacity of the circulatory system and the ability of the woman to withstand blood loss at delivery. Elevation of the hematocrit indicates hemoconcentration of blood, which occurs with edema or dehydration. A low hemoglobin, in the absence of other evidence of bleeding, suggests anemia. Blood may be typed and crossmatched if the woman is in a high-risk category. A serology test for syphilis is obtained if one has not been done in the last three months or if an antepartal serology result was positive.

In many hospitals, the admission process also includes signing a delivery permit, fingerprinting the woman for the infant records, and fastening an identification bracelet to her wrist.

Depending on how rapidly labor is progressing, the nurse notifies the clinician before or after completing the admission procedures. The report should include the following information: cervical dilatation and effacement, station, presenting part, status of the membranes, contraction pattern, FHR, vital signs that are not in the normal range, the woman's wishes, and her reaction to labor.

Nursing management of labor is influenced by the physical, psychologic, and cultural data obtained during admission.

## DX Essential Nursing Diagnoses to Consider

### The Birth Process

During admission:

  Anxiety

  Pain

  Knowledge deficit

During labor and birth:

  Pain

  Altered family processes

  Anxiety

  Impaired physical mobility

  Ineffective breathing pattern

  Ineffective individual coping

  Knowledge deficit

  Decreased cardiac output

  Fluid volume deficit

  Altered tissue perfusion

  Potential for infection

  Potential for injury

## • NURSING PLAN AND IMPLEMENTATION DURING THE FIRST STAGE OF LABOR

After the nursing assessment and diagnosis steps have been completed, the nurse creates a plan of care arranged around nursing goals.

## ● *Integration of Cultural Beliefs*

Knowledge of values, customs, and practices of different cultures is as important during labor as it is in the prenatal period. Without this knowledge, a nurse is less likely to understand a woman's behavior and may impose personal values and beliefs upon a woman. As cultural sensitivity increases, so does the likelihood of providing high-quality care.

In the following sections, brief general information is given regarding possible cultural responses to labor. It is difficult to present even a brief discussion in a clear, non-judgmental way, because once a statement is made it may appear stereotypical and some may feel it is not reflective of all people in a group. The following exaggerated example may present a stereotypical picture of how some individuals may view a North American woman's response to birth: The white Protestant North American woman brings a picture to use as a focal point during labor and places it on the wall at the foot of the bed. She practices Lamaze breathing techniques and uses a red sucker to provide moisture for her mouth during breathing. She frequently removes all of her clothes during transition and will give birth on her hands and knees. Although the preceding somewhat exaggerated example is not a reflection of what every woman in this group will want during childbirth, there are some aspects that individual women would like. It is difficult to give examples and not assume that they are pertinent to ALL women in that particular group. Within every culture each person is an individual with his or her own belief and value system. General information about any culture or belief system needs to be used as a knowledge and base; then assessments of the individual are made to determine individual needs and desires.

### *MODESTY*

Modesty is an important consideration for women regardless of the cultural grouping; however, some women may be more uncomfortable with the degree of exposure needed for some procedures during labor and the birth process. Some women may be particularly uncomfortable when men are present and feel more comfortable with women; others may be uncomfortable with exposure of personal body parts regardless of the gender of the examiner or person who assists them. The nurse needs to be observant of the woman's responses to examinations and procedures and to provide the draping and privacy that the woman needs. It is more prudent to assume that embarrassment will occur with exposure and take measures to provide privacy than to assume that it will not matter to the woman to be exposed during procedures. Some Asian women are not accustomed to male physicians and attendants. Modesty is of great concern, and exposure of as little of the woman's body as possible is strongly recommended.

### PAIN EXPRESSION

The manner that a woman chooses to deal with the discomfort of labor varies widely. Some women may seem to turn inward and remain very quiet during the whole process. They speak only to ask others to leave the room or cease conversation. Others may be very vocal, ranging from counting out loud, moaning quietly, crying, or cursing loudly. They may also turn from side to side or change positions on a frequent basis. In Asian cultures it is important for individuals to act in a way that will not bring shame on the family. Therefore, the Asian woman may not express pain outwardly for fear of shaming herself and her family (Hollingsworth et al 1980). Mexican-American women, by contrast, may be more expressive during labor. One way they may express pain and suffering is through groaning and moaning (Murillo-Rohde 1979). Another behavior of laboring Mexican-American women is to keep their mouths closed for fear of making the uterus rise. They are to yell only when they exhale (Kay 1978).

### CULTURAL BELIEFS: SOME EXAMPLES

In looking at specific practices related to position, food, and drink during labor, obvious differences between cultures are apparent. In most non-European societies uninfluenced by Westernization, women assume an upright position in childbirth. For example, Hmong women who have emigrated from Laos to our country report that squatting during childbirth is common in their culture (LaDu 1985). Some traditional Native American women give birth in upright positions. For example, the Pueblo woman gives birth on her knees, the Zuni woman kneels or squats while a midwife kneads her abdomen, and in some tribes teas made of juniper twigs may be given to relax the woman (Higgins and Wayland 1981).

Hmong women have special customs regarding childbirth. The beginning of labor signifies the beginning of a transition and entails certain dietary restrictions. The woman may want to be active and may be able to move about during labor. The husband is frequently present and actively involved in providing comfort. During labor the woman usually prefers only "hot" foods and warm water to drink. Traditionally, the woman prefers that the amniotic membranes not be ruptured until just before birth. It is thought that the escape of fluid at this time makes the birth easier. She may choose to kneel or squat for the birth of her baby. As soon as the baby is born, an egg needs to be soft-boiled and given to the mother to eat to restore her energy. During the postpartum period the mother prefers "warm" foods, such as chicken prepared with warm water and warm rice (Morrow 1986).

Vietnamese women also follow prescribed customs during pregnancy and birth (Calhoun 1986). While in labor, the woman usually maintains self-control and may smile throughout the labor. She may prefer to walk about during labor and to deliver in a squatting position. She may avoid drinking cold water and prefer fluids at room temperature. The newborn is protected from praise to prevent jealousy.

In working with women from another culture, an awareness of historical beliefs and practices helps the nurse understand their behavior. In many cases, certain old practices are retained either in part or in full. An awareness of cultural values is also necessary, since specific behavior is often dictated by these traditional views.

## ● Support of the Adolescent During Birth

Each adolescent in labor is different. The nurse must assess what each client brings to the experience by asking the following questions:

● Has the young woman received prenatal care?

● What are her attitudes and feelings about the pregnancy?

● Who will attend the birth and what is the person's relationship to her?

● What preparation has she had for the experience?

● What are her expectations and fears regarding labor and delivery?

● How has her culture influenced her?

● What are her usual coping mechanisms?

● Does she plan to keep the newborn?

Any adolescent who has not had prenatal care requires close observation during labor. Fetal well-being is established by fetal monitoring. Adolescent women are at highest risk for pregnancy and labor complications and must be monitored intensively.

The nurse should be alert to any physiologic complications of labor in the adolescent. The young woman's prenatal record is carefully reviewed for risks. The adolescent is screened for pregnancy-induced hypertension (PIH), cephalopelvic disproportion (CPD), anemia, drugs ingested during pregnancy, sexually transmitted disease, and size-date discrepancies.

The support role of the nurse depends on the woman's support system during labor. The young woman may not be accompanied by someone who will stay with her during childbirth. Whether she has a support person or not, it is important for the nurse to establish a trusting relationship with the young woman. In this way, the nurse can help her maintain control and understand what is happening to her. Establishing rapport without recrimination for possible inappropriate behavior is essential. The adolescent who is given positive reinforcement for "work well done" will leave the experience with increased self-esteem, despite the emotional problems that may accompany her situation.

If a support person does accompany the adolescent, that person also needs the nurse's encouragement and support. The nurse must explain changes in the young woman's behavior and substantiate her wishes. Hospital rules that exclude people under age 16 years may be waived to allow a young father-to-be to remain with the adolescent woman. The nursing staff should reinforce the adolescents' feelings that they are wanted and important.

The adolescent who has taken childbirth education classes is generally better prepared than the adolescent who has had no preparation. The nurse must keep in mind, however, that the younger the adolescent, the less she may be able to participate actively in the process.

The very young adolescent (under age 14) has fewer coping mechanisms and less experience to draw on than her older counterparts have. Because her cognitive development is incomplete, the younger adolescent may have fewer problem-solving capabilities. Her ego integrity may be more threatened by the experience, and she may be more vulnerable to stress and discomfort.

The very young woman needs someone to rely on at all times during labor. She may be more childlike and dependent than older teens. The nurse must be sure that instructions and explanations are simple and concrete. During the transition phase, the young teenager may become withdrawn and unable to express her need to be nurtured. Touch, soothing encouragement, and measures to maintain her comfort help her maintain control and meet her needs for dependence. During the second stage of labor, the young adolescent may feel as if she is losing control and may reach out to those around her. By remaining calm and giving directions, the nurse helps her control feelings of helplessness.

The middle adolescent (age 14–16 years) often attempts to remain calm and unflinching during labor. If unable to break through the teenager's stoic barrier, the nurse needs to rise above frustration and realize that a caring attitude will still affect the young woman.

Many older adolescents feel that they "know it all," but they may be no more prepared for childbirth than younger counterparts. The nurse's reinforcement and nonjudgmental manner will help them save face. If the adolescent has not taken classes, she may require preparation and explanations. The older teenager's response to the stresses of labor, however, is similar to that of the adult woman.

Even if the adolescent is planning to relinquish her newborn, she should be given the option of seeing and holding the infant. She may be reluctant to do this at first, but the grieving process is facilitated if the mother sees the infant. However, seeing or holding the newborn should be the young woman's choice. (See Chapter 28 for further discussion of the relinquishing mother and the adolescent parent.)

## ● *Promotion of Comfort*

The first step in planning care for the woman in the first stage of labor is to identify factors that may contribute to discomfort. These factors include uncomfortable positions, diaphoresis, continual leaking of amniotic fluid, a full bladder, a dry mouth, anxiety, and fear. Nursing interventions can minimize the effects of these factors. These interventions are described later in this section.

There are many types of responses to pain. The most frequent physiologic manifestations are increased pulse and respiratory rates, dilated pupils, and increased blood pressure and muscle tension. In labor, these reactions are transitory because the pain is intermittent. Increased muscle tension is most significant because it may impede the progress of labor. Women in labor frequently tighten skeletal muscles voluntarily during a contraction and remain motionless. Grimacing is also common. Verbal statements relating to pain and requests for intervention usually mean that the woman has reached her tolerance level. Vocalization may take many forms during the first stage of labor. A grunting sound typically accompanies the bearing-down effort during the second stage of labor.

Some women desire body contact during a contraction and may reach out to grasp the supporting person. As the intensity of the contraction increases with the progress of labor, the woman is less aware of the environment and may have difficulty hearing verbal instructions. The pattern of coping with labor contractions varies from the use of highly structured breathing techniques to loud vocalizations. Irritability and refusal of touch are common responses to the discomfort of the second stage of labor. The tense and frightened woman is more likely to lose control during any stage of labor.

A decrease in the intensity of discomfort is one of the goals of nursing support during labor. Nursing measures used to decrease pain include:

● Ensuring general comfort

● Decreasing anxiety

● Providing information

● Using specific supportive relaxation techniques

● Administering pharmacologic agents as ordered by the physician

### GENERAL COMFORT

General comfort measures are of utmost importance throughout labor. By relieving minor discomforts the nurse helps the woman use her coping mechanisms to deal with pain.

The woman should be encouraged to assume any position that she finds the most comfortable. A side-lying position is generally the most advantageous for the laboring woman, although frequent position changes seem to achieve more efficient contractions (Roberts et al 1983). Care should be taken that all body parts are supported, with the joints slightly flexed. For instance, when the woman is in a side-lying position, pillows may be placed against her chest and under the uppermost arm. A pillow or folded bath blanket is placed between her knees to support the uppermost leg and relieve tension or muscle strain. A pillow placed at the woman's midback also helps provide support. If the woman is more comfortable on her back, the head of the bed should be elevated to relieve the pressure of the uterus on the vena cava. Pillows may be placed under each arm and under the knees to provide support. Since a pregnant woman is at increased risk for thrombophlebitis, excessive pressure behind the knee and calf should be avoided and frequent assessment of pressure points needs to be made. Back rubs and frequent changes of position contribute to comfort and relaxation.

Diaphoresis and the constant leaking of amniotic fluid can dampen the woman's gown and bed linen. Fresh, smooth, dry bed linen promotes comfort. To avoid having to change the bottom sheet following rupture of the membranes, the nurse may replace chux at frequent intervals. The perineal area should be kept as clean and dry as possible to promote comfort as well as to prevent infection. A full bladder adds to the discomfort during a contraction and may prolong labor by interfering with the descent of the fetus. The bladder should be kept as empty as possible. Even though the woman is voiding, urine may be retained because of the pressure of the fetal presenting part. A full bladder can be detected by palpation directly over the symphysis pubis. Some of the regional procedures for analgesia during labor contribute to the inability to void, and catheterization may be necessary.

The woman may experience dryness of the oral mucous membranes. A lemon glycerine swab, popsicles, ice chips, or a wet 4 × 4 sponge may relieve the discomfort. Some prepared childbirth programs advise the woman to bring suckers to help combat the dryness that occurs with some of the breathing patterns.

Some women feel discomfort from cold feet. They may bring socks or slippers to wear to increase their comfort.

### HANDLING ANXIETY

The anxiety experienced by women entering labor is related to a combination of factors inherent to the process. A moderate amount of anxiety about the pain enhances the woman's ability to deal with the pain. An excessive degree of anxiety decreases her ability to cope with the pain.

Two ways to decrease anxiety that is not related to pain are to give information, which eases fear of the unknown, and to establish rapport with the couple, which helps them preserve their personal integrity. In addition to being a good listener, the nurse must demonstrate genuine concern for the laboring woman. Remaining with the woman as much as possible conveys a caring attitude and dispels fears of abandonment. Praise for correct breathing, relaxation efforts, and pushing efforts not only encourages repetition of the behavior but also decreases anxiety about the ability to cope with labor (Stephany 1983).

## CLIENT TEACHING

Providing information about the nature of the discomfort that will occur during labor is important. Stressing the intermittent nature and maximum duration of the contractions can be most helpful. The woman can cope with pain better when she knows that a period of relief will follow. Describing the type of discomfort and specific sensations that will occur as labor progresses helps the woman recognize these sensations as normal and expected when she does experience them.

During the second stage, the woman may interpret rectal pressure as a need to move her bowels. The instinctive response is to tighten muscles rather than bear down (push). A sensation of splitting apart also occurs in the latter part of the second stage, and the woman may be afraid to bear down. The woman who expects these sensations and understands that bearing down contributes to progress at this stage is more likely to do so.

Descriptions of sensations should be accompanied with information on specific comfort measures (Simkin 1982). Some women experience the urge to push during transition when the cervix is not fully dilated and effaced. This sensation can be controlled by panting, and instructions should be given prior to the time that panting is required.

A thorough explanation of surroundings, procedures, and equipment being used also decreases anxiety, thereby reducing pain (Frink and Chally 1984). Attachment to an electronic monitor can produce fear, because equipment of this type is associated with critically ill people. The beeps, clicks, and other strange noises should be explained, and a simplified explanation of the monitor strip should be given. The nurse can emphasize that the use of the monitor provides a more accurate way to assess the well-being of the fetus during the course of labor. In addition, the nurse can show the woman and her coach how the monitor can help them use controlled breathing techniques to relieve pain. The monitor may indicate the beginning of a contraction just seconds before the woman feels it. The woman and coach can learn how to read the tracing to identify the beginning of the contraction.

## SUPPORTIVE RELAXATION TECHNIQUES

Tense muscles increase resistance to the descent of the fetus and contribute to maternal fatigue. This fatigue increases pain perception and decreases the woman's ability to cope with the pain. Comfort measures, massage, techniques for decreasing anxiety, and client teaching can contribute to relaxation. Adequate sleep and rest are also important. The laboring woman needs to be encouraged to use the periods between contractions for rest and relaxation. A prolonged prodromal phase of labor may have prohibited sleeping. An aura of excitement naturally accompanies the onset of labor, making it difficult for the woman to sleep even though the contractions are mild and infrequent.

Distraction is another method of increasing relaxation and coping with discomfort. During early labor, conversation or activities such as light reading, cards, or other games serve as distractions. One technique that is effective for relieving moderate pain is to have the woman concentrate on a pleasant experience she has had in the past.

Touch is another type of distraction (Figure 16.1). Although some women regard touching as an invasion of privacy or threat to their independence, others want to touch and be touched during a painful experience. Nurses can make themselves available to the woman who desires touch. The nurse can place a hand on the side of the bed within the woman's reach. The person who needs touch will reach out for contact, and the nurse can pick up and follow through with this behavioral cue.

Visualization techniques enhance relaxation; with this method the woman visualizes her body relaxing, or the perineum relaxing (Nichols and Humenick 1988).

Mild to moderate abdominal discomfort during contractions may be relieved or lessened by effleurage. Back pain associated with labor may be relieved more effectively by firm pressure on the lower back or sacral area. To apply firm pressure, the nurse places her hand or a rolled, warmed towel or blanket in the small of the woman's back.

In addition to the measures just described, the nurse can enhance the woman's relaxation by providing encouragement and support for her controlled breathing techniques.

## CONTROLLED BREATHING

Controlled breathing may help the laboring woman. Used correctly, it increases the woman's pain threshold, permits relaxation, enhances the woman's ability to cope with the uterine contractions, and allows the uterus to function more efficiently.

Women usually learn Lamaze breathing in prenatal classes and practice it a number of weeks before delivery (see Table 16.1). If the woman has not learned Lamaze or another controlled breathing technique, teaching her may be difficult when she is admitted in active labor. In this instance, the nurse can teach abdominal and pant-pant-blow breathing. In abdominal breathing, the woman moves the abdominal wall upward as she inhales and downward as she exhales. This method tends to lift the abdominal wall off

## Table 16.1 Nursing Support of Breathing Techniques

Determine which breathing method the woman (couple) has learned. Provide encouragement as needed in maintaining breathing pattern. Provide support to the labor coach and assist as needed.

### LAMAZE BREATHING PATTERN CUES

#### FIRST-LEVEL BREATHING

Pattern begins and ends with a cleansing breath (in through the nose and out through pursed lips as if cooling a spoonful of hot food). While inhaling through the nose and exhaling through pursed lips, slow breaths are taken moving only the chest. The rate should be approximately 6–9/minute or 2 breaths/15 seconds. The coach or nurse may assist by reminding the woman to take a cleansing breath and then the breaths could be counted out if needed to maintain pacing. The woman inhales as someone counts "one one thousand, two one thousand, three one thousand, four one thousand." Exhalation begins and continues through the same count.

*First-level breathing pattern for use during uterine contractions. The pattern begins and ends with a cleansing breath (CB).*

#### SECOND-LEVEL BREATHING

Pattern begins and ends with a cleansing breath. Breaths are then taken in and out silently through the mouth at approximately four breaths/five seconds. The jaw and entire body needs to be relaxed. The rate can be accelerated to 2–2½ breaths/second. The rhythm for the breaths can be counted out as "one and two and one and two and . . ." with the woman exhaling on the numbers and inhaling on *and*.

*Second-level breathing pattern.*

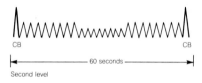

#### THIRD-LEVEL BREATHING

Pattern begins and ends with a cleansing breath. All breaths are rhythmical, in and out through the mouth. Exhalations are accompanied by a "Hee" or "Hoo" sound in a varying pattern, which begins as 3:1 (Hee Hee Hee Hoo) and can change to 2:1 (Hee Hee Hoo) or 1:1 (Hee Hoo) as the intensity of the contraction changes. The rate should not be more rapid than 2–2½/second. The rhythm of the breaths would match a "one and two and . . ." count.

*Third-level breathing pattern. Darkened "spike" represents Hoo.*

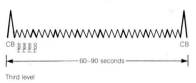

### ABDOMINAL BREATHING PATTERN CUES

The abdomen moves outward during inhalation and downward during exhalation. The rate remains slow with approximately 6–9 breaths/minute.

*Breathing sequence for abdominal breathing.*

### QUICK METHOD

When the woman has not learned a particular method and is in active phase of labor, the nurse may teach her a combination of two patterns. Abdominal breathing may be used until labor is more advanced. Then a more rapid pattern can be used consisting of two short blows from the mouth followed by a longer blow. (This pattern is called "pant pant blow" even though all exhalations are a blowing motion.)

*Pant-pant-blow breathing pattern.*

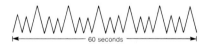

the contracting uterus and thus may provide some pain relief. The breathing is deep and rhythmical. As transition approaches, the woman may feel the need to breathe more rapidly. To avoid hyperventilation, which may occur with deep abdominal breathing, the woman can use the pant-pant-blow breathing pattern.

As the woman uses her breathing technique, the nurse can assess and support the interaction between the woman

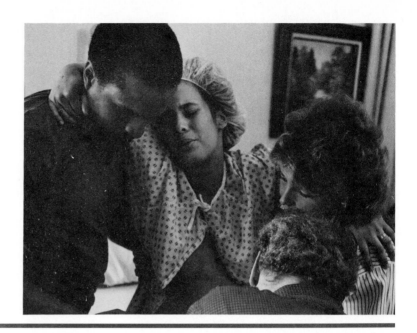

*Figure 16.1  The woman's partner provides support and encouragement during labor.*

and her coach or support person. In the absence of a coach, the nurse helps the laboring woman by helping to identify the beginning of each contraction and encouraging her as she breathes through each contraction. Continued encouragement and support with each contraction throughout labor have immeasurable benefits.

**Hyperventilation** may occur when a woman breathes very rapidly over a prolonged period of time. Hyperventilation is the result of an imbalance of oxygen and carbon dioxide (that is, too much carbon dioxide is exhaled, and too much oxygen remains in the body). The signs and symptoms of hyperventilation are tingling or numbness in the tip of nose, lips, fingers, or toes; dizziness; spots before the eyes; or spasms of the hands or feet (carpal-pedal spasms). If hyperventilation occurs, the woman should be encouraged to slow her breathing rate and to take shallow breaths. With instruction and encouragement, many women are able to change their breathing to correct the problem. Encouraging the woman to relax and counting out loud for her so she can pace her breathing during contractions are also helpful. If the signs and symptoms continue or become more severe (that is, if they progress from numbness to spasms), the woman can breathe into a paper surgical mask or a paper bag until symptoms abate. Breathing into a mask or bag causes rebreathing of carbon dioxide. The nurse should remain with the woman to reassure her.

In some instances, analgesics and/or regional anesthetic blocks may be used to enhance comfort and relaxation during labor. See Chapter 17 for a discussion of analgesia and anesthesia. Table 16.2 summarizes labor progress, possible responses of the laboring woman, and support measures.

## ● PROVISION OF CARE IN THE FIRST STAGE OF LABOR

After the admission process is completed, the nurse can help the laboring woman and her partner become comfortable with the surroundings. The nurse can also assess their individual needs and plans for this experience. As long as there are no contraindications (such as vaginal bleeding or ROM with the fetus unengaged), the woman may be encouraged to ambulate. Many women feel much more at ease and comfortable if they can move around and do not have to remain in bed. In addition, ambulation may decrease the need for analgesics, shorten labor, and decrease the incidence of FHR abnormalities (Carr 1980, McKay 1980).

The nurse will need to evaluate physical parameters of the woman and her fetus. Maternal temperature is monitored every four hours unless the temperature is over 37.5° C (99.6° F); if it is, it must be taken every two hours. Blood pressure, pulse, and respirations are monitored every hour. If the woman's blood pressure is over 140/90 mm Hg or her pulse is more than 100, the physician or nurse-midwife must be notified. The blood pressure and pulse are then reevaluated more frequently. Uterine contractions are palpated for frequency, intensity, and duration. The FHR is auscultated every 30–60 minutes as long as it remains between 120–160 beats/min. The FHR should be auscultated throughout one contraction and for about 15 seconds after the contraction to assure that there are no decelerations. If the FHR is not in the 120–160 range and/or decelerations are heard, continuous electronic monitoring is recommended (see Table 16.3).

## Table 16.2  Normal Progress, Psychologic Characteristics, and Nursing Support During First and Second Stages of Labor

| Phase | Cervical dilatation | Uterine contractions | Woman's response | Support measures |
|---|---|---|---|---|
| STAGE 1 | | | | |
| Latent phase | 1–4 cm | Every 15–30 min, 15–30 sec duration Mild intensity | Usually happy, talkative, and eager to be in labor Exhibits need for independence by taking care of own bodily needs and seeking information | Establish rapport on admission and continue to build during care. Assess information base and learning needs. Be available to consult regarding breathing technique if needed; teach breathing technique if needed and in early labor. Orient family to room, equipment, monitors, and procedures. Encourage woman and partner to participate in care as desired. Provide needed information. Assist woman into position of comfort; encourage frequent change of position; and encourage ambulation during early labor. Offer fluids/ice chips. Keep couple informed of progress. Encourage woman to void every one to two hours. Assess need for and interest in using visualization to enhance relaxation and teach if appropriate. |
| Active phase | 4–7 cm | Every three to five min, 30–60 sec duration Moderate intensity | May experience feelings of helplessness; exhibits increased fatigue and may begin to feel restless and anxious as contractions become stronger; expresses fear of abandonment Becomes more dependent as she is less able to meet her needs | Encourage woman to maintain breathing patterns; provide quiet environment to reduce external stimuli. Provide reassurance, encouragement, support; keep couple informed of progress. Promote comfort by giving backrubs, sacral pressure, cool cloth on forehead, assistance with position changes, support with pillows, effleurage. Provide ice chips, ointment for dry mouth and lips. Encourage to void every one to two hours. |

*(continues)*

### Table 16.2 Normal Progress, Psychologic Characteristics, and Nursing Support During First and Second Stages of Labor (*continued*)

| Phase | Cervical dilatation | Uterine contractions | Woman's response | Support measures |
|---|---|---|---|---|
| STAGE 1 (*continued*) | | | | |
| Transition | 8–10 cm | Every two to three min, 45–90 sec duration Strong intensity | Tires and may exhibit increased restlessness and irritability; may feel she cannot keep up with labor process and is out of control Physical discomforts Fear of being left alone May fear tearing open or splitting apart with contractions | Encourage woman to rest between contractions; if she sleeps between contractions, wake her at beginning of contraction so she can begin breathing pattern (increases feeling of control). Provide support, encouragement, and praise for efforts. Keep couple informed of progress; encourage continued participation of support persons. Promote comfort as listed above but recognize many women do not want to be touched when in transition. Provide privacy. Provide ice chips, ointment for lips. Encourage to void every one to two hours. |
| STAGE 2 | Complete | Every 1½–2 min, 60–90 sec duration Strong intensity | May feel out of control, helpless, panicky | Assist woman in pushing efforts. Encourage woman to assume position of comfort. Provide encouragement and praise for efforts. Keep couple informed of progress. Provide ice chips. Maintain privacy as woman desires. |

### Table 16.3 Nursing Assessments in the First Stage

| Phase | Mother | Fetus |
|---|---|---|
| Latent | Blood pressure, pulse, respirations q 1 hr if in normal range Temperature q 4 hr unless over 37.5°C (99.6°F) or membranes ruptured, then q 1 hr Uterine contraction q 30 minutes | FHR q 30 min if normal characteristics present (average variability, baseline in the 120–160 BPM range, without late or variable decelerations). Note fetal activity. If electronic fetal monitor in place assess for reactive NST. |
| Active | Blood pressure, pulse, respirations q 1 hr if in normal range Uterine contractions q 30 min | FHR q 15 min if normal characteristics are present. |
| Transition | Blood pressure, pulse, respiration q 30 min | FHR q 15 minutes if normal characteristics are present. |

The laboring woman may be feeling some discomfort during contractions. The nurse can assist with diversions or by repositioning the woman. The woman may begin to use her breathing method during contractions (see the preceding discussion of management of pain).

The nurse should offer fluids in the form of clear liquids and/or ice chips at frequent intervals. Because gastric-emptying time is prolonged during labor, solid foods are usually avoided.

## ACTIVE PHASE

During this phase, the contractions have a frequency of three to five minutes, a duration of 30–60 seconds, and a moderate intensity. Contractions need to be palpated every 15–30 minutes. As the contractions become more frequent and intense, vaginal exams are done to assess cervical dilatation and effacement and fetal station and position. During the active phase, the cervix dilates from 4 to 7 cm, and vaginal discharge and bloody show increase. Maternal blood pressure, pulse, and respirations should be monitored every hour (unless elevated as previously noted). The FHR is auscultated and evaluated every 15 minutes.

A woman who has been ambulatory up to this point may now wish to sit in a chair or on a bed (see Figure 16.2). If the woman wants to lie on the bed, she is encouraged to assume a side-lying position. The nurse can assist her to a position of comfort and may place pillows to support her body. To increase comfort, the nurse can give back rubs or effleurage, or place a cool cloth on the woman's forehead or across her neck. Because vaginal discharge increases, the nurse needs to change the chux frequently. Washing the perineum with warm soap and water removes secretions and increases comfort.

If the amniotic membranes have not ruptured previously, they may during this phase. When the membranes rupture, the nurse notes the color and odor of the amniotic fluid and the time of rupture, and immediately auscultates the FHR. The fluid should be clear with no odor. Fetal stress leads to intestinal and anal sphincter relaxation, and meconium may be released into the amniotic fluid. Meconium turns the fluid greenish-brown. Whenever the nurse notes meconium-stained fluid, an electronic monitor is applied to continuously assess the FHR. The time of rupture is noted because current practice suggests that delivery should occur within 24 hours of ROM. An additional concern is prolapse of the umbilical cord that occurs when membranes rupture and the fetus is not engaged. The concern is that the amniotic fluid coming through the cervix will propel the umbilical cord through the cervix (prolapsed cord). The FHR is auscultated because a drop in the rate might indicate an undetected prolapsed cord. Immediate intervention is necessary to remove pressure on a prolapsed umbilical cord (see Chapter 18). See Table 16.4 for additional deviations from normal.

## TRANSITION

During transition, the contraction frequency is every two to three minutes, duration is 60–90 seconds, and intensity is strong. Cervical dilatation increases from 8 to 10

### Table 16.4 Deviations from Normal Labor Process Requiring Immediate Intervention

| Problem | Immediate action |
| --- | --- |
| Woman admitted with vaginal bleeding or history of painless vaginal bleeding | 1. Do not perform vaginal examination.<br>2. Assess FHR.<br>3. Evaluate amount of blood loss.<br>4. Evaluate labor pattern.<br>5. Notify clinician immediately. |
| Presence of greenish amniotic fluid | 1. Continuously monitor FHR.<br>2. Evaluate dilatation status of cervix and determine whether umbilical cord is prolapsed.<br>3. Maintain woman on complete bed rest.<br>4. Notify physician/nurse-midwife immediately. |
| Absence of FHR and fetal movement | 1. Notify physician/nurse-midwife.<br>2. Provide emotional support to laboring couple (woman has an idea that "something is wrong"). |
| Prolapse of umbilical cord | 1. Relieve pressure on cord manually.<br>2. Continuously monitor FHR; watch for changes in FHR pattern.<br>3. Notify physician/nurse-midwife. |
| Woman admitted in advanced labor; delivery imminent | 1. Proceed directly to delivery room.<br>2. Obtain necessary information:<br>  a. Physician's/nurse-midwife's name<br>  b. Bleeding problems<br>  c. Obstetric problems<br>  d. FHR and maternal vital signs, if possible<br>  e. Length of labor and last time she ate<br>3. Direct ancillary personnel to telephone physician/nurse-midwife. *Do not leave woman alone.*<br>4. Provide support to couple. |

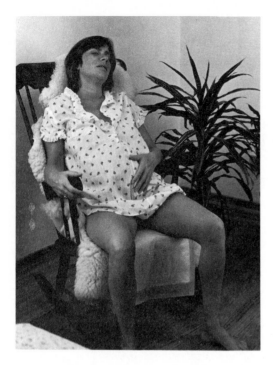

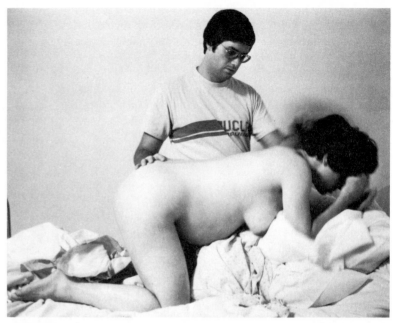

*Figure 16.2  As long as no contraindications exist, the laboring woman is encouraged to choose a position of comfort. The nurse modifies her assessments and interventions as necessary.*

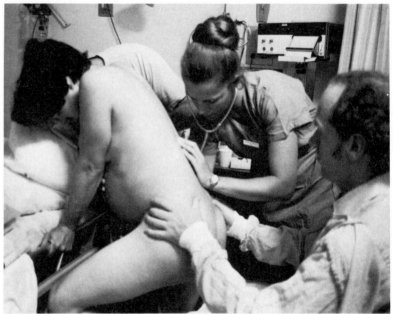

cm, effacement is complete (100%), and there is usually a heavy amount of bloody show. Contractions are palpated at least every 15 minutes. Sterile vaginal examinations are done more frequently because this stage of labor usually is accompanied by rapid change. Maternal blood pressure, pulse, and respirations are taken at least every 30 minutes, and FHR is auscultated every 15 minutes.

Comfort measures become very important in this phase of labor, but continual assessment is required to intervene appropriately. The woman may rapidly change from wanting a back rub and other "hands-on" care to wanting to be left completely alone. The support person and the nurse need to follow her cues and change interven-

tions as needed. Because the woman is breathing more rapidly, the nurse can increase her comfort by offering small spoons of ice chips to moisten her mouth or applying petroleum jelly to dry lips. The nurse can encourage the woman to rest between contractions. If analgesics have been administered, a quiet environment enhances the quality of rest between contractions. The nurse can awaken the woman just before another contraction begins so that she can begin her breathing.

Some women have difficulty maintaining control during this time and need help with their breathing. Either the support person or the nurse can breathe along with the woman during each contraction to help her maintain her pattern. It is helpful to encourage her and assure her that she is doing a good job. The woman will begin to feel increased rectal pressure as the fetal presenting part moves down the birth canal. The nurse encourages the woman to refrain from pushing until the cervix is completely dilated. This measure helps prevent cervical edema.

## ● NURSING PLAN AND IMPLEMENTATION DURING THE SECOND STAGE OF LABOR

### ● Provision of Care in the Second Stage

The second stage is reached when the cervix is completely dilated (10 cm). The uterine contractions continue as in the transition phase. Frequent sterile vaginal examinations are done to assess progress. Maternal pulse, blood pressure, and FHR are assessed every 5–15 minutes; some protocols recommend assessment after each contraction (see Table 16.5). The woman feels an uncontrollable urge to push (bear down). The nurse can help by encouraging her and by assisting with positioning (see Figure 16.3). The woman can be propped up with pillows to a semireclining position.

When the contraction begins, the nurse tells the woman to take two short breaths, then to take a third breath and hold it while pulling back on her knees and pushing down with her abdominal muscles. Some women prefer to exhale slightly, called *exhale breathing,* while pushing to avoid the physiologic effects of the Valsalva maneuver. With this method, the woman takes several deep breaths and then holds her breath for five to six seconds. Then, through slightly pursed lips, she exhales slowly every five to six

| Table 16.5 Nursing Assessments in the Second Stage | |
| --- | --- |
| **Mother** | **Fetus** |
| Blood pressure, pulse, respirations q 5–15 min | FHR after each contraction |
| Just before delivery BP between each contraction | |
| Uterine contraction palpated continuously | |

seconds while continuing to hold her breath. The woman takes another breath and continues exhale breathing and pushing during the contraction (McKay 1981).

A nullipara is usually prepared for birth when perineal bulging is noted. A multipara usually progresses much more quickly, so she may be prepared for the birth when the cervix is dilated 7–8 cm. As the birth approaches, the woman's partner or support person also prepares for the birth. (See Essential Facts to Remember—Indications of Imminent Birth.)

### ● Promotion of Comfort in the Second Stage

Most of the comfort measures that have been used during the first stage remain appropriate at this time. Cool cloths to the face and forehead may help provide cooling as the woman is involved in the intense physical exertion of pushing. The woman may feel hot and want to remove

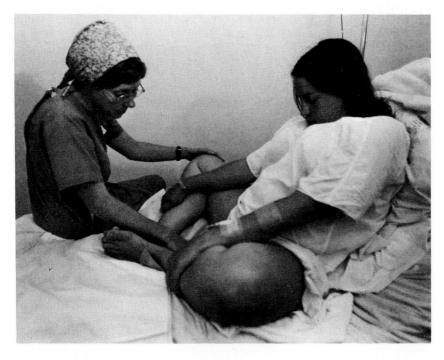

*Figure 16.3  The nurse provides support during pushing efforts.*

## Essential Facts to Remember

### Indications of Imminent Birth

Birth is imminent if the woman shows the following changes:

Bulging of the perineum

Uncontrollable urge to bear down

Increased bloody show

some of the covering. Care still needs to be taken to provide privacy even though covers are removed. The woman can be encouraged to rest and "let all muscles go" during the period between contractions. The nurse and support person(s) can assist the woman into a pushing position with each contraction to further conserve energy. Sips of fluids or ice chips may be used to provide moisture and relieve dryness of the mouth.

### PREPARATIONS IN THE BIRTHING ROOM

Couples often choose the **birthing room** for labor and delivery because of the more relaxed atmosphere maintained there. Not having to transfer a woman from the room where she has labored to a different room for delivery contributes tremendously to a relaxed atmosphere for both the woman and the nursing staff. It also avoids an uncomfortable transfer from one bed to another just before delivery. The needed equipment and supplies are brought to the birthing room when the birth is imminent.

Birthing rooms usually have birthing beds that can be adapted for delivery by removing a small section near the foot. Stirrups are available if needed or desired. In settings where birth is monitored by nurse-midwives, an ordinary double bed is often found, which prevents the use of stirrups.

There are many other factors that facilitate the relaxed, nonmedical atmosphere in the birthing room. Other family members may be in attendance in addition to the support person. They are not usually required to change into scrub attire. Good handwashing technique is required of all staff, but often they do not wear caps and masks. Sterile gloves for the physician/nurse-midwife and sterile equipment are still common, but the physician/nurse-midwife does not usually put on a sterile gown, and the use of sterile drapes is kept to a minimum. Even medical interventions for a normal birth seem minimized in a birthing room in contrast to the delivery room setting. Currently concern regarding AIDS has resulted in the use of universal precautions during birth. Health care professionals may wear gloves, aprons, and goggles.

### PREPARATIONS IN THE DELIVERY ROOM

When the birth is to occur in a delivery room, the woman will need to be transferred from the labor room shortly before birth. In some facilities the woman will be moved in her labor bed. In other facilities, the woman may be transferred from the labor bed to a cart (gurney) and then to a delivery table. No matter which transfer technique is used, safety must be provided by raising the side rails into a locked position.

Another priority is to provide privacy and preserve modesty for the laboring woman as she is pushed from her room to the delivery room. The woman is usually involved in her pushing efforts and may throw the covers off. Although she may be unaware of others at this time, after delivery she may be embarrassed that others were able to see her.

After being wheeled into the delivery room, the labor bed or transfer cart must be carefully supported against the birthing bed. This ensures the woman's safety during the transfer.

It is important that the woman move from one bed to another between contractions. During the contraction, the woman feels increased discomfort and may be involved in pushing efforts. Perineal bulging may be occurring, which adds to the discomfort and difficulty in moving. All of these factors together make moving very uncomfortable. If birth seems imminent, it is safer for the woman to deliver in her labor bed. Transfer to the delivery bed is then delayed until after the baby has been delivered and the cord has been clamped and cut.

During transfer and preparation of the woman for delivery, the woman's partner or support person is also preparing for delivery. In most facilities, the support person is required to don scrub suit, disposable boots, and perhaps cap and mask before entering the delivery room. In some facilities the nurse wears a disposable cap and mask; in other areas, no additional clothing is now required (other than the scrub suit that is donned when starting the work hours). The physician/nurse-midwife may don a sterile gown, sterile gloves, disposable hat and gloves, or some combination of this clothing.

## • Assisting the Couple and Physician/Nurse-Midwife During Birth

### MATERNAL BIRTHING POSITIONS

The woman is usually positioned for delivery on a bed, birthing chair, or delivery table. The position that the woman assumes is determined not only by her individual wishes but also by the physician/nurse-midwife.

Stirrups, if used, are padded to alleviate pressure, and both legs should be lifted simultaneously to avoid strain on

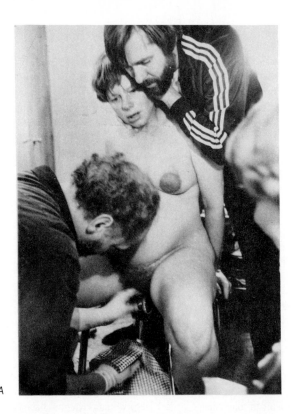

A

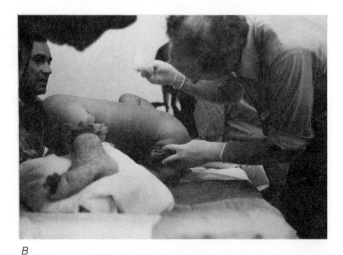

B

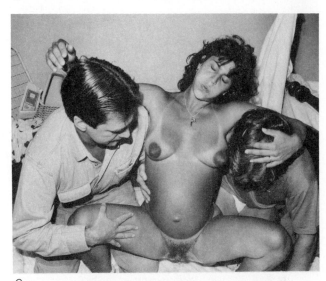

C

Figure 16.4 Birthing positions. Clockwise from upper left: (**A**) Birthing stool. (**B**) Side-lying birth. Note that the woman's upper leg is supported by her partner. (**C**) Supported squatting position used in the second stage of labor. (**D**) Use of a bar to provide support when in the squatting position. (All photos by Suzanne Arms Wimberley except photo **D**, which is used with permission of Northwest Quality Innovations, Inc.)

abdominal, back, and perineal muscles. The stirrups should be adjusted to fit the woman's legs. The feet are supported in the stirrup holders. The height and angle of the stirrups are adjusted so there is no pressure on the back of the knees or the calf, which might cause discomfort and post-partal vascular problems. The delivery table or bed is elevated 30° to 60° to help the woman bear down, and handles are provided so she may pull back on them.

The upright posture for labor and delivery was considered normal in most societies until modern times. Squatting, kneeling, standing, and sitting were variously selected for birth by women. Only within the last two hundred years has the recumbent position become more usual in the Western world. Its use in this century has been reinforced because of the convenience it offers in applying new technology. The lithotomy position has thus become the conventional manner in which North American women give birth in hospitals. In searching for alternative positions, consumers and professionals alike are refocusing on the comfort of the laboring woman rather than on the convenience of the physician/nurse-midwife (see Figure 16.4 and Table 16.6).

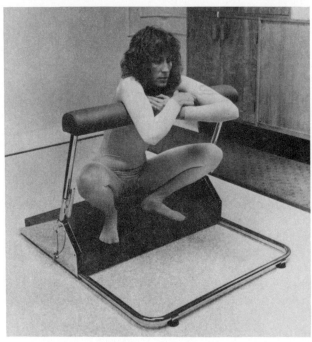

D

## Table 16.6 Comparison of Birthing Positions

| Position | Advantages | Disadvantages | Nursing implications |
|---|---|---|---|
| Sitting in birthing chair | Gravity aids descent and expulsion of infant.<br>Does not compromise venous return from lower extremities.<br>Chair can be tilted to various degrees.<br>Woman can view birth process. | If woman is short, sitting with legs spread may increase tension on perineum, which may lead to lacerations.<br>Position of body, legs, and feet cannot be altered.<br>Potential for increased blood loss (Shannahan and Cottrell 1985). | Encourage woman to tilt the chair to increase her comfort.<br>Assess for pressure points on legs. |
| Semi-Fowler's | Does not compromise venous return from lower extremities.<br>Woman can view birth process. | If legs are positioned wide apart, relaxation of perineal tissues is decreased. | Assess that upper torso is evenly supported.<br>Increase support of body by changing position of bed or using pillows as props. |
| Left lateral Sims' | Does not compromise venous return from lower extremities.<br>Increased perineal relaxation and decreased need for episiotomy.<br>Appears to prevent rapid descent. | It is difficult for the woman to see the birth if she desires. | Adjust position so that the upper leg lies on the bed (scissor fashion) or is supported by the partner or by pillows. |
| Squatting | Size of pelvic outlet is increased.<br>Gravity aids descent and expulsion of newborn.<br>Second stage may be shortened (McKay 1984). | May be difficult to maintain balance while squatting. | Help woman maintain balance.<br>Use a squatting bar if available. |
| Sitting in birthing bed | Gravity aids descent and expulsion of the fetus.<br>Does not compromise venous return from lower extremities.<br>Woman can view the birth process.<br>Leg position may be changed at will. | | Assure that legs and feet have adequate support. |

## CLEANSING THE PERINEUM

After the woman has been positioned for the birth, her vulvar and perineal area is cleansed to increase her comfort and to remove the bloody discharge that is present prior to the actual birth. An aseptic technique such as the one that follows is recommended.

After thoroughly washing her hands, the nurse opens the sterile prep tray, dons sterile gloves, and cleanses the woman's vulva and perineum with the cleansing solution (Figure 16.5). Some agency policies dictate the area be rinsed with sterile water. Beginning with the mons, the area is cleansed up to the lower abdomen. The second sponge is used to cleanse the inner groin and thigh of one leg, and the third one is used to cleanse the other leg, moving outward to avoid carrying material from surrounding areas to the vaginal outlet. The last three sponges are used to cleanse the labia and vestibule with one downward sweep each. The used sponges are then discarded.

The labor coach is given a stool to sit on if desired. Both the woman and the coach are kept informed of procedures and progress and are supported throughout the birth.

The woman's blood pressure and the FHR are monitored between contractions, and the contractions are palpated until the birth. The nurse continues to assist the woman in her pushing efforts.

In addition to assisting the woman and her partner, the nurse also assists the physician or nurse-midwife in preparing for the birth. The physician or nurse-midwife dons a sterile gown and gloves and places sterile drapes over the woman's abdomen and legs. An episiotomy may

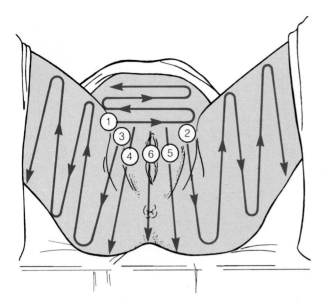

*Figure 16.5  Cleansing the perineum prior to birth. The nurse follows the numbered diagram, using a new sponge for each area.*

be done just before birth if there is a need for one. See the discussion of episiotomy in Chapter 19.

The woman is encouraged to push with the contractions until the fetal chin clears the perineum. Then she is asked to pant to avoid too rapid a delivery of the fetal head. While supporting the fetal head, the physician or nurse-midwife assesses whether the umbilical cord is around the fetal neck and removes it if it is, and then suctions the mouth and nose with a bulb syringe. The mouth is suctioned first to prevent reflex inhalation of mucus when the sensitive nares is touched with the bulb syringe tip. The woman is encouraged to push again as the rest of the body is born. Figures 16.6 to 16.15 depict the birth experience of one family.

## ● PROVISION OF INITIAL CARE TO THE NEWBORN

The physician/nurse-midwife places the newborn on the mother's abdomen or in the radiant heated unit. The newborn is maintained in a modified Trendelenburg position. This position aids drainage of mucus from the nasopharynx and trachea by gravity. The newborn is dried immediately. Warmth can be maintained by placing warmed blankets over the newborn or placing the newborn in skin-to-skin contact with the mother. If the newborn is in a radiant heated unit, he or she is dried, placed on a dry blanket, and left uncovered under the radiant heat. Because radiant heat warms the outer surface of objects, a newborn wrapped in blankets will receive no benefit from radiant heat.

The newborn's nose and mouth are suctioned with a bulb syringe as needed.

Most immediate care of the newborn can be accomplished while the newborn is in the parent's arms or in the radiant heated unit.

## APGAR SCORING SYSTEM

The Apgar scoring system (Table 16.7) was designed in 1952 by Dr. Virginia Apgar. The purpose of the **Apgar score** is to evaluate the physical condition of the newborn at birth and the immediate need for resuscitation. The newborn is rated one minute after birth and again at five minutes and receives a total score ranging from 0 to 10 based on the following criteria:

1.  The *heart rate* is auscultated or palpated at the junction of the umbilical cord and skin. This is the most important assessment. A newborn heart rate of less than 100 beats/min indicates the need for immediate resuscitation.

2.  The *respiratory effort* is the second most important Apgar assessment. Complete absence of respirations is termed *apnea*. A vigorous cry indicates adequate respirations.

3.  The *muscle tone* is determined by evaluating the degree of flexion and resistance to straightening of the extremities. A normal newborn's elbows and hips are flexed, with the knees positioned up toward the abdomen.

4.  The *reflex irritability* is evaluated by stroking the baby's back along the spine, or by flicking the soles of the feet. A cry merits a full score of 2. A grimace is 1 point, and no response is 0.

### Table 16.7  The Apgar Scoring System

| Sign | Score 0 | Score 1 | Score 2 |
|---|---|---|---|
| Heart rate | Absent | Slow—below 100 | Above 100 |
| Respiratory effort | Absent | Slow—irregular | Good crying |
| Muscle tone | Flaccid | Some flexion of extremities | Active motion |
| Reflex irritability | None | Grimace | Vigorous cry |
| Color | Pale blue | Body pink, blue extremities | Completely pink |

Source: Apgar V: The newborn (Apgar) scoring system, reflections and advice. *Pediatr Clin North Am* August 1966; 13:645.

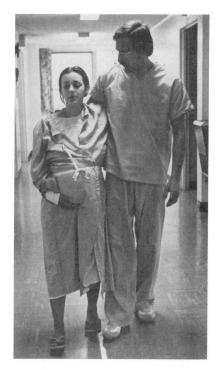

Figure 16.6   Woman and her husband walking in the hospital during labor.

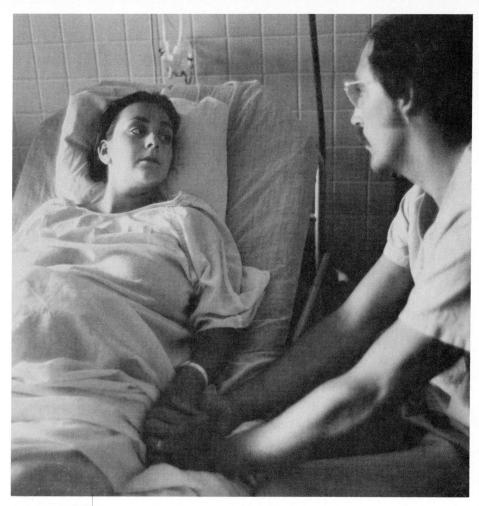

Figure 16.7   The husband coaches his wife during a contraction.

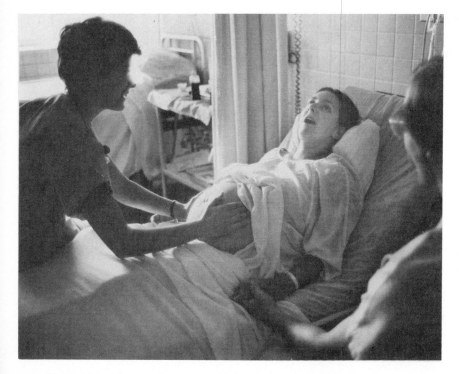

Figure 16.8   The attending nurse-midwife assesses a contraction.

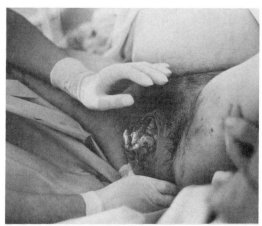

Figure 16.9   The baby's head is crowning.

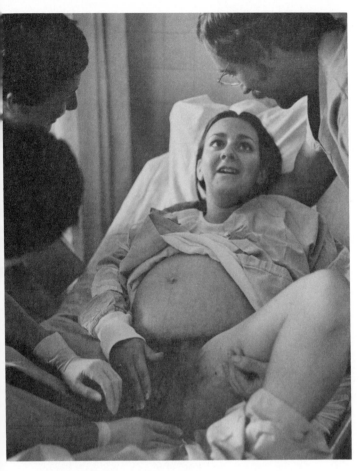

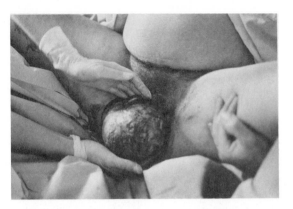

Figure 16.11 *The nurse-midwife holds the baby's head as it is born.*

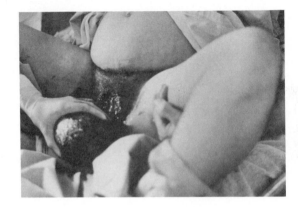

Figure 16.10 *The mother can feel her baby's head crowning.*

Figure 16.12 *The baby's head is born.*

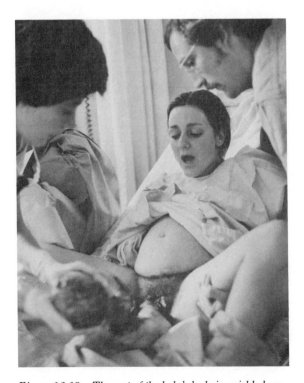

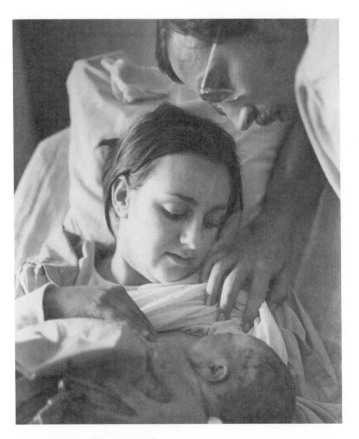

Figure 16.13 *The rest of the baby's body is quickly born.*

Figure 16.14 *The new family*

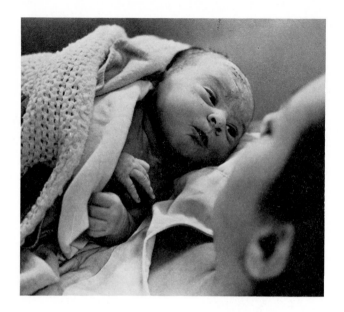

*Figure 16.15   The baby gets acquainted with his mother.*

5. The *skin color* is inspected for cyanosis and pallor. Generally, newborns have blue extremities, and the rest of the body is pink, which merits a score of 1. This condition is termed *acrocyanosis* and is present in 85% of normal newborns at one minute after birth. A completely pink newborn scores a 2 and a totally cyanotic, pale infant is scored 0. Newborns with darker skin pigmentation will not be pink in color. Their skin color is assessed for pallor and acrocyanosis, and a score is selected based on the assessment.

A score of 8–10 indicates a newborn in good condition who requires only nasopharyngeal suctioning and perhaps some oxygen near the face (called "blow-by" oxygen). If the Apgar score is below 8, resuscitative measures may need to be instituted. See the discussion in Chapter 24.

## CARE OF UMBILICAL CORD

If the clinician has not placed some type of cord clamp (Figure 16.16) on the newborn's umbilical cord, it is the responsibility of the nurse to do so. Before applying the cord clamp, the nurse examines the cut end for the presence of two arteries and one vein. The umbilical vein is the largest vessel, and the arteries are seen as smaller vessels. The number of vessels is recorded on the delivery room and newborn records. The cord is clamped approximately ½–1 inch from the abdomen to allow room between the abdomen and clamp as the cord dries. Abdominal skin must not be clamped, as this will cause necrosis of the tissue. The most common types of cord clamps include the plastic Hollister cord clamp, the metal Hesseltine clamp,

and the cord bander. The Hollister clamp is removed in the newborn nursery approximately 24 hours after the cord has dried. The rubber band that remains on the umbilical cord stump if a cord bander is used will remain in place until the cord falls off.

## PHYSICAL ASSESSMENT OF NEWBORN BY NURSE

An abbreviated systematic physical assessment is performed by the nurse in the birthing area to detect any abnormalities (Table 16.8). First, the size of the newborn and the contour and size of the head in relationship to the rest of the body are noted. The newborn's posture and movements indicate tone and neurologic functioning.

The skin is inspected for discoloration, presence of

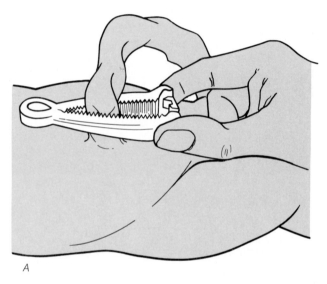

A

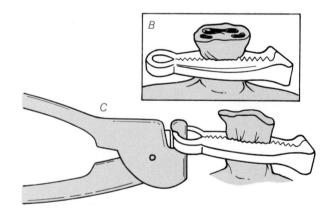

*Figure 16.16   Hollister cord clamp. (**A**) Clamp is positioned ½–1 inch from the abdomen and then secured. (**B**) Cut cord. The one vein and two arteries can be seen. (**C**) Plastic device for removing clamp after cord has dried. After the clamp is cut, the nurse grasps the clamp on either side of the cut area and gently separates the Hollister clamp.*

## Table 16.8   Initial Newborn Evaluation

| Assess | Normal findings |
|---|---|
| Respirations | Rate 30–60, irregular<br>No retractions, no grunting |
| Apical pulse | Rate 120–160 and somewhat irregular |
| Temperature | Skin temp above 97.8°F (36.5°C) |
| Skin color | Body pink with bluish extremities (acrocyanosis) |
| Umbilical cord | Two arteries and one vein |
| Gestational age | Should be 38–42 weeks to remain with parents for extended time |
| Sole creases | Sole creases that involve the heel |

In general expect: scant amount of vernix on upper back, axilla, groin, lanugo only on upper back; ears with incurving of upper ⅔ of pinnae and thin cartilage that springs back from folding; male genitalia—testes palpated in upper or lower scrotum; female genitalia—labia majora larger, clitoris nearly covered.

In the following situations, newborns should generally be stabilized rather than remaining with parents in the birth area for an extended period of time:

*Apgar is less than 8 at one minute and less than 9 at five minutes, or a baby requires resuscitation measures (other than whiffs of oxygen).*
Respirations are below 30 or above 60, with retractions and/or grunting.
Apical pulse is below 120 or above 160 with marked irregularities.
Skin temperature is below 97.8°F (36.5°C).
Skin color is pale blue, or there is circumoral pallor.
Baby is less than 38 or more than 42 weeks' gestation.
Baby is very small or very large for gestational age.
There are congenital anomalies involving open areas in the skin (meningomyelocele).

vernix caseosa and lanugo, and evidence of trauma and desquamation. Vernix caseosa is a white, cheesy substance found normally on newborns. It is absorbed within 24 hours after delivery. Vernix is abundant on preterm infants and absent on postterm newborns. A large quantity of fine hair (lanugo) is often seen on preterm newborns, especially on their shoulders, foreheads, backs, and cheeks. Desquamation of the skin is seen in postterm newborns.

The nares are observed for flaring. As the newborn cries, the palate can be inspected for cleft palate. The presence of mucus in the nose and mouth can be assessed and removed with the bulb syringe as needed. The chest is inspected for respiratory rate and the presence of retractions. If retractions are present, the newborn is assessed for grunting or stridor. A normal respiratory rate is 30–40 per minute. The lungs may be auscultated bilaterally for breath sounds. Absence of breath sounds on one side could mean pneumothorax. Rales may be heard immediately after birth because a small amount of fluid may remain in the lungs; this fluid will be absorbed. Rhonchi indicate aspiration of oral secretions. If there is excessive mucus or respiratory distress, the nurse suctions the newborn with a DeLee suction. (See Procedure 16.1, DeLee Suction, and Figure 16.17.)

The elimination of urine or meconium is noted and recorded on the newborn record.

### NEWBORN IDENTIFICATION

To ensure correct identification, the nurse gives the mother and the newborn matching identification bands in the delivery room. One bracelet is placed on the mother's wrist. Two bracelets are placed on the newborn—one on the wrist and one on the ankle. The newborn bands must be applied snugly to prevent their loss.

Most hospitals footprint the newborn and fingerprint the mother for further identification purposes. To prepare the newborn for footprinting, the nurse wipes the soles of both the newborn's feet to remove any vernix caseosa.

### ● Assisting with Leboyer Birth

In a conventional delivery, the newborn is subjected to extreme changes in sensory input—bright lights, voices, suctioning, and being quickly dried and placed in blankets. In 1975 Frederick Leboyer introduced a birthing technique that eases the newborn's transition to extrauterine life.

In the **Leboyer method,** the lights in the delivery

## Procedure 16.1

## DeLee Suction

| Objective | Nursing Action | Rationale |
|---|---|---|
| Clear secretions from newborn's nose and/or oropharynx. | Put on disposable gloves for suctioning the newborn. | |
| | Tighten the lid on the DeLee mucus trap collection bottle (Figure 16.17). | Avoids spillage of secretions and prevents air from leaking out of lid. |
| | Place the whistle tip into a tubing connected to low suction on a wall suction unit; insert other end of tubing in newborn's nose or mouth approximately 3–5 in. | Provides suction. Clears nasopharynx. |
| | Continue suction as tube is removed. | Gives gentle suction. Avoids redepositing secretions in newborn's nasopharynx. Facilitates removal of secretions. |
| | Continue reinserting tube and providing suction for as long as: 1. Secretions are being removed. 2. Newborn continues to have depressed respirations. 3. Movement of secretion can be heard with respiratory effort by auscultation of lungs. | |
| | Occasionally the tube may be passed into the newborn's stomach to remove secretions or meconium that was swallowed before birth; if this action is needed, insert tube into newborn's mouth and then into the stomach. | If meconium was present in amniotic fluid, the baby may have swallowed some. Secretions and/or meconium aspirate may be removed from newborn's stomach to decrease incidence of aspiration of stomach contents. |
| | Provide suction and continue suction as tube is removed. | |

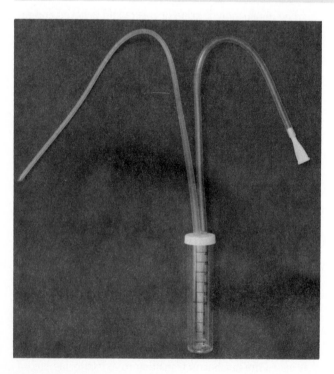

*Figure 16.17   DeLee suction trap*

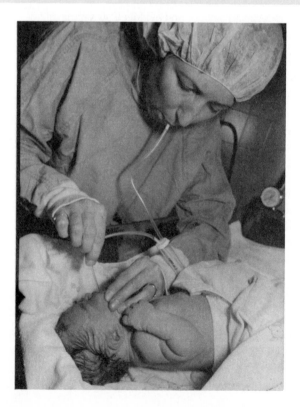

room are dimmed, and the noise level, including talking, is kept to a minimum. After delivery the newborn is placed on his or her stomach on the mother's bare abdomen. The mother is encouraged to gently stroke and touch the newborn in a massaging motion.

Clamping of the umbilical cord is delayed until all pulsations have ceased out of respect for the innate rhythms of the new life. Leboyer (1976) believes that this delay helps the newborn's initial respiratory efforts and shelters the newborn from anoxia at the time of birth. After the umbilical cord is clamped, the newborn is gently and slowly placed in a water bath that has been warmed to 98–99° F. The newborn remains in the bath until he or she is completely relaxed. The warm water recreates the temperature and weightlessness of the womb. Following the bath the infant is carefully and gently dried and wrapped in layers of warm blankets.

Critics of the Leboyer method question the ability of the physician/nurse-midwife to quickly assess maternal and/or neonatal complications or calculate Apgar scores in a dimly lit room. Traditional practitioners have expressed concern about the possibility of high neonatal bilirubin levels when cord clamping is delayed. Hypothermia as a result of the bath is also cited as a risk of the Leboyer method. On the other hand, proponents and couples themselves cite the advantages: increased participation by the father in the birth—particularly when he gives the bath—and the serenity of the birth experience.

## • NURSING PLAN AND IMPLEMENTATION DURING THE THIRD AND FOURTH STAGES

### • Provision of Care in the Third Stage

After birth, the physician or nurse-midwife prepares for the delivery of the placenta (see Chapter 14). The following signs suggest placental separation:

1. The uterus rises upward in the abdomen because the placenta settles into the lower uterine segment.
2. As the placenta moves downward, the umbilical cord lengthens.
3. A sudden trickle or spurt of blood appears.
4. The shape of the uterus changes from a disk to a globe.

While waiting for these signs, the nurse palpates the uterus to check for ballooning of the uterus caused by uterine relaxation and subsequent bleeding into the uterine cavity.

After the placenta has separated, the woman may be asked to bear down to aid delivery of the placenta.

Oxytocics are frequently given at the time of the delivery of the placenta, so the uterus will contract and bleeding will be minimized. Oxytocin (Pitocin), 10 units, may be added to an intravenous infusion or given by slow intravenous push. Some physicians may order methylergonovine maleate (Methergine), 0.2 mg, intramuscularly. In addition to administering the ordered medications, the nurse assesses and records maternal blood pressure before and after administration of oxytocics. (For further information, refer to the Drug Guides—Oxytocin in Chapter 19 and Methylergonovine Maleate in Chapter 26.)

### • Provision of Care in the Fourth Stage

After the delivery of the placenta, the physician or nurse-midwife inspects the placental membranes to make sure they are intact and that all cotyledons are present. This inspection is especially important with Duncan placentas because there is an increased risk that placental fragments are left in the uterus. If there is a defect or a part missing from the placenta, a manual uterine examination is done.

The time of delivery of the placenta and the mechanism (Schultze or Duncan) are noted on the delivery record.

The vagina and cervix are inspected for lacerations, and any necessary repairs are made. The episiotomy may be repaired now if it has not been done previously. (See further discussion of episiotomy in Chapter 19.) The fundus of the uterus is palpated; normal position is at the midline and below the umbilicus. A displaced fundus may be caused by a full bladder or blood collected in the uterus. The uterus may be emptied of blood by grasping it with one hand anteriorly and posteriorly and squeezing.

The uterine fundus is palpated at frequent intervals to ensure that it remains firmly contracted. The maternal blood pressure is monitored at 5–15-minute intervals to detect any changes. An increase in blood pressure may be due to oxytocic drugs. A decrease may be associated with excessive blood loss.

The nurse washes the woman's perineum with gauze squares and warmed solution and dries the area with a sterile towel before placing the maternity pads. If stirrups have been used the woman's legs are removed from the stirrups at the same time to avoid muscle strain. The legs may be bicycled to help circulation return. The woman remains in the same bed or is transferred to a recovery room bed, and the nurse helps her don a clean gown. The mother may feel cold and begin shivering. She can be covered with a warmed bath blanket and a second blanket. The nurse ensures that the mother, father, and newborn are provided with time to begin the attachment process. (See Chapter 26 for further discussion of attachment.)

During the recovery period (one to four hours) the woman is monitored closely. Deviations from normal in vital signs require frequent checking. Blood pressure should return to the prelabor level due to an increased volume of blood returning to the maternal circulation from the uteroplacental shunt. Pulse rate should be slightly lower than it

## Table 16.9  Maternal Adaptations Following Birth

| Characteristic | Normal finding |
| --- | --- |
| Blood pressure | Should return to prelabor level |
| Pulse | Slightly lower than in labor |
| Uterine fundus | In the midline at the umbilicus or one to two fingerbreadths below the umbilicus |
| Lochia | Red (rubra), small to moderate amount (from spotting on pads to ¼–½ of pad covered in 15 minutes); should not exceed saturation of one pad in first hour |
| Bladder | Nonpalpable |
| Perineum | Smooth, pink, without bruising or edema |
| Emotional state | Wide variation, including excited, exhilarated, smiling, crying, fatigued, verbal, quiet, pensive, and sleepy |

tion. The nurse palpates the bladder to determine whether it is distended. The bladder fills rapidly with the extra fluid volume returned from the uteroplacental circulation (and with fluid received intravenously, if given during labor and birth). The postpartal woman may not realize that her bladder is full because trauma to the bladder and urethra during childbirth and the use of regional anesthesia decreases bladder tone and the urge to void.

All measures should be taken to enable the mother to void. A warm towel placed across the lower abdomen or warm water poured over the perineum may relax the urinary sphincter and thus facilitate voiding. If the woman is unable to void, catheterization is necessary.

The perineum is inspected for edema and hematoma formation. An ice pack often reduces the swelling and alleviates the discomfort of an episiotomy.

Frequently women have tremors in the immediate postpartal period. This shivering response may be caused by a difference in internal and external body temperatures (higher temperature inside the body than on the outside). Another theory is that the woman is reacting to the fetal cells that have entered the maternal circulation at the placental site. A heated bath blanket placed next to the woman tends to alleviate the problem.

was during labor. Baroreceptors cause a vagal response, which slows the pulse. A rise in the blood pressure may be a response to oxytocic drugs or may be caused by PIH. Blood loss may be reflected by a lowered blood pressure and a rising pulse rate (see Table 16.9).

The fundus should be firm at the umbilicus or lower and in the midline. It is palpated (Figure 16.18) but not massaged unless it is soft (boggy). If it becomes boggy or appears to rise in the abdomen, the fundus is massaged until firm; then the nurse exerts firm pressure on the fundus in an attempt to express retained clots. During all aspects of fundal massage, the nurse uses one hand to provide support for the lower portion of the uterus.

The nurse inspects the bloody vaginal discharge for amount and charts it as minimal, moderate, or heavy and with or without clots. This discharge, or **lochia rubra,** should be bright red. A soaked perineal pad contains approximately 100 mL of blood. If the perineal pad becomes soaked in a 15-minute period or if blood pools under the buttocks, continuous observation is necessary. When the fundus is firm, a continuous trickle of blood may signal laceration of the vagina or cervix, or an unligated vessel in the episiotomy. See Essential Facts to Remember—Immediate Postdelivery Danger Signs.

If the fundus rises and displaces to the right, the nurse must be concerned about two factors. First, as the uterus rises, the uterine contractions become less effective and increased bleeding may occur. Second, the most common cause of uterine displacement is bladder disten-

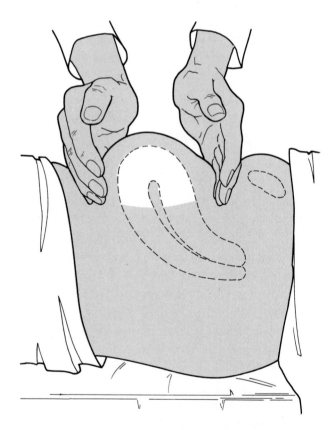

*Figure 16.18  Suggested method of palpating the fundus of the uterus during the fourth stage. The left hand is placed just above the symphysis pubis, and gentle downward pressure is exerted. The right hand is cupped around the uterine fundus.*

The couple may be tired, hungry, and thirsty. Some agencies serve the couple a meal. The tired mother will probably drift off into a welcomed sleep. The father should also be encouraged to rest, since his supporting role is tiring physically and mentally. The mother is usually transferred from the birthing unit to the postpartal or mother-baby area after two hours or more, depending on agency policy and whether the following criteria are met:

- Stable vital signs
- No bleeding
- Nondistended bladder
- Firm fundus
- Sensations fully recovered from any anesthetic agent received during delivery

## ● *Enhancing Attachment*

Dramatic evidence indicates that the first few hours and even minutes after birth are an important period for the **attachment** of mother and infant (Klaus and Kennell 1982). Separation during this period not only delays attachment but may affect maternal and child behavior over a much longer period.

Klaus and Kennell (1982) believe the bonding experience can be enhanced by at least 30–60 minutes of early contact in privacy. If this period of contact can occur during the first hour after birth, the newborn will be in the quiet state and able to interact with parents by looking at them. Newborns also turn their heads in response to a spoken voice. (See Chapter 21 for further discussion of newborn states.)

The first parent-newborn contact may be brief (a few minutes) to be followed by a more extended contact after uncomfortable procedures (delivery of the placenta and suturing of the episiotomy) are completed. When the newborn is returned to the mother, she can be assisted to begin breast-feeding if she so desires. The nurse can help the mother to a more comfortable position for holding the infant and breast-feeding. Even if the newborn does not actively nurse, he or she can lick, taste, and smell the mother's skin. This activity by the newborn stimulates the maternal release of prolactin, which promotes the onset of lactation.

Darkening the birthing or delivery room by turning out most of the lights causes newborns to open their eyes and gaze around. This in turn enhances eye-to-eye contact with the parents. (*Note:* If the physician or nurse-midwife needs a light source, the spotlight can be left on.) Treatment of the newborn's eyes may also be delayed. Many parents who establish eye contact with the newborn are content to quietly gaze at their infant. Others may show more active involvement by touching and/or inspecting the newborn. Some mothers talk to their babies in a high-pitched voice, which seems to be soothing to newborns. Some couples verbally express amazement and pride when they see they have produced a beautiful, healthy baby. Their verbalization enhances feelings of accomplishment and ecstasy. Figure 16.19 shows a new parent establishing bonds with his newborn son.

Both parents need to be encouraged to do whatever they feel most comfortable doing. Some parents prefer only limited contact with the newborn immediately after birth and instead desire private time together in a quiet environment. In spite of the current zeal for providing immediate attachment opportunities, nursing personnel need to be aware of parents' wishes. The desire to delay interaction with the newborn does not necessarily imply a decreased ability of the parents to bond to their newborn (see Chapter 26 for further discussion of parent-newborn attachment).

## Essential Facts to Remember

### Immediate Postdelivery Danger Signs

In the immediate postdelivery recovery period, the following conditions should be reported to the physician or nurse-midwife:

Hypotension

Tachycardia

Uterine atony

Excessive bleeding

Hematoma

## *One Family's Story*

*Allison and Scott Jones are expecting their first child. During the pregnancy, they have attended prenatal classes and made special preparations in anticipation of using the birthing room at their local hospital. The pregnancy has proceeded without difficulty or problems.*

*When labor begins, they go to the hospital and are greeted by Marie Carlson, a nurse in the birthing center. Ms Carlson helps Allison and Scott get settled and completes the admission process. Allison is having contractions every two to three minutes lasting 45 seconds, and cervical dilatation is 5 cm. She is breathing with the contractions and is excited that the day of birth is at hand.*

*Ms Carlson works to provide a comfortable, unhurried atmosphere. She is already acquainted with the Joneses because they have attended the prenatal classes that she teaches. She is familiar with their level of knowledge and will now*

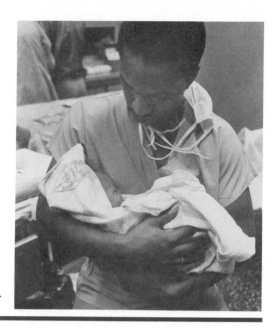

*Figure 16.19   A father holds his newborn son.*

work to support them as labor progresses. She notes that Allison and Scott are working well together in timing contractions and using relaxation techniques and breathing methods. Ms Carlson completes her physical assessment, then talks with the couple about the progress. Ms Carlson leaves, letting the Joneses know she is available whenever they need her. She has found that parents who use the birthing room are well prepared and that she may not need to stay quite so close. She returns periodically to assess progress and to see how the Joneses are coping with the labor. As long as all is going well, she allows the couple privacy. She has notified the physician, who is now on the way to the hospital, of Allison's admission and labor status.

As Allison proceeds into transition, Ms Carlson notes that the Joneses need more encouragement and support, so she stays in constant attendance. She assesses maternal, fetal, and labor status and keeps the Joneses informed of their progress.

Dr JG Grey comes in to see the Joneses and stays close by because the labor is progressing rapidly. Toward the end of the transition, Ms Carlson prepares the equipment to be used during the birth. She assists Allison in her pushing efforts when the cervix has completely dilated. During the birth, she assists Allison, Scott, and Dr Grey. The birth is monitored in the same unhurried manner. Ms Carlson assesses the physical parameters and offers continuing support as Allison gives birth to a baby girl of healthy appearance. Ms Carlson assesses the newborn quickly and then places her in her mother's arms.

The postdelivery recovery period is monitored closely so that any problems can be identified. Allison is recovering without problems and is eager to learn more about her new daughter. Ms Carlson talks to the Joneses to assess their level of knowledge and provides information that is needed. She does a physical assessment of the newborn and explains the findings to the Joneses. She assists Allison as she breast-feeds her baby for the first time. Ms Carlson continues frequent assessments of the mother and baby.

During the recovery period, she provides quiet time for the new family to be together and get acquainted.

A few hours after birth, Ms Carlson assists the Joneses as they prepare for early discharge. She will be making a visit to the Joneses' home the next morning to assess the mother and newborn and to provide information and continued support.

## • NURSING PLAN AND IMPLEMENTATION DURING PRECIPITOUS BIRTH

Occasionally labor progresses so rapidly that the maternity nurse is faced with the task of assisting in the actual birth of the baby. This is called a **precipitous birth**. The attending maternity nurse has the primary responsibility for providing a physically and psychologically safe experience for the woman and her baby.

A woman whose physician or nurse-midwife is not present may feel disappointed, frightened, abandoned, angry, and cheated. She may fear what is going to happen and feel that everything is out of control. In working with the woman the nurse provides support by keeping her informed about the labor progress and assuring her that the nurse will stay with her. If birth is imminent, the nurse must not leave the mother alone. Auxiliary personnel can be directed to contact the physician or nurse-midwife and to retrieve the emergency birth pack ("precip pack"). An emergency birth pack should be readily accessible to the birthing rooms. A typical pack contains the following items:

1. A small drape that can be placed under the woman's buttocks to provide a sterile field

2. A bulb syringe to clear mucus from the newborn's mouth

3. Two sterile clamps (Kelly or Rochester) to clamp the umbilical cord before applying a cord clamp

4. Sterile scissors to cut the umbilical cord

5. A sterile umbilical cord clamp, either Hesseltine or Hollister

6. A baby blanket to wrap the newborn in after birth

7. A package of sterile gloves

As the materials are being gathered, the nurse must remain calm. The woman is reassured by the composure of the nurse and feels that the nurse is competent.

The nurse assists in the precipitous birth as follows. The woman is encouraged to assume a comfortable position. If time permits, the nurse scrubs her hands with soap and water and puts on sterile gloves. Sterile drapes are placed under the woman's buttocks.

At all times during the birth, the nurse provides suggestions such as when to maintain a controlled breathing pattern and when to push, supports the woman's efforts, and provides reassurance.

The nurse may place an index finger inside the lower portion of the vagina and the thumb on the outer portion of the perineum and gently massage the area to aid in stretching of perineal tissues and to help prevent perineal lacerations. This is called "ironing the perineum."

When the infant's head crowns, the nurse instructs the woman to pant, which decreases her urge to push. The nurse checks whether the amniotic sac is intact. If it is, the nurse tears the sac so the newborn will not breathe in amniotic fluid with the first breath.

With one hand, the nurse applies gentle pressure against the fetal head to prevent it from popping out rapidly. *The nurse does not hold the head back forcibly.* Rapid birth of the head may result in tears in the woman's perineal tissues. In the fetus the rapid change in pressure within the fetal head may cause subdural or dural tears. The nurse supports the perineum with the other hand and allows the head to be born between contractions.

As the woman continues to pant, the nurse inserts one or two fingers along the back of the fetal head to check for the umbilical cord. If there is a **nuchal cord** (umbilical cord around the neck), the nurse bends her fingers like a fish hook, grasps the cord, and pulls it over the baby's head. It is important to check that the cord is not wrapped around more than one time. If the cord is tightly looped and cannot be slipped over the baby's head, two clamps are placed on the cord, the cord is cut between the clamps, and the cord is unwound.

Immediately after birth of the head, the mouth, throat, and nasal passages are suctioned. The nurse places one hand on each side of the head and exerts gentle downward traction until the anterior shoulder passes under the symphysis pubis. At this time, gentle upward traction helps the birth of the posterior shoulder. The nurse then instructs the woman to push gently so that the rest of the body can be born quickly. The newborn must be supported as it emerges.

The newborn is held at the level of the uterus to facilitate blood flow through the umbilical cord. The combination of amniotic fluid and vernix makes the newborn very slippery, so the nurse must be careful to avoid dropping the newborn. The nose and mouth of the newborn are suctioned again, using a bulb syringe. The nurse then dries the newborn to prevent heat loss.

As soon as the nurse determines that the newborn's respirations are adequate, the infant can be placed on the mother's abdomen. The newborn's head should be slightly lower than the body to aid drainage of fluid and mucus. The weight of the newborn on the mother's abdomen stimulates uterine contractions, which aid in placental separation. The umbilical cord should not be pulled.

The nurse is alert for signs of placental separation (slight gush of dark blood from the vagina, lengthening of the cord, or a change in uterine shape from discoid to globular). When these signs are present, the mother is instructed to push so that the placenta can be delivered. The nurse inspects the placenta to determine whether it is intact.

The nurse checks the firmness of the uterus. The fundus may be gently massaged to stimulate contractions and to decrease bleeding. Putting the newborn to breast also stimulates uterine contractions through release of oxytocin from the pituitary gland.

The umbilical cord may now be cut. Two sterile clamps are placed approximately 1–3 inches from the newborn's abdomen. The cord is cut between them with sterile scissors. A sterile cord clamp (Hollister or Hesseltine) can be placed adjacent to the clamp on the newborn's cord, between the clamp and the newborn's abdomen. The clamp *must not* be placed snugly against the abdomen, because the cord will dry and shrink.

The area under the mother's buttocks is cleaned, and her perineum is inspected for lacerations. Bleeding from lacerations may be controlled by pressing a clean perineal pad against the perineum and instructing the woman to keep her thighs together.

If the physician's arrival is delayed or if the newborn is having respiratory distress, the newborn should be transported immediately to the nursery. *The newborn must be properly identified before he or she leaves the birth area.*

## ● Record Keeping

The following information is noted and placed on a delivery record:

1. Position of fetus at birth
2. Presence of cord around neck or shoulder (nuchal cord)
3. Time of birth
4. Apgar scores at one and five minutes after birth
5. Sex of newborn
6. Time of delivery of the placenta
7. Method of placental expulsion
8. Appearance and intactness of placenta
9. Mother's condition
10. Any medications that were given to mother or newborn (per agency protocol)

## ● EVALUATION

Evaluation provides an opportunity to determine the effectiveness of nursing care. As a result of comprehensive nursing care during the intrapartal period the following outcomes may be anticipated:

- The mother's physical and psychologic well-being has been maintained and supported.

- The baby's physical and psychologic well-being has been protected and supported.

- The couple have had input into the birth process and have participated as much as they desired.

- The mother and her baby have had a safe birth.

## ESSENTIAL CONCEPTS

- **Admission to the birth setting involves assessment of many physiologic and psychologic factors. The information gained helps the nurse establish priorities of care.**

- **Before care is begun it is important to explain what will be done, the reasons, potential benefits and risks, and possible alternatives if appropriate. This helps the woman determine what happens to her body.**

- **Behavioral responses to labor vary with the phase of labor, the preparation the woman has had, and her previous experience, cultural beliefs, and developmental level.**

- **The adolescent has special needs in the birth setting. Her developmental needs require specialized nursing care.**

- **Each woman's cultural beliefs affect her needs for privacy, expression of discomfort, and expecta-**

tions for the birth and the role she wishes the father to play in the birth event.

- **The laboring woman's comfort may be increased by general comfort measures, supportive relaxation techniques, methods of handling anxiety, controlled breathing, and support by a caring person.**

- **The laboring woman fears being alone during labor. Even if there is a support person available, the woman's anxiety will be decreased when the nurse remains with her.**

- **Maternal birthing positions include a wide variety of possibilities, from side-lying to sitting, squatting, and lying flat.**

- **Immediate assessments of the newborn include evaluation of the Apgar score and an abbreviated physical assessment. These early assessments help determine the need for resuscitation and whether the newborn's adaptation to extrauterine life is progressing normally. The newborn who is not experiencing problems may remain with the parents for an extended period of time following birth.**

- **Immediate care of the newborn following birth also includes maintenance of respirations, promotion of warmth, prevention of infection, and accurate identification.**

- **The new parents and their baby are given time together as soon as possible after birth.**

- **Nursing assessments continue after the birth and are important to assure that normal physiologic adaptations are happening after birth.**

### References

Apgar V: The newborn (Apgar) scoring system: Reflections and advice. *Pediatr Clin North Am* August 1966; 13:645.

Calhoun MA: The Vietnamese woman: Health/illness attitudes and behaviors. In: *Women, Health and Culture.* Stern PN (editor). Washington DC: Hemisphere, 1986.

Carr KC: Obstetric practices which protect against neonatal morbidity: Focus on maternal position in labor and birth. *Birth Fam J* Winter 1980; 7:249.

Frink BB, Chally P: Managing pain responses to cesarean childbirth. *Am J Mat Child Nurs* July/August 1984; 9(4):270.

Higgins PG, Wayland JR: Labour and delivery in North America. *Nurs Times* September 1981 (Midwifery Suppl) 77.

Hollingsworth AO et al: The refugees and childbearing: What to expect. *RN* November 1980; 43:45.

Kay MA: The Mexican American. In: *Culture Childbearing Health Professionals.* Clark AL (editor). Philadelphia: Davis, 1978.

Klaus MH, Kennell JH: *Parent-Infant Bonding,* 2nd ed. St. Louis: Mosby, 1982.

LaDu EB: Childbirth care for Hmong families. *Am J Mat Child Nurs* November/December 1985; 10:382.

Leboyer F: *Birth Without Violence.* New York: Knopf, 1976.

Mahan CS, McKay S: Preps and enemas: Keep or discard? *Contemp OB/GYN* November 1983; 22(5):241.

McKay SR: Maternal position during labor and birth: A reassessment. *J Obstet Gynecol Neonatal Nurs* 1980; 9:288.

McKay SR: Second stage labor: Has tradition replaced safety? *Am J Nurs* 1981; 81:1061.

McKay SR: Squatting: An alternate position for the second stage of labor. *Am J Mat Child Nurs* May/June 1984; 8:181.

Morrow K: Transcultural midwifery: Adapting to Hmong birthing customs in California. *J Nurse-Midwifery* November/December 1986; 31:285.

Murillo-Rohde I: Cultural sensitivity in the care of the Hispanic patient. *Wash State J Nurs* 1979 (Special Suppl):25.

Nichols FH, Humenick SS: *Childbirth Education: Practice, Research and Theory.* Philadelphia: Saunders, 1988.

Roberts JE, Mendez-Bauer C, Wodell DA: The effects of maternal position on uterine contractility and efficiency. *Birth* Winter 1983; 10(4):243.

Shannahan MB, Cottrell BH: Effect of birth chair on duration of second stage labor, fetal outcome and maternal blood loss. *Nurs Res* March/April 1985; 34:89.

Simkin P: Preparing parents for second stage. *Birth* Winter 1982; 9(4):229.

Stephany T: Supporting the mother of a patient in labor. *J Obstet Gynecol Neonatal Nurs* September/October 1983; 12(5):345.

## Additional Readings

Cottrell BH, Shannahan MK: A comparison of fetal outcome in birth chair and delivery table births. *Res Nurs Health* 1987; 10(4):239.

Flagler S: Maternal role competence. *West J Nurs Res* 1988; 10(3):274.

Gilson GJ et al: Expectant management of premature rupture of membranes at term in a birthing center setting. *J Nurse-Midwifery* May/June 1988; 33(3):134.

Goldman B: Home Birth: "We did it, all of us." *Can Med Assoc J* 1988; 139(8):773.

Isenberg SJ et al: Source of the conjunctival bacterial flora at birth and implications for ophthalmia neonatorum prophylaxis. *Am J Ophthalmol* 1988; 106(4):458.

Lomas J et al: The labor and delivery satisfaction index: The development and evaluation of a soft outcome measure. *Birth* September 1987; 14(3):125.

McKay S, Mahan C: How can aspiration of vomitus in obstetrics best be prevented? *Birth* December 1988; 15(4):222.

McKay S, Mahan C: Modifying the stomach contents of laboring women: Why and how; success and risks. *Birth* December 1988; 15(4):213.

Nodine PM, Robert J: Factors associated with perineal outcome during childbirth. *J Nurse-Midwifery* May/June 1987; 32(3):123.

Poma PA: Pregnancy in Hispanic women. *J Nat Med Assoc* 1987; 79:929.

Roberts J et al: A descriptive analysis of involuntary bearing down efforts during the expulsive phase of labor. *J Obstet Gynecol Neonatal Nurs* January/February 1987; 16(1):48.

Shearer M: Commentary: How well does the LADSI measure satisfaction with labor and delivery? *Birth* September 1987; 14(3):130.

Vansintejan GA, Glaser WA: Wibangbe: The making of a documentary about the training and supervision of traditional birth attendants in Zaire. *J Nurse-Midwifery* November/December 1988; 33(6):280.

Weller, RH, Eberstein IW, Bailey M: Pregnancy wantedness and maternal behavior during pregnancy. *Demography* 1987; 24(3):407.

# 17

# Maternal Analgesia and Anesthesia

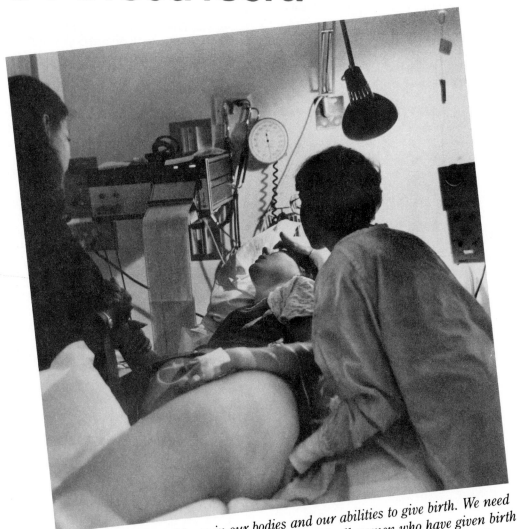

*What we need is confidence in our bodies and our abilities to give birth. We need to reclaim the past by feeling our connection with all women who have given birth before us, and know that our bodies know and are equal to the task at hand.*
(Pregnant Feelings)

## Objectives

● Describe the use of systemic drugs to promote pain relief during labor.

● Identify the major types of regional analgesia and anesthesia, including area affected, advantages, disadvantages, techniques, and nursing implications.

● Discuss the complications of regional anesthesia that may occur.

● Describe the major inhalation and intravenous anesthetics used to provide general anesthesia.

● Describe the major complications of general anesthesia.

## Key Terms

caudal block
epidural block
local infiltration
paracervical block
pudendal block
regional anesthesia
spinal block

The management of pain during childbirth is an important aspect of the health care of the childbearing woman. Pain relief measures vary from breathing techniques, effleurage, and positive reinforcement (discussed in Chapter 16), to regional nerve blocks. The type of analgesics and anesthetics used during each woman's labor and delivery will depend on the preferences of the woman and the physician or nurse-midwife as well as the physical condition of the mother and fetus.

## ● SYSTEMIC DRUGS

The goal of pharmacologic pain relief during labor is to provide maximal analgesia at minimal risk for the mother and fetus. To reach this goal, clinicians must consider a number of factors:

● All systemic drugs used for pain relief during labor cross the placental barrier by simple diffusion, but some drugs cross more readily than others.

● Drug action in the body depends on the rate at which the substance is metabolized by liver enzymes and excreted by the kidneys.

● High drug doses remain in the fetus for long periods because the fetal liver enzymes and kidney excretion are inadequate to metabolize analgesic agents.

## ● Nursing Care

Nursing interventions directed toward pain relief begin with nonpharmacologic measures such as providing information, support, and physical comfort. Back rubs, the application of cool cloths, and encouragement as the woman practices breathing techniques are examples of comfort measures. Some laboring women need no further interventions. However, for other women, the progression of labor brings increasing discomfort that interferes with their ability to perform breathing techniques and maintain a sense of control. In this instance, pharmacologic analgesics may be used to decrease discomfort, increase relaxation, and reestablish the woman's sense of control.

Because analgesic drugs affect the woman, fetus, and contraction pattern, the nurse must assess the following areas before administering medication:

## MATERNAL ASSESSMENT

- The woman is willing to receive medication after being advised about it.
- Vital signs are stable.

## FETAL ASSESSMENT

- The fetal heart rate (FHR) is between 120 and 160 beats/minute, and no late or variable decelerations are present.
- Short-term variability is present and long-term variability is average.
- The fetus exhibits normal movement and accelerations are present with fetal movement.
- The fetus is at term.
- Meconium staining is not present.

## ASSESSMENT OF LABOR

- Contraction pattern is well established.
- The cervix is dilated at least 4–5 cm in nulliparas and 3–4 cm in multiparas.
- The fetal presenting part is engaged.
- There is progressive descent of the fetal presenting part. No complications are present.

If these normal parameters are not present further assessment will be necessary.

The general guidelines for administering analgesic drugs are as follows:

1. The woman is in an individual labor/birthing room.
2. The environment is free from sensory stimuli, such as bright lights, noise, and irrelevant conversation, to allow the woman to focus on the drug action.
3. An explanation of the effects of the medication is given, including how long the effects will last and how the drug will make the woman feel. See Essential Facts to Remember—What Women to Know About Pain Relief Medication.
4. The woman is encouraged to empty her bladder prior to administration of the drug.
5. The baseline FHR and maternal vital signs are recorded on nurse's notes and on the monitor strip prior to administration.
6. The physician/nurse-midwife's written order is checked, and the medication prepared and signed out on the narcotic or control sheet.
7. The woman is asked again if she is allergic to any medication and her arm band is checked for identification.

## Essential Facts to Remember

### What Women Need to Know About Pain Relief Medications

Before receiving medications, the woman should understand:

- Type of medication administered
- Route of administration
- Expected effects of medication
- Implications for fetus/neonate
- Safety measures needed (for example, remain in bed with side rails up)

8. The drug is administered by the route ordered, using correct technique.
9. The side rails are pulled up for safety, and the reason explained to the woman.
10. The medication, dosage, time, route, and site of administration are charted on the nurse's notes and on the monitor strip.
11. The FHR is monitored to assess the effects of the medication on the fetus, and the woman is evaluated for signs that the analgesic agent is having the desired effect.
12. The woman is not left alone. If no family member is present and it is necessary for the nurse to leave, the woman should be given a short explanation and assurances that the nurse will be available when needed.

There is no completely safe and satisfactory method of pain relief. Analgesia, when judiciously used, can be beneficial to the laboring woman and do little harm to the fetus. The woman who is free from fear and who has confidence in the medical and nursing personnel usually has a relatively comfortable first stage of labor and requires a minimum of medication. A positive, supportive, caring attitude on the part of the professional nurse and the expectant parents is an essential aspect of pain relief.

## ● Analgesics

### MEPERIDINE HYDROCHLORIDE

Meperidine hydrochloride (Demerol) is a narcotic analgesic frequently used for obstetric analgesia.

The intravenous route is preferred to intramuscular injection because it results in prompt, smooth, and more predictable action. In order to reduce the total drug dose necessary to achieve the desired analgesic effect, McDonald (1985) recommends titrated intravenous administration. Using this technique, the initial dose is 25 mg injected through a 25-gauge needle over a period of approximately one minute. Smaller intravenous doses are subsequently given as necessary to maintain analgesia. See Drug Guide—Meperidine Hydrochloride for further discussion and nursing implications.

## BUTORPHANOL TARTRATE

Butorphanol tartrate (Stadol) is a synthetic analgesic. It effectively relieves moderate to severe pain. The exact mechanism of the drug is unknown, but it is thought to act on the subcortical portion of the central nervous system.

The recommended initial dose is 2 mg intramuscularly

---

## ◈ Drug Guide

# Meperidine Hydrochloride (Demerol)

### Overview of Obstetrical Action

Meperidine hydrochloride is a narcotic analgesic that interferes with pain impulses at the subcortical level of the brain. In addition, it enhances analgesia by altering the physiologic response to pain, suppressing anxiety and apprehension, and creating a euphoric feeling. Meperidine hydrochloride is used during labor to provide analgesia. Peak analgesia occurs in 40 to 60 minutes with intramuscular and in five to seven minutes with intravenous administration. Duration is two to four hours. Administration after labor has reached the active phase does not appear to delay labor or decrease uterine contraction frequency or duration. Meperidine HCl crosses the placental barrier and appears in the fetus one to two minutes after maternal intravenous injection (Briggs et al 1986).

*Route, Dosage, Frequency*
*IM:* 50 to 100 mg every three to four hours

*IV:* 25 to 50 mg by slow intravenous push every three to four hours

*Maternal Contraindications*
Hypersensitivity to meperidine, asthma

Central nervous system (CNS) depression

Respiratory depression

Fetal distress

Preterm labor if delivery is imminent

Hypotension

Respirations <12 per minute

Concurrent use with anticonvulsants may increase depressant effects

*Maternal Side Effects*
Respiratory depression

Nausea and vomiting, dry mouth

Drowsiness, dizziness, flushing

Transient hypotension

Tachycardia, palpitations

Convulsions (Karch and Boyd 1989)

*Effect on Fetus/Neonate*
Neonatal respiratory depression may occur if delivery occurs 60 minutes or longer after administration of the drug to the mother; incidence of respiratory depression peaks at two to three hours after administration (Briggs et al 1986).

Neonatal hypotonia, lethargy, interference of thermoregulatory response.

Neurologic and behavioral alterations for up to 72 hours after delivery; presence of meperidine in neonatal urine up to three days following delivery (Briggs et al 1986).

May have depressed attention and social responsiveness for first six weeks of life (Briggs et al 1986).

### Nursing Considerations

Assess the woman's history, labor and fetal status, maternal blood pressure, and respirations to identify contraindications to administration.

Intramuscular doses should be injected deeply to avoid irritation to subcutaneous tissue.

Intravenous doses should be diluted and administered slowly.

Provide for the woman's safety by instructing her to remain on bed rest, by keeping side rails up, and placing call bell within reach.

Evaluate effect of drug (comfort and relaxation are enhanced, woman is able to rest between contractions).

Observe for maternal side effects.

Observe newborn for respiratory depression; be prepared to initiate resuscitative measures and administer antagonist naloxone if needed.

every three to four hours. If it is given intravenously, however, the dosage is reduced.

Butorphanol tartrate has limited respiratory depressant effects, but, in individuals with respiratory diseases, the respiratory depression may be pronounced. Other side effects include sedation, nausea, dizziness, and a clammy, sweaty sensation.

It has a potential to elevate cerebrospinal fluid pressure. Because butorphanol has a weak narcotic antagonistic activity, it may cause withdrawal symptoms in individuals who have been receiving opiates.

The specific antidote is naloxone (Narcan), which may be given intravenously, intramuscularly, or subcutaneously.

## ● Narcotic Antagonists

Narcotic antagonists counteract the respiratory depressant effects of the opiate-type narcotics. The most commonly used narcotic antagonists include levallorphan tartrate (Lorfan) and naloxone.

### LEVALLORPHAN

The narcotic antagonist levallorphan tartrate is effective only against neonatal respiratory depression caused by narcotic analgesics. This antagonist acts by competing with narcotics in the respiratory center receptors and by displacing the narcotic molecules from the receptor sites. If the receptors are not occupied solely by narcotics, this antagonist agent produces respiratory depression by occupying these sites. Therefore, levallorphan increases depression caused by barbiturates, tranquilizers, and other sedative drugs.

When a narcotic antagonist is needed, levallorphan 1 mg may be administered to the laboring woman intravenously, five to ten minutes before delivery to prevent respiratory depression of the newborn.

### NALOXONE

Naloxone exhibits little pharmacologic activity in the absence of narcotics. Naloxone is an antagonist with little or no agonistic effect.

Unlike levallorphan, naloxone can be used to reverse the mild respiratory depression following small doses of opiates. The drug is useful for respiratory depression caused by fentanyl, alpha-prodine, morphine, and meperidine as well as pentazocine and butorphanol (American Society of Hospital Pharmacists 1985). *Naloxone is the drug of choice when the depressant is unknown because it will cause no further depression.* Although the agent may be given to the mother prior to delivery, many physicians feel it is preferable to wait and administer naloxone to the depressed infant. In this way the exact dose is known and the

infant's response to the agent can be readily assessed. For neonatal dosage see Drug Guide—Narcan in Chapter 24.

When naloxone is given, other resuscitative measures and trained personnel should be readily available. The duration of the drug is shorter than the analgesic drug it is acting as an antagonist for, so the nurse must be alert to the return of respiratory depression and the need for repeated doses. Naloxone should be given with caution in women with known or suspected opiate dependency because it may precipitate severe withdrawal.

## ● Ataractics

Ataractic drugs do not relieve pain but do decrease apprehension and anxiety, relieve nausea, and enhance the effects of narcotics. Ataractics frequently used in labor include promethazine hydrochloride (Phenergan), hydroxyzine hydrochloride (Vistaril), and diazepam (Valium).

## ● Sedatives

The principal use of barbiturates in current obstetric practice is in false labor or in the early stages of beginning labor. An oral dose of secobarbital (Seconal) or pentobarbital (Nembutal) promotes relaxation and allows the woman to sleep a few hours. The woman can then enter the active phase of labor in a more relaxed and rested state.

## ● REGIONAL ANESTHESIA

**Regional anesthesia** is achieved by injecting local anesthetic agents so that they come into direct contact with nervous tissue. The methods most commonly used in labor are paracervical block, peridural block (lumbar epidural and caudal), subarachnoid block (spinal for cesarean birth, low spinal for vaginal delivery—also known as *saddle block*), pudendal block, and local infiltration (see Table 17.1). The nerve blocks are accomplished by a single injection or continuously by means of an in-dwelling plastic catheter.

Regional anesthesia has gained widespread popularity in recent years and is particularly compatible with the goals of psychoprophylactic preparation for childbirth. In general, the advantages of a regional anesthesia are as follows:

1. Relief from discomfort is complete in the area blocked.

2. Depression of maternal vital signs rarely occurs.

3. Aspiration of gastric contents is virtually eliminated if no additional sedative was administered.

4. Administration at the optimal time does not significantly alter the course of labor.

5. The woman remains alert and able to participate in the birth.

## Table 17.1 Summary of Regional Blocks

| Type of block | Administration | When given | Effect of block | Major disadvantages | Nursing considerations |
|---|---|---|---|---|---|
| Paracervical | Local anesthetic agent injected transvaginally adjacent to the outer rim of cervix | When in active labor; may be repeated | Relieves pain of cervical dilatation, does not anesthetize lower vagina or perineum | Associated with fetal bradycardia | Assess maternal BP and pulse and FHR. Assure continuous FHR tracing. Assess maternal bladder. |
| Epidural block | Local anesthetic injected into epidural space | When in active labor; may be used as a continuous block | Relieves discomfort of uterine contractions and fetal descent and anesthetizes the perineum | Maternal hypotension | Assess maternal BP and pulse and FHR for baseline. Use electronic fetal monitor (EFM) for continuous tracing. Assess maternal BP, pulse every one to two min during the first 15 min after the injection and every 10–15 min until stable. Assess bladder at frequent intervals for distention past birth. Delay ambulation until all motor control has returned. Assess for orthostatic hypotension. |
| Spinal block | Local anesthetic agent injected into spinal fluid in the spinal canal | Given late in the second stage for vaginal birth; may be used as anesthesia for cesarean birth | Anesthesia for birth (vaginal or cesarean) | Maternal hypotension, headache, need to remain flat for 6–12 hr after birth | Assess maternal vital signs (VS) and FHR for baseline. Assist with positioning during administration. Assess for presence of uterine contraction and inform anesthesiologist. Place wedge under right hip to tip uterus off vena cava. Assess maternal BP and pulse and FHR every two to five min until stable. Continue to monitor contractions. Provide safety and prevent injury when moving woman. Maintain bedrest for 6–12 hr following birth. |

*(continues)*

## Table 17.1 Summary of Regional Blocks *(continued)*

| Type of block | Administration | When given | Effect of block | Major disadvantages | Nursing considerations |
|---|---|---|---|---|---|
| Pudendal block | Local anesthetic agent injected around pudendal nerve | In late second stage (just prior to the birth of the infant) | Perineal anesthesia for birth and episiotomy repair | Broad ligament hematoma | Provide support. Assess for development of hematoma. |
| Local infiltration | Local anesthetic injected in perineal tissues | At time of birth (just prior to the birth of the infant) | Perineal anesthesia for repair of episiotomy or lacerations | Large amounts of local used | Provide support. Assess for perineal trauma (swelling, bruising). |

The disadvantages include:

1. A high degree of skill is required for proper administration of most regional anesthetics.

2. Failures such as no effect or unilateral or incomplete anesthesia can occur even when the agents are administered by experienced clinicians.

3. Some agents have side effects.

4. Systemic toxic reactions to these agents are more common than to agents used for general anesthesia.

Prerequisites for the administration of regional anesthetics are knowledge of the anatomy and physiology of pertinent structures, techniques of administration, the pharmacology of local anesthetics, and potential complications. With the exception of nurse anesthetists and nurse-midwives, who may perform procedures for which they have been trained, nurses in the United States may *not* legally administer anesthetic agents. This restriction applies to the reinjection of agents through in-dwelling catheters. However, the nurse must have an adequate knowledge of all aspects of regional anesthesia to provide support and to give appropriate reinforcing explanations to the woman. The nurse who has a thorough understanding of the techniques and agents can also provide more efficient assistance to the administrator. Client safety is increased when the nurse recognizes complications and immediately initiates appropriate intervention.

Pain associated with the first stage of labor can be relieved by blocking the sensory nerves supplying the uterus with the techniques of paracervical and peridural (lumbar epidural and caudal) blocks. Pain associated with the second stage and birth can be alleviated with pudendal, peridural, and subarachnoid (spinal, low spinal, and saddle) blocks (Figure 17.1).

### ● Regional Anesthetic Agents

Two types of local anesthetic agents are currently available—the ester and amide types. The ester type includes procaine hydrochloride (Novocain), chloroprocaine hydrochloride (Nesacaine), and tetracaine hydrochloride (Pentocaine). Esters are rapidly metabolized; therefore, toxic maternal levels are not as likely to be reached, and placental transfer to the fetus is prevented. Amide types include lidocaine hydrochloride (Xylocaine), mepivacaine hydrochloride (Carbocaine), and bupivacaine hydrochloride (Marcaine). Amide types are more powerful and longer-acting agents. They readily cross the placenta, can be measured in the fetal circulation, and affect the fetus for a prolonged period.

Regional anesthetic agents block the conduction of nerve impulses from the periphery to the central nervous system. Although the mechanism of their action is not fully understood, the smaller the fiber, the more sensitive it is to local anesthetics. The small fibers that conduct the sensations of pain, temperature, pressure, and touch can be blocked without affecting the large, heavily myelinated fibers that continue to maintain muscle tone, position sense, and motor function (Albright et al 1986).

Absorption of local anesthetics depends primarily on the vascularity of the area of injection. The agents also contribute to increased blood flow by causing vasomotor paralysis. Higher concentration of drugs causes greater vasodilatation. Good maternal physical condition or a high metabolic rate aids absorption. Malnutrition, dehydration, electrolyte imbalance, and cardiovascular and pulmonary problems lower the threshold for toxic effects. The pH of tissues affects the rate of absorption, which has implications for fetal complications. The addition of vasoconstrictors such as epinephrine delays absorption and prolongs the anesthetic effect. Recent studies have demonstrated that epinephrine decreases uteroplacental blood flow, making it an undesirable additive in many situations. The breakdown of local anesthetics in the body is accomplished by the liver and plasma esterase, with the resulting substance being eliminated by the kidneys.

*The weakest concentration and the smallest amount necessary to produce the desired results are advocated.*

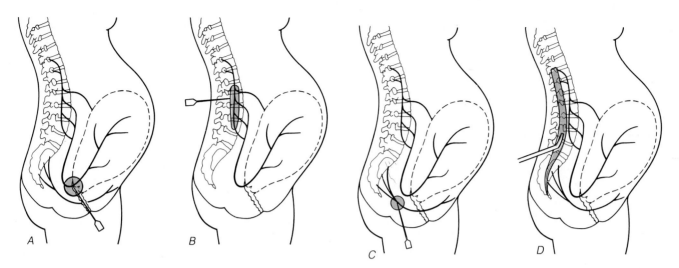

*Figure 17.1   Schematic diagram showing pain pathways and sites of interruption: (**A**) Paracervical block: Relief of uterine pain only. (**B**) Lumbar sympathetic block: Relief of uterine pain only. (**C**) Pudendal block: Relief of perineal pain. (**D**) Lumbar epidural block: Dark area demonstrates peridural space and nerves affected, and white tube represents continuous plastic catheter. (From Bonica JJ:* Principles and Practice of Obstetric Analgesia and Anesthesia. *Philadelphia: Davis, 1972, pp 492, 512, 521, and 614.)*

## ADVERSE MATERNAL REACTIONS

Reactions to local anesthetic agents range from mild symptoms to cardiovascular collapse. Mild reactions include palpitations, vertigo, tinnitus, apprehension, confusion, headache, and a metallic taste in the mouth. Moderate reactions include more severe degrees of mild symptoms plus nausea and vomiting, hypotension, and muscle twitching, which may progress to convulsions and loss of consciousness. The severe reactions are sudden loss of consciousness, coma, severe hypotension, bradycardia, respiratory depression, and cardiac arrest. Local toxic effects on tissues may also result from high concentrations of the agents. Because of the possibility of adverse reactions, especially hypotension, anesthetic agents should not be used unless an intravenous line is in place.

## ● Paracervical Block

A **paracervical block** is the result of a local anesthetic agent injected transvaginally adjacent to the outer rim of the cervix. The agent may be administered during the active phase of labor. This measure relieves the pain of cervical dilatation but does not anesthetize the lower vagina or perineum (Figure 17.2).

Paracervical block has several disadvantages. The vascularity of the injection area increases the possibility of rapid absorption, with resulting systemic toxic reaction. Hematomas may occur as a result of uterine vessel damage. In addition, fetal bradycardia frequently occurs. Because of the high incidence of fetal bradycardia and de-

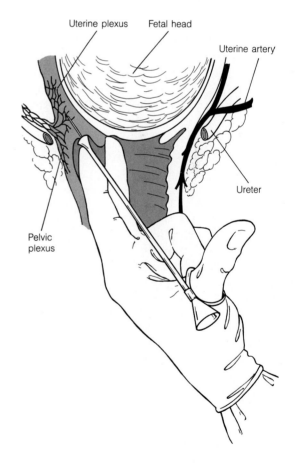

*Figure 17.2   Technique for paracervical block from needle in place at appropriate distance beyond guide (From Bonica JJ:* Principles and Practice of Obstetric Analgesia and Anesthesia. *Philadelphia: Davis, 1972, p 515.)*

creased variability, paracervical blocks are no longer in common use.

## ● Lumbar Epidural Block

A lumbar **epidural block** provides regional anesthesia during the first and second stages of labor. The area of the body affected depends on the amount of anesthetic that is injected.

The epidural (peridural) space is a potential space between the ligamentum flavum and the dura mater. The space extends from the base of the skull to the end of the sacral canal (Figure 17.3). Access to the space may be through the lumbar or caudal area. A lumbar epidural block is most frequently continuous, providing analgesia and anesthesia from active labor through episiotomy repair (Figure 17.4).

Once a woman is in active labor, a small amount of local anesthetic agent injected in the lumbar epidural space will relieve the discomfort of uterine contractions. A larger dose is given late in the first stage to extend anesthesia to the vagina, relieving the pain caused by the descent of the fetus. An additional dose may be given to provide anesthesia in the perineum during birth.

Advantages of the lumbar epidural block include:

1. It may be given in active phase of labor.
2. Provides effective and often complete relief of pain/discomfort from uterine contractions and cervical dilatation.
3. Enhances rest and relaxation.
4. Enhances woman's ability to cope because the source of discomfort is removed.

The lumbar epidural block has several disadvantages:

1. Considerable skill is required to administer epidural blocks.
2. A larger amount of anesthetic agent is required and the dura mater may be punctured, resulting in an inadvertent spinal anesthesia.
3. Maternal hypotension and resulting FHR late decelerations may occur.
4. Perineal relaxation may interfere with fetal rotation and the ability to bear down, and a forceps delivery may be needed.

Epidural anesthesia is contraindicated when maternal hemorrhage is present or likely to occur, when there is local infection at the site of injection (such as pilonidal cyst), and when there is central nervous system, cardiac, or pulmonary disease.

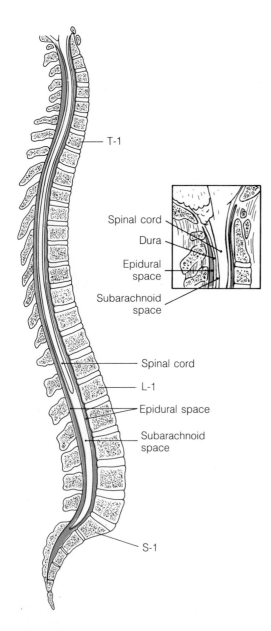

*Figure 17.3  Epidural space*

### NURSING ROLE

The nurse assesses the maternal vital signs and the FHR for a baseline. The procedure and expected results are explained, and the woman's questions are answered. The woman is positioned on her left side, shoulders parallel, with her legs slightly flexed; or she may be assisted to a sitting position, with her back arched and her feet supported on a stool. As the anesthetic agent is injected the woman may feel a burning, prickly, or warm sensation in her legs. Maternal blood pressure and pulse must be taken every one to two minutes during the first 15 minutes after the injection and every 10–15 minutes thereafter until they are stable. The most common side effect of epidural anesthesia is hypotension. Some clinicians attempt to prevent hypotension by infusing 500–1000 mL of solution in-

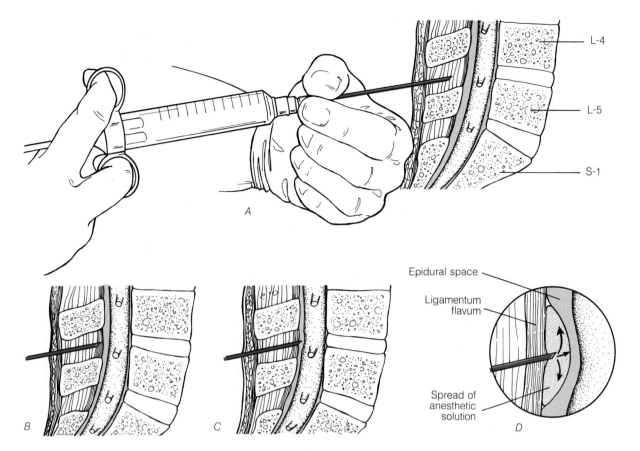

L-4

L-5

S-1

*A*

*B*

*C*

Epidural space

Ligamentum
flavum

Spread of
anesthetic
solution

*D*

*Figure 17.4    Technique for epidural block: (A) Proper position of insertion, (B) Needle in the ligamentum flavum, (C) Tip of needle in epidural space, (D) Force of injection pushing dura away from tip of needle. (From Bonica JJ:* Principles and Practice of Obstetric Analgesia and Anesthesia. *Philadelphia: Davis 1972, p 631.)*

travenously at a rapid rate. If hypotension occurs, the nurse assists with corrective measures such as positioning the woman in a left side-lying position, increasing the flow rate of the intravenous infusion, and administering oxygen. The FHR should be assessed continuously during any hypotensive episode.

The bladder is assessed at frequent intervals because the epidural block lessens the urge to urinate. During the second stage of labor, the woman may also require more assistance with pushing, since she cannot feel her contractions and does not experience the urge to push.

Headache (as occurs with spinal blocks) is *not* a side effect of epidural anesthesia, because the dura mater of the spinal canal has not been penetrated and there is no leakage of spinal fluid. Therefore, lying flat for a prescribed number of hours after delivery is not required. Ambulation should be delayed, however, until the anesthesia has worn off. This may take several hours, depending on the agent and the total dose. Motor control of the legs is weak but not totally absent after delivery. Return of

complete sensation and the ability to control the legs are essential before ambulation is attempted.

To assess sensation the nurse can touch various parts of the woman's legs to determine if the touch can be felt. Motor control may be evaluated by asking the woman to raise her knees, to lift her feet (one at a time) off the bed, and/or to dorsiflex her foot. Even though assessments may indicate that sensation and motor control have returned, care should be taken to support the woman as she stands. The nurse needs to be ready to support the woman's weight and quickly return her to bed if motor control is inadequate. In addition, blood pressure assessments assist the nurse in determining the safety of ambulation. Blood pressure is assessed while the woman is lying down, then sitting in the bed. As long as the blood pressure values remain stable (no evidence of orthostatic hypotension), a standing blood pressure is assessed. It is advisable to have additional assistance when the woman stands for the first time, to maintain safety. See Nursing Care Plan— Regional Anesthesia for further nursing actions.

*(Text continues on page 466.)*

# Nursing Care Plan

## Regional Anesthesia—Lumbar Epidural

### Client Assessment

#### Nursing History

Maternal information
1. Allergies to drugs (especially anesthetic agents)
2. Psychologic status
   a. What kind of anesthesia does woman want and what kind will she accept?
   b. Does she understand the procedure?
   c. What does she expect it to accomplish?
   d. Is she able to cope with the labor process, and can she follow directions?
3. Prenatal preparation and education
   a. Type of childbirth classes
   b. Degree of involvement in preparation classes
4. Presence of disease states
   a. Cardiovascular disorders
   b. Pulmonary disorders
   c. CNS disorders
   d. Metabolic problems
5. Course of current pregnancy
6. Support person available

Fetal information
1. Gestational age
   a. Calendar dates
   b. Ultrasound
2. Status of fetus
   a. Stability of FHR
   b. Result of assessments of fetal well-being

#### Physical Examination

1. Maternal vital signs and FHR to establish baselines
2. Estimation of pregnant uterus (Leopold's maneuver to determine fetal size, presentation, and position)
3. Quality of contractions
   a. Frequency
   b. Duration
   c. Intensity
4. Vaginal examination to determine
   a. Status of cervix
      (1) Dilatation
      (2) Effacement
   b. Maternal-fetal pelvic relationship
      (1) Presentation and position
      (2) Station of presenting part
   c. Rate of progress in labor
5. Determination whether site to be used for injection is free from infection

#### Diagnostic Studies

1. No specific tests required for mother
2. Fetal scalp blood samples if fetal distress occurs

#### Analysis of Nursing Priorities

1. Maintaining a safe environment for the mother and fetus
2. Continuous monitoring of maternal status to detect and treat potential problems
3. Continuous monitoring of fetal status for same reason
4. Promoting thorough understanding of procedure through education of both parents

| Nursing Diagnosis/Client Goals | Nursing Interventions | Rationale/Evaluation |
| --- | --- | --- |
| **Nursing Diagnosis:**<br><br>Pattern 8: Knowing<br>Knowledge deficit related to regional anesthetic and analgesia | Determine current knowledge level. | **Rationale:**<br><br>Determination of woman's current knowledge level and factors that affect learning allows nurse to provide individualized teaching. |
| **Client Goal:**<br><br>Woman will be able to discuss the regional block, as measured by ability to verbalize:<br><br>● Type of regional block<br>● Expected effect<br>● Possible adverse effects<br>● Alternatives to regional block<br>● Expected nursing care | Evaluate factors related to learning such as primary language spoken, ability to hear and interpret information, and/or presence of anxiety, which may affect ability to process information. | Understanding of the anticipated effects, side effects, and nursing care will help woman be informed and participate in decision making. |

# Nursing Care Plan

## Regional Anesthesia—Lumbar Epidural *(continued)*

| Nursing Diagnosis/Client Goals | Nursing Interventions | Rationale/Evaluation |
|---|---|---|
| | Provide information regarding:<br>● Reason for the block<br>● Effect of the block<br>● Possible side effects<br>● Possible alternative pain relief measures<br>● Associated nursing care that may be expected | |
| | | **Evaluation:**<br>Woman is able to discuss the regional block and has no further questions. |
| **Nursing Diagnosis:**<br>Pattern 1: Exchanging<br>Potential for injury to mother and fetus related to hypotension secondary to vasodilation and pooling of blood in the extremities | Have legal consents signed.<br>Have woman empty bladder.<br>Begin intravenous fluids.<br>Initiate intravenous infusion. | **Rationale:**<br>Regional anesthesia interferes with woman's urge to void.<br>Intravenous fluids maintain adequate hydration and provide systemic access in the event of maternal hypotension or other untoward events. |
| **Client Goal:**<br>Woman will not experience hypotension as measured by:<br>Blood pressure (BP) remains above 90/60.<br>Pulse remains in 60–80 range. | Overhydrate the woman receiving an epidural block with 500–1000 mL fluid prior to procedure.<br><br>Dextrose-free solution is recommended. | Increased intravenous fluid intake increases blood volume and increases cardiac output to help minimize hypotension.<br><br>Rapid infusion of fluids containing dextrose causes fetal hyperglycemia with rebound hypoglycemia in the first two hours after birth. |
| | Position woman correctly for procedure (see text for proper positioning for individual procedures).<br><br>Assess maternal status:<br>1. Obtain baseline vital signs before any anesthetic agent is given.<br>2. Monitor blood pressure every five min for 30 min following administration of anesthetic agent.<br>3. Monitor pulse and respiration. | Baseline reading allows more complete evaluation of maternal status.<br>Hypotension is a frequent complication of regional anesthesia.<br><br>Pulse may slow following spinal anesthesia due to decreased venous return, decreased venous pressure, and decreased right heart pressure. Respiratory paralysis is a potential complication of regional anesthesia. |

*(continues)*

## Nursing Care Plan

### Regional Anesthesia—Lumbar Epidural (continued)

| Nursing Diagnosis/Client Goals | Nursing Interventions | Rationale/Evaluation |
| --- | --- | --- |
| | Monitor fetal status:<br>1. Use fetal monitoring to establish a baseline reading of FHR.<br>2. Monitor FHR continuously. | Maternal hypotension may interfere with fetal oxygenation and is evidenced by fetal bradycardia. |
| | Observe, record, and report complications of anesthesia, including hypotension, fetal distress, respiratory paralysis, changes in uterine contractility, decrease in voluntary muscle effort, trauma to extremities, nausea and vomiting, loss of bladder tone, and spinal headache. | |
| | Observe, record, and report symptoms of hypotension, including systolic pressure <100 mm Hg or a 25% fall in systolic pressure, apprehension, restlessness, dizziness, tinnitus, headache. | |
| | Institute treatment measures:<br>1. Place woman with head flat and foot of bed elevated. | Gravity increases venous filling of the heart and the pulmonary blood volume; the result is an increase in stroke volume and cardiac output with a rise in blood pressure. |
| | 2. Increase IV fluid rate. | Blood volume increases and circulation improves. |
| | 3. Administer $O_2$ by face mask. | Oxygen content of circulating blood increases. |
| | 4. Administer vasopressors as ordered. | Vasoconstriction occurs; vasopressors are not used in pregnant women unless absolutely necessary because they may further compromise the fetus. |
| | Specific interventions for treatment of hypotension following peridural anesthesia:<br>1. Raise knee gatch on bed.<br>2. Manually displace uterus laterally to left.<br>3. Administer $O_2$ by face mask at 6–10 L/min.<br><br>4. Increase rate of IV fluids.<br>5. Keep woman supine for 5–10 min following administration of block to allow drug to diffuse bilaterally; after 5–10 min position woman on side. | Increases venous return (vena cava is usually to the right).<br>Face mask is method of choice, because woman in labor breathes through her mouth. |
| | Specific interventions for hypotension following spinal anesthesia:<br>1. Administer $O_2$ by face mask at 6–10 L/min.<br>2. Manually displace uterus to left.<br>3. Increase rate of IV fluids.<br>4. Place legs in stirrups. | BP drops following spinal anesthesia, probably because of paralysis of the sympathetic vasoconstrictor fibers to blood vessels.<br>Increases venous return. |

## *Nursing Care Plan*

## Regional Anesthesia—Lumbar Epidural *(continued)*

| Nursing Diagnosis/Client Goals | Nursing Interventions | Rationale/Evaluation |
|---|---|---|
| | Observe, record, and report fetal bradycardia (FHR < 120/min) and loss of beat-to-beat variability. | Maternal hypotension causes decreased blood circulation to fetus and results in fetal hypoxia. |
| | Institute treatment measures for maternal hypotension. (Note: Paracervical blocks commonly cause a drop in FHR for a short period of time.) | Amide group of anesthetic agents (bupivacaine, mepivacaine, and lidocaine) have potential to produce direct fetal myocardial depression; bradycardia may be caused by reduced placental blood flow. |
| | | **Evaluation:** |
| | | Woman remains normotensive. FHR is between 120 and 160; accelerations are present with fetal movement; no variable or late deceleration. |
| **Nursing Diagnosis:** | | **Rationale:** |
| Pattern 1: Exchanging Decreased cardiac output related to sympathetic blockade | Monitor uterus for onset of a contraction. | Uterine contraction during injection of anesthetic agent may increase upward spread to a higher level than desired. |
| **Client Goal:** | Converse with woman during test dose. | Altered sensorium may indicate a complication. |
| Woman remains normotensive as measured by BP in 110/80 to 138/88 range. | Assist with injection and taping of catheter. | Catheter must be securely taped to prevent displacement. |
| | Monitor maternal BP, pulse, and respiration every five minutes for 20–30 minutes. | Local anesthetic agent causes sympathetic blockade, may cause other complications. Regimen must also be followed after every reinjection. |
| | | **Evaluation:** |
| | | Woman is normotensive. |
| **Nursing Diagnosis:** | | **Rationale:** |
| Pattern 1: Exchanging Impaired gas exchange in fetus due to anesthetic agent | Observe, record, and report symptoms of hypotension: BP < 100 mm Hg or 25% fall in systolic pressure, nausea, and apprehension. | Maternal hypotension will decrease oxygenation of fetus. Early detection and immediate treatment decrease hypoxia in fetus. |
| **Client Goal:** | If hypotension occurs institute treatment measures: | |
| FHR is 120–160, with average variability, no late or variable decelerations or accelerations with fetal movement or scalp stimulation. | 1. Place woman with head flat and foot of bed elevated, left lateral position. | Gravity increases venous return to heart, increasing pulmonary blood volume; result is an increase in stroke volume and cardiac output with a rise in BP. |
| | 2. Increase IV fluid rate. | Blood volume increases and circulation improves. |
| | 3. Administer $O_2$ by face mask at 6–10 L/min. | Increases oxygen content of circulating blood; mask is method of choice because woman in labor tends to breathe through her mouth. |

*(continues)*

# Nursing Care Plan

## Regional Anesthesia—Lumbar Epidural (continued)

| Nursing Diagnosis/Client Goals | Nursing Interventions | Rationale/Evaluation |
|---|---|---|
| | 4. Administer vasopressor as ordered. | Vasoconstriction occurs; used only when BP cannot be maintained by other means. |
| | Monitor BP and pulse following delivery. | Hypotension due to anesthetic agent may be delayed in onset. |
| | Explain possible delayed effects of anesthetic agents on fetus. | Anesthetic agents may produce neonatal neurobehavioral effects that could interfere with bonding. |
| | Assist woman to assume left lateral position. | Left lateral position prevents compression of vena cava, assisting venous return from extremities. |
| | Monitor and record BP and pulse every 15 to 20 minutes. | Early detection and treatment of hypotension can minimize effect on the fetus. |
| | Monitor FHR continuously. | Local anesthetic agents may cause loss of variability and late decelerations. |
| | | **Evaluation:** |
| | | FHR remains 120–160, with average variability, and no late or variable decelerations. |
| **Nursing Diagnosis:** | | **Rationale:** |
| Pattern 1: Exchanging Altered patterns of urinary elimination related to effects of epidural | Assess bladder and encourage woman to void at frequent intervals. | Urinary retention frequently accompanies epidural block; client may be unaware of need to void. |
| **Client Goal:** | Catheterize if necessary. | Client has been overhydrated and distention may (1) impede progress of labor, (2) increase chance of bladder trauma, and (3) cause lack of postpartum bladder tone. |
| Woman will have normal urinary elimination as measured by: <br> ● Bladder is not distended. <br> ● Urination occurs without difficulty. <br> ● No urinary retention is present. | | Anesthetic agents may decrease frequency of contractions. <br> Return of uncomfortable contractions is an indication of need for reinjection of epidural catheter. <br> Optimal time is prior to the return of painful contractions. |
| | | **Evaluation:** |
| | | Woman's bladder remains empty, no bladder distention is present. |
| **Nursing Diagnosis:** | | **Rationale:** |
| Pattern 1: Exchanging Potential for injury to mother related to decreased motor control | Assess progress of labor: increase in frequency and duration of contractions, observe for increase in show, perform vaginal examinations. | Woman who chooses epidural wants to experience and participate in labor and delivery. |

## Nursing Care Plan

### Regional Anesthesia—Lumbar Epidural *(continued)*

| Nursing Diagnosis/Client Goals | Nursing Interventions | Rationale/Evaluation |
|---|---|---|
| **Client Goal:**<br>The woman's extremities will be supported during movement.<br><br>**Client Goal:**<br>The woman will verbalize need for assistance as measured by her using the call light to request assistance when ambulating. | Inform woman of progress in labor. Provide reassurance throughout labor. During second stage of labor coordinate woman's pushing effort with increased uterine pressure of contractions.<br><br>Assist with "sitting dose" reinjection for delivery.<br><br>Support extremities during movement. Position legs securely in stirrups (or on table for cesarean delivery).<br><br>Ensure woman understands need for assistance with ambulation. | Loss of sensation may decrease awareness of the urge to push and the ability to push. Pushing without contraction will be ineffective and cause maternal exhaustion.<br><br>Additional anesthesia is necessary for perineal relaxation, delivery, and episiotomy repair.<br><br>Epidural block should not produce motor paralysis but the client may not have full control of extremities.<br><br>Motor control of the legs may be weak following epidural. Ambulation is delayed until complete sensation and ability to control legs has returned.<br><br>**Evaluation:**<br>The woman's extremities are supported during movement. Woman asks for assistance during ambulation in early postpartum period. |
| **Nursing Diagnosis**<br>Pattern 1: Exchanging<br>Potential for injury related to toxic systemic reaction<br><br>**Client Goal:**<br>Woman will remain free of signs and symptoms of toxic systemic reaction as measured by no evidence of:<br><br>● Excitement<br>● Disorientation<br>● Incoherent speech<br>● Nausea<br>● Vomiting<br>● Loss of consciousness<br>● Severe hypotension<br>● Bradycardia<br>● Respiratory or cardiac arrest | Observe for and report symptoms of toxic reaction: excitement, disorientation, incoherent speech, muscle twitching, nausea and vomiting, and convulsions or severe reactions of sudden loss of consciousness, severe hypotension, bradycardia, respiratory depression, and cardiac arrest.<br><br>Small, more frequent doses of analgesic agent are recommended to avoid severe reactions.<br><br>Institute treatment immediately:<br>1. Support ventilation.<br>2. Increase IV fluids.<br>3. Administer muscle relaxant for convulsions as ordered.<br>4. Be prepared for respiratory and cardiac resuscitation. | **Rationale:**<br>Larger volume of anesthetic agent used with epidural increases likelihood of toxic reaction.<br><br><br>Immediate treatment will lessen the effects of toxic systemic reactions on fetus.<br><br><br>**Evaluation:**<br>Woman remains free of signs and symptoms. |

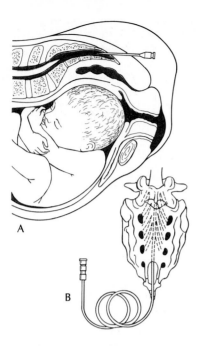

Figure 17.5   Caudal technique: (A) Placement of needle in caudal canal, (B) Plastic catheter in caudal canal. (Reprinted with permission of Ross Laboratories, Columbus, OH 43216. From Clinical Education Aid No. 17.)

## ● Caudal Block

A **caudal block** is achieved by injecting a local anesthetic into the epidural space. The resulting anesthesia relieves the discomfort of uterine contractions. There is also loss of sensation in the cervix, the lower vagina, and the perineal area (Figure 17.5).

### NURSING CARE

The nursing implications of the caudal block are much the same as those of the lumbar epidural block. The exception is that the woman is placed in a lateral Sims position for administration of the agent.

## ● Subarachnoid Block (Spinal, Low Spinal)

In a subarachnoid block (**spinal block**), a local anesthetic agent is injected directly into the spinal fluid in the spinal canal to provide anesthesia for vaginal delivery and cesarean birth (see Figure 17.6). A subarachnoid block is given late in the second stage, when the fetal head is on the perineum. The technique of administration varies depending on whether the block is being given for a cesarean or vaginal delivery.

The disadvantages include a fairly high incidence of hypotension after the block, the need for the woman to remain flat for 6–12 hours after the block, and possible headache afterward.

Contraindications for subarachnoid block include severe hypovolemia, central nervous system disease, infection at the site of puncture, and severe hypotension or hypertension. In addition, the woman may not wish to have the spinal procedure.

### NURSING CARE

The nurse assesses maternal vital signs and the FHR to establish a baseline. The procedure and expected effect are explained to the woman, and any questions are answered. Before this block is given, the woman must sign a consent form. Because this block is given late in the second stage, the woman will be on the delivery bed. The nurse helps the woman sit on the side of the bed and put her feet on a stool. The woman places her arms between her knees, bows her head, and arches her back to widen the intervertebral spaces. The nurse supports the woman in this position and palpates the uterus to identify the beginning of uterine contractions. The clinician injects the anesthetic agent between contractions. If the anesthetic agent is injected during a contraction, the level of anesthesia is higher and may compromise respiration. After the woman returns to a lying position, the nurse places a rolled towel under her right hip so that the uterus is displaced

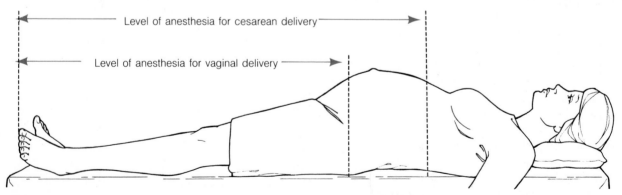

Figure 17.6   Levels of anesthesia for vaginal and cesarean birth (Reprinted with permission of Ross Laboratories, Columbus, OH 43216. From Clinical Education Aid No. 17.)

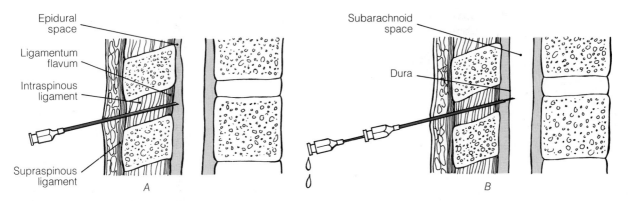

*Figure 17.7 Double needle technique for spinal injection: (**A**) Large needle in epidural space, (**B**) 25–26-gauge needle in larger needle entering the spinal canal. (From Bonica JJ: Principles and Practice of Obstetric Analgesia and Anesthesia. Philadelphia: Davis, 1972, p 563.)*

slightly to the left. Maternal blood pressure, pulse, and FHR are assessed every two to five minutes until the woman is stable. In the absence of maternal hypotension or toxic reaction, the subarachnoid block has no direct effect on the fetus (Figure 17.7).

The nurse continues to monitor uterine contractions and instructs the woman to bear down because she will not experience the urge to do so. The block affects the pushing effort to such an extent that forceps are frequently required to assist delivery. After delivery, temporary motor paralysis of the woman's legs is not uncommon. The nurse exercises great care when moving the woman from the delivery bed to protect her from injury. The woman remains flat in bed for 6–12 hours following the block. The woman may not regain sensation and control of her bladder for 8–12 hours and may need to be catheterized.

## ● Pudendal Block

A **pudendal block,** administered by a transvaginal or transperineal method, intercepts signals to the pudendal nerve. The pudendal block provides perineal anesthesia for the latter part of the first stage, the second stage of labor, delivery, and episiotomy repair. The pudendal block stops the pain of perineal distention but not the discomfort of uterine contractions (Figure 17.8).

The disadvantages of the pudendal block include possible broad ligament hematoma, perforation of the rectum, and trauma to the sciatic nerve.

### NURSING CARE

The nurse explains the procedure and the expected effect and answers any questions. Pudendal block does not alter maternal vital signs or FHR; thus, additional assessments are not necessary.

## ● LOCAL INFILTRATION ANESTHESIA

**Local infiltration** of perineal tissues is achieved by injecting an anesthetic agent into the subcutaneous tissue in a fanlike pattern (Figure 17.9). Local anesthetics are generally used at the time of birth for episiotomy repair.

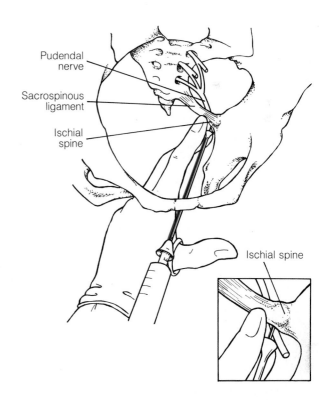

*Figure 17.8 Technique for pudendal block: Inset shows needle extending beyond guide. (Modified from Bonica JJ: Principles and Practice of Obstetric Analgesia and Anesthesia. Philadelphia: Davis, 1972, p 495.)*

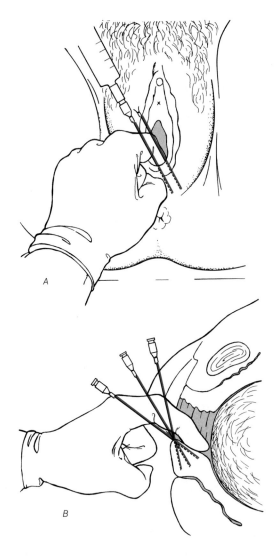

*Figure 17.9   Local infiltration anesthesia: (**A**) Technique of local infiltration for episiotomy and repair, (**B**) Technique of local infiltration showing fan pattern for the fascial planes. (From Bonica JJ:* Principles and Practice of Obstetric Analgesia and Anesthesia. *Philadelphia: Davis, 1972, p 505.)*

A disadvantage of local infiltration is that large amounts of local anesthetic must be used.

### NURSING CARE

The nurse explains the procedure and the expected effect and answers any questions. Local anesthetic agents have no effect on maternal vital signs or FHR; thus, additional assessments are unnecessary.

## ● GENERAL ANESTHESIA

The goal of obstetric anesthesia is to provide maximal pain relief with minimal side effects to the woman and her fetus. Anesthetic techniques and drugs should be selected to meet their needs. A general anesthesia may be needed for cesarean birth and for surgical intervention with some obstetric complications. The method used to achieve general anesthesia may be intravenous injection, inhalation of anesthetic agents, or a combination of both methods.

The leading cause of obstetric anesthetic death is regurgitation and aspiration of gastric contents. The physiologic changes in the gastrointestinal tract during pregnancy include decreased gastric motility and delayed gastric emptying. The gastric contents are highly acid and produce chemical pneumonitis if aspirated. Every childbearing woman should be viewed as having a stomachful of hydrochloric acid. Prophylactic antacid therapy prior to general anesthesia has become common practice in the last decade.

Clear antacids such as sodium citrate may be given 15–30 minutes prior to scheduled cesarean delivery to decrease gastric pH (Steude and de Rosayro 1988). There still remains a problem with gastric volume even when the pH has been decreased. Cimetidine (Tagamet) and ranitidine (Zantac) are being used to block production of gastric secretions, thereby reducing gastric volume. These agents were administered to over 10,000 women with no significant side effects in mother or infant (Moore et al 1984). Ranitidine, with a longer duration of action and lack of inhibition of hepatic drug metabolism, is the agent of choice (Moore et al 1984).

Because of the risk of aspiration the use of mask anesthesia without placement of an endotracheal tube can no longer be justified (Albright et al 1986, Devore 1985). In order to prevent possible regurgitation during intubation, the simplest and most effective method is to apply cricoid pressure. During the process of rapid induction of anesthesia, an assistant applies cricoid pressure as the woman loses consciousness. This is accomplished by depressing the cricoid cartilage 2 to 3 cm posteriorly so that the esophagus is occluded. Figure 17.10 shows the appropriate technique. Instead of using the other hand to support the neck, which helps avoid anatomical distortion, Crawford (1982) recommends that a firm foam rubber block be used. It is important to note that cricoid pressure should be increased if active retching occurs and in any case pressure should not be released until the cuffed endotracheal tube is in place.

Prior to induction of anesthesia, the mother should have a wedge placed under the right hip to displace the uterus and avoid vena caval compression in the supine position. She should also be preoxygenated with either three to five minutes of 100% oxygen or with four deep breaths of 100% oxygen in 15 seconds. Morris and Dewan (1985) found the latter to be as effective as breathing oxygen for three minutes. Of course intravenous fluids should be initiated so that access to the intravascular system is immediately available. The woman who has been in prolonged labor may also need to be hydrated if an infusion was not previously in place.

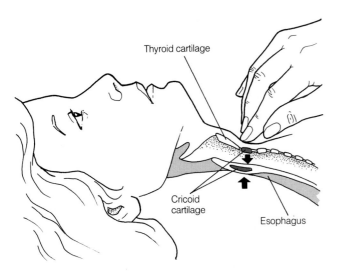

*Figure 17.10    Proper position for fingers in applying cricoid pressure*

## Inhalation Anesthetics
### NITROUS OXIDE

Nitrous oxide is the oldest analgesic and anesthetic gaseous agent. Induction is rapid and pleasant; it is nonirritating and nonexplosive and disturbs physiologic functioning less than any other agent (Albright et al 1986). The main obstetric uses of nitrous oxide are as an analgesic during the second stage of labor, as an induction agent or supplement to more potent inhalation anesthetics, and as a part of balanced anesthesia.

### HALOTHANE (FLUOTHANE)

Halothane is frequently used as a general anesthetic. Induction with this agent is smooth, rapid, safe, and predictable. It does cause depression of respiration and irritability of cardiac tissue, resulting in arrhythmias. Only a moderate degree of muscle relaxation is produced. Halothane increases blood flow to the uterus and does not contribute to uterine relaxation when used in low doses.

## Intravenous Anesthetics

Thiopental sodium (Pentothal) is an ultrashort-acting barbiturate, which means that it exerts its effect rapidly and has a brief duration of action (Julien 1984). Thiopental sodium produces narcosis within 30 seconds after intravenous administration. Induction and emergence from its effects are smooth, pleasant, and with little incidence of nausea and vomiting.

Thiopental sodium is most frequently used for induction and as an adjunct to other more potent anesthetics.

## Balanced Anesthesia

A trend in vaginal delivery requiring anesthesia or cesarean birth is *balanced anesthesia*. Balanced anesthesia is induced by several different agents administered through different routes. Since no single anesthetic agent is suitable for all people in all situations, the combined use of several agents and techniques increases effectiveness and client safety. In this way, each agent is used for a specific purpose. Furthermore, because of the combined effect, much smaller amounts of the agents can be given than if they were used alone.

An example of balanced anesthesia is the use of an intravenous barbiturate (thiopental sodium) for sedation and rapid pleasant induction, then halothane or another general anesthetic agent and oxygen inhaled through a face mask for analgesia and anesthesia. Intravenous succinylcholine chloride may be given to produce muscle relaxation. The purpose of balanced anesthesia is to obtain the maximum benefit from each agent and technique with a minimum of side effects for the woman and newborn.

## Complications of General Anesthesia

The primary dangers of general anesthesia are as follows:

### FETAL DEPRESSION

Most general anesthetic agents reach the fetus in about two minutes. The depression in the fetus is directly proportional to the depth and duration of the anesthesia. The long-term significance of fetal depression in a normal delivery has not been determined. The poor fetal metabolism of general anesthetic agents is similar to that of analgesic agents administered during labor. General anesthesia is not advocated when the fetus is considered to be at high risk, particularly in premature delivery.

### UTERINE RELAXATION

The majority of general anesthetic agents cause some degree of uterine relaxation.

### VOMITING AND ASPIRATION

Pregnancy results in decreased gastric motility, and the onset of labor halts the process almost entirely. Food eaten hours earlier may remain undigested in the stomach. The nurse must find out when the laboring woman last ate and record this information on the client's chart and on her anesthesia record.

Even when food and fluids have been withheld, the gastric juice produced during fasting is highly acidic and can produce chemical pneumonitis if aspirated. Such pneumonitis is known as Mendelson's syndrome. The signs and symptoms are chest pain, respiratory embarrassment, cyanosis, fever, and tachycardia. It has become common procedure to administer an antacid during labor to neutralize the gastric contents.

Vomiting and aspiration of undigested food or acidic gastric juice occurs most frequently during emergence from general anesthesia. Sellick's maneuver of applying cricoid pressure to compress the esophagus, thereby occluding the lumen to avoid regurgitation of stomach contents into the pharynx and trachea, is frequently practiced. Every nurse in the labor and delivery unit should be trained in the proper technique for applying cricoid pressure. All delivery room suites should have emergency equipment available to deal with complications such as aspiration.

## ESSENTIAL CONCEPTS

● Pain relief during labor may be enhanced by psychoprophylactic methods and administration of analgesics and regional anesthesia blocks.

● The goal of pharmacologic pain relief during labor is to provide maximal analgesia with minimal risk for the mother and fetus.

● The optimal time for administering analgesia is determined after making a complete assessment of many factors. An analgesic agent is generally administered to nulliparas when the cervix has dilated 5 to 6 cm and to multiparas when the cervix has reached 3 to 4 cm dilatation.

● Analgesic agents include meperidine and butorphanol.

● Narcotic antagonists counteract the respiratory depressant effect of the opiate narcotics by acting at specific receptor sites in the CNS. These drugs include levallorphan and naloxone.

● Regional analgesia and anesthesia are achieved by injecting local anesthetic agents into an area that will bring the agent into direct contact with nerve tissue. Methods most commonly used in childbearing include peridural block (lumbar epidural), subarachnoid block (spinal, low spinal, or saddle block), pudendal block, and local infiltration.

● Two types of local anesthetic agents used in regional blocks are amide and ester groups. The amides are absorbed quickly and can be found in maternal blood within minutes after administration, while the esters are metabolized more rapidly and have only limited placental transfer.

● Untoward reactions of the woman to local anesthetic agents range from mild symptoms, such as palpitations, to cardiovascular collapse.

● The goal of general anesthesia is to provide maximal pain relief with minimal side effects to the woman and her fetus.

● Complications of general anesthesia include fetal depression, uterine relaxation, vomiting, and aspiration.

● The choice of analgesia and anesthesia for the high-risk woman and fetus requires careful evaluation.

## References

Albright GA, Joyce TH, Stevenson DK: *Anesthesia in Obstetrics,* 2nd ed. Boston: Butterworth, 1986.

American Society of Hospital Pharmacists: Bupivacaine hydrochloride. In: *Drug Information 85.* Bethesda, MD: 1985, p 1475.

Briggs GC, Freeman RK, Yaffe SJ: *Drugs in Pregnancy and Lactation,* 2nd ed. Baltimore: Williams and Wilkins, 1986.

Crawford JS: The "contracrecoid" cuboid aid to tracheal intubation, correspondence. *Anesthesia* 1982; 37:345.

Devore JS: Analgesia and anesthesia for delivery. In: *Gynecology and Obstetrics.* Vol 2. Sciarra JL, Dilts PV, Gerbie AB (editors). Philadelphia: Harper and Row, 1985.

Julien RM: *Understanding Anesthesia.* Menlo Park, CA: Addison-Wesley, 1984.

Karch A, Boyd E: *Handbook of Drugs and the Nursing Process.* Philadelphia: Lippincott, 1989.

McDonald JS: Anesthesia and the high risk fetus. Chapter 91 in: *Gynecology and Obstetrics.* Sciarra JL, Depp R, Eschenback DA (editors). Philadelphia: Harper and Row, 1985.

Moore A et al: Spinal fluid kinetics of morphine. *Clin Pharmacol Ther* January 1984; 35:40.

Morris MC, Dewan D: Pre-oxygenation for cesarean section: A comparison of two techniques. *Anesthesiology* 1985; 62:827.

Steude GM, de Rosayro M: Analgesia and anesthesia for delivery. Chapter 66 in: *Gynecology and Obstetrics.* Vol 2. Sciarra JL (editor), Dilts PV (assoc editor). Philadelphia: Harper and Row, 1988.

## Additional Readings

Dale S: The role of the anaesthetic nurse in obstetric anaesthesia. *NATNEWS* 1988; 25(3):10.

Davies JM et al: Infections and the parturient: Anaesthetic considerations. *Can J Anaesth* 1988; 35(3, Part 1):270.

Giuffre M et al: Patient-controlled analgesia in clinical pain research measurement. *Nurs Res* July/August 1988; 37(4):254.

McKay S, Mahan C: Modifying the stomach contents of laboring women: Why and how; success and risks. *Birth* December 1988; 15(4):213.

McKay S, Mahan C: How can aspiration of vomitus in obstetrics best be prevented? *Birth* December 1988; 15(4):222.

Redick LF: Anesthesia for twin delivery. *Clin Perinatol* 1988; 15(1):107.

# 18

## Intrapartal Family at Risk

*When I found I was pregnant the first time, I was amazed. When I found I was pregnant the second time, I thought "How can that be? We don't 'do it' that often." (Having a child can really affect your sex life.) When I found out I was pregnant the third time, and that we were expecting twins, I just felt tired.*

## Objectives

● Describe the psychologic factors that may contribute to complications during labor and birth.

● Discuss dysfunctional labor patterns.

● Summarize various types of fetal malposition and malpresentation and possible associated problems.

● Discuss the nursing care that is indicated in the event of fetal distress.

● Discuss intrauterine fetal death including etiology, diagnosis, management, and the nurse's role in assisting the family.

● Compare abruptio placentae and placenta previa.

● Identify variations that may occur in the umbilical cord and insertion into the placenta.

● Delineate the effects of pelvic contractures on labor and delivery.

● Discuss complications of the third and fourth stages.

## Key Terms

abruptio placentae
amniotic fluid embolism
cephalopelvic disproportion (CPD)
dystocia
hydramnios
macrosomia
oligohydramnios
persistent/occiput-posterior position
placenta previa
postdate pregnancy
precipitous labor
premature rupture of membranes (PROM)
preterm labor
prolonged labor

The successful completion of the 40-week gestational period requires the harmonious functioning of four components: the psyche, powers, passenger, and passage. (These components are described in depth in Chapter 14.) The psyche is the intellectual and emotional processes of the pregnant woman as influenced by heredity and environment and includes her feelings about pregnancy and motherhood. The powers are the myometrial forces of the contracting uterus. The passenger includes all the products of conception: the fetus, placenta, cord, membranes, and amniotic fluid. The passage comprises the vagina, introitus, and bony pelvis. Disruptions in any of the four components may affect the others and cause **dystocia** (abnormal or difficult labor).

## ● USING THE NURSING PROCESS WITH INTRAPARTAL FAMILIES AT RISK

The nursing process forms a basis for the provision of nursing care to the woman and her family when there are problems associated with the pregnancy.

### ● Nursing Assessment

The nurse collects information regarding the woman's history and correlates it with known information regarding predisposing factors. The history helps the nurse identify pertinent assessments that need to be made.

### ● Nursing Diagnosis

The nurse looks for cues that may suggest the woman is at risk for problems during the intrapartal period. Sometimes subtle clues may be the only indication of a developing problem. The nurse operates on her or his knowledge of normal labor and delivery, and thus is able to identify problems quickly.

The nurse organizes the data and assessment information into nursing diagnoses that are appropriate for a woman at risk in the intrapartal period. Nursing diagnoses that may apply include:

● Knowledge deficit related to the possible implications and problems associated with intrapartal problems

● Potential for injury to the fetus related to decreased blood supply, secondary cord compression, problems during labor, or birth trauma

● Ineffective individual coping related to unanticipated problems in labor and/or birth

● Fear related to unknown outcome of the labor and birth

## ● Nursing Plan and Implementation

After nursing diagnoses are identified, the nurse identifies nursing interventions to prevent or treat designated client problems. The nurse uses basic nursing skills and special intrapartal interventions to provide nursing care to the intrapartal family at risk.

## ● Evaluation

Evaluation of the woman's response to care and the effectiveness of the nursing interventions is an ongoing process. As a result of evaluation, the nurse may revise the plan of care or add other nursing interventions.

## ● CARE OF THE WOMAN AT RISK DUE TO EXCESSIVE ANXIETY AND FEAR

The anxiety, fear, and pain associated with labor may lead to a vicious cycle of increased fear and anxiety because of continued central pain perception. This enhances catecholamine release, which in turn increases physical distress and results in myometrial dysfunction. Ineffectual labor may occur (Lederman et al 1985).

## ● Medical Therapy

The medical therapy for anxiety and fear is directed by the individual circumstances of each laboring woman. The obstetrician may first use communication and sharing of information in an attempt to allay anxiety. When needed, pharmacologic measures such as ataractics or sedatives may be ordered to help the woman feel more calm.

## ● Nursing Assessment

Unless birth is imminent or severe complications exist, the nurse begins the assessment by reviewing the woman's background. Factors such as age, parity, marital and socioeconomic status, culture, and knowledge and understanding of the labor process contribute to the woman's psychologic response to labor.

As labor progresses, the nurse is alert for the woman's verbal and nonverbal behavioral responses to the pain and anxiety coexisting with labor. The woman who is agitated and seems uncooperative, or is too quiet and compliant, may require further appraisal for anxiety. Verbal statements such as "Is everything okay?" "I'm really nervous," or "What's going on?" usually indicate some degree of anxiety and concern. Other women may be irritable, require frequent explanations, or repeat the same questions. The nurse further observes for nonverbal cues including a tense posture, clenched hands, or pain out of context to the stage of labor. Recognizing the impact of fatigue on pain and anxiety is another important nursing observation.

## ● Nursing Diagnosis

Nursing diagnoses that may apply to the woman with excessive fear or anxiety include:

● Anxiety related to stress of the labor process

● Fear related to unknown outcome of labor

● Ineffective individual coping related to inability to use relaxation techniques during labor

## ● Nursing Plan and Implementation
### ANTICIPATORY EDUCATION DURING THE PRENATAL PERIOD

Nursing research demonstrates that education is effective in minimizing the stress accompanying labor. Research findings generally indicate that women who participate in prenatal classes benefit by maintaining better control in labor, decreasing their use of ataractics and analgesics, manifesting more positive attitudes, and experiencing feelings of anticipation rather than fear (Genest 1981, Sasmor et al 1981).

Antepartal classes provide relevant information about the developmental and psychologic changes that can be expected during childbirth and teach relaxation strategies to reduce the anxiety and pain of labor. Couples learn coping mechanisms in the form of physical and emotional comfort measures, controlled breathing exercises, and relaxation techniques.

### PROVISION OF SUPPORT DURING LABOR AND BIRTH

Prepared couples should be offered support and encouragement by the nurse as they employ the techniques they have learned. If the mother begins to lose control, the nurse can often assist the partner in helping the mother regain control. If anxiety is evident, the nurse should acknowledge and alleviate it, if possible, through comfort measures (see Chapter 16).

Unprepared couples can be taught many of these activities at the time of admission, especially if active labor has not begun. Clear but succinct information about the labor process, medical procedures, the environment, simple breathing exercises, and relaxation techniques can be given, thereby preventing or relieving some apprehension and fear. Even a woman in active labor who has had no prior preparation can achieve a great deal of relaxation from physical comfort measures, touch, constant attention, therapeutic interaction, and, possibly, analgesics.

The nurse's ability to help the woman and her partner cope with the stress of labor is directly related to the rapport established between them. By employing a calm, caring, confident, nonjudgmental approach, the nurse not only is able to acknowledge the anxiety, but also often is able to identify the source of the distress. Once the causative factors are known, the appropriate interventions, such as information, comfort measures, touch, or therapeutic communication, can be implemented.

## ● Evaluation

Anticipated outcomes of nursing care include the following:

- The woman experiences a decrease in physiologic signs of stress and an increase in psychologic comfort.
- The woman is able to use effective coping mechanisms to manage her anxiety in labor.
- The woman's fear is decreased.
- The woman is able to verbalize feelings regarding her labor.

## ● CARE OF THE WOMAN WITH DYSFUNCTIONAL LABOR

Complications of the powers involve problems with the frequency, duration, and intensity of contractions, and/or the resting tone of the uterus between contractions. These problems lead to a dysfunctional labor and can be associated with additional complications, such as maternal exhaustion, dehydration, increased risk of infection, and fetal complications.

## ● Hypertonic Labor Patterns

In hypertonic labor patterns, ineffectual uterine contractions of poor quality occur in the latent phase of labor, and the resting tone of the myometrium increases. Contractions usually become more frequent, but their intensity may decrease (Figure 18.1, *B*). The contractions are painful but ineffective in dilating and effacing the cervix, and a prolonged latent phase may result.

Maternal implications of hypertonic labor include:

- Increased discomfort due to uterine muscle cell anoxia
- Fatigue as pattern continues and no labor progress results

- Dehydration and increased incidence of infection if labor is prolonged
- Stress on coping abilities

Fetal-neonatal implications include:

- Early fetal distress because contractions and increased resting tone interfere with the uteroplacental exchange
- Prolonged pressure on the fetal head, which may result in cephalhematoma, caput succedaneum, or excessive molding (Figure 18.2).

### MEDICAL THERAPY

Management of hypertonic labor may include bed rest and sedation to promote relaxation and to reduce pain. Oxytocin is not administered to a woman suffering from hypertonic uterine activity because it is likely to accentuate the abnormal labor pattern (Pritchard et al 1985). If the hypertonic pattern continues and develops into prolonged latent phase, an oxytocin infusion and/or amniotomy may be used as treatment methods (see Chapter 19). These methods are instituted only after cephalopelvic disproportion (CPD) and fetal malpresentation have been ruled out. When an oxytocin infusion is used to stimulate uterine contractions, the physician/nurse-midwife needs to assure that vaginal birth is possible; in other words, the maternal pelvis must be large enough for the fetus to pass through. If the maternal pelvic diameters are less than average, or if the fetus is particularly large or is in a malpresentation or malposition, then **cephalopelvic disproportion** (CPD) is said to be present. In the presence of CPD labor will not be stimulated because vaginal birth is not possible.

### NURSING ASSESSMENT

The relationship between the intensity of pain being experienced and the degree to which the cervix is dilating and effacing should be evaluated as a part of the labor assessment. Whether anxiety is having a deleterious effect on labor progress should also be noted, especially if the mother is a primigravida or is postterm. Evidence of increasing frustration and discouragement on the part of the mother and her partner may become apparent as labor ensues and their birth plan cannot be followed.

### NURSING DIAGNOSIS

Nursing diagnoses that may apply to the woman in hypertonic labor include:

- Pain related to woman's inability to relax secondary to hypertonic uterine contractions

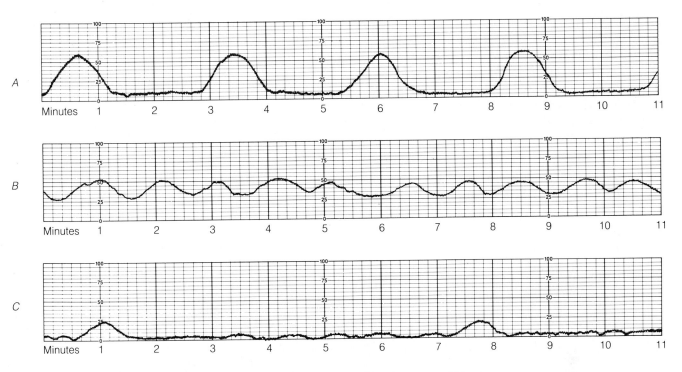

*Figure 18.1   Comparison of labor patterns:* **(A)** *Normal uterine contraction pattern. Note contraction frequency is every three minutes, duration is 60 seconds. The baseline resting tone is below 10 mm Hg.* **(B)** *Hypertonic uterine pattern. Note in this example the contraction frequency is every one minute, duration is 50 seconds (which allows only a 10-second rest between contractions), intensity increases approximately 25 mm Hg during the contraction, and the resting tone of the uterus is increased.* **(C)** *Hypotonic uterine contraction pattern. Note in this example the contraction frequency is every seven minutes with some uterine activity between contractions, duration is 50 seconds, and intensity increases approximately 25 mm Hg during contractions.*

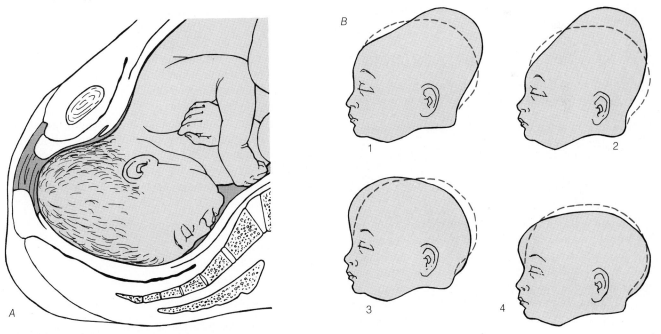

*Figure 18.2   Effects of labor on the fetal head:* **(A)** *Caput succedaneum formation. The presenting portion of the scalp area is encircled by the cervix during labor, causing swelling of the soft tissue.* **(B)** *Molding of the fetal head in cephalic presentations:* **(1)** *occiput anterior,* **(2)** *occiput posterior,* **(3)** *brow,* **(4)** *face.*

## Essential Nursing Diagnoses to Consider

**Dysfunctional Labor (Hypertonic, Hypotonic, or Prolonged Labor Pattern)**

Anxiety

Fatigue

Fear

Impaired physical mobility

Ineffective individual coping

Knowledge deficit

Potential for infection

Potential fluid volume deficit

Powerlessness

Sleep pattern disturbance

Spiritual distress

Urinary retention

- Ineffective individual coping related to ineffectiveness of breathing techniques to relieve discomfort
- Anxiety related to slow labor progress
- Knowledge deficit related to lack of understanding regarding dysfunctional labor patterns

For additional nursing diagnoses see Essential Nursing Diagnoses to Consider—Dysfunctional Labor.

### NURSING PLAN AND IMPLEMENTATION

#### Provision of Comfort and Support to the Laboring Woman and Her Partner

The woman experiencing a hypertonic labor pattern will probably be very uncomfortable because of the increased force of contractions. Her anxiety level and that of her partner may be high. The nurse attempts to reduce the woman's discomfort and promote a more effective labor pattern.

The nurse may wish to try a change of position for the woman; lateral position may correct the hypertonic pattern. Comfort measures include mouth care, effleurage, back rub, and change of linens. If sedation is ordered, the nurse ensures that the environment is conducive to relaxation. The labor coach may also need assistance in helping the woman cope. A calm understanding approach by the nurse offers the woman and her partner further support. Provision of information about the cause of the hypertonic labor pattern and assurances that the woman is not overreacting to the situation are also important nursing actions.

#### Promotion of Maternal-Fetal Physical Well-Being

Fluid balance must be maintained through adequate hydration. Urine ketones should be monitored hourly. The couple should be informed of labor progress.

Nursing measures in the event of fetal-neonatal distress are given in the Nursing Care Plan—Fetal Distress.

#### Client Education

The laboring woman needs to have information about the dysfunctional labor pattern and the possible implications for herself and her baby. Information will help relieve anxiety and thereby increase relaxation and comfort. The nurse needs to explain treatment methods and offer opportunities for questions.

### EVALUATION

Anticipated outcomes of nursing care include:

- The woman experiences a more effective labor pattern.
- The woman has increased comfort and decreased anxiety.
- The woman and her partner are able to cope with the labor.
- The woman and her partner understand the labor pattern and its possible implications.

## • Hypotonic Labor Patterns

A hypotonic labor pattern usually occurs in the active phase of labor, although it may occur in the latent phase. When this pattern occurs in the active phase, it usually develops after labor has been well established. Hypotonic labor is characterized by fewer than two to three contractions in a ten-minute period (Figure 18.1, *C*).

Hypotonic labor may occur when the uterus is overstretched from a twin gestation or in the presence of a large fetus, hydramnios, and grandmultiparity. Bladder or bowel distention and CPD may also be associated with this pattern.

Maternal implications of hypotonic labor patterns include:

- Intrauterine infection if labor is prolonged
- Postpartal hemorrhage from insufficient uterine contractions following delivery
- Maternal exhaustion
- Stress on coping abilities

Fetal-neonatal implications include:

- Fetal distress, due to prolonged labor pattern
- Fetal sepsis from maternal pathogens that ascend from the birth canal

## Nursing Care Plan

### Fetal Distress

#### Client Assessment

**Nursing History**

Assess client for presence of predisposing factors:
1. Preexisting maternal diseases
2. Maternal hypotension, bleeding
3. Placental abnormalities

**Physical Examination**

Asphyxia is suggested when one or more of the following are present:

1. FHR decelerations, decreased variability, tachycardia followed by bradycardia
2. Presence of meconium in amniotic fluid
3. Fetal scalp blood pH determination $\leq 7.20$

**Diagnostic Studies**

Maternal hemoglobin and hematocrit
Urinalysis

| Nursing Diagnosis/Client Goals | Nursing Interventions | Rationale/Evaluation |
|---|---|---|
| **Nursing Diagnosis:**<br><br>Pattern 1: Exchanging<br>Decreased cardiac output in fetus related to decreased uteroplacental perfusion secondary to maternal hypotension, circulating blood volume, and vasoconstriction associated with PIH<br><br>**Client Goal:**<br><br>The FHR will remain in the range of 120–160 with average variability, accelerations with fetal movement, and no late or variable decelerations. | Observe and record the signs of fetal asphyxia: | **Rationale:**<br><br>Fetal asphyxia implies hypoxia (reduction in $P_{O_2}$), hypercapnia (elevation of $P_{CO_2}$), and acidosis (lowering of blood pH). Anaerobic glycolysis (breakdown of glycogen) takes place in the presence of hypoxia, and the end product of this process is lactic acid, resulting in metabolic acidosis. |
| | 1. Presence of meconium in amniotic fluid | Fetal hypoxic episode leads to increased intestinal peristalsis and anal sphincter relaxation resulting in meconium release. |
| | 2. Decreased variability | Variability of FHR depends on intact sympathetic and parasympathetic nervous systems. When variability decreases, it indicates the fetus is no longer able to react or compensate for changes in the uterine environment. |
| | 3. Late decelerations in FHR | Vagal stimulation elicited through hypoxic brain tissues causes bradycardia. |
| | 4. Fetal hyperactivity | Fetus may initially become hyperactive in an attempt to increase circulation. |
| | Initiate following interventions:<br>1. Administer $O_2$ to the woman with tight face mask at 6–10 L/min, per physician order. | Administration of $O_2$ may increase amount of oxygen available for transport to fetus. Tight face mask is used because laboring woman tends to breathe through her mouth. |
| | 2. Change maternal position (lateral, left side preferred). | Changed maternal position may relieve compression of the maternal vena cava and the cord, thereby facilitating $O_2$ exchange. |

*(continues)*

# Nursing Care Plan

## Fetal Distress (continued)

3. Correct maternal hypotension if present:
   a. Administer IV fluids.
   b. Assess any maternal bleeding; if present, replace circulatory fluids.

Lowered maternal blood pressure or circulating blood volume affects $O_2$ exchange gradient of maternal-placental-fetal unit.

4. Decrease uterine contractions; if oxytocin is infusing, decrease infusion rate or discontinue oxytocin.

Increased uterine tone decreases exchange at placental site and decreases fetal recovery time following contractions.

Assist with testing to evaluate fetal status:
1. Prepare equipment for fetal blood sampling.

Evaluate fetal acidotic state. Hypoxia causes increase in lactic acid and results in acidosis, which causes a drop in the pH of the fetal blood (normal pH is 7.25–7.30); other tests that may be done on fetal blood sample are $O_2$ pressure (normal 18–22 mm Hg), $CO_2$ pressure (normal 48–50 mm Hg), base deficit (normal 0–10 mg/L)

2. Prepare woman for immediate delivery (may be vaginal or cesarean birth).

### Evaluation:

The FHR is within normal limits.

### Nursing Diagnosis:

Pattern 1: Exchanging
Altered tissue perfusion in fetus related to impaired blood flow through umbilical cord related to cord compression

### Client Goal:

The FHR will remain in the range of 120–160 with average variability, accelerations with fetal movement, and no late or variable decelerations.

Observe and note variable decelerations of FHR. If variable deceleration lasts longer than 30 sec, change maternal position; if necessary, follow interventions listed under fetal asphyxia.
Relieve pressure on umbilical cord.

### Rationale:

Umbilical vessels may be partially or completely occluded by compression of the cord; cord may prolapse through cervix and vagina, or compression may occur when the cord is trapped between a fetal part and the bony pelvis; transient episodes of compression are reflected by variable decelerations (decelerations that are unrelated to uterine contractions).

### Evaluation:

The FHR is within normal limits.

### Nursing Diagnosis:

Pattern 1: Exchanging
Altered tissue perfusion in fetus related to impaired blood flow through the umbilical cord related to prolapsed cord

### Client Goal:

The FHR will remain in the range of 120–160 with average variability, accelerations with fetal movement, and no late or variable declerations.

Evaluate for presence of predisposing factors:
1. Abnormalities in presentation: breech, shoulder, transverse lie
2. Rupture of membranes
3. Multiple gestation
4. Preterm gestation
Observe for prolapse of the cord externally through vaginal introitus. While doing vaginal exam, evaluate for presence of cord, which feels like rope and pulsates.

### Rationale:

Occult or obvious prolapse of the cord may cause severe decrease in oxygen transfer; failure to relieve pressure may result in fetal death.

Emergency measures for a prolapsed cord are aimed at immediately relieving compression and establishing fetal blood/oxygen circulation.

*(continues)*

# Nursing Care Plan

## Fetal Distress (continued)

Institute emergency measures for prolapse of cord:
1. Manually exert pressure on the presenting part; this must be done continuously; woman may be maintained in supine position, Trendelenburg position, knee-chest position, or on her side with a pillow to elevate her hips.
2. If occult prolapse is suspected, change maternal position to side-lying position.
3. Notify physician/nurse-midwife immediately.

**Evaluation:**

The FHR is within normal limits.

**Nursing Diagnosis:**

Pattern 9: Feeling
Fear related to knowledge of fetal distress

**Client Goal:**

The woman will have opportunity to ask questions and will verbalize whether she receives support.

Inform woman of fetal status.
Explain treatment plan.
Provide accurate information.

**Rationale:**

Anxiety is decreased when factual information is provided.

**Evaluation:**

The woman verbalizes understanding of current problem and has no further questions.

## MEDICAL THERAPY

Improving the quality of the uterine contractions while ensuring a safe outcome for the woman and her baby are the goals of therapy.

Prior to initiating treatment for hypotonic labor, the physician validates the adequacy of pelvic measurements and completes tests to establish gestational age if there is any question about fetal maturity. After CPD, fetal malpresentation, and fetal immaturity have been ruled out, oxytocin (Pitocin) may be given intravenously via an infusion pump to improve the quality of uterine contractions. Intravenous fluid is useful to maintain adequate hydration and prevent maternal exhaustion. Amniotomy may be done to stimulate the labor process.

An improvement in the quality of uterine contractions is demonstrated by noticeable progress in the labor process. If the labor pattern does not become effective, or if other complications develop, further interventions, including cesarean delivery, may be necessary.

## NURSING ASSESSMENT

Assessing contractions (for frequency and intensity), maternal vital signs, and fetal heart rate (FHR) provides the nurse with data to evaluate maternal-fetal status. The nurse is also alert for signs and symptoms of infection and dehydration. Because of the stress associated with a prolonged labor, observing the woman and her partner's degree of success with their coping mechanisms is also important.

## NURSING DIAGNOSIS

Nursing diagnoses that may apply to the woman in hypotonic labor include:

- Pain related to inability to cope with uterine contractions secondary to dysfunctional labor
- Knowledge deficit related to lack of information regarding dysfunctional labor

## NURSING PLAN AND IMPLEMENTATION

### Promotion of Maternal-Fetal Physical Well-Being

Nursing measures include frequent monitoring of contractions, maternal vital signs, and FHR. If meconium is present in the amniotic fluid, observing fetal status closely becomes more critical. Maintaining an intake and output record provides a way of determining maternal hydration or dehydration. The woman should be encouraged to void every two hours, and her bladder should be checked for distention. Because her labor may be prolonged, the woman must continue to be monitored for signs of infection (elevated temperature, chills, changes in characteristics of amniotic fluid). Vaginal examinations should be kept to a minimum. The nursing implications of oxytocin infusion are presented in Drug Guide—Oxytocin in Chapter 19.

### Provision of Emotional Support

The nurse assists the woman and her partner to cope with the frustration of a lengthy labor process. A warm, caring approach is coupled with techniques to reduce anxiety.

### Client Education

The teaching plan must include information regarding the dysfunctional labor process and implications for the mother and baby. Disadvantages of and alternatives to treatment also need to be discussed and understood.

## EVALUATION

Anticipated outcomes of nursing care include:

● The woman maintains comfort during labor.

● The woman understands the type of labor pattern that is occurring and the treatment plan.

## ● Prolonged Labor

Labor lasting more than 24 hours is termed **prolonged labor.** In these cases, the latent and/or active phase is prolonged.

Prolonged labor is more common in women who have never had children (nulliparas). The principal causes are CPD, malpresentations, malpositions, uterine contraction dysfunction, and cervical dystocia. Other influencing factors are overuse of analgesics, anesthetics, and sedatives in the latent phase of labor.

Maternal implications of prolonged labor include:

● Exhaustion

● Intrauterine infection

● Third stage and postpartum bleeding from inadequate uterine contractions

Fetal-neonatal implications include:

● Fetal distress

● Increased risk of infection

● Prolapse of the cord after rupture of membranes (ROM) if presenting part is not well engaged

● Cephalhematoma and/or caput succedaneum

## MEDICAL THERAPY

Monitoring of prolonged labor begins with identification of any causal factors. Treatment depends on these factors and may include stimulating labor through the intravenous administration of oxytocin and/or performing an amniotomy. Hydration is maintained with intravenous fluids. Sedatives or analgesics may be given to increase rest and relaxation and to decrease anxiety. In the event of serious maternal or fetal distress or CPD, a cesarean delivery is usually done.

## NURSING ASSESSMENT

Monitoring maternal-fetal status is a primary nursing responsibility. The FHR patterns are assessed for signs of distress, including subtle tachycardia followed by bradycardia, late decelerations, and decreasing variability. Amniotic fluid is observed for meconium staining and signs of infection. The nurse evaluates labor progress by considering the pattern of the contractions, the degree of cervical dilatation and effacement, and descent. Ongoing assessment of maternal hydration occurs throughout labor. If the woman is receiving oxytocin (Pitocin) therapy, the nurse watches maternal-fetal response to the treatment closely.

## NURSING DIAGNOSIS

Nursing diagnoses that may apply to the woman with prolonged labor include:

● Pain related to prolonged time in labor

● Ineffective individual coping related to ineffectiveness of breathing techniques to relieve discomfort and anxiety

● Potential for infection related to increased need for invasive assessments secondary to extended time in labor

## NURSING PLAN AND IMPLEMENTATION
### Promotion of Maternal-Fetal Physical Well-Being

The nurse completes assessments pertinent to prolonged labor. The nurse calculates fluid intake and output and checks urine for presence of ketones to gain information about the maternal hydration state.

Following birth, the mother should be closely monitored for signs and symptoms of hemorrhage, shock, and infection. The fetus should be observed for signs of sepsis, cerebral trauma, and cephalhematoma. Nursing actions for fetal distress are given in the Nursing Care Plan—Fetal Distress.

### Provision of Emotional Support

Helping the woman and her partner deal with the anxiety and frustration associated with prolonged labor is another important nursing responsibility. The nurse offers support, encouragement, and information as appropriate. Comfort measures such as helping the woman change position, providing for oral hygiene and skin care, or applying cool washcloths to the forehead may help the woman relax. The involvement of the woman's partner in her care may reduce her anxiety, and the nurse encourages this involvement.

## EVALUATION

Anticipated outcomes of nursing care include:

- The woman maintains comfort during the labor.
- The woman and her partner are able to cope with the hypotonic pattern.
- The woman and fetus have had the risk of infection reduced.

## ● Precipitous Labor

**Precipitous labor** is labor that lasts for less than three hours. Contributing factors in precipitous labor are (a) multiparity, (b) large pelvis, (c) previous precipitous labor, and (d) a small fetus in a favorable position. One or more of these factors, plus strong contractions, result in a rapid transit of the infant through the birth canal (Pritchard et al 1985).

Precipitous labor and precipitous delivery are not the same. A *precipitous delivery* is an unexpected, sudden, and often unattended birth. See Chapter 16 for discussion of emergency delivery.

Maternal implications of precipitous labor include:

- Increased risk of uterine rupture from intense contractions
- Loss of coping abilities
- Lacerations of the cervix, vagina, and perineum due to rapid descent and delivery of the fetus
- Postpartal hemorrhage due to undetected lacerations and/or inadequate uterine contractions after delivery

Fetal-neonatal implications include:

- Fetal distress and/or hypoxia from decreased uteroplacental circulation due to intense uterine contractions
- Cerebral trauma from rapid descent through birth canal

## MEDICAL THERAPY

Any woman with a history of precipitous labor requires close medical monitoring and preparation for an emergency delivery to facilitate a safe outcome for the mother and fetus. Drugs such as magnesium sulfate have been used in cases of precipitous labor. Tocolytic agents such as ritodrine may also prove effective (Pritchard et al 1985).

## NURSING ASSESSMENT

During the intrapartal nursing assessment, the nurse can identify a woman at increased risk of precipitous labor (for example, a previous history of precipitous or short labor places a woman at risk). During the labor the presence of one or both of the following factors may indicate potential problems:

- Accelerated cervical dilatation and fetal descent
- Intense uterine contractions with little uterine relaxation between contractions

## NURSING DIAGNOSIS

Nursing diagnoses that may apply to the woman with precipitous labor include:

- Potential for injury related to rapid labor and birth
- Pain related to rapid labor process

## NURSING PLAN AND IMPLEMENTATION

If the woman has a history of precipitous labor, she is closely monitored, and an emergency delivery pack is kept at hand. The physician is informed of any unusual findings on the Friedman graph (Chapter 15). The nurse stays in constant attendance if at all possible. Comfort and rest may be promoted by assisting the woman to a comfortable position, providing a quiet environment, and administering sedatives as needed. Information and support are given before and after the delivery.

To avoid hyperstimulation of the uterus and possible precipitous labor during oxytocin administration, the nurse should be alert to the dangers of oxytocin overdosage (see Drug Guide—Oxytocin, Chapter 19). If the woman who is receiving oxytocin develops an accelerated labor pattern, the oxytocin is discontinued immediately, and the woman is turned on her left side to improve uterine perfusion. Oxygen may be started to increase the available oxygen in the maternal circulating blood; this increases the amount available for exchange at the placental site.

## EVALUATION

Anticipated outcomes of nursing care include:

- The woman and her baby remain injury free during birth.
- The woman has increased comfort during the birth process.

# ● CARE OF THE WOMAN WITH PREMATURE RUPTURE OF MEMBRANES

**Premature rupture of membranes (PROM)** is spontaneous rupture of the membranes and leakage of amniotic fluid prior to the onset of labor. Preterm PROM is defined as rupture of membranes less than 259 days (37 weeks) from the start of the last menstrual period. PROM is associated with maternal age of 35 years or greater, multiparity, incompetent cervix, damage to the cervix by surgical instrumentation, and low weight gain (Flood and Naeye 1984).

Maternal implications of PROM include:

● Intrauterine infection due to ascending pathogens

● Increased stress regarding the condition of the child if rupture occurs prior to term

● Prolonged hospitalization if the fetal gestational age is less than 37 weeks

Fetal-neonatal implications include risk of:

● Fetal sepsis due to ascending pathogens

● Malpresentation

● Prolapse of the umbilical cord

● Increased perinatal morbidity and mortality

## ● Medical Therapy

Gestational age of the fetus and the presence or absence of maternal infection determine the management of PROM.

After confirming with Nitrazine Paper and a microscopic examination (ferning test) that the membranes have ruptured, the gestational age of the fetus is calculated. Single or combination methods of calculation may be used, including Nägele's rule, fundal height, ultrasound to measure the fetal biparietal diameter (BPD), and amniocentesis to identify lung maturity. If maternal signs and symptoms of infection are evident, antibiotic therapy (usually by intravenous infusion) is initiated immediately, and the fetus is delivered vaginally or by cesarean birth regardless of the gestational age. Upon admission to the nursery the neonate is assessed for sepsis and placed on antibiotics. Chapter 24 provides further information about the neonate with sepsis.

Management of PROM in the absence of infection and gestation of less than 37 weeks is usually conservative. The woman is hospitalized on bed rest. On admission complete blood cell count (CBC) and urinalysis are obtained. Continuous electronic fetal monitoring may be ordered at the beginning of treatment but usually is discontinued after a few hours, unless membranes are ruptured or the fetus is estimated to be very low birth weight (VLBW). Mater-nal blood pressure (BP), pulse, and temperature, and FHR are assessed every four hours. A white blood cell count (WBC) is ordered daily. Vaginal exams are avoided to decrease the chance of infection. As the gestation approaches 34 weeks, an amniocentesis may be done weekly to evaluate lecithin/sphingomyelin (L/S) and phosphatidylglycerol (PG). After initial treatment and observation, some women may be followed at home. The woman is advised to continue bed rest (with bathroom privileges); monitor her temperature four times a day; avoid intercourse, douches, or tampons; and have a WBC every other day (Oxorn 1986, Danforth and Scott 1986). The woman is advised to contact her physician and return to the hospital if she has fever, uterine tenderness and/or contractions, increased leakage of fluid, or a foul vaginal discharge.

Opinions as to the efficacy of administering glucocorticoids (betamethasone or dexamethasone) prophylactically for PROM are sharply divided (Creasy and Resnik 1989, Avery and Burket 1986). When gestation is between 34 and 36 weeks, medical practice has been to delay delivery for 24 hours to allow natural elevation of maternal-fetal blood glucocorticoids, thereby contributing to fetal lung maturity. If gestation is between 28 and 32 weeks and labor can be delayed for 24 to 48 hours, betamethasone (Celestone) is frequently given. Glucocorticoids are not administered in the presence of uterine infection. (See Drug Guide—Betamethasone.) In research by Simpson and Harbert (1984), no difference was noted in the occurrence of respiratory distress syndrome (RDS) in the preterm neonate because of the administration of glucocorticoids. Another study (Garite et al 1981) found no reduction in the incidence of RDS and also discovered an increased incidence of neonatal and maternal sepsis when glucocorticoids were given.

Some researchers suggest a short-term saline solution infusion into the amniotic cavity to treat variable or prolonged fetal heart decelerations once they appear (Nageotte et al 1985). When these researchers infused warmed (37° C) sterile normal saline through a uterine pressure catheter, they found a decreased incidence of variable decelerations and improvement of metabolic state at delivery.

## ● Nursing Assessment

Determining the duration of the rupture of the membranes is a significant component of the intrapartal assessment. The nurse asks the woman when her membranes ruptured and when labor began, because the risk of infection may be directly related to the time involved. Gestational age is determined to prepare for the possibility of a preterm delivery. The nurse observes the mother for signs and symptoms of infection, especially by reviewing her WBC, temperature, and pulse rate and the character of her amniotic fluid. If the mother has a fever, hydration status should be checked. When a preterm or cesarean

# ✿ Drug Guide

## Betamethasone (Celestone Solupan®)

### Overview of Maternal-Fetal Action

"Betamethasone is a glucocorticoid which acts to accelerate fetal lung maturation and prevent hyaline membrane disease by inhibiting cell mitosis, increasing cell differentiation, promoting selected enzymatic actions, and participating in the storage and secretion of surfactant" (Bishop 1981). The best results are obtained when the fetus is between 30 and 32 weeks' gestation. The drug may be used as early as 26 weeks and as late as 34 weeks (Briggs et al 1986).

To obtain optimal results, delivery should be delayed for at least 24 hours after the end of treatment. If delivery does not occur, the effect of the drug disappears in about one week. A female fetus seems more likely than a male to obtain the most prophylactic effect (Briggs et al 1986).

### Route, Dosage, Frequency
Prenatal maternal intramuscular administration of 12 mg of betamethasone is given once a day for two days. Repeated treatment will be needed on a weekly basis until 34 weeks of gestation (unless delivery occurs).

### Contraindications
Inability to delay birth for 48 hours

L/S ratio of 2:1

Presence of a condition that necessitates immediate delivery (eg, maternal bleeding)

Presence of maternal infection, diabetes mellitus, hypertension

Concomitant use of tocolytic agents, which may increase risk of maternal pulmonary edema (Bishop 1981)

Gestational age greater than 34 weeks

### Maternal Side Effects
Bishop (1981) reports that suspected maternal risks include (a) initiation of lactation, (b) increased risk of infection, (c) augmentation of placental insufficiency in hypertensive women, (d) gastrointestinal bleeding, (e) inability to use estriol levels to assess fetal status, (f) pulmonary edema when used concurrently with tocolytics (such as ritodrine).

May cause $Na^+$ retention, $K^+$ loss, weight gain, edema, indigestion

Increased risk of infection if PROM present (Briggs et al 1986).

### Effects on Fetus/Neonate
Lowered cortisol levels between one and eight days following delivery (Giacoia and Yaffe 1982)

Possible suppression of aldosterone levels up to two weeks following delivery (Giacoia and Yaffe 1982)

Hypoglycemia

Increased risk of neonatal sepsis (Briggs et al 1986)

Animal studies have shown serious fetal side effects such as reduced head circumference, reduced weight of the fetal adrenal and thymus glands, and decreased placental weight (Briggs et al 1986). Human studies have not observed these effects, however.

### Nursing Considerations

Assess for presence of contraindications.

Provide education regarding possible side effects.

Administer deep into gluteal muscle, avoid injection into deltoid (high incidence of local atrophy).

Periodically evaluate BP, pulse, weight, and edema.

Assess lab data for electrolytes.

---

birth is anticipated, the nurse evaluates the coping abilities of the woman and her partner.

## ● Nursing Diagnosis

Nursing diagnoses that may apply to the woman with premature rupture of the membranes include:

● Potential for infection related to premature rupture of membranes

● Impaired gas exchange in the fetus related to compression of the umbilical cord secondary to prolapse of the cord

● Ineffective individual coping related to unknown outcome of the pregnancy

## ● Nursing Plan and Implementation
### PROMOTION OF MATERNAL-FETAL PHYSICAL WELL-BEING

Nursing actions should focus on the woman, her partner, and the fetus. The time her membranes ruptured and the time of labor onset are recorded. The nurse observes the woman for signs and symptoms of infection by frequently monitoring her vital signs (especially temperature and pulse), describing the character of the amniotic fluid, and reporting elevated WBC to the physician/nurse-midwife. Uterine activity and fetal response to the labor are evaluated, but vaginal exams are not done unless absolutely necessary. Comfort measures may help promote rest and relaxation. The nurse must also ensure that hydration is maintained, particularly if the woman's temperature is elevated.

### CLIENT EDUCATION

Provision of education is another important aspect of nursing care. The couple needs to understand the implications of PROM and all treatment methods. It is important to address side effects and alternative treatments. The couple needs to know that although the membranes are ruptured, fluid continues to be produced.

### PROVISION OF PSYCHOLOGIC SUPPORT

Providing psychologic support for the couple is critical. The nurse may reduce anxiety by listening empathetically, relaying accurate information, and providing explanations of procedures. Preparing the couple for a cesarean birth, a preterm neonate, and the possibility of fetal or neonatal demise may be necessary.

## ● Evaluation

Anticipated outcomes of nursing care include:

● The woman's risk of infection and cord prolapse are decreased.

● The couple understands the implications of PROM and all treatments and alternative treatments.

● The pregnancy is maintained without trauma to the mother or her baby.

## ● CARE OF THE WOMAN AT RISK DUE TO PRETERM LABOR

Labor that occurs between 20 and 38 weeks of pregnancy is referred to as **preterm labor.** The incidence of preterm labor is 5%–10% and prematurity of the fetus accounts for approximately 75% of neonatal morbidity and mortality (Hollander 1987).

Preterm labor may be caused by fetal, maternal, or placental factors. Premature rupture of the membranes occurs in 20% to 30% of the cases of preterm labor. In the other 70% to 80% of cases, no known cause has been identified (Danforth and Scott 1986). Maternal factors include cardiovascular or renal disease, diabetes, preeclampsia-eclampsia, abdominal surgery, a blow to the abdomen, uterine anomalies, cervical incompetence, maternal infection (especially urinary tract infection [UTI]), and maternal use of drugs such as cocaine. Uterine manipulation or displacement during abdominal surgery may contribute to the early onset of labor. Fetal factors include multiple pregnancy, hydramnios, and fetal infection.

Other cases reveal a strong correlation between preterm delivery and low socioeconomic status (education, income, occupation) and/or history of preterm births.

Risk-scoring tools help identify a large proportion of pregnant women who are at risk for preterm delivery. Table 7.1 presents one system for determining the risk of spontaneous preterm delivery.

Maternal implications of preterm labor include:

● Increased stress related to the baby's condition

● Stress of unplanned hospitalization

● Administration of additional medications

Fetal-neonatal implications include:

● Increased morbidity and mortality

● Increased risk of trauma during delivery

● Immature organ systems that may be incompatible with life

## ● Medical Therapy

Women who are at risk for preterm labor are taught to recognize the symptoms associated with preterm labor. If any symptoms are present, the woman is encouraged to notify her physician/nurse-midwife immediately. Immediate diagnosis is necessary to stop preterm labor before it advances to a stage at which intervention will be ineffective. Some clinicians use weekly cervical exams to assist in detecting early cervical changes associated with preterm labor (Holbrook et al 1987).

Diagnosis of preterm labor is confirmed by two contractions lasting at least 30 seconds in a 15-minute period and by cervical dilatation and effacement.

Labor is not interrupted if one or more of the following conditions are present:

● Active labor with cervical dilatation of 4 cm or more

● Presence of severe pregnancy-induced hypertension (PIH), which creates risk for the woman if the pregnancy continues

● Fetal complications (isoimmunization, gross anomalies)

● Prolonged rupture of membranes

● Hemorrhage

● Fetal death

The drugs currently in use to arrest preterm labor are ritodrine (Yutopar), terbutaline sulfate (Brethine), and magnesium sulfate. See Drug Guide—Ritodrine.

Magnesium sulfate has long been used in treatment of PIH and has been gaining favor in the treatment of preterm labor because it is effective and has fewer side ef-

 *Drug Guide*

# Ritodrine (Yutopar)

## Overview of Action in Obstetrics

Ritodrine is a sympathomimetic $\beta_2$-adrenergic agonist. It exerts its effect on Type II beta receptors, which are found in uterine smooth muscle, bronchioles, and diaphragm. Stimulation of Type II receptors results in uterine relaxation, bronchodilation, vasodilation, and muscle glycogenolysis. As muscles in the vessel walls relax, hypotension is induced. The body compensates by increasing maternal heart rate and pulse pressure.

Ritodrine causes a potassium shift, which may cause hypokalemia. There may also be an increase in blood glucose and plasma insulin levels and stimulation of glycogen release from muscles and the liver (NAACOG 1984). Ritodrine is FDA-approved for use in treatment of preterm labor.

### Route, Dosage, Frequency

Add 150 mg of ritodrine to 500 mL IV fluid and administer as a piggyback to a primary IV. The resulting dilution is 0.3 mg/mL. Note: Some authorities recommend a saline solution and others believe a dextrose solution reduces the incidence of pulmonary edema (Niebyl 1986). The initial dose is 0.1 mg/min (20 mL/hr on an adult infusion pump). The dose is increased 0.05 mg/min (10 mL/hr on an adult infusion pump) every ten minutes until contractions cease. Maximum dosage is 0.35 mg/min (70 mL/hr on an adult infusion pump). When contractions cease, the infusion rate may be decreased by 0.5 mg/min (10 mL/hr on an adult infusion pump). The infusion may be maintained at a low rate for a period of hours to assure that contractions do not begin again. Before the intravenous infusion is discontinued, PO administration is begun (Shortridge 1983, Yutopar Drug Information 1984).

NOTE: Current studies are being conducted using lower doses of ritodrine (Hollander 1987). See your agency protocols for further information.

Gonik and Creasy (1986) recommend administration of oral ritodrine 30 minutes before ending IV ritodrine. The initial PO dose is 10–20 mg every two hours, and the time between doses may be increased to three to four hours based on uterine response and maternal pulse. The maternal pulse is maintained in the 90–100 beats/min range.

This dosage can be administered safely to a maximum of 120 mg over 24 hours. The length of therapy varies.

Current research is directed toward the use of a single injection of ritodrine for other obstetric problems. Rapid relaxation of the uterus may be needed in the presence of tetanic contractions and cord prolapse (Ingemarsson et al 1985b). It has also been suggested for use with fetal bradycardia to improve the heart rate (Ingemarsson et al 1985a) and to inhibit labor in order to manage fetal distress (Caritis et al 1985).

### Maternal Contraindications

Preterm labor accompanied by cervical dilatation greater than 4 cm, chorioamnionitis, severe preeclampsia-eclampsia, severe bleeding, fetal death, significant intrauterine growth retardation (IUGR) contraindicate use of ritodrine, as do any of the following:

Hypovolemia, uncontrolled hypertension

Pulmonary hypertension

Cardiac disease, arrhythmias

Diabetes mellitus (use with caution)

Concurrent therapy with glucocorticoids (use with caution)

Gestation less than 20 weeks

### Maternal Side Effects

Tachycardia, occasionally premature ventricular contractions (PVCs), increased stroke volume, slight increase in systolic and decrease in diastolic pressure, palpitations, tremors, nervousness, nausea and vomiting, headache, erythema, hypotension, shortness of breath (Bealle et al 1985)

Decreased peripheral vascular resistance, which lowers diastolic pressure → widening of pulse pressure

Hyperglycemia (usually peaks within three hours after initiation of therapy) (Hankins and Hauth 1985)

Metabolic acidosis

Hypokalemia (causes internal redistribution)

Pulmonary edema in women treated concurrently with glucocorticoids, and who have fluid overload (Benedetti 1983)

Increased concentration of lactate and free fatty acids

ST segment depression, T wave flattening, prolongation of QT interval (Hendricks et al 1986)

Increase in plasma volume as indicated by decreases in hemoglobin, hematocrit, and serum albumin levels (Philipsen et al 1985)

Possible neutropenia with long-term IV therapy (Wang and Davidson 1986)

Caritis (1988) notes early-onset side effects of chest pain, tachycardia, hypotension, shortness of breath, and vomiting are probably associated with infusion rate and plasma concentration. Late-onset side effects of fluid retention, decreasing hematocrit, and pulmonary edema are probably related to duration of therapy, total fluid intake, and total drug administered.

*(continues)*

## ⚡ Drug Guide

## Ritodrine (Yutopar) *(continued)*

*Effects on Fetus/Neonate*

Fetal tachycardia, cardiac dysrhythmias

Increased serum glucose concentration

Fetal acidosis

Fetal hypoxia

Neonatal hypoglycemia, hypocalcemia, ↑ WBC

Neonatal paralytic ileus, irritability, tremors

Neonatal hypotension at birth

May decrease incidence of neonatal respiratory distress syndrome (Lipshitz 1981)

### Nursing Considerations

Position woman in left side-lying position to increase placental perfusion and decrease incidence of hypotension.

Complete a history and assessment to identify possible presence of infection and maternal-fetal contraindications to treatment.

Explain procedure, which will include electronic fetal monitor, IV, frequent assessments, possible use of cardiac monitor, blood samples, intake and output, and daily weight, and potential for development of side effects, especially increase in pulse and fetal heart rate.

Monitor uterine activity and fetal heart rate by electronic fetal monitor.

Assess maternal BP and pulse every 15 minutes while dosage is being increased and every 30 minutes while on maintenance IV (Shortridge 1983). As long as dosage is being increased, some agency protocols recommend taking maternal BP and pulse prior to dose increase. Notify physician if maternal pulse >120 beats/min. (Note: Expect increase of 20–40 beats/min. Maternal pulse may exceed 120 beats/min for a brief period of time [NAACOG 1984].)

Assess respiratory rate and auscultate breath sounds with maternal vital signs. Note signs of pulmonary edema (rales and rhonchi). When oral therapy is begun, maternal BP, pulse, and respirations may be taken with each PO dose.

Monitor FHR with maternal assessments (Note: Expect increase of approximately 10 beats/min. The rate should not exceed 180 beats/min. Notify physician of rate >180 beats/min).

Apply antiembolism stockings to prevent pooling of blood in extremities.

Encourage passive range of motion in legs every one to two hours.

Assess hydration status by evaluating intake/output, skin turgor, mucous membranes, and urine concentration.

Maintain intake and output records. Intake is usually limited to 2500 mL/day (Gonik and Creasy 1986) and 90–100 mL/hr (Shortridge 1983).

Assess output every hour until contractions cease, then every four hours (Shortridge 1983).

Weigh daily at same time after woman has emptied bladder, using same scales and same clothing.

Observe woman closely for problems associated with hypokalemia (muscle weakness, cardiac arrhythmia) and pulmonary edema (dyspnea, wheezing, coughing, rales or rhonchi, or tachypnea). Discontinue therapy if pulmonary edema or cardiac problems develop.

Assess lab data regarding electrolytes, glucose, and WBC.

Have $\beta$ blocking agent available as antidote for betasympathomimetic therapy. Propranolol (Inderal) 0.25 mg IV is usually used (Shortridge 1983). It should be given by a physician and injected over at least one minute to reduce the potential for lowering the blood pressure and precipitating cardiac standstill. Cardiac monitoring should be continuous.

Provide psychosocial support. The threat of preterm labor produces anxiety. Provide information and counseling for the woman and partner, and encourage questions. Assist them in making life-style changes such as more frequent rest periods, cessation of employment, and possible changes in sexual activity. If woman is discharged on oral therapy, teach her to take medications on time to ensure optimum effect, to observe for signs of preterm labor, and to assess her pulse with each dose. The woman needs to report pulse above 120, palpitations, tremors, agitation, nervousness, chest pain, and any difficulty breathing.

If birth occurs when woman is on ritodrine therapy, assess newborn for presence of side effects (NAACOG 1984).

It is recommended to discontinue ritodrine in the presence of any of the following: Maternal heart rate above 140 beats/min or fetal heart rate above 200 beats/min, more than six maternal or fetal premature ventricular contractions/min, maternal systolic pressure above 180 mm Hg or diastolic below 40 mm Hg, chest pain, shortness of breath (Bealle et al 1985).

fects than β sympathomimetics. The usual recommended loading dose is 4 g bolus IV over 20 minutes. The constant dose is then 2 g/hr. The dose may be increased by 1 g/hr every 30 minutes until contractions cease or a serum magnesium concentration of 6–8 mg/dL is obtained. After contractions cease, the infusion is decreased to the lowest effective rate to maintain tocolysis and a serum magnesium concentration in the range of 6–8 mg/dL (Hollander 1987). The therapy is continued for 12 hours. The maternal serum level that is important for tocolysis seems to be 6–8 mg/dL or 4–7 mEq/L (Wilkins et al 1986). Side effects with the loading dose may include flushing, a feeling of warmth, headache, nausea, and dizziness. Other side effects include lethargy and sluggishness, decreased muscle tone (eg, diplopia), impaired deep tendon reflexes, decreased respirations, and cardiac arrythmias (Hollander 1987). See Drug Guide—Magnesium Sulfate on page 314 for other side effects. Fetal side effects may include hypotonia that persists for one or two days following birth (Wilkins et al 1986).

In comparison with IV ritodrine, magnesium sulfate has no recognizable effect on systolic or diastolic blood pressure (mean blood pressure is maintained and uteroplacental perfusion is maintained), does not alter maternal heart rate (though it may cause a slight decrease in the fetal heart rate), has no effect on cardiac output, and only slightly increases placental blood flow (Thiagarajah et al 1985).

Long-term oral therapy may be accomplished with magnesium oxide, magnesium peroxide, or magnesium gluconate. The therapeutic dose is usually 250 to 450 mg every three hours. This dose maintains a maternal serum level of 2 to 2.5 mg, which is usually sufficient to prevent uterine contractions (Niebyl 1986).

Two new drugs may soon be used in the treatment of preterm labor. Hexaprenaline, another β-mimetic drug, has less effect on maternal pulse and BP and FHR than ritodrine (Niebyl 1986). In some health care centers prostaglandin synthesis inhibitors (PSI) such as indomethacin (Indocin) are being investigated and used in selected instances. Early research indicates maternal side effects, such as oliguria and vasoconstriction, and potential fetal side effects, such as premature closure of ductus arteriosus, have been reported (Knight 1986).

Research is also being conducted on the use of calcium channel blockers such as nitrendipine and nifedipine to inhibit preterm labor (Sakamoto and Huszar 1986, Veille et al 1986).

An additional treatment may be recommended. Administration of glucocorticoids helps the lungs of the preterm infant to mature. If glucocorticoids are given more than 24 hours before delivery, the incidence of respiratory distress syndrome is reduced. Dexamethasone (Decadron) or betamethasone may be administered intramuscularly to the woman, and delivery is delayed at least 24 hours if possible.

When labor cannot be arrested, plans for delivery are made. A cesarean delivery is usually performed to protect the fetal head from excessive trauma (head compression) during delivery and to minimize the risk of intraventricular hemorrhage. There is some controversy concerning the optimal delivery method, especially for VLBW (501–1500 g) babies. Some researchers believe that the incidence of intraventricular hemorrhage is more likely to be associated with fetal hypoxia and acidosis than with head compression during delivery (Morales and Koerten 1986, Welch and Bottoms 1986). Regardless of the delivery method, qualified personnel who can assist the respiratory effort of the preterm infant should be present at birth.

● *Nursing Assessment*

During the antepartal period, the nurse identifies the woman at risk for preterm labor by noting the presence of predisposing factors. During the intrapartal period, the nurse assesses the progress of labor and the physiologic impact of labor on the mother and fetus. The key nursing assessments during ritodrine therapy are listed in Table 18.1.

**Table 18.1 Key Nursing Assessments During Ritodrine Therapy**

| Time interval | Assessment |
| --- | --- |
| **DURING INITIAL IV THERAPY AND INCREASES IN INFUSION RATE** | |
| Every 10 or 15 minutes | FHR and maternal BP, pulse, and respirations. Auscultate lung sounds for rales and rhonchi. Be alert for complaints of dyspnea, chest tightness. Uterine activity. |
| Every hour | Assess output (should be over 30 cc/hr or match intake). Assess intake (should not exceed 90–100 mL/hr). |
| **DURING MAINTENANCE IV THERAPY** | |
| Every 30 minutes | Maternal BP, pulse, and respirations; FHR; lung sounds; uterine activity. |
| Every 4 hours | Intake and output. |
| **DURING PO THERAPY** | |
| Before each dose | Maternal BP, pulse, and respirations; FHR; lung sounds. |
| Every 4–8 hours | Intake and output. |
| Whenever lab work results are available, evaluate $K^+$ (for hypokalemia), hemoglobin, and hematocrit (for signs of hemodilution, which, together with hypokalemia, may be associated with pulmonary edema). | |

## ● Nursing Diagnosis

Nursing diagnoses that may apply to the woman with preterm labor include:

- Knowledge deficit related to causes, identification, and treatment of preterm labor
- Fear related to early labor and delivery
- Ineffective individual coping related to need for constant attention to pregnancy

See Essential Nursing Diagnoses to Consider—Preterm Labor for additional nursing diagnoses.

## ● Nursing Plan and Implementation

### EDUCATION FOR SELF-CARE

Once the woman at risk for preterm labor has been identified, she must be educated about the importance of preventing the onset of labor. Increasing the woman's awareness of the subtle symptoms of preterm labor is one of the most important teaching objectives of the nurse. The signs and symptoms of preterm labor include (Creasy and Resnick 1989):

- Uterine contractions that occur every ten minutes or less
- Mild, menstrual-like cramps felt low in the abdomen
- Feelings of pelvic pressure (constant or intermittent) that may feel like the baby pressing down
- Low backache, which may be constant or intermittent
- A change in the vaginal discharge (an increase in amount, a change to more clear and watery, or a pinkish tinge)
- Abdominal cramping with or without diarrhea

The woman is also taught to evaluate contraction activity once or twice a day. She does so by lying down tilted to one side with a pillow behind her back for support. The woman places her fingertips on the fundus of the uterus, which is above the umbilicus (navel). She checks for contractions (hardening or tightening in the uterus) for about one hour. It is important for the pregnant woman to know that uterine contractions occur occasionally throughout the pregnancy. If they occur every ten minutes for one hour, however, the cervix could begin to dilate and labor could ensue.

The nurse ensures that the woman knows when to report signs and symptoms. If contractions occur every ten minutes (or less) for one hour, if any of the other signs and symptoms are present for one hour, or if clear fluid begins leaking from the vagina, the woman should telephone her physician/nurse-midwife, clinic, or hospital birthing unit and make arrangements to be checked for ongoing labor.

Care givers need to be aware that the woman is knowl-edgeable and attuned to changes in her body, and her call must be taken seriously. When a woman is at risk for preterm labor, she may have many episodes of contractions and other signs or symptoms. If she is treated positively, she will feel freer to report problems as they arise.

Preventive self-care measures are also very important. The nurse has a vital role in communicating self-care measures (see Table 18.2).

## PROMOTION OF MATERNAL-FETAL PHYSICAL WELL-BEING DURING LABOR

Provision of supportive nursing care to the woman in preterm labor is important during hospitalization. This care consists of promoting bed rest, monitoring vital signs (especially blood pressure and respirations), measuring intake and output, and continuous monitoring of FHR and uterine contractions. Placing the woman on her left side facilitates maternal-fetal circulation. Vaginal examinations are kept to a minimum. If tocolytic agents are being administered, the mother and fetus are monitored closely for any adverse effects.

### Table 18.2  Self-Care Measures to Prevent Preterm Labor

Rest two or three times a day lying on your left side.

Drink 2 to 3 quarts of water or fruit juice each day. Avoid caffeine drinks. Filling a quart container and drinking from it will eliminate the need to keep track of numerous glasses of fluid.

Empty your bladder at least every two hours during waking hours.

Avoid lifting heavy objects. If other small children are in the home, work out alternatives for picking them up, such as sitting on a chair and having them climb on your lap.

Avoid prenatal breast preparation such as nipple rolling or rubbing nipples with a towel. This is not meant to discourage breast-feeding but to avoid the potential increase in uterine irritability.

Pace necessary activities to avoid overexertion.

Sexual activity may need to be curtailed or eliminated.

Find pleasurable ways to boost the spirits to help compensate for limitations of activities.

Try to focus on one day or one week at a time rather than longer periods of time.

If on bed rest, get dressed each day and rest on a couch rather than becoming isolated in the bedroom.

Source: Prepared in consultation with Susan Bennett, RN, ACCE, Coordinator of the Prematurity Prevention Program.

# Essential Nursing Diagnoses to Consider

## Preterm Labor

Altered family processes

Altered patterns of urinary elimination: Urinary frequency, urgency

Altered sexuality patterns

Anticipatory grieving

Anxiety

Fatigue

Fear

Impaired gas exchange

Impaired physical mobility

Ineffective family coping

Ineffectual individual coping

Knowledge deficit

Noncompliance

Potential fluid volume deficit

Potential for infection

Powerlessness

Sleep pattern disturbance

Spiritual distress

## PROVISION OF EMOTIONAL SUPPORT TO THE FAMILY

Whether preterm labor is arrested or proceeds, the woman and her partner experience intense psychologic stress. Decreasing the anxiety associated with the unknown and the risk of a preterm neonate is a primary aim of the nurse.

Providing emotional support for the woman and her partner during preterm labor and delivery is also important. Common behavioral responses include feelings of anxiety and guilt about the possibility that the pregnancy will terminate early. With empathetic communication, the nurse can facilitate the expression of these feelings, thereby helping the couple identify and implement coping mechanisms. The nurse also keeps the couple informed about the labor progress, the treatment regimen, and the status of the fetus so that their full cooperation will be elicited. In the event of imminent vaginal or cesarean delivery, the couple should be offered brief but ongoing explanations to prepare them for the actual birth process and the events following the birth.

## • Evaluation

Anticipated outcomes of nursing care include:

- The woman understands the cause, identification, and treatment of preterm labor.
- The woman's fears about early labor and delivery are lessened.
- The woman feels comfortable in her ability to cope with her situation and has resources to call on.
- The woman understands self-care measures and can identify characteristics that need to be reported to her care giver.
- The woman and her baby have a safe labor and birth.

## • CARE OF THE WOMAN WITH POSTDATE PREGNANCY

Postdate pregnancy has become recognized as an important problem. While many pregnancies extend beyond the anticipated due date, the true postdate pregnancy is associated with increased risk for asphyxia and trauma in the fetus.

**Postdate pregnancy** is one that extends more than 294 days or 42 weeks past the first day of the last menstrual period. Approximately 12% of women give birth after 294 days (41 full weeks), and only one third of these are truly postdate (Freeman 1986).

Maternal implications of postdate pregnancy include:

- Physiologic risks are minimal.
- Psychologic stress is increased as due date is passed and concern for the baby increases.

Fetal implications include:

- Decreased perfusion from the placenta may occur.
- Oligohydramnios may be present, which increases the risk of cord compression.
- Meconium aspiration is eight times more likely (Usher et al 1988).
- Perinatal mortality increases for the small, immature, growth-retarded fetus (Eden et al 1987).

## • Medical Therapy

Therapies that may be used when postdate pregnancy is suspected include weekly or twice weekly nonstress test (NST) and/or contraction stress test (CST), and fetal biophysical profile to provide information regarding fetal status.

## • Nursing Assessment

Assessment of the woman with postdate pregnancy usually occurs in the birth setting. The nurse needs to stay alert for evidence of variable decelerations of the FHR, which are associated with cord compression due to the oligohydramnios. Meconium may be present and would be evident when the amniotic membranes rupture. The woman's knowledge base regarding the condition, implications for her baby, risks, and possible interventions needs to be assessed.

## Nursing Diagnosis

Possible nursing diagnoses include:

- Knowledge deficit related to lack of information regarding postdate pregnancy
- Fear related to the unknown outcome for the baby
- Ineffective individual coping related to anxiety regarding the status of the baby

## Nursing Plan and Implementation
### PROMOTION OF FETAL WELL-BEING

The woman may be taught to assess fetal activity each day to become more familiar with fetal movement and to detect any decrease in movement. (See Chapter 13 for further discussion of fetal movement records.)

While in the birth setting, the fetal heart rate is monitored by continuous electronic monitoring. The FHR tracing is evaluated frequently for signs of distress.

### PROVISION OF EMOTIONAL SUPPORT TO THE MOTHER

Women with pregnancies that extend past the due date frequently report that they would like more support from nursing personnel. In a recent study (Campbell 1986), women reported that they felt increased stress and anxiety and had more difficulty coping. Encouragement, support, and recognition of the woman's anxiety were all identified as helpful strategies by health personnel.

### CLIENT EDUCATION

The woman needs to have information regarding the postdate pregnancy. The implications and associated risks for the baby need to be addressed as well as possible treatment plans. The woman and her partner need opportunities to ask questions and clarify information.

## Evaluation

Anticipated outcomes of nursing care include:

- The woman has knowledge regarding the postdate pregnancy.
- The woman and her partner feel supported and able to cope with the postdate pregnancy.

- Fetal status is maintained, any abnormalities are quickly identified, and supportive measures are initiated.

## CARE OF THE WOMAN WITH A RUPTURED UTERUS

A ruptured uterus is the tearing of previously intact uterine muscles or of an old uterine scar. The rupture can be caused by a weakened cesarean scar, usually from a "classic" incision; obstetric trauma; mismanagement of oxytocin induction or augmentation; CPD; and congenital defects of the birth canal.

The signs and symptoms of a complete rupture include excruciating pain and cessation of contractions. Vaginal hemorrhage may occur, but vaginal bleeding is usually not profuse. Massive intraperitoneal hemorrhage and hematomas of the broad ligament are hidden sources of bleeding and may account for the scant vaginal bleeding. The woman exhibits signs of hypovolemic shock, and the fetal heart stops beating.

Maternal implications of ruptured uterus include:

- Development of profound shock and risk of maternal death
- Abdominal surgery and possible hysterectomy
- Prolonged hospitalization for intensive care and recuperation
- Loss of the expected baby

Fetal-neonatal implications include:

- Fetal asphyxia and death

## Medical Therapy

In the presence of a threatened or actual rupture, emergency surgical intervention is performed to save the mother and her baby. Delivery is by cesarean birth. If the rupture (uterine tear) is small, the physician may be able to repair it. If the rupture is large, the physician may do a hysterectomy.

## Nursing Care

The nurse may be the one to identify the signs of uterine rupture. The nurse monitors vital signs, evaluates maternal hemorrhage, and quickly mobilizes the staff for an emergency laparotomy or cesarean birth. When the physiologic needs of the woman are met, the nurse can focus on the emotional needs of the family. The family must have a clear understanding of the procedure and its implications for future childbearing. In addition, if fetal death has occurred, the couple should be given an opportunity to grieve and allowed to see their infant if they desire.

# ● CARE OF THE WOMAN AND FETUS AT RISK DUE TO FETAL MALPOSITION

**Persistent occiput-posterior** (OP) position of the fetus is probably one of the most common complications encountered during childbirth. If the fetus is in this position, the occiput of the fetal head is directed toward the back of the maternal pelvis. The fetus may remain in this position throughout labor and birth, or it may rotate (or change) to an occiput-anterior (OA) position during birth.

Maternal implications of occiput-posterior position include:

● Risk of third- or fourth-degree perineal lacerations during birth

● Risk of extension of a midline episiotomy

Fetal implications include:

● No increased risk of fetal mortality unless labor is prolonged or an operative delivery is performed

## ● Medical Therapy

Medical treatment focuses on close monitoring of the maternal and fetal status and labor progress to determine whether vaginal or cesarean birth is the safer delivery method. According to Pritchard et al (1985), vaginal birth is possible as follows:

1. Await spontaneous delivery
2. Forceps delivery with the occiput directly posterior
3. Forceps rotation of the occiput to the anterior position and delivery (Scanzoni's maneuver)
4. Manual rotation to the anterior position followed by forceps delivery

If the pelvis is roomy and the perineum is relaxed, as found in grandmultiparity, the fetus may have no particular problem delivering spontaneously in the occiput-posterior position. If, however, the perineum is rigid, the second stage of labor may be prolonged. A prolonged second stage is one that lasts over an hour in multiparas and two hours or more in nulliparas. In the event of a prolonged second stage with arrest of descent due to occiput-posterior position, a midforceps or manual rotation may be done if no CPD is present. In cases of CPD, cesarean birth is the treatment of choice.

## ● Nursing Assessment

Signs and symptoms of a persistent occiput-posterior position are a dysfunctional labor pattern, a prolonged active phase, secondary arrest of dilatation or arrest of descent, and complaints of intense back pain by the laboring woman. The back pain is caused by the fetal occiput compressing the sacral nerves. Further assessment may reveal a depression in the maternal abdomen above the symphysis. Fetal heart tones will be heard far laterally on the abdomen, and on vaginal examination one will find the wide diamond-shaped anterior fontanelle in the anterior portion of the pelvis. This fontanelle may be difficult to feel because of molding of the fetal head.

## ● Nursing Diagnosis

Nursing diagnoses that may apply to women with persistent occiput posterior include:

● Pain related to back discomfort secondary to occiput posterior position

● Ineffective individual coping related to unanticipated discomfort and slow progress in labor

## ● Nursing Plan and Implementation
### FACILITATION OF FETAL POSITION CHANGE

Changing maternal posture has been used for many years to enhance rotation of OP or occiput-transverse (OT) to OA. The woman may be placed on one side and then asked to move to the other side as the fetus begins to rotate. This side-lying position may promote rotation; it also enables the support persons to apply counterpressure on the sacral area to decrease discomfort. A knee-chest position provides a downward slant to the vaginal canal, directing the fetal head downward on descent. Andrews and Andrews (1983) suggest that a hands and knees position is often effective in rotating the fetus. In addition to maintaining a hands and knees position on the bed, the woman may do pelvic rocking, and the support person may perform firm stroking motions on the abdomen. The stroking begins over the fetal back and swings around to the other side of the abdomen. After the fetus has rotated, the woman lies in a Sims' position on the side opposite the fetal back. Although Andrews and Andrews (1983) suggest that further research is warranted, these maternal position changes appear to be a safe, simple, and economical way to assist the change of fetal position.

## ● Evaluation

Anticipated outcomes of nursing care include:

● The woman's discomfort is decreased.

● The woman and her partner understand comfort measures and position changes that may assist her.

● The woman's coping abilities are strengthened.

● The woman and her partner feel supported and encouraged.

# ● CARE OF THE WOMAN AND FETUS AT RISK DUE TO FETAL MALPRESENTATION

Fetal malpresentations include brow, face, breech, shoulder (transverse lie), and compound presentation.

## ● Brow Presentation

In a brow presentation, the forehead of the fetus becomes the presenting part. The fetal neck is hyperextended instead of flexed, with the result that the fetal head enters the birth canal with the widest diameter of the head (occipitomental) foremost (see Figure 18.3).

The brow presentation occurs more often in the multipara than the nullipara and is thought to be due to lax abdominal and pelvic musculature.

Maternal implications of brow presentation include:

● Cesarean birth in the presence of CPD

● Cesarean birth if the brow presentation does not convert to an occiput presentation

Fetal-neonatal implications include:

● Increased risk of fetal mortality from infection due to prolonged labor and/or injuries received during vaginal delivery

● Possibility of trauma during a vaginal birth, including tentorial tears, cerebral and neck compression, and damage to the trachea and larynx

## MEDICAL THERAPY

As long as dilatation and descent are occurring, active interference is not necessary. In the presence of labor problems but no CPD, a manual conversion may be attempted. In the presence of failed conversions, CPD, or secondary arrest of labor, cesarean birth is the management of choice.

## NURSING ASSESSMENT

Leopold's maneuvers reveal a cephalic prominence on the same side at the fetal back. A brow presentation can be detected on vaginal examination by palpation of the diamond-shaped anterior fontanelle on one side and orbital ridges and root of the nose on the other side.

## NURSING DIAGNOSIS

Nursing diagnoses that may apply to a woman with a brow presentation include:

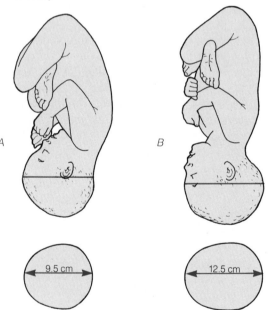
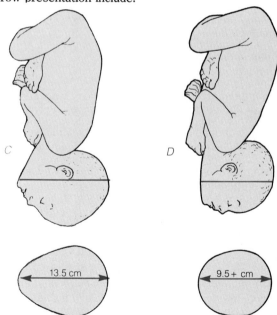

*Figure 18.3  Types of cephalic presentation: **(A)** The occiput is the presenting part because the head is flexed and the fetal chin is against the chest. The largest anteroposterior (AP) diameter that presents and passes through the pelvis is approximately 9.5 cm. **(B)** Military presentation. The head is neither flexed nor extended. The presenting AP diameter is approximately 12.5 cm. **(C)** Brow presentation. The largest diameter of the fetal head (approximately 13.5 cm) presents in this situation. **(D)** Face presentation. The AP diameter is 9.5 cm. (From Danforth DN, Scott JR [editors]: Obstetrics and Gynecology, 5th ed. Philadelphia: Lippincott, 1986.)*

- Knowledge deficit related to the possible maternal-fetal effects of brow presentation
- Potential for injury to the fetus related to pressure on fetal structures secondary to brow presentation

## NURSING PLAN AND IMPLEMENTATION

### Promotion of Maternal-Fetal Physical Well-Being

Nursing management of abnormal cephalic presentations includes close observation of the woman for labor aberrations and of the fetus for signs of distress. The fetus should be observed closely during labor for signs of hypoxia as evidenced by late decelerations and bradycardia.

### Provision of Emotional Support to the Family

The nurse may need to explain the position to the laboring couple or to interpret what the physician/nurse-midwife has told them. The nurse should stay close at hand to reassure the couple, inform them of any changes, and assist them with labor-coping techniques.

In face and brow presentation, the appearance of the newborn may be affected. The couple may need help in beginning the attachment process because of the newborn's facial appearance. After the infant is inspected for gross abnormalities, the pediatrician and nurse can assure the couple that the facial edema and excessive molding are only temporary and will subside in three or four days.

### EVALUATION

Anticipated outcomes of nursing care include:

- The woman and her partner understand the implications and associated problems of brow presentation.
- The mother and her baby have a safe labor and delivery.

## ● Face Presentation

In a face presentation, the face of the fetus is the presenting part (Figure 18.4; also see Figure 18.3, **D**). The fetal head is hyperextended even more than in the brow presentation. Face presentation occurs most frequently in multiparas, in preterm delivery, and in the presence of anencephaly.

Maternal implications of face presentation include:

- Increased risk of CPD and prolonged labor
- With prolonged labor, increased risk of infection

Fetal-neonatal implications include:

- Postdelivery edema and bruising, giving the newborn a distorted appearance

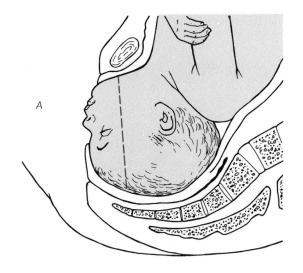

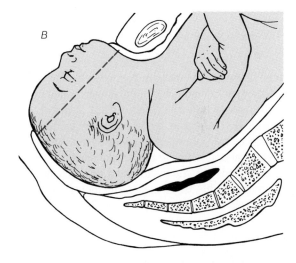

*Figure 18.4   Mechanism of birth in mentoanterior position: (A) The submentobregmatic diameter at the outlet. (B) The fetal head is born by movement of flexion.*

- As in the brow presentation, possible swelling of the neck and internal structures due to trauma during descent

### MEDICAL THERAPY

If no CPD is present, if the chin (mentum) is anterior, and if the labor pattern is effective, the woman may deliver vaginally (Figure 18.4). Mentum posteriors can become wedged on the anterior surface of the sacrum (Figure 18.5). In this case, as well as in the presence of CPD, cesarean birth is the management of choice.

### NURSING ASSESSMENT

When performing Leopold's maneuvers, the nurse finds that the back of the fetus is difficult to outline, and a

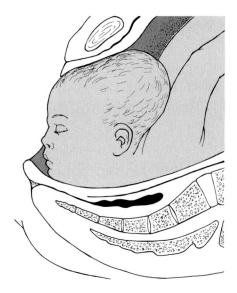

*Figure 18.5 Mechanism of birth in mentoposterior position. Fetal head is unable to extend farther. The face becomes impacted.*

deep furrow can be palpated between the hard occiput and the fetal back (Figure 18.6). Fetal heart tones can be heard on the side where the fetal feet are palpated. It may be difficult to determine by vaginal examination whether a breech or face is presenting, especially if facial edema is already present. During the vaginal examination, palpation of the saddle of the nose and the gums should be attempted. When assessing engagement, the nurse must remember that the face has to be deep within the pelvis before the biparietal diameters have entered the inlet.

### NURSING DIAGNOSIS

Nursing diagnoses that may apply to the woman with a fetus in face presentation include:

- Fear related to unknown outcome of the labor
- Potential for injury to the newborn's face related to edema secondary to the birth process

### NURSING PLAN AND IMPLEMENTATION
#### Promotion of Maternal-Fetal Well-Being

Nursing interventions are the same as for the brow presentation.

### EVALUATION

Anticipated outcomes of nursing care include:

- The woman and her partner understand the implications and associated problems of face presentation.
- The mother and her baby have a safe labor and birth.

### ● Breech Presentation

The exact cause of breech presentation (Figure 18.7) is unknown. This malpresentation occurs in 3% to 4% of all pregnancies and has a threefold to tenfold increase in perinatal morbidity and mortality in comparison to cephalic presentation (Mazor et al 1985). Breech presentation is frequently associated with preterm birth, placenta previa, hydramnios, multiple gestation, and grandmultiparity. The fetus in breech presentation is three times more likely to have congenital anomalies than a fetus in cephalic presentation (Mazor et al 1985). Because of the increased incidence of congenital anomalies, an ultrasound may be done late in pregnancy to identify fetal problems or the presence of placenta previa (Mazor et al 1985).

Material implications of breech presentation include:

- Cesarean delivery may be done.

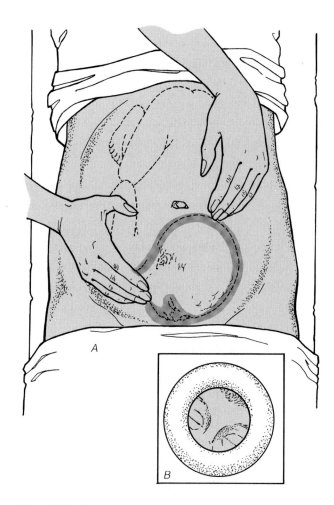

*Figure 18.6 Face presentation: (A) Palpation of the maternal abdomen with the fetus in right mentum posterior (RMP). (B) Vaginal examination may permit palpation of facial features of the fetus.*

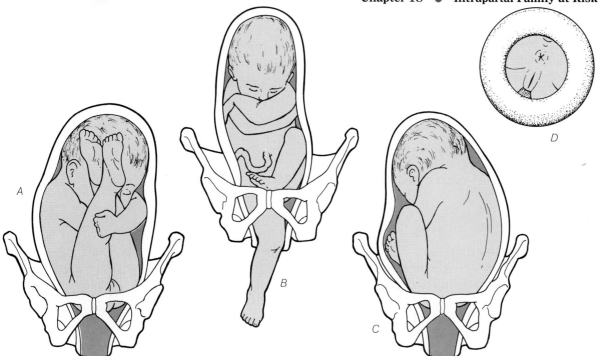

*Figure 18.7   Breech presentation: (A) Frank breech. (B) Incomplete (footling) breech.*
*(C) Complete breech in (LSA) position. (D) On vaginal examination, the nurse may feel the*
*anal sphincter. The tissue of the fetal buttocks feels soft.*

Fetal-neonatal implications include:

- Higher perinatal mortality rate (five times greater for breech infants than for cephalic infants)

- Increased risk of prolapsed cord, especially in incomplete breeches, because space is available between the cervix and presenting part

- Increased risk of cervical cord injuries due to hyperextension of the fetal head during vaginal delivery

- Increased risk of birth trauma, including intracranial hemorrhage, spinal cord injuries, brachial plexus palsy, and fracture of the upper extremities (Collea 1984)

## MEDICAL THERAPY

Some clinicians may do an external version between the thirty-seventh week of pregnancy and the time that labor begins. If the version is successful and the fetus remains in cephalic presentation, a vaginal delivery is anticipated. If the version is unsuccessful, a cesarean birth is usually selected.

## NURSING ASSESSMENT

Frequently it is the nurse who first recognizes a breech presentation. On palpation the hard vertex is felt in the fundus and ballottement of the head can be done independently of the fetal body. The wider sacrum is palpated in the lower part of the abdomen. If the sacrum has not descended, on ballottement the entire fetal body will move. Furthermore, fetal heart tones (FHTs) are usually auscultated above the umbilicus. Passage of meconium from compression of the infant's intestinal tract on descent is common.

The nurse is particularly alert for a prolapsed umbilical cord, especially in incomplete breeches, because space is available between the cervix and presenting part through which the cord can slip. If the infant is small and the membranes rupture, the danger is even greater. This is one reason why any woman admitted to the labor and delivery suite with a history of ruptured membranes should not be ambulated until a full assessment, including vaginal examination, is performed.

## NURSING DIAGNOSIS

Nursing diagnoses that may apply to a woman with a breech presentation include:

- Impaired gas exchange in the fetus related to interruption in umbilical blood flow secondary to compression of the cord

- Knowledge deficit related to the implications and associated complications of breech presentation on the mother and fetus

## NURSING PLAN AND IMPLEMENTATION

### Promotion of Maternal-Fetal Physical Well-Being

During labor it is important for the nurse to continue to make frequent assessments to evaluate fetal and maternal status. The nurse needs to be aware of the associated problems of breech presentation and look for subtle clues of beginning problems. The nurse provides teaching and information regarding the breech presentation and the nursing care needed.

### Assistance During Vaginal Delivery

Although many infants in breech presentations are delivered by cesarean birth, a few are born vaginally. The nurse should include Piper forceps as a part of the delivery table setup. During the birth process, the nurse may have to assist in the support of the infant's body if the physician elects to use forceps. The circulating nurse should monitor the FHR closely during the delivery.

If the family and physician elect a cesarean birth, the nurse intervenes as with any cesarean birth.

## EVALUATION

Anticipated outcomes of nursing care include:

● The woman and her partner understand the implications and associated problems of breech presentation.

● The mother and baby have a safe labor and delivery.

● Major complications are recognized early and corrective measures are instituted.

## ● Transverse Lie (Shoulder Presentation)

A transverse lie occurs in approximately one in 300–400 deliveries (Danforth and Scott 1986). Maternal conditions associated with a transverse lie are grandmultiparity with relaxed uterine muscles, placenta previa, hydramnios, and preterm labor (Figure 18.8).

Maternal implications of transverse lie include:

● Dysfunctional labor
● Uterine rupture
● Cesarean birth

Fetal-neonatal implications include:

● Increased risk of prolapsed cord

## MEDICAL THERAPY

With a viable fetus at term in the transverse lie, the

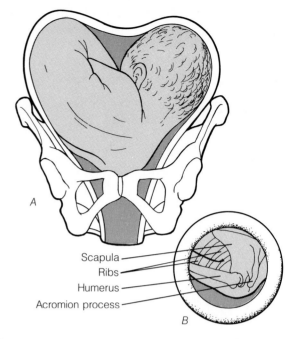

Scapula
Ribs
Humerus
Acromion process

B

*Figure 18.8   Transverse lie: (A) Shoulder presentation. (B) On vaginal examination the nurse may feel the acromion process as the fetal presenting part.*

immediate goal is a safe birth. External version for vaginal delivery may be attempted if the following criteria are met:

● There is no indication for rapid termination of labor.
● The fetus is highly movable.
● Contractions are not strong and frequent.
● There is no CPD.
● The membranes are intact.
● There is an adequate amount of amniotic fluid.
● Placenta previa has been ruled out.

When the required criteria are met, attempts at external version are appropriate prior to the onset of labor or in early labor. (See discussion in Chapter 19.)

## NURSING CARE

The nurse can identify a transverse lie by inspection and palpation of the abdomen, by auscultation of FHTs in the midline of the abdomen (not conclusive), and by vaginal examination.

On palpation no fetal part is felt in the fundal portion of the uterus or above the symphysis. The head may be palpated on one side and the breech on the other. Fetal heart tones are usually auscultated just below the midline of the umbilicus. On vaginal examination, if a presenting part is palpated, it is the ridged thorax or possibly an arm that is compressed against the chest.

The primary nursing actions are to assist in the interpretation of the fetal presentation and to provide information and support to the couple. The nurse assesses maternal and fetal status frequently and prepares the woman for an operative birth. The nurse explains to the parents the need for cesarean and the assessments and care surrounding a cesarean. (See Chapter 19 for further information regarding teaching with cesarean birth.)

## ● Compound Presentation

A compound presentation is one in which there are two presenting parts such as occiput and fetal hand; occiput and fetal foot; or breech and fetal hand. Some compound presentations resolve themselves spontaneously, but others require additional manipulation at delivery.

## ● CARE OF THE WOMAN AND FETUS AT RISK DUE TO DEVELOPMENTAL ABNORMALITIES
## ● Macrosomia

Fetal **macrosomia** occurs when a neonate weighs more than 4000 g at birth. This condition is more common among offspring of large parents and diabetic women and in cases of grandmultiparity and postmaturity.

Maternal implications of macrosomia include:

- Risk of CPD
- Risk of dysfunctional labor
- Soft tissue laceration during delivery
- Increased incidence of postpartal hemorrhage

Fetal-neonatal implications include:

- Cerebral trauma
- Excessive trauma to the fetal head
- Shoulder dystocia during delivery
- Increased risk of upper brachial plexus injury (McFarland et al 1986)

### MEDICAL THERAPY

The occurrence of maternal and fetal problems associated with excessively large infants may be somewhat lessened by identifying macrosomia prior to the onset of labor. If a large fetus is suspected, the maternal pelvis should be evaluated carefully. An estimation of fetal size can be made by palpating the crown–rump length of the fetus in utero, but the greatest errors in estimation occur on both ends of the spectrum—the macrosomic fetus and the very small fetus. Fundal height can give some clue. Ultrasound or x-ray pelvimetry may give further information about fetal size. Whenever the uterus appears excessively large,

hydramnios, an oversized fetus, or multiple pregnancies must be considered as possible causes.

When fetal weight is estimated to be 4500+ g and there is any abnormality of the labor pattern, a cesarean should be considered (Acker et al 1985, O'Leary 1986).

Unfortunately, in some situations a diagnosis of an oversized fetus is not made until numerous attempts to deliver the newborn have not been successful. If shoulder dystocia occurs and delivery cannot be completed by various maneuvers, the physician may find it necessary to fracture the clavicles to save the neonate's life. Appropriate pediatric and anesthesia support must be available to reduce the sequelae of the traumatic birth.

### NURSING CARE

The nurse assists in identifying women who are at risk for a large fetus or those who exhibit signs of macrosomia. Because these women are prime candidates for dystocia and its complications, the nurse frequently assesses the FHR for indications of fetal distress and evaluates the rate of cervical dilatation and fetal descent.

The presence of a protraction and/or arrest disorder may be associated with an increased incidence of shoulder dystocia (Acker et al 1986).

The nurse should use the Friedman graph to monitor labor closely for dysfunction. The fetal monitor is applied for continuous fetal evaluation. Early decelerations could mean disproportion at the bony inlet. Any sign of labor dysfunction or fetal distress should be reported to the physician.

The nurse provides support for the laboring woman and her partner and information regarding the implications and possible associated problems. During the birth, the nurse continues to provide support and encouragement to the couple.

The nurse inspects macrosomic neonates after delivery for skull fractures, cephalhematoma, and Erb palsy and informs the nursery of any problems. If the nursery staff is aware of a difficult delivery, the newborn will be observed more closely for cerebral and neurologic damage.

Postpartally, the nurse checks the uterus for potential atony and the maternal vital signs for deviations suggesting shock.

## ● Hydrocephalus

In hydrocephalus, 500–1000 mL of cerebrospinal fluid accumulates in the ventricles of the fetal brain. When this occurs before delivery, severe CPD results because of the enlarged cranium of the fetus.

With the use of ultrasound during pregnancy, diagnosis of this fetal abnormality is more likely. Once the woman is in labor, hydrocephalus should be suspected if labor contractions progress yet the fetal head does not enter the birth canal. If a hydrocephalic fetus is in vertex presentation, the person doing a vaginal examination will feel wide suture lines and a globular cranium.

Maternal implications of hydrocephalus include obstruction of labor, with resulting uterine rupture.

Fetal-neonatal implications: The outlook for the fetus is questionable. If hydrocephalus is identified early in the gestation, intrauterine surgery may be performed to place a shunt, thereby preventing excessive accumulation of fluid in the fetal head. This surgery is not currently available to all mothers in all parts of the country.

If enlargement of the fetal head continues, the fetus-neonate is usually brain damaged and may die during delivery or shortly afterward. Frequently, other congenital malformations, such as myelomeningocele, accompany this condition.

### MEDICAL THERAPY

Medical intervention is directed toward delivering the fetus by the least traumatic means. It is important to know the degree of hydrocephalus and whether other anomalies or abnormalities are present that would make it very unlikely that the baby could live after the birth. When anomalies that are incompatible with life are present, the decision regarding the method of birth needs to be discussed between the physician and the parents. A cesarean birth may give the newborn the best chance, but if the predicted chance of survival is very small, or if the fetus is already dead, a cesarean birth unnecessarily increases the risk to the mother. The decisions regarding method of delivery are not easy; they are best made by the parents and health care providers together.

### NURSING CARE

The nurse performing abdominal palpation discovers the presence of a hard mass just above the symphysis; this is the unengaged head. If the presentation is breech, it is difficult on external palpation to distinguish between the breech and an enlarged head. An ultrasound is indicated in the presence of breech presentations to evaluate the cranium. Vaginal examination with a vertex presentation reveals wide suture lines and a globular cranium.

Additional nursing assessments focus on the information needs of the woman and her partner. It is also important to assess their emotional state in order to provide support.

The nurse helps the couple cope with the crisis and to deal with their grief (see discussion in Chapter 28).

The nurse assists with diagnostic procedures and interprets the findings if the couple has questions after conversations with the physician. The type of assistance at delivery will depend on the method chosen.

## ● CARE OF THE WOMAN WITH A TWIN PREGNANCY

As discussed in Chapter 3, two fetuses that develop from one fertilized ovum are categorized as monozygotic (identical) twins. Dizygotic (fraternal) twins, the result of the fertilization of two separate ova, are not identical. If the twins are of the same sex, the placenta is examined in the pathology laboratory to determine whether the twins are monozygotic or dizygotic.

According to Pritchard et al (1985), the incidence of monozygotic twins has no correlation with race, heredity, age, parity, or fertility therapy. However, these factors figure significantly in the incidence of dizygotic twins.

During the prenatal period, any fetal growth, movement, or heart tone findings not in keeping with gestational age should lead the examiner to suspect a multiple gestation. Ultrasound examination can provide a positive diagnosis.

### ● Maternal Implications

Early in the pregnancy, spontaneous abortions are more common, possibly because of genetic defects, poor placental development, or poor implantation. The woman may experience more physical discomfort during her pregnancy, such as shortness of breath, dyspnea on exertion, backaches, and pedal edema. Other associated problems include increased incidence of PIH, maternal anemia, hydramnios, and placenta previa.

Complications during labor include abnormal fetal presentations; preterm labor; inadequate uterine contractions due to overstretching of the myometrium; abruptio placentae before labor begins, during labor with ROM, or after birth of the first twin; and increased risk of postpartal hemorrhage due to decreased uterine tone.

### ● Fetal-Neonatal Implications

The perinatal mortality rate is four times greater for the first twin and five times greater for the second twin than for a singleton baby. Fetal problems include decreased intrauterine growth rate for each fetus, increased incidence of fetal anomalies, increased risk of preterm labor, and the associated problems of a preterm baby, and abnormal presentations (Collea 1984).

### ● Medical Therapy

The goals of medical care are the promotion of normal fetal development for both fetuses, preventing the delivery of preterm fetuses, and diminishing fetal trauma during labor.

Once the presence of twins has been detected, preventing and treating problems that infringe on the development and birth of normal fetuses is a significant medical activity. Prenatal care is comprehensive. The woman's visits are more frequent than those of the woman with one fetus. The childbearing woman needs to understand nutritional implications, assessment of fetal activity, signs of preterm labor, and danger signs.

Serial ultrasounds are done to assess the growth of each fetus and to provide early recognition of IUGR. A program of bed rest is usually advised beginning in the 26th week. Some physicians believe that bed rest in the lateral position enhances uterine–placental–fetal blood flow and decreases the risk of preterm labor (Gilstrap et al 1987). Others question the value of bed rest, especially for the prevention of uterine contractions, which seem to precede preterm labor (Newman et al 1986).

Testing usually begins at 30 to 34 weeks' gestation and may include NST, fetal biophysical profile, and in some instances CST. A reactive NST is associated with good fetal outcome if birth occurs within one week of the testing. The NST is done every three to seven days until birth or until results become nonreactive (Polin and Frangipane 1986). If the NST is nonreactive, some physicians recommend a CST, while others avoid this test because of the associated risk of stimulating preterm labor (Lodeiro et al 1986). The fetal biophysical profile is also accurate in assessing fetal status with twin pregnancies. Some researchers have found that a fetal biophysical score of 8 is associated with a reactive NST and suggest that both of these tests do not need to be done at the same time (Lodeiro et al 1986).

Intrapartal management and assessment require careful attention to maternal and fetal status. The mother should have an IV in place with a large bore needle. Anesthesia and cross-matched blood should be readily available. The twins are monitored by electronic fetal monitoring. The labor may progress very slowly or very quickly.

The decision regarding method of delivery may not be made until labor occurs, and the method depends on a variety of factors. The presence of maternal complications such as placenta previa, abruptio placentae, or severe PIH usually indicates the need for cesarean birth. Fetal factors such as severe IUGR, preterm birth, fetal anomalies, fetal distress, or unfavorable fetal position or presentation also require cesarean delivery.

Any combination of presentations and positions can occur with twins (Figure 18.9). Approximately 50% of twins are delivered by cesarean, which is chosen in the hope of reducing complications for the twins, especially birth asphyxia (Bell et al 1986).

● *Nursing Care*

Antepartally, the woman may need counseling about diet and daily activities. The nurse can help her plan meals to meet her increased needs. An increase of 300 calories

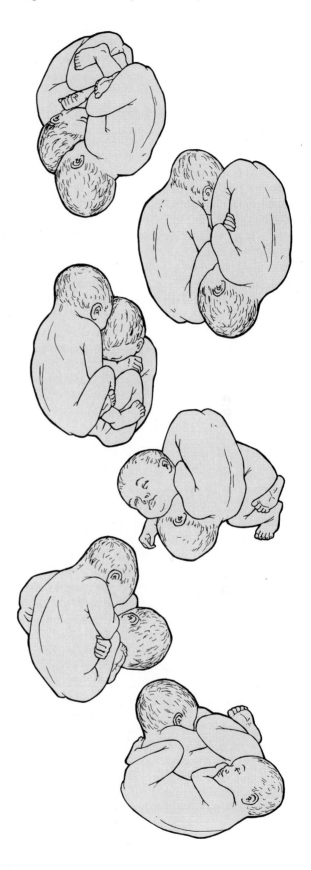

*Figure 18.9  Types of twin presentations*

or more over the recommended daily dietary allowance established by the Food and Nutrition Board of the National Research Council is advised for uncomplicated pregnancy (see Table 10.1). The daily intake of protein should be increased as much as 1.5 g/kg of body weight. Daily iron supplements of 60–80 mg and an additional 1 mg of folic acid are recommended.

Counseling about daily activities may include encouraging the woman to plan frequent rest periods during the day. The rest period will have optimal effects if the woman rests in a side-lying position (which increases uteroplacental blood flow) and elevates the lower legs and the feet to reduce edema. Back discomfort may be relieved by pelvic rocking, maintaining good posture, and using good body mechanics when lifting objects or moving about.

During labor, both fetuses are assessed by auscultation or electronic monitoring. Care is taken to identify the location of each twin's FHR so that changes in rate can be evaluated. Signs of distress must be identified immediately. The woman's labor is assessed for dysfunctional patterns.

After birth the nurse must prepare to receive two neonates instead of one. This means a duplication of everything, including resuscitation equipment, radiant warmers, and newborn identification papers and bracelets. Two staff members should be available for newborn resuscitation.

## ● CARE OF THE WOMAN AND FETUS IN THE PRESENCE OF FETAL DISTRESS

When the oxygen supply is insufficient to meet the physiologic demands of the fetus, fetal distress results. The condition may be acute, chronic, or a combination of both. A variety of factors may contribute to fetal distress. The most common are related to cord compression and uteroplacental insufficiency associated with placental abnormalities and preexisting maternal disease. If the resultant hypoxia persists and metabolic acidosis follows, the situation is potentially life threatening to the fetus.

The most common initial signs of fetal distress are meconium-stained amniotic fluid (in a vertex presentation) and decelerations in FHR. Fetal scalp blood samples demonstrating a pH value of 7.20 or less provide a more sophisticated indication of fetal problems and are generally obtained when questions about fetal status arise. (For further discussion see p 414.)

A variety of factors may contribute to fetal distress. The most common are related to cord compression, uteroplacental insufficiency, and preexisting maternal disease.

### ● Maternal Implications

Indications of fetal distress greatly increase the psychologic stress a laboring woman must face. The professional staff may become so involved in assessing fetal status and initiating corrective measures that they fail to give explanation and emotional support to the woman and her partner. It is imperative to provide full explanations of the problem and comfort to the couple. In many instances, if delivery is not imminent, the woman must undergo cesarean delivery. This method of birth may be a source of fear for the couple and of frustration, too, if they prepared for a shared vaginal birth experience.

### ● Fetal-Neonatal Implications

Prolonged fetal hypoxia may lead to mental retardation or cerebral palsy and ultimately to fetal death.

### ● Medical Therapy

When there is evidence of possible fetal distress, treatment is centered on relieving the hypoxia and minimizing the effects of anoxia on the fetus. Initial interventions include changing the mother's position and administering oxygen by mask at 6 to 10 L per minute. If electronic fetal monitoring has not yet been used, it is usually instituted at this time. If oxytocin is in use, it should be discontinued. Fetal scalp blood samples are taken.

### ● Nursing Care

The nurse reviews the woman's prenatal history to anticipate the possibility of fetal distress. When the membranes rupture, it is important to assess FHR and to observe for meconium staining. As labor progresses, the nurse is particularly alert for even subtle changes in the FHR pattern and the fetal scalp pH, if available. Reports by the mother of increased or greatly decreased fetal activity may also be associated with fetal distress. For further discussion of FHR patterns and characteristics, see Chapter 15.

Additional information regarding nursing interventions is presented in the Nursing Care Plan—Fetal Distress.

## ● CARE OF THE FAMILY AT RISK DUE TO INTRAUTERINE FETAL DEATH

Fetal death, often referred to as fetal demise, accounts for one half of the perinatal mortality after 20 weeks' gestation. Intrauterine fetal death (IUFD) results from unknown causes or a number of physiologic maladaptations including preeclampsia-eclampsia, abruptio placentae, placenta previa, diabetes, infection, congenital anomalies, and isoimmune disease.

Prolonged retention of the fetus may lead to maternal development of disseminated intravascular coagulation (DIC) (also referred to as consumption coagulopathy).

After the release of thromboplastin from the degenerating fetal tissues into the maternal bloodstream, the extrinsic clotting system is activated, triggering the formation of multiple tiny blood clots. Fibrinogen and factors V and VII are subsequently depleted, and the woman begins to display symptoms of DIC. Fibrinogen levels begin a linear descent three to four weeks after the death of the fetus and continue to decrease without appropriate medical intervention.

## ● Medical Therapy

Abdominal x-ray examination may reveal Spalding's sign, an overriding of the fetal cranial bones. In addition, maternal estriol levels fall. Diagnosis of IUFD is confirmed by absence of heart action on real-time ultrasonography (Pitkin 1987).

The goals of therapy are to deliver the fetus within two weeks of fetal death and to assist the family with the grieving process. In 75% of these circumstances, spontaneous labor begins within two weeks of the fetal death (Quilligan 1987). Artificial rupture of the membranes is avoided because of the risk of introducing infection. If labor does not begin, oxytocin or prostaglandins may be administered to induce labor.

## ● Nursing Assessment

Cessation of fetal movement reported by the mother to the nurse is frequently the first indication of fetal death. It is followed by a gradual decrease in the signs and symptoms of pregnancy. Fetal heart tones are absent, and fetal movement is no longer palpable. Once fetal demise is established, the nurse assesses the family's ability to adapt to their loss. Open communication between the mother, her partner, and the health team members contributes to a more realistic understanding of the medical condition and its associated treatments. The nurse may discuss prior experiences the family has had with stress and what they feel were their coping abilities at that time. Determining what social supports and resources the family has is also important.

## ● Nursing Diagnosis

Nursing diagnoses that may apply include:

● Dysfunctional grieving related to an actual loss

● Altered family processes related to loss of a family member

● Ineffective individual coping related to depression in response to loss of child

● Ineffective family coping related to death of a child

● Anxiety related to death of a child

## ● Nursing Plan and Implementation

### PROVISION OF EMOTIONAL SUPPORT TO THE FAMILY

The parents of a stillborn infant suffer a devastating experience, precipitating an intense emotional trauma. During the pregnancy, the couple has already begun the attachment process, which now must be terminated through the grieving process. The behaviors that couples exhibit while mourning may be associated with the five stages of grieving described by Elizabeth Kübler-Ross (1969). Often the first stage is *denial* of the death of the fetus. Even when the initial health care provider suspects fetal demise, the couple is hoping that a second opinion will be different. Some couples may not be convinced of the death until they view and hold the stillborn infant. The second stage is *anger*, resulting from the feelings of loss, loneliness, and perhaps guilt. The anger may be projected at significant others and health team members, or it may be omitted when the death of the fetus is sudden and unexpected. *Bargaining*, the third stage, may or may not be present depending on the couple's preparation for the death of the fetus. If death is anticipated the couple may wish they could change the circumstances through an action on their part. For instance, they might say "If only our child could live we promise we'll be good parents." If the death is unanticipated, the couple may have no time for bargaining. In the fourth stage, *depression* is evidenced by preoccupation, weeping, and withdrawal. Physiologic postpartal depression appearing 24 to 48 hours after delivery may compound the depression of grief. The final stage is *acceptance*, which involves the process of resolution. This is a highly individualized process that may take months to complete.

In some facilities, a checklist is used to make sure important aspects of working with the parents are addressed. The checklist becomes a communication tool between staff members to share information particular to this couple (Beckey et al 1985, Carr and Knupp 1985). Such a checklist might include the following items:

● When the fetal death is known before admission, inform the admission department and nursing staff so that inappropriate remarks are not made.

● Allow the woman and her partner to remain together as much as they wish. Provide privacy by assigning them to a private room.

● Stay with the couple and do not leave them alone and isolated.

● As much as possible, have the same nurse provide care to increase the support for the couple. Develop a care plan to provide for continuity of care.

● Have the most experienced labor and delivery nurse auscultate for fetal heart tones. This avoids the searching that a more inexperienced nurse might feel compelled to do. Avoid the temptation to listen again "to make sure" (Whitaker 1986).

● Listen to the couple; do not offer explanations. They require solace without minimizing the situation.

● Facilitate the woman and her partner's participation in the labor and delivery process. When possible, allow them to make decisions about who will be present and what ritual will occur during the birth process. Allow the woman to make the decision regarding whether to have sedation during labor and delivery. Provide a quiet supportive environment; ideally the labor and delivery should occur in a labor room or possibly a birthing room rather than the delivery room.

● Give parents accurate information regarding plans for labor and birth.

● Provide ongoing opportunities for the couple to ask questions.

● Arrange for the woman to be assigned to a room that is away from new mothers and babies. Let the woman decide if she wants to be on another unit. If early discharge is an option, allow the family to make that selection.

● Encourage the couple to experience the grief that they feel. Accept the weeping and depression. A couple may have intense feelings that they are unable to share with each other. Encourage them to talk together and allow emotions to show freely.

● Give the couple an opportunity to see and hold the stillborn infant in a private quiet location. (Advocates of seeing the stillborn believe that viewing assists in dispelling denial and enables the couple to progress to the next step in the grieving process.) If they choose to see their stillborn infant, prepare the couple for what they will see by saying "the baby is cold," "the baby is blue," "the baby is bruised," or other appropriate statements.

● Some families may elect to bathe or dress their stillborn; support them in their choice.

● Take a photograph of the infant, and let the family know it is available if they want it now or some time in the future.

● Offer a card with footprints, crib card, ID band, and possibly a lock of hair to the parents. These items may be kept with the photo if the parents do not want them at this time (Beckey et al 1985).

● Prepare the couple for returning home. If there are siblings, each will progress through age-appropriate grieving. Provide the parents with information about normal mourning reactions, both psychologic and physiologic.

● Furnish the mother with educational materials that discuss the changes she will experience in returning to the nonpregnant state.

● Provide information about community support groups including group name, contact person if possible, and phone number. Use materials such as the book *When Hello Means Goodbye* by Schwiebert and Kirk (1985).

● Contact religious support systems if parents desire.

● Discuss further care of stillborn baby (dress, rituals).

● Remember it is not so important to "say the right words." The caring support and human contact that a couple receives is important and can be conveyed through silence and your presence.

The nurse experiences many of the same grief reactions as the parents of a stillborn infant. It is important to have support persons and colleagues available for counseling and support.

● *Evaluation*

Anticipated outcomes of nursing care include:

● The family members express their feelings about the death of their baby.

● The family participates in decisions regarding whether to see their baby and in other decisions regarding the baby.

● The family has resources available for continued support.

● The family knows the community resources available and has names and phone numbers to use if they choose.

● The family is moving into and through the grieving process.

● CARE OF THE WOMAN AND FETUS AT RISK DUE TO PLACENTAL PROBLEMS

The most common types of placental problems are abruptio placentae, placenta previa, and abnormalities in placental formation and structure. Because the placenta is very vascular, problems are usually associated with maternal and possibly fetal hemorrhage. Abruptio placentae is a major emergency in labor and delivery and requires rapid, effective interventions. Although placenta previa is primarily an antepartal problem, it is presented here for the sake of comparison. Causes and sources of hemorrhage are highlighted in Essential Facts to Remember—Causes and Sources of Hemorrhage.

# Essential Facts to Remember

## Causes and Sources of Hemorrhage

| Causes and Sources | Signs and Symptoms |
|---|---|
| ***Antepartal Period*** | |
| Abortion | Vaginal bleeding<br>Intermittent uterine contractions<br>Rupture of membranes |
| Placenta previa | Painless vaginal bleeding after seventh month |
| Abruptio placentae<br>Marginal (partial) | Vaginal bleeding; no increase in uterine pain |
| Central (severe) | No vaginal bleeding<br>Extreme tenderness of abdominal area<br>Rigid, boardlike abdomen<br>Increase in size of abdomen |
| ***Intrapartal Period*** | |
| Placenta previa | Bright red vaginal bleeding |
| Abruptio placentae | Same signs and symptoms as listed for the types of abruptio placentae |
| Uterine atony in stage III | Bright red vaginal bleeding, ineffectual contractility |
| ***Postpartal Period*** | |
| Uterine atony | Boggy uterus<br>Dark vaginal bleeding<br>Presence of clots |
| Retained placental fragments | Boggy uterus<br>Dark vaginal bleeding<br>Presence of clots |
| Lacerations of cervix or vagina | Firm uterus<br>Bright red vaginal bleeding |

## ● Abruptio Placentae

Separation of the placenta from the site of implantation on the uterine wall prior to delivery of the infant is called **abruptio placentae.** The incidence varies according to the population studied and the diagnostic criteria used, which accounts for rates that vary from 1 in 86 to 1 in 750 (Pritchard et al 1985). Whether the incidence has stabilized or declined over the last two to three decades is not readily apparent. It is clear, however, that the risk of

recurrence in subsequent pregnancies is as much as 30 times the risk in the general population (Green 1984).

The cause of abruptio placentae is largely unknown. Theories have been proposed relating its occurrence to decreased blood flow to the placenta through the sinuses during the last trimester. Excessive intrauterine pressure caused by hydramnios or multiple pregnancy, maternal hypertension, cigarette smoking, alcohol ingestion, increased maternal age and parity, trauma, and sudden changes in intrauterine pressure (as with amniotomy) have been suggested as contributing factors.

Abruptio placentae is subdivided into three types (Figure 18.10).

● *Central.* In this situation, the placenta separates centrally, and the blood is trapped between the placenta and the uterine wall. Entrapment of the blood results in concealed bleeding.

● *Marginal.* In this case, the blood passes between the fetal membranes and the uterine wall and escapes vaginally (also called marginal sinus rupture).

● *Complete.* Massive vaginal bleeding is seen in the presence of total separation.

The signs and symptoms of these three types of placental abruption are given in the Essential Facts to Remember—Differential Signs and Symptoms of Abruptio Placentae and Placenta Previa. In severe cases of central abruptio placentae, the blood invades the myometrial tissues between the muscle fibers. This occurrence accounts for the uterine irritability that is a significant sign of abruptio placentae. If hemorrhage continues, eventually the uterus turns entirely blue. After birth of the neonate, the uterus contracts poorly. This condition is known as *Couvelaire uterus* and frequently necessitates hysterectomy.

As a result of the damage to the uterine wall and the retroplacental clotting with central abruption, large amounts of thromboplastin are released into the maternal blood supply. This in turn triggers the development of DIC and resultant hypofibrinogenemia. Fibrinogen levels, which are ordinarily elevated in pregnancy, may drop in minutes to the point at which blood will no longer coagulate due to the separation of the placenta.

## MATERNAL IMPLICATIONS

Maternal mortality is approximately 6%. Problems following birth depend in large part on the severity of the intrapartal bleeding, coagulation defects (DIC), hypofibrinogenemia, and time between separation and birth. Moderate to severe hemorrhage results in hemorrhagic shock, which may prove fatal to the mother if it is not reversed. In the postpartal period, mothers who have suffered this disorder are at risk for hemorrhage and renal failure due to

## Essential Facts to Remember

### Differential Signs and Symptoms of Abruptio Placentae and Placenta Previa

| Abruptio Placentae | | | Placenta Previa |
|---|---|---|---|
| *Central* | *Marginal* | *Complete* | |
| No overt bleeding from vagina | Dark red vaginal bleeding | Massive vaginal bleeding | Bright red bleeding |
| Rigid abdomen | Nonrigid abdomen | Rigid abdomen | Nonrigid abdomen |
| Acute pain in abdominal area | Tenderness over uterus | Acute pain in abdominal area | No pain |
| Decreased blood pressure | Decreased blood pressure | Profound shock | Effect on blood pressure and pulse depends on amount of bleeding |

shock, vascular spasm, intravascular clotting, or a combination of the three.

### FETAL-NEONATAL IMPLICATIONS

Perinatal mortality associated with premature separation of the placenta is about 15%. In severe cases, in which most of the placenta has separated, infant mortality is 100%. In less severe separation, fetal outcome depends on the level of maturity. The most serious complications in the neonate arise from preterm labor, anemia, and hypoxia. If fetal hypoxia progresses unchecked, irreversible brain damage or fetal demise may result. With thorough assessment and prompt action on the part of the health team, fetal and maternal outcomes can be improved.

### MEDICAL THERAPY

Because of the risk of DIC, evaluating the results of coagulation tests is imperative. In DIC, fibrinogen levels and platelet counts are usually decreased; prothrombin times and partial thromboplastin times are normal to prolonged. If the values are not markedly abnormal, serial testing may be helpful in establishing an abnormal trend that is indicative of coagulopathy. Another very sensitive test determines fibrin degradation products levels; these values rise with DIC.

After establishing the diagnosis, emphasis is placed on maintaining the cardiovascular status of the mother and developing a plan for effecting the delivery of the fetus. Which birth method is selected depends on the condition of the woman and fetus; in many circumstances, cesarean birth may be the safest option.

If the separation is mild and gestation is near term, labor may be induced and the fetus delivered vaginally with as little trauma as possible. If the induction of labor by rupture of membranes and oxytocin infusion by pump does not initiate labor within eight hours, a cesarean birth is usually done. A longer delay would increase the risk of increased hemorrhage, with resulting hypofibrinogenemia. Supportive treatment to decrease risk of DIC includes typing and cross-matching for blood transfusions (at least three units), clotting mechanism evaluation, and intravenous fluids.

In cases of moderate to severe placental separation, a cesarean delivery is done after hypofibrinogenemia has been treated by intravenous infusion of cryoprecipitate or plasma. Vaginal delivery is impossible in the event of a Couvelaire uterus, because the uterus would not contract properly in labor. Cesarean birth is necessary in the face of severe hemorrhage to allow an immediate hysterectomy to save both woman and fetus.

The hypovolemia that accompanies severe abruptio placentae is life threatening and must be combated with whole blood. If the fetus is alive but in distress, emergency cesarean birth is the method of choice. With a stillborn fetus, vaginal birth is preferable unless shock from hemorrhage is uncontrollable. Intravenous fluids of a balanced salt solution such as lactated Ringer's are given through a 16- or 18-gauge cannula (Pritchard et al 1985). Central venous pressure (CVP) monitoring may be needed to evaluate intravenous fluid replacement. A normal CVP of 10 cm $H_2O$ is the goal (Berkowitz 1983). The CVP is evaluated hourly, and results are communicated to the physician. Elevations of CVP may indicate fluid overload and pulmonary edema. The hematocrit is maintained at 30% through the administration of packed red cells and/or whole blood (Berkowitz 1983).

Laboratory testing is ordered to provide ongoing data regarding hemoglobin, hematocrit, and coagulation status. A clot observation test may be done at the bedside to evaluate coagulation status. A glass tube containing 5 mL of maternal blood is inverted four to five times. If a clot

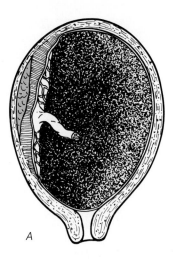 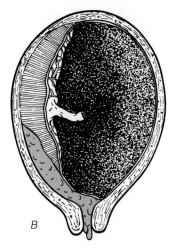 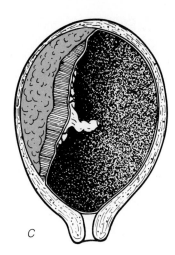

*Figure 18.10   Abruptio placentae: (A) Central abruption with concealed hemorrhage. (B) Marginal abruption with external hemorrhage. (C) Complete abruption. (Reprinted with permission of Ross Laboratories, Columbus, OH 43216. From Clinical Education Aid no. 12.)*

fails to form in six minutes, a fibrinogen level of less than 150 mg/dL is suspected. If a clot is not formed in 30 minutes, the fibrinogen level may well be less than 100 mg/dL. A clot observation test may be completed by a physician or a nurse.

Measures are taken to stimulate labor to prevent DIC. An amniotomy may be performed and oxytocin stimulation is given to hasten delivery. Progressive dilatation and effacement usually occur (Pritchard et al 1985).

## NURSING CARE

Electronic monitoring of the uterine contractions and resting tone between contractions provides information regarding the labor pattern and effectiveness of the oxytocin induction. Since uterine resting tone is frequently increased with abruptio placentae, it must be evaluated frequently for further increase. Abdominal girth measurements may be ordered hourly and are obtained by placing a tape measure around the maternal abdomen at the level of the umbilicus. Another method of evaluating uterine size, which increases as more bleeding occurs at the site of abruption, is to place a mark at the top of the uterine fundus. The distance from the symphysis pubis to the mark may be evaluated hourly.

For nursing diagnoses and further nursing care, see Nursing Care Plan—Hemorrhage.

## ● Placenta Previa

In **placenta previa,** the placenta is implanted in the lower uterine segment instead of in the upper portion of the uterus. This implantation may be on a portion of the lower segment or over the internal cervical os. As the lower uterine segment contracts and dilates in the later weeks of pregnancy, the placental villi are torn from the uterine wall, thus exposing the uterine sinuses at the placental site. Bleeding begins, but because its amount depends on the number of sinuses exposed, initially it may be either scanty or profuse.

The cause of placenta previa is unknown. Statistically it occurs in about one in every 167 deliveries, with 20% being complete, and it is more common in multiparas (Pritchard et al 1985). Women with a previous history of placenta previa as well as those who have undergone a low cervical cesarean delivery appear to be at greater risk.

Other factors associated with placenta previa are increased incidences of IUGR, placenta accreta, and breech and transverse lie positions (Danforth and Scott 1986).

The types of placenta previa are as follows (Figure 18.11):

● *Low-lying or marginal placenta previa.* The placental edge is attached very close to but does not cover the internal os.

● *Partial placenta previa.* A small portion of the placenta covers the internal os.

● *Complete or total placenta previa.* The placenta totally covers the internal os.

## FETAL-NEONATAL IMPLICATIONS

The prognosis for the fetus depends on the extent of placenta previa. Changes in the FHR and meconium staining of the amniotic fluid may be apparent. In a profuse bleeding episode, the fetus is compromised and does suffer some hypoxia. FHR monitoring is imperative when the woman is admitted, particularly if a vaginal birth is antici-

# Nursing Care Plan

## Hemorrhage

### Client Assessment

#### Nursing History

Identify factors predisposing to hemorrhage:
1. Presence of preeclampsia-eclampsia (PIH)
2. Overdistention of the uterus
   a. Multiple pregnancy
   b. Hydramnios
3. Grandmultiparity
4. Advanced age
5. Uterine contractile problems
   a. Hypotonicity
   b. Hypertonicity
6. Painless vaginal bleeding after seventh month
7. Presence of hypertension
8. Presence of diabetes
9. History of previous hemorrhage or bleeding problems, blood coagulation defects, abortions
10. Retained placental fragments
11. Cervical and/or vaginal lacerations

Determine religious preference to establish whether client will permit a blood transfusion.

#### Physical Examination

Severe abdominal pain (central abruptio placentae)

External or concealed bleeding (see Essential Facts to Remember—Differential Signs and Symptoms of Abruptio Placentae and Placenta Previa).

Painless vaginal hemorrhage (placenta previa)

Shock symptoms (decreased blood pressure, increased pulse, pallor)

Uterine tetany or uterine atony

Portwine amniotic fluid with abruptio placentae

Degree of hemorrhage

Changes in FHR

#### Diagnostic Studies

Hemoglobin and hematocrit

Type and cross-match

Fibrinogen levels

---

### Nursing Diagnosis/Client Goal

#### Nursing Diagnosis:

Pattern 1: Exchanging
Altered tissue perfusion (renal, cerebral, and peripheral) secondary to excessive blood loss

#### Client Goal:

The woman will maintain adequate tissue perfusion as measured by:
- BP between 110/70 and 138/88
- Pulse rate 60–90
- Urine output > 30 cc/hr
- Skin warm and nonclammy

### Nursing Interventions

Observe, record, and report blood loss.

Evaluate woman experiencing decrease in blood volume using following parameters:
1. Monitor rate and quality of respirations continuously.

2. Measure pulse rate.

3. Assess pulse quality by direct palpation.
   Determine pulse deficit by comparing apical-radial rates.

4. Compare present BP with woman's baseline BP; note pulse pressure.

### Rationale/Evaluation

#### Rationale:

Monitoring the amount of blood loss aids in determining appropriate interventions.

Initially respiratory rate increases as a result of sympathoadrenal stimulation, resulting in increased metabolic rate; pain and anxiety may cause hyperventilation.

Increased pulse rate is an effect of increased epinephrine.

Reflects circulatory status.

Thready pulse indicates vasoconstriction and reflects decreased cardiac output; peripheral pulses may be absent if vasoconstriction is intense.

Bounding pulse may indicate overload.

Hypotension indicates loss of large amount of circulatory fluid or lack of compensation in circulatory system.

As cardiac output decreases, there is usually a fall in pulse pressure.
Peripheral vasoconstriction may make accurate readings difficult.

# Nursing Care Plan

## Hemorrhage *(continued)*

| Nursing Diagnosis/Client Goal | Nursing Interventions | Rationale/Evaluation |
|---|---|---|
| | 5. Monitor urine output (decrease to less than 30 mL/hr is sign of shock):<br>a. Insert Foley catheter.<br>b. Measure output hourly.<br>c. Measure specific gravity to determine concentration of urine. | Vasoconstrictor effect of norepinephrine decreases blood flow to kidneys, which decreases glomerular filtration rate and the output of urine.<br>Inability to concentrate urine may indicate renal damage from vasoconstriction and decreased blood perfusion. |
| | 6. Inspect skin for presence of following:<br>a. Pallor and cyanosis:<br>*Pallor* in brown-skinned persons appears yellowish-brown; black-skinned individuals appear ashen gray; generally pallor may be observed in mucous membranes, lips, and nail beds.<br>*Cyanosis* is assessed by inspecting lips, nail beds, conjunctiva, palms, and soles of feet at regular intervals; evaluate capillary refilling by pressing on nail bed and observing return of color; compare by testing your own nail bed.<br>b. Coldness<br>c. Clamminess | Skin reflects amount of vasoconstriction. Pallor is determined by intensity of vasoconstriction.<br><br><br><br><br>Cyanosis occurs when the amount of unoxygenated hemoglobin in the blood is ≤5 g/dL blood.<br><br><br>Produced by slow blood flow. |
| | Evaluate state of consciousness frequently. | |
| | Measure CVP: normal CVP is 5–10 cm H$_2$O. | Caused by sympathetic stimulation of sweat glands.<br>Diminished cerebral blood flow causes restlessness and anxiety; as shock progresses, state of consciousness decreases.<br>Provides estimation of volume of blood returning to heart and ability of both chambers in right heart to propel blood. Low CVP indicates a decrease in the circulating volume of blood (hypovolemia). |
| | Assess amount of blood loss:<br>1. Count pads.<br>2. Weigh pads and chux (1 g = 1 mL blood approximately).<br>3. Record amount in a specific amount of time (for example, 50 mL bright red blood on pad in 20 min). | In obstetric clients, blood is replaced according to estimates of actual blood loss, rather than using parameters of increased and decreased BP. |
| | Hypovolemia:<br>Relieve decreased blood pressure by administration of whole blood. | Hypotension results from decreased blood volume. |
| | While waiting for whole blood to be available, infuse isotonic fluids, plasma, plasma expanders, or serum albumin. | Degree of hypovolemia may be assessed by CVP, hemoglobin, and hematocrit. |

*(continues)*

# Nursing Care Plan

## Hemorrhage (continued)

| Nursing Diagnosis/Client Goal | Nursing Interventions | Rationale/Evaluation |
|---|---|---|
| | Marginal abruptio placentae:<br>If abruptio placentae is diagnosed, nurse and physician will:<br>1. Evaluate blood loss.<br><br>2. Assess uterine contractile pattern and tenderness.<br>3. Monitor maternal vital signs.<br>4. Assess fetal status.<br>5. Assess cervical dilatation and effacement.<br>6. Rule out placenta previa.<br>7. Perform amniotomy and begin oxytocin infusion if labor does not start immediately or is ineffective.<br><br>Central abruptio placentae with severe blood loss:<br>1. Perform same assessments as for marginal abruptio placentae.<br>2. Monitor CVP.<br>3. Replace blood loss.<br>4. Effect immediate delivery.<br>5. Observe for signs and symptoms of disseminated intravascular coagulation (DIC). | Bleeding often stops as shock develops but resumes as circulation is restored. Provides information on type of abruption and maternal and fetal status.<br><br><br><br><br><br><br><br><br>**Evaluation:**<br>The woman maintains normal tissue perfusion. |
| **Nursing Diagnosis:**<br><br>Pattern 1: Exchanging<br>Potential altered tissue perfusion related to blood loss secondary to uterine atony following birth<br><br>**Client Goal:**<br><br>The woman's uterus will remain well contracted in the midline and below the umbilicus. | 1. Assess contractility of uterus and amount of vaginal bleeding.<br>2. Postpartally, massage uterus every 15 min for one hour, every 30 min for one hour, every 60 min for two to four hours. Evaluate more frequently if uterus is boggy or not in the midline. Administer oxytocin per protocol or physician/nurse-midwife order. | **Rationale:**<br><br>Muscle fibers that have been overstretched or overused do not contract well; contraction of muscle fibers over open placental site is essential; slight relaxation of uterus muscle fibers leads to continuous oozing of blood.<br><br>**Evaluation:**<br><br>The woman's uterus remains firm, in the midline, and below the umbilicus. |
| **Nursing Diagnosis:**<br><br>Pattern 9: Feeling<br>Fear related to concern for own personal status and the baby's safety<br><br>**Client Goal:**<br><br>The woman will have opportunities to verbalize concern. | Keep woman informed of present status.<br>Provide accurate information.<br>Provide opportunities for questions.<br>Establish trusting relationship.<br>Encourage woman to participate in decision making if at all possible. | **Rationale:**<br><br>As hemorrhage occurs, the safety of the mother and baby are threatened. Anxiety and fear may be lessened somewhat when the woman is informed, understands what is happening, and has some part in the decision-making process.<br><br>**Evaluation:**<br><br>The woman verbalizes questions and receives support. |

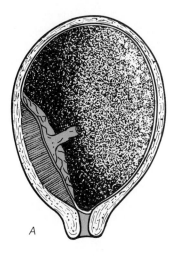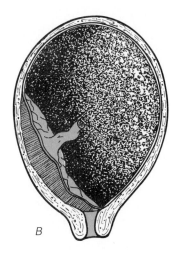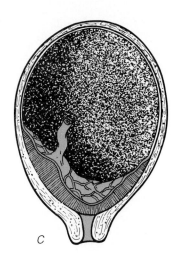

*Figure 18.11    Placenta previa: (A) Low placental implantation. (B) Partial placenta previa. (C) Total placenta previa. (Reprinted with permission of Ross Laboratories, Columbus, OH 43216. From Clinical Education Aid no. 12.)*

pated. This is important because the presenting part of the fetus may obstruct the flow of blood from the placenta or umbilical cord. If fetal distress occurs, cesarean birth is indicated.

After birth, blood sampling should be done to determine whether the intrauterine bleeding episodes of the woman have caused anemia in the newborn.

## MEDICAL THERAPY

The goal of medical care is to identify the cause of bleeding and to provide treatment that will ensure delivery of a mature newborn. Indirect diagnosis is made by localizing the placenta through tests that require no vaginal ex-

amination. The most commonly employed diagnostic test is the ultrasound scan (Figure 18.12). If placenta previa is ruled out, a vaginal examination can be performed with a speculum to determine the cause of bleeding (such as cervical lesions).

Direct diagnosis of placenta previa can be made only by feeling the placenta inside the cervical os. However, such an examination may cause profuse bleeding due to tearing of tissue in the cotyledons of the placenta. Because of the danger of bleeding, a vaginal examination should be performed only if ultrasound is not available, the pregnancy is near term, and there is profuse vaginal bleeding. The examination may be done using a double setup procedure. In this situation, it must be determined whether the

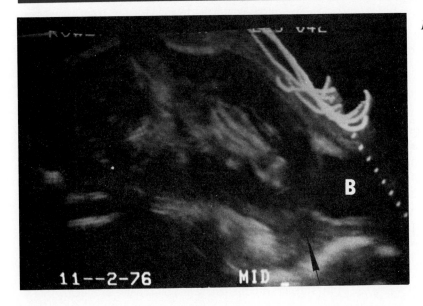

*Figure 18.12    Ultrasound of placenta previa*

cause of the bleeding is placenta previa or advanced labor with copious bloody show (which is normal). *Double setup* means that the delivery room is set up for the vaginal examination and normal vaginal birth and for a cesarean birth should placenta previa be present and the examination precipitates brisk bleeding. Adequate personnel must be present to respond to treatment decisions.

The differential diagnosis of placental or cervical bleeding takes careful consideration. Partial separation of the placenta may also present with painless bleeding, and a true placenta previa may not demonstrate overt bleeding until labor begins, thus confusing the diagnosis. Another important fact to note is that the causes of slight-to-moderate antepartal bleeding episodes in 20% to 25% of women are never accurately diagnosed.

Care of the women with painless late gestational bleeding depends on (a) the week of gestation during which the first bleeding episode occurs and (b) the amount of bleeding. If the pregnancy is less than 37 weeks' gestation, expectant management is employed to delay delivery until about 37 weeks' gestation to allow the fetus to mature. Expectant management involves stringent regulation of the following:

1. Bed rest with bathroom privileges only as long as the woman is not bleeding
2. No rectal or vaginal exams
3. Monitoring of blood loss, pain, and uterine contractility
4. Evaluating FHTs with external monitor
5. Monitoring of vital signs
6. Complete laboratory evaluation: hemoglobin, hematocrit, Rh factor, and urinalysis
7. Intravenous fluid (lactated Ringer's) with drip rate monitored
8. Two units of cross-matched blood available for transfusion

If frequent, recurrent, or profuse bleeding persists, or if fetal well-being appears threatened, a cesarean birth may be performed before 37 weeks.

## NURSING ASSESSMENT

Assessment of the woman with placenta previa must be ongoing to prevent or treat complications that are potentially lethal to the mother and fetus. Painless, bright red vaginal bleeding is the best diagnostic sign of placenta previa. If this sign should develop during the last three months of a pregnancy, placenta previa should always be considered until ruled out by examination. The first bleeding episode is generally scanty. If no rectal or vaginal examinations are performed, it often subsides spontaneously. However, each subsequent hemorrhage is more profuse.

The uterus remains soft, and if labor begins, it relaxes fully between contractions. The FHR usually remains stable unless profuse hemorrhage and maternal shock occur. As a result of the placement of the placenta, the fetal presenting part is often unengaged, and transverse lie is common.

Blood loss, pain, and uterine contractility are appraised by the nurse from both subjective and objective perspectives. Maternal vital signs and the results of blood and urine tests provide the nurse with additional data about the woman's condition. FHR is evaluated with an external fetal monitor. Another pressing nursing responsibility is observing and verifying the family's ability to cope with the anxiety associated with an unknown outcome.

## NURSING DIAGNOSIS

Nursing diagnoses that may apply are presented in the Nursing Care Plan—Hemorrhage.

## NURSING PLAN AND IMPLEMENTATION
### Preparation for Double Setup Procedure

Before a double setup procedure is performed, the laboring couple should be physiologically and psychologically prepared for possible surgery (Chapter 19). A whole-blood setup should be readied for intravenous infusion and a patent intravenous line established before any intrusive procedures are undertaken. The maternal vital signs should be monitored every 15 minutes in the absence of hemorrhage and every five minutes with active hemorrhage. The external tocodynamometer should be connected to the maternal abdomen to monitor uterine activity continuously.

### Promotion of Physical Well-Being

The nurse continues to monitor the woman and her fetus to determine the status of the bleeding and to determine the mother's and baby's responses. Vital signs, intake and output, and other pertinent assessments must be made frequently. The nurse evaluates the electronic monitor tracing to evaluate the fetal status.

### Provision of Emotional Support to the Family

Emotional support for the family is an important nursing care goal. When active bleeding is occurring, the assessments and management must be directed toward physical support. However, emotional aspects need to be addressed simultaneously. The nurse can explain the assessments being completed and the treatment measures that need to be done. Time can be provided for questions, and the nurse can act as an advocate in obtaining information for the family. Emotional support can also be offered by staying with the family and by the use of touch.

### Promotion of Neonatal Physiologic Adaptation

The newborn's hemoglobin, cell volume, and erythrocyte count should be checked immediately and then monitored closely. The newborn may require oxygen and administration of blood.

### Provision of Care to the Woman with Bleeding

Additional information regarding nursing care is addressed in the Nursing Care Plan—Hemorrhage.

### EVALUATION

Anticipated outcomes of nursing care include:

- The cause of hemorrhage is recognized promptly and corrective measures are taken.
- The woman's vital signs remain in the normal range.
- The woman and her baby have a safe labor and birth.
- Any other complications are recognized and treated early.
- The family understands what has happened and the implications and associated problems of placenta previa.

## ● Other Placental Problems

Other problems of the placenta are presented in Table 18.3 and in Figure 18.13.

## ● CARE OF THE WOMAN AND FETUS WITH A PROLAPSED UMBILICAL CORD

A prolapsed umbilical cord results when the umbilical cord precedes the fetal presenting part. When this occurs, pressure is placed on the umbilical cord, as it is trapped between the presenting part and the maternal pelvis. Consequently, the vessels carrying blood to and from the fetus are compressed (see Figure 18.14).

Prolapse of the cord may occur with rupture of the membranes if the presenting part is not well engaged in the pelvis.

## ● Maternal Implications

Although a prolapsed cord does not directly precipitate physical alterations in the woman, her immediate concern for the baby creates enormous stress. The woman may need to deal with some unusual interventions, a cesarean delivery, and in some circumstances, death of the baby.

## ● Fetal-Neonatal Implications

Compression of the cord results in decreased blood flow and leads to fetal distress. If labor is occurring, the cord is compressed further with each contraction. If the pressure on the cord is not relieved, the fetus will die.

## Table 18.3  Placental and Umbilical Cord Variations

| Placental variation | Maternal implications | Fetal-neonatal implications |
|---|---|---|
| **SUCCENTURIATE PLACENTA** | | |
| One or more accessory lobes of fetal villi will develop on the placenta. | Postpartal hemorrhage from retained lobe | |
| **CIRCUMVALLATE PLACENTA** | | |
| A double fold of chorion and amnion form a ring around the umbilical cord on the fetal side of the placenta. | Increased incidence of late abortion, antepartal hemorrhage, and preterm labor | Fetal death |
| **BATTLEDORE PLACENTA** | | |
| The umbilical cord is inserted at or near the placental margin. | Increased incidence of preterm labor and bleeding | Prematurity, fetal distress |
| **VELAMENTOUS INSERTION OF THE UMBILICAL CORD** | | |
| The vessels of the umbilical cord divide some distance from the placenta in the placental membranes. | Hemorrhage if one of vessels is torn | Fetal distress, hemorrhage |

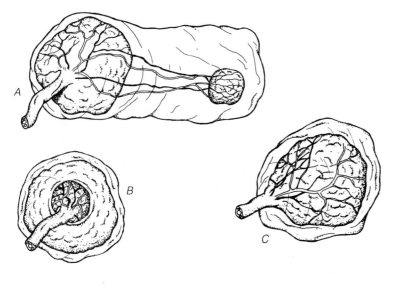

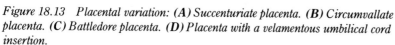

*Figure 18.13   Placental variation: (A) Succenturiate placenta. (B) Circumvallate placenta. (C) Battledore placenta. (D) Placenta with a velamentous umbilical cord insertion.*

## ● Medical Therapy

Preventing the occurrence of prolapse of the cord is the preferred medical approach. If the prolapse does happen, relieving the compression on the cord is critical to fetal outcome. The medical and nursing team must work together to facilitate delivery.

Bed rest is indicated for all laboring women with a history of ruptured membranes, until engagement with no cord prolapse has been documented. Furthermore, at the time of spontaneous rupture of membranes or amniotomy, the FHR should be auscultated for at least a full minute and again at the end of a contraction and after a few contractions. If fetal bradycardia is detected on the auscultation, the woman should be examined to rule out a cord prolapse. In the presence of cord prolapse, electronic monitor tracings show severe, moderate, or prolonged variable decelerations with baseline bradycardia. If these patterns are found, the woman is examined vaginally.

If a loop of cord is discovered, the gloved fingers are left in the vagina, and attempts are made to lift the fetal head off the cord to relieve compression until the physician arrives. This is a life-saving measure. Oxygen is begun, and FHR is monitored to see if the cord compression is adequately relieved.

The force of gravity can be employed to relieve the compression. The woman assumes the knee-chest position or the bed is adjusted to the Trendelenburg position and the woman should be transported to the delivery or operating room in this position. The nurse must remember that the cord may be occultly prolapsed with an actual loop extending into the vagina or lying alongside the presenting part. It may be pulsating strongly or so weakly that it is difficult to determine on palpation of the cord whether the fetus is alive.

## ● Nursing Care

Because there are few outward signs of cord prolapse, each pregnant woman is advised to call her physician or nurse-midwife when the membranes rupture and to go to the office, clinic, or birthing facility. A sterile vaginal examination determines if there is danger of cord prolapse. If the presenting part is well engaged, the risk of cord prolapse is minimal, and ambulation may be encouraged. If the presenting part is not well engaged, bed rest is recommended to prevent cord prolapse. See Essential Nursing Diagnoses to Consider—Prolapse of the Umbilical Cord for possible nursing diagnoses.

Because cord prolapse can be associated with fetal death, some physicians and nurse-midwives may insist that bed rest be maintained after rupture of membranes regardless of fetal engagement. This can lead to conflict if the laboring woman and her partner do not hold the same opinions. The nurse can ease this situation by helping communication between the physician or nurse-midwife and the couple.

During labor, any alteration of FHR or presence of meconium in the amniotic fluid indicates the need to assess for the presence of cord prolapse. Vaginal birth is possible with prolapsed cord if:

● The cervix is completely dilated.

● Pelvic measurements are adequate.

## Essential Nursing Diagnoses to Consider

### Prolapse of the Umbilical Cord

Altered tissue perfusion (fetal)

Anticipatory grieving

Anxiety

Fear

Impaired gas exchange (fetal)

Ineffective family coping

Ineffectual individual coping

Knowledge deficit

Potential for infection

Potential for injury

Powerlessness

Spiritual distress

If these conditions are not present, cesarean birth is the method of choice. The woman is taken to the delivery room while the examiner continues to relieve the pressure on the cord until the infant has been delivered.

## ● CARE OF THE WOMAN AND FETUS AT RISK DUE TO AMNIOTIC FLUID-RELATED COMPLICATIONS

## ● Amniotic Fluid Embolism

In the presence of a small tear in the amnion or chorion high in the uterus, a small amount of amniotic fluid may leak into the chorionic plate and enter the maternal circulation as an **amniotic fluid embolism.** The fluid can also enter at areas of placental separation or cervical tears. Under pressure from the contracting uterus, the fluid is driven into the maternal system. The more debris in the amniotic fluid (such as meconium), the greater the maternal problems.

### MATERNAL IMPLICATIONS

This condition frequently occurs during or after the birth when the woman has had a difficult, rapid labor. Suddenly she experiences respiratory distress, circulatory collapse, acute hemorrhage, and cor pulmonale as the embolism blocks the vessels of the lungs. The woman exhibits a sudden onset of dyspnea, cyanosis, cardiovascular collapse, shock, and coma. If she survives for more than one hour, she has a 50% chance of developing DIC caused by thromboplastin-like material in the amniotic fluid. This results in massive hemorrhage.

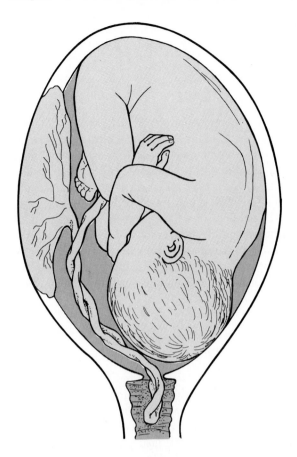

*Figure 18.14   Prolapse of the umbilical cord*

Maternal mortality is approximately 85% (Duff 1984). In suspected cases in which women survive, it is difficult to determine whether an amniotic fluid embolism actually occurred since specific tests are not available.

### FETAL-NEONATAL IMPLICATIONS

Delivery must be facilitated immediately to obtain a live birth. In many cases, the birth has already occurred, or the fetus can be delivered vaginally with forceps. If labor has been tumultuous (very strong, frequent contractions), the fetus may suffer problems associated with dysfunctional labor.

### MEDICAL THERAPY

The goals of medical therapy are to maintain oxygenation, support the cardiovascular system and blood pressure, and assess coagulopathy (Clark 1986).

Any woman exhibiting chest pain, dyspnea, cyanosis, frothy sputum, tachycardia, hypotension, and massive hemorrhage needs the cooperation of every member of the health team if her life is to be saved. Medical interventions are supportive. Recovery is contingent on the return of the mother's cardiovascular and respiratory stability. If necessary, the delivery is assisted to enhance the health of the newborn.

## NURSING CARE

Every delivery room should be equipped with a working oxygen unit. In the absence of the physician, the nurse administers oxygen under positive pressure until medical help arrives. An intravenous line is quickly established. If respiratory and cardiac arrest occurs, cardiopulmonary resuscitation (CPR) is initiated immediately.

The nurse readies the equipment necessary for blood transfusion and for the insertion of the CVP line. As the blood volume is replaced, using fresh whole blood to provide clotting factors, the CVP is monitored frequently. In the presence of cor pulmonale, fluid overload could easily occur.

## ● Hydramnios

**Hydramnios** (also called polyhydramnios) occurs when there is over 2000 mL of amniotic fluid. The exact cause of hydramnios is unknown; however, it often occurs in cases of major congenital anomalies. It is postulated that a major source of amniotic fluid is found in special amnion cells that lie over the placenta (Danforth and Scott 1986). During the second half of the pregnancy, the fetus begins to swallow and inspire amniotic fluid and to urinate, which contributes to the amount present. In cases of hydramnios, no pathology has been found in the amniotic epithelium. However, hydramnios is associated with fetal malformations that affect the fetal swallowing mechanism and neurologic disorders in which the fetal meninges are exposed in the amniotic cavity. This condition is also found in cases of anencephaly, in which the fetus is thought to urinate excessively due to overstimulation of the cerebrospinal centers. When monozygotic twins manifest hydramnios, it is possible that the twin with the increased blood volume urinates excessively. The weight of the placenta has been found to be increased in some cases of hydramnios, indicating that increased functioning of the placental tissue may be contributory.

There are two types of hydramnios: chronic and acute. In the chronic type, the fluid volume gradually increases. Most cases are of this variety. In acute cases, the volume increases rapidly over a period of a few days.

## MATERNAL IMPLICATIONS

When the amount of amniotic fluid is over 3000 mL, the woman experiences shortness of breath and edema in the lower extremities from compression of the vena cava. Milder forms of hydramnios occur more frequently and are associated with minimal symptoms. Hydramnios is associated with such maternal disorders as diabetes and Rh sensitization and with multiple gestations.

Antepartally, if the amniotic fluid is removed rapidly, abruptio placentae can result from too sudden a change in the size of the uterus. Because of overdistention of uterine muscles, uterine dysfunction can occur intrapartally, and the incidence of postpartal hemorrhage increases.

## FETAL-NEONATAL IMPLICATIONS

Fetal malformations and premature delivery are common with hydramnios; thus perinatal mortality is high. Prolapsed cord can occur when the membranes rupture, a further complication for the fetus. The incidence of malpresentations is also increased.

## MEDICAL THERAPY

Hydramnios is managed with supportive treatment unless the intensity of the woman's distress and symptoms dictate otherwise.

If the accumulation of amniotic fluid is severe enough to cause maternal dyspnea and pain, hospitalization and removal of the excessive fluid are required. This can be done vaginally or by amniocentesis. The dangers of performing the technique vaginally are prolapsed cord and the inability to remove the fluid slowly. If amniocentesis is performed, it should be done with the aid of sonography to prevent inadvertent damage to the fetus and placenta. The fluid should be removed slowly to prevent abruption (Pritchard et al 1985).

## NURSING CARE

Hydramnios should be suspected when the fundal height increases out of proportion to the gestational age. As the amount of fluid increases, the nurse may have difficulty palpating the fetus and auscultating the FHR. In more severe cases, the maternal abdomen appears extremely tense and tight on inspection. On sonography, large spaces can be identified between the fetus and the uterine wall. An anencephalic infant or a dilated fetal stomach resulting from esophageal atresia may also be identified, and multiple gestations may be confirmed. An x-ray fetogram will also show a radiolucent area of space and any fetal skeletal defects.

When amniocentesis is performed, it is vital to maintain sterile technique to prevent infection. The nurse can offer support to the couple by explaining the procedure to them. The nurse assists the clinician in interpreting sonographic findings.

If the fetus has been diagnosed with a congenital defect in utero or is born with the defect, psychologic support is needed to assist the family. Often the nurse collaborates with social services to offer the family this additional help.

## ● *Oligohydramnios*

**Oligohydramnios,** in which the amount of amniotic fluid is severely reduced and concentrated, is a rare maternal finding. The exact cause of this condition is unknown. It is found in cases of postmaturity, with IUGR secondary to placental insufficiency, and in fetal conditions associated with renal and urinary malfunction. If oligohydramnios occurs in the first part of pregnancy, there is a danger of fetal adhesions (one part of the fetus may adhere to another part). Pulmonary hypoplasia has been found, theoretically due to lack of fluid inhaled in the terminal air sacs (Pritchard et al 1985). An increased incidence of major anomalies involving major organ systems and low five-minute Apgar scores has also been found (Bastide et al 1986). The perinatal mortality rate is more than doubled.

### MATERNAL IMPLICATIONS

Labor can be dysfunctional, and progress is slow.

### FETAL-NEONATAL IMPLICATIONS

Fetal hypoxia may occur due to umbilical cord compression.

At this time there is no recommended treatment for oligohydramnios. Some clinicians are considering a warm saline infusion into the uterus but this is not standard practice. During labor, the fetus is at increased risk of cord compression due to decreased amniotic fluid, so the care givers need to be particularly alert for variable decelerations of the fetal heart rate.

## ● CARE OF THE WOMAN WITH CEPHALOPELVIC DISPROPORTION (CPD)

The passage includes the maternal bony pelvis, beginning at the pelvic inlet and ending at the pelvic outlet, and the maternal soft tissues within these anatomic areas. A contracture (narrowed diameter) in any of the described areas can result in CPD if the fetus is larger than the pelvic diameters. Abnormal fetal presentations and positions occur in CPD as the fetus attempts to accommodate to its passage.

The gynecoid and anthropoid pelvic types usually are adequate for vertex delivery, but the android and platypelloid types predispose to CPD. Certain combinations of types also can result in pelvic diameters inadequate for vertex delivery. (See Chapter 3 for a description of pelvis types and their implications for childbirth.)

## ● *Types of Pelvic Contractures*

*Contracture of the pelvic inlet* is indicated by a diagonal conjugate less than 11.5 cm. The primary risk is that the narrowed diameter will not permit engagement of the fetal presenting part. If engagement does occur, the fetus may assume a malpresentation, such as face or shoulder.

The management of inlet contractures begins with assessment of the pelvic configuration, the size and presentation of the fetus, uterine activity, cervical dilatation, and any problems during previous labors and deliveries. These findings influence the decision to proceed with a trial labor or to do a cesarean delivery.

*Contractures of the midpelvis* are more common than inlet contractures. Although a satisfactory method of measuring the midpelvis manually does not exist, prominent spines, converging pelvic walls, or a narrow sacrosciatic notch can be ascertained on vaginal examination. Midpelvis contractures cause transverse arrest of the head, leading to potentially difficult midforceps delivery.

The treatment goal is to allow the natural forces of labor to push the biparietal diameter of the fetal head beyond the potential interspinous obstruction.

A bulging perineum and crowning indicate that the obstruction has been passed.

*Contractures of the outlet* and midpelvis almost always occur simultaneously (Mengert and Steer 1984). A diameter of less than 8 cm between the inner surfaces of the ischial tuberosities constitutes an outlet contracture. Whether vaginal delivery can occur depends on the woman's measurements and fetal size.

## ● *Implications of Pelvic Contractures*
### MATERNAL IMPLICATIONS

Labor is prolonged in the presence of CPD. Membrane rupture can result from the force of the unequally distributed contractions being exerted on the fetal membranes. In obstructed labor, where the fetus cannot descend, uterine rupture can occur. With delayed descent, necrosis of maternal soft tissues can result from pressure exerted by the fetal head. Eventually, necrosis can cause fistulas from the vagina to other nearby structures. Difficult forceps deliveries can also result in damage to maternal soft tissue.

### FETAL-NEONATAL IMPLICATIONS

If the membranes rupture and the fetal head has not entered the inlet, there is a danger of cord prolapse. Excessive molding and/or overriding of the sutures may occur. A large caput succedaneum (see Chapter 21) may form. If the labor and delivery are particularly difficult, skull fracture and/or intracranial hemorrhage may occur.

## MEDICAL THERAPY

The goal of medical treatment is to assess the maternal pelvis accurately and determine whether CPD is present.

Fetopelvic relationships can be appraised by x-ray pelvimetry when the pregnancy is at term or in early labor. The x-ray pelvimetry provides measurements for the maternal pelvic inlet, midpelvis, and outlet; degree of fetal descent; and selected diameters of the fetal head.

When pelvimetry is used in combination with ultrasonography, the mechanisms of labor are even more predictable.

In addition to x-ray pelvimetry, assessment techniques such as careful manual examination of the pelvis and the technique of magnetic resonance imaging (MRI) are used to identify inadequate diameters and determine the treatment plan (Silbar 1986).

When the pelvic diameters are borderline or questionable, a trial of labor (TOL) may be advised. In this process, the woman continues to labor and careful, frequent assessments of cervical dilatation and fetal descent are made by the physician and nurse. As long as there is continued progress, the TOL continues. If progress ceases, the decision for a cesarean birth is made.

## NURSING CARE

The adequacy of the maternal pelvis for a vaginal delivery should be assessed intrapartally as well as antepartally. During the intrapartal assessment, the size of the fetus and its presentation, position, and lie must also be considered. (See Chapter 15 for intrapartal assessment techniques.)

The nurse should suspect CPD when labor is prolonged, cervical dilatation and effacement are slow, and engagement of the presenting part is delayed.

The couple may need support in coping with the stresses of this complicated labor. The nurse should keep the couple informed of what is happening and explain the procedures that are being used. This knowledge reassures the couple that measures are being taken to resolve the problem.

Nursing actions during the TOL are similar to care during any labor with the exception that the assessments of cervical dilatation and fetal descent are more frequent. Contractions should be monitored continuously, and the labor progress may be charted on the Friedman graph. The fetus should also be monitored continuously. Any signs of fetal distress are reported to the physician immediately.

The mother may be positioned in a variety of ways to increase the pelvic diameters. Sitting or squatting increases the outlet diameters and may be effective in instances where there is failure of or slow fetal descent. Changing from one side to the other and/or maintaining a hands and knees position may assist the fetus in occiput posterior position to change to an occiput anterior. The mother may instinctively want to assume one of these positions. If not, the nurse may encourage a change of position.

## ● CARE OF THE WOMAN AT RISK DUE TO POSTPARTAL HEMORRHAGE

Postpartal hemorrhage is a loss of blood in excess of 500 mL in the first 24 hours following delivery. Immediate postpartal hemorrhage is most commonly caused by uterine atony and lacerations of the vagina and cervix.

## ● Retained Placenta

The placenta should be delivered within 30 minutes of the birth of the infant. If it is not, or if hemorrhage occurs after the birth of the newborn but before delivery of the placenta, the cause is frequently a retained placenta. In this instance, the physician observes the firmness of the fundus and administers fundal massage if needed. When the placenta is ready to separate, fundal massage helps to express (deliver) the placenta. If signs of placental separation have not occurred, the physician manually removes the placenta by inserting a gloved hand into the uterus and placing the fingers at the placental margin. Then the placenta is gently separated from the uterine wall. During this procedure, the other hand remains on the uterine fundus, externally.

After delivery of the placenta, the consistency of the fundus is assessed. If it is boggy and bleeding continues, vigorous massage is instituted. Oxytocics (Pitocin, Methergine, or Ergotrate) may be given. If the bleeding persists, the physician undertakes bimanual uterine compression. If intravenous infusion is not already occurring, a line is established, and oxytocin is added at a rapid rate. Blood transfusions may be ordered. Oxygen at 6–10 L/min is given by face mask. The physician manually checks the uterine cavity for retained placental fragments and also inspects the cervix and vagina for lacerations. The combination of bimanual compression, oxytocics, and blood transfusion is usually effective. The fundus should be assessed frequently for the next few hours to see that it remains contracted.

## ● Placenta Accreta

*Placenta accreta*, a type of retained placenta, is very serious because the chorionic villi attach directly to the myometrium of the uterus. Placenta accreta cannot be manually removed from the uterus as described above. An abdominal hysterectomy is usually required to control bleeding.

## Uterine Atony

Relaxation of the uterus (or insufficient contractions) following birth can frequently be anticipated in the presence of the following:

● Overdistention of the uterus due to multiple fetuses, macrosomic fetus, or hydramnios

● Dysfunctional labor that has already indicated the uterus is contracting in an other-than-normal pattern

● Oxytocin stimulation or augmentation during labor

● Use of anesthetics that produce uterine relaxation

● Distention of the bladder

Hemorrhage from uterine atony may be slow and steady rather than sudden and massive. The blood may escape from the vagina or collect in the uterus. Because of the increased blood volume associated with pregnancy, changes in maternal blood pressure and pulse may not occur until blood loss has been significant.

After delivery of the placenta, the fundus should be palpated to assure that it is firm and well contracted. If it is not firm, vigorous massage should be instituted. Oxytocics may be given.

## Retained Placental Fragments

Hemorrhage from retained placental fragments is not usually a cause of immediate postpartal hemorrhage but tends to be a major cause of later postpartal bleeding. To prevent this type of hemorrhage, the placenta should be inspected after delivery for evidence of missing pieces or cotyledons. The membranes should be inspected for absent sections or for vessels that traverse from the edge of the placenta outward along the membranes, which may indicate placenta succenturiate (an accessory portion attached to the main placenta by an artery and vein) and a retained lobe. The uterine cavity may be checked for retained placental fragments or membranes.

## Inversion of Uterus

Uterine inversion occurs when the uterus turns inside out during the third stage of labor. This rare occurrence can be caused by a lax uterine wall coupled with undue tension on an umbilical cord when the placenta has not separated. Forceful pressure on the fundus with a dilated cervix and sudden emptying of the uterine contents may be contributing factors. Maternal bleeding with shock is rapid and profound.

### MEDICAL THERAPY

The physician manually replaces the uterus by grasping the vaginal mass, spreading the cervical ring with the fingers and thumb, and steadily forcing the fundus upward. The patient is often placed under deep anesthesia. Occasionally tocolytic agents are given (Oxorn 1986).

### NURSING CARE

Nursing interventions should be directed at management of shock. Volume replacement should be a priority. The nurse starts an intravenous infusion and sees that a blood sample is collected for type and cross-matching. The nurse monitors blood pressure and pulse rate every five minutes until the anesthesiologist arrives and is ready to assume this duty.

Careful monitoring of intake and output is vital. An indwelling catheter is usually inserted into the bladder after the uterus is replaced. The uterus should be assessed frequently to ensure it remains contracted.

## CARE OF THE WOMAN WITH GENITAL TRACT TRAUMA

## Hematoma

The most common site of a genital tract hematoma is the lateral vaginal wall in the area of the ischial spines. If the hematoma is 3 cm or less and does not enlarge, it does not require therapy. A hematoma that continues to enlarge may allow enough blood loss to cause shock, sensations of intense internal pressure, and severe pain. In this instance, the hematoma should be drained, and the bleeding point located and ligated (Work 1982).

Nursing measures are directed first toward further assessment when the patient complains of intense pressure and pain in the perineal or rectal area. The perineum should be inspected for bruising or areas of swelling. Maternal blood pressure and pulse are assessed.

Signs and symptoms of shock in the presence of a well-contracted uterus and no visible vaginal blood loss should alert the nurse to the possibility of hematoma. The hematoma may be palpated by gentle rectal exam, although this procedure may be quite uncomfortable for the woman. After alerting the physician, the nurse continues to monitor vital signs and may initiate intravenous fluids if hypovolemic shock is developing.

## Perineal Lacerations

A laceration of the perineal tissues may occur when the perineal tissues have been stretched too much or the episiotomy has been extended. Lacerations of the vagina and perineum are classified as first, second, third, or fourth degree (Pritchard et al 1985).

● First-degree lacerations involve the perineal skin and vaginal mucosa.

- Second-degree lacerations include underlying fascia and muscle in addition to the skin and vaginal mucosa.

- Third-degree lacerations include all of the above and extend to the anal sphincter.

- Fourth-degree lacerations include all of the above and tear through the anal sphincter extending up the rectal wall.

Lacerations are repaired by suturing. Nursing measures begin with careful assessment of the perineum for swelling and bruising. Cold packs may be applied to increase comfort. In the postpartum period, additional comfort measures include sitz baths, use of a perineal light, and topical anesthetic spray to the perineum.

# ESSENTIAL CONCEPTS

- Stress, anxiety, and fear have a profound effect on labor, particularly when complications occur that imply maternal or fetal jeopardy.

- A hypertonic labor pattern is characterized by painful contractions that are not effective in effacing and dilating the cervix. It usually leads to a prolonged latent phase.

- Hypotonic labor patterns begin normally and then progress to infrequent, less intense contractions. If there are no contraindications, IV oxytocin is used as treatment.

- Prolonged labor lasts more than 24 hours.

- Precipitous labor is extremely rapid labor that lasts for less than three hours. It is associated with an increased risk to the mother and newborn infant.

- Spontaneous rupture of the membranes prior to labor is called premature rupture of the membranes. Associated problems include amnionitis and prolapse of the umbilical cord.

- Preterm labor occurs between 20 and 37 weeks of completed pregnancy. The major problems are associated with the extrauterine adaptation of the preterm infant due to lack of development and immaturity of major organ systems.

- The occiput posterior position of the fetus during labor prolongs the labor process, causes severe back discomfort in the laboring woman, and predisposes her to vaginal and perineal trauma and lacerations during birth.

- The types of fetal malpresentations include face, brow, breech, and shoulder.

- A fetus/newborn weighing more than 4000 g is termed macrosomic. Problems may occur during labor, delivery, and in the early neonatal period.

- Preventing and treating problems that infringe on the development and delivery of normal fetuses are significant medical-nursing activities once the presence of twins has been detected.

- Intrauterine fetal death poses a major nursing challenge to provide support and caring for the parents.

- Major bleeding problems in the intrapartal period are abruptio placentae and placenta previa.

- Abruptio placentae is the separation of the placenta from the side of the uterus prior to birth of the infant. Abruptio placentae may be central, marginal, or complete.

- Placenta previa occurs when the placenta implants low in the uterus near or over the cervix. A low-lying or marginal placenta is one that lies near the cervix. In partial placenta previa part of the placenta lies over the cervix. In complete placenta previa the cervix is completely covered.

- Prolapsed umbilical cord results when the umbilical cord precedes the fetal presenting part. When this occurs pressure is placed on the umbilical cord and blood flow to the fetus is diminished.

- Amniotic fluid embolism occurs when a bolus of amniotic fluid enters the maternal circulation and then enters the maternal lungs. Maternal mortality is very high with this complication.

- Hydramnios (also called polyhydramnios) occurs when there is over 2000 mL of amniotic fluid contained within the amniotic membranes. Hydramnios is associated with fetal malformations that affect fetal swallowing, and with maternal diabetes mellitus, Rh sensitization, and multiple gestations.

- Oligohydramnios is present when there is a severely reduced volume of amniotic fluid. Oligohydramnios is associated with IUGR, with postmaturity, and with fetal renal or urinary malfunctions. The fetus is more likely to experience variable decelerations because the amniotic fluid is insufficient to keep pressure off the umbilical cord.

- Cephalopelvic disproportion (CPD) occurs when there is a narrowed diameter in the maternal pelvis. The narrowed diameter is called a contracture and it may occur in the pelvic inlet, the midpelvis, or the outlet. If pelvic measurements are borderline, a trial of labor (TOL) may be attempted.

Failure of cervical dilatation and/or fetal descent would then necessitate a cesarean birth.

● Postpartal hemorrhage is a blood loss of more than 500 mL in the first 24 hours after birth. Postpartal hemorrhage is caused by uterine atony (relaxation of the uterus), retention of placental fragments, and lacerations of the cervix or vagina.

● A hematoma may occur in the lateral vaginal wall during the birth. The woman may complain of intense pressure and/or pain in the rectal area. Signs and symptoms of shock may be present.

● ● ● ● ● ● ● ● ● ● ● ● ● ● ● ● ● ● ● ● ● ● ● ● ● ● ● ● ● ● ●

## References

Acker DB, Sachs BP, Friedman EA: Risk factors for shoulder dystocia. *Obstet Gynecol* 1985; 66:762.

Acker DB, Sachs BP, Friedman EA: Risk factors for shoulder dystocia in the average-weight infant. *Obstet Gynecol* 1986; 67:614.

Andrews CM, Andrews EC: Nursing, maternal postures, and fetal positions. *Nurs Res* 1983; 32:6.

Avery MD, Burket BA: Effect of perineal massage on the incidence of episiotomy and perineal laceration in a nurse-midwifery service. *J Nurse-Midwifery* May/June 1986; 31:128.

Bastide A et al: Ultrasound evaluation of amniotic fluid: Outcome of pregnancies with severe oligohydramnios. *Am J Obstet Gynecol* April 1986; 154:895.

Bealle MH et al: A comparison of ritodrine, terbutaline, and magnesium sulfate for the suppression of preterm labor. *Am J Obstet Gynecol* 1985; 153:854.

Beckey RD et al: Development of a perinatal grief checklist. *J Obstet Gynecol Neonatal Nurs* May/June 1985; 14:194.

Bell D et al: Birth asphyxia, trauma, and mortality in twins: Has Cesarean section improved outcome? *Am J Obstet Gynecol* 1986; 154:235.

Benedetti TJ: Maternal complications of parenteral β-sympathomimetic therapy for premature labor. *Am J Obstet Gynecol* 1983; 145:1.

Berkowitz RL: *Critical Care of the Obstetric Patient.* New York: Churchill Livingstone, 1983.

Bishop EH: Acceleration of fetal pulmonary maturity. *Obstet Gynecol* 1981; 58(Suppl):48.

Briggs GC, Freeman RK, Yaffe SJ: *Drugs in Pregnancy and Lactation,* 2nd ed. Baltimore: Williams and Wilkins, 1986.

Campbell B: Overdue delivery: Its impact on mothers-to-be. *Am J Mat Child Nurs* May/June 1986; 11:170.

Caritis SN: A pharmacologic approach to the infusion of ritodrine. *Am J Obstet Gynecol* 1988; 158:380.

Caritis SN, Lin LS, Wong LK: Evaluation of the pharmacodynamics and pharmacokinetics of ritodrine when administered as a loading dose. *Am J Obstet Gynecol* 1985; 152:1026.

Carr D, Knupp SF: Grief and perinatal loss: A community hospital approach to support. *J Obstet Gynecol Neonatal Nurs* March/April 1985; 14:130.

Clark SL et al: Squamous cells in the maternal pulmonary circulation. *Am J Obstet Gynecol* January 1986; 154:104.

Collea JV: Choosing a method for breech delivery. *Contemp OB/GYN* April 1984; 23:27.

Creasy RK, Resnik R: *Maternal Fetal Medicine: Principles and Practice.* Philadelphia: Saunders, 1989.

Danforth DN, Scott JR: *Obstetrics and Gynecology,* 5th ed. Philadelphia: Lippincott, 1986.

Duff P: Defusing the dangers of amniotic fluid embolus. *Contemp OB/GYN* August 1984; 24:127.

Eden RD et al: Perinatal characteristics of uncomplicated postdate pregnancies. *Obstet Gynecol* 1987; 69:296.

Flood B, Naeye RL: Factors that predispose to premature rupture of the fetal membranes. *J Obstet Gynecol* March/April 1984; 13:119.

Freeman RK: Problems of postdate pregnancy. *Contemp OB/GYN* October 1986; 28:73.

Garite TJ et al: Prospective randomized study of corticosteroids in the management of premature rupture of the membranes and premature gestation. *Am J Obstet Gynecol* 1981; 141:508.

Genest M: Preparation for childbirth—Evidence for efficacy: A review. *J Obstet Gynecol Neonatal Nurs* 1981; 10:82.

Giacoia GP, Yaffe S: Perinatal pharmacology. Chapter 100 in: Sciarra JL (editor): *Gynecology and Obstetrics.* Vol 3. Philadelphia: Harper and Row, 1982.

Gilstrap LC et al: Twins: Prophylactic hospitalization and ward rest at early gestational age. *Obstet Gynecol* 1987; 69:578.

Gonik B, Creasy RK: Preterm labor: Its diagnosis and management. *Am J Obstet Gynecol* 1986; 154:3.

Green JR: Placental abnormalities: Placenta previa and abruptio placentae. In *Maternal Fetal Medicine: Principles and Practice.* Creasy RK, Resnik R (editors). Philadelphia: Saunders, 1989.

Hankins GD, Hauth JC: A comparison of the relative toxicities of beta-sympathomimetic tocolytic agents. *Am J Perinatol* October 1985; 2:338.

Hendricks SK, Keroes J, Katz M: Electrocardiographic changes associated with ritodrine-induced maternal tachycardia and hypokalemia. *Am J Obstet Gynecol* 1986; 154:921.

Holbrook H et al: Evaluation of the weekly cervical examination in a preterm birth prevention program. *Am J Perinatol* 1987; 4(3):240.

Hollander DI: Magnesium sulfate and ritodrine hydrochloride: A randomized comparison. *Am J Obstet Gynecol* 1987; 156:631.

Ingemarsson I et al: Single injection of terbutaline in term labor. I. Effect on fetal pH in cases with prolonged bradycardia. *Am J Obstet Gynecol* 1985a; 153:859.

Ingemarsson I et al: Single injection of terbutaline in term labor. II. Effect on uterine activity. *Am J Obstet Gynecol* 1985b; 153:865.

Knight A: PSIs—tocolytics of last resort? *Contemp OB/GYN* January 1986; 27:191.

Kübler-Ross E: *On Death and Dying.* New York: Macmillan, 1969.

Lederman RP et al: Anxiety and epinephrine in multiparous women in labor: Relationship to duration in labor and fetal heart pattern. *Obstet Gynecol* 1985; 153:870.

Lipshitz J: Beta-adrenergic agonists. *Semin Perinatol* July 1981; 5:252.

Lodeiro JG et al: Fetal biophysical profile in twin gestations. *Obstet Gynecol* 1986; 67:824.

Mazor M, Hagay ZJ, Biale Y: Fetal malformations associated with breech delivery. *J Reprod Med* 1985; 30:884.

McFarland LV et al: Erb/Duchenne's palsy: A consequence of fetal macrosomia and method of delivery. *Obstet Gynecol* 1986; 68:784.

Mengert WF, Steer CM: Pelvic capacity. Chapter 53 in: *Gynecology and Obstetrics*. Vol 2. Sciarra JL (editor). Philadelphia: Harper and Row, 1984.

Morales WJ, Koerten J: Obstetric management and intraventricular hemorrhage in very-low-birth-weight infants. *Obstet Gynecol* 1986; 68:35.

NAACOG: Preterm labor and tocolytics. *OGN Nurs Practice Resource* September 1984; 10.

Nageotte MP et al: Prophylactic intrapartum amnioinfusion in patients with preterm premature rupture of membranes. *Am J Obstet Gynecol* 1985; 153:557.

Newman RB et al: Uterine activity during pregnancy in ambulatory patients: Comparison of singleton and twin gestations. *Am J Obstet Gynecol* 1986; 154(3):530.

Niebyl J (moderator): Symposium: Tocolytics: When and how to use them. *Contemp OB/GYN* June 1986; 27:146.

O'Leary JA: Shoulder dystocia: An ounce of prevention. *Contemp OB/GYN* 1986; 27(4):78.

Oxorn H: *Human Labor and Birth*. 5th ed. New York: Appleton-Century-Crofts, 1986.

Philipsen T et al: Pulmonary edema following ritodrine cases with prolonged bradycardia. *Am J Obstet Gynecol* 1985; 153:859.

Pitkin RM: Fetal death: Diagnosis and management. *Am J Obstet Gynecol* September 1987; 157:583.

Polin JI, Frangipane WL: Current concepts in management of obstetric problems for pediatricians: II. Modern concepts in management of multiple gestation. *Ped Clin North Am* 1986; 33(3):649.

Pritchard JA, MacDonald PC, Grant NF: *Williams Obstetrics*. 17th ed. Norwalk, CT: Appleton-Century-Crofts, 1985.

Quilligan EJ: *Current Therapy in Obstetrics and Gynecology*. Philadelphia: Saunders, 1987.

Sakamoto H, Huszar G: Pharmacologic levels of nitrendipine do not affect actin-myosin interaction in the human uterus and placenta. *Am J Obstet Gynecol* 1986; 154:402.

Sasmor JL et al: Childbirth education in 1980. *J Obstet Gynecol Neonatal Nurs* 1981; 10:155.

Schwiebert P, Kirk P: *When Hello Means Goodbye*. Oregon Health Sciences University, 1985.

Shortridge LA: Using ritodrine hydrochloride to inhibit preterm labor. *Am J Mat Child Nurs* January/February 1983; 8:58.

Silbar EL: Factors related to the increasing cesarean section rates for cephalopelvic disproportion. *Am J Obstet Gynecol* May 1986; 154:1095.

Simpson GF, Harbert GM Jr: Use of betamethasone in management of preterm gestation with rupture of membranes. *Am J Obstet Gynecol* August 1984; 66:168.

Thiagarajah S, Harbert GM, Bourgeois FJ: Magnesium sulfate and ritodrine hydrochloride: Systemic and uterine hemodynamic effects. *Am J Obstet Gynecol* November 1985; 153:666.

Usher RH et al: Assessment of fetal risk in postdate pregnancies. *Am J Obstet Gynecol* 1988; 158:259.

Veille JC et al: The effect of a calcium channel blocker (nifedipine) in uterine blood flow in the pregnant goat. *Am J Obstet Gynecol* 1986; 154:1160.

Wang R, Davidson BJ: Ritodrine-induced neutropenia. *Am J Obstet Gynecol* 1986; 154:924.

Welch RA, Bottoms SF: Reconsideration of head compression and intraventricular hemorrhage in the vertex very-low-birth-weight fetus. *Obstet Gynecol* 1986; 68:29.

Whitaker CM: Death before birth. *Am J Nurs* February 1986; 86:156.

Wilkins IA et al: Long-term use of magnesium sulfate as a tocolytic agent. *Obstet Gynecol* 1986; 67:38S.

Work BA: Caring for genital tract birth trauma. *Contemp OB/GYN* 1982; 20:82.

Yutopar Drug Information Insert. Astra Pharmaceutical Products, Westborough, MA, 1984.

## Additional Readings

Brar HS et al: Maternal and fetal blood flow velocity waveforms in patients with preterm labor: Effect of tocolytics. *Obstet Gynecol* August 1988; 72(2):209.

Brooten D et al: Anxiety, depression, and hostility in mothers of preterm infants. *Nurs Res* July/August 1988; 37(4):213.

Conti MT, Eutropius L: Preventing UTIs: What works? *Am J Nurs* March 1987; 87:307.

Curtis P, Safransky N: Rethinking oxytocin protocols in the augmentation of labor. *Birth* December 1988; 15(4):199.

Davis DL, Stewart M, Harmon RJ: Perinatal loss: Providing emotional support for bereaved parents. *Birth* December 1988; 15(4):242.

Fortney JA, Kennedy KI, Laufe LE: Management of breech presentations in developing country hospitals. *Trop Doctor* 1987; 17:34.

Gilson GJ et al: Expectant management of premature rupture of membranes at term in a birthing center setting. *J Nurse-Midwifery* May/June 1988; 33(3):134.

Herbert WN, Owen HG, Collins ML: Autologous blood storage in obstetrics. *Obstet Gynecol* August 1988; 72(2):166.

McKay S, Mahan C: How can aspiration of vomitus in obstetrics best be prevented? *Birth* December 1988; 15(4):222.

McKay S, Mahan C: Modifying the stomach contents of laboring women: Why and how; success and risks. *Birth* December 1988; 15(4):213.

Sadler ME: When your patient's baby dies before birth. *RN* August 1987; 28.

Thomson M: Unexplained differences in first stage labor duration in primiparas at North American and European hospitals. *Birth* December 1988; 15(4):205.

Wilson D: An overview of sexually transmissible diseases in the perinatal period. *J Nurse-Midwifery* May/June 1988; 33(3):115.

# 19

# Obstetric Procedures:
# The Role of the Nurse

*As women in childbirth we bring our complete selves to the experience: body, mind, emotions, habits, past experiences, lessons to be learned . . . a woman births as she lives, expressing this continuity of birth within the rest of a woman's life. (Birthing Normally: A Personal Growth Approach to Childbirth)*

## Objectives

- Relate the various methods of version to the nursing interventions for each method.

- Discuss the use of amniotomy in current maternity care.

- Compare methods for inducing labor, explaining their advantages and disadvantages.

- Describe the types of episiotomies performed, the rationale for each, and the associated nursing interventions.

- Summarize the indications for forceps delivery and types of forceps that may be used.

- Discuss the use of vacuum extraction including indications, procedure, complications, and related nursing interventions.

- Explain the indications for cesarean birth, impact on the family unit, preparation and teaching needs, and associated nursing interventions.

## Key Terms

amniotomy
episiotomy
induction of labor
vaginal birth after cesarean (VBAC)
version

The use of operative and other obstetric procedures has increased in recent years. More childbearing women are being identified as high risk, and these births need to be assisted to reduce the possible dangers to the woman and newborn. In addition, certain obstetric procedures are performed to accommodate the wishes of the expectant family or the physician.

Obstetric procedures discussed in this chapter are versions, amniotomy, induction of labor, episiotomy, forceps delivery, vacuum extraction, and cesarean birth.

## CARE OF THE WOMAN DURING VERSION

**Version** is the alteration of fetal position by abdominal or intrauterine manipulation to achieve a more favorable fetal position for birth.

## External or Cephalic Version

The fetus can be rotated from a breech or transverse position to cephalic position by external abdominal manipulation. This version may be done before term (40 weeks' gestation) and is more successful in multiparous women with relaxed abdominal walls.

The prerequisites for cephalic version are as follows (Pritchard et al 1985, VanDorsten et al 1981):

1. The presenting part must not be engaged.
2. The abdominal wall must be thin enough to permit accurate palpation.
3. The uterine wall must not be irritable.
4. There must be a sufficient quantity of amniotic fluid in the uterus, and the membranes must be intact.
5. There must be a reactive nonstress test (NST).

Contraindications include the following (Danforth and Scott 1986):

1. Cephalopelvic disproportion (CPD) that would prevent a vaginal birth
2. Third-trimester bleeding
3. Low implantation of the placenta
4. Previous uterine surgery
5. Multiple gestation
6. Oligohydramnios
7. Nonreactive NST
8. History of premature labor

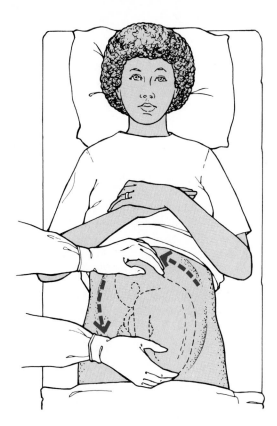

*Figure 19.1    External (or cephalic) version of fetus. A new technique involves pressure on the fetal head and buttocks so that the fetus completes a "backward flip" or "forward roll."*

Before an external or cephalic version, the woman receives ritodrine intravenously to relax the uterus. Under continuous fetal monitoring, the fetus is turned from breech to vertex presentation (Figure 19.1).

## ● Role of the Nurse

As the woman is admitted, the nurse begins her assessment by validating that no contraindications to the version are present. Maternal vital signs and fetal heart rate (FHR) are assessed and the NST is done to ascertain reactivity of the FHR. Maternal vital signs are assessed prior to the version and every five minutes throughout the procedure and for 30 minutes following it. The fetus is monitored continuously with ongoing evaluation of the FHR.

The nurse completes the assessments previously discussed. Assessments of the maternal-fetal response to the β-mimetic are also done (see Drug Guide—Ritodrine, Chapter 18, p 485). The nurse also provides information for the woman and her partner.

### CLIENT TEACHING

The admission period and time when the initial NST is performed are excellent opportunities for educating the woman. The woman should be encouraged to express her

understanding and expectations of the procedure, verbalize her fears, and ask questions. The possibility of failure of the procedure and operative intervention if the fetus becomes distressed should be discussed. Explaining what will occur in either of these circumstances will better prepare the woman if intervention becomes necessary.

## ● Internal or Podalic Version

Internal or podalic version is used to rotate a fetus in a vertex or transverse position to a breech position. The only indication for this is for the delivery of the second twin (Pritchard et al 1985). In this procedure, after the first twin is delivered, the physician reaches into the uterine cavity, grasps one or both feet of the second twin and draws them through the cervix.

## ● CARE OF THE WOMAN DURING LABOR INDUCTION

The American College of Obstetrics and Gynecology (ACOG) defines **induction of labor** as the deliberate initiation of uterine contractions prior to their spontaneous onset. The procedure may be either elective or medically indicated because of the presence of a maternal and/or fetal problem.

*Elective induction* is defined by the Food and Drug Administration (FDA) as "the initiation of labor for the convenience of an individual with a term pregnancy who is free of medical indications." The advisability of elective induction is questionable because of the associated maternal risks and the possibility of delivering a preterm infant (US Dept HEW 1978).

*Medically indicated induction* may be considered in the presence of diabetes mellitus, renal disease, severe pregnancy-induced hypertension (PIH), abruptio placentae, premature rupture of membranes (PROM), postterm pregnancy, severe fetal hemolytic disease, and intrauterine fetal death.

## ● Contraindications

All contraindications to spontaneous labor and vaginal delivery are contraindications to induction (Niswander 1985, Pritchard et al 1985).

The major maternal contraindications are:

● Client refusal

● Previous uterine incision

● CPD

● Presence of herpesvirus type 2

● Placenta previa centrally located

● Overdistention of the uterus (hydramnios, multiple gestation)

The major fetal contraindications are:

● Severe fetal distress or positive contraction stress test (CST)

● Preterm fetus

● Breech or transverse presentation

Before an induction is attempted, assessment must indicate that both the woman and the unborn child are ready for labor. This assessment includes evaluation of fetal maturity and cervical readiness.

## ● Labor Readiness

### FETAL MATURITY

Gestational age of the fetus can be determined throughout the gestational period by ultrasound examination. Amniotic fluid studies also provide important information on fetal maturity. (See Chapter 13 for a discussion of methods to assess fetal maturity.)

### CERVICAL READINESS

The findings of vaginal examinations help determine whether cervical changes favorable to induction have occurred. Bishop (1964) developed a prelabor scoring system that has proved helpful in predicting the inducibility of women (Table 19.1). Components evaluated are cervical dilatation, effacement, consistency, and position as well as the station of the fetal presenting part. A score of 0, 1, 2, or 3 is given to each assessed characteristic. The higher the total score for all the criteria, the more likely it is that labor will ensue. The lower the total score, the higher the failure rate. A favorable cervix is the most important criterion for a successful induction.

The presence of a cervix that is anterior, soft, more than 50% effaced, and dilated at least 3 cm, with the fetal head at +1 station or lower is favorable for a successful induction (Danforth and Scott 1986).

## ● Methods

The most frequently used methods of induction are amniotomy, intravenous oxytocin infusion, or both.

### AMNIOTOMY

**Amniotomy,** the artificial rupturing of membranes (AROM), is probably the most common operative procedure in obstetrics. Amniotomy is often performed after active labor begins. The procedure is thought to shorten labor because when the hard fetal head comes in better contact with the cervix during contractions, dilatation occurs more quickly.

Possible problems associated with amniotomy are:

1. Maternal intrauterine infection and fetal infection due to introduction of bacteria or prolonged rupture of membranes (ROM)

2. Increased incidence of early decelerations during labor because of the increased pressure on the fetal head

3. Prolapsed umbilical cord, which may occur when the amniotic fluid escapes from the uterus and when the presenting part is not well engaged

The mechanism by which amniotomy stimulates labor is unknown. However, under favorable conditions, which include cervical readiness and position of the fetal head against the lower segment and dipping into the pelvis, about 80% of women at term go into active labor within 24 hours after amniotomy (Danforth and Scott 1986).

The advantages of amniotomy as a method of labor induction are as follows:

1. The contractions elicited are similar to those of spontaneous labor.

2. There is usually no risk of hypertonus or rupture of the uterus.

## Table 19.1  Prelabor Status Evaluation Scoring System

| Factor | Assigned value | | | |
| | 0 | 1 | 2 | 3 |
| --- | --- | --- | --- | --- |
| Cervical dilatation | Closed | 1–2 cm | 3–4 cm | 5 cm or more |
| Cervical effacement | 0%–30% | 40%–50% | 60%–70% | 80% or more |
| Fetal station | −3 | −2 | −1, 0 | +1, or lower |
| Cervical consistency | Firm | Moderate | Soft | |
| Cervical position | Posterior | Midposition | Anterior | |

Source: Bishop EH: Pelvic scoring for elective inductions. *Obstet Gynecol* 1964; 24:266.

3. The woman does not require as close surveillance as in oxytocin infusion.
4. Fetal monitoring is facilitated because amniotomy does not interfere with the following:
   a. Scalp blood sampling for pH determinations
   b. Scalp electrode application
   c. Intrauterine catheter placement
5. The color and composition of amniotic fluid can be evaluated.

The disadvantages of amniotomy are:

1. During the procedure there is a risk of compression of the umbilical cord (McKay and Mahan 1983).
2. Once an amniotomy is done, delivery must occur regardless of subsequent findings that suggest delaying birth.
3. The danger of a prolapsed cord is increased.
4. There is a risk of infection from ascending organisms.
5. Compression and molding of the fetal head are increased.
6. Labor may not be successfully induced, resulting in cesarean delivery.

### AROM Procedure

While performing a sterile vaginal examination, the physician introduces an amnihook (or other rupturing device) into the vagina. A small tear is made in the amniotic membrane. Following rupture of the membranes, amniotic fluid is allowed to escape.

The nurse explains the AROM procedure to the woman. The fetal presentation, position, and station are assessed because amniotomy is usually delayed until engagement has occurred. The woman is positioned in a semireclining position and draped to provide privacy. The FHR is assessed just prior to and immediately after the amniotomy, and the two FHR assessments are compared. If there are marked changes, the nurse should check for prolapse of the cord. The amniotic fluid is inspected for amount, color, odor, and the presence of meconium or blood. The perineal area is cleansed and dried after the procedure. The chux should be changed frequently to maintain comfort. Because there is now an open pathway for organisms to ascend into the uterus, strict sterile technique must be observed during vaginal examinations. In addition, the number of vaginal examinations must be kept to a minimum in order to reduce the chance of introducing an infection, and the woman's temperature should be monitored every two hours.

### PROSTAGLANDIN ADMINISTRATION

In some centers, prostaglandin gel PGE$_2$ is being used to ripen the cervix and induce labor. The gel is placed in a diaphragm, which is inserted into the vagina and placed against the cervix. The gel may be removed if side effects, such as hypertonus or hyperactivity of the uterus, nausea, and vomiting, develop. Prostaglandin gel may also be administered in suppository form. The suppository is placed in the posterior vaginal fornix (Macer et al 1984). Research is currently being conducted to determine if the administration of prostaglandins is safe and effective.

### OXYTOCIN INFUSION

Intravenous administration of oxytocin is an effective method of initiating uterine contractions (inducing labor). It may also be used to augment labor (enhance contractions that are ineffective). A primary line of 1000 mL electrolyte solution (for example, 5% dextrose in lactated Ringer's) is started intravenously. To prepare the secondary line, 1000 mL of matching solution is prepared by adding 10 units of Pitocin. The secondary line is regulated by an infusion pump and is connected as closely as possible to the primary venipuncture site.

During administration, the goal is to achieve contractions every two to three minutes of good intensity, each of which lasts 40–50 seconds. The uterus should relax to normal baseline tone between contractions.

Oxytocin induction is not without some risks. Rapid progression of infusion rates or continuance of a particular rate without adequate assessment of the uterine contractions may lead to hyperstimulation of the uterus, fetal distress due to decreased placental perfusion, a rapid labor and birth with the danger of cervical or perineal lacerations, or uterine rupture. Water intoxication may occur if large doses are given in electrolyte-free solution over a prolonged period of time (Niswander 1985).

### ● Role of the Nurse

Constant observation and accurate assessments are mandatory to provide safe, optimal care for both woman and fetus. Baseline data (maternal temperature, pulse, respiration, blood pressure, and FHR) should be obtained before beginning the infusion. A fetal monitor is used to provide continuous data. Many institutions recommend obtaining a 15-minute recording before the infusion is started to obtain baseline data on uterine contractions and FHR. Before each advancement of the infusion rate, assessments of the following should be made:

● Maternal blood pressure and pulse
● Rate and reactivity of the FHR tracing (any bradycardia or decelerations are noted)
● Contraction status, frequency, intensity, duration, and resting tone between contractions

During the induction, urinary output is assessed to identify any problems with retention, fluid deficit, and pos-

# 🔬 Drug Guide

## Oxytocin (Pitocin)

### Overview of Obstetric Action

Oxytocin (Pitocin) exerts a selective stimulatory effect on the smooth muscle of the uterus and blood vessels. Oxytocin affects the myometrial cells of the uterus by increasing the excitability of the muscle cell, increasing the strength of the muscle contraction, and supporting propagation of the contraction (movement of the contraction from one myometrial cell to the next). Its effect on the uterine contraction depends on the dosage used and on the excitability of the myometrial cells. During the first half of gestation, little excitability of the myometrium occurs and the uterus is fairly resistant to the effects of oxytocin. However, from midgestation on, the uterus responds increasingly to exogenous intravenous oxytocin. When at term, cautious use of diluted oxytocin, administered intravenously, results in a slow rise of uterine activity.

The circulatory half-life of oxytocin is three to four minutes, but the uterine effects last 20–30 minutes.

The effects of oxytocin on the cardiovascular system can be pronounced. There may be an initial decrease in the blood pressure, but with prolonged administration, a 30% increase in the baseline blood pressure may be noted. Cardiac output and stroke volume are increased. With doses of 20 mU/min or above, the antidiuretic effect of oxytocin results in a decrease of free water exchange in the kidney and a marked decrease in urine output (Marshall 1985).

Oxytocin is used to induce labor at term and to augment uterine contractions in the first and second stages of labor. Oxytocin may also be used immediately after delivery to stimulate uterine contraction and thereby control uterine atony.

Oxytocin is not thought to cross the placenta because of its molecular weight and the presence of oxytocinase in the placenta (Giacoia and Yaffe 1982). Oxytocin has an antidiuretic effect.

*Route, Dosage, Frequency*

*For induction of labor:* Add 10 units Pitocin (1 mL) to 1000 mL of intravenous solution. (The resulting concentration is 10 mU oxytocin per 1 mL of intravenous fluid.) Using an infusion pump, administer IV, starting at 0.5 mU/min to 1 mU/min and increasing the rate stepwise every 30–60 minute interval until good contractions (every two to three minutes, each lasting 40–60 seconds) are achieved. The maximum rate is 20–40 mU/minute and 90% of patients respond with 16 mU/min or less (NAACOG 1988).

| | |
|---|---|
| 0.5 mU/min = 3 mL/hr | 8 mU/min = 48 mL/hr |
| 1.0 mU/min = 6 mL/hr | 10 mU/min = 60 mL/hr |
| 1.5 mU/min = 9 mL/hr | 12 mU/min = 72 mL/hr |
| 2 mU/min = 12 mL/hr | 15 mU/min = 90 mL/hr |
| 4 mU/min = 24 mL/hr | 18 mU/min = 108 mL/hr |
| 6 mU/min = 36 mL/hr | 20 mU/min = 120 mL/hr |

Protocols may vary from one agency to another.

*For augmentation of labor:* Prepare and administer IV Pitocin as for labor induction. Increase rate until labor contractions are of good quality. The flow rate is gradually increased at no less than every 30 minutes. Most patients achieve cervical dilatation with doses of less than 13 mU/min (NAACOG 1988). In some settings, or in a situation when limited fluids may be administered, a more concentrated solution may be used. When 10 U Pitocin is added to 500 mL IV solution the resulting concentration is 1 mU/min = 3 mL/hr. If 10 U Pitocin is added to 250 mL IV solution the concentration is 1 mU/min = 1.5 mL/hr.

*For administration after delivery of placenta:* One dose of 10 units Pitocin (1 mL) is given intramuscularly or by slow intravenous push or added to IV fluids for continuous infusion.

---

sibility of the development of water intoxication. As contractions are established, vaginal examinations are done to evaluate cervical dilatation, effacement, and station. The frequency of vaginal examinations primarily depends on the number of pregnancies and on characteristics of the contractions. For example, a nullipara who has contractions every five to seven minutes, each lasting 30 seconds, and who does not perceive her contractions does not usually require a vaginal examination. When her contractions are every two to three minutes, lasting 50–60 seconds with good intensity, a vaginal examination will be needed to evaluate her progress.

For additional information on nursing interventions, see Drug Guide—Oxytocin, and Nursing Care Plan—Induction of Labor.

Oxytocin may be given intravenously for augmentation of labor; see Drug Guide—Oxytocin for further discussion.

### CLIENT TEACHING

Aspects to address during client teaching include: the purpose and procedure for the induction, nursing care that will be provided, assessments during the induction procedure, comfort measures, and a review of breathing techniques that may be used during labor.

# 🔬 Drug Guide

## Oxytocin (Pitocin) *(continued)*

*Maternal Contraindications*
Severe preeclampsia-eclampsia

Predisposition to uterine rupture (in nullipara over 35 years of age, paragravida 4 or more, overdistention of the uterus, previous major surgery of the cervix or uterus)

Cephalopelvic disproportion

Malpresentation or malposition of the fetus, cord prolapse

Preterm infant

Rigid, unripe cervix; total placenta previa

Presence of fetal distress

*Maternal Side Effects*
Hyperstimulation of the uterus results in hypercontractility, which in turn may cause the following:

Abruptio placentae

Impaired uterine blood flow → fetal hypoxia

Rapid labor → cervical lacerations

Rapid labor and delivery → lacerations of cervix, vagina, perineum, uterine atony, fetal trauma

Uterine rupture

Water intoxication (nausea, vomiting, hypotension, tachycardia, cardiac arrhythmia) can occur if oxytocin is given in electrolyte-free solution or at a rate exceeding 20 mU/min.

Hypotension can occur with rapid IV bolus administration postpartum.

*Effect on Fetus/Neonate*
Fetal effects are primarily associated with the presence of hypercontractility of the maternal uterus. Hypercontractility causes a decrease in the oxygen supply to the fetus, which is reflected by irregularities and/or decrease in FHR.

Hyperbilirubinemia can also occur.

### Nursing Considerations

Explain induction of augmentation procedure to woman.

Apply fetal monitor and obtain 15-minute tracing and NST to assess FHR before starting IV oxytocin.

For induction or augmentation of labor, start with primary IV and piggy-back secondary IV with oxytocin into the primary line, close to the venipuncture site.

Assure continuous fetal and uterine contraction monitoring.

Assess FHR, maternal blood pressure, pulse, and uterine contraction frequency, duration, and resting tone before each increase in oxytocin infusion rate.

Record all assessments and IV rate on monitor strip and on woman's chart.

Record all client activities (such as change of position, vomiting), procedures done (amniotomy, sterile vaginal examination), and administration of analgesics on monitor strip to allow for interpretation and evaluation of tracing.

Assess cervical dilatation as needed.

Apply nursing comfort measures.

Discontinue IV oxytocin infusion and infuse primary solution when (a) fetal distress is noted (bradycardia, late or variable decelerations, meconium staining); (b) uterine contractions are more frequent than every two minutes; (c) duration of contractions exceeds more than 90 seconds (NAACOG 1988); or (d) insufficient relaxation of the uterus between contractions or a steady increase in resting tone are noted; in addition to discontinuing IV oxytocin infusion, turn client to side and administer oxygen by tight face mask at 6–10 L/min; notify physician.

## ● CARE OF THE WOMAN DURING AN EPISIOTOMY

An **episiotomy** is a surgical incision of the perineal body extending downward from the vaginal opening. It is done with sharp scissors with rounded points. The purposes of an episiotomy are to prevent lacerations, to minimize stretching of the perineal tissues, and to decrease trauma to the fetal head during the descent and delivery (Bromberg 1986, Varner 1986).

The routine use of episiotomies is becoming an increasingly controversial issue. Various authors have found no evidence to support the reasons for episiotomies just listed (Banta and Thacker 1982, Buekens et al 1985, Thacker and Banta 1983, Varner 1986). However, most medical textbooks still advocate the prophylactic use of this procedure.

A regional or local block is given in preparation for the episiotomy. The episiotomy is performed just before birth of the infant when the presenting part is beginning to crown but before there is excessive stretching of the perineal tissues. The incision begins at the midline and may be extended down the midline through the perineal body, or it
*(Text continues on page 531.)*

# Nursing Care Plan

## Induction of Labor

### Client Assessment

#### Nursing History

Previous pregnancies
Present pregnancy course
Childbirth preparation
Estimated gestational age

#### Physical Examination

1. Examination of pregnant uterus (Leopold's maneuvers to determine fetal size and position)

2. Vaginal examination to evaluate cervical readiness
   a. Ripe cervix: Feels soft to the examining finger, is located in a medial to anterior position, is more than 50% effaced, and is 2–3 cm dilated
   b. Unripe cervix: Feels firm to the examining finger, is long and thick, perhaps in a posterior position, with little or no dilatation

3. Presence of contractions
4. Membranes intact or ruptured
5. Fetal size (Leopold's maneuvers, ultrasound)
6. Fetal readiness
7. CPD evaluation
8. Maternal vital signs and FHR before beginning induction

#### Diagnostic Studies

Fetal maturity tests (L/S ratio, creatinine concentrations, ultrasonography)
Maternal blood studies (complete blood cell count [CBC], hemoglobin, hematocrit, blood type, Rh factor)
Urinalysis

| Nursing Diagnosis/Client Goals | Nursing Interventions | Rationale/Evaluation |
| --- | --- | --- |
| **Nursing Diagnosis:**<br><br>Pattern 8: Knowing<br>Knowledge deficit related to induction procedure | Assess the woman's feelings regarding induction. She may ask, "Will this work?" "How long will it take?" "Will it hurt more?"<br><br>Assess knowledge base regarding the induction process.<br>Provide needed information (for example, when the cervix is ripe, contractions should begin in 30–60 minutes); length of labor depends on a number of factors.<br><br>Assess knowledge of breathing techniques; if woman does not have a method to use, teach breathing techniques before starting oxytocin infusion. | **Rationale:**<br><br>Woman may be apprehensive about what will happen, or feel a sense of failure that she cannot "go into labor by herself."<br><br>After assessing knowledge base, appropriate information can be given to allay apprehension.<br><br><br><br>Use of breathing techniques during contractions will help relaxation; although a woman may be apprehensive about induction, teaching a new breathing method will be easier before contractions are present. |
| **Client Goal:**<br><br>The woman will discuss the induction procedure, the benefits, and the potential risks. | | **Evaluation:**<br><br>The woman is able to discuss the induction procedure and has no further questions. |

| Nursing Diagnosis/Client Goals | Nursing Interventions | Rationale/Evaluation |
| --- | --- | --- |
| **Nursing Diagnosis:**<br><br>Pattern 1: Exchanging<br>Decreased cardiac output related to positional changes and the weight of the uterus on the vena cava | Position woman on her side; encourage her to avoid supine position.<br>Monitor maternal blood pressure (BP) and pulse and FHR every 15–20 minutes. | **Rationale:**<br><br>Side-lying position maintains optimal blood flow to uterus and placenta. |

# Nursing Care Plan

## Induction of Labor (continued)

| Nursing Diagnosis/Client Goals | Nursing Interventions | Rationale/Evaluation |
|---|---|---|
| **Client Goal:**<br><br>The woman will maintain vital signs within normal range with no significant increase or decrease. | If she becomes hypotensive:<br>1. Keep the woman on her side, may change to other side.<br>2. Discontinue oxytocin infusion and increase flow rate of main line.<br>3. Increase rate of primary IV.<br>4. Monitor FHR.<br>5. Notify physician.<br>6. Assess for cause of hypotension. | Initial hypotension is secondary to peripheral vasodilatation induced by oxytocin, which causes diminished blood supply to placenta and resultant decrease in $O_2$ supply to fetus. Actions are directed toward improving blood flow and oxygenation of tissues. |
| | | **Evaluation:**<br><br>The woman's vital signs remain within normal limits. |
| **Nursing Diagnosis:**<br><br>Pattern 1: Exchanging<br>Altered tissue perfusion (placenta) related to hypertonic contraction pattern | Apply monitor to obtain 15 minutes of tracing prior to starting induction. | **Rationale:**<br><br>Establishes baseline data. |
| | Administer oxytocin in electrolyte solution. | Oxytocin has slight antidiuretic effect, especially when administered in electrolyte-free solutions. |
| **Client Goal**<br><br>The woman will maintain normal contraction pattern as measured by:<br>● Frequency of 2½–3 minutes<br>● Duration of about 60 sec<br>● Relaxation of uterus between contractions | Monitor and record fluid intake and output. Monitor for nausea, vomiting, hypotension, tachycardia, cardiac arrhythmias. | Provides information on hydration status. These are signs and symptoms of water intoxication; they must be differentiated from other problems. |
| | Monitor FHR by continuous electronic fetal monitoring. Obtain 15-minute tracing prior to beginning induction to evaluate fetal status; *do not* start infusion or advance rate (if induction has already begun) if FHR is not in range of 120–160 beats/min, if decelerations are present, or if variability decreases. | Will provide continuous data regarding fetal response to induction. |
| | Evaluate maternal BP and pulse before beginning induction and then before each increase in infusion rate; do not advance infusion rate in presence of maternal hypertension or hypotension or radical changes in pulse rate. | To establish baseline data and to assess client response in induction; client status may change rapidly. |
| | Evaluate contraction frequency, duration, and intensity prior to each increase in infusion rate. | Evaluates uterine response to induction. |
| | *Do not* increase rate of infusion if contractions are every two to three minutes, lasting 40–60 seconds, with moderate intensity. | Desired effect has been obtained. Further increase in rate may produce hypertonic labor pattern (contractions with frequency of less than two min, for example more than five contractions in ten min or a duration of longer than 75–90 sec). |

*(continues)*

# Nursing Care Plan

## Induction of Labor (continued)

| Nursing Diagnosis/Client Goals | Nursing Interventions | Rationale/Evaluation |
|---|---|---|
| | Discontinue oxytocin infusion if:<br>1. Contractions are more frequent than every two minutes.<br>2. Contraction duration exceeds 75–90 seconds.<br>3. Uterus does not relax between contractions. | Uterus is being overstimulated and serious complications may develop for woman and fetus. |
| | Increase oxytocin IV infusion rate every 20 minutes until adequate contractions are achieved; do *not* exceed an infusion rate of 20 mU/min.<br>(Note: protocols directing how often oxytocin is increased may vary from 20–30 minutes. See American College of Obstetrics and Gynecology [ACOG] guidelines and agency protocol.) | Uterine response to oxytocin may be individualized. |
| | Check infusion pump to assure oxytocin is infusing; check whether pump is on, chamber refills and empties, level of fluid in IV bottle becomes lower; if problem is found, correct it, and restart infusion at beginning dose.<br>Check piggy-back connection to primary tubing to assure solution is not leaking | Oxytocin may not be infusing due to pump, mechanical, or human error. |
| | Evaluate cervical dilatation by vaginal examination with each oxytocin dosage increase after labor is established. | When cervix responds by stretching or pulling, *do not* increase oxytocin dosage; overdosage may occur, causing rapid labor with possible cervical lacerations and fetal damage; when there is no change in the cervix, additional oxytocin is needed. |
| | Observe contraction frequency and duration. In presence of contractions lasting over 90 seconds:<br>1. Discontinue oxytocin infusion.<br>2. Assess maternal status.<br>3. Assess fetal status. | Contractions lasting over 90 seconds with decreased resting tone may result in fetal hypoxia.<br>Ruptured uterus or abruptio placentae can result from drug-induced tumultuous labor.<br>(Note: Terms hyperstimulation, hypertonic labor pattern, and tumultuous labor are used interchangeably.) |
| | Monitor FHR continuously (normal range is 120–160/min).<br>In episodes of bradycardia (< 120 beats/min) lasting for more than 30 sec, administer $O_2$ by face mask at 6–10 L/min.<br>Stop oxytocin infusion.<br>Position woman on left side if quick recovery of FHR does not occur. | $O_2$ deficiency may occur over a long period of time; in cases of placental insufficiency or cord compression, compensated tachycardia may be evoked. |
| | Carefully evaluate fetal tachycardia (> 160 beats/min).<br>Sustained tachycardia may necessitate discontinuation of oxytocin infusion.<br>Assess for presence of meconium staining. | Persistent fetal tachycardia causes more prominent $O_2$ deficiency (hypoxia) and $CO_2$ increase in fetal blood. Vasoconstriction occurs, with increased fetal blood flow through coronary arteries, brain, and placenta; this increased de- |

## Nursing Care Plan

### Induction of Labor *(continued)*

| Nursing Diagnosis/Client Goals | Nursing Interventions | Rationale/Evaluation |
| --- | --- | --- |
| | | mand on myocardial performance leads to cardiac decompensation if oxygen exchange is impaired and hypoxia continues. Fetal hypoxia may also cause central vasomotor center to release adrenal catecholamines; at term, this enhances depolarization of cardiac pacemaker cells, which will result in direct bradycardia. Bradycardia or subsequent reflex tachycardia temporarily remedies the $O_2$ deficiency. |
| | | **Evaluation:** The woman's contraction pattern is established with contractions every two to three minutes, lasting about 60–75 sec with relaxation of the uterus between contractions. |
| **Nursing Diagnosis:** Pattern 9: Feeling Pain related to uterine contractions | Provide support to woman as she uses breathing techniques. | Contractions may build up more quickly with oxytocin induction. |
| | Encourage use of effluerage, back rub, and other supportive measures. Assess need for analgesia or anesthesia. | Techniques help maintain relaxation and thereby decrease pain sensation. After labor is well established, analgesia or epidural anesthesia may be given without delaying progress. |
| **Client Goal:** The woman will maintain her breathing pattern and a relaxed state during contractions. | | **Evaluation:** The woman maintains breathing pattern and a sense of control during labor. |

may extend at a 45° angle in a mediolateral direction to the right or left (Figure 19.2). A midline episiotomy is preferred if the perineum is of adequate length and no difficulty during birth is anticipated, because blood loss is less, the incision is easy to repair, and the incision heals with less discomfort. The major disadvantage is that the midline incision may extend through the anal sphincter and rectum. In the presence of a short perineum or an anticipated difficult delivery, a mediolateral episiotomy provides more room for delivery and decreases the possibility of a traumatic extension into the rectum. The mediolateral episiotomy may be complicated by greater blood loss, a longer healing period, and more discomfort postpartally.

The episiotomy is usually performed with regional or local anesthesia but may be performed without anesthesia in emergency situations. It is generally proposed that as crowning occurs, the distention of the tissues causes numbing. Adequate anesthesia must be given for the repair.

Repair of the episiotomy (episiorrhaphy) and any lacerations is accomplished either during the period between delivery of the neonate and before delivery of the placenta or after the delivery of the placenta.

### ● Role of the Nurse

The woman needs to be supported during the repair as she may feel some pressure sensations. In the absence of adequate anesthesia, she may feel pain. Placing a hand

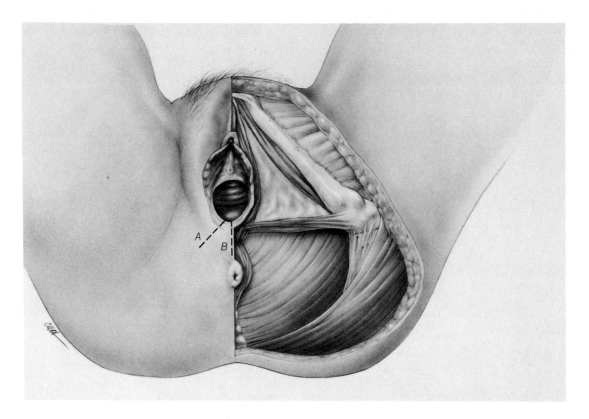

*Figure 19.2   The two most common types of episiotomies are midline and mediolateral: (A) Right mediolateral, (B) Midline.*

on her shoulder and talking with her can provide comfort and distraction from the repair process. If the woman is having more discomfort than she can comfortably handle, the nurse needs to act as an advocate in communicating the woman's needs to the physician/nurse-midwife. At all times the woman needs to be the one who decides whether the amount of discomfort is tolerable, and she should never be told "This doesn't hurt." She is the person experiencing the discomfort, and her evaluation must be respected. If there are just a few (three to five) stitches left, she may choose to forego more local anesthesia, but she should be given the choice.

The type of episiotomy and type of suture used (usually chromic catgut 00 or 000) are recorded on the delivery record. This information should also be included in a report to the recovery room, so that adequate assessments can be made and relief measures can be instituted if necessary.

Pain relief measures may begin immediately after delivery with application of an ice pack to the perineum. For optimal effect the ice pack should be applied for 20 to 30 minutes and removed for at least 20 minutes before being reapplied. The perineal tissues should be assessed frequently to prevent injury from the ice pack.

## CLIENT TEACHING

The nurse provides information regarding comfort  measures that may be used. After the fourth stage is completed, warm sitz baths (101°F to 105°F) are recommended to increase circulation to the area and promote healing. The use of cool sitz baths is currently being investigated, with some women reporting increased pain relief from using a lukewarm sitz bath to which ice chips have been added (Ramler and Roberts 1986, Varner 1986). The episiotomy site should be inspected every 15 minutes during the first hour after delivery and thereafter daily for redness, swelling, tenderness, and hematomas. Mild analgesic sprays and oral analgesics are ordered as needed. The mother will need instruction in perineal hygiene care and may need instructions about use of the analgesic spray. (See Chapter 26 for additional discussion of relief measures.)

## • CARE OF THE WOMAN DURING FORCEPS DELIVERY

Forceps may be used to provide traction, to rotate the fetus, or both. There are two types of forceps deliveries.

The delivery is termed *outlet forceps delivery* when the fetal head is visible on the perineum without spreading the labia. When the fetal head is higher than the level of the ischial spines, delivery is termed a *midforceps delivery*. Before a midforceps delivery can be performed, the lower part of the fetal head must be at the level of the ischial spines, and the biparietal diameter must have entered the inlet (engagement). Most midforceps deliveries involve rotation of the fetus from an occiput-posterior (OP) or occiput-transverse (OT) position to an occiput-anterior position. *High forceps deliveries* (application of forceps before engagement of the fetal head) are no longer done because they are extremely dangerous for the woman and the fetus.

## ● Indications

Forceps may be used electively to shorten the second stage of labor by sparing the women the pushing effort, or when regional or general anesthesia has affected the woman's motor innervation and she cannot push effectively. They are also advocated in preterm infant delivery (Pritchard et al 1985).

## ● Complications

Maternal complications may include lacerations of the birth canal and perineum and increased bleeding. Fetal complications usually arise as a result of pressure on the tissues of the fetal head, which may cause edema or bruising. Incorrect placement of the forceps may also result in bruising, edema, and temporary paralysis of an area of the newborn's face. A difficult forceps delivery may result in cerebral edema or brachial plexus palsy in the newborn. In light of questions about the method that provides the best outcome for the fetus and the current medicolegal climate, a cesarean delivery is frequently chosen over midforceps (Laube 1986).

## ● Prerequisites for Forceps Application

Use of forceps requires complete dilatation of the cervix and knowledge of the exact position and station of the fetal head. The membranes must be ruptured to allow a firm grasp on the fetal head. The presentation must be vertex or face with the chin anterior, and the head must be engaged, preferably on the perineum. *Under no circumstances should there be any CPD.*

## ● Role of the Nurse

The nurse can explain the procedure briefly to the woman if she is awake. With adequate regional anesthesia, she should feel some pressure but no pain. The woman is encouraged to maintain breathing techniques to prevent her from pushing during application of the forceps (Figure 19.3). The nurse monitors contractions and with each contraction the physician will provide traction as the woman pushes. The nurse should monitor the FHR continuously until the delivery. It is not uncommon to observe bradycardia as traction is being applied to the forceps. Bradycardia results from head compression and is transient in nature.

The newborn is inspected for bruising and edema to the tissues of the face and head. Assessments for cerebral trauma and brachial plexus palsy are particularly important if there was a difficult forceps delivery.

### CLIENT TEACHING

The nurse answers questions and reiterates explanations that the physician provided. Nursing assessments of the woman and her newborn are reviewed. Opportunities are provided for questions.

## ● CARE OF THE WOMAN DURING VACUUM EXTRACTION

In vacuum extraction, suction is used to help deliver the fetal head. The vacuum extractor is composed of a soft silicone cup attached by tubes to a suction bottle (pump). The suction cup, which comes in various sizes, is placed against the fetal occiput. The pump is used to create negative pressure (suction) inside the cup. Traction is applied in coordination with uterine contractions and the fetal head is delivered (Figure 19.4).

The most common indication for use of the vacuum extractor is a prolonged first stage of labor. Other indications include: (a) fetal distress, (b) malpositions such as OP or OT, and (c) maternal complications such as cardiopulmonary disease, shock, PIH, and abruptio placentae (Greis et al 1981). Contraindications for use of the vacuum extractor include the presence of CPD, or face or breech presentation.

The theoretical advantages of the vacuum extractor are a great reduction in intracranial pressure during traction and no impingement on maternal soft tissue (Pritchard et al 1985). Risks of vacuum extraction may include abrasion of the fetal scalp and cephalohematoma (Fall et al 1986).

## ● Role of the Nurse

During the procedure, the woman is informed about what is happening. If adequate regional anesthesia has been administered, the woman feels only pressure during the procedure. The FHR should be auscultated every five minutes or more frequently. The nurse should be ready to release the suction quickly in the event that the cup accidentally slips off during traction ("pull off") to prevent damage to the maternal tissues. Parents need to be in-

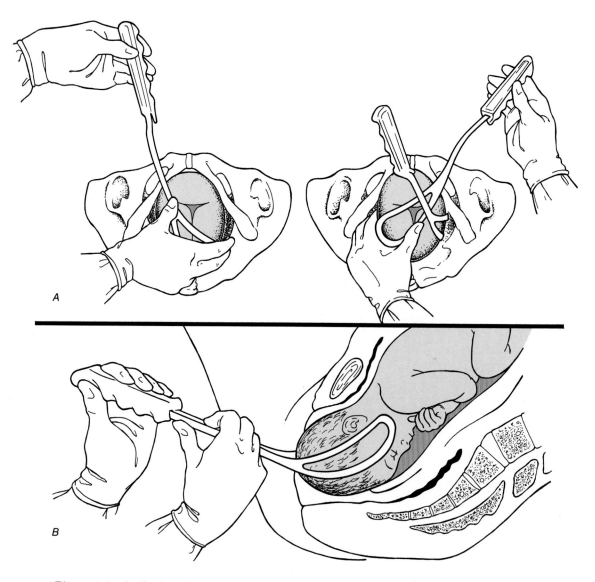

*Figure 19.3   Application of forceps in occiput anterior (**OA**) position: (**A**) The left blade is inserted along the left side wall of the pelvis over the parietal bone. (**B**) The right blade is inserted along the right side wall of the pelvis over the parietal bone. (**C**) With correct placement of the blades, the handles lock easily. During contractions, traction is applied to the forceps in a downward and outward direction to follow the birth canal.*

formed that the caput on the baby's head will disappear in a few hours.

Assessment of the newborn should include inspection and continued observation for cerebral trauma and soft tissue necrosis.

### CLIENT TEACHING

Aspects to be addressed include the sensations that the woman will feel during the vacuum extraction and the possible effects on the newborn.

## ● CARE OF THE FAMILY DURING CESAREAN BIRTH

Cesarean birth is the delivery of the infant through an abdominal and uterine incision. Technologic and medical advancements have altered the attitude toward cesarean birth from a "procedure of last resort" to an "alternative birth method." In the United States the incidence of cesarean birth has increased from 5.5% in 1970 to approximately 27%–30% in 1988 (Queenan et al 1988).

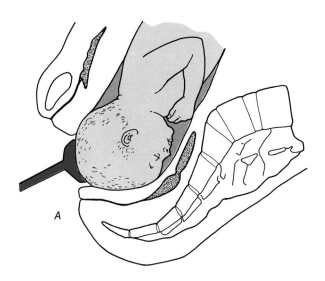

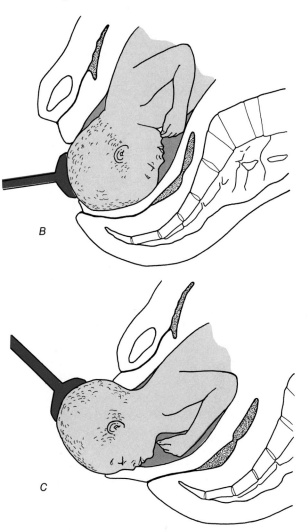

*Figure 19.4    Vacuum extractor traction: (**A**) Traction outward and posteriorly. (**B**) Traction outward and horizontally. (**C**) Traction outward and anteriorly.*

## • Indications for Cesarean Birth

Cesarean births are performed in cases of breech presentation, fetal distress, dysfunctional labor, and uteroplacental insufficiency from maternal disease conditions (Westgren and Paul 1985). The most commonly occurring indication for cesarean birth is dystocia caused by CPD. Other indications for this procedure include breech presentation, prolapsed cord, placenta previa, abruptio placentae, intrauterine growth retardation (IUGR), prolonged ROM, genital herpes, prematurity, fetal distress, and occasionally tumors blocking the vagina.

## • Maternal Mortality and Morbidity

Maternal mortality is two to four times greater in cesarean deliveries than vaginal deliveries (Petitti 1985). Mortality is less than one per 1000 (Willson 1988) and is most often due to anesthesia accidents and/or underlying medical conditions such as cardiac disease, renal disease, diabetes, or severe PIH.

Major complications resulting from cesarean birth include hemorrhage, injury to the bladder or intestines, trauma to the ovaries, endometritis, infection of the incision, and urinary tract infection (UTI). Elevated temperature occurs in 29%–85% of women after cesarean birth (Elliott 1984). The risk to the fetus of a traumatic vaginal birth must be weighed against the risk of maternal morbidity.

## • Surgical Techniques
### SKIN INCISIONS

The skin incision for a cesarean delivery is either transverse (Pfannenstiel) or vertical and is not indicative of the type of incision made into the uterus. The transverse incision is made across the lowest and narrowest part of the abdomen. Since the incision is made just below the pubic hair line, it is almost invisible after healing. The limitation of this type of skin incision is that it does not allow for extension of the incision if needed. Since it usually requires more time, this incision is used when time is not of the essence (eg, with CPD or failure to progress and no fetal or maternal distress). The vertical incision is made between the navel and the symphysis pubis. This type of incision is quicker and is therefore preferred in cases of fetal distress and preterm or macrosomic infants. A variation of the vertical incision is the paramedian (just off center). This incision allows for stronger scar formation and is recommended for obese women (Morrison and Wiser 1986). The type of skin incision is determined by time factor, client preference, or physician preference.

### UTERINE INCISIONS

The type of uterine incision is contingent on the need for the cesarean. The choice of incision affects the woman's opportunity for a subsequent vaginal delivery and her risks of a ruptured uterine scar with a subsequent pregnancy.

The two major types of uterine incisions are in the lower uterine segment or in the upper segment of the uterine corpus.

The lower uterine segment incision most commonly used is a transverse incision, although a vertical incision may also be used (Figure 19.5). The *transverse incision* is preferred for the following reasons (Danforth and Scott 1986, Morrison and Wiser 1986, Pritchard et al 1985):

1. The lower segment is the thinnest portion of the uterus and involves less blood loss.
2. It requires only moderate dissection of bladder from underlying myometrium.
3. It is easier to repair.
4. The site is less likely to rupture during subsequent pregnancies.
5. There is a decreased chance of adherence of bowel or omentum to the incision line.

The disadvantages are:

1. It takes longer to make and repair this incision.
2. It is limited in size because of the presence of major blood vessels on either side of the uterus.
3. It has a greater tendency to extend laterally into the uterine vessels.

4. The incision may stretch and become a thin window, but it usually does not create problems clinically until a subsequent labor ensues.

The *lower uterine segment vertical incision* is preferred for multiple gestation, abnormal presentation, placenta previa, fetal distress, and preterm and macrosomic fetuses. Disadvantages of this incision include:

1. The incision may extend downward into the cervix.
2. More extensive dissection of the bladder is needed to keep the incision in the lower uterine segment.
3. If it extends upward into the upper segment, hemostasis and closure is more difficult.
4. The chance of rupture with subsequent labor is increased (Danforth and Scott 1986, Morrison and Wiser 1986, Pritchard et al 1985).

One other incision, the *classic incision,* was the method of choice for many years but is used infrequently now. This vertical incision was made into the upper uterine segment. There was more blood loss, and it was more difficult to repair. Most important, there was an increased risk of uterine rupture with subsequent pregnancy, labor, and delivery because the upper uterine segment is the most contractile portion of the uterus.

## ● Vaginal Birth After Cesarean Delivery

In North America, elective repeat cesarean births are common following a primary cesarean, and in 1988 approximately one in 20 babies was delivered by repeat cesarean. However **vaginal birth after cesarean (VBAC)** is gain-

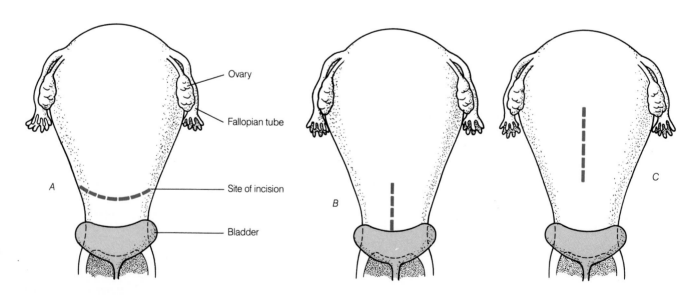

*Figure 19.5   Incisions in lower uterine segment: (**A**) Transverse (Kerr incision).*
*(**B**) Vertical (Sellheim incision). (**C**) Classic.*

ing acceptance in cases of nonrecurring indications (for example, cord accident, placenta previa, fetal distress). This trend had been influenced by consumer demand and a growing body of evidence suggesting that a properly conducted vaginal delivery after a cesarean poses less risk for maternal and neonatal mortality and morbidity than does a repeat cesarean (Porreco and Meier 1984).

Although there is no clear argument on guidelines for VBAC, the general principles are the following (Flamm 1985, Porreco and Meier 1985):

1. Early in the pregnancy the woman and physician/nurse-midwife discuss the options for a trial of labor and VBAC to allow for questions, planning, and increased opportunity for shared decision making.

2. Contraindications for vaginal delivery (such as CPD, placenta previa, abruptio placentae, and medical/obstetrical complications) are ruled out.

3. Previous medical records are available to substantiate a low segment uterine incision and whether previous problems occurred. A classic uterine incision would preclude a VBAC.

4. The VBAC is conducted in a fully equipped facility with emergency equipment and personnel readily available.

5. Blood products are readily available.

6. Oxytocin is used judiciously.

7. Regional anesthesia is considered, and if it is used, the woman is carefully assessed.

8. Continuous electronic monitoring equipment is available for monitoring the contractile pattern and the fetal heart rate.

## ● *Anesthesia for Cesarean Birth*

There is no perfect anesthetic for cesarean birth. Each has its advantages, disadvantages, possible risks, and side effects. Goals for anesthesia administration include safety, comfort, and emotional satisfaction for the client. There are two classifications of anesthesia for cesarean delivery: general, and conduction (spinal and epidural). See Chapter 17 for further discussion.

## ● *Role of the Nurse*
### PREPARATION FOR CESAREAN BIRTH

Cesarean birth is an alternative method of childbirth. Given that one out of every five or six births is a cesarean, preparation for this possibility should be an integral part of every childbirth education curriculum. (See the discussion in Chapter 11.) Ideally, all couples should be encouraged to discuss the possibility of a cesarean birth with their phy-

sician or nurse-midwife. They can also discuss their specific needs and desires. Their preferences may include the following:

● Participating in the choice of anesthetic

● Father (or significant other) being present during the procedures and/or birth

● Father (or significant other) being present in the recovery or postpartum room

● Audio recording and/or taking pictures of the birth

● Delayed instillation of eye drops to promote eye contact between parent and infant in the first hours after birth

● Physical contact or holding the newborn while on the delivery table and/or in the recovery room (if the mother cannot hold the newborn the father can hold the baby for her)

● Breast-feeding on the delivery table and/or in the recovery room

Information that couples need about cesarean birth includes:

● Events in the preparatory phase

● Description or viewing of the birthing room/surgical suite

● Types of anesthesia for birth and analgesia available postpartum

● Sensations that may be experienced

● Roles of significant others

● Interaction with neonate

● Immediate recovery phase

● Postpartal phase

The context in which this information is given should be "birth-oriented" rather than surgery-oriented.

Additional client teaching is presented in the Nursing Care Plan—Cesarean Birth.

### PREPARATION FOR EMERGENCY CESAREAN BIRTH

In reality, a couple is frequently ill prepared for the possibility of a cesarean birth. Childbirth attendants sometimes wait until the last minute to inform the woman of the need for a cesarean under the guise of "sparing the couple undue anxiety." Ironically, the woman's reaction to this delayed approach is not only excessive anxiety but also anger, shock, and resentment resulting in a state of crisis or panic (Cox and Smith 1982). By contrast, the mutual decision approach between the physician and the woman keeps the family fully informed as developments occur. The physi-
*(Text continues on page 540.)*

# Nursing Care Plan

## Cesarean Birth

### Client Assessment

#### Nursing History

Present pregnancy course
Estimated gestational age
Childbirth preparation
Sensitivity to medications and anesthetic agents
Past bleeding problems

#### Physical Examination

1. Fetal size, fetal status (FHR), and fetal maturity

2. Lung and cardiac status

3. Complete physical examination prior to administration of anesthetic

#### Diagnostic Studies

CBC
Hemoglobin and hematocrit
Type and cross-match for two units whole blood
Rh
Prothrombin time
Testing for syphilis
Urinalysis

| Nursing Diagnosis/Client Goals | Nursing Interventions | Rationale/Evaluation |
|---|---|---|
| **Nursing Diagnosis:**<br><br>Pattern 8: Knowing<br>Knowledge deficit related to the cesarean birth | Integrate cesarean birth information into childbirth preparation classes.<br>Emphasize the similarities between vaginal and cesarean delivery.<br>Minimize perceptions of "normal" versus "abnormal" birth. | **Rationale:**<br><br>Couples may deny the possibility of an unplanned cesarean birth.<br>Preparatory needs are basically the same for all couples anticipating childbirth.<br>A good knowledge base will allow for adaptive coping responses should they deliver in either manner. |
| **Client Goal:**<br><br>The woman will discuss the cesarean birth procedure as measured by:<br>● Reason for cesarean<br>● Preoperative preparation<br>● Postoperative care measures such as turn, cough, deep breathe, and need for frequent monitoring by nursing personnel | Provide factual information.<br><br>Encourage couple to discuss with obstetrician the approach and birth preferences in the event of a vaginal or cesarean birth. | Information enables couples to make choices and participate in their birth experience.<br><br>Opportunity to discuss needs and desires minimizes unrealistic expectations, disappointment, and/or feelings of loss; promotes understanding of options, beliefs of birth attendant, and hospital policies; and allows couple to do anticipatory problem solving and develop effective coping behaviors. |
| | Encourage expression of feelings. | Enables couple to work through fears, ambivalent or unresolved feelings, and grief associated with loss of vaginal birth. |
| | Assess reaction to and interpretation of past cesarean birth experiences. | Identifies need for information and opportunity to work through fears or unresolved feelings. |
| | Encourage the development of mutual support by couples sharing their experiences and common concerns. | Decreases sense of being "different" or "alone" by realizing that their fears and concerns are not unique and feelings of anger or guilt are normal. |
| | Describe preoperative procedure:<br>● Abdominal prep<br>● Insertion of in-dwelling bladder catheter<br>● Insertion of IV | Explanation of pre- and postoperative measures decreases client anxiety and increases the woman's ability to participate in care. |

# Nursing Care Plan

## Cesarean Birth *(continued)*

| Nursing Diagnosis/Client Goals | Nursing Interventions | Rationale/Evaluation |
|---|---|---|
| | Teach postoperative measures:<br>● How to deep breathe and cough<br>● Need for frequent position changes<br>● Frequency of monitoring vital signs | |
| | Create a safe, nonthreatening environment for couples to work through unresolved negative feelings. | Negative feelings may contribute to distortion of information, impede learning, and affect expectations of upcoming birth experience. |
| | Encourage couples to identify events that would make this birth experience more positive. | Allow for anticipatory problem solving, and enhance ability to meet goals and expectations for birth event. |
| | Cover most salient points of what to anticipate:<br>● What is going to happen to the woman's body and how it will feel<br>● What and why specific procedures will be done<br>● How to handle discomfort associated with procedures | Knowing what to expect increases coping capability. |
| | Provide couple with brief period of privacy. | They need an opportunity to pool their coping strengths to deal with the anxiety of the situation. |
| | Inquire if couple has any questions about the decision. | Give opportunity for further clarification. |
| | Prepare woman in increments, giving information and rationale for each procedure. | Crisis-altered cognitive grasp leads to information not being heard or misinterpreted. |
| | Avoid silence. | Silence is often interpreted by the client as frightening and/or negative. |
| | Employ eye contact and therapeutic touch. | Convey a feeling of caring and reality orientation. |
| | | **Evaluation:**<br>Woman is able to discuss cesarean birth and associated pre- and postoperative care. |
| **Nursing Diagnosis:**<br><br>Pattern 1: Exchanging<br>Impaired gas exchange related to decreased air exchange secondary to shallow breathing with incisional pain and ineffective cough | Teach deep breathing and coughing.<br>Teach abdominal splinting while deep breathing and coughing.<br>Assess lung sounds.<br><br>Explain that she will be turned every two hours. | **Rationale:**<br>Promotes good air exchange.<br>Provides support and decreases pain.<br>Provides data on respiratory status.<br><br>Provides aeration of lungs and assists in preventing pulmonary complications. |

*(continues)*

## Nursing Care Plan

### Cesarean Birth (continued)

| Nursing Diagnosis/Client Goals | Nursing Interventions | Rationale/Evaluation |
|---|---|---|
| **Client Goal:**<br>The woman will maintain effective respiratory function as measured by:<br>• Respirations between 14 and 20 per min<br>• Secretions removed from respiratory tract | | **Evaluation:**<br>The woman is able to discuss the need for position changes and can demonstrate deep breathing and coughing. |
| **Nursing Diagnosis:**<br>Pattern 9: Feeling<br>Pain related to incision and uterine involution | Administer analgesic medications.<br>Provide quiet environment to enhance rest. | **Rationale:**<br>Provides relief of pain.<br>Promotes comfort. |
| **Client Goal:**<br>The woman will have increased comfort as measured by:<br>• Woman states pain has lessened.<br>• Woman able to relax and rest. | Provide comfort measures such as:<br>• Change position and support body parts.<br>• Back rub.<br>• Therapeutic touch.<br>• Use music.<br>• Modify environment. | Identified comfort measures.<br>Use gate control theory.<br><br>**Evaluation:**<br>The woman has decreased pain. |
| **Nursing Diagnosis:**<br>Pattern 1: Exchanging<br>Altered tissue perfusion related to excessive blood loss secondary to inadequate contraction of the uterus after delivery | Evaluate firmness and position of fundus.<br>Palpate fundus after pain medication is administered to promote patient comfort.<br><br>Fundus may be palpated from side of abdomen to avoid placing pressure on vertical incision. | **Rationale:**<br>Monitor involution.<br>Palpation of fundus causes discomfort to the woman and is frequently neglected and therefore becomes increasingly important.<br><br>Avoid tenderness at incisional site. |

cian presents all the facts, suggests alternatives, and describes likely outcomes of nonintervention, allowing the expectant parents to participate in the decision making. The opportunity to make choices and have control over their birthing experience is the major factor influencing a couple's positive perception of the event (Affonso and Stichler 1980).

The period preceding surgery must be used to its greatest advantage. The couple needs some time and privacy to assimilate the information given to them and to pull together their strength to face this new crisis. It is imperative that care givers utilize their most effective communication skills. The woman often interprets silence as indi-

cating danger for her and her fetus, or she may think that the clinician is angry at her "failure" to perform (Affonso 1981). The woman may experience panic or fear. She may be confused and numb to instructions. The physician must address the salient points regarding what the couple may anticipate during the next few hours. Asking "What questions do you have about the decision?" gives the couple an opportunity for further clarification. The woman is best prepared in increments; she is given her information and the rationale for each procedure before it is begun. Before a procedure, the woman should be told (a) what the nurse or clinician is going to do, (b) why it is being done, and (c) what sensations she may experience. This allows the

## Nursing Care Plan

### Cesarean Birth *(continued)*

| Nursing Diagnosis/Client Goals | Nursing Interventions | Rationale/Evaluation |
|---|---|---|
| | Evaluate lochia. | Lochia progresses from rubra to serosa to alba. Increase in flow indicates inefficient contraction of uterus and/or subinvolution. |
| **Client Goal:** The woman will maintain normal tissue perfusion as measured by: <br>● No excessive blood loss <br>● Uterus remains contracted, in midline and below umbilicus <br>● Skin warm, dry, and nonclammy <br>● Normotensive | | **Evaluation:** The woman remains normotensive, uterus is well contracted in the midline and below the umbilicus, and blood loss is not excessive. |
| **Nursing Diagnosis:** Pattern 3: Relating <br>Altered parenting | Provide information about the baby as soon as possible. | **Rationale:** Interaction may be impaired because of recovery from anesthesia and discomfort in first few hours after birth. |
| **Client Goal:** The parents will have opportunities to interact with their baby and will move into a positive attachment. | Provide opportunities for the parents to be with the baby as soon as possible. Provide opportunities to discuss feelings about the cesarean birth and the woman's self-image as a mother. | Feelings of failure associated with birthing experience can be generalized to ability to assume mothering role. |
| | | **Evaluation:** The woman is interacting with her newborn and engaging in care-taking behaviors. |

woman to give informed consent to the procedure. The woman experiences a sense of control, and therefore less helplessness and powerlessness.

Often the phenomenon of memory lapse is more pronounced during crisis or panic states. "Missing pieces" are unremembered events or segments of time. Although not unique to cesarean birth, this phenomenon contributes to a sense of loss or missing out for the woman. Her inability to remember may contribute to feelings of depression or anger. It is important for the delivery nurse to visit the woman during the postpartal period to fill in the "missing pieces" by reviewing the birth with the woman.

Preparation of the woman for surgery involves more

than the procedures of establishing intravenous lines and urinary catheter or doing an abdominal prep. As discussed previously, good communication skills are useful in helping the woman stay in control. For some women therapeutic touch and eye contact do much to maintain reality orientation and control. These measures reduce anxiety for the woman during the stressful preparatory period. The nurse should continually assess how the woman is perceiving the event and coping with her apprehension (Leach and Sproule 1984, Lipson 1984).

Before the surgery, the woman is given nothing by mouth, an abdominal and perineal prep is done (from below breasts to the pubic region), and an in-dwelling catheter to dependent drainage is inserted to prevent bladder distention and obstructed delivery. The woman must sign a consent form for surgery. At least two units of whole blood are readied for administration. An intravenous line is started, with an adequate size needle to permit blood administration, and preoperative medication may be ordered. The pediatrician should be notified, and adequate preparation made to receive the infant. The nurse should make sure that the infant warmer is functional and that appropriate resuscitation equipment is available. The nurse assists in positioning the woman on the operating table. The FHR should be ascertained before surgery and during preparation, since fetal hypoxia can result from supine maternal hypotension. The operating table may be adjusted so it slants slightly to one side. This helps relieve the pressure of the gravid uterus on the vena cava and lessens the incidence of supine maternal hypotension. The suction should be in working order, and the urine collection bag should be positioned under the operating table to ensure proper drainage of urine.

## PARTICIPATION OF THE FATHER

There are conflicting opinions and policies about fathers in the delivery room during a cesarean birth. It is interesting that the reasons for excluding them are similar to those once given for excluding fathers from attending vaginal birth. Examples of these opinions, which have since been proved to be invalid, include concerns about the father fainting, emotional trauma, increased risk of law suits or infection, and so on. The National Institutes of Health (NIH) Cesarean Birth Task Force (1980), after considering this issue, concluded that "in spite of the widespread fears of adverse effects . . . there is no evidence of harm from fathers' participation." The position statement by the American College of Obstetrics and Gynecology (ACOG) states that they "cannot perceive strong medical indications or contraindications to the presence of fathers in the operating suite" (Affonso 1981). In fact, the father's presence during the cesarean procedure leads to a more positive evaluation of the birth experience later by both the mother and the father (Affonso 1981). In addition, when the father is present for the birth, the mother requires less postpartal medication for pain, experiences less loneliness, and is less anxious about the baby's health. It is important to note that not all fathers desire to be present during birth, and some women would prefer that the father was not present. The couple needs to be free to choose what they prefer.

When the father attends the cesarean birth, he wears a surgical gown and mask as do others in the operating suite. A stool can be placed at the bedside near the woman's head. The father can sit nearby to provide physical touch, visual contact, and verbal reassurance to his partner.

Other measures can be taken to promote the partici-

pation of the father who is not allowed or chooses not to be present during the birth. They are:

1. Allowing the father to be near the delivery room where he can hear the newborn's first cry

2. Encouraging the father to carry or accompany the infant to the nursery for the initial assessment

3. Involving the father in postpartal care in the recovery room

In addition to meeting the emotional and informational needs of the expectant parents, other nursing functions are carried out to assure physiologic support and safety of the woman and neonate.

After birth of the infant the nurse assists the pediatrician with physiologic support of the neonate. After the infant's condition is stable, he or she should be shown to the woman if she is awake. The circulating nurse helps apply the dressing to the incision and, with the aid of other staff, transfers the woman to the recovery room.

The physical care of the woman in the immediate recovery period assumes the highest priority because her physiologic processes need to stabilize following surgery. However, psychologic aspects of nursing care are also very important. The nurse provides support to the woman through the way that the nursing care is organized and communicated to her. The nurse gives explanations for all assessments, maintains rapport with the woman, and helps her with the difficult tasks that are part of this recovery period. If the woman's condition permits (vital signs are stable and the woman is awake), the mother and infant may spend time together and the mother may even wish to breast-feed. Women need to be supported in their decisions regarding interactions with support persons and the baby. Some women may wish to be alone and need to devote all their energy to this initial recovery time; others may want other people and the baby with them. These decisions are based on personal preferences of the woman and also on the type of anesthesia that is used.

## IMMEDIATE POSTPARTAL RECOVERY PERIOD

The postpartal recovery room must be equipped with suction and oxygen to ensure a patent airway and to protect from respiratory obstruction due to secretions. The recovery room nurse should check the woman's vital signs every five minutes until they are stable, then every 15 minutes for an hour, then every 30 minutes until she is discharged to the postpartal floor. The nurse should remain with the woman until she is stable.

The dressing and perineal pad must be checked every 15 minutes for at least an hour, and the fundus should be gently palpated to determine whether it is remaining firm. The fundus may be palpated from the side while the incision is supported with the other hand. Oxytocin is usually administered intravenously to promote the contractility of the uterine muscles. If the woman has been under general anesthesia, she should be positioned on her side to facilitate drainage of secretions, turned, and assisted with coughing and deep breathing every two hours for at least 24 hours. If she has received a spinal anesthetic, the level of anesthesia should be checked every 15 minutes until sensation has fully returned. The nurse monitors intake and output and observes the urine for bloody tinge, which could mean surgical trauma to the bladder. The physician prescribes medication, which should be administered as needed, to relieve the mother's pain and nausea. Facilitation of parent-infant interaction following birth and post-partal care is discussed in Chapter 26.

# ESSENTIAL CONCEPTS

● **An external (or cephalic) version may be done after 37 weeks' gestation to change a breech presentation to a cephalic. The benefits of the version are that a lower-risk vaginal delivery may be anticipated. The version is accomplished with the use of tocolytics to relax the uterus. An internal podalic version is used only when needed during the vaginal birth of a second twin.**

● **Amniotomy (AROM) is probably the most common procedure in obstetrics. The risks are prolapse of the umbilical cord and infection.**

● **Indicated induction of labor is done for many reasons. The methods include amniotomy, prostaglandins, and oxytocin infusion.**

● **Nursing responsibilities are heightened during an induced labor.**

● **An episiotomy may be done just prior to delivery of the fetus. Although in this country it is very prevalent, it is becoming more controversial.**

● **Forceps deliveries can be low outlet or midforceps. Low outlet forceps are the most common and are associated with few maternal-fetal complications. Midforceps are associated with more complications but when needed are an important aid to delivery.**

● **A vacuum extractor is a soft pliable cup attached to suction that can be applied to the fetal head and used in much the same way as forceps.**

● **At least one in five births is now accomplished by cesarean birth. The increase in the cesarean birth rate has been influenced by many factors.**

**The nurse has a vital role in providing information, support, and encouragement to the couple participating in a cesarean birth.**

● **Vaginal birth after cesarean (VBAC) is becoming more popular and the success rate is more than 60%. Overcoming the old fears of uterine rupture is a high priority for both the parents and the medical community.**

## References

Affonso DD: *Impact of Cesarean Childbirth.* Philadelphia: Davis, 1981.

Affonso DD, Stichler JF: Cesarean birth: Women's reactions. *Am J Nurs* March 1980; 80:468.

Banta D, Thacker SB: The risks and benefits of episiotomy: A review. *Birth* Spring 1982; 9:25.

Bishop EH: Pelvic scoring for elective inductions. *Obstet Gynecol* 1964; 24:266.

Bromberg MH: Presumptive maternal benefits of routine episiotomy. A literature review. *J Nurse-Midwifery* 1986; 31:121.

Buekens P et al: Episiotomy and third degree tears. *Br J Obstet Gynaecol* 1985; 92:820.

Cox BE, Smith EC: The mother's self-esteem after a cesarean delivery. *Am J Mat Child Nurs* September/October 1982; 7:309.

Danforth DN, Scott JR: *Obstetrics and Gynecology,* 5th ed. Philadelphia: Harper and Row, 1986.

Elliott JP: Lavage to prevent postcesarean infection. *Contemp OB/GYN* May 1984; 23(5):43.

Fall O et al: Forceps or vacuum extractor? A comparison of effects on the newborn. *Acta Obstet Gynaecol Scand* 1986; 65:75.

Flamm BL: Vaginal birth after cesarean section: Controversies old and new. *Clin Obstet Gynecol* December 1985; 28:735.

Giacoia GP, Yaffe S: Perinatal pharmacology. Chapter 100 in: *Gynecology and Obstetrics.* Vol. 3. Sciarra JL (editor). Philadelphia: Harper and Row, 1982.

Greis JB et al: Comparison of maternal and fetal effects of vacuum extraction with forceps or cesarean deliveries. *Obstet Gynecol* May 1981; 57:571.

Laube DW: Forceps delivery. *Clin Obstet Gynecol* June 1986; 29:286.

Leach L, Sproule V: Meeting the challenge of cesarean births. *J Obstet Gynecol Neonatal Nurs* May/June 1984; 13(3):191.

Lipson JG: Repeat cesarean births: Social and psychological issues. *J Obstet Gynecol Neonatal Nurs* May/June 1984; 13(3):157.

Macer J, Buchanan D, Yonekura ML: Induction of labor with prostaglandin E$_2$ vaginal suppositories. *Obstet Gynecol* May 1984; 63(5):644.

Marshall C: The art of induction/augmentation of labor. *J Obstet Gynecol Neonatal Nurs* January/February 1985; 14:22.

McKay S, Mahan CS: How worthwhile are membrane stripping and amniotomy? *Contemp OB/GYN* December 1983; 22(6):173.

Morrison JC, Wiser WL: Cesarean birth: Surgical techniques. Chapter 83 in: *Gynecology and Obstetrics.* Vol 2. Sciarra JL (editor). Hagerstown, MD: Harper and Row, 1986.

NAACOG OGN Practice Resource. The nurse's role in induction/augmentation of labor. Washington DC: January 1988.

NIH Cesarean Birth Task Force. National Institute of Child Development statement on cesarean childbirth. US Department of Health and Human Services, Building HHH, Rm 447F8, Washington, DC 20201, 1980.

Niswander KR: Induction of labor. Chapter 71 in: *Gynecology and Obstetrics*. Vol 2. Sciarra JL (editor). Hagerstown, MD: Harper and Row, 1985.

Petitti DB: Maternal mortality and morbidity with cesarean section. *Clin Obstet Gynecol* 1985; 28:763.

Porreco RP, Meier PR: Repeat cesarean—Mostly unnecessary. *Contemp OB/GYN* September 1985; 24(3):55.

Pritchard JA, MacDonald PC, Gant NF: *Williams Obstetrics,* 17th ed. New York: Appleton-Century-Crofts, 1985.

Queenan JT et al: Symposium: Today's high C/S rate: Can we reduce it? *Contemp Ob/Gyn* July 1988; 32:154.

Ramler D, Roberts J: A comparison of cold and warm sitz baths for relief of postpartum perineal pain. *J Obstet Gynecol Neonatal Nurs* November/December 1986; 15:471.

Thacker SB, Banta HB: Benefits and risks of episiotomy: An interpretive review of the English language literature, 1860–1980. *Obstet Gynecol Surv* 1983; 38:322.

US Department of Health, Education, and Welfare: New restrictions on oxytocin use. *Food and Drug Administration Bulletin.* Vol 8. October/November 1978.

VanDorsten JP et al: Randomized control trial of external cephalic version with tocolysis in late pregnancy. *Am J Obstet Gynecol* October 1981; 141:417.

Varner MW: Episiotomy: Techniques and indications. *Clin Obstet Gynecol* June 1986; 29:309.

Westgren M, Paul RH: Delivery of the low birth weight infant by cesarean section. *Clin Obstet Gynecol* December 1985; 28:752.

Willson JR: The conquest of cesarean section-related infections: A progress report. *Obstet Gynecol* 1988; 72:519.

## Additional Readings

Fawcett J, Henklein JC: Antenatal education for cesarean birth: Extension of a field test. *J Obstet Gynecol Neonatal Nurs* 1987; 16:61.

Hag CL: Vaginal birth after cesarean delivery. *Am Fam Phys* 1988; 37(6):167.

Herbert WN, Owen HG, Collins ML: Autologous blood storage in Obstetrics. *Obstet Gynecol* August 1988; 72(2):166.

Laros RK, Dattel BJ: Management of twin pregnancy: The vaginal route is still safe. *Am J Obstet Gynecol* 1988; 158(6, Part 1):1330.

Legino LF et al: Third- and fourth-degree perineal tears: 50 years' experience at a university hospital. *J Reprod Med* 1988; 33(5):423.

Nodine PM, Robert J: Factors associated with perineal outcome during childbirth. *J Nurse-Midwifery* May/June 1987; 32(3):123.

Poma PA: Pregnancy in Hispanic women. *J Nat Med Assoc* 1987; 79:929.

Sadovsky E, Aboulafia Y, Ohel G: Managing breech delivery. *Contemp OB/GYN* July 1987; 30(1):47.

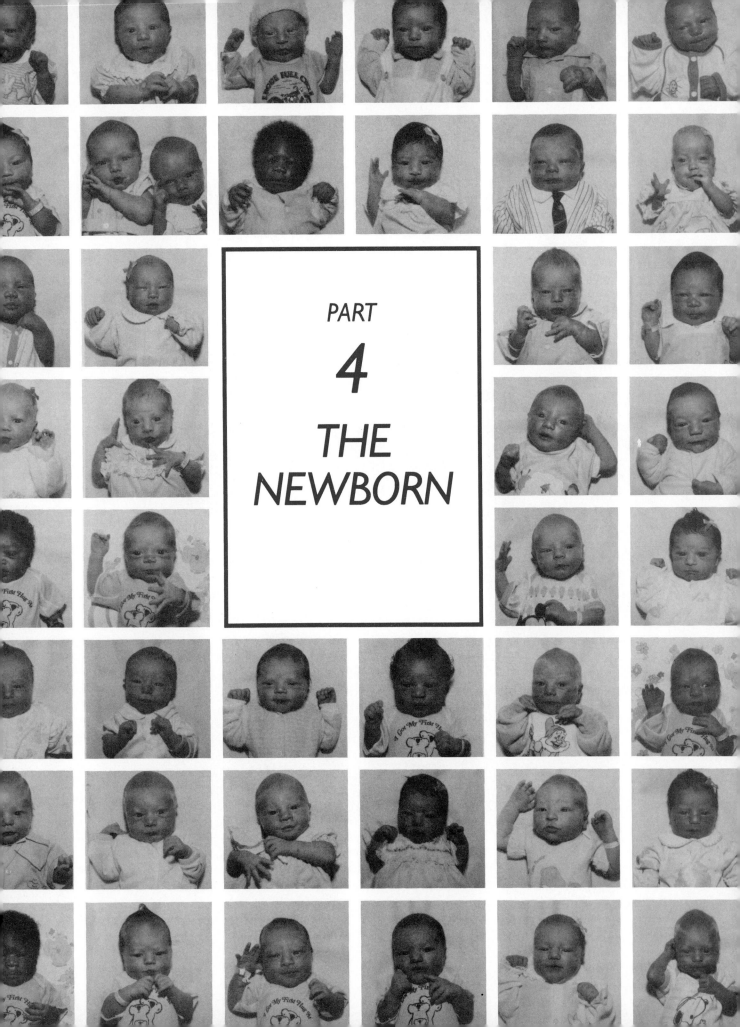

PART

*4*

*THE
NEWBORN*

# 20

# Physiologic Responses of the Newborn to Birth

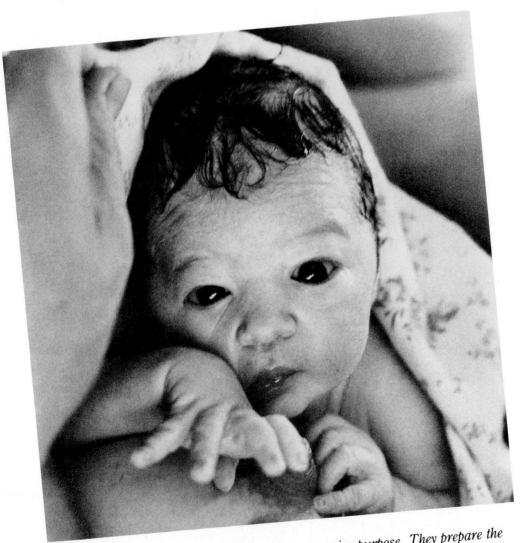

*The incredible attributes of the newborn have a major purpose. They prepare the baby for interaction with the family and for life in the world. (The Amazing Newborn)*

## Objectives

● Summarize the cardiovascular and respiratory changes that occur during the transition to extrauterine life.

● Summarize the major mechanisms of heat loss in the newborn and how the newborn produces heat.

● Describe the functional abilities of the newborn's gastrointestinal tract and liver.

● Explain the steps involved in conjugation and excretion of bilirubin in the newborn.

● Discuss the reasons why the newborn develops jaundice.

● Identify three reasons why the newborn's kidneys have difficulty in maintaining fluid and electrolyte balance.

● List the immunologic responses available to the newborn.

● Describe how various factors affect the newborn's blood values.

● Describe the normal sensory/perceptual abilities seen in the newborn period.

## Key Terms

active acquired immunity
brown adipose tissue (BAT)
cardiopulmonary adaptation
conduction
convection
evaporation
habituation
meconium
orientation
passive acquired immunity
periodic breathing
physiologic anemia of infancy
physiologic jaundice
radiation
self-quieting ability
surfactant
thermal neutral zone (TNZ)

The neonatal period includes the time from birth through the twenty-eighth day of life. During this period, the newborn adjusts from intrauterine to extrauterine life. The nurse must be knowledgeable about a newborn's normal biopsychosocial adaptations to recognize deviations from it.

To begin life as an independent being, the neonate must immediately establish pulmonary ventilation in conjunction with marked circulatory changes. These radical and rapid changes are crucial to the maintenance of life. In contrast, all other neonatal body systems can change their functions or establish themselves over a prolonged period of time.

## ● RESPIRATORY ADAPTATIONS

The following must occur to establish respiratory function:

1. Extrauterine respiratory movements begin.
2. Air entry overcomes opposing forces so that the lungs expand.
3. Some air remains in the alveoli during expiration, thus preventing lung collapse. (The amount of air remaining is called the functional residual capacity.)
4. Pulmonary blood flow increases, and cardiac output is redistributed.

Although the previous events occur at birth, certain intrauterine factors also enhance the newborn's ability to breathe.

## ● Intrauterine Factors Supporting Respiratory Function

### FETAL LUNG DEVELOPMENT

The respiratory system is in a continuous state of development during fetal life, and the development continues into the neonatal period. During the first 20 weeks of gestation, development is limited to the differentiation of pulmonary, vascular, and lymphatic structures.

At 20 to 24 weeks alveolar ducts begin to appear, followed by primitive alveoli at 24 to 28 weeks.

During weeks 20–24 the alveolar epithelial cells begin to differentiate into type 1 cells (structures necessary for gas exchange) and type 2 cells (structures that provide for the synthesis and storage of *surfactant*). **Surfactant** is composed of a group of surface-active phospholipids, of which one component, lecithin, is the most critical for alveolar stability.

At 28–32 weeks of gestation, the number of type 2 cells increases further, and surfactant is produced by a choline pathway within the type 2 cells. Surfactant production by this pathway peaks at about 35 weeks of gestation, and remains high until term, paralleling late fetal lung development. At this time, the lungs are structurally developed enough to permit maintenance of good lung expansion and adequate exchange of gases (Avery 1987).

Clinically, the peak production of surfactant by the choline pathway corresponds closely with the marked decrease in incidence of idiopathic respiratory distress syndrome for babies born after 35 weeks of gestation. Production of sphingomyelin remains constant throughout gestation. The neonate born before the lecithin/sphingomyelin (L/S) ratio is 2:1 will have varying degrees of respiratory distress. (See discussion of L/S ratio in Chapter 24.)

## FETAL BREATHING MOVEMENTS

The ability of the neonate to breathe air immediately upon exposure to extrauterine life appears to be the consequence of weeks of intrauterine practice. Fetal breathing movements (FBM) occur as early as 11 weeks' gestation. Goldstein and Reid (1980) propose that FBM are essential for development of chest wall muscles (including the diaphragm) and to a lesser extent for regulating lung fluid volume and therefore lung growth.

## ● Initiation of Breathing

To maintain life, the lungs must function immediately after birth. Two radical changes must take place for the lungs to function:

1. Pulmonary ventilation must be established through lung expansion following birth.
2. A marked increase in the pulmonary circulation must occur.

The first breath of life—the gasp in response to chemical, tactile, thermal, and mechanical changes associated with birth—initiates the serial opening of the alveoli. Thus begins the transition from a fluid-filled environment to an air-breathing, independent, extrauterine life.

## CHEMICAL STIMULI

An important chemical stimulator that contributes to the onset of breathing is transitory asphyxia of the fetus and newborn. Elevation in $P_{CO_2}$ and decrease in pH and $P_{O_2}$ are the natural outcome of normal vaginal birth with cessation of placental gas exchange and umbilical cord pulsation, and cutting of the cord. These changes, which are present in all newborns to some degree, stimulate the aortic and carotid chemoreceptors, initiating impulses that trigger the medulla's respiratory center. Although brief periods of asphyxia are a significant stimulator, prolonged asphyxia is abnormal and acts as a central nervous system depressant.

## THERMAL STIMULI

The significant decrease in environmental temperature after birth (from 98.6°F to 70–75°F or 37°C to 21–23.9°C) is a major stimulus for initiation of breathing. As nerve endings in the skin are stimulated, the newborn responds with rhythmic respirations. Normal temperature changes that occur at birth are apparently within acceptable physiologic limits. Excessive cooling may result in profound depression and evidence of cold stress (see Chapter 24).

## SENSORY AND PHYSICAL STIMULI

As the fetus moves from a quiet environment to one of sensory abundance, a number of physical and sensory influences help respiration begin. They include the numerous tactile, auditory, and visual stimuli of birth. Historically, vigorous stimulation was provided by slapping the buttocks or heels of the newborn, but today greater emphasis is placed on gentle physical contact. Thoroughly drying the infant, for example, provides stimulation in a far more comforting way and decreases heat loss.

## MECHANICAL EVENTS

During the latter half of gestation, the fetal lungs produce fluid continuously. This secretion fills the lungs almost completely, expanding the air spaces. Some of the lung fluid drains out of the lungs into the amniotic fluid and is then swallowed by the fetus.

Secretion of lung fluid diminishes 48 hours before onset of labor. However, approximately 80 to 110 mL of fluid remains in the respiratory passages of a normal term fetus at the time of birth. This fluid must be removed from the lungs to permit adequate movement of air.

The primary mechanical events that initiate respiration involve the removal of fluid from the lungs as the baby passes through the birth canal. As the fetal chest is compressed, increasing intrathoracic pressure, approximately one third of the fluid is squeezed out of the lungs. After the birth of the newborn's trunk, the chest wall recoils. This chest recoil is thought to produce a small, passive inspiration of air (negative intrathoracic pressure sucks air in), which is drawn into the lungs to replace the fluid

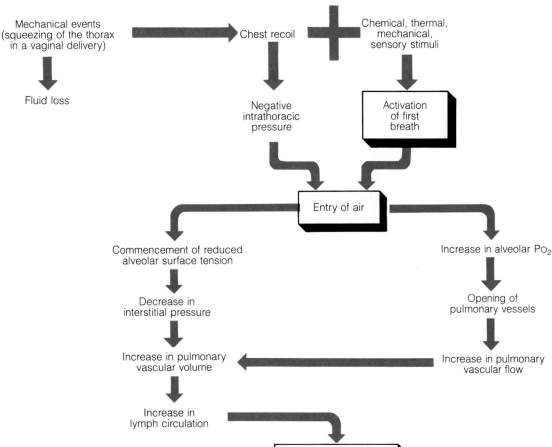

Mechanical events
(squeezing of the thorax
in a vaginal delivery)

Chemical, thermal,
mechanical,
sensory stimuli

Chest recoil

Fluid loss

Negative
intrathoracic
pressure

Activation
of first
breath

Entry of air

Commencement of reduced
alveolar surface tension

Increase in alveolar $P_{O_2}$

Decrease in
interstitial pressure

Opening of
pulmonary vessels

Increase in pulmonary
vascular volume

Increase in pulmonary
vascular flow

Increase in
lymph circulation

Promotion of
adequate oxygenation

*Figure 20.1   Initiation of respiration in the neonate*

that was squeezed out. After this first inspiration, the newborn exhales, with crying, against a partially closed glottis, creating a positive intrathoracic pressure. On inspiration, the diaphragm descends, creating greater pressure within the alveoli than outside. Fluid flows from the alveoli across the alveolar membranes into the pulmonary interstitial tissue.

With each succeeding breath, the lungs expand. Since the protein concentration is higher in the pulmonary capillaries, the interstitial fluid passes by osmosis into the capillaries and lymphatics. As pulmonary vascular resistance decreases, pulmonary blood flow increases, and more fluid is absorbed into the bloodstream. In the normal term newborn, movement of lung fluid to the interstitial tissue is rapid, but movement into lymph and blood vessels may take several hours (Korones 1986).

Some of the inspired air is also forced into the proximal airways. An air-liquid interface (the surface boundary between these two components) is created between the smaller airways and alveoli. About 70% of the alveoli fluid is reabsorbed within two hours of birth, and it is com-

pletely absorbed within 12 to 24 hours of birth (Korones 1986). Figure 20.1 summarizes the initiation of respiration.

Although the initial expiration should clear the airways of accumulated fluid and permit further inspiration, some clinicians feel it is wise to suction mucus and fluid from the newborn's mouth and oropharynx. They use a DeLee or bulb syringe as soon as the newborn's head and shoulders are delivered and again as the newborn adapts to extrauterine life and stabilizes (see Procedure 16.1, p 442 and Chapter 16).

Problems associated with lung clearance and/or initiation of respiratory activity may be caused by a variety of factors. The lymphatics may be underdeveloped, thus decreasing the rate at which the fluid is absorbed from the lungs. Complications that occur antenatally or during labor and birth can interfere with adequate lung expansion, resulting in increased pulmonary vascular resistance, and decreased blood flow. These complications include inadequate compression of the chest wall in a very small neonate, the absence of chest wall compression in the neonate delivered by cesarean birth, or severe asphyxia at birth.

## Factors Opposing the First Breath

Three major factors may oppose the initiation of respiratory activity: (1) alveolar surface tension, (2) viscosity of lung fluid within the respiratory tract, and (3) degree of lung compliance.

Because of alveolar surface tension, there is a constant tendency for surfaces to collapse into each other. Surfactant reduces the attracting force between moist alveolar surfaces.

Surfactant promotes lung expansion by preventing the alveoli from completely collapsing with each expiration and increases lung *compliance* (the ability of the lung to fill with air easily). When surfactant is decreased, compliance is also decreased and the pressure needed to expand the lungs with air increases. Resistive forces of the lung filled with viscous fluid, combined with the small radii of the airways, necessitates pressures of 40–80 cm of water to initially open the lung. The first breath usually establishes a functional residual capacity (FRC) that is 30% to 40% of the fully expanded lung volume. This FRC allows alveolar sacs to remain partially expanded on expiration. The remaining air in the lung after expiration decreases the need for continuous high pressures for following breaths. Subsequent breaths require only 6 to 8 cm $H_2O$ pressure to open alveoli during inspiration. Therefore, the first breath of life is usually the most difficult.

## Cardiopulmonary Physiology

With the onset of respiration, the functions of the cardiovascular and respiratory systems become interrelated, hence the term **cardiopulmonary adaptation.** As air enters the lungs, $Po_2$ rises in the alveoli, which stimulates the relaxation of the pulmonary arteries and triggers a decrease in the pulmonary vascular resistance. At the same time, the lowered surface tension decreases interstitial pressure. As pulmonary vascular resistance decreases, the vascular flow in the lung increases by 20%, followed by an increase over the birth level of up to 85% at seven hours of life and 100% at 24 hours of life. This greater blood volume to the lungs contributes to the conversion from fetal circulation to newborn circulation.

After pulmonary circulation is established, blood is distributed throughout the lung, although the alveoli may or may not be fully open. For adequate oxygenation to occur, sufficient blood must be delivered by the heart to the lungs. It is important to remember that shunting of blood is common in the early newborn period. This bidirectional blood flow, or right-to-left shunting through the ductus arteriosus, may divert a significant amount of blood away from the lungs, depending on the pressure changes of respiration, crying, and the cardiac cycle. This shunting in the newborn period is also responsible for the unstable transitional period to neonatal respiratory functions.

## Oxygen Transport

The transportation of oxygen to the peripheral tissues depends on the type of hemoglobin in the red blood cell. In the fetus and neonate, a variety of hemoglobins exist, the most significant being fetal hemoglobin (Hb F) and adult hemoglobin (Hb A). Approximately 70%–90% of hemoglobin in the fetus and neonate is of the fetal variety. The greatest difference between Hb F and Hb A is related to the transport of oxygen.

In the newborn, the greater affinity of Hb F for oxygen causes a shift to the left in the oxygen dissociation curve. Since more oxygen is bound to Hb F, the oxygen saturation in the newborn's blood is greater than in the adult's, but the amount of oxygen available to the tissues is less. This is beneficial prenatally, because the fetus must maintain adequate oxygen uptake in the presence of very low oxygen tension (umbilical venous $Po_2$ cannot exceed the uterine venous $Po_2$). Because of this phenomenon, hypoxia in the neonate is particularly difficult to recognize because of the high concentration of oxygen in the blood. Clinical manifestations of cyanosis are lacking until low blood levels of oxygen are present. Shifts to the left in the curve also may be caused by alkalosis (increased pH) and hypothermia. Acidosis, hypercarbia, and hyperthermia may cause the oxygen dissociation curve to shift to the right.

## Maintaining Respiratory Function

The ability of the lung to maintain oxygen (oxygenation) and carbon dioxide exchange (ventilation) is influenced by such factors as lung compliance and airway resistance. Lung compliance is influenced by the elastic recoil of the lung tissue and by anatomic variation. Anatomic differences between the neonate and the adult influence lung compliance. The infant has a relatively large heart, as well as mediastinal structures that reduce available lung space. The large abdomen further encroaches on the high diaphragm to decrease lung space. Anatomically, the neonatal chest is equipped with weak intercostal muscles, a rigid rib cage with horizontal ribs, and a high diaphragm that restricts the space available for lung expansion. Ventilation is also limited by airway resistance, which depends on the radii, length, and number of airways.

## Characteristics of Neonatal Respiration

Normal neonatal respiration rate is 30–50 breaths/min. Initial respirations may be largely diaphragmatic, with shallow and irregular depth and rhythm. Additionally, they are primarily abdominal and synchronous with the chest movement. Short periods of apnea are to be expected. When the breathing pattern is characterized by pauses

| Table 20.1 Fetal and Neonatal Circulation | | |
|---|---|---|
| **System** | **Fetal** | **Neonatal** |
| Pulmonary blood vessels | Constricted with very little blood flow; lungs not expanded | Vasodilation and increased blood flow; lungs expanded; increased oxygen stimulates vasodilation. |
| Systemic blood vessels | Dilated with low resistance; blood mostly in placenta | Arterial pressure rises due to loss of placenta; increased systemic blood volume and resistance. |
| Ductus arteriosus | Large with no tone; blood flow from pulmonary artery to aorta | 1. Reversal of blood flow. Now from aorta to pulmonary artery due to increased left atrial pressure.<br>2. Ductus is sensitive to increased oxygen and body chemicals and begins to constrict. |
| Foramen ovale | Patent with large blood flow from right atrium to left atrium | Increased pressure in left atrium attempts to reverse blood flow and shuts one-way valve. |

lasting 5–15 seconds, **periodic breathing** is occurring. Periodic respiration is rarely associated with differences in skin color or heart rate changes, nor does it have prognostic significance. Tactile or other sensory stimulation increases the inspired oxygen and converts periodic breathing patterns to normal breathing patterns. Neonatal sleep states particularly influence respiratory patterns. With deep sleep, the pattern is reasonably regular. Periodic breathing occurs with rapid-eye-movement (REM) sleep, and grossly irregular breathing is evident with motor activity, sucking, and crying.

The neonate is an obligatory nose breather, and any obstruction will cause respiratory distress, so it is important to keep the throat and nose clear. Immediately after birth and for the first two hours after birth, respiratory rates of 60 to 70 breaths per minute are normal. Some initial dyspnea or cyanosis may also be normal. Any increased use of the intercostal muscle (retracting) may indicate respiratory distress. See Chapter 24 and Table 24.4, p 704 for the signs of respiratory distress. After the newborn is two hours of age, if the respiration rate drops below 30/min or exceeds 60/min when the infant is at rest, or if dyspnea or cyanosis occur, the physican should be notified.

## • CARDIOVASCULAR ADAPTATIONS

As described earlier, blood flow to the lungs increases with the first respirations of the normal newborn. This greater blood volume contributes to the conversion from fetal circulation to neonatal circulation.

## • Fetal-Neonatal Transition Circulation

During fetal life, blood with higher oxygen content is diverted to the heart and brain. Blood in the descending aorta is less oxygenated and supplies the kidney and intestinal tract. Limited amounts of blood, pumped from the right ventricle toward the lungs, enter the pulmonary vessels. In the fetus, increased pulmonary resistance forces most of this blood through the ductus arteriosus into the descending aorta (see Table 20.1). Expansion of the lungs with the first breath decreases the pulmonary vascular resistance, and the clamping of the cord raises systemic vascular resistance and left atrial pressure. This physiologic mechanism marks the transition from fetal to neonatal circulation and shows the interplay of cardiovascular and respiratory systems (Figure 20.2). Five major areas of change occur in cardiopulmonary adaptation.

1. *Increased aortic pressure and decreased venous pressure.* When the cord is cut, the placental vascular bed is eliminated and the intravascular space is reduced. Consequently, aortic (systemic) blood pressure is increased. At the same time, when the newborn is separated from the placenta, blood return via the inferior vena cava is decreased, resulting in a small decrease in pressure within the venous circulation.

2. *Increased systemic pressure and decreased pulmonary artery pressure.* With the loss of the low-resistance placenta, pressure increases in the systemic circulation, resulting in greater systemic resistance.

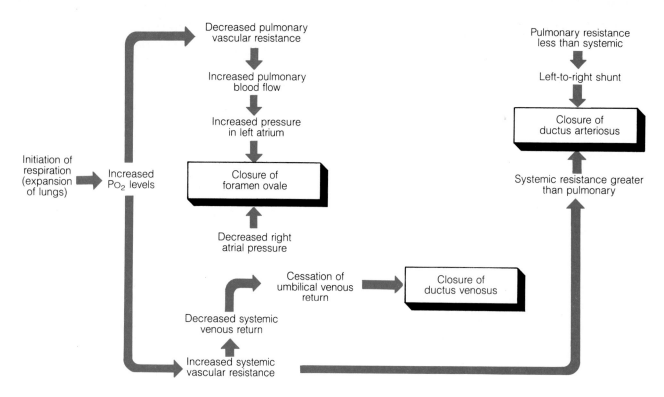

*Figure 20.2   Transitional circulation: conversion from fetal to neonatal circulation*

At the same time, lung expansion promotes increased pulmonary blood flow, and the increased blood $P_{O_2}$ associated with initiation of respirations produces vasodilation of pulmonary blood vessels. The combination of increased pulmonary blood flow and vasodilation results in decreased pulmonary artery resistance. As a result of opening the vascular beds, the systemic vascular pressure decreases, causing perfusion of the other body systems.

3. *Closure of the foramen ovale.* Closure of the foramen ovale is a function of atrial pressures. In utero, pressure is greater in the right atrium, and the foramen ovale is open. Decreased pulmonary resistance and increased pulmonary blood flow result in increased pulmonary venous return into the left atrium, thereby increasing left atrial pressure slightly. The decreased pulmonary vascular resistance also causes a decrease in right atrial pressure. The pressure gradients are now reversed, left atrial pressure is greater, and the foramen ovale is functionally closed. Although the foramen ovale closes one to two hours after birth, a slight right-to-left shunting may occur in the early neonatal period. Any increase in pulmonary resistance may result in reopening of the foramen ovale, causing a right-to-left shunt. Permanent closure occurs within several months.

4. *Closure of the ductus arteriosus.* Initial elevation of the systemic vascular pressure above the pulmonary vascular pressure increases pulmonary blood flow by causing a reversal of the flow through the ductus arteriosus. Blood now flows from the aorta into the pulmonary artery. Furthermore, although the presence of oxygen causes the pulmonary arterioles to dilate, an increase in blood $P_{O_2}$ triggers the opposite response in the ductus arteriosus—it constricts.

    In utero, the placenta provides prostaglandin $E_2$, which causes ductus vasodilation. With the loss of the placenta and increased pulmonary blood flow, prostaglandin $E_2$ levels drop, leaving the active constriction by $P_{O_2}$ unopposed. If the lungs fail to expand or if $P_{O_2}$ levels drop, the ductus remains patent. Fibrosis of the ductus occurs within three weeks after birth, but functional closure is accomplished within 15 hours after birth.

5. *Closure of the ductus venosus.* Although the mechanism of initiating closure of the ductus venosus is not known, it appears to be related to mechanical pressure changes after severing of the cord, redistribution of blood, and cardiac output. Closure of the bypass forces perfusion of the liver. Anatomic fibrosis occurs within 3–7 days (Korones 1986) (Figure 20.3).

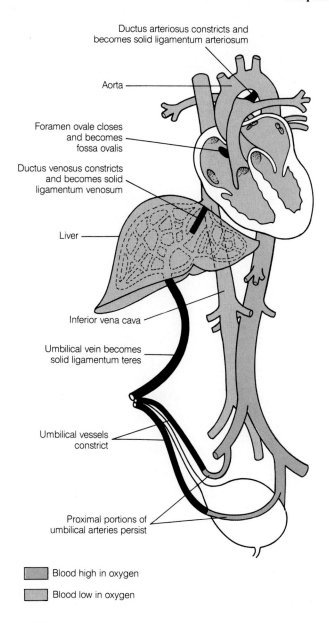

Ductus arteriosus constricts and
becomes solid ligamentum arteriosum

Aorta

Foramen ovale closes
and becomes
fossa ovalis

Ductus venosus constricts
and becomes solid
ligamentum venosum

Liver

Inferior vena cava

Umbilical vein becomes
solid ligamentum teres

Umbilical vessels
constrict

Proximal portions of
umbilical arteries persist

Blood high in oxygen

Blood low in oxygen

*Figure 20.3   Major changes that occur in the newborn's circulatory system (From Hole JW:* Human Anatomy and Physiology, *2nd ed. Dubuque, IA: Brown, 1981 p 757.)*

## • Characteristics

### HEART RATE

Shortly after the first cry and the advent of cardiopulmonary circulation, the newborn heart rate accelerates to 175–180 beats/min. Thereafter, the rate follows a fairly uniform course, slowing to 115 beats/min at four to six hours of life, then rising and plateauing at approximately 120 beats/min at 12–24 hours of life (Smith and Nelson 1976). The range of the heart rate in the full-term neonate is 100 beats per minute while asleep and 120 to 150 while awake. Resting heart rates are as low as 70 to 90 beats per minute, and rates as high as 180 while crying have

been reported as normal. Apical pulse rates should be obtained by auscultation for a full minute, preferably when the neonate is asleep. Peripheral pulses should also be evaluated to detect any lags or unusual characteristics.

### BLOOD PRESSURE

During the newborn period, the blood pressure tends to be the highest immediately after birth, and then descends to its lowest level about three hours after. By days 4–6 of life, the blood pressure rises to a level approximately the same as the initial level (Smith and Nelson 1976). Blood pressure is particularly sensitive to the changes in blood volume that occur in the transition to neonatal circulation (Figure 20.4).

Blood pressure values during the first 12 hours of life vary with the birth weight. In the full-term resting neonate, the average blood pressure is 74/47 mm Hg; in the preterm newborn, it averages 64/39 mm Hg. Crying may cause an elevation of 20 mm Hg in both the systolic and diastolic blood pressure, thus accurate measurement is more likely in the quiet newborn. The measurement of blood pressure is best accomplished by using the Doppler technique or a 1- to 2-inch cuff and a stethoscope over the brachial artery.

### HEART MURMURS

Murmurs are usually produced by turbulent blood flow. Murmurs may be heard when blood flows across an abnormal valve or across a stenosed valve, when there is an atrial septal or ventricular septal defect, or when there

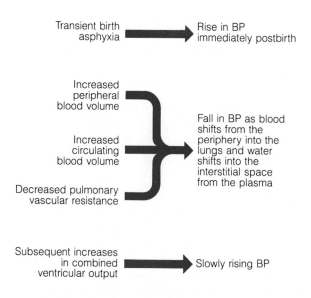

Transient birth asphyxia → Rise in BP immediately postbirth

Increased peripheral blood volume

Increased circulating blood volume

Decreased pulmonary vascular resistance

} Fall in BP as blood shifts from the periphery into the lungs and water shifts into the interstitial space from the plasma

Subsequent increases in combined ventricular output → Slowly rising BP

*Figure 20.4   Response of blood pressure (BP) to neonatal changes in blood volume*

is increased flow across a normal valve. A transient murmur is often heard in newborns before the ductus arteriosus closes completely.

## CARDIAC WORKLOAD

Prior to birth, the right ventricle does approximately two thirds of the cardiac work, resulting in increased size and thickness of the right ventricle at birth. After birth the left ventricle must assume a larger share of the cardiac workload, and must increase in size and thickness (Avery and Taeusch 1984). This may explain why left-sided heart defects are less tolerable than right-sided lesions after birth.

## ● HEMATOPOIETIC SYSTEM

Fetal erythrocytes are larger than those present at birth but fewer in number. After birth, the red blood cell (RBC) count gradually increases as cell size decreases. Neonatal RBCs have a life span of 80–100 days, approximately two thirds the life span of an adult's RBC. In neonatal red blood cells, about 5% of the RBCs retain their nucleus.

In the first days of life, hematocrit may rise by 1–2 g/dL above fetal levels as a result of placental transfusion, low oral fluid intake, and diminished extracellular fluid volume. By one week postnatally, peripheral hemoglobin is comparable to fetal blood counts. The hemoglobin level declines progressively thereafter (Avery 1987), creating a phenomenon known as **physiologic anemia of infancy.**

Leukocytosis is a normal finding because the trauma of birth stimulates increased production of neutrophils during the first week of life. Neutrophils then decrease to 35% of the total leukocyte count by two weeks of age. Eventually, lymphocytes become the predominant type of leukocyte and the total white blood count falls.

Blood volume of the term infant is estimated to be 80 to 85 mL/kg of body weight. The true amount of blood volume varies based on the amount of placental transfusion received. The concentration of serum electrolytes in the blood indicates the fluid and electrolyte status of the baby. See Table 20.2 for normal term newborn electrolyte and blood values. Hematologic values in the newborn are affected by several factors, including:

*The site of the blood sample.* Hemoglobin and hematocrit levels taken simultaneously are significantly higher in capillary blood than in venous blood. Sluggish peripheral blood flow creates red blood cell stasis, thereby increasing their concentration in the capillaries. Because of this, blood samples taken from venous blood sites are more accurate.

### Table 20.2  Normal Term Newborn Blood Values

| Laboratory data | Normal range |
| --- | --- |
| Hemoglobin | 15–20 g/dL |
| Hematocrit | 43%–61% |
| White blood cell count (WBC) | 10,000–30,000/mm$^3$ |
| Neutrophils | 40%–80% |
| Immature WBC | 3%–10% |
| Platelets | 100,000–280,000/mm$^3$ |
| Reticulocytes | 3%–6% |
| Blood volume | 82.3 mL/kg (third day after early cord clamping) 92.6 mL/kg (third day after delayed cord clamping) |
| Sodium mmol/L | 124–156 |
| Potassium mmol/L | 5.3–7.3 |
| Chloride mmol/L | 90–111 |
| Calcium mg/dL | 7.3–9.2 |
| Glucose mg/dL | 40–97 |

*Delayed cord clamping and the normal shift of plasma to the extravascular spaces.* Neonatal hemoglobin and hematocrit values are higher when a placental transfusion occurs postnatally. Placental vessels contain about 100 mL of blood at term, most of which can be transfused into the newborn by holding the newborn below the level of the placenta and by late clamping of the cord. Blood volume increases by 40% to 60% with late cord clamping (Korones 1986). The increase is reflected by a rise in hemoglobin level and an increase in the hematocrit to 65% about 48 hours after birth (compared with 48% when the cord is clamped immediately). For greatest accuracy, the initial hemoglobin and hematocrit levels should be measured in the cord blood, although this is not a routine practice.

*Gestational age.* There appears to be a positive association between increasing gestational age, higher red blood cell numbers, and greater hemoglobin concentration. This means that the gestational age of the newborn influences the values.

*Prenatal and/or perinatal hemorrhage.* Occurrence of significant prenatal or perinatal bleeding decreases the hematocrit level and causes hypovolemia.

# ● *TEMPERATURE REGULATION*

Temperature regulation is the maintenance of thermal balance by the dissipation of heat to the environment (heat loss) at a rate equal to the production of heat. Newborns are *homeothermic;* they attempt to stabilize their internal body temperatures within a narrow range in spite of significant temperature variations in their environment.

Thermoregulation in the newborn is closely related to the rate of metabolism and oxygen consumption. Within a specific environmental temperature range, called the thermal neutral zone (TNZ), the rates of oxygen consumption and metabolism are minimal and internal body temperature is maintained because of thermal balance (see Table 20.3). For an unclothed full-term neonate, the range of the TNZ is an ambient temperature of 32–34° C (89.6–93.2° F). The limits for an adult are 26–28° C (78.8–82.4° F). Thus, the normal newborn requires higher environmental temperatures to maintain a thermal neutral environment.

Several neonatal characteristics affect the establishment of a TNZ. One of these is the decreased sub-

## Table 20.3 Neonatal Thermal Environmental Temperatures*

| Age and weight | Range of temperature (°C)† | Age and weight | Range of temperature (°C)† |
|---|---|---|---|
| **0–6 HOURS** | | **72–96 HOURS** | |
| Under 1200 g | 34.0–35.4 | Under 1200 g | 34.0–35.0 |
| 1200–1500 g | 33.9–34.4 | 1200–1500 g | 33.0–34.0 |
| 1501–2500 g | 32.8–33.8 | 1501–2500 g | 31.1–33.2 |
| Over 2500 (and >36 weeks) | 32.0–33.8 | Over 2500 (and >36 weeks) | 29.8–32.8 |
| **6–12 HOURS** | | **4–12 DAYS** | |
| Under 1200 g | 34.0–35.4 | Under 1500 g | 33.0–34.0 |
| 1200–1500 g | 33.5–34.4 | 1501–2500 g | 31.0–33.2 |
| 1501–2500 g | 32.2–33.8 | Over 2500 (and >36 weeks) | |
| Over 2500 (and >36 weeks) | 31.4–33.8 | 4–5 days | 29.5–32.6 |
| **12–24 HOURS** | | 5–6 days | 29.4–32.3 |
| Under 1200 g | 34.0–35.4 | 6–8 days | 29.0–32.2 |
| 1200–1500 g | 33.3–34.3 | 8–10 days | 29.0–31.8 |
| 1501–2500 g | 31.8–33.8 | 10–12 days | 29.0–31.4 |
| Over 2500 (and >36 weeks) | 31.0–33.7 | **12–14 DAYS** | |
| **24–36 HOURS** | | Under 1500 g | 32.6–34.0 |
| Under 1200 g | 34.0–35.0 | 1500–2500 g | 31.0–33.2 |
| 1200–1500 g | 33.1–34.2 | Over 2500 (and >36 weeks) | 29.0–30.8 |
| 1501–2500 g | 31.6–33.6 | **2–3 WEEKS** | |
| Over 2500 (and >36 weeks) | 30.7–33.5 | Under 1500 g | 32.2–34.0 |
| **36–48 HOURS** | | 1500–2500 g | 30.5–33.0 |
| Under 1200 g | 34.0–35.0 | **3–4 WEEKS** | |
| 1200–1500 g | 33.0–34.1 | Under 1500 g | 31.6–33.6 |
| 1501–2500 g | 31.4–33.5 | 1500–2500 g | 30.0–32.7 |
| Over 2500 (and >36 weeks) | 30.5–33.3 | **4–5 WEEKS** | |
| **48–72 HOURS** | | Under 1500 g | 31.2–33.0 |
| Under 1200 g | 34.0–35.0 | 1500–2500 g | 29.5–32.2 |
| 1200–1500 g | 33.0–34.0 | **5–6 WEEKS** | |
| 1501–2500 g | 31.2–33.4 | Under 1500 g | 30.6–32.3 |
| Over 2500 g (and >36 weeks) | 30.1–33.2 | 1500–2500 g | 29.0–31.8 |

*Adapted from Scopes and Ahmed (1966). For his table, Scopes had the walls of the incubator one to two degrees warmer than the ambient air temperatures.
†Generally speaking, the smaller infants in each weight group will require a temperature in the higher portion of the temperature range. Within each time range, the younger the infant, the higher the temperature required.

Source: Klaus MH, Fanaroff AA: *Care of the High-Risk Neonate,* 3rd ed. Philadelphia: Saunders, 1986, p. 103.

cutaneous fat and thin epidermis of the newborn. Blood vessels are closer to the skin than those of an adult. Therefore, the circulating blood is influenced by changes in environmental temperature, and in turn influences the hypothalamic temperature-regulating center.

The flexed posture of the term infant decreases the surface area exposed to the environment, thereby reducing heat loss. Other neonatal characteristics such as size and age may also affect the establishing of a TNZ. Preterm small for gestational age (SGA) neonates require higher environmental temperatures to achieve a thermal neutral environment, while a larger, well-insulated newborn may be able to cope with lower environmental temperature. If the environmental temperature falls below the lower limits of the TNZ, the neonate responds with increased oxygen consumption and metabolism, which results in greater heat production. Prolonged exposure to the cold may result in depleted glycogen stores and acidosis. Oxygen consumption can also increase when the environmental temperature is above the TNZ.

## ● *Heat Loss*

A newborn is at a distinct disadvantage in maintaining a normal temperature. With a larger body surface in relation to mass and a limited amount of insulating subcutaneous fat, the newborn loses about four times the heat of an adult (Danforth and Scott 1986). Because of the risk of hypothermia and possible cold stress, minimizing heat loss in the newborn after birth is imperative (see Chapter 16, p 437 and Chapter 22, p 617 for nursing measures).

Two major routes of heat loss are from the internal core of the body to the body surface and from the external surface to the environment. Usually the core temperature is 0.5° C higher than the skin temperature, resulting in continuous transfer of heat to the surface. The greater the difference in temperatures between core and skin, the more rapid the transfer. Heat loss from the body surface to the environment takes place in four ways—convection, radiation, evaporation, and conduction.

● **Convection** is the loss of heat from the warm body surface to the cooler air currents. Air-conditioned rooms, oxygen by mask, and removal from an incubator for procedures done without an overhead warmer increase convective heat loss of the neonate.

● **Radiation** losses occur when heat transfers from the heated body surface to cooler surfaces and objects not in direct contact with the body. The walls of a room or of an incubator are potential causes of heat loss by radiation, even if the ambient temperature of the isolette is within the thermal neutral range for that infant.

● **Evaporation** is the loss of heat incurred when water is converted to a vapor. The newborn is particularly prone to lose heat by evaporation immediately after birth when the infant is wet with amniotic fluid and during baths.

● **Conduction** is the loss of heat to a cooler surface by direct skin contact. Chilled hands, cool scales, cold examination tables, and cold stethoscopes can cause loss of heat by conduction.

After birth, the highest losses of heat generally result from radiation and convection because of the newborn's large body surface compared with weight, and from thermal conduction because of the marked difference between core temperature and skin temperature. The newborn can respond to the cooler environmental temperature with adequate peripheral vasoconstriction, but this mechanism is less effective because of the minimal amount of fat insulation present, the large body surface, and ongoing thermal conduction. Because of these factors, minimizing the baby's heat loss and preventing hypothermia are imperative. Nursing measures for preventing hypothermia can be found in Chapter 22.

## ● *Heat Production*

When exposed to a cool environment, the newborn requires additional heat. The neonate has several physiologic mechanisms that increase heat production, or *thermogenesis*. These include increased basal metabolic rate, muscular activity, and chemical thermogenesis (also called *nonshivering thermogenesis*).

Nonshivering thermogenesis (NST), an important mechanism of heat production unique to the newborn, uses the infant's stores of **brown adipose tissue (BAT)** (also called *brown fat*). Brown adipose tissue is the primary source of heat in the cold-stressed neonate. It first appears in the fetus at about 26–30 weeks of gestation and continues to increase until two to five weeks after the birth of a full-term infant, unless the fat is depleted by cold stress. BAT is deposited in the midscapular area, around the neck, and in the axillas, with deeper placement around the trachea, esophagus, abdominal aorta, kidneys, and adrenal glands (Figure 20.5). BAT constitutes 2%–6% of the newborn's total body weight. Brown fat receives its name from its dark color, which is due to its enriched blood supply, dense cellular content, and abundant nerve endings.

The large numbers of brown fat cells increase the speed with which triglycerides are metabolized to produce heat. In addition, brown fat's rich blood supply enhances distribution of heat throughout the body, and its nerve supply initiates metabolic activity. The brown fat is metabolized and used within several weeks of birth (Korones 1986).

Hypoxia and the effect of certain drugs (such as meperidine) may prevent metabolism of brown fat. Me-

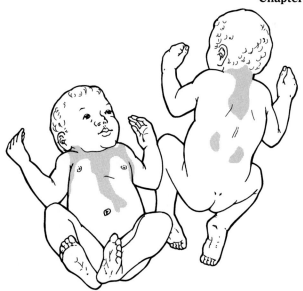

*Figure 20.5   The distribution of brown adipose tissue (brown fat) in the neonate (Adapted from Davis V: Structure and function of brown adipose tissue in the neonate.* J Obstet Gynecol Neonatal Nurs *November/December 1980; 9:364.)*

peridine given to the laboring woman leads to a greater fall in the newborn's body temperature during the neonatal period. It is important to remember that neonatal hypothermia prolongs and increases the effects of many analgesic and anesthetic drugs in the neonate.

Nonshivering thermogenesis occurs when skin receptors perceive a drop in the environmental temperature and in response transmit sensations to the central nervous system, which in turn stimulates the sympathetic nervous system.

Thermographic studies of newborns exposed to cold show an increase in the skin heat over the neonate's brown fat deposits between 1 and 14 days of age. If the brown fat supply has been depleted, the metabolic response to cold will be limited or lacking. A decrease in the environmental temperature of 2° C (36° F) is a drop sufficient to double the oxygen consumption of a term neonate (Avery and Taeusch 1984).

The normal term neonate is usually able to cope with the increase in basal metabolism, but the preterm neonate may be unable to increase ventilation to the necessary level of oxygen consumption. As a consequence, maintaining an optimal thermal environment is an absolute necessity to prevent neonatal cold stress and the resulting metabolic physiologic responses. (See Chapter 24 for discussion of cold stress.)

Shivering, a muscular activity common in the cold adult, is rarely seen in the newborn, although it has been observed at ambient temperatures of 15° C (59° F) or less. If an infant shivers, his or her metabolic rate has already doubled. The extra muscular activity does little to produce needed heat.

# ● HEPATIC ADAPTATION

In the newborn, the liver is frequently palpable 2 to 3 cm below the right costal margin. It is relatively large and occupies about 40% of the abdominal cavity. The neonatal liver plays a significant role in iron storage, carbohydrate metabolism, conjugation of bilirubin, and coagulation.

## ● Iron Storage and Red Blood Cell Production

Neonatal iron stores are determined by total body hemoglobin content and length of gestation. If the mother's iron intake during pregnancy has been adequate, the infant will have stored enough iron to last until the fifth month of neonatal life. At this time, foods containing iron or iron supplements must be given to prevent anemia in the infant.

## ● Carbohydrate Metabolism

Neonatal carbohydrate reserves are relatively low. One third of this reserve is in the form of liver glycogen. Glucose, stored as glycogen in the fetal liver starting during weeks 9–10 of gestation (Korones 1986), is the major source of energy for the fetus. At term, neonatal glycogen stores are twice those of an adult.

Glucose is the main source of energy in the first few hours (four to six) after birth. The blood glucose level falls rapidly and then stabilizes at values of 50–60 mg/dL for several days; by the third postnatal day, values increase to 60–70 mg/dL. Blood glucose levels are influenced by a balance between liver glucose output and peripheral uptake and by body temperature, insulin concentration, and muscular activity.

The newborn enters an energy crunch at the time of birth with the removal of the maternal glucose supply and the increased energy expenditure associated with the birth process and extrauterine life. Fuel sources are consumed at a faster rate because of the work of breathing, loss of heat when exposed to cold, activity, and activation of muscle tone.

If the fetus or neonate experiences hypoxia, the glycogen stores are used and may be depleted to meet metabolic requirements. As stores of liver and muscle glycogen and blood glucose decrease, the neonate compensates by changing from a predominantly carbohydrate metabolism to fat metabolism. Energy is derived from fat and protein as well as from carbohydrates. The amount and availability of these fuel sources depend on constraints imposed by immature metabolic pathways (lack of specific enzymes or hormones) in the first few days of life.

## • Conjugation of Bilirubin

*Conjugation* of bilirubin is the conversion of yellow lipid-soluble pigment into water-soluble pigment. Unconjugated (indirect) bilirubin is a breakdown product derived from hemoglobin that is released from lysed red blood cells and from heme pigments found in cell elements (nonerythrocyte bilirubin). Unconjugated bilirubin is not in ex-

cretable form and is a potential toxin. Total serum bilirubin is the sum of direct (conjugated) and indirect bilirubin.

The fetus does not conjugate bilirubin because unconjugated bilirubin can cross the placenta to be excreted. Fetal unconjugated bilirubin is normally excreted by the placenta in utero, so total bilirubin at birth is usually less than 3 mg/dL unless an abnormal hemolytic process has been present. Postnatally, the infant must conjugate bilirubin (convert a lipid-soluble pigment into a water-soluble pigment) in the liver, producing a rise in serum bilirubin in the first few days of life.

Unconjugated albumin-bound bilirubin is taken up by the liver cells. Since albumin does not transfer into the liver cells, the bilirubin must be transferred to two other intracellular binding proteins labeled Y and Z. These determine the amount of bilirubin held in a liver cell for processing and consequently the potential amount of bilirubin uptake into the liver. The clearance and conjugation of bilirubin depend on the glucuronyl transferase enzyme. Activity of this enzyme results in the attachment of unconjugated bilirubin to glucuronic acid (product of liver glycogen), producing conjugated, direct bilirubin. Direct bilirubin is excreted into the tiny bile ducts, then into the common duct and duodenum. The conjugated bilirubin then progresses down the intestines, where bacteria transform it into urobilinogen. This product is not reabsorbed but is excreted as a yellow-brown pigment in the stools.

The newborn liver has relatively less glucuronyl transferase activity at birth and in the first few weeks of life than an adult liver. This reduction in activity predisposes the newborn to decreased conjugation of bilirubin and increased susceptibility to jaundice.

Even after the bilirubin has been conjugated and bound, it can be converted back to unconjugated bilirubin by enterohepatic circulation. In the intestines β-glucuronidase enzyme acts to split off (deconjugate) the bilirubin from glucuronic acid if it has not first been reduced by gut bacteria to urobilinogen; the free bilirubin is reabsorbed through the intestinal wall and brought back to the liver via portal vein circulation. This recycling of the bilirubin and decreased ability to clear bilirubin from the system are prevalent in babies who have very high β-glucuronidase activity levels as well as delayed bacterial colonization of the gut (see Figure 20.6).

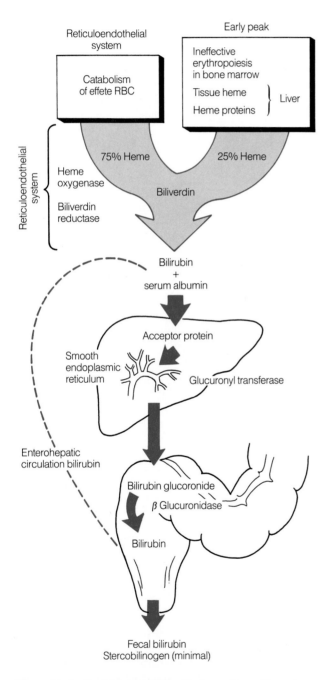

*Figure 20.6   Conjugation of bilirubin in newborns (From Avery GB:* Neonatology: Pathophysiology and Management of the Newborn. *3rd ed. Philadelphia: Lippincott, 1987, p 541.)*

## • Physiologic Jaundice— Icterus Neonatorum

**Physiologic jaundice** is caused by accelerated destruction of fetal RBCs, impaired conjugation of bilirubin, and increased bilirubin reabsorption from the intestinal tract. This condition does not have a pathologic basis, but rather is a normal biologic response of the newborn.

Oski (1984) describes six factors whose interactions may give rise to physiologic jaundice:

1. *Increased amounts of bilirubin delivered to the liver.* The increased blood volume due to delayed cord clamping combined with accelerated RBC destruction leads to an increased bilirubin level in the blood. A proportionately larger amount of nonerythrocyte bilirubin is formed in the neonate. Therefore, newborns have two to three times greater production or breakdown of bilirubin.

2. *Defective uptake of bilirubin from the blood.* Inadequate formation of hepatic binding proteins results in higher bilirubin levels, as seen in hypoproteinemia.

3. *Defective conjugation of the bilirubin.* Decreased glucuronyl-transferase activity results in greater bilirubin values, as in Crigler-Najjar syndrome.

4. *Defect in bilirubin excretion.* A congenital infection may cause impaired excretion. Delay in introduction of bacterial flora and decreased intestinal motility can also delay excretion.

5. *Inadequate hepatic circulation.* Decreased oxygen supplies to the liver associated with neonatal hypoxia or congenital heart disease lead to a rise in the bilirubin level.

6. *Increased reabsorption of bilirubin from the intestine.* Reduced bowel motility, intestinal obstruction, or delayed passage of meconium increases the circulation of bilirubin in the enterohepatic pathway, thereby resulting in higher bilirubin values.

About 50% of full-term neonates and 80% of preterm neonates exhibit physiologic jaundice on about the second or third day after birth. The characteristic yellow color results from increased levels of unconjugated bilirubin, which are a normal product of RBC breakdown and reflect a temporary inability of the body to eliminate bilirubin. The signs of physiologic jaundice appear *after* the first 24 hours postnatally. This differentiates physiologic jaundice from pathologic jaundice (Chapter 24), which is clinically seen at birth or within the first 24 hours of postnatal life.

During the first week, unconjugated bilirubin levels in physiologic jaundice should not exceed 12 to 12.5 mg/dL in the full-term or preterm newborn (Sills and Coen 1984). Peak bilirubin levels are reached between days 3 and 5 in the full-term infant and between days 5 and 6 in the preterm infant. These values are established for European and American newborns. Chinese, Japanese, Korean, and American Indian neonates have considerably higher bilirubin levels that persist for longer periods with no apparent ill effects (Oski 1984).

Nursery environment, including lighting, hinders the early detection of the degree and type of jaundice. Pink walls and artificial lights mask the beginning of jaundice in newborns. Daylight assists the observer in early recognition by eliminating distortions caused by artificial light.

The following nursery procedures are designed to decrease the probability of high bilirubin levels:

● The infant's body temperature is maintained at 36.4° C (97.6° F) or above, since chilling results in acidosis. Acidosis in turn decreases available serum albumin–binding sites, weakens albumin-binding powers, and causes elevated unconjugated bilirubin levels.

● Stool is monitored for amount and characteristics. Bilirubin is eliminated in the feces; inadequate stooling may result in reabsorption and recycling of bilirubin. Early breast-feeding is encouraged because the laxative effect of colostrum increases excretion of stool.

● Early feedings are also encouraged to promote intestinal elimination and bacterial colonization, and to provide caloric intake necessary for formation of hepatic binding proteins.

If jaundice is suspected, the nurse can quickly assess the neonate's coloring by pressing his or her skin with a finger. As the blanching occurs, the nurse can observe the yellow coloring. If jaundice becomes apparent, nursing care is directed toward keeping the neonate well hydrated and promoting intestinal elimination. For specific nursing management and therapies, see p 725.

Physiologic jaundice may be very upsetting to parents; they require emotional support and thorough explanation of the condition. Necessary hospitalization of the newborn for a few additional days may also be disturbing to parents. They should be encouraged to provide for the emotional needs of their newborn by continuing to feed, hold, and caress the infant. If the mother is discharged, the parents should be encouraged to return for feedings and feel free to telephone or visit whenever possible. In many instances, the mother, especially if she is breast-feeding, may elect to remain hospitalized with her infant; this decision should be supported. As an alternative to extended hospitalization, some newborns are treated in home phototherapy programs (Jaundiced babies . . . 1984).

## BREAST-FEEDING JAUNDICE

Breast-feeding is implicated in prolonged jaundice in some newborns. According to Korones (1986), 1% to 5% of newborns being breast-fed will develop breast-feeding jaundice. The breast-fed jaundiced newborn's bilirubin level begins to rise about the fourth day after the mother's milk has come in. The level peaks at two to three weeks of age and may reach 20 to 25 mg/dL without intervention (Oski 1984).

It is theorized that some women's breast milk may contain several times the normal concentration of certain

## Essential Facts to Remember

### Jaundice

#### Physiologic Jaundice

- Physiologic jaundice occurs *after* the first 24 hours of life.
- During first week of life, bilirubin should not exceed 12 mg/dL.
- Bilirubin levels peak at three to five days in term infants.

#### Breast-Milk Jaundice

- Bilirubin levels begin to rise about the fourth day after mature breast milk comes in.
- Peak of 20–25 mg/dL is reached at two to three weeks of age.
- It may be necessary to interrupt nursing for a short period when bilirubin reaches 20 mg/dL.

free fatty acids. These free fatty acids may inhibit the conjugation of bilirubin or increase lipase activity, which disrupts the red blood cell membrane. Increased lipase activity enhances absorption of bile across the GI tract membrane, thereby increasing the enterohepatic circulation of bilirubin. In the past it was thought that the breast milk of women whose newborns have breast-feeding jaundice contained an enzyme that inhibited glucuronyl transferase.

Newborns with breast milk jaundice appear well, and at present there is an absence of documented kernicterus with this type of jaundice. Even so, it is suggested that traditional guidelines should be followed (Neville and Neifert 1983). Interruption of nursing may be advised if bilirubin reaches presumed toxic levels of approximately 20 mg/dL or if the interruption is necessary to establish the cause of the hyperbilirubinemia (Oski 1984). Within 24 to 36 hours after discontinuing breast-feeding, the newborn's serum bilirubin levels begin to fall dramatically, returning to normal levels in four to eight days.

Many physicians believe that breast-feeding may be resumed once other causes of jaundice have been ruled out and breast-feeding is determined to be the cause. The bilirubin concentration may rise 1 to 3 mg/dL with a subsequent decline (Oski 1984). Nursing mothers need encouragement and support in their desire to nurse their infants, assistance and instruction regarding pumping and expressing milk during the interrupted nursing period, and reassurance that nothing is wrong with their milk or mothering abilities. (See Essential Facts to Remember—Jaundice.)

## ● Coagulation

The liver plays an important part in blood coagulation during fetal life and continues this function to some degree during the first few months following birth. Coagulation factors II, VII, IX, and X (synthesized in the liver) are activated under the influence of vitamin K and therefore are considered vitamin K-dependent. The absence of normal flora needed to synthesize vitamin K in the normal newborn gut results in low levels of vitamin K and creates a transient blood coagulation deficiency between the second and fifth day of life. From a low point at about two to three days after birth, these coagulation factors rise slowly, but do not approach normal adult levels until nine months of age or later. Increasing levels of these vitamin K-dependent factors indicate a response to dietary intake and bacterial colonization of the intestines. Although usually no clinical consequences arise, an injection of vitamin K (Aqua-MEPHYTON) is given prophylactically on the day of birth to combat the deficiency. (Hemorrhagic disease of the newborn is discussed in more depth in Chapter 24.) Other coagulation factors having low cord blood levels in normal newborns are XI, XII, and XIII. Fibrinogen and factors V and VIII are near adult ranges (Oski and Naiman 1982).

Platelet counts at birth are in the same range as for adults, but newborns may manifest mild transient platelet aggregation functioning defect. This platelet defect is accentuated by phototherapy (Hatch and Sumner 1981).

Prenatal maternal therapy with phenytoin sodium (Dilantin) or phenobarbital also causes abnormal clotting studies and neonatal bleeding in the first 24 hours after birth. Infants born to mothers receiving coumarin (warfarin) compounds may bleed because these agents cross the placenta and accentuate existing vitamin K-dependent factor deficiencies.

## ● GASTROINTESTINAL ADAPTATION

By 36–38 weeks of fetal life, the gastrointestinal system is fully mature, with enzymatic activity and the ability to transport nutrients. The term neonate has adequate intestinal and pancreatic enzymes to digest most simple carbohydrates, proteins, and fats.

The carbohydrates requiring digestion in the newborn are usually disaccharides (lactose, maltose, and sucrose). Lactose is the primary carbohydrate in the breast-feeding newborn and is generally easily digested and well absorbed. The only enzyme lacking is pancreatic amylase, which remains relatively deficient during the first few months of life. Therefore, newborns have trouble digesting starches (changing more complex carbohydrates into maltose).

Although proteins require more digestion than carbohydrates, they are well digested and absorbed from the neonatal intestine.

The neonate digests and absorbs fats less efficiently because of the minimal activity of the pancreatic enzyme lipase. The neonate excretes about 10%–20% of the dietary fat intake, compared with 10% for the adult. The newborn absorbs the fat in breast milk more completely than the fat in cows' milk because breast milk consists of more medium-chain triglycerides and contains lipase. (See Chapter 23 for further discussion of infant nutrition.) In utero, swallowing is accompanied by gastric emptying and peristalsis of the fetal intestinal tract. By the end of gestation, in preparation for extrauterine life, peristalsis becomes much more pronounced.

Air enters the stomach immediately after birth. The small intestine is filled within 2–12 hours and the large bowel within 24 hours. The salivary glands are immature at birth, and the infant produces little saliva until about age three months. The newborn's stomach has a capacity of about 50–60 mL. It empties intermittently, starting within a few minutes of the beginning of a feeding. Two to four hours after feeding, the stomach is completely empty. The newborn's gastric pH is equal to an adult's, but stomach contents become less acidic in about a week and remain less acid than those of adults for two to three months.

The cardiac sphincter is immature, as is nervous control of the stomach, so some regurgitation may be noted in the neonatal period. Regurgitation of the first few feedings during the first day or two of life can usually be lessened by avoiding overfeeding and by burping the newborn well during and after the feeding.

When no other signs and symptoms are evident, vomiting is often self-limiting and ceases within the first few days of life. However, vomiting or continuous regurgitation should be observed closely. If the neonate has swallowed bloody or purulent amniotic fluid, lavage may be indicated to relieve the problem.

Adequate digestion and absorption are essential for neonatal growth and development. If optimal nutritional support is available, postnatal growth ideally should parallel intrauterine growth; that is, after 30 weeks of gestation, the fetus gains 30 g per day and adds 1.2 cm to body length daily. To gain weight at the intrauterine rate, the term neonate requires 120 calories per kilogram per day. Following birth, caloric intake is often insufficient for weight gain until the neonate is five to ten days old. During this time, there may be a weight loss of 5%–10%. Failure to lose weight when caloric intake is inadequate may indicate fluid retention. Shift of intracellular water to extracellular space and insensible water loss account for the 5%–10% weight loss.

Normal term neonates pass meconium within 12 hours of life or at least within 48 hours (Avery and Tauesch 1984). **Meconium** is formed in utero from the amniotic fluid and its constituents, with intestinal secretions and

## Essential Facts to Remember

### Physiologic Adaptations to Extrauterine Life

- Periodic breathing may be present.
- Desired skin temperature 36–36.5° C (96.8–97.7° F), stabilizes four to six hours after birth.
- Desired blood glucose level reaches 60–70 mg/dL by third postnatal day.
- Stools (progresses from):

  Meconium (thick, tarry, dark green)
  Transitional stools (thin, brown to green)
  Breast-fed infants (yellow gold, soft, or mushy)
  Bottle-fed infants (pale yellow, formed, and pasty)

shed mucosal cells. It is recognized by its thick, tarry, dark green appearance. Transitional (thin brown to green) stools consisting of part meconium and part fecal material are passed for the next day or two, after which the stools become entirely fecal. Generally, the stools of a breast-fed newborn are pale yellow (but may be pasty green); they are more liquid and more frequent than those of formula-fed neonates, whose stools are paler. Frequency of bowel movement varies, but ranges from one every two to three days to as many as ten daily. (See Essential Facts to Remember—Physiologic Adaptations to Extrauterine Life.)

## ● URINARY ADAPTATIONS
## ● Kidney Development and Function

Certain physiologic features of the newborn's kidneys are important to consider when looking at the newborn's ability to handle body fluids and excrete urine.

1. The term newborn's kidneys have a full complement of functioning nephrons.

2. The glomerular filtration rate of the newborn's kidney is low in comparison with the adult rate. Because of this physiologic inefficiency, the newborn's kidney is unable to dispose of water rapidly when necessary.

3. The juxtamedullary portion of the nephron has limited capacity to reabsorb $Na^+$ and $H^+$ and concentrate urine. The limitation of tubular reabsorption can lead to inappropriate loss of substances present in the glomerular filtrate, such as amino acids and bicarbonate.

Full-term newborns are less able than adults to concentrate urine (reabsorb water back into the blood) because the tubules are short and narrow. There is a greater capacity for glomerular filtration than for tubular reabsorption-secretion. Although feeding practices may affect the osmolarity of the urine, the maximum concentrating ability of the newborn is a specific gravity of 1.025. The inability to concentrate urine is due to the limited excretion of solutes (principally sodium, potassium, chloride, bicarbonate, urea, and phosphate) in the growing newborn. The ability to concentrate urine fully is attained by three months of age.

Since the newborn has difficulty concentrating urine, the effect of excessive insensible water loss or restricted fluid intake is unpredictable. The newborn kidney is also limited in its dilutional capabilities. Maximal dilution ability is a specific gravity of 1.001. Concentrating and dilutional limitations of renal function are important considerations in monitoring fluid therapy to avoid dehydration and over-hydration.

## Characteristics of Newborn Urinary Function

Many newborns void immediately after birth and it goes unnoticed. Among normal newborns, 92% void by 24 hours after birth and 99% void by 48 hours (Fanaroff and Martin 1987). A newborn who has not voided by 72 hours should be assessed for adequacy of fluid intake, bladder distention, restlessness, and symptoms of pain. Appropriate clinical personnel should be notified.

The initial bladder volume is 6 to 44 mL of urine. Unless edema is present, normal urinary output is often limited, and the voidings are scanty until fluid intake increases. (The fluid of edema is eliminated by the kidneys, so infants with edema have a much higher urinary output.) The first two days postnatally, the newborn voids two to six times daily, with a urine output of 30 to 60 mL per day. The newborn subsequently voids 5 to 25 times every 24 hours, with a volume of 30 to 50 mL/kg per day.

Following the first voiding, the newborn's urine frequently appears cloudy (due to mucus content) and has a high specific gravity, which decreases as fluid intake increases. Occasionally pink stains ("brick dust spots") ap-

pear on the diaper. These are caused by urates and are innocuous. Blood may occasionally be observed on the diapers of female infants. This *pseudomenstruation* is related to the withdrawal of maternal hormones. Males may have bloody spotting from a circumcision. In the absence of apparent causes for bleeding, the clinician should be notified. Normal urine during early infancy is straw-colored and almost odorless, although odor occurs when certain drugs are given or when infection is present. Table 20.4 contains urinalysis values of the normal newborn.

## • IMMUNOLOGIC ADAPTATIONS

The newborn possesses varying degrees of nonspecific and specific immunity. The nonspecific mechanism is *opsonization,* the coating of invasive bacteria to ready them for ingestion by phagocytes. Specific immunity is provided by *immunoglobulins,* a type of antibody secreted by lymphocytes and plasma cells into the body fluids.

The cells that constitute the immune system appear early in fetal life, but usually are not fully activated until sometime after birth. Opsonization, for example, is impaired at birth. Albumin and globulin, however, are present throughout the last trimester of gestation.

Of the three major types of immunoglobulins primarily involved in immunity—IgG, IgA, and IgM—only IgG crosses the placenta. The pregnant woman forms antibodies in response to illness or immunization. This process is called **active acquired immunity.** When IgG antibodies are transferred to the fetus in utero, **passive acquired immunity** results, since the fetus does not produce the antibodies itself. IgG is very active against bacterial toxins.

Because the maternal immunoglobin is transferred primarily during the third trimester, preterm infants (especially those born prior to 34 weeks) may be more susceptible to infection. In general, newborns have immunity to tetanus, diphtheria, smallpox, measles, mumps, poliomyelitis, and a variety of other bacterial and viral diseases. The period of resistance varies: Immunity against common viral infections such as measles may last four to eight months, whereas immunity to certain bacteria may disappear within four to eight weeks.

The normal newborn does produce antibodies in response to an antigen, but not as effectively as an older child would. It is customary to begin immunization at two months of age, and then the infant can develop active acquired immunity.

IgM immunoglobulins are produced in response to blood group antigens, gram-negative enteric organisms, and some viruses in the expectant mother. Because IgM does not normally cross the placenta, most or all is produced by the fetus beginning at 10–15 weeks' gestation. Elevated levels of IgM at birth may indicate placental leaks

| Table 20.4 Newborn Urinalysis Values |
| --- |
| Protein <5–10 mg/dL |
| WBC <2–3 |
| RBC 0 |
| Casts 0 |
| Bacteria 0 |

or, more commonly, antigenic stimulation in utero. Consequently, elevations suggest that the infant was exposed to an intrauterine infection such as syphilis or a TORCH infection. (For in-depth discussion see Table 24.7.) The lack of available maternal IgM in the newborn also accounts for the infant's susceptibility to gram-negative enteric organisms such as *E coli*.

The functions of IgA immunoglobulins are not fully understood. IgA appears to provide protection mainly on secreting surfaces such as the respiratory tract, gastrointestinal tract, and eyes. Serum IgA does not cross the placenta and is not normally produced by the fetus in utero. Unlike the other immunoglobulins, IgA is not affected by gastric action. Colostrum, the forerunner of breast milk, is very high in the secretory form of IgA. Consequently, it may be of significance in providing some passive immunity to the infant of a breast-feeding mother (Charles and Larsen 1984). Newborns begin to produce secretory IgA in their intestinal mucosa at about four weeks after birth.

# NEUROLOGIC AND SENSORY/PERCEPTUAL FUNCTIONING

The newborn's brain is about one quarter the size of an adult's, and myelination of nerve fibers is incomplete. Unlike the cardiovascular or respiratory systems, which undergo tremendous changes at birth, the nervous system is minimally influenced by the actual birth process.

Because many biochemical and histologic changes have yet to occur in the newborn's brain, the postnatal period is considered a time of risk in regard to the development of the brain and nervous system. For neurologic development—including development of intellect—to proceed, the brain and other nervous system structures must mature in an orderly, unhampered fashion.

## Intrauterine Factors Influencing Newborn Behavior

The newborn responds to and interacts with the environment in a predictable pattern of behavior that is somewhat shaped by his or her intrauterine experience. This intrauterine experience is affected by intrinsic factors such as maternal nutrition and external factors such as the mother's physical environment. Depending on the newborn's intrauterine experience, neonatal behavioral responses to various stresses vary from dealing quietly with the stimulation, to becoming overreactive and tense, to a combination of the two.

Brazelton (1975, 1977) found a positive association between newborn behavior and nutritional status of the pregnant woman. Newborns with higher birth weight attended and responded to visual and auditory cues and exhibited more mature motor activity than low-birth-weight newborns.

Factors such as exposure to intense auditory stimuli in utero can eventually be manifested in the behavior of the newborn. For example, the fetal heart rate initially increases when the pregnant woman is exposed to an auditory stimuli, but repetition of the stimuli leads to decreased FHR. Thus the newborn who was exposed to intense noise during fetal life is significantly less reactive to loud sounds postnatally.

## Characteristics of Newborn Neurologic Function

Partially flexed extremities with the legs near the abdomen is the usual position of the normal newborn. When awake, the newborn may exhibit purposeless, uncoordinated bilateral movements of the extremities.

The organization and the quality of the newborn's motor activity are influenced by a number of factors including the following (Brazelton 1984):

- Sleep-alert states
- Presence of environmental stimuli, such as heat, light, cold, and noise
- Conditions causing a chemical imbalance, such as hypoglycemia
- Hydration status
- State of health
- Recovery from the stress of labor and birth

Eye movements are observable during the first few days of life. An alert neonate is able to fixate on faces and brightly colored objects. If a bright light shines in the newborn's eyes, the blinking response is elicited.

The cry of the newborn should be lusty and vigorous. High-pitched cries, weak cries, or no cries are all causes for concern.

Growth of the newborn's body progresses in a cephalocaudal (head-to-toe), proximal-distal fashion. The newborn is somewhat hypertonic; that is, there is resistance to extending the elbow and knee joints. Muscle tone should be symmetrical. Diminished muscle tone and flaccidity may indicate neurologic dysfunction.

Specific symmetrical deep tendon reflexes can be elicited in the newborn. Plantar flexion is present. Other reflexes, including the Moro, grasping, rooting, and sucking reflexes are characteristic of neurologic integrity.

The performance of complex behavioral patterns is reflective of neonatal integrity. Neonates who can bring a hand to their mouth may be demonstrating motor coordination as well as a self-quieting technique, thus increasing the complexity of the behavioral response. Neonates also possess complex, organized defensive motor patterns as exhibited by the ability to remove an obstruction, such as a cloth across the face.

# Behavioral States of the Newborn

The behavior of the newborn can be divided into two categories, the sleep state and the alert state (Prechtl and Beintema 1964, Brazelton 1984). These postnatal behavioral states are similar to those that have been identified during pregnancy (Nijhuis et al 1982, Tuck 1986). Subcategories are identified under each major category.

## SLEEP STATES

The sleep states are as follows:

1. *Deep or quiet sleep.* Deep sleep is characterized by closed eyes with no eye movements; regular, even breathing; and jerky motions or startles at regular intervals. Behavioral responses to external stimuli are likely to be delayed. Startles are rapidly suppressed, and changes in state are not likely to occur.

2. *Active REM.* Irregular respirations, eyes closed with REM, irregular sucking motions, minimal activity, and irregular but smooth movement of the extremities can be observed in active REM sleep. Environmental and internal stimuli initiate a startle reaction and a change of state.

Sleep cycles in the neonate have been recognized and defined according to duration. The length of the cycle depends on the age of the neonate. At term, REM active sleep and quiet sleep occur in intervals of 45–50 minutes. About 45%–50% of the total sleep of the neonate is active sleep, 35%–45% is quiet (deep) sleep, and 10% of sleep is transitional between these two periods. It is hypothesized that REM sleep stimulates the growth of the neural system. Over a period of time, the neonate's sleep-wake patterns become diurnal; that is, the infant sleeps at night and stays awake during the day. (See Chapter 21 for a short discussion of Brazelton's assessment of neonatal states.)

## ALERT STATES

In the first 30 to 60 minutes after birth, many neonates display a quiet alert state, characteristic of the first period of reactivity (Saigal et al 1981). About 12 to 18 hours after birth, the infant is again alert when the second period of reactivity occurs. (A further description of these two periods of reactivity is found on p 616.) These periods of alertness tend to be short the first two days after birth to allow the baby to recover from the birth process. Subsequently, alert states are of choice or of necessity (Braz-

elton 1984). Increasing choice of wakefulness by the newborn indicates a maturing capacity to achieve and maintain consciousness. Heat, cold, and hunger are but a few of the stimuli that can cause wakefulness by necessity. Once the disturbing stimuli are removed, sleep tends to recur.

The following are subcategories of the alert state (Brazelton 1984):

1. *Drowsy or semidozing.* The behaviors common to the drowsy state are open or closed eyes, fluttering eyelids, semidozing appearance, and slow, regular movements of the extremities. Mild startles may be noted from time to time. Although the reaction to a sensory stimulus is delayed, a change of state often results.

2. *Wide awake (quiet alert).* In the wide-awake state, the neonate is alert and follows and fixates on attractive objects, faces, or auditory stimuli. Motor activity is minimal, and the response to external stimuli is delayed.

3. *Active awake.* The eyes are open and motor activity is quite intense with thrusting movements of the extremities in the active-awake state. Environmental stimuli cause increase in startles or motor activity, but individual reactions are difficult to distinguish because of generalized high activity level.

4. *Crying.* Intense crying is accompanied by jerky motor movements. Crying serves several purposes for the newborn. It may be a distraction from disturbing stimuli such as hunger and pain. Fussiness often allows the neonate to discharge energy and reorganize behavior. Most important, crying elicits an appropriate response of help from the parents.

# Behavioral/Sensory Capacities of the Newborn

**Habituation** is the newborn's ability to process and respond to visual and auditory stimulation. For example, when a bright light is flashed into the neonate's eyes, the initial response is blinking, constriction of the pupil, and perhaps a slight startle reaction. However, with repeated stimulation, the newborn's response repertoire gradually diminishes and disappears. The capacity to ignore repetitious disturbing stimuli is a neonatal defense mechanism readily apparent in the noisy, well-lighted nursery.

**Orientation** is the newborn's ability to be alert to, to follow, and to fixate on complex visual stimuli that are appealing and attractive. The newborn prefers the human face and eyes and bright shiny objects. As the face or object comes into the line of vision, the neonate responds with bright, wide eyes, still limbs, and fixed staring. This intense visual involvement may last several minutes, dur-

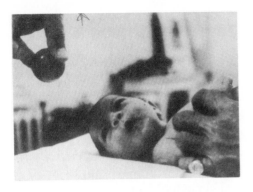

*Figure 20.7   Head turning to follow (From Avery ME, Taeusch HW:* Schaffer's Diseases of the Newborn. *Philadelphia: Saunders, 1984, p 71. Reprinted by permission.)*

ing which time the neonate is able to follow the stimulus from side to side. Figure 20.7 illustrates this response. The newborn uses this sensory capacity to become familiar with family, friends, and surroundings (Figure 20.8).

**Self-quieting ability** refers to newborns' ability to use their own resources to quiet and comfort themselves. Their repertoire includes hand-to-mouth movements, sucking on a fist or tongue, and attending to external stimuli. Neurologically impaired newborns are unable to use self-quieting activities and require more frequent comforting from care givers when stimulated.

## AUDITORY CAPACITY

The newborn responds to auditory stimulation with a definite, organized behavior repertoire. The stimulus used to assess auditory response should be selected to match the state of the newborn. A rattle is appropriate for light sleep, a voice for an awake state, and a clap for deep sleep. As the neonate hears the sound, the cardiac rate rises, and a minimal startle reflex may be observed. If the sound is appealing, the newborn will become alert and search for the site of the auditory stimulus.

## OLFACTORY CAPACITY

Neonates are able to distinguish their mothers' breast pads from those of other mothers by one week postnatally (Brazelton 1984). Apparently this phenomenon is related to the neonate's ability to select by smell.

## TASTE AND SUCKING

The newborn responds differently to varying tastes. Sugar, for example, increases sucking. Sucking pattern variations also exist in newborns fed cows' milk or human breast milk (Brazelton 1984). When breast-feeding, the neonate sucks in bursts with frequent regular pauses. The bottle-fed newborn tends to suck at a regular rate with infrequent pauses.

When awake and hungry, the neonate displays rapid

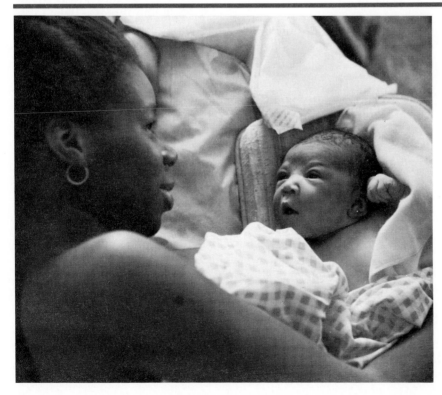

*Figure 20.8   Mother and baby gaze at each other. This quiet, alert state is the optimal state for interaction between baby and parents.*

searching motions in response to the rooting reflex. Once feeding begins, the newborn establishes a sucking pattern according to the method of feeding. Finger sucking is not only present postnatally, but in utero. The neonate frequently uses sucking as a self-quieting activity, which assists in the development of self-regulation.

## TACTILE CAPACITY

The neonate is very sensitive to being touched, cuddled, and held. Often a mother's first response to an upset or crying newborn is touching or holding. Swaddling, placing a hand on the infant's abdomen, or holding the arms to prevent a startle reflex are other methods of soothing the newborn. The settled neonate is then able to attend to and interact with the environment. \

● ● ● ● ● ● ● ● ● ● ● ● ● ● ● ● ● ● ● ● ● ● ● ● ● ● ● ●

# ESSENTIAL CONCEPTS

● **Establishing pulmonary ventilation and the resulting cardiovascular changes are essential for extrauterine survival.**

● **The production of surfactant is crucial to keeping the lungs expanded during expiration by reducing alveolar surface tension.**

● **Neonatal respiration is initiated primarily by chemical and mechanical events in association with thermal and sensory stimulation.**

● **The characteristics of newborn respirations differ from adult respirations because the newborn is an obligatory nose breather. Respirations move from being primarily shallow, irregular, and diaphragmatic to synchronous abdominal and chest breathing.**

● **Periodic breathing is normal, and newborn sleep states affect breathing patterns.**

● **The status of the cardiopulmonary system may be measured by evaluating the heart rate, blood pressure, cardiac output, and presence or absence of murmurs.**

● **Oxygen transport in the newborn is significantly affected by the presence of greater amounts of Hb F (fetal hemoglobin) than Hb A (adult hemoglobin); Hb F holds oxygen easier but releases it to the body tissues only at low $Po_2$ levels.**

● **Blood values in the newborn are modified by several factors such as site of the blood sample, gestational age, prenatal and/or perinatal hemor-**rhage, and the timing of the clamping of the umbilical cord.

● **Blood glucose level should reach 60 to 70 mg/dL by the third postnatal day.**

● **The newborn is considered to have established thermoregulation when oxygen consumption and metabolic activity are minimal.**

● **Excessive heat loss occurs from radiation and convection because of the newborn's larger surface area when compared to weight, and from thermal conduction because of the marked difference between core temperature and skin temperature.**

● **The primary source of heat in the cold-stressed newborn is brown adipose fat.**

● **The normal newborn possesses the ability to digest and absorb nutrients necessary for neonatal growth and development.**

● **The newborn's liver plays a crucial role in iron storage, carbohydrate metabolism, conjugation of bilirubin, and coagulation.**

● **The newborn's stools change from meconium (thick, tarry, dark green) to transitional stools (thin, brown-to-green) and then to the distinct forms for either breast-fed newborns (yellow-gold, soft, or mushy) or bottle-fed newborns (pale yellow, formed, and pasty).**

● **Controversy continues to exist about the relationship of breast-feeding and the development of prolonged jaundice.**

● **The neonatal kidney is characterized by a decreased rate of glomerular flow, limited tubular reabsorption, limited excretion of solutes, and limited ability to concentrate urine. Most newborns void by between 24 and 48 hours of extrauterine life.**

● **The immune system in the newborn is not fully activated until sometime after birth, but the newborn does possess some specific and nonspecific immunologic abilities.**

● **Neurologic and sensory/perceptual functioning in the newborn is evident from the newborn's interaction with the environment, presence of synchronized motor activity, and well-developed sensory capacities.**

● **The behavioral states in the neonate can be divided into sleep states and alert states.**

● ● ● ● ● ● ● ● ● ● ● ● ● ● ● ● ● ● ● ● ● ● ● ● ● ● ● ●

# References

Avery GB: *Neonatology: Pathophysiology and Management of the Newborn,* 3rd ed. Philadelphia: Lippincott, 1987.

Avery, ME, Taeusch HW (editors): *Schaffer's Diseases of the Newborn,* 5th ed. Philadelphia: Saunders, 1984.

Brazelton TB et al: Biomedical variables and neonatal performance of Guatemalan infants. Presented to American Academy of Cerebral Palsy, New Orleans, 1975.

Brazelton TB et al: The behavior of nutritionally deprived Guatemalan neonates. *Dev Med Child Neurol* 1977; 19:364.

Brazelton TB: Neonatal behavior and its significance. In: *Schaffer's Diseases of the Newborn.* Avery ME, Taeusch HW (editors). Philadelphia: Saunders, 1984.

Charles D, Larsen B: How colostrum and milk protect the newborn. *Contemp Obstet Gynecol* 1984; 24(1):143.

Danforth DH and Scott R (editors): *Obstetrics and Gynecology,* 5th ed. Philadelphia: Harper and Row, 1986.

Fanaroff AA, Martin RJ: *Neonatal-Perinatal Medicine,* 4th ed. St Louis: Mosby, 1987.

Goldstein JD, Reid LM: Pulmonary hypoplasia resulting from phrenic nerve agenesis and diaphragmatic amyoplasia. *J Pediatr* 1980; 97:282.

Jaundiced babies bloom with home phototherapy. *Am J Nurs* 1984; 84(7):871.

Jaundiced babies bloom with home phototherapy. *Am J Nurs* 1984; 84(7):871.

Korones SB: *High Risk Newborn Infants: The Basis for Intensive Care Nursing,* 4th ed. St Louis: Mosby, 1986.

Neville MC, Neifert MR: *Lactation: Physiology, Nutrition, and Breastfeeding.* New York: Plenum Press, 1983.

Nijhuis JG et al: Are there behavioral states in the human fetus? *Early Human Dev* 1982; 6:177.

Oski FA: Physiologic jaundice. In: *Schaffer's Diseases of the Newborn.* Avery ME, Taeusch HW (editors). Philadelphia: Saunders, 1984.

Oski FA, Naiman JL: *Hematologic Problems in the Newborn,* 3rd ed. Philadelphia: Saunders, 1982.

Prechtl HFR, Beintema DL: *The Neurological Examination of the Full-Term Newborn Infant.* London: William Heinemann, 1964.

Saigal S et al: Observations on the behavioral state of newborn infants during the first hour of life. *Am J Obstet Gynecol* March 15 1981; 139:716.

Scopes J, Ahmed I: Range of critical temperatures in sick and premature newborn babies. *Arch Dis Child* 1966; 41:417.

Sills JA, Coen RW: The neonate. In: *Maternal Fetal Medicine.* Creasy RK, Resnik R (editors). Philadelphia: Saunders, 1984.

Smith CA, Nelson NM: *The Physiology of the Newborn Infant,* 4th ed. Springfield, IL: Thomas, 1976.

Tuck SM: Ultrasound monitoring of fetal behavior. *Ultrasound Med Biol* April 1986; 12:307.

## Additional Readings

Avery ME, Fletcher BD, Williams RG: *The Lung and Its Disorders in the Newborn Infant,* 4th ed. Philadelphia: Saunders, 1981.

Bernhardt J: Sensory capabilities of the fetus. *Am J Mat Child Nurs* 1987; 12(1):44.

Chess S, Thomas A: Temperamental differences: A critical concept in child health care. *Pediatric Nurs* May/June 1985; 11:167.

Choi EC, Hamilton RK: The effects of culture on mother-infant interaction. *J Obstet Gynecol Neonatal Nurs* 1986; 15(3):256.

Daze AM, Scanlon JW: *Neonatal Nursing.* Baltimore: University Park Press, 1985.

Dierker LJ, Rosen MG: Studying life before birth: The human brain develops. *P/N* 1986; 10(4):10.

Dodman N: Newborn temperature control. *Neonatal Netw* 1987; 5(6):19.

Heck LJ et al: Serum glucose levels in term neonates, during the first 48 hours of life. *J Pediatr* January 1987; 110:119.

Koldvsky O: Perinatal adaptation of gastrointestinal tract functions in man. *P/N* 1987; 11(1):31.

Martin RG: Drug disposition in the neonate. *Neonatal Netw* 1986; 4(4):14.

Ruchala P: The effect of wearing head coverings on the axillary temperatures of infants. *Am J Mat Child Nurs* July/August 1985; 10:240.

Saul K, Warburton D: Increased incidence of early onset hyperbilirubinemia in breast-fed versus bottle-fed infants. *J Perinatol* 1984; 4(3):36.

Tan KL: Blood pressure in full term healthy neonates. *Clin Pediatr* January 1987; 26:21.

# 21

# Nursing Assessment of the Newborn

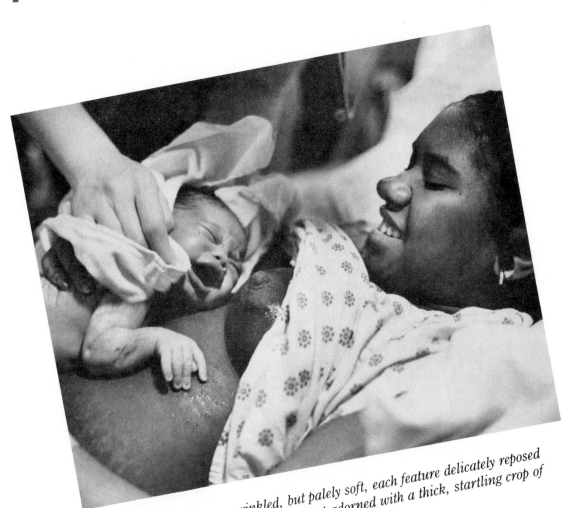

She was not red nor even wrinkled, but palely soft, each feature delicately reposed in its right place, and she was not bald but adorned with a thick, startling crop of black hair. (Margaret Drabble, The Millstone)

## Objectives

● Describe the normal physical and behavioral characteristics of the newborn.

● Summarize the components of a complete newborn assessment.

● Explain the various components of the gestational age assessment.

● Describe the neurologic and/or neuromuscular characteristics of the newborn and the reflexes that may be present at birth.

● Describe the categories of the neonatal behavioral assessment.

## Key Terms

acrocyanosis
Brazelton's neonatal behavioral assessment
caput succedaneum
cephalhematoma
chemical conjunctivitis
Epstein's pearls
Erb-Duchenne paralysis
erythema toxicum
gestational age assessment tools
harlequin sign
milia
molding
mongolian spots
Moro reflex
mottling
nevus flammeus (port-wine stain)
nevus vasculosus (strawberry mark)
pseudomenstruation
rooting reflex
skin turgor
subconjunctival hemorrhage
telangiectatic nevi (stork bites)
thrush
tonic neck reflex
vernix caseosa

Unlike the adult, the newborn communicates needs primarily by behavior. Because the nurse is the most consistent observer of the newborn, he or she must be able to interpret this behavior into information about the neonate's condition and to respond with appropriate nursing interventions. This chapter focuses on the assessment of the neonate and on interpretation of the findings.

Assessment of the newborn is a continuous process designed to evaluate development and adjustments to extrauterine life. In the delivery room, the Apgar scoring procedure (see Chapter 16 for in-depth discussion) and careful observation of the neonate form the basis of assessment and are correlated with information such as:

● Maternal prenatal care history

● Birthing history

● Maternal analgesia and anesthesia

● Complications of labor or birth

● Treatment instituted immediately after birth, in conjunction with determination of clinical gestational age

● Consideration of the classification of newborns by weight and gestational age and by neonatal mortality risk

● Physical examination of the newborn

The nurse incorporates data from these sources with the assessment findings during the first one to four hours after birth to formulate a plan for nursing intervention.

## ● TIMING OF NEWBORN ASSESSMENTS

The first 24 hours of life are significant because during this period the newborn makes the critical transition from intrauterine to extrauterine life. The risk of mortality and morbidity is statistically high during this period. Assessment of the infant is essential to ensure that the transition is proceeding successfully.

There are three major assessments of newborns while they are in the birth facility. The first assessment is done immediately after birth in the birthing area to determine the need for resuscitation or other interventions. The newborn who is stable can stay with the parents after birth to initiate early attachment. The newborn who has complications is taken to the nursery for further evaluation and intervention.

A second evaluation is done in the first one to four hours after birth as part of the routine admission procedures. During this assessment, the nurse carries out a brief physical examination to evaluate the newborn's adaptation to extrauterine life and to estimate gestational age. Any problems that place the newborn at risk are assessed further during this time.

Prior to discharge, a physician or nurse-practitioner does a complete physical examination. A behavioral assessment is also done at this time.

This chapter presents the procedures for estimating gestational age and performing the complete physical examination and behavioral assessment. Chapter 16, p 440 discusses the immediate postdelivery assessment. Chapter 22, p 613 describes the brief assessment performed during the first four hours of life.

## • PARENTAL INVOLVEMENT

The various neonatal assessments and the data obtained from them are only as effective as the degree to which the findings are shared with the parents and incorporated into the interaction between parents and infant. Parents must be included in the assessment process from the moment of their child's birth. The Apgar score and its meaning should be explained immediately to the parents. As soon as possible, the parents should be a part of the physical and behavioral assessments. The examiner should emphasize the uniqueness of their infant.

The nurse can encourage the parents to identify the unique behavioral characteristics of their infant and to learn nurturing activities. Attachment is promoted when parents are allowed to explore their infant in private, identifying individual physical and behavioral characteristics. The nurse's supportive responses to the parents' questions and observations are essential throughout the assessment process. With the nurse's help, attachment and the beginning of interactions between family members are established.

## • ESTIMATION OF GESTATIONAL AGE

The nurse must establish the newborn's gestational age in the first four hours after birth so that careful attention can be given to age-related problems. Traditionally, the gestational age of a neonate was determined from the date of the pregnant woman's last menstrual period. This method was accurate only 75% to 85% of the time. Because of the problems that develop with the newborn who is preterm or whose weight is inappropriate for gestational age, a more accurate system was developed to evaluate the newborn. Once learned, the procedure can be done in a few minutes.

Clinical **gestational age assessment tools** have two components: external physical characteristics and neurologic and/or neuromuscular development evaluations. Physical characteristics generally include sole creases, amount of breast tissue, amount of lanugo, cartilagenous development of the ear, testicular descent, and scrotal rugae or labial development. These objective clinical criteria are not influenced by labor and birth and do not change significantly within the first 24 hours after birth.

During the first 24 hours of life, the newborn's nervous system is unstable; thus, neurologic evaluation findings based on reflexes or assessments dependent on the higher brain centers may not be reliable. If the neurologic findings drastically deviate from the gestational age derived by evaluation of the external characteristics, a second assessment is done in 24 hours.

The neurologic assessment components (excluding reflexes) are the most useful in assessing neonates of less than 34 weeks' gestation. Between 26 and 34 weeks, neurologic changes are significant, whereas significant physical changes are less evident. The important neurologic changes consist of replacement of extensor tone by flexor tone in a *caudocephalad* (tail-to-head) progression. Neurologic examination facilitates assessment of functional or physiologic maturation in addition to physical development.

Of the current gestational assessment aids, Dubowitz and Dubowitz's tool is the most thoroughly documented and validated way to assess intrauterine growth alterations and preterm neonates. This assessment tool lists physical characteristics and neuromuscular tone components to be assessed upon admission to the nursery.

Ballard's *estimation of gestational age* by maturity rating is a simplified version of the Dubowitz tool. The Ballard tool omits some of the neuromuscular tone assessments such as head lag, ventral suspension (which is difficult to assess in the very ill neonate), and leg recoil. The scoring method of Ballard's tool is much like that of the Dubowitz tool; each physical and neuromuscular finding is given a value, and the total score is matched to a gestational age (Figure 21.1). The maximum score on the Ballard's tool is 50, which corresponds to a gestational age of 44 weeks.

For example, upon completing a gestational assessment of a one-hour-old newborn, the nurse gives a score of 3 to all the physical characteristics, for a total of 18, and gives a score of 3 to all the neuromuscular assessments, for a total neurologic score of 18. The physical characteristics score of 18 is added to the neurologic score of 18 for a total score of 36, which correlates with 38+ weeks' gestation. Since all infants vary slightly in the development of physical characteristics and maturation of neurologic function, there will be greater variance in each of these scores instead of all being 3, as in the example.

Both these tools lose accuracy when neonates of less than 28 weeks' or over 43 weeks' gestation are assessed. An additional tool is Brazie and Lubchenco's "Clinical Estimation of Gestational Age" (Appendix E). Some nurseries use the physical characteristics component of this tool as an initial assessment for all neonates admitted to the nursery.

In carrying out gestational age assessments, the nurse should keep in mind that some maternal conditions such as pregnancy-induced hypertension (PIH) and diabetes may affect certain gestational assessment components and warrant further study. Maternal diabetes, although it

## Estimation of Gestational Age by Maturity Rating
Symbols: X=First exam    O=Second exam

### Neuromuscular Maturity

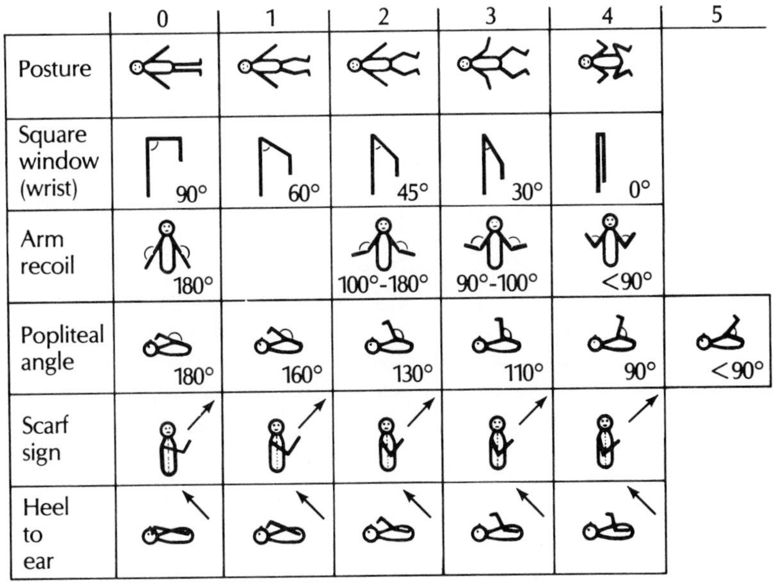

|  | 0 | 1 | 2 | 3 | 4 | 5 |
|---|---|---|---|---|---|---|
| Posture | | | | | | |
| Square window (wrist) | 90° | 60° | 45° | 30° | 0° | |
| Arm recoil | 180° | | 100°–180° | 90°–100° | <90° | |
| Popliteal angle | 180° | 160° | 130° | 110° | 90° | <90° |
| Scarf sign | | | | | | |
| Heel to ear | | | | | | |

Gestation by dates _____ wks.

Birth date _____ Hour _____ am/pm

APGAR _____ 1 min _____ 5 min

| Score | Wks |
|---|---|
| 5 | 26 |
| 10 | 28 |
| 15 | 30 |
| 20 | 32 |
| 25 | 34 |
| 30 | 36 |
| 35 | 38 |
| 40 | 40 |
| 45 | 42 |
| 50 | 44 |

### Physical Maturity

|  | 0 | 1 | 2 | 3 | 4 | 5 |
|---|---|---|---|---|---|---|
| Skin | gelatinous red, transparent | smooth pink, visible veins | superficial peeling and/or rash, few veins | cracking pale area, rare veins, | parchment, deep cracking, no vessels | leathery, cracked, wrinkled |
| Lanugo | none | abundant | thinning | bald areas | mostly bald | |
| Plantar creases | no crease | faint red marks | anterior tansverse crease only | creases on anterior 2/3 of sole | creases cover entire sole | |
| Breast | barely percept. | flat areola, no bud | stippled areola, 1–2 mm bud | raised areola, 3–4 mm bud | full areola, 5–10 mm bud | |
| Ear | pinna flat, stays folded | sl. curved pinna, soft with slow recoil | well-curv. pinna, soft but ready recoil | formed and firm with instant recoil | thick cartilage, ear stiff | |
| Genitals (male) | scrotum empty, no rugae | | testes descending, few rugae | testes down, good rugae | testes pendulous, deep rugae | |
| Genitals (female) | prominent clitoris and labia minora | | majora and minora equally prominent | majora large, minora small | clitoris and minora completely covered | |

*Figure 21.1   Newborn maturity rating and classification (From Ballard JL et al: A simplified assessment of gestational age. Classification of the low-birth-weight infant. In Klaus MH: Pediatr Res 1977; 11:374. Figure adapted from Sweet AY, Fanaroff AA: Care of the High-Risk Infant. Philadelphia: Saunders, 1977, p 47.)*

appears to accelerate fetal growth, seems to retard maturation. Maternal hypertensive states, which retard growth, seem to speed maturation.

Newborns of preeclamptic-eclamptic women suffer a poor correlation with the criteria involving active muscle tone and edema criteria. Babies with respiratory distress syndrome tend to be flaccid and edematous and to assume a "frogleg" posture. These characteristics affect the scoring of the neuromuscular components of the assessment tool.

## ● *Assessment of Physical Characteristics*

The nurse first evaluates observable characteristics without disturbing the infant. Selected physical characteristics common to both gestational assessment tools are presented here in the order in which they might be evaluated most effectively:

1. *Resting posture,* although a neuromuscular component, should be assessed as the infant lies undisturbed on a flat surface (Figure 21.2).
2. *Skin* in the preterm neonate appears thin and transparent, with veins prominent over the abdomen early in gestation. As term approaches, the skin

appears opaque because of increased subcutaneous tissue. Disappearance of the protective vernix caseosa promotes skin desquamation and is commonly seen in postmature infants.

3. *Lanugo,* a fine hair covering, decreases as gestational age increases. The amount of lanugo is greatest at 28–30 weeks and then disappears, first from the face, then from the trunk and extremities.
4. *Sole (plantar) creases* are reliable indicators of gestational age in the first 12 hours of life. After this, the skin of the foot begins drying, and superficial creases appear. Development of sole creases begins at the top (anterior) portion of the sole and, as gestation progresses, proceeds to the heel (Figure 21.3). Peeling may also occur. Plantar creases vary with race. Black newborns' sole creases may be less developed at term.
5. The *areola* is inspected and the *breast bud tissue* is gently palpated by application of the forefinger and middle finger to the breast area and is measured in centimeters or millimeters (Figure 21.4). At term gestation, the tissue will measure between 0.5 and 1 cm (5 to 10 mm). During the assessment the

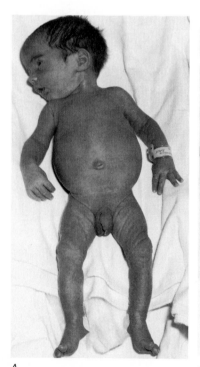
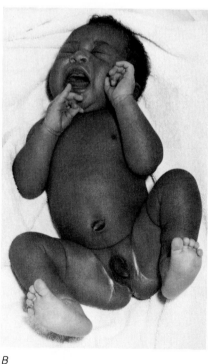
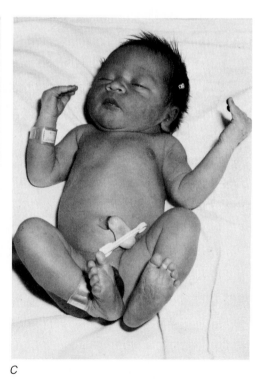

A    B    C

*Figure 21.2    Resting posture: (A) Infant exhibits beginning of flexion of the thigh. The gestational age is approximately 31 weeks. Note the extension of the upper extremities. (B) Infant exhibits stronger flexion of the arms, hips, and thighs. The gestational age is approximately 35 weeks. (C) The full-term infant exhibits hypertonic flexion of all extremities. (From Dubowitz L, Dubowitz V: The Gestational Age of the Newborn. Menlo Park, CA: Addison-Wesley, 1977.)*

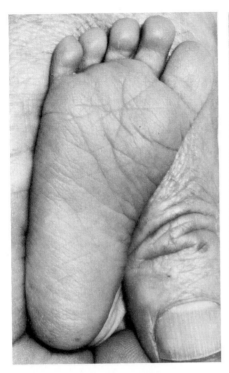
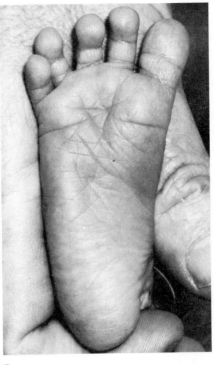
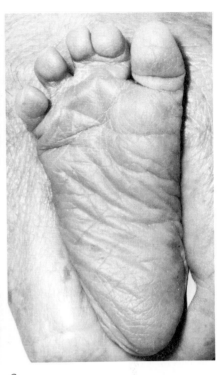

A        B        C

*Figure 21.3 Sole creases: (A) Infant has a few sole creases on the anterior portion of the foot. Note the slick heel. The gestational age is approximately 35 weeks. (B) Infant has a deeper network of sole creases on the anterior two thirds of the sole. Note the slick heel. The gestational age is approximately 37 weeks. (C) The full-term infant has deep sole creases down to and including the heel as the skin loses fluid and dries after birth; sole (plantar) creases can be seen even in preterm newborns. (From Dubowitz L, Dubowitz V: Gestational Age of the Newborn. Menlo Park, CA: Addison-Wesley, 1977.)*

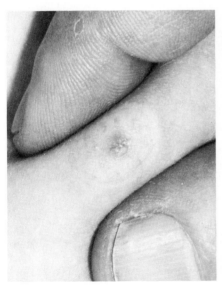
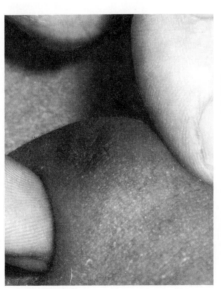
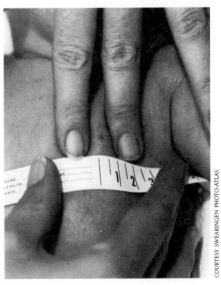

A        B        C

*Figure 21.4 Breast tissue: (A) Newborn has a visible raised area. On palpation the area is 4 mm. The gestational age is 38 weeks. (B) Newborn has 10 mm breast tissue area. The gestational age is 40 to 44 weeks. (C) Gently compress the tissue between middle and index finger and measure the tissue in centimeters or millimeters. Absence of or decreased breast tissue often indicates premature or SGA newborn. (From Dubowitz L, Dubowitz V: Gestational Age of the Newborn. Menlo Park, CA: Addison-Wesley, 1977; Swearingen PL: The Addison-Wesley Photo-Atlas of Nursing Procedures. Menlo Park, CA: Addison-Wesley, 1984.)*

nipple should not be grasped because skin and subcutaneous tissue will prevent accurate estimation of size. The nurse may also cause trauma to the breast tissue if this procedure is not done gently.

As gestation progresses, the breast tissue mass and areola enlarge. However, a large breast tissue mass can occur as a result of conditions other than advanced gestational age. The infant of a diabetic mother tends to be large for gestational age (LGA) and the accelerated development of breast tissue is a reflection of subcutaneous fat deposits. Small for gestational age (SGA) term or postterm newborns may have used subcutaneous fat (which would have been deposited as breast tissue) to survive in utero; as a result, their lack of breast tissue may indicate a gestational age of 34 to 35 weeks, even though other factors indicate a *term* or *postterm* neonate.

6. *Ear form and cartilage distribution* develop with gestational age. The cartilage gives the ear its shape and substance (Figure 21.5). In a newborn of less than 34 weeks' gestation the ear is relatively shapeless and flat; it has little cartilage, so the ear folds over on itself and remains folded. By approximately 36 weeks' gestation, some cartilage and slight incurving of upper pinna are present, and the pinna springs back slowly when folded. (This response is tested by holding the top and bottom of the pinna together with the forefinger and thumb and then releasing it, or by folding the pinna of the ear forward against the side of the head, releasing it, and observing the response.) By term, the newborn's pinna is firm, stands away from the head, and springs back quickly from the folding.

7. *Male genitals* are evaluated for size of the scrotal sac, the presence of rugae, and descent of the testes (Figure 21.6). Prior to 36 weeks, the scrotum has few rugae, and the testes are palpable in the inguinal canal. By 36–38 weeks, the testes are in the upper scrotum, and rugae have developed over the anterior portion of the scrotum. By term, the testes are generally in the lower scrotum, which is pendulous and covered with rugae.

8. The appearance of the *female genitals* depends in part on subcutaneous fat deposition and therefore relates to fetal nutritional status (Figure 21.7). The clitoris varies in size and occasionally is so large that it is difficult to identify the sex of the infant. This may be caused by adrenogenital syndrome, which causes the adrenals to secrete excessive amounts of androgen and other hormones. At 30 to 32 weeks' gestation, the clitoris is prominent, and the labia majora are small and widely separated. As gestational age increases, the labia majora increase in size. At 36 to 40 weeks, they nearly cover the

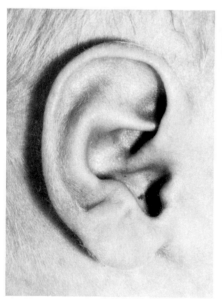
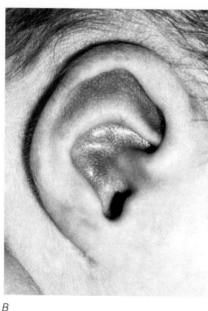
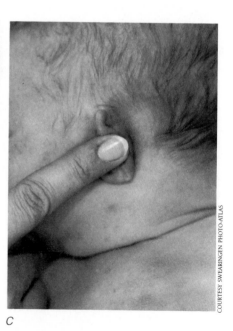

A  B  C

COURTESY SWEARINGEN PHOTO-ATLAS

*Figure 21.5  Ear form and cartilage: (A) The ear of the infant at approximately 36 weeks' gestation shows incurving of the upper two thirds of the pinna. (B) Infant at term shows well-defined incurving of the entire pinna. (C) If the auricle stays in the position in which it is pressed, or returns slowly to its original position, it usually means the gestational age is less than 38 weeks. (From Dubowitz L, Dubowitz V: Gestational Age of the Newborn. Menlo Park, CA: Addison Wesley, 1977; Swearingen PL: The Addison-Wesley Photo-Atlas of Nursing Procedures. Menlo Park, CA: Addison-Wesley, 1984.)*

clitoris. At 40 weeks and beyond, the labia majora cover the labia minora and clitoris.

Other physical characteristics assessed by some gestational age scoring tools include the following:

1. *Vernix* covers the preterm newborn. The postterm infant has no vernix. After noting vernix distribution, the birthing area nurse dries the newborn to prevent evaporative heat loss, thus disturbing the vernix. The birthing area nurse must communicate to the neonatal nurse the amount of vernix and the areas of vernix coverage.

2. *Hair* of the preterm infant has the consistency of matted wool or fur and lies in bunches rather than in the silky, single strands of the term newborn's hair.

3. *Skull firmness* increases as the fetus matures. In a term newborn the bones are hard, and the sutures are not easily displaced. The nurse should not attempt to displace the sutures forceably.

4. *Nails* appear and cover the nail bed at about 20 weeks' gestation. Nails extending beyond the fingertips may be indicative of a postterm newborn.

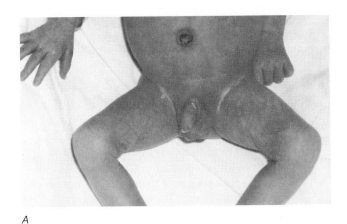

A

B

*Figure 21.6 Male genitals: (A) A preterm infant's testes are not within the scrotum. The scrotal surface has few rugae. (B) Term infant's testes are generally fully descended. The entire surface of the scrotum is covered by rugae. (From Dubowitz L, Dubowitz V:* Gestational Age of the Newborn. *Menlo Park, CA: Addison-Wesley, 1977; Swearingen PL:* The Addison-Wesley Photo-Atlas of Nursing Procedures. *Menlo Park, CA: Addison-Wesley, 1984.)*

COURTESY SWEARINGEN PHOTO-ATLAS

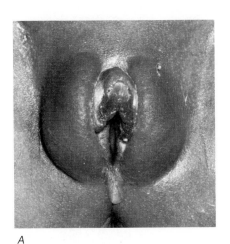

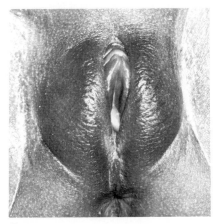

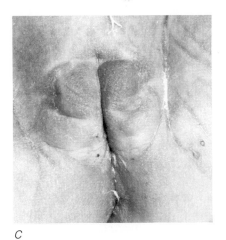

A

B

C

*Figure 21.7 Female genitals: (A) Infant has a prominent clitoris. The labia majora are widely separated, and the labia minora, viewed laterally, would protrude beyond the labia majora. The gestational age is 30 to 36 weeks. (B) The clitoris is still visible; the labia minora are now covered by the larger labia majora. The gestational age is 36 to 40 weeks. (C) The term infant has well developed, large labia majora that cover both the clitoris and the labia minora. (From Dubowitz L, Dubowitz V:* Gestational Age of the Newborn. *Menlo Park, CA: Addison-Wesley, 1977.)*

## ● Assessment of Neuromuscular Maturity Characteristics

The central nervous system of the human fetus matures at a fairly constant rate. Specific neurologic parameters correlated to gestational age have been established. Tests have been designed to evaluate neurologic status as manifested by neuromuscular tone development. In the fetus, neuromuscular tone develops from the lower to the upper extremities. The neurologic evaluation requires more manipulation and disturbances than the physical evaluation of the neonate.

The neuromuscular evaluation (refer to Figure 21.1) is best performed when the infant has stabilized. The following characteristics are evaluated:

1. The *square window sign* is elicited by flexing the neonate's hand toward the ventral forearm. The angle formed at the wrist is measured (Figure 21.8).

2. *Recoil* is a test of flexion development. Because flexion first develops in the lower extremities, recoil is first tested in the legs. The neonate is placed on his or her back on a flat surface. With a hand on the neonate's knees and while manipulating the hip joint, the nurse places the neonate's legs in flexion, then extends them parallel to each other and flat on the surface. The response to this maneuver is recoil of the neonate's legs. According to gestational age, they may not move or they may return slowly or quickly to the flexed position.

    Arm recoil is tested by flexion at the elbow and extension of the arms at the newborn's side.

While the baby is in the supine position, the nurse completely flexes both elbows, holds them in this position for five seconds, extends the arms at the baby's side, and releases them. Upon release, the elbows of a full-term newborn form an angle of less than 90° and rapidly recoil back to flexed position. The elbows of preterm newborns have slower recoil time and form a less-than-90° angle. Arm recoil is also slower in healthy but fatigued newborns after birth; therefore arm recoil is best elicited after the first hour of birth when the baby has had time to recover from the stress of birth.

3. The *popliteal angle* (degree of knee flexion) is determined with the newborn supine and flat. The thigh is flexed on the abdomen/chest, and the nurse places the index finger of the other hand behind the newborn's ankle to extend the lower leg until resistance is met. The angle formed is then measured. Results vary from no resistance in the very immature infant to an 80° angle in the term infant.

4. The *scarf sign* is elicited by placing the neonate supine and drawing an arm across the chest toward the infant's opposite shoulder until resistance is met. The location of the elbow is then noted in relation to the midline of the chest (Figure 21.9).

5. The *heel-to-ear extension* is performed by placing the infant in a supine position and then gently drawing the foot toward the ear on the same side until resistance is felt. Both the popliteal angle and the proximity of foot to ear are assessed. In a very

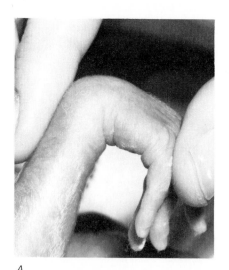
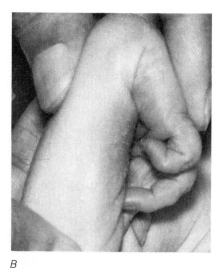
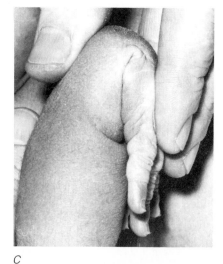

A

B

C

*Figure 21.8   Square window sign: (A) This angle is 90° and suggests an immature newborn of 28 to 32 weeks' gestation. (B) A 30° angle is commonly found from 38 to 40 weeks' gestation.*

*(C) A 0° angle occurs from 40 to 42 weeks. (From Dubowitz L, Dubowitz V: Gestational Age of the Newborn. Menlo Park, CA: Addison-Wesley, 1977.)*

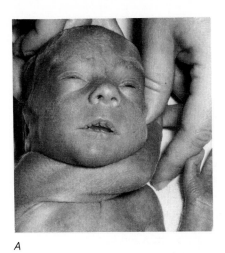

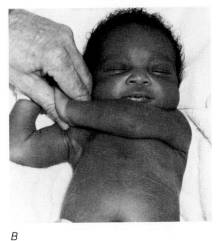

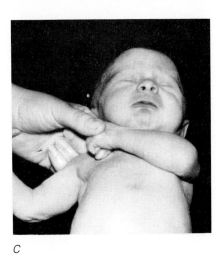

A

B

C

*Figure 21.9  Scarf sign: (A) No resistance is noted until after 30 weeks' gestation. The elbow can be readily moved past the midline. (B) The elbow is at midline at 36 to 40 weeks' gestation.*

*(C) Beyond 40 weeks' gestation, the elbow will not reach the midline. (From Dubowitz L, Dubowitz V: Gestational Age of the Newborn. Menlo Park, CA: Addison-Wesley, 1977.)*

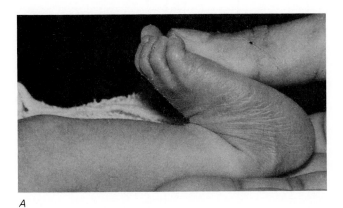

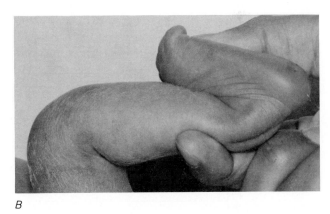

A

B

*Figure 21.10  Ankle dorsiflexion: (A) A 45° angle is indicative of 32 to 36 weeks' gestation. A 20° angle is indicative of 36 to 40 weeks' gestation. (B) An angle of 0° is common at gestational age*

*of 40 weeks or more. (From Dubowitz L, Dubowitz V: Gestational Age of the Newborn. Menlo Park, CA: Addison-Wesley, 1977.)*

immature infant, the leg will remain straight and the foot will go to the ear or beyond. Maneuvers involving the lower extremities of newborns who had frank breech presentation should be delayed to allow for resolution of leg positioning (Ballard et al 1979).

6.  *Ankle dorsiflexion* is determined by flexing the ankle on the shin. The examiner uses a thumb to push on the sole of the neonate's foot while the fingers support the back of the neonate's leg. Then the angle formed between the foot and the interior leg is measured (see Figure 21.10). This sign can be influenced by intrauterine position and congenital deformities.

7.  Head lag (*neck flexors*) is measured by pulling the

neonate to a sitting position and noting the degree of head lag. Total lag is common in infants up to 34 weeks' gestation, whereas postmature infants (42 weeks) will hold their head in front of their body line.

8.  Ventral suspension (*horizontal position*) is evaluated by holding the infant prone on the examiner's hand. The position of head and back and degree of flexion in the arms and legs are then noted. Some flexion of arms and legs indicates 36–38 weeks' gestation; fully flexed extremities, with head and back even, are characteristic of a term neonate.

9.  *Major reflexes* such as sucking, rooting, grasping, Moro, tonic neck, and others are evaluated and scored. (See p 593.)

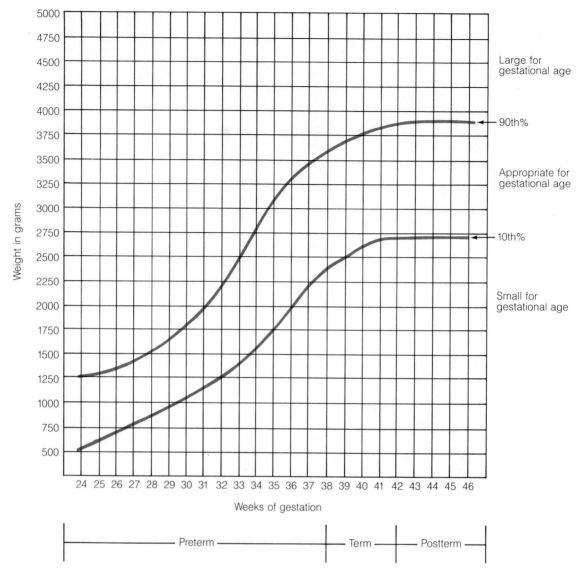

*Figure 21.11    Classification of newborns by birth weight and gestational age. The newborn's birth weight and gestational age are placed on the graph. The newborn is then classified as large for gestational age, appropriate for gestational age, or small for gestational age.*

Determination of gestational age (see p 570) and correlation with birth weight (Figure 21.11) enables the nurse to assess the infant more accurately and to anticipate possible physiologic problems. This information is then used in conjunction with a complete physical examination to determine priorities and to establish a plan of care appropriate to the individual infant.

# ● PHYSICAL ASSESSMENT

After the initial determination of gestational age and related potential problems, a more extensive physical assessment is done. The nursing student is expected to be able to do most of the assessments, although she or he may not be required to know all the alterations and possible causes. The nurse should choose a warm, well-lighted area that is free of drafts. Completing the physical assessment in the presence of the parents provides an opportunity to acquaint them with their unique newborn. The examination should be performed in a systematic, head-to-toe manner and all findings recorded. When assessing the physical and neurologic status of the newborn, the nurse should first consider general appearance and then proceed to specific areas.

A guide for systematically assessing the newborn appears on pp 596–609. Normal findings, alterations, and related causes are presented and correlated with suggested nursing responses. The findings are typical for a full-term newborn.

## ● General Appearance

The newborn's head is disproportionately large for the body. The center of the baby's body is the umbilicus rather than the symphysis pubis, as in the adult. The body appears long and the extremities short. The flexed position that the neonate maintains contributes to the apparent shortness of the extremities. The hands are tightly clenched. The neck looks short because the chin rests on the chest. Newborns have a prominent abdomen, sloping shoulders, narrow hips, and rounded chests. They tend to stay in a flexed position similar to the one maintained in utero and will offer resistance when the extremities are straightened. After a breech birth, the feet are usually dorsiflexed, and it may take several weeks for the newborn to assume typical newborn posture.

## ● Weight and Measurements

The normal full-term Caucasian newborn has an average birth weight of 3405 g (7 lb, 8 oz), whereas black, Asian, and Native American newborns are usually somewhat smaller. Other factors that influence weight are age and size of parents, health of mother, and the interval between pregnancies. After the first week and for the first six months, the neonate's weight will increase about 198 g (7 oz) weekly.

Approximately 70%–75% of the neonate's body weight is water. During the initial newborn period (the first three or four days), there is a physiologic weight loss of about 5%–10% for term infants because of fluid shifts. This weight loss may reach 15% for preterm infants. Large babies may also tend to lose more weight because of greater fluid loss in proportion to birth weight. If weight loss is greater than expected, clinical reappraisal is indicated. Factors contributing to weight loss include small fluid intake resulting from delayed breast-feeding or a slow adjustment to the formula, increased volume of meconium excreted, and urination. Weight loss may be marked in the presence of temperature elevation because of associated dehydration.

The length of the normal newborn is difficult to measure because the legs are flexed and tensed. To measure length, the nurse should place infants flat on their backs with legs extended as much as possible (Figure 21.12). The average length is 50 cm (20 in), with the range being 45–55 cm (18–22 in). The newborn will grow approximately an inch a month for the next six months. This is the period of most rapid growth.

At birth, the newborn's head is one third the size of an adult's head. The circumference of the newborn's head is 32–37 cm (12½–14½ in). For accurate measurement, the

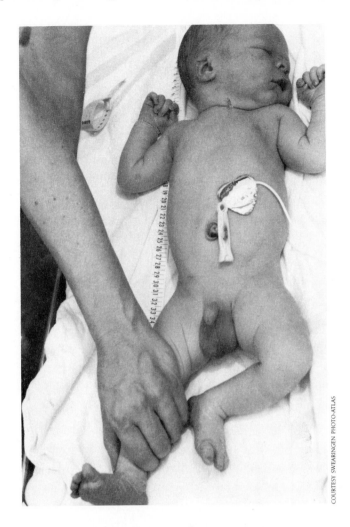

*Figure 21.12 Measuring the length of a newborn (From Swearingen PL: The Addison-Wesley Photo-Atlas of Nursing Procedures. Menlo Park, CA: Addison-Wesley, 1984.)*

tape is placed over the most prominent part of the occiput and brought to just above the eyebrows (Figure 21.13, **A**). The circumference of the newborn's head is approximately 2 cm greater than the circumference of the newborn's chest at birth and will remain in this proportion for the next few months. (Factors that alter this measurement are discussed on p 582.)

The average circumference of the chest at birth is 32 cm (12.5 in). Chest measurements should be taken with the tape measure at the lower edge of the scapulas and brought around anteriorly directly over the nipple line (Figure 21.13, **B**). The abdominal circumference or girth may also be measured at this time by placing the tape around the newborn's abdomen at the level of the umbilicus, with the bottom edge of the tape at the top edge of the umbilicus. (See Essential Facts to Remember—Measurements.)

## Essential Facts to Remember

### Measurements

#### Weight

Average: 3405 g (7 lb, 8 oz)

Range: 2500–4000 g (5 lb, 8 oz–8 lb, 13 oz)

Weight is influenced by racial origin and maternal age and size

Physiologic weight loss: 5%–10% for term infants, up to 15% for preterm infants

Growth: 7 oz (198 g) per week for first six months

#### Length

Average: 50 cm (20 in)

Range: 45–55 cm (18–22 in)

Growth: 1 inch (2.5 cm) per month for first six months.

#### Head Circumference

32–37 cm (12½–14½ in)

Approximately 2 cm larger than chest circumference

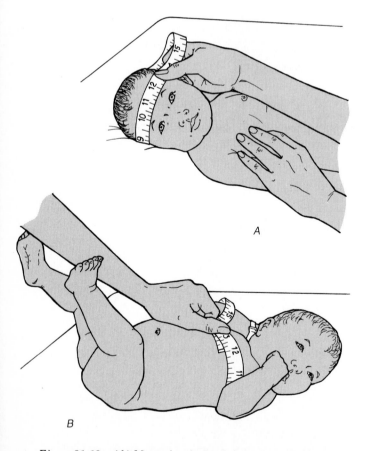

*Figure 21.13* **(A)** *Measuring the head circumference of the newborn.* **(B)** *Measuring the chest circumference of the newborn.*

## ● Temperature

Initial assessment of the newborn's temperature is critical. In utero, the temperature of the fetus is about the same as or slightly higher than the expectant mother's. When the baby enters the outside world, his or her temperature can suddenly drop as a result of exposure to cold drafts and the skin's heat-loss mechanisms.

If no heat conservation measures are instituted, the normal term newborn's deep body temperature falls 0.1°C (0.2°F) per minute; skin temperature lowers 0.3°C (0.5°F) per minute. Marked decrease in skin temperature occurs within ten minutes after exposure to room air (Korones 1986). The temperature should stabilize within 8 to 12 hours. Temperature should be monitored when the newborn is admitted to the nursery and at four-hour intervals until stable, then once every eight-hour shift (AAP 1988). Many institutions use a continuous probe, or measurements are obtained every 15 to 30 minutes for the first hour, then each hour for four hours. (See Chapter 20 for a discussion of the physiology of temperature regulation.)

Body temperature can be assessed either by the rectum, axilla, or skin. Rectal temperature is assumed to be the closest approximation to core temperature, but this depends on the depth of the thermometer insertion. Normal rectal temperature is 36.6°C to 37.2°C (97.8° to 99°F). The rectal route is not recommended as a routine method as it may predispose to rectal mucosal irritation and increase chances of perforation (AAP 1988). If the temperature is taken rectally, the nurse holds the thermometer in the rectum for five minutes (Figure 21.14, *A*). Rectal temperatures were previously advocated to detect imperforate anus, but nurses can make this assessment by observing the newborn's stools.

Axillary temperature reflects body temperature and the body's compensatory response to the thermal environment. Axillary temperatures are recommended as an alternative to rectal temperatures. Axillary temperatures are reliable as a close estimation of the rectal temperature (Korones 1986). In preterm and term newborns, there is less than 0.10°C (0.20°F) difference between the two sites. If the axillary method is used, the thermometer must remain in place at least three minutes unless an electronic thermometer is used (Figure 21.14, *B*). Normal axillary temperature ranges from 36.5°C to 37°C (97.7°F to 98.6°F). Axillary temperatures can be misleading because the friction caused by apposition of the inner arm skin and upper chest wall and the nearness of brown fat to the probe may elevate the temperature.

The best measure of skin temperature is by means of continuous skin probe rather than axillary temperature, especially for small newborns or newborns maintained in incubators or under radiant warmers. Normal skin temperature is 36°C to 36.5°C (96.8°F to 97.7°F). Skin tem-

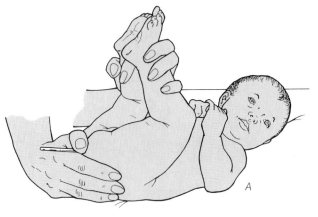

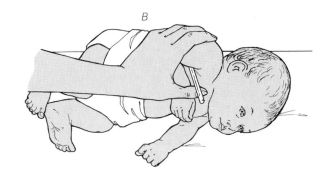

*Figure 21.14   (A) The rectal thermometer must be held in place for five minutes and the legs supported. (B) The axillary temperature should be taken for three minutes. The newborn's arm should be tightly but gently pressed against the thermometer and the newborn's side as illustrated.*

perature assessment allows time for initiation of interventions prior to a more serious fall in core temperatures.

Temperature instability, a deviation of more than 1°C (2°F) from one reading to the next, or a subnormal temperature may indicate an infection. In contrast to an elevated temperature in older children, an increased temperature in a newborn may indicate reactions to too much covering, too hot a room, or dehydration. Dehydration, which tends to increase body temperature, occurs in newborns whose feedings have been delayed for any reason. Newborns respond to overheating (temperature greater than 37.5°C or 99.5°F) by increased restlessness and eventually by perspiration. The perspiration is initially seen on the head and face, then on the chest.

## ● Skin Characteristics

The skin of the newborn should be pink-tinged or ruddy in color and warm to the touch. The ruddy color results from increased concentration of red blood cells in the blood vessels and from limited subcutaneous fat deposits.

## ACROCYANOSIS

**Acrocyanosis** (bluish discoloration of the hands and feet) may be present in the first two to six hours after birth. This condition is due to poor peripheral circulation, which results in vasomotor instability and capillary stasis, especially when the newborn is exposed to cold. If the central circulation is adequate, the blood supply should return quickly when the skin is blanched with a finger. (See Color Plate V.)

**Mottling** (lacy pattern of dilated blood vessels under the skin) occurs as a result of general circulation fluctuations. It may last several hours to several weeks or may come and go periodically.

## HARLEQUIN SIGN

**Harlequin sign** (clown) color change is occasionally noted: A deep red color develops over one side of the infant's body while the other side remains pale, so that the skin resembles a clown's suit. This color change results from a vasomotor disturbance in which blood vessels on one side dilate while the vessels on the other side constrict. It usually lasts from 1–20 minutes. Affected neonates may have single or multiple episodes.

## JAUNDICE

*Jaundice* is first detectable on the face (where skin overlies cartilage) and the mucous membranes of the mouth. It is evaluated by blanching the tip of the nose, the forehead, the sternum, or the gum line. This procedure must be carried out in appropriate lighting. If jaundice is present, the area will appear yellowish immediately after blanching. Another area to assess for jaundice is the sclera. Evaluation and determination of the cause of jaundice must be initiated immediately to prevent possibly serious sequelae. For detailed discussion of causes and assessment of jaundice see Chapter 24.

## ERYTHEMA NEONATORUM TOXICUM

**Erythema toxicum** is a perifollicular eruption of lesions that are firm, vary in size from 1 to 3 mm, and consist of a white or pale yellow papule or pustule with an erythematous base. The rash may appear suddenly, usually over the trunk and diaper area, and is frequently widespread. (See Color Plate XII.) The lesions do not appear on the palms of the hands or the soles of the feet. The peak incidence is at 24 to 48 hours of life. The cause is unknown and no treatment is necessary. Some clinicians feel it may be caused by irritation from clothing. The lesions disappear in a few hours or days. If a maculopapular rash appears and there is a question whether it is erythema toxicum, a smear of the aspirated papule will show numerous eosinophils on staining and no bacteria will be cultured.

## SKIN TURGOR

**Skin turgor** is assessed to determine hydration status, the need to initiate early feedings, and the presence of any infectious processes. The usual place to assess skin turgor is over the abdomen. Skin should be elastic (return to original shape).

## VERNIX CASEOSA

**Vernix caseosa,** a whitish cheeselike substance, covers the fetus while in utero and lubricates the skin of the newborn. The skin of the term or postterm infant has less vernix and is frequently dry, and peeling is common, especially on the hands and feet.

## MILIA

**Milia,** which are exposed sebaceous glands, appear as raised white spots on the face, especially across the nose. (See Color Plate VIII.)

## FORCEPS MARKS

Forceps marks may be present after a difficult forceps birth. The newborn may have reddened areas over the cheeks and jaws. It is important to reassure the parents that these will disappear, usually within one or two days. Transient facial paralysis resulting from the forceps pressure is a rare complication.

## ● Birthmarks

### TELANGIECTATIC NEVI

**Telangiectatic nevi,** or **"stork bites,"** appear as pale pink or red spots and are frequently found on the eyelids, nose, lower occipital bone, and nape of the neck. (See Color Plate IX.) These lesions are common in light-complexioned neonates and are more noticeable during periods of crying. These areas blanch easily, have no clinical significance, and usually fade by the second birthday.

### MONGOLIAN SPOTS

**Mongolian spots** are macular areas of bluish-black pigmentation found on the dorsal area and the buttocks. (See Color Plate VII.) They are common in Asian and black infants and newborns of other dark-skinned races. They gradually fade during the first or second year of life.

### NEVUS FLAMMEUS

**Nevus flammeus** or **port-wine stain,** is a capillary angioma directly below the epidermis. It is a nonelevated, sharply demarcated, red-to-purple dense area of capillaries. (See Color Plate X.) The size and shape are variable, but it commonly appears on the face. It does not grow in size, does not fade with time, and does not blanch as a rule. In the black infant, the nevus flammeus appears jet black in color. The birthmark may be concealed by using an opaque cosmetic cream. If convulsions and other neurologic problems accompany the nevus flammeus, it is suggestive of Sturge-Weber syndrome with involvement of the fifth cranial nerve.

### NEVUS VASCULOSUS

**Nevus vasculosus,** or **"strawberry mark,"** is a capillary hemangioma. It consists of newly formed and enlarged capillaries in the dermal and subdermal layers. It is a raised, clearly delineated, dark red, rough-surfaced birthmark commonly found in the head region. Such marks usually grow (often rapidly) for several months and become fixed in size by eight months. They then begin to shrink and start to resolve spontaneously several weeks to months after peak growth is reached. Except in rare cases, they are completely gone by the time the child is 7 years old. Parents can be told that resolution is heralded by a pale purple or gray spot on the surface of the hemangioma. The best cosmetic effect is achieved when the lesions are allowed to resolve spontaneously.

Birthmarks are frequently a cause of concern for parents. The mother may be especially anxious, fearing that she is to blame ("Is my baby 'marked' because of something I did?"). Guilt feelings are common in the presence of misconceptions about the cause. Birthmarks should be identified and explained to the parents. By providing appropriate information about the cause and course of birthmarks, the nurse frequently relieves the fears and anxieties of the family.

## ● Head

### GENERAL APPEARANCE

The newborn's head is large (approximately one fourth of the body size), with soft, pliable skull bones. The head may appear asymmetrical in the newborn of a vertex delivery. This asymmetry, called **molding,** is caused by overriding of the cranial bones during labor and birth (Figure 21.15). Within a few days after birth, the overriding usually diminishes and the suture lines become palpable. Because head measurements are affected by molding, a second measurement is indicated a few days after birth. The heads of breech-born newborns and those born by elective cesarean are characteristically round and well shaped since pressure was not exerted on them during birth. Any extreme differences in head size may indicate microcephaly or hydrocephalus. Variations in the shape, size, or appearance of the head measurements may be due

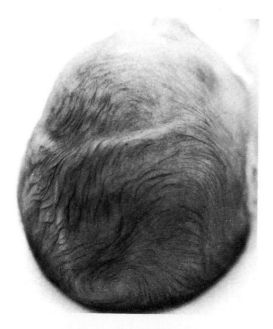

*Figure 21.15    Overlapped cranial bones produce a visible ridge in a small, premature infant. Easily visible overlapping does not often occur in term infants. (From Korones SB:* High-Risk Newborn Infants, *4th ed. St Louis: Mosby, 1986.)*

to *craniostenosis* (premature closure of the cranial sutures) and *plagiocephaly* (asymmetry caused by pressure on the fetal head during gestation).

Two *fontanelles* ("soft spots") may be palpated on the infant's head. Fontanelles, which are openings at the juncture of the cranial bones, can be measured with the fingers. Accurate measurement necessitates that the examiner's finger be measured in centimeters. The assessment should be carried out with the newborn in sitting position and not crying. The diamond-shaped *anterior fontanelle* is approximately 3–4 cm long by 2–3 cm wide. It is located at the juncture of the frontal and parietal bones. The *posterior fontanelle,* smaller and triangular, is formed by the parietal bones and the occipital bone. The fontanelles will be smaller immediately after birth than several days later because of molding. The anterior fontanelle closes within 18 months, whereas the posterior fontanelle closes within 8–12 weeks.

The fontanelles are a useful indicator of the newborn's condition. The anterior fontanelle may swell when the newborn cries or passes a stool, or may pulsate with the heartbeat, which is normal. A bulging fontanelle usually signifies increased intracranial pressure, and a depressed fontanelle indicates dehydration. The sutures between the cranial bones should be palpated for amount of overlapping.

In addition to being inspected for degree of molding and size, the head should be evaluated for soft tissue edema and bruising.

## CEPHALHEMATOMA

**Cephalhematoma** is a collection of blood resulting from ruptured blood vessels between the surface of a cranial bone (usually parietal) and the periosteal membrane. The scalp in these areas feels loose and slightly edematous. These areas emerge as defined hematomas between the first and second day. Although external pressure may cause the mass to fluctuate, it does not increase in size when the infant cries. Cephalhematomas may be unilateral or bilateral and do not cross suture lines. They are relatively common in vertex births and may disappear within two to three weeks or very slowly over subsequent months. Figure 21.16 shows a cephalhematoma.

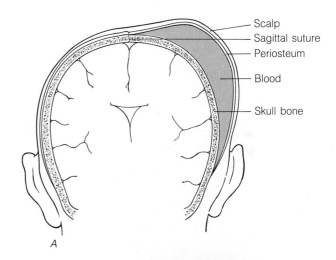

Scalp
Sagittal suture
Periosteum
Blood
Skull bone

*A*

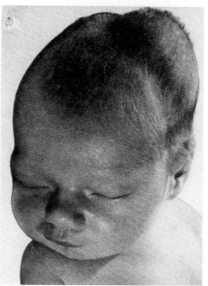

*B*

*Figure 21.16    Cephalhematoma is a collection of blood between the surface of a cranial bone and the periosteal membrane. This is a cephalhematoma over the left parietal bone. (Photo reproduced with permission from Porter EL, Craig JM:* Pathology of the Fetus and Infant, *3rd ed. Chicago: Year Book Medical Publishers, 1975.)*

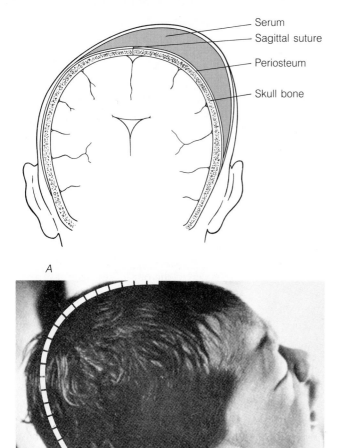

Serum
Sagittal suture
Periosteum
Skull bone

*A*

*B*

*Figure 21.17  Caput succedaneum is a collection of fluid (serum) under the scalp. (Photo courtesy Mead Johnson Laboratories, Evansville, IN.)*

## CAPUT SUCCEDANEUM

**Caput succedaneum** is a localized, easily identifiable soft area of the scalp, generally resulting from a long and difficult labor or vacuum extraction. The sustained pressure of the presenting part against the cervix results in compression of local blood vessels, and venous return is slowed. This causes an increase in tissue fluids, an edematous swelling, and occasional bleeding under the periosteum. The caput may vary from a small area to a severely elongated head. The fluid in the caput is reabsorbed within 12 hours or a few days after birth. Caputs resulting from vacuum extractors are sharply outlined, circular areas up to 2 cm thick. They disappear more slowly than naturally occurring edema. It is possible to distinguish between a cephalhematoma and a caput because the caput overrides suture lines (Figure 21.17), whereas the cephalhematoma,

because of its location, never crosses a suture line. Caput succedaneum is present at birth, whereas cephalhematoma is not. See Essential Factors to Remember—Comparison of Cephalhematoma and Caput Succedaneum.

## ● *Face*

The newborn's face is well designed to help the infant suckle. Sucking (fat) pads are located in the cheeks, and a labial tubercle (sucking callus) is frequently found in the center of the upper lip. The chin is recessed, and the nose is flattened. The lips are sensitive to touch, and the sucking reflex is easily initiated.

Symmetry of the eyes, nose, and ears is evaluated. See the Neonatal Physical Assessment Guide, p 599, for deviations in symmetry and variations in size, shape, and spacing of facial features. Facial movement symmetry should be assessed to determine presence of facial palsy.

Facial paralysis appears when the newborn cries; the affected side is immobile and the palpebral (eyelid) fissure widens (Figure 21.18). Paralysis may result from forceps birth or pressure on the facial nerve from the maternal pelvis during birth. Facial paralysis usually disappears within a few days to three weeks.

### EYES

The eyes of the Caucasian neonate are a blue- or slate-blue gray. Scleral color tends to be bluish because of its relative thinness. The infant's eye color usually is established at approximately three months, although it may change any time up to one year. Dark-skinned neonates tend to have dark eyes at birth.

The eyes should be checked for size, equality of pupil

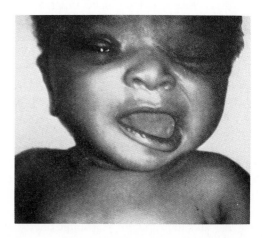

*Figure 21.18  Facial paralysis. Paralysis of the right side of the face from injury to right facial nerve. (Courtesy of Dr Ralph Platow. In: Potter EL, Craig JM:* Pathology of the Fetus and Infant, *3rd ed. Chicago: Year Book Medical Publishers, 1975.)*

## Essential Facts to Remember

### Comparison of Cephalhematoma and Caput Succedaneum

#### Cephalhematoma

Collection of blood between cranial (usually parietal) bone and periosteal membrane
Does not cross suture lines
Does not increase in size with crying
Appears on first and second day
Disappears after two to three weeks or may take months

#### Caput Succedaneum

Collection of fluid, edematous swelling
Crosses suture lines
Present at birth or shortly thereafter
Reabsorbed within 12 hours or a few days after birth

size, reaction of pupils to light, blink reflex to light, and edema and inflammation of the eyelids. The eyelids are usually edematous during the first few days of life because of the birth and the instillation of silver nitrate or sometimes erythromycin in the newborn's eyes. **Chemical conjunctivitis** may also appear a few hours after the instillation of the ophthalmic drops but disappears without treatment in one to two days. If infectious conjunctivitis exists, the infant has the same purulent exudate as in chemical conjunctivitis, but it is caused by staphylococci or a variety of gram-negative bacteria and requires treatment with ophthalmic antibiotics. Onset is usually after the second day. Edema of the orbits or eyelids may persist for several days until the neonate's kidneys can evacuate the fluid.

Small **subconjunctival hemorrhages** appear in about 10% of newborns and are commonly found on the sclera. These are caused by the changes in vascular tension or ocular pressure during birth. They will remain for a few weeks and are of no pathologic significance. Parents need reassurance that the infant is not bleeding from within the eye and that vision will not be impaired.

The neonate may demonstrate transient strabismus caused by poor neuromuscular control of eye muscles (Figure 21.19). It gradually regresses in three to four months. The "doll's eye" phenomenon is also present for about ten days after birth. As the newborn's head position is changed to the left and then to the right, the eyes move to the opposite direction. This results from underdeveloped integration of head-eye coordination.

The nurse should observe the neonate's pupils for opacities or whiteness. Congenital cataracts should be suspected in infants of mothers with a history of rubella, cytomegalic inclusion disease, or syphilis.

The cry of the neonate is commonly tearless because the lacrimal structures are immature at birth and are not usually fully functional until the second month of life. Some babies may produce tears during the neonatal period. Poor oculomotor coordination and absence of accommodation limit visual abilities, but the newborn does have peripheral vision and can fixate on near objects (9–12 in) for short periods (Ludington-Hoe 1983). The newborn can perceive faces, shapes, and colors and begins to show visual preferences early. The neonate blinks in response to bright lights, to a tap on the bridge of the nose (glabellar reflex), or to a light touch on the eyelids. Pupillary light reflex is also present. Examination of the eye is best accomplished by rocking the newborn from an upright position to the horizontal a few times or by other methods that will elicit an opened-eye response.

### NOSE

The neonate's nose is small and narrow. Infants are characteristically nose breathers for the first few months of life. The newborn generally removes obstructions by sneezing. Nasal patency is assured if the neonate breathes easily with mouth closed. If respiratory difficulty occurs, the nurse checks for choanal atresia (congenital occlusion blocking passageway between nose and pharynx).

The newborn has the ability to smell after the nasal passages are cleared of amniotic fluid and mucus. This ability is demonstrated by the search for milk. Infants will turn their heads toward the milk source, whether bottle or breast.

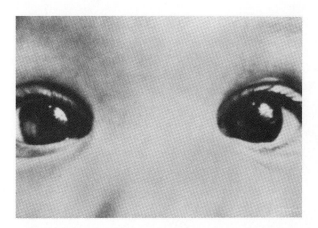

*Figure 21.19  Transient strabismus may be present in the newborn due to poor neuromuscular control. (Courtesy Mead Johnson Laboratories, Evansville, IN.)*

## MOUTH

The lips of the newborn should be pink, and a touch on the lips should produce sucking motions. Saliva is normally scant. The taste buds are developed prior to birth, and the newborn can easily discriminate between sweet and bitter.

The easiest way to completely examine the mouth is to gently stimulate infants to cry by depressing their tongue, thereby causing them to open the mouth fully. It is extremely important to observe the entire mouth to look for a cleft palate, which can be present even in the absence of a cleft lip. The examiner places a clean index finger along the hard and soft palates to feel for any openings (Figure 21.20).

Occasionally, an examination of the gums will reveal *precocious teeth* on the lower central incisor. If they appear loose, they should be removed to prevent aspiration.

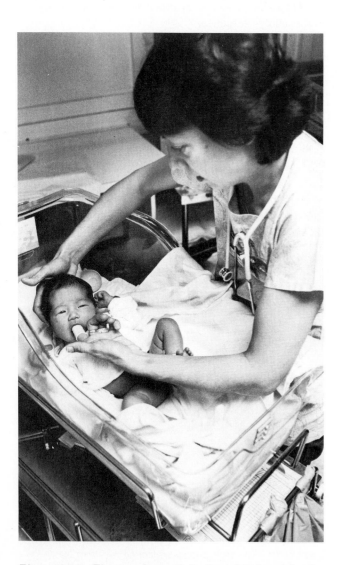

*Figure 21.20  The nurse inserts index finger into the newborn's mouth and feels for any openings along the hard and soft palates.*

Gray-white lesions (*inclusion cysts*) on the gums may be confused with teeth. On the hard palate and gum margins, **Epstein's pearls,** small glistening white specks (keratin-containing cysts) that feel hard to the touch are often present. These usually disappear in a few weeks and are of no significance. **Thrush** may appear as white patches that look like milk curds adhering to the mucous membranes and that cause bleeding when removed. Thrush is caused by *Candida albicans,* often acquired from an infected vaginal tract during birth or if the mother uses poor hand washing, and is treated with a preparation of nystatin (Mycostatin).

A neonate who is *tongue-tied* has a ridge of frenulum tissue attached to the underside of the tongue at varying lengths from its base, causing a heart shape at the tip of the tongue. "Clipping the tongue," or cutting the ridge of tissue, is not recommended. This ridge does not affect speech or eating, but cutting does create an entry for infection.

Transient nerve paralysis resulting from birth trauma may be manifested by asymmetrical mouth movements when the neonate cries or by difficulty with sucking and feeding.

## EARS

The ears of the newborn should be soft and pliable and should recoil readily. In the normal newborn, the top of the ear (pinna) should be parallel to the outer and inner canthus of the eye. The ears should be inspected for shape, size, position, and firmness of ear cartilage. *Low-set ears* are characteristic of many syndromes and may indicate chromosomal abnormalities (especially trisomies 13 and 18), mental retardation, and/or internal organ abnormalities, especially bilateral renal agenesis as a result of embryologic developmental deviations (Figure 21.21). *Preauricular skin tags* may be present. They are ligated at the base and allowed to slough off.

Following the first cry, the newborn's hearing becomes acute as mucus from the middle ear is absorbed and the eustachian tube becomes aerated. Risk factors (Duara et al 1986) associated with potential hearing loss include:

- The presence of hearing loss in any family member prior to the age of 50 years

- Serum bilirubin level greater than 20 mg/dL for the full-term newborn

- Suspected maternal rubella infection during pregnancy, resulting in congenital rubella syndrome

- Congenital defects of the ear, nose, or throat

- Small neonatal size, particularly less than 1500 g at birth

- Perinatal asphyxia

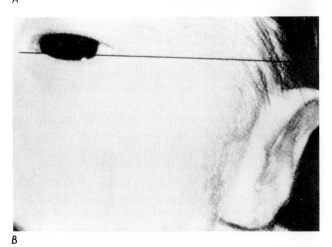

*Figure 21.21  The position of the external ear may be assessed by drawing a line across the inner and outer canthus of the eye to the insertion of the ear. (A) Normal position. (B) True low-set. (Courtesy Mead Johnson Laboratories, Evansville, IN.)*

The newborn's hearing is evaluated by response to loud or moderately loud noises unaccompanied by vibrations. The sleeping neonate should stir or awaken in response to the nearby sounds.

## • Neck

A short neck, creased with skin folds, is characteristic of the normal newborn. Because muscle tone is not well developed, the neck cannot support the full weight of the head, which rotates freely. The head lags considerably when the neonate is pulled from a supine to a sitting position, but the prone infant is able to raise the head slightly. The neck is palpated for masses and presence of lymph nodes and is inspected for webbing. Adequacy of range of motion and neck muscle function is determined by fully extending the head in all directions. Injury to the sternocleidomastoid muscle (congenital torticollis) must be considered in the presence of neck rigidity.

The clavicles are evaluated for evidence of fractures, which occasionally occur during difficult deliveries or in neonates with broad shoulders. The normal clavicle is straight. If fractured, a lump and a grating sensation (crepitus) during movements may be palpated along the course of the side of the break. The Moro reflex (p 593) is also elicited to evaluate bilateral equal movement of the arms. If the clavicle is fractured, the response will be demonstrated only on the unaffected side.

## • Chest

The thorax is cylindrical at birth, and the ribs are flexible. The general appearance of the chest should be assessed. A protrusion at the lower end of the sternum, called the *xiphoid cartilage*, is frequently seen. It is under the skin and will become less apparent after several weeks as the infant accumulates adipose tissue.

Engorged breasts occur frequently in male and female newborns. This condition, which occurs by the third day, is a result of maternal hormonal influences and may last up to two weeks (Figure 21.22). The infant's breast should not be massaged or squeezed, because this practice may cause a breast abscess. Extra or *supernumerary nipples* are occasionally noted below and medial to the true nipples. These harmless pink spots vary in size and do not contain glandular tissue (Korones 1986). Accessory nipples can be differentiated from a pigmented nevi (mole) by placing the fingertips alongside the accessory nipple and pulling the adjacent tissue laterally. The accessory nipple will appear dimpled. At puberty the accessory nipple may darken.

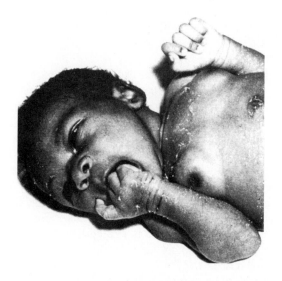

*Figure 21.22  Breast hypertrophy (From Korones SB: High-Risk Newborn Infants, 4th ed. St. Louis: Mosby, 1986.)*

## ● Cry

The neonate's cry should be strong, lusty, and of medium pitch. A high-pitched, shrill cry is abnormal and may indicate neurologic disorders or hypoglycemia. Cries vary in length from three to seven minutes after consoling measures are used. The neonate's cry is an important method of communication and alerts caretakers to changes in his or her condition and needs.

## ● Respiration

Normal breathing for a term newborn is predominantly diaphragmatic, with associated rising and falling of the abdomen during inspiration and expiration. Any signs of respiratory distress, nasal flaring, intercostal or xiphoid retraction, expiratory grunt or sigh, seesaw respirations, or tachypnea (sustained respirations greater than 60 per minute) should be noted. Hyperextension (chest appears high) or hypoextension (chest appears low) of the anteroposterior diameter of the chest should also be noted. Both the anterior and posterior chest are auscultated. Some breath sounds are heard better when the newborn is crying, but localization and identification of breath sounds are difficult in the newborn. Because sounds may be transmitted from the unaffected lung to the affected lung, the absence of breath sounds cannot be diagnosed. Air entry may be noisy in the first couple of hours until lung fluid resolves, especially in cesarean births.

## ● Heart

Heart rates can be as rapid as 180 beats per minute in newborns and fluctuate a great deal. Normal range is 120 to 150 beats per minute. Auscultation provides the nurse with valuable assessment data. The heart is examined for rate and rhythm, position of the apical impulse, and heart sound intensity.

The pulse rate is variable and follows the trend of respirations in the neonatal period. The pulse rate is influenced by physical activity, crying, state of wakefulness, and body temperature. Auscultation is performed over the entire heart region (precordium), below the left axilla, and below the scapula. Apical pulse rates are obtained by auscultation for a full minute, preferably when the neonate is asleep.

The placement of the heart in the chest should be determined when the neonate is in a quiet state. The heart is relatively large at birth and is located high in the chest, with its apex somewhere between the fourth and fifth intercostal space.

A shift of heart tones in the mediastinal area to either side may indicate pneumothorax, dextrocardia (heart placement on the right side of the chest), or a diaphragmatic hernia. The experienced nurse can diagnose these and many other problems early with a stethoscope. Normally, the heart beat has a "toc tic" sound. A slur or slushing sound (usually after the first sound) may indicate a *murmur*. Although 90% of all murmurs are transient and are considered normal (Korones 1986), they should be observed closely by a physician.

In newborns, a low-pitched, musical murmur heard just to the right of the apex of the heart is fairly common. Occasionally, significant murmurs will be heard, including the murmur of a patent ductus arteriosus, aortic or pulmonary stenosis, or small ventricular septal defect. See Chapter 24 for a discussion of congenital heart defects.

Peripheral pulses (brachial, femoral, pedal) are also evaluated to detect any lags or unusual characteristics. Brachial pulses are palpated bilaterally for equality and compared with the femoral pulses. Femoral pulses are palpated by applying gentle pressure with the middle finger over the femoral canal (Figure 21.23). Decreased or absent femoral pulses indicate coarctation of the aorta and require additional investigation. A wide difference in blood pressure between the upper and lower extremities also indicates coarctation. The measurement of blood pressure is best accomplished by using the Doppler technique or a 1–2 inch cuff and a stethoscope over the brachial artery.

Blood pressure is becoming a routine measurement on newborns, especially if they are having distress, are premature, or are suspected of cardiac anomaly. If cardiac anomaly is suspected, palpate blood pressure in all four extremities. For pertinent aspects of vital signs, see Essential Facts to Remember—Vital Signs.

## ● Abdomen

Without disturbing the infant, the nurse can learn a great deal about the newborn's abdomen. It should be cylindrical and protrude slightly. A certain amount of laxness of the abdominal muscles is normal. A scaphoid appearance suggests the absence of abdominal contents. No cyanosis should be present, and few if any blood vessels should be apparent to the eye. There should be no gross distention or bulging. The more distended the abdomen, the tighter the skin becomes, with engorged vessels appearing. Distention is the first sign of many of the abnormalities found in the gastrointestinal tract.

Prior to palpation of the abdomen, the presence or absence of bowel sounds should be auscultated in all four quadrants. Palpation can cause a transient decrease in intensity of the bowel sounds.

Abdominal palpation should be done systematically. The nurse palpates each of the four abdominal quadrants and moves in a clockwise direction until all four quadrants have been palpated for softness, tenderness, and the presence of masses.

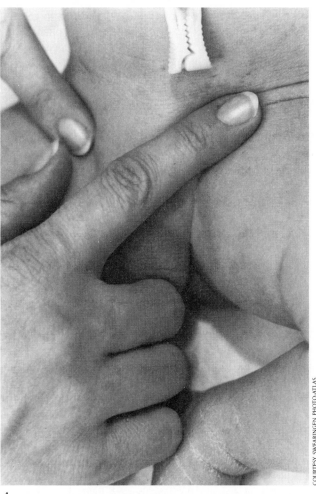

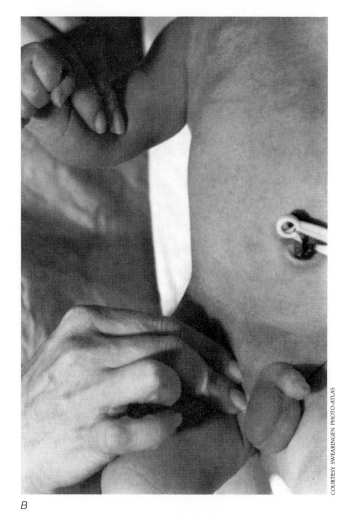

COURTESY SWEARINGEN PHOTO-ATLAS

COURTESY SWEARINGEN PHOTO-ATLAS

*A*

*B*

*Figure 21.23* *(A) Bilaterally palpate the femoral arteries for rate and intensity of the pulses. Press fingertip gently at the groin as shown. (B) Compare the femoral pulses to the brachial pulses by palpating the pulses simultaneously for comparison of rate and* *intensity. (From Swearingen PL:* The Addison-Wesley Photo-Atlas of Nursing Procedures. *Menlo Park, CA: Addison-Wesley, 1984.)*

## ● Umbilical Cord

Initially the umbilical cord is white and gelatinous in appearance, with the two umbilical arteries and one umbilical vein readily apparent. Because a single umbilical artery is frequently associated with congenital anomalies, the vessels should be counted as part of the newborn assessment. The cord begins drying within one or two hours of birth and is shriveled and blackened by the second or third day. Within seven to ten days, it sloughs off, although a granulating area may remain for a few days longer.

Cord bleeding is abnormal and may result because the cord was inadvertently pulled or because the cord clamp was loosened. Foul-smelling drainage is also abnormal and is generally caused by infection. Such infection requires immediate treatment to prevent the development of septicemia. If the neonate has a patent urachus (abnormal connection between the umbilicus and bladder), moistness or draining urine may be apparent at the base of the cord.

## ● Genitals
### FEMALE INFANTS

The labia majora, labia minora, and clitoris are examined, and the nurse notes the size of each as appropriate for gestational age. A vaginal tag or hymenal tag is often evident and will usually disappear in a few weeks. During the first week of life, the neonate may have a vaginal discharge composed of thick whitish mucus. This discharge, which can become tinged with blood, is referred to as **pseudomenstruation** and is caused by the withdrawal of maternal hormones. Smegma, a white cheeselike substance, is often present under the labia.

## Essential Facts to Remember

### Vital Signs

**Pulse**

120–150 beats/min
During sleep as low as 100 beats/min; if crying, up to 180 beats/min
Apical pulse is counted for one (1) full minute

**Respirations**

30–50 respirations/min
Predominantly diaphragmatic but synchronous with abdominal movements
Respirations are counted for one (1) full minute

**Blood Pressure**

80–60/45–40 mm Hg at birth
100/50 mm Hg at day 10

**Temperature**

Axillary: 36.5–37° C (97.7–98.6° F)
Skin: 36–36.5° C (96.8–97.7° F)
Rectal: 36.6–37.2° C (97.8–99° F)

### MALE INFANTS

The penis is inspected to determine whether the urinary orifice is correctly positioned. *Hypospadias* occurs when the urinary meatus is located on the ventral surface of the penis. It occurs most commonly in whites in the United States. *Phimosis* is a condition commonly occurring in newborn males in which the opening of the prepuce is narrowed and the foreskin cannot be retracted over the glans. This condition may interfere with urination, so the adequacy of the urinary stream should be evaluated.

The scrotum is inspected for size and symmetry and should be palpated to verify the presence of both testes and to rule out cryptorchidism (failure of testes to descend). The testes are palpated separately between the thumb and forefinger, with the thumb and forefinger of the other hand placed together over the inguinal canal. Scrotal edema and discoloration are common in breech births. *Hydrocele* (a collection of fluid surrounding the testes in the scrotum) is common in newborns and should be identified.

### • Anus

The anal area is inspected to verify that it is patent and has no fissure. Imperforate anus and rectal atresia may be ruled out by a digital examination. The passage of the first meconium stool is also noted. Atresia of the gastrointestinal tract or meconium ileus with resultant obstruction must be considered if the infant does not pass meconium in the first 24 hours of life.

### • Extremities

Extremities are examined for gross deformities, extra digits or webbing, clubfoot, and range of motion. The normal neonate's extremities appear short, are generally flexible, and move symmetrically.

### ARMS AND HANDS

Nails extend beyond the fingertips in term infants. Fingers and toes should be counted. *Polydactyly* is the presence of extra digits on either the hands or the feet. Polydactyly is more common in blacks. If the infant has polydactyly and the parents do not, a dominant genetic disorder can be ruled out. *Syndactyly* refers to fusion (webbing) of fingers or toes. Hands should be inspected for normal palmar creases. A single palmar crease, called *simian line* (see Figure 4.18), is frequently present in children with Down syndrome. (See Chapter 4 for further discussion.)

*Brachial palsy,* which is partial or complete paralysis of portions of the arm, results from trauma to the brachial plexus during a difficult birth. It occurs most commonly when strong traction is exerted on the head of the neonate in an attempt to deliver a shoulder lodged behind the symphysis pubis in the presence of shoulder dystocia. Brachial palsy may also occur during a breech birth if an arm becomes trapped over the head and traction is exerted.

The portion of the arm affected is determined by the nerves damaged. **Erb-Duchenne paralysis** involves damage to the upper arm (fifth and sixth cervical nerves) and is the most common type. Injury to the eighth cervical and first thoracic nerve roots and the lower portion of the plexus produces the relatively rare *lower arm injury*. The *whole arm type* results from damage to the entire plexus.

With Erb-Duchenne paralysis (Erb's palsy) the infant's arm lies limply at the side. The elbow is held in extension, with the forearm pronated. The infant is unable to elevate the arm, and the Moro reflex cannot be elicited on the affected side (Figure 21.24). When lower arm injury occurs, paralysis of the hand and wrist results; complete paralysis of the limb occurs with the whole arm type.

Treatment involves passive range-of-motion exercises to prevent muscle contractures and to restore function. The nurse should carefully instruct the parents in the correct method of performing the exercises and provide for supervised practice sessions. In more severe cases, splinting of the arm is indicated until the edema decreases. The arm is held in a position of abduction and external rotation with the elbow flexed 90°. The "Statue of Liberty" splint is commonly used, although similar results are ob-

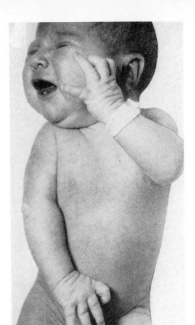

*Figure 21.24 Erb's palsy resulting from injury to the fifth and sixth cervical roots of brachial plexus (Photo reproduced with permission from Potter EL, Craig JM: Pathology of the Fetus and Infant, 3rd ed. Chicago: Year Book Medical Publishers, 1975.)*

tained by attaching a strip of muslin to the head of the crib and tying the other end around the wrist, thereby holding the arm up.

Prognosis is related to the degree of nerve damage resulting from trauma and hemorrhage within the nerve sheath. Complete recovery occurs within a few months with minimal trauma. Moderate trauma may result in some partial paralysis. Recovery is unlikely with severe trauma, and muscle wasting may develop.

## LEGS AND FEET

The legs of the newborn should be of equal length, with symmetrical skin folds. *Ortolani's maneuver* is performed to rule out the possibility of congenital hip dysplasia. With the baby supine, the nurse places thumbs on the inner thighs and fingers on the outer aspect of the neonate's leg from the knee to the head of the femur. The legs are flexed, then abducted and pressed downward. If a clunk is felt under the index finger and there is resistance to abduction, a dislocation exists (Figure 21.25).

The feet are then examined for evidence of clubfoot. Intrauterine position frequently causes the feet to appear

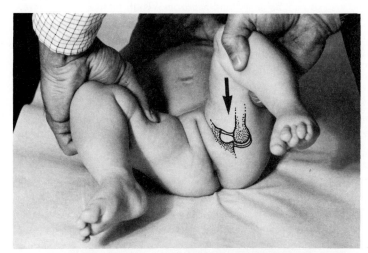

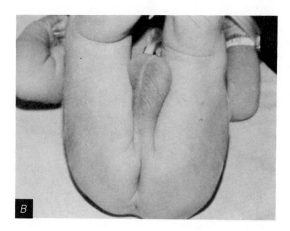

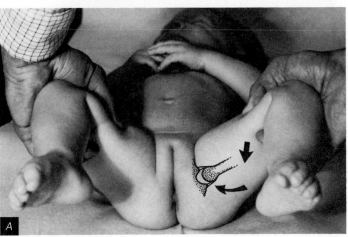

*Figure 21.25 Congenital dislocation of the right hip. (A) Ortolani's maneuver puts downward pressure on the hip and then inward rotation. If the hip is dislocated, this will force the femoral head over the acetabular rim with a noticeable "clunk." (B) Dislocated right hip in a young infant as seen on gross inspection. (From Smith DW: Recognizable Patterns of Human Deformation. Philadelphia: Saunders, 1981.)*

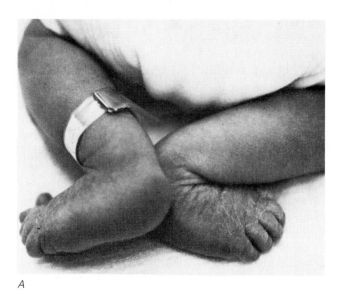

*A*

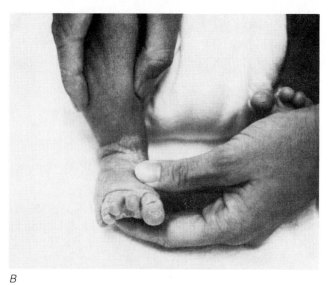

*B*

*Figure 21.26 (A) Bilateral talipes equinovarus seen with infant in supine position. (B) To determine the presence of clubfoot, the* *nurse moves the foot to the midline. Resistance indicates true clubfoot.*

to turn inward (Figure 21.26). If the feet can easily be returned to the midline by manipulation (positional clubfoot) no treatment is indicated. Further investigation is indicated when the foot will not turn to a midline position or align readily. This is considered a "true" clubfoot.

## ● Back

With the neonate prone, the nurse examines the back. The spine should appear straight and flat, since the lumbar and sacral curves do not develop until the infant begins to sit. The base of the spine is then examined for a dermal sinus. The nevus philosus ("hairy nerve") is only occasionally found at the base of the spine in newborns, but it is significant because it is frequently associated with spina bifida.

## ● Assessment of Neurologic Status

The neurologic examination assesses the intactness of the neonatal nervous system. It should begin with a period of observation, noting the general physical characteristics and behaviors of the newborn. Important behaviors to assess are the state of alertness, resting posture, cry, and quality of muscle tone and motor activity.

Partially flexed extremities with the legs abducted to the abdomen is the usual position of the neonate. When awake, the newborn may exhibit purposeless, uncoordinated bilateral movements of the extremities. If these movements are absent, minimal, or obviously asymmetrical, neurologic dysfunction should be suspected. Eye movements are observable during the first few days of life. An alert neonate is able to fixate on faces and brightly col-

ored objects. If a bright light shines in the newborn's eyes, the blinking response is elicited. The cry of the newborn should be lusty and vigorous. High-pitched cries, weak cries, or no cries are all causes for concern.

Muscle tone is evaluated with the head of the neonate in a neutral position as various parts of the body are passively moved. The newborn is somewhat hypertonic; that is, resistance to extending the elbow and knee joints should be noted. Muscle tone should be symmetrical. Diminished muscle tone and flaccidity require further evaluation.

Neonatal tremors are common in the full-term infant and must be evaluated to differentiate them from a convulsion. A fine jumping of the muscle is likely to be a central nervous system disorder and requires further evaluation. Tremors may also be related to hypoglycemia or hypocalcemia. Neonatal seizures may consist of no more than chewing or swallowing movements, deviations of the eyes, rigidity, or flaccidity because of central nervous system immaturity.

Specific deep tendon reflexes can be elicited in the neonate but have limited value unless they are obviously asymmetrical. The knee jerk is brisk; a normal ankle clonus may involve three or four beats. Plantar flexion is present.

The central nervous system of the newborn is immature and characterized by a variety of reflexes. Because the newborn's movements are uncoordinated, methods of communication are limited, and control of bodily functions is drastically limited, the reflexes serve a variety of purposes. Some are protective (blink, gag, sneeze), some aid in feeding (rooting, sucking), and some stimulate human interaction (grasping). Neonatal reflexes and general neurologic activities should be carefully assessed.

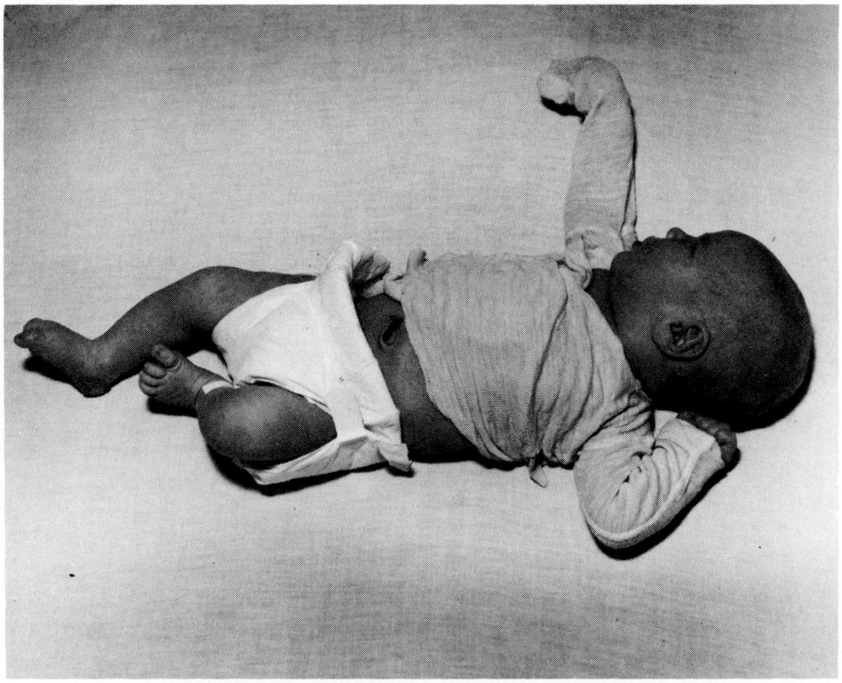

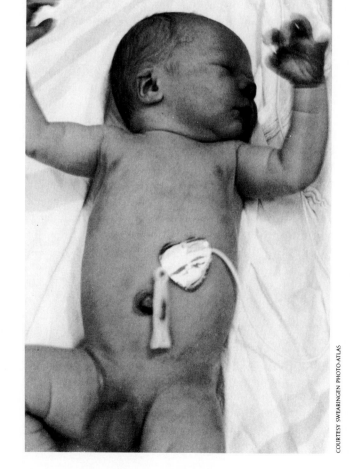

Figure 21.27  *Tonic neck reflex*

The most common reflexes found in the normal neonate are the following:

● *Tonic neck reflex*. The **tonic neck reflex** (*fencer
position*) is elicited when the neonate is supine and the
head is turned to one side. In response, the extremities
on the same side straighten, whereas on the opposite
side they flex (Figure 21.27). This reflex may not be
seen during the early neonatal period, but once it appears it persists until about the third month.

● *Moro reflex*. The **Moro reflex** is elicited when the
neonate is startled by a loud noise or is lifted slightly
above the crib and then suddenly lowered. In response, the infant straightens arms and hands outward while the knees flex. Slowly the arms return to
the chest, as in an embrace. The fingers spread,
forming a C, and the infant may cry (Figure 21.28).

● *Grasp reflex*. If the newborn's palm is stimulated with
a finger or object, the newborn grasps and holds it
firmly enough to be lifted momentarily from the crib
(Figure 21.29).

● *Rooting reflex*. The **rooting reflex** is elicited when
the side of the infant's mouth or cheek is touched. In
response, the newborn turns toward that side and

*Figure 21.28  Moro reflex (From Swearingen PL: The Addison-
Wesley Photo-Atlas of Nursing Procedures. Menlo Park, CA:
Addison-Wesley, 1984.)*

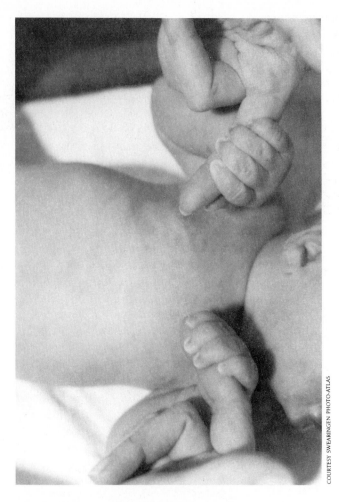

COURTESY SWEARINGEN PHOTO-ATLAS

*Figure 21.29   Grasping reflex (From Swearingen PL:* The Addison-Wesley Photo-Atlas of Nursing Procedures. *Menlo Park, CA: Addison-Wesley, 1984.)*

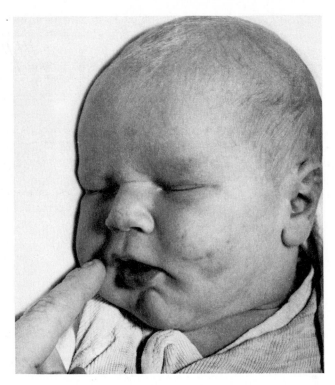

*Figure 21.30   Rooting reflex*

opens the lips to suck (if not fed recently) (Figure 21.30).

- *Sucking reflex.* When an object is placed in the neonate's mouth or anything touches his or her lips a sucking reflex is elicited.

- *Babinski reflex.* Hyperextension of all toes occurs when the lateral aspect of the sole is stroked from the heel upward across the ball of the foot.

- *Trunk incurvation.* When the infant is prone, stroking the spine causes the pelvis to turn to the stimulated side.

In addition to these reflexes, the infant can blink, yawn, cough, sneeze, and draw back from pain (protective reflexes). Neonates can even move a little on their own. When placed on their stomachs, they push up and try to crawl (*prone crawl*). When he or she is held upright with one foot touching a flat surface, the neonate puts one foot in front of the other and walks (*stepping reflex*) (Figure

21.31). This reflex is more pronounced at birth and is lost in four to five months.

The Neonatal Physical Assessment Guide summarizes the stimulus for and response of the common newborn reflexes.

Brazelton (1984) recommends the following steps as a means of assessing central nervous system integration:

1. Insert a clean finger into the newborn's mouth to elicit a sucking reflex.

2. As soon as the neonate is sucking vigorously, assess hearing and vision responses by noting sucking changes in the presence of a light, a rattle, and a voice.

3. The neonate should respond with a brief cessation of sucking followed by continuous sucking with repetitious stimulation.

This examination demonstrates auditory and visual integrity as well as the ability for complex behavioral interactions.

## • NEONATAL PHYSICAL ASSESSMENT

Following is a guide for systematically assessing the newborn. Normal findings, alterations, and related causes are presented, in correlation with suggested nursing responses. The findings are typical for a full-term neonate.

**Plate I**    Beginnings . . .

**Plate II**    Linea nigra

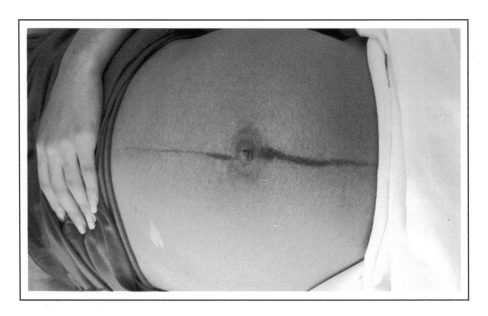

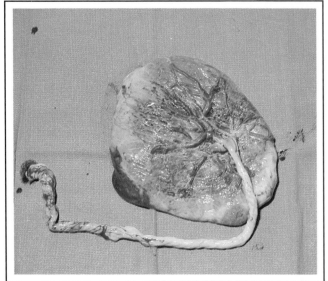

**Plate III**    Fetal side of placenta

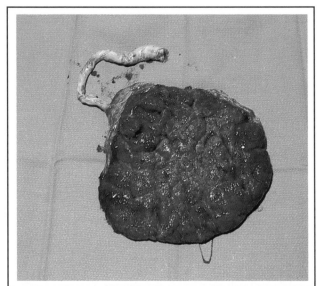

**Plate IV**    Maternal side of placenta

**Plate V**    Acrocyanosis

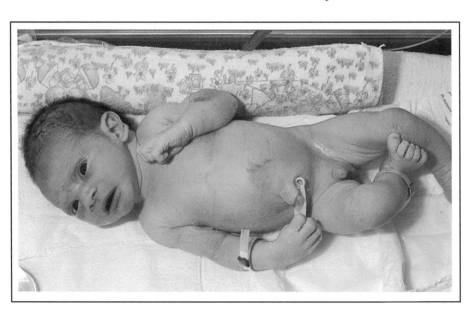

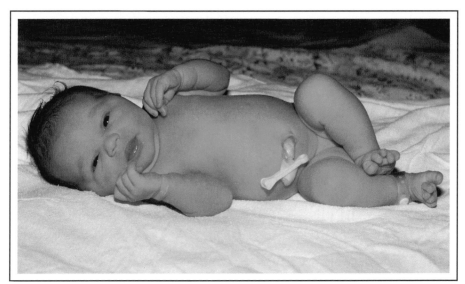

**Plate VI**      Normal newborn

**Plate VII**      Mongolian spots

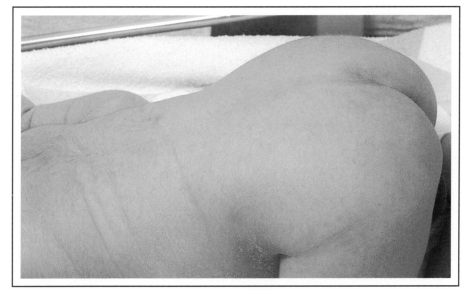

**Plate VIII**      Facial milia

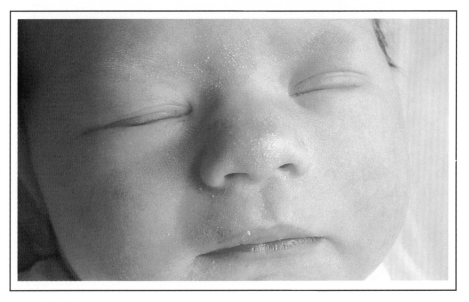

**Plate IX**    Stork bites

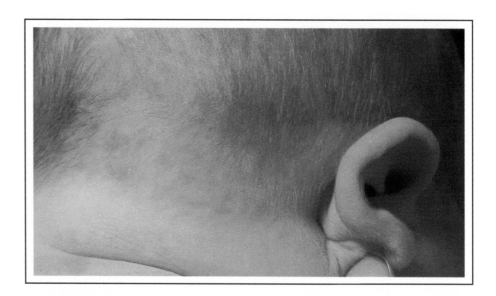

**Plate X**    Portwine stain

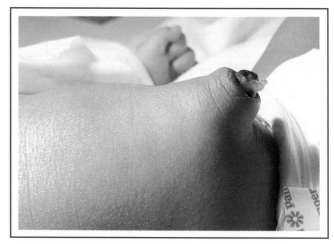

**Plate XI**    Umbilical hernia

**Plate XII**    Erythema toxicum

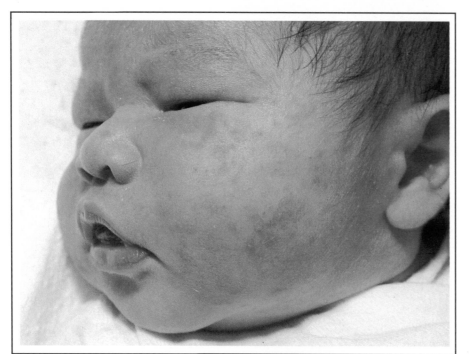

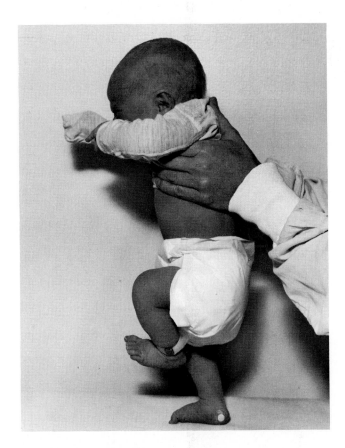

*Figure 21.31   The stepping reflex disappears after about one month.*

# ● NEONATAL BEHAVIORAL ASSESSMENT

Two conflicting forces influence parents' perceptions of their infant. One is the parents' preconceptions, based on hopes and fears, of what their newborn will be like. The other is their initial reaction to the infant's temperament, behaviors, and physical appearance. Nurses can assist parents in identifying their baby's specific behaviors.

Brazelton (1973) developed a tool that has revolutionized our understanding and perception of the newborn's capabilities and responses, permitting us to recognize each infant's individuality. **Brazelton's neonatal behavioral assessment** tool provides valuable guidelines for assessing the newborn's state changes, temperament, and individual behavior patterns. It provides a means by which the health care provider, in conjunction with the parents (primary care givers), can identify and understand the individual newborn's states. Parents learn which responses, interventions, or activities best meet the special needs of their infant, and this understanding fosters positive attachment experiences.

The assessment tool attempts to identify the newborn's repertoire of behavioral responses to the environ-ment and also documents the infant's neurologic adequacy and capabilities. The examination usually takes 20 to 30 minutes.

Some items are scored according to the newborn's response to specific stimuli. Others, such as consolability and alertness, are scored as a result of continuous behavioral observations throughout the assessment. (For a complete discussion of all test items and maneuvers, the student is referred to Brazelton 1973.)

Generally the tool is set up so that the midpoint is the norm for most items. The Brazelton assessment tool differs from most in that the newborn's score is determined not on the average performance but on the best. Since the first few days after birth are a period of behavioral disorganization, the complete assessment should be done on the third day after delivery. Every effort should be made to elicit the best response. This may be accomplished by repeating tests at different times or by testing during situations that facilitate the best possible response, such as when parents are alerting their babies by holding, cuddling, rocking, or singing to them.

The assessment of the newborn should be carried out initially in a quiet, dimly or softly lit room, if possible. The newborn's state of consciousness should be determined, because scoring and introduction of the test items are correlated with the sleep or awake state. The newborn's state depends on physiologic variables, such as the amount of time from the last feeding, positioning, environmental temperature, and health status; presence of such external stimuli as noises and bright lights; and the wake-sleep cycle of the infant. An important characteristic of the neonatal period is the *pattern of states,* as well as the transitions from one state to another. The pattern of states is a predictor of the infant's receptivity and ability to respond to stimuli in a cognitive manner. Babies learn best in a quiet, alert state and in an environment that is supportive and protective and that provides appropriate stimuli.

The nurse should observe the newborn's sleep-wake patterns (as discussed in Chapter 22) and the rapidity with which the newborn moves from one state to another, ability to be consoled, and ability to diminish the impact of disturbing stimuli. The following questions may provide the nurse with a framework for assessment:

- Does the newborn's response style and ability to adapt to stimuli indicate a need for parental interventions that will alert the newborn to the environment so that he or she can grow socially and cognitively?

- Are parental interventions necessary to lessen the outside stimuli, as in the case of the baby who responds to sensory input with intensity?

- Can the baby control the amount of sensory input that he or she must deal with?

*(Text continues on page 608.)*

# Neonatal Physical Assessment Guide

| Assessment and Normal Findings | Alterations and Possible Causes* | Nursing Responses to Data Base† |
|---|---|---|
| **Vital Signs** | | |
| Blood pressure (BP)<br>At birth: 80–60/45–40 mm Hg<br>Day 10: 100/50 mm Hg (may be unable to measure diastolic pressure with standard sphygmomanometer) | Low BP (hypovolemia, shock) | Monitor BP in all cases of distress, prematurity, or suspected anomaly.<br>Low BP; refer to physician immediately so measures to improve circulation are begun. |
| Pulse: 120–150 beats/min (if asleep 100/min; if crying, up to 180/min) | Weak pulse (decreased cardiac output)<br><br>Bradycardia (severe asphyxia)<br><br>Tachycardia (over 160 beats/min at rest) (infection, central nervous system [CNS] problems) | Assess skin perfusion by blanching (capillary refill test).<br>Correlate finding with BP assessments; refer to physician.<br>Carry out neurologic and thermoregulation assessments. |
| Respirations<br>30–50 breaths/min<br>Synchronization of chest and abdominal movements<br>Diaphragmatic and abdominal breathing | Tachypnea (pneumonia, respiratory distress syndrome [RDS])<br>Rapid, shallow breathing (hypermagnesemia due to large doses given to mothers with PIH)<br>Respirations below 30 breaths/min (maternal anesthesia or analgesia) | Identify sleep-wake state; correlate with respiratory pattern.<br>Evaluate for all signs of respiratory distress; report findings to physician. |
| Transient tachypnea | Expiratory grunting, subcostal and substernal retractions; flaring of nares (respiratory distress); apnea (cold stress, respiratory disorder) | |
| Crying<br>Strong and lusty<br>Moderate tone and pitch<br>Cries vary in length from three to seven minutes after consoling measures are used | High-pitched, shrill (neurologic disorder, hypoglycemia)<br>Weak or absent (CNS disorder, laryngeal problem) | Discuss neonate's use of cry for communication.<br>Assess and record abnormal cries. |
| Temperature<br>Axilla 36.5–37° C (97.7–98.6° F)<br>Rectal 36.6–37.2° C (97.8–99° F); 36.8° C (98.8° F) desired<br>Heavier neonates tend to have higher body temperatures | Elevated temperature (room too warm, too much clothing or covers, dehydration, sepsis, brain damage)<br>Subnormal temperature (brain stem involvement, cold)<br>Swings of more than 2° F from one reading to next or subnormal temperature (infection) | Notify physician of elevation or drop.<br>Counsel parents on possible causes of elevated or low temperatures, appropriate home-care measures, when to call physician.<br>Teach parents how to take rectal and/or axillary temperature; assess parents' information regarding use of thermometer; provide teaching as needed. |
| Weight<br>2500–4000 g (5–8.75 lb) | <2748 g (<6 lb) = SGA or preterm infant<br>>4050 g (>9 lb) = LGA or infants of diabetic mothers (IDMs) | Plot weight and gestational age to identify high-risk infants.<br>Ascertain body build of parents.<br>Counsel parents regarding appropriate caloric intake. |
| Within first three to four days, normal weight loss of 5%–10%<br>Large babies tend to lose more due to greater fluid loss in proportion to birth weight except IDMs | Loss greater than 15% (small fluid intake, loss of meconium and urine, feeding difficulties) | Notify physician of net losses or gains.<br>Calculate fluid intake and losses from all sources (insensible water loss, radiant warmers, and phototherapy lights). |

*Possible causes of alterations are placed in parentheses.
† This column provides guidelines for further assessment and initial nursing interventions.

## Neonatal Physical Assessment Guide *(continued)*

| Assessment and Normal Findings | Alterations and Possible Causes* | Nursing Responses to Data Base† |
|---|---|---|
| **Length**<br>45 cm (18 in) to 55 cm (22 in)<br>Grows 10 cm (3 in) during first three months | Less than 45 cm (congenital dwarf)<br>Short/long bones proximally (achondroplasia)<br>Short/long bones distally (Ellis-Van Creveld syndrome) | Assess for other signs of dwarfism.<br>Determine other signs of skeletal system adequacy.<br>Plot progress at subsequent well-baby visits. |
| **Posture**<br>Body usually flexed, hands tightly clenched, neck appears short as chin rests on chest<br>In breech births, feet are usually dorsiflexed | Only extension noted, inability to move from midline (trauma, hypoxia, immaturity)<br>Constant motion | Record spontaneity of motor activity and symmetry of movements.<br>If parents express concern about neonate's movement patterns, reassure and evaluate further if appropriate. |
| **Skin**<br>Color<br>  Color consistent with racial background | Pallor of face, conjunctiva (anemia, hypothermia, anoxia) | Discuss with parents common skin color variations to allay fears. |
|   Pink-tinged or ruddy color over face, trunk, extremities | Beefy red (hypoglycemia, immature vasomotor reflexes, polycythemia) | Document extent and time of occurrence of color change. |
|   Common variations: acrocyanosis, circumoral cyanosis, or harlequin color change | Meconium staining (fetal distress)<br>Icterus (hemolytic reaction from blood incompatibility, sepsis) | Obtain Hb and hematocrit values.<br>Assess for respiratory difficulty.<br>Differentiate between physiologic and pathologic jaundice. |
|   Mottled when undressed | Cyanosis (choanal atresia, CNS damage or trauma, respiratory or cardiac problem, cold stress) | Assess degree of (central or peripheral) cyanosis and possible causes; refer to physician. |
|   Minor bruising over buttocks in breech presentation and over eyes and forehead in facial presentations | | Discuss with parents cause and course of minor bruising related to labor and birth. |
| Texture<br>  Smooth, soft, flexible; may have dry, peeling hands and feet | Generalized cracked or peeling skin (SGA or postterm; blood incompatibility; metabolic, kidney dysfunction) | Report to physician. |
| | Seborrhea-dermatitis (cradle cap)<br>Absence of vernix (postmature)<br>Yellow vernix (bilirubin staining) | Instruct parents to shampoo the scalp and anterior fontanelle area daily with soap; rinse well; avoid use of oil. |
| Turgor<br>  Elastic, returns to normal shape after pinching | Maintains tent shape (dehydration) | Assess for other signs and symptoms of dehydration. |
| Pigmentation<br>  Clear; milia across bridge of nose or forehead will disappear within a few weeks | | Advise parents not to pinch or prick these pimplelike areas. |
|   Café-au-lait spots (one or two) | Six or more (neurologic disorder such as Van Recklinghausen disease, cutaneous neurofibromatosis) | |

*Possible causes of alterations are placed in parentheses.
† This column provides guidelines for further assessment and initial nursing interventions.

*(continues)*

# Neonatal Physical Assessment Guide (continued)

| Assessment and Normal Findings | Alterations and Possible Causes* | Nursing Responses to Data Base† |
|---|---|---|
| Mongolian spots common in dark-skinned infants over dorsal area and buttocks | | Assure parents of normalcy of this pigmentation; it will fade in first year or two. |
| Erythema toxicum | Impetigo (group A β-hemolytic streptococcus or *Staphylococcus aureus* infection) | If impetigo occurs, instruct parents about hand-washing and linen precautions during home care. |
| Telangiectatic nevi birthmarks | Hemangiomas:<br>Nevus flammeus (port-wine stain)<br>Nevus vascularis (strawberry hemangioma)<br>Cavernous hemangiomas | Collaborate with physician.<br>Counsel parents about birthmark's progression to allay misconceptions.<br>Record size and shape of hemangiomas.<br>Refer for follow-up at well-baby clinic. |
| Rashes | Rashes (infection) | Assess location and type of rash (macular, papular, vesicular).<br>Obtain history of onset, prenatal history, and related signs and symptoms. |
| Petechiae of head or neck (breech presentation, cord around neck) | Generalized petechiae (clotting abnormalities) | Determine cause; advise parents if further health care is needed. |
| **Head** | | |
| General appearance, size, movement<br>Round, symmetrical, and moves easily from left to right and up and down; soft and pliable | Asymmetrical, flattened occiput on either side of head (plagiocephaly)<br>Head held at angle (torticollis)<br>Unable to move head side-to-side (neurologic trauma) | Instruct parents to change infant's sleeping positions frequently.<br><br>Determine adequacy of all neurologic signs. |
| Circumference: 32–37 cm (12.5–14.5 in); 2 cm greater than chest circumference<br>Head one fourth of body size | Extreme differences in size may be: microencephaly (Cornelia de Lange syndrome, cytomegalic inclusion disease (CID), rubella, toxoplasmosis, chromosome abnormalities), hydrocephalus (meningomyelocele, achondroplasia), anencephaly (neural tube defect)<br>Head is 3 cm or more larger than chest circumference (preterm, hydrocephalus) | Measure circumference from occiput to frontal area using metal or paper tape.<br>Measure chest circumference using metal or paper tape and compare to head circumference.<br>Record measurements on growth chart.<br>Reevaluate at well-baby visits. |
| Common variations:<br>Molding<br>Breech and cesarean newborns' heads are round and well shaped | Cephalhematoma (trauma during birth, persists up to three weeks)<br>Caput succedaneum (long labor and birth; disappears in one week) | Reassure parents regarding common manifestations due to birth process and when they should disappear. |
| Fontanelles<br>Palpation of juncture of cranial bones<br>Anterior fontanelle; 3–4 cm long by 2–3 cm wide, diamond-shaped | Overlapping of anterior fontanelle (malnourished or preterm infant) | Discuss normal closure times with parents and care of "soft spots" to allay misconceptions. |
| Posterior fontanelle; 1–2 cm at birth, triangle-shaped | Premature closure of sutures (craniostenosis)<br>Late closure (hydrocephalus) | Refer to physician.<br>Observe for signs and symptoms of hydrocephalus. |
| Slight pulsation | Moderate to severe pulsation (vascular problems) | Refer to physician. |

*Possible causes of alterations are placed in parentheses.
† This column provides guidelines for further assessment and initial nursing interventions.

## Neonatal Physical Assessment Guide *(continued)*

| Assessment and Normal Findings | Alterations and Possible Causes* | Nursing Responses to Data Base† |
|---|---|---|
| Moderate bulging noted with crying, stooling, or pulsations with heartbeat | Bulging (increased intracranial pressure, meningitis)<br>Sunken (dehydration) | Evaluate hydration status. |
| **Hair** | | |
| Texture<br>Smooth with fine texture variations (Note: variations dependent on ethnic background) | Coarse, brittle, dry hair (hypothyroidism)<br>White forelock (Waardenburg syndrome) | Instruct parents regarding routine care of hair and scalp. |
| Distribution<br>Scalp hair high over eyebrows (Spanish-Mexican hairline begins mid-forehead and extends down back of neck) | Low forehead and posterior hairlines may indicate chromosomal disorders. | Assess for other signs of chromosomal aberrations.<br>Refer to physician. |
| **Face** | | |
| Symmetrical movement of all facial features, normal hairline, eyebrows and eyelashes present | | Assess and record symmetry of all parts, shape, regularity of features, sameness or differences in features. |
| Spacing of features<br>Eyes at same level; nostrils equal size, cheeks full, and sucking pads present | Eyes wide apart—ocular hypertelorism (Apert syndrome, cri-du-chat, Turner syndrome) | Observe for other signs and symptoms indicative of disease states or chromosomal aberrations. |
| Lips equal on both sides of midline | Abnormal face (Down syndrome, cretinism, gargoylism) | |
| Chin recedes when compared to other bones of face | Abnormally small jaw—micrognathia (Pierre Robin syndrome, Treacher Collins syndrome) | Maintain airway.<br>Initiate surgical consultation and referral. |
| Movement<br>Makes facial grimaces | Inability to suck, grimace, and close eyelids (cranial nerve injury) | Initiate neurologic assessment and consultation. |
| Symmetrical when resting and crying | Asymmetry (paralysis of facial cranial nerve) | Assess and record symmetry of all parts, shape, regularity of features, sameness or differences in features. |
| **Eyes** | | |
| General placement and appearance<br>Bright and clear; even placement; slight nystagmus | Gross nystagmus (damage to third, fourth, and sixth cranial nerves) | |
| Concomitant strabismus | Constant and fixed strabismus | Reassure parents that strabismus is considered normal up to six months. |
| Move in all directions<br>Blue- or slate-blue gray | Lack of pigmentation (albinism)<br>Brushfield spots (may indicate Down syndrome) | Discuss with parents any necessary eye precautions.<br>Assess for other signs of Down syndrome. |
| Brown color at birth in dark-skinned infants | | Discuss with parents that permanent eye color is usually established by three months of age. |

*Possible causes of alterations are placed in parentheses.
† This column provides guidelines for further assessment and initial nursing interventions.

*(continues)*

## Neonatal Physical Assessment Guide (continued)

| Assessment and Normal Findings | Alterations and Possible Causes* | Nursing Responses to Data Base† |
|---|---|---|
| **Eyelids**<br>Position: above pupils but within iris, no drooping | Elevation or retraction of upper lid (hyperthyroidism)<br><br>"Setting sun" (hydrocephalus), ptosis (congenital or paralysis of oculomotor muscle) | Assess for signs of hydrocephalus and hyperthyroidism.<br>Evaluate interference with vision in subsequent well-baby visits. |
| Eyes on parallel plane<br>Epicanthal folds in Asian and 20% of Caucasian newborns | Upward slant in non-Asians (Down syndrome)<br>Epicanthal folds (Down syndrome, cri-du-chat syndrome) | Assess for other signs of Down syndrome. |
| **Movement**<br>Blink reflex in response to light stimulus | | |
| **Inspection**<br>Edematous for first few days of life, resulting from birth and instillation of silver nitrate (chemical conjunctivitis); no lumps or redness | Purulent drainage (infection); infectious conjunctivitis (staphylococcus or gram-negative organisms)<br>Marginal blepharitis (lid edges red, crusted, scaly) | Initiate good hand washing.<br>Refer to physician.<br>Evaluate infant for seborrheic dermatitis; scales can be removed easily. |
| **Cornea**<br>Clear<br>Corneal reflex present | Ulceration (herpes infection); large cornea or corneas of unequal size (congenital glaucoma)<br>Clouding, opacity of lens (cataract) | Refer to ophthalmologist.<br>Assess for other manifestations of congenital herpes; institute nursing care measures. |
| **Sclera**<br>May appear bluish in newborn, then white; slightly brownish color frequent in blacks | True blue sclera (osteogenesis imperfecta) | Refer to physician. |
| **Pupils**<br>Pupils equal in size, round, and react to light by accommodation | Anisocoria—unequal pupils (CNS damage)<br>Dilation or constriction (intracranial damage, retinoblastoma, glaucoma)<br>Pupils nonreactive to light or accommodation (brain injury) | Refer for neurologic examination. |
| Slight nystagmus in infant who has not learned to focus<br>Pupil light reflex demonstrated at birth or by three weeks of age | Nystagmus (labyrinthine disturbance, CNS disorder) | |
| **Conjunctiva**<br>Chemical conjunctivitis<br>Subconjunctival hemorrhage | Pale color (anemia) | Obtain hematocrit and hemoglobin.<br>Reassure parents that chemical conjunctivitis will subside in one to two days and subconjunctival hemorrhage disappears in a few weeks. |
| Palpebral conjunctiva (red but not hyperemic) | Inflammation or edema (infection, blocked tear duct) | |

*Possible causes of alterations are placed in parentheses.
† This column provides guidelines for further assessment and initial nursing interventions.

## Neonatal Physical Assessment Guide (continued)

| Assessment and Normal Findings | Alterations and Possible Causes* | Nursing Responses to Data Base† |
|---|---|---|
| Vision<br>20/150<br>Tracks moving object to midline<br>Fixed focus on objects at a distance of about 7 in; may be difficult to evaluate in newborn<br>Prefers faces, geometric designs, and black and white to colors | Cataracts (congenital infection) | Record any questions about visual acuity and initiate follow-up evaluation at first well-baby checkup. |
| Lashes and lacrimal glands<br>Presence of lashes (lashes may be absent in preterm infants) | No lashes on inner two thirds of lid (Treacher Collins syndrome); bushy lashes (Hurler syndrome); long lashes (Cornelia de Lange syndrome) | |
| Cry commonly tearless | Excessive tearing (plugged lacrimal duct, natal narcotic withdrawal) | Demonstrate to parents how to milk blocked tear duct.<br>Refer to ophthalmologist if tearing is excessive before third month of life. |
| **Nose** | | |
| Appearance of external nasal aspects<br>May appear flattened as a result of delivery process | Continued flat or broad bridge of nose (Down syndrome) | Arrange consultation with specialist. |
| Small and narrow in midline; even placement in relationship to eyes and mouth | Low bridge of nose; beaklike nose (Apert syndrome, Treacher Collins syndrome)<br>Upturned (Cornelia de Lange syndrome) | Initiate evaluation of chromosomal abnormalities. |
| Patent nares bilaterally (nose breathers) | Blockage of nares (mucus and/or secretions) | Inspect for obstruction of nares. |
| Sneezing common to clear nasal passages | Flaring nares (respiratory distress)<br>Choanal atresia | |
| Identifies odors, appears to smell breast milk | No response to stimulating odors | Inspect for obstruction of nares. |
| **Mouth** | | |
| Function of facial, hypoglossal, glossopharyngeal, and vagus nerves<br>Symmetry of movement and strength | Mouth draws to one side (transient seventh cranial nerve paralysis due to pressure in utero or trauma during birth, congenital paralysis) | Initiate neurologic consultation.<br>Administer eye care if eye on affected side is unable to close. |
| | Fishlike shape (Treacher Collins syndrome) | |
| Presence of gag, swallowing, coordinated with sucking reflexes<br>Adequate salivation | Suppressed or absent reflexes | Evaluate other neurologic functions of these nerves. |
| Palate (soft and hard)<br>Hard palate dome-shaped<br>Uvula midline with symmetrical movement of soft palate | High-steepled palate (Treacher Collins syndrome) | |

*Possible causes of alterations are placed in parentheses.
† This column provides guidelines for further assessment and initial nursing interventions.

(continues)

## Neonatal Physical Assessment Guide (continued)

| Assessment and Normal Findings | Alterations and Possible Causes* | Nursing Responses to Data Base† |
|---|---|---|
| Palate intact, sucks well when stimulated | Clefts in either hard or soft palate (polygenic disorder) | Initiate a surgical consultation referral. |
| Epithelial (Epstein's) pearls appear on mucosa | | Assure parents that these are normal in newborn and will disappear at two or three months of age. |
| Esophagus patent; some drooling common in newborn | Excessive drooling or bubbling (esophageal atresia) | Test for patency of esophagus. |
| **Tongue** | | |
| Free-moving in all directions, midline | Lack of movement or asymmetrical movement<br>Tongue-tied | Further assess neurologic functions.<br>Test reflex elevation of tongue when depressed with tongue blade. |
| | Deviations from midline (cranial nerve damage) | Check for signs of weakness or deviation. |
| Pink color, smooth to rough texture, noncoated | White cheesy coating (thrush)<br>Tongue has deep ridges | Differentiate between thrush and milk curds.<br>Reassure parents that tongue pattern may change from day to day. |
| Tongue proportional to mouth | Large tongue with short frenulum (cretinism, Down syndrome, other syndromes) | Evaluate in well-baby clinic to assess development delays.<br>Initiate referrals. |
| **Ears** | | |
| External ear | | |
| Without lesions, cysts, or nodules | Nodules, cysts, or sinus tracts in front of ear<br>Adherent earlobes | Evaluate characteristics of lesions.<br>Counsel parents to clean external ear with washcloth only; discourage use of cotton-tip applicators. |
| | Preauricular skin tags | Refer to physician for ligation. |
| Hearing | | |
| With first cry, eustachian tubes are cleared | | |
| Absence of all risk factors | Presence of one or more risk factors | Assess history of risk factors for hearing loss. |
| Attends to sounds; sudden or loud noise elicits Moro reflex | No response to sound stimuli (deafness) | Test for Moro reflex. |
| **Neck** | | |
| Appearance | | |
| Short, straight, creased with skin folds | Abnormally short neck (Turner syndrome)<br>Arching or inability to flex neck (meningitis, congenital anomaly) | Report findings to physician. |
| Posterior neck lacks loose extra folds of skin | Webbing of neck (Turner syndrome, Down syndrome, trisomy 18) | Assess for other signs of the syndromes. |
| Clavicles | | |
| Straight and intact | Knot or lump on clavicle (fracture during difficult delivery) | Obtain detailed labor and birth history; apply figure-8 bandage. |
| Moro reflex elicitable | Unilateral Moro reflex response on unaffected side (fracture of clavicle, brachial palsy, Erb-Duchenne paralysis) | Collaborate with physician. |

*Possible causes of alterations are placed in parentheses.
† This column provides guidelines for further assessment and initial nursing interventions.

## Neonatal Physical Assessment Guide *(continued)*

| Assessment and Normal Findings | Alterations and Possible Causes* | Nursing Responses to Data Base† |
|---|---|---|
| Symmetrical shoulders | Hypoplasia | |
| **Chest** | | |
| Appearance and size | | Measure at level of nipples after exhalation |
| Circumference: 32.5 cm, 1–2 cm less than head | | |
| Wider than it is long | | |
| Normal shape without depressed or prominent sternum | Funnel chest (congenital or associated with Marfan syndrome) | Determine adequacy of other respiratory and circulatory signs. |
| Lower end of sternum (xiphoid cartilage) may be protruding; is less apparent after several weeks | Continued protrusion of xiphoid cartilage (Marfan syndrome, "pigeon chest") | Assess for other signs and symptoms of various syndromes. |
| Sternum 8 cm long | Barrel chest | |
| Expansion and retraction | | |
| Bilateral expansion | Unequal chest expansion (pneumonia, pneumothorax respiratory distress) | Assess respiratory effort regularity, flaring of nares, difficulty on both inspiration and expiration. |
| No intercostal, subcostal, or supracostal retractions | Retractions (respiratory distress) | Record and consult physician. |
| Auscultation | | |
| Breath sounds are louder in infants | Decreased breath sounds (decreased respiratory activity, atelectasis, pneumothorax) | Perform assessment and report to physician any positive findings. |
| Chest and axilla clear on crying | Increased breath sounds (resolving pneumonia or in cesarean births) | |
| Bronchial breath sounds (heard where trachea and bronchi closest to chest wall, above sternum and between scapulae) | | |
| Bronchial sounds bilaterally | Adventitious or abnormal sounds (respiratory disease or distress) | |
| Air entry clear | | |
| Rales may indicate normal newborn atelectasis | | |
| Cough reflex absent at birth, appears in two or more days | | |
| Breasts | | |
| Flat with symmetrical nipples | Lack of breast tissue (preterm or SGA) | |
| Breast tissue diameter 5 cm or more at term | | |
| Distance between nipples 8 cm | | |
| Breast engorgement occurs on third day of life; liquid discharge may be expressed in term infants | Breast abscesses | Reassure parents of normalcy of breast engorgement. |
| Nipples | Supernumerary nipples | |
| | Dark-colored nipples | |
| **Heart** | | |
| Auscultation | | |
| Location: lies horizontally, with left border extending to left of midclavicle | | |
| Regular rhythm and rate | Arrhythmia (anoxia), tachycardia, bradycardia | Refer all arrhythmia and gallop rhythms. |

*Possible causes of alterations are placed in parentheses.
† This column provides guidelines for further assessment and initial nursing interventions.

*(continues)*

# Neonatal Physical Assessment Guide *(continued)*

| Assessment and Normal Findings | Alterations and Possible Causes* | Nursing Responses to Data Base† |
|---|---|---|
| Determination of point of maximal impulse (PMI)<br>  Usually lateral to midclavicular line at third or fourth intercostal space | Malpositioning (enlargement, abnormal placement, pneumothorax, dextrocardia, diaphragmatic hernia) | Initiate cardiac evaluation. |
| Functional murmurs<br>No thrills | Location of murmurs (possible congenital cardiac anomaly) | Evaluate murmur: location, timing, and duration; observe for accompanying cardiac pathology symptoms; ascertain family history. |
| Horizontal groove at diaphragm shows flaring of rib cage to mild degree | Marked rib flaring (vitamin D deficiency)<br>Inadequacy of respiratory movement | Initiate cardiopulmonary evaluation; assess pulses and blood pressures in all four extremities for equality and quality. |
| **Abdomen** | | |
| Appearance<br>  Cylindrical with some protrusion; appears large in relation to pelvis; some laxness of abdominal muscles<br>  No cyanosis, few vessels seen<br>  Diastasis recti—common in black infants | Distention, shiny abdomen with engorged vessels (gastrointestinal abnormalities, infection, congenital megacolon)<br>Scaphoid abdominal appearance (diaphragmatic hernia)<br>Increased or decreased peristalsis (duodenal stenosis, small bowel obstruction)<br>Localized flank bulging (enlarged kidneys, ascites, or absent abdominal muscles) | Examine abdomen thoroughly for mass or organomegaly.<br>Measure abdominal girth.<br>Report deviations of abdominal size.<br>Assess other signs and symptoms of obstruction.<br><br>Refer to physician. |
| Umbilicus<br>  No protrusion of umbilicus (protrusion of umbilicus common in black infants)<br>  Bluish white color<br>  Cutis navel (umbilical cord projects); granulation tissue in navel | Umbilical hernia<br>Patent urachus (congenital malformation)<br>Omphalocele<br>Gastroschisis<br>Redness or exudate around cord (infection)<br>Yellow discoloration (hemolytic disease, meconium staining) | Measure umbilical hernia by palpating the opening and record; it should close by one year of age; if not, refer to physician.<br>Instruct parents on cord care and hygiene. |
| Two arteries and one vein apparent<br>Begins drying one to two hours after birth<br>No bleeding<br>Auscultation and percussion<br>Soft bowel sounds heard shortly after birth; heard every 10–30 sec | Single umbilical artery (congenital anomalies)<br><br><br>Bowel sounds in chest (diaphragmatic hernia)<br>Absence of bowel sounds<br>Hyperperistalsis (intestinal obstruction) | Collaborate with physician.<br><br>Assess for other signs of dehydration and/or infection. |
| Femoral pulses<br>  Palpable, equal, bilateral | Absent or diminished femoral pulses (coarctation of aorta) | Monitor blood pressure in upper and lower extremities. |
| Inguinal area<br>  No bulges along inguinal area<br>  No inguinal lymph nodes felt | Inguinal hernia | Initiate referral.<br>Continue follow-up in well-baby clinic. |

*Possible causes of alterations are placed in parentheses.
† This column provides guidelines for further assessment and initial nursing interventions.

## Neonatal Physical Assessment Guide (continued)

| Assessment and Normal Findings | Alterations and Possible Causes* | Nursing Responses to Data Base† |
|---|---|---|
| **Bladder** <br> Percusses 1–4 cm above symphysis <br> Emptied about three hours after birth; if not, at time of birth <br> Urine—inoffensive, mild odor | Failure to void within 24–48 hours after birth <br> Exposure of bladder mucosa (exstrophy of bladder) <br> Foul odor (infection) | Check if baby voided at birth. <br> Consult with clinician; obtain urine specimen if infection is suspected. |
| **Genitals** <br> Gender clearly delineated | Ambiguous genitals | Refer for genetic consultation. |
| **Male** <br> Penis <br> Slender in appearance, 2.5 cm long, 1 cm wide at birth <br> Normal urinary orifice, urethral meatus at tip of penis | Micropenis (congenital anomaly) <br> Meatal atresia | Observe and record first voiding. |
|  | Hypospadias, epispadias | Collaborate with physician in presence of abnormality. |
| Noninflamed urethral opening | Urethritis (infection) | Palpate for enlarged inguinal lymph nodes and record painful urination. |
| Foreskin adheres to glans; prepuce can be retracted beyond urethral opening | Ulceration of meatal opening (infection, inflammation) | Evaluate whether ulcer is due to diaper rash; counsel regarding care. |
| Uncircumcised foreskin tight for two to three months | Phimosis—if still tight after three months | Instruct parents on how to care for uncircumcised penis. |
| Circumcised <br> Erectile tissue present |  | Teach parents how to care for circumcision. |
| Scrotum <br> Skin loose and hanging or tight and small; extensive rugae and normal size <br> Normal skin color <br> Scrotal discoloration common in breech | Large scrotum containing fluid (hydrocele) <br> Red, shiny scrotal skin (orchitis) | Shine a light through scrotum (transilluminate) to verify diagnosis. |
| Testes <br> Descended by birth; not consistently found in scrotum | Undescended testes (cryptorchidism) | If testes cannot be felt in scrotum, gently palpate femoral, inguinal, perineal, and abdominal areas for presence. |
| Testes size 1.5–2 cm at birth | Enlarged testes (tumor) <br> Small testes (Klinefelter syndrome or adrenal hyperplasia) | Refer and collaborate with physician for further diagnostic studies. |
| **Female** <br> Mons <br> Normal skin color; area pigmented in dark-skinned infants <br> Labia majora cover labia minora; symmetrical size appropriate for gestational age | Hematoma, lesions | Evaluate for recent trauma. |
| Clitoris <br> Normally large in newborn <br> Edema and bruising in breech birth | Hypertrophy (hermaphroditism) |  |

*Possible causes of alterations are placed in parentheses.
† This column provides guidelines for further assessment and initial nursing interventions.

*(continues)*

# Neonatal Physical Assessment Guide (continued)

| Assessment and Normal Findings | Alterations and Possible Causes* | Nursing Responses to Data Base† |
|---|---|---|
| **Vagina** | | |
| Urinary meatus and vaginal orifice visible (0.5 cm circumference) | Inflammation; erythema and discharge (urethritis) | Collect urine specimen for laboratory examination. |
| Vaginal tag or hymenal tag disappears in a few weeks | Congenital absence of vagina | Refer to physician. |
| Discharge; smegma under labia | Foul-smelling discharge (infection) | Collect data and further evaluate reason for discharge. |
| Bloody or mucoid discharge | Excessive vaginal bleeding (blood coagulation defect) | |
| **Buttocks and Anus** | | |
| Buttocks symmetrical | Pilonidal dimple | Examine for possible sinus. Instruct parents about cleansing this area. |
| Anus patent and passage of meconium within 24–48 hours after birth | Imperforate anus, rectal atresia (congenital gastrointestinal defect) | Evaluate extent of problems. Initiate surgical consultation. Perform digital examination to ascertain patency, if patency uncertain. |
| No fissures, tears, or skin tags | Fissures | |
| **Extremities and Trunk** | | |
| Short and generally flexed; extremities move symmetrically through range of motion but lack full extension | Unilateral or absence of movement (spinal cord involvement) Fetal position continued or limp (anoxia, CNS problems, hypoglycemia) | Review birth record to assess possible cause. |
| All joints move spontaneously; good muscle tone, of flexor type, birth to two months | Spasticity when infant begins using extensors (cerebral palsy, lack of muscle tone, "floppy baby" syndrome) | Collaborate with physician. |
| Arms | | |
| Equal in length | Brachial palsy (difficult delivery) | Report to clinician. |
| Bilateral movement | Erb-Duchenne paralysis | |
| Flexed when quiet | Muscle weakness, fractured clavicle Absence of limb or change of size (phocomelia, amelia) | |
| Hands | | |
| Normal number of fingers | Polydactyly (Ellis-Van Creveld syndrome) Syndactyly—one limb (developmental anomaly) Syndactyly—both limbs (genetic component) | Report to clinician. |
| Normal palmar crease | Simian line on palm (Down syndrome) | |
| Normal size hands | Short fingers and broad hand (Hurler syndrome) | |
| Nails present and extend beyond fingertips in term infant | Cyanosis and clubbing (cardiac anomalies) Nails long (postterm) | |

*Possible causes of alterations are placed in parentheses.
† This column provides guidelines for further assessment and initial nursing interventions.

## Neonatal Physical Assessment Guide *(continued)*

| Assessment and Normal Findings | Alterations and Possible Causes* | Nursing Responses to Data Base† |
|---|---|---|
| **Spine**<br>C-shaped spine<br>Flat and straight when prone<br>Slight lumbar lordosis<br>Easily flexed and intact when palpated<br>At least half of back devoid of lanugo<br>Full-term infant in ventral suspension should hold head at 45° angle, back straight | Spina bifida occulta (nevus pilosus)<br>Dermal sinus<br>Myelomeningocele<br>Head lag, limp, floppy trunk (neurologic problems) | Evaluate extent of neurologic damage; initiate care of spinal opening. |
| **Hips**<br>No sign of instability | Sensation of abnormal movement, jerk, or snap of hip dislocation | Examine all newborn infants for dislocated hip prior to discharge from hospital. |
| Hips abduct to more than 60° | | If this is suspected, refer to orthopedist for further evaluation.<br>Reassess at well-baby visits. |
| **Inguinal and buttock skin creases**<br>Symmetrical inguinal and buttock creases | Asymmetry (dislocated hips) | Refer to orthopedist for evaluation, counsel parents regarding symptoms of concern and discuss therapy. |
| **Legs**<br>Legs equal in length<br>Legs shorter than arms at birth | Shortened leg (dislocated hips)<br>Lack of leg movement (fractures, spinal defects) | Refer to orthopedist for evaluation.<br>Counsel parents regarding symptoms of concern and discuss therapy. |
| **Feet**<br>Foot is in straight line<br>Positional clubfoot—based on position in utero<br>Fat pads and creases on soles of feet | Talipes equinovarus (true clubfoot) | Discuss differences between positional and true clubfoot with parents.<br>Teach parents passive manipulation of foot.<br>Refer to orthopedist if not corrected by three months of age. |
| Talipes planus (flat feet) normal under three years of age | | Reassure parents that flat feet are normal in infant. |
| **Neuromuscular** | | |
| **Motor function**<br>Symmetrical movement and strength in all extremities | Limp, flaccid, or hypertonic (CNS disorders, infection, dehydration, fracture) | Appraise newborn's posture and motor functions by observing activities and motor characteristics. |
| May be jerky or have brief twitchings | Tremors (hypoglycemia, hypocalcemia, infection, neurologic damage) | Evaluate electrolyte imbalance and neurologic functioning. |
| Head lag not over 45° | Delayed or abnormal development (preterm, neurologic involvement) | |
| Neck control adequate to maintain head erect briefly | Asymmetry of tone or strength | |
| **Reflexes**<br>**Blink**<br>Stimulated by flash of light, response is closure of eyelids | Damage to cranial nerve | |

*Possible causes of alterations are placed in parentheses.
† This column provides guidelines for further assessment and initial nursing interventions.

*(continues)*

## Neonatal Physical Assessment Guide (continued)

| Assessment and Normal Findings | Alterations and Possible Causes* | Nursing Responses to Data Base† |
|---|---|---|
| **Pupillary reflex**<br>Stimulated by flash of light, response is constriction of pupil | Damage to cranial nerve | |
| **Moro**<br>Response to sudden movement or loud noise should be one of symmetrical extension and abduction of arms with fingers extended; then return to normal relaxed flexion<br>Infant lying on back: slightly raised head suddenly released; infant held horizontally, lowered quickly about 6 in, and stopped abruptly<br>Fingers form a C<br>Present at birth, disappears by six months of age | Asymmetry of body response (fractured clavicle, injury to brachial plexus)<br>Consistent absence (brain damage) | Discuss normality of this reflex in response to loud noises and/or sudden movements. |
| **Rooting and sucking**<br>Turns in direction of stimulus to cheek or mouth; opens mouth and begins to suck rhythmically when finger or nipple is inserted into mouth; difficult to elicit after feeding; disappears by four to seven months of age<br>Sucking is adequate for nutritional intake and meeting oral stimulation needs; disappears by 12 months | Poor sucking or easily fatigable (preterm; breast-fed infants of barbiturate-addicted mothers)<br>Absence of response (preterm, neurologic involvement, depressed infants) | Evaluate strength and coordination of sucking.<br>Observe neonate during feeding and counsel parents about mutuality of feeding experience and neonate's responses. |
| **Palmar grasp**<br>Fingers grasp adult finger when palm is stimulated and hold momentarily; lessens at three to four months of age | Asymmetry of response (neurologic problems) | Evaluate other reflexes and general neurologic functioning. |

*Possible causes of alterations are placed in parentheses.
† This column provides guidelines for further assessment and initial nursing interventions.

The behaviors and the sleep-wake states in which they are assessed are categorized as follows:

*Habituation.* The infant's ability to diminish or shut down innate responses to specific repeated stimuli, such as a rattle, bell, light, or pinprick to heel, is assessed.

*Orientation to inanimate and animate visual and auditory assessment stimuli.* How often and where the newborn attends to auditory and visual stimuli are observed. The infant's orientation to the environment is determined by an ability to respond to clues given by others and by a natural ability to fix on and to follow a visual object horizontally and vertically. This capacity and parental appreciation of it are important for positive communication between infant and parents; the parents' visual (*en face*) and auditory (soft, continuous voice) presence stimulates their infant to orient to them. Inability or lack of response may indicate visual or auditory problems. It is important for parents to know that their infant can turn to voices by three days of age and can become alert at different times with a varying degree of intensity in response to sounds.

*Motor activity.* Several components are evaluated. Motor tone of the newborn is assessed in the most characteristic state of responsiveness. This summary assessment includes overall use of tone as the neonate responds to being handled—whether during spontaneous activity, prone placement, or horizontal holding—and overall assessment of body tone as the neonate reacts to all stimuli.

## Neonatal Physical Assessment Guide *(continued)*

| Assessment and Normal Findings | Alterations and Possible Causes* | Nursing Responses to Data Base† |
|---|---|---|
| **Plantar grasp**<br>Toes curl downward when sole of foot is stimulated; lessens by eight months | Absent (defects of lower spinal column) | |
| **Stepping**<br>When held upright and one foot touching a flat surface, will step alternately; disappears at four to five months of age | Asymmetry of stepping (neurologic abnormality) | Evaluate muscle tone and function on each side of body.<br>Refer to specialist. |
| **Babinski**<br>Fanning and extension of all toes when one side of sole is stroked from heel upward across ball of foot | Absence of response (low spinal cord defects) | Refer for further neurologic evaluation. |
| **Tonic neck**<br>Fencer position—when head is turned to one side, extremities on same side extend and on opposite side flex; this reflex may not be evident during early neonatal period; disappears at three to four months of age<br>Response often more dominant in leg than in arm | Absent after one month of age or persistent asymmetry (cerebral lesion) | |
| **Prone crawl**<br>While on abdomen, neonate pushes up and tries to crawl | Absence or variance of response (preterm, weak or depressed infants) | Evaluate motor functioning.<br>Refer to specialist. |
| **Trunk incurvation**<br>In prone position, stroking of spine causes pelvis to turn to stimulated side | Failure to rotate to stimulated side (neurologic damage) | |

*Possible causes of alterations are placed in parentheses.
† This column provides guidelines for further assessment and initial nursing interventions.

*Variations.* Frequency of alert states, state changes, color changes (throughout all states as examination progresses), activity, and peaks of excitement are assessed.

*Self-quieting activity.* Assessment is based on how often, how quickly, and how effectively newborns can use their resources to quiet and console themselves when upset or distressed. Considered in this assessment are such self-consolatory activities as putting hand to mouth, sucking on a fist or the tongue, and attuning to an object or sound. The infant's need for outside consolation must also be considered, for example, seeing a face; being rocked, held, or dressed; using a pacifier; and having extremities restrained.

*Cuddliness or social behaviors.* This area encompasses the infant's need for and response to being held. Also considered is how often the newborn smiles. These behaviors influence the parents' self-esteem and feelings of acceptance or rejection. Cuddling also appears to be an indicator of personality. Cuddlers appear to enjoy, accept, and seek physical contact; are easier to placate; sleep more; and form earlier and more intense attachments. Noncuddlers are active, restless, have accelerated motor development, and are intolerant of physical restraint. Smiling, even as a grimace reflex, greatly influences parent-infant feedback. Parents identify this response as positive.

# ESSENTIAL CONCEPTS

● A perinatal history, determination of gestational age, physical examination, and behavior assessment forms the basis for complete newborn assessment.

● The common physical characteristics included in the gestational age assessment are: skin, lanugo, sole (plantar) creases, breast tissue and size, ear form and cartilage, and genitalia.

● The neuromuscular components of gestational age scoring tools are usually posture, square window sign, popliteal angle, arm recoil, heel to ear, and scarf sign.

● By assessing the physical and neuromuscular components of a gestational age tool, the nurse can determine the gestational age of the newborn.

● After determining the gestational age of the baby, the nurse can assess how the newborn will make the transition to extrauterine life and anticipate potential physiologic problems.

● In-depth knowledge of normal newborn physical characteristics and common variations is essential for the newborn nurse.

● Normal ranges for vital signs assessed in the newborn are: Heart rate—120–150 beats/min; respirations—30–60 respirations/min; axillary temperature—36.5°C—37°C (97.7°F–98.6°F), or skin temperature—36°C–36.5°C (96.8°F–97.7°F), or rectal temperature—36.6°C–37.2°C (97.8°F–99°F); and blood pressure at birth of 80–60/45–40 mm Hg.

● Normal newborn measurements include: Weight range 2950–3515 g (6 lb, 8 oz–7 lb, 2 oz), with weight dependent on maternal size and age; length range 45.8–52.3 cm (18–20.5 in); and head circumference range of 33–35 cm (13–14 in)—aproximately 2 cm larger than the chest circumference.

● Commonly elicited newborn reflexes are tonic neck, Moro, grasp, rooting, sucking, and blink.

● An important role of the nurse during the physical and behavioral assessments of the newborn is to teach parents about their newborn and involve them in their baby's care. This facilitates the parents' identification of their newborn's uniqueness and allays their concerns.

## References

AAP Committee on Fetus and Newborn and ACOG Committee on Obstetrics: *Guidelines for Perinatal Care.* Evanston IL: American Academy of Pediatrics, 1988.

Ballard JL et al: A simplified score for assessment of fetal maturation of newly born infants. *J Pediatr* November 1979; 95:769.

Brazelton T: *The Neonatal Behavioral Assessment Scale.* Philadelphia: Lippincott, 1973.

Brazelton T: Neonatal behavior and its significance. In: *Schaeffer's Diseases of the Newborn.* Avery ME, Taeusch HW (editors). Philadelphia: Saunders, 1984.

Duara S et al: Neonatal screening with auditory brainstem responses: Results of a follow-up audiometry and risk factor evaluation. *J Pediatr* 1986; 108(2):276.

Korones, SB: *High-Risk Newborn Infants,* 4th ed. St. Louis: Mosby, 1986.

Ludington-Hoe SM: What can newborns really see? *Am J Nurs* 1983; 83:1286.

## Additional Readings

Budreau G: Postnatal cranial molding and infant attractiveness: Implications for nursing. *Neonatal Netw* April 1987; 5:13.

Haddock B, Vincent P, Merow D: Axillary and rectal temperatures of full-term neonates: Are they different? *Neonatal Netw* 1986; 5(1):36.

Judd JM: Assessing the newborn from head to toe. *Nurs* 1985; 15:12.

Klaus M, Klaus PH: *The Amazing Newborn.* Reading, MA: Addison-Wesley, 1985.

Korones SB: The normal neonate: Assessment of early physical findings. In: *Gynecology and Obstetrics.* Vol 2. Sciarra J et al (editors). Hagerstown, MD: Harper and Row, 1985.

Lascari AD: "Early" breast-feeding jaundice: Clinical significance. *J Pediatr* January 1986; 108:156.

Scanlon JW et al: *A System of Newborn Physical Examination.* Baltimore: University Park Press, 1979.

Sendak MJ, Harris AP: Neonatal pulse oximetry in the delivery room: Review of recent investigations. *P/N* 1987; 11(1):8.

Stephen SB, Sexton PR: Neonatal axillary temperatures: Increases in readings over time. *Neonatal Netw* 1987; 5(6):25.

White PL et al: Comparative accuracy of recent abbreviated methods of gestational age determination. *Clin Pediatr* 1980; 19(5):319.

Zachman RD et al: Neonatal blood pressure at birth by the Doppler method. *Am Heart J* January 1986; 111:189.

# The Normal Newborn: Needs and Care

*When our daughter was laid in my arms right after birth she was so delicate. I had not dared to hope that we would be blessed with a girl because there were so few girls in my husband's family. Our two-year-old niece was the first girl in 107 years, so I had pretty much decided that another boy would be just fine. But here she was, right here in my arms.*

## Objectives

● Summarize the essential areas of information to be obtained about a newborn's birth experience and immediate postnatal period.

● Explain the physiologic and behavioral responses of newborns during periods of reactivity and possible interventions needed.

● Discuss the major nursing considerations and activities to be carried out during the first four hours after birth (admission and transitional period) and subsequent daily care.

● Identify the assessments and activities that should be included in a daily care plan for a normal newborn.

● Determine common parental concerns regarding their newborns.

● Describe the topics and related content to be included in parent education classes on newborn/infant care.

● Identify the information to be included in discharge planning with parents.

## Key Terms

circumcision
newborn screening tests
parent-infant attachment
periods of reactivity

At the moment of birth, numerous physiologic adaptations begin to take place in the newborn's body. Because of these dramatic changes, newborns require close observation to determine how smoothly they are making the transition to extrauterine life. Newborns also require care that enhances their chances of making the transition successfully.

The two broad goals of nursing care during this period are to promote the physical well-being of the newborn and to promote the establishment of a well-functioning family unit. The first goal is met by providing comprehensive care to the newborn while he or she is in the nursery. The second goal is met by teaching parents how to care for their new baby and by supporting their parenting efforts so that they feel confident and competent. Thus, the nurse should be knowledgeable about family adjustments that need to be made, as well as the health care needs of the newborn. With such a background, the nurse can provide comprehensive care and promote the establishment of a well-functioning family unit. It is important that new parents return home with the positive feeling that they have the support, information, and skills to care for their child. Equally important is the need for the family to begin a unique relationship between family members and the new child. The cultural and social expectations of individual families and communities affect the way in which normal newborn care is carried out.

## ● USING THE NURSING PROCESS DURING THE NORMAL NEWBORN PERIOD

## ● Nursing Assessment

Assessment during the neonatal period gives the nurse an opportunity to identify any actual or potential physical problems facing the newborn. Careful assessment of the general characteristics, variations, and responses of the newborn helps the nurse differentiate between normal physiologic adaptations and abnormal findings that require further evaluation. Individual temperament and behavior patterns need to be assessed. These assessments are discussed in detail in Chapter 21.

During the newborn assessment, the nurse determines the presence of any psychosocial factors that may affect the family's ability to integrate its newest member. The nurse's assessment should reveal the extent of the family's need for information, support, and instruction about child care. Identifying the family's strengths is just as important as identifying problems because these strengths can be incorporated in the care plan. To perform an accurate family assessment, the nurse must be knowledgeable about the characteristics of the expanding family.

An accurate assessment is essential during this period, since the plan of care is based on the findings of the assessment. If the assessment is inadequate, the plan of care will most likely be ineffective as well. The newborn's successful transition to extrauterine life may ultimately depend on the nurse's ability to identify physiologic needs correctly. The family's ability to meet the physical and psychologic needs of the newborn may be affected by the nurse's accuracy in identifying their strengths and weaknesses.

Assessment is performed on a daily basis while the newborn is present on the birthing unit. The daily assessment period is an opportune time for parent education. The nurse can explain the newborn's physiologic and behavioral changes and responses as the assessment proceeds.

## ● Nursing Diagnosis

Nursing diagnoses are based on an analysis of the findings of the assessment. Physiologic alterations of the newborn form the basis of many nursing diagnoses, as does the family's incorporation and care of their new baby. Nursing diagnoses that may apply to the newborn and family include:

- Ineffective airway clearance related to mucus obstruction
- Altered patterns of urinary elimination related to circumcision
- Altered nutrition: less than body requirements related to limited nutritional/fluid intake
- Pain related to heel sticks for blood glucose and hematocrit
- Knowledge deficit related to lack of experience in infant care
- Knowledge deficit related to decision about male circumcision
- Altered parenting related to the need to integrate the newborn into the family unit

Identification, prioritization, and documentation of the nursing diagnoses are essential for developing a thoughtful, systematic plan of care.

## ● Nursing Plan and Implementation

Even though most newborns are healthy, every newborn has physiologic needs that must be met. The family

also has needs, which are usually psychologic and educational. To meet these needs in an organized fashion, the neonatal nurse must develop a plan of care based on the assessment findings and nursing diagnoses.

A nursing care plan is important to ensure consistent and comprehensive care. Even though most newborns and their mothers remain in the birthing unit for a brief period, they may have several nurses administering care during their stay. When there is one care plan implemented by all personnel caring for the family, the goals of care are more likely to be achieved. Redundancy or missed interventions are less likely, and parent education can proceed at a steady pace, even though different nurses are teaching.

## ● Evaluation

Through ongoing observations nurses evaluate whether the newborn's body systems are successfully maturing and adapting to extrauterine life. This evaluation is based on knowledge of the expected cardiovascular, pulmonary, renal, and neurologic changes that occur in the days immediately following birth.

To evaluate the daily nursing care given to the newborn, the nurse notes whether complications have developed in the baby. The success of parent education can be evaluated by how well the parents perform baby care measures and how comfortable they feel in caring for their baby.

## ● NURSING ASSESSMENT DURING THE FIRST FOUR HOURS

Nursing assessments of the general characteristics, variations, and responses of each newborn reveal how extrauterine adaptation is proceeding. Based on their findings, nurses can individualize their care to meet the needs of each newborn.

## ● Admission Assessment Procedures

After the baby is admitted to the health care facility, the admission assessment procedures are carried out to ensure that the newborn's adaptation to extrauterine life is proceeding normally.

If the initial assessment indicates that the newborn is not at risk, routine admission procedures are performed in the presence of the parents in the birthing area. The admission care measures may be carried out by the nurse or by the parents with the nurse in attendance to educate and support the parents. Other interventions may be delayed until the newborn has been transferred to an observational nursery.

As discussed in Chapter 20, the newborn's physiologic adaptations to extrauterine life occur rapidly. All the body

## Essential Facts to Remember

### Timing and Types of Newborn Assessments

Assessment of the newborn is performed in three phases:

1. Immediately after birth, the nurse determines need for resuscitation or if newborn is stable and can be placed with parents to initiate early attachment/bonding.

2. Assessment within one to four hours after birth:

   - Progress of newborn's adaptation to extrauterine life
   - Determination of gestational age
   - Ongoing assessment for high-risk problems

3. Assessment within first 24 hours or prior to discharge:

   - Perform complete physical examination. (Depending on agency protocol, the nurse may complete some components on her own, with a physician or nurse practitioner completing the exam prior to discharge.)
   - Determine behavioral state organization abilities.

systems are affected. Thus the newborn requires close monitoring during the first few hours of life so that any deviation from normal can be identified immediately.

During the assessment in the first four hours after birth, the nurse focuses on the newborn's physiologic adaptations. A complete physical examination is done later by the physician or nurse practitioner, usually within the first 24 hours of life or just prior to discharge (see Chapter 21 and Essential Facts to Remember—Timing and Types of Newborn Assessments).

If the newborn is transferred to an observational nursery for the first four-hour assessment, the nurse receiving the infant first checks and confirms the newborn's identification. The birthing area nurse who carries the baby to the nursery communicates via a concise verbal report all significant information regarding the newborn. The essential data to be reported and recorded as part of the newborn's chart include the following:

1. *Condition of the newborn.* Essential information includes the newborn's Apgar scores at one and five minutes, resuscitative measures required in the delivery room, vital signs, voidings, and passing of meconium. Complications to be noted are excessive mucus, delayed spontaneous respirations or responsiveness, abnormal number of cord vessels, and obvious physical abnormalities.

2. *Labor and birth record.* A copy of the labor and birth record should go with the newborn to the nursery. The record has all the significant data about the birth, such as duration, course, and status of mother and fetus throughout labor and birth. Analgesia or anesthesia administered to the mother is also noted. The birthing nurse takes particular care to note any variation or difficulties such as prolonged rupture of membranes, meconium in amniotic fluid, signs of fetal distress during labor, nuchal cord (cord around the newborn's neck at birth), and use of forceps.

3. *Antepartal history.* Any maternal problems that may have compromised the fetus in utero such as preeclampsia, recent infections, or a history of maternal substance abuse are to be considered in the newborn's assessment. Information about maternal age, estimated date of delivery (EDD), previous pregnancies, and existing siblings is also included.

4. *Parent-infant interaction information.* Parental opportunities to hold their newborn and their desires regarding care, such as rooming-in, circumcision, and the type of feeding, are noted. Information about other children in the home, available support systems, and interactional patterns within each family unit assists in providing comprehensive care.

If no neonatal distress is apparent, the nurse proceeds with the admission assessment by taking the newborn's vital signs and performing actions to maintain body temperature and a clear airway. The initial temperature may be taken by the axillary method, which is safer than the rectal method and correlates closely with rectal temperature in the newborn (Mayfield et al 1984). Normal axillary temperature is 36.5° C to 37° C (97.7° F–98.6° F). Some hospitals still choose to use a rectal thermometer for the initial temperature, theorizing that rectal patency can be assessed simultaneously. Successful alternative methods sometimes used for assessing anal patency are digital examination or use of a sterile, flexible rubber catheter. Patency can also be assessed by observing the newborn having a bowel movement.

Once the initial temperature assessment is made, the core temperature is monitored either by obtaining an axillary temperature at intervals or by placing a skin sensor on the newborn for continuous reading. The usual skin sensor placement site is on the newborn's abdomen (Figure 22.1), but placement on the upper thigh or arm gives a reading more closely correlated with the mean body temperature (Avery and Taeusch 1984). The axillary temperature should be monitored every hour for the first four hours and then once every four hours until 24 hours from birth.

The apical pulse and respirations are monitored every 15 to 30 minutes for one hour and then every one to two hours until stable. The apical pulse is best assessed while the newborn is at rest. The newborn's respirations may be irregular and still be normal.

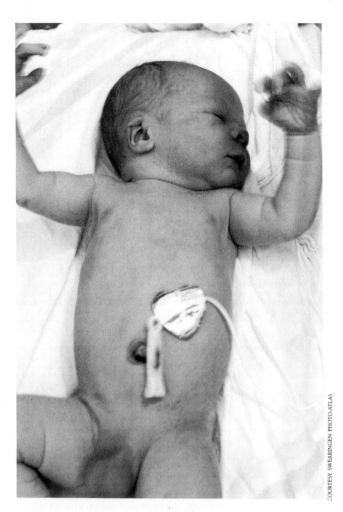

*Figure 22.1    Temperature monitoring for newborns: A skin thermal sensor is placed on the newborn's abdomen, upper thigh, or arm and secured with porous tape or a foil-covered foam pad. (From Swearingen P:* The Addison-Wesley Photo-Atlas of Nursing Procedures. *Menlo Park, CA: Addison-Wesley, 1984.)*

*Figure 22.2    Blood pressure measurement using the Dinamap and Doppler devices: The cuff can be applied to either the neonate's upper arm or thigh. (From Swearingen P:* The Addison-Wesley Photo-Atlas of Nursing Procedures. *Menlo Park, CA: Addison-Wesley, 1984.)*

Blood pressure is monitored by auscultation, by palpation, or by Doppler or Dinamap instrument (Figure 22.2). If a Dinamap or Doppler device is used, the newborn's extremities must be immobilized during the assessment, and the cuff should cover two thirds of the upper arm or upper leg. Movement, crying, and inappropriate cuff size can give inaccurate measurements of the blood pressure.

The newborn is weighed in grams and pounds. Parents understand weights stated in pounds and ounces (Figure 22.3). The scales are covered each time an infant is weighed to prevent cross-infection and heat loss from conduction. The newborn is measured; the measurements are recorded in both centimeters and inches. Three routine measurements are (a) length, (b) circumference of the head, and (c) circumference of the chest. In some facilities, abdominal girth may also be measured. The nurse rapidly assesses the baby's color, muscle tone, alertness, and general state. Basic assessments for estimating gesta-

tional age are done and the physical assessment is completed. (For more in-depth discussion of newborn assessments see Chapter 21.)

A hematocrit and blood glucose evaluation is routinely done on all newborns in many institutions (see Procedure 24.2).

The initial assessment during the first four hours after birth serves as a basis for establishing nursing diagnoses regarding the infant and setting priorities for care and family education needs (Haun et al 1984). In many settings, the father accompanies the newborn to the nursery. This is an excellent opportunity for him to get to know his child as well as an excellent opportunity for the astute nurse to take note of the father's bonding process and comfort level with the newborn. The nurse must be aware that the father may be overwhelmed by the unfamiliar nursery setting. However, he may benefit from observing and interacting with the nurse who cares for his child.

## Essential Facts to Remember

### Signs of Newborn Transition

Normal findings for the newborn during the first few hours of life include:

Pulse: 120–150 beats/min
  During sleep as low as 100 beats/min
  If crying, up to 180 beats/min
Respirations: 30–60 respirations/min
  Predominantly diaphragmatic but synchronous with abdominal movements
Temperature: Axillary: 36.5–37° C (97.7–98.6° F)
  Skin: 36–36.5° C (96.8–97.7° F)
Dextrostix: Greater than 45 mg %
Hematocrit: Less than 65%–70% central venous sample

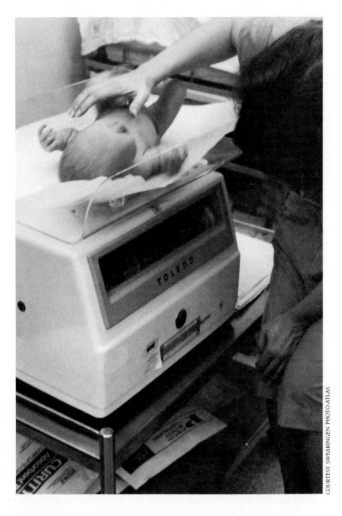

*Figure 22.3  Weighing of newborns: The scale is balanced before each weight, with the protective pad in place. The care giver's hand is poised above the infant as a safety measure. (Swearingen P: The Addison-Wesley Photo-Atlas of Nursing Procedures. Menlo Park, CA: Addison-Wesley, 1984.)*

## • Periods of Reactivity

The nurse must be able to assess accurately the newborn's physiologic adaptation and behavior during the transitional periods (see Essential Facts to Remember—Signs of Newborn Transition). The baby usually shows a predictable pattern of behavior during the first several hours after birth, characterized by two **periods of reactivity** separated by a sleep phase.

### FIRST PERIOD OF REACTIVITY

This phase lasts approximately 30 minutes after birth. During this phase the baby is awake and active and may appear hungry and have a strong sucking reflex. This is a natural opportunity to initiate breast-feeding if this is the mother's choice. Bursts of random, diffuse movements alternating with relative immobility may occur. Respirations are rapid, as high as 80 breaths/min, and there may be retraction of the chest, transient flaring of the nares, and grunting. The heart rate is rapid and irregular. Bowel sounds are absent.

### SLEEP PHASE

The newborn's activity gradually diminishes, and the heart rate and respirations decrease as the baby enters the sleep phase. First sleep usually occurs an average of three hours after birth and may last from a few minutes to two to four hours. During this period, the newborn will be difficult to awaken and will show no interest in sucking. Bowel sounds become audible, and cardiac and respiratory rates return to baseline values.

### SECOND PERIOD OF REACTIVITY

The newborn is again awake and alert. This phase lasts four to six hours in the normal newborn. Physiologic responses are variable during this stage. The heart and respiratory rates increase; however, the nurse must be alert for apneic periods, which may cause a drop in the heart rate. The newborn must be stimulated to continue breathing during such times. The newborn may become mildly cyanotic or mottled during these fluctuations. Production of respiratory and gastric mucus increases, and the newborn responds by gagging, choking, and regurgitating.

Continued close observation and intervention is required to maintain a clear airway during this period of reactivity. Positioning on the side and nasal suctioning with a bulb syringe or a DeLee mucus trap may also be necessary (see Figure 16.17). The gastrointestinal tract becomes more active. The first meconium stool is frequently passed during this second active stage, and the initial voiding may also occur at this time. The newborn will indicate readiness for feeding by such behaviors as sucking, rooting, and swallowing. If feeding was not initiated in the first period of reactivity, it should be done at this time. See the section on feeding, p 619, for further discussion of this first feeding.

## ● NURSING DIAGNOSIS

Nursing diagnoses that may apply to the newborn and family during the first four hours of life are presented in Essential Nursing Diagnoses to Consider—The Newborn and Family. Many of these nursing diagnoses and associated interventions must be identified and implemented very quickly during this period.

## ● NURSING PLAN AND IMPLEMENTATION DURING ADMISSION

In addition to continuously observing and assessing the newborn during the admission period, the nurse makes a plan that centers around the baby's need to remain under observation. The nurse assesses the newborn's ability to maintain a clear airway, maintain body temperature, maintain stable vital signs, demonstrate normal neurologic status and no observable complications, and tolerate the first feeding. Fulfillment of these criteria indicates a successful beginning adaptation to extrauterine life. The baby is moved to a regular nursery or to rooming-in. This transfer usually takes place between 6 and 12 hours after birth.

If 24 hours have passed and the first voiding and passage of stool has not occurred, the nurse continues the normal observation routine while also assessing for abdominal distention, status of bowel sounds, hydration, fluid intake, and temperature stability.

## ● Maintenance of a Clear Airway

The nurse positions the newborn on his or her side. If necessary, a bulb syringe (see Figure 22.10) or DeLee suction is used to remove mucus from the nasal passages and oral cavity. Another routine but controversial practice in some institutions is use of the DeLee catheter to remove mucus from the stomach to help prevent possible aspiration. This practice can cause vagal nerve stimulation, which can result in bradycardia and apnea in the unstabilized newborn.

## ● Maintenance of a Neutral Thermal Environment

A neutral thermal environment is essential to minimize the newborn's need to use calories to maintain body

## Essential Nursing Diagnoses to Consider

### The Newborn and Family

Ineffective airway clearance
Ineffective breathing pattern
Ineffective thermoregulation
Decreased cardiac output
Altered tissue perfusion (peripheral)
Hypothermia
Fluid volume deficit
Pain
Potential for infection
Potential for injury
Altered parenting
Knowledge deficit

heat in the optimal range of 36.5°C to 37.0°C (97.7°F–98.6°F). If the newborn becomes hypothermic, the body's response can lead to metabolic acidosis, hypoxia, and shock (Kemp et al 1982).

A neutral thermal environment is best achieved by performing the newborn assessment and interventions with the newborn unclothed and under a radiant warmer. The thermostat of the radiant warmer is controlled by the thermal skin sensor taped to the newborn's abdomen, upper thigh, or arm. The sensor indicates when the newborn's temperature exceeds or falls below the acceptable temperature range. The nurse should be aware that leaning over the newborn may block the radiant heat waves from reaching the newborn.

It is common practice in some institutions to cover the neonate's head with a stockinette or knit cap to prevent further heat loss in addition to placing the baby under a radiant warmer. A study by Ruchala (1985) suggests that a head covering should be used while the baby is outside the radiant warmer but not when the newborn is under the radiant warmer (to avoid a barrier effect).

When the newborn's temperature is normal and vital signs are stable (about two to four hours after birth), the baby has historically been given a sponge bath. However, this admission bath may be postponed for some hours if the newborn's condition dictates or the parents desire it. The sponge bath and shampoo are done quickly to minimize heat loss. The bath takes place while the baby is either under the radiant warmer or in the bassinet in the parents' room. The temperature is rechecked after the bath and if it is stable, the newborn is dressed, wrapped, and placed in an open crib at room temperature. If the

## 🔬 Drug Guide

# Vitamin K$_1$ Phytonadione (AquaMEPHYTON)

### Overview of Neonatal Action

Phytonadione is used in prophylaxis and treatment of hemmorhagic disease of the newborn. It promotes liver formation of the clotting factors II, VII, IX, and X. At birth the neonate does not have the bacteria in the colon that are necessary for synthesizing fat-soluble vitamin K$_1$, therefore the newborn may have decreased levels of prothrombin during the first five to eight days of life reflected by a prolongation of prothrombin time.

### Route, Dosage, Frequency

Intramuscular injection is given in the lateral thigh muscle. A one-time only prophylactic dose of 0.5–1.0 mg is given in the delivery room or upon admission to the newborn nursery. May need to repeat six to eight hours later, especially if mother received anticoagulants during pregnancy.

### Neonatal Side Effects

Pain and edema may occur at injection site. Possible allergic reactions such as rash and urticaria may also occur.

### Nursing Considerations

Observe for bleeding (usually occurs on second or third day). Bleeding may be seen as generalized ecchymoses or bleeding from umbilical cord, circumcision site, nose, or gastrointestinal tract. Results of serial PT and PTT should be assessed.

Observe for jaundice and kernicterus, especially in preterm infants.

Observe for signs of local inflammation.

---

baby is unable to maintain his or her axillary temperature at 36.5° C (97.7° F) or more, the newborn is returned to the warmer.

The nurse starts measures to prevent neonatal heat loss, such as using heat shields, keeping the infant dry and covered, and avoiding placement on cool surfaces or the use of cold instruments. The infant is also protected from drafts, open windows or doors, or air conditioners. Blankets and clothing are stored in a warm place. (See discussion on nonshivering thermogenesis and the mechanism of heat loss in Chapter 20.)

## • Prevention of Complications of Hemorrhagic Disease of Newborn

A prophylactic injection of vitamin K$_1$ phytonadione may be given to prevent hemorrhage, which can occur due to low prothrombin levels in the first few days of life (see the accompanying Drug Guide—Vitamin K$_1$ Phytonadione). The potential for hemorrhage is considered to result from the absence of gut bacterial flora, which influences the production of vitamin K in the newborn (see Chapter 24 for further discussion). Controversy exists over whether the administration of vitamin K may predispose the newborn to significant hyperbilirubinemia. However, Pritchard et al (1985) indicate there is no evidence to support this concern as long as a standard dose of 1 mg is given. Recently some people have questioned whether research supports giving vitamin K to newborns who have had a nontraumatic birth.

The vitamin K injection is given intramuscularly in the middle one third of the vastus lateralis muscle located in the lateral aspect of the thigh (Figure 22.4). An alternate site is the rectus femoris muscle in the anterior aspect of the thigh. However, this site is near the sciatic nerve and femoral artery and should be used with caution (Figure 22.5).

## • Prevention of Infection

The nurse is also responsible for giving the legally required prophylactic eye treatment for *Neisseria gonorrhoeae*, which may have infected the newborn during the birth process. At present, 1% silver nitrate, 0.5% erythromycin, and 1% tetracycline given topically are all acceptable for prophylaxis of newborn eye gonorrheal infections (AAP 1988). Silver nitrate may still be the best treatment in areas where chlamydial infections are low and if penicillinase-producing *Neisseria gonorrhoeae* (PPNG) is present. In the U.S., where chlamydial infections are more common than gonococcal infections, erythromycin or tetracycline ointments are preferable (AAP 1988). (See Drug Guide—Erythromycin [Ilotycin].)

To instill silver nitrate, the nurse punctures the wax container of 1% silver nitrate with a sterile needle, pulls down the infant's lower eyelid, and administers one or two drops into the lower conjunctival sac (Figure 22.6). With erythromycin, a 1–2 cm ribbon is spread over the lower conjunctival sac. After instillation, the eye is closed to spread the medication. The other eye is treated in the

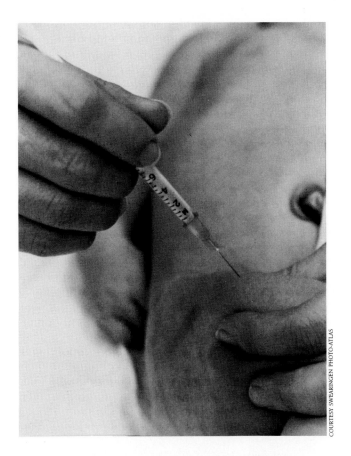

COURTESY SWEARINGEN PHOTO-ATLAS

*Figure 22.4 Procedure for Vitamin K injection: Bunch the tissue of the upper thigh (vastus lateralis muscle) and quickly insert the needle at a 90° angle to the thigh. Aspirate, then slowly inject the solution to distribute the medication evenly and minimize the baby's discomfort. Remove the needle and massage the site with an alcohol swab. (From Swearingen P:* The Addison-Wesley Photo-Atlas of Nursing Procedures. *Menlo Park, CA: Addison-Wesley, 1984.)*

same manner. The American Academy of Pediatrics (1988) recommends that the eyes not be flushed after instillation of silver nitrate. The skin around the newborn's eye should be wiped to prevent staining of the skin.

Silver nitrate and the other medications can cause chemical conjunctivitis, and silver nitrate has a higher incidence of this effect. Chemical conjunctivitis causes the newborn some discomfort and may interfere with the baby's ability to focus on the parents' faces. The resulting edema, inflammation, and discharge may cause concern if the parents have not been given information that the side effects will clear in 24 to 48 hours and that this prophylactic eye treatment is necessary for the newborn's wellbeing.

During the first 24 hours of life, the nurse is constantly alert for signs of distress. If the newborn is with the parents during this period, extra care must be taken in their education so that they can maintain their newborn's temperature, recognize the hallmarks of physiologic dis-

tress, and know how to respond immediately to signs of respiratory problems. (See Essential Facts to Remember—Signs of Neonatal Distress.) Their repertoire of responses includes nasal and oral suctioning, vigorous fingertip stroking of the newborn's spine to stimulate respiratory activity, positioning, and resuscitative measures if necessary.

## ● Initiation of First Feeding

The timing of the first feeding varies depending on whether the newborn is to be breast-fed or bottle-fed. Mothers who choose to breast-feed their newborns may seek to put their baby to the breast while in the birthing or recovery area. This practice should be encouraged since successful, long-term breast-feeding during infancy appears to be related to beginning breast-feedings in the first few hours of life (Beske and Garvis 1982). Bottle-fed babies usually begin the first feedings by five hours of age, during the second period of reactivity, when they awaken and appear hungry.

Signs indicating newborn readiness for the first feeding are: active bowel sounds, absence of abdominal distention, and a lusty cry that quiets with rooting and sucking behaviors when a stimulus is placed near the lips.

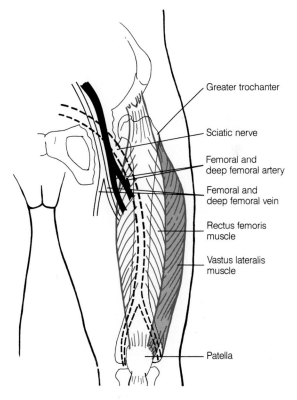

Greater trochanter

Sciatic nerve

Femoral and deep femoral artery

Femoral and deep femoral vein

Rectus femoris muscle

Vastus lateralis muscle

Patella

*Figure 22.5 Injection sites: The middle third of the vastus lateralis muscle is the preferred site for intramuscular injection in the newborn. The middle third of the rectus femoris is an alternate site, but its proximity to major vessels and the sciatic nerve necessitates caution during injection.*

## Essential Facts to Remember

### Signs of Neonatal Distress

The most common signs of distress in the newborn are the following:

- Increased rate (more than 60/min) or difficult respirations
- Sternal retractions
- Excessive mucus
- Facial grimacing
- Cyanosis (generalized)
- Abdominal distention or mass
- Lack of meconium elimination within 24 hours of birth
- Inadequate urine elimination
- Vomiting of bile-stained material
- Unusual jaundice of the skin

## • Facilitation of Parent-Infant Attachment

Eye-to-eye contact between the parents and baby is extremely important during the early hours after birth, when the newborn is in the first period of reactivity. The newborn is alert during this time, the eyes are wide open, and often direct eye contact is made with human faces within optimal range for visual acuity (7 to 8 inches). It is theorized that this eye contact is an important foundation in establishing attachment in human relationships (Klaus and Klaus 1985). Consequently the prophylactic eye medication is often delayed to provide an opportunity for this period of eye contact between parents and their newborn, thus facilitating the attachment process. The nurse also must be immediately available to support the family during the attachment process.

## • NURSING ASSESSMENT FOR DAILY NEWBORN CARE

Routine daily assessments vary among birthing facilities and from shift to shift. However, the following are as-

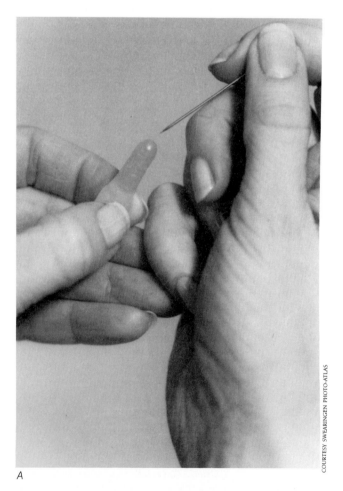

A

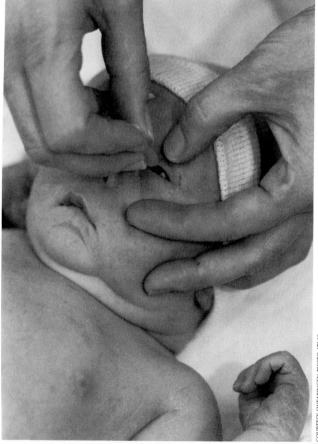

B

*Figure 22.6 Silver nitrate instillation: (A) Wax container is punctured with a needle. (B) One or two drops of 1% silver nitrate solution is instilled (or when antibiotic ointment is used a 1–2 cm ribbon is placed) in each lower conjunctival sac. (From Swearingen P: The Addison-Wesley Photo-Atlas of Nursing Procedures. Menlo Park, CA: Addison-Wesley, 1984.)*

COURTESY SWEARINGEN PHOTO-ATLAS

COURTESY SWEARINGEN PHOTO-ATLAS

# Drug Guide

## Erythromycin (Ilotycin) Ophthalmic Ointment

### Overview of Neonatal Action

Erythromycin (Ilotycin) is used as prophylactic treatment of ophthalmia neonatorum, which is caused by the bacteria *Neisseria gonorrhoeae*. Preventive treatment of gonorrhea in the newborn is required by law. Erythromycin is also effective against ophthalmic chlamydial infections. It is either bacteriostatic or bactericidal, depending on the organisms involved and the concentration of drug.

### *Route, Dosage, Frequency*

Ophthalmic ointment is instilled as a narrow ribbon or strand, ½-inch long, along the lower conjunctival surface of each eye, starting at the inner canthus. It is instilled only once in each eye. Administration may be done in the birthing area or later in the nursery so that eye contact is facilitated and the bonding process is not interrupted.

### *Neonatal Side Effects*

Sensitivity reaction; may interfere with ability to focus and may cause edema and inflammation. Side effects usually disappear in 24–48 hours.

### Nursing Considerations

Wash hands immediately prior to instillation to prevent introduction of bacteria.

Do not irrigate the eyes after instillation.

Observe for hypersensitivity.

---

sessed daily while the newborn baby is in the birthing setting:

- *Vital signs.* These are taken once a shift or more, depending on the newborn's status.

- *Weight.* The baby should be weighed at the same time each day for accurate comparisons. A weight loss of up to 10% for term infants is expected during the first week of life. This is the result of limited intake, loss of excess extracellular fluid, and passage of meconium. Parents should be told about the expected weight loss, the reason for it, and the expectations for regaining the birth weight.

- *Skin color.* Changes in skin color may indicate the need for closer assessment of temperature, cardiopulmonary status, hematocrit, and bilirubin levels.

- *Intake/output.* Fluid intake and voiding and stooling patterns are recorded.

- *Umbilical cord.* The cord is assessed for signs of hemorrhage or infection, such as oozing and foul smell.

- *Circumcision.* The circumcision is assessed for signs of hemorrhage and infection. The first voiding after a circumcision is also a significant assessment in order to evaluate for possible urinary obstruction due to trauma and edema.

- *Newborn nutrition.* Caloric and fluid intake are recorded. The nurse is also responsible for assessing the mother's skill and education needs regarding breast-feeding or bottle-feeding.

- *Parent education.* The nurse assesses the parent's knowledge of newborn and infant care. The nurse also assesses whether the parent's learning needs can be met in a group setting or require individual teaching. For further discussion see p 623.

- *Attachment.* Ongoing attachment between newborn and parents is assessed. Some indications of possible difficulties in attachment are verbalizations indicating disappointment with the newborn and lack of eye contact and physical comforting behaviors. Attachment is promoted by encouraging all family members to be involved with the new member of the family.

## ● NURSING DIAGNOSIS

Nursing diagnoses that may apply to the newborn and family in the provision of daily newborn care are presented in the Essential Nursing Diagnoses to Consider—Daily Newborn Care.

## ● NURSING PLAN AND IMPLEMENTATION OF DAILY NEWBORN CARE
## ● *Maintenance of Cardiopulmonary Function*

The newborn should always be placed in a prone or propped, side-lying position when left unattended to pre-

## Essential Nursing Diagnoses to Consider

### Daily Newborn Care

Ineffective airway clearance

Potential for hypothermia

Impaired skin integrity

Altered patterns of urinary elimination

Constipation

Potential for infection

Altered nutrition: less than body requirements

Knowledge deficit

Altered health maintenance

Family coping: potential for growth

Altered family processes

Altered parenting

vent aspiration and facilitate drainage of mucus. A bulb syringe is kept within easy reach should the baby need oral-nasal suctioning. If the newborn has respiratory difficulty, the airway is cleared. Vigorous fingertip stroking of the baby's spine will frequently stimulate respiratory activity. A cardiorespiratory monitor can be used on newborns who are not being observed at all times and are at risk for decreased respiratory or cardiac function. Indicators of risk are pallor, cyanosis, a ruddy color, apnea, or other signs of instability.

### ● Maintenance of Neutral Thermal Environment

Every effort is made to maintain the newborn's temperature within the normal range. The nurse must make certain the newborn is undressed and exposed to the air as little as possible. A stockinette or knit head covering should be used for the small newborn who has less subcutaneous fat to act as insulation in maintaining body heat. The ambient temperature of the room where the newborn is kept should be monitored routinely and kept at approximately 37.8° C (70° F). Parents should be advised to dress the newborn in one more layer of clothing than is necessary for an adult to maintain thermal comfort. A newborn whose temperature falls below optimal levels will use calories to maintain body heat rather than for growth. Chilling also decreases the affinity of serum albumin for bilirubin, thereby increasing the likelihood of newborn jaundice.

A newborn who is overheated will increase activity and respiratory rate in an attempt to cool the body.

Both measures deplete caloric reserves. In addition, the increased respiratory rate leads to increased insensible fluid loss.

### ● Promotion of Adequate Hydration and Nutrition

Nutrition is addressed in depth in Chapter 23. Adequate hydration is enhanced by maintaining a neutral thermal environment and by offering early and frequent feedings. Early feedings promote gastric emptying and increase peristalsis, thereby decreasing the potential for hyperbilirubinemia by decreasing the amount of time fecal material is in contact with beta glucuronidase in the small intestine. This enzyme is capable of freeing the bilirubin from the feces, allowing bilirubin to be reabsorbed into the vascular system.

Excessive handling of the newborn can cause an increase in the newborn's metabolic rate and caloric use. The nurse should be alert to the baby's subtle cues of fatigue. These include turning the head away from eye contact, decrease in muscle tension and activity in the extremities and neck, and loss of eye contact, which may be manifested by fluttering or closure of the eyelids. The nurse quickly ceases stimulation when signs of fatigue emerge. The nurse's care should demonstrate to the parents the need for awareness of newborn cues and the use of periods of alertness in the baby for contact and stimulation.

### ● Prevention of Complications and Promotion of Safety

Pallor may be an early sign of hemorrhage and must be reported to the physician. The newborn is placed on a cardiorespiratory monitor to permit continuous assessment. If cyanosis develops and is unrelieved by administration of oxygen, it is likely the newborn is in hypovolemic shock, which necessitates emergency interventions and Trendelenburg positioning. All newborns are at risk from hemorrhage, but this is especially true following a circumcision procedure.

Infection in the nursery is best prevented by requiring that all personnel having direct contact with newborns follow a three-minute scrub procedure at the beginning of each shift. The hands must also be washed well before and after contact with every newborn or after touching any soiled surface such as the floor or one's hair or face. Parents are often instructed to use an antiseptic hand cleaner before touching the baby as well. Anyone with an infection should refrain from working with newborns until the infection has cleared. Some agencies ask fathers, siblings, and grandparents to wear a gown over their street clothes and to wash their hands before handling the newborn.

It is essential to verify the identity of the newborn, by comparing the numbers and names on the identification bracelets of mother and newborn before giving a baby to a parent. Other safety issues are specifically covered later in the sections on circumcision, positioning and handling, bathing, nail care, and safety considerations.

## ● *Enhancement of Parent-Infant Attachment and Parental Knowledge of Infant Care*

**Parent-infant attachment** is promoted by encouraging all family members to be involved with the new member of the family. Specific interventions are examined in depth in Chapter 26.

To meet parent needs for information, the nurse who is responsible for the daily care of the mother and newborn should assume the primary responsibility for education. Nearly every contact with the parents presents an opportunity for sharing information that can facilitate the parents' sense of competence in newborn care. The nurse also needs to recognize and respect the fact that there are many good ways to provide safe baby care. The parents' methods of giving care should be reinforced rather than contradicted, unless their care methods are harmful to the newborn.

The information that follows is provided to increase the nurse's knowledge of infant care and can also be used to meet parents' needs for information.

### OPPORTUNITIES FOR PARENT TEACHING

Parents may be familiar with handling and caring for infants or this may be their first time to interact with a newborn. If they are new parents, the sensitive nurse gently teaches them by example and instructions geared to their needs and previous knowledge about the various aspects of newborn care.

The nurse observes how parents interact with their infant during feeding and caregiving activities. Rooming-in, even for a short time, offers opportunities for the nurse to provide information and evaluate whether the parents are comfortable with changing diapers, wrapping, handling, and feeding their newborn. Do both parents get involved in the infant's care? Is the mother depending on someone else to help her at home? Does the mother give excuses for not wanting to be involved in her baby's care? ("I am too tired," "My stitches hurt," or "I will learn later.") All these considerations need to be taken into account when evaluating the educational needs of the parents.

Several methods may be used to teach parents about newborn care. Daily child care classes are a nonthreatening way to convey general information. Individual instruction is helpful to answer specific questions or to clarify an item that may have been confusing in class (Figure 22.7). Discharge planning is essential to verify the mother's knowledge when she leaves the hospital. Follow-up calls after discharge lend added support by providing another opportunity for mothers to have their questions answered.

The essential areas to be covered by a nurse in educating parents before discharge are described in the following sections.

### *Positioning and Handling*

Methods of positioning and handling the newborn are demonstrated to parents if needed. As the parents provide care, the nurse can instill parental confidence by giving them positive feedback. If the parents encounter prob-

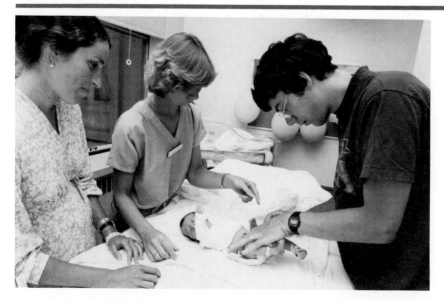

*Figure 22.7 Individualizing parent education: Father returns demonstration of diapering his daughter.*

lems, the nurse can suggest alternatives and serve as a role model.

How to pick up a newborn is one of the first concerns of anyone who has not handled many babies. When the infant is in the side-lying position, he or she is easily picked up by sliding one hand under the baby's neck and shoulders and the other hand under the buttocks or between the legs, then gently lifting the newborn from the crib. This technique provides security and support for the head (which the newborn is unable to support until three or four months of age).

After the baby is out of the crib, one of the following holds may be used (Figure 22.8). The *cradle hold* is frequently used during feeding. It provides a sense of warmth and closeness, permits eye contact, frees one of the nurse's or parent's hands, and provides security because the cradling protects the newborn's body. Extra security is provided by gripping the thigh with the hand while the arm supports the infant's body. The *upright position* provides security and a sense of closeness and is ideal for burping the infant. One hand should support the neck and shoulders, while the other hand holds the buttocks or is placed between the newborn's legs. The *football hold* frees one of the care giver's hands and permits eye contact. This hold is ideal for shampooing, carrying, or breast-feeding. It frees the mother to talk on the telephone, answer the door at home, or do the myriad tasks that await her attention.

The newborn infant is most frequently positioned on the side with a rolled blanket or diaper behind for support (Figure 22.9). This position aids drainage of mucus and allows air to circulate around the cord. It is also more comfortable for the newly circumcised male. After feeding the newborn is placed on the right side to aid digestion and to prevent aspiration; this position makes it easier to expel air bubbles from the stomach. Once the cord is healed, many babies prefer to lie prone. Newborns have enough head control to turn their heads side to side to prevent suffocation. The infant's position should be changed periodically during the early months of life, because neonatal skull bones are soft, and flattened areas may develop if the newborn consistently lies in one position. Babies should not be left in a supine position when unattended due to the danger of aspiration.

### Nasal and Oral Suctioning

Most babies are obligatory nose breathers for the first months of life. They generally maintain air passage patency by coughing or sneezing. During the first few days of life, however, the newborn has increased mucus, and gentle suctioning with a bulb syringe may be indicated. The nurse can demonstrate the use of the bulb syringe in the nose and mouth and have the parents do a return demonstration. The parents should repeat this demonstration before discharge so they will feel more confident and comfortable with the procedure. Care should be taken to only apply gentle suction so nasal bleeding does not occur.

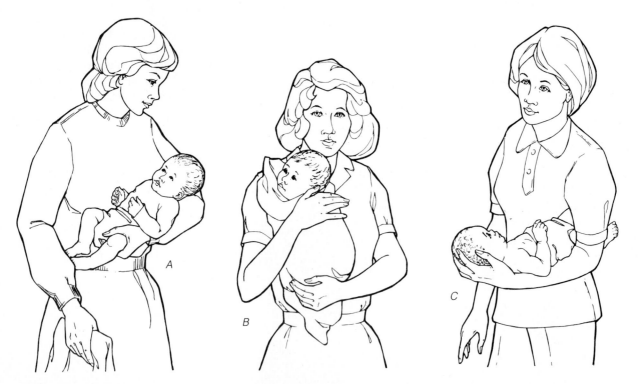

*Figure 22.8  Various positions for holding an infant: (A) Cradle hold. (B) Upright position. (C) Football hold.*

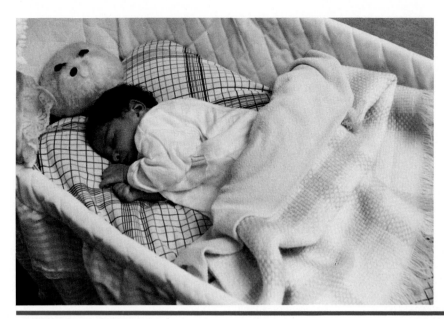

Figure 22.9  The most common sleeping position of the newborn is on the side. The little girl shown here does not need the additional support provided by a rolled blanket since she is no longer a newborn.

To suction the newborn, the bulb syringe is compressed (to expel the air), then the tip is placed in the nostril, and the bulb is permitted to reexpand slowly as the nurse or parent releases the compression on the bulb (Figure 22.10). The drainage is then compressed out of the bulb onto a tissue. The bulb syringe may also be used in the mouth if the newborn is spitting up and unable to handle the excess secretions. The bulb is compressed, the tip of the bulb syringe is placed about 1 inch in on one side of the infant's mouth, and compression is released. This draws up the excess secretions. The procedure is repeated on the other side of the mouth. The center back of the baby's mouth is avoided because suction in this area might stimulate the gag reflex. The bulb syringe should be washed in warm, soapy water and rinsed in warm water after each use. A bulb syringe should always be kept near the newborn.

Parents have a great fear that their baby will choke and may be relieved if they know how to take action if such an event occurs. They should be advised to turn the newborn's head to the side as soon as there is any indication of gagging or vomiting.

### Bathing

An actual bath demonstration is the best way for the nurse to provide information to parents. Because excess bathing and use of soap will dry out the baby's sensitive skin, bathing should be done every other day or twice a week. Sponge baths are recommended for the first two weeks or until the umbilical cord completely falls off and has healed.

Supplies (see Table 22.1) can be kept in a plastic bag or some type of container to eliminate the necessity of

Figure 22.10  Nasal and oral suctioning: The bulb is compressed, then the tip is placed either in the mouth or nose; the bulb is released. (From Swearingen P: The Addison-Wesley Photo-Atlas of Nursing Procedures. Menlo Park, CA: Addison-Wesley, 1984.)

| Table 22.1 Bath Supplies |
| --- |
| Washcloths |
| Towels |
| Blanket |
| Unperfumed mild soap (eg, Neutrogena) |
| Shampoo |
| Petroleum jelly or A and D ointment |
| Rubbing alcohol |
| Cotton balls |
| Diapers |
| Clean clothes |

hunting for them each time. The mother may want to use a small plastic tub, a clean kitchen or bathroom sink, or a large bowl. Expensive baby tubs are not necessary, but some parents may prefer to purchase them.

Before starting, if no one else is at home, the parent may want to take the phone off the hook and put a sign on the door to prevent being disturbed. Having someone home during the first few baths will be helpful because that person can get items that were forgotten and provide moral support. The room should be warm and free of drafts.

*Sponge Bath* After the supplies are gathered, the tub (or any of the containers mentioned above) is filled with water that is warm to the touch. The water temperature is tested with an elbow or forearm. Parents may also choose to purchase a thermometer to help them determine when the bath water is at approximately 37.8° C (100° F) and safe to use. Soap should not be added to the water. The infant should be wrapped in a blanket, with a T-shirt and diaper on. This helps keep the newborn warm and secure.

To start the bath, the parents wrap a washcloth around the index finger once. Each eye is gently wiped from inner to outer corner. This direction is the way eyes naturally drain, and wiping in this direction prevents irritation of the eyes. A different portion of the washcloth is used for each eye to prevent cross-contamination. Cotton balls can also be used for this purpose, using a new one for each eye.

The ears are washed next by wrapping the washcloth once around an index finger and gently cleaning the external ear and behind the ear. Cotton swabs are never used in the ear canal because it is possible to put the swab too far into the ear and damage the ear drum. In addition, the swab may pack any discharge farther down into the ear canal.

The remainder of the baby's face is then wiped with the soap-free washcloth. Many babies start to cry at this point. The face should be washed every day and the mouth and chin wiped off after each feeding.

The neck is washed carefully but thoroughly with the washcloth. Soap may now be used. Formula or breast milk and lint collect in the skin folds of the neck, so it may be helpful to sit the baby up, supporting the neck and shoulders with one hand while washing the neck with the other hand.

The baby's T-shirt is now removed and the blanket unwrapped. The chest, back, and arms are wet with the washcloth. The parent may then lather the hands with soap and wash the baby's chest, back, and arms. Wetting the cord is avoided, if possible, because it delays drying. Soap is rinsed off with the wet washcloth, and the upper part of the body is dried with a towel or blanket. The baby's upper body is then wrapped with a dry clean blanket to prevent a chill.

Next the infant's legs are unwrapped, wet with the washcloth, lathered, rinsed, and well dried. If the infant has dry skin, a *small* amount of lotion or ointment (A and D ointment) may be used. Ointments are thought to be better than lotions for dry cracked feet and hands. Baby oil is not recommended, as it clogs skin pores. Powders are not currently recommended. Some believe they aggravate dry skin and others avoid powders because of the possible danger of inhalation.

Both baby oil and baby powder can cause serious respiratory problems if inhaled. Parents should be warned of this danger and advised to take measures to prevent these substances from being aspirated by the baby. If parents want to use powder, advise them to select one that is talc free. The powder should be shaken into the parent's hand and then placed on the infant rather than shaking the powder directly over the baby.

The genital area is cleaned daily with soap and water and with water after each wet or dirty diaper. Girls are washed from the *front* of the genital area toward the rectum to avoid fecal contamination of the urethra and thus to the bladder. Newborn girls often have a thick, white mucous discharge or a slight bloody discharge from their vaginal area. This discharge is normal for the first one to two weeks of age and should be wiped off with a damp cloth at diaper changes.

Parents of uncircumcised baby boys should cleanse the penis daily. Even minimal retraction of the foreskin is not advised. Baby boys who have been circumcised need daily gentle cleansing. A very wet washcloth is rubbed over a bar of soap. The washcloth is squeezed above the baby's penis, letting the soapy water run over the circumcision site. The area is rinsed off with plain warm water and patted dry. A small amount of petroleum jelly or bactericidal ointment may be put on the circumcised area, but excessive amounts may block the meatus and should be avoided. It is important to avoid using ointments if a plastibell is in place. Use of ointments may cause the plastibell ring to slip off the penis too early.

Baby powder (or cornstarch) is not recommended for diaper rash. Baby powder may cake with urine and irritate the infant's perineal area. Cornstarch may promote fungal infection. Ointments that provide a barrier, such as zinc oxide, A and D ointment, or petroleum jelly are more effective for diaper rash. If the ointment does not help the rash, parents using disposable diapers should try another brand of diaper. If cloth diapers are used, a different detergent or fabric softener may alleviate the problem. If the rash persists, parents should discuss the problem with a nurse practitioner or physician because it may be due to a yeast or fungal infection.

The umbilical cord should be kept clean and dry. The close proximity of the umbilical vessels makes the cord a common portal for infection. Various preparations such as triple dye, alcohol, hexachlorophene, Betadine, and Bacitracin are used for cord care in newborn nurseries to promote drying and provide a bactericidal effect. Triple dye may be used and seems to be a highly effective anti-staphylococcal agent (Andrich and Golden 1984). At discharge, most parents are advised to clean the area around the cord with a cotton ball and alcohol (70% isopropyl) two to three times a day until the cord is completely gone and the stump is healed. The cord stump generally falls off in 7 to 14 days. The diaper should be folded down to allow air to circulate around the cord. The care provider should be consulted if bright red bleeding or puslike drainage occurs or if the area remains unhealed two to three days after the cord stump has sloughed off. See Teaching Guide—What to Tell Parents About Home Cord Care.

The last step in bathing is washing the infant's hair (some suggest doing this step first). The newborn is swaddled in a dry blanket, leaving only the head exposed, and held in the football hold with the head tilted slightly downward to prevent water running in the eyes. Water should be brought to the head by a cupped hand. The hair is moistened and lathered with a small amount of shampoo. A *very* soft brush may be used to massage the shampoo over the entire head. The brush may be used over the soft spots. The hair is then rinsed and toweled dry. Oils or lotions are not used on the newborn's head unless there is evidence of cradle cap. Moistening the scaly area with lotion a half an hour or more before shampooing softens the crusts or scales and makes it easier to remove them. To assist in preventing cradle cap, the infant's hair should be brushed every day and the hair washed during baths.

**Tub Baths** The infant may be put in a tub after the cord has fallen off and the circumcision site is healed (approximately two weeks) (Figure 22.11). Infants usually enjoy a tub bath more than a sponge bath, although some newborns cry during either type.

*Figure 22.11   Tub bath: When bathing the infant, it is important to support the head. Note that the cord site has healed on this 2-week-old baby.*

Only 3 or 4 inches of water is needed in the tub. To prevent slipping, a washcloth is placed in the bottom of the tub or sink, or the baby can be brought into a tub with the parent.

The face is washed in the same manner as for a sponge bath. The parent then places the newborn in the tub using the cradle hold and grasping the distal thigh. The neck is supported by the parent's elbow in the cradle position. An alternative hold is to support the newborn's head and neck with the parent's forearm while grasping the distal shoulder and arm.

Because wet infants are slippery, some parents have found that pulling a cotton sock (with the holes cut out for the fingers) over their arm will prevent the baby from slipping.

The body may be washed with a soapy washcloth or hand. To wash the baby's back, the parent places his or her noncradling hand on the infant's chest with the thumb under the infant's arm closest to the parent. Gently tipping

# Teaching Guide
## What to Tell Parents About Home Cord Care

**Assessment** The nurse focuses on the parents' previous experience with newborns and their understanding of what the umbilical cord is and what naturally happens during the first few weeks after birth.

**Nursing Diagnosis** The essential nursing diagnoses would probably be: Knowledge deficit related to home care of the umbilical cord and potential for infection related to contamination of umbilical cord.

**Nursing Plan and Implementation** The teaching plan will include information about the need for daily cleansing, expected changes in the umbilical cord, and demonstration of actual procedure for care of the umbilical cord.

**Parent Goals** At the completion of the teaching session the parents will be able to:

1. State the normal changes in the umbilical cord.
2. List the signs of infection of the cord.
3. Demonstrate proper cord care.

---

## Teaching Plan

### Content

Clean the cord and skin around base of cord with a cotton ball or Q-tip. Lift cord stump and squeeze alcohol from soaked cotton ball down onto the cord. With a Q-tip, swab around base of cord to clean away any drainage, since bacteria grows on dried drainage. Cord care should be done at least two to three times a day or with each diaper change. Baby may cry when the cold alcohol touches the tummy; there are no nerve ends in the cord. No tub baths until cord falls off in 7–14 days.

Fold diapers below umbilical cord to air-dry cord. Wet or soiled diapers slow drying process and increase possibility of infection.

Check cord each day for any odor, oozing of yellow puslike material, or reddened areas around the cord. Area around cord may also be tender. Report to health care provider any signs of infection.

Normal changes in cord: Cord should look dark and dry up, falling off at about 7–14 days after birth. A little drop of blood may appear on the diaper as the cord is about to fall off. Never pull the cord or attempt to loosen it.

### Teaching Method

*Discussion*
   Use of poster showing cleaning techniques, position of diapers, and colored pictures of signs of infection.
   Demonstration of cord cleaning.

---

**Evaluation** The nurse presented the information and demonstrated the proper procedure for cord care. Parents were able to identify the signs of infection and normal changes seen in the cord prior to its falling off and carried out proper cord care procedure prior to baby's discharge.

the baby forward onto the supporting hand frees the cradling arm to wash the back of the baby. After the bath the baby is lifted out of the tub in the cradle position, dried well, and wrapped in a dry blanket. The hair can then be washed in the same way as for a sponge bath.

### Nail Care

The nails of the newborn are seldom cut in the hospital. During the first days of life, the nails may adhere to the skin of the fingers, and cutting is contraindicated. Within a week the nails separate from the skin and frequently break off. If the nails are long or if infants are scratching themselves, the nails may be trimmed. This is most easily done while infants sleep. Nails should be cut straight across using adult cuticle scissors or blunt-ended infant cuticle scissors.

### Wrapping the Newborn

Wrapping helps the newborn maintain body temperature and provides a feeling of closeness and security. When wrapping, a blanket is placed on the crib (or secure surface) in the shape of a diamond. The top corner of the blanket is folded down slightly, and the baby's body is placed with the head at the upper edge of the blanket. The right corner of the blanket is wrapped around the infant and tucked under the left side (not too tightly—newborns need a little room to move). The bottom corner is then pulled up to the chest, and the left corner is wrapped around the baby's right side (Figure 22.12).

### Dressing the Newborn

Newborns need to wear a T-shirt, diaper (plastic pants if using cloth diapers), and a sleeper. On a fairly cool day, they should also be wrapped in a light blanket while being fed. A good rule of thumb is for the parent to add one more light layer of clothing than the parent is wearing. Infants should wear hats outdoors to protect their sensitive ears from drafts. Their eyes should be protected if it is breezy. An infant may be covered with a blanket in air-conditioned buildings. The blanket should be unwrapped or removed when inside a warm building.

At home the amount of clothing the infant wears is determined by the temperature. Families who maintain the home at 60–65° F should dress the infant more warmly than those who maintain the temperature at 70–75° F.

Parents must also be advised of the ease with which a baby's skin can burn when exposed to the sun. To prevent sunburn the baby should remain shaded, wear a light layer of clothing, or be protected with a sunscreen product.

Diaper shapes vary and are subject to personal preference (Figure 22.13). Prefolded and disposable diapers are usually rectangular. Diapers may also be triangular or kite-folded. Extra material is placed in front for boys and toward the back for girls to aid in absorbency.

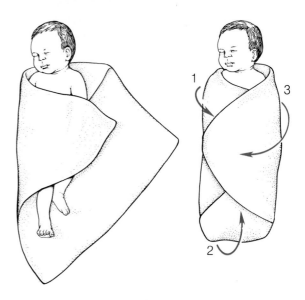

*Figure 22.12    Steps used for wrapping a baby*

Baby clothing should be laundered separately using a mild soap or detergent. Diapers may be presoaked prior to washing. All clothing should be rinsed twice to remove soap and residue and to decrease the possibility of rash. Some infants may not tolerate the use of clothing treated with fabric softeners; in this case softeners should be avoided.

### Temperature Assessment

The nurse must demonstrate for parents how to take rectal and axillary temperatures. A return demonstration  is an effective way to evaluate their understanding. The nurse shows them how to shake down a thermometer before inserting it.

When parents take a rectal temperature, the infant should be supine with the legs held up in one hand, exposing the rectum. The end of the rectal thermometer is lubricated with water-soluble lubricant, and the thermometer is inserted just until the silver bulb is covered, approximately half an inch. The thermometer is held in place five minutes. A baby is never left alone with a thermometer in place and the adult must maintain a hold on the thermometer at all times. Some pediatricians feel that rectal temperatures are more accurate and prefer that parents take temperatures this way. Parents may be more receptive to taking axillary temperatures and should make their preferences known to the care giver.

To take an axillary temperature, the thermometer is placed under one of the infant's arms, making sure that the bulb of the thermometer is underneath the armpit. It is held in place three to four minutes (Figure 21.14, **B**). A parent only needs to take the newborn's temperature when any signs of illness are present. See Essential Facts to Remember—When Parents Should Call Their Health Care Provider.

## Essential Facts to Remember

### When Parents Should Call Their Health Care Provider

If any of the following signs are present, parents need to call their health care provider:

- Temperature above 38.4° C (101° F) rectally or below 36.1° C (97° F) rectally
- More than one episode of projectile vomiting
- Refusal of two feedings in a row
- Lethargy (listlessness), difficulty waking the baby
- Cyanosis with or without a feeding
- Absence of breathing longer than 15 seconds
- Two consecutive green, watery stools after baby is one week old
- No wet diapers for 18–24 hours

When parents find their infant has a temperature, they may expect to give an antipyretic such as Tylenol (acetaminophen). All parents should be advised to avoid giving any form of aspirin to their infants for any illness that may be viral. Use of aspirin in viral illnesses has been linked to Reye syndrome in children. Flu, colds, teething, constipation, diarrhea, and other common ailments and their management should be discussed with the clinician before they occur. When analgesic and/or antipyretic medication is needed, clinicians frequently advise acetaminophen drops.

### Stools and Urine

The appearance and frequency of newborn's stools  can cause concern for parents. The nurse prepares parents by discussing and showing pictures of meconium stools and transitional stools, and by describing the difference between breast-milk and formula stools. Although each baby develops his or her own stooling patterns, parents can be given an idea of what to expect. Parents should be told that:

- Breast-fed babies may have six to ten small, loose yellow stools per day or only one stool every few days.

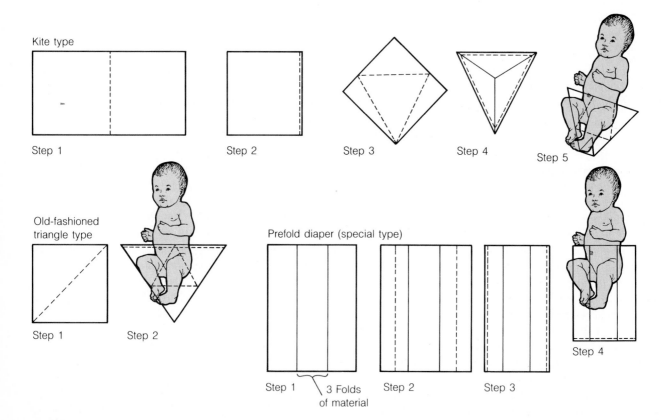

Figure 22.13   Three basic diaper shapes. Dotted lines indicate folds.

● Formula-fed babies may only have one or two stools a day, which are more formed and yellow or yellow-brown.

The parents may also be shown pictures of a constipated stool (small, pelletlike) and diarrhea (loose, green, or perhaps blood-tinged). Parents should understand that a green color is common in transitional stools so that transitional stools are not confused with diarrhea the first week of a newborn's life.

Constipation may be an indication that the baby needs additional fluid intake. Parents may try offering additional water in an attempt to reverse the constipation.

Babies normally void (urinate) five to eight times per day. Less than five to eight wet diapers a day may indicate the newborn needs more fluids.

### Sleep and Activity

Perhaps nothing is more individual to each neonate than the sleep-activity cycle. It is important for the nurse to recognize the individual variations of each newborn and to assist parents as they develop sensitivity to their infant's communication signals and rhythms of activity and sleep. (See Table 22.2.)

The newborn demonstrates several different sleep-wake states after the initial periods of reactivity described earlier. It is not uncommon for a neonate to sleep almost continuously for the first two to three days following birth, awakening only for feedings every three to four hours. Some newborns bypass this stage of deep sleep and may require only 12–16 hours of sleep. The parents need to know that this is normal.

*Quiet sleep* is characterized by regular breathing and no movement except for sudden body jerks. During this sleep state, normal household noise will not awaken the infant. In the *active sleep state,* the newborn has irregular breathing and fine muscular twitching. The newborn may cry out during sleep, but this does not mean he or she is uncomfortable or awake. Unusual household noise may awaken the infant more easily in this state; however, the newborn will quickly go back to sleep.

*Wide awake* is a state in which newborns are quietly involved with the environment. They watch a moving mobile, smile, and, as they become older, discover and play with their hands and feet.

When infants become uncomfortable due to wet diapers, hunger, or cold, they enter the *active awake and crying state.* In this state, the cause of the crying should be identified and eliminated. Sometimes parents are frustrated as they try to identify the external or internal stimuli that are causing the angry, hurt crying. Parents can be told that, by moving the baby toward an upright position where the baby can look around and explore the environment with his or her eyes, the baby's state will change from crying to quiet alert (Klaus and Klaus 1985).

For the newborn, crying is the only means of vocally expressing needs. Parents and care givers learn to distinguish different tones and qualities of the neonate's cry. The amount of crying is highly individual. Some babies will cry as little as 15–30 minutes in 24 hours or as long as two hours every 24 hours. When crying continues after causes such as discomfort or hunger are eliminated, the newborn may be comforted by swaddling or by rocking and other reassuring activity. Excessive crying should be noted and assessed, taking other factors into consideration. After the first two to three days, newborns settle into patterns that are individual to each infant and family. Parents can be reassured that they will not spoil the newborn by picking her or him up and cuddling. Cessation of crying in this situation indicates the parents have been successful in soothing the baby.

### Circumcision

**Circumcision** is a surgical procedure in which the prepuce, an epithelial layer covering the penis, is separated from the glans penis and is excised. This permits exposure of the glans for easier cleaning. Circumcision is the most frequent surgical procedure performed on babies.

The parents make the decision about circumcision for their newborn male child. In most cases the choice is based on cultural, social, and family tradition. New evidence suggesting that medical indications for circumcision exist (*San Francisco Chronicle* 1989) may also influence parental decisions. To guarantee informed consent, parents should be informed about possible long-term medical effects of circumcision and noncircumcision during the prenatal period.

In the past, this procedure was recommended for all newborn males. Starting in the mid-1960s, however, use of circumcision declined, and the American Academy of Pediatrics (AAP) Committee on Fetus and Newborn (1988) stated that there were no valid medical reasons for routine newborn circumcision and did not recommend the procedure. In March of 1989 the AAP reversed this recommendation, concluding that, "newborn circumcision has potential medical benefits and advantages, as well as disadvantages and risks" (*San Francisco Chronicle* 1989).

Circumcision was originally a rite of the Jewish religion. The practice gained widespread cultural acceptance in the United States but is done infrequently in many European countries. Many parents choose circumcision because they want the infant to have a similar physical appearance to the father or the majority of other children, or they may feel that it is expected by society (Harris 1986).

Another frequently cited reason for circumcising newborn males is to prevent the need for anesthesia, hospitalization, pain, and trauma should the procedure be needed later in life. Pritchard et al (1985) noted that only 5% to 10% of males are estimated to be in this category.

## Table 22.2 Infant State* Chart (Sleep and Awake States)

| Sleep states | Characteristics of state | | | | | Implications for caregiving |
|---|---|---|---|---|---|---|
| | Body activity | Eye movements | Facial movements | Breathing pattern | Level of response | |
| Deep sleep | Nearly still except for occasional startle or twitch | None | Without facial movements, except for occasional sucking movement at regular intervals | Smooth and regular | Only very intense and disturbing stimuli will arouse infants. | Care givers trying to feed infant in deep sleep will probably find the experience frustrating. Infants will be unresponsive, even if care givers use disturbing stimuli (flicking feet) to arouse infants. Infants may only arouse briefly and then become unresponsive as they return to deep sleep. If care givers wait until infants move to a higher, more responsive state, feeding or caregiving will be much more pleasant. |
| Light sleep | Some body movements | Rapid eye movement (REM): Fluttering of eyes beneath closed eyelids | May smile and make brief fussy or crying sounds | Irregular | More responsive to internal and external stimuli. When these stimuli occur, infants may remain in light sleep or move to drowsy state. | Light sleep makes up the highest proportion of newborn sleep and usually precedes wakening. Due to brief fussy or crying sounds made during this state, care givers who are not aware that these sounds occur normally may think it is time for feeding and may try to feed infants before they are ready to eat. |
| Drowsy | Activity level variable, with mild startles interspersed from time to time; movements usually smooth | Eyes open and close occasionally, are heavy-lidded with dull, glazed appearance | May have some facial movements; often there are none and the face appears still | Irregular | Infants react to sensory stimuli although responses are delayed. State change after stimulation frequently noted. | From the drowsy state infants may return to sleep or awaken further. In order to wake them care givers can provide something for infants to see, hear, or suck, as this may arouse them to quiet alert state, a more responsive state. Infants left alone without stimuli may return to a sleep state. |
| Quiet alert | Minimal | Brightening and widening of eyes | Faces have bright, shining, sparkling looks | Regular | Infants attend most to environment, focusing attention on any stimuli that are present. | Infants in this state provide much pleasure and positive feedback for care givers. Providing something for infants to see, hear, or suck will often maintain a quiet alert state in the first few hours after birth. Most newborns commonly experience a period of intense alertness before going into a long sleeping period. |

| Table 22.2 | Infant State* Chart (Sleep and Awake States) *(continued)* | | | | | |

| | **Characteristics of state** | | | | | |
|---|---|---|---|---|---|---|
| **Sleep states** | **Body activity** | **Eye movements** | **Facial movements** | **Breathing pattern** | **Level of response** | **Implications for caregiving** |
| Active alert | Much body activity; may have periods of fussiness | Eyes open with less brightening | Much facial movement; faces not as bright as in alert state | Irregular | Increasingly sensitive to disturbing stimuli (hunger, fatigue, noise, excessive handling). | Care givers may intervene at this stage to console and to bring infants to a lower state. |
| Crying | Increased motor activity with color changes | Eyes may be tightly closed or open | Grimaces | More irregular | Extremely responsive to unpleasant external or internal stimuli. | Crying is the infant's communication signal. It is a response to unpleasant stimuli from the environment or from within infants (fatigue, hunger, discomfort). Crying tells us infants have been reached. Sometimes infants can console themselves and return to lower states. At other times they need help from care givers. |

*State* is a group of characteristics that regularly occur together: body activity, eye movements, facial movements, breathing pattern, and level of response to external stimuli (eg, handling) and internal stimuli (eg, hunger).

Source: Adapted from Barnard K et al: Parent-infant relationships. Module 3, series 1. *The First Six Hours of Life.* The National Foundation/March of Dimes, 1978, p 21.

Circumcision should not be performed if the newborn is premature or compromised, has a known bleeding problem, or is born with a genitourinary defect such as hypospadias or epispadias, which may necessitate the use of the foreskin in future surgical repairs (Pritchard et al 1985).

Parents must be informed about potential risks and outcomes of circumcision. Hemorrhage, infection, difficulty in voiding, separation of the edges of the circumcision, discomfort, and restlessness are early potential problems. Later there is the risk that the glans and urethral meatus can become irritated and inflamed from contact with ammonia from urine. Ulcerations and progressive stenosis may develop. Adhesions, entrapment of the penis, and damage to the urethra are all potential complications that could require surgical correction (Gibbons 1984). A growing number of researchers are validating that the newborn feels pain during the procedure and parents need to be aware of this when making their decision about the procedure for their baby.

Recent studies suggest that circumcision provides advantages as well as risks, including prevention of urinary tract infections in infants and cancer of the penis in adults,

and inhibition of many sexually transmitted diseases. The rate of cervical cancer in sexual partners of circumcised men has also been found to be lower than that in partners of uncircumcised men (*San Francisco Chronicle* 1989).

Parents who are doubtful about their ability to use good hygienic practices in caring for their uncircumcised male infant and child require information from the nurse. They should be told that the foreskin and glans are two similar layers of cells that separate from each other. The separation process begins prenatally and is normally completed at between three and six years of age. In the process of separation, sterile sloughed cells build up between the layers. This buildup looks similar to the smegma secreted after puberty, but it is harmless. Occasionally during the daily bath, the parents can gently test for retraction. If retraction has occurred, daily gentle washing of the glans with soap and water is sufficient to maintain adequate cleanliness (Gibbons 1984). The child should be taught to incorporate this practice into his daily self-care activities.

If circumcision is to be done, the procedure is not usually done until the day before discharge when the newborn is well stabilized and there is less chance of cold stress and bleeding. The parents may also choose to have the circum-

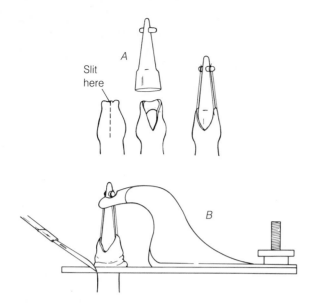

Slit here

A

B

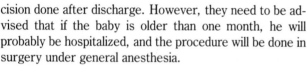

Figure 22.14   Circumcision using the Yellen or Gomco clamp: (A) The prepuce is drawn over the cone and (B) the clamp is applied. Pressure is maintained for three to five minutes, and then the excess prepuce is cut away.

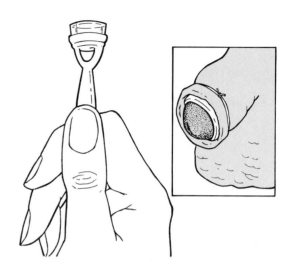

Figure 22.15   Circumcision using the Plastibell: The bell is fitted over the glans. A suture is tied around the bell's rim and the excess prepuce is cut away. The plastic rim remains in place for three to four days until healing takes place. The bell may be allowed to fall off or removed if still in place after eight days.

cision done after discharge. However, they need to be advised that if the baby is older than one month, he will probably be hospitalized, and the procedure will be done in surgery under general anesthesia.

The nurse's responsibilities during a circumcision are to determine if the parents have any further questions about the procedure, to ensure that the circumcision permit is signed, and to help ensure that the parents' decision was an informed one. The nurse can ask the parents to explain circumcision and the possible complications.

The nurse gathers the equipment and prepares the newborn by removing the diaper and placing him on a circumcision board or some other type of restraint. In the Jewish ceremonies, the infant is held by the parent or other relative and given wine as soon as the procedure is completed.

There are a variety of techniques for circumcision (Figures 22.14, 22.15), and all produce minimal bleeding. During the procedure, the nurse assesses the newborn's response. One consideration is pain experienced by the newborn. Some physicians use local anesthesia for this procedure. Successful pain relief has been achieved with the use of lidocaine to block the penile dorsal nerve.

The nurse can provide comfort measures such as lightly stroking the baby's head and talking to him. Following the circumcision he should be held and comforted by a parent (Lubchenco 1980) or the nurse. The nurse must be alert to any cues that these measures are overstimulating the newborn instead of comforting him. Such cues are turning away of the head, increased generalized body

movement, skin color changes, hyperalertness, and hic-coughing (D'Apolito 1984).

After the circumcision a small petroleum jelly gauze strip is applied to help control bleeding and to keep the diaper from adhering to the site in all procedures except the Plastibell. The petroleum jelly gauze is left in place for one to two days. It need not be changed unless it becomes contaminated with stool. A and D ointment may be used instead of petroleum jelly. A large amount is placed on the penis at each diaper change or at least four to five times a day for at least 48 hours.

The baby's voiding is assessed for amount, adequacy of stream, and presence of blood. If bleeding does occur, light pressure is applied intermittently to the site with a sterile gauze pad, and the physician is notified. The newborn may cry when he voids. He should be positioned on his side with the diaper fastened loosely to prevent undue pressure. He may remain fussy for several hours and be less interested in feedings.

Before discharge, the parents should be instructed to observe the penis for bleeding or possible signs of infection. A whitish yellow exudate around the glans is granulation tissue. It is normal and not indicative of an infection. The exudate may be noted for about two or three days, and should not be removed.

The parents should be instructed to squeeze water gently over the penis and pat it dry after each diaper change. The diaper is loosely fastened for two to three days, because the glans remains tender for this length of time.

If the Plastibell is used, parents are informed that it will remain in place for three or four days and then fall off. If it is still in place after eight days, it may require manual removal by the clinician (Gibbons 1984).

## ● NURSING DIAGNOSIS

Nursing diagnoses that may apply to the newborn and family in preparation for discharge are presented in Essential Nursing Diagnoses to Consider—Newborn Discharge from the Birthing Center.

## ● NURSING PLAN AND IMPLEMENTATION FOR DISCHARGE

The nurse can do much to assist parents in feeling comfortable with newborn care. By discussing with parents how to meet their newborn's needs and ensure his or her safety, the nurse can get the new family off to a good start. The nurse also plays a vital role in fostering parent-infant attachment.

In addition to the information the nurse provides to parents during their stay in the birthing site, the nurse should provide information about safety, the newborn screening program, and follow-up care before the mother and baby are discharged.

## ● Safety Considerations

The nurses can be an excellent role model for parents in the area of safety. Newborns should always be positioned on the stomach or side with a blanket rolled up behind them. Correct use of the bulb syringe must be demonstrated. The baby should never be left alone anywhere but in the crib. The mother is reminded that while she and the newborn are together in the hospital, she should never leave the baby alone because newborns spit up frequently the first day or two after birth.

Accidents are the number one cause of death in children, with car accidents causing the most deaths, followed by poisonings. Half of the children killed or injured in automobile accidents could have been protected by the use of federally approved car seats. Newborns should go home from the hospital in a car seat (not infant carrier seat).

The seat should be positioned to face the rear of the car until the baby is a year old or weighs 20 pounds. At this time the bone structure is adequately mineralized and better able to withstand a forward impact in a five-point harness restraint belt. Children should always ride in a car seat until they are four years old (depending on the size of the child), no matter how short the trip. In many states, the use of car seats for children up to the age of four is mandatory.

## Essential Nursing Diagnoses to Consider

### Newborn Discharge from the Birthing Center

Altered family process
Knowledge deficit
Potential for injury
Altered health maintenance

Newborns do not need pillows or stuffed animals in the crib while they sleep; these items could cause suffocation.

## ● Newborn Screening Program

Before the newborn and mother are discharged from the hospital, parents are informed about the normal screening tests for newborns and should be told when to return to the hospital or clinic to have the tests completed. **Newborn screening tests** detect disorders that cause mental retardation, physical handicaps, or death if left undiscovered. Inborn errors of metabolism usually can be detected within one to two weeks after birth and important treatment begun before any damage has occurred. The disorders that can be identified from a drop of blood obtained by a heel stick on the second or third day are galactosemia, homocystinuria, hypothyroidism, maple syrup urine disease, phenylketonuria (PKU), and sickle cell anemia. Parents should be instructed that a second blood specimen will be required from the newborn after 7–14 days, when the disorder should be identifiable. However, it must be clarified that an abnormal test result is not diagnostic. More definitive tests must be performed to verify the results (Avery and Taeusch 1984). If additional tests are positive, treatment is initiated. These conditions may be treated by dietary means or by administration of missing hormones. The inborn conditions cannot be cured, but they can be treated. Although they are not contagious, they may be inherited (Chapter 24, p 740).

## ● Follow-Up Care

Each newborn will have variations in normal physiologic responses. Parents need to learn how to interpret these changes in their child. To assist parents in caring for their newborn at home, some physicians encourage pediatric prenatal visits so that this contact is established before the birth (Sprunger and Preece 1981). Public health nurses have long been involved as guides in newborn care and parent education (Lauri 1981). Hospitals are now expanding their primary care functions to the new family to include one home visit by the primary nurse who cared for the family in the hospital. The hospital nursery staff may also make themselves available as a 24-hour telephone resource for the new mother who needs additional support and consultation during the first few days at home with her newborn.

Routine well-baby visits should be scheduled with the clinic, pediatric nurse practitioner, or physician.

Parents should be taught all necessary caregiving methods before discharge. A checklist may be helpful to see if the teaching has been completed. The nurse needs to review all areas for understanding and questions with the mother, without rushing, taking time to answer all queries. The mother should have the physician's phone number, address, and any specific instructions. Having the nursery phone number is also reassuring to a new mother. The parents are encouraged to call with questions.

## ● Documentation

The final step of discharge planning is documentation. Any concerns of the parents or nurse are noted. The nurse records which demonstrations and/or classes the mother and/or father attended and their expressed understanding of the instructions given to them.

Parent education is a wonderful aspect of family-centered maternity care. The nurse who takes the time to get the family off to a good start can feel satisfied that the best care is being provided for all members of the family.

## One Family's Story

*Nancy Pachelli, a 29-year-old research chemist, had given birth to a daughter, Maria, during the night. When her nurse, Jeanne Osaki, was completing her morning postpartum assessment, Nancy talked about her fears. She told Ms. Osaki that she was delighted to have a little girl but was rather scared, too. Nancy said that both she and her husband, Randy, were only children who had never done any babysitting as teenagers. They had moved to the area recently when both were offered better jobs, but neither had any family close by. She said, "People assume that because I'm older and have a career I somehow know about child care, but I don't. Do you know, I can't remember ever changing a diaper and neither can Randy. My mother is going to fly out this weekend to help me but our HMO discharges women 12 hours after delivery. That means that by tonight I'll be on my own. What am I going to do?"*

*Jeanne Osaki showed Nancy how to change a diaper and offered some tips about holding her baby. She also observed Nancy to assess problems areas. Jeanne realized that Nancy*

*was bright and eager and quickly incorporated any recommendations Jeanne made. Jeanne praised Nancy when she provided effective care for Maria and made several suggestions as Nancy attempted breast-feeding. Nancy said that her first attempt to feed Maria had been a limited success because the infant was sleepy and only sucked briefly. This time the baby nursed a little longer.*

*Randy Pachelli arrived shortly after breakfast and changed his first diaper under Nancy's direction. Ms. Osaki told the couple that the hospital TV channel had regularly scheduled programs on various aspects of child care and suggested they watch the next one. She also advised that they attend the bath class. They did both. Jeanne Osaki recognized that, despite their efforts to learn, the Pachellis were still feeling somewhat overwhelmed. When Althea Robbins, the nurse-midwife from the health maintenance organization (HMO), arrived to make rounds, Jeanne advised her of the couple's anxiety and recommended that they receive a home visit.*

*Ms. Robbins talked with the couple and told them of Jeanne Osaki's recommendation. She explained that the HMO offered home visits as part of their maternity care for couples who wished that service. The Pachellis expressed their desire for a visit and an appointment was scheduled for the next morning.*

*Throughout the day Ms. Osaki organized Nancy Pachelli's care so that Nancy had time to rest and time to learn. She spent time with the couple, discussing various aspects of the puerperium and of newborn care. She gave them encouragement and support as they cared for Maria. She also provided them with a series of pamphlets and instructional aids, and told them about an area support group for breast-feeding mothers. Before they were discharged she completed the teaching checklist and gave them the mother-baby unit phone number in case they had questions.*

*When changing the baby the evening after her discharge, Nancy noticed that there was a drop of blood on Maria's diaper. She called the unit and the evening nurse explained about pseudomenstruation. The next morning a visiting nurse from the HMO arrived. She observed Mrs. Pachelli during feeding and discussed concerns the couple had. She scheduled a follow-up visit for two days later and advised the couple to keep a list of questions.*

*By the time of her follow-up visit, Nancy had several questions on her list but was feeling increasingly confident. She and the nurse decided that further home visits were not necessary.*

*Ten days later Nancy Pachelli, accompanied by Maria, saw Althea Robbins at her first postpartum visit. The baby was content and growing and Nancy handled her with ease. Nancy told Althea how much she appreciated the support they had received from the nurses. She said, "I always thought of nurses as taking care of sick people. I never realized that nurses really are teachers, too."*

# ● EVALUATION

When evaluating the nursing care provided during the newborn period, the following outcomes may be anticipated.

● Newborn baby's adaptation to extrauterine life is supported and complete.

● Baby's physiologic and psychologic integrity is supported.

● Parent-newborn feeding pattern will be satisfactorily established.

● Parents demonstrate safe techniques for caring for their baby.

● Parents express understanding of bonding process and display attachment behaviors.

● Parents verbalize developmentally appropriate behavioral expectations of and follow-up care for their baby.

## ESSENTIAL CONCEPTS

● The overall goal of newborn nursing care is to provide comprehensive care while promoting the establishment of a well-functioning family unit.

● The period immediately following birth, during which adaptation to extrauterine life occurs, requires close monitoring to identify any deviations from normal.

● The first period of reactivity lasts for 30 minutes after birth. The newborn is alert and hungry at this time, making this a natural opportunity to promote attachment.

● The second period of reactivity requires close monitoring by the nurse as apnea, decreased heart rate, gagging, choking, and regurgitation are likely to occur and require nursing intervention.

● Nursing goals during the first four hours after birth (admission period) are to: maintain a clear airway, maintain a neutral thermal environment, prevent hemorrhage and infection, initiate oral feedings, and facilitate attachment.

● The newborn is routinely given prophylactic vitamin K to prevent possible hemorrhagic disease of the newborn.

● Prophylactic eye treatment for *Neisseria gonorrhoeae* is legally required on all newborns.

● Nursing goals in daily newborn care include maintenance of cardiopulmonary function, mainte-

nance of neutral thermal environment, promotion of adequate hydration and nutrition, prevention of complications, promotion of safety, and enhancement of attachment and parental knowledge of infant care.

● Essential daily care includes assessments of the vital signs, weight, overall color, intake/output, umbilical cord and circumcision, newborn nutrition, parent education, and attachment.

● The physician should be notified if there is evidence of bright red bleeding or puslike drainage near the cord stump or if the umbilicus remains unhealed.

● Following a circumcision the newborn must be observed closely for signs of bleeding, inability to void, and signs of infection.

● Signs of illness in newborns include: temperature above 38.4° C (101° F) or below 36.1° C (97° F), more than one episode of projectile vomiting, refusal of two feedings in a row, lethargy, cyanosis, and absence of breathing for longer than 15 seconds.

● Newborn screening for galactosemia, homocystinuria, hypothyroidism, maple syrup urine disease, phenylketonuria, and sickle cell anemia is done on all newborns in the first one to three days, with a second blood specimen drawn after 7 to 14 days.

## References

American Academy of Pediatrics. *Guidelines for Perinatal Care,* 2nd ed. Chicago, IL: American Academy of Pediatrics, 1988.

Andrich M, Golden S: Umbilical cord care. *Clin Pediatr* 1984; 23:342.

Avery M, Taeusch Jr H: *Schaffer's Diseases of the Newborn,* 5th ed. Philadelphia: Saunders, 1984.

Beske E, Garvis M: Important factors in breast feeding success. *Am J Mat Child Nurs* May/June 1982; 7:174.

D'Apolito K: The neonate's response to pain. *Am J Mat Child Nurs* July/August 1984; 9:256.

Gibbons M: Circumcision: The controversy continues. *Pediatr Nurs* March/April 1984; 10:103.

Harris CC: Cultural values and the decision to circumcise. *IMAGE* Fall 1986; 18–98.

Haun N, Porter E, Chance G: Care of the normal neonate. *Canad Nurs* October 1984; 80:37.

Kemp C, Silver H, O'Brien D: *Current Pediatric Diagnosis and Treatment,* 7th ed. Los Altos, CA: Lange, 1982.

Klaus M, Klaus P: *The Amazing Newborn.* Menlo Park, CA: Addison-Wesley, 1985.

Lauri S: The public health nurse as a guide in infant child care and education. *J Adv Nurs* 1981; 6–297.

Lubchenco LO: Routine neonatal circumcision: A surgical anachronism. *Clin Obstet Gynecol* 1980; 23:1135.

Mayfield S et al: Temperature measurement in term and preterm neonates. *J Pediatr* February 1984; 104:271.

Pediatricians change minds on circumcision. *San Francisco Chronicle* March 6, 1989, pp A1, A20.

Pritchard J, MacDonald P, Gant N: *Williams Obstetrics,* 17th ed. East Norwalk, CT: Appleton-Century-Crofts, 1985.

Ruchala P: The effect of wearing head covering on the axillary temperatures of infants. *Am J Mat Child Nurs* July/August 1985; 10:240.

Sprunger LW, Preece EW: Use of pediatric prenatal visits by family physicians. *J Fam Pract* 1981; 13:1007.

## Additional Readings

Chess S, Thomas A: Temperamental differences: A critical concept in child health care. *Pediatr Nurs* May/June 1985; 11:167.

Choi ES, Hamilton RK: The effects of culture on mother-infant interaction. *J Obstet Gynecol Neonatal Nurs* May/June 1986; 15:256.

Cunningham N et al: Infant carrying, breastfeeding, and mother-infant relations, letter. *Lancet* February 1987; 1:379.

Hayden GF et al: Providing free samples of baby items to newly delivered parents. An unintentional endorsement? *Clin Pediatr* March 1987; 26:14.

Lincoln GA: Neonatal circumcision: Is it needed? *J Obstet Gynecol Neonat Nurs* November/December 1986; 15:463.

Osborn LM et al: Hygiene care in uncircumcised infants. *Pediatrics* March 1981; 67:365.

Panwar S: Introducing family-centered care for mothers and newborns. *Nursing Management* November 1986; 17:45.

Pelosi MA, Apuzzio J: Making circumcision safe and painless. *Contemp OB/GYN* 1984; 24:42.

Sandstrom I: Ophthalmia neonatorum with special reference to chlamydia trachomatis: Diagnosis and treatment. *Acta Paediatr Scand* 1986; 330(Suppl):4.

Tedder JI: Newborn circumcision. *J Obstet Gynecol Neonat Nurs* January/February 1987; 16:42.

Tomlinson PS: Father involvement with first-born infants: Interpersonal and situational factors. *Pediatr Nurs* March/April 1987; 13:101.

Wagner T, Hindi-Alexander M: Hazards of baby powder. *Pediatr Nurs* March/April 1984; 10:124.

# 23

# Newborn Nutrition

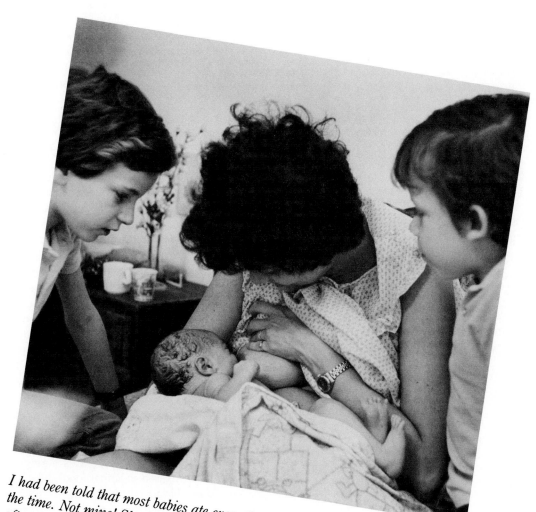

*I had been told that most babies ate every three or four hours and slept the rest of the time. Not mine! She wanted to nurse every two hours, and sometimes more often than that. Sometimes she would sleep for an hour, sometimes for fifteen minutes. I loved her, but I also felt consumed by her needs. It was hard to adjust to the fact that I couldn't get anything finished, whether it was an article I was reading or folding the laundry. At the end of the day I would realize I hadn't accomplished anything. Once I accepted the fact that I was not going to function at my old efficient rate (at least for a while) and stopped feeling guilty about what I wasn't getting done, I felt freer to enjoy the time I was spending with my baby. (The New Our Bodies, Ourselves)*

## Objectives

● Compare the nutritional value and composition of breast milk and formula preparations.

● Identify the benefits of breast-feeding for both mother and infant.

● Develop guidelines for helping both breast-feeding and bottle-feeding mothers to feed their infants successfully.

● Delineate nursing responsibilities for client education about problems the breast-feeding mother may encounter at home.

● Describe an appropriate process for weaning an infant from breast-feeding.

● Discuss the use of supplemental foods in the diet of infants under one year old.

● Discuss the advantages/disadvantages of breast-feeding and formula feeding.

## Key Terms

colostrum
letdown reflex
mature milk
oxytocin
prolactin
transitional milk
weaning

Feeding their newborn is an exciting, satisfying, and often worrisome task for parents. Meeting this essential need of their new child helps parents strengthen their attachment to their child and fosters their self-images as nurturers and providers. Whether a woman chooses to breast-feed or bottle-feed, she can be reassured that she can adequately meet her infant's needs. Questions may arise, however, and the nurse works with the woman to help her develop skill in her chosen method. The nurse provides information, assists the parent, and answers questions as necessary. In every interaction it is the nurse's responsibility to support the parents and increase rather than decrease the family's sense of confidence.

## ● NUTRITIONAL NEEDS OF THE NEWBORN

The newborn's diet must supply nutrients to meet the rapid rate of physical growth and development. A neonatal diet should include protein, carbohydrate, fat, water, vitamins, and minerals, and provide adequate calories. Recommendations shown in Table 23.1 are all based on limited research data but give generalizations about requirements for optimal nutrition for the first year of life.

The calories (50–55 cal/lb/day or 110–120 cal/kg/day) in the newborn's diet are divided among protein, carbohydrate, and fat and should be adjusted according to the infant's weight. Protein is needed for rapid cellular growth and maintenance. The fat portion of the diet provides calories, regulates fluid and electrolyte balance, and develops the neonatal brain and neurologic system. Water requirements are high (64–73 mL/lb/day or 140–160 mL/kg/day) in the newborn because of an inability to concentrate urine. Fluid needs are further increased in illness or hot weather. The iron intake of the infant will be affected by accumulation of iron stores during the fetal life, and the mother's iron and other food intake if she is breast-feeding. Ascorbic acid (usually in the form of fruit juices) and meat, poultry, and fish, are known to enhance absorption of iron in the mother. See Essential Facts to Remember—Newborn Caloric and Fluid Needs.

## ● Breast Milk

Three types of milk are produced during the establishment of lactation: (a) colostrum, (b) transitional milk, and (c) mature milk. **Colostrum** is a yellowish or creamy-appearing fluid that is thicker than later milk and contains more protein, fat-soluble vitamins, and minerals. It also contains high levels of immunoglobulins, which may be a source of immunity for the newborn. Colostrum production begins early in pregnancy and may last for several days after birth. However, in most cases colostrum is replaced by transitional milk within two to four days after birth. **Transitional milk** is produced from the end of colostrum production until approximately two weeks postpartum. This milk contains lactose, water-soluble vitamins, elevated levels of fat, and more calories than colostrum.

The final milk produced, **mature milk,** has a high percentage of water. Although it appears similar to skim milk and may cause mothers to question whether their milk is "rich enough," mature breast milk provides 20 kcal/ounce, as do most prepared formulas. However, the percentage of calories derived from protein is lower in breast milk than in formulas, with a greater proportion of calories being derived from carbohydrates in the form of lactose (Pipes 1985). The nitrogen wastes of protein metabolism are less in breast-fed babies and are less taxing on the immature kidneys.

The American Academy of Pediatrics (1988) recommends breast milk as the optimal food for the first four to six months of life. The advantages that breast-feeding provides to newborns and infants are generally immunologic, nutritional, and psychosocial.

Secretory IgA, which is present in colostrum and breast milk, has antiviral, antibacterial, and antigenic-inhibiting properties, and their benefits extend into the infant and toddler period (Gulick 1986). It is theorized that the immature intestine allows large molecules, such as those found in cow's milk, to cross the small intestine mucosa. Secretory IgA plays a role in decreasing the permeability of the intestine to these macromolecules. Other properties in colostrum and breast milk that act to inhibit the growth of bacteria and/or viruses are *Lactobacillus*

## Essential Facts to Remember

### Newborn Caloric and Fluid Needs

- Caloric intake: 50–55 cal/lb/day or 110–120 cal/kg/day
- Fluid requirements: 64–73 mL/lb/day or 140–160 mL/kg/day
- Weight gain: First six months—1 oz/day
  Second six months—0.5 oz/day

*bifidus,* lysozymes, lactoperoxidase, lactoferrin, transferrin, and various immunoglobulins or antibodies. Immunoglobulins to the poliomyelitis virus are also present in the breast milk of immune mothers. Due to the fact that breast milk may inhibit the desired intestinal infection and immune response of the infant, some clinics suggest that breast-feedings be withheld for 30 to 60 minutes following the administration of the Sabin oral polio vaccine. Breast milk is also known to be nonallergenic.

Breast milk is composed of lactose, lipids, polyunsaturated fatty acids, and amino acids, especially taurine, and has a whey to casein protein ratio that facilitates the digestion, absorption, and full use of breast milk compared to formulas (Gulick 1986). Some researchers feel the high concentration of cholesterol and the balance of amino acids in breast milk make it the best food for myelination and neurologic development. It is also suggested that high cholesterol levels in breast milk may stimulate the production of enzymes that lead to more efficient metabolism of cholesterol, thereby reducing its long-term harmful effects on the cardiovascular system (Anholm 1986).

The iron found in breast milk, even though much lower in concentration than that in prepared formulas, is much more readily and fully absorbed and is sufficient to meet the infant's iron needs.

The American Academy of Pediatrics (1988) states that there is generally no need to give supplemental iron to breast-fed newborns before the age of six months. Supplemental iron may be detrimental to the ability of breast milk to protect the newborn by interfering with lactoferrin, an iron-binding protein that enhances the absorption of iron and has anti-infective properties.

Another advantage of breast milk is that all its components are delivered to the infant in an unchanged form, and vitamins are not lost through processing and heating. If the breast-feeding mother is taking daily multivitamins and her diet is adequate, the only supplements necessary are vitamin D and fluoride until the infant is six months old. Because of the poor passage of fluoride into breast milk, infants should receive supplemental fluoride to be started shortly after birth (American Academy of Pediatrics Com-

| Table 23.1 Nutritional Needs of the Normal Newborn | | |
|---|---|---|
| | **At birth** | **At one year** |
| Calories | 120/kg/day | 100/kg/day |
| Protein | 1.9 g/100 kcal* | 1.7 g/100 kcal* |
| Fat | 30%–55% of total calories | 30%–50% of total calories |
| Carbohydrate | 35%–55% of total calories | 35%–55% of total calories |
| Water | 330 mL† | 700 mL |

*Estimated to be approximately equivalent to levels in breast milk.
†Approximately.

Source: Adapted from information contained in Eckstein EF: *Food, People, and Nutrition.* Westport, CT: AV Publishing, 1980.

mittee on Nutrition 1985). If the mother's diet or vitamin intake is inadequate or questionable, care givers may choose to prescribe additional vitamins for the infant.

The psychosocial advantages of breast-feeding are primarily those associated with attachment. Breast-feeding enhances attachment by providing the opportunity for frequent, direct skin contact between the newborn and the mother. The newborn's sense of touch is highly developed at birth and is a primary means of communication. The tactile stimulation associated with breast-feeding can communicate warmth, closeness, and comfort. The increased closeness provides both newborn and mother with the opportunity to learn each other's behavioral cues and needs. The mother's sense of accomplishment in being able to satisfy her baby's needs for nourishment and comfort is enhanced when the newborn sucks vigorously, and is satiated and calmed by the breast-feeding. Some mothers prefer breast-feeding as a means of extending the close, unique, nourishing relationship between mother and baby that existed prior to delivery. In the event of a twin birth, breast-feeding not only is possible but also enhances the mother's individualization and attachment to each newborn. The fantasized single baby is replaced more readily with the reality of two individual babies when the mother has close and frequent contact with each (Gromada 1981). Other advantages that have been cited associate breast-feeding with improved language and cognitive development as well as scholastic ability (Anholm 1986).

One disadvantage of breast-feeding is that most drugs taken by the mother are transmitted through breast milk and may cause harm to the infant (see Appendix G for specific drugs and their possible effects on the neonate). Jaundice caused by breast milk may be another reason to interrupt breast-feeding. Breast-feeding can normally be resumed after 48 hours without resulting in further hyperbilirubinemia.

A mother's poor nutritional, physical, or mental health or a personal aversion to breast-feeding may be contraindications to nursing. Difficulty in maintaining milk supply, concern over the adequacy of the breast milk to meet the newborn's needs, sore nipples, resumption of a heavy work schedule, and constant demands on her time are other reasons a mother discontinues breast-feeding. Lack of support and encouragement from health care providers or family may also contribute to a woman's decision to stop breast-feeding.

Opinion varies as to the advisability of continuing breast-feeding during a pregnancy. Some feel the nutritional demands on the pregnant mother are too great and advocate gradual weaning. Others suggest that with adequate rest, a proper diet, and strong emotional support, continued breast-feeding during pregnancy is a valid choice. The practice of nursing one infant throughout pregnancy and then breast-feeding both infants after birth is called *tandem nursing* (Lawrence 1980). When pregnancy occurs, the decision is best made on an individual basis after considering maternal health and motivation and the age of the first child.

Even though many mothers obtain information about breast-feeding from written sources, family and friends, and Le Leche League, the nurse needs to be a ready source of information, encouragement, and support as well. The nurse can be helpful during the time when parents are deciding whether to breast-feed, after the birth process when breast-feedings are just being established, and after the family returns home.

## ● *Bottle-Feeding*

Although breast-feeding is rising in popularity, formula feeding is a viable and nurturing choice (Neifert 1986). Formula feeding can also meet the goal of successful growth of the baby. The closeness and warmth that can occur during breast-feeding is also an integral part of bottle-feeding. An advantage of bottle-feeding is that both parents can share equally in this nurturing, caring experience with their baby. Numerous types of commercially prepared lactose formulas meet the nutritional needs of the infant. Some of the most common formulas are Similac, Enfamil, and SMA. These milk formulas contain different amounts of amino acids: tyrosine and phenylalanine are more prevalent in formula milk; the taurine present in breast milk is absent in cow's milk formula. Bottle-fed babies do gain weight faster than breast-fed babies because of the higher protein in commercially prepared formula than in human milk.

Bottle-fed infants up to six months of age can gain as much as 1 ounce per day and tend to regain their birth weight by ten days after birth (Pipes 1985). Healthy breast-fed babies, however, gain approximately ½ ounce per day in the first six months of life (Stahl and Guida 1984) and tend to regain their birth weight by about 14 days postpartum. Formula-fed infants generally double their weight within three and a half to four months, whereas nursing infants double their weight at about five months of age.

Formulas contain mostly saturated fatty acids, whereas breast milk is higher in unsaturated fatty acids. Calcium, sodium, and chloride occur in higher concentrations in some commercially made formulas, which may be detrimental to the newborn's kidneys. Their immature state may not be ready to handle such high loads of solutes. This high solute load may also lead to thirst in the formula-fed infant, causing overfeeding and possible obesity (Evans and Glass 1979).

Another potential problem with formulas is an allergic reaction in the newborn. The small intestine of the infant is permeable to macromolecules such as those found in cow's milk and milk-based formulas. The introduction of formula's foreign protein may cause an allergy that may be exhibited by spitting up and decreased appetite. (See Essential Facts to Remember—Pros and Cons of Breast- and Bottle-Feeding.)

# Essential Facts to Remember

## Pros and Cons of Breast- and Bottle-Feeding

| Breast | Bottle |
| --- | --- |

### Newborn's Health

Colostrum is rich in antibodies until baby's own immune system is established.

Mother's milk is almost always tolerated by baby. Breast milk proteins are easily digested and fats well absorbed.

Baby can't overeat, limits self to natural weight. No need to empty bottle.

Some babies are allergic to certain formulas. Trial and error may be necessary.

Formula is linked to an increased number of GI and respiratory infections.

More air may be ingested into stomach, causing gas, cramps, and spitting up.

### Composition

Higher levels than formula contains of lactose, cystine, and cholesterol, which are necessary for brain and nerve growth.

Perfect balance of proteins, carbohydrates, fats, vitamins, and minerals.

Made to be as close to human milk as possible, but nutrients not as biodegradable. Contains adequate vitamins and minerals.

### Purity

Pure and as free from foreign materials as whatever the mother consumes.

No storage, sanitation, or spoilage unless pumped milk is not refrigerated. Frozen milk can be safely kept for at least one month.

Formula companies comply with federal guidelines for sterility and quality.

Ready-to-drink formula has an expiration date and shelf half-life even if unopened. Once mixed, powdered formula should be used within 24 hours.

### Cost

Costs are minimal, including the cost of two or three nursing bras, cloth or disposable nursing pads used for about first six weeks, breast cream to prevent and/or treat sore and cracked nipples, manual or electric breast pump, and the cost of a well-balanced diet for the mother. No waste with breast milk.

Expenses include cost of bottles or disposable nursers with plastic liners, nipples, nipple caps, and a heat-resistant mixing container. Formula is a major expense, especially when baby takes 24 oz or four bottles a day.

### Convenience

Mother can feed whenever baby needs; milk is at perfect temperature.

If baby is only on breast milk, mother is tied down and can't miss too many feedings. She risks decreasing her supply if she supplements.

Engorgement can cause discomfort. Certain clothes can make nursing discreetly difficult.

Mother has more freedom to come and go rather than timing her trips from home based on baby's feeding schedule.

Requires frequent trips to store or buying formula in large quantities.

Night feedings are more disruptive. Preparation time is about the same as for making iced tea.

### Emotional Aspects

Pleasant way to nurture—skin-to-skin contact enhances closeness. Nursing has calming effect on baby, who hears familiar sound of mother's heartbeat and smells her scent.

Mother may be embarrassed, nervous, or have aversion to breast-feeding, especially in public.

Father is left out of nurturing experience for first three months if baby is breast-fed exclusively.

Same degree of intimacy as with breast if mother or father holds baby close, smiles, and snuggles during feedings.

Mother may be more at ease with bottle than with offering breast.

Father equal partner in nurturing and feeding experience.

*Source: Adapted from Lesko W and Lesko M:* The Maternity Source Book. *New York: Warner Books, 1984, p 284–87.*

Clinicians recommend iron-fortified formulas or supplements when bottle-feeding with non–iron fortified formulas, as iron deficiency anemia is still very prevalent. Seven milligrams of iron per day is the recommended iron dosage. However, the nurse must be aware that excess iron in the diet may interfere with the baby's natural ability to defend against disease (Picciano and Deering 1980). Parents also need to be informed about the constipation that sometimes results from iron-enriched formula and about various methods of alleviating the constipation.

Many companies make an enriched formula that is similar to breast milk. These formulas all have sufficient levels of carbohydrate, protein, fat, vitamins, and minerals to meet the newborn's nutritional needs.

The American Academy of Pediatrics recommends that infants be given breast milk or formula rather than whole milk until one year of age. However, the American Academy of Pediatrics Committee on Nutrition (1985) has more recently noted that no research studies to date have identified any conclusive evidence of harm to the infant who is given modified whole cow's milk along with adequate supplementary feedings after age six months. Table 23.2 compares the components of breast milk, unmodified cow's milk, and a commercially standardized formula used for normal, healthy newborns.

Neither unmodified cow's milk nor skim milk is an acceptable alternative for newborn feeding. The protein content in cow's milk is too high (50%–75% more than human milk), is poorly digested, and may cause bleeding of the gastrointestinal tract. Unmodified cow's milk is also inadequate in vitamins. Skim milk lacks adequate calories, fat content, and essential fatty acids necessary for proper development of the neonate's neurologic system. It provides excessive protein and also causes problems as a result of altered osmolarity. Nutritionists advise against use of unmodified cow's milk or skim milk for children under two years of age.

## ● NEWBORN FEEDING

### ● Initial Feeding

The time when the first feeding is given should be determined by the physiologic and behavioral cues of the newborn. The nurse should assess for active bowel sounds, absence of abdominal distention, and a lusty cry, which quiets and is replaced with rooting and sucking behaviors when a stimulus is placed near the lips. These signs are indicators that the newborn is hungry and physically ready to tolerate the feeding. Assessment of the newborn's physiologic status is of primary and ongoing concern to the nurse throughout the first feeding.

The initial feeding provides an opportunity to assess whether the baby's upper gastrointestinal tract is patent and ensure that the suck-swallow mechanism is coordi-nated. Feedings may need to be delayed or prohibited if hydramnios (indicating tracheoesophageal fistula; see Chapter 24 for further discussion) is noted at delivery or if a cleft palate, respiratory distress, cyanosis, or abdominal distention are present. In cases of esophageal atresia, the feeding is taken well initially, but as the esophageal pouch fills, the feeding is quickly regurgitated unchanged by stomach contents. If a fistula is present, the infant gags, chokes, regurgitates mucus, and may become cyanotic as fluid passes through the fistula into the lungs.

It is the practice in some birthing centers to offer the bottle-fed newborn an initial feeding of sterile water approximately one to six hours after birth (Coen and Koffler 1987). Glucose water should not be used, since it will damage the newborn's lung tissue if aspirated (Avery 1987). The sterile water feeding provides an opportunity for the nurse to assess the effectiveness of the newborn's suck, swallow, and gag reflexes. A softer nipple made for preterm infants may be used if the newborn appears to tire easily. Extreme fatigue coupled with rapid respiration and circumoral cyanosis may indicate cardiovascular complications and should be assessed further.

It is not unusual for the neonate to regurgitate some mucus and water following a feeding even though it was taken without difficulty. Consequently, the newborn is positioned on the right side after a feeding to aid drainage and is observed carefully.

Mothers who plan to breast-feed can nurse their newborns immediately following birth. This practice provides stimulation for milk production and aids in maternal-newborn attachment. If the newborn appears to have difficulty nursing, the sterile water feeding by the nurse allows an opportunity for assessment. If the water feeding is taken without difficulty and retained, the mother may resume breast-feeding. In formula-fed newborns, after a few successful swallows of sterile water, glucose water or formula may be substituted to give needed sugar and prevent hypoglycemia. The newborn may take 15–30 mL at this first feeding. The newborn's stomach will be filled within three to five minutes of strong sucking at the breast or bottle.

### ● Establishing a Feeding Pattern

Following the initial feeding with water for bottle-fed babies or breast milk for breast-fed babies, mothers should feed their babies when they seem hungry. An "on demand" feeding program facilitates each baby's own rhythm and may be less traumatic to mother's nipples, while not causing excessive weight gain (Lesko 1984).

Breast milk is rapidly digested by the newborn, who may desire to nurse every two to three hours initially, with one or two feedings during the night.

Rooming-in permits the mother to feed the infant as needed. When rooming-in is not available, a supportive

## Table 23.2 Composition of Mature Breast Milk, Unmodified Cow's Milk, and a Routine Infant Formula

| Composition/dL | Mature breast milk | Cow's milk | Routine formula (20 cal) with iron |
|---|---|---|---|
| Calories | 75.0 | 69.0 | 67.0 |
| Protein, g | 1.1 | 3.5 | 1.5 |
| Lactalbumin % | 80 | 18 | 60 |
| Casein % | 20 | 82 | 40 |
| Water, mL | 87.1 | 87.3 | 90 |
| Fat, g | 4.5 | 3.5 | 3.8 |
| Carbohydrate, g | 7.1 | 4.9 | 7.0 |
| Ash, g | 0.21 | 0.72 | 0.34 |
| Minerals | | | |
| Na, mg | 16.0 | 50.0 | 21.0 |
| K, mg | 51.0 | 144.0 | 69.0 |
| Ca, mg | 33.0 | 118.0 | 46.0 |
| P, mg | 14.0 | 93.0 | 32.0 |
| Mg, mg | 4.0 | 13.0 | 5.3 |
| Fe, mg | 0.05 | Tr. | 1.3 |
| Zn, mg | 0.15 | 0.4 | 0.42 |
| Vitamins | | | |
| A, IU | 182.0 | 140.0 | 210.0 |
| C, mg | 5.0 | 1.0 | 5.3 |
| D, IU | 2.2 | 4.2 | 42.3 |
| E, IU | 0.18 | 0.04 | 0.83 |
| Thiamin, mg | 0.01 | 0.03 | 0.04 |
| Riboflavin, mg | 0.04 | 0.17 | 0.06 |
| Niacin, mg | 0.2 | 0.1 | 0.7 |
| Curd size | Soft Flocculent | Firm Large | Mod. firm Mod. large |
| pH | Alkaline | Acid | Acid |
| Anti-infective properties | + | ± | − |
| Bacterial content | Sterile | Nonsterile | Sterile |
| Emptying time | More rapid | | |

Source: Avery GB: *Neonatology*, 3rd ed. Philadelphia: Lippincott, 1987, p 1192.

nursing staff and flexible nursery policies will allow the mother to feed on demand when the infant is hungry. Nothing is more frustrating to a new mother than attempting to nurse a newborn who is sound asleep because he or she is either not hungry or exhausted from crying. Once lactation is established and the family is home, a feeding pattern agreeable to both mother and child is usually established.

Formula-fed newborns may awaken for feedings every two to five hours but are frequently satisfied with feedings every three to four hours. Because formula is digested more slowly, the bottle-fed infant may go longer between feedings but should not go longer than four hours. The bottle-fed baby may begin skipping the night feeding within about six weeks. This is very individualized depending on the size and development of the infant.

Both breast-fed and bottle-fed infants experience growth spurts at certain times and require increased feeding. The mother of a breast-fed infant may meet these increased demands by nursing more frequently to increase her milk supply; however, it will take about 24 hours for the milk supply to increase adequately to meet the new demand. A slight increase in feedings will meet the needs of the formula-fed infant.

Providing nourishment for her newborn is a major concern of the new mother. Her feelings of success or failure may influence her self-concept as she assumes her maternal role. With proper instruction, support, and encouragement from professional persons, feeding becomes a source of pleasure and satisfaction to both parents and infant.

Table 23.3 can be used to assist parents in identifying their baby's cues indicating hunger and satiation.

## • PROMOTION OF SUCCESSFUL INFANT FEEDING

Parents may see feeding their baby as the center of the relationship between themselves and this new family member. Whether the mother has chosen to bottle-feed or breast-feed, the nurse can help the mother have a successful experience while in the hospital and during the early days at home. Feeding and caring for newborns may be routine tasks for the nurse, but the success or nonsuccess that a mother achieves the first few times may determine her feelings about herself as an adequate mother.

As an expression of personality, the response of the newborn to caring is important. A parent may interpret the newborn's behavior as rejection, which may alter the progress of parent-child relationships. A parent may also interpret the sleepy infant's refusal to suck or inability to retain formula as evidence of parental incompetence. Likewise, the breast-feeding mother may deduce that the newborn does not like her if he or she fails to take her nipple readily. Conversely, infants pick up messages from the muscular tension of those holding them. Parents need to know that it is not unusual for babies not to nurse well for the first days.

A nurse who is sensitive to the needs of the mother can form a relationship with her that permits sharing of knowledge about techniques and emotions connected with the feeding experience. Breast-feeding women frequently express disappointment in the help given to them by hospital nurses, saying they would like more encouragement, support, and practical information about feeding their newborn (Beske and Garvis 1982). This desire and need also applies to nonnursing mothers. To adequately assist breast-feeding mothers, the nurse must have a sound understanding of the "physiology of breast-feeding." Consistency in teaching by nurses is also essential. A new mother becomes very frustrated if she is shown a number of different methods of feeding her newborn.

The decision by the mother about whether to breast-feed or bottle-feed is usually made by the sixth month of pregnancy and often even before conception. This decision is frequently based on the influences of relatives (especially the father and maternal grandmother) (Beske and Garvis 1982), friends, and social customs rather than on knowledge about the nutritional and psychologic needs of herself and her newborn. With the technologic advances in formula production and the availability of knowledge about breast-feeding techniques, the mother should be confident that the choice she makes will promote normal growth and development of her newborn.

If the mother makes the decision to breast-feed at the time of birth without prenatal preparation or support from her partner or other members of her family, she may encounter difficulty. It is necessary for the nurse to find out before delivery whether the woman really wants to breast-feed or has made the decision based on social or family pressures (Mullett 1982).

The nurse's primary responsibility is to support the feeding method decision and to help the family achieve a

| Table 23.3 | Infant Feeding Behaviors | | |
|---|---|---|---|
| **Age** | **Hunger behavior** | **Feeding behavior** | **Satiety behavior** |
| Birth to 13 weeks (0–3 months) | Cries; hands fisted; body tense | Rooting reflex; medial lip closure; strong suck reflex; suck-swallow pattern; tongue thrust and retraction; palmomental reflex, gags easily, needs burping | Withdraws head from nipple; falls asleep; hands relaxed; relief of body tension |
| 14–24 weeks (4–6 months) | Eagerly anticipates; grasps and draws bottle to mouth; reaches with open mouth | Aware of hands; generalized reaching; intentional hand to mouth; tongue elevation; lips purse at corners—pucker; shifts food in mouth—prechewing; tongue protrudes in anticipation of nipple; tongue holds nipple firm; tongue projection strong; suck strength increases; coughs and chokes easily; preference for tastes | Tosses head back; fusses or cries; covers mouth with hands; ejects food; distracted by surroundings |

Source: Mott S, Fazekas N, James S: *Nursing Care of Children and Families*. Menlo Park, CA: Addison-Wesley, 1985, p 216.

positive result. No woman should be made to feel inadequate or superior because of her choice in feeding. There are advantages and disadvantages to breast- and bottle-feeding, but positive bonds in parent-child relationships may be developed with either method.

Immediately before feeding, the mother should be made as comfortable as possible. Preparations may include voiding, washing her hands, and assuming a position of comfort.

Depending on the newborn's level of hunger, the parents may want to use the time before feeding to get acquainted with their infant. The presence of the nurse during part of this time to answer questions and provide reinforcement of parenting skills will be helpful for the family.

For the sleepy baby, a period of playful activity—such as gently rubbing the feet and hands or adjusting clothing and loosening coverings to expose the infant to room air—may increase alertness so that, when the feeding is initiated, the infant is ready and sucks eagerly. It may allow the active newborn an opportunity to calm down so that he or she can find and grasp the nipple effectively. After the feeding, when the infant is satisfied and asleep, parents may explore the characteristics unique to their newborn. Hospital routines must be flexible enough to allow this time for the family. Rooming-in offers spontaneous, frequent encounters for the family and provides opportunities to practice handling skills, thereby increasing confidence in care after discharge. It may also allow for demand rather than scheduled feeding times, and this should be encouraged.

## ● Cultural Considerations in Infant Feeding

Breast-feeding has been the traditional feeding method for most cultures. However, bottle-feeding has become extremely popular, much to the dismay of older members of some cultures. Navajo elders, for instance, believe that breast-feeding ensures respect and obedience because the child remains close to the mother, while the bottle-fed infant will be more disobedient (Clark 1981).

Western practices encourage the new mother to breast-feed as soon as possible, but in many cultures (for example, Mexican American, Navajo, Filipino, and Vietnamese) colostrum is not offered to the newborn. Breast-feeding begins only after the milk flow is established. Interestingly, a group of Vietnamese mothers who delayed breast-feeding until the third day after delivery had no difficulty breast-feeding (Ward et al 1981).

In many Asian cultures the newborn is given boiled water until the mother's milk flows. The newborn is fed on demand and cries are responded to immediately. If the crying continues, evil spirits may be blamed and a priest's blessing may be necessary. Although many of the Hmong women of Laos combine breast-feeding with some bottle-feeding, they find it unacceptable to express their milk or pump their breasts. Thus other methods of providing relief should be suggested if breast engorgement develops (LaDu 1985).

In the black American culture there is much emphasis on feeding. Solid foods are introduced early and may even be added to the infant's formula. For the traditional Mexican American, a fat baby is considered a healthy baby and infants are fed on demand. "Spoiling" is encouraged and a colicky baby may be given mint or olive oil for relief. These are but a few of the cultural practices related to feeding. The nurse should make a point of learning about other practices if she/he will be working with mothers from various cultures.

## ● Breast-Feeding
### LACTATION

The female breast is divided into 15 to 24 lobes separated from one another by fat and connective tissue. These lobes are subdivided into lobules, composed of small units called *alveoli* where milk is synthesized. The lobules have a system of lactiferous ductiles that join larger ducts and eventually open onto the nipple surface. During pregnancy, the increased levels of estrogen stimulate breast development in preparation for lactation.

Following birth the levels of estrogen and progesterone drop rapidly, and the anterior pituitary begins to secrete **prolactin.** This hormone promotes milk production by stimulating the alveolar cells of the breast. **Oxytocin,** secreted by the posterior pituitary when the infant sucks on the mother's nipple, triggers the **letdown reflex** and a flow of milk results.

The letdown reflex can be stimulated by the newborn's sucking, presence, or cry, or even by maternal thoughts about her baby. It may also occur during sexual orgasm because oxytocin is released. Conversely, the mother's lack of self-confidence, or fear of, embarrassment about, or pain connected with breast-feeding may prevent the milk from being ejected into the duct system. Milk production is decreased with repeated inhibition of the letdown reflex. Failure to empty the breasts frequently and completely also decreases production. As milk accumulates and is not withdrawn, the buildup of pressure in the alveoli suppresses secretion.

Once lactation is well established, prolactin production decreases. Oxytocin and sucking continue to be the facilitators of milk production. The release of oxytocin in response to the infant's suckling is beneficial to the new mother. Oxytocin stimulates uterine contraction and thus promotes rapid involution of the uterus.

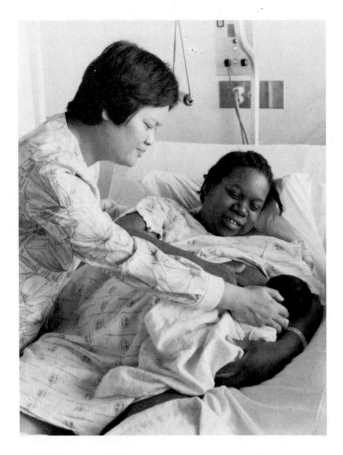

*Figure 23.1 For many mothers, the nurse's support and knowledge are instrumental in establishing successful breast-feeding.*

## EDUCATION FOR BREAST-FEEDING SELF-CARE

The nurse caring for the breast-feeding mother should help the woman achieve independence and success in her feeding efforts (Figure 23.1). Prepared with a knowledge of the anatomy and physiology of the breast and lactation, the components and positive effects of breast milk, and techniques of breast-feeding, the nurse can help the woman and her family use their own resources to achieve a successful experience. The objectives involved in breast-feeding are (a) to provide adequate nutrition, (b) to establish an adequate milk supply, and (c) to prevent trauma to the nipples. All teaching is aimed toward these goals.

### Procedures for Breast-Feeding

The newborn who is breast-feeding should be put to breast as soon as possible, depending on the situation of birth. Colostrum has sufficient nutrients to satisfy the infant until milk is established in two to four days. Establishment of lactation depends on the strength of the infant's suck and the frequency of nursing.

Positioning of the baby at the breast is a critical factor. The entire body of the infant should be turned toward the mother's breast, with the mouth adjacent to the nipple. The nipple should be directed straight into the mouth, and as much of the areola as possible should be included so that, as the baby sucks, the jaws compress the ducts that are directly beneath the areola (Figure 23.2). To do this, the mother holds her breast with her thumb placed on the upper portion of the breast and the remainder of her fingers cupped under her breast. She then lightly brushes the infant's lips with the nipple. Through the rooting reflex, the infant can locate the nipple. The mother should avoid stimulating both cheeks, which only confuses the hungry infant.

If the mother does not have a prominent or everted nipple, she may try rolling the nipple between her thumb and forefinger or stretching the nipple by pressing in and outward around the nipple prior to the feeding. Nurses should avoid the temptation to substitute a regular nipple shield to correct nipple positions. The shield tends to confuse the baby, as the artificial nipples on the shields are softer and easier to feed from, and the baby may refuse the human nipple when it is reoffered. This problem, termed "nipple confusion," may also be avoided if sterile water or dextrose and water feedings are not routinely

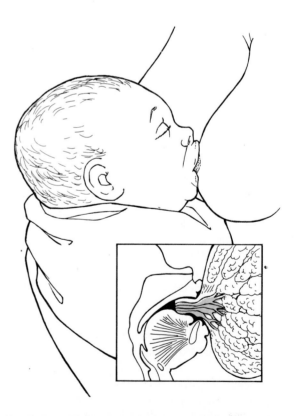

*Figure 23.2 To nurse effectively, it is important that the infant's mouth cover the majority of the areola to compress the ducts below. (Courtesy Ross Laboratories, Columbus, OH.)*

given to breast-feeding infants. The other problem with nipple shields is that the baby may not get enough milk. If nipple confusion occurs, the woman should discontinue all artificial nipples (including pacifiers) and patiently help her baby learn to grasp her breast nipple. Use of breast pumps starts milk flowing and draws the nipple out. Also, use of the football hold facilitates infant grasp of the nipple, as well as offering the nipple when the baby is alert enough to nurse and not frantically upset and hungry (Neifert 1986).

Following feedings, the nipples should be assessed for trauma so that corrections may be made in position and technique for the next feeding. Current literature suggests that imposing time limits for breast-feeding (five minutes, then seven minutes, etc) is not helpful in preventing nipple soreness as was previously believed (deCarvalho et al 1984, L'Esperance and Frantz 1985). Furthermore, since letdown may take up to three minutes to occur, in the first few days at least, artificial time limits may actually interfere with successful feeding. In working to avoid undue nipple trauma it is important, then, to be certain that the nipple is properly positioned, that the infant's mouth covers a large portion of the areola, and that the position of the infant is varied from one feeding to another.

The mother is encouraged to alternate the breast she offers to the infant first at each feeding. A convenient way for the mother to remember which breast to begin with is to fasten a small safety pin to the bra cup on that side. Generally the infant will empty the breasts during a feeding.

If a full breast appears to be occluding the infant's nares, the mother should either lift the breast slightly or gently press the breast away from the nares. Pressure must be gentle to avoid inadvertently pulling the breast from the infant's mouth. If positioned correctly, light pressure against the tip of the nose causes the nares to open.

The mother is instructed in techniques for breaking suction prior to removing the infant from the breast. By inserting a finger into the infant's mouth beside the nipple, she can break the suction, and the nipple may be removed without trauma. Burping between feedings on each breast and at the end of the feeding continues to be necessary. If the infant has been crying, it is also advisable to burp before beginning feeding.

The cesarean birth mother needs support so that the infant does not rest on her abdomen for long periods of time. If she is breast-feeding, she may be more comfortable lying on her side with a pillow behind her back and one between her legs. The nurse can position the newborn next to the woman's breast and place a rolled towel or small pillow behind the infant for support. The mother will initially need assistance turning from side to side and burping the newborn. She may prefer to breast-feed sitting up with a pillow on her lap and the infant resting on the pillow rather than directly on her abdomen. It may be helpful to place a rolled pillow under the arm supporting the infant's head.

Initially more milk is produced than is required by the infant. Later the amount of milk will be produced to meet nutritional need, manifested through sucking. Milk may tend to leak until demand meets supply. The mother should expect and deal with this by using breast pads without plastic in her bra to absorb the milk. She should be cautioned to remove wet pads frequently to avoid infection or irritation to the nipples. The mother can also use pressure, for instance, arms across breasts or hands over breasts to stop leaking.

The use of supplementary feedings for the breast-feeding infant may weaken or confuse the sucking reflex and may interfere with successful outcome. Often parents are concerned because they have no visual assurance regarding the amount consumed. The mother may be reassured about adequacy of intake if she listens for sounds of swallowing while the baby is nursing. In addition, if the infant gains weight and has six or more wet diapers a day, he or she is receiving adequate amounts of milk. Activity levels and intervals between feedings may also indicate how satisfied the infant is. Parents should know that, because breast milk is more easily digested than formulas, the breast-fed infant becomes hungry sooner. Thus the frequency of breast-feedings may be greater, particularly after discharge, when maternal fatigue or excitement may decrease milk supply temporarily. Increasing the frequency of feedings alleviates problems during these periods. The parents may also expect the infant to demand more frequent nursing during periods when growth spurts are expected, such as 10 days to 2 weeks, 5 to 6 weeks, 2½ to 3 months, and 4½ to 6 months (Riordan 1983).

### Expression of Milk

The mother may be taught to express her milk manually and freeze it for bottle-feeding if she will be absent for a scheduled feeding. Breast milk should be frozen in plastic bottles or plastic bags; if glass bottles are used, the antibodies will adhere to the sides of the bottle and their benefits will be lost. Manual expression to relieve maternal discomfort and to maintain the milk supply is advisable if the mother must go several hours without feeding. The mother's milk supply will decrease unless the breasts are emptied regularly.

Milk may be expressed by hand or by using a breast pump. To express her milk manually, the woman first washes her hands, and then massages her breast to stimulate letdown. To massage her breast, the woman grasps the breast with both hands at the base of the breast near the chest wall. Using the palms of her hands she then firmly slides her hands toward her nipple. She repeats this process several times. She is then ready to begin hand expression. The woman generally uses her left hand for her right breast and right hand for her left breast. However, some women find it preferable to use the hand on the same

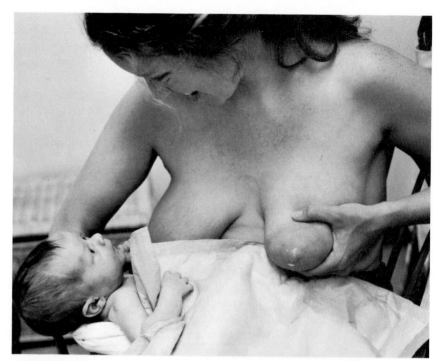

*Figure 23.3   Hand position for manual expression of milk*

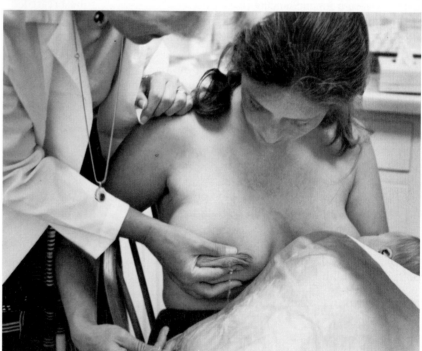

*Figure 23.4   Manual expression of milk*

side as the breast (right hand for right breast). The nurse should encourage the woman to use the method she finds most effective. She grasps the areola with her thumb on the top and her first two fingers on the lower portion (Figure 23.3). Without allowing her fingers to slide on her skin, she pushes inward toward the chest and then squeezes her fingers together while pulling forward on the areola (Figure 23.4). She can use a container to catch any fluid

that is squeezed out. She then repositions her hand by rotating it slightly so that she can repeat the process. She continues to reposition her hand and repeat the process to empty all the milk sinuses.

Hand or electric breast pumps are useful for building and maintaining a milk supply when the infant is not able to nurse (premature infant, ill infant, infant with breast milk jaundice, mother on medications that are excreted in the breast milk) or for the working mother who regularly misses certain feedings (Figure 23.5). Hand pumps are more portable, can be purchased by the mother, and are less expensive. Electric pumps are more efficient but are bulky and expensive. They may be rented in many areas. Breast pumps work by suction to express the milk. Some have collection systems for easy milk saving. Many agencies have a variety of pumps available and provide instruction on correct methods of pumping the breasts. Videotapes or photographs are also useful in demonstrating the process to new mothers.

### External Supports

La Leche League is an organized group of volunteers who work to provide education about breast-feeding and assistance to women who are breast-feeding infants. They sponsor activities, have printed material available, offer one-to-one counseling to mothers with questions or problems, and provide group support to breast-feeding mothers.

Numerous books and pamphlets are also available to help the breast-feeding mother. The mother needs the support of all family members, her physician/nurse-midwife, pediatrician or pediatric nurse practitioner, and all nursing personnel because it is often the attitudes of these people that ultimately lead the woman to success or failure.

### Prescription Drugs and Breast-Feeding

Many medications, when administered to the mother, are secreted in the milk. These include salicylates, bromides, antibiotics, most alkaloids, some cathartics, alcohol, and the majority of addicting drugs (Pritchard et al 1985). The mother should receive information about this and should also be instructed to inform her physician that she is nursing, should she require medical treatment at a later time. Clinicians who do not routinely care for obstetric or pediatric clients may not be familiar with the effects on breast milk of the drugs they prescribe and may need to consult the obstetrician. The positive and negative effects of the medication on the woman and her infant must be considered carefully.

## SELECTED POTENTIAL PROBLEMS IN BREAST-FEEDING

Many women stop nursing because the problems encountered seem to have no solutions. Anticipatory guidance about remedies and solutions to the problems is the nurse's role. This allows the mother to provide her infant with the nutritional and emotional experience that she has planned for during the pregnancy.

Breast-feeding problems include nipple inversion; inadequate letdown, which may be due to overfatigue; nipple

*Figure 23.5   Hand-held breast pump*

soreness; faulty newborn sucking behaviors; cracked nipples; breast engorgement; and plugged ducts (caked breasts). Table 23.4 summarizes self-care measures the nurse can suggest to a woman with a breast-feeding problem.

### Nipple Soreness

The mother should be told that some soreness often occurs initially with breast-feeding and that the problem will clear as soon as the letdown reflex is established. The infant should not be switched to bottle-feeding or have feedings delayed as this will only cause engorgement and more soreness.

Because the area of greatest stress to the nipple is in line with the newborn's chin and nose, nipple soreness may be decreased by encouraging the mother to rotate positions when feeding the infant. Figure 23.6 illustrates the cradle hold, football hold, and maternal side-lying positions. Changing positions alters the focus of greatest stress and promotes more complete breast emptying.

## Table 23.4 Self-Care Measures for the Woman with Breast-Feeding Problems

### NIPPLE INVERSION

Use Hoffman's exercises antepartally to increase protractility (see Chapter 8).
Use special breast shields such as Woolrich or Eschmann.
Use hand to shape nipple when beginning to nurse.
Apply ice for a few minutes prior to feeding to improve nipple erection.
If all else fails, use nipple shield for a few minutes until nipple becomes erect, then switch to regular nursing.

### INADEQUATE LETDOWN

Massage breasts prior to nursing.
Feed in a quiet, private place, away from distraction.
Take a warm shower before nursing to relax and stimulate letdown.
Apply warm compresses for 20 minutes before nursing.
Use relaxation techniques and focus on letdown.
Drink water, juice, or noncaffeinated beverages before and during feeding.
Avoid overfatigue by resting when baby sleeps, feeding while lying down, and having quiet time alone.
Develop a conditioned response by establishing a routine for starting feedings.
Allow the baby sufficient time (at least 10 to 15 minutes per side) to trigger the letdown reflex.
If all else fails, obtain a prescription for oxytocin nasal spray (to be used only for a day or so) from the health care provider.
Make time for change of activity, such as a walk or time for a favorite activity.

### NIPPLE SORENESS

Ensure that infant is correctly positioned at breast.
Rotate breast-feeding positions (see Figure 23.6).
Use finger to break suction before removing infant from the breast.
Hold baby close when feeding to avoid undue pulling on nipple.
Don't allow baby to sleep with nipple in mouth.
Nurse more frequently.
Begin nursing on less sore breast.
Apply ice to nipples and areola for a few minutes prior to feeding.
Protect nipples to prevent skin breakdown:
  Clean milk gently from nipple with warm water.
  Allow nipples to air dry, or dry nipples with hair dryer set to low heat, or expose nipples to sunlight, initially for 30 seconds then increasing to three minutes.

### NIPPLE SORENESS (continued)

If clothing rubs nipples, use ventilated shields to keep clothing away from skin.
Lightly apply protective substance such as lanolin, Massé Breast Cream, Eucerin cream, or A and D ointment between feedings. Avoid duct openings at end of nipple. If infant objects to taste, wash substance off before next feeding.
Remove plastic from breast pads to facilitate air circulation.
Apply tea bags soaked in warm water.
Change breast pads frequently.
Nurse long enough to empty breasts completely.

### CRACKED NIPPLES

Use interventions discussed under sore nipples.
Inspect nipples carefully for cracks or fissures.
Use a nipple shield if it is helpful; some women find it contributes to their discomfort.
Temporarily stop nursing on the affected breast and hand express milk for a day or two until cracks heal.
Maintain healthy diet. Protein and vitamin C are essential for healing.
Use a mild analgesic such as acetaminophen for discomfort.
Consult health care providers if signs of infection develop (see Chapter 27).

### BREAST ENGORGEMENT

Nurse frequently (every 1½ to 3 hours).
Wear a well-fitting supportive bra at all times.
Take a warm shower or apply warm compresses to trigger letdown.
Massage breasts and then hand express some milk to soften the breast so the infant can "latch on."
Breast-feed long enough to empty breast.
Alternate starting breast.
Take a mild analgesic 20 minutes before feeding if discomfort is pronounced.

### PLUGGED DUCTS (CAKED BREASTS)

Nurse frequently and for long enough to empty the breasts completely.
Rotate feeding position.
Massage breasts prior to feeding, in a warm shower when possible.
Maintain good nutrition and adequate fluid intake.

---

Nipple soreness may also develop if the infant develops faulty sucking habits. An infant may retract the tongue rather than positioning it correctly under the breast. Consequently the tongue does not act as a cushion and the infant's jaw may bruise the nipple. Soreness may also develop if the infant falls asleep with the breast in his or her mouth. This leads to problems because of continuous negative pressure on the nipple (L'Esperance and Frantz 1985).

Occasionally the infant grasps only the nipple in his or her mouth. Vigorous sucking produces little milk because the milk sinuses under the areola are not compressed. This results in a frustrated infant and marked soreness for the mother. The problem is overcome by positioning the infant with as much areola as possible in his or her mouth.

Nipple soreness is especially pronounced during the first few minutes of the feeding. If the mother is not expecting this, she may become discouraged and quickly

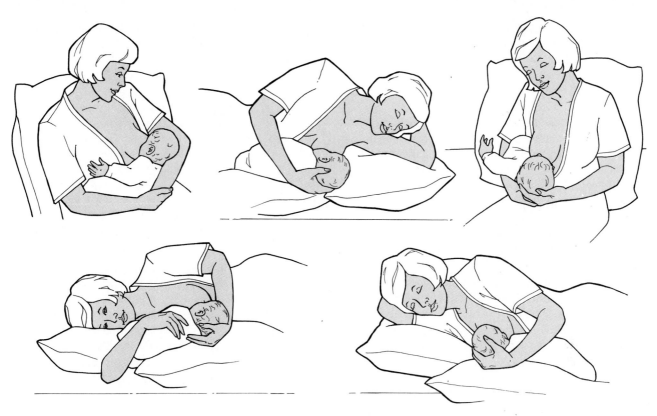

*Figure 23.6    Examples of breast-feeding position changes to facilitate thorough breast emptying and prevent nipple soreness.*

stop. The letdown reflex may take a few minutes to activate, and it may not occur if the mother stops nursing too quickly. The problem is compounded if the infant does not empty the mammary ducts; the infant is unsatisfied, and the possibility of breast engorgement increases.

Because nipple soreness can also result from an overeager infant, the mother may find it helpful to nurse more frequently. This helps ease the vigorous sucking of a ravenous infant.

### Cracked Nipples

Nipple soreness is frequently coupled with cracked nipples. Whenever a breast-feeding mother complains of soreness, the nipples must be carefully examined for fissures or cracks, and the mother should be observed during breast-feeding to see whether the infant is correctly positioned at the breast. If the positioning is correct and cracks exist, interventions are necessary. The mother's first reaction may be to cease nursing on the sore breast, but this may aggravate the problem if engorgement and plugged ducts result. Relief measures are described in Table 23.4.

### Breast Engorgement

About the time their milk initially comes in, many women complain of feelings of engorgement. Their breasts are hard, painful, and warm and appear taut and shiny. At first this fullness is caused by venous congestion due to the increased vascularity in the breasts. Later the problem may be compounded by the pressure of accumulating milk. Relief measures are described in Table 23.4.

### Plugged Ducts

Some mothers experience plugging of one or more ducts, especially in conjunction with or following engorgement. This is often referred to as caked breasts. Manifested as an area of tenderness or "lumpiness" in an otherwise well woman, plugging may be relieved by the use of heat and massage.

### BREAST-FEEDING AND THE WORKING MOTHER

Often a mother returning to work elects to continue breast-feeding her infant. This decision requires planning on her part and family encouragement and assistance. She will find this easier to accomplish if she has six to eight weeks at home to establish lactation before returning to work. She should use this time to accustom her infant to taking supplemental feedings from a bottle. This permits others to care for the baby while the mother works. A few days before returning to work she can begin manually expressing and freezing her milk for her infant's use while she is gone. At work it will be necessary for her to pump her breasts during lunch or coffee breaks to avoid the discomfort of full breasts. Because milk production follows the principle of supply and demand, if breasts are not pumped, the milk supply will decrease.

Sometimes a mother has a flexible schedule and can return home to nurse at lunch time or have the baby brought to her. If this is not possible, the infant may be fed expressed milk or a supplemental bottle of formula. If the mother is expressing milk at work for use the next day, she must be certain to keep it refrigerated and use it within 48 hours. Breast milk can be frozen in plastic bottles or bags and stored for up to six months.

To maintain an adequate milk supply the working mother must pay special attention to her fluid intake. She can ensure an adequate intake by drinking extra fluid at each break and whenever possible during the day. In addition, it is helpful to nurse more on weekends, to nurse during the night, to eat a nutritionally sound diet, and to continue manual expression or pumping when not nursing (Reifsnider and Myers 1985).

Night nursing presents a dilemma in that it may help a working mother maintain her milk supply but may also contribute to fatigue. Some women choose to have the infant sleep with them so that breast-feeding is more easily accomplished. Other women find it difficult to sleep soundly when the infant is in the same bed. For the mother who works long hours or has a rigid work schedule, the best alternative may be to limit breast-feeding to morning and evening feedings with supplemental feedings at other times. This choice allows her to maintain a close relationship with the infant and provides some of the unique benefits of breast milk.

### WEANING

The decision to wean the baby from the breast may be made for a variety of reasons including family or cultural pressures, changes in the home situation, pressure from the woman's partner, or a personal opinion about when **weaning** should occur. For the woman who is comfortable with breast-feeding and well-informed about the process, the appropriate time to wean her infant will become evident if she is sensitive to the child's cues. Often weaning falls between periods of great developmental activity for the child. Thus weaning commonly occurs at 8 to 9 months, 12 to 14 months, 18 months, 2 years, and 3 years of age. Within our society, however, weaning commonly occurs before the child is nine months old, although it may occur any time from soon after birth to four years of age (Lauwers and Woessner 1983).

If weaning is timed to respond to the child's cues, and if the mother is comfortable with the timing, it can be accomplished with less difficulty than if the process is begun before both mother and child are ready emotionally. Nevertheless, weaning is a time of emotional separation for mother and baby; it may be difficult for them to give up the closeness of their nursing sessions. The nurse who is understanding about this possibility can help the mother see that her infant is growing up and plan other comforting, consoling, and play activities to replace breast-feeding. A gradual approach is the easiest and most comforting way to wean the child from breast-feedings. Other activities can enhance the parent-infant attachment process.

During weaning, the mother should substitute one cup-feeding or bottle-feeding for one breast-feeding session over a couple of days to a week so that her breasts gradually produce less milk. Eliminating the breast-feedings associated with meals first facilitates the mother's ability to wean the infant as satiation with food lessens the desire for milk (Bishop 1985). Over a period of several weeks she should substitute more cup-feedings or bottle-feedings for breast-feedings. Many mothers continue to nurse once a day in the early morning or late evening for several months until the milk supply is gone. The slow method of weaning prevents breast engorgement and allows infants to alter their eating methods at their own rates.

## • Bottle-Feeding: Education for Self-Care

The mother who has chosen to bottle-feed her infant  should be encouraged to assume a comfortable position with adequate arm support so she can easily hold her infant. Most women cradle their infants in the crook of the arm close to the body, which provides the intimacy and cuddling so essential to an infant. With the great emphasis placed on successful breast-feeding, the teaching needs of the bottle-feeding new mother may be overlooked. If she has had only limited experience in feeding infants, she may need some guidelines to feed her newborn successfully. The following important principles should be included in the teaching provided:

1. Bottles should always be held, not propped. Positional otitis media may develop when the infant is fed horizontally, because milk and nasal mucus may block the eustachian tube. Holding the infant provides a rest for the feeder, social and close physical contact for the baby, and an opportunity for parent-child interaction and bonding (Figure 23.7).

2. The nipple should have a hole big enough to allow milk to flow in drops when the bottle is inverted. Too large an opening may cause overfeeding or regurgitation because of rapid feeding. If feeding is too fast, the nipple should be changed and the infant should be helped to eat more slowly by stopping the feeding frequently for burping and cuddling.

*Figure 23.7 An infant is supported comfortably during bottle-feeding.*

3. The nipple should be pointed directly into the mouth, and should be on top of the tongue. The nipple should be full of liquid at all times to avoid ingestion of extra air, which decreases the amount of feeding and increases discomfort.

4. The infant should be burped at intervals, preferably at the middle, or at about every ½ oz at the first few feedings, and at the end of the feeding. The infant who seems to swallow a great deal of air while sucking may need more frequent burping. In addition, if the infant has cried before being fed, air may have been swallowed, and the infant should be burped before beginning to feed or after taking just enough to calm down. Burping is done by holding the infant upright on the shoulder or by holding the infant in a sitting position on the feeder's lap with chin and chest supported on one hand. The back is then gently patted or stroked with the other hand. Too-

frequent burping may confuse a newborn who is attempting to coordinate sucking, swallowing, and breathing simultaneously.

5. Newborns frequently regurgitate small amounts of feedings and the mother may require reassurance that this is normal. Initially it may be due to excessive mucus and gastric irritation from foreign substances in the stomach from birth. Later, regurgitation may result when the infant feeds too rapidly and swallows air. It may also occur when the infant is overfed and the cardiac sphincter allows the excess to be regurgitated. Because this is a common occurrence, experienced mothers and nurses generally keep a "burp cloth" available. Although regurgitation is normal, vomiting or a forceful expulsion of fluid is not. When it occurs, further evaluation is indicated, especially if other symptoms are present.

6. Infants should be encouraged but not forced to feed and should be allowed to set their own pace once feedings are established. Overfeeding can result in infant obesity. During early feedings, however, the infant may need simple tactile stimulation—such as gently rubbing feet and hands, adjusting clothing, and loosening coverings—to maintain adequate sucking for a sufficient time to complete a full feeding.

Formula preparation and sterilization techniques are always important to discuss with families. Cleanliness remains an essential component but sterilization is necessary only if the water source is questionable. (Procedure 23.1 describes methods of sterilization.) Bottles may be effectively prepared in dishwashers (nipples may be weakened by the temperature of dishwashers and therefore should be washed thoroughly by hand with soap and water and rinsed well) or washed thoroughly in warm soapy water and rinsed well. Tap water, if from an uncontaminated source, may be used for mixing powdered formulas, which are less expensive than the concentrated or ready-to-use prepared formulas.

Bottles may be prepared individually or up to one day's supply of formula may be prepared at one time. Extra bottles are stored in the refrigerator and should be warmed slightly before feeding. To prevent infection, it is important for unused portions of bottles to be discarded after each feeding. Ready-to-use disposable bottles of formula are very convenient, but are also expensive.

Parents need to be advised that putting an infant to bed with a bottle of formula or juice or allowing the infant to breast-feed intermittently while sleeping beside the mother through the night may foster tooth decay and ear infections. Cavities are prevented by the saliva bathing the teeth and washing away the cariogenic materials. The flow of saliva diminishes rapidly once the infant has fallen asleep, and the milk or juice is left in contact with the teeth. The

## Procedure 23.1

# Methods of Bottle Sterilization

| Terminal Sterilization | Aseptic Method of Sterilization |
| --- | --- |
| Advantages:<br>1. Safest, most efficient method<br>2. More easily learned<br><br>Disadvantages:<br>1. Prolonged cooling period (one to two hr)<br>2. Not suitable for disposable bottles<br><br>Procedure:<br>1. Assemble equipment and wash hands.<br>2. Thoroughly wash bottles, caps, and nipples in warm soapy water; squeeze some water through the nipple holes to rid them of accumulated milk; rinse well.<br>3. Wash the lid of the formula can (if using a liquid) and prepare formula according to directions.<br>4. Fill the bottles with the desired amount of formula and loosely apply the nipples and caps; one or two bottles of water may be prepared at the same time.<br>5. Place the prepared bottles in a large kettle or bottle sterilizer and add the appropriate amount of water (as specified on the sterilizer or 2–3 in if a kettle is used).<br>6. Cover the sterilizer, bring the water to a gentle boil and then boil for 25 min.<br>7. Remove from heat but let the bottles remain in the sterilizer with the lid on until the sides of the pan are cool to the touch.<br>8. Remove the bottles, tighten the lids, and refrigerate until needed. | Advantages:<br>1. May be modified for use with disposable bottles<br><br>Disadvantages:<br>1. Difficult to learn, contamination more likely<br><br>Procedure:<br>1. Same as steps 1 and 2 of terminal method.<br>2. Place all equipment needed (bottles, nipples, caps, can opener, tongs, measuring pitcher, and spoon) in a large kettle or sterilizer; cover with water and boil for five min.<br>3. In another pan boil the amount of water necessary to make the formula (boil for five min).<br>4. Drain the water from the sterilizer pan and let the equipment cool for a few minutes.<br>5. Remove the measuring pitcher, being certain to touch only the handle.<br>6. Using the sterilized can opener, open a can of formula after first washing the lid with soapy water and rinsing well; pour the formula into the prepared measuring pitcher and add the correct amount of boiled water; mix with the prepared spoon.<br>7. Using tongs, remove the bottles from the sterilizer and fill them with the desired amount of formula; (one or two bottles of water may also be prepared by boiling enough additional water).<br>8. Using the tongs, set the nipples on the bottles, then, touching only the edges, apply the caps.<br>9. Refrigerate until needed.<br><br>To modify for disposable bottles:<br><br>Complete all steps as directed except *do not boil the bottles* with the other equipment and allow the water to cool for 15–20 min before preparing the formula (the plastic bag may melt if the formula is too hot). |

subsequent decay is referred to as bottle mouth syndrome. It is believed ear infections are more likely to occur when the infant feeds in a horizontal position, allowing the milk to pool near the pharyngeal opening to the eustachian tube. To avoid both of these conditions, parents should be encouraged to hold the infant during feedings, spend quiet time comforting and consoling the infant, and then place the drowsy infant in the crib without a bottle.

Parents need to be advised that the infant needs extra water between meals when solid food is added because the solute load on the infant's kidneys will be increased. Juices,

however, add extra calories to the diet and often are delayed until the infant is 9 to 12 months old and can drink from a cup.

## ● NUTRITIONAL ASSESSMENT OF THE INFANT

During the early months of life, the food offered to and consumed by infants will be instrumental in their proper growth and development.

At each well-child visit the nurse assesses the nutritional status of the newborn. Assessment should include four components:

- Nutritional history from the parent
- Weight gain since the last visit
- Growth chart percentiles
- Physical examination

The nutritional history reports the type, amount, and frequency of milk and supplemental foods being given to the infant on a daily basis. The healthy formula-fed infant should generally gain 1 ounce per day for the first six months of life and 0.5 ounce per day for the second six months. Healthy breast-fed babies may fall within these weight gain parameters but may also be normal while gaining 0.5 ounce per day for the first six months (Stahl and Guida 1984). Individual charts show the infant's growth with respect to height, weight, and head circumference. The important consideration is that infants continue to grow at their own individual rates.

For the breast-feeding mother who is concerned about whether her infant is getting adequate nutrition, the nurse can recommend looking for an appearance of weight gain and counting the number of wet diapers in a 24-hour period. Six wet diapers or more in a day indicates adequate nutrition is being attained in the totally breast-fed infant. If additional water is ingested, the count will be higher. The presence of urine can most accurately be assessed when the diaper is free of feces. This is most likely prior to feedings. The gastrocolic reflex often stimulates stooling following a feeding. For the anxious parent, another means of reassurance of adequate intake and output is to keep a record of the frequency and duration of feedings and the exact number of wet and/or soiled diapers. Keeping a record tends to give the worried parent a sense of control and a tangible indication on which to rule out or base concern (Humphrey 1985).

The physical examination will assist in identifying any nutritional disorders. Edema, dermatitis, cheilosis, or bleeding gums may be caused by excess protein intake, riboflavin deficiency, niacin deficiency, or vitamin C deficiency, respectively. Iron deficiency should be suspected in a pale, diaphoretic, irritable infant who is obese and consumes more than 35 to 40 ounces of formula per day (Driggers 1980).

By calculating the nutritional needs of infants, the nurse can recommend a diet that supplies appropriate nutrition for infant growth and development. This assessment is especially helpful in counseling mothers of infants under six months of age in view of the tendency to add too many supplemental foods or offer too much formula to infants of this age. Clinicians generally advise that an infant not be given more than 32 ounces of formula in one day. If additional calories are needed, supplemental foods should

### Table 23.5  Average Recommended Levels of Caloric Intake*

| Birth to 3 months | 55 calories/lb |
| 3–6 months | 52 calories/lb |
| 6–9 months | 50 calories/lb |
| 9–12 months | 47 calories/lb |

*Caloric needs may vary up to 10% for individual infants on a day-to-day basis. This would amount to only a 2 to 3 ounce variation in amount of formula per day.

Source: *Recommended Dietary Allowances,* 8th ed. Washington, DC: National Academy of Sciences, 1980.

be added to the diet. Conversely, if the caloric intake is adequate or excessive, formula alone gives the infant enough calories and introduction of solid foods can be delayed until later.

When an infant's caloric intake and weight gain is found to be excessive, clinicians do not advise putting the infant on a weight reduction diet, because tissue growth is rapid during this period and must be supported. The appropriate advice is to provide a maintenance caloric intake as a means of allowing the infant to maintain weight while growing in length and age.

Identification of appropriate nutritional intake can be done by comparing the infant's dietary intake with the desired caloric intake, weight, age, and the number of calories needed by the infant. Most commercial formulas prescribed for the normal healthy newborn contain 20 calories per ounce. If the infant is eating solids, the caloric value of those foods must be determined and included in the calculation of nutritional intake. With knowledge of the amount of calories needed per day by the infant according to weight and using Table 23.5, the nurse can counsel the parents about how many ounces per day the child needs to meet caloric requirements. The following case study shows the effectiveness of these assessments.

## One Baby's Feeding Story

*Jamie, age one week, is visited at home by the nurse associated with a health maintenance organization (HMO). Jamie is Mrs Adams's first child, and Mrs Adams is concerned about whether Jamie is getting adequate nourishment. Jamie weighed 7 pounds at birth and has regained her birth weight after an 11-ounce (10%) loss. Mrs Adams reports that Jamie takes 3 ounces of formula (20 cal/oz) at each of seven feedings during a 24-hour period, does not spit up any formula, and has eight to ten wet diapers a day.*

(continues)

## Nursing Assessment

*Using Table 23.6, the nurse calculates one-week-old Jamie's dietary needs as follows:*

*Jamie's weight = 7 lb*

*24-hr caloric need: 7 lb × 55 cal/lb = 385 cal/lb*

*Needed 20 cal/oz formula for 24 hr = 385 cal ÷ 20 cal/oz = 19 oz*

*Jamie's 24-hr intake = 21 ounces (20 cal/ounce) = 420 calories*

## Nursing Diagnosis

● *Altered nutrition: more than body requirements related to formula intake that is greater than necessary to meet Jamie's growth needs*

● *Knowledge deficit related to assessing adequacy of food intake*

## Plan and Implementation

*Encourage Mrs Adams to offer Jamie 2¾ ounces of formula at each of the seven feedings a day.*

*Using Table 23.3, advise Mrs Adams of cues that indicate hunger and satiation, ie, baby withdraws head from nipple and falls asleep.*

*Explore alternative methods for providing comfort to a newborn.*

*Discuss with Mrs Adams the signs that indicate Jamie is receiving adequate nutrition and fluids.*

## Evaluation

*On a follow-up well-baby visit, Jamie is weighed and is gaining 1 oz/day. Jamie continues to have eight to ten wet diapers a day and is alert and responsive.*

## ESSENTIAL CONCEPTS

● The newborn needs 50 to 55 cal/lb/day and 2 to 2.5 ounces of water/lb/day.

● Infants should receive formula or breast milk until one year of age.

● The use of skim milk, cow's milk with lowered fat content, or unmodified cow's milk is not recommended for children under two years old.

● Mature breast milk and commercially prepared formulas (unless otherwise noted) provide 20 cal/ounce.

● Signs indicating newborn readiness for the first feeding are: active bowel sounds, absence of abdominal distention, and a lusty cry that quiets with rooting and sucking behaviors when a stimulus is placed near the lips.

● Formula-fed infants regain their birth weight by ten days of age and gain 1 ounce/day for the first six months and 0.5 ounce/day for the second six months; birthweight is doubled at 3.5 to 4 months of age. Healthy breast-fed babies gain approximately 0.5 ounce/day in the first six months of life, regain their birth weight by about 14 days of age, and double their birth weight at approximately five months of age.

● Formula-fed infants need no vitamin or mineral supplements other than iron, if it is not already in the formula, and they need fluoride if it is not obtained in the water system.

● The bottle-feeding mother may require assistance with feeding and burping her infant. She will also benefit from information about feeding schedules, types of formula, and the like.

● Breast-feeding mothers should be encouraged to ensure that the infant is correctly positioned at breast, with a large portion of the areola in his or her mouth. The mother is advised to rotate positions to ensure that all ducts are emptied.

● To prevent sore nipples the nurse can encourage the breast-feeding mother to allow her breasts to air dry after feeding.

● The breast-feeding mother needs to increase her caloric intake by about 200 calories. It is also essential that she consume adequate amounts of liquid to promote milk production.

● Breast-fed infants need supplements of vitamin D and fluoride. However, there is no need to give supplemental iron to breast-fed infants before six months of age.

● A disadvantage of breast-feeding is that most drugs taken by the mother are transmitted through breast milk.

● Breast-fed infants are probably getting adequate nutrition if they are gaining weight and have at least six wet diapers a day when not receiving additional water supplements.

● Formula intake should not exceed 32 ounces in 24 hours. If additional calories are needed, supplemental foods should be added to the diet.

● After six months, supplemental foods should be added to the diet starting with small amounts and adding one new food every three to seven days.

## References

American Academy of Pediatrics, Committee on Fetus and Newborn: *Guidelines for Perinatal Care,* 2nd ed. Elk Grove Village, IL: AAP, 1988.

American Academy of Pediatrics, Committee on Nutrition: *Pediatric Nutrition Handbook,* 2nd ed. Elk Grove Village, IL: AAP, 1985.

Anholm P: Breast feeding: A preventive approach to health care in infancy. *Issues Comp Pediatr Nurs* 1986; 9:1.

Avery G: *Neonatology,* 3rd ed. Philadelphia: Lippincott, 1987.

Beske JE, Garvis M: Important factors in breastfeeding success. *Am J Mat Child Nurs* May/June 1982; 7:174.

Bishop W: Weaning the breastfed toddler or preschooler. *Pediatr Nurs* May/June 1985; 11:211.

Clark AL: *Culture and Childrearing.* Philadelphia: Davis, 1981.

Coen RW, Koffler H: *Primary Care of the Newborn.* Boston: Little, Brown, 1987.

deCarvalho M et al: Does the duration and frequency of early breastfeeding affect nipple pain? *Birth* Summer 1984; 11:81.

Driggers D: Infant nutrition made simple. *Am Fam Physician* 1980; 22:113.

Evans H, Glass L: Breastfeeding: Advantages and potential problems. *Pediatr Ann* 1979; 8:110.

Gromada K: Maternal-infant attachment: The first step toward individualizing twins. *Am J Mat Child Nurs* March/April 1981; 6:129.

Gulick E: Infant health and breastfeeding. *Pediatr Nurs* January/February 1986; 12:51.

Humphrey N: Common questions about breastfeeding. *Children's Nurse* February 1985; 3:1.

LaDu EB: Childbirth care for Hmong families. *Am J Mat Child Nurs* November/December 1985; 10:382.

Lauwers J, Woessner C: *Counseling the Nursing Mother.* Wayne, NJ: Avery, 1983.

Lawrence RA: *Breastfeeding: A Guide for the Medical Profession.* St Louis: Mosby, 1980.

Lesko W, Lesko M: *The Maternity Sourcebook.* New York: Warner Books, 1984.

L'Esperance C, Frantz K: Time limitation for early breastfeeding. *J Obstet Gynecol Neonatal Nurs* March/April 1985; 14:114.

Mullett SE: Helping mothers breast-feed. *Am J Mat Child Nurs* 1982; 7:178.

Neifert M: *Dr. Mom: A Guide to Baby and Child Care.* New York: Signet, 1986.

Picciano M, Deering R: The influence of feeding regimens on iron status during infancy. *Am J Clin Nutr* 1980; 33:746.

Pipes P: *Nutrition in Infancy and Childhood,* 3rd ed. St Louis: Mosby, 1985.

Pritchard JA, MacDonald PC, Gant N: *Williams Obstetrics,* 17th ed. New York: Appleton-Century-Crofts, 1985.

Reifsnider E, Myers ST: Employed mothers can breastfeed, too! *Am J Mat Child Nurs* July/August 1985; 10:256.

Riordan J: *A Practical Guide to Breastfeeding.* St. Louis: Mosby, 1983.

Stahl M, Guida D: Slow weight gain in the breast-fed infant: Management options. *Pediatr Nurs* March/April 1984; 10:117.

Ward BG et al: Vietnamese refugees in Adelaide: An obstetric analysis. *Med J Aust* 1981; 1:72.

## Additional Readings

Balkam JAJ: Guidelines for drug therapy during lactation. *J Obstet Gynecol Neonatal Nurs* January/February 1986; 15:65.

Beall MH: Breastfeeding: Some drug admonitions. *Contemp OB/GYN* February 1987; 29:49.

Boyer DB: Serum indirect bilirubin levels and meconium passage in early fed normal newborns. *Nurs Res* May/June 1987; 36:174.

Hot milk in cool bottles . . . microwave oven. *Emerg Med* January 30 1987; 19:109.

Janas LM et al: Quantities of amino acids ingested by human milk-fed infants. *J Pediatrics* November 1986; 109:802.

Jones D: Breast-feeding practices. *Nurs Times* January 21–27 1987; 83:56.

Jordan PL: Breastfeeding as a risk factor for fathers. *J Obstet Gynecol Neonatal Nurs* March/April 1986; 15:94.

Meier P, Anderson GC: Responses of small preterm infants to bottle- and breast-feeding. *Am J Mat Child Nurs* March/April 1987; 12:97.

Morse JM et al: Minimal breastfeeding. *J Obstet Gynecol Neonatal Nurs* July/August 1986; 15:333.

Niebyl JR: Making the breastfeeding decision. *Contemp OB/GYN* September 1986; 28:43.

Position of the American Dietetic Association: Promotion of breastfeeding. *J Am Diet Assoc* November 1986; 86:1580.

Scrimshaw SCM et al: Factors affecting breastfeeding among women of Mexican origin or descent in Los Angeles. *Am J Pub Health* April 1987; 77:467.

# 24

# The Newborn at Risk

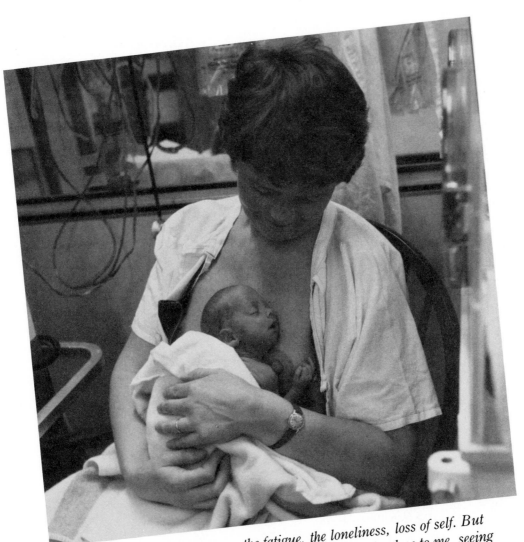

*I had heard about the negatives—the fatigue, the loneliness, loss of self. But nobody told me about the wonderful parts: holding my baby close to me, seeing her first smile, watching her grow and become more responsive day by day. How can I describe the way I felt when she stroked my breast while nursing, or looked into my eyes or arched her eyebrows like an opera singer? This was the deepest connection I'd felt to anybody. Sometimes the intensity almost frightened me. For the first time I cared about somebody else more than myself, and I would do anything to nurture and protect her. (The New Our Bodies, Ourselves)*

## Objectives

● Compare the physiologic needs and complications of the preterm, postterm, small-for-gestational-age, and large-for-gestational-age infant and the underlying etiology of the various complications.

● Differentiate between postmaturity and placental insufficiency syndrome and explain why infants with these conditions sometimes require care similar to that for a preterm infant.

● Based on the labor record, Apgar score, and observable physiologic indicators, identify infants in need of resuscitation and the appropriate method of resuscitation.

● Based on clinical manifestations, differentiate the various types of respiratory distress (hyaline membrane disease, transient tachypnea of the newborn, and meconium aspiration syndrome) in the neonate.

● Identify the components of nursing care of an infant with respiratory distress syndrome.

● Differentiate between physiologic and pathologic jaundice based on onset, cause, possible sequelae, and specific management.

● Explain the set of circumstances that must be present for the development of erythroblastosis and ABO incompatibility and the nurse's role in the care of an infant with hemolytic disease.

● Use nursing assessment and diagnosis to identify nursing responsibilities in caring for the neonate receiving phototherapy or an exchange transfusion.

● Describe the nursing assessment of clinical manifestations that would lead the nurse to suspect neonatal sepsis.

● Relate the consequences of maternal syphilis, gonorrhea, AIDS, or herpesvirus to the management of the infant in the neonatal period.

● Discuss selected metabolic abnormalities (including cold stress, hypoglycemia, and hypocalcemia), their effects on the neonate, and the nursing implications.

● Discuss selected hematologic variations and the nursing implications associated with each problem.

● Identify the nursing assessments that would make the nurse suspect a congenital cardiac defect during the early neonatal period.

● Discuss the nursing assessments of and initial interventions in selected congenital anomalies.

## Key Terms

cold stress
drug dependent infants
erythroblastosis fetalis
exchange transfusion
fetal alcohol syndrome (FAS)
hemolytic disease of the newborn
hydrops fetalis
hyperbilirubinemia
hypoglycemia
inborn errors of metabolism
infant of diabetic mother (IDM)
intrauterine growth retardation (IUGR)
jaundice
kernicterus
large for gestational age (LGA)
meconium aspiration syndrome (MAS)
phenylketonuria (PKU)
phototherapy
polycythemia
postterm infant
preterm infant
respiratory distress syndrome (RDS)
sepsis neonatorum
small for gestational age (SGA)

Within the last 20 years, the field of neonatology has expanded greatly. In response to increasing knowledge about the neonate, many levels of nursery care have evolved: special care; transitional care; and low-, medium-, and high-risk care. The nurse is an important care giver in all these nurseries. As a member of the multidisciplinary health care team, the nurse has contributed the high-touch, human care necessary in a high-tech perinatal environment.

In addition to the availability of high-level newborn care, other factors that influence the outcome for these at-risk infants include birth weight, gestational age, type and length of newborn illness, and environmental and maternal factors.

## • IDENTIFICATION OF AT-RISK NEWBORNS

An at-risk newborn is one susceptible to illness (morbidity) or even death (mortality) because of dysmaturity, immaturity, physical disorders, or complications of birth. In most cases, the infant is the product of a pregnancy involving one or more predictable risk factors, including the following:

- Low socioeconomic level of the mother
- Exposure to environmental dangers such as toxic chemicals
- Preexisting maternal conditions such as heart disease or diabetes
- Obstetric factors such as age or parity
- Medical conditions related to pregnancy such as prenatal maternal infection
- Obstetric complications such as abruptio placentae

Various risk factors and their specific effects on the pregnancy outcome are listed in Table 7.1.

Because these factors and the perinatal risks associated with them are known, the birth of many high-risk neonates can often be anticipated and prepared for through adequate prenatal care. The pregnancy can be closely monitored, treatment can be instituted as necessary, and arrangements can be made for birth to occur at a facility with appropriate equipment and personnel to care for both mother and baby.

Identification of at-risk infants cannot always be made before labor, since the course of labor and birth or how the infant will withstand the stress of labor is not known prior to the actual process. Thus during labor, fetal heart monitoring has played a significant role in detecting infants in distress.

Immediately after birth a valuable tool in identifying the high-risk neonate is the Apgar score. The lower the Apgar score at five minutes after birth, the higher the percentage of neurologic abnormalities (such as cerebral palsy) seen after one year. The percentage also increases significantly as birth weight decreases (Korones 1986).

The newborn classification and neonatal mortality risk chart is another useful tool in identifying newborns at risk (Figure 24.1). Before this classification tool was developed, birth weight of less than 2500 g was the sole criterion for determination of immaturity. It was eventually recognized that an infant could weigh more than 2500 g but be immature. Conversely, an infant less than 2500 g might be functionally at term or beyond. Thus, birth weight and gestational age together became the criteria used to assess neonatal maturity and mortality risk.

According to the newborn classification and neonatal mortality risk chart, *gestation* is divided as follows:

- Preterm = 0–37 (completed) weeks
- Term = 38–41 (completed) weeks
- Postterm = 42 + weeks

As shown in Figure 24.1, large-for-gestational-age (LGA) infants are those above the curved line labeled 90%. Appropriate-for-gestational-age (AGA) infants are those between the lines labeled 10th percentile and 90th percentile. Small-for-gestational-age (SGA) infants are those below the curved line labeled 10th percentile. A newborn is assigned to a category depending on birth weight and gestational age. For example, a newborn classified as Pr SGA is preterm and small for gestational age. The full-term newborn whose weight is appropriate for gestational age is classified F AGA.

*Neonatal mortality risk* is the chance of death within the neonatal period. As indicated in Figure 24.1, the neonatal mortality risk decreases as both gestational age and birth weight increase. Infants who are preterm and small for gestational age have the highest neonatal mortality risk. The mortality for LGA infants has decreased at most perinatal centers because of improved management of diabetes in pregnancy and increased recognition of potential problems with LGA infants.

Neonatal morbidity can be anticipated based on birth weight and gestational age. In Figure 24.2 the infant's birth weight is located in the vertical column, and the gestational age in weeks is found horizontally. The area where the two meet on the graph identifies commonly occurring prob-

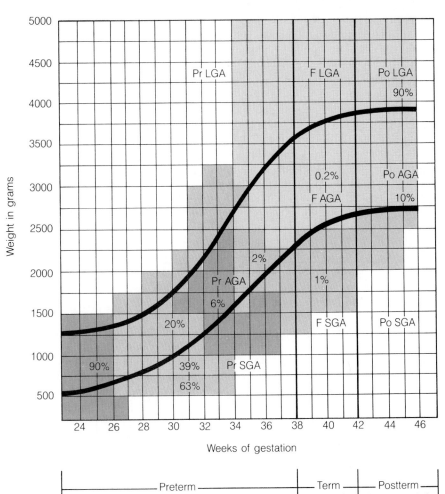

*Figure 24.1   Newborn classification and neonatal mortality risk chart (From Koops BL, Morgan LP, Battaglia FC: Neonatal mortality risk in relationship to birth weight and gestational age. J Pediatr 1982; 101(6):969.)*

lems. This tool assists in determining the needs of particular infants for special observation and care. For example, an infant of 2000 g at 40 weeks' gestation should be carefully assessed for evidence of fetal distress, hypoglycemia, congenital anomalies, congenital infection, and polycythemia.

## ● USING THE NURSING PROCESS FOR AT-RISK NEWBORNS
### ● Nursing Assessment

Assessment of the at-risk newborn is an ongoing nursing process. It begins with the history of the newborn, which includes family and maternal history and other factors that may influence in utero development.

In the birthing area the nurse correlates the Apgar scores and careful observation with information about the duration of labor, maternal analgesia and anesthesia, and complications of the labor and birth process. Assessment continues when the newborn is admitted to the nursery.

All previous assessments, Apgar scores, and treatments immediately after birth are evaluated in conjunction with the physical assessment of the newborn. As discussed in Chapter 21, the physical examination includes all of the following:

● Complete head-to-toe assessment, observing for cardiorespiratory function, temperature, and congenital anomalies

● Clinical determination of gestational age

● Classification of the baby as AGA, SGA, or LGA and correlation with the morbidity risk for the specific classification (Figure 24.2).

### ● Nursing Diagnosis

Many of the nursing diagnoses for at-risk newborns are based on careful analysis of the assessment data and center on alterations in physiologic process, the newborns' response to procedures or stimuli, and the psychosocial needs of these newborns and their parents. Nursing diagnoses that may apply to the newborn and family are presented here:

- Impaired gas exchange related to respiratory distress secondary to fluid aspiration or surfactant deficiency

- Altered nutrition: less than body requirements related to inadequate fluid intake

- Ineffective thermoregulation related to hypothermia secondary to inadequate subcutaneous tissue

The psychosocial needs of these newborns and their parents may be addressed in such nursing diagnoses as:

- Ineffective family coping related to birth of potentially ill newborn

- Knowledge deficit related to potential long-term developmental outcomes secondary to at-risk newborn complications

## ● Nursing Plan and Implementation

When all the data are gathered and analyzed, the care plan is developed. Nursing care of the at-risk newborn depends on minute-to-minute observations of the changes in

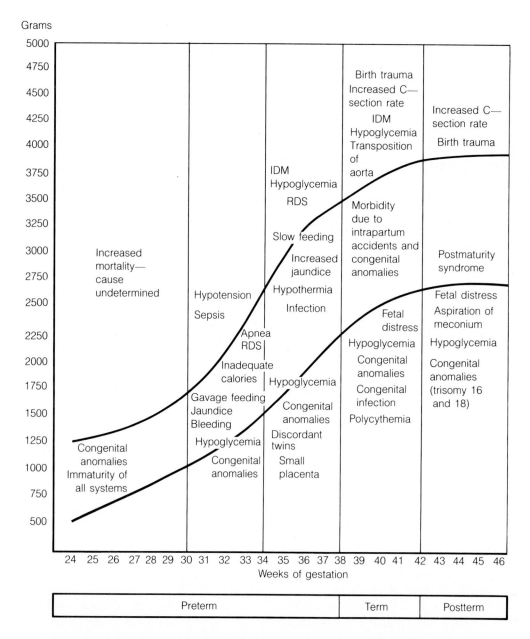

*Figure 24.2   Neonatal morbidity by birth weight and gestational age (From Lubchenco LO:* The High Risk Infant. *Philadelphia: Saunders, 1976, p 122.)*

the neonate's physiologic status. It is essential to a baby's survival that the neonatal nurse understand the basic physiologic principles that guide nursing management of the at-risk neonate. The organization of nursing care must be directed toward:

- Decreasing physiologically stressful situations
- Constantly observing for subtle signs of change in clinical condition
- Interpreting laboratory data and coordinating interventions
- Conserving the infant's energy, especially in frail, debilitated newborns
- Providing for developmental stimulation and sleep cycle
- Assisting the family in developing attachment behaviors

## • Nursing Evaluation

The success of the care plan is confirmed by continuous assessments of the neonate's behavior, communication with family and health team members, and use of diagnostic measures.

The at-risk newborn is the newest member of a family, so it is imperative to incorporate the parents into the plan of care. They must be kept informed of their newborn's condition and progress, involved in care, and given frequent opportunities to interact with their newborn and voice their fears and concerns. They should also be assisted in learning about their baby and how to care for their baby. The nurse should make every effort to evaluate on an ongoing basis how the family is being incorporated into the care of their newborn and how they are adjusting to this new member of the family.

## • CARE FOR THE SMALL-FOR-GESTATIONAL-AGE (SGA) NEWBORN

A **small-for-gestational-age (SGA)** newborn is any newborn who at birth is at or below the tenth percentile (intrauterine growth curves) on the newborn classification chart (Figure 24.1). It should be noted that intrauterine growth charts are influenced by altitude and ethnicity. When assigning SGA classification to a newborn, birth weight charts should be based on the local population into which the newborn is born (Guidelines for Perinatal Care 1988). An SGA newborn may be preterm, term, or postterm. Other terms used to designate a growth-retarded newborn include *intrauterine growth retarded* (IUGR), *small for dates* (SFD), and *dysmature*. For this discussion, *SGA* and *IUGR* will be used interchangeably.

Between 3% and 7% of all pregnancies are complicated by IUGR. SGA infants have a five-fold increase in perinatal asphyxia and an eight-fold higher perinatal mortality than normal infants (Brar and Rutherford 1988).

## • Causes of Intrauterine Growth Retardation (IUGR)

The causes of IUGR may be maternal, placental, or fetal factors and may not be apparent antenatally. Intrauterine growth is linear in the normal pregnancy from approximately 28 to 38 weeks' gestation. After 38 weeks, growth is variable, depending on the growth potential of the fetus and placental function. The most common causes of growth retardation are:

- *Malnutrition.* Maternal nutrition does not significantly influence the birth weight of the neonate unless starvation occurs during the last trimester of pregnancy. Before the third trimester, the nutritional supply to the fetus far exceeds its needs. Only in the third trimester is maternal nutrition a limiting factor in fetal growth.
- *Vascular complications.* Complications associated with pregnancy-induced hypertension (PIH), chronic hypertensive vascular disease, and advanced diabetes mellitus cause diminished blood flow to the uterus.
- *Maternal disease.* Maternal heart disease, alcoholism, narcotic addiction, sickle cell anemia, phenylketonuria (PKU), and asymptomatic pyelonephritis are associated with SGA.
- *Maternal factors.* SGA is associated with such maternal factors as small stature, primiparity, grand multiparity, smoking, lack of prenatal care, age (<16 years or >40 years), and low socioeconomic class—which usually results in poor health care, poor education, and poor living conditions.
- *Environmental factors.* Such factors include high altitude, x-rays, and maternal use of drugs such as antimetabolites, anticonvulsants, and trimethadione, which have teratogenic effects.
- *Placental factors.* Placental conditions such as infarcted areas, abnormal cord insertions, placenta previa, or thrombosis may affect circulation to the fetus, which becomes more deficient with increasing gestational age.
- *Fetal factors.* Congenital infections (rubella, toxoplasmosis) or malformations, multiple pregnancy (twins, triplets), sex (female neonate), chromosomal syndromes, and inborn errors of metabolism can predispose a fetus to IUGR.

Antenatal identification of fetuses suffering IUGR is the first step in the detection of common disorders of the

SGA infant. The perinatal history of maternal conditions and examination of the placenta and the newborn are important in determining this at-risk newborn.

## ● Patterns of IUGR

Growth occurs in two ways—increase in cell number and cell size. If insult occurs early during the critical period of organ development in the fetus, fewer new cells are formed, organs are small, and organ weight is subnormal. In contrast, growth failure that begins later in pregnancy does not affect the total number of cells but only their size. The organs are normal, but their size is diminished.

Two varying clinical pictures of SGA newborns have been described. They are characterized by either *symmetric* (proportional) IUGR or *asymmetric* (disproportional) IUGR.

*Symmetric IUGR* is caused by long-term maternal conditions (such as chronic hypertension, severe malnutrition, chronic intrauterine infection, substance abuse, and anemia) or fetal genetic abnormalities (Brar and Rutherford 1988). Symmetric IUGR can be noted by ultrasound in the first half of the second trimester with its onset prior to 32 weeks' gestation. In symmetric IUGR there is chronic prolonged retardation of growth in size of organs, weight, length, and, in severe cases, head circumference.

*Asymmetric IUGR* is associated with an acute compromise of uteroplacental blood flow. Some associated causes are placental infarcts, PIH, and poor weight gain in pregnancy. The growth retardation is usually not evident before the third trimester because, although weight is decreased, length and head circumference remain appropriate for that gestational age.

Birth weight is reduced below the tenth percentile, whereas head size may be between the fifteenth and the ninetieth percentile.

Asymmetric SGA neonates are particularly at risk for perinatal asphyxia, pulmonary hemorrhage, hypocalcemia, and hypoglycemia in the neonatal period (Teberg et al 1988).

Despite growth retardation, physiologic maturity develops according to gestational age. Therefore, the SGA newborn may be more physiologically mature than the preterm AGA newborn and less predisposed to complications of prematurity such as respiratory distress syndrome and hyperbilirubinemia. The SGA newborn's chances for survival are better because of organ maturity, although this newborn still faces many other potential difficulties in the newborn period as well as long-term problems.

## ● Common Complications of the SGA Newborn

The complications occurring most frequently in the SGA neonate are the following:

1. Perinatal asphyxia—chronic hypoxia in utero, which leaves little reserve to withstand the demands of labor and birth. Thus, intrauterine asphyxia occurs with its potential systemic problems.

2. Aspiration syndromes—gasping secondary to in utero hypoxia can cause aspiration of amniotic fluid into the lower airways, or can lead to relaxation of the anal sphincter with passage of meconium. This results in meconium aspiration with first breaths after birth.

3. Heat loss—decreased ability to conserve heat results from diminished subcutaneous fat (used for survival in utero), depletion of brown fat in utero, and large surface area. The surface area is diminished somewhat because of the flexed position assumed by the SGA infant.

4. Hypoglycemia—high metabolic rate (secondary to heat loss), poor liver glycogen stores, and inhibited gluconeogenesis lead to low blood sugar levels.

5. Hypocalcemia—calcium depletion secondary to birth asphyxia and preterm birth.

6. Polycythemia—a physiologic response to in utero chronic hypoxic stress.

Infants who have significant IUGR tend to have a poor prognosis, especially when born before 37 weeks' gestation. Factors contributing to poor outcome for these infants are as follows:

● *Congenital malformations.* Congenital malformations occur 10 to 20 times more frequently in SGA infants than in AGA infants. The more severe the IUGR, the greater the chance for malformation as a result of impaired mitotic activity and cellular hypoplasia.

● *Intrauterine infections.* When IUGR infants are exposed to intrauterine infections such as rubella and cytomegalovirus, they are profoundly affected by direct invasion of the brain and other vital organs by the offending virus.

● *Continued growth difficulties.* It is generally agreed that SGA newborns tend to be shorter than newborns of the same gestational age but will have appropriate size growth. Miller (1985) reports that asymmetrical IUGR infants can be expected to catch up in weight to normal growth infants by three to six months of age. Symmetric SGA infants reportedly have varied growth potential but tend not to catch up to their peers. It is important to remember that the rate of growth during the newborn's first year of life remains the best predictor of later growth potential (Avery and Taeusch 1984).

● *Learning difficulties.* Often SGA newborns exhibit poor brain development and subsequent failure to catch up, and minimal cerebral dysfunction is not uncommon. Dysfunction is characterized by hyperactivity, short attention span, and poor fine motor coordination (reading, writing, and drawing). Poor scholastic performance is also a common problem (Parkinson et al 1981). Some hearing loss and speech defects also occur.

Korones (1986) reported that SGA newborns born into families of high socioeconomic levels do as well as their peers at age 10 to 12 years while, at the same age, SGA neonates from families of low socioeconomic levels function below their peers. This finding suggests that the environment of the symmetrical SGA neonate can play a vital role in long-term outcome.

## ● Medical Therapy

The goal of medical therapy is early recognition and implementation of medical management of the potential problems associated with SGA babies.

## ● Nursing Assessment

The nurse is responsible for assessing gestational age and identifying signs of potential complications associated with SGA infants.

All body parts of the symmetric IUGR infant are in proportion, but they are below normal size for the baby's gestational age. Therefore the head does not appear overly large or the length excessive in relation to the other body parts. These newborns are generally vigorous (Korones 1986).

The asymmetric IUGR infant appears long, thin, and emaciated, with loss of subcutaneous fat tissue and muscle mass. The baby has loose skin folds; dry, desquamating skin; and a thin and often meconium-stained cord. The head appears relatively large (although it approaches normal size) because the chest size and abdominal girth are decreased. The baby may have a vigorous cry and appear deceptively alert (Figure 24.3).

## ● Nursing Diagnosis

Nursing diagnoses that may apply are included in the Nursing Care Plan—Small-for-Gestational-Age Newborn.

## ● Nursing Plan and Implementation

Hypoglycemia, the most common metabolic complication of IUGR, produces such sequelae as central nervous system (CNS) abnormalities and mental retardation. In addition to hypoglycemia, conditions such as asphyxia, hyperviscosity, and cold stress may also affect the baby's outcome. Meticulous attention to physiologic parameters is essential for immediate nursing management and reduction of long-term disorders (see Nursing Care Plan—Small-for-Gestational-Age Newborn).

The long-term needs of the SGA newborn include

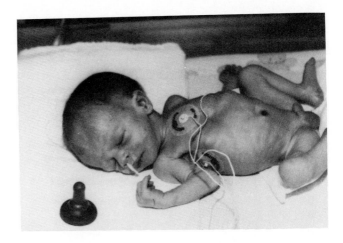

*Figure 24.3   The infant with symmetric IUGR appears long, thin, and emaciated. The gestational age of the infant shown here is 41 weeks. He weighed approximately 1560 g at birth.*

scrupulous follow-up evaluation of patterns of growth and possible disabilities that may later interfere with learning or motor functioning. Long-term follow-up care is especially necessary for those infants with congenital malformations, congenital infections, and obvious sequelae from physiologic problems. In addition, the parents of the IUGR neonate need support, because a positive atmosphere can enhance the baby's growth potential and the child's ultimate outcome. (See Chapter 28 for further discussion of families facing childbearing crises.)

## ● CARE OF THE LARGE-FOR-GESTATIONAL-AGE (LGA) NEWBORN

A **large-for-gestational-age (LGA)** neonate is one whose birth weight is at or above the ninetieth percentile on the intrauterine growth curve (at any week of gestation). The majority of infants categorized as LGA have been found to be so categorized because of miscalculation of dates due to postconceptual bleeding (Korones 1986). Careful gestational age assessment is essential to identify the potential needs and problems of such infants.

The best-known condition associated with excessive fetal growth is maternal diabetes (Classes A–C); however, only a minority of large newborns are born to diabetic mothers. The cause of the majority of cases of LGA newborns is unclear, but certain factors or situations have been found to correlate with their birth.

● Genetic predisposition is correlated to the prepregnancy weight and to weight gain during pregnancy. Large parents tend to have large infants.

● Multiparous women have three times the number of LGA infants as primigravidas.

*(Text continues on page 672.)*

## Nursing Care Plan

### Small-for-Gestational-Age Newborn

## Client Assessment

### Nursing History

**MATERNAL FACTORS:**

Vascular—PIH, chronic hypertension, advanced diabetes

Preexisting diseases—heart disease, alcoholism, narcotic addiction, sickle cell anemia, PKU

Primiparity, smoking, lack of prenatal care, low socioeconomic level, very young or old

Environmental factors—high altitude, x-rays, maternal drug use (antimetabolics, anticonvulsants)

**PLACENTAL FACTORS**—infarcts, placenta previa

**FETAL FACTORS:**

Congenital infections

Multiple pregnancy

Inborn errors of metabolism

Chromosomal syndrome

### Physical Examination

Large-appearing head in proportion to chest and abdomen

Loose dry skin

Scarcity of subcutaneous fat, with emaciated appearance

Long, thin appearance

Sunken abdomen

Sparse scalp hair

Anterior fontanelle may be depressed

May have vigorous cry and appears alert

Birth weight below tenth percentile

### Diagnostic Studies

Blood glucose and Dextrostix

Hematocrit

Total bilirubin level

Calcium levels

Chest x-rays

| Nursing Diagnosis/Client Goals | Nursing Interventions | Rationale/Evaluation |
| --- | --- | --- |
| **Nursing Diagnosis:**<br><br>Pattern 1: Exchanging<br>Impaired gas exchange related to aspiration of meconium | Auscultate breath sounds q 4 hr.<br>Suction endotracheal tube q 3–4 hr.<br>Give oxygen prior to suction as needed.<br>Ensure chest physiotherapy is done as indicated. | **Rationale:**<br><br>In utero, hypoxia causes relaxation of anal sphincter and reflex gasping of meconium.<br>Maintain airway patency. |
| **Client Goal:**<br><br>Baby's respirations will be 30–50/min with no periods of apnea, intermittent cyanosis, sternal retractions, grunting, or nasal flaring. | Observe for worsening signs of respiratory distress such as generalized cyanosis; worsening retractions, grunting, and nasal flaring, as evidenced by Silverman respiratory index; sustained tachypnea; apnea episodes; inequality of breath sounds; presence of rales and rhonchi. Administer oxygen per order for relief of respiratory distress signs (see p 713 for nursing care and treatment of meconium aspiration, infant resuscitation).<br>Implement treatment plan by respiratory distress.<br><br>Monitor glucose levels by Dextrostix. | <br><br>Respiratory distress increases consumption of glucose.<br><br>**Evaluation:**<br><br>Baby's respirations and respiratory effort are within normal range and show no worsening signs of respiratory distress. |

# Nursing Care Plan

## Small-for-Gestational-Age Newborn *(continued)*

| Nursing Diagnosis/Client Goals | Nursing Interventions | Rationale/Evaluation |
|---|---|---|
| **Nursing Diagnosis:**<br><br>Pattern 1: Exchanging<br>Ineffective thermoregulation related to decreased subcutaneous fat<br><br>**Client Goal:**<br><br>Baby will maintain skin temperature between 36.1 and 36.7°C (97–98°F). | Provide neutral thermal zone (NTZ) range for infant based on postnatal weight.<br><br>Use skin probe to maintain skin temperature at 36–36.5°C.<br><br>Obtain axillary temps and compare to registered skin probe temp q 2 hr and PRN. If discrepancy exists, evaluate potential cause.<br><br>Adjust and monitor incubator or radiant warmer to maintain skin temperature.<br><br>Minimize heat losses and prevent cold stress by:<br>1. Warming and humidifying oxygen without blowing over face in order to avoid increasing oxygen consumption<br>2. Keeping skin dry<br>3. Keeping isolettes, radiant warmers, and cribs away from windows and cold external walls and out of drafts<br>4. Avoiding placing infant on cold surfaces such as metal treatment tables, cold x-ray plates<br>5. Padding cold surfaces with diapers and using radiant warmers during procedures<br>6. Warming blood for exchange transfusions.<br><br>Monitor for signs and symptoms of cold stress: decreased temperature, lethargy, pallor (for further discussion see p 693) | **Rationale:**<br><br>Neutral thermal environment charts used for preterm baby must be altered for SGA newborns.<br><br>Diminished subcutaneous fat and a large body surface compared to body weight predispose SGA baby to thermoregulation problems.<br><br>Discrepancies between axillary and skin probe monitor temp may be due to mechanical causes or the burning of brown fat.<br><br>SGA infant has increased heat loss due to decreased available brown fat stores for heat production and less fat insulation.<br><br><br>Cold stress increases oxygen requirements.<br><br>**Evaluation:**<br><br>Baby's temperature will be stable and maintained within normal limits. |
| **Nursing Diagnosis:**<br><br>Pattern 1: Exchanging<br>Potential for injury to tissues related to decreased glycogen stores and impaired gluconeogenesis | Monitor Dextrostix per SGA protocol and report values <45 mg/dL<br><br>Observe, record, and report signs of hypoglycemia: cyanosis, lethargy, jitteriness, seizure activity, and apnea.<br><br>Notify physician if values are low. Monitor vital signs q 2 hr PRN. | **Rationale:**<br><br>Combined with depletion of glycogen stores, impaired gluconeogenesis predisposes SGA infants to profound hypoglycemia within first two days of life.<br><br>Hypoglycemia causes CNS irritability. |

*(continues)*

# Nursing Care Plan

## Small-for-Gestational-Age Newborn (continued)

| Nursing Diagnosis/Client Goals | Nursing Interventions | Rationale/Evaluation |
| --- | --- | --- |
| **Client Goal:**<br><br>Baby will have Dextrostix of greater than 45 mg/dL, no signs of respiratory distress, and will be alert and active. | Initiate feeding schedule for SGA newborns per agency protocol. Monitor Dextrostix.<br><br>Provide glucose intake either through early enteral feeding (before four hr) or by IV per physician's order.<br>See further discussion of hypoglycemia on p 717.<br><br>Record I & O, monitor IV rate and site hourly. | Frequent monitoring of Dextrostix assists in identifying decreasing glucose levels.<br><br>Provision of glucose through early feedings (begin before four hr of age), or IV, maintains needed glucose levels.<br><br>Decreasing glucose is reflected in lethargy, decreased appetite.<br><br>**Evaluation:**<br><br>Baby will have normal blood glucose levels. |
| **Nursing Diagnosis:**<br><br>Pattern 1: Exchanging<br>Altered nutrition: less than body requirements related to SGA's increased metabolic rate<br><br>**Client Goal:**<br><br>Baby will not lose more than 2% weight, takes formula without tiring, and gains weight. | Initiate test water feeding at one hr of age, then proceed to 5% glucose/water. Move early to formula feeding q 2–3 hr.<br><br>Supplement oral feedings with intravenous intake per orders.<br><br>Use concentrated formulas that supply more calories in less volume, such as Similac 24.<br><br>Promote growth by providing caloric intake of 120–150 cal/kg/day in small amounts. Monitor and record signs of respiratory distress or fatigue occurring during feedings.<br><br>Supplement gavage or nipple feedings with intravenous therapy per physician order until oral intake is sufficient to support growth.<br><br>Begin nipple feeding slowly, such as nipple feed once per day, nipple feed once per shift, and then nipple feed every other feeding.<br><br>Monitor daily weight with anticipation of small amount of weight loss when nipple feedings start. | **Rationale:**<br><br>Sterile water is desirable for first feedings because it causes fewer pulmonary complications in the presence of aspiration of feeding.<br><br>SGA newborns require more calories/kg for growth because of increased metabolic activity and oxygen consumption secondary to increased percentage of body weight made up by visceral organs.<br><br>Small, frequent feedings of high caloric formula are used because of limited gastric capacity and decreased gastric emptying.<br><br>Small, frequent feedings decrease fatigue associated with feeding.<br><br>Adequate nutritional intake promotes growth and prevents such complications as metabolic catabolism and hypoglycemia.<br><br>Gavage feedings require less energy expenditure on the part of the newborn.<br><br>Nipple feeding, an active rather than passive intake of nutrition, requires energy expenditure, burning of calories, and potential weight loss.<br><br>**Evaluation:**<br><br>Baby will gain weight and tolerate nipple feedings without tiring. |

# Nursing Care Plan

## Small-for-Gestational-Age Newborn *(continued)*

| Nursing Diagnosis/Client Goals | Nursing Interventions | Rationale/Evaluation |
| --- | --- | --- |

### Nursing Diagnosis:

Pattern 1: Exchanging
Altered tissue perfusion related to increased blood viscosity

### Client Goals:

Baby's hemoglobin will be less than 22 g/dL, hematocrit less than 65%; baby will show no signs of respiratory distress, cyanosis, or tachycardia.

Obtain central hematocrit on admission.

Monitor, record, and report symptoms, including:
1. Decrease in peripheral pulses, discoloration of extremity, alteration in activity or neurologic depression, renal vein thrombosis with decreased urine output, hematuria, or proteinuria in thromboembolic conditions
2. Tachycardia or congestive heart failure
3. Respiratory distress syndrome, cyanosis, tachypnea, increased oxygen need, labored respirations, or hemorrhage in respiratory system

Watch for other signs of increased hematocrit such as hyperbilirubinemia.

Assist with partial plasma exchange.

### Rationale:

Exact etiology of polycythemia in SGA is not known but is thought to be a physiologic response to chronic hypoxia with increased erythropoietin production.

Polycythemia is defined as a central venous hematocrit above 65%–70% in the first week of life. Hyperviscosity is resultant "thickness" of red-cell rich blood so that its ability to perfuse the tissues is disturbed due to thickness and decrease in deformability of cells.
Symptoms are caused by poor perfusion of tissues.

As the increased red blood cells begin to break down, hyperbilirubinemia may present.

Partial plasma exchange decreases blood volume and blood viscosity to less than 60%.

### Evaluation:

Baby has normal hemoglobin and hematocrit and shows no signs of respiratory distress.

### Nursing Diagnosis:

Pattern 3: Relating
Potential altered parenting related to prolonged separation of baby and parents secondary to illness

### Client Goals:

Baby's parents will touch, hold, and participate in the baby's care and talk about the future of their baby.

Include parents in determining infant's plan of care and encourage their participation. Encourage parents to visit frequently. Provide opportunities for parents to touch, hold, talk to, and care for infant. Determine the type and amount of appropriate sensory stimulation and implement sensory stimulation program.

### Rationale:

Parent-infant bonding begins in first few hours or days following birth of an infant. SGA infants experience prolonged periods of separation from their parents, which necessitates intervention to ensure parent-infant bonding.

Support emotionally the psychologic well-being of family, including positive parent-infant bonding and sensory stimulation of infant.

### Evaluation:

Baby's parents have bonded with infant, are involved in the care, and have realistic expectations about the baby.

*(continues)*

## Nursing Care Plan

## Small-for-Gestational-Age Newborn *(continued)*

| Nursing Diagnosis/Client Goals | Nursing Interventions | Rationale/Evaluation |
|---|---|---|
| **Nursing Diagnosis:**<br><br>Pattern 8: Knowing<br>Knowledge deficit (parental) concerning care of newborn at home<br><br>**Client Goals:**<br><br>Baby's parents will ask about taking her or him home and will participate in discharge planning, attend necessary classes on infant care, and ask about when to call the doctor and follow-up needs. | Prepare for discharge by instructing parents in such areas as feeding techniques, formula preparation (including bottle sterilization), and breast-feeding; bathing, diapering, and hygiene; rectal temperature monitoring; administration of vitamins; sibling rivalry; care of complications and preventing exposure to infections; normal elimination patterns, normal reflexes and activity, and how to promote normal growth and development without being overprotective; returning for continued medical care; and availability of community resources if indicated. | **Rationale:**<br><br>Parents should receive the same postpartum teaching as any parent taking a new infant home.<br>Parents need to understand the changes to expect in color of the infant's stool and number of bowel movements plus odor from bottle- or breast-feeding in order to avoid unnecessary concern. Preterm infants usually do not require referral to community agencies such as visiting nurse associations unless there is a specific problem requiring assistance. Infants with congenital abnormalities, feeding problems, or resolving complications with infections, or mothers unable to cope with defective infants are examples of conditions requiring referral to community resources.<br><br>**Evaluation:**<br><br>Baby's parents verbalize how to take care of their baby at home and know when to return for follow-up and when to call their health care provider. |

- Male infants are traditionally larger than female infants.
- Infants with erythroblastosis fetalis, Beckwith-Wiedemann syndrome, or transposition of the great vessels are usually large.

The increase in the LGA infant's body size is characteristically proportional, although head circumference and body length are in the upper limits of intrauterine growth. The exception to this rule is the infant of the diabetic mother, whose body weight increases only in proportion to length.

### • Common Complications of the LGA Newborn

Common disorders of the LGA infant include:

- *Birth trauma because of cephalopelvic disproportion* (CPD). Often these infants have a biparietal diameter greater than 10 cm or a fundal height measurement greater than 42 cm without the presence of hydramnios. Because of their excessive size, there are more breech presentations and shoulder dystocias. These complications may result in asphyxia, fractured clavicles, brachial palsy, facial paralysis, phrenic nerve palsy, depressed skull fractures, and intracranial bleeding.

- *Increased incidence of cesarean births due to fetal size.* These births are accompanied by all the risk factors associated with cesarean deliveries.

- *Hypoglycemia, polycythemia, and hyperviscosity.* These disorders are most often seen with erythroblastosis fetalis and Beckwith-Wiedemann syndrome and in infants of diabetic mothers.

### • Nursing Care

The perinatal history, in conjunction with ultrasonic measurement of fetal skull and gestational age testing, is important in identifying an at-risk LGA newborn. Nursing care is directed toward early identification and immediate treatment of the common disorders. Essential components of the nursing assessment are monitoring vital signs and screening for hypoglycemia and polycythemia. The nursing care involved in the complications associated with LGA newborns applies to the care needed by the infant of a diabetic mother and will be discussed in the next section.

# ● CARE OF THE INFANT OF A DIABETIC MOTHER (IDM)

**Infants of diabetic mothers (IDMs)** are considered at risk and require close observation the first few hours to the first few days of life. Mothers with severe diabetes or diabetes of long duration (type 1, or White's classes D–F, associated with vascular complications) may give birth to SGA infants. The typical IDM (type 1, or White's classes B and C), however, is LGA. He or she is fat, macrosomic, and plethoric (Figure 24.4). The cord and placenta are also large.

The infant is not edematous since IDMs have decreased total body water, particularly in the extracellular spaces. Their excessive weight is due to visceral organomegaly, cardiomegaly, and increased body fat. The only organ not affected is the brain.

The excessive fetal growth of the IDM is caused by exposure to high levels of maternal glucose, which readily crosses the placenta. The fetus responds to these high glucose levels with increased insulin production and hyperplasia of the pancreatic beta cells. The main action of the insulin is to facilitate the entry of glucose into muscle and fat cells in a function similar to a cellular growth hormone. Once in the cells, glucose is converted to glycogen and stored. Insulin also inhibits the breakdown of fat to free fatty acids, thereby maintaining lipid synthesis, increasing the uptake of amino acids, and promoting protein synthesis. Insulin is an important regulator of fetal growth and metabolism.

# ● Common Complications of the IDM

Although IDMs are usually large, they are immature in physiologic functions and exhibit many of the problems of the preterm infant. The complications most often seen in an IDM are:

● *Hypoglycemia.* After birth the most common problem of an IDM is hypoglycemia. Even though the high maternal blood supply is lost, this newborn continues to produce high levels of insulin, which deplete the blood glucose within hours after birth. IDMs also have less ability to release glucagon and catecholamines, which normally stimulate glucagon breakdown and glucose release. The incidence of hypoglycemia in IDMs varies from 2% to 75%. The wide range in incidence is thought to be due to the degree of success in controlling the maternal diabetes, differences in maternal blood sugars at the time of birth, length of labor, the

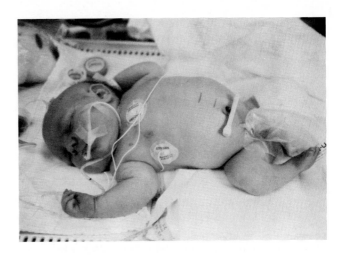

*Figure 24.4  Macrosomic infant of diabetic mother. X-ray examination of this infant revealed caudal regression of the spine.*

class of maternal diabetes, and early versus late feedings of the newborn.

● *Hypocalcemia.* Tremors are the obvious clinical sign of hypocalcemia. This may be due to the IDM's increased incidence of prematurity and to the stresses of difficult pregnancy, labor, and birth, which predispose any infant to hypocalcemia. Also, diabetic women tend to have higher calcium levels at term, causing possible secondary hypoparathyroidism in their infants (Korones 1986).

● *Hyperbilirubinemia.* This condition may be seen at 48 to 72 hours after birth. It may be caused by slightly decreased extracellular fluid volume, which increases the hematocrit level. Enclosed hemorrhages resulting from complicated vaginal birth may also cause hyperbilirubinemia. There may also be an increase in rate of bilirubin production in the presence of polycythemia.

● *Birth trauma.* Since most IDMs are LGA, trauma may occur during labor and birth (see p 672).

● *Polycythemia.* This condition may be caused by the decreased extracellular volume in IDMs. Current research centers on the fact that hemoglobin $A_{1c}$ binds oxygen, which decreases the oxygen available to the fetal tissues. This tissue hypoxia stimulates increased erythropoietin production, which increases the hematocrit level (Shannon et al 1986).

● *Respiratory distress.* This complication occurs especially in newborns of White's classes A–C diabetic mothers. Increasing evidence suggests that IDMs may have normal levels of the phospholipids that make up surfactant, which leads others to theorize that the composition of the lipids themselves is altered in the lungs of IDMs (Avery and Taeusch 1984). Other researchers (Duara et al 1985) theorize that fetal hyperinsulinemia may block normal maturation of basal lung areas. RDS does not appear to be a problem for infants born of diabetic mothers in White's classes D–F; instead, the stresses of poor uterine blood supply may lead to increased production of steroids, which accelerates lung maturation.

● *Congenital birth defects.* These may include transposition of the great vessels, ventricular septal defect, patent ductus, small left colon syndrome, and caudal regression syndrome.

## ● Medical Therapy

The goal of medical therapy is the early detection of and intervention in the problems associated with being born an IDM. Key prenatal management is directed toward control of maternal hyperglycemia, which minimizes the common complications of IDMs: pulmonary problems, macrosomia, polycythemia, and hypoglycemia.

Because the onset of hypoglycemia occurs at two hours of age in IDMs (with a spontaneous rise to normal levels by four to six hours), blood glucose determinations should be done on cord blood and at 1, 2, 4, 6, 12, and 24 hours of age (Korones 1986).

IDMs who are symptomatic should be given 10% to 15% glucose intravenously immediately after birth at the volume of fluids necessary for the hydration of the infant. The rate of 4 to 6 mg/kg/min usually maintains normoglycemia in the IDM (Avery 1987). Once the blood glucose has been stable for 24 hours, the solution is then decreased in concentration with careful attention to the neonate's blood glucose level. Dextrose (25% to 50%) as a rapid infusion is contraindicated because it may lead to severe rebound hypoglycemia following an initial brief increase in glucose level.

## ● Nursing Diagnosis

Nursing diagnoses that may apply to IDMs include:

● Altered nutrition: less than body requirements related to increased glucose metabolism secondary to hyperinsulinemia

● Impaired gas exchange related to respiratory distress secondary to impaired production of surfactant

● Ineffective family coping related to the illness of the baby

## ● Nursing Plan and Implementation
### PROMOTION OF PHYSICAL WELL-BEING

Nursing care of the IDM is directed toward early detection and ongoing monitoring of hypoglycemia (by doing glucose tests) and polycythemia (by obtaining central hematocrits). Specific nursing interventions for hypoglycemia and polycythemia are presented later in this chapter. In caring for the IDM baby, the nurse assesses for signs of respiratory distress, hyperbilirubinemia, birth trauma, and congenital anomalies. Close and ongoing nursing assessments and care are essential in decreasing the potential harmful effects of the problems associated with being an IDM.

### PROMOTION OF FAMILY ADAPTATION

Education of parents is directed toward prevention of macrosomia and resultant fetal-neonatal problems by better diabetic control for future pregnancies. Parents are advised that with prompt care, most IDMs' neonatal problems have no significant sequelae.

## ● Evaluation

Anticipated outcomes of nursing care include:

● The IDM is free of respiratory distress and metabolic alterations.

● The parents understand the effects of DM on the baby and preventive steps they can initiate to decrease the impact of maternal diabetes on subsequent fetuses.

● The parents verbalize their concerns surrounding their baby's health problems and understand the rationale behind management of their newborn.

## ● CARE OF THE POSTTERM INFANT

The **postterm infant** is any infant delivered after 42 weeks' gestation (product of a prolonged pregnancy). In the past, the terms *postterm* and *postmature* were used interchangeably. Currently the term *postmature* is used only when the infant is delivered after 42 weeks of gestation and also demonstrates characteristics of the postmaturity syndrome (Hendriksen 1985).

Prolonged pregnancy occurs in approximately 5%–10% of all pregnancies (Losh and Duhring 1987). The cause of postterm pregnancy is not completely understood, but several factors are known to be associated with it, including primiparity, high multiparity mothers (greater than four), and a history of prolonged pregnancies (Affonso and Harris 1980). Many pregnancies classified as prolonged are thought to be due to inaccurate obstetrical dates.

Most babies born as a result of prolonged pregnancy are of normal size and health; some keep on growing after term and are over 4000 g, which supports the premise that the postterm fetus can remain well nourished. Intrapartal problems for these healthy but large fetuses are CPD and shoulder dystocia. At birth about 5% of postterm newborns show signs of postmaturity syndrome (Oxorn 1986). The major portion of the following discussion will address the fetus who is not tolerating the prolonged pregnancy, is suffering from uteroplacental compromise to blood flow and resultant hypoxia, and is considered to have postmaturity syndrome.

## ● Common Complications of the Postmature Syndrome Newborn

The truly postmature infant is at high risk for morbidity and has a mortality rate two to three times greater than term infants. The majority of deaths occur during labor, since by that time the fetus has used up necessary reserves. Because of decreased placental function, oxygenation and nutrition transport are impaired, leaving the fetus prone to hypoglycemia and asphyxia when the stresses of labor begin. Problems in surviving postmature infants are thus a result of inadequate placental function, decreased reserves, and the stress of labor. The most common disorders of the postmature infant are:

● Hypoglycemia, from nutritional deprivation and resultant depleted glycogen stores

● Meconium aspiration in response to hypoxia in utero

● Polycythemia due to increased production of red blood cells (RBCs) in response to hypoxia

● Congenital anomalies of unknown cause

● Seizure activity because of hypoxic insult

● Cold stress because of loss or poor development of subcutaneous fat

The long-term effects of postmaturity syndrome are unclear. At present, studies do not agree on the effect of postmaturity syndrome on weight gain and IQ scores.

## ● Medical Therapy

The goal of medical therapy is identification and management of the postmature newborn's potential problems.

Antenatal management is directed at differentiating the fetus who has postmaturity syndrome from the fetus who at birth is large, well-nourished, and equally alert and has experienced an equally long gestation. Table 24.1 depicts a system that attempts to distinguish in utero the fetus who may have postmaturity syndrome and requires intervention from the healthy fetus who is tolerating the prolonged (postterm) pregnancy.

Antenatal tests that can be done to evaluate fetal status and determine obstetrical management include fetal ultrasound, and the nonstress test (NST) and contraction stress test (CST). These tests and their use in postterm pregnancy are discussed in more depth in Chapters 13 and 18.

If the amniotic fluid is meconium stained, the baby's airway should be suctioned by the clinician prior to delivery of the chest and trunk and before the baby takes its first breath to minimize the chance of meconium aspiration syndrome. For detailed discussion of medical management and nursing assessments and care, see p 712.

**Table 24.1  Evaluation of Fetal Status in True Prolonged Pregnancy**$^*$

| Clinical parameters | Positive | Guarded | Negative |
|---|---|---|---|
| Uterine size | Increasing | No increase | Decreasing |
| Amniotic fluid volume | Appropriate | Diminished | Oligohydramnios |
| Fetal activity | Unchanged | Diminished | Absent |
| Maternal weight | Increasing | Decreasing | |
| Estriol levels | Stable/increasing | Chronically low | Decrease ≥ 35% |
| Ultrasound (growth-adjusted sonographic age) | Maintenance of growth percentile | Decrease in growth percentile | Cessation of growth |
| Nonstress test | Reactive | Nonreactive: spontaneous variables | Spontaneous late deceleration |
| Oxytocin challenge test | Negative | Ambiguous: variable decelerations | Positive |
| Intrapartum monitoring | Baseline 100–140 beats/min, normal pattern, variability of 6–15 beats/min | Baseline >150 beats/min, decreased variability, variable decelerations | Baseline >150 beats/min, absent variability, repetitive late decelerations |

Source: Hobart JM, Depp R: Prolonged pregnancy. In: *Gynecology and Obstetrics*. Vol. 3. Sciarra JL (editor). Philadelphia: Harper and Row, 1982. p 5.

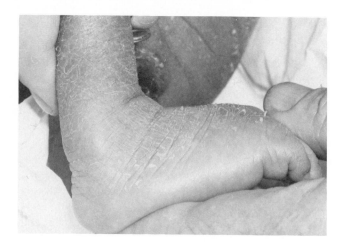

*Figure 24.5  Postterm infant demonstrates deep cracking and peeling of skin. (From Dubowitz L, Dubowitz V:* Gestational Age of the Newborn. *Menlo Park, CA: Addison-Wesley, 1977.)*

Hypoglycemia is monitored by serial glucose determinations. The baby may be placed on glucose infusions or given early feedings if respiratory distress is not present. Postmature newborns are often voracious eaters.

Peripheral and central hematocrits are tested to assess the presence of polycythemia. Oxygen is provided for respiratory distress. A partial exchange transfusion may be necessary to prevent adverse sequelae such as hyperviscosity.

## ● Nursing Assessment

The newborn with postmaturity syndrome appears alert. This wide-eyed, alert appearance is not necessarily a positive sign as it may indicate chronic intrauterine hypoxia.

The infant has dry, cracking, parchmentlike skin without vernix or lanugo (Figure 24.5). Fingernails are long, and scalp hair is profuse. The infant's body appears long and thin. The wasting involves depletion of previously stored subcutaneous tissue, causing the skin to be loose. Fat layers are almost nonexistent.

Postmature newborns frequently have meconium staining, which colors the nails, skin, and umbilical cord. The varying shades (yellow to green) of meconium staining can give some clue about whether the expulsion of meconium was a recent or chronic, long-standing event.

Prolonged pregnancy itself is not responsible for the postmaturity syndrome. The previously described characteristics of the postmature newborn are primarily caused by a combination of advanced gestational age, placental insufficiency, and continued exposure to amniotic fluid (Clifford 1957).

## ● Nursing Diagnosis

Nursing diagnoses that may apply to the postmature newborn include:

- Potential for injury (cellular) related to hypothermia secondary to decreased liver glycogen and brown fat stores
- Altered nutrition: less than body requirements related to increased use of glucose secondary to in utero stress
- Impaired gas exchange in the lungs and at the cellular level related to airway obstruction from potential meconium aspiration in utero

## ● Nursing Plan and Implementation

Nursing interventions are primarily supportive measures. They include the following:

- Observation of cardiopulmonary status, since the stresses of labor are poorly tolerated and severe asphyxia can ensue at birth
- Provision of warmth to counterbalance poor response to cold stress and decreased liver glycogen and brown fat stores
- Frequent monitoring of blood glucose and initiation of early feeding (at one or two hours of age) or intravenous glucose per physician order
- Observation for the common disorders identified earlier and institution of nursing care and medical management as ordered

### PROVISION OF EMOTIONAL SUPPORT TO THE PARENTS

The nurse encourages parents to express their feelings and fears regarding the newborn's condition and potential long-term problems.

## ● Evaluation

Anticipated outcomes of nursing care include:

- The postterm newborn establishes effective respiratory function.
- The postmature baby is free of metabolic alterations (hypoglycemia) and maintains a stable temperature.

## ● CARE OF THE PRETERM (PREMATURE) NEWBORN

A **preterm infant** is any infant born before 38 weeks' gestation. The length of gestation and thus the level of maturity vary even in the "premature" population. Figure 24.6 shows a preterm newborn.

The incidence of preterm births in the United States ranges from 7% of white newborns to 14% to 15% of non-

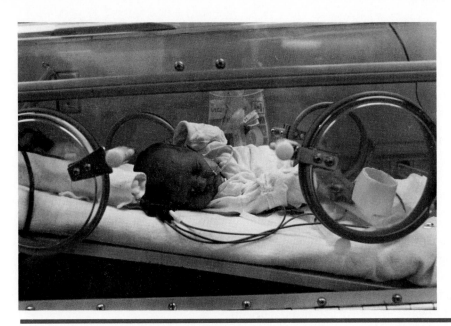

*Figure 24.6  Preterm infant*

whites. The causes of preterm labor are poorly under-stood, but more and more of the factors that influence preterm labor and delivery are being identified (see Chapter 18 for a discussion of preterm labor and delivery).

With the help of modern technology, some babies under 500 g and between 23 and 26 weeks' gestation are surviving. But the mortality rates are the highest among these newborns.

## • Physiologic Considerations

The major problem of the preterm newborn is variable immaturity of all systems. The degree of immaturity depends on the length of gestation. For example, newborns of 32 weeks' gestation can be expected to exhibit more immaturity than newborns of 36 weeks' gestation. Maintenance of the preterm newborn falls within narrow physiologic parameters. "Catch-up care" is usually not possible if ground is lost in initial management. Improper physiologic management (or lack of management) adds stress and feeds the vicious cycle of physiologic deterioration.

The preterm infant must travel the same complex pathway from intrauterine to extrauterine life as the term newborn. Because of immaturity, the preterm newborn is unable to make this transition as smoothly. This section considers physiologic and nutritional factors associated with prematurity.

### RESPIRATORY AND CARDIAC PHYSIOLOGY AND CONSIDERATIONS

The preterm infant's lungs are not fully mature and ready to take over the process of oxygen and carbon dioxide exchange without assistance until 37–38 weeks' gesta-tion. Critical factors in the development of respiratory distress include:

1.  The preterm infant's inability to produce adequate amounts of surfactant. (See Chapter 20 for discussion of respiratory adaptation and development.) When surfactant is decreased, compliance (ability of the lung to fill with air easily) is also lessened and the inspiratory pressure needed to expand the lungs with air increases.

2.  In the preterm infant, the muscular coat of pulmonary blood vessels is incompletely developed. Because of this, the pulmonary arterioles do not constrict as well in response to decreased oxygen levels (Avery 1987). Lower pulmonary vascular resistance leads to left-to-right shunting of blood through the ductus arteriosus back into the lungs.

3.  The ductus arteriosus usually responds to rising oxygen levels by vasoconstriction; in the preterm infant, who has higher susceptibility to hypoxia, the ductus may remain open. A patent ductus increases the blood volume to the lungs, causing pulmonary congestion, increased respiratory effort, and higher oxygen use.

### THERMOREGULATION

Maintaining a normal body temperature in the preterm infant presents a nursing challenge. Heat loss is a major problem that the nurse can do much to prevent. Two limiting factors in heat production, however, are the availability of glycogen in the liver (glycogen stores are primarily laid down during the third trimester) and the amount of brown fat available for metabolism (the preterm infant does not have a full supply of brown fat). If the baby is chilled after birth, both glycogen and brown fat stores are metabolized rapidly for heat production, leaving the newborn with no reserves in the event of future stress. Since the muscle mass is small in preterm infants, and muscular activity is diminished (they are unable to shiver), little heat is produced.

Heat loss occurs as a result of several physiologic and anatomic factors:

1. The preterm baby has a much larger ratio of body surface to body weight. This means that the infant's ability to produce heat (body weight) is much less than the potential for losing heat (surface area). The loss of heat in a preterm infant weighing 1500 g is five times greater per unit of body weight than in an adult (Korones 1986).

2. The preterm baby has very little subcutaneous fat, which is the human body's insulation. Without adequate insulation, heat is easily conducted from the core of the body (warmer temperature) to the surface of the body (cooler temperature). Heat is lost from the body as the blood vessels, which lie close to the skin surface in the preterm infant, transport blood from the body core to the subcutaneous tissues.

3. The posture of the preterm baby is another important factor influencing heat loss. Flexion of the extremities decreases the amount of surface area exposed to the environment; extension increases the surface area exposed to the environment and thus increases heat loss. The gestational age of the infant influences the amount of flexion, from completely hypotonic and extended at 28 weeks to strong flexion displayed by 36 weeks

In summary, the more preterm an infant the less able he or she is to maintain heat balance. Prevention of heat loss by providing a neutral thermal environment is one of the most important considerations in nursing management of the preterm infant (Noerr 1984). Cold stress, with its accompanying severe complications, can be prevented (see p 692).

## NUTRITION AND FLUID REQUIREMENTS

Providing adequate nutrition and fluids for the preterm infant is a major concern of the health care team. Early feedings are extremely valuable in maintaining normal metabolism and lowering the possibility of such complications as hypoglycemia, hyperbilirubinemia, hyperkalemia, and azotemia. However, the preterm infant is at risk for complications that may develop because of immaturity of the digestive system.

Since the basic structure of the gastrointestinal (GI) tract is formed early in gestation, the preterm infant is able to take in suitable nourishment. However, the ability to digest and absorb food efficiently develops later in gestation. As a result of GI immaturity, the preterm neonate has the digestive and absorption problems listed below:

● Limited ability exists to convert certain essential amino acids to nonessential amino acids. Certain amino acids, such as histidine, taurine, and cysteine, are essential to the preterm infant but not to the term infant (American Academy of Pediatrics 1985).

● Kidney immaturity causes an inability to handle the increased osmolarity of formula protein. The preterm infant requires a higher concentration of whey protein than casein.

● Difficulty absorbing saturated fats occurs because of decreased bile salts and pancreatic lipase. Severe illness of the newborn may also prevent intake of adequate nutrients.

● Lactose digestion may not be fully functional during the first few days of a preterm's life. The preterm neonate can digest and absorb most simple sugars.

● Deficiency of calcium and phosphorus may exist since two thirds of these minerals are deposited in the last trimester. As a result the preterm infant is prone to rickets and significant bone demineralization.

Oral caloric intake necessary for growth in an uncompromised healthy preterm neonate is 120–150 kcal/kg/day. In addition to relatively high caloric needs, the preterm neonate requires more protein (3–4 g/kg/day) than the term neonate.

### Formula for Preterm Neonates

The composition of the "best-suited formula" for the preterm infant is a subject of much discussion and research. Breast milk as the primary source of nutrition for the preterm infant has also been a topic of recent debate and research (McCormick 1984).

It is now known that the quality as well as the quantity of protein ingested is important to the small preterm infant. To meet these needs, several higher-calorie, higher-protein formulas are available that meet the preterm infant's nutritional demands, yet do not overtax the concentration abilities of the immature kidneys.

Most preterm formulas contain protein with a whey/casein ratio of 60/40 (a similar proportion to that found in breast milk) and a caloric value of 24 calories per ounce. Similac Special Care and Enfamil Premature Formula are specially formulated for preterm neonates. Preterm formulas also need to contain medium chain triglycerides (MCT), and additional amino acids such as cysteine. The preterm neonate also needs calcium and vitamin D supplements to increase mineralization of bones. Multivitamins

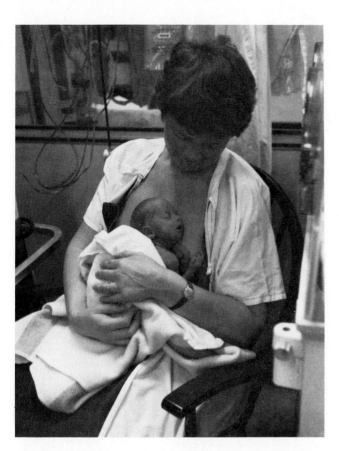

*Figure 24.7   Mother visits intensive care unit to breast-feed her preterm infant. Skin-to-skin contact is especially beneficial for small, sick, or preterm babies.*

and vitamin E are required if the diet is high in MCT and if the infant is fed a formula with iron.

Breast milk is widely used to feed preterm infants. Besides its many benefits for the infant, it allows the mother to contribute to her infant's well-being (Figure 24.7). It is a nursing responsibility to inform mothers of their option to breast-feed if they choose to do so. The nurse should be aware of the advantages and possible disadvantages of breast-feeding, such as slower growth rate, hyponatremia, and lactose intolerance, if breast milk is the sole source of food.

Additional factors that influence the preterm neonate's nutrition are the immaturity of the renal system (inability to concentrate urine), immaturity of the respiratory system (weak or absent cough), and immaturity of the neurologic system (poor suck, gag, and swallow reflexes).

Nutritional intake is considered adequate when there is consistent weight gain of 20–30 g per day. Initially, no weight gain may be noted for several days, but total weight loss should not exceed 15% of the total birth weight or more than 1%–2% per day. Some institutions add the criteria of head circumference growth and increase in body length of 1 cm/week, once the neonate is stable.

## Essential Facts to Remember

### Nutrition of the Preterm Infant

- Initially requires 80–100 mL/kg/day; may need more fluid if of lower birth weight
- Requires 120–150 cal/kg/day oral intake for growth
- Requires supplemental multivitamins, vitamin E, folic acid, and calcium
- Desired weight gain of 20–30 g/day
- Desired initial weight loss of only 1%–2%/day

Feeding regimens are established based on the weight and estimated stomach capacity of the neonate. In many instances it is necessary to supplement the oral feedings with parenteral fluids to maintain adequate hydration and caloric intake.

Calculation of fluid requirements must take into account both the weight of the neonate and postnatal age. In the preterm infant, more fluid is lost through the skin than in term infants because of decreased insulating fat and blood vessels close to the surface. In addition, higher environmental temperature, phototherapy, and radiant warmers may increase fluid loss an additional 50%.

Recommendations for fluid therapy in the preterm infant are approximately 80–100 mL/kg/day for day 1; 100–120 mL/kg/day for day 2; and 120–150 mL/kg/day by day 3 of life. These amounts may be increased up to 200 mL/kg/day if the infant is very small, receiving phototherapy, or under a radiant warmer. The infant may need less fluid if a heat shield is used, the environment is more humid, or humidified oxygen is being provided. (See Essential Facts to Remember—Nutrition of the Preterm Infant.)

### Methods of Feeding

The preterm infant is fed by various methods depending on the infant's gestational age, health and physical condition, and neurologic status. The two most common oral feeding methods are nipple and gavage feeding.

***Nipple Feeding***   Preterm infants who have a coordinated suck and swallow reflex and those showing continued weight gain may be fed by nipple. To avoid excessive expenditure of energy a soft nipple is usually used.

***Gavage Feeding***   Preterm infants who do not have coordinated swallow or suck reflexes require gavage feeding. Gavage feeding is also used when infants are losing weight because of the energy expenditure secondary to nippling. See Procedure 24.1.

## Procedure 24.1

## Gavage Feeding

| Objective | Nursing Action | Rationale |
| --- | --- | --- |
| Ensure smooth accomplishment of the procedure. | Gather necessary equipment including: <br> 1. No. 5 or No. 8 Fr feeding tube <br> 2. 10–30 mL syringe <br> 3. ¼-in paper tape <br> 4. Stethoscope <br> 5. Appropriate formula <br> 6. Small cup of sterile water <br><br> Explain procedure to parents. | Considerations in choosing size of catheter include size of the infant, area of insertion (oral or nasal), and rate of flow desired. The very small infant (less than 1600 g) requires a 5 Fr feeding tube; an infant greater than 1600 g may tolerate a larger tube. Orogastric insertion is preferred over nasogastric insertion as most infants are obligatory nose breathers. If nasogastric insertion is used, a No. 5 catheter should be used to minimize airway obstruction. The size of the catheter will influence the rate of flow. The syringe is used to aspirate stomach contents prior to feeding, to inject air into the stomach for testing tube placement, and for holding measured amount of formula during feeding. Tape is used to mark tube for insertion depth as well as for securing tube during feeding. Stethoscope is needed to auscultate rush of air into stomach when testing tube placement. <br> Sterile water may be used to lubricate feeding tube when inserted nasally. With oral insertion, there are enough secretions in the mouth to lubricate the tube adequately. The cup of sterile water may also be used to test for placement by placing the end of the tube into the water to check for air bubbles from the lungs. However, this test may not be accurate as air may also be present in the stomach (Avery 1987). |
| Insert tube accurately into stomach. | Position infant on back or side with head of bed elevated. <br><br> Take the tube from package and measure the distance from the tip of the ear to the nose to the xiphoid process, and mark the point with a small piece of paper tape (Figure 24.8). | This position allows easy passage of the tube. <br><br> This measuring technique ensures enough tubing to enter stomach. |

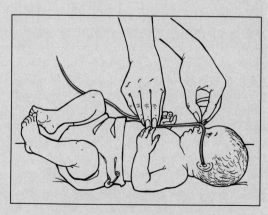

*Figure 24.8  Measuring gavage tube length*

# Procedure 24.1

## Gavage Feeding *(continued)*

| Objective | Nursing Action | Rationale |
|---|---|---|

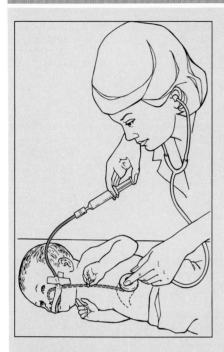

*Figure 24.9  Auscultation for placement of gavage tube*

Introduce formula into stomach without complication.

**Nursing Action (column 2):**

If inserting tube nasally, lubricate tip in cup of sterile water. Shake excess drops to prevent aspiration.

Stabilize infant's head with one hand, and pass the tube via the mouth (or nose) into the stomach, to the point previously marked. If the infant begins coughing or choking or becomes cyanotic or aphonic, remove the tube immediately.

If no respiratory distress is apparent, lightly tape tube in position, draw up 0.5–1.0 mL of air in syringe, and connect it to tubing. Place stethoscope over the epigastrium and briskly inject the air (Figure 24.9).

Aspirate stomach contents with syringe, and note amount, color, and consistency. Return residual to stomach unless ordered to discard it.

If only a clear fluid or mucus is found upon aspiration and if any question exists as to whether the tube is in the stomach, the aspirate can be tested for pH.

Hold infant for feeding or position on right side if infant cannot be held.

Separate syringe from tube, remove plunger from barrel, reconnect barrel to tube, and pour formula into syringe.

Elevate syringe 6–8 in over infant's head. Allow formula to flow at slow, even rate.

Continue adding formula to syringe until desired volume has been absorbed. Then rinse tubing with 2–3 mL sterile water.

Remove tube by loosening tape, folding the tube over on itself, and quickly withdrawing it in one smooth motion. If tube is to be left in, position it so that infant is unable to remove it.

**Rationale (column 3):**

Water should be used, as opposed to an oil-based lubricant, in case the tube is inadvertently passed into a lung.

Any signs of respiratory distress signal likelihood that tube has entered trachea. Orogastric insertion is less likely to result in passage into the trachea than nasogastric insertion.

Nurse should hear a sudden rush of air as tube enters stomach.

Residual formula should be evaluated as part of the assessment of infant's tolerance of gavage feedings. It is not discarded, unless particularly large in volume or mucoid in nature, because of the potential for causing an electrolyte imbalance.

Stomach aspirate tests in the 1–3 range for pH.

Positioning on side decreases the risk of aspiration in case of emesis during feeding.

Feeding should be allowed to flow in by gravity. It should not be pushed in under pressure with a syringe.

Raising column of fluid increases force of gravity. Nurse may need to initiate flow of formula by inserting plunger of syringe into barrel just until formula is seen to enter feeding tube. Rate should be regulated to prevent sudden stomach distention, with possibility of vomiting and aspiration.

Rinsing tube ensures that infant receives all of formula. It is especially important to rinse tube if it is going to be left in place, because this decreases risk of clogging and bacterial growth in tube.

Folding tube over on itself minimizes potential for aspiration of fluid which would otherwise flow from tubing as it passes epiglottis. A tube left in place should be replaced at least every 24 hours.

*(continues)*

## Procedure 24.1

### Gavage Feeding (continued)

| Objective | Nursing Action | Rationale |
|---|---|---|
| Maximize feeding pleasure of infant. | Whenever possible hold infant during gavage feeding. If it is too awkward to hold infant during feeding, be sure to take time for holding afterward. | Feeding time is important to infant's tactile sensory input. |
| | Offer a pacifier to infant during feeding. | Infants fed for long periods by gavage can lose their sucking reflex. Sucking during feeding comforts and relaxes infant, making formula flow more easily. One study showed that infants allowed to suck during feedings were able to nipple sooner and were discharged earlier than a control group of infants who did not suck during tube feedings. |

An alternative method of feeding is transpyloric feeding. This feeding method should be done only in specially equipped and staffed high-risk nurseries since it can cause perforation of the stomach or intestines. Preterm infants who cannot tolerate any oral (enteral) feedings may be given nutrition by total parenteral nutrition (hyperalimentation).

Because of general immaturity, the preterm infant is susceptible to the following feeding problems:

1. Marked danger of aspiration and its associated complications because of the infant's poorly developed gag reflex, incompetent esophageal cardiac sphincter, and poor sucking and swallowing reflexes.

2. Small stomach capacity, which limits the amount of fluid that can be introduced to meet the infant's high caloric needs.

3. Decreased absorption of essential nutrients because of immaturity, malabsorption, and nutritional loss associated with vomiting and diarrhea.

4. Fatigue associated with sucking, which may lead to increased basal metabolic rate, increased oxygen requirements, and possible necrotizing enterocolitis (NEC).

5. Feeding intolerance and NEC due to diminished blood flow to the intestinal tract because of shock or prolonged hypoxia at birth.

### RENAL PHYSIOLOGY

The kidneys of the preterm infant are immature in comparison with those of the full-term infant. This situation poses clinical problems in the management of fluid and electrolyte balance. Specific characteristics of the preterm infant include the following:

1. The glomerular filtration rate (GFR) is lower due to decreased renal blood flow. Decreased GFR also occurs in severe respiratory distress and perinatal asphyxia. The more preterm the newborn, the less the GFR. Anuria and/or oliguria may be observed in the preterm infant after severe asphyxia with associated hypotension.

2. The preterm infant's kidneys are limited in their ability to concentrate urine or to excrete excess amounts of fluid. This means that if excess fluid is administered, the infant is at risk for fluid retention and overhydration. If too little is administered, the infant will become dehydrated because of the inability to retain adequate fluid.

3. The kidneys of the preterm infant will begin excreting glucose (glycosuria) at a lower serum glucose level than occurs in the adult. Therefore, glycosuria with hyperglycemia is common (Oh 1981)

4. The buffering capacity of the kidney is less, predisposing the infant to metabolic acidosis. Bicarbonate is excreted at a lower serum level, and excretion of acid is accomplished more slowly. Therefore, after periods of hypoxia or insult, the kidneys require a longer time to excrete the lactic acid that accumulates. Sodium bicarbonate is frequently required to treat the metabolic acidosis.

5. The immaturity of the renal system affects the infant's ability to excrete drugs. Because excretion time is longer, many drugs are given at less frequent

intervals in the preterm infant (that is, every 12 hours instead of every eight hours). Urine output must be carefully monitored when the infant is receiving nephrotoxic drugs such as gentamicin, nafcillin, and others. In the event of poor urine output, drugs can become toxic in the infant much more quickly than in the adult.

## REACTIVITY PERIODS AND BEHAVIORAL STATES

Because of the immaturity of all systems in comparison to those of the full-term neonate, the preterm infant's periods of reactivity are delayed. The very ill infant may be hypotonic and unreactive for several days, so these periods of reactivity may not be observed at all.

As the preterm newborn grows and the condition stabilizes, it becomes increasingly possible to identify behavioral states and traits unique to each infant. This is a very important part of nursing management of the high-risk infant. The nurse can help parents learn their infant's cues for interaction.

Preterm infants tend to be more disorganized in their sleep-wake cycles and are unable to attend as well to the human face and objects in the environment. Neurologically, their responses are weaker (sucking, muscle tone, states of arousal) than full-term infants' responses (Gorski et al 1979).

By observing each baby's patterns of behavior and responses, especially sleep-wake states, the nurse can teach parents optimal times for interacting with their newborn.

## ● Common Complications of Prematurity

The preterm neonate is at risk for many complications secondary to the immaturity of various body systems in addition to those already discussed. The most common of these complications are briefly described here and discussed in more detail later in the chapter:

1. *Apnea.* Cessation of breathing for more than 20 seconds. It is thought to be primarily a result of neuronal immaturity, a factor that contributes to the tendency for irregular breathing patterns in preterm infants. When cyanosis and bradycardia (heart rate less than 100 beats/min) are also present, these periods are called apneic episodes or spells (Avery 1987).

2. *Patent ductus arteriosus.* Failure of ductus arteriosus to close due to decreased pulmonary arteriole musculature and hypoxemia.

3. *RDS.* Respiratory distress results from inadequate surfactant production.

4. *Intraventricular hemorrhage.* Up to 35 weeks' gestation the preterm's brain ventricles are lined by the germinal matrix, which is highly susceptible to hypoxic events. The germinal matrix is very vascular, and these blood vessels rupture in the presence of hypoxia.

5. *Hypocalcemia.* The preterm infant lacks adequate amounts of calcium secondary to early birth and growth needs.

6. *Hypoglycemia.* The preterm infant's decreased brown fat and glycogen stores and increased metabolic needs predispose this infant to hypoglycemia.

7. *Necrotizing enterocolitis.* This condition occurs when blood flow to the gastrointestinal tract is decreased secondary to shock or prolonged hypoxia.

8. *Anemia.* The preterm infant is at risk for anemia because of the rapid rate of growth required, shorter red blood cell life, excessive blood sampling, decreased iron stores, and deficiency of vitamin E.

9. *Hyperbilirubinemia.* Immature hepatic enzymatic function decreases conjugation of bilirubin, resulting in increased bilirubin levels.

10. *Infection.* The preterm infant is more susceptible to infection than term infants. Most of the neonate's immunity is acquired in the last trimester. Therefore the preterm infant has decreased antibodies available for protection.

## ● Long-Term Needs and Outcome

The care of the preterm infant and the family does not stop on discharge from the nursery. Follow-up care is extremely important because many developmental problems are not noted until the infant is older and begins to demonstrate motor delays or sensory disability.

Within the first year of life, preterm infants face higher mortality than term infants. Causes of death include sudden infant death syndrome (SIDS) (which occurs about five times more frequently in the preterm infant), respiratory infections, and neurologic defects. Morbidity is also much higher among preterm infants, with those weighing less than 1500 g at highest risk for long-term complications.

The most common long-term problems observed in preterm infants include:

● *Retrolental fibroplasia (RLF) or retinopathy of prematurity (ROP).* In spite of new technology and the ability to monitor arterial oxygen closely, RLF and resulting loss of eyesight continue to occur in the preterm infant.

● *Bronchopulmonary dysplasia (BPD).* Long-term lung disease is a result of damage to the alveolar epithelium secondary to positive pressure respirator therapy and high oxygen concentration. These infants have long-term dependence on oxygen therapy and an increased incidence of respiratory infection during their first few years of life.

- *Speech defects.* The most frequently observed speech defects involve delayed development of receptive and expressive ability that may persist into the school years.

- *Neurologic defects.* The most common neurologic defects include cerebral palsy, hydrocephalus, seizure disorders, lower IQ scores, and learning disabilities. However, the socioeconomic climate and family support systems are extremely important influences on the child's ultimate school performance in the absence of major neurologic defects (Vohr and Coll 1985).

    When evaluating the infant's abilities and disabilities, it is important for parents to understand that developmental progress must be evaluated from the expected date of birth, not from the actual date of birth. Developmental level cannot be evaluated based on chronologic age. In addition, the parents need the consistent support of health care professionals in the long-term management of their infant to promote the highest quality of life possible.

- *Sensorineural hearing loss.* Preterm infants are still at risk for hearing loss, especially those with severe asphyxia or recurrent apnea in the neonatal period. Hyperbilirubinemia and ototoxic drugs such as gentamicin and furosemide (Lasix) are also known to contribute to hearing loss in the newborn, depending on multiple factors such as renal function, age, and duration of treatment (Eviator 1984).

## • Nursing Assessment

Accurate assessment of the physical characteristics and gestational age of the preterm newborn is imperative to anticipate the special needs and problems of this baby. Physical characteristics vary greatly depending on the gestational age, but the following characteristics are frequently present:

- Color—usually pink or ruddy but may be acrocyanotic; observe for cyanosis, jaundice, pallor, or plethora

- Skin—reddened, translucent, blood vessels readily apparent, lack of subcutaneous fat

- Lanugo—plentiful, widely distributed

- Head size—appears large in relation to body

- Skull—bones pliable, fontanelle smooth and flat

- Ears—minimal cartilage, pliable, folded over

- Nails—soft, short

- Genitals—small; testes may not be descended

- Resting position—flaccid, froglike

- Cry—weak, feeble

- Reflexes—poor sucking, swallowing, and gag

- Activity—jerky, generalized movements (seizure activity is abnormal)

Determination of gestational age in preterm newborns requires knowledge and experience in administering gestational assessment tools. The tool used should be specific, reliable, and valid. For a discussion of gestational age assessment tools, see Chapter 21, p 570.

## • Nursing Diagnosis

Nursing diagnoses that may apply to the preterm newborn include:

- Impaired gas exchange related to newborn respiratory distress secondary to immature pulmonary vasculature

- Ineffective breathing pattern: apnea related to immature central nervous system

- Altered nutrition: less than body requirements related to weak suck and swallow reflexes

- Fluid volume deficit related to dehydration secondary to high insensible water losses

- Ineffective family coping related to anger/guilt at having delivered a premature baby

## • Nursing Plan and Implementation

### MAINTENANCE OF RESPIRATORY FUNCTION

There is increased danger of respiratory obstruction in preterm newborns because their bronchi and trachea are so narrow that mucus can obstruct the airway. The nurse must maintain patency through judicious suctioning.

Positioning of the newborn can also affect respiratory function. The nurse should slightly elevate the infant's head to maintain the airway. Because the newborn has weak neck muscles and cannot control head movement, the nurse should ensure that this head position is maintained. The nurse should avoid placing the infant in the supine position because the newborn has difficulty raising the chest due to weak chest and abdominal muscles. The prone position is best for facilitating chest expansion. Weak or absent cough or gag reflexes increase the chance of aspiration in the premature newborn. The nurse should ensure that the infant's position facilitates drainage of mucus or regurgitated formula.

The nurse monitors heart and respiratory rates with cardiorespiratory monitors and observes the newborn to identify alterations in cardiopulmonary status. Nursery nurses must be alert to signs of respiratory distress, including:

- Cyanosis—serious sign when generalized
- Tachypnea—sustained respiratory rate greater than 60/min after first four hours of life
- Retractions
- Expiratory grunting
- Flaring nostrils
- Apneic episodes
- Presence of rales or rhonchi on auscultation
- Inadequate breath sounds

The nurse who observes any of these alterations records and reports them for further evaluation. If respiratory distress occurs, the nurse administers oxygen per physician order to relieve hypoxemia. If hypoxemia is not treated immediately, it may result in patent ductus arteriosus or metabolic acidosis. If oxygen is administered to the newborn, the nurse monitors the oxygen concentration with devices such as the transcutaneous oxygen monitor ($tcPO_2$) or the pulseoximeter. Monitoring of oxygen concentration in the baby's blood is essential since hyperoxemia can lead to blindness (retinopathy of prematurity).

The nurse must also consider respiratory function during feeding. To prevent aspiration and increased energy expenditure and oxygen consumption, the nurse must ensure that the infant's gag and suck reflexes are intact before initiating oral feedings. To minimize oxygen consumption, the body temperature must be maintained around $36.5°C \pm 0.2°C$ ($97.7°F \pm 0.5°F$).

## MAINTENANCE OF NEUTRAL THERMAL ENVIRONMENT

Provision of a neutral thermal environmental minimizes the oxygen consumption expended to maintain a normal core temperature; it also prevents cold stress and facilitates growth by decreasing the calories needed to maintain body temperature. The preterm infant's immature central nervous system provides poor temperature control, and stores of brown fat are decreased. A small infant (<1200 g) can lose 80 cal/kg/day through radiation of body heat.

The nurse can minimize heat loss and temperature instability effects by taking the following measures:

1. Warm and humidify oxygen without blowing it over the face to avoid increasing oxygen consumption.
2. Place the baby in a double-walled Isolette, and use a heat shield over small preterm infants.
3. Avoid placing the baby on cold surfaces such as metal treatment tables and cold x-ray plates; pad cold surfaces with diapers and use radiant warmers during procedures; and warm hands before handling the baby to prevent heat transfer via convection/conduction.

4. Warm the blood before exchange transfusions.
5. Keep the skin dry and place a cap on the baby's head to prevent heat loss via evaporation. (The head makes up 25% of the total body size).
6. Keep Isolettes, radiant warmers, and cribs away from windows and cold external walls and out of drafts to prevent heat loss by radiation.
7. Use a skin probe to monitor the baby's skin temperature. The temperature should be 36°C to 37°C (96.8°F to 97.7°F). Temperature fluctuations indicate hypothermia or hyperthermia.

## MAINTENANCE OF FLUID AND ELECTROLYTE STATUS

Maintenance of hydration is accomplished by providing adequate intake based on the neonate's weight, gestational age, chronologic age, and volume of sensible and insensible water losses. Adequate fluid intake should provide sufficient water to compensate for increased insensible losses and to provide the amount needed for renal excretion of metabolic products. Insensible water losses can be minimized by providing a neutral thermal environment.

The nurse evaluates the hydration status of the baby by assessing and recording signs of dehydration. Signs of dehydration include sunken fontanelle, loss of weight, poor skin turgor (skin returns to position slowly), dry oral mucous membranes, decreased urine output, and increased specific gravity (>1.013). The nurse must also identify signs of overhydration by observing the newborn for edema or excessive weight gain and by comparing urine output with fluid intake.

The preterm infant should be weighed at least once daily at the same time each day. Weight change is one of the most sensitive indicators of fluid balance.

Intake and output is measured accurately. A comparison of intake and output measurements over an eight-hour or 24-hour period provides important information about renal function and fluid balance. Assessment of patterns and whether they show a net gain or loss over several days is also essential to fluid management. Blood serum levels and pH should be monitored to evaluate for electrolyte imbalances.

Accurate hourly intake calculations should be maintained when administering intravenous fluids. Since the preterm infant is unable to excrete excess fluid, it is important to maintain the correct amount of intravenous fluid to prevent fluid overload. This can be accomplished by using neonatal or pediatric infusion pumps. To prevent electrolyte imbalance and dehydration, care must be taken to give the correct IV solutions and volumes and concentrations of formulas. Urine specific gravity and pH are obtained periodically. Urine osmolality provides an indication of hydration, although this factor must be correlated with other assessments (for example, serum sodium). Hydration is considered adequate when the urine output is 1 to 3 cc/kg/hr.

## PREVENTION OF INFECTION

The nurse is responsible for minimizing the preterm newborn's exposure to pathogenic organisms. The preterm newborn is susceptible to infection because of an immature immune system and thin and permeable skin. Invasive procedures, techniques such as umbilical catheterization and mechanical ventilation, and prolonged hospitalization place the infant at greater risk for infection.

Strict hand washing, reverse isolation, and use of equipment for only one infant help minimize exposure of the preterm newborn to infectious agents. Many intensive care nurseries require a two- to three-minute scrub using iodined antibacterial solutions, which decrease growth of gram-positive cocci and gram-negative rod organisms. Other specific nursing interventions include limiting visitors; requiring visitors to wash their hands; and maintaining strict aseptic practices when changing intravenous tubing and solutions (IV solutions and tubing should be changed every 24 hours), administering parenteral fluids, and assisting with sterile procedures. Isolettes and radiant warmers should be changed weekly. There should be minimal use or avoidance of chemical skin preps and tape, which may cause skin trauma.

If infection (sepsis) occurs in the preterm newborn, the nurse may be the first to identify the subtle clinical signs associated with infection. The nurse informs the clinician of the findings immediately and implements the treatment plan per clinician orders in the presence of infection. For specific nursing care required for the newborn with an infection, see p 739.

## PROVISION OF ADEQUATE NUTRITION AND PREVENTION OF FATIGUE DURING FEEDING

The first feedings may be sterile water in small amounts given every two to three hours. These small amounts are increased slowly by one to two mL. Formula or breast milk (with or without fortifiers to increase caloric content) is incorporated into the feedings slowly; initially it may be at quarter strength, then half strength, and so on. This is done to avoid overtaxing the digestive capacity of the preterm newborn.

Special formulas (eg, Similac Special Care, Enfamil Premature Formula) are used to meet the caloric needs of the preterm newborn. These special formulas are concentrated to supply more calories in less volume. Small, frequent feedings of high-calorie formula are used because the newborn has limited gastric capacity and decreased gastric emptying.

The feeding method depends on the feeding abilities and health status of the preterm newborn; see the discussion of various feeding methods. Both nipple and gavage methods are initially supplemented with intravenous therapy until oral intake is sufficient to support growth. Growth usually occurs when 120 to 150 cal/kg/day are provided, and this prevents metabolic catabolism and hypoglycemia. Growth is evaluated by an increase in weight, length, and body measurements.

The nurse must be watchful for any signs of respiratory distress or fatigue during feedings. Prior to each feeding, the nurse measures abdominal girth and auscultates the abdomen to determine the presence and quality of bowel sounds. Such assessments promote early detection of abdominal distention and decreased peristaltic activity, which may indicate necrotizing enterocolitis (NEC) or paralytic ileus. The nurse also checks for residual formula in the stomach prior to feeding. This is done when the newborn is fed by gavage or transpyloric method or in the presence of abdominal distention in a nipple-fed newborn. The presence of residual formula is an indication of intolerance to the type or amount of feeding or the increase in amount of feeding. Residual formula is usually readministered because digestive processes have already been initiated.

Preterm newborns who are ill or fatigue easily with nipple feedings are usually fed by gavage or transpyloric feeding. The infant is essentially passive with these methods, thus conserving energy and calories. As the baby matures, gavage feedings are replaced with nipple feedings to assist in strengthening the sucking reflex and meeting oral and emotional needs. The nurse establishes a nipple-feeding program that is begun and progresses slowly, such as one nipple feeding per day, then one nipple feeding per shift, and then a nipple feeding every other feeding. Daily weights are monitored because often there is a small weight loss when nipple feedings are started. After feedings, the baby is placed on the right side (with support to maintain this position) or on the abdomen. These positions enhance gastric emptying and decrease the change of aspiration if regurgitation occurs. Gastroesophageal reflux is not uncommon in preterm newborns.

The nurse involves the parents in feeding their preterm baby. This is essential to the development of attachment between parents and infant. In addition, such involvement increases parental knowledge about the care of their infant and helps them cope with the situation.

## PROMOTION OF PARENT-INFANT ATTACHMENT

Preterm newborns are generally separated from their parents for prolonged periods. Illness or complications may be detected in the first few hours or days following birth. The resultant interruption in parent-newborn bonding necessitates intervention to ensure successful attachment of parent and child.

Nurses should take measures to promote positive parental feelings toward the newborn. Photographs of the baby are given to parents to have at home or to the mother if she is in a different hospital. The infant's first name is placed on the Isolette as soon as it is known to help the parents feel that their infant is a unique and special person. The telephone number of the nursery and/or intensive care unit and names of staff members are given to parents so that they have access to information about their baby at any time of day or night. Equipment and therapies are explained to parents, and the explanations are repeated as often as necessary to familiarize them with the treatment and decrease their anxiety.

Parents are included in determining the baby's plan of care. Early involvement in the care and decisions regarding their baby provides parents with realistic expectations for their baby. Their daily participation (if possible) is encouraged, as are early and frequent visits. The nurse provides opportunities for parents to touch, hold, talk to, and care for the baby. Parents are started with simple tasks, based on the nurse's assessment of the parent's skill and coping abilities. Early success in performing simple tasks builds parents' confidence in their care-taking abilities.

## PROMOTION OF SENSORY STIMULATION

Within the past 20 years, increased attention has been given to the infant's need for sensory stimulation. Evidence suggests that the infant who receives tactile, kinesthetic, and auditory stimulation has fewer apneic spells, decreased stooling, improved weight gain, and advanced central nervous system (CNS) functioning (Klaus and Kennell 1982).

With prolonged separation and the neonatal intensive care unit (NICU) environment, individualized baby sensory stimulation programs are necessary. The nurse plays a key role in determining the appropriate type and amount of sensory (visual, tactile, and auditory) stimulation.

Research into the unique behavioral characteristics of the preterm infant highlights many responses that reflect disorganization of the autonomic system. This work suggests that some preterm infants are not developmentally able to deal with more than one sensory input at a time. The Assessment of Preterm Infant Behavior (APIB) scale (Als et al 1982) identifies the individual preterm newborn behaviors according to five areas of development. The preterm baby's behavioral reactions to stimulation are observed, and developmental interventions are then based on reducing stress and optimizing the newborn's behavioral organization (Cole and Frappier 1985). Parents are ideally equipped to meet the baby's need for stimulation. Stroking, rocking, cuddling, singing, and talking can all be an integral part of the baby's care. Visual stimulation in the form of mobiles and en face interaction with the care giver are also important. Teaching the parents to read behavioral cues will help them move at their infant's own pace when providing stimulation.

## PREPARATION FOR DISCHARGE

Parents of preterm babies should receive the same postpartal teaching as any parent taking a new infant home. In preparing for discharge, parents are encouraged to spend time just before discharge caring directly for their baby. This familiarizes the parents with their baby's behavior patterns and helps them establish realistic expectations about the infant.

Discharge instruction includes breast- and bottle-feeding techniques, formula preparation (including bottle sterilization), and vitamin administration. Mothers of preterm babies desiring to breast-feed are taught to pump their breasts to keep the milk flowing and provide milk even before discharge. This activity (pumping) allows breast-feeding after discharge from the hospital. Information on bathing, diapering, hygiene, and normal elimination patterns is given. Parents should be told to expect changes in the color of the baby's stool, number of bowel movements, and timing of elimination when the infant is switched from bottle- to breast-feeding. This information can prevent unnecessary concern by the parents. Normal growth and development patterns, reflexes, and activity for preterm infants are discussed. Care of the preterm infant with complications, prevention of infections, and the need for continued medical follow-up are emphasized.

Families with preterm infants usually do not need to be referred to community agencies, such as visiting nurse assistance. Referral may be necessary if the infant has severe congenital abnormalities, feeding problems, or complications with infections or respiratory problems, or if the parents seem unable to cope with an at-risk baby. Parents of preterm infants can benefit from meeting with others in a similar situation to share common experiences and concerns. Nurses can refer parents to support groups sponsored by the hospital or by others in the community.

## • Evaluation

Anticipated outcomes of nursing care include:

- The preterm newborn is free of respiratory distress and establishes effective respiratory function.

- The preterm newborn gains weight and shows no signs of fatigue and/or aspiration during feedings.

- The parents are able to verbalize their anger and guilt feelings about the birth of a preterm baby and show attachment behavior such as frequent visits and growing confidence in their participatory care activities.

# CARE OF THE NEWBORN OF A SUBSTANCE-ABUSING MOTHER

The newborn of an alcoholic or drug-dependent woman will also be alcohol- or drug-dependent. After birth, when an infant's connection with the maternal blood supply is severed, the neonate suffers withdrawal. In addition, the drugs ingested by the mother may be teratogenic, resulting in congenital anomalies.

## Alcohol Dependency

The **fetal alcohol syndrome** (FAS) described by Jones and colleagues (1973) refers to a series of malformations frequently found in infants born to women who have been chronic severe alcoholics. It has been estimated that the complete FAS syndrome occurs in one or two live births per 1000 with a partial expression frequency at about three to five live births per 1000 (Abel 1985).

Controversy surrounds the exact cause of FAS. Although it is known that ethanol freely crosses the placenta to the fetus, it is still not known whether the alcohol alone or the break-down products of alcohol cause the damage. Alcohol itself may not harm the fetus but rather the breakdown product acetaldehyde, which is cytotoxic and teratogenic (Tanmer 1985). Pregnant women with inherited acquired defects of mitochondrial aldehyde dehydrogenase may have acetaldehyde levels well over the danger limit (35 mol/L) for their fetus, even after modest alcohol intake (Dunn et al 1979). This may explain why "social drinking" can sometimes cause adverse fetal effects, while heavy drinking may have no effect at all on the fetus.

Studies have shown alcohol-induced uterine vessel vasoconstriction, which exposes the fetus to hypoxia (Altura et al 1982).

Other factors in conjunction with alcohol may contribute to the teratogenic effects. These factors include drugs (diazepam, nicotine, and caffeine), in addition to poor diet and low socioeconomic status (Chasnoff 1986). Cavdar (1984) suggests that severe zinc deficiency produced by overconsumption of alcohol may be the major factor leading to dysmorphogenesis. This might also account for the association of immune deficiency with FAS, since zinc plays a crucial role in cell-mediated immune functions.

### LONG-TERM COMPLICATIONS

The long-term prognosis for the FAS neonate is less than favorable. Most infants with FAS are growth-deficient at birth and do not demonstrate postnatal catch-up growth (Chasnoff 1986). In fact most FAS infants are evaluated for failure to thrive. It has been found that decreased adipose tissue is a constant feature of persons with FAS.

These infants have a delay in the normal progression of oral feeding development but have a normal progression of oral motor function. Many FAS infants nurse poorly and have persistent vomiting until six to seven months of age. They have difficulty adjusting to solid foods and show little spontaneous interest in food (Streissguth and LaDue 1985).

Central nervous system dysfunctions are the most common and serious problem associated with FAS. Most children exhibiting FAS are mildly to severely mentally retarded. The more abnormal the facial features, the lower the IQ scores. Providing a better environment for FAS infants has not been found to have an influence on IQ (Iosub et al 1981), which indicates that the brain damage occurred prenatally. These children are often hyperactive and show a high incidence of speech and language abnormalities indicative of CNS disorders.

### MEDICAL THERAPY

Prevention of alcohol-induced complications is the foremost goal of medical therapy. This can be accomplished by educating the pregnant woman about the risks of alcohol ingestion and having the woman eliminate, or at least significantly reduce, her alcohol intaken (Rosett et al 1983, Larsson et al 1985).

The medical goal during the neonatal period is the management of CNS dysfunction and withdrawal. Seizures are treated with phenobarbital or diazepam.

### NURSING ASSESSMENT

Newborns with FAS show the following characteristics:

- *Abnormal structural development and CNS dysfunction,* including mental retardation, microcephaly, and hyperactivity.

- *Growth deficiencies.* Infants with FAS are often IUGR with weight, length, and head circumference being affected. These infants continue to show a persistent postnatal growth deficiency, with weight being more affected than linear growth.

- *Distinctive facial abnormalities.* These include short palpebral fissures, midfacial and maxillary hypoplasia, micrognathia, hypoplastic upper lip, and diminished or absent philtrum.

- *Associated anomalies.* Abnormalities affecting cardiac (primarily septal), ocular, renal, and skeletal (especially involving joints, such as congenital dislocated hips) systems are often noted.

- *Sensorineural hearing loss* has also been documented (Church and Gerkin 1988).

Withdrawal symptoms of the alcohol-dependent neonate have been documented in children with normal facial features as well as in those with the typical features of FAS (Coles et al 1984). These symptoms include tremors, seizures, sleeplessness, unconsolable crying, abnormal reflexes, activeness with little ability to maintain alertness and attentiveness to environment, abdominal distention, and exaggerated mouthing behaviors such as hyperactive rooting and increased nonnutritive sucking (Clarren et al 1985).

Signs and symptoms of withdrawal often appear within 6 to 12 hours and at least within the first three days of life. Seizures after the neonatal period are rare. Alcohol dependence in the infant is physiologic, not psychologic.

### NURSING DIAGNOSIS

Nursing diagnoses that may apply to the FAS newborn include:

- Altered nutrition: less than body requirements related to decreased food intake and hyperirritability

- Potential for injury related to seizure activity secondary to CNS dysfunction or chemical dependence

- Ineffective family coping related to potential developmental delay and/or guilt over the diagnosis

### NURSING PLAN AND IMPLEMENTATION

#### Promotion of Physical Well-Being

The nurse's awareness of the signs and symptoms of fetal alcohol effects is important in structuring and guiding nursing care. Nursing care of the FAS newborn is aimed at avoiding heat loss, protecting the infant from injury during seizures, administering medications such as phenobarbital or diazepam to limit convulsions, monitoring intravenous fluid therapy, and reducing environmental stimuli. The FAS baby is most comfortable in a quiet, dimly lit environment. Because of their feeding problems, these infants require extra time and patience during feedings.

Mothers should be informed that breast-feeding is not contraindicated but that excessive alcohol consumption may intoxicate the newborn and inhibit the letdown reflex. The nurse must monitor the newborn's vital signs closely and observe for evidence of seizure activity and respiratory distress.

#### Promotion of Family Adaptation

Infants affected by maternal alcohol abuse are also at risk psychologically. Restlessness, sleeplessness, agitation, resistance to cuddling or holding, and frequent crying can be frustrating to parents as their efforts to relieve the distress are unrewarded. Feeding dysfunction can also result in frustrations for the care giver and digestive upsets for the infant. Frustration may cause the parents to punish the baby or result in the unconscious desire to "stay away from the infant." Either outcome may create an unstable family environment, and result in the infant's failure to thrive.

The nurse should focus on providing support for the parents and reinforcing positive parenting activity. Prior to discharge, parents are provided with opportunities to provide baby care so that they can feel confident in their interpretations of their baby's cues and ability to meet the baby's needs. Referring the family to social services and visiting nurse or public health nurse associations is essential for the well-being of the infant. Follow-up care and teaching can strengthen the parents' skill and coping abilities and help them create a stable, healthy environment for their family.

### EVALUATION

Anticipated outcomes of nursing care include:

- The FAS newborn is able to tolerate feedings and gain weight.

- The FAS infant's hyperirritability and/or seizures are controlled and the baby has suffered no physical injuries.

- The parents are able to identify the special needs of their newborn and accept outside assistance as needed.

## • Drug Dependency

**Drug-dependent infants** are predisposed to a number of problems. Since almost all narcotic drugs cross the placenta and enter the fetal circulation, the fetus can develop problems in utero and/or soon after birth.

The greatest risks to the fetus of the drug-dependent mother are:

- Intrauterine asphyxia—often a direct result of fetal withdrawal secondary to maternal withdrawal. Fetal withdrawal is accompanied by hyperactivity with increased oxygen consumption, which, if not adequately compensated, can lead to fetal asphyxia. Moreover, narcotic-addicted women tend to have a higher incidence of PIH, abruptio placentae, and placenta previa, resulting in placental insufficiency and fetal asphyxia.

- Intrauterine infection—particularly sexually transmitted disease and hepatitis—is often connected with the pregnant addict's life-style. Such infections can involve the fetus.

- Alterations in birth weight—may depend on the type of drug the mother uses. Women using predominantly heroin have infants of lower birth weight who are SGA, whereas women maintained on methadone have higher-birth-weight infants, some of whom are LGA (Merker et al 1985).

- Low Apgar scores—may be related to the intrauterine asphyxia or the medication the woman received during labor. The use of a narcotic antagonist (nalorphine or naloxone) to reverse respiratory depression is contraindicated, as it may precipitate acute withdrawal in the infant.

## COMMON COMPLICATIONS OF THE DRUG-ADDICTED NEWBORN

The newborn of a woman who abused drugs during her pregnancy is predisposed to the following problems:

- *Respiratory distress.* The addicted newborn frequently suffers respiratory stress, mainly meconium-aspiration pneumonia and transient tachypnea. Meconium aspiration is usually secondary to increased oxygen consumption and activity experienced by the fetus during intrauterine withdrawal. Transient tachypnea may develop secondary to the inhibitory effects of narcotics on the reflex responsible for clearing the lungs. Respiratory distress syndrome occurs less in heroin-addicted newborns even in the presence of prematurity because they have tissue-oxygen unloading capabilities comparable to those of a six-week-old term infant. In addition, heroin stimulates production of glucocorticoids via the anterior pituitary gland.

- *Jaundice.* Newborns of methadone-addicted women may develop jaundice due to prematurity. Heroin contributes to early maturity of the liver, leading to a lower incidence of hyperbilirubinemia for these babies.

- *Congenital anomalies.* The incidence of anomalies of the genitourinary and cardiovascular systems is slightly increased in infants of drug-addicted mothers.

- *Behavioral abnormalities.* Babies exposed to cocaine have poor state organization and decreased interactive behaviors when tested with the Brazelton Neonatal Behavioral Assessment Scale (Chasnoff 1986).

- *Withdrawal.* The most significant postnatal problem of the drug-addicted newborn is that of narcotic withdrawal (usually from heroin or methadone). The onset of the withdrawal manifestations usually occurs within the first 72 hours after birth. For heroin-addicted newborns a majority of withdrawal symptoms are seen within the first 24 to 48 hours. For newborns exposed to barbiturates, symptoms may be delayed for several days. Withdrawal for cocaine-addicted infants may occur four to five days after birth. For methadone-addicted infants, withdrawal may be delayed two to three weeks but can occur earlier. In most cases, the withdrawal manifestations peak in the newborn about the third day and subside by the fifth to seventh day. There is an increased frequency of withdrawal in infants born to women maintained on more than 50 mg of methadone. Women on methadone doses of less than 20 mg/day at the time of delivery have reduced incidence of neonatal withdrawal (Chasnoff 1986).

## LONG-TERM COMPLICATIONS

The physical and mental development of infants of drug-addicted mothers falls within normal limits up to two years of age. Although these infants demonstrate higher incidence of gastrointestinal and respiratory illnesses, it is believed these are related not to narcotic addiction but to lack of education regarding proper infant care, feeding, and hygiene. Another important problem is the high incidence of SIDS (sudden infant death syndrome) among newborns born to opiate-addicted mothers, with infants born to cocaine-addicted mothers having even higher risk (Chasnoff 1986). The occurrence of SIDS may be even higher in those infants who have moderate-to-severe postnatal withdrawal.

## MEDICAL THERAPY

The goal of medical therapy is prevention through prenatal management (see Chapter 12) and pharmacologic management of neonatal narcotic withdrawal. For optimal fetal and neonatal outcome, the narcotic-addicted woman should receive complete prenatal care as soon as possible. She should be started on a methadone program with a reduction in dosage to 20 mg or less, if possible. The aim of methadone maintenance during pregnancy is the prevention of heroin use. The dose of methadone used for maintenance should be sufficient to ensure this goal even if the dose is greater than 20 mg. It is not recommended that the woman be withdrawn completely from narcotics while pregnant since this induces fetal withdrawal with poor newborn outcomes.

About 50% of newborns of addicted mothers experience withdrawal symptoms severe enough to require treatment. Drugs to control withdrawal symptoms are phenobarbital or paregoric. Nutritional support is important in light of the increase in energy expenditure that withdrawal may entail. The American Academy of Pediatrics (1983) recommends use of a formula that supplies 24 calories per ounce to provide 150 to 250 cal/kg/day.

## NURSING ASSESSMENT

Early identification of the newborn needing medical or pharmacologic interventions decreases the incidence of mortality and morbidity. During the newborn period, nursing assessment focuses on:

- Discovering the mother's last drug intake and dosage level. This is accomplished through the perinatal history and laboratory tests.

- Assessing the complications related to intrauterine withdrawal such as SGA, intrauterine asphyxia, and prematurity.

- Identifying the signs and symptoms of newborn drug withdrawal, which can be classified in five groups:

1. Central nervous system signs
   a. Hyperactivity
   b. Hyperirritability (persistent high-pitched cry)
   c. Increased muscle tone
   d. Exaggerated reflexes
   e. Tremors, seizures
   f. Sneezing, hiccups, yawning
   g. Short, unquiet sleep
   h. Fever
2. Respiratory signs
   a. Tachypnea
   b. Excessive secretions
3. Gastrointestinal signs
   a. Disorganized, vigorous suck
   b. Vomiting
   c. Drooling
   d. Sensitive gag reflex
   e. Hyperphagia
   f. Diarrhea
   g. Abdominal cramping
4. Vasomotor signs
   a. Stuffy nose, yawning, sneezing
   b. Flushing
   c. Sweating
   d. Sudden, circumoral pallor
5. Cutaneous signs
   a. Excoriated buttocks, knees, elbows
   b. Facial scratches
   c. Pressure point abrasions

Although many of the signs and symptoms of narcotic withdrawal are similar to those seen with hypoglycemia and hypocalcemia, glucose and calcium values are reported to be within normal limits for these infants (Chasnoff 1986).

## NURSING DIAGNOSIS

Nursing diagnoses that may apply to drug-dependent newborns include:

- Fluid volume deficit, and altered nutrition: less than body requirements related to vomiting and diarrhea, uncoordinated suck and swallow reflex, hypertonia secondary to withdrawal

- Pain related to skin excoriation over bony prominences secondary to constant activity

- Altered parenting related to hyperirritable behavior

## NURSING PLAN AND IMPLEMENTATION
### Promotion of Physical Well-Being

Care of the drug-dependent newborn is based on reducing withdrawal symptoms and promoting adequate respiration, temperature, and nutrition. Specific nursery care measures include:

- Temperature regulation
- Careful monitoring of pulse and respirations every 15 minutes until stable; stimulation if apnea occurs
- Small frequent feedings, especially in the presence of vomiting, regurgitation, and diarrhea
- Intravenous therapy as needed
- Medications as ordered, such as phenobarbital, paregoric, diazepam (Valium), or chlorpromazine hydrochloride (Thorazine). Methadone should not be given because of possible neonatal addiction to it
- Proper positioning on the right side to avoid possible aspiration of vomitus or secretions
- Observation for problems of SGA or LGA newborns
- Swaddling to minimize injury

### Promotion of Family Adaptation

Parents should be prepared for what they can expect for the first few months at home. At the time of discharge the mother should be instructed to anticipate mild jitteriness and irritability in the newborn, which may persist from 8 to 16 weeks, depending on the initial severity of the withdrawal. The nurse should help the mother learn feeding techniques and comforting measures. Parents are to be counseled regarding available resources, such as support groups, and signs and symptoms that indicate the need for further care. Ongoing evaluation is necessary because of the potential for long-term problems.

## EVALUATION

Anticipated outcomes of nursing care include:

- The newborn tolerates feedings, gains weight, and has a decreased number of stools.
- The parents learn ways to comfort their newborn.
- The parents are able to cope with their frustrations and begin to use outside resources as needed.

## • CARE OF THE NEWBORN WITH COLD STRESS

**Cold stress** is excessive heat loss resulting in the use of compensatory mechanisms (increased respirations and nonshivering thermogenesis) to maintain core body temperature. Heat loss that results in cold stress occurs in the newborn through the mechanisms of evaporation, convection, conduction, and radiation. (See Chapter 20, p 556 for types of heat loss.) Heat loss at the time of birth that

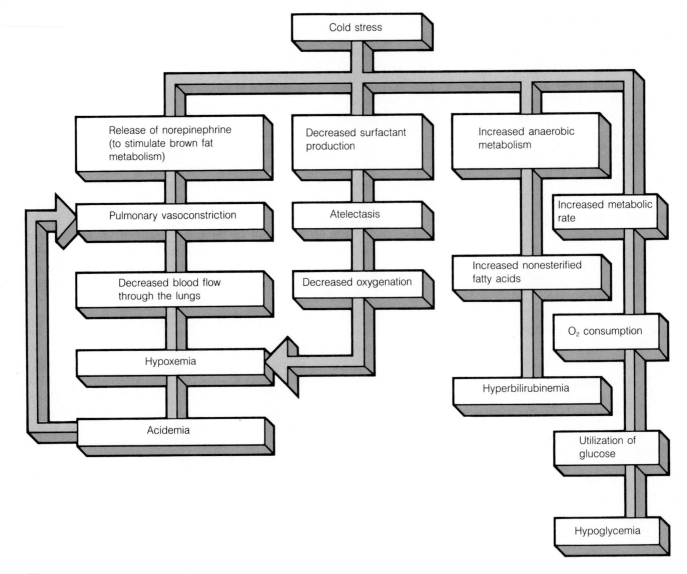

*Figure 24.10  Cold stress schematic*

leads to cold stress can play a significant role in the severity of RDS and the ultimate outcome for the infant.

The amount of heat lost by an infant depends to a large extent on the actions of the nurse or care giver. Both preterm and SGA newborns are at risk for cold stress because they have decreased adipose tissue, brown fat stores, and glycogen available for metabolism.

As discussed in Chapter 20, the newborn infant's major source of heat production in nonshivering thermogenesis (NST) is brown fat metabolism. This metabolism is impaired in the presence of several conditions including hypoxemia (Po₂ less than 50), intracranial hemorrhage or any CNS abnormality, and hypoglycemia (<40 mg%).

When these conditions occur, the infant's temperature should be monitored more closely and the neutral thermal environment conscientiously maintained. The nurse must recognize these conditions and treat them as soon as possible.

The metabolic consequences of cold stress can be devastating and potentially fatal to an infant. Oxygen requirements are raised, glucose use increases, acids are released into the bloodstream, and surfactant production decreases. The effects are graphically depicted in Figure 24.10.

● *Nursing Assessment*

The nurse observes for signs of cold stress. These include increased respirations, decrease in skin temperature, decrease in peripheral perfusion, appearance of hypoglycemia, and the possible development of metabolic acidosis.

Skin temperature assessments are used because initial response to cold stress is vasoconstriction, resulting in a decrease in skin temperature; therefore, monitoring rectal temperature is not satisfactory. A decrease in rectal temperature represents long-standing cold stress with decompensation in the infant's ability to maintain core body temperature.

If a decrease in skin temperature is noted, the nurse determines whether hypoglycemia is present. Hypoglycemia is a result of the metabolic effects of cold stress and is suggested by glucose strip values below 45 mg/mL, tremors, irritability or lethargy, apnea, or seizure activity.

## • Nursing Care

If cold stress occurs, the following nursing interventions should be initiated:

● The newborn is warmed slowly since rapid temperature elevation may cause apnea.

● Skin temperature is monitored every 15 minutes to determine if the infant's temperature is increasing.

● The infant is placed and maintained in a neutral thermal environment.

The presence of anaerobic metabolism is assessed and interventions initiated for the resulting metabolic acidosis. Attempts to burn brown fat increase oxygen consumption, lactic acid levels, and metabolic acidosis. Hypoglycemia may be reversed by adequate glucose intake. See p 720 for interventions.

## • CARE OF THE NEWBORN WITH AIDS

An increasing number of newborns are being born with or acquiring AIDS in the newborn period or early infancy. Perinatal and neonatal modes of transmission have been identified as transplacental, breast-feeding, and /or contaminated blood. For discussion of fetal/neonatal AIDS characteristics see Chapter 12.

Since June 1981, 851 cases of children with AIDS under age 13 have been reported to the Centers for Disease Control (CDC). Of the total 851 cases, 76.5% of the children were born to parents with or at risk of AIDS and 60% of these children have died (CDC 1988). Eighty-five percent of the 851 children were under five years of age when diagnosed. Perinatally acquired AIDS, if acquired during early gestation, usually presents clinically at two to four months of age (Berry 1988). Early identification of babies with or at risk for AIDS is essential in the newborn period. Diagnosis may be made by doing an ELISA test followed by the Western Blot test. These tests show antibodies to the AIDS virus; some false positives can occur in infants who still have maternal antibodies in their blood. Therefore, babies should be retested after six months of age. Opportunistic diseases such as gram-negative sepsis are the primary cause of mortality.

## • Nursing Assessment

Many newborns with AIDS are premature and/or SGA and show failure to thrive during neonatal and infant life. They can show signs and symptoms of disease within days of delivery. Signs that may be seen in the newborn period include: failure to thrive, enlarged spleen and liver, swollen glands, interstitial pneumonia (rarely seen in adults), recurrent GI (diarrhea and weight loss) and urinary system infections, chronic cough, evidence of Epstein-Barr virus, developmental delays, neurologic deficits and/or microcephaly (Berry 1988). Some cranial and facial stigmas have been associated with AIDS contracted in utero (Klug 1986). These features are: prominent boxlike forehead, increased distance between inner canthuses of the eyes, mild obliquity of the eyes, flattened nasal bridge, prominent triangular philtrum, and patulous lips.

## • Nursing Diagnosis

Nursing diagnoses that may apply to the infant with AIDS include:

● Altered nutrition: less than body requirements related to formula intolerance and inadequate intake

● Impaired skin integrity related to chronic diarrhea

● Potential for infection related to AIDS immunosuppression

● Impaired physical mobility related to decreased neuromuscular development

● Altered growth and development related to lack of attachment and stimulation

● Altered parenting related to diagnosis of AIDS

## • Nursing Care

AIDS newborn nursing care involves normal newborn care or the care required for a newborn in a NICU. In addition, the nurse must include care for a newborn suspected of having a blood-borne infection, as with hepatitis B. The major goals of nursing care involve providing for comfort, keeping the newborn well nourished and protected from opportunistic infections, and facilitating growth, development, and attachment. See Essential Facts to Remember—Issues for Care Givers to Infants with AIDS.

### PARENT EDUCATION

Hand washing is crucial when caring for newborns  with AIDS. Parents should be taught proper hand-washing technique. Nutrition is essential since failure to thrive and weight loss are common. Small, frequent feedings and food supplementation are helpful. The nurse should discuss sanitary formula preparation with parents. The baby should not be put to bed with juice or formula because of

# Essential Facts to Remember

## Issues for Care Givers to Infants with AIDS

| | |
|---|---|
| Resuscitation | For suctioning, use a bulb syringe, mucus extractor, or meconium aspirator with wall suction on low setting. |
| Admission care | To remove blood from baby's skin, give warm water, mild soap bath as soon as possible after admission. |
| Hand washing | Thorough hand washing is indicated before and after caring for infant. Hands must be washed immediately if potentially contaminated with blood or body fluids. |
| Gowns | Long-sleeved gowns are indicated when at bedside. |
| Gloves | Gloves are indicated when touching blood or body fluids, ie, changing diapers. Gloves should also be worn when handling newborns before and during their initial baths. |
| Mask | Not routinely needed. Masks are indicated if mouth is likely to come in contact with body fluids (eg, when caring for intubated or coughing child who has copious secretions) or if caretaker feels she is infectious, thereby posing risk to infant. |
| Goggles | Not routinely needed. Goggles are indicated if eyes are likely to come in contact with body fluids (eg, when caring for intubated or coughing child who has copious secretions). If glasses are worn, goggles are not necessary. |
| Needles and syringes | Care should be taken to avoid needlestick injuries. Used needles should not be recapped or bent; they should be placed in a prominently labeled, puncture-resistant plastic container designed specifically for such disposal and belonging specifically to that infant. After the infant is discharged, the container is discarded. |
| Specimens | Blood and other specimens should be double-bagged and/or sealed in an impervious container and labeled "blood/body fluids precautions." |
| Equipment and linen | Articles contaminated with blood or body fluids should be discarded or bagged according to isolation protocol of institution and labeled "blood/body fluids precautions" before being sent for decontamination and reprocessing. |
| Body fluid spills | Blood and body fluid spills should be cleaned promptly with a solution of 5.25% sodium hypochlorite (household bleach) diluted 1:10 with water. |
| Breast milk storage | Individually bag each child's milk container. |
| Education and support | Provide education and psychological support for family and staff. Care givers who avoid contact with baby at risk or who overdress in unnecessary isolation garb subtly exacerbate an already difficult family situation. Information resources include the National AIDS Hotline (1-800-342-2437). |
| Exempted personnel | Immunologically compromised staff (pregnant women may be included in this group) and possibly infectious staff members should not care for these infants. |

*Adapted from Inglis AD and Lozano M: AIDS and the neonatal ICU.* Neonatal Network *December 1986; p 39; and Berry RK: Home care of the child with AIDS.* Pediatric Nursing *July/August 1988; 14(4):341–44.*

potential bacteria growth. Unpasteurized milk and milk products must not be used since they are associated with intestinal infections (salmonella).

Parents need to be alert to the signs of feeding intolerance such as increasing regurgitation, abdominal distention, and loose stools. The newborn should be weighed three times a week.

Prompt diaper changing and perineal care can prevent or minimize diaper rash and promote comfort. It is impor-

tant to remember that the diaper-changing area in the home should be separate from the food preparation and serving areas. Disposable diapers are recommended over cloth diapers (Berry 1988). The diapers are to be placed in plastic bags, sealed, and placed in the garbage can daily. Disposable gloves are worn when changing diapers or cleaning the diaper area, especially in the presence of diarrhea. Good skin care is essential to prevent skin rashes.

The baby should have his or her own skin care items,

towels, and washcloths. Most clothing and linens can be washed with other household laundry. Linen that is visibly soiled with blood or body fluids should be kept separate and washed separately in hot sudsy water with household bleach. Diaper-changing areas should be cleaned with a 1:10 dilution of household bleach after each diaper change. Toys should be kept as clean as possible, and they should not be shared with other children. Toys should be checked for sharp edges to prevent scratches.

Parents should be instructed on what signs of infection to be alerted to and when to call their health care provider. Topical mycostatin ointment is used for diaper rashes and oral mycostatin for oral thrush. If diarrhea occurs, the baby requires frequent perineal care and fluid replacements. Antidiarrheal medications are often ineffective. Irritability may be the first sign of fever. Rectal temperatures should be avoided, as they may stimulate diarrhea. Tepid water sponging, fluids, and antipyretics are of use in managing fever.

Parents and family members need to be reassured that there are no documented cases of people contracting AIDS from routine care of infected babies. Emotional support for the family is essential because of the stress and social isolation they may face. Because of these stresses, attachment may not occur and/or the infant may suffer from lack of sensory and tactile stimulation. Babies should be held for feedings and benefit from frequent, gentle touch. Auditory stimulation may also be provided using music or tapes of parents' voices. Families should be informed about support groups, available counseling, and information resources.

## ● CARE OF THE NEWBORN AT RISK DUE TO ASPHYXIA

Neonatal asphyxia results from circulatory, respiratory, and biochemical factors.

Circulatory patterns that accompany asphyxia indicate an inability to make the transition to extrauterine circulation—in effect a return to fetal circulatory patterns. Failure of lung expansion and establishment of respiration rapidly produces hypoxia (decreased $Pao_2$), acidosis (decreased pH), and hypercarbia (increased $Pco_2$). These biochemical changes result in pulmonary vasoconstriction, with retention of high pulmonary vascular resistance, hypoperfusion of the lungs, and a large right-to-left shunt through the ductus arteriosus. The foramen ovale opens (as right atrial pressure exceeds left atrial pressure), and blood flows from right to left.

Biochemical changes that occur in asphyxia contribute to these circulatory changes. The most serious biochemical abnormality is a change from aerobic to anaerobic metabolism in the presence of hypoxia. This results in the accumulation of lactate and the development of metabolic acidosis. A concomitant respiratory acidosis may also occur due to a rapid increase in $Pco_2$ during asphyxia. In response to hypoxia and anaerobic metabolism, the amounts of free fatty acids and glycerol in the blood increase. Glycogen stores are also mobilized to provide a continuous glucose source for the brain. Rapid use of hepatic and cardiac stores of glycogen may occur during an asphyxial attack.

The neonate is supplied with several protective mechanisms against hypoxial insults (Klaus and Fanaroff 1986): a relatively immature brain and a resting metabolic rate less than that observed in the adult, an ability to mobilize substances within the body for anaerobic metabolism and use the energy more efficiently, and an intact circulatory system able to redistribute lactate and hydrogen ion in tissues still being perfused. Unfortunately, severe prolonged hypoxia will overcome these protective mechanisms, resulting in brain damage or death of the neonate.

The newborn who is apneic at birth requires immediate resuscitative efforts. The need for resuscitation can be anticipated if specific risk factors are present during the pregnancy or labor and birth period.

## ● Risk Factors Predisposing to Asphyxia

Need for resuscitation may be anticipated if the mother demonstrates the risk factors antepartally and intrapartally described in Tables 7.1 and 15.1. Neonatal risk factors for resuscitation are:

- Fetal heart rate changes
- Difficult birth
- Fetal blood loss
- Apneic episode unresponsive to tactile stimulation
- Cardiac arrest
- Inadequate ventilation

Particular attention must be paid to at-risk pregnancies during the intrapartal period. Labor and delivery are asphyxiating processes and often the at-risk fetus has less tolerance to the stress of labor and birth. At times no risk factors prenatally may be apparent.

## ● Medical Therapy

The initial goal of medical management is to identify the fetus at risk for asphyxia, so that resuscitative efforts can begin at birth.

Fetal biophysical assessment (see Chapter 13, p 353) and monitoring (fetal and maternal pH and blood gases) during the intrapartal period may help identify fetal distress. If fetal distress is present, appropriate measures can be taken to deliver the fetus immediately, before major damage occurs, and to treat the asphyxiated newborn.

Fetal scalp blood sampling (p 478), may indicate asphyxic insult and related degree of fetal acidosis if considered in relation to stage of labor, uterine contractions, and ominous fetal heart rate (FHR) patterns. Normal fetal pH ranges from 7.3 to 7.35. The pH falls gradually during the first stage of labor. During the second stage and birth, it decreases more drastically. The stress of labor causes an intermittent decrease in exchange of gases in the placental intervillous space, which causes a fall in pH and fetal acidosis. The acidosis is primarily metabolic rather than respiratory, because exchange of $CO_2$ is more rapid than exchange of hydrogen ions in the placenta.

During labor, a fetal pH of 7.25 or higher is considered normal. A pH value of 7.21–7.24 is considered as "preacidosis." A pH value of 7.20 or less is considered an ominous sign of fetal asphyxia (Bowen et al 1986). However, low fetal pH without associated hypoxia can be caused by maternal acidosis secondary to prolonged labor, dehydration, and maternal lactate production. Simultaneous testing of maternal venous pH and fetal pH may help to rule out contributing maternal acidosis or to identify maternal alkalosis, which might result in a false normal fetal pH in the presence of fetal compromise.

The treatment of fetal/newborn asphyxia is resuscitation. The goal of resuscitation is to provide an adequate airway with expansion of the lungs, to decrease the $P_{CO_2}$ and increase the $P_{O_2}$, to support adequate cardiac output, and to minimize oxygen consumption by reducing heat loss (Avery and Taeusch 1984).

Initial resuscitative management of the neonate is extremely important. The infant should be kept in a head-down position prior to the first gasp to avoid aspiration of the oropharyngeal secretions. The oropharynx and nasopharynx must be suctioned immediately. Clearing the nasal and oral passages of fluid that may obstruct the air-way establishes a patent airway. Suction is always performed before resuscitation so that mucus, blood, and meconium, are not aspirated into the lungs.

After the first few breaths, the infant is kept in a flat position under a radiant heat source and is dried quickly to maintain skin temperature at about 36.5°C (97.7°F). Drying is also a good stimulation to breathing. Heat loss through evaporation is tremendous during the first few minutes of life. The temperature of a wet 1500 g baby in a 16°C (62°F) delivery room drops 1°C every three minutes. Hypothermia increases oxygen consumption and increases the hypoxic insult and may lead to severe acidosis and development of respiratory distress.

Appraisal of the infant's need for resuscitation begins at the time of birth. The time of the first gasp, first cry, and onset of sustained respirations should be noted in order of occurrence. The Apgar score (p 437) is important in determining the severity of neonatal depression and the immediate course of necessary action (Table 24.2).

Breathing is established by employing the simplest form of resuscitative measures initially, with progression to more complicated methods as required.

1. Simple stimulation is provided by rubbing the back.

2. If respirations have not been initiated or are inadequate (gasping or occasional respirations), the lungs must be inflated with positive pressure. The mask is positioned securely on the face (over nose and mouth, avoiding the eyes) with head in "sniffing" or neutral position (Figure 24.11). Hyperextension of the infant's neck will obstruct the trachea. An airtight connection is made between the infant's face and the mask (thus allowing the bag to inflate). The lungs are inflated rhythmically by squeezing the bag. Oxygen

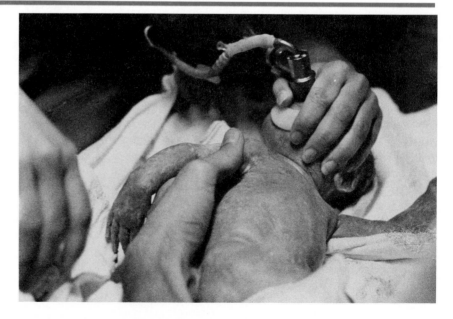

*Figure 24.11  Resuscitation of infant with bag and mask. Note that the mask covers the nose and mouth and the head is in a neutral position.*

## Table 24.2 Guidelines for Resuscitation of the Neonate

| Apgar score | Heart rate | Arterial blood pH* | Appearance | Resuscitative measures |
|---|---|---|---|---|
| 9 or 10 | >100 | 7.30–7.40 (normal) | Regular respirations; flexed extremities; cries in response to flicking of soles of feet; may be dusky or show acrocyanosis | Place under radiant heat source and dry immediately; gently suction airway. |
| 7 or 8 | 60–100 | 7.20–7.29 (slight acidosis) | Decreased tone, cyanotic, or dusky and dyspneic; respirations may be shallow, irregular, or gasping; heart rate is normal; fair response to flicking of sole | Dry and place under warmer; give oxygen near face. |
| 5 or 6 | 60–100 | 7.10–7.19 (moderate acidosis) | Same as for Apgar 7 or 8 | Dry and place under warmer; clear airway and stimulate through drying process. If still not improved, place in "sniff" position and begin ventilation (100% $O_2$) with bag and mask, using pressure of 30 cm $H_2O$ at rate of 30–50 per min. If difficulty persists, reevaluate maternal history of drug administration, especially if heart rate responds to ventilation but there is no spontaneous respiration. Give narcotic antagonist (Narcan) if indicated. Mildly depressed newborns will usually develop regular spontaneous respirations within five minutes. If tracheal aspiration reveals blood or meconium, directly visualize with laryngoscope and suction as needed before administering positive pressure. |
| 3 or 4 | <60 | 7.00–7.09 (marked acidosis) | White and limp, little or no respiratory effort Jaw is slack during suctioning | For Apgar 3–4: Dry under warmer; clear airway; consider immediate intubation. |
| 0 to 2 | <60 | <7.00 (severe acidosis) | Same as for Apgar 3 or 4 | Hold $O_2$ near face during intubation. Ventilate after direct visualization with laryngoscope and appropriate suctioning. Check breath sounds. If heart rate remains low (0–<60), immediately institute external cardiac massage. Correction of hypotension is usually via umbilical vein. Obtain blood gas values (pH, $Pco_2$, $Po_2$) and BP. |

*Correlations of Apgar score and arterial blood pH adapted from Sailing E: Technical and theoretical problems in electronic monitoring of the human fetal heart. *Int J Gynecol Obstet* 1972; 10:211, and from Korones S: *High-Risk Newborn Infants: The Basis for Intensive Nursing Care,* 3rd ed. St Louis: Mosby, 1986.

can be delivered at 100% with an anesthesia or Laerdal bag and adequate liter flow, whereas an Ambu or Hope bag delivers only 40% oxygen, unless it has been adapted. In addition, it may not be possible to maintain adequate inspiratory pressure with Ambu or Hope bags. In a crisis situation it is crucial that 100% $O_2$ be delivered with adequate pressure.

3. The rise and fall of the chest is observed for proper ventilation. Air entry and heart rate are checked by auscultation. Manual resuscitation is coordinated with any voluntary efforts. The rate of ventilation should be between 30 and 50 breaths per minute. Pressure should be less than 30 cm of $H_2O$. If ventilation is adequate, the chest moves with each inspiration, bilateral breath sounds are audible, and the lips and mucous membranes become pink. If color and heart rate fail to respond to ventilatory efforts, poor or improper placement of an endotracheal tube may be the cause; if the neonate is intubated properly, failure to respond may result from pneumothorax, diaphragmatic hernia, or hypoplastic lungs (Potter's syndrome). Distention of the stomach is controlled by inserting a nasogastric tube for decompression.

4. Intubation is rarely needed. Most newborns can be resuscitated by bag and mask ventilation.

Once breathing has been established, the heart rate should increase to over 100 beats/min. If the heart is less than 60 beats/min, external cardiac massage is begun. (Cardiac massage is commenced immediately if there is no detectable heart beat.)

1. The infant is positioned *properly* on a firm surface.

2. The resuscitator uses two fingers, or may stand at the foot of the infant and place both thumbs at the junction of the middle and lower third of the sternum, with the fingers wrapped around and supporting the back.

3. The sternum is depressed approximately two thirds of the distance to the vertebral column (1.0–1.5 cm), at a rate of 80 to 100 beats per minute.

4. A 3:1 ratio of heartbeat (cardiac massage) to assisted ventilation is used.

Drugs that should be available in the birthing area include those needed in the treatment of shock, cardiac arrest, and narcosis. Oxygen, because of its effective use in ventilation, is the drug most often used.

If by five minutes after birth the neonate has not responded to the resuscitation with spontaneous respirations and a heart rate above 100 beats per minute, it may be necessary to correct the acidosis and provide the myocardium with glucose. The most accessible route for administering medications is the umbilical vein. In a severely asphyxiated neonate, sodium bicarbonate (2 to 4 mEq/kg) is given to correct severe metabolic acidosis. If bradycardia is profound, epinephrine (0.01 mL/kg of a 1:10,000 solution) is given through the umbilical vein catheter, the peripheral IV, or the endotracheal tube (if an IV has not been started yet). Bradycardia can also be treated with atropine (0.03 mg/kg intravenously). Calcium gluconate (1 or 2 mL/kg of a 10% solution) intravenously is used for arrhythmias, poor cardiac output despite adequate ventilation, and severe hypocalcemia or hyperkalemia. Dextrose can be given to correct hypoglycemia. Usually a 10% dextrose in water intravenous solution is sufficient to prevent or treat hypoglycemia in the birthing area. Naloxone hydrochloride (0.02 mg/mL neonatal solution intravenously or intramuscularly), a narcotic antagonist, is used to reverse narcotic depression. See Drug Guides—Sodium Bicarbonate and Naloxone.

In the advent of shock (low blood pressure or poor peripheral perfusion) the neonate should be given a volume expander. Fresh frozen plasma, plasminate, packed red blood cells, and whole blood can also be used for volume expansion and treatment of shock.

## ● Nursing Assessment

Communication between the obstetric office or clinic and the birthing area nurse facilitates the identification of potential newborns in need of resuscitation. Upon arrival of the woman in the birthing area, the nurse should have the antepartal record and should note any contributory perinatal history factors and assess present fetal status. As labor progresses, nursing assessments include ongoing monitoring of FHR and its response to contractions, assisting with fetal scalp blood sampling, and observing for the presence of meconium in the amniotic fluid. In addition, the nurse should alert the resuscitation team and the practitioner responsible for care of the neonate of any potential high-risk laboring women.

## ● Nursing Diagnosis

Nursing diagnoses that may apply to the newborn with asphyxia include:

● Ineffective breathing pattern related to lack of spontaneous respirations at birth secondary to in utero asphyxia

● Decreased cardiac output related to impaired oxygenation

● Ineffective family coping related to baby's lack of spontaneous respirations at birth and fear of losing their newborn

## ● Nursing Plan and Implementation
### PREPARATION OF RESUSCITATION EQUIPMENT

Following identification of possible high-risk situations, the next step in effective resuscitation is assembling the necessary equipment and ensuring proper functioning (See Table 24.3). It is desirable to provide for pH and blood gas determination as well. Necessary equipment includes a radiant warmer that provides a servocontrolled

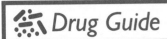 *Drug Guide*

# Sodium Bicarbonate

### Overview of Neonatal Action

Sodium bicarbonate is an alkalizing agent. It buffers hydrogen ions caused by accumulation of lactic acid from anaerobic metabolism occurring during hypoxemia. Sodium bicarbonate thereby raises the blood pH, reversing the metabolic acidosis. Sodium bicarbonate should *only* be used to correct severe metabolic acidosis in asphyxiated newborns once adequate ventilation has been established (Avery 1987).

Note: Sodium bicarbonate dissociates in solution into sodium ion and carbonic acid, which can split into water and carbon dioxide. The carbon dioxide must be eliminated via the respiratory tract.

*Route, Dosage, Frequency*
For resuscitation and severe asphyxiation: intravenous push via umbilical vein catheter for quick infusion. Dosage is 2 mEq/K: 4 mL of 0.5 mEq/mL (4.2%) or 2 mL of mEq/mL (8.4%). 8.4% solution diluted at least 1:1 with sterile water to decrease the osmolarity (Benitz and Tatro 1988); infuse at rate no faster than 1 mEq/kg/min (Avery 1987). Can repeat every 15 minutes if needed for total of four doses. For marked metabolic acidosis: a pH of less than 7.05 and a base deficit of 15 mEq/L or more should be corrected using a 0.5 mEq/mL solution of sodium bicarbonate at a rate of 1 mEq/kg/min or slower. Calculate total dosage by the following formula:
   mEq = 0.3 × weight (kg) × base deficit in mEq/L

*Neonatal Contraindications*
Inadequate respiratory ventilation that causes a rise in $P_{CO_2}$ and a decrease in pH

Presence of edema; metabolic or respiratory alkalosis; and hypocalcemia, anuria, or oliguria

*Neonatal Side Effects*
Hypernatremia, hyperosmolarity, fluid overload

Intracranial hemorrhage (rapid infusion of bicarbonate increases serum osmolarity, causing a shift of interstitial fluid into the blood and capillary rupture) (Benitz and Tatro 1988)

### Nursing Considerations

Assess for any contraindications.

Monitor intake and output rates.

Assess adequacy of ventilation by monitoring respiratory status, rate, and depth; ventilate as necessary.

Dilute bicarbonate prior to administration into umbilical vein catheter (for resuscitation) or peripheral IV to prevent sloughing of tissue.

Evaluate effectiveness of drug by monitoring arterial blood gases for $P_{CO_2}$, bicarbonate concentration, and pH determination.

Sodium bicarbonate is incompatible with acidic solutions.

Administration with calcium creates precipitates.

---

overhead radiant heat source (a thermostatic mechanism that is taped to the infant's abdomen triggers the radiant warmer to turn on or off in order to maintain a level of thermoneutrality), and an open bed for easy access to the newborn. It is essential that the nurse keep the infant warm. The infant is dried quickly to prevent evaporative heat loss and is placed under the radiant warmer.

Resuscitative equipment in the birthing room must be sterilized after each use. In the high-risk nursery the need for resuscitation may occur at any time.

Equipment reliability must be maintained before an emergency arises. The nurse inspects all equipment—bag and mask, oxygen and flow meter, laryngoscope, suction machines—for damaged or nonfunctioning parts before a birth or assembly at the infant's bedside. A systematic check of the emergency cart and equipment should be a routine responsibility of each shift.

## PROVISION AND DOCUMENTATION OF RESUSCITATION

Training and knowledge about resuscitation are vital to personnel in the birth setting for both normal and high-risk births. Since resuscitation is at least a two-person effort, the nurse should call for assistance so that there is adequate staff available. The resuscitative efforts should be recorded on the newborn's chart so that all members of the health care team will have access to this information.

## PARENT EDUCATION

Birth room resuscitation is particularly distressing for the parents. If the need for resuscitation is anticipated, the parents should be assured that a team will be present at the birth to care specifically for their infant. As soon as sta-

## Table 24.3   Newborn Resuscitation Equipment

1. Radiant warmer

2. Stethoscope

3. Bag (that can deliver 100% oxygen)

4. Mask (two mask sizes: one preterm and one newborn)

5. Tubing and pressure gauges for bag

6. Oxygen, flow meter, and provision for warmth and humidification

7. Suction equipment
   a. DeLee trap
   b. Bulb syringe
   c. Mechanical suction apparatus
   d. Suction catheters (No. 5, 6, and 8 Fr)

8. Intubation equipment
   a. Magill forceps
   b. Endotracheal tubes—sizes 2.5, 3.0, 3.5, 4.0 mm (fitted with adapter)
   c. Wire stylets for tubes
   d. Laryngoscope handle with two blades—size 0 (premature), size 1 (newborn)
   e. Four extra batteries
   f. Two extra bulbs

9. Nasogastric tube (for decompression of stomach)

10. Infant plastic airway

11. K-Y lubricating jelly

12. Benzoin

13. Cotton applicators

14. Adhesive tape

15. Scissors

16. Safety pins (for attachments)

17. Syringes (tuberculin, 3, 5, and 10 mL)

18. Umbilical artery catheter tray (No. 3.5 and 5 Fr catheters)

19. IV solution and tubing

20. Drugs (solutions)
    a. Sodium bicarbonate (0.5 mEq/mL)
    b. Epinephrine (0.01 mL/kg of 1:10,000 solution)
    c. Dextrose and water (D/W) (10% D/W for IV for hypoglycemia)
    d. Calcium gluconate (10% solution)
    e. Narcan (0.02 mg/mL neonatal solution)
    f. Volume expanders (plasma or human plasma protein fraction [plasminate])
    g. Normal saline (for suctioning)
    h. Atropine (0.4 mg/0.5 mL)

21. Blood pressure cuff and gauge or pressure transducer

22. Doppler (to measure blood pressure)

23. ECG electrodes and heart rate monitor

bilization is accomplished, a member of the interdisciplinary team should discuss the infant's condition with the parents. The parents may have many fears about the need for resuscitation and the condition of their infant following the resuscitation.

## • Evaluation

Anticipated outcomes of nursing care include:

• The risk of asphyxia is promptly identified, and intervention is started early.

• The newborn's metabolic and physiologic processes are stabilized, and recovery is proceeding without further complications.

• The parents can verbalize the reason for resuscitation and what was done to resuscitate their newborn.

• The parents can verbalize their fears about the resuscitation process and potential implications for their baby's future.

## • CARE OF THE NEWBORN WITH RESPIRATORY DISTRESS

One of the severest conditions to which the newborn may fall victim is respiratory distress—an inappropriate respiratory adaptation to extrauterine life. The nursing care of a baby with respiratory distress requires understanding of the normal pulmonary and circulatory physiology, the pathophysiology of the disease process, clinical manifestations, and supportive and corrective therapies. Only with this knowledge can the nurse make appropriate observations concerning responses to therapy and development of complications. Unlike the verbalizing adult client, the newborn communicates needs only by behavior. The neonatal nurse interprets this behavior as clues about the individual baby's condition.

## • Idiopathic Respiratory Distress Syndrome (Hyaline Membrane Disease)

**Respiratory distress syndrome (RDS),** also referred to as *hyaline membrane disease* (HMD), is a complex disease affecting primarily preterm infants and accounts for approximately 7000 deaths per year in the United States alone. The syndrome occurs more frequently in premature white infants than in black infants and almost twice as often in males as in females.

The factors precipitating the pathologic changes of RDS have not been determined, but two main factors are associated with its development:

## ⚡ Drug Guide

# Naloxone Hydrochloride (Narcan)

### Overview of Neonatal Action

Naloxone hydrochloride (Narcan) is used to reverse respiratory depression due to acute narcotic toxicity. It displaces morphinelike drugs from receptor sites on the neurons; therefore, the narcotics can no longer exert their depressive effects. Naloxone reverses narcotic-induced respiratory depression, analgesia, sedation, hypotension, and pupillary constriction (Berkowitz et al 1981).

### Route, Dosage, Frequency

Intravenous dose is 0.01 mg/kg, usually through umbilical vein, although naloxone can be given intramuscularly. Neonatal dose is supplied as 0.02 mg/mL solution (0.5–1.0 mL for preterms and 2 mL for full-terms). Reversal of drug depression occurs within one to two minutes. The duration of action is variable (minutes to hours) and depends on amount of drug present and rate of excretion; usually the effect lasts approximately four hours (Bhatt et al 1987). Dose may be repeated in five minutes. If no improvement after two or three doses, naloxone administration should be discontinued. If initial reversal occurs, repeat dose as needed.

### Neonatal Contraindications

Must be used with caution in infants of narcotic-addicted mothers as it may precipitate acute withdrawal syndrome.

Respiratory depression resulting from nonmorphine drugs such as sedatives, hypnotics, anesthetics, or other nonnarcotic CNS depressants.

### Neonatal Side Effects

Excessive doses may result in irritability and increased crying, and possibly prolongation of PTT.

Tachycardia

### Nursing Considerations

Monitor respirations closely—rate and depth.

Assess for return of respiratory depression when naloxone effects wear off and effects of longer-acting narcotic reappear.

Have resuscitative equipment, $O_2$, and ventilatory equipment available.

Monitor bleeding studies.

Naloxone hydrochloride is incompatible with alkaline solutions.

---

1. *Prematurity.* All preterm newborns—whether AGA, SGA, or LGA—and especially IDMs are at risk for RDS. The incidence of RDS increases with the degree of prematurity, with most deaths occurring in newborns weighing less than 1500 g. The maternal and fetal factors resulting in preterm labor and birth, complications of pregnancy, cesarean birth (indications for), and familial tendency are all associated with RDS.

2. *Asphyxia.* Asphyxia, with a corresponding decrease in pulmonary blood flow, may interfere with surfactant production

Development of RDS indicates a failure to synthesize lecithin, which is required to maintain alveolar stability. Upon expiration this instability increases atelectasis, which causes hypoxia and acidosis. These inhibit surfactant production and cause pulmonary vasoconstriction. The resulting lung instability causes the biochemical problems of hypoxemia (decreased $P_{O_2}$), hypercarbia (increased $P_{CO_2}$), and acidemia (decreased pH), which further increases pulmonary vasoconstriction and hypoperfusion. The cycle of

events of RDS leading to eventual respiratory failure is diagrammed in Figure 24.12.

Because of these pathophysiologic conditions, the neonate must expend increasing amounts of energy to reopen the collapsed alveoli with every breath, so that each breath becomes as difficult as the first. The progressive expiratory atelectasis upsets the physiologic homeostasis of the pulmonary and cardiovascular systems and prevents adequate gas exchange. Lung compliance decreases, which accounts for the difficulty of inflation, labored respirations, and the increased work of breathing.

The physiologic alterations of RDS produce the following complications:

1. *Hypoxia.* Hypoxia produces physiologic complications and consequences that increase the hypoxia and decrease pulmonary perfusion. As a result of hypoxia, the pulmonary vasculature constricts, pulmonary vascular resistance increases, and pulmonary blood flow is reduced. Increased pulmonary vascular resistance may precipitate a return to fetal circulation as the ductus opens and blood flow is shunted around

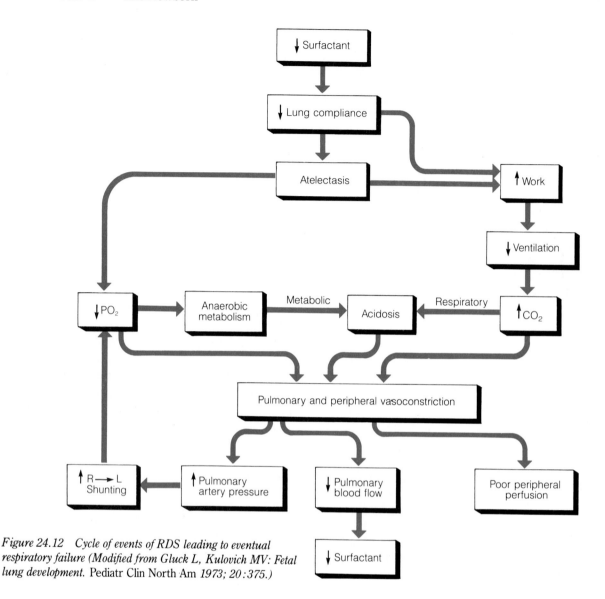

*Figure 24.12   Cycle of events of RDS leading to eventual respiratory failure (Modified from Gluck L, Kulovich MV: Fetal lung development.* Pediatr Clin North Am *1973; 20:375.)*

the lungs. Hypoxia also causes impairment or absence of metabolic response to cold, reversion to anaerobic metabolism resulting in lactate accumulation (acidosis), and impaired cardiac output, which decreases perfusion to vital organs.

2. *Respiratory acidosis.* Increased $PCO_2$ and decreased pH are results of alveolar hypoventilation. Carbon dioxide retention and resultant respiratory acidosis are the measures of ventilatory inadequacy, so that persistently rising $PCO_2$ and decrease in pH are poor prognostic signs of pulmonary function and adequacy.

3. *Metabolic acidosis.* Decreased pH and decreased bicarbonate levels may be results of impaired delivery of oxygen at the cellular level. Because of the lack of oxygen, the neonate begins an anaerobic pathway of metabolism, with an increase in lactate levels and a resultant base deficit. As the lactate

levels increase, the pH becomes acidotic (decreased pH), and the buffer base decreases in an attempt to compensate and maintain acid-base homeostasis.

The classic radiologic picture of RDS is diffuse reticulogranular density (bilaterally), with portions of the air-filled tracheobronchial tree outlined by the opaque ("white-out") lungs (air-bronchogram). The progression of radiologic findings parallels the pattern of resolution of RDS (four to seven days) and the time of surfactant reappearance.

## MEDICAL THERAPY

The primary goal of prenatal management is the prevention of preterm birth through aggressive treatment of preterm labor and possible administration of glucocorticoids to enhance fetal lung development (see p 483). The goals of postnatal therapy are maintenance of adequate

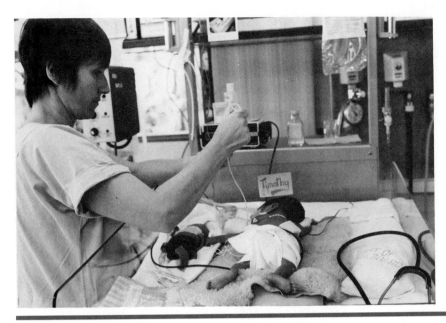

*Figure 24.13 Infant on a respirator*

oxygenation and ventilation, correction of acid-base abnormalities, and provision of the supportive care required to maintain homeostasis.

Supportive medical management consists of ventilatory therapy, transcutaneous oxygen and carbon dioxide monitoring, correction of acid-base imbalance, environmental temperature regulation, adequate nutrition, and protection from infection. Ventilatory therapy is directed toward prevention of hypoventilation and hypoxia. Mild cases of RDS may require only increased humidified oxygen concentrations. Use of continuous positive airway pressure (CPAP) may be required in moderately afflicted

infants. Severe cases of RDS require mechanical ventilatory assistance, with positive end-expiratory pressure (PEEP) (Figure 24.13).

## NURSING ASSESSMENT

Increasing cyanosis, tachypnea, grunting respirations, nasal flaring, and significant retractions are characteristics of the disease. Table 24.4 reviews clinical findings associated with respiratory distress. The Silverman-Andersen index (Figure 24.14) may be helpful in evaluating the signs of respiratory distress.

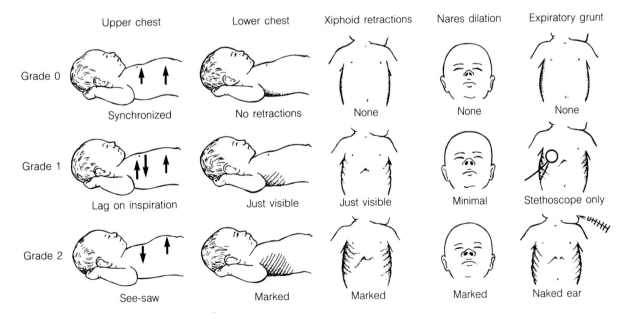

*Figure 24.14 Evaluation of respiratory status using the Silverman-Andersen index (From Nursing Inservice Aid no 2. Ross Laboratories, Columbus, Ohio; and Silverman WA, Andersen DH: Pediatrics 1956; 17:1, copyright © 1956, American Academy of Pediatrics.)*

## Table 24.4   Clinical Assessments Associated with Respiratory Distress

| Clinical picture | Significance |
| --- | --- |
| **SKIN** | |
| Color | |
| Pallor or mottling | Represents poor peripheral circulation due to systemic hypotension and vasoconstriction and pooling of independent areas (usually in conjunction with severe hypoxia). |
| Cyanosis (bluish tint) | Depends on hemoglobin concentration, peripheral circulation, intensity and quality of viewing light, and acuity of observer's color vision; frankly visible in advanced hypoxia; central cyanosis is most easily detected by examination of mucous membranes and tongue. |
| Jaundice (yellow discoloration of skin and mucous membranes due to presence of unconjugated [indirect] bilirubin) | Metabolic aberrations (acidosis, hypercarbia, asphyxia) of respiratory distress predispose to dissociation of bilirubin from albumin-binding sites and deposition in the skin and central nervous system. |
| Edema (presents as slick, shiny skin) | Characteristic of preterm infant because of low total protein concentration with decrease in colloidal osmotic pressure and transudation of fluid; edema of hands and feet frequently seen within first 24 hours and resolved by fifth day in infant with severe RDS. |
| **RESPIRATORY SYSTEM** | |
| Tachypnea (normal respiratory rate 30–50/min; elevated respiratory rate 60+/min) | Increased respiratory rate is the most frequent and easily detectable sign of respiratory distress after birth; a compensatory mechanism that attempts to increase respiratory dead space to maintain alveolar ventilation and gaseous exchange in the face of an increase in mechanical resistance. As a decompensatory mechanism it increases work load and energy output (by increasing respiratory rate), which causes increased metabolic demand for oxygen and thus increase in alveolar ventilation (of already over-stressed system). During shallow, rapid respirations, there is increase in dead space ventilation, thus decreasing alveolar ventilation. |
| Apnea (episode of nonbreathing of more than 20 sec in duration; periodic breathing, a common "normal" occurrence in preterm infants, is defined as apnea of 5–10 sec alternating with 10–15 sec periods of ventilation) | Poor prognostic sign; indicative of cardiorespiratory disease, CNS disease, metabolic alterations, intracranial hemorrhage, sepsis, or immaturity; physiologic alterations include decreased oxygen saturation, respiratory acidosis, and bradycardia. |
| Chest | Inspection of thoracic cage includes shape, size, and symmetry of movement. Respiratory movements should be symmetrical and diaphragmatic; asymmetry reflects pathology (pneumothorax, diaphragmatic hernia). Increased anteroposterior diameter indicative of air-trapping (meconium aspiration syndrome). |
| Labored respirations (Silverman-Andersen chart in Figure 24.14 indicates severity of retractions, grunting, and flaring, which are signs of labored respirations) | Indicative of marked increase in work of breathing. |
| Retractions (inward pulling of soft parts of chest cage—suprasternal, substernal, intercostal, subcostal—at inspiration) | Reflect significant increase in negative intrathoracic pressure necessary to inflate stiff, noncompliant lung; infants attempt to increase lung compliance by using accessory muscles; markedly decreases lung expansion; seesaw respirations are seen when chest flattens with inspiration and abdomen bulges; retractions increase work and $O_2$ need of breathing, so that assisted ventilation may be necessary due to exhaustion. |
| Flaring nares (inspiratory dilation of nostrils) | Compensatory mechanism that attempts to lessen resistance of narrow nasal passage. |

**Table 24.4   Clinical Assessments Associated with Respiratory Distress** *(continued)*

| Clinical picture | Significance |
| --- | --- |
| **RESPIRATORY SYSTEM** *(continued)* | |
| Expiratory grunt (Valsalva maneuver in which infant exhales against closed glottis, thus producing audible moan) | Produces increase in transpulmonary pressure, which decreases or prevents atelectasis, thus improving oxygenation and alveolar ventilation; intubation should not be attempted unless infant's condition is rapidly deteriorating, because it prevents this maneuver and allows aveoli to collapse. |
| Rhythmic movement of body with labored respirations (chin tug, head bobbing, retractions of anal area) | Result of use of abdominal and other respiratory accessory muscles during prolonged forced respirations. |
| Ausculation of chest reveals decreased air exchange with harsh breath sounds or fine inspiratory rales; rhonchi may be present. | Decrease in breath sounds and distant quality may indicate interstitial or intrapleural air or fluid. |
| **CARDIOVASCULAR SYSTEM** | |
| Continuous systolic murmur may be audible | Patent ductus arteriosus is common occurrence with hypoxia, pulmonary vasoconstriction, right-to-left shunting, and congestive heart failure. |
| Heart rate usually within normal limits (fixed heart rate may occur with a rate of 110–120/min) | Fixed heart rate indicates decrease in vagal control. |
| Point of maximal impulse usually located at fourth to fifth intercostal space, left sternal border | Displacement may reflect dextrocardia, pneumothorax, or diaphragmatic hernia. |
| **HYPOTHERMIA** | Inadequate functioning of metabolic processes that require oxygen to produce necessary body heat. |
| **MUSCLE TONE** | |
| Flaccid, hypotonic, unresponsive to stimuli | May indicate deterioration in neonate's condition and possible CNS damage, due to hypoxia, acidemia, or hemorrhage. |
| Hypertonia and/or seizure activity | |

## NURSING DIAGNOSIS

Nursing diagnoses that may apply are included in the Nursing Care Plan—Newborn with Respiratory Distress Syndrome.

## NURSING PLAN AND IMPLEMENTATION

Based on clinical parameters the neonatal nurse implements therapeutic approaches to maintain physiologic homeostasis and provides supportive care to the newborn with RDS (see Nursing Care Plan—Newborn with Respiratory Distress Syndrome).

Methods of transcutaneous monitoring and nursing interventions are included in Table 24.5.

The nursing care of infants on ventilators or with umbilical artery catheters will not be discussed here. These infants have severe respiratory distress and are cared for in intensive care nurseries by nurses with special knowledge and training.

## • Transient Tachypnea of the Newborn (Type 2 Respiratory Distress Syndrome)

Some newborns, primarily AGA preterm, and near-term infants, develop progressive respiratory distress that resembles classic RDS. These infants have usually had some intrauterine or intrapartal asphyxia caused by maternal oversedation, cesarean birth, maternal bleeding, prolapsed cord, breech, or birth maternal diabetes. The resultant effect on the neonate is failure to clear the airway of lung fluid, mucus, and other debris or an excess of fluid in the lungs due to aspiration of amniotic or tracheal fluid.

Usually little or no difficulty is experienced at the onset of breathing. However, shortly after admission to the transition nursery, expiratory grunting, flaring of the nares, and mild cyanosis may be noted in the infant breathing room air. Tachypnea is usually present by six hours of age, with respiratory rates as high as 100 to 140 breaths per minute.

*(Text continues on page 712.)*

## Table 24.5 Transcutaneous Monitors

| Type | Function and rationale | Nursing interventions |
|------|------------------------|----------------------|
| **TcPo$_2$**<br><br>Measures oxygen diffusion across the skin<br><br>Clark electrode is heated to 43°C (preterm) or 44°C (term) to warm the skin beneath the electrode and promote diffusion of oxygen across the skin surface. Po$_2$ is measured when oxygen diffuses across the capillary membrane, skin, and electrode membrane (Cohen 1984). | When transcutaneous monitors are properly calibrated and electrodes are appropriately positioned they will provide reliable, continuous, noninvasive measurements of Po$_2$, Pco$_2$, and oxygen saturation. Readings vary when skin perfusion is decreased.<br><br>Reliable as trend monitor. Frequent calibration necessary to overcome mechanical drift.<br><br>Following membrane change, machine must "warm-up" one hour prior to initial calibration; otherwise, after turning it on, it must equilibrate for 30 min prior to calibration.<br><br>When placed on infant values will be low until skin is heated; approximately 15 min required to stabilize.<br><br>Second-degree burns are rare but can occur if electrodes remain in place too long.<br><br>Decreased correlations noted with older infants (related to skin thickness); with infants with low cardiac output (decreased skin perfusion); and with hyperoxic infants.<br><br>The adhesive that attaches the electrode may abrade the fragile skin of the preterm infant.<br><br>May be used for both pre- and postductal monitoring of oxygenation for observations of shunting. | Use TcPo$_2$ to monitor trends of oxygenation with routine nursing care procedures.<br><br>Clean electrode surface to remove electrolyte deposits; change solution and membrane once a week.<br><br>Allow machine to stabilize before drawing arterial gases; note reading when gases are drawn and use values to correlate.<br><br>Ensure airtight seal between skin surface and electrode; place electrodes on clean, dry skin on upper chest, abdomen, or inner aspect of thigh; avoid bony prominences.<br><br>Change skin site and recalibrate at least every four hours; inspect skin for burns; if burns occur, use lowest temperature setting and change position of electrode more frequently.<br><br>Adhesive discs may be cut to a smaller size or skin prep may be used under the adhesive circle only; allow membrane to touch skin surface at center. |
| **PULSE OXIMETER**<br><br>Monitors beat-to-beat arterial oxygen saturation.<br><br>Microprocessor measures saturation by the absorption of red and infrared light as it passes through tissue. Changes in absorption related to blood pulsation through vessel determine saturation and pulse rate (Epstein et al 1985). | Calibration is automatic.<br><br>Less dependent on perfusion than TcPo$_2$ and TcPco$_2$; however, functions poorly if peripheral perfusion is decreased due to low cardiac output.<br>Much more rapid response time than TcPo$_2$ —offers "real-time" readings.<br><br>Can be located on extremity, digit, or palm of hand leaving chest free, not affected by skin characteristics.<br>Requires understanding of oxyhemoglobin dissociation curve.<br><br>Pulse oximeter reading of 85%–90% reflects clinically safe range of saturation.<br><br>Extreme sensitivity to movement; decreases if average of seventh or fourteenth beat is selected rather than beat-to-beat.<br><br>Poor correlation with extreme hyperoxia. | Understand and use oxyhemoglobin dissociation curve.<br><br>Monitor readings and correlate with arterial blood gases.<br><br>Use disposable cuffs (reusable cuffs allow too much ambient light to enter and readings may be inaccurate). |

## Nursing Care Plan

# Newborn with Respiratory Distress Syndrome

## Client Assessment

### Nursing History

Preterm delivery

Gestational history: Recent episodes of fetal or intrapartal stress (maternal hypotension, bleeding, maternal and resultant fetal oversedation), severe fetal lung circulation compromise

Neonatal history: Birth asphyxia resulting in acute hypoxia, exposure to hypothermia

Familial tendency

Low Apgar, requiring bag and mask resuscitation in birthing area

### Physical Examination

At birth or within two hours, rapid development initially of tachypnea (over 60 respirations/min), expiratory grunting (audible), or subcostal/intercostal retractions

Followed by flaring of nares on inspiration, cyanosis and pallor, signs of increased air hunger (apneic spells, hypotonus), rhythmic movement of body and labored respirations, chin tug

Auscultation: Initially breath sounds may be normal; then decreased air exchange with harsh breath sounds and, upon deep inspiration, rales; later a low-pitched systolic murmur indicates patent ductus

Increasing oxygen concentration requirements to maintain adequate $Po_2$ levels

### Diagnostic Studies

Arterial blood gases (indicating respiratory failure): $Pao_2$ less than 50 mm Hg while breathing 100% $O_2$, and $Pco_2$ above 60 mm Hg

X-ray: Diffuse reticulogranular density bilaterally, with air-filled tracheobronchial tube outlined by opaque lungs (air bronchogram); atelectasis/hypoexpansion in severe cases.

Clinical course worsens first 24–48 hours after birth and persists for more than 24 hours

Dextrostix

| Nursing Diagnosis/Client Goals | Nursing Interventions | Rationale/Evaluation |
|---|---|---|
| **Nursing Diagnosis:**<br><br>Pattern 1: Exchanging<br>Impaired gas exchange related to inadequate lung surfactant<br><br>**Client Goals:**<br><br>Baby's respirations will be 30–50/min, regular, and without apneic periods.<br>Baby's oxygen requirement and work of breathing will diminish.<br><br>Baby's need for assisted ventilation will be noted early. | Determine baseline of respiratory effort, ventilatory adequacy—observation of chest wall movement, skin, mucous membranes, color; estimation of degree and equality of air entry by auscultation, arterial blood gases, and pH determination.<br><br>Maintain on respiratory and cardiac monitors—note rates every 30–60 min or more often as indicated by the severity of infant's distress.<br>Check and calibrate all monitoring and measuring devices every eight hr.<br>Calibrate oxygen devices to 21% and 100% $O_2$ concentrations.<br>Monitor oxygen concentrations at least every hour.<br><br>Administer oxygen by oxygen hood (a small transparent head hood that contains an inlet and carbon dioxide outlet) (Figure 24.15). | **Rationale:**<br><br>Alveoli of normal infant remain stable during expiration due to presence of surfactant. Alveoli of infant with RDS lack surfactant and collapse with expiration. Values used to determine adequate oxygenation—normal $Pao_2$ 50–70 mm Hg. Adequate ventilation—normal $Paco_2$ 35–45 mm Hg. Acid-base balance—normal pH 7.35–7.45.<br><br>Alveolar atelectasis and intrapulmonary shunting results in poor gas exchange, hypoxemia, hypercarbia, and acid-base derangements.<br>Grunting, a compensatory mechanism, increases transpulmonary pressure, overcomes high surface tension, forces and prevents atelectasis, and thus enables improved oxygenation and a rise in $Pao_2$.<br><br>Provides a constant oxygen environment. Incubators are not recommended for long-term oxygen delivery since the concentration is difficult to regulate and fluctuates when portholes are opened for care giving. |

*(continues)*

# Nursing Care Plan

## Newborn with Respiratory Distress Syndrome (continued)

| Nursing Diagnosis/Client Goals | Nursing Interventions | Rationale/Evaluation |
|---|---|---|

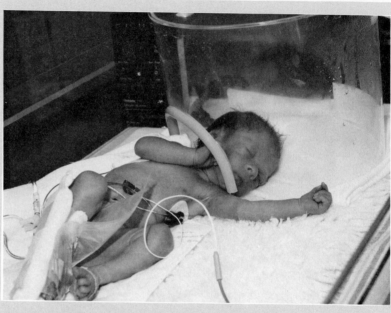

Figure 24.15 Infant in oxygen hood

Maintain stable oxygen concentration by increasing or decreasing oxygen by 5%–10% increments and then obtain arterial blood gases.

Stable concentration of oxygen is necessary to maintain $Pao_2$ within normal limits (50–70 mm Hg). Sudden increase or decrease in $O_2$ concentration may result in disproportionate increase or decrease in $Pao_2$ due to vasoconstriction in response to hypoxemia.

Monitor:
1. Color (pink), cyanosis (central or acrocyanosis), duskiness, pallor
2. Respiratory effort (evaluation at rest), rate of respirations, patterns (apnea, periodic breathing), quality (easy, unlabored; abdominal, labored), auscultation (site of breath sounds—overall or part of lung fields—describe quality of breath sounds every one to two hr), accompanying sounds with respiratory effort (change from previous observations)
3. Activity—less active, flaccid, lethargic, unresponsive, increased activity, restless, irritable; inability to tolerate exertion, crying, sucking, or nursing care activity
4. Circulatory response (evaluate at rest); rate, regularity, and rhythm of heart rate; periods of bradycardia; alterations of blood pressure

Observations of clinical condition are taken serially for comparison and changes.

Observations should be taken while infant is receiving oxygen and with any oxygen adjustment.

Return $O_2$ concentration to previous levels if there is deterioration in neonate's condition or drop below desired transcutaneous oxygen monitor (TCM) levels.

Any deterioration of clinical condition with oxygen adjustments (usually a decrease in ambient oxygen concentration) indicates inability of neonate to compensate for hypoxia.

## Nursing Care Plan

### Newborn with Respiratory Distress Syndrome *(continued)*

| Nursing Diagnosis/Client Goals | Nursing Interventions | Rationale/Evaluation |
| --- | --- | --- |
| | Repeat arterial blood gases (keep $PaO_2$ 50–70 mm Hg). Gases should be done within 15–20 min after any change in ambient $O_2$ concentration or after inspiratory or expiratory pressure changes. | |
| | Record and report clinical observations and action taken. | |
| | Maintain stable environment prior to collection of arterial blood gas sample: | |
| | 1. Maintain constant $O_2$ concentration at least 15–20 min before sample. | Accurate arterial blood determinations are essential in management of any infant receiving oxygen, because presence or absence of cyanosis is unreliable. |
| | 2. Avoid any disturbances of infant 15 min before gases are drawn. | Crying or struggling may cause hyperventilation or breath holding and may increase shunting of blood. |
| | Do not suction; if suction is absolutely necessary, delay blood sample. | |
| | Maintain temperature of sample (pH should be measured at body temperature). | Use of temporal, radial, or brachial arteries takes skill, is time-consuming, and may have serious consequences; therefore, most common technique for sampling is through umbilical artery catheter. |
| | Provide arterial blood gas setup (a 3 mL syringe with heparinized solution and a heparinized tuberculin syringe) to obtain blood sample. | |
| | After blood sample is taken, recheck flow through line to assure patency and prevent establishment of clot. | |
| | Replace blood used to clear line. | Total blood volume of infant is small; blood removed to clear catheter must be returned to prevent hypovolemia, anemia. |
| | Use heparinized flush solution before restarting IV solution to prevent clots in the line. | |
| | Assess need for assisted ventilatory measures. Criteria for assisted ventilation: 1. Apnea 2. Hypoxia ($PaO_2$ <50 mm Hg) 3. Hypercarbia ($PaCO_2$ >60 mm Hg) 4. Respiratory acidosis (pH <7.20) | Application of CPAP or PEEP produces same stabilization force on alveoli as grunting does and produces same effect—improved oxygenation and rise in $PaO_2$. |
| | Have ventilatory support equipment available. | |
| | Administer ventilator care per agency protocol. | Delivery of CPAP or PEEP can only be done by use of nasal prongs, nasopharyngeal tube, or oral intubation. |

*(continues)*

## Nursing Care Plan

### Newborn with Respiratory Distress Syndrome (continued)

| Nursing Diagnosis/Client Goals | Nursing Interventions | Rationale/Evaluation |
| --- | --- | --- |

**Evaluation:**

Baby's respiratory status is improving and need for assisted ventilation was identified and met.

**Nursing Diagnosis:**

Pattern 1: Exchanging
Altered nutrition: less than body requirements related to increased metabolic needs of stressed infant

**Client Goals:**

Baby will not have greater than 2% weight loss, will have greater than 40 mg % glucose, and will progress to oral feedings.

Maintain IV rate at prescribed level; record type and amount of fluid infused hourly. Use infusion pump. Observe vital signs for signs of too-rapid infusion. Maintain normal urine output (1–3 mL/kg/hr). Maintain specific gravity of urine between 1.006 and 1.012.
Take daily weights.

Manage route of IV administration.
With umbilical catheter: Protect catheter from strain or tension. Restrain as necessary. Prevent dislodgement of catheter. Always keep catheter and stopcock on top of bed linens so they are easily visible.

Observe for occlusion of vessels by clot and for vasospasm—discoloration of skin, discoloration of toes or feet (blanching or cyanosis). If discoloration occurs, contralateral foot may be wrapped with warm cloth, but this is controversial. Removal of catheter is preferred (Korones 1986).

Observe for signs of infection or sepsis: temperature instability, drainage, redness or foul odor from cord, lethargy, irritability, vomiting, poor feeding, hypotonia.

Peripheral IV in scalp or extremity vein: Prepare equipment, insert IV in vein, and restrain infant.

If vessel chosen is an artery, it pulsates. Place peripheral IV in vein (which doesn't pulsate).

Maintain proper placement of IV.

Advance as soon as possible from intravenous to oral feedings. Gavage or nipple feedings are used, and IV is used as supplement (discontinued when oral intake is sufficient) (see Procedure 24.1).

Provide adequate caloric intake: amount of intake, type of formula, route of administration, and need for supplementation of intake by other routes.

**Rationale:**

Fluids are provided to sick neonate by intravenous route and are calculated to replace sensible and insensible water losses as well as evaporative losses due to tachypnea.
Overload of circulatory system by too much or too rapid administration of fluid causes pulmonary edema and cardiac embarrassment that may be fatal.

Greater nutritional fluid is required because of energy needed to cope with stress. Stressed infants are predisposed to hypoglycemia because of increased metabolic demands as well as reduced glycogen stores and decreased ability to convert fat and protein to glucose.

Vasospasm in unwrapped foot will be relieved by treatment, and the discoloration will disappear and toes will be pink. If discoloration persists, clot may be occluding vessel—catheter must be removed, or loss of extremity is possible.

Very small arteries may not pulsate and arterial area will blanch if saline is infused.

Ability to aspirate blood and/or easily inject small amount of saline indicates patent IV. Infiltration is evaluated by area of edema and redness about site, inability to obtain blood on aspiration, or difficulty in injecting solution.

Calories are essential to prevent catabolism of body proteins and metabolic acidosis due to starvation or inadequate caloric intake.

## Nursing Care Plan

## Newborn with Respiratory Distress Syndrome (continued)

| Nursing Diagnosis/Client Goals | Nursing Interventions | Rationale/Evaluation |
| --- | --- | --- |
| | Monitor for hypocalcemia.<br><br>Monitor for hypoglycemia: Dextrostix below 45 mg %, urine screening for glucose. | Hypocalcemia and hypoglycemia result from delayed or inadequate caloric intake and stress.<br><br>**Evaluation:**<br><br>Baby maintains normal glucose levels, follows normal weight curves and is tolerating oral feedings. |
| **Nursing Diagnosis:**<br><br>Pattern 1: Exchanging<br>Potential for infection related to invasive procedures<br><br>**Client Goals:**<br><br>Baby will maintain a stable temperature and blood pressure. Baby's respiratory status improves. | See section on sepsis nursing care.<br><br>Pay careful attention to infection control by cleaning and replacing nebulizers/humidifiers at least every 24 hr; use sterile tubing and replace every 24 hr; use sterile distilled water. | **Rationale:**<br><br>Decreased lung expansion predisposes to atelectasis and secondary superimposed infections.<br><br>The warm, moist environment found in Isolettes and with $O_2$ equipment promotes growth of microorganisms.<br><br>**Evaluation:**<br><br>Baby will be free of infection or infection is treated. |
| **Nursing Diagnosis:**<br><br>Pattern 1: Exchanging<br>Ineffective thermoregulation related to increased respiratory effort secondary to RDS<br><br>**Client Goals:**<br><br>Baby will maintain a stable temperature. Baby will not become hypoglycemic, cyanotic, or have periods of bradycardia or apnea. | Observe infant for temperature instability and signs of increased oxygen consumption (need for increased $O_2$ concentration) and metabolic acidosis.<br><br>Maintain neutral thermal environment.<br><br><br><br>Use servocontrol to maintain constant temperature regulation.<br><br>Warm all inspired gases.<br>Place a thermometer in the oxygen hood and document the temperature of the delivered gas with vital signs. Oxyhood and Isolette temperature should be maintained in the infant's neutral thermal range.<br>Place thermometer in-line of ventilatory circuit and maintain inspired gas at 34–35°C.<br>Use heat shields for small infants. | **Rationale:**<br><br>Cold stress increases oxygen consumption and promotes pulmonary vasoconstriction. This leads to hypoxia and acidosis, which further depress surfactant production.<br><br>Cold stress leads to chemical thermogenesis (burning brown fat to maintain body temperature), which increases $O_2$ needs in an already compromised infant.<br><br><br><br>Cold air/oxygenation blown in face of newborn is source of cold stress and is stimulus for increased consumption of oxygen and increased metabolic rate.<br><br><br><br><br><br>Heat shields will prevent heat loss by convection and reduce insensible water losses.<br><br>**Evaluation:**<br><br>Baby's temperature was within normal limits. Signs of cold stress are absent or minimized. |

## MEDICAL THERAPY

The goal of medical management is to identify the type of respiratory distress and to institute treatment.

Initial x-ray findings may be identical to those showing RDS within the first three hours. However, radiographs of infants with transient tachypnea usually reveal a generalized overexpansion of the lungs (hyperaeration of alveoli), which is identifiable principally by flattened contours of the diaphragm. Dense perihilar streaks (increased vascularity) radiate from the hilar region and represent engorgement of the lymphatics, which are needed to clear alveolar fluid upon initiation of air breathing.

Ambient oxygen concentrations as high as 70% may be required to correct the cyanosis initially. Thereafter, oxygen requirements usually decrease over the first 48 hours, unlike infants with RDS, whose requirements increase during this time.

The infants should be improving by 24 to 48 hours, except for modest $O_2$ dependence (less than 30%). The duration of the clinical course of transient tachypnea is approximately four days (96 hours). Early acidosis, both respiratory and metabolic (with moderate elevations of $P_{CO_2}$), is easily corrected. Ventilatory assistance is rarely needed, and most of these infants survive.

If progressive deterioration occurs to the extent that assisted ventilation is required, a diagnosis of superimposed sepsis must be considered and treatment measures initiated. For nursing actions, see the Nursing Care Plan—Newborn with Respiratory Distress Syndrome.

## • CARE OF NEWBORN WITH MECONIUM ASPIRATION SYNDROME

The presence of meconium in amniotic fluid indicates an asphyxial insult to the fetus. The physiologic response to asphyxia is increased intestinal peristalsis, relaxation of the anal sphincter, and passage of meconium into the amniotic fluid.

Approximately 10% of all pregnancies will have meconium-stained fluid. This fluid may be aspirated into the tracheobronchial tree in utero or during the first few breaths taken by the newborn; this aspiration is called **Meconium Aspiration Syndrome (MAS)**. This syndrome primarily affects term, SGA, and postterm newborns, and those that have experienced a prolonged labor.

Presence of meconium in the lungs produces a ball-valve action (air is allowed in but not exhaled), so that alveoli overdistend; rupture with pneumomediastinum or pneumothorax is a common occurrence. The meconium also initiates a chemical pneumonitis in the lung with oxygen and carbon dioxide trapping and hyperinflation. Secondary bacterial pneumonias are common. Clinical manifestations of MAS include: (a) fetal hypoxia in utero a few days or a few minutes prior to birth, indicated by a sudden increase in fetal activity followed by diminished activity, slowing of fetal heart rate or weak and irregular heartbeat, and meconium staining of amniotic fluid; and (b) presence of signs of distress at birth, such as pallor, cyanosis, apnea, slow heartbeat, and low Apgar scores (below 6) at one and five minutes. As the victims of intrauterine asphyxia, meconium-stained neonates or newborns who have aspirated meconium are often depressed at birth and require resuscitation to establish adequate respiratory effort.

After the initial resuscitation, the severity of clinical symptoms correlates with the extent of aspiration. Mechanical ventilation is frequently required from birth due to immediate signs of distress (generalized cyanosis, tachypnea, and severe retractions). An overdistended, barrel-shaped chest with increased anteroposterior diameter is common. Auscultation reveals diminished air movement with prominent rales and rhonchi. Abdominal palpation may reveal a displaced liver due to diaphragmatic depression secondary to the overexpansion of the lungs (Nugent 1983). Yellowish staining of the skin, nails, and umbilical cord is usually present, especially in postterm newborns.

## • Medical Therapy

The combined efforts of the obstetrician and pediatrician are needed to prevent MAS. The most effective form of preventive management is outlined as follows:

1.  After the head of the neonate is delivered and the shoulders and chest are still in the birth canal, the nasopharynx and oropharynx are suctioned with a DeLee catheter. This is called "suctioning on the perineum." The same procedure of suctioning immediately after the head is born is used with a cesarean birth. The DeLee suction is connected to the wall suction to decrease the possibility of AIDS transmission.

2.  Immediately after birth, intubation of the neonate and direct suctioning of the trachea through an endotracheal tube is performed.
    a.  The resuscitator places his or her mouth over the endotracheal tube and sucks on the tube as it is withdrawn from the trachea (a paper mask is placed over the tube to prevent inhalation of meconium by the resuscitator or wall suction is used).
    b.  If meconium is suctioned from the trachea, the neonate is reintubated and suctioned until the airway is cleared.

c. It is recommended that the neonate not be lavaged with normal saline once intubated, as this procedure forces the meconium into the small airways.

If the newborn is not adequately suctioned on the perineum, respiratory or resuscitative efforts will push meconium into the airway and into the lungs. Stimulation of the neonate is avoided to minimize respiratory movements. Further resuscitative efforts as indicated follow the same principles mentioned earlier in this Chapter. Resuscitated neonates should be immediately transferred to the nursery for closer observation. An umbilical arterial line may be used for direct monitoring of arterial blood pressures; blood sampling for pH, and blood gases; and infusion of intravenous fluids, blood, or medications.

Treatment usually involves high ambient oxygenation and controlled ventilation. Low positive end-expiratory pressures (PEEP) are desired to avoid air leaks. Unfortunately, high pressures may be needed to cause sufficient expiratory expansion of obstructed terminal airways or to stabilize airways that are weakened by inflammation so that the most distal atelectatic alveoli are ventilated. Systemic blood pressure and pulmonary blood flow must be maintained. Intravenous tolazoline (Priscoline) or isoproterenol (Isuprel) may be used to increase the pulmonary blood flow by overcoming the arterioles' vasoconstriction and pulmonary vasospasm, which has created a right-to-left cardiopulmonary shunt. Tolazoline must be used with extreme caution as dramatic falls in blood pressure can occur.

Treatment also includes chest physiotherapy (chest percussion, vibration, and drainage) to remove debris. Prophylactic antibiotics are frequently given. Bicarbonate may be necessary for several days for severely ill newborns. Mortality in term or postterm infants is very high, because they are so difficult to oxygenate.

## ● Nursing Assessment

During the intrapartal period, the nurse should observe for signs of fetal hypoxia and meconium staining of amniotic fluid. At birth, the nurse assesses the newborn for signs of distress. During the ongoing assessment of the newborn, the nurse carefully observes for complications such as pulmonary air leaks; anoxic cerebral injury manifested by cerebral edema and/or convulsions; anoxic myocardial injury evidenced by congestive heart failure or cardiomegaly; disseminated intravascular coagulation (DIC) resulting from hypoxic hepatic damage with depression of liver-dependent clotting factors; anoxic renal damage demonstrated by hematuria, oliguria, or anuria; fluid overload; sepsis secondary to bacterial pneumonia; and any signs of intestinal necrosis from ischemia, including gastrointestinal obstruction or hemorrhage.

## ● Nursing Diagnosis

Nursing diagnoses that may apply to the newborn with meconium aspiration syndrome include:

● Impaired gas exchange related to presence of respiratory distress secondary to aspiration of meconium and amniotic fluid during birth

● Altered nutrition: less than body requirements related to respiratory distress and increased energy requirements

● Ineffective family coping related to life-threatening illness in term newborn

## ● Nursing Plan and Implementation
### PREVENTION OF MECONIUM ASPIRATION

Initial interventions are aimed primarily at prevention of the aspiration by assisting with the removal of the meconium from the infant's naso- and oropharynx prior to the first extrauterine breath.

### PROMOTION OF PHYSICAL WELL-BEING

When significant aspiration occurs, therapy is supportive with the primary goals of maintaining appropriate gas exchange and minimizing complications. Nursing interventions after resuscitation should include: maintenance of adequate oxygenation and ventilation, temperature regulation, glucose strip test at two hours of age to check for hypoglycemia, observation of intravenous fluids, calculation of necessary fluids (which may be restricted in first 48–72 hours due to cerebral edema), and provision of caloric requirements.

## ● Evaluation

Anticipated outcomes of nursing care include:

● The risk of MAS is promptly identified and early intervention is initiated.

● The newborn is free of respiratory distress and metabolic alterations.

● The parents verbalize their concerns about their baby's health problem/survival and understand the rationale behind management of their newborn.

## ● CARE OF THE NEWBORN WITH CONGENITAL HEART DEFECT

The incidence of congenital heart defects is 7.5 per 1000 live births. They account for one third of the deaths caused by congenital defects in the first year of life. Because accurate diagnosis and surgical treatment are now available, many such deaths can be prevented. Nurses need knowledge of congenital heart disease to detect deviations from normal and to initiate interventions.

# Overview of Congenital Heart Defects

Factors that might influence development of congenital heart malformation can be classified as environmental or genetic. Infections of the pregnant woman, such as rubella, coxsackie B, and influenza, have been implicated. Thalidomide, steroids, alcohol, lithium, and some anticonvulsants have been shown to cause malformations of the heart. Seasonal spraying of pesticides has also been linked to an increase in congenital heart defects. Clinicians are also beginning to see cardiac defects in infants of PKU mothers who do not follow their diets.

Infants born with chromosomal abnormalities have a higher incidence of cardiovascular anomalies. Infants with Down syndrome and trisomy 13/15 and 16/18 frequently have heart lesions. Increased incidence and risk of recurrence of specific defects occur in families.

It is customary to describe congenital malformations of the heart as either *acyanotic*—those that do not present with cyanosis—or *cyanotic*—those that do present with cyanosis. If an opening exists between the right and left sides of the heart, blood will normally flow from the area of greater pressure (left side) to the area of lesser pressure (right side). This process is referred to as left-to-right shunt and does not produce cyanosis because oxygenated blood is being pumped out to the systemic circulation. If pressure in the right side of the heart, due to obstruction of normal flow, exceeds that in the left side, unoxygenated blood will flow from the right side to the left side of the heart and out into the system. This right-to-left shunt causes cyanosis. If the opening is large, there may be a bidirectional shunt with mixing of blood in both sides of the heart, which also produces cyanosis.

The common cardiac defects seen in the first six days of life are left ventricular outflow obstructions (mitral stenosis, aortic stenosis, or atresia), hypoplastic left heart, coarctation of the aorta, patent ductus arteriosus (PDA, the most common defect), transposition of the great vessels, tetralogy of Fallot, and large ventricular septal defect or atrial septal defects (see Figure 24.16). Table 24.6 presents the clinical manifestations and medical/surgical management of these cardiac defects.

# Nursing Assessment

The primary goal of the neonatal nurse is early identification of cardiac defects and initiation of referral to the physician. The three most common manifestations of cardiac defect are cyanosis, detectable heart murmur, and congestive heart failure signs (tachycardia, tachypnea, diaphoresis, hepatomegaly, and cardiomegaly).

Nursing assessment of the following signs and symptoms assists in identifying the newborn with a cardiac problem.

1. Tachypnea—reflects increased pulmonary blood flow
2. Dyspnea—caused by increased pulmonary venous pressure and blood flow; can also cause chest retractions, wheezing
3. Color—ashen, gray, or cyanotic
4. Difficulty in feeding—requires many rest periods before finishing even 1 or 2 ounces
5. Diaphoresis—beads of perspiration over the upper lip and forehead; may accompany feeding fatigue
6. Stridor or choking spells
7. Failure to gain weight
8. Heart murmur—may not be heard in left-to-right shunting defects since the pulmonary pressure in the newborn is greater than pressure in the left side of the heart in the early newborn period
9. Hepatomegaly—in right-sided heart failure caused by venous congestion in the liver
10. Tachycardia—pulse over 160, may be as high as 200
11. Cardiac enlargement.

# Nursing Diagnosis

Nursing diagnoses that may apply to the newborn with cardiac defect include:

- Altered tissue perfusion related to decrease in circulating oxygen
- Ineffective breathing pattern related to fatigue
- Altered nutrition: less than body requirements related to increased energy expenditure
- Knowledge deficit of parents related to cardiac anomaly and future implications for care

# Nursing Plan and Implementation

## MAINTENANCE OF CARDIOPULMONARY STATUS

When the baby has dyspnea or cyanosis, oxygen must be given by an oxygen hood, tent, mask, cannula, or oxygen prongs. Mist is often ordered, which requires the use of an oxygen hood or tent. Oxygen administration should always be accompanied by humidity, and the air should be warmed to decrease the drying effects of cold, dry oxygen. Vital signs are carefully monitored for evidence of tachycardia, tachypnea, expiratory grunting, and retractions.

## Table 24.6   Cardiac Defects of the Early Newborn Period

| Congenital heart defect | Clinical findings | Medical/surgical management |
|---|---|---|
| **ACYANOTIC** | | |
| Patent ductus arteriosus (PDA)<br>　↑ in females, maternal rubella, RDS, <1500 g preterm newborns, high-altitude births | Harsh grade 2–3 machinery murmur upper left sternal border (LSB) just beneath clavicle<br>　↑ difference between systolic and diastolic pulse pressure<br>Can lead to right heart failure and pulmonary congestion<br>　↑ left atrial (LA) and left ventricular (LV) enlargement, dilated ascending aorta<br>　↑ pulmonary vascularity | Indomethacin—0.2 mg/kg orally (prostaglandin inhibitor)<br>Surgical ligation<br>Use of $O_2$ therapy and blood transfusion to improve tissue oxygenation and perfusion<br>Fluid restriction and diuretics |

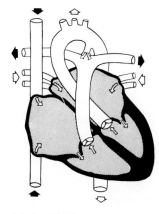

*Figure 24.16 (**A**) The patent ductus arteriosus is a vascular connection that, during fetal life, short-circuits the pulmonary vascular bed and directs blood from the pulmonary artery to the aorta.*

| | | |
|---|---|---|
| Atrial septal defect (ASD)<br>　↑ in females and Down syndrome | Initially frequently asymptomatic<br>Systolic murmur 2nd left intercostal space (LICS)<br>With large ASD, diastolic rumbling murmur lower left sternal (LLS) border<br>Failure to thrive, upper respiratory infection (URI), poor exercise tolerance | Surgical closure with patch or suture |
| Ventricular septal defect (VSD)<br>　↑ in males | Initially asymptomatic until end of first month or large enough to cause pulmonary edema<br>Loud, blowing systolic murmur 3rd–4th intercostal space (ICS) pulmonary blood flow<br>Right ventricular hypertrophy<br>Rapid respirations, growth failure, feeding difficulties<br>Congestive right heart failure at 6 weeks–2 months of age | Follow medically—some spontaneously close<br>Use of lanoxin and diuretics in congestive heart failure (CHF)<br>Surgical closure with Dacron patch |
| Coarctation of aorta<br>Can be preductal or postductal | Absent or diminished femoral pulses<br>Increased brachial pulses<br>Late systolic murmur left intrascapular area<br>Systolic BP in lower extremities<br>Enlarged left ventricle<br>Can present in CHF at 7–21 days of life | Surgical resection of narrowed portion of aorta |

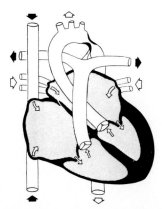

*Figure 24.16 (**B**) Coarctation of the aorta is characterized by a narrowed aortic lumen. The lesion produces an obstruction to the flow of blood through the aorta, causing an increased left ventricular pressure and work load.*

*(continues)*

## Table 24.6   Cardiac Defects of the Early Newborn Period *(continued)*

| Congenital heart defect | Clinical findings | Medical/surgical management |
|---|---|---|
| CYANOTIC | | |
| Tetralogy of Fallot<br>(Most common cyanotic heart defect)<br>Pulmonary stenosis<br>VSD<br>Overriding aorta<br>Right ventricular hypertrophy | May be cyanotic at birth or within first few months of life<br>Harsh systolic murmur LSB<br>Crying or feeding increases cyanosis and respiratory distress<br>X-ray: Boot-shaped appearance secondary to small pulmonary artery<br>Right ventricular enlargement | Prevention of dehydration intercurrent infections<br>Alleviation of paroxysmal dyspneic attacks<br>Palliative surgery to increase blood flow to the lungs<br>Corrective surgery—resection of pulmonic stenosis, closure of VSD with Dacron patch |

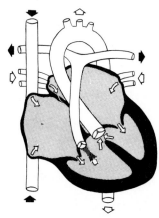

*Figure 24.16 (**C**) Tetralogy of Fallot. The severity of symptoms depends on the degree of pulmonary stenosis, the size of the ventricular septal defect, and the degree to which the aorta overrides the septal defect.*

| | | |
|---|---|---|
| Transposition of great vessels (TGA)<br>(↑ females, IDMs, LGAs) | Cyanosis at birth or within three days<br>Possible pulmonic stenosis murmur<br>Right ventricular hypertrophy<br>Polycythemia<br>"Egg on its side" x-ray | Prostaglandin E to vasodilate ductus to keep it open<br>Initial surgery to create opening between right and left side of heart if none exists<br>Total surgical repair—usually the Mustard procedure |

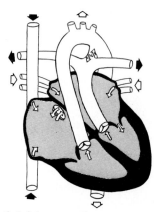

*Figure 24.16 (**D**) Complete transposition of great vessels. This anomaly is an embryologic defect caused by a straight division of the bulbar trunk without normal spiraling. As a result, the aorta originates from the right ventricle, and the pulmonary artery from the left ventricle. An abnormal communication between the two circulations must be present to sustain life. (All illustrations from* Congenital Heart Abnormalities. Clinical Education Aid no. 7. *Ross Laboratories, Columbus, Ohio.)*

| | | |
|---|---|---|
| Hypoplastic left heart syndrome | Normal at birth—cyanosis and shocklike congestive heart failure develop within a few hours to days<br>Soft systolic murmur just left of the sternum<br>Diminished pulses<br>Aortic and/or mitral atresia<br>Tiny, thick-walled left ventricle<br>Large, dilated, hypertrophied right ventricle<br>X-ray: Cardiac enlargement and pulmonary venous congestion | Currently no effective corrective treatment |

Morphine sulfate, a dose of 0.05 mg/kg of body weight, can be used if the infant is markedly irritable. Morphine is thought to decrease peripheral and pulmonary vascular resistance, which results in decreased tachypnea. Infants in congestive heart failure are more comfortable in a semi-Fowler's position.

The nurse provides for rest by administering a sedative as required. Organizing nursing care is a key to decreasing energy requirements and providing periods of rest.

### PARENT EDUCATION

After the baby is stabilized and gaining weight, decisions are made about ongoing care and surgical interventions. The parents need careful and complete explanations and the opportunity to take part in decision making. They also require ongoing emotional support.

## ● Evaluation

Anticipated outcomes of nursing care of newborns with congenital heart defects include:

- The newborn's oxygen consumption and energy expenditure are minimal while at rest and during feedings.

- Newborn is protected from additional stresses such as infection, cold stress, and dehydration.

- Parents verbalize their concerns surrounding their baby's health maintenance and understand the rationale for follow-up care.

## ● CARE OF THE NEWBORN WITH HYPOGLYCEMIA

**Hypoglycemia** is the most common metabolic disorder occurring in LGA, SGA, and preterm AGA infants. The pathophysiology of hypoglycemia differs for each classification.

AGA preterm infants have not been in utero a sufficient time to store glycogen and fat. Therefore, they have very low glycogen and fat stores and a decreased ability to carry out gluconeogenesis (Fantazia 1984). This situation is further aggravated by increased use of glucose by the tissues (especially the brain and heart) during stress and illness (chilling, asphyxia, sepsis, and RDS).

Infants of Class A–C or type 1 diabetic mothers (diagnosed, suspected, or gestational diabetics) have increased stores of glycogen and fat. Circulating insulin and insulin responsiveness are also higher. Because the high in utero glucose loads stop at birth, the neonate experiences rapid and profound hypoglycemia. The SGA infant has used up glycogen and fat stores because of intrauterine malnutrition and has a blunted hepatic enzymatic response with

which to use glucose. Any newborn who is stressed at birth (from asphyxia or cold) also quickly uses up available glucose stores and becomes hypoglycemic.

Hypoglycemia is defined as a blood glucose below 30 mg/dL in the first 72 hours and below 40 mg/dL after the first three days. It may also be defined as a glucose strip (Dextrostix) result below 45 mg/dL when corroborated with laboratory blood glucose value (see Procedure 24.2).

## ● Medical Therapy

The goal of management includes early identification of hypoglycemia through observation and screening of newborns at risk. The newborn may be asymptomatic, or any of the following may occur:

- Lethargy, jitteriness
- Poor feeding
- Vomiting
- Pallor
- Apnea, irregular respirations, respiratory distress, cyanosis
- Hypotonia, possible loss of swallowing reflex
- Tremors, jerkiness, seizure activity
- High-pitched cry

Differential diagnosis of an infant with nonspecific hypoglycemic symptoms includes determining if the infant has any of the following:

- CNS disease
- Sepsis
- Metabolic aberrations
- Polycythemia
- Congenital heart disease
- Drug withdrawal
- Temperature instability
- Hypocalcemia

Aggressive treatment is recommended after a single low blood glucose value if the infant manifests any of these symptoms.

Provision of adequate caloric intake is important. Early formula feeding or breast-feeding is one of the major preventive approaches. If early feeding or intravenous glucose is started to meet the recommended fluid and caloric needs, the blood glucose is likely to remain above the hypoglycemic level. Intravenous infusions of a dextrose solution (5%–10%) begun immediately after birth should prevent hypoglycemia. However, in the very small AGA infant infusions of 10% dextrose solution may cause hyperglycemia to develop, requiring an alteration in the glucose con-

## Procedure 24.2

## Glucose Strip Test

| Objective | Nursing Action | Rationale |
|---|---|---|
| Ensure quick, efficient completion of procedure. | Gather the following equipment:<br>1. Lancet (do not use needles)<br>2. Alcohol swabs<br>3. 2 × 2 sterile gauze squares<br>4. Small Band-Aid<br>5. Glucose strips and bottle | All necessary equipment must be ready to ensure that blood sample is collected at time and in manner necessary. Do not use needles because of danger of nicking periosteum. Warm heel for five to ten sec prior to heel stick with a warm wet towel to facilitate flow of blood. |
| | Select clear, previously unpunctured site. Clean site by rubbing vigorously with 70% isopropyl alcohol swab, followed by dry gauze square. Grasp lower leg and heel so as to impede venous return slightly. | Selection of previously unpunctured site minimizes risk of infection and excessive scar formation. Friction produces local heat, which aids vasodilation.<br>Impeding venous return facilitates extraction of blood sample from puncture site. |
| Minimize trauma at puncture site. | Dry site completely before lancing. | Alcohol is irritating to injured tissue and may also produce hemolysis. |
| | With quick piercing motion, puncture lateral heel with blade, being careful not to puncture too deeply. Avoid the darkened areas shown in Figure 24.17. Toes are acceptable sites if necessary. | The lateral heel is the site of choice because it precludes damaging the posterior tibial nerve and artery, plantar artery, and important longitudinally oriented fat pad of the heel, which in later years could impede walking.<br>This is especially important for infant undergoing multiple heel stick procedures. Optimal penetration is 4 mm. |

*Figure 24.17   Glucose strip test (heel stick)*

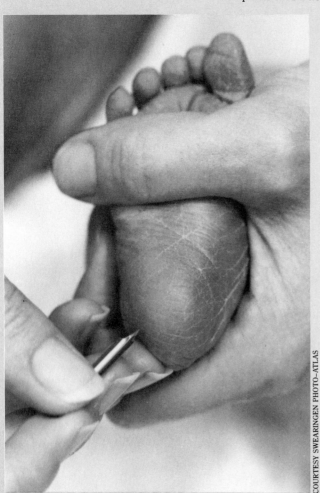

COURTESY SWEARINGEN PHOTO–ATLAS

# Procedure 24.2

## Glucose Strip Test *(continued)*

| Objective | Nursing Action | Rationale |
|---|---|---|
| Ensure accurate blood sampling. | After puncture has been made, remove first drop of blood with sterile gauze square and proceed to collect subsequent drops of blood onto glucose strip, ensuring that it is a stand-up drop of blood on strip (Figure 24.18) | The first drop is usually discarded because it tends to be minutely diluted with tissue fluid from puncture. |

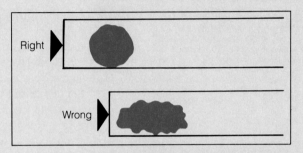

*Figure 24.18   Glucose strip drop of blood*

| | | |
|---|---|---|
| | Wait 60 seconds (apply Band-Aid while waiting), then rinse blood gently from stick under a steady stream of running water (Figure 24.19). Compare immediately against color chart on side of bottle. <br> Record results on vital signs sheet or on back of graph. Report immediately any findings under 45 mg/dL or over 175 mg/dL. | For accurate results, directions must be followed closely, and reagent strips must be fresh. False low readings may be caused by: <br> 1. Timing <br> 2. Washing (chemical reaction can be washed off) <br> 3. Squeezing foot, causing tissue fluid dilution |

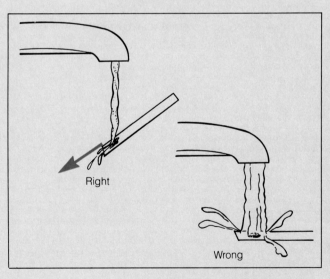

*Figure 24.19   Glucose test strip rinse*

| Prevent excessive bleeding. | Apply folded gauze square to puncture site and secure firmly with bandage. <br><br> Check puncture site frequently for first hour after sample | A pressure dressing should be applied to puncture site to stop bleeding. <br><br> Active infants sometimes kick or rub their dressings off and can bleed profusely from puncture site, especially if bandage becomes moist or is rubbed excessively against crib sheet. |

centration. Infants require 6 to 10 mg/kg/min of glucose to maintain normal glucose concentrations (Avery and Taeusch 1984). Therefore, an intravenous glucose solution should be calculated based on body weight of the infant, with blood glucose tests to determine adequacy of the infusion treatment.

A rapid infusion of 25% to 50% dextrose is contraindicated because it may lead to profound rebound hypoglycemia following an initial brief increase. Hypoglycemia resulting from hyperinsulinemia may be helped by administration of long-acting epinephrine. Epinephrine promotes glycogen conversion to glucose; it is also an anti-insulin agent. In more severe cases of hypoglycemia, corticosteroids may be administered. It is thought that steroids enhance gluconeogenesis from noncarbohydrate protein sources (Avery 1987).

The prognosis for untreated hypoglycemia is poor. It may result in permanent, untreatable CNS damage or death.

## • Nursing Assessment

The objective of assessment is to identify newborns at risk and to screen symptomatic infants. For newborns who are diagnosed as having hypoglycemia, assessment is ongoing with careful monitoring of glucose values. Glucose strips, urine dipsticks, and urine volume (above 1–3 mL/kg/hr) are evaluated frequently for osmotic diuresis and glycosuria.

## • Nursing Diagnosis

Nursing diagnoses that may apply to the newborn with hypoglycemia are:

- Altered nutrition: less than body requirements related to increased glucose use secondary to physiologic stress
- Ineffective breathing pattern related to tachypnea and apnea
- Pain related to frequent heel sticks for glucose monitoring

## • Nursing Plan and Implementation
### MONITORING OF GLUCOSE LEVELS

When caring for a preterm AGA infant the nurse should monitor blood glucose levels using glucose strips or laboratory determinations every four to eight hours for the first day of life, and daily or as necessary thereafter. The IDM should be monitored hourly for the first several hours after birth as this is the time when precipitous falls in glucose are most likely. In the SGA newborn, symptoms usually appear between 24 and 72 hours of age; occasionally they may begin as early as three hours of age. Infants who are below the tenth percentile on the intrauterine growth curve should have blood sugar assessments at least every eight hours until four days of age or more frequently if any symptoms develop.

Calculation of glucose requirements and maintenance of intravenous glucose will be necessary for any symptomatic infant with low serum glucose levels. Careful attention to glucose monitoring is again required when the transition from intravenous to oral feedings is attempted. Titration of intravenous glucose may be required until the infant is able to take adequate amounts of formula or breast milk to maintain a normal blood sugar level.

### DECREASING PHYSIOLOGIC STRESS

The method of feeding greatly influences glucose and energy requirements. In addition, the therapeutic nursing measure of nonnutritive sucking during gavage feedings has been reported to increase the baby's daily weight gain and lead to earlier nipple feeding and discharge (Field et al 1982). Nonnutritive sucking may also lower activity levels, which allows newborns to conserve their energy stores. Activity can increase energy requirements; crying alone can double the baby's metabolic rate. Establishment and maintenance of a neutral thermal environment has a potent influence on the newborn's metabolism. The nurse pays careful attention to environmental conditions, physical activity, and organization of care and integrates these factors into delivery of nursing care. The nurse identifies any discrepancies between the baby's caloric requirements and received calories and weighs the newborn daily at consistent times, preferably before a feeding. Only then can findings of unusual losses or gains, as well as the pattern of weight gain, be considered reliable.

## • Evaluation

Anticipated outcomes of nursing care include:

- The risk of hypoglycemia is promptly identified, and intervention is started early.
- The newborn's metabolic and physiologic processes are stabilized, and recovery is proceeding without sequelae.
- The parents verbalize their concerns about their baby's health problem and understand the rationale behind management of their newborn.

## • CARE OF THE NEWBORN WITH JAUNDICE

The most common abnormal physical finding in neonates is **jaundice** (icterus). Jaundice develops from deposit of the yellow pigment *bilirubin* in lipid tissues. Unconjugated bilirubin is a break-down product derived primarily from hemoglobin that is released from lysed red blood cells and heme pigments found in cell elements (nonerythrocyte bilirubin).

Fetal unconjugated bilirubin is normally cleared by the placenta in utero, so total bilirubin at birth is usually less than 3 mg/dL unless an abnormal hemolytic process has been present. Postnatally, the infant must conjugate bilirubin (convert a lipid-soluble pigment into a water-soluble pigment) in the liver, producing a rise in serum bilirubin in the first days of life.

The rate and amount of conjugation depends on the rate of hemolysis, on the maturity of the liver, and on albumin-binding sites. See Chapter 20, p 558 for discussion of conjugation of bilirubin. A normal, healthy, full-term infant's liver is usually mature enough and producing enough glucuronyl transferase that total serum bilirubin levels do not reach pathologic levels (above 12 mg/dL in the blood).

## ● *Pathophysiology*

Serum albumin-binding sites are usually sufficient to meet the normal demands. However, certain conditions tend to decrease the sites available. Fetal or neonatal asphyxia decreases the binding affinity of bilirubin to albumin as acidosis impairs the capacity of albumin to hold bilirubin. Hypothermia and hypoglycemia release free fatty acids that dislocate bilirubin from albumin. Maternal use of sulfa drugs or salicylates interferes with conjugation or interferes with serum albumin-binding sites by competing with bilirubin for these sites.

A number of bacterial and viral infections (cytomegalic inclusion disease, toxoplasmosis, herpes, syphilis) can affect the liver and produce jaundice. **Hyperbilirubinemia** (elevation of bilirubin level) may also result from blood disorders such as polycythemia (twin-to-twin transfusion, large placental transfer of blood), or enclosed hemorrhage (cephalhematoma, bleeding into internal organs, ecchymoses). Increased hemolysis due to conditions such as sepsis, hemolytic disease of the newborn, or an excessive dose of vitamin K may also cause elevated bilirubin levels.

The bilirubin level at which an infant is harmed varies, but at that level the infant may suffer neurologic defects and eventually death. While the mechanism of bilirubin-produced neuronal injury is uncertain, evidence indicates that high concentrations of unconjugated bilirubin can be neurotoxic (Avery and Taeusch 1984). Unconjugated bilirubin has a high affinity for extravascular tissue such as fatty tissue (subcutaneous tissue) and the brain. Thus bilirubin not bound to albumin can cross the blood-brain barrier and damage the cells of the CNS and produce kernicterus. **Kernicterus** (meaning "yellow nucleus") refers to the deposition of unconjugated bilirubin in the basal ganglia of the brain and to the symptoms of neurologic damage that follow untreated hyperbilirubinemia. The classic bilirubin encephalopathy of kernicterus most commonly found with blood group incompatibility is virtually unknown today due to aggressive treatment with phototherapy and exchange transfusions.

Kernicterus, usually associated with unconjugated bilirubin levels of over 20 mg/dL in normal term infants and over 10 mg/dL in sick preterm newborns, has been noted at autopsy in both types of babies at lower levels. The risk of kernicterus at lowered bilirubin levels has been associated with asphyxia, acidosis, and low serum albumin levels. Current therapy can reduce the incidence of kernicterus encephalopathy but cannot distinguish all infants who are at risk.

Late complications may include cerebral palsy (de Vries et al 1985), impaired or absent hearing, learning difficulties (Brooten et al 1985), and mental retardation.

Certain prenatal and perinatal factors predispose the newborn to hyperbilirubinemia. During pregnancy, maternal conditions that predispose to neonatal hyperbilirubinemia include hereditary spherocytosis, diabetes, intrauterine infections (TORCH and gram-negative bacilli) that stimulate production of maternal isoimmune antibodies, and drug ingestion (sulfas, salicylates, novobiocin, diazepam, oxytocin).

## ● *Causes of Hyperbilirubinemia*

A primary cause of hyperbilirubinemia is **hemolytic disease of the newborn** secondary to Rh incompatibility. Thus the pregnant woman who is Rh-negative or who has blood type O should be asked about outcomes of any previous pregnancies and her history of blood transfusion. Prenatal amniocentesis with spectrophotographic examination may be indicated in some cases. Cord blood from neonates is evaluated for bilirubin level, which should not exceed 5 mg/dL. Neonates of Rh-negative and O-blood type mothers are carefully assessed for appearance of jaundice and levels of serum bilirubin.

Isoimmune hemolytic disease, also known as **erythroblastosis fetalis,** occurs after transplacental passage of a maternal antibody that predisposes fetal and neonatal red blood cells to early destruction. Jaundice, anemia, and compensatory erythropoiesis result. Immature red blood cells—erythroblasts—are found in large numbers in the blood, hence the designation erythroblastosis fetalis. **Hydrops fetalis,** the most severe form of erythroblastosis fetalis, occurs when maternal antibodies attach to the Rh antigen of the fetal red blood cells, making them susceptible to destruction by phagocytes. The fetal system responds by increased erythropoiesis within foci in the placenta and extramedullary sites, and hyperplasia of the bone marrow. Rapid and early destruction of erythrocytes results in a marked increase of immature red blood cells—erythroblasts—that do not have the functional capabilities of mature cells.

If anemia is severe, as seen in hydrops fetalis, cardiomegaly with severe cardiac decompensation and hepatosplenomegaly occur. Severe generalized massive edema (*anasarca*) and generalized fluid effusion into the pleural cavity (hydrothorax), pericardial sac, and peritoneal cavity (ascites) develop. Jaundice is not present until later because the bili pigments are being excreted through the placenta into the maternal circulation. Severe anemia is also responsible for hemorrhage in pulmonary and other tissues. The hydropic hemolytic disease process is also characterized by hyperplasia of the fetal zone of the adrenal cortex and pancreatic islets. Hyperplasia of the pancreatic islets predisposes the infant to neonatal hypoglycemia similar to that of IDMs. These infants also have increased bleeding tendencies due to associated thrombocytopenia and hypoxic damage to the capillaries. Hydrops is a frequent cause of intrauterine death among infants with Rh disease. In rare cases, the grossly enlarged edemic fetal body and placenta may cause uterine rupture.

ABO incompatibility may result in jaundice, although it rarely results in hemolytic disease severe enough to be clinically diagnosed and treated. Hepatosplenomegaly may be found occasionally in newborns with ABO incompatibility, but hydrops fetalis and stillbirth are rare.

The best treatment for hemolytic disease is prevention. Prenatal identification of the fetus at risk for Rh or ABO incompatibility will allow prompt treatment. See Chapter 12 for discussion of in utero management of this condition.

Certain neonatal conditions predispose to hyperbilirubinemia: polycythemia (central hematocrit 65% or more), pyloric stenosis, obstruction or atresia of the biliary duct or of the lower bowel, low-grade urinary tract infection, sepsis, hypothyroidism, enclosed hemorrhage (cephalhematoma, large bruises), asphyxia neonatorum, hypothermia, acidemia, and hypoglycemia. Hepatitis from intrauterine infections or metabolic liver disease elevates the level of conjugated bilirubin.

Neonates born with congenital biliary duct atresia have a poor prognosis; about two thirds have an inoperable lesion and succumb during the first three years of life. The prognosis for a newborn with hyperbilirubinemia depends on the extend of the hemolytic process and the underlying cause. Severe hemolytic disease results in fetal and early neonatal death from the effects of anemia—cardiac decompensation, edema, ascites, and hydrothorax. Hyperbilirubinemia that is not aggressively treated may lead to kernicterus. The resultant neurologic damage is responsible for death, cerebral palsy, mental retardation, sensory difficulties, or to a lesser degree, perceptual impairment, delayed speech development, hyperactivity, muscle incoordination, or learning difficulties (Klaus and Fanaroff 1986).

## • Medical Therapy

The goals of medical management are prompt identification of infants at risk for jaundice based on perinatal and neonatal history, laboratory tests to identify the cause of the jaundice, and prompt treatment to prevent the neurologic damage that can result from hyperbilirubinemia.

In the presence of one or more of the predisposing factors, laboratory determination should be made of the maternal and neonatal blood types for Rh or ABO incompatibility. Other necessary laboratory evaluations are Coombs' test, serum bilirubin levels (direct, indirect, and total), hemoglobin, reticulocyte percentage, and white cell count.

Neonatal hyperbilirubinemia of any origin must be considered pathologic (Avery and Taeusch 1984) if any of the following criteria are met:

1.  Clinically evident jaundice in the first 24 hours of life
2.  Serum bilirubin concentration rising by more than 5 mg/dL per day
3.  Total serum bilirubin concentrations exceeding 12.9 mg/dL in term infants or 15 mg/dL in preterm babies (since preterm newborns have less subcutaneous fat, bilirubin may reach higher levels before it is visible)
4.  Conjugated bilirubin concentrations greater than 2 mg/dL
5.  Persistence of clinical jaundice beyond seven days in term infants or beyond 14 days in preterm infants

Initial diagnostic procedures are aimed at differentiating jaundice resulting from increased bilirubin production, impaired conjugation or excretion, increased intestinal reabsorption, or a combination of these factors. The Coombs' test is performed to determine whether jaundice is due to hemolytic disease.

If the hemolytic process is due to Rh sensitization, laboratory findings reveal the following: (a) an Rh-positive neonate with a positive Coombs' test, (b) increased erythropoiesis with many immature circulating red blood cells (nucleated blastocysts), (c) anemia, in most cases, (d) elevated levels (5 mg/dL or more) of bilirubin in cord blood, and (e) a reduction in albumin-binding capacity. Maternal data may include an elevated anti-Rh titer and spectrophotometric evidence of fetal hemolytic process.

The Coombs' test can be either indirect or direct. The indirect Coombs' test measures the amount of Rh-positive antibodies in the mother's blood. Rh-positive red blood cells are added to the maternal blood sample. If the mother's serum contains antibodies, the Rh-positive red blood cells will agglutinate (clump) when rabbit immune antiglobulin is added, and the test results are labeled positive.

The direct Coombs' test reveals the presence of antibody-coated (sensitized) Rh-positive red blood cells in the neonate. Rabbit immune antiglobulin is added to the neonatal blood cells specimen. If the neonatal red blood cells agglutinate, they have been coated with maternal antibodies, and the test result is positive.

The direct Coombs' test on the neonate's cells may be

negative or mildly positive, but the indirect Coombs' test, when using the neonate's serum on adult red blood cells, may be strongly positive. This finding indicates that the neonate's red blood cells are not coated with the antibody; however, the antibody is present in the neonate's serum.

If the hemolytic process is due to ABO incompatibility, laboratory findings reveal an increase in recticulocytes. The resulting anemia is usually not significant during the neonatal period and is rare later on. The direct Coombs' test may be negative or mildly positive, while the indirect Coombs' test may be strongly positive. Infants with a direct Coombs' positive test have increased incidence of jaundice with bilirubin levels in excess of 10 mg/dL. Increased numbers of spherocytes (spherical, plump, mature erythrocytes) are seen on a peripheral blood smear. Increased numbers of spherocytes are not seen on smears from Rh disease infants.

Regardless of the cause of hyperbilirubinemia, management is directed toward preventing anemia and minimizing the consequences of hyperbilirubinemia.

Treatment has four goals:

- Alleviating the anemia
- Removing maternal antibodies and sensitized erythrocytes
- Increasing serum albumin levels
- Reducing the levels of serum bilirubin

Therapeutic methods of management of hyperbilirubinemia include phototherapy, exchange transfusion, infusion of albumin, and drug therapy. If hemolytic disease is present, it may be treated by phototherapy, exchange transfusion, and drug therapy. When determining the appropriate management of hyperbilirubinemia due to hemolytic disease, the three variables that must be taken into account are the newborn's (1) serum bilirubin level, (2) birth weight, and (3) age in hours. If a neonate has hemolysis with an unconjugated bilirubin level of 14 mg/dL, weighs less than 2500 g (birth weight), and is 24 hours old or less, an exchange transfusion may be the best management. However, if that same neonate is over 24 hours of age, phototherapy may be the treatment of choice to prevent the possible complication of kernicterus (Figure 24.20).

| Serum bilirubin mg/dL | Birth weight | <24 hrs. | 24–48 hrs. | 49–72 hrs. | >72 hrs. |
|---|---|---|---|---|---|
| <5 | All | | | | |
| 5–9 | All | Phototherapy if hemolysis | | | |
| 10–14 | <2500 g | Exchange if hemolysis | Phototherapy | Phototherapy | Phototherapy |
| 10–14 | >2500 g | Exchange if hemolysis | Phototherapy | Investigate bilirubin > 12 mg | Investigate bilirubin > 12 mg |
| 15–19 | <2500 g | Exchange | Exchange | Exchange | Consider exchange |
| 15–19 | >2500 g | Exchange | Exchange | Exchange | Phototherapy |
| 20 + | All | Exchange | Exchange | Exchange | Exchange |

☐ Observe   ▨ Investigate jaundice

*Figure 24.20  Therapy for isoimmune hemolytic disease in the neonate. Phototherapy is used after any exchange transfusion. If the following conditions are present, treat the neonate as if in the next higher bilirubin category; perinatal asphyxia, respiratory distress, metabolic acidosis (ph 7.25 or below), hypothermia (temperature below 35°C), low serum protein (5 g/dL or less), birth weight less than 1500 g, or signs of clinical or CNS deterioration. (From Avery GB: Neonatology, 2nd ed. Philadelphia: Lippincott, 1981, p 511.)*

## PHOTOTHERAPY

**Phototherapy** may be used alone or in conjunction with exchange transfusion to reduce serum bilirubin levels. Exposure of the neonate to high-intensity light (a bank of fluorescent light bulbs or bulbs in the blue-light spectrum) decreases serum bilirubin levels in the skin. Phototherapy reduces serum bilirubin by facilitating biliary excretion of unconjugated bilirubin. This occurs when light absorbed by the tissue converts unconjugated bilirubin to two isomers called photobilirubin. The photobilirubin moves from the tissues to the blood by a diffusion mechanism. In the blood it is bound to albumin and transported to the liver. It moves into the bile and is excreted into the duodenum for removal with feces without requiring conjugation by the liver (Avery and Taeusch 1984). The photodegradation products formed when light oxidizes bilirubin can be excreted in the urine. Phototherapy plays an important role in preventing a rise in bilirubin levels but does not alter the underlying cause of jaundice, and hemolysis may continue to produce anemia.

It is generally accepted that phototherapy should be started at 4 to 5 mg/dL below the calculated exchange level for each infant. Sick neonates of less than 1000 g should have phototherapy instituted at a bilirubin concentration of 5 mg/dL. Some authors have recommended initiating phototherapy "prophylactically" in the first 24 hours of life in high-risk, very-low-birth-weight infants. However, a recent study (Curtis-Cohen et al 1985) has demonstrated no alteration in the course of hyperbilirubinemia in infants who received prophylactic phototherapy compared with infants in whom phototherapy was begun at a bilirubin concentration of 5 mg/dL. Sick preterm infants who are at least 1500 g should have phototherapy instituted when the bilirubin level is 10 mg/dL. Any neonate with a bilirubin level of 20 mg/dL or above should have an exchange transfusion regardless of weight or age.

## EXCHANGE TRANSFUSION

**Exchange transfusion** is the withdrawal and replacement of the neonate's blood with donor blood. Early or immediate exchange transfusion is indicated in the presence of the following conditions:

- Anti-Rh titer of greater than 1:16 in the mother
- Severe hemolytic disease in a previous newborn
- Clinical hemolytic disease of the newborn at birth or within the first 24 hours
- Positive direct Coombs' test
- Cord serum levels of conjugated (direct) bilirubin greater than 3.5 mg/dL in the first week
- Serum unconjugated bilirubin levels greater than 2.0 mg/dL in the first 48 hours

- Hemoglobin less than 12 g/dL or infants with hydrops at birth

Exchange transfusion is used to treat anemia with red blood cells that are not susceptible to maternal antibodies, remove sensitized red blood cells that would be lysed soon, remove serum bilirubin, and provide bilirubin-free albumin and increase the binding sites for bilirubin. In Rh incompatibility, fresh (under two days old) group O, Rh-negative whole blood, or packed red blood cells, is chosen. This type of blood contains no A or B antigens or Rh antigens; therefore the maternal antibodies still present in the neonate's blood will not cause hemolysis of the transfused blood. Packed cells are used if the infant is anemic. Citrate-phosphate-dextrose (CPD) blood is preferred because it presents less of an acid load to the infant.

In case of ABO incompatibility, group O with Rh-specific cells and low titers of anti-A and anti-B donor blood is used, not the infant's blood type, since donor blood contains no antigens to further stimulate maternal antibodies.

Every four to eight hours after the transfusion, bilirubin determinations are made. Repeat exchange may be necessary if the serum bilirubin level rises at a rate of 0.5–1.0 mg/dL/hr (Avery 1987) or if the bilirubin level exceeds 20 mg/dL. Daily hemoglobin estimates should be obtained until stable, and hemoglobin determinations every two weeks for two months are valuable.

## DRUG THERAPY

Phenobarbital is capable of stimulating the liver's production of enzymes that increase conjugation of bilirubin and its excretion. This drug is effective only if given to the pregnant woman over several days prior to two weeks before delivery.

Postnatal drug therapy is of limited value in term infants. It takes three to seven days to show any effect and may take much longer in preterm infants. The use of phenobarbital postnatally for the treatment of hyperbilirubinemia is controversial because the side effects (lethargy with poor feedings) may outweigh the benefits, and preterm newborns may not respond at all.

## • Nursing Assessment

Assessment is aimed at identifying prenatal and perinatal factors that predispose to development of jaundice and identifying jaundice as soon as it is apparent. Clinically, ABO incompatibility presents as jaundice and occasionally as hepatosplenomegaly. Hydrops is rare. Hemolytic disease of the newborn is suspected if the placenta is enlarged, if the newborn is edematous with pleural and pericardial effusion plus ascites, if pallor or jaundice is noted during the first 24 to 36 hours, if hemolytic anemia is diagnosed, or if the spleen and liver are enlarged. The nurse carefully notes changes in behavior and observes for evidence of bleeding. If laboratory tests indicate elevated bilirubin levels, the nurse checks the newborn for jaundice about every two hours and records observations.

To check for jaundice, the nurse should blanch the skin over a bony prominence (forehead, nose, or sternum) by pressing firmly with the thumb. After pressure is released, if jaundice if present, the area appears yellow before normal color returns. The nurse should check oral mucosa and the posterior portion of the hard palate and conjunctival sacs for yellow pigmentation in darker-skinned babies. Assessment in daylight gives best results as pink walls and surroundings may mask yellowish tints and yellow light makes differentiation of jaundice difficult. The time of onset of jaundice is recorded and reported. If jaundice appears, careful observation of the increase in depth of color and of the infant's behavior is mandatory.

The newborn's behavior is assessed for neurologic signs of kernicterus, which are rare but may include hypotonia, diminished reflexes, lethargy, seizures, or opisthotonic posturing.

## ● Nursing Diagnosis

Nursing diagnoses that may apply are included in the Nursing Care Plan—Newborn with Jaundice.

## ● Nursing Plan and Implementation
### PROMOTION OF EFFECTIVE PHOTOTHERAPY

Ideally the entire skin surface of the newborn is exposed to the light. Minimal covering is applied over the genitals and buttocks to expose maximum skin surface while protecting the bedding. Phototherapy success is measured every 12 hours or with daily serum bilirubin levels. The lights must be turned off while drawing blood for serum bilirubin levels. Because it is not known if phototherapy injures the delicate eye structures, particularly the retina, the nurse should apply eye patches over the newborn's closed eyes during exposure (Figure 24.21). Phototherapy is discontinued and the eye patches are removed at least once per shift to assess the eyes for the presence of conjunctivitis. Patches are also removed to allow eye contact during feeding (social stimulation) or when parents are visiting (parental attachment).

The irradiance level at the skin determines the effectiveness of the phototherapy. The desired level of irradiance is 5 to 6 microwatts per square centimeter per nanometer. Most phototherapy units will provide this level of irradiance 42 to 45 cm below the lamps. Irradiance levels can be increased slightly as indicated. The nurse can use a photometer to measure and maintain the levels at between 4 and 8.5 microwatts per square centimeter (Avery and Taeusch 1984).

The neonate's temperature is monitored to prevent hyperthermia or hypothermia. The newborn will require additional fluids to compensate for the increased water loss through the skin and loose stools. Loose stools and increased urine output are the results of increased bilirubin excretion. The infant must be observed for signs of dehydration (Braune and Lacey 1983).

A transient bronze discoloration of the skin may occur with phototherapy when the infant has elevated direct serum bilirubin levels or liver disease. As a side effect of phototherapy, some newborns develop a maculopapular rash. In addition to assessing the neonate's skin color for jaundice and bronzing, the nurse examines the skin for developing pressure areas. The neonate should be repositioned at least every two hours to permit the light to reach all skin surfaces, to prevent pressure areas, and to vary the stimulation to the infant. The nurse keeps track of the number of hours each lamp is used so that each can be replaced before its effectiveness is lost.

*(Text continues on page 730.)*

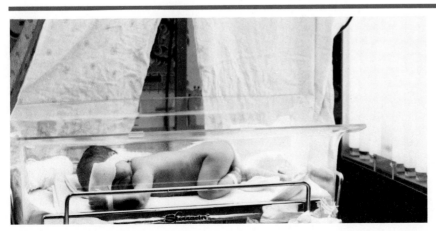

*Figure 24.21 Infant receiving phototherapy. The phototherapy light is positioned over the Isolette. The infant is undressed to expose as much skin as possible. Bilateral eye patches are always used during phototherapy.*

## *Nursing Care Plan*

### Newborn with Jaundice

---

**Client Assessment**

#### Nursing History

*Maternal*
ABO incompatibility
Rh negative
Diabetes
Presence of infection, such as syphilis, cytomegalovirus, rubella, toxoplasmosis
Presence of familiar blood dyscrasias such as spherocytosis, G-6-PD deficiency
Medications: Novobiocin, sulfonamides, and salicylates interfere with conjugation or compete for serum albumin-binding sites
Number and outcome of previous pregnancies
Condition at birth and current health status of other children

*Paternal*
Rh factor—negative or positive

*Delivery*
Enlarged placenta (larger than one seventh of neonate's weight)
Delayed clamping of umbilical cord
Traumatic delivery

*Neonate*
Enclosed hemorrhage, hematoma, large bruises, intracranial bleeding
Bacterial and/or viral infections can affect liver and thus decrease glucuronyl transferase activity
Polycythemia (central hematocrit of 65% or more)
Biliary atresia, cystic fibrosis (inspissated bile)
Congenital hypothyroidism
Conditions that decrease available albumin-binding sites:
1. Fetal or neonatal asphyxia decreases binding affinity of bilirubin to albumin.
2. Chilling and hypoglycemia create fatty acids to compete for binding sites.
3. Preterm neonates tend to have lower serum albumin levels and therefore less albumin to bind to.

#### Physical Examination

Generalized edema with pleural and pericardial effusion

Pallor or jaundice noted in first 24–36 hours

May have enlargement of spleen or liver

Changes in behavior (lethargy, irritability)

Dark, concentrated urine

Hypoactive bowel sounds

Presence of hematomas or large bruises (assess for other signs of enclosed bleeding)

Excessive ecchymosis or petechiae

Meconium passage may be delayed

#### Diagnostic Studies

Coombs' test—direct on baby, indirect on mother's blood

Total bilirubin level

Indications for exchange transfusion:
In ABO incompatibility, serum bilirubin levels greater than 20 mg/dL (full-term) and 15 mg/dL (preterm)
In Rh incompatibility, serum bilirubin greater than 20 mg/dL (term) greater than 15 mg/dL (large preterms), and greater than 13 mg/dL (less than 1250 g preterms)

Total serum protein (provides measure of binding capacity)

Complete blood cell count (CBC)—assess anemia and polycythemia

Peripheral smear—evaluate red blood cells for immaturity or abnormality

Blood glucose

$CO_2$ combining power

Reticulocyte count

Kleihauer-Betke test

Transcutaneous jaundice meter

---

| Nursing Diagnosis/Client Goals | Nursing Interventions | Rationale/Evaluation |
| --- | --- | --- |
| **Nursing Diagnosis:**<br><br>Pattern 1: Exchanging<br>Impaired tissue integrity related to predisposing factors associated with hyperbilirubinemia | Evaluate baby's history for predisposing factors for hyperbilirubinemia. | **Rationale:**<br><br>Early identification of risk factors enables the nurse to monitor babies for early signs of hyperbilirubinemia.<br>Acidosis, hypoxia, hypothermia, etc increase the risk of hyperbilirubinemia at lower bilirubin levels. |

# Nursing Care Plan

## Newborn with Jaundice (continued)

| Nursing Diagnosis/Client Goals | Nursing Interventions | Rationale/Evaluation |
|---|---|---|
| **Client Goal:**<br><br>Babies at risk for jaundice and early signs of jaundice will be identified. | Observe color of amniotic fluid at time of rupture of membranes.<br><br>Assess baby for developing jaundice in daylight if possible.<br><br>1. Observe sclera.<br><br><br>2. Observe skin color and assess by blanching.<br><br>3. Check oral mucosa, posterior portion of hard palate, and conjunctival sacs for yellow pigmentation in dark-skinned newborns.<br><br>Report jaundice occurring within 24 hours of birth. | Amber-colored amniotic fluid is indicative of hyperbilirubinemia.<br><br>Early detection is affected by nursery environment. Artificial lights (with pink tint) may mask beginning of jaundice.<br><br>Most visible sign of hyperbilirubinemia is jaundice noted in skin, sclera, or oral mucosa. Onset is first seen on face.<br><br>Blanching the skin leaves a yellow color to the skin immediately after pressure is released.<br><br>Underlying pigment of dark-skinned people may normally appear yellow.<br><br>**Evaluation:**<br><br>Baby's jaundice is identified early. |
| **Nursing Diagnosis:**<br><br>Pattern 1: Exchanging<br>Potential for injury related to reabsorption of bilirubin secondary to decreased stooling<br><br>**Client Goal:**<br><br>Baby will start feedings within four to six hr after birth, have active bowel sounds, and begin to pass meconium stools. | Initiate feedings within four to six hr after delivery or per protocol. | **Rationale:**<br><br>Early feeding stimulates digestive enzymes involved in establishing gut bacterial flora and decreased enterohepatic circulation.<br><br>**Evaluation:**<br><br>Baby tolerates feedings and passes meconium. |
| **Nursing Diagnosis:**<br><br>Pattern 1: Exchanging<br>Fluid volume deficit secondary to phototherapy<br><br>**Client Goal:**<br><br>Baby will have good skin turgor, clear amber urine output of 1–3 cc/kg/hr, six to eight wet diapers/day, and will maintain weight. | Offer feedings every two to four hr.<br><br><br><br>Provide 25% extra fluid intake.<br><br>Assess for dehydration:<br>1. Poor skin turgor<br>2. Depressed fontanelles<br>3. Sunken eyes<br>4. Decreased urine output<br>5. Weight loss<br>6. Changes in electrolytes<br><br>Monitor intake and output (I & O). | **Rationale:**<br><br>Adequate hydration increases peristalsis and excretion of bilirubin.<br><br><br><br>Replace fluid losses due to watery stools, if under phototherapy.<br><br>Phototherapy treatment may cause liquid stools and increased insensible water loss, which increases risk of dehydration. |

*(continues)*

# Nursing Care Plan

## Newborn with Jaundice (continued)

| Nursing Diagnosis/Client Goals | Nursing Interventions | Rationale/Evaluation |
|---|---|---|
| | Weigh daily.<br>Report signs of dehydration. | Prevents fluid overload. |
| | Administer IV fluids<br>1. Monitor flow rates.<br>2. Assess insertion site for signs of infection. | IV fluids may be used if baby is dehydrated or in presence of other complications. IV may be started if exchange transfusion is to be done. |
| | | **Evaluation:**<br>Baby tolerates oral feedings and is adequately hydrated. |
| **Nursing Diagnosis:**<br>Pattern 1: Exchanging<br>Potential for injury related to use of phototherapy | Cover baby's eyes with eye patches while under phototherapy lights. Cover testes/penis in male infants. | **Rationale:**<br>Protects retina from damage due to high intensity light and testes from damage from heat. |
| **Client Goal:** | Make certain that the eyelids are closed prior to applying eyepatches. | Prevents corneal abrasions. |
| Baby will not have any corneal irritation/drainage, skin breakdown, or major fluctuations in temperature. | Remove baby from under phototherapy and remove eye patches during feedings. | Provides visual stimulation and facilitates attachment behaviors. |
| | Inspect eyes each shift for conjunctivitis, drainage, and corneal abrasions due to irritation from eye patches. | Prevents or facilitates prompt treatment of purulent conjunctivitis. |
| | Administer thorough perianal cleansing with each stool or change of perianal protective covering. | Frequent stooling increases risk of skin breakdown. Prevents infection. |
| | Provide minimal coverage—only of diaper area. | Provides maximal exposure. Shielded areas become more jaundiced, so maximum exposure is essential. |
| | Use paper face mask after removing nose strip. | Metal strip can burn baby's skin when heated by the lights. |
| | Avoid the use of oily applications on the skin. | |
| | Reposition baby q 2 hours. | Provides equal exposure of all skin areas and prevents pressure areas. |
| | Observe for bronzing of skin. | Bronzing is related to use of phototherapy with increased direct bilirubin levels or liver damage; may last for two to four months. |
| | Place plexiglass shield between baby and light. | |
| | Monitor baby's skin and core temperature frequently until temperature is stable. | Hypothermia and hyperthermia are common complications of phototherapy. Hypothermia results from exposure to lights, subsequent radiation, and convection losses. |
| | Check axillary temperature with readings on servo-controlled unit on Isolette. | Hyperthermia may result from the increased environmental heat. |

# Nursing Care Plan

## Newborn with Jaundice *(continued)*

| Nursing Diagnosis/Client Goals | Nursing Interventions | Rationale/Evaluation |
| --- | --- | --- |
| | Regulate Isolette temperature as needed. | Additional heat from phototherapy lights frequently causes a rise in the baby's and the Isolette's temperatures. Fluctuations in temperature may occur in response to radiation and convection. |
| | | **Evaluation:** Baby's eyes are protected, skin is intact, and baby maintains a stable temperature. |
| **Nursing Diagnosis:** Pattern 7: Perceiving Sensory/perceptual alterations related to neurologic damage secondary to kernicterus **Client Goal:** Baby will not show signs of altered biorhythms, hypotonia, temperature instability, spasticity, lethargy, poor sucking reflex. | Monitor any neurologic/behavioral changes in baby by taking vital signs every two hr. Report any changes promptly. Closely assess infant's daily patterns to detect notable changes in food ingestion, bowel and urine and sleeping and waking rhythms, irritability. Report signs of worsening condition (kernicterus): 1. Hypotonia, lethargy, poor sucking reflex, hypertonicity 2. Spasticity and opisthotonus 3. Temperature instability 4. Gradual appearance of extrapyramidal signs 5. Impaired or absent hearing Monitor laboratory studies as indicated: 1. Direct and indirect bilirubin 2. $CO_2$ 3. Reticulocyte count 4. Hematocrit and hemoglobin (H & H) total serum protein | **Rationale:** Baby may develop green, watery stools and green urine due to excretion of bilirubin byproducts. Changes in biologic rhythms caused by phototherapy are unclear and may indicate signs of worsening condition. Deposition of bilirubin in brain leads to development of symptoms of kernicterus. Note: Treatment may be more aggressive in presence of neonatal complications such as asphyxia, respiratory distress, metabolic acidosis, hypothermia, low serum protein, sepsis, signs of CNS deterioration (Avery 1987). **Evaluation:** Baby's neurologic status is within normal limits. |
| **Nursing Diagnosis:** Pattern 8: Knowing Knowledge deficit related to causes of and care of baby with hyperbilirubinemia **Client Goals:** Parents will be informed of baby's disease process, rationale for treatments, and expected outcome. Mother will understand the reason for temporary discontinuation of breast-feeding, how to pump her breasts, and how to reinstate breast-feeding. | Provide explanation of: 1. Infant's condition 2. Treatment modalities, causative and contributing factors of jaundice and hyperbilirubinemia 3. Reasons that mother may be asked to cease breast-feeding temporarily | **Rationale:** Parents may not understand what is happening or why. Physician preference of treatment modalities may vary. Parents may not understand why their newborn is not receiving a treatment that another with the same condition is receiving. The etiology of breast milk jaundice remains uncertain. The serum bilirubin levels begin to fall within 48 hr after discontinuation of breast-feeding. Opinion of physicians varies regarding the need for discontinuing breast-feeding. |

*(continues)*

## Nursing Care Plan

### Newborn with Jaundice *(continued)*

| Nursing Diagnosis/Client Goals | Nursing Interventions | Rationale/Evaluation |
|---|---|---|
| | Assist mother to pump her breasts to maintain her milk supply. Give explanation of equipment being used and changes in bilirubin levels. Allow parents an opportunity to ask questions; reinforce or clarify information as needed. | Mother may need support and information to restart breast-feeding. If breast-feeding is temporarily discontinued, assess mother's knowledge of pumping her breasts and provide information and support as needed. |
| | | **Evaluation:** Parents understand the process of jaundice and rationale behind treatments. |
| **Nursing Diagnosis:** Pattern 3: Relating Potential altered parenting related to parenting a baby with jaundice | Encourage parents to provide tactile stimulation during feeding and diaper changes. | **Rationale:** Neonate has normal needs for tactile stimulation. |
| **Client Goals:** Parents will provide care and stimulation for their baby. | Provide cuddling and eye contact during feedings and talk to baby frequently. Encourage parents to come into nursery for feedings and to touch their baby. | Provides comforting and decreased sensory deprivation. Presence of equipment may discourage parents from interacting with neonate. |
| | | **Evaluation:** Parents are involved in the care of their baby and the bonding process occurs. |

### PROMOTION OF EFFECTIVE EXCHANGE TRANSFUSION

The nurse's responsibilities during exchange transfusion are to: assemble equipment, prepare the baby, assist the physician during the procedure, and maintain a careful record of all events. After the procedure the nurse observes the newborn for complications from the transfusion and clinical signs of hyperbilirubinemia and neurologic damage (Procedure 24.3).

### NURSING GOAL: PROVISION OF TEACHING AND EMOTIONAL SUPPORT TO FAMILIES

Many parents must face the mother's discharge while the neonate remains in the hospital for treatment of hyperbilirubinemia. The terms *jaundice, hyperbilirubinemia, exchange transfusion,* and *phototherapy* may sound frightening and threatening. Some parents may feel guilty and think they have caused the problem. On occasion, a multidisciplinary team (eg, nurse, obstetrician, pediatrician, clergyman, genetic counselor, psychologist) may collaborate to help the parents cope with the situation. Under stress, parents may not be able to "hear" or understand the physician's first explanations. The nurse must expect that the parents will need explanations repeated and clarified and that they may need help voicing their questions and fears. Eye and tactile contact with the neonate is encouraged. The nurse can coach parents when they visit with the baby. Parents are kept informed of their infant's condition and are encouraged to return to the hospital or telephone at any time so that they can be fully involved in the care of their infant. (See the Nursing Care Plan—Newborn with Jaundice.)

### • CARE OF THE NEWBORN WITH HEMORRHAGIC DISEASE

Several transient coagulation-mechanism deficiencies normally occur in the first several days of a newborn's life. Foremost among these is a slight decrease in the level of prothrombin, resulting in a prolonged clotting time during

## Procedure 24.3

## Nursing Responsibilities During Exchange Transfusion*

| Objective | Nursing Action | Rationale |
|---|---|---|
| Prepare infant. | 1. Identify baby. | To prepare correct infant. |
| | 2. Keep newborn NPO for four hr preceding exchange transfusion or aspirate stomach. | To decrease chance of regurgitation and aspiration by neonate. |
| | 3. May administer salt-poor albumin (1 g/kg body weight) one hr before exchange transfusion. | To increase binding of bilirubin. Do not give to severely anemic or edemic neonate or to neonate with congestive heart failure, because of hazard of hypervolemia. |
| | 4. Assess vital signs. | To provide a baseline. |
| | 5. Position neonate in supine position, soft restraints; provide warmth under radiant warmer and have warm blankets available. | To provide maximum visualization, thermoregulation and prevent chilling. |
| | 6. Clean abdomen by scrubbing. | To reduce number of bacteria present. |
| | 7. Attach monitor leads to infant. | To assess pulse and respiration. |
| Prepare equipment. | 1. Have resuscitation equipment available (oxygen, bag and mask, intubation equipment, 10% glucose IV solution and sodium bicarbonate). | To provide life support measures if necessary. |
| | 2. Obtain blood and check it with physician for type, Rh, and age. | To ensure using correct blood. |
| | 3. Attach blood tubing. | To allow infusion. |
| | 4. Apply blood warmer. | To reduce chill. |
| | 5. Open exchange transfusion and umbilical vein trays. Pour prep solution into basins. | To maintain sterility |
| | 6. Prepare gown and gloves for physician. | |
| Monitor infant status before and during procedure. | Assess pulse, respirations, color, and activity state. | To recognize possible problems such as apnea, bradycardia, cardiac arrhythmia, or arrest and provide data on neonate's response to treatment. |
| Record blood exchange and medications used. | 1. Using blood exchange sheet, record time, amount of blood in, amount of blood out, medications and baby's response, and any other pertinent information. | Donor blood is given at rate of 170 mL/kg of body weight. It replaces 85% of infant's own blood. |
| | 2. Inform physician when 100 mL of blood has been used. | Calcium gluconate is given IV after each 100 mL of blood if indicated to decrease cardiac irritability. |

*Exchange transfusion is a therapeutic procedure for hyperbilirubinemia of any etiology.

*(continues)*

## Procedure 24.3

### Nursing Responsibilities During Exchange Transfusion* (continued)

| Objective | Nursing Action | Rationale |
|---|---|---|
| Assess neonate response after transfusion. | After the exchange, carefully monitor the following for 24–48 hr:<br>1. Vital signs<br>2. Neurologic signs (lethargy, increased irritability, jitteriness, convulsion)<br>3. Amount and color of urine (hematuria)<br>4. Presence of edema<br>5. Signs of necrotizing enterocolitis<br>6. Infection or hemorrhage at infusion site<br>7. Signs of increasing jaundice<br>8. Neurologic signs of kernicterus<br>9. Calcium, glucose, and bilirubin levels<br>10. Other complications such as hypokalemia, septicemia, shock, and thrombosis | To provide information on status of neonate and identification of complications such as hypocalcemia, hyperkalemia, hypernatremia, hypoglycemia and acidosis, sepsis, shock, thrombus, formation, and transfusion mismatch reaction. |
| Prepare blood samples. | Label tubes and send to laboratory with appropriate laboratory slips. | To follow routines of your institution. |
| | Retype and cross-match 2 units of blood two hours postexchange. | To provide for possible future exchange. |

*Exchange transfusion is a therapeutic procedure for hyperbilirubinemia of any etiology.

the initial week of life. Vitamin K is required for the liver to form prothrombin (factor II) and proconvertin (factor VII) for blood coagulation. Vitamin K, a fat-soluble vitamin, may be obtained from food, but it is usually synthesized by bacteria in the colon, and consequently a dietary source is unnecessary. However, intestinal flora are practically nonexistent in newborns, so they are unable to synthesize vitamin K.

Bleeding due to vitamin K deficiency generally occurs on the second or third day of life, but it may occur earlier in babies of mothers treated with phenytoin sodium (Dilantin) or phenobarbital. These drugs impair vitamin K activity, and bleeding may be seen at birth. Coumarin compounds are vitamin K antagonists that can cross the placenta. Thus the baby exposed to maternal coumarin can also manifest bleeding in the first 24 hours of life. Bleeding may also occur in babies receiving parenteral nutrition without adequate vitamin K additives (1 mg/week).

Bleeding from the nose, umbilical cord, circumcision site, gastrointestinal tract, and scalp, as well as generalized ecchymoses may be seen. Internal hemorrhage may occur.

This disorder can be completely prevented by the prophylactic use of an injection of vitamin K. A dose of 1 mg of AquaMEPHYTON is given as part of newborn care imme-

diately following birth, and consequently the disease is rarely seen today (see Drug Guide, Chapter 22). Larger doses are contraindicated because they may result in the development of hyperbilirubinemia.

## • CARE OF THE NEWBORN WITH ANEMIA

Neonatal anemia is often difficult to recognize by clinical evaluation alone. Mean hemoglobin in a full-term newborn is 17 g/dL, slightly higher than in prematures, in whom the mean hemoglobin is 16 g/dL. Infants with hemoglobin values of less than 14 mg/dL (term) and 13 g/dL (preterm) are usually considered anemic. The most common causes of neonatal anemia are blood loss, hemolysis, and impaired red blood cell production.

Blood loss (hypovolemia) occurs in utero from placental bleeding (placenta previa or abruptio placentae). Intrapartal blood loss may be fetomaternal, fetofetal, or the result of umbilical cord bleeding. Birth trauma to abdominal organs or the cranium may produce significant blood loss, and cerebral bleeding may occur due to hypoxia.

Excessive hemolysis of red cells is usually a result of blood group incompatibilities but may be due to infections.

The most common cause of impaired red cell production is a deficiency in G-6-PD, which is genetically transmitted. Anemia and jaundice are the presenting signs.

A condition known as **physiologic anemia** exists as a result of the normal gradual drop in hemoglobin for the first 6 to 12 weeks of life. Theoretically, the bone marrow stops production of red blood cells as a response to the elevated oxygenation of extrauterine respirations. When the amount of hemoglobin becomes lower, reaching levels of 10 to 11 g/dL at about 6 to 12 weeks of age, the bone marrow begins production of RBCs again, and the anemia disappears.

Anemia in preterm newborns occurs earlier and reversal by bone marrow is initiated at lower levels of hemoglobin (7–9 g/dL). The preterm baby's hemoglobin reaches a low sooner (four to eight weeks after birth) than does a term newborn's (six to twelve weeks) because preterm red blood cell survival time is shorter compared to term newborn survival time because the rate of growth in preterms is relatively rapid, and because a vitamin E deficiency is common in small preterm newborns.

## ● Medical Therapy

The goal of management is early identification and correction of anemia. Hematologic problems can be anticipated based on the obstetric history and clinical manifestations. The age at which anemia is first noted is also of diagnostic value.

Clinically, anemic infants are very pale in the absence of other symptoms of shock and usually have abnormally low red blood cell counts. In acute blood loss, symptoms of shock may be present, such as pallor, low arterial blood pressure, and a decreasing hematocrit value. The initial laboratory workup should include hemoglobin and hematocrit measurements, reticulocyte count, examination of peripheral blood smear, bilirubin determinations, direct Coombs' test of infant's blood, and examination of maternal blood smear for fetal erythrocytes (Kleihauer-Betke test). Medical management depends on the severity of the anemia and whether blood loss is acute or chronic. The baby should be placed on constant cardiac and respiratory monitoring. Mild or slow chronic anemia may be treated adequately with iron supplements alone or with iron-fortified formulas. Frequent determinations of hemoglobin, hematocrit, and bilirubin levels (in hemolytic disease) are essential. In severe cases of anemia, transfusions are the treatment of choice.

## ● Nursing Care

The nurse assesses the newborn for symptoms of anemia (pallor). If the blood loss is acute, the baby may exhibit signs of shock. Continued observations will be necessary to identify physiologic anemia as the preterm newborn grows. Signs of compromise include poor weight gain, tachycardia, tachypnea, and apneic episodes.

The nurse promptly reports any symptoms indicating anemia or shock. The amount of blood drawn for all laboratory tests should be recorded so that total blood removed can be assessed and replaced by transfusion when necessary. If the newborn exhibits signs of shock, the nurse may need to begin necessary interventions.

## ● CARE OF THE NEWBORN WITH POLYCYTHEMIA

**Polycythemia** is a condition in which blood volume and hematocrit values are increased. A common problem in low-risk nurseries, polycythemia affects 2% to 17% of newborns (Nantze 1985). It is observed more commonly in SGA and full-term infants than in preterm neonates.

An infant is considered polycythemic when the central venous hematocrit value is greater than 65%–70%, or the venous hemoglobin level is greater than 22 g/dL during the first week of life (Avery 1987).

Several conditions predispose the neonate to polycythemia:

1. At the time of birth an excessive volume of placental blood may transfuse into the infant before the cord is cut, resulting in a blood volume increase.

2. During gestation an increased amount of blood may cross the placenta to the infant (maternofetal transfusion), resulting in increased blood volume after birth.

3. A twin-to-twin transfusion may occur, in which one twin receives less blood and becomes anemic, and the other twin receives an excess amount of blood resulting in polycythemia.

4. Increased red blood cell production may occur in utero in response to chronic fetal distress in SGA, IDM, or postmature infants and secondary to conditions of PIH and placenta previa

Other conditions that present with polycythemia are chromosomal anomalies such as trisomy 21, 18, and 13; endocrine disorders such as hypoglycemia and hypocalcemia; and births at altitudes over 5000 feet.

## ● Medical Therapy

The goal of therapy is to reduce the central venous hematocrit to less than 60% in symptomatic infants. Treatment of asymptomatic infants is more controversial, but most authorities agree that these newborns benefit from prophylactic exchanges. To decrease the red cell mass, the symptomatic infant receives a partial exchange transfusion in which blood is removed from the infant and replaced millimeter for millimeter with fresh plasma. Supportive treatment of presenting symptoms is required until resolution. This usually occurs spontaneously following the partial exchange transfusion.

## ● Nursing Assessment

The nurse assesses, records, and reports symptoms of polycythemia. The nurse also does an initial screening of the newborn's hematocrit on admission to the nursery.

Many infants are asymptomatic, but as symptoms develop they are related to the increased blood volume, hyperviscosity (thickness) of the blood, and decreased deformability of red blood cells, all of which result in poor perfusion of tissues. The infants have a characteristic plethoric (ruddy) appearance. The most common symptoms observed include:

- Tachycardia and congestive heart failure due to the increased blood volume

- Respiratory distress with grunting, tachypnea, and cyanosis; increased oxygen need; or hemorrhage in respiratory system due to pulmonary venous congestion, edema, and hypoxemia

- Hyperbilirubinemia due to increased numbers of red blood cells hemolysed

- Decrease in peripheral pulses, discoloration of extremities, alteration in activity or neurologic depression, renal vein thrombosis with decreased urine output, hematuria, or proteinuria due to thromboembolism

- Seizures due to decreased perfusion of the brain and increased vascular resistance secondary to sluggish blood flow, which can result in neurologic or developmental problems

## ● Nursing Care

The nurse must observe closely for the signs of distress or change in vital signs during the partial exchange. The nurse must assess carefully for potential complications resulting from the exchange such as transfusion overload (may result in congestive heart failure), irregular cardiac rhythm, bacterial infection, hypovolemia, and anemia.

Parents need specific explanations about polycythemia and its treatment. The newborn needs to be reunited with the parents as soon after the exchange as the baby's status permits.

## ● CARE OF THE NEWBORN WITH HYPOCALCEMIA

Calcium is transported across the placenta in increasing amounts during the third trimester of pregnancy. This predisposes the infant who is born preterm to have lower serum calcium levels in the neonatal period. This risk is increased in the presence of perinatal asphyxia, trauma, and hypotonia, and with the use of bicarbonate in treating acidosis. IDMs and infants of mothers with hyperparathyroidism are also at higher risk for hypocalcemia. Hypocalcemia is a common occurrence in the intrapartally asphyxiated neonate in the first two to three days of life due to a delay in oral feedings, which results in less intestinal absorption of calcium. Hypocalcemia is also associated with the practice of administering low-calcium or calcium-free intravenous therapy management.

Serum calcium levels should be monitored in at-risk newborns. Normal serum calcium levels range from 8.0 to 10.5 mg/dL. Hypocalcemia refers to serum calcium levels less than 7 mg/dL or ionized calcium concentrations less than 3 to 3.5 mg/dL. An electrocardiogram (ECG) measurement of the Q-T interval will assist in the diagnosis.

## ● Medical Therapy

Identification of at-risk and/or symptomatic newborns with screening for hypocalcemia is the first consideration of preventive management.

Emergency treatment of symptomatic newborns with intravenous calcium salts will normalize serum concentrations and minimize complications. Initial treatment of symptomatic hypocalcemia is intravenous therapy. Intravenous 10% calcium gluconate may be administered as a continuous infusion or in intermittent slow pushes. Intravenous push doses of calcium gluconate should not exceed 2 mL/kg at any one time. Doses may be repeated as necessary three or four times in 24 hours.

Maintenance calcium will be given either parenterally or orally. Oral calcium glubionate or calcium gluconate may be used for maintenance. Low-phosphorus milk may be used in the treatment of asymptomatic hypocalcemia.

Treatment for hypocalcemia is usually necessary for only four or five days unless other complications exist. Calcium levels should be monitored every 12 to 24 hours and the dose should be tapered off gradually.

## ● Nursing Assessment

Nursing assessment is aimed at identifying at-risk newborns, monitoring serum calcium levels, and closely observing for symptoms.

Schedules for screening serum calcium levels for various at-risk groups have been recommended and are as follows: IDMs at 6, 12, 24, and 48 hours of age; infants suffering from intrapartal asphyxia at 3, 6, and 12 hours of age; preterm newborns less than 1000 g at six hours; and preterm newborns less than 1500 g at 12 hours of age. Healthy preterm newborns greater than 1500 g who are taking milk feedings need not be monitored (Cloherty and Stark 1985).

The symptoms of hypocalcemia are nonspecific and are seen in conjunction with other disorders. The signs and symptoms that may be observed are:

- Apnea
- Cyanotic episodes
- High-pitched cry
- Twitching, jitteriness
- Seizures (local or generalized)
- Abdominal distention
- Edema

## Nursing Care

The nurse must keep in mind several precautions when administering calcium gluconate intravenously:

1. When giving an intravenous push, calcium must be injected very slowly over a period of at least ten minutes, or no more than 1 mL per minute. The heart rate must be monitored, and if bradycardia or other cardiac arrhythmias occur, the infusion must be discontinued immediately.

2. When calcium is administered as a continuous drip, the heart rate must also be monitored constantly. Calcium must not be mixed with other medications such as phosphate or bicarbonate in the line as the mixture may precipitate.

3. The intravenous site must be observed closely for signs of infiltration, as calcium is very damaging to the tissues. If extravasation at the site of infusion occurs, necrosis and sloughing of the tissue is likely.

4. If the calcium is administered through an umbilical arterial catheter, the tip of the catheter should be far enough from the heart that calcium is not injected directly into the heart. If an umbilical venous catheter is used, the tip must be in the inferior vena cava to avoid necrosis of the liver.

Continued observation and monitoring of serum levels will be required during the transition from intravenous to oral maintenance therapy and again when calcium supplementation is tapered off.

## CARE OF THE NEWBORN WITH INFECTION

Neonates up to one month of age are particularly susceptible to infection, referred to as **sepsis neonatorum,** caused by organisms that do not cause significant disease in older children. Incidence of severe infection is 0.5 to 2 per 1000 live newborns.

One predisposing factor is prematurity. The general debilitation and underlying illness often associated with prematurity necessitates invasive procedures such as umbilical catheterization, intubation, resuscitation, ventilatory support, and monitoring. Even full-term infants are susceptible because their immunologic systems are immature. They lack the complex factors involved in effective phagocytosis and the ability to localize infection or to respond with a well-defined recognizable inflammatory response.

Maternal antepartal infections such as rubella, toxoplasmosis, cytomegalic inclusion disease, and herpes may cause congenital infections and resulting disorders in the newborn. Intrapartal maternal infections, such as amnionitis and those resulting from premature rupture of membranes and precipitous delivery, are sources of neonatal infection. Passage through the birth canal and contact with the vaginal flora (β-hemolytic streptococci, herpes, listeria, and gonococci) expose the infant to infection (see Table 24.7). With infection anywhere in the fetus or newborn, the adjacent tissues or organs are very easily penetrated, and the blood-brain barrier is ineffective. Septicemia is more common in males, except for those infections caused by group B β-hemolytic streptococcus.

At present, gram-negative organisms (especially *E coli*, Aerobacter, *Proteus,* and *Klebsiella*) and the gram-positive organism β-hemolytic streptococcus are the most common causative agents. Pseudomonas is a common fomite contaminant of ventilatory support and oxygen therapy equipment.

Protection of the newborn from infections starts prenatally and continues throughout pregnancy and delivery. Prenatal prevention should include maternal screening for venereal disease and monitoring of rubella titers in women who are negative. Intrapartally, sterile technique is essential, smears from genital lesions are taken, and placenta and amniotic fluid cultures are obtained if amnionitis is suspected. If genital herpes is present toward term, cesarean birth may be indicated. Local eye treatment with silver nitrate or an antibiotic ophthalmic ointment is given to all newborns to prevent gonococcal damage.

## Medical Therapy

Infants with a history of possible exposure to infection in utero (for example, premature rupture of membranes [PROM] more than 24 hours before delivery or questionable maternal history of infection) should have cultures (gastric aspirate and ear canal) taken as soon after birth as possible. Cultures are obtained before antibiotic therapy is begun.

1. Two blood cultures are obtained from different peripheral sites. They are taken from a peripheral rather than an umbilical vessel, because catheters have yielded false positives resulting from contamination. The skin is prepared by cleaning with an antiseptic solution, such as one containing iodine,

## Table 24.7 Maternally Transmitted Newborn Infections

| Infection | Nursing assessment | Nursing plan and implementation |
|---|---|---|
| **GROUP B STREPTOCOCCUS** 1–2% colonized with one in ten developing disease Early onset—usually within hours of delivery or within first week Late onset—one week to three months | Severe respiratory distress (grunting and cyanosis). May become apneic or demonstrate symptoms of shock. Meconium-stained amniotic fluid seen at birth. | Early assessment of clinical signs necessary. Assist with x-ray—shows aspiration pneumonia or hyaline membrane disease (HMD). Immediately obtain blood, gastric aspirate, external ear canal and nasopharynx cultures. Administer antibiotics, usually aqueous penicillin or ampicillin combined with gentamicin as soon as cultures are obtained. Early assessment and intervention are essential to survival. Initiate referral to evaluate for blindness, deafness, learning or behavioral problems. |
| **SYPHILIS** Spirochetes cross placenta after 16–18th week of gestation | Check perinatal history for positive maternal serology. Assess infant for: Elevated cord serum IgM and FTA-ABS IgM Rhinitis (snuffles) Fissures on mouth corners and excoriated upper lip Red rash around mouth and anus Copper-colored rash over face, palms, and soles Irritability Generalized edema, particularly over joints; bone lesions; painful extremities Hepatosplenomegaly, jaundice Congenital cataracts SGA and failure to thrive | Initiate isolation techniques until infants have been on antibiotics for 48 hours. Administer penicillin. Provide emotional support for parents because of their feelings about mode of transmission and potential long-term sequelae. |
| **GONORRHEA** | Assess for: Ophthalmia neonatorum (conjunctivitis) Purulent discharge and corneal ulcerations Neonatal sepsis with temperature instability, poor feeding response, and/or hypotonia, jaundice | Administer 1% silver nitrate solution or ophthalmic antibiotic ointment (see Drug Guide—Erythromycin [Ilotycin]) or, in lieu of silver nitrate, penicillin. Initiate follow-up referral to evaluate any loss of vision. |

and allowed to dry; the specimen is obtained with a sterile needle/syringe.

2. Spinal fluid culture is done following a spinal tap.

3. Urine culture is best obtained from a specimen obtained by a suprapubic bladder aspiration.

4. Skin cultures are taken of any lesions or drainage from lesions or reddened areas.

5. Nasopharyngeal, rectal, ear canal, and gastric aspirate cultures may be obtained.

Other laboratory investigations include a complete blood count, chest x-ray examination, serology, and gram stains of cerebrospinal fluid, urine, skin exudate, and umbilicus. White blood count (WBC) with differential may indicate the presence or absence of sepsis. A level of 30,000 WBC may be normal in the first 24 hours of life, while a low WBC may be indicative of sepsis. A low neutrophil count and a high band count indicate that an infection is present. Stomach aspirate should be sent for culture and smear if a gonococcal infection or amnionitis are sus-

## Table 24.7 Maternally Transmitted Newborn Infections *(continued)*

| Infection | Nursing assessment | Nursing plan and implementation |
|---|---|---|
| **HERPES TYPE 2** | Small cluster vesicular skin lesions over all the body. Check perinatal history for active herpes genital lesions. Disseminated form—DIC, pneumonia, hepatitis with jaundice, hepatosplenomegaly, and neurologic abnormalities. Without skin lesions, see fever or subnormal temperature, respiratory congestion, tachypnea and tachycardia. | Carry out careful hand washing and gown and glove isolation with linen precautions. Administer intravenous vidarabine (Vira A) or acyclovir (Zovirax). Initiate follow-up referral to evaluate potential sequelae of microcephaly, spasticity, seizures, deafness, or blindness (Hanshaw et al 1985). Encourage parental rooming-in and touching of their newborn. Show parents appropriate hand-washing procedures and precautions to be used at home if mother's lesions are active (Haggerty 1985). Obtain throat, conjunctiva, cerebral spinal fluid (CSF), blood, urine, and lesion cultures to identify herpesvirus type 2 antibiotics in serum IgM fraction. Cultures positive in 24–48 hours. |
| **MONILIAL INFECTION (THRUSH)** | Assess buccal mucosa, tongue, gums, and inside the cheeks for white plaques (seen five to seven days of age). Check diaper area for bright red, well-demarcated eruptions. Assess for thrush periodically when newborn is on long-term antibiotic therapy. | Differentiate white plaque areas from milk curds by using cotton tip applicator (if it is thrush, removal of white areas causes raw bleeding areas). Maintain cleanliness of hands, linen, clothing, diapers and feeding apparatus. Instruct breast-feeding mothers on treating their nipples with nystatin. Administer gentian violet (1%–2%) swabbed on oral lesions one hour after feeding, or nystatin instilled in baby's oral cavity and on mucosa. Swab skin lesions with topical nystatin. Discuss with parents that gentian violet stains mouth and clothing. Avoid placing gentian violet on normal mucosa; causes irritation. |
| **CHLAMYDIA TRACHOMATIS** | Assess for perinatal history of preterm birth. Symptomatic newborns present with pneumonia—conjunctivitis after three to four days. Chronic follicular conjunctivitis (corneal neovascularization and conjunctival scarring). | Instill ophthalmic erythromycin (See Drug Guide—Erythromycin [Ilotycin]). Initiate follow-up referral for eye complications. |

pected. Serum IgM levels are elevated (normal level less than 20 mg/dL) in response to transplacental infections. If available, counterimmuno-electrophoresis tests for specific bacterial antigens are done. Evidence of congenital infections may be seen on skull x-ray films for cerebral calcifications (cytomegalovirus, toxoplasmosis), on bone x-ray films (syphilis, cytomegalovirus), and in serum-specific IgM levels (rubella). Cytomegalovirus infection is best diagnosed by urine culture.

Because neonatal infection causes high mortality, ther-apy is instituted before results of the septic workup are obtained. A combination of two broad spectrum antibiotics in large doses is given until culture with sensitivities is received.

After the pathogen and its sensitivities are determined, appropriate specific antibiotic therapy is begun. Combinations of penicillin or ampicillin and kanamycin have been used in the past, but new kanamycin-resistant enterobacteria and penicillin-resistant staphylococcus necessitate increasing use of gentamicin.

## Table 24.8   Neonatal Sepsis Antibiotic Therapy

| Drug | Dose | Route | Schedule | Comments |
|---|---|---|---|---|
| Ampicillin | 50–100 mg/kg/day | IM or IV | Every 12 hours* <br> Every 8 hours† | Effective against gram-positive microorganisms and majority of *E coli* strains. |
| Cefotaxime | 100–150 mg/kg/day | IM or IV | Every 12 hours* <br> Every 8 hours† | Active against most major pathogens in infants; effective against aminoglycoside-resistant organisms; achieve CSF bactericidal activity; lack of ototoxicity and nephrotoxicity; wide therapeutic index (levels not required); resistant organisms can develop rapidly if used extensively; ineffective against pseudomonas, listeria. |
| Gentamicin | 5.0–7.5 mg/kg/day | IM or IV | Every 12 hours* <br> Every 8 hours† | Effective against gram-negative rods and staphylococci; may be used instead of kanamycin against penicillin-resistant staphylococci and *E coli* strains and *Pseudomonas aeruginosa*. May cause ototoxicity and nephrotoxicity. Need to follow serum levels. Must never be given as IV push. Must be given over at least 30–60 min. In presence of oliguria or anuria, dose must be decreased or discontinued. In infant less than 1000 g, dosage interval may be as long as 24 hours. Monitor serum levels before administration of second dose. |
| Methicillin | 50–100 mg/kg/day | IM or IV | Every 12 hours* <br> Every 6–8 hours† | Effective against penicillinase-resistant staphylococci |
| Nafcillin | 50–100 mg/kg/day | IM or IV | Every 12 hours* <br> Every 6 hours† | Effective against penicillinase-resistant staphylococci. |
| Penicillin G (aqueous crystalline) | 50,000–125,000 U/kg/day | IM or IV | Every 12 hours* <br> Every 8 hours† | Initial sepsis therapy effective against most gram-positive microorganisms except resistant staphylococci; can cause heart block in infants. |

*Up to seven days of age.
†Greater than seven days of age.

The possibility of rotating aminoglycosides has been suggested to prevent development of resistance (McCracken 1985). Use of cephalosporins and, in particular, cefotaxime, has emerged as an alternative to aminoglycoside therapy in the treatment of neonatal infections. Duration of therapy varies from 7 to 14 days (Table 24.8). If cultures are negative and symptoms subside, antibiotics may be discontinued after three days. Supportive physiologic care may be required to maintain respiratory, hemodynamic, nutritional, and metabolic homeostasis.

● *Nursing Assessment*

Symptoms are most often noticed by the nurse during daily care of the neonate rather than during the infant's sporadic contact with the physician. The infant may deteriorate rapidly in the first 12 to 24 hours after birth if β-hemolytic streptococcal infection is present, with signs and symptoms mimicking RDS. On the other hand, the onset of sepsis may be more gradual with more subtle signs and symptoms. The most common symptoms observed include:

1. Subtle behavioral changes—the infant "isn't doing well" and is often lethargic or irritable (especially after first 24 hours) and hypotonic. Color changes may include pallor, duskiness, cyanosis, or a "shocky" appearance. Skin is cool and clammy.

2. Temperature instability, manifested by either hypothermia (recognized by a decrease in skin temperature) or hyperthermia (elevation of skin temperature) necessitating a corresponding increase

or decrease in Isolette temperature to maintain neutral thermal environment.

3. Poor feeding, evidenced by a decrease in total intake, abdominal distention, vomiting, poor sucking, lack of interest in feeding, and diarrhea.

4. Hyperbilirubinemia.

5. Onset of apnea.

Signs and symptoms may suggest CNS disease (jitteriness, tremors, seizure activity), respiratory system disease (tachypnea, labored respirations, apnea, cyanosis), hematologic disease (jaundice, petechial hemorrhages, hepatosplenomegaly), or gastrointestinal disease (diarrhea, vomiting, bile-stained aspirate, hepatomegaly). A differential diagnosis is necessary because of the similarity of symptoms to other more specific conditions.

## ● *Nursing Diagnosis*

Nursing diagnoses that may apply to the infant with sepsis neonatorum include:

● Potential for infection related to tachypnea, lethargy, and temperature instability secondary to immature immunologic system

● Fluid volume deficit related to feeding intolerance

● Ineffective family coping related to present illness resulting in prolonged hospital stay

## ● *Nursing Plan and Implementation*
### PREVENTION OF INFECTION

In the nursery, environmental control and prevention of acquired infection is the responsibility of the neonatal nurse. The nurse must promote strict hand-washing technique for all who enter the nursery, including nursing colleagues; physicians; laboratory, x-ray, and inhalation technicians; and parents. The nurse must be prepared to assist in the aseptic collection of specimens for laboratory investigations. Scrupulous care of equipment—changing and cleaning of incubators at least every seven days, removal and sterilization of wet equipment every 24 hours, prevention of cross-use of linen and other equipment, periodic cleaning of sinkside equipment such as soap containers, and special care with the open radiant warmers (access without prior hand washing is much easier than with the closed incubator)—will prevent fomite contamination or contamination through improper hand washing of debilitated, infection-prone newborns. An infected neonate can be effectively isolated in an incubator and receive close observation. Visiting of the nursery area by unnecessary personnel should be discouraged.

### PROVISION OF ANTIBIOTIC THERAPY

The nurse administers antibiotics as ordered by the clinician. It is the nurse's responsibility to be knowledgeable about the following:

● The proper dose to be administered, based on the weight of the newborn

● The appropriate route of administration, as some antibiotics cannot be given intravenously

● Admixture incompatibilities since some antibiotics are precipitated by intravenous solutions or by other antibiotics

● Side effects and toxicity

### PROMOTION OF PHYSICAL WELL-BEING

In addition to antibiotic therapy, physiologic supportive care is essential in caring for a septic infant. The nurse should:

● Observe for resolution of symptoms or development of other symptoms of sepsis

● Maintain neutral thermal environment with accurate regulation of humidity and oxygen administration.

● Provide respiratory support: Administer oxygen and observe and monitor respiratory effort.

● Provide cardiovascular support: Observe and monitor pulse and blood pressure; observe for hyperbilirubinemia, anemia, and hemorrhagic symptoms.

● Provide adequate calories, because oral feedings may be discontinued due to increased mucus, abdominal distention, vomiting, and aspiration.

● Provide fluids and electrolytes to maintain homeostasis.

● Detect and treat metabolic disturbances, a common occurrence.

● Observe for the development of hypoglycemia, hyperglycemia, acidosis, hyponatremia, and hypocalcemia.

### PROVISION OF SUPPORT AND EDUCATION TO PARENTS

Restriction of parent visits has not been shown to  have any effect on the rate of infection and may indeed be harmful for the newborn's psychologic development. With instruction and guidance from the nurse, both parents should be allowed to handle the baby and participate in daily care. Support to the parents is crucial. They need to be informed of the newborn's prognosis as treatment continues and to be involved in care as much as possible. They also need to understand how infection is transmitted.

## ● Evaluation

Anticipated outcomes of nursing care include:

● The risks for development of sepsis are identified early, and immediate action is taken to minimize the development of the illness.

● Appropriate use of aseptic technique protects the newborn from further exposure to illness.

● The baby's symptoms are relieved, and the infection is treated.

● The parents verbalize their concerns about their baby's illness and understand the rationale behind the management of their newborn.

## ● CARE OF THE NEWBORN WITH CONGENITAL ANOMALIES

The birth of a baby with a congenital defect places both newborn and family at risk. Many congenital anomalies can be life threatening if not corrected within hours after birth; others are very visible and cause the families emotional distress. Table 24.9 identifies some of the more common anomalies and their early management and nursing care in the neonatal period.

## ● CARE OF THE NEWBORN WITH INBORN ERRORS OF METABOLISM

**Inborn errors of metabolism** are a group of hereditary disorders that are transmitted by mutant genes and result in an enzyme defect that blocks a metabolic pathway and leads to an accumulation of metabolites that are toxic to the infant. Most of the disorders are transmitted by an autosomal recessive gene, requiring two heterozygous parents to produce a homozygous infant with the disorder. Heterozygous parents carrying some inborn errors of metabolism disorders can be identified by special tests, and some inborn errors of metabolism can be detected in utero.

The detection of many inborn errors of metabolism is now accomplished neonatally through newborn screening programs. These programs principally test for disorders associated with mental retardation.

**Phenylketonuria (PKU)** is the most common of the amino acid disorders. Newborn screenings have set its incidence at about one in 10,000 live births worldwide (Naylor 1985). The highest incidence is noted in white populations from northern Europe and the United States. It is rarely observed in African, Jewish, or Japanese people.

Phenylalanine is an essential amino acid used by the body for growth, and in the normal individual any excess is converted to tyrosine. The newborn with PKU lacks this converting ability, which results in an accumulation of phe-

nylalanine in the blood. Phenylalanine produces two abnormal metabolites, phenylpyruvic acid and phenylacetic acid, which are eliminated in the urine, producing a musty odor. Excessive accumulation of phenylalanine and its abnormal metabolites in the brain tissue leads to progressive mental retardation.

*Maple syrup urine disease (MSUD)* is an inborn error of metabolism and, when untreated, is a rapidly progressing and often fatal disease caused by an enzymatic defect in the metabolism of the branched chain amino acids leucine, isoleucine, and valine.

*Homocystinuria* is a disorder caused by a deficiency of the enzyme cystathionine B synthase, which produces a block in the normal conversion of methionine to cystine.

*Galactosemia* is an inborn error of carbohydrate metabolism in which the body is unable to use the sugars galactose and lactose. Enzyme pathways in liver cells normally convert galactose and lactose to glucose. In galactosemia, one step in that conversion pathway is absent, either because of the lack of the enzyme galactose l-phosphate uridyl transferase, or because of the lack of the enzyme galactokinase. High levels of unusable galactose circulate in the blood, which causes cataracts, brain damage, and hepatomegaly (Smith 1980).

Another disorder frequently included in mandatory newborn screening blood tests is *congenital hypothyroidism*. An inborn enzymatic defect, lack of maternal dietary iodine, or maternal ingestion of drugs that depress or destroy thyroid tissue can cause congenital hypothyroidism.

The incidence of metabolic errors is relatively low, but for affected infants and their families these disorders pose a threat to survival and frequently require lifelong treatment.

## ● Medical Therapy

A blood test (called the Guthrie blood test) for PKU is required of all newborns by law in most states. The Guthrie test, done before discharge, is a simple screening tool that uses a drop of blood collected from a heel stick and placed on filter paper. The Guthrie test should be done at least 24 hours, but preferably 72 hours, after the initiation of feedings containing the usual amounts of breast milk or formula. Phenylalanine is found in milk, so its metabolites begin to build up in the PKU baby once milk feedings are initiated.

High-risk newborns should be receiving a 60% milk intake with no more than 40% of their total intake coming from nonprotein intravenous fluids. The PKU testing of high-risk newborns should be deferred for at least 48 hours after hyperalimentation is initiated. Hospitals and birthing centers frequently discharge mother and infant 24 to 48 hours after delivery. It is vital that the parents understand the need for the screening procedure, and a follow-up check is necessary to confirm that the test was done.

(Text continues on page 744.)

## Table 24.9   Congenital Anomalies: Identification and Care in Newborn Period

| Congenital anomaly | Nursing assessments | Nursing goals and interventions |
| --- | --- | --- |
| Congenital hydrocephalus | Enlarged head<br>Enlarged or full fontanelles<br>Split or widened sutures<br>"Setting sun" eyes<br>Head circumference >90% on growth chart | Assess presence of hydrocephalus: Measure and plot occipital-frontal baseline measurements, then measure head circumference once a day.<br>Check fontanelle for bulging and sutures for widening.<br>Assist with head ultrasound and transillumination.<br>Maintain skin integrity: Change position frequently.<br>Clean skin creases after feeding or vomiting.<br>Use sheepskin pillow under head.<br>Postoperatively, position head off operative site.<br>Watch for signs of infection. |
| Choanal atresia | Occlusion of posterior nares<br>Cyanosis and retractions at rest<br>Snorting respirations<br>Difficulty breathing during feeding<br>Obstruction by thick mucus | Assess patency of nares: Listen for breath sounds while holding baby's mouth closed and alternately compressing each nostril.<br>Assist with passing feeding tube to confirm diagnosis.<br>Maintain respiratory function: Assist with taping airway in mouth to prevent respiratory distress.<br>Position with head elevated to improve air exchange. |
| Cleft lip | Unilateral or bilateral visible defect<br>May involve external nares, nasal cartilage, nasal septum, and alveolar process<br>Flattening or depression of midfacial contour (Figure 24.22) | Provide nutrition: Feed with special nipple.<br>Burp frequently (increased tendency to swallow air and reflex vomiting).<br>Clean cleft with sterile water (to prevent crusting on cleft prior to repair).<br>Support parental coping: Assist parents with grief over loss of idealized baby.<br>Encourage verbalization of their feelings about visible defect.<br>Provide role model in interacting with infant.<br>(Parents internalize others' responses to their newborn.) |

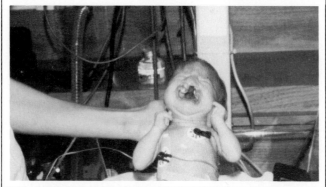

*Figure 24.22   Cleft abnormality involving both hard and soft palate and unilateral cleft lip*

| | | |
| --- | --- | --- |
| Cleft palate | Fissure connecting oral and nasal cavity<br>May involve uvula and soft palate<br>May extend forward to nostril involving hard palate and maxillary alveolar ridge<br>Difficulty in sucking<br>Expulsion of formula through nose (Figure 24.22) | Prevent aspiration/infection: Place prone or in side-lying position to facilitate drainage.<br>Suction nasopharyngeal cavity (to prevent aspiration or airway obstruction).<br>During neonatal period, feed in upright position with head and chest tilted slightly backward (to aid swallowing and discourage aspiration).<br>Provide nutrition: Feed with special nipple that fills cleft and allows sucking. Also decreases change of aspiration through nasal cavity.<br>Clean mouth with water after feedings.<br>Burp after each ounce (tend to swallow large amounts of air).<br>Thicken formula to provide extra calories.<br>Plot weight gain patterns to assess adequacy of diet.<br>Provide parental support: Refer parents to community agencies and support groups. Encourage verbalization of frustrations as feeding process is long and frustrating.<br>Praise all parental efforts.<br>Encourage parents to seek prompt treatment for URI and teach them ways to decrease URI. |

*(continues)*

## Table 24.9  Congenital Anomalies: Identification and Care in Newborn Period
*(continued)*

| Congenital anomaly | Nursing assessments | Nursing goals and interventions |
|---|---|---|
| Tracheoesophageal fistula (type 3) | History of maternal hydramnios<br>Excessive mucous secretions<br>Constant drooling<br>Abdominal distention beginning soon after birth<br>Periodic choking and cyanotic episodes<br>Immediate regurgitation of feeding<br>Clinical symptoms of aspiration pneumonia (tachypnea, retractions, rhonchi, decreased breath sounds, cyanotic spells)<br>Failure to pass nasogastric tube (Figure 24.23) | Maintain respiratory status and prevent aspiration:<br>Withhold feeding until esophageal patency is determined.<br>Quickly assess patency before putting to breast in birth area.<br>Place on low intermittent suction to control saliva and mucus (to prevent aspiration pneumonia).<br>Place in warmed, humidified Isolette (liquefies secretions facilitating removal).<br>Elevate head of bed 20°–40° (to prevent reflux of gastric juices).<br>Keep quiet (crying causes air to pass through fistula and to distend intestines causing respiratory embarrassment).<br>Maintain fluid and electrolyte balance: Give fluids to replace esophageal drainage and maintain hydration.<br>Provide parent education: Explain staged repair—provision of gastrostomy and ligation of fistula, then repair of atresia.<br>Keep parents informed; clarify and reinforce physician's explanations regarding malformation, surgical repair, pre- and postoperative care, and prognosis (knowledge is ego strengthening).<br>Involve parents in care of infant and in planning for future; facilitate touch and eye contact (to dispel feelings of inadequacy, increase self-esteem and self-worth, and promote incorporation of infant into family). |

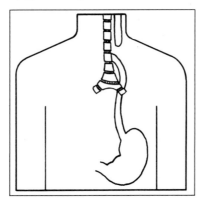

*Figure 24.23   The most frequently seen type of congenital tracheoesophageal fistula and esophageal atresia*

| Congenital anomaly | Nursing assessments | Nursing goals and interventions |
|---|---|---|
| Diaphragmatic hernia | Difficulty initiating respirations<br>Gasping respirations with nasal flaring and chest retraction<br>Barrel chest and scaphoid abdomen<br>Asymmetrical chest expansion<br>Breath sounds may be absent, usually on left side<br>Heart sounds displaced to right<br>Spasmodic attacks of cyanosis and difficulty in feeding<br>Bowel sounds may be heard in thoracic cavity (Figure 24.24) | Maintain respiratory status: Immediately administer oxygen.<br>Initiate gastric decompression.<br>Place in high semi-Fowler's position (to use gravity to keep abdominal organ's pressure off diaphragm).<br>Turn to affected side to allow unaffected lung expansion.<br>Carry out interventions to alleviate respiratory and metabolic acidosis.<br>Assess for increased secretions around suction tube (denotes possible obstruction).<br>Aspirate and irrigate tube with air or sterile water. |

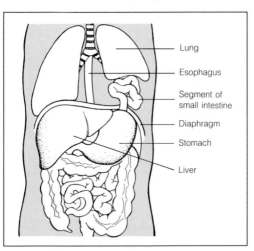

Lung

Esophagus

Segment of small intestine

Diaphragm

Stomach

Liver

*Figure 24.24   Diaphragmatic hernia. Note compression of the lung by the intestine on the affected side.*

**Table 24.9   Congenital Anomalies: Identification and Care in Newborn Period**
*(continued)*

| Congenital anomaly | Nursing assessments | Nursing goals and interventions |
|---|---|---|
| Omphalocele | Herniation of abdominal contents into base of umbilical cord<br>May have an enclosed transparent sac covering | Maintain hydration and temperature:<br>Provide D₅LR and albumin for hypovolemia.<br>Place infant in sterile bag up to above defect.<br>Cover sac with moistened sterile gauze and place plastic wrap over dressing (to prevent rupture of sac and infection).<br>Initiate gastric decompression by insertion of nasogastric tube attached to low suction (to prevent distention of lower bowel and impairment of blood flow).<br>Prevent infection and trauma to defect.<br>Position to prevent trauma to defect.<br>Administer broad-spectrum antibiotics. |
|  | Saclike cyst containing meninges, spinal cord, and nerve roots in thoracic and/or lumbar area (Figure 24.25).<br>Myelomeningocele directly connects to subarachnoid space so hydrocephalus often associated<br>No response or varying response to sensation below level of sac<br>May have constant dribbling of urine<br>Incontinence or retention of stool<br>Anal opening may be flaccid | Prevent trauma and infection.<br>Position on abdomen or on side and restrain (to prevent pressure and trauma to sac).<br>Meticulously clean buttocks and genitals after each voiding and defecation (to prevent contamination of sac and decrease possibility of infection).<br>May put protective covering over sac (to prevent rupture and drying).<br>Observe sac for oozing of fluid or pus.<br>Credé bladder as ordered (to prevent urinary stasis).<br>Assess amount of sensation and movement below defect.<br>Observe for complications:<br>Obtain occipital-frontal circumference baseline measurements, then measure head circumference once a day (to detect hydrocephalus).<br>Check fontanelle for bulging. |
| Imperforate anus, congenital dislocated hip, and clubfoot | See discussion in Chapter 21, p 591 | Identify defect and initiate appropriate referral early. |

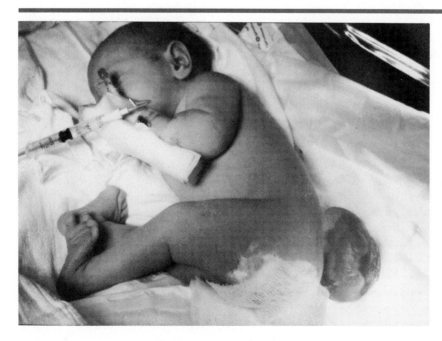

*Figure 24.25   Newborn with lumbar meningocele (Courtesy of Dr Paul Winchester.)*

Because it is possible to do the testing on an infant with PKU before the phenylalanine concentration rises and thus miss the diagnosis, some states routinely request a repeat test at 10 to 14 days. When the Guthrie blood test is performed early, during the first three to four days of life, a phenylalanine blood level of about 4 to 6 mg/dL is considered a presumptive positive; but only one in 20 to 30 infants with this level are true positives (Wasserman and Gromisch 1981).

Some states simultaneously test all hospitalized newborns for MSUD, homocystinuria, and PKU during the first three to four days of life. Diagnosis of MSUD is made by analyzing blood levels of leucine, isoleucine, and valine. Confirmation of the diagnosis depends on blood assay for the enzyme oxidative decarboxylase.

In several states newborn screening includes an enzyme assay for galactose l-phosphate uridyl transferase; this test, however, does not detect galactosemia if it is caused by a deficiency of the enzyme galactokinase.

For hypothyroidism, immediate and appropriate thyroid replacement therapy is established based on newborn screening and laboratory data. Frequently, premature infants of less than 30 weeks' gestation have low $T_4$ or thyroid stimulating hormone (TSH) values when compared with normal values of term infants. This may reflect the premature's inability to bind thyroid. Management includes frequent laboratory monitoring and adjustment of thyroid medication to accommodate growth and development of the child. With adequate treatment, children remain free of symptoms, but if the condition is untreated, stunted growth and mental retardation occur.

## ● Nursing Assessment

The clinical picture of a PKU baby involves a normal appearing newborn, most often with blond hair, blue eyes, and fair complexion. Decreased pigmentation may be related to the competition between phenylalanine and tyrosine for the available enzyme, tyrosinase. Tyrosine is needed for the formation of melanin pigment and the hormones epinephrine and thyroxin. Without treatment, the infant fails to thrive, and develops vomiting and eczematous rashes. By about six months of age, the infant exhibits behaviors indicative of mental retardation and other CNS involvement, including seizures and abnormal electroencephalogram (EEG) patterns.

Newborns with MSUD have feeding problems and neurologic signs (seizures, spasticity, opisthotonus) during the first week of life. A maple syrup odor of the urine is noted and, when ferric chloride is added to the urine, its color changes to gray-green.

Homocystinuria varies in its presentation, but the more common characteristics are skeletal abnormalities, dislocation of ocular lenses, intravascular thromboses, and mental retardation. Abnormalities occur because of the toxic effects of the accumulation of methionine and the metabolite homocystine in the blood.

Clinical manifestations of galactosemia include vomiting, diarrhea, hepatosplenomegaly, jaundice, and mental retardation. The condition is frequently associated with anemia, sepsis, and cataracts in the neonatal period. Except for cataracts and mental retardation, those findings are reversible when galactose is excluded from the diet. Mental retardation can be prevented by early diagnosis and careful dietary management.

A large tongue, umbilical hernia, cool and mottled skin, low hairline, hypotonia, and large fontanelles are frequently associated with congenital hypothyroidism. Early symptoms include prolonged neonatal jaundice, poor feeding, constipation, low-pitched cry, poor weight gain, inactivity, and delayed motor development.

## ● Nursing Diagnosis

Nursing diagnoses that may apply to the newborn with an inborn error of metabolism are:

● Knowledge deficit related to special dietary management required secondary to inborn error of metabolism

● Ineffective family coping related to parental guilt secondary to hereditary nature of disease

## ● Nursing Plan and Implementation
### NEWBORN SCREENING

Newborn screening for several inborn errors of metabolism is mandatory in many states. It is the nurse's responsibility to obtain the heel stick blood on the filter paper prior to discharge of the baby. The first filter paper test screens for PKU, homocystinuria, MSUD, galactosemia, and sickle cell anemia. A second blood specimen is usually required at 7 to 14 days after birth, but the nurse must remember that this second blood specimen tests only for PKU.

Some clinicians have the parents perform a diaper test for PKU. At about six weeks of age, the parent should take a freshly wet diaper and press the prepared test stick against the wet area. They note the color of the test stick, record the color on the prepared sheet, and mail the form back to the physician. A green color reaction is positive and indicates probable PKU.

### PARENT EDUCATION—DIETARY MANAGEMENT

Nursing responsibilities include prompt and appropriate dietary management of the newborn with an inborn error of metabolism. Once identified, an afflicted PKU infant can be treated by a special diet that limits ingestion of phenylalanine. Special formulas low in phenylalanine, such as Lofenalac, are available. Special food lists are helpful for parents of a PKU child. If treatment is begun before three months of age, CNS damage can be minimized.

Controversy exists about when, if ever, the special diet should be terminated. Because of the rigidity and severe limitations of the low phenylalanine diet, many clinicians terminate the special diet at six years of age. Brain size does not dramatically increase after age 6, but myelination continues actively through adolescence and to some extent possibly through 40 years of age. The effect of high phenylalanine levels on continued development of the brain after six years is not known (Schuett et al 1980).

Female children with PKU are now living longer and may bear children. There is a 95% risk of producing a child with mental retardation if the mother with PKU is not on a low-phenylalanine diet during pregnancy. It is recommended that the woman reinstate her low phenylalanine diet a few months before becoming pregnant (Rohr et al 1987).

Dietary management of MSUD must be initiated immediately with a formula that is low in the branched-chain amino acids leucine, isoleucine, and valine (Sarett 1979).

Infants with homocystinuria are managed on a diet that is low in methionine but supplemented with cystine and pyridoxine (vitamin $B_6$). With early diagnosis and careful management, mental retardation may be prevented.

Galactosemia is treated by the use of a galactose-free formula, such as Nutramigen (a protein hydrolysate process formula), a meat-base formula, or a soybean formula. As the infant grows, parents must be educated not only to avoid giving their child milk and milk products but also to read all labels carefully and avoid any foods containing dry milk products.

Parents of affected newborns should be referred to support groups. The nurse should also ensure that parents are informed about centers that can provide them with information about biochemical genetics and dietary management.

## ● Evaluation

Anticipated outcomes of nursing care include:

● The risk of inborn errors of metabolism is promptly identified, and early intervention is initiated.

● The parents verbalize their concerns about their baby's health problems, long-term care needs, and potential outcomes.

● The parents are aware of available community health resources and use them as indicated.

## ESSENTIAL CONCEPTS

● Early identification of potential high-risk fetuses through assessment of prepregnant, prenatal, and intrapartal factors facilitates strategically timed nursing observations and interventions.

● High-risk neonates, whether they are premature, SGA, LGA, postterm, or infant of a diabetic or substance-addicted mother, have many similar problems, although their problems are based on different physiologic processes.

● Small-for-gestational-age newborns are associated with perinatal asphyxia and resulting aspiration syndrome, hypothermia, hypoglycemia, hypocalcemia, polycythemia, congenital anomalies, and intrauterine infections. Long-term problems include continued growth and learning difficulties.

● Large-for-gestational-age newborns are at risk for birth trauma as a result of cephalopelvic disproportion, hypoglycemia, polycythemia, and hyperviscosity.

● Infants of diabetic mothers are at risk for hypoglycemia, hypocalcemia, hyperbilirubinemia, polycythemia, and respiratory distress due to delayed maturation of their lungs.

● Postterm newborns frequently encounter the following intrapartal problems: CPD (shoulder dystocia) and birth traumas, hypoglycemia, polycythemia, meconium aspiration, cold stress, and possible seizure activity. Long-term complications may involve poor weight gain and low IQ scores.

● The common problems of the preterm newborn are a result of the baby's immature body systems. Potential problem areas include respiratory distress (respiratory distress syndrome), patent ductus arteriosus, hypothermia and cold stress, feeding difficulties and necrotizing enterocolitis, marked insensible water loss and loss of buffering agents through the kidneys, infection, anemia of prematurity, apnea and intraventricular hemorrhage, retinopathy of prematurity, and behavioral state disorganization. Long-term needs and problems include bronchopulmonary dysplasia, speech defects, sensorineural hearing loss, and neurologic defects.

● Newborns of alcohol dependent mothers are at risk for physical characteristic alterations and the long-term complications of feeding problems; CNS dysfunction, including lower IQ, hyperactivity, and language abnormalities; and congenital anomalies.

● Newborns born to drug-dependent mothers experience drug withdrawal as well as respiratory distress, jaundice, congenital anomalies, and behavioral abnormalities. With early recognition and intervention, the potential long-term physiologic and emotional consequences of these difficulties can be avoided or at least lessened in severity.

● Newborn conditions that commonly present with respiratory distress and require oxygen and ventilatory assistance are hyaline membrane disease, meconium aspiration syndrome, transient tachypnea of the newborn, and persistent pulmonary hypertension of the newborn.

● Cold stress sets up the chain of physiologic events of hypoglycemia, pulmonary vasoconstriction, hyperbilirubinemia, respiratory distress, and metabolic acidosis. Nurses are responsible for early detection and initiation of treatment for hypoglycemia.

● Cardiac defects are a significant cause of morbidity and mortality in the newborn period. Early identification and nursing and medical care of newborns with cardiac defects is essential to the improved outcome of these infants. Care is directed toward lessening the work load of the heart and decreasing oxygen and energy consumption.

● Differentiation between pathologic and physiologic jaundice is the key to early and successful intervention.

● Nursing assessment of the septic newborn involves identification of very subtle clinical signs that are also seen in other clinical disease states.

● Inborn errors of metabolism such as galactosemia, PKU, homocystinuria, and maple syrup urine disease are usually included in a newborn screening program designed to prevent mental retardation through dietary management and medication.

● The nursing care of the neonate with special problems involves the understanding of normal physiology, the pathophysiology of the disease process, clinical manifestations, and supportive or corrective therapies. Only with this theoretical background can the nurse make appropriate observations concerning responses to therapy and development of complications.

● Neonates communicate needs only by their behavior; the neonatal nurse, through objective observations and evaluations, interprets this behavior into meaningful information about the infant's condition.

● The nurse is the facilitator for interdisciplinary communication with the parents, identifying their understanding of their infant's care and their needs for emotional support.

● Parents of at-risk newborns need support from nurses and health care providers to understand the special needs of their baby and to feel comfortable in an overwhelmingly strange environment.

● ● ● ● ● ● ● ● ● ● ● ● ● ● ● ● ● ● ● ● ● ● ● ● ● ● ● ● ● ● ●

## References

Abel EL: Prenatal effects of alcohol on growth: A brief overview. *Fed Proc* 1985; 44:2318.

Affonso DD, Harris TR: Postterm pregnancy: Implications for mother and infant, challenge for the nurse. *J Obstet Gynecol Neonatal Nurs* 1980; 9:139.

Als H et al: Assessment of preterm infant behavior (APIB). In: *Theory and Research in Behavioral Pediatrics*. Fitzgerald HE, Lester BM, Yogman MW (editors). Vol 1. New York: Plenum, 1982.

Altura BM et al: Alcohol produces spasms of human umbilical blood vessels: Relationship of fetal alcohol syndrome (FAS). *Eur J Pharmacol* 1982; 86:311.

American Academy of Pediatrics Committee on Nutrition: Nutritional needs of low-birthweight infants. *Pediatrics* 1985; 75(5):976.

American Academy of Pediatrics: Report: Neonatal drug withdrawal. *Pediatrics* 1983; 72:895.

Ampola MG: *Metabolic Diseases in Pediatric Practice,* Boston: Little, Brown, 1982.

Avery GB (editor): *Neonatology,* 3rd ed. Philadelphia: Lippincott, 1987.

Avery ME, Taeusch HW (editor): *Schaffer's Diseases of the Newborn,* 5th ed. Philadelphia: Saunders, 1984.

Benitz WE and Tatro DS: *The Pediatric Drug Handbook.* Chicago: Year Book Medical Publishers, 1988.

Berkowitz RL et al: *Handbook for Prescribing Medications During Pregnancy.* Boston: Little, Brown, 1981.

Berry RK: Home care of the child with AIDS. *Pediatr Nurs* July/August 1988; 14(4):341–44.

Bhatt DR et al: *Neonatal Drug Formulary.* California Perinatal Association, 1987.

Bowen LW et al: Maternal-fetal pH difference and fetal scalp pH as predictors of neonatal outcome. *Obstet Gynecol* 1986; 67:487.

Brar HS, Rutherford SE: Classification of intrauterine growth retardation. *Sem Perinatol* January 1988; 12(1):2–10.

Braune KW, Lacey L: Common hematologic problems of the immediate newborn period: *J Obstet Gynecol Neonat Nurs* 1983; 12 (Suppl):19s.

Brooten D et al: Breast-milk jaundice. *J Obstet Gynecol Neonat Nurs* 1985; 14:220.

Cavdar AO: Fetal alcohol syndrome, malignancies, and zinc deficiency. *J Pediatr* 1984; 105(2):335.

Centers for Disease Control: *AIDS Weekly Surveillance Report—United States.* February 22, 1988. Atlanta, GA: CDC.

Chasnoff IJ: *Drug Use in Pregnancy—Mother and Child.* Boston: MTP Press, 1986.

Church MW and Gerkin KP: Hearing disorders in children with fetal alcohol syndrome: Findings from case reports. *Pediatrics* August 1988; 82(2):147.

Clarren SK, Bowden DM, Astley S: The brain in the fetal alcohol syndrome. *Alcohol Health Res World* Fall 1985, p 20.

Clifford S: Postmaturity. *Adv Pediatr* 1957; 9:13.

Cloherty JP, Stark AR (editors): *Manual of Neonatal Care,* 2nd ed. Boston: Little, Brown, 1985.

Cohen MA: Transcutaneous oxygen monitoring for sick neonates. *Am J Mat Child Nurs* 1984; 9:324.

Cole JG, Frappier PA: Infant stimulation reassessed: A new approach to providing care for the preterm infant. *J Obstet Gynecol Neonatal Nurs* 1985; 14(6):471.

Coles CD et al: Neonatal ethanol withdrawal: Characteristics in clinically normal, nondysmorphic neonates. *J Pediatr* 1984; 105(3):445.

Curtis-Cohen M et al: Randomized trial of prophylactic phototherapy in the infant with very low birth weight. *J Pediatr* 1985; 107:121.

deVries LS et al: Relationship of serum bilirubin levels to ototoxicity and deafness in high-risk low-birth-weight infants. *Pediatrics* 1985; 76:351.

Duara S et al: A newly recognized profile in neonatal lung disease with maternal diabetes. *Am J Radiol* 1985; 144:637.

Dunn PM et al: Metronidazole and the fetal alcohol syndrome. *Lancet* July 1979; 2:144.

Epstein MF et al: Estimation of $Paco_2$ by two noninvasive methods in the critically ill newborn infant. *J Pediatr* 1985; 106:282.

Eviator L: Evaluation of hearing in the high-risk infant. *Clin Perinatol* 1984; 11(1):153.

Fantazia D: Neonatal hypoglycemia. *J Obstet Gynecol Neonatal Nurs* September/November 1984; 13(5):297.

Field T et al: Nonnutritive sucking during tube feedings: Effects on preterm neonates in an intensive care unit. *Pediatrics* 1982; 70(3):381.

Gorski PA et al: Stages of behavioral organization in the high-risk neonate: Theoretical and clinical considerations. *Semin Perinatol* 1979; 3:61.

*Guidelines for Perinatal Care.* Chicago: American Academy of Pediatrics and American College of Obstetricians and Gynecologists, 1988.

Haggerty L: TORCH: A literature review and implications for practice. *J Obstet Gynecol Neonatal Nurs* 1985; 14:124.

Hanshaw JB et al (editors): *Viral Diseases of the Fetus and Newborn.* Philadelphia: Saunders, 1985.

Hendriksen A: Prolonged pregnancy: A literature review. *J Nurs-Midwifery* 1985; 39(1):33.

Hobart JM, Depp R: Prolonged pregnancy. In *Gynecology and Obstetrics.* Vol 3. Sciarra JL (editor). Philadelphia: Harper and Row, 1982.

Inglis AD, Lozano M: AIDS and the neonatal ICU. *Neonatal Network* December 1986; p 39.

Iosub S et al: Fetal alcohol syndrome revisited. *Pediatrics* October 1981; 68:475.

Jones KL et al: Pattern of malformation in offspring of chronic alcoholic mothers. *Lancet* June 1973; 1:1267.

Klaus MH, Fanaroff AA: *Care of the High-Risk Neonate.* Philadelphia: Saunders, 1986.

Klaus MH, Kennell JH: *Maternal-Infant Bonding,* 2nd ed. St Louis: Mosby, 1982.

Klug RM: AIDS beyond the hospital. *Am J Nurs* October 1986; (Part 2):1126.

Korones SB: *High-Risk Newborn Infants: The Basis for Intensive Care Nursing,* 4th ed. St Louis: Mosby, 1986.

Larsson G, Bohlin AB, Tunell R: Prospective study of children exposed to variable amounts of alcohol in utero. *Arch Dis Child* 1985; 60:316.

Losh DP and Durhing JL: Management of postdates pregnancy. *AFP* August 1987; 36(2):184–194.

McCormick A: Special considerations in the nursing care of the very-low-birth-weight infant. *J Obstet Gynecol Neonatal Nurs* 1984; 13(6):357.

McCracken GH: Use of third-generation cephalosporins for treatment of neonatal infections. *Am J Dis Child* 1985; 139:1079.

Merker L, Higgins P, Kinnard E: Assessing narcotic addiction in neonates. *Pediatr Nurs* May/June 1985; p 177.

Miller HC: Prenatal factors affecting intrauterine growth retardation. *Clin Perinatol* June 1985; 12:307.

Nantze D: Hyperviscosity-polycythemia syndrome. *Neonatal Netw* October 1985; 4:8.

Naylor EW: Recent developments in neonatal screening. *Sem Perinatol* April 1985; 9(3):232.

Noerr B: Nursing care to maintain neonatal thermoregulation. *Critical Care Nurse* March/April 1984; 4(2):103.

Nugent J: Acute respiratory care of the newborn. *J Obstet Gynecol Neonatal Nurs* 1983; 12(suppl):31s.

Oh W: Renal functions and clinical disorders in the neonate. *Clin Perinatol* 1981; 4:321.

Oxorn H: *Human Labor and Birth,* 5th ed. Norwalk, CT: Appleton-Century-Crofts, 1986.

Parkinson CE, Wallis S, Harvey D: School achievement and behavior of children who were small-for-dates at birth. *Dev Med Child Neurol* 1981; 23:41.

Rohr FJ et al: New England maternal PKU project: Prospective study of untreated and treated pregnancies and their outcomes. *J Pediatr* 1987; 110(3):391.

Rosett HL et al: Patterns of alcohol consumption and fetal development. *Obstet Gynecol* 1983; 61:539.

Sarett HP: *Products for Dietary Management of Inborn Errors of Metabolism and Other Special Feeding Problems.* Evansville, IN: Mead Johnson, 1979.

Schuett VE et al. Diet discontinuation policies and practices of PKU clinics in the United States. *Am J Pub Health* 1980; 70(5):498.

Shannon K et al: Erythropoiesis in infants of diabetic mothers. *Ped Res* 1986; 20(2):161.

Smith EJ: Galactosemia: An inborn error of metabolism. *Nurse Pract* March/April 1980; 5:8.

Streissguth AP, La Due RA: Psychological and behavioral effects in children prenatally exposed to alcohol. *Alcohol Health & Res World* Fall 1985; 10:6.

Tanmer JE: Disposition of ethanol in maternal venous blood and the amniotic fluid. *J Obstet Gynecol Neonatal Nurs* 1985; 14(6):484.

Teberg AJ, Walther FJ, Pena IC: Mortality, morbidity, and outcome of the small-for-gestational age infant. *Sem Perinatol* January 1988; 12(1):84.

Vohr BR, Coll CT: Neurodevelopmental and school performance of very low-birth-weight infants: A seven-year longitudinal study. *Pediatrics* 1985; 76(3):345.

Wasserman E, Gromisch DS: *Survey of Clinical Pediatrics,* 7th ed. New York: McGraw-Hill, 1981.

## Additional Readings

Adamkin DH: Use of intravenous fat emulsions. Part 2. *Perinatal/Neonatal* July/August 1986; 10:48.

Anderson GC, Marks EA, Wahlberg V: Kangaroo care for premature infants. *Am J Nurs* July 1986; 807.

Armentrout D: Attitudes/beliefs/feelings held by neonatal nurses toward the care and management of fetal-infants. *Neonatal Network* February 1986; 4:21.

Boyes SM: AIDS virus in breast milk: A new threat to neonates and donor milk banks. *Neonatal Network* April 1987; 5:37.

Budreau G: Postnatal cranial molding and infant attractiveness: Implications for nursing. *Neonatal Network* April 1987; 5:13.

Cagle CS: Access to prenatal care and prevention of low birth weight. *Am J Mat Child Nurs* July/August 1987; 12:235.

Chasnoff IJ et al: Cocaine use in pregnancy. *N Engl J Med* September 1985; 313:666.

Doberczak TM et al: One-year follow-up of infants with abstinence associated seizures. *Arch Neurol* June 1988; 45:649.

Eden RD et al: Perinatal characteristics of uncomplicated postdate pregnancies. *Obstet Gynecol* March 1987; 69:296.

Gates E: Obstetrical decision making in the delivery of the extremely premature infant. *Neonatal Network* February 1986; 4:7.

Kauffman RE: Therapeutic intervention to prevent intracerebral hemorrhage in preterm infants. *J Pediatr* 1986; 108:323.

Linton PT: Behavioral development of the premature infant. *Perinatal/Neonatal* July/August 1986; 10:27.

Little BB: Cocaine use in pregnant women in a large public hospital. *Am J Perinatol* July 1988; 5(3):206.

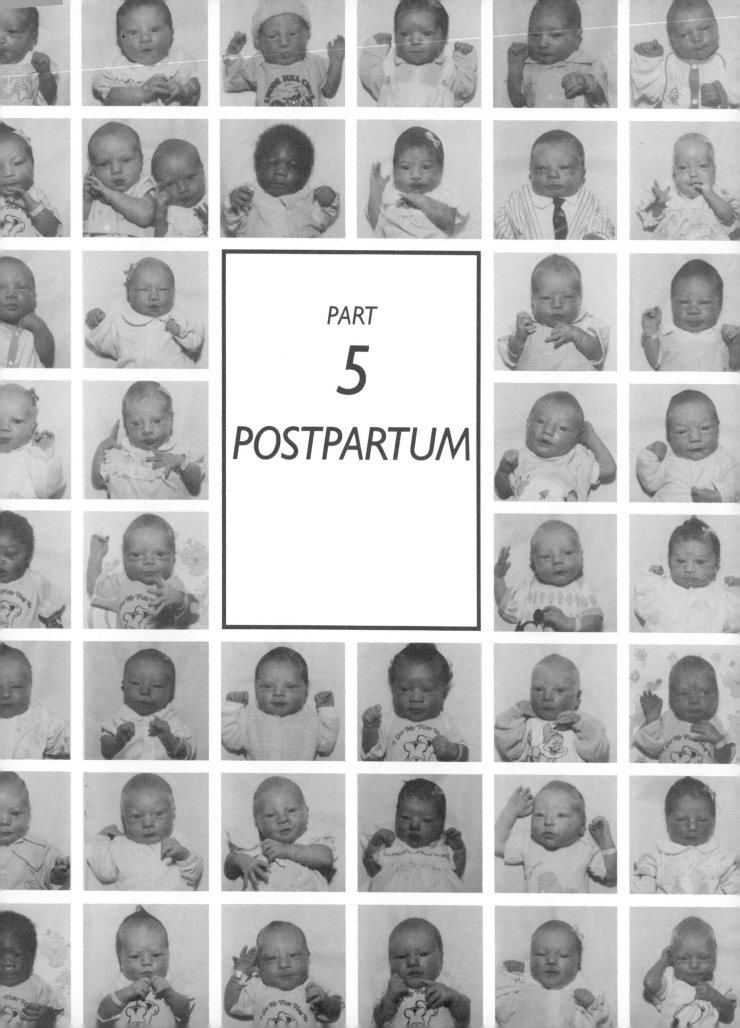

# PART

# 5

# POSTPARTUM

# 25

# Postpartal Adaptation and Nursing Assessment

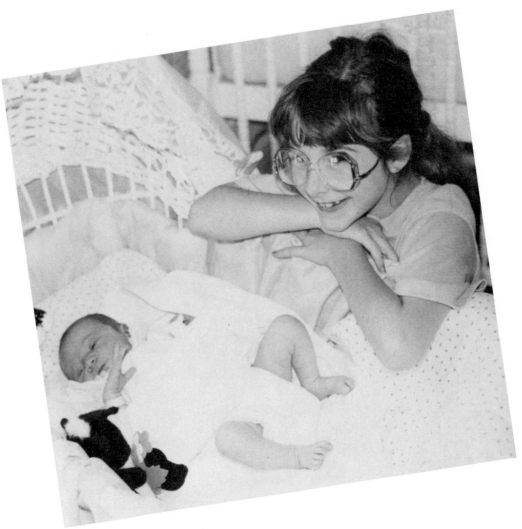

*I love being a big sister!*

## Objectives

● Describe the basic physiologic changes that occur in the postpartal period as a woman's body returns to its prepregnant state.

● Discuss the psychologic adjustments that normally occur during the postpartal period.

● Summarize the factors that influence the development of parent-infant attachment.

● Delineate a normal postpartal assessment.

## Key Terms

afterpains
boggy uterus
carunculae myrtiformes
diastasis recti abdominis
en face
engrossment
episiotomy
fourth trimester
fundus
involution
lochia
lochia alba
lochia rubra
lochia serosa
postpartum blues
puerperium

The **puerperium**, or postpartal period, is the period during which the woman adjusts, physically and psychologically, to the process of childbirth. It begins immediately after delivery and continues for approximately six weeks or until the body has returned to a near prepregnant state. The puerperium is often referred to as the "fourth trimester." Although the time span is less than three months, this title demonstrates the idea of continuity.

This chapter describes the physiologic and psychologic changes that occur postpartally and the basic aspects of a thorough postpartal assessment.

## ● POSTPARTAL PHYSICAL ADAPTATIONS

Comprehensive nursing assessment is based on a sound understanding of the normal anatomic and physiologic processes of the puerperium. These processes involve the reproductive organs and other major body systems.

## ● Reproductive Organs
### INVOLUTION OF THE UTERUS

The term **involution** is used to describe the rapid reduction in size and the return of the uterus to a normal condition similar to its prepregnant state.

Following separation of the placenta, the decidua of the uterus is irregular, jagged, and varied in thickness. The spongy layer of the decidua is cast off as lochia, while the inner layer forms the basis for the development of new endometrium. Except at the placental site, this process takes about three weeks. Bleeding from the larger uterine vessels of the placental site is controlled by compression of the retracted uterine muscle fibers. The clotted blood is gradually absorbed by the body. Some of these vessels are eventually obliterated and replaced by new vessels with smaller lumens.

Rather than forming a fibrous scar in the decidua, the placental site heals by a process of exfoliation. In this process, the site is undermined by the growth of the endometrial tissue both from the margins of the site and from the fundi of the endometrial glands left in the basal layer of the site. The infarcted superficial tissue then becomes necrotic and is sloughed off.

Exfoliation is a very important aspect of involution. If healing of the placental site left a fibrous scar, the area

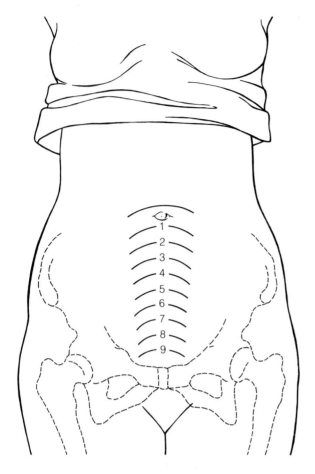

*Figure 25.1   Involution of the uterus: The height of the fundus decreases about one fingerbreadth (approximately 1 cm) each day.*

available for future implantation would be limited, as would the number of possible pregnancies.

The uterus gradually decreases in size as the cells grow smaller and the hyperplasia of pregnancy reverses. Protein material in the uterine wall is broken down and absorbed. The process is basically one of cell size reduction rather than a radical decrease in cell number.

Factors that retard uterine involution include prolonged labor, anesthesia or excessive analgesia, difficult delivery, grandmultiparity, a full bladder, and incomplete expulsion of the products of conception. Factors that enhance involution include an uncomplicated labor and birth, complete expulsion of the products of conception, breast-feeding, and early ambulation.

## CHANGES IN FUNDAL POSITION

Immediately following the delivery of the placenta, the uterus contracts to the size of a large grapefruit. The **fundus** is situated in the midline midway between the symphysis pubis and the umbilicus (Figure 25.1). The walls of the contracted uterus are in close proximity and the uter-

ine blood vessels are firmly compressed by the myometrium. Within 6–12 hours after birth, the fundus of the uterus rises to the level of the umbilicus. A fundus that is above the umbilicus and is boggy (feels soft and spongy rather than firm and well contracted) is associated with excessive uterine bleeding. As blood collects and forms clots within the uterus, the fundus rises; firm contractions of the uterine muscles are interrupted, causing a **boggy uterus**. When the fundus is higher than expected and is not in the midline (usually deviated to the right), distention of the bladder should be suspected.

After birth the top of the fundus remains at the level of the umbilicus for about a day and then descends into the pelvis approximately one finger breadth on each succeeding day.

If the mother is breast-feeding, the release of endogenous oxytocin from the posterior pituitary in response to suckling hastens this process. Within ten days the uterus is again a pelvic organ and cannot be palpated above the symphysis (Varney 1987). Barring complications, the uterus approaches its prepregnant size and location by five to six weeks.

## LOCHIA

The uterus rids itself of the debris remaining after birth through a discharge called **lochia**, which is classified according to its appearance and contents. **Lochia rubra** is dark red in color. It occurs for the first two to three days and contains epithelial cells, erythrocytes, leukocytes, shreds of decidua, and occasionally fetal meconium, lanugo, and vernix caseosa. Lochia should not contain large clots; if it does the cause should be investigated without delay. **Lochia serosa** follows from about the third until the tenth day. It is a pinkish color and is composed of serous exudate (hence the name), shreds of degenerating decidua, erythrocytes, leukocytes, cervical mucus, and numerous microorganisms. Gradually the red blood cell component decreases, and a creamy or yellowish discharge persists for an additional week or two. This final discharge is termed **lochia alba**, and is composed primarily of leukocytes, decidual cells, epithelial cells, fat, cervical mucus, cholesterol crystals, and bacteria. When the lochia stops, the cervix is considered closed, and chances of infection ascending from the vagina to the uterus decrease.

Like menstrual discharge, lochia has a musty, stale odor that is not offensive. Foul-smelling lochia suggest infection and should be assessed promptly.

The total volume of lochia is 240–270 mL and the daily volume gradually declines. Discharge is heavier in the morning due to pooling in the vagina and uterus. The amount of lochia may also be increased by exertion or breast-feeding.

Evaluation of lochia is necessary not only to determine the presence of hemorrhage but also to assess uterine involution. The type, amount, and consistency of lochia determine the stage of healing of the placental site, and a progressive change from bright red at birth to dark red to pink to white/clear discharge should be observed. Persistent discharge of lochia rubra or a return to lochia rubra indicates subinvolution or late postpartal hemorrhage (see Chapter 27).

### CERVICAL CHANGES

Following birth the cervix is flabby and formless and may appear bruised. The external os is markedly irregular and closes slowly. It admits two fingers for a few days following birth, but by the end of the first week it will admit only a fingertip.

The shape of the external os is permanently changed by the first childbearing. The characteristic dimplelike os of the nullipara changes to the lateral slit (fish-mouth) os of the multipara. After significant cervical laceration or several lacerations, the cervix may appear lopsided.

### VAGINAL CHANGES

Following birth the vagina appears edematous and may be bruised. Small superficial lacerations may be evident and the rugae have been obliterated. The apparent bruising is due to pelvic congestion and will quickly disappear. The hymen, torn and jagged, heals irregularly, leaving small tags called the **carunculae myrtiformes.**

The size of the vagina decreases and rugae return within three weeks. Tone and contractility of the vaginal orifice may be improved by perineal tightening exercises (Kegel's). The labia majora and labia minora are more flaccid in the woman who has born a child than in the nullipara.

### PERINEAL CHANGES

During the early postpartal period the soft tissue in and around the perineum may appear edematous with some bruising. If an episiotomy is present, the edges should be drawn together. Occasionally ecchymosis occurs, and this may delay healing.

## ● Recurrence of Ovulation and Menstruation

Approximately 40% of nonnursing mothers resume menstruation in six weeks, while 90% resume within 24 weeks after birth. Of these, approximately 50% ovulate during the first cycle. At 12 weeks after birth about 45% of the lactating primiparas are menstruating. Among nursing mothers 80% have one or more anovulatory cycles before the first ovulatory one (Easterling and Herbert 1986).

## ● Abdomen

Following birth the stretched abdominal wall appears loose and flabby, but it will respond to exercise within two to three months. In the grandmultipara, in the woman in whom overdistention of the abdomen has occurred, or in the woman with poor muscle tone before pregnancy, the abdomen may fail to regain good tone and will remain flabby. **Diastasis recti abdominis**, a separation of the abdominal muscle, may occur with pregnancy, especially in women with poor abdominal muscle tone. If diastasis occurs, part of the abdominal wall has no muscular support but is formed only by skin, subcutaneous fat, fascia, and peritoneum. If rectus muscle tone is not regained, support may be inadequate during future pregnancies. This may result in a pendulous abdomen and increased maternal backache. Fortunately, diastasis responds well to exercise. (See p 785 for a discussion of postpartal exercises.)

Striae (stretch marks), which are caused by stretching and rupture of the elastic fibers of the skin, are red to purple at the time of birth. These gradually fade and after a time appear as silver or white streaks.

## ● Lactation

During pregnancy, breast development in preparation for lactation results from the influence of both estrogen and progesterone. After birth, the interplay of maternal hormones leads to the establishment of milk production. This process is described in detail in the section on breastfeeding.

## ● Gastrointestinal System

Hunger following birth is common, and the mother may enjoy a light meal. She may also be quite thirsty and will drink large amounts of fluid. This helps replace fluids lost in labor, in the urine, and through perspiration.

The bowels tend to be sluggish following birth due to decreased abdominal muscle tone. Women who have had an episiotomy may tend to delay elimination for fear of increasing their pain or in the belief that their stitches will be torn if they bear down. In refusing or delaying the bowel movement, the woman may cause increased constipation and more pain when bowel elimination finally occurs.

## ● Urinary Tract

The postpartal woman has an increased bladder capacity, swelling and bruising of the tissue around the urethra, decreased sensitivity to fluid pressure, and a decreased sensation of bladder filling. Consequently, she is at risk for overdistention, incomplete emptying, and a buildup of residual urine. Women who have had an anesthetic block have inhibited neural functioning of the bladder and are more susceptible to bladder distention, difficulty voiding, and bladder infections.

Puerperal diuresis causes rapid filling of the bladder. Thus adequate bladder elimination is an immediate concern. If stasis exists, chances increase that a urinary tract infection will develop. A full bladder may also increase the tendency toward uterine relaxation by displacing the uterus and interfering with contractility, all of which may lead to hemorrhage.

In the absence of infection, the dilated ureters and renal pelves will return to prepregnant size by the end of the sixth week.

## ● Vital Signs

A temperature of up to 38°C (100.4°F) may occur after birth as a result of the exertion and dehydration of labor. After the first 24 hours, the woman should be afebrile and any temperature of 38°C (100.4°F) or greater would suggest infection.

Blood pressure readings should remain stable after birth. A decrease may indicate physiologic readjustment to decreased intrapelvic pressure, or it may be related to uterine hemorrhage. Blood pressure elevations, especially when accompanied by headache, suggest pregnancy-induced hypertension (PIH), and the woman should be evaluated further.

Puerperal bradycardia with rates of 50–70 beats/min commonly occurs during the first six to ten days of the postpartal period. It may be related to decreased cardiac effort, the decreased blood volume following placental separation, contraction of the uterus, and increased stroke volume. Tachycardia occurs less frequently and is related to increased blood loss or difficult, prolonged labor and birth.

## ● Blood Values

The blood values should return to the prepregnant state by the end of the postpartal period. Pregnancy-associated activation of coagulation factors may continue for variable amounts of time. This condition, in conjunction with trauma, immobility, or sepsis, predisposes the woman to development of thromboembolism.

Leukocytosis often occurs, with white blood counts of 15,000–20,000/mL. Hemoglobin and hematocrit levels may be difficult to interpret in the first two days following birth because of the changing blood volume. In general, a decrease of two percentage points from the hematocrit done on admission to the birthing unit indicates a blood loss of 500 mL (Varney 1987).

Hemoglobin and hematocrit values should approximate or exceed prelabor values within two to six weeks as normal concentrations are reached. As extracellular fluid is excreted, hemoconcentration occurs with a related rise in hematocrit.

## ● Weight Loss

An initial weight loss of about 10–12 lb occurs as a result of the birth of infant, placenta, and amniotic fluid. Puerperal diuresis accounts for the loss of an additional 5 lb during the early puerperium. By the sixth to eighth week after birth, the woman has returned to approximately her prepregnant weight if she has gained the average 25–30 pounds.

## ● Postpartal Chill

Frequently the mother experiences a shaking chill immediately after birth, which is related to a nervous response or to vasomotor changes. If not followed by fever, this chill is not of clinical concern, but it is uncomfortable for the woman. The woman's comfort may be increased by covering her with a warmed blanket and encouraging her to relax. The mother may also find a warm beverage helpful. Later in the puerperium, chill and fever indicate infection and require further evaluation.

## ● Postpartal Diaphoresis

The elimination of excess fluid and waste products via the skin during the puerperium produces greatly increased perspiration. Diaphoretic episodes frequently occur at night, and the woman may awaken drenched with perspiration. This perspiration is not significant clinically, but the mother should be protected from chilling.

## ● Afterpains

**Afterpains** more commonly occur in multiparas than primiparas and are caused by intermittent uterine contractions. Although the uterus of the primipara usually remains consistently contracted, the lost tone of the multiparous uterus results in alternate contraction and relaxation. This phenomenon also occurs if the uterus has been markedly distended, as with a multiple pregnancy or hydramnios, or if clots or placental fragments were retained. These afterpains may cause the mother severe discomfort for two to three days following birth. The administration of oxytocic agents stimulates uterine contraction and increases the discomfort of the afterpains. Because endogenous oxytocin is released when the infant suckles, breast-feeding also increases the severity of the afterpains. The nursing mother may find it helpful to take a mild analgesic approximately one hour before feeding her infant. An analgesic is also helpful at bedtime if the afterpains interfere with the mother's rest.

## ● POSTPARTAL PSYCHOLOGIC ADAPTATIONS

### ● Maternal Role

Reva Rubin (1961) has identified two stages of emotional adjustment that occur in the postpartal period as the woman reverses the inward focus that characterized labor and slowly resumes her normal role and functions. During this period the woman also accepts the new responsibilities resulting from the birth of her child. The *taking-in phase* lasts for two to three days following birth and is characterized by maternal passivity and dependence. The mother is hesitant about making decisions and somewhat preoccupied with her own needs. Food and sleep are major concerns for her.

The *taking-hold phase* begins on the second or third day after birth as the mother resumes control of her life. She may be concerned about control of her bodily functions such as elimination. If she is breast-feeding she may worry about the quality of her milk and her ability to nurse her baby. She requires assurance that she is doing well as a mother. If her baby spits up following a feeding she may see this occurrence as a personal failure. She may also feel demoralized by the fact that nurses handle her baby proficiently while she still feels unsure and tentative.

A study by Martell and Mitchell (1984) suggests that today's new mothers tend to be less dependent and better able to assume self-care responsibilities early in the postpartum period. Gay et al (1988) and Martell and Mitchell (1984) suggest that nurses should examine Rubin's concepts carefully and more skeptically in light of current trends in maternity care. It will be interesting to see what further study brings to this subject.

More recently, research has focused on the attainment of the maternal role. *Maternal role attainment* is the process by which a woman learns mothering behaviors and becomes comfortable with her identity as a mother. The formation of a maternal identity indicates that the woman has attained the maternal role. Formation of a maternal identity occurs with each child a woman bears. As the mother grows to know this child and forms a relationship with her or him, the mother's maternal identity gradually, systematically evolves and she "binds in" to the infant (Rubin 1984).

Maternal role attainment occurs in four stages (Mercer 1985). (The formal and informal stages of maternal attainment correspond with the taking-in and taking-hold stages previously identified by Rubin [1961]):

1.  The *anticipatory stage* occurs during pregnancy. The woman looks to role models, especially her own mother, for examples of how to mother.

2.  The *formal stage* begins when the child is born. The woman is still influenced by the guidance of others and tries to act as she believes others expect her to act.

3.  The *informal stage* begins when the mother begins to make her own choices about mothering. The woman begins to develop her own style of mothering and finds ways of functioning that work well for her.

4.  The *personal stage* is the final stage of maternal role attainment. When the woman reaches this stage, she is comfortable with the notion of herself as "mother."

In most cases maternal role attainment occurs within three to ten months following birth. Social support, the woman's age and personality traits, the temperament of her infant, and the family's socioeconomic status all influence the woman's success in attaining the maternal role.

The postpartum woman faces a number of challenges as she adjusts to her new role. For many women, finding time for themselves is one of the greatest challenges. It is often difficult for the new mother to find time to read a book, talk to her partner, or even eat a meal without interruption! Women also report feelings of incompetence because they have not mastered all aspects of the mothering role. Often they are unsure of what to do in a given situation. The next greatest challenge involves fatigue due to sleep deprivation. The demands of nighttime care are tremendously draining, especially if the woman has other children at home. One challenge faced by the new mother involves the feeling of responsibility that having a child brings. Women experience a sense of lost freedom, an awareness that they will never again be quite as carefree as they were before becoming mothers. Finally, mothers cite the infant's behavior as a problem, especially when the child is about eight months old. Stranger anxiety may be developing, the infant may begin crawling and getting into things, teething may cause fussiness, and the baby's tendency to put everything in his or her mouth requires constant vigilance by the parent (Mercer 1985).

All too often postpartum nurses are unaware of the long-term adjustments and stresses that the childbearing family faces as its members adjust to new and different roles. Nurses can help by providing anticipatory guidance about the realities of being a mother. Agencies should have literature available for reference at home. Ongoing parenting groups also give parents an opportunity to discuss problems and become comfortable in new roles.

### ● Postpartum Blues

The **postpartum blues** consist of a transient period of depression that often occurs during the first few days of the puerperium. It may be manifested by tearfulness, anorexia, difficulty in sleeping, and a feeling of letdown. This depression frequently occurs while the woman is still hospitalized, but it may occur at home, too. Psychologic adjustments and hormonal factors are thought to be the main cause, although fatigue, discomfort, and overstimulation may play a part.

## ● Development of Parent-Infant Attachment

A mother's first interaction with her infant is influenced by many factors, including participation in her family of origin, her relationships, the stability of her home environment, the communication patterns she developed, and the degree of nurturing she received as a child. These factors have shaped the self she has become. Certain characteristics of that self are also important:

- *Level of trust.* What level of trust has this mother developed in response to her life experiences? What is her philosophy of childrearing? Will she be able to treat her infant as a unique individual with changing needs that should be met as much as possible?

- *Level of self-esteem.* How much does she value herself as a woman and as a mother? Does she feel generally able to cope with the adjustments of life?

- *Capacity for enjoying oneself.* Is the mother able to find pleasure in everyday activities and human relationships?

- *Interest in and adequacy of knowledge about childbearing and childrearing.* What beliefs about the course of pregnancy, the capacities of newborns, and the nature of her emotions may influence her behavior at first contact with her infant and later?

- *Her prevailing mood or usual feeling tone.* Is the woman predominantly content, angry, depressed, or anxious? Is she sensitive to her own feelings and those of others? Will she be able to accept her own needs and to obtain support in meeting them?

- *Reactions to the present pregnancy.* Was the pregnancy planned? Did it go smoothly? Were there ongoing life events that enhanced her pregnancy or depleted her reserves of energy?

By the time of birth each mother has developed an emotional orientation of some kind to the fetus based on these factors, as well as a physical awareness of the fetus within her and her fantasy images and perceptions.

### INITIAL ATTACHMENT BEHAVIOR

A fairly regular pattern of maternal behaviors is exhibited at first contact with a normal newborn. In a progression of touching activities, the mother proceeds from fingertip exploration of the newborn's extremities toward palmar contact with larger body areas and finally to enfolding the infant with the whole hand and arms. The time taken to accomplish these steps varies from minutes to days, depending, it appears, on the timing of the first con-

*Figure 25.2* En face *position*

tact, the clothing barriers present, and the physical condition of the baby. Maternal excitement and elation tend to increase during the time of the initial meeting. The mother also increases the proportion of time spent in the **en face** position (Figure 25.2). She arranges herself or the newborn so that she has direct face-to-face and eye-to-eye contact. There is an intense interest in having the infant's eyes open. When the eyes are open, the mother characteristically greets the newborn and talks in high-pitched tones to him or her.

In most instances the mother relies heavily on her senses of sight, touch, and hearing in getting to know what her baby is really like. She tends also to respond verbally to any sounds emitted by the newborn, such as cries, coughs, sneezes, and grunts. The sense of smell may also be involved, although this possibility has not yet been adequately studied.

In addition to acting on and interacting with the newborn, the mother is undergoing her own emotional reactions to the whole happening and, more specifically, to the baby as she perceives him or her. The frequency of the "I can't believe" reaction leads to the speculation that human gains as well as losses may initially be met with a degree of shock, disbelief, and denial. A feeling of emotional distance from the newborn is quite common: "I felt he was a stranger." On the other hand, feelings of connectedness between the newborn and the rest of the family can be expressed in positive or negative terms: "She's got your cute nose, Daddy" or "Oh, God, no! He looks just like the first one, and he was an impossible baby." A mother's facial expressions or the frequency and content of her questions may demonstrate concerns about the infant's general condition or normality, especially if her pregnancy was complicated or if a previously delivered baby was not normal.

What are the characteristic behaviors of a newborn? Unless care is taken to effect a gentle birth, a number of harsh stimuli assault the senses of the newly born neonate. The newborn is probably suctioned, held with head down somewhat, exposed to bright lights and cool air, and in some way cleaned. The infant usually responds by crying. In fact, newborns are typically stimulated to cry to reassure the caretakers that they are well and normal. When newborns no longer need to concentrate most of their energy in physical and physiologic response to the immediate crisis of birth, they are able to lie quietly with eyes open, looking about, moving limbs occasionally, making sucking motions, possibly attempting to get hand to mouth. Placed in appropriate proximity to the mother, the neonate appears to focus briefly on her face and to attend to her voice repeatedly in the first moments.

During the first few days following her infant's birth, the new mother applies herself to the task of getting to know her baby. This is termed the *acquaintance phase*. If the infant gives clear behavioral cues about needs, the infant's responses to mothering will be predictable, which will make the mother feel effective and competent. Other behaviors that make an infant more attractive to caretakers are smiling, grasping a finger, nursing eagerly, cuddling, and being easy to console.

During this time the newborn is also becoming acquainted. Within a few days after birth, infants show signs of recognizing recurrent situations and responding to changes in routine. To the extent that the world is their mother, it can be said that they are actively acquainting themselves with her.

During the *phase of mutual regulation* mother and infant seek to deal with the issue of the degree of control to be exerted by each partner in their relationship. In this phase of adjustment, a balance is sought between the needs of the mother and the needs of the infant. The most important consideration is that each should obtain a good measure of enjoyment from the interaction. During the mutual adjustment phase negative maternal feelings are likely to surface or intensify. Because "everyone knows that mothers love their babies," these negative feelings often go unexpressed and are allowed to build up. If they are expressed, the response of friends, relatives, or health care personnel is often to deny the feelings to the mother: "You don't mean that." Some negative feelings are normal in the first few days following delivery, and the nurse should be supportive when the mother vocalizes these feelings.

When mutual regulation arrives at the point where both mother and infant primarily enjoy each other's company, reciprocity has been achieved. **Reciprocity** is an interactional cycle that occurs simultaneously between mother and infant. It involves mutual cuing behaviors, expectancy, rhythmicity, and synchrony. The development of reciprocity between a mother and her infant is evidence of the bond of attachment that has formed between them. It enables the mother to let go of the infant she knew as a fetus during pregnancy. A new relationship now develops with an individual who has a unique character and who evokes a response entirely different from the fantasy response of pregnancy. When reciprocity is synchronous, the interaction between mother and infant is mutually gratifying and is sought and initiated by both partners. They find pleasure and delight in each other's company and grow in mutual love.

### FATHER-INFANT INTERACTIONS

Traditionally, the primary role of the expectant father has been one of support for the pregnant woman. Commitment to family-centered maternity care, however, fostered interest in understanding the feelings and experiences of the new father. Evidence suggests that the father has a strong attraction to his newborn and that the feelings he experiences are similar to the mother's feelings of attachment (Figure 25.3). The characteristic sense of absorption, preoccupation, and interest in the infant demonstrated by fathers during early contact with their infants has been termed **engrossment**.

### SIBLINGS AND OTHERS

Recent work with infants has shown that they are capable of maintaining a number of strong attachments without loss of quality. These attachments may include siblings, grandparents, aunts, and uncles. The social setting and personality of the individual seem to be significant factors in the development of multiple attachments. The advent of open visiting hours and rooming-in permits siblings and grandparents to participate in the attachment process.

### ● Cultural Influences in the Postpartal Period

Many cultures emphasize certain postpartal routines or rituals for mother and baby. Frequently, these are designed to restore harmony or the hot-cold balance of the body. For many Mexican Americans, black Americans,

## Postpartal Physical Assessment Guide

| Assess/Normal Findings | Alterations and Possible Causes* | Nursing Responses to Data† |
|---|---|---|
| **Vital Signs** | | |
| Blood pressure (BP): Should remain consistent with baseline BP during pregnancy | High BP (PIH, essential hypertension, renal disease, anxiety)<br>Drop in BP (may be normal; uterine hemorrhage) | Evaluate history of preexisting disorders and check for other signs of PIH (edema, proteinuria).<br>Assess for other signs of hemorrhage (↑ pulse, cool clammy skin). |
| Pulse: 50–90 beats/min<br>May be bradycardia of 50–70 beats/min | Tachycardia (difficult labor and delivery, hemorrhage) | Evaluate for other signs of hemorrhage (↓ BP, cool clammy skin). |
| Respirations: 16–24/min | Marked tachypnea (respiratory disease) | Assess for other signs of respiratory disease. |
| Temperature: 36.2–38°C (98–100.4°F) | After first 24 hr, temperature of 38°C (100.4°F) or above suggests infection | Assess for other signs of infection; notify physician/nurse-midwife. |
| **Breasts** | | |
| General appearance: Smooth, even pigmentation, changes of pregnancy still apparent; one may appear larger | Reddened area (mastitis) | Assess further for signs of infection. |
| Palpation: Depending on postpartum day—may be soft, filling, full or engorged | Palpable mass (caked breast, mastitis)<br>Engorgement (venous stasis)<br>Tenderness, heat, edema (engorgement, caked breast, mastitis) | Assess for other signs of infection: If blocked duct consider heat, massage, position change for breast-feeding.<br>Assess for further signs.<br>Report mastitis to physician/nurse-midwife. |
| Nipples: Supple, pigmented, intact; become erect when stimulated | Fissures, cracks, soreness (problems with breast-feeding), not erectile with stimulation (inverted nipples) | Reassess technique; recommend appropriate interventions. |
| **Abdomen** | | |
| Musculature: Abdomen may be soft, have a "doughy" texture; rectus muscle intact | Separation in musculature (diastasis recti abdominis) | Evaluate size of diastasis; teach appropriate exercises for decreasing the separation. |
| Fundus: Firm, midline; following appropriate schedule of involution | Boggy (full bladder, uterine bleeding) | Massage until firm; assess bladder and have woman void if needed; attempt to express clots when firm.<br>If bogginess remains or recurs, report to physician/nurse-midwife. |
| May be tender when palpated | Constant tenderness (infection) | Assess for evidence of endometritis. |
| **Lochia** | | |
| Scant to moderate amount, earthy odor; no clots | Large amount, clots (hemorrhage)<br>Foul-smelling lochia (infection) | Assess for firmness, express additional clots; begin peri-pad count.<br>Assess for other signs of infection; report to physician/nurse-midwife. |
| Normal progression:<br>First 1–3 days—rubra<br>Days 3–10—serosa (alba seldom seen in hospital) | Failure to progress normally or return to rubra from serosa (subinvolution) | Report to physician/nurse-midwife. |

*Possible causes of alterations are placed in parentheses.
†This column provides guidelines for further assessment and initial nursing actions.

## Postpartal Physical Assessment Guide (continued)

| Assess/Normal Findings | Alterations and Possible Causes* | Nursing Responses to Data† |
|---|---|---|
| **Perineum** | | |
| Slight edema and bruising in intact perineum | Marked fullness, bruising, pain (vulvar hematoma) | Assess size; apply ice glove or ice pack; report to physician/nurse-midwife. |
| Episiotomy: No redness, edema, ecchymosis, or discharge; edges well approximated | Redness, edema, ecchymosis, discharge, or gaping stitches (infection) | Encourage sitz baths, review perineal care, appropriate wiping techniques. |
| Hemorrhoids: None present; if present, should be small and nontender | Full, tender, inflamed hemorrhoids | Encourage sitz baths, side-lying position; tucks pads, anesthetic ointments, manual replacement of hemorrhoids; stool softeners, increased fluid intake |
| **Costo Vertebral Angle (CVA) Tenderness** | | |
| None | Present (kidney infection) | Assess for other symptoms of urinary tract infection (UTI); obtain clean catch urine; report to physician/nurse-midwife. |
| **Lower Extremities** | | |
| No pain with palpation; negative Homan's sign | Positive findings (thrombophlebitis) | Report to physician/nurse-midwife. |
| **Elimination** | | |
| Urinary output: Voiding in sufficient quantities at least every four to six hr; bladder not palpable | Inability to void (urinary retention) Symptoms of urgency, frequency, dysuria (UTI) | Employ nursing interventions to promote voiding; if not successful obtain order for catheterization. Report symptoms of UTI to physician/nurse-midwife. |
| Bowel elimination: Should have normal bowel movement by second or third day after birth | Inability to pass feces (constipation due to fear of pain from episiotomy, hemorrhoids, perineal trauma) | Encourage fluids, ambulation, roughage in diet; sitz baths to promote healing of perineum; obtain order for stool softener. |

*Possible causes of alterations are placed in parentheses.
†This column provides guidelines for further assessment and initial nursing actions.

and Asians, cold is avoided after birth. This prohibition includes cold air, wind, and all water (even if heated). Dietary changes also reflect the need to avoid cold foods and restore the balance between hot and cold (Horn 1981).

The nurse caring for a mother during the postpartal period carefully assesses the family's beliefs and practices and adapts to them whenever possible. Family members can be encouraged to bring preferred food and drink, and client care can be modified somewhat to accommodate traditional beliefs.

The extended family frequently plays an essential role during the puerperium. The grandmother is often the primary helper to the mother and her newborn. She brings wisdom and experience, allowing the new mother time to rest, as well as giving her ready access to someone who can help with problems and concerns as they arise. It is imperative to include members who have authority in the family. Visiting rules may be waived to allow family members or authority figures access to the mother and newborn. These practices show respect, and the nurse may gain an ally in the care of the mother and baby, especially if the mother follows the advice of her cultural mentor. Nurses can work for a blending of old and new behaviors to meet the goals of all concerned.

## ● POSTPARTAL NURSING ASSESSMENT

Comprehensive care is based on a thorough assessment that identifies individual needs or potential problems. (See the accompanying Postpartal Physical Assessment Guide.)

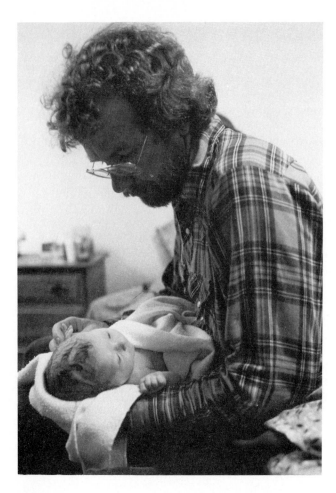

*Figure 25.3   The bond between father and infant develops.*

## • Risk Factors

The emphasis on ongoing assessment and client education during the puerperium is designed to meet the needs of the childbearing family and to detect and treat possible complications. Table 25.1 identifies factors that may place the new mother at risk during the postpartal period. The nurse uses this knowledge during the assessment and is particularly alert for possible complications that may occur in an individual because of identified risk factors.

## • Physical Assessment

Several principles should be remembered in preparing for and completing the assessment of the postpartal woman.

- Select the time that will provide the most accurate data. Palpating the fundus when the woman has a full bladder, for example, may give false information about the progress of involution.

### Table 25.1   Postpartal High-Risk Factors

| Factors | Maternal implications |
|---|---|
| PIH (Preeclampsia-eclampsia) | ↑ Blood pressure<br>↑ Central nervous system (CNS) irritability<br>↑ Need for bedrest → ↑ risk thrombophlebitis |
| Diabetes | Need for insulin regulation<br>Episodes of hypoglycemia or hyperglycemia<br>↓ Healing |
| Cardiac disease | ↑ Maternal exhaustion |
| Cesarean birth | ↑ Healing needs<br>↑ Pain from incision<br>↑ Risk infection<br>↑ Length of hospitalization |
| Overdistention of uterus (multiple gestation, hydramnios) | ↑ Risk hemorrhage<br>↑ Risk anemia<br>↑ Stretching of abdominal muscles<br>↑ Incidence and severity of afterpains |
| Abruptio placentae or placenta previa | Hemorrhage → anemia<br>↓ Uterine contractility after delivery → ↑ infection risk |
| Precipitous labor (<3 hours) | ↑ Risk lacerations to birth canal → hemorrhage |
| Prolonged labor (>24 hours) | Exhaustion<br>↑ Risk hemorrhage<br>Nutritional and fluid depletion<br>↑ Bladder atony and/or trauma |
| Difficult birth | Exhaustion<br>↑ Risk perineal lacerations<br>↑ Risk hematomas<br>↑ Risk hemorrhage → anemia |
| Extended period of time in stirrups at time of birth | ↑ Risk thrombophlebitis |
| Retained placenta | ↑ Risk hemorrhage<br>↑ Risk infection |

- An explanation of the purpose of regular assessment should be given to the woman.
- The woman should be relaxed, and the procedures should be done as gently as possible to avoid unnecessary discomfort.
- The data obtained should be recorded and reported as clearly as possible.

## *Essential Facts to Remember*

### Common Postpartal Concerns

Several postpartal occurrences cause special concern for mothers. The nurse will frequently be asked about the following events:

| Source of Concern | Explanation |
|---|---|
| Gush of blood that sometimes occurs when she first arises | Due to pooling of blood in vagina. Gravity causes blood to flow out when she stands. |
| Night sweats | Normal physiologic occurrence that results as body attempts to eliminate excess fluids that were present during pregnancy. May be aggravated by plastic mattress pad. |
| Afterpains | More common in multiparas. Due to contraction and relaxation of uterus. Increased by oxytocins, breast-feeding. Relieved with mild analgesics and time. |
| "Large stomach" after birth and failure to lose all weight gained during pregnancy | Products of conception account for only a portion of the weight gained during pregnancy. The remainder takes approximately six weeks to lose. Abdomen also appears large to ↓ tone. Postpartal exercises will help. |

While the nurse is performing the physical assessment, she should also be teaching the woman. For example, when the nurse is assessing breast milk production, the letdown reflex and breast self-examination can be discussed. Mothers are very receptive to instruction on postpartal abdominal tightening exercises when the nurse assesses the woman's fundal height and diastasis. The assessment also provides an excellent time to teach her about the body's postpartal physical and anatomic changes as well as danger signs to report. (See Essential Facts to Remember—Common Postpartal Concerns.) Since the time the woman spends in the postpartum unit is often limited, nurses should use every available opportunity for client education regarding self-care. One of the best opportunities comes during the normal postpartal assessment. To assist nurses in recognizing these opportunities, examples of client teaching during the assessment have been incorporated.

### BREASTS

Beginning with the breasts, the nurse should first assess the fit and support provided by the bra. The nurse provides information about how to select a supportive bra. A properly fitting bra provides support to the breasts and helps maintain breast shape by limiting stretching of supporting ligaments and connective tissue. If the mother is breast-feeding, the straps of the bra should be cloth, not elastic, and easily adjustable. The back should be wide and have at least three rows of hooks to adjust for fit. Traditional nursing bras have a fixed inner cup and a separate half cup that can be unhooked for breast-feeding while continuing to support the breast. Purchasing a bra one size

too large during pregnancy will usually result in a good fit because the breasts increase in size with milk production.

The bra is then removed so the breasts can be examined. The nurse notes the size and shape of the breasts and any abnormalities, reddened areas, or engorgement. The breasts are also lightly palpated for softness, slight firmness associated with filling, firmness associated with engorgement, warmth, or tenderness. The nipples are assessed for fissures, cracks, soreness, or inversion. The nurse teaches the woman the characteristics of the breast and explains how to recognize problems such as fissures or cracks.

The nonnursing mother is assessed for evidence of breast discomfort, and relief measures are taken if necessary. (See discussion of lactation suppression in the nonnursing mother on p 783.) Breast assessment findings for a nursing woman may be recorded as follows: Breasts soft, filling, no evidence of nipple tenderness or cracking.

### ABDOMEN AND FUNDUS

Before examination of the abdomen, the woman should void. This practice assures that a full bladder is not causing displacement of the uterus or any uterine atony; if atony is present, other causes must be investigated.

The nurse determines the relationship of the fundus to the umbilicus and also assesses the firmness of the fundus. The nurse notes whether the fundus is in the midline or displaced to either side of the abdomen. The most common cause of displacement is a full bladder, thus this finding requires further assessment. The results of the assessment should then be recorded. (See Procedure 25.1.)

While completing the assessment, the nurse teaches

# Procedure 25.1

## Assessing the Fundus

| Objective | Nursing Action | Rationale |
|---|---|---|
| Prepare woman. | Explain procedure; have the woman void; position woman flat in bed with head comfortably positioned on a pillow; if the procedure is uncomfortable, woman may flex legs. | Having the woman void assures that a full bladder is not causing any uterine atony. Having woman flat prevents falsely high assessment of fundal height. Flexing the legs relaxes the abdominal muscles. The uterus may be tender if frequent massage has been necessary. |
| Determine uterine firmness. | Gently place one hand on the lower segment of the uterus; using the side of the other hand, palpate the abdomen until the top of the fundus is located. Determine whether the fundus is firm. If it is not firm, massage until firm. | Provides support for uterus. Provides a larger surface for palpation and is less uncomfortable for the woman. A firm fundus indicates that the muscles are contracted and bleeding will not occur. |
| Determine the height of the fundus. | Measure the height of the top of the fundus in fingerbreadths. (See Figure 25.4.) | Fundal height gives information about the progress of involution. |

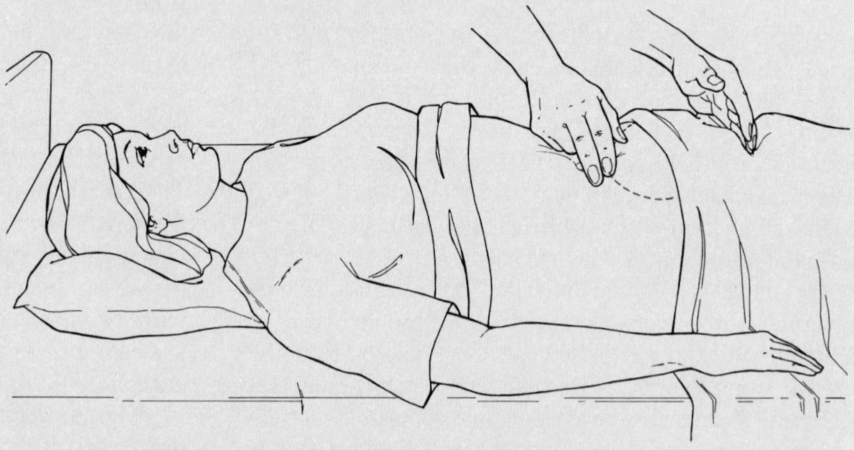

*Figure 25.4   Measurement of descent of fundus: The fundus is located two fingerbreadths below the umbilicus.*

| Objective | Nursing Action | Rationale |
|---|---|---|
| Ascertain position. | Determine whether fundus is deviated from the midline. If not in midline, locate position. Evaluate bladder for distention. Ascertain voiding pattern; use measuring device to measure urine output for next few hours (until normal elimination status is established). | Fundus may be deviated when bladder is full. |
| Correlate uterine status with lochia. | Observe lochia for amount, presence of clots, color, and odor. | As normal involution occurs, the lochia decreases in amount and changes from rubra to serosa. Increased amounts of lochia may be associated with uterine relaxation; failure to progress to next type of lochia may indicate uterine relaxation or infection. |
| Record findings. | Fundal height is recorded in fingerbreadths; example: 2 FB ↓ U; 1 FB ↑ U. | Allows for consistency of reporting among care givers. |
|  | If massage had been necessary it could be recorded as: Uterus: Boggy → firm c̄ light massage. |  |

the woman about fundal position. The mother can be assisted in gently massaging her fundus to determine firmness.

Following the uterine assessment and prior to assessing the lochia, the nurse examines for diastasis recti. The separation in the rectus muscle is evaluated according to its length and width. The separation is palpated first just below the umbilicus, and the width is ascertained. Then the separation is palpated for length toward the symphysis pubis and toward the xiphoid process. If palpation is difficult due to abdominal relaxation, the woman is asked to lift her head unassisted by the nurse. This action contracts the rectus muscles and more clearly defines their edges.

Methods of charting these results vary from institution to institution. Some prefer recording the diastasis measured from the umbilicus down and then from the umbilicus up:

Diastasis: U ↓ 4 cm by 1 cm
U ↑ 2 cm by 1 cm

Others prefer recording the entire length:

Diastasis: 6 cm by 1 cm

Either method is acceptable.

In the woman who has had a cesarean birth, the abdominal incision should be inspected for any signs of infection, including drainage, foul odor, or redness. During the assessment, the nurse teaches the woman about her incision. Characteristics of normal healing may be reviewed and signs of infection discussed.

## LOCHIA

The next aspect to be evaluated is the lochia, which is assessed for character, amount, odor, and the presence of clots. During the first one to three days the lochia should be rubra. A few small clots are normal and occur as a result of blood pooling in the vagina. However, the passage of numerous or large clots is abnormal, and the cause should be investigated immediately. After two to three days, the lochia becomes serosa.

Lochia should never exceed a moderate amount, such as four to eight peri-pads daily, with an average of six. However, because this is influenced by an individual woman's pad-changing practices, she should be questioned about the length of time the current pad has been in use, whether the amount is normal, and whether any clots were passed prior to this examination, such as during voiding. If heavy bleeding is reported but not seen, the woman is asked to put on a clean perineal pad and is then reassessed in one hour (Figure 25.5). Clots and heavy bleeding may be caused by uterine relaxation (atony) or retained placental fragments and require further assessment. Because of the evacuation of the uterine cavity during cesarean birth, women with such surgery usually have less

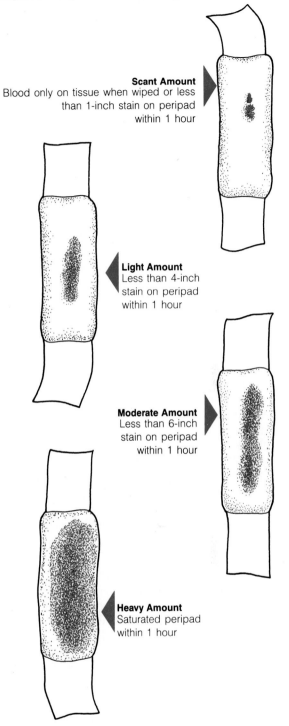

**Scant Amount**
Blood only on tissue when wiped or less than 1-inch stain on peripad within 1 hour

**Light Amount**
Less than 4-inch stain on peripad within 1 hour

**Moderate Amount**
Less than 6-inch stain on peripad within 1 hour

**Heavy Amount**
Saturated peripad within 1 hour

*Figure 25.5  Suggested guideline for assessing lochia volume (From Jacobson H: A standard for assessing lochia volume.* Am J Mat Child Nurs *May/June 1985; 10:175.)*

lochia after the first 24 hours than mothers who deliver vaginally. If the woman is at increased risk for bleeding, or is actually experiencing heavy flow of lochia rubra, the physician may also order methylergonovine maleate (Methergine). See Drug Guide—Methergine, p 776.

The odor of the lochia is nonoffensive and never foul. If foul odor is present, so is an infection.

The amount of lochia is charted first, followed by character. For example:

- Lochia: moderate amount rubra
- Lochia: small rubra/serosa

Client teaching that may be addressed during assessment of the lochia may center on normal changes that can be expected in the amount and color of the flow. Hygienic measures may be reviewed if appropriate. The timing of teaching hygienic practices should be approached delicately as should the content to be included. When the nurse approaches the teaching with the goals of promoting comfort, enhancing tissue healing, and preventing infection, value-laden statements regarding personal beliefs about the need for cleanliness or control of body odor are avoided.

## PERINEUM

The perineum is inspected with the woman lying in a Sims' position. The buttock is lifted to expose the perineum and anus. If an **episiotomy** was done or a laceration required suturing, the wound is assessed. The state of healing is evaluated by observing for redness, edema, ecchymosis, discharge, and approximation—the REEDA scale (Davidson 1974). (See Table 27.1.)

After 24 hours some edema may still be present, but the skin edges should be "glued" together (well approximated) so that gentle pressure does not separate them. Gentle palpation should elicit minimal tenderness and there should be no hardened areas suggesting infection. Ecchymosis interferes with normal healing, as does infection.

Foul odors associated with drainage indicate infection. Further observation of the incision for warmth, tenderness, edema, and separation should also be made.

The nurse next assesses the state of any hemorrhoids present around the anus for size, number, and pain or tenderness.

During the assessment, the nurse talks with the woman to determine the effectiveness of comfort measures that have been used. The nurse provides teaching about the episiotomy. Some women do not thoroughly understand what an episiotomy is and where it is, and may believe that the stitches must be removed as with other types of surgery. Frequently, when women fear that the stitches must be removed manually, they are afraid to ask about them. As the nurse explains the findings of her assessment, information about the episiotomy, its location, and signs that are being assessed can be addressed. In addition, the nurse can casually add that the sutures are special, and that they dissolve slowly over the next few weeks as the tissues heal. By the time the sutures are dissolved the tissues are strong and the incision edges will not separate

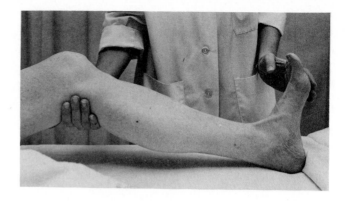

*Figure 25.6  Homan's sign: With the woman's knee flexed to decrease the risk of embolization, the nurse dorsiflexes the foot. Pain in the foot or leg is a positive Homan's sign.*

rate. This is also an opportunity to teach comfort measures that may be used (see Chapter 26).

An example of charting a perineal assessment might be: Midline episiotomy; no edema, tenderness, or ecchymosis present. Skin edges well approximated. Patient reports pain relief measures are controlling discomfort.

## LOWER EXTREMITIES

If thrombophlebitis occurs, the most likely site will be in the woman's legs. To assess for this, her legs should be stretched out straight and should be relaxed. The foot is then grasped and sharply dorsiflexed. No discomfort or pain should be present. If pain is elicited, the nurse-midwife or physician is notified that the woman has a positive Homan's sign (Figure 25.6). The pain is caused by inflammation of the vessel. The legs are also evaluated for edema. This may be done by comparing both legs, since usually only one leg is involved. Any areas of redness, tenderness, and increased skin temperature should also be noted.

Early ambulation is an important aspect in the prevention of thrombophlebitis. Most women are able to be up shortly after birth. The cesarean birth client requires passive range of motion exercises until she is ambulating more freely.

Client teaching associated with assessment of the lower extremities focuses on the signs and symptoms of thrombophlebitis. In addition, the nurse may review self-care measures to promote circulation, and measures to prevent thrombophlebitis, such as ambulation, avoiding pressure behind the knees, and avoiding using the knee gatch on the bed and crossing the legs.

Results of the assessment are usually contained in a summary nursing note. If tenderness and warmth have been noted, they might be recorded as follows: Tenderness, warmth, and slight redness noted on posterior aspect of left calf—positive Homan's. Woman advised to avoid pressure to this area; lower leg elevated and moist heat applied per agency protocol. Call placed to Dr Smith to report findings.

## VITAL SIGNS ASSESSMENT

Alterations in vital signs may indicate complications, so they are assessed at regular intervals. The blood pressure should remain stable, while the pulse often shows a characteristic slowness that is no cause for alarm. Pulse rates return to prepregnant norms very quickly unless complications arise.

Temperature elevations (less than 38°C [100.4°F]) due to normal processes should last for only a few days and should not be associated with other clinical signs of infection. Any elevation should be evaluated in light of other signs and symptoms. The woman's history should also be carefully reviewed to identify other factors, such as premature rupture of membranes (PROM) or prolonged labor, which might increase the incidence of infection in the genital tract.

The nurse informs the woman of the results of the vital signs assessment. Information regarding the normal changes in blood pressure and pulse can be provided. This may be an opportunity to assess whether the mother knows how to assess her own and her infant's temperature and how to read a thermometer.

## NUTRITIONAL STATUS

Determination of postpartal nutritional status is based primarily on information provided by the mother and on direct assessment. During pregnancy the recommended daily dietary allowances call for increases in calories, proteins, and most vitamins and minerals. After delivery, the nonnursing mother's dietary requirements return to prepregnancy levels (Food and Nutrition Board 1980).

Visiting the mothers during mealtime provides an opportunity for unobtrusive nutritional assessment and counseling. The nonnursing mother should be advised about the need to reduce her caloric intake by about 300 cal and to return to prepregnancy levels for other nutrients. The nursing mother, on the other hand, should increase her caloric intake by about 200 cal over the pregnancy requirements. Basic discussion will prove helpful, followed by referral as needed. In all cases, literature on nutrition should be provided so that the woman will have a source of information following discharge. (See Essential Facts to Remember—Encouraging Healthful Nutrition.)

The dietitian should be informed of any mother whose cultural or religious beliefs require specific foods. Appropriate meals can then be prepared for her. Many women, especially those who gained excessively, are interested in losing weight after birth. The dietitian can design weight-reduction diets to meet nutritional needs and food preferences. The nurse may also refer women with unusual eating habits or numerous questions about good nutrition to the dietitian.

## Essential Facts to Remember

### Encouraging Healthful Nutrition

Encourage the woman to have daily:

Four servings of milk
Three servings of meat
Four servings of fruit-vegetable
Four servings of whole grain

New mothers are also advised that it is common practice to prescribe iron supplements for four to six weeks after delivery. The hematocrit is then checked at the postpartal visit to detect any anemia.

As a part of the nutritional assessment, the nurse can provide teaching about the nutritional needs of the woman during the postpartal period. See Essential Facts to Remember—Facts About Nutrition, and the discussion in Chapter 10.

## ELIMINATION

During the hours after birth the nurse carefully monitors a new mother's bladder status. A boggy uterus, a displaced uterus, or a palpable bladder are signs of bladder distention and require nursing intervention.

The postpartal woman should be encouraged to void every four to six hours. The bladder should be assessed for distention until the woman demonstrates complete emptying of the bladder with each voiding. The nurse may employ techniques to facilitate voiding, such as helping the woman out of bed to void or pouring warm water on the perineum. Catheterization is required when the bladder is distended and the woman cannot void or if no voiding has occurred in eight hours. The cesarean birth mother may have an in-dwelling catheter inserted prophylactically. The same assessments should be made in evaluating bladder emptying once the catheter is removed.

During the physical assessment the nurse elicits information from the woman regarding the adequacy of her fluid intake, whether she feels she is emptying her bladder completely when she voids, and any signs of urinary tract infection (UTI) she may be experiencing.

In the same way the nurse obtains information about the new mother's intestinal elimination and any concerns she may have about it. Many mothers fear that the first bowel movement will be painful and possibly even damaging if an episiotomy has been done. Stool softeners may be ordered to increase bulk and moisture in the fecal material and to allow more comfortable and complete evacuation. Constipation is avoided to prevent pressures on sutures that may increase discomfort. Encouraging ambulation, forcing fluids, and providing fresh fruits and roughage in the diet enhance bowel elimination and assist the woman in reestablishing her normal bowel pattern.

During the assessment the nurse may provide information regarding postpartum diuresis and why the woman may be emptying her bladder so frequently. The need for additional fluid intake with suggestions of specific amounts may be helpful. Signs of retention and overflow voiding are discussed, and symptoms of UTI may be reviewed with the mother at this time if it seems an appropriate moment for teaching. Methods of assisting bowel elimination may be reviewed and opportunities for the woman to ask questions are provided.

### REST AND SLEEP STATUS

As part of the postpartal assessment, the nurse evaluates the amount of rest a new mother is getting. If the woman reports difficulty sleeping at night, cause should be determined. If it is simply the strange hospital environment, a warm drink, backrub, or mild sedative may prove helpful. Appropriate nursing measures are indicated if the woman is bothered by normal postpartal discomforts such as afterpains, diaphoresis, or episiotomy or hemorrhoidal pain.

A daily rest period should be encouraged and hospital activities should be scheduled to allow time for napping.

## • Psychologic Assessment

Adequate assessment of the mother's psychologic adjustment is an integral part of postpartal evaluation. This assessment focuses on the mother's general attitude, feelings of competence, available support systems, and caregiving skills. It also evaluates her fatigue level, sense of satisfaction, and ability to accomplish her developmental tasks.

Fatigue is often a highly significant factor in a new mother's apparent disinterest in her newborn. Frequently the woman is so tired from a long labor and birth that everything seems to be an effort. To avoid inadvertently classifying a very tired mother as one with a potential attachment problem, the nurse should do the psychologic assessment on more than one occasion. After a nap the new mother is often far more receptive to her infant and her surroundings.

Some new mothers have little or no experience with infants and may feel totally overwhelmed. They may show these feelings by asking questions and reading all available material or by becoming passive and quiet because they simply cannot deal with their feelings of inadequacy. Unless a nurse questions the woman about her plans and previous experience in a supportive, nonjudgmental way, one might conclude that the woman was disinterested, withdrawn, or depressed. Problem clues might include excessive continued fatigue, marked depression, excessive preoccupation with physical status and/or discomfort, evidence of low self-esteem, lack of support systems, marital problems, inability to care for or nurture the newborn, and current family crises (such as illness, unemployment, and so on). These characteristics frequently indicate a potential for maladaptive parenting, which may lead to child abuse or neglect (physical, emotional, intellectual) and cannot be ignored. Referrals to public health nurses or other available community resources may provide greatly needed assistance and alleviate potentially dangerous situations.

## • Assessment of Early Attachment

If attachment is accepted as a desired outcome of nursing care, a nurse in any of the various postpartal settings can periodically observe and note progress toward attachment. The following questions can be addressed in the course of nurse-client interaction:

1. Is the mother attracted to her newborn? To what extent does she seek face-to-face contact and eye contact? Has she progressed from fingertip touch, to palmar contact, to enfolding the infant close to her own body? Is attraction increasing or decreasing? If the mother does not exhibit increasing attraction, why not? Do the reasons lie primarily within her, in the baby, or in the environment?

2. Is the mother inclined to nurture her infant? Is she progressing in her interactions with her infant? Has she selected a rooming-in arrangement if it is available?

3. Does the mother act consistently? If not, is the source of unpredictability within her or her infant?

4. Is her mothering intelligently carried out? Does she seek information and evaluate it objectively? Does she develop solutions based on adequate knowledge of valid data? Does she evaluate the effectiveness of her maternal care and make appropriate adjustments?

5. Is she sensitive to the newborn's needs as they arise? How quickly does she interpret her infant's behavior and react to cues? Does she seem happy and satisfied with the infant's responses to her efforts? Is she pleased with feeding behaviors? How much of this ability and willingness to respond is related to the baby's nature and how much to her own?

6. Does she seem pleased with her baby's appearance and sex? Is she experiencing pleasure in interaction

with her infant? What interferes with the enjoyment? Does she speak to the baby frequently and affectionately? Does she call him or her by name? Does she point out family traits or characteristics she sees in the newborn?

7. Are there any cultural factors that might modify the mother's response? For instance, is it customary for the grandmother to assume most of the child-care responsibilities while the mother recovers from childbirth?

When these questions are addressed and the facts have been assembled by the nurse, the nurse's intuitive feelings and formal background of knowledge should combine to answer three more questions: Is there a problem in attachment? What is the problem? What is its source? Each nurse can then devise a creative approach to the problem as it presents itself in the context of a unique developing mother-infant relationship.

## DATA BASE: THE FOURTH TRIMESTER

The first several postpartal weeks have been termed the fourth trimester to stress the idea of continuity as the family adjusts to having a new member and as the woman's body returns to an essentially prepregnant state. During this period the woman must accomplish certain physical and developmental tasks:

● Restoring physical condition

● Developing competence in caring for and meeting the needs of her infant

● Establishing a relationship with her new child

● Adapting to altered life-styles and family structure resulting from the addition of a new member

The new mother may have an inadequate or incorrect understanding of what to expect during the early postpartal weeks. She may be concerned with restoring her figure and surprised because of continuing physical discomfort from sore breasts, episiotomy, or hemorrhoids. Fatigue is perhaps her greatest yet most underestimated problem during the early weeks. This may be aggravated if she has no extended family support or if there are other young children at home.

Developing skill and confidence in caring for an infant may be especially anxiety provoking for a new mother. As she struggles to establish a mutually acceptable pattern with her baby, small unanticipated concerns may seem monumental. The woman may begin to feel inadequate and, if she lacks support systems, isolated.

Nurses have been in the forefront of health providers in attempting to improve the care currently existing during the postpartal period. Many obstetricians and nurse practitioners now routinely see all postpartal women one to two weeks after birth in addition to the routine six-week checkup. This extra visit provides an opportunity for physical assessment as well as assessment of the mother's psychologic and informational needs.

## Follow-Up Care

Follow-up care for the postpartal woman may be accomplished by home visits, follow-up phone calls, or postpartal classes. A home visit two to three days after discharge permits accurate assessment and teaching. It is especially useful for women who took advantage of early discharge policies and left the hospital after 24 hours or less.

The follow-up telephone call is usually initiated by a nurse from the postpartal unit of the agency where the mother delivered. It is made during the first week after discharge and is designed to provide assessment and care if necessary, to reinforce knowledge and provide additional teaching, and to make referrals if indicated.

Postpartal classes are becoming more common as care givers recognize the continuing needs of the childbearing family. A series of structured classes may focus on topics such as parenting, postpartal exercise, or nutrition, or there may be loosely structured group sessions that address concerns of mothers as they arise. Such classes offer chances for the new mother to socialize, share her concerns, and receive encouragement. Because babysitting arrangements may be difficult or expensive, it is desirable to provide child care for newborns and siblings, or in some instances, infants may remain with mothers in the class.

## Two- and Six-Week Examinations

The routine physical assessment, which can be made rapidly, focuses on the woman's general appearance, breasts, reproductive tract, bladder and bowel elimination, and any specific problems or complaints. (See the accompanying Postpartal Physical Assessment Guide—Two Weeks and Six Weeks After Birth.) In addition, conversation is used to determine nutrition patterns, fatigue level, family adjustment, and psychologic status of the mother (see the Postpartal Psychologic Assessment Guide). Any problems with child care are explored, and referral to a pediatric nurse practitioner or pediatrician is made if needed. Available community resources, including Public Health Department follow-up visits, are mentioned when appropriate. If not already discussed, teaching about family planning is appropriate at this time, and information regarding birth control methods is provided.

*(Text continues on page 772.)*

## Postpartal Physical Assessment Guide

### Two Weeks and Six Weeks After Birth

| Assess/Normal Findings | Alterations and Possible Causes* | Nursing Responses to Data† |
|---|---|---|
| **Vital Signs** | | |
| Blood pressure: Return to normal prepregnant level | Elevated blood pressure (anxiety, essential hypertension, renal disease) | Review history, evaluate normal baseline; refer to physician/nurse-midwife if necessary. |
| Pulse: 60–90 beats/min (or prepregnant normal rate) | Increased pulse rate (excitement, anxiety, cardiac disorders) | Count pulse for full minute, note irregularities; marked tachycardia or beat irregularities require additional assessment and possible physician/nurse-midwife referral. |
| Respirations: 16–24/min | Marked tachypnea or abnormal patterns (respiratory disorders) | Evaluate for respiratory disease; refer to physician/nurse-midwife if necessary. |
| Temperature: 36.2°C–37.6°C (98°F–99.6°F) | Increased temperature (infection) | Assess for signs and symptoms of infection or disease state. |
| **Weight** | | |
| Two weeks: Probable weight loss of 14–20+ lb | Little or no weight loss (fluid retention, subinvolution, poor dietary habits) | Evaluate dietary habits and nutritional state; review blood pressure to evaluate fluid retention or blood losses. |
| Six weeks: Returning to normal prepregnant weight | Retained weight (poor dietary habits) | Determine amount of daily exercise. Provide dietary teaching. Refer to dietitian if necessary for additional dietary counseling. |
| | Extreme weight loss (excessive dieting) | Discuss appropriate diets; refer to dietitian for additional counseling if necessary. |
| **Breasts** | | |
| Nonnursing:<br>  Two weeks: May have mild tenderness; small amount of milk may be expressed; breasts returning to prepregnant size<br>  Six weeks: Soft, with no tenderness; return to prepregnant size | Some engorgement (incomplete suppression of lactation)<br>Redness; marked tenderness (mastitis)<br>Palpable mass (tumor) | Engorgement usually seen when no medication has been given to suppress lactation or may occur after lactation suppression medication is stopped. Advise client to wear a supportive well-fitted bra, avoid hot showers, etc; evaluate for signs and symptoms of mastitis (rare in nonnursing mothers). |
| Nursing:<br>  Full, with prominent nipples; lactation established | Cracked, fissured nipples (feeding problems)<br>Redness, marked tenderness, or even abscess formation (mastitis)<br>Palpable mass (full milk duct, tumor) | Counsel about nipple care.<br>Evaluate client condition, evidence of fever; refer to physician/nurse-midwife for initiation of antibiotic therapy, if indicated.<br>Opinion varies as to value of breast examination for nursing mothers; some feel a nursing mother should examine her breasts monthly, after feeding, when breasts are empty; if palpable mass is felt, refer to physician for further evaluation. |

*Possible causes of alterations are placed in parentheses.
†This column provides guidelines for further assessment and initial nursing interventions.

# Postpartal Physical Assessment Guide

## Two Weeks and Six Weeks After Birth (continued)

| Assess/Normal Findings | Alterations and Possible Causes* | Nursing Responses to Data† |
|---|---|---|
| | | For breast inflammation instruct the mother to:<br>1. Keep breast empty by frequent feeding.<br>2. Rest when possible.<br>3. Take aspirin for pain.<br>4. Force fluids.<br>If symptoms persist for more than 24 hours, instruct her to call her physician/nurse-midwife. |
| **Abdominal Musculature** | | |
| Two weeks: Improved firmness, although "bread dough" consistency is not unusual, especially in multipara<br>Striae pink and obvious | Marked diastasis recti (relaxation of muscles) | Evaluate exercise level; provide information on appropriate exercise program. |
| Cesarean incision healing | Drainage, redness, tenderness, pain, edema (infection) | Evaluate for infection; refer to physician/nurse-midwife if necessary. |
| Six weeks: Muscle tone continues to improve; striae may be beginning to fade, may not achieve a silvery appearance for several more weeks; linea nigra fading | | |
| **Elimination Pattern** | | |
| Urinary tract:<br>Return to prepregnant urinary elimination routine | Urinary incontinence, especially when lifting, coughing, laughing, and so on (urethral trauma, cystocele) | Assess for cystocele; instruct in appropriate muscle tightening exercises; refer to physician/nurse-midwife. |
| | Pain or burning when voiding, urgency and/or frequency, pus or white blood cells (WBC) in urine, pathogenic organisms in culture (urinary tract infection) | Evaluate for urinary tract infection; obtain clean catch urine; refer to physician/nurse-midwife for treatment if indicated. |
| Routine urinalysis within normal limits (proteinuria disappeared) | Sugar or ketone in urine—may be some lactose present in urine of breast-feeding mothers (diabetes) | Evaluate diet; assess for signs and symptoms of diabetes; refer to physician/nurse-midwife. |
| Bowel habits:<br>Two weeks: May still be some discomfort with defecation, especially if client had severe hemorrhoids or 3° extension | Severe constipation or pain when defecating (trauma or hemorrhoids) | Discuss dietary patterns; encourage fluid, adequate roughage.<br>Continue use of stool softener if necessary to prevent pain associated with straining; continue sitz baths, periods of rest for severe hemorrhoids; assess healing of episiotomy and/or lacerations; severe constipation may require administration of laxatives, stool softeners, and an enema. |
| Six weeks: Return to normal prepregnancy bowel elimination | Marked constipation | See above. |
| | Fecal incontinence or constipation (rectocele) | Assess for evidence of rectocele; instruct in muscle tightening exercises; refer to physician/nurse-midwife. |

*Possible causes of alterations are placed in parentheses.
† This column provides guidelines for further assessment and initial nursing interventions.

(continues)

# Postpartal Physical Assessment Guide

## Two Weeks and Six Weeks After Birth (continued)

| Assess/Normal Findings | Alterations and Possible Causes* | Nursing Responses to Data† |
|---|---|---|
| **Reproductive Tract** | | |
| Lochia: | | |
| Two weeks: Lochia alba, scant amounts, fleshy odor | Foul odor, excessive in amounts (infection)<br>Return to lochia rubra or persistence of lochia rubra or serosa | Assess for evidence of infection and/or subinvolution; culture lochia; refer to physician/nurse-midwife. |
| Six weeks: No lochia, or return to normal menstruation pattern | See above | See above. |
| Pelvic examination: | | |
| Two weeks: Uterus no longer palpable abdominally; external os closed; uterine muscles still somewhat lax and uterus may be displaced; introitus of vagina still lacking tone—gapes when intraabdominal pressure is increased by coughing or straining<br>Episiotomy and/or lacerations healing; no signs of infection | External cervical os open, uterus not decreasing appropriately (subinvolution, infection)<br>Evidence of redness, tenderness, poor tissue approximation in episiotomy and/or laceration (wound infection) | Assess for evidence of subinvolution and/or infection; refer to physician/nurse-midwife if indicated. |
| Six weeks: almost returned to prepregnant size with almost completely restored muscle tone | Continued flow of lochia, some opening of cervical os, failure to decrease appropriately in size (subinvolution) | Assess for evidence of subinvolution and/or infection; refer to physician for further evaluation and for dilatation and curettage if necessary.<br>Cervix completely closed with only transverse slit apparent |
| Good return of muscle tone to pelvic floor | Marked relaxation of pelvic floor muscles (uterine prolapse) | Assess for evidence of uterine prolapse; discuss appropriate perineal exercises; refer to physician/nurse-midwife if indicated. |
| Papanicolaou test: Negative | Test results show atypical cells | Refer to physician/nurse-midwife for further evaluation and treatment. |
| **Hemoglobin and Hematocrit Levels** | | |
| Six weeks: Hb 12 g/dL<br>Hct 37% ± 5% | Hb < 12 g/dL<br>Hct 32% (anemia) | Assess nutritional status, begin (or continue) supplemental iron; for marked anemia (Hb 9g/dL) additional assessment and/or physician/nurse-midwife referral may be necessary. |

*Possible causes of alterations are placed in parentheses.
† This column provides guidelines for further assessment and initial nursing interventions.

# Postpartal Psychologic Assessment Guide

| Assess/Normal Findings | Alterations and Possible Causes* | Nursing Responses to Data† |
|---|---|---|
| **Attachment** | | |
| Bonding process demonstrated by soothing, cuddling, and talking to infant; appropriate feeding techniques; eye-to-eye contact; calling infant by name. | Failure to bond demonstrated by lack of behaviors associated with bonding process, calling infant by nickname that promotes ridicule, inadequate infant weight gain, infant is dirty, hygienic measures are not being maintained, severe diaper rash, failure to obtain adequate supplies to provide infant care (malattachment). | Provide counseling; talk with the woman about her feelings regarding the infant; provide support for the caretaking activities that are being performed; refer to public health nurse for continued home visits. |
| Parent interacts with infant and provides soothing, caretaking activities. | Parent is unable to respond to infant needs (inability to recognize needs, inadequate education and support, fear, family stress). | Provide support for caretaking activities observed; provide information regarding caretaking activities, such as responding to infant cry; methods of wrapping infant; methods of soothing the infant such as swaddling, rocking, increasing stimuli by singing to the infant or decreasing stimuli by putting infant to rest in quiet room; methods of holding the infant; differences in the cry. Identify support system such as friends, neighbors; provide information regarding community resources and support groups. |
| Parents are feeling more comfortable and successful with the parent role. | Evidence of stress and anxiety (difficulty moving into or dealing with the parent role). | Provide support and encouragement; provide information regarding progression into parent role and assist parents in talking through their feelings; refer to community resources and support groups. |
| Woman is in the informal or personal stage of maternal role attainment. | Woman is still greatly influenced by others, has not developed an image or style of her own (woman remains in the anticipatory stage). | Provide role modeling for the woman in working through problem solving with the infant; provide encouragement as she thinks through decisions and develops her sense of problem solving; encourage her to make decisions regarding infant care. |
| **Adjustment to Parental Role** | | |
| Parents are coping with new roles in terms of division of labor, financial status, communication, readjustment of sexual relations, and adjusting to new daily tasks. | Inability to adjust to new roles (immaturity, inadequate education and preparation, ineffective communication patterns, inadequate support, current family crisis). | Provide counseling; refer to parent groups. |
| **Education** | | |
| Mother understands self-care measures. | Inadequate knowledge of self-care (inadequate education). | Provide education and counseling. |
| Parents are knowledgeable regarding infant care. | Inadequate knowledge of infant care (inadequate education). | |
| Siblings are adjusting to new baby. | Excessive sibling rivalry. | |
| Parents have chosen a method of contraception. | Birth control method not chosen. | |

*Possible causes of alterations are placed in parentheses.
†This column provides guidelines for further assessment and initial nursing interventions.

In ideal situations a family approach involving the father, infant, and possibly other siblings would permit a total evaluation and provide an opportunity for all family members to ask questions and express concerns. In addition, disturbed family patterns might be more readily diagnosed and therapy instituted to prevent future problems of neglect or abuse.

## ESSENTIAL CONCEPTS

● **The uterus involutes rapidly, primarily through a reduction in cell size.**

● **Involution is assessed by measuring fundal height. The fundus is at the level of the umbilicus within a few hours after delivery and should decrease by approximately one fingerbreadth per day.**

● **The placental site heals by a process of exfoliation, so no scar formation occurs.**

● **Lochia progresses from rubra to serosa to alba and is assessed in terms of type, quantity, and characteristics.**

● **The abdomen may be flabby initially. Diastasis recti should be measured.**

● **Constipation may develop postpartally due to decreased tone, limited diet, and denial of the urge to defecate due to fear of pain.**

● **Decreased bladder sensitivity, increased capacity, and postpartal diuresis may lead to problems with bladder elimination. Frequent assessment and prompt intervention are indicated. A fundus that is boggy but does not respond to massage, is higher than expected, or deviates to the side usually indicates a full bladder.**

● **Postpartally a healthy woman should be normotensive and afebrile. Bradycardia is common.**

● **Postpartally the WBC is often elevated. Activation of clotting factors predisposes the woman to thrombus formation.**

● **Psychologic adaptations are traditionally described as taking-in and taking-hold.**

● **Postpartal cultural practices are often based on a belief in a balance between hot and cold.**

● **Postpartal assessment should be completed in a systematic way, usually cephalocaudally. It provides a tremendous opportunity for informal client teaching.**

## References

Davidson N: REEDA: Evaluating postpartum healing. *J Nurse-Midwifery* 1974; 9(2):6.

Easterling WE, Herbert WNP: The puerperium. In: *Obstetrics and Gynecology*, 5th ed. Danforth DN, Scott JR (editors). Philadelphia: Lippincott, 1986.

Food and Nutrition Board, National Academy of Sciences—National Research Council: *Recommended Dietary Allowances*, 9th ed. Washington DC, 1980.

Gay JT, Edgil AE, Douglas AB: Reva Rubin Revisited. *J Obstet Gynecol Neonatal Nurs* November/December 1988; 17(6):394.

Horn BM: Cultural concepts and postpartal care. *Nurs Health Care* 1981; 2:516.

Martell LK, Mitchell SK: Rubin's puerperal change reconsidered. *J Obstet Gynecol Neonatal Nurs* May/June 1984; 13(3):145.

Mercer RT: The process of maternal role attainment over the first year. *Nurs Res* July/August 1985; 34:198.

Rubin R: Puerperal change. *Nurs Outlook* 1961; 9:753.

Rubin R: *Maternal Identity and the Maternal Experience.* New York: Springer, 1984.

Varney H: *Nurse Midwifery*, 2nd ed. Boston: Blackwell Scientific Publications, 1987.

## Additional Readings

Bliss-Holtz VJ, Hughes CB: Prenatal concerns for learning infant care studied. *N J Nurse* 1988; 18(5):12.

Boissonnault JS, Blaschak MJ: Incidence of diastasis recti abdominis during the childbearing year. *Phys Ther* 1988; 68(7):1082.

Flagler S: Maternal role competence. *West J Nurs Res* 1988; 10(3):274.

Johnston PK: Counseling the pregnant vegetarian. *Am J Clin Nutr* 1988; 48(3 Suppl):901.

Kimball AM et al: Preliminary report of an identification mission for safe motherhood, Senegal: Putting the M back in M.C.H. *Int J Gynaecol Obstet* 1988; 26(2):181.

Konard CJ: Helping mothers integrate the birth experience. *Am J Mat Child Nurs* July/August 1987; 12(4):249.

Lindell SG: Education for childbirth: A time for change. *J Obstet Gynecol Neonatal Nurs* 1988; 17(2):108.

Lutwak RA, Ney AM, White JE: Maternity nursing and Jewish law. *Am J Mat Child Nurs* January/February 1988; 13:44.

McInerney PA: European cultural childbirth practices. *Nurs RSA* 1988; 3(3):35.

Mercer RT et al: Effect of stress on family functioning during pregnancy. *Nurs Res* 1988; 37(5):268.

Muhlen-Schulte L, Wade K: Intervention in childbirth and neonatal responsiveness. *Commun Health Stud* 1988; 12(1):69.

Olds DL et al: Improving the life-source development of socially disadvantaged mothers: A randomized trial of nurse home visitation. *Am J Pub Health* November 1988; 78(11):1436.

Poma PA: Pregnancy in Hispanic women. *J Nat Med Assoc* 1987; 79:929.

Ruff CC: How well do adolescents mother? *Am J Mat Child Nurs* July/August 1987; 12(4):249.

Weller, RH, Eberstein IW, Bailey M: Pregnancy wantedness and maternal behavior during pregnancy. *Demography* 1987; 24(3):407.

# 26

## The Postpartal Family: Needs and Care

*I remember so clearly the day I brought my firstborn home from the hospital. My husband dropped me off and then had to return to work. I sat in the living room with my new son and tried to envision the future. How would this small person change our lives? I know now that, though it is sometimes frustrating to be a parent, it is infinitely enriching, too.*

## Objectives

● Relate the use of nursing diagnoses to the findings of the "normal" postpartum assessment and analysis.

● Delineate nursing responsibilities for client education during the early postpartum period.

● Discuss appropriate nursing interventions to meet identified nursing goals for the childbearing family.

● Compare the nursing needs of a woman who experienced a cesarean birth with the needs of a woman who gave birth vaginally.

● Summarize the nursing needs of the childbearing adolescent during the postpartum period.

● Describe possible approaches to follow-up nursing care for the childbearing family.

## Key Term

engorgement

Certain premises form the basis of effective nursing care during the postpartal period.

● The best postpartal care is family centered and disrupts the family unit as little as possible. This approach uses the family's resources to support an early and smooth adjustment to the newborn by all family members.

● Knowledge of the range of normal physiologic and psychologic adaptations occurring during the postpartal period allows the nurse to recognize alterations and initiate interventions early. Communicating information about postpartal adaptations to the family facilitates their adjustment to their situation.

● Nursing care is aimed at accomplishing specific goals that ultimately meet individual needs. These goals are formulated after careful assessment and consideration of factors that could influence the outcome of care.

This chapter describes how the nurse can use the nursing process effectively to plan and provide care. Specific nursing responses to the mother's physical needs and the family's psychosocial needs are described at length.

## ● USING THE NURSING PROCESS DURING THE POSTPARTAL PERIOD

Often standardized nursing care plans provide the written guidelines for a nurse's action during the postpartal period. Each family is different, however, and the nurse may need to modify interventions to meet a family's needs. Whether a predetermined care plan exists or not, using the nursing process can help the nurse individualize the approach to families and determine priorities.

## ● Nursing Assessment

The postpartal assessment focuses on three interrelated areas of concern—the mother's physical changes and psychologic adjustments, the education needs of the parents, and the family's adjustment to the newest member. During the postpartal assessment, the nurse identifies the strengths of the woman or family as well as actual and potential problems that may influence maternal or family well-being. Ultimately, the assessment findings influence the plan of care.

The assessment period can also be used as a forum for client education. For example, as the postpartal nurse identifies physical changes in the mother, he or she explains them to the woman and her partner. As the nurse assesses the parents' skill in handling the new baby, he or she offers information or provides demonstrations that will enhance the parents' competence.

## ● Nursing Diagnosis

For most postpartal women, physical recovery goes smoothly and is considered a healthy process. Because of this perception, it is all too common for care givers to think that the woman and her family have no "real" needs and thus that no care plan is needed. Nothing could be further from the truth. Every member of the family has needs, although they may not be obvious, especially if they are psychologic or educational.

The postpartal family's needs, which should be identified during assessment, are the basis for developing nursing diagnoses. Once a nursing diagnosis is made and recorded, systematic action, as delineated in a nursing care plan, can be taken to meet the identified need.

Many nurses have suggested that nursing diagnoses are difficult to make in a wellness setting because of their emphasis on "problems." Stolte (1986) suggests that in some cases resorting to the identification of potential problems may create an artificial situation. She advocates an approach that enables the nurse to identify strengths (called "positive diagnoses") as well as needs or problems. One possible "positive nursing diagnosis" is "Progressive acquisition of maternal role behaviors related to seeking and gaining experience in child care" (p 14). This type of diagnosis focuses on a woman's strengths while permitting the nurse to take action to foster further progress in a specific area.

Many agencies that use nursing diagnoses prefer to use the NANDA list exclusively. Consequently, physiologic alterations form the basis of many postpartal diagnoses. Examples of such diagnoses are:

● Constipation related to fear of tearing stitches and/or pain
● Altered patterns of urinary elimination related to dysuria.

## ● Nursing Plan and Implementation

Many women remain on a postpartum unit for only a short time, so it is often feasible to assign a woman's care to the same nurse. However, time off and shift changes still make it imperative to develop and record a specific care plan. Implementation of the plan by all personnel caring for the postpartal woman promotes consistency, progress in client education, and more effective ongoing assessment and evaluation. An important component of nursing care is client teaching, which is given high priority by many agencies. Sophisticated, detailed forms and guide-lines are often available to assist in health teaching. Such tools are a useful adjunct but cannot take the place of the nurse's client-specific plan.

## ● Evaluation

Nursing evaluation on the postpartum unit enables the nurse to refine or modify the care plan based on its effectiveness and/or changes in the woman's status. Evaluation tends to be the most overlooked step of the nursing process, yet the nurse cannot provide quality care without determining whether interventions have been effective.

## ● NURSING ASSESSMENT

The nurse completes assessments of the new family and analyzes the data obtained. Cues are identified and additional assessments may be made as needed. See Chapter 25 for thorough discussion of the postpartal assessment.

## ● NURSING DIAGNOSIS

The nurse can anticipate that for many women with a low-risk postpartal period, certain nursing diagnoses such as those discussed previously and possibly those presented in Essential Nursing Diagnosis to Consider—The Postpartal Period will be used. After completing the assessment and diagnosis steps of the nursing process, the nurse creates a plan of care arranged around nursing goals.

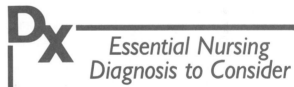

## Essential Nursing Diagnosis to Consider

### The Postpartal Period

Altered family processes
Altered patterns of urinary elimination: Urinary retention
Altered tissue perfusion
Anxiety
Bathing/hygiene self-care deficit
Constipation
Family coping: Potential for growth
Impaired physical mobility
Ineffective individual coping
Knowledge deficit
Pain
Potential for infection
Potential fluid volume deficit

## Essential Facts to Remember

### Position of the Uterine Fundus Following Birth

- Immediately after birth: The top of the fundus is in the midline about midway between the symphysis pubis and umbilicus.
- Six to twelve hours after birth: The top of the fundus is in the midline and at the level of the umbilicus.
- One day after birth: The top of the fundus remains in the midline at the level of the umbilicus.
- Second day after birth and thereafter: The top of the fundus remains in the midline and descends about one fingerbreadth per day.

## ● NURSING PLAN AND IMPLEMENTATION DURING THE POSTPARTAL PERIOD
## ● Promotion of Maternal Physical Well-Being

Maternal physical well-being is promoted by monitoring the status of the uterus, monitoring vital signs on a regular schedule, and providing medications as needed for women with problems involving the Rh factor, women who are not rubella immune, and women with some degree of anemia following childbirth.

### MONITORING UTERINE STATUS

The nurse completes an assessment of the uterus as discussed in Chapter 25. The assessment interval is every 15 minutes for the first hour after childbirth, every 30 minutes for the next hour, and then hourly for approximately two hours. After that, the nurse monitors uterine status at the beginning of each shift (every eight hours) or

## ⚕ Drug Guide

### Methylergonovine Maleate (Methergine)

#### Overview of Obstetric Action

Methylergonovine maleate is an ergot alkaloid that stimulates smooth muscle tissue. Because the smooth muscle of the uterus is especially sensitive to this drug, it is used postpartally to stimulate the uterus to contract. This contraction clamps off uterine blood vessels and prevents hemorrhage. In addition, the drug has a vasoconstrictive effect on all blood vessels, especially the larger arteries. This may result in hypertension, particularly in a woman whose blood pressure is already elevated.

#### Route, Dosage, and Frequency
Methergine has a rapid onset of action and may be given intramuscularly, orally, or intravenously.

Usual IM dose: 0.2 mg following delivery of the placenta. The dose may be repeated every two to four hours if necessary.

Usual oral dose: 0.2 mg every four hours (six doses).

Usual IV dose: Because the adverse effects of Methergine are far more severe with IV administration, this route is seldom used. If Methergine is given intravenously, the rate should *not* exceed 0.2 mg/min and the client's blood pressure should be monitored continuously.

#### Maternal Contraindications
Pregnancy, hepatic or renal disease, cardiac disease, and hypertension contraindicate this drug's use (Karch and Boyd 1989).

#### Maternal Side Effects
Hypertension (particularly when administered IV), nausea, vomiting, headache, bradycardia, dizziness, tinnitus, abdominal cramps, palpitations, dyspnea, chest pain, and allergic reactions may be noted.

#### Effects on Fetus/Neonate
Because Methergine has a long duration of action and can thus produce tetanic contractions, it should never be used during pregnancy as it may result in fetal trauma or death.

#### Nursing Considerations

1. Monitor fundal height and consistency and the amount and character of the lochia.
2. Assess the blood pressure before administration and routinely throughout drug administration.
3. Observe for adverse effects or symptoms of ergot toxicity.

## Essential Facts to Remember

### Normal Characteristics of Lochia

- Lochia rubra is red and is present for the first two to three days.
- Lochia serosa is pinkish red and is present from the third to the tenth day.
- Lochia alba is creamy white and is present from the 11th to about the 21st day.

### Table 26.1 Changes in Lochia That Cause Concern

| Change | Possible problem | Nursing actions |
| --- | --- | --- |
| Presence of clots | Inadequate uterine contractions that allow bleeding from vessels at the placental site | Assess location and firmness of fundus. Assess voiding pattern. Record and report findings. |
| Persistent lochia rubra | Inadequate uterine contractions | Assess location and firmness of fundus. Assess activity pattern. Assess for signs of infection. Record and report findings. |

more frequently if problems arise such as bogginess, positioning out of midline, heavy lochia flow, or the presence of clots. See Essential Facts to Remember—Position of the Uterine Fundus Following Birth.

Medications may be ordered to promote uterine contractions. See Drug Guide—Methylergonovine Maleate (Methergine).

The amount, consistency, color, and odor of the lochia is monitored on an ongoing basis. See Essential Facts to Remember—Normal Characteristics of Lochia. Changes in lochia that need to be assessed further, documented, and reported to the physician/nurse-midwife are presented in Table 26.1.

### RUBELLA VACCINE

Women who have a rubella titer of less than 1:10 are usually given rubella vaccine in the postpartal period. If the woman is not rubella immune and is also Rh negative and receives RhoGAM, there is some question regarding whether the RhoGAM will interfere with the production of antibodies to rubella (Varney 1987). At this time, most physicians/nurse-midwives would continue to order rubella vaccine and would repeat the rubella titer in a few weeks to determine immunity. (See Table 26.2)

### Education for Self-Care

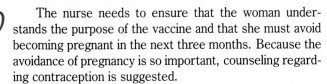

The nurse needs to ensure that the woman understands the purpose of the vaccine and that she must avoid becoming pregnant in the next three months. Because the avoidance of pregnancy is so important, counseling regarding contraception is suggested.

### RHOGAM

All Rh-negative women who meet specific criteria should receive RhoGAM within 72 hours after childbirth. See discussion of criteria on p 323.

### Education for Self-Care

The Rh-negative woman needs to understand the implications of her Rh-negative status in future pregnancies. The nurse provides opportunities for questions.

## ● Promotion of Comfort and Relief of Pain

Discomfort may be present to varying degrees in the postpartal woman. Potential sources of discomfort include an edematous perineum; an episiotomy, perineal laceration, or extension; vaginal hematoma, engorged hemorrhoids, or engorged breasts with sore nipples.

### RELIEF OF PERINEAL DISCOMFORT

There are many nursing interventions available for the relief of perineal discomfort. Prior to selecting a method, the nurse needs to have assessed the perineum to determine the degree of edema, etc. It is also important to ask the woman if there are special measures that she feels will be particularly effective, or to offer her choices when possible. It is important to cleanse the hands prior to and immediately following all relief measures. At all times, it is important to remember hygienic practices such as moving from the front (area of the symphysis pubis) to the back (area around the anus) of the perineum. This is important to remember while placing ice packs, placing perineal pads, and applying topical anesthetics or pain relief products. Avoiding contamination between the anal area and the urethral/vaginal area is important to prevent infection.

## Table 26.2 Essential Information for Common Postpartum Drugs

| Drug | Dose/route | Indication | Adverse effects | Nursing implications |
|---|---|---|---|---|
| Deladumone OB (contains 360 mg testosterone enanthate and 16 mg estradiol valerate) Drug class: Androgen, hormone | 2 cc deep IM at the beginning of the second stage of labor or just prior to the birth of the baby | Suppress lactation | Hirsutism, hoarseness, deepening of voice, facial hair growth, discomfort at injection site | Determine if woman has known sensitivity to androgens; presence of liver, cardiac, or kidney disease. Administer deep IM. POSSIBLE NURSING DIAGNOSES RELATED TO DRUG THERAPY Knowledge deficit regarding the drug therapy Body image disturbance related to androgenic effects of drug |
| TACE (chlorotrianisene) Drug class: Nonsteroidal synthetic estrogen, hormone | One of the following regimens: 12 mg PO TID for seven days or 50 mg PO every six hours for six doses or 72 mg PO BID for two days Administer first dose within eight hours of birth | Suppress lactation | Nausea and vomiting, abdominal cramps, headache, thrombophlebitis, photosensitivity, migraine headache, depression, pulmonary emboli | Determine if woman has sensitivity or prior problems with estrogens or contraindications to the use of estrogens (hypertension, history of migraine headaches). Observe diabetic women closely (may increase insulin requirements); observe women at risk for thrombophlebitis. CLIENT TEACHING Inform client about name of drug, expected action, possible side effects, that drug is excreted in breast milk, need to take all pills that are ordered, possibility that engorgement may occur a few days after she finishes taking the pills (Varney 1987). POSSIBLE NURSING DIAGNOSES RELATED TO DRUG THERAPY Knowledge deficit regarding drug therapy Personal identity disturbance related to androgenic effects of drug |

### Ice Pack

If an episiotomy is done at the time of birth, an ice pack is generally applied to reduce edema and provide numbing of the tissues, which promotes comfort. In some agencies, chemical ice bags are used. These are usually activated by folding both ends toward the middle. Inexpensive ice bags may be made by filling a disposable glove with ice chips or crushed ice and then taping the top of the glove. The disposable glove needs to first be rinsed under running water to remove any powder that may be present, and then wrapped in an absorbent towel or washcloth before placing it against the perineum. To attain the maximum effect of this cold treatment, the ice pack should remain in place approximately 20 minutes and then be re-moved for about ten minutes before replacing it. Care needs to be taken to protect the perineum from burns caused by contact with the ice pack.

**Education for Self-Care** The nurse provides information regarding the purpose of the ice pack, anticipated effects, benefits, and possible problems, and how to prepare an ice pack for home use if edema is present and early discharge is planned.

### Sitz Bath

The warmth of the water in the sitz bath provides comfort, decreases pain, and promotes circulation to the tissues, which promotes healing and reduces the incidence

## Table 26.2  Essential Information for Common Postpartum Drugs *(continued)*

| Drug | Dose/route | Indication | Adverse effects | Nursing implications |
|---|---|---|---|---|
| Empirin #3 (325 mg aspirin and 30 mg codeine) Drug class: Narcotic analgesic | Usual adult dose: One to two tablets PO every four hours PRN | For relief of mild to moderate pain | Aspirin: Nausea, dyspepsia, epigastric discomfort, dizziness Codeine: respiratory depression, apnea, light-headedness, dizziness, nausea, sweating, dry mouth, constipation, facial flushing, suppression of cough reflex, ureteral spasm, urinary retention, pruritis | Determine if woman is sensitive to aspirin or codeine; has history of impaired hepatic or renal function. Monitor bowl sounds, respirations, urine output. Administer with food or after meals if GI upset occurs; encourage woman to drink one full glass (240 mL) with the tablet to reduce the risk of the tablet lodging in the esophagus. **CLIENT TEACHING** Inform client about name of drug, expected action, possible side effects, that it is secreted in breast milk (Note: Some physician/nurse-midwives may avoid ordering this medication for nursing mothers), and review safety measures (assess for dizziness, use side rails, call for assistance when getting out of bed and ambulating, report to nurse any signs of adverse effects); ask if she has any questions. **POSSIBLE NURSING DIAGNOSES RELATED TO DRUG THERAPY** Knowledge deficit regarding the drug therapy Potential for injury related to dizziness secondary to effect of drug |

*(continues)*

of infection. Sitz baths may be ordered TID and PRN. The nurse prepares the sitz bath by cleansing the sitz tub or portable sitz. Water at 102–105°F is added. The woman is instructed to remain in the sitz for 20 minutes. Care needs to be taken during the first sitz bath as the warm moist heat and warm environment may cause the woman to faint. Placing a call bell well within reach and checking on the woman at frequent intervals will increase her comfort and maintain safety. The woman needs to be observed at frequent intervals for signs that she may faint, such as dizziness, a floaty or spacy feeling, or difficulty hearing. It is important for the woman to have a clean unused towel to pat dry her perineum after the sitz and to have a clean perineal pad to apply.

***Education for Self-Care***   The nurse provides information regarding the purpose and use of the sitz bath, anticipated effects, benefits and possible problems, and

safety measures to prevent injury from fainting, slipping, or excessive water temperature. Home use of sitz baths may be recommended for the woman with an extensive episiotomy, and the woman may use a portable sitz or her bathtub. It is important for the nurse to emphasize that in using a bathtub, only 4–6 inches of water is drawn, the temperature of the water needs to be assessed, and the water is used only for the sitz and not for bathing. If a tub bath is taken, the water should be released, the tub cleansed, and new water drawn prior to the sitz to prevent infection.

### Perineal Heat Lamp

A perineal heat lamp provides dry heat, which drys the perineal tissues, and warmth, which increases circulation to promote healing and comfort. Heat lamps are usually ordered TID PRN. The woman's perineum is cleansed to

## Table 26.2 Essential Information for Common Postpartum Drugs *(continued)*

| Drug | Dose/route | Indication | Adverse effects | Nursing implications |
|---|---|---|---|---|
| Percoset (contains 325 mg acetaminophen and 5 mg oxycodone) Drug class: Narcotic analgesic | One to two tablets PO every four hours PRN | For moderate to moderately severe pain Can be used in aspirin-sensitive women | Acetaminophen: Hepatotoxicity, headache, rash, hypoglycemia Oxycodone: Respiratory depression, apnea, circulatory depression, euphoria, facial flushing, constipation, suppression of cough reflex, ureteral spasm, urinary retention | Determine if woman is sensitive to acetaminophen or codeine; has bronchial asthma, respiratory depression, convulsive disorder. Observe woman carefully for respiratory depression if given with barbiturates or sedative/hypnotics. Consider that postcesarean-birth woman may have depressed cough reflex, so teaching and encouragement to deep breathe and cough is needed. Monitor bowel sounds, urine and bowel elimination. CLIENT TEACHING Teaching should include name of drug, expected effect, possible adverse effects, that drug is secreted in the breast milk, encouragement to report any signs of adverse effects immediately. POSSIBLE NURSING DIAGNOSES RELATED TO DRUG THERAPY Altered breathing patterns: depression Constipation Urinary retention |

prevent drying of secretions on the perineum and to remove any ointments or perineal sprays. The lamp is placed approximately 12 inches from the perineum and usually contains a 60-watt light bulb.

***Education for Self-Care*** The nurse provides information about the use and purpose of the heat lamp treatment. Safety information regarding the placement of the lamp and reminders not to move the lower extremities close to the lamp are important to avoid burns. Many of the heat lamps are rather cumbersome, and it is difficult to find a storage spot in the mother's room; however, they should NEVER be placed on the floor for storage between uses.

### Topical Agents

Topical anesthetics such as Dermoplast aerosol spray or Americain spray may be used to relieve perineal discomfort. The woman is advised to apply the anesthetic following a sitz bath or perineal care. Because of the danger of tissue burns she must be cautioned not to apply anesthetic before using a heat lamp.

Witch hazel compresses may be used to relieve perineal discomfort and edema. Nupercainal ointment or TUCKS may be ordered for relief of hemorrhoidal pain. It is important for the nurse to emphasize the need for the woman to wash her hands before and after using the topical treatments.

***Education for Self-Care*** The nurse provides information regarding the anesthetic spray or topical agent. The woman needs to understand the purpose, use, anticipated effects, benefits, and possible problems associated with the product. Demonstration of application by the nurse can be combined with teaching. A return demonstration is a useful method of evaluating the woman's understanding.

### Perineal Care

Perineal care after each elimination cleans the perineum and helps promote comfort. Many agencies provide "peri bottles" that the woman can use to squirt warm tap water over her perineum following elimination. To cleanse her perineum, the woman should use moist antiseptic towelettes or toilet paper in a blotting (patting) motion and

## Table 26.2 Essential Information for Common Postpartum Drugs *(continued)*

| Drug | Dose/route | Indication | Adverse effects | Nursing implications |
|------|-----------|-----------|-----------------|---------------------|
| Rubella virus vaccine, live (Meruvax 2) | Single dose vial, inject subcutaneously in outer aspect of the upper arm | Stimulate active immunity against rubella virus | Burning or stinging at the injection site; about two to four weeks later may have rash, malaise, sore throat, or headache | Determine if woman has sensitivity to neomycin (vaccine contains neomycin); is immunosuppressed, or has received blood transfusions (not to be administered within three months of blood transfusion, plasma transfusion, or serum immune globulin). Note: If a woman is to receive both RhoGAM and rubella, there is a possibility that the formation of antibodies to rubella may be suppressed by the RhoGAM injection. Most physicians will go ahead and order both injections and retest for maternal rubella immune status in about three months (Varney 1987). |
| | | | | CLIENT TEACHING |
| | | | | Name of drug, expected effect, possible adverse effects, possible comfort measures to use if adverse effects occur; rubella titer will be assessed in about three months. Instruct woman to AVOID PREGNANCY FOR THREE MONTHS following vaccination. Provide information regarding contraceptives and their use. |
| | | | | POSSIBLE NURSING DIAGNOSES RELATED TO DRUG THERAPY |
| | | | | Knowledge deficit regarding drug therapy<br>Knowledge deficit regarding types and use of contraceptives<br>Pain related to rash and malaise |

*(continues)*

should start at the front (area just under the symphysis pubis) and proceed toward the back (area around the anus), to prevent contamination from the anal area. In addition, to prevent contamination the perineal pad should be applied from front to back (attach front edge to special belt first, then back edge; place the front portion against the perineum first).

***Education for Self-Care*** The nurse demonstrates how to cleanse the perineum and assists the woman as necessary. Additional information regarding the use of perineal pads may be offered. The pads need to be placed snugly against the perineum but should not produce pressure. If the pad is worn too loosely, it may rub back and forth, irritating perineal tissues and causing contamination between the anal area and vaginal area. Occasionally, a woman may not ever have used a perineal pad or belt and will need additional assistance in using them during the postpartal period.

## RELIEF OF HEMORRHOIDAL DISCOMFORT

Some mothers experience hemorrhoidal pain after giving birth. Relief measures include the use of sitz baths, anesthetic ointments, rectal suppositories, or witch hazel pads applied directly to the anal area. The woman may be taught to digitally replace external hemorrhoids in her rectum. She may also find it helpful to maintain a side-lying position when possible and to avoid prolonged sitting. The mother is encouraged to maintain an adequate fluid intake,

## Table 26.2 Essential Information for Common Postpartum Drugs *(continued)*

| Drug | Dose/route | Indication | Adverse effects | Nursing implications |
|---|---|---|---|---|
| RhoGAM (Rh immune globulin specific for D antigen) | Postpartum: One vial IM within 72 hours of birth Antepartal: One vial microdose RhoGAM IM at 28 weeks in Rh-negative women; after amniocentesis, spontaneous or therapeutic abortion, or ectopic pregnancy | Prevention of sensitization to the Rh factor in Rh-negative women and to prevent hemolytic disease in the newborn in subsequent pregnancies<br><br>Mother must be: Rh negative Not previously sensitized to Rh factor Infant must be: Rh positive Direct antiglobulin negative | Soreness at injection site | Confirm criteria for administration are present. Assure correct vial is used for the client (each vial is cross-matched to the specific woman and must be carefully checked). Inject entire contents of vial.<br><br>CLIENT TEACHING<br><br>Name of drug, expected action, possible side effects; report soreness at injection site to nurse; woman should carry information regarding Rh status and dates of RhoGAM injections with her at all times; explain use of RhoGAM with subsequent pregnancies.<br><br>POSSIBLE NURSING DIAGNOSES RELATED TO DRUG THERAPY<br><br>Knowledge deficit related to the need for RhoGAM and future implications Pain related to soreness at injection site |
| Seconal Sodium (secobarbital sodium) Drug Class: Sedative, short-acting barbiturate | 100 mg PO at bedtime | Promote sleep | Somnolence, confusion, ataxia, vertigo, nightmares, hypoventilation, bradycardia, hypotension, nausea, vomiting, rashes | Determine if woman has sensitivity to barbiturates, or respiratory distress. Monitor respirations, blood pressure, pulse. Modify environment to increase relaxation and promote sleep. Monitor for drug interaction if woman also is taking tranquilizers, or TACE.<br><br>CLIENT TEACHING<br><br>Name of drug, expected effect, possible adverse effects, safety measures (siderails, use call bell, ask for assistance when out of bed); medication is secreted in breast milk.<br><br>POSSIBLE NURSING DIAGNOSES RELATED TO DRUG THERAPY<br><br>Potential for injury related to possible ataxia or vertigo Altered thought processes related to drug-induced confusion Knowledge deficit regarding drug therapy |

and stool softeners are administered to ensure greater comfort with bowel movements. The hemorrhoids usually disappear a few weeks after birth if the woman did not have them prior to her pregnancy.

### AFTERPAINS

Afterpains are the result of intermittent uterine contractions. A primipara may not experience afterpains because her uterus is able to maintain a contracted state. Multiparous women and those who have had a multiple pregnancy or hydramnios frequently experience discomfort from afterpains as the uterus intermittently contracts. The nurse can suggest the woman lie prone with a small pillow under the lower abdomen. The woman needs to be told that the discomfort may feel intensified for about five minutes but then will diminish greatly if not completely. The prone position applies pressure to the uterus and therefore stimulates contractions. When the uterus maintains a constant contraction, the afterpains cease. Additional nursing interventions may be to encourage a sitz bath (for warmth), positioning, ambulation, or administration of an analgesic agent. For breast-feeding mothers, a mild analgesic administered an hour before feeding will promote comfort and enhance maternal-infant interaction. (See Table 26.2.)

#### Education for Self-Care

The nurse provides information about the cause of afterpains and methods to decrease discomfort. Any medications that are ordered will be explained, along with expected effect, benefits and possible side effects, and any special considerations such as the possibility of dizziness or sleepiness with particular medications.

### DISCOMFORT FROM IMMOBILITY

Discomfort may also be caused by immobility. The woman who has been in stirrups for any length of time may experience muscular aches from such extreme positioning. It is not unusual for women to experience joint pains and muscular pain in both arms and legs, depending on the effort they exerted during the second stage of labor.

Early ambulation is encouraged to help reduce the incidence of complications such as constipation and thrombophlebitis. It also helps promote a feeling of general well-being.

The nurse assists the woman the first few times she gets up during the postpartal period. Fatigue, effects of medications, loss of blood, and possibly even lack of food intake may result in feelings of dizziness or faintness when the woman stands up. Because this may be a problem during the woman's first shower, the nurse should remain in the room, check the woman frequently, and have a chair close by in case she becomes faint. During this first shower

the nurse instructs the woman in the use of the emergency call button in the bathroom; if she becomes faint during a future shower, she can call for assistance.

#### Education for Self-Care

The nurse provides information about ambulation and the importance of monitoring any signs of dizziness or weakness.

### EXCESSIVE PERSPIRATION

Postpartal diaphoresis may cause discomfort for new mothers. The nurse can offer a fresh dry gown and bed linens to enhance comfort. Some women may feel refreshed by a shower. It is important to consider cultural practices and realize that some Mexican American and Asian women may prefer not to shower in the first few days following birth. Because diaphoresis also may lead to increased thirst, the nurse can offer fluids as the woman desires. Again, cultural practices are important to consider. Caucasian women may prefer iced water and Asian women may prefer water at room temperature. It is important for the nurse to ascertain the woman's wishes rather than operate solely from the nurse's own value/cultural belief system.

#### Education for Self-Care

The nurse provides information regarding the normal physiologic occurrence of the diaphoresis and methods to increase comfort.

## ● *Suppression of Lactation in the Nonnursing Mother*

Lactation may be suppressed through drug therapy and mechanical inhibition. The drugs used are hormones that inhibit the secretion of prolactin. However, because many of these drugs, such as chlorotrianisene (TACE), are estrogen-based medications and are associated with an increased incidence of thromboembolic disease, most practitioners prescribe them much less frequently than formerly. A newer, nonhormonal lactation suppressant, bromocriptine mesylate (Parlodel) is now available. See the accompanying Drug Guide—Bromocriptine (Parlodel).

Because bromocriptine is expensive and not always completely successful in suppressing lactation, mechanical methods of lactation suppression are becoming increasingly popular. Although signs of engorgement do not usually occur until the second or third postpartum day, prevention of engorgement is best accomplished by beginning nonpharmaceutical methods of lactation suppression as soon as possible after birth. Ideally this involves having the woman begin wearing a supportive, well-fitting bra within six hours after birth. The bra is worn continuously until

# 🔆 Drug Guide

## Bromocriptine (Parlodel)

### Overview of Obstetric Action

Bromocriptine is a dopamine agonist that acts to suppress lactation by stimulating the production of prolactin-inhibiting factor at the hypothalamic level. This results in decreased secretion of prolactin by the pituitary gland. The drug may also directly inhibit the pituitary by preventing the release of prolactin from the hormone-producing cells (Foster 1982). When administered postpartally it helps suppress milk production and decrease breast leakage and pain. It may also be used for suppression after lactation has already begun.

### Route, Dosage, and Frequency

The usual dose is 2.5 mg orally two times per day. The total daily dose generally does not exceed 7.5 mg. The medication is usually taken for two to three weeks. Research regarding the efficacy of parenteral administration suggests that a single intramuscular dose of a microencapsulated form of bromocriptine may be effective in suppressing lactation when administered following birth. This would be useful following obstetric surgery or for women experiencing severe vomiting (Peters et al 1986).

### Maternal Contraindications
Maternal hypotension, desire to breast-feed, pregnancy.

### Maternal Side Effects
Hypotension is the primary side effect. To prevent problems associated with hypotension, administration should be delayed until the new mother's vital signs are stable. Other side effects include nausea, headache, dizziness, and occasionally faintness and vomiting.

### Nursing Considerations

Administration should be delayed until maternal blood pressure is stable. Blood pressure should be carefully monitored if bromocriptine is administered concurrently with any antihypertensives. Taking bromocriptine with meals may help decrease the possibility of nausea. Early resumption of ovulation has occurred in women taking bromocriptine; the woman should be informed of this and receive information about contraceptives (Foster 1982).

---

lactation is suppressed (usually about five days) and is removed only for showers (Wong and Stepp-Gilbert 1985). The bra provides support and eases the discomfort that can occur with tension on the breasts because of fullness. A snug breast binder may be used if the woman does not have a bra available or if she finds the binder more comfortable. Ice packs should be applied over the axillary area of each breast for 20 minutes four times daily. This, too, should be begun soon after birth. Ice is also useful in relieving discomfort if engorgement occurs.

### EDUCATION FOR SELF-CARE.

The mother is advised to avoid any stimulation of her breasts by her baby, herself, breast pumps, or her sexual partner until the sensation of fullness has passed (usually about one week). Such stimulation will increase milk production and delay the suppression process. Heat is avoided for the same reason, and the mother is encouraged to let shower water flow over her back rather than her breasts. Suppression takes only a few days in most cases, but small amounts of milk may be produced up to a month after birth. In some instances, lactation is suppressed until the

woman stops taking bromocriptine, and then engorgement occurs.

### BREAST DISCOMFORT

Breast **engorgement** may be a source of pain for the postpartal woman. Specific nursing interventions for the bottle-feeding mother are discussed in Chapter 23.

## • Promotion of Rest and Graded Activity

Following birth a woman may feel exhausted and in need of rest. In other cases she may be euphoric and full of psychic energy immediately after birth, ready to relive the experience of birth repeatedly. The nurse can provide a period for airing of feelings and then encourage a period of rest.

Physical fatigue often affects other adjustments and functions of the new mother. For example, fatigue can reduce milk flow, thereby increasing problems with establishing breast-feeding. Energy is also needed to make the psychologic adjustments to a new infant and to assume new roles. Adjustments are most smoothly accomplished when adequate rest is obtained. Nurses can encourage rest by organizing their activities to avoid frequent interruptions for the woman. Rest times should be provided before encounters with the newborn if rooming-in is not used.

## POSTPARTAL EXERCISES

The woman should be encouraged to begin simple exercises while in the hospital and continue them at home. She is advised that increased lochia or pain means she should reevaluate her activity and make necessary alterations. Most agencies provide a booklet describing suggested postpartal activities. (Exercise routines vary for women undergoing cesarean birth or tubal ligation following delivery.) See Figure 26.1 for a description of some commonly used exercises.

## RESUMPTION OF ACTIVITIES

Ambulation and activity may gradually increase after birth. The new mother should avoid heavy lifting, excessive stair climbing, and strenuous activity. One or two daily naps are essential and are most easily achieved if the mother sleeps when her baby does.

By the second week at home, light housekeeping may be resumed. Although it is customary to delay returning to work for six weeks, most women are physically able to resume practically all activities by four to five weeks. Delaying returning to work until after the final postpartal examination will minimize the possibility of problems.

## ● Promotion of Maternal Psychologic Well-Being

The birth of a child, with the changes in role and the increased responsibilities it produces, is a time of emotional stress for the new mother. During the early puerperium she is emotionally labile, and mood swings and tearfulness are common.

Initially the mother may repeatedly discuss her experiences in labor and birth. This allows the mother to integrate her experiences. If she feels that she did not cope well with labor, she may have feelings of inadequacy and may benefit from reassurance that she did well.

During this time the new mother must also adjust to the loss of her fantasized child and accept the child she has borne. This may be more difficult if the child is not of the desired sex or if he or she has birth defects.

During the *taking-in* period the mother is focused on bodily concerns and may not be fully ready to learn about personal and infant care. However, because early discharge is common, classes and information should be offered and printed handouts provided for reference as questions arise at home.

During the *taking-hold* phase the mother becomes concerned about her ability to be a successful parent. During this time the mother requires reassurance that she is effective. She also tends to be more receptive to teaching and demonstration designed to assist her in mothering successfully.

The depression and weepiness that characterize the "postpartum blues" are often a surprise for the new mother. She requires reassurance that these feelings are normal, an explanation about why they occur, and a supportive environment that permits her to cry without feeling guilty.

## ● Promotion of Effective Parent Education

Meeting the educational needs of the new mother and her family is one of the primary challenges facing the postpartum nurse. Each woman has educational needs that vary based on age, background, experience, and expectations. The steps of the nursing process provide a useful tool for identifying and meeting educational needs following delivery.

The nurse first assesses the learning needs of the new mother through observation, and tactfully phrased questions. For example, "What plans have you made for handling things when you get home?" will elicit a response of several words and may provide the opportunity for some information sharing and guidance. Some agencies also use checklists of common concerns for new mothers. The woman can check those that are of interest to her.

Teaching should then be planned and implemented to provide learning experiences in a logical, nonthreatening way. Postpartal units use a variety of approaches, including handouts, formal classes, videotapes, and individual interaction. Regardless of the technique, timing is important. The new mother is more receptive to teaching during the taking-hold phase, when she is ready to assume responsibility for her own care and that of her newborn. Unfortunately, many women are discharged during the taking-in phase. Because of this, many units provide printed material for new mothers to consult if questions arise at home.

Teaching should include information on role change and psychologic adjustments as well as skills. Anticipatory guidance can help prepare new parents for the many changes they experience with a new family member.

Information is also essential for women with specialized educational needs: the mother who has had a cesarean birth, the parents of twins, the parents of an infant with congenital anomalies, and so on. Nurses who are attuned to these individual problems can begin providing guidance as soon as possible.

Evaluation may take several forms: return demonstrations, question and answer sessions, and even formal evaluation tools. Follow-up phone calls after discharge provide additional evaluative information and continue the helping process for the family.

## ● *Promotion of Family Wellness*

The promotion of family wellness involves several areas of concern. These include a satisfactory maternity experience, the need for follow-up care for mother and infant, and birth control. The new or expanding family may also have needs for information about adjustment of siblings and resuming sexual relations.

### *ROOMING-IN*

The emphasis on family-centered maternity care must be continued in the postpartal period. The practice of

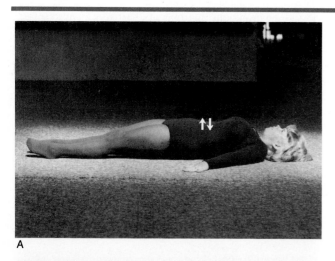

A

B

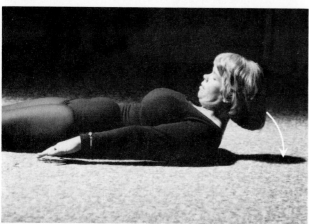

C

D

*Figure 26.1   Postpartal exercises. Begin with five repetitions two or three times daily and gradually increase to ten repetitions. First day: (A) Abdominal breathing. Lying supine, inhale deeply, using the abdominal muscles. The abdomen should expand. Then exhale slowly through pursed lips, tightening the abdominal muscles. (B) Pelvic rocking. Lying supine with arms at sides, knees bent and feet flat, tighten abdomen and buttocks and attempt to flatten back on floor. Hold for a count of ten, then*

*arch the back, causing the pelvis to "rock." On second day add: (C) Chin to chest. Lying supine with no pillow, legs straight, raise head and attempt to touch chin to chest. Slowly lower head. (D) Arm raises. Lying supine, arms extended at 90° angle from body, raise arms so they are perpendicular and hands touch. Lower slowly. On fourth day add: (E) Knee rolls. Lying supine with knees bent, feet flat, arms extended to the side, roll knees slowly to one side, keeping shoulders flat. Return to original* rooming-in provides increased opportunities for parent-child interaction.

In rooming-in the newborn shares the mother's unit, and they are cared for together. This enables the mother to have time to bond with her baby and learn to care for him or her in a supportive environment. Rooming-in is especially conducive to a self-demand feeding schedule for both breast-feeding and bottle-feeding babies. It also allows the father to participate in the care of his new child.

The rooming-in policy must be flexible enough to permit the mother to return the baby to the nursery if she finds it necessary because of fatigue or physical discomfort. Many agencies also return the infants to a central nursery at night so the mothers can get more rest.

Rooming-in provides an excellent opportunity for family bonds to grow. With rooming-in, father, mother, infant, and often siblings can begin functioning as a family unit immediately.

## REACTIONS OF SIBLINGS

Sibling visitation helps meet the needs of both the siblings and their mother. A visit to the hospital reassures children that their mother is well and still loves them. It

E

F

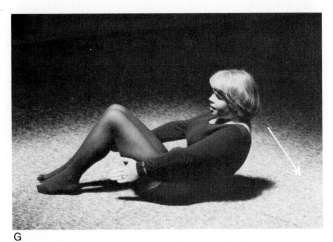

G

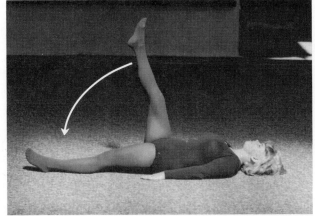

H

*position and roll to opposite side. (F) Buttocks lift. Lying supine, arms at sides, knees bent, feet flat, slowly raise the buttocks and arch the back. Return slowly to starting position. On sixth day add: (G) Abdominal tighteners. Lying supine, knees bent, feet flat, slowly raise head toward knees. Arms should extend along either side of legs. Return slowly to original position. (H) Knee to abdomen. Lying supine, arms at sides, bend one knee and thigh until foot touches buttocks. Straighten leg and lower it slowly.*

*Repeat with other leg. After two to three weeks, more strenuous exercises such as sit-ups and side leg raises may be added as tolerated. Kegel exercises, begun antepartally, should be done many times daily during postpartum to restore vaginal and perineal tone.*

also provides an opportunity for the children to become familiar with the new baby. For the mother the pangs of separation are lessened as she interacts with her children and introduces them to the newest family member.

Although the parents have prepared their children for the presence of a new brother or sister, the actual arrival of the infant in the home necessitates some adjustments. If small children are waiting at home, it is helpful if the father carries the baby inside. This practice keeps the mother's arms free to hug and touch her older children. Many mothers bring a doll home with them for an older child. The child cares for the doll alongside his or her mother or father, thereby identifying with the parent. This identification helps decrease anger and the need to regress for attention.

Parents may also provide supervised times when older children can hold the new baby and perhaps even help with a bottle-feeding. The older children feel a sense of accomplishment and learn tenderness and caring—qualities appropriate for both males and females. The nurse can help the parents come up with ways to show the other children that they, too, are valued and have their own places in the family.

## RESUMPTION OF SEXUAL RELATIONS

Previously couples were discouraged from engaging in sexual intercourse until six weeks postpartum. Currently the couple is advised to abstain from intercourse until the episiotomy is healed and the lochial flow has stopped (usually by the end of the third week). Because the vaginal vault is "dry" (hormone poor), some form of lubrication such as K-Y jelly may be necessary during intercourse. The female-superior or sidelying coital positions may be preferable because they allow the woman to control the depth of penile penetration.

Breast-feeding couples should be forewarned that during orgasm milk may spurt from the nipples due to the release of oxytocin. Some couples find this pleasurable, others choose to have the woman wear a bra during sex. Nursing the baby prior to lovemaking may reduce the chance of milk release.

Other factors may serve as deterrents to fully satisfactory sexual experience: the baby's crying may "spoil the mood"; the woman's changed body may be repulsive to her or her partner; maternal sleep deprivation may interfere with a mutually satisfying experience; and the woman's physiologic response to sexual stimulation may be changed due to hormonal changes (this lasts about three months). With anticipatory guidance during the prenatal and postpartal periods, the couple can be forewarned of potential temporary problems. Anticipatory guidance is enhanced if the couple can discuss their feelings and reactions as they are experienced. See Teaching Guide—What to Tell New Parents About Resumption of Sexual Activity.

## • Promotion of Parent-Infant Attachment

Nursing interventions to enhance the quality of parent-infant attachment should be designed to promote feelings of well-being, comfort, and satisfaction. Following are some suggestions for ways of achieving this:

1. Determine the childbearing and childrearing goals of the infant's mother and father and adapt them wherever possible in planning nursing care for the family. This includes giving the parents choices about their labor and birth experience and their initial time with their new infant.

2. Postpone eye prophylaxis to facilitate eye contact between parents and their newborn.

3. Provide time in the first hour after birth for the new family to become acquainted, with as much privacy as possible.

4. Arrange the health care setting so that the individual nurse-client relationship can be developed and maintained. A primary nurse can develop rapport and assess the mother's strengths and needs.

5. Encourage the parents to involve the siblings in integrating the infant into the family by bringing them to the hospital for sibling visits.

6. Use anticipatory guidance from conception through the postpartal period to prepare the parents for expected problems of adjustment.

7. Include parents in any nursing intervention, planning, and evaluation. Give choices whenever possible.

8. Initiate and support measures to alleviate fatigue in the parents.

9. Help parents to identify, understand, and accept both positive and negative feelings related to the overall parenting experience.

10. Support and assist parents in determining the personality and unique needs of their infant. Whenever possible, rooming-in should be available. This practice gives the mother a chance to learn her infant's normal patterns and develop confidence in caring for him or her. It also allows the father more uninterrupted time with his infant in the first days of life. If mother and baby are doing well and if help is available for the mother at home, early discharge permits the family to begin establishing their life together.

# Teaching Guide
## What to Tell New Parents About Resumption of Sexual Activity

**Assessment**  The nurse assesses the readiness of the couple to discuss the resumption of their personal and sexual life together.

**Nursing Diagnosis**  The essential nursing diagnosis will probably be: Knowledge deficit related to resumption of sexual activity.

**Nursing Plan and Implementation**  The teaching plan will consist of establishing rapport with the couple in order to promote an environment that is conducive for teaching and discussion. It is helpful to provide privacy during the teaching session so that the couple feels free to ask questions and discuss freely without interruption.

**Client Goals**  At the completion of the teaching the couple will be able to:

1. Discuss the changes in the woman's body that affect sexual activity
2. Discuss the length of time that is advised before resumption of sexual activity
3. Discuss information needed to make contraceptive choices

## Teaching Plan

### Content

Present information regarding the changes that may affect sexual activity:

    Tenderness of vagina and perineum
    Dryness of vagina
    Presence of lochia
    Healing process
    Breast engorgement and tenderness
    Escape of milk during sexual activity

Discuss the length of time lochia will persist and time needed for healing process. Provide opportunity for couple to ask questions about contraceptives. Provide information about available choices and benefits and disadvantages of each method. Refer to physician/nurse-midwife for additional information if needed.

### Teaching Method

*Discussion*

*Discussion*
    *Have samples of different types of contraceptives to examine.*
    *Provide pamphlets on particular contraceptive methods.*

**Evaluation**  The nurse may evaluate the learning by providing time for discussion and for questions. If the couple has indicated they will use a particular type of contraceptive, the nurse may ask them about aspects of that method to ascertain they have correct complete information.

## One Family's Story

*Elena Rodriquez was an 18-year-old, Spanish-speaking only, primapara who had recently moved to the United States from Mexico with her husband, Raoul, age 20. Raoul spoke English fairly well and acted as interpreter for Elena. Elena's sister, Theresa, and her husband, Joseph Gallegos, a native of Arizona, were sponsors for the couple. Joseph had a small but successful construction company, and Raoul worked there as a carpenter. Theresa and Raoul attended the birth of Ramon Joseph Rodriguez and both provided great support for Elena.*

*County Hospital, where Elena gave birth, was a large urban teaching hospital. The city had a sizable Spanish-speaking population, and many of the staff spoke the language.*

*Alice Warren, a nursing student who spoke Spanish fluently, was assigned to care for Elena on the morning following the birth. Alice soon noted that, although Elena was polite and answered Alice's questions, she seemed upset and distracted. Finally Elena blurted out that the preceding evening she had been examined by several male doctors on rounds. When Elena had walked in the halls earlier she noticed that many doctors were on the floor. Elena had been extremely embarrassed to be examined by so many men and was afraid that it would happen again. Alice realized that Elena was modest and had indeed been very embarrassed. She quickly discussed the situation with her instructor and team leader. The three decided that Alice should discuss the situation with the chief resident, Tim Erikson. Tim was sensitive to Elena's need and agreed with Alice's suggestion that one physician, preferably a woman, be assigned to Elena. Tim had second-year resident Sandy Ryan take the case and skipped Elena on rounds.*

*Elena was quite relieved, and, as she relaxed, became very responsive to teaching. Alice helped her with breast-feeding and showed her how to diaper Ramon.*

*When Theresa arrived she sought out Alice's instructor and told the instructor how much she appreciated all Alice had done to provide good care for Elena. She told the instructor that Elena and her family would be living with the Gallegos family until they were able to afford a place of their own. Theresa had arranged to take a few days off from work to be home with Elena, so things were well-organized at home.*

*The following morning Alice reviewed the items on the postpartum teaching list a final time and also gave Elena some postpartum literature printed in Spanish. She then had Elena do a return demonstration of basic aspects of infant care such as bathing. Alice and Elena spent time discussing potential problems such as fatigue. Alice also tactfully included information about sexual issues.*

*When Raoul arrived to get Elena, he told Alice that Elena had been very afraid of having her baby in a "foreign" hospital. However, the experience had been wonderful, and she felt confident of her ability to care for her son.*

## ● NURSING PLAN AND IMPLEMENTATION FOR CESAREAN BIRTH

After a cesarean birth the new mother has postpartal needs similar to those of her counterparts who delivered vaginally. Because she has undergone major abdominal surgery, the woman's nursing care needs are also similar to those of other surgical clients.

The chances of pulmonary infection are increased due to immobility after the use of narcotics and sedatives, and because of the altered immune response in postoperative patients. For this reason, the woman is encouraged to cough and deep breathe every two to four hours while awake for the first few days following cesarean delivery.

Leg exercises are also encouraged every two hours until the woman is ambulating. They increase circulation and help prevent thrombophlebitis and also aid intestinal mobility by tightening abdominal muscles.

Monitoring and management of the woman's pain experience is carried out during the postpartum period. Sources of pain include incisional pain, gas pain, referred shoulder pain, periodic uterine contractions (afterbirth pains), and pain from voiding, defecation, or constipation.

Nursing interventions are oriented toward preventing or alleviating pain or helping the woman cope with pain. The nurse should undertake the following measures:

● Administer analgesics as needed, especially during the first 24–72 hours. Their use will relieve the woman's pain and enable her to be more mobile and active.

● Offer comfort through proper positioning, backrubs, oral care, and the reduction of noxious stimuli such as noise and unpleasant odors.

● Encourage the presence of significant others, including the newborn. This practice provides distraction from the painful sensations and helps reduce the woman's fear and anxiety.

● Encourage the use of breathing, relaxation, and distraction (for example, stimulation of cutaneous tissue) techniques taught in childbirth preparation class.

Abdominal distention may produce marked discomfort for the woman during the first postpartal days. Measures to prevent or minimize gas pains include leg exercises, abdominal tightening, ambulation, avoiding carbonated or very hot or cold beverages, avoiding the use of straws, and providing a high-protein, liquid diet for the first 24–48 hours. Medical intervention for gas pain includes the use of suppositories and enemas and encouraging the woman to lie on her left side. Lying on the left side allows the gas to rise from the descending colon to the sigmoid colon so that it can be expelled more readily.

The nurse can minimize discomfort and promote satisfaction as the mother assumes the activities of her new role. Instruction and assistance in assuming comfortable positions when holding and/or breast-feeding the infant will do much to increase her sense of competence and comfort.

Signs of depression, anger, or withdrawal may indicate a grief response to the loss of the fantasized birth experience. Fathers as well as mothers may experience feelings of "missing out," guilt, or even jealousy toward another couple who had a vaginal birth. The cesarean birth couple needs the opportunity to tell their story repeatedly to work through these feelings. The nurse can provide factual information about their situation and support the couple's effective coping behaviors.

By the second or third day the cesarean birth mother moves into the taking-hold phase and is usually receptive to learning how to care for herself and her infant. Special emphasis should be given to home management. She should be encouraged to let others assume responsibility for housekeeping and cooking. Fatigue not only prolongs recovery but interferes with breast-feeding and mother-infant interaction.

The cesarean birth mother usually does extremely well postoperatively. Most women are ambulating by the day after the surgery. Usually by the third postpartal day the incision can be covered with plastic wrap so the woman can shower, which seems to provide a mental as well as physical lift. Most women are discharged by the fifth or sixth postoperative day, although some go home as early as the fourth day after birth.

## ● *Promotion of Parent-Infant Interaction After Cesarean Birth*

Many factors associated with cesarean birth may hinder successful and frequent maternal-infant interaction. These include the physical condition of the mother and newborn and maternal reactions to stress, anesthesia, and medications. The mother and her infant may be separated after birth because of hospital routines, prematurity, or neonatal complications. A healthy infant born by uncomplicated cesarean delivery is no more fragile than a vaginally delivered newborn. However, some agencies automatically place cesarean-birth infants in the high-risk nursery for a time, thereby causing anxiety for the parents and interfering with parent-infant interaction.

The presence of the father or significant other during the birth process positively influences the woman's perception of the birth event (Marut and Mercer 1979). Not only does his or her presence reduce the woman's fears, but it enhances her sense of control. It also enables the couple to share feelings and respond to one another with touch and eye contact. Later, they have the opportunity to relive the experience and fill in any gaps or missing pieces. This is especially valuable if the mother has had general anesthesia. The father or significant other can take pictures, hold the infant, and foster the discovery process by directing the mother's attention to the details of the infant.

The perception of and reactions to a cesarean birth experience depend on how the woman defines that experience. Her reality is what she perceives it to be. If the woman's attitude is more positive than negative, successful resolution of subsequent stressful events is more likely. Because the definition of events is transitory in nature, the possibility of change and growth is present. Often the mothering role is perceived as an extension of the childbearing role. Inability to fulfill expected childbearing behavior (vaginal birth) may lead to parental feelings of role failure and frustration. The nurse can help families alter their negative definitions of cesarean birth, and bolster and encourage positive perceptions.

## ● *NURSING PLAN AND IMPLEMENTATION FOR THE POSTPARTAL ADOLESCENT*

The adolescent mother has special postpartal needs, depending on her level of maturity, support systems, and cultural background. The nurse needs to assess maternal-infant interaction, roles of support people, plans for discharge, knowledge of childrearing, and plans for follow-up care. It is imperative to have a community health service be in touch with the woman shortly after discharge.

Contraception counseling is an important part of teaching. The incidence of repeat pregnancies during adolescence is high. The younger the adolescent, the more likely she is to become pregnant again.

The nurse has many opportunities for teaching the adolescent about her newborn in the postpartal unit. Because the nurse is a role model, the manner in which she handles the newborn greatly influences the young mother. The father should be included in as much of the teaching as possible.

A newborn examination done at the bedside gives the adolescent information about her baby's health and shows her proper methods of handling an infant. Because adolescent mothers tend to focus their interaction in the physical domain, they need to learn the importance of verbal, visual, and auditory stimulation as well. The nurse can also use this time to give information about infant behavior. Parents who have some idea of what to expect from their infant will be less frustrated with the newborn's behavior.

The adolescent mother appreciates positive feedback about her fine newborn and her developing maternal responses. This praise and encouragement will increase her confidence and self-esteem.

Group classes for adolescent mothers should include infant care skills, information about growth and development, infant feeding, well-baby care, and danger signals in the ill newborn.

Ideally, teenage mothers should visit adolescent clinics

## Essential Facts to Remember

### Signs of Postpartal Complications

After discharge, a woman should contact her physician/nurse-midwife if any of the following develop:

- Sudden persistent or spiking fever
- Change in the character of the lochia—foul smell, return to bright red bleeding, excessive amount
- Evidence of mastitis, such as breast tenderness, reddened areas, malaise
- Evidence of thrombophlebitis, such as calf pain, tenderness, redness
- Evidence of urinary tract infection, such as urgency, frequency, burning on urination
- Continued severe or incapacitating postpartal depression

where mother and newborn are assessed for several years after birth. In this way, the woman's enrollment in classes on parenting, need for vocational guidance, and school attendance can be followed closely. School systems offering classes for young mothers are an excellent way of helping adolescents finish school and learn how to parent at the same time.

## ● NURSING PLAN AND IMPLEMENTATION REGARDING DISCHARGE INFORMATION

Ideally, preparation for discharge begins from the moment a woman enters the hospital to give birth. Nursing efforts should be directed toward assessing the couple's knowledge, expectations, and beliefs and then providing anticipatory guidance and teaching accordingly. Since teaching is one of the primary responsibilities of the postpartum nurse, many agencies have elaborate teaching programs and classes. Before the actual discharge, however, the nurse should spend time with the couple to determine if they have any last-minute questions. In general, discharge teaching should include at least the following information:

1. The woman should contact her care giver if she develops any of the signs of possible complications. (See Essential Facts to Remember—Signs of Postpartal Complications.)
2. The woman should review the literature she has received that explains recommended postpartum

exercises, the need for adequate rest, the need to avoid overexertion initially, and the recommendation to abstain from sexual intercourse until lochia has ceased. The woman may take either a tub bath or shower and may continue sitz baths at home if she desires.

3. The woman should be given the phone number of the postpartum unit and should be encouraged to call if she has any questions, no matter how simple.
4. The woman should receive information on local agencies and/or support groups, such as La Leche League and Mothers of Twins, that might be of particular assistance to her.
5. Both breast-feeding and bottle-feeding mothers should receive information geared to their specific nutritional needs. They should also be told to continue their vitamin and iron supplements until their postpartal examination.
6. The woman should have a scheduled appointment for her postpartal examination and for her infant's first well-baby examination before they are discharged.
7. The mother should clearly understand the correct procedure for obtaining copies of her infant's birth certificate.
8. The new parents should be able to provide basic care for their infants and should know when to anticipate that the cord will fall off; when the infant can have a tub bath; when the infant will need his or her first immunizations; and so on. They should also be comfortable feeding and handling the baby, and should be aware of basic safety considerations, including the need for using a car seat whenever the infant is in a car.
9. The parents should also be aware of signs and symptoms in the infant that indicate possible problems and who they should contact about them.

The nurse can also use this final period to reassure the couple of their ability to be successful parents. She can stress the infant's need to feel loved and secure. She can also urge parents to talk to each other and work together to solve any problems that may arise.

Follow-up visits are mentioned when appropriate. If not already discussed, teaching about family planning is appropriate at this time, and information regarding birth control methods is provided.

In ideal situations a family approach involving the father, infant, and possibly other siblings would permit a total evaluation and provide an opportunity for all family members to ask questions and express concerns. In addition, disturbed family patterns might be more readily diagnosed and therapy instituted to prevent future problems of neglect or abuse.

## EVALUATION

As a result of comprehensive nursing care the post-partal family will achieve the following outcomes:

- The mother will have increased comfort and learn pain relief measures.
- The mother will be rested and will understand how to add more activity over the next few days and weeks.
- The mother's physiologic and psychologic well-being have been supported.
- The mother understands self-care measures.
- The new parents understand how to care for their baby.
- The new parents have had opportunities to form attachment with their baby.
- The cesarean mother has been supported and received safe care.

## ESSENTIAL CONCEPTS

- Nursing diagnoses can be used effectively in caring for women postpartally.
- Postpartum discomfort may be due to a variety of factors, including engorged breasts, an edematous perineum, an episiotomy or extension, engorged hemorrhoids, or hematoma formation.
- Various self-care approaches are helpful in promoting comfort.
- Lactation suppression may be accomplished by mechanical techniques or by administering the medication bromocriptine. Because of the increased risk of thrombus formation, estrogen-based medications are rarely used.
- The new mother requires opportunities to discuss her childbirth experience with an empathetic listener.
- The first day or two following birth are marked by maternal behaviors that are more dependent and comfort oriented. Then the woman becomes more independent and ready to assume responsibility.
- Rooming-in provides the childbearing family with opportunities to interact with their new member during the first hours and days of life. This enables the family to develop some confidence and skill in a "safe" environment.

- Sexual intercourse may resume once the episiotomy has healed and lochia has stopped. Couples should be forewarned of possible changes; for example, the vagina may be "dry," the level of desire may be influenced by fatigue, or the woman's breasts may leak milk during orgasm.
- Following cesarean birth a woman has the nursing care needs of a surgical client in addition to her needs as a postpartum client. She may also require assistance in working through her feelings if the cesarean delivery was unexpected.
- Postpartally the nurse evaluates the adolescent mother in terms of her level of maturity, available support systems, cultural background, and existing knowledge and then plans care accordingly.
- Prior to discharge the couple should be given any information necessary for the woman to provide appropriate self-care. They should have a beginning skill in caring for their newborn and should be familiar with warning signs of possible complications for mother or baby. Printed information is valuable in helping couples deal with questions that may arise at home.
- Because of the trend toward early discharge, follow-up care is more important than ever. Many approaches are used, especially home visits and telephone follow-up.

### References

Foster S. Bromocriptine: Suppressing lactation. *MCN* March/April 1982; 7:99.

Karch A, Boyd E: *Handbook of Drugs*. Philadelphia: Lippincott, 1989.

Marut J, Mercer R: Comparison of primiparas' perceptions of vaginal and cesarean births. *Nurs Res* May 1979; 28:260.

Peters F et al: Inhibition of lactation by a long-acting bromocriptine. *Obstet Gynecol* 1986; 67:82.

Stolte K: Nursing diagnosis and the childbearing woman. *Am J Mat Child Nurs* 1986; 13:13.

Varney H: *Nurse Midwifery*, 2nd ed. Boston: Blackwell Scientific, 1987.

Wong S, Stepp-Gilbert E: Lactation suppression: Nonpharmaceutical versus pharmaceutical method. *J Obstet Gynecol Neonatal Nurs* July/August 1985; 14:302.

### Additional Readings

Alexander GR, Cornely DA: Prenatal care utilization: Its measurement and relationship to pregnancy outcomes. *Am J Prev Med* 1987; 3(5):243.

Cartwright A: Unintended pregnancies that lead to babies. *Soc Sci Med* 1988; 27(3):249.

Chalmers B: The Pedi woman's experiences of childbirth and early parenthood: A summary of major findings. *Curationis* 1988; 11(1):12.

Fawcett J, Tulman L, Myers ST: Development of the inventory of functional status after childbirth. *J Nurse-Midwifery* November/December 1988; 33 (6):252.

Flagler S: Maternal role competence. *West J Nurs Res* 1988; 10(3):274.

Gerlach C, Schmid M: Second skill educational development of personnel for a single-room maternity care system. *JOGNN* 1988; 17:388.

Mercer RT et al: Effect of stress on family functioning during pregnancy. *Nurs Res* 1988; 37(5):268.

Olds DL et al: Improving the life-course development of socially disadvantaged mothers: A randomized trial of nurse home visitation. *Am J Pub Health* November 1988; 78(11):1436.

Poma PA: Pregnancy in Hispanic women. *J Nat Med Assoc* 1987; 79:929.

Weller RH, Eberstein IW, Bailey M: Pregnancy wantedness and maternal behavior during pregnancy. *Demography* 1987; 24(3):407.

# 27

# The Postpartal Family at Risk

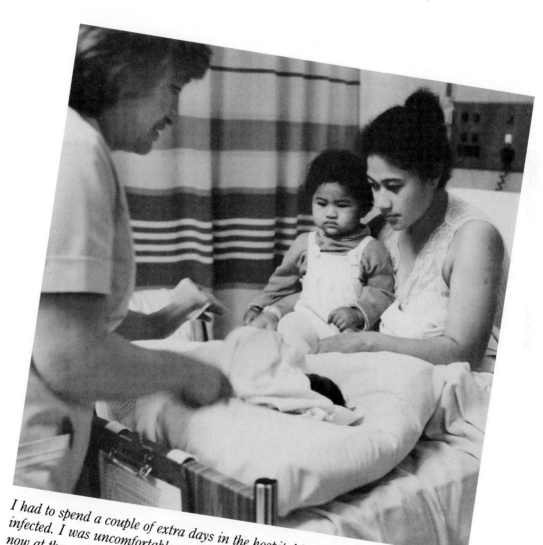

*I had to spend a couple of extra days in the hospital because my stitches got infected. I was uncomfortable and frustrated that something would go wrong now at the end after such a smooth pregnancy. But my son came to visit and friends called, and I survived. I am amazed, though, at how much that unexpected setback bothered me.*

## Objectives

● Summarize the causes of and appropriate nursing interventions for hemorrhage during the postpartal period.

● Compare the causative factors, pathophysiology, and nursing interventions of different puerperal infections.

● Discuss causative factors, pathophysiology, and nursing interventions for thromboembolic disease of the puerperium.

● Contrast puerperal cystitis and pyelonephritis and their implications for maternal nursing care.

● Differentiate disorders of the breast and complications of lactation.

● Identify the possible precipitating factors associated with puerperal psychiatric disorders.

## Key Terms

early postpartal hemorrhage
endometritis
late postpartal hemorrhage
mastitis
oophoritis
pelvic cellulitis (parametritis)
peritonitis
puerperal morbidity
pulmonary embolism
salpingitis
subinvolution
thrombophlebitis
uterine atony

The puerperium is often thought of as a smooth, uneventful transition time—and usually it is. However, the nurse must be aware of problems that may develop postpartally and their implications for the childbearing family.

This chapter deals with the broad area of maternal complications during the puerperium. It emphasizes application of the nursing process to meet the needs of the woman experiencing such complications.

## ● USING THE NURSING PROCESS WITH WOMEN AT RISK DURING THE POSTPARTAL PERIOD

When providing care to the childbearing woman during the postpartal period, the nurse uses the nursing process to make ongoing assessments and detect, as early as possible, the development of any complications. When a potential problem is noted, the nurse analyzes the data; formulates appropriate nursing diagnoses; and develops, implements, and evaluates a plan of care. Often the care will be provided in a collaborative way as the nurse works with other members of the health care team.

## ● Nursing Assessment

Because complications can develop in the postpartal period, the postpartal nurse should make ongoing assessment a major priority. Such assessment is especially important because the nurse is often the first person to detect a developing complication. If a complication does develop, assessment remains important to determine the effectiveness of therapy and to detect any signs that the problem is worsening.

## ● Nursing Diagnosis

The nurse analyzes the information gained from assessment, formulates appropriate nursing diagnoses, and develops appropriate client goals. If, for example, the nurse is caring for a woman who complains of dysuria, the nurse first reviews the woman's history. The nurse learns that the woman was catheterized twice during labor for bladder distention and was also catheterized during the third hour after childbirth. The woman reports that she does not feel that she is fully emptying her bladder. The nurse cannot palpate the bladder suprapubically. The woman has no costovertebral angle (CVA) tenderness but her temperature is 100.8°F. She is unable to produce another urine specimen so the nurse offers her additional fluids. The nurse then formulates the nursing diagnosis, "altered patterns of urinary elimination related to dysuria secondary to possible bladder infection."

## Nursing Plan and Implementation

Once the data have been analyzed and the diagnosis established, the nurse develops and implements a care plan. In the case of the woman with dysuria, the nurse notifies the physician that the woman may be developing cystitis and obtains an order for a clean-catch urine for culture. The nurse explains what is occurring to the woman and may administer a mild analgesic, or obtain an order for an antispasmodic if he or she believes the woman is also experiencing bladder spasms.

## Evaluation

The nurse evaluates the effectiveness of the plan of care. For example, in the preceding situation the woman was relieved to learn that the nurse took her problem seriously. After receiving the antispasmodic, the woman was able to provide a clean-catch urine specimen, which revealed that the woman did have cystitis. Antibiotic therapy was begun. The nurse concluded that the plan had been effective thus far, but discussions with the woman revealed that a new nursing diagnosis was necessary; knowledge deficit related to a lack of understanding of self-care measures to help prevent urinary tract infection (UTI). The nurse then began planning an approach to meet this identified need.

Thus the process is cyclic, building on assessment, logical analysis, and well-planned and implemented intervention, followed by evaluation and modification as necessary.

# CARE OF THE WOMAN WITH POSTPARTAL HEMORRHAGE

Puerperal hemorrhage has been divided into early and late postpartal hemorrhage. **Early postpartal hemorrhage** (or immediate postpartal hemorrhage) occurs when blood loss is greater than 500 mL in the first 24 hours after delivery. **Late postpartal hemorrhage** (delayed postpartal hemorrhage) occurs after the first 24 hours.

## Early Postpartal Hemorrhage

The main causes of early postpartal hemorrhage are uterine atony, lacerations of the genital tract, and retained placenta or placental fragments. Certain factors predispose to hemorrhage: (a) overdistention of the uterus due to hydramnios, a large infant, or multiple gestation; (b) grand multiparity; (c) use of anesthetic agents (especially halothane) to relax the uterus; (d) trauma due to obstetric procedures such as midforceps delivery, intrauterine manipulation, or forceps rotation; (e) a prolonged labor or a very rapid labor; (f) use of oxytocin to induce or to augment labor; (g) uterine infection; and (h) maternal malnutrition, anemia, pregnancy-induced hypertension (PIH), or history of hemorrhage.

In most cases the clinician can predict when a woman is at risk for hemorrhage. The key to successful management is prevention. Prevention begins with adequate nutrition, good prenatal care, and early diagnosis and management of any complications that may arise. Traumatic procedures should be avoided, and delivery should take place in a facility that has blood immediately available. Any woman at risk should be typed and cross-matched for blood and have intravenous lines in place. Excellent labor management and delivery technique is imperative.

Uterine atony and retained placenta are discussed in this section. Lacerations are considered in Chapter 18.

### UTERINE ATONY

**Uterine atony,** the relaxation of the uterus (or insufficient contractions) following birth, can frequently be anticipated in the presence of (a) overdistention of the uterus that occurs with multiple fetuses, macrosomic fetus, or hydramnios; (b) dysfunctional labor that has already indicated the uterus is contracting in an abnormal pattern; (c) oxytocin stimulation or augmentation during labor; and (d) the use of anesthesia that produces uterine relaxation. Hemorrhage from uterine atony may be slow and steady rather than sudden and massive. The blood may escape the vagina or collect in the uterus. Because of the increased blood volume associated with pregnancy, changes in maternal blood pressure and pulse may not occur until blood loss has been significant.

After delivery of the placenta, the fundus should be palpated to assure that it is firm and well contracted. If it is not firm, vigorous massage should be instituted until the uterus contracts. Oxytocics (Pitocin or Methergine) may be given. If the bleeding persists, the physician undertakes bimanual uterine compression, which consists of using one gloved hand to massage the uterine fundus externally while the other gloved hand is inserted into the vagina and the closed fist is pressed against the uterus (Figure 27.1,*A*). With this procedure the uterus is compressed and massaged and hemorrhage can usually be controlled. Oxygen is administered by mask. Blood transfusion may be ordered. If these $F_2$ measures are not successful, 15-methylprostaglandin $F_2$ (Prostin 15M) may be administered intramuscularly to stimulate powerful, sustained contractions. The dose may be repeated within 90 minutes, and again as necessary. The side effects, such as

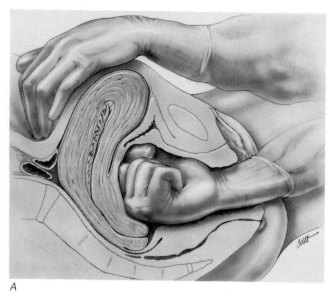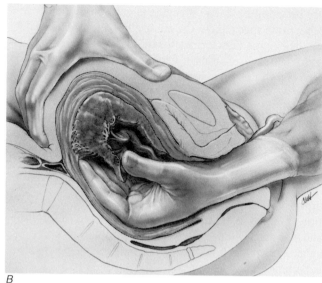

A

B

*Figure 27.1 (**A**) Manual compression of the uterus and massage with the abdominal hand usually will effectively control hemorrhage from uterine atony. (**B**) Manual removal of the placenta: The fingers are alternately abducted, adducted, and advanced until the placenta is completely detached. (Adapted from Pritchard JA, MacDonald PC, Gant NF:* Williams' Obstetrics, *17th ed. New York: Appleton-Century-Crofts, 1985.)*

nausea, vomiting, and diarrhea, are unpleasant and are often treated with medication. Other side effects include fever, flushing, and elevated diastolic blood pressure. If, despite these measures, bleeding persists, other causes such as placenta accreta or cervical laceration should be considered (Few 1987).

### RETAINED PLACENTA

Hemorrhage may occur after the birth of the newborn but before delivery of the placenta. In this instance, the physician observes the firmness of the fundus and administers fundal massage if needed. When the placenta is ready to separate, delivery of the placenta is enhanced by massaging the fundus. If signs of placental separation have not occurred, the physician manually removes the placenta by inserting a gloved hand into the uterus and placing the fingers at the placental margin. Then the placenta is gently separated from the uterine wall. During this procedure, the other hand remains on the uterine fundus, externally (Figure 27.1, **B**). After delivery of the placenta, the consistency of the fundus is assessed. If it is boggy and bleeding continues, the interventions for uterine atony are performed.

### • Late Postpartal Hemorrhage

Late postpartal hemorrhage is most frequently caused by retained placental fragments. Hemorrhage from this cause may occur in the hours following the fourth stage of

labor or may not develop for a day or two. Placental fragments are occasionally retained for a week or longer.

### • Medical Therapy

To prevent late postpartum hemorrhage from retained placental fragments, the placenta should be inspected after delivery for evidence of missing pieces or cotyledons. The uterine cavity may also be checked for retained placental fragments or membranes.

Often a boggy uterus postpartally is the first indication of late postpartum hemorrhage. Usually therapy consists of a continuous intravenous infusion of fluids and oxytocin. If the woman's blood pressure is normal, methylergonovine or ergonovine may be used. If this treatment is not effective or if a placental fragment is retained for several days, curettage is indicated, together with the administration of antibiotics to prevent infection.

### • Nursing Assessment

Careful evaluation of the woman's prenatal history and ongoing assessment during labor and birth will help identify factors that put the woman at risk for postpartal hemorrhage. Periodic assessment for evidence of vaginal bleeding is a major nursing responsibility during the postpartal period. This is done by visual assessment, by pad counts, or by weighing of the perineal pad. A boggy uterus that does not stay contracted without constant massage is atonic, whereas a uterus that does not *involute* (return to normal size) appropriately should be investigated for possible retained placental tissue and infection.

### NURSING DIAGNOSIS

Examples of nursing diagnoses that may apply when a woman experiences postpartal hemorrhage are included in Essential Nursing Diagnoses to Consider—Postpartal Hemorrhage.

### NURSING PLAN AND IMPLEMENTATION

Regular assessment of fundal height and firmness will alert the nurse to the possible development or recurrence of hemorrhage. The nurse massages a boggy uterus until firm and, if it appears larger than anticipated, attempts to express clots. If the woman seems to have a slow, steady, free flow of blood the nurse begins to weigh the perineal pads and monitors the woman's vital signs closely to detect the development of hypovolemic shock.

If the woman is bleeding more profusely the nurse administers oxygen by face mask. The nurse also administers medications as ordered and assesses their effectiveness. Intravenous oxytocin will probably be continued for several hours if bleeding is severe. Urinary output is measured to determine the adequacy of fluid replacement.

Because blood loss may cause anemia, the nurse assesses for evidence of pallor or fatigue, and reviews the results of the hematocrit determination. The nurse also encourages the woman to obtain adequate rest and helps

## Essential Facts to Remember

### Signs of Postpartal Hemorrhage

The nurse must suspect postpartal hemorrhage or hematoma formation if a woman complains of any of the following:

- Excessive or bright red bleeding
- A boggy fundus that does not respond to massage
- Abnormal clots
- Any unusual pelvic discomfort or backache
- High temperature

her plan activities so that rest is possible. With this in mind the nurse should find ways to promote maternal-infant attachment while being cognizant of the health needs of the mother. In addition to helping the mother as needed in caring for the newborn, the nurse can work with the woman's partner and family to find ways to help the mother cope.

### Education for Self-Care

Due to current trends, the mother may be discharged  any time after four hours postbirth. Because hemorrhage may develop after discharge, she and her support persons should receive clear, preferably written, explanations of the normal postpartum course and signs of complications. Instructions for assessing fundal height and consistency and for massaging the fundus should be included. The woman and her family are advised to contact her care giver if any of the signs of postpartal hemorrhage occur (see Essential Facts to Remember—Signs of Postpartal Hemorrhage).

### EVALUATION

Anticipated outcomes of nursing care include the following:

- Signs of postpartal hemorrhage are detected quickly and managed effectively.
- Maternal-infant attachment is maintained successfully.
- The woman is able to identify abnormal changes that might occur following discharge and understands the importance of notifying her care giver if they develop.

## ● Hematomas

Hematomas are usually the result of injury to a blood vessel without noticeable trauma to the superficial tissue. Hematomas occur following spontaneous as well as forceps deliveries. The most frequently observed hema-

## Essential Nursing Diagnoses to Consider

### Postpartal Hemorrhage

Altered tissue perfusion

Decreased cardiac output

Fatigue

Fear

Fluid volume deficit

Impaired gas exchange

Ineffective breast-feeding

Knowledge deficit

Potential activity intolerance

Potential fluid volume deficit

Potential for injury

tomas are of the vagina and vulva. The soft tissue in the area offers no resistance, and hematomas containing 250–500 mL of blood may develop rapidly. Within the vagina, the lateral wall, especially in the area of the ischial spines, is a common site of hematoma formation. Hematomas may also develop in the upper portion of the vagina or may occur upward into the broad ligament.

## MEDICAL THERAPY

Small vulvar hematomas may be treated with the application of ice packs and continued observation. Large hematomas generally require surgical intervention to evacuate the clot. General anesthesia is usually required, and if the hematoma is not accessible vaginally, a laparotomy must be performed. Antibiotics and transfusions may also be indicated.

## NURSING ASSESSMENT

Often, the woman complains of severe vulvar pain (pain that seems out of proportion or excessive), usually from her "stitches," or of severe rectal pressure. On examination, the large hematoma appears as a unilateral, tense, fluctuant bulging mass at the introitus or within the labia majora. With smaller hematomas the nurse may note unilateral bluish or reddish discoloration of the skin of the perineum. The area feels firm and is painful to the touch. The nurse should estimate the size of the hematoma so that increasing size will be quickly noted.

Hematomas can develop in the upper portion of the vagina. In this case, besides pain, the woman may have difficulty voiding because of pressure on the urethra or meatus. Diagnosis is confirmed through careful vaginal examination.

Hematomas that occur upward into the broad ligament may be more difficult to detect. The woman may complain of severe lateral uterine pain, flank pain, or abdominal distention. Occasionally the hematoma can be discovered with high rectal examination or with abdominal palpation although these procedures may be quite uncomfortable for the woman. If the bleeding continues, signs of anemia may be noted.

Signs and symptoms of shock in the presence of a well-contracted uterus and no visible vaginal blood loss may also alert the nurse to the possibility of a hematoma.

## NURSING DIAGNOSIS

Nursing diagnoses that may apply when a woman develops a hematoma postpartally include:

● Potential for injury related to tissue damage secondary to prolonged pressure from a large vaginal hematoma

● Pain related to tissue trauma secondary to hematoma formation

## NURSING PLAN AND IMPLEMENTATION

If birth was long or traumatic, the postpartal nurse can promote comfort and decrease the possibility of hematoma formation by applying an ice pack to the woman's perineum during the first hour after birth. In addition, if a hematoma develops, sitz baths will aid fluid absorption once the bleeding has been controlled and will promote comfort, as will the judicious use of analgesics.

## EVALUATION

Anticipated outcomes of nursing care include:

● Hematoma formation is avoided; if it does occur, it is detected quickly and managed successfully.

● The woman's discomfort is relieved effectively.

● Tissue damage is avoided or minimized.

## ● Subinvolution

**Subinvolution** of the uterus occurs when the uterus fails to follow the normal pattern of involution but instead remains enlarged. Retained placental fragments and infection are the most frequent causes. With subinvolution the fundus is higher in the abdomen than expected. In addition, lochia often fails to progress from rubra to serosa to alba. Lochia may remain rubra or return to rubra several days postpartum. Leukorrhea and backache may occur if infection is the cause. Subinvolution is most commonly diagnosed during the routine postpartal examination at four to six weeks. The woman may relate a history of irregular or excessive bleeding, or describe the symptoms listed previously. Diagnosis is made when an enlarged, softer-than-normal uterus is palpated with bimanual examination. Treatment involves oral administration of methylergonovine (Methergine) 0.2 mg every three to four hours for 24 to 48 hours. When metritis is present, antibiotics are also administered. If this treatment is not effective or if the cause is believed to be retained placental fragments, curettage is indicated (Pritchard et al 1985).

## ● CARE OF THE WOMAN WITH A POSTPARTAL REPRODUCTIVE TRACT INFECTION

Puerperal infection is an infection of the reproductive tract associated with childbirth. Because infection accounts for a large percentage of postpartal morbidity, it is useful to remember the definition of **puerperal morbidity** published by the Joint Committee on Maternal Welfare:

Temperature of 100.4°F (38.0°C) or higher, the temperature to occur on any two of the first ten postpartum days, exclusive of the first 24 hours, and to be taken by mouth by a standard technique at least four times a day.

However, recent findings indicate that the definition's exclusion of the first 24 hours may not be accurate (Easterling and Herbert 1986). Moreover, since many women are discharged within the first day after delivery, the definition is of limited value in many cases.

## ● Causative Factors

The vagina and cervix of pregnant women usually contain pathogenic bacteria sufficient to cause infection. Generally, other factors must be present, however, for infection to occur. Premature rupture of membranes (PROM) allows organisms to ascend into the uterus and is a major factor in the development of infection postpartally. In addition, the placental site, episiotomy, lacerations, abrasions, and any operative incisions are all potential portals for bacterial entrance and growth. Hematomas are easily infected and enhance the possibility of sepsis. Tissue that has been compromised through trauma is less able to marshal the necessary forces to combat infection. Other factors predisposing the woman to infection include frequent vaginal examinations, lapses in aseptic technique, anemia, intrauterine manipulation, hemorrhage, cesarean birth, retained placental fragments, and faulty perineal care.

Approximately 70% of puerperal infections are caused by anaerobic bacteria. The most common anaerobes involved include bacteriodes (all species), peptococcus, and *Clostridium perfringens.*

Aerobic bacteria, especially group A beta hemolytic streptococci and *Escherichia coli,* are also responsible for postpartal infection. *E coli* may be introduced as a result of contamination of the vulva or reproductive tract from feces during labor and delivery. Group A beta hemolytic streptococci may be transmitted from the skin or nasopharynx of the woman herself, or more probably from an external source such as personnel or equipment. Other aerobic bacteria implicated in puerperal infections include *Klebsiella, Proteus mirabilis, Pseudomonas, Staphylococcus aureus,* and *Neisseria gonorrhoeae* (Eschenbach and Wager 1980).

## ● Types of Infections
### LOCALIZED INFECTIONS

A less severe complication of the puerperium is the localized infection of the episiotomy or of lacerations to the perineum, vagina, or vulva. Wound infection of the abdominal incision site following cesarean birth is also possible. The skin edges become reddened, edematous, firm, and tender. The skin edges then separate, and purulent material, sometimes mixed with sanguineous liquid, drains from the wound. The woman may complain of localized pain and

dysuria and may have a low-grade fever (less than 101°F or 38.3°C). If the wound abscesses or is unable to drain, high temperature and chills may result.

## ENDOMETRITIS (METRITIS)

**Endometritis,** an inflammation of the endometrium, may occur postpartally. After delivery of the placenta, the placental site provides an excellent culture medium for bacterial growth. The remaining portion of the decidua is also susceptible to pathogenic bacteria because of its thinness (approximately 2 mm) and its hypervascularity. The cervix may also be a bacterial breeding ground because of the multiple small lacerations attending normal labor and birth.

In mild cases of endometritis the woman will generally have discharge that is scant (or profuse), bloody, and foul smelling. In more severe cases, the symptoms may include uterine tenderness and jagged, irregular temperature elevation, usually between 38.3°C (101°F) and 40°C (104°F). Tachycardia, chill, and evidence of subinvolution may be noted. Although foul-smelling lochia is cited as a classic sign of endometritis, with infection caused by beta hemolytic streptococcus the lochia may be scant and odorless (Pritchard et al 1985).

## SALPINGITIS AND OOPHORITIS

Occasionally, bacteria may spread into the lumen of the fallopian tubes, producing infection in the tubes (**salpingitis**) and ovaries (**oophoritis**). Most often caused by a gonorrheal infection, such infection generally becomes apparent between 9 and 15 days postpartally. Symptoms include bilateral (or unilateral) lower abdominal pain, high temperature, and tachycardia. If tubal closure results, sterility may ensue (Vorherr 1982).

## PELVIC CELLULITIS (PARAMETRITIS) AND PERITONITIS

**Pelvic cellulitis** (**parametritis**) refers to infection involving the connective tissue of the broad ligament and, in more severe forms, the connective tissue of all the pelvic structures. It is generally spread by way of the lymphatics in the uterine wall, but may also occur if pathogenic organisms invade a cervical laceration that extends upward into the connective tissue of the broad ligament. This laceration then serves as a direct pathway that allows the pathogens already in the cervix to spread into the pelvis. **Peritonitis** refers to infection involving the peritoneum.

A pelvic abscess may form in the case of puerperal peritonitis and most commonly is found in the uterine ligaments, cul-de-sac of Douglas, and the subdiaphragmatic space. Pelvic cellulitis may be a secondary result of pelvic vein thrombophlebitis. This condition occurs when the clot

| Table 27.1 | | REEDA Scale Used to Evaluate Healing | | | |
|---|---|---|---|---|---|
| **Points** | **Redness** | **Edema** | **Ecchymosis** | **Discharge** | **Approximation** |
| **0** | None | None | None | None | Closed |
| **1** | Within 0.25 cm of incision bilaterally | Perineal, less than 1 cm from incision | Within 0.25 cm bilaterally or 0.5 cm unilaterally | Serum | Skin separation 3 mm or less |
| **2** | Within 0.5 cm of incision bilaterally | Perineal and/or vulvar, between 1 to 2 cm from incision | Between 0.25 to 1 cm bilaterally or between 0.5 to 2 cm unilaterally | Serosanguineous | Skin and subcutaneous fat separation |
| **3** | Beyond 0.5 cm of incision bilaterally | Perineal and/or vulvar, greater than 2 cm from incision | Greater than 1 cm bilaterally or 2 cm unilaterally | Bloody, purulent | Skin, subcutaneous fat, and fascial layer separation |
| Score: _____ | | _____ | _____ | _____ | _____ <br> Total _____ |

Source: Davidson N: REEDA: Evaluating postpartum healing. *J Nurse Midwifery* 1974; 19:7.

becomes infected and the wall of the vein breaks down from necrosis, spilling the infection into the connective tissues of the pelvis.

A woman suffering from parametritis may demonstrate a variety of symptoms, including marked high temperature (102°F–104°F or 38.9°C–40°C), chills, malaise, lethargy, abdominal pain, subinvolution of the uterus, tachycardia, and local and referred rebound tenderness. If peritonitis develops, the woman will be acutely ill with severe pain, marked anxiety, high fever, rapid, shallow respirations, pronounced tachycardia, excessive thirst, abdominal distention, nausea, and vomiting.

## ● *Medical Therapy*

Diagnosis of the infection site and causative pathogen is accomplished by careful history and complete physical examination, blood work, cultures of the lochia (although this may be of limited value since multiple organisms are usually present), and urinalysis to rule out urinary tract infection. When a localized infection develops it is treated with antibiotic creams, sitz baths, and analgesics as necessary for pain relief. If an abscess has developed or a stitch site is infected, the suture is removed and the area is allowed to drain.

Metritis is treated by the administration of antibiotics. The route and dosage are determined by the severity of the infection. Severe infection warrants the administration of parenteral antibiotics. Careful monitoring is also necessary to prevent the development of a more serious infection.

Parametritis and peritonitis are treated with intravenous antibiotics. Broad spectrum antibiotics effective against the most commonly occurring causative organisms are chosen initially pending the results of culture and sensitivity reports. If multiple organisms are present, the approach to antibiotic therapy remains empirical. If no improvement is observed, the antibiotic is changed.

The development of an abscess is frequently heralded by the presence of a palpable mass and may be confirmed with ultrasound. An abscess usually requires incision and drainage to avoid rupture into the peritoneal cavity and the possible development of peritonitis. Following drainage of the abscess, the cavity may be packed with iodoform gauze to promote drainage and facilitate healing.

The woman with a severe systemic infection is acutely ill and may require care in an intensive care unit. Supportive therapy will include maintenance of adequate hydration with intravenous fluids, analgesics, ongoing assessment of the infection, and possibly continuous nasogastric suctioning if paralytic ileus develops.

## ● *Nursing Assessment*

The woman's perineum should be inspected at least twice daily for signs of early developing infection. The REEDA scale helps the nurse remember to consider redness, edema, ecchymosis, discharge, and approximation (see Table 27.1).

Fever, malaise, abdominal pain, foul-smelling lochia, tachycardia, and other signs of infection should be noted and reported immediately so that treatment can be instituted.

## ● *Nursing Diagnosis*

For nursing diagnoses that might apply, see the Nursing Care Plan—Puerperal Infection.

# Nursing Care Plan

## Puerperal Infection

### Client Assessment

#### Nursing History

1. Predisposing health factors include:
   a. Malnutrition
   b. Anemia
   c. Debilitated condition

2. Predisposing factors associated with labor and birth include:
   a. Prolonged labor
   b. Hemorrhage
   c. Premature and/or prolonged rupture of membranes
   d. Soft tissue trauma
   e. Invasive techniques (eg, internal monitoring, frequent vaginal exams)
   f. Operative procedures
   g. Maternal exhaustion

#### Physical Examination

1. Localized episiotomy infections may present with the following signs and symptoms:
   a. Complaints of unusual degree of discomfort, localized pain
   b. Reddened edematous lesion
   c. Purulent drainage, sanguineous drainage
   d. Failure of skin edges to approximate
   e. Fever (generally below 38.3°C or 101°F)
   f. Dysuria

2. Endometritis
   a. Mild case may be asymptomatic or characterized only by low-grade fever, anorexia, and malaise
   b. More severe cases may demonstrate:
      (1) Fever of 101–103°F+
      (2) Anorexia, extreme lethargy
      (3) Chills

   (4) Rapid pulse (tachycardia)
   (5) Lower abdominal pain or uterine tenderness
   (6) Lochia—appearance varies depending on causative organism: may appear normal, be profuse, bloody, and foul smelling, may be scant and serosanguineous to brownish and foul smelling
   (7) Severe afterpains
   (8) Vomiting, diarrhea
   (9) Uterine subinvolution

3. Pelvic cellulitis (parametritis)
   a. Signs and symptoms of severe infection (see previous discussion of endometritis)
   b. Severe abdominal pain, usually lateral to the uterus on one or both sides and apparent with both abdominal palpation and pelvic examination

4. Puerperal peritonitis
   a. Symptoms just described plus severe abdominal pain
   b. Abdominal rigidity, guarding, rebound tenderness
   c. Possible vomiting and diarrhea
   d. Tachycardia, shallow respirations, anxiety
   e. Marked bowel distention if paralytic ileus develops, absent bowel sounds

#### Diagnostic Studies

1. Elevated white blood count (WBC), although it may be within normal puerperal limits (5000–15,000/mm$^3$) initially
2. Culture of intrauterine material to reveal causative organism
3. Urine culture to rule out an asymptomatic urinary tract infection (should be normal)
4. Elevated sedimentation rate
5. Bimanual examination
6. Ultrasonography

| Nursing Diagnosis/Client Goals | Nursing Interventions | Rationale/Evaluation |
|---|---|---|

**Nursing Diagnosis:**

Pattern 1: Exchanging
Potential for injury related to the spread of infection

**Client Goal:**

Woman will not suffer injury from infection as evidenced by: return of temperature to normal range, WBC count in normal range for postpartum client. If localized infection—decreased redness, edema, ecchymosis, drainage; wound edges approximated. If systemic infection—absence of malaise, uterine tenderness, foul-smelling lochia, fever, elevated WBC, abdominal pain, chills, lethargy, tachycardia, abdominal rigidity.

Evaluate history for factors that would retard wound healing.

Employ principles of medical asepsis in hand washing, disposal of contaminated material, etc.
Promote normal wound healing by using:
1. Sitz baths two to four times daily for 10–15 min
2. Peri-light two to three times daily for 10–15 min
3. Peri-care following elimination
4. Frequent changing of peri-pads
5. Early ambulation
6. Diet high in protein and vitamin C
7. Fluid intake to 2000 mL/day

**Rationale:**

Careful evaluation of client history enables the nurse to identify those women who are at risk for infection and for delayed wound healing.

Infection may be spread through direct contact with bacteria on hands, contaminated material, etc.
Warm water is cleansing, promotes healing through increased vascular flow to affected area, and is soothing to woman. Peri-care promotes removal of urine and fecal contaminants from perineum. Changing pads frequently decreases the media for bacterial growth. Ambulation promotes drainage of lochia. These nutrients are essential for satisfactory wound healing.

*(continues)*

## Nursing Care Plan

### Puerperal Infection (*continued*)

| Nursing Diagnosis/Client Goals | Nursing Interventions | Rationale/Evaluation |
|---|---|---|
| | Evaluate degree of healing using the REEDA scale (Table 27.1). Report signs and symptoms of wound infection, including:<br>1. Redness<br>2. Edema<br>3. Excessive pain<br>4. Inadequate approximation of wound edges<br>5. Purulent drainage<br>6. Fever, anorexia, malaise<br>Obtain culture from wound site and administer antibiotics, per physician order. | REEDA scale provides consistent, objective tool for evaluation of wound healing. Wound infection produces characteristic signs and symptoms that reflect the body's response to the invading organism. |
| | Increase wound drainage by:<br>1. Assisting physician in opening wound for drainage, when indicated<br>2. Anticipating packing of a cavity greater than 2–3 cm with iodoform gauze | Antibiotic therapy based on knowledge of causative organism is treatment of choice for localized infection.<br>Abscesses may develop when infected material accumulates in closed body cavity.<br>Iodoform packing maintains patency of opening so drainage can continue. |
| | Report signs of progressive infection such as uterine subinvolution, foul-smelling lochia, uterine tenderness, severe lower abdominal pain, fever, elevated WBC, malaise, chills, lethargy, tachycardia, nausea and vomiting, abdominal rigidity. | More severe infections such as endometritis, pelvic cellulitis, or peritonitis can develop and produce characteristic signs as the body responds systemically to the invading pathogens. |
| | Administer IV fluids and antibiotics as ordered | IV fluids maintain adequate hydration; antibiotics are the treatment of choice to combat the infection. |
| | Maintain semi-Fowler's position. | Promotes comfort and helps prevent spread of infection. |
| | Monitor vital signs at least q 4 h and more frequently if they are significantly abnormal. | Tachycardia and fever occur because the body's metabolic rate increases in response to its efforts to combat infection. A profound systemic infection can produce septic shock with ↓ blood pressure (BP) and ↑ respirations. |
| | Monitor intake and output, urine specific gravity, and level of hydration as ordered. | Vigorous fluid and electrolyte therapy is necessary not only because of vomiting and diarrhea, but also because both fluid and electrolytes become sequestered in lumen and wall of bowel. |
| | Maintain continuous nasogastric suction per physician order. | Continuous nasogastric suction is used to decompress the bowel when paralytic ileus complicates the course and results in cessation of gastrointestinal (GI) motility. |
| | Transfer woman to intensive care if indicated by her condition. | Woman with peritonitis is in critical condition, and quality of nursing care this patient receives will weigh the balance between recovery and demise. |
| | | **Evaluation:**<br>Therapy and supportive measures are effective and woman does not suffer injury from infection. |

# Nursing Care Plan

## Puerperal Infection *(continued)*

| Nursing Diagnosis/Client Goals | Nursing Interventions | Rationale/Evaluation |
|---|---|---|
| **Nursing Diagnosis:**<br><br>Pattern 9: Feeling<br>Pain related to the presence of infection<br><br>**Client Goal:**<br><br>Woman will obtain relief of pain as evidenced by her verbal expressions of comfort, ability to sleep, reduction in tachycardia. | Promote comfort through:<br>1. Adequate periods of rest<br>2. Judicious use of analgesics and antipyretics<br>3. Provision of emotional support<br>4. Use of supportive nursing measures such as backrubs, instruction in relaxation techniques, maintenance of cleanliness, provision of diversional activities | **Rationale:**<br><br>Comfort is essential to enable the woman to rest and recover.<br><br>**Evaluation:**<br><br>Woman states she is free of pain. She is able to rest well and is coping emotionally with her infection. |
| **Nursing Diagnosis:**<br><br>Pattern 3: Relating<br>Potential altered parenting related to delayed parent-infant attachment secondary to woman's malaise and other symptoms of infection<br><br>**Client Goal:**<br><br>Woman will bond with her infant as evidenced by her ability to feed her infant successfully, her involvement in her infant's care, her demonstration of affectionate behaviors, and her expressions of positive thoughts about her baby. | Promote and maintain mother-infant interaction:<br>1. Provide opportunities for the mother to see and hold her infant.<br>2. Encourage the mother to feed the infant if she feels able. Assist mother with feeding when IV is in place.<br>3. If breast-feeding mother is unable to nurse, assist her in pumping her breasts to maintain milk production.<br>4. Encourage partner/support person to discuss infant with woman and to become involved in infant's care if the woman is not able to do so.<br>5. Provide pictures of the infant for the mother's bedside.<br>6. Encourage verbalization of anxieties, fears, and concerns.<br><br>Assess breast-feeding infant's mouth for signs of thrush, a common side effect of antibiotics taken by the mother. Treatment should be initiated, but breast-feeding need not be stopped. | **Rationale:**<br><br>Critically ill woman may become very depressed not only from disease process but also because her anticipated postpartal course is now denied to her, and she may interpret this as a failure of her ability to mother her infant.<br>Success at infant feeding generally enhances the woman's outlook and encourages mother-infant interaction.<br><br>Assists woman to feel involved with her infant and reassures her that her baby is receiving care and love.<br><br><br>Thrush, a monilial infection caused by *Candida albicans,* often occurs when normal oral flora are destroyed by antibiotic therapy.<br><br>**Evaluation:**<br><br>The woman bonds well with her newborn and potential altered parenting is avoided. |
| **Nursing Diagnosis:**<br><br>Pattern 8: Knowing<br>Knowledge deficit related to a lack of understanding of condition and its treatment<br><br>**Client Goal:**<br><br>Woman will be able to discuss her condition, its treatment, and her care needs following discharge. | Provide information regarding predisposing factors, signs and symptoms, and treatment.<br>Discuss the value of a nutritious diet in promoting healing<br>Review hygiene practices such as correct wiping after voiding, hand washing, etc, to prevent the spread of infection.<br>Discuss home care routines following postpartal infection. | **Rationale:**<br><br>Women have the right and responsibility to be actively involved in their own health care to the extent that they are able. To be an active participant the woman needs appropriate information.<br><br>**Evaluation:**<br><br>Woman is able to describe her condition and its implications. She cooperates with therapy and asks appropriate questions. |

## • Nursing Plan and Implementation

During the puerperium the nurse teaches the woman self-care measures that are helpful in preventing infection. The woman should understand the importance of perineal care, good hygiene practices to prevent contamination of the perineum (including wiping from front to back and changing perineal pads after going to the bathroom), and thorough hand washing. Sitz baths are cleansing and promote healing also. Adequate fluid intake coupled with a diet high in protein and vitamin C, which are necessary for wound healing, also helps prevent infection.

If the woman is seriously ill the nurse administers antibiotics as ordered, monitors the woman's vital signs and intake and output, and meets her comfort and hygiene needs. Ongoing assessment is indicated to detect subtle changes in the woman's condition. The nurse also promotes maternal-infant attachment, which may be difficult when the woman is acutely ill. Pictures and information about the newborn as well as brief visits are helpful in promoting attachment.

### PREPARATION FOR DISCHARGE

The woman with puerperal infection may need assistance when she is discharged. If the family cannot provide this home assistance, a referral is needed. The community health/visiting nurse service can be contacted as soon as puerperal infection is diagnosed so that the nurse can meet with the woman for a family and home assessment and development of a home care plan.

The family needs instruction in care of the newborn and a well-baby appointment should be scheduled. The mother should be instructed regarding activity, rest, medications, diet, and signs and symptoms of complications, and she should be scheduled for a return medical visit.

## • Evaluation

Anticipated outcomes of nursing care include the following:

- The infection is quickly identified and treated successfully without further complications.

- The woman understands the infection and the purpose of therapy; she cooperates with any ongoing antibiotic therapy if indicated following discharge.

- Maternal-infant attachment is maintained.

## • CARE OF THE WOMAN WITH THROMBOEMBOLIC DISEASE

Thromboembolic disease occurs in approximately 1% of women with vaginal birth and in 2% to 10% of women undergoing cesarean birth (Vorherr 1982). Although the disease may also occur antepartally, it is generally considered a postpartal complication. *Venous thrombosis* refers to thrombus formation in a superficial or deep vein with the accompanying risk that a portion of the clot might break off and result in pulmonary embolism. When the thrombus is formed in response to inflammation in the vein wall, it is termed **thrombophlebitis.** In this type of thrombosis the clot tends to be more firmly attached and therefore is less likely to result in embolism. In *noninflammatory venous thrombosis* (also called phlebothrombosis) the clot tends to be more loosely attached and the risk of embolism is greater. The main factors responsible for this type of thrombosis are venous stasis, vascular anoxia, and endothelial damage (Vorherr 1982).

Factors contributing directly to the development of thromboembolic disease postpartally include (a) increased amounts of certain blood clotting factors; (b) postpartal thrombocytosis (increased quantity of circulating platelets) and their increased adhesiveness; (c) release of thromboplastin substances from the tissue of the decidua, placenta, and fetal membranes; and (d) increased amounts of fibrinolysis inhibitors. Predisposing factors are (a) obesity, increased maternal age, and high parity; (b) anesthesia and surgery with possible vessel trauma and venous stasis due to prolonged inactivity; (c) previous history of venous thrombosis; (d) maternal anemia, hypothermia, or heart disease; and (e) use of estrogen for suppression of lactation.

## • Superficial Thrombophlebitis

Superficial thrombophlebitis is far more common postpartally than during pregnancy. Often the clot involves the saphenous veins. This disorder is more common in women with preexisting varices, although it is not limited to these women. Symptoms usually become apparent about the third or fourth postpartal day: tenderness in a portion of the vein, some local heat and redness, absent or low-grade fever, and occasionally slight elevation of the pulse. Treatment involves application of local heat, elevation of the affected limb, bed rest and analgesics, and the use of elastic support hose. Anticoagulants are usually not necessary unless complications develop. Pulmonary embolism is extremely rare. Occasionally the involved veins have incompetent valves, and as a result, the problem may spread to the deeper leg veins, such as the femoral vein.

## • Deep Vein Thrombophlebitis

Deep leg vein thrombophlebitis is more frequently seen in women with a history of thrombosis. Certain obstetric complications such as hydramnios, PIH, and operative birth are associated with an increased incidence.

Clinical manifestations may include edema of the ankle and leg, and an initial low-grade fever often followed by

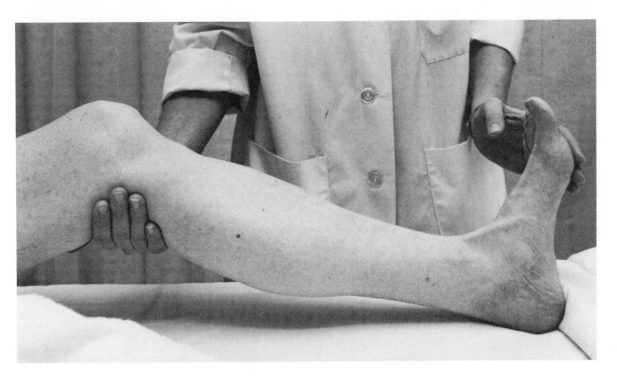

*Figure 27.2 Homan's sign: With the woman's knee flexed to decrease the risk of embolization, the nurse dorsiflexes the foot. Pain in the foot or leg is a positive Homan's sign.*

high temperature and chills. Depending on the vein involved, the woman may complain of pain in the popliteal and lateral tibial areas (popliteal vein), entire lower leg and foot (anterior and posterior tibial veins), inguinal tenderness (femoral vein), or pain in the lower abdomen (iliofemoral vein). The Homan's sign (Figure 27.2) may or may not be positive, but pain often results from calf pressure. Because of reflex arterial spasm, sometimes the limb is pale and cool to the touch—the so-called milk leg or *phlegmasia alba dolens*—and peripheral pulses may be decreased.

Septic pelvic thrombophlebitis may develop in conjunction with infections of the reproductive tract and is more common in women who have had a cesarean birth. The classic sign is fever of unknown origin. However, when the ovarian vein is involved, lower abdominal pain also occurs. If untreated, tachycardia, nausea, ileus, and elevated white count usually develop (Fagnant and Monif 1987).

## MEDICAL THERAPY

Because cases are seldom clear-cut, diagnosis involves a variety of approaches, such as client history and physical examination, occlusive cuff impedence plethysmography (IPG), Doppler ultrasonography, and contrast venography. In questionable cases, contrast venography provides the most accurate diagnosis of deep vein thrombophlebitis. Unfortunately, venography is not practical for multiple examinations or prospective screening and may itself induce phlebitis.

Treatment involves the administration of intravenous heparin, using an infusion pump to permit continuous, accurate infusion of medication. Bed rest is required, and analgesics are given as necessary to relieve discomfort. The woman is often given antibiotic therapy. In most cases thrombectomy is not necessary.

Once the symptoms have subsided (usually in several days), the woman may begin ambulation while wearing elastic support stockings. At this point, anticoagulant therapy is usually changed to sodium warfarin, which the woman continues on for two to six months at home. While on warfarin, prothrombin times are assessed periodically to maintain correct dosage levels.

## NURSING ASSESSMENT

The nurse carefully assesses the woman's history for factors predisposing to thrombophlebitis. In addition, the nurse is alert to any complaints of pain in the legs, inguinal area, or lower abdomen because such pain may indicate deep vein thrombosis. The nurse also assesses the woman's legs for evidence of edema, temperature change, or pain with palpation.

## NURSING DIAGNOSIS

Nursing diagnoses that may apply to a postpartal woman with thrombophlebitis are found in the Nursing Care Plan—Thrombophlebitis.

# Nursing Care Plan

## Thrombophlebitis

### Client Assessment

#### Nursing History

1. Predisposing factors include:
   a. Increased maternal age
   b. Obesity
   c. Increased parity
   d. Prolonged labor with associated pressure of the fetal head on the pelvic veins
   e. PIH
   f. Heart disease
   g. Hypercoagulability of the early puerperium
   h. Anemia
   i. Immobility
   j. Hemorrhage
   k. Previous history of venous thrombosis

2. Initiating factors may include:
   a. Trauma to deep leg veins due to faulty positioning for delivery
   b. Operative delivery, including cesarean birth
   c. Abortion
   d. Postpartal pelvic cellulitis

#### Physical Examination

1. Superficial thrombophlebitis
   a. Tenderness along the involved vein
   b. Areas of palpable thrombosis
   c. Warmth and redness in the involved area

2. Deep vein thrombophlebitis
   a. Positive Homan's sign (pain occurs when foot is dorsiflexed while leg is extended)
   b. Tenderness and pain in affected area
   c. Fever (initially low, followed by high fever and chills)
   d. Edema in affected extremity
   e. Pallor and coolness in affected limb
   f. Diminished peripheral pulses

#### Diagnostic Studies

Thrombophlebitis
a. Doppler ultrasonography demonstrates increased circumference of affected extremity
b. Occlusive cuff IPG
c. Venography confirms diagnosis

| Nursing Diagnosis/Client Goals | Nursing Interventions | Rationale/Evaluation |
|---|---|---|
| **Nursing Diagnosis:**<br><br>Pattern 1: Exchanging<br>Potential for injury related to obstructed venous return<br><br>**Client Goal:**<br><br>Client will not experience any injury, as evidenced by absence of pain, edema, and pallor; pulses will be palpable; ambulation will be possible; and anticoagulant overdose will be avoided. | Report signs and symptoms of developing thrombophlebitis (see client assessment section of nursing care plan).<br><br>Maintain bed rest and warm, moist soaks as ordered.<br>Administer intravenous heparin as ordered, by continuous intravenous drip, heparin lock, or subcutaneously including:<br>1. Monitor IV or heparin lock site for signs of infiltration.<br>2. Obtain Lee-White clotting times or partial thromboplastin time (PTT) per physician order and review prior to administering heparin.<br>3. Observe for signs of anticoagulant overdose with resultant bleeding, including:<br>  a. Hematuria<br>  b. Epistaxis<br>  c. Ecchymosis<br>  d. Bleeding gums<br><br>4. Provide protamine sulfate, per physician order, to combat bleeding problems related to heparin overdosage. | **Rationale:**<br><br>Early detection of developing thrombophlebitis permits prompt treatment. As the thrombus increases in size, signs of obstruction also increase.<br><br>Bed rest is ordered to decrease possibility that portion of clot will dislodge and cause pulmonary embolism. Warmth promotes blood flow to affected area.<br>Heparin does not dissolve clot but is administered to prevent further clotting. It is safe for breast-feeding mothers because heparin is not excreted in mother's milk.<br><br><br><br><br><br><br><br>Protamine sulfate is heparin antagonist, given intravenously, which is almost immediately effective in counteracting bleeding complications caused by heparin overdose. |

# Nursing Care Plan

## Thrombophlebitis *(continued)*

| Nursing Diagnosis/Client Goals | Nursing Interventions | Rationale/Evaluation |
|---|---|---|
| | Immediately report the development of any signs of pulmonary embolism, including:<br>1. Sudden onset of severe chest pain, often located substernally<br>2. Apprehension and sense of impending catastrophe<br>3. Cough (may be accompanied by hemoptysis)<br>4. Tachycardia<br>5. Fever<br>6. Hypotension<br>7. Diaphoresis, pallor, weakness<br>8. Shortness of breath<br>9. Neck vein engorgement<br>10. Friction rub and evidence of atelectasis upon auscultation<br>Initiate or support any emergency treatment. | Pulmonary embolism is major complication of thrombophlebitis. Signs and symptoms may occur suddenly and require immediate emergency treatment; prognosis is related to size and location of embolism. |
| | Initiate progressive ambulation following the acute phase; provide properly fitting elastic stockings prior to ambulation.<br>Obtain prothrombin time (PT) and review prior to beginning warfarin. Repeat periodically per physician order. | Elastic stockings or "TEDs" help prevent pooling of venous blood in lower extremities.<br>PT is the test most commonly used to monitor the blood of clients receiving warfarin.<br><br>**Evaluation:**<br>The woman recovers fully and injury is avoided. |
| **Nursing Diagnosis:**<br>Pattern 9: Feeling<br>Pain related to tissue hypoxia and edema secondary to vascular obstruction<br><br>**Client Goal:**<br>Woman will obtain relief of pain as evidenced by verbal expressions of comfort and ability to rest and sleep. | Administer analgesics as ordered for relief of pain.<br>Provide supportive nursing comfort measures such as backrubs, provision of quiet time for sleep, diversional activities.<br>Maintain limb in elevated position. | **Rationale:**<br>Analgesics act to relieve pain and enable the woman to rest.<br><br>Elevation of affected limb promotes venous return and helps decrease edema.<br><br>**Evaluation:**<br>Woman states that pain is relieved and that she is able to rest comfortably. |

*(continues)*

# Nursing Care Plan

## Thrombophlebitis *(continued)*

| Nursing Diagnosis/Client Goals | Nursing Interventions | Rationale/Evaluation |
|---|---|---|
| **Nursing Diagnosis:**<br><br>Pattern 3: Relating<br>Potential altered parenting related to decreased maternal-infant interaction secondary to bed rest and IVs<br><br>**Client Goal:**<br><br>Woman will develop bonds of attachment with her infant as evidenced by her ability to feed her infant successfully, her involvement in her infant's care, her demonstration of affectionate behaviors, and verbal expressions of positive thoughts about her baby. | Maintain mother-infant attachment when mother is on bed rest:<br>1. Provide frequent contacts for mother and infant; modified rooming-in is possible if the crib is placed close to the mother's bed and nurse checks often to help mother lift or move infant.<br>2. Encourage mother to feed baby. Breast-feeding mothers may nurse; for acutely ill mothers it may be necessary to pump the breasts.<br>3. Provide photos of infant if contact is limited. | **Evaluation:**<br>Woman successfuly develops bonds of attachment with her infant. |
| **Nursing Diagnosis:**<br><br>Pattern 3: Relating<br>Altered family processes related to illness of family member<br><br>**Client Goal:**<br><br>Woman and her family will cope effectively with her illness as evidenced by frequent visits from partner (and other family members, including siblings), verbalized plans for handling family tasks and for coping when woman is discharged, and expressions of assurance by woman that the family will deal effectively with her illness. | 1. Encourage woman to express her concerns to her partner. Assist couple in planning ways to manage while woman is hospitalized and after her discharge.<br>2. Encourage partner or support person to bring other children to hospital to visit mother and meet new sibling.<br>3. Encourage partner or support person to bring in family pictures. Encourage phone calls.<br>4. Contact social services if indicated to obtain additional assistance for family if needed. | **Rationale:**<br>Illness of any family member impacts the entire family. This is especially true when the family situation is such that the mother is the primary nurturer and she is absent. Family members attempt to continue their own roles while also assuming the tasks of the missing member. This can result in crisis.<br><br>**Evaluation:**<br>Woman expresses assurance that family misses her but is coping effectively. Family is able to discuss plans for coping following the woman's discharge. |
| **Nursing Diagnosis:**<br><br>Pattern 8: Knowing<br>Knowledge deficit related to the thrombophlebitis, its treatment, preventive measures, and the medication, warfarin<br><br>**Client Goal:**<br><br>Woman will understand her condition, its treatment, and long-term implications as evidenced by her ability to discuss the condition and answer questions about her care and responsibilities. | 1. Discuss ways of avoiding circulatory stasis such as avoiding prolonged standing or sitting; avoiding crossing legs.<br>2. Review need to wear support stockings and to plan for rest periods with legs elevated.<br>3. Discuss the use of warfarin, its side effects, possible interactions with other medications, and need to have dosage assessed through periodic checks of the prothrombin time.<br>4. Discuss signs of bleeding including:<br>  a. Hematuria<br>  b. Epistaxis<br>  c. Ecchymosis<br>  d. Bleeding gums | **Rationale:**<br>Such discussion is essential to help the woman understand the condition, her medication, and its implications. She must have a clear understanding to be able to provide effective self-care.<br><br>**Evaluation:**<br>Woman is able to discuss her condition, its treatment, preventive measures, and long-term implications. |

## NURSING PLAN AND IMPLEMENTATION

Because trauma is often a factor in the development of thrombophlebitis, the nurse avoids sources of trauma such as prolonged use of stirrups. If used, stirrups should be well padded and properly positioned. Early ambulation is encouraged and the use of the knee-gatch on the bed is avoided. Following a cesarean birth, women are encouraged to do leg exercises regularly.

Once heparin therapy is instituted, the nurse assesses for evidence of bleeding related to heparin and keeps the heparin antagonist, protamine sulfate, readily available. The nurse also monitors the woman closely for signs of pulmonary embolism.

### Education for Self-Care

The woman is instructed to avoid prolonged standing or sitting because they contribute to venous stasis. She is also instructed to avoid crossing her legs because of the pressure it causes. Walking is acceptable because it promotes venous return.

Women who are discharged on warfarin must understand the purpose of the medication and be alert for signs of bleeding. Certain medications such as aspirin and nonsteroidal anti-inflammatory drugs increase anticoagulant activity and should be avoided. In fact, the woman should check for possible medication interaction before taking any medication while on warfarin. She should also have vitamin K available in case bleeding occurs, and may choose to wear a Medic Alert bracelet in case of emergency.

Warfarin is excreted in the breast milk and thus may present problems for breast-feeding mothers. Women who wish to continue nursing may be maintained at home on low doses of subcutaneous heparin since heparin is not excreted in breast milk.

## EVALUATION

Anticipated outcomes of nursing care include the following:

- If thrombophlebitis develops, it is detected quickly and managed successfully without further complications.
- At discharge the woman is able to explain the purpose, dosage regimen, and necessary precautions associated with any prescribed medications such as anticoagulants.
- The woman can discuss self-care measures and ongoing therapies (such as the use of elastic stockings) that are indicated.
- The woman has bonded successfully with her newborn and is able to care for her or him effectively.

## • Pulmonary Embolism

A sudden onset of dyspnea accompanied by sweating, pallor, cyanosis, confusion, systemic hypotension, cough (with or without hemoptysis), tachycardia, shortness of breath, fever, and increased jugular pressure may indicate **pulmonary embolism.** Chest pain that mimics heart attack, coupled with the woman's verbalized fear of imminent death and complaint of pressure in the bowel and rectum, should alert the nurse to the extensive size of the embolus. A friction rub and evidence of atelectasis may be noted upon auscultation. A gallop (heart) rhythm may be present even if respiratory inspiration is normal, although smaller emboli may present with only transient syncope, tightness of the chest, or unexplained fever.

Even x-ray films and electrocardiogram (ECG) changes and laboratory data are not always reliable. If a case of pulmonary embolism is suspected, prompt treatment should begin even in the absence of corroborative data. If the embolism is small and heparin therapy is begun quickly, the chance of survival is excellent. However, when a large thrombus occludes a major pulmonary vessel, death may occur before therapy can even begin.

Therapy involves the administration of a variety of intravenous medications, such as meperidine hydrochloride to relieve the pain, lidocaine to correct any arrhythmias, and drugs such as papaverine hydrochloride and aminophylline to reduce spasms of the bronchi and coronary and pulmonary vessels (Vorherr 1982). Oxygen is administered and heparin infusion is begun. In severe cases an embolectomy may be necessary, although fibrinolytic therapy with medications (such as streptokinase) that lyse clots may be tried first.

## • CARE OF THE WOMAN WITH A URINARY TRACT INFECTION (UTI)

The postpartal woman is at increased risk of developing urinary tract problems due to the normal postpartal diuresis, increased bladder capacity, decreased bladder sensitivity from stretching and/or trauma, and possible inhibited neural control of the bladder following the use of general or regional anesthesia.

Emptying the bladder is vital. Women who have not sufficiently recovered from the effects of anesthesia cannot void spontaneously, and catheterization is necessary.

Retention of residual urine, bacteria introduced at the time of catheterization, and a bladder traumatized by birth combine to provide an excellent environment for the development of cystitis.

# ● *Overdistention*

Overdistention occurs postpartally when, as a result of the predisposing factors previously identified, the woman is unable to empty her bladder.

## MEDICAL THERAPY

Overdistention, if discovered in the recovery room, is often managed by draining the bladder with a straight catheter as a one-time measure. If the overdistention recurs or is diagnosed later in the postpartal period, an indwelling catheter is generally ordered for 24 hours.

## NURSING ASSESSMENT

The overdistended bladder appears as a large mass, reaching sometimes to the umbilicus and displacing the uterine fundus upward. There is increased vaginal bleeding, the fundus is boggy, and the woman may complain of cramping as the uterus attempts to contract.

## NURSING DIAGNOSIS

Nursing diagnoses that may apply when a woman has difficulties due to overdistention include:

● Potential for infection related to urinary stasis secondary to overdistention
● Altered patterns of urinary elimination related to overdistention

## NURSING PLAN AND IMPLEMENTATION

Diligent monitoring of the bladder during the recovery period and preventive health measures greatly reduce the chances for overdistention of the bladder. Encouraging the mother to void spontaneously and assisting her to use the toilet, if possible, or the bedpan, if she has received conductive anesthesia, prevent the largest percentage of overdistention.

If catheterization becomes necessary, careful aseptic technique should be used during catheter insertion. Because of the trauma and edema associated with birth, catheterization can be uncomfortable postpartally, and the nurse should be careful and gentle in performing the procedure. If the amount of urine drained from the bladder reaches 900–1000 mL, the catheter should be clamped, the Foley balloon inflated, and the catheter taped to the woman's leg. After an hour the catheter may be unclamped and placed on gravity drainage. The physician should be notified. When the in-dwelling catheter is removed, a urine specimen is often sent to the lab.

# ● *Cystitis (Lower Urinary Tract Infection)*

*E coli* causes 73%–90% of the cases of postpartal cystitis (bladder inflammation) and pyelonephritis (Vorherr 1982). In most cases the infection ascends the urinary tract from the urethra to the bladder and then to the kidneys because vesiculoureteral reflux forces contaminated urine into the renal pelvis.

## MEDICAL THERAPY

When cystitis is suspected in the puerperium, a clean-catch midstream urine sample is obtained for microscopic examination, culture, and sensitivity tests. Taking a catheterized specimen is avoided when possible because of the increased risk of infection. When the bacterial concentration is greater than 100,000 microorganisms per milliliter of fresh urine, infection is generally present; counts between 10,000 and 100,000 are suggestive, particularly if clinical symptoms are noted.

Treatment is theoretically delayed until urine culture and sensitivity reports are available. In the clinical setting, however, antibiotic therapy is often begun immediately using one of the short-acting sulfonamides, or in the case of sulfa allergy, ampicillin. Then, if indicated, the antibiotic can be changed (Pritchard et al 1985). Antispasmodics may be given to relieve discomfort.

# ● *Pyelonephritis (Upper Urinary Tract Infection)*

Pyelonephritis is an inflammation of the renal pelvis that is usually the result of infection. In most cases the infection has ascended from the lower urinary tract. It occurs more commonly on the right, although both kidneys may be affected. If untreated, the renal cortex may be damaged and kidney function impaired.

## MEDICAL THERAPY

With pyelonephritis, bed rest, forced fluids, and broad spectrum antibiotics are prescribed immediately. The antibiotics can be changed if the culture so indicates. Intake and output are measured. If nausea and vomiting are severe, fluids are given intravenously. Antispasmodics and analgesics are given to relieve discomfort. The woman usually continues to take antibiotics for two to four weeks after clinical and bacteriologic response. A clean-catch urine culture should be obtained two weeks after completion of therapy and then periodically for the next two years.

## NURSING ASSESSMENT

Symptoms of cystitis often appear two to three days after birth. The initial symptoms of cystitis may include frequency, urgency, dysuria, and nocturia. Hematuria and suprapubic pain may be present. A slightly elevated temperature may occur, but systemic symptoms are often absent.

When a UTI progresses to pyelonephritis, systemic symptoms usually occur, and the woman becomes acutely ill. Symptoms include chills, high fever, flank pain (unilateral or bilateral), nausea, and vomiting, in addition to all the signs of lower UTI. Costovertebral pain also may be elicited. Urine culture and sensitivity are obtained to identify the causative organism.

## NURSING DIAGNOSIS

Nursing diagnoses that may apply if a woman develops a UTI postpartally include:

● Pain related to dysuria secondary to cystitis

● Knowledge deficit related to a lack of understanding of the potential long-term effects of pyelonephritis

## NURSING PLAN AND IMPLEMENTATION

Prevention is important in dealing with UTI. Regular, complete bladder emptying, instruction on proper wiping techniques to avoid fecal contamination of the meatus, good perineal care, and frequent changing of perineal pads all decrease chances of infection.

### Education for Self-Care

At home the woman should follow the recommendations listed above. She should be advised to maintain a good fluid intake, to void following sexual intercourse (to wash contaminants from the meatal area), and to wear cotton crotch underwear to facilitate air circulation. A woman with pyelonephritis must understand the potential seriousness of the condition and monitor herself for any symptoms of UTI.

## EVALUATION

Anticipated outcomes of nursing care include the following:

● Signs of UTI are detected quickly and the condition is treated successfully.

● The woman incorporates self-care measures to prevent the recurrence of UTI as part of her personal hygiene routine.

● The woman cooperates with any long-term therapy or follow-up.

● Maternal-infant attachment is maintained and the woman is able to care for her newborn effectively.

## ● CARE OF THE WOMAN WITH MASTITIS

**Mastitis** refers to an inflammation of the breast generally caused by *Staphylococcus aureus* and primarily seen in breast-feeding mothers. Because symptoms seldom occur before the second to fourth week postpartally, nurses often are not fully aware of how uncomfortable and acutely ill the woman may be.

The infection usually begins when bacteria invade the breast tissue. Often the tissue has been traumatized in some way (fissured or cracked nipples, overdistention, manipulation, or milk stasis) and is especially susceptible to pathogenic invasion. The most common source of the bacteria is the infant's nose and throat, although other sources include the hands of the mother or hospital personnel or the woman's circulating blood.

### ● Medical Therapy

Diagnosis is usually based on the symptoms, physical examination, and a culture and sensitivity of the breast milk. Treatment involves the administration of appropriate antibiotics, use of analgesics to ease discomfort, and local application of heat.

Current literature suggests that the mother should nurse frequently (every one to two hours) while infected to prevent milk stasis and engorgement, both of which are associated with increased risk of infection and the development of abscess (Easterling and Herbert 1986, Niebyl 1985). However, some agencies prefer to have the mother cease nursing while acutely ill and pump her breasts to prevent engorgement. Breast-feeding is resumed after the mother is afebrile and receiving antibiotics.

Occasionally the process of mastitis continues and a frank abscess develops. The mother's milk and any drainage from the nipple is then cultured and antibiotic therapy is modified if sensitivity reports indicate the organism is resistant to the current antibiotic. In addition, it is usually necessary to incise and drain the area and pack it with sterile gauze. The packing is gradually decreased to permit proper healing.

Often the breast is covered with a sterile surgical dressing, making breast-feeding impossible. If possible, the dressing should be applied so that the woman can continue to breast-feed or pump her breast, thereby avoiding engorgement. Once the dressings, drains, and packing have been removed and the incisions are healing well, careful breast-feeding may resume, closely supervised by the experienced nurse.

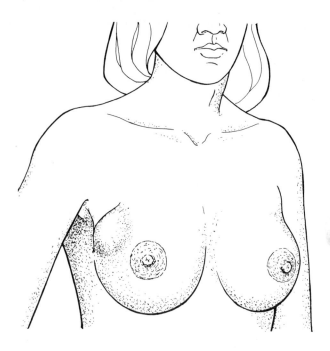

*Figure 27.3 Mastitis: Erythema and swelling are present in the upper outer quadrant of the breast. Axillary lymph nodes are enlarged and tender.*

## ● Nursing Assessment

Once the infection develops, the woman may have a high temperature, chills, malaise, tachycardia, and headache. The breasts may be very tender, have a reddened and warm area, feel firm to the touch, or show areas of lumpiness (Figure 27.3).

## ● Nursing Diagnosis

Nursing diagnoses that may apply to the woman with mastitis include:

● Knowledge deficit related to appropriate breast-feeding practices

● Pain related to the development of mastitis

## ● Nursing Plan and Implementation

Prevention of mastitis is far simpler than therapy. Meticulous hand washing by all personnel is the primary measure in preventing epidemic nursery infections and subsequent maternal mastitis. Prompt attention to mothers who have blocked milk ducts eliminates stagnant milk as a growth medium for bacteria. Frequent breast-feeding of the infant usually prevents mastitis.

### EDUCATION FOR SELF-CARE

Since mastitis usually develops following discharge, the woman should be given information about signs and symptoms in the discharge information. If symptoms develop the woman should breast-feed frequently, increase her fluid intake, rest in bed, and employ measures to determine whether she has a plugged duct or mastitis. (See discussion in Chapter 23.) If improvement does not occur within 12 to 14 hours or if fever persists, the woman should consult her physician, who will usually order an antibiotic (Ogle and Davis 1988).

To promote complete breast emptying, the woman can nurse on the affected breast first. If that is uncomfortable she can nurse on the opposite breast until let-down occurs and then switch to the affected breast. Application of heat to the affected breast using warm compresses may help the discomfort. In addition, some women find it soothing to lie on their side in a tub of hot water with the affected breast immersed and floating.

The nurse should stress to the woman that factors contributing to the development of mastitis include inadequate emptying of the breasts, improper positioning of the infant at breast, ineffectual sucking, breast engorgement or overdistention (such as when a mother skips feedings or the infant begins sleeping through the night), plugged ducts, or pressure constriction from a poorly fitting bra. Fatigue and stress are also contributing factors (Ogle and Davis 1988).

If women are having difficulty with breast-feeding they may find it helpful to seek advice from a support group such as La Leche League or a lactation consultant.

## ● Evaluation

Anticipated outcomes of nursing care include the following:

● The woman's mastitis is detected early and treated successfully.

● The woman can continue breast-feeding if she chooses.

● The woman understands self-care measures she can employ to prevent the recurrence of the mastitis.

## ● CARE OF THE WOMAN WITH A POSTPARTAL PSYCHIATRIC DISORDER

Many different types of psychiatric problems may be encountered in the puerperium but only rarely is the disorder serious. Approximately 70% to 80% of women experience a transient depression during the first week, most commonly on the third postpartal day (Easterling and Herbert 1986). This transient depression is usually accompanied by tearfulness and is a self-limiting, brief episode.

When psychiatric illness occurs after childbirth, one or several of the following signs are usually present: depression, delusions, confusion, mania, delirium, hallucinations, anxiety, and sexual dysfunction. Occasionally, violent behavior forms part of the clinical picture; sometimes this violence is directed against the infant. Approximately one in 1000 term pregnancies is followed by psychiatric problems sufficiently severe to require hospitalization (Hamilton 1982).

Depression is the most common type of psychiatric disorder seen after childbirth. Depression may be triggered by a variety of factors including (a) unwanted or unplanned pregnancy, (b) unfaithful partner, (c) recent loss of a support person or close friend, (d) worries about the health of the fetus or the newborn, (e) sexual rejection by the partner during pregnancy, (f) separated or single marital status, and (g) major or severe illness of another child (Mozley 1985). It tends to peak about six weeks postbirth, although symptoms may arise earlier. In addition to feelings of sadness, the woman may experience feelings of failure, self-accusatory thoughts, depression, inability to cope with the infant, and exhaustion. Suicidal thinking may be present, which poses a true danger to the woman. Treatment is generally directed at relief of symptoms, and hospitalization may be indicated if the woman seems capable of harming herself.

In some women postpartal psychosis has a more subtle onset and may be characterized by increasing hostility and anger, fearfulness, anxiety, and aversion to sexual activity. The woman often suffers from insomnia. Agitation, confusion, delusions, hallucinations, and labile affect are common (Daw 1988). Unfortunately, this type of disturbance frequently culminates in an act of violence, such as child abuse.

It is important to consider contributing factors to postpartal psychiatric disorders, because one fourth of women with a history of postpartal mental illness experience recurrence after a subsequent pregnancy. Contributing factors include (a) a chronic history of inability to deal with life's crises; (b) a traumatic relationship with the woman's own mother, especially during childhood; (c) self-defensive or conflicting motives for the pregnancy itself; (d) external variables such as prolonged infertility prior to pregnancy, physical complications during pregnancy or labor and birth, problems or abnormalities with the infant; (e) concomitant life stresses, such as poverty, a recent family member's death, or home or job change (Barglow 1982).

## ● Medical Therapy

Treatment of mild postpartal psychiatric disorders usually is achieved on an outpatient basis, although medication or hospitalization is indicated in some cases. Postpartum blues are handled with reassurance, education, and empathy. Depression is treated by educating the woman and her family, reducing stressors, and increasing her socialization. Antidepressant medications are often ordered. True psychosis requires hospitalization with treatment, including the use of antipsychotic medication and, in some cases,

electroconvulsive therapy (Daw 1988). If the mother appears to have rejected her infant, it is never wise to compel her to care for her or him, as this forces the woman to deal with feelings of guilt, shame, and hostility that may overwhelm her and endanger the infant.

## ● Nursing Assessment

The nurse observes the woman for signs of depression, which may be manifested by tearfulness, exhaustion, and statements indicating feelings of failure and self-accusation. Behavior and verbalizations that are bizarre or seem to indicate a potential for violence against herself or others, including the infant, should be reported as soon as possible for further evaluation.

## ● Nursing Diagnosis

Possible nursing diagnoses that may apply to a woman with a postpartum psychiatric disorder include:

- Ineffective individual coping related to postpartum depression
- Potential altered parenting related to child neglect secondary to postpartum psychosis

## ● Nursing Plan and Implementation

Although a history of psychiatric problems is not always indicative of current problems, the nurse should be aware of any previous or current emotional problems. In providing daily care the nurse is often the first to note patterns of behavior that suggest possible depression or other psychiatric problems.

If care givers have any doubts about the woman's stability, a referral may be made to the public health service so that follow-up care is possible. In this way problems can be identified before they become major obstacles to the woman's or her infant's emotional health.

## ● Evaluation

Anticipated outcomes of nursing care include the following:

- Signs of potential postpartal disorders are detected quickly and therapy is implemented.
- The newborn is cared for effectively by the father or another support person until the mother is able to do so.

## ESSENTIAL CONCEPTS

● The main causes of early postpartal hemorrhage are uterine atony, lacerations of the vagina and cervix, and retained placental fragments.

● Late postpartal hemorrhage is most often caused by retained placental fragments.

● The nurse should assess the woman regularly for signs of hemorrhage during the postpartum period.

● Complaints of severe vulvar pain are often the first indication that a vulvar hematoma is developing. Vaginal hematomas may cause pain and difficulty voiding. Complaints of lateral uterine pain or flank pain may indicate that a hematoma of the broad ligament is developing.

● The most common postpartal infection is endometritis, an infection that is limited to the uterine cavity. An infection involving the peritoneal cavity, peritonitis, may be life threatening and requires vigorous therapy and skilled nursing care.

● Thromboembolic disease originating in the veins of the leg, thigh, or pelvis may occur in the antepartum or postpartum periods and carries with it the potential for creating a pulmonary embolus.

● A postpartal woman is at increased risk for developing urinary tract problems due to normal postpartal diuresis, increased bladder capacity, decreased bladder sensitivity from stretching and/or trauma, and, possibly, inhibited neural control of the bladder following the use of anesthetic agents.

● Mastitis is an inflammation of the breast caused by *Staphylococcus aureus* and is primarily seen in breast-feeding women. Symptoms seldom occur before the second to fourth postpartal week.

● Although many different types of psychiatric problems may be encountered in the postpartal period, depression is the most common. Episodes occur frequently in the week after childbirth and are typically transient.

● The normal puerperium is a dynamic period during which major changes must take place. When nurses are keenly aware of these normal physiologic and psychologic changes, they can quickly assess when deviations occur in the involutional process. These deviations place additional stress on the body, creating a risk situation for the mother that necessitates immediate intervention and evaluation.

### References

Barglow P: Postpartum mental illness: Detection and treatment. In: *Gynecology and Obstetrics.* Vol 2. Sciarra JL (editor). Philadelphia: Harper and Row, 1982.

Daw JL: Postpartum depression. *South Med J* February 1988; 81:207.

Easterling WE, Herbert WNP: The puerperium. In: *Obstetrics and Gynecology,* 5th ed. Danforth DN, Scott JR (editors). Philadelphia: Harper and Row, 1986.

Eschenbach D, Wager G: Puerperal infections. *Clin Obstet Gynecol* 1980; 23(4):1003.

Fagnant RJ, Monif RG: Uncovering and correcting septic pelvic thrombophlebitis. *Contemp OB/GYN* February 1987; 29:129.

Few BJ: Prostaglandin $F_2$ for treating severe postpartum hemorrhage. *Am J Mat Child Nurs* May/June 1987; 12:169.

Hamilton JA: Puerperal psychoses. In: *Gynecology and Obstetrics.* Vol 2. Sciarra JL (editor). Philadelphia: Harper and Row, 1982.

Mozley P: Predicting postpartum depression. *Contemp OB/GYN* May 1985; 5:173.

Niebyl JR: When the nursing mother has mastitis. *Contemp OB/GYN* July 1985; 26:31.

Ogle KS, Davis S: Mastitis in lactating women. *J Fam Practice* 1988; 26(2):139.

Pritchard JA, MacDonald PC, Gant NF: *Williams' Obstetrics,* 17th ed. New York: Appleton-Century-Crofts, 1985.

Vorherr H: Puerperium: Maternal involutional changes—management of puerperal problems and complications. In: *Gynecology and Obstetrics.* Vol 2. Sciarra JL (editor). Philadelphia: Harper and Row, 1982.

### Additional Readings

Duff P: Diagnosing and treating post-C/S endometritis. *Contemp OB/GYN* March 1987; 29:129.

Gjerdingen DK et al: Postpartum mental and physical problems. How common are they? *Postgrad Med* December 1986; 80:133.

Hill PD: Effects of heat and cold on the perineum after episiotomy/laceration. *J Obstet Gynecol Neonatal Nurs* March/April 1989; 18:124.

Hillard PA: Postpartum hemorrhage. *Parents* January 1987; 62:104.

Schneider GT: A postpartum emergency—necrotizing fasciitis. *Contemp OB/GYN* February 1988; 31:109.

Soper DE et al: Abbreviated antibiotic therapy for the treatment of postpartum endometritis. *Obstet Gynecol* January 1987; 69:127.

Theesen K et al: Pharmacology: Caring for the depressed OB patient. *Contemp OB/GYN* February 1989; 33:122.

Zuckerman BS et al: Maternal depression: A concern for pediatricians. *Pediatrics* January 1987; 179:110.

# 28
# Families in Crisis: Nursing Care

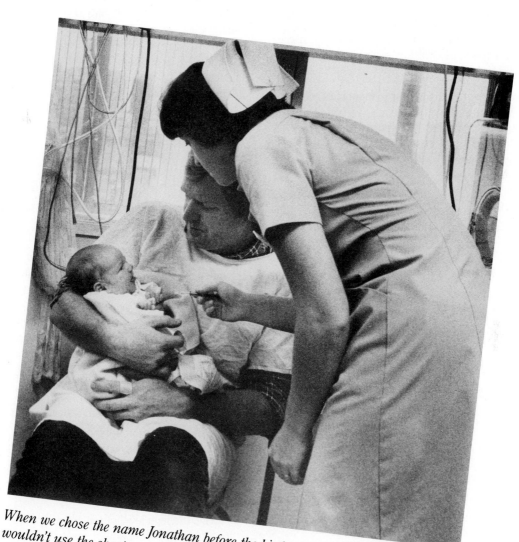

*When we chose the name Jonathan before the birth of our son, I thought I wouldn't use the shorter versions of the name. However, in the hospital, people referred to him by nicknames. They always talked about Jonny, or asked me how Jon was. I was pleased to hear these names. He sounded like a real person even though he had so many problems and was dying. (When Pregnancy Fails)*

## Objectives

● Compare the process of crisis intervention to the nursing process.

● Identify specific assessment strategies to predict which families will need additional support to avert or resolve a crisis.

● Describe the stages of the grieving process.

● Discuss the nurse's role in assisting the family that loses an infant.

● Identify the needs of and nursing support for family members who must deal with the birth of a high-risk infant or infant with a defect.

● Discuss the role of the nurse in the resolution of the following postpartal crises: malattachment, relinquishment of the infant, adolescent parenting, child abuse, and single-parent families.

## Key Terms

acute grief
chronic grief
crisis intervention
grief
grief work
loss
modeling
reciprocal inhibition

**M**aternity nurses deal with families suffering from a variety of crises, ranging from birth of a child with a congenital anomaly to unwanted pregnancy and relinquishment of the child. The nurse who is familiar with the signs of crisis and methods of intervention can help identify and avert or resolve the crises of individuals and families. Nurses who are able to identify crisis situations can make referrals as well as explain a woman's situation to other members of the health care team. In addition to being a therapeutic agent, the nurse can serve as the primary coordinator of the intervention program for the family.

A crisis is potentially growth promoting or emotionally destructive for those involved. How a family meets a crisis depends on the personalities of those involved, the family structure, and previously existing problems. It is also determined by the family's experience with crises and patterns of problem solving.

## ● USING THE NURSING PROCESS WITH FAMILIES AT RISK

### ● Nursing Assessment

Through the process of assessment, nurses and other health care professionals are responsible for identifying families at risk. Assessment should reveal crisis or precrisis states, and by further questioning, nurses can determine the family's ability to cope with the crisis.

The answers to the following questions will help determine the effects of the crisis on the family:

● To what extent has the crisis disrupted the family's normal life pattern?

● Has the family's economic status been affected?

● Can family members handle the responsibilities involved in the activities of daily living—for example, eating or personal hygiene?

● Does the family or a family member seem to be on the brink of despair?

● Has the high level of tension distorted one or more individual's perception of reality?

● Is the family's usual support system present, absent, or exhausted?

● What are the resources of the nurse or agency in relation to the family's assessed needs?

# ● *Nursing Diagnosis*

Essential data are identified from the answers to these and related questions. This information is used to determine the goals of the intervention plan and formulate nursing diagnoses. Nursing diagnoses of families at risk center on their psychologic feelings and needs. Nursing diagnoses that may apply include:

- Ineffective family coping related to the perinatal loss of fetus or newborn
- Altered parenting related to birth of an at-risk newborn
- Knowledge deficit related to normal grief and loss process
- Anxiety related to loss of self-esteem secondary to birth of at-risk baby

# ● *Nursing Plan and Implementation*

An effective intervention plan has the following features (Hoff 1988).

- Focuses on the immediate concrete problem
- Considers the family's functional level and dependency needs
- Is appropriate to the family's culture and life-style
- Includes all family members and significant others
- Is practical, has a specified time frame, and is concrete
- Is dynamic and renegotiable
- Includes an arrangement for follow-up contact

## METHODS OF INTERVENTION

Depending on the family's ability to accept and adjust to the situation causing the crisis, the nurse may find one or more of the following intervention methods helpful.

### Anticipatory Guidance

Anticipatory guidance of both expectant families and families with newborns can help prevent crisis. Whether the pregnancy and infant are normal or high risk, anticipatory guidance can give families the knowledge they need to understand and cope with the situation. Clients will feel more in control if they know what to expect.

The nurse's role as health educator is good preparation for this intervention. Before birth, parents may need to discuss the emotional and physical changes that accompany pregnancy. They want to know what to expect during labor and birth, and, if the pregnancy is high risk, how to prevent further complications and increase the infant's chances for survival and health. Postpartal families are more concerned with infant care. If the child is not healthy, they want information about special problems to expect and medical care that is required.

### Modeling

**Modeling** is using the behaviors of others as examples by role playing or having the client talk with someone who has mastered a similar crisis. This is an especially effective strategy if the crisis concerns a mother feeling inadequate about her parenting skills. As the mother watches the nurse caring for the infant in a relaxed and comfortable manner, she is encouraged to incorporate these behaviors into her way of functioning.

### Relaxation Techniques

Relaxation techniques are especially valuable for parents who respond to stress with increased tension, feelings of helplessness, withdrawal from caretaking responsibilities, or abusive behaviors. Relaxation techniques are based on the principle of **reciprocal inhibition**, meaning that it is impossible to feel relaxed and tense at the same time. With guidance from the nurse, clients can learn to do relaxation exercises on their own.

The three primary components of relaxation techniques are breathing techniques, muscle relaxation, and imagery. A relaxation exercise may incorporate one or more of these components.

### Crisis Intervention

**Crisis intervention** is perhaps the most important skill that a nurse can use to help families at risk. Crisis intervention is a form of psychotherapy that focuses on the immediate crisis. It is not necessary to know the history or personalities of the people involved. The therapist's role is direct, active, and participating.

The techniques of crisis intervention are relatively simple and do not require extensive training. Since most crises last no longer than four to six weeks, usually one to four crisis intervention sessions are enough.

The primary goals of crisis intervention are to help the client deal with the crisis, regain his or her equilibrium, grow from the experience, and improve coping skills. The specific problem-solving steps involved in situational crisis intervention as outlined by Aguilera and Messick (1986) are similar to the steps of the nursing process.

The first objective in *assessment* of the individual and the problem is to define the situation clearly and identify the crisis-precipitating event. Assessment is then made of the client's perception of the event (whether realistic or distorted), the client's support system, and his or her coping skills.

When the assessment of the immediate crisis is complete, a plan of intervention is developed. This plan is based on how much the crisis has disrupted the individual's or family's life and the feelings of those involved. Tentative approaches are proposed to the individual, examined for their usefulness, and used to restore the person at least to the precrisis level of equilibrium.

The type of *intervention* used by the maternity nurse depends on the nurse's knowledge base about crisis and on his or her flexibility, creativity, and interpersonal skills. The nurse should know the limits of his or her skills and should refer the client to appropriate professionals when that limit is reached.

Therapeutic aspects of crisis counseling include:

● Empathetic listening

● Exploring a client's coping mechanisms

● Identifying and expanding the client's support system

● Encouraging release of tension through nondestructive means such as crying or physical activity

The nurse should be able to assess the potential for destructive behavior toward self or others. This information should be obtained in a gentle but direct way. Using words such as *suicide* will not suggest ideas that are not already being entertained by someone in crisis. If the nurse believes that the client is at risk for destructive behavior, the nurse must notify appropriate agencies that can help the client.

Intervention may include one or more of the following techniques:

● Interpretation and confrontation

● Encouraging the person to express and explore her or his feelings in order to bring those feelings out into the open

● Reassurance and feedback about progress

● Self-disclosure by the counselor

● Assistance in problem solving

Group therapy may be an effective way to avert or resolve a client's crisis. The nurse working with maternity clients does not have to be a trained psychotherapist to use groups effectively. Groups are often an ideal format in which to provide anticipatory guidance about child care or allow parents to express their concerns. Parents who have a preterm infant or child with a congenital anomaly often find the support and shared information from a group of parents in the same situation absolutely invaluable.

No matter how well trained in crisis intervention techniques, a nurse cannot perceive the meaning of a crisis to an individual unless he or she has some understanding of that person's world. Awareness of sociocultural values and attitudes will make any intervention more effective.

## ● Evaluation

*Evaluation* is an ongoing process throughout planning and intervention. Various approaches are tried and discarded or modified depending on their success. The adaptive coping mechanisms that the family has used successfully are reinforced.

## ● LOSS AND GRIEF

Many crises affecting families postpartally involve loss and grief related to fetal/newborn death or loss of "normal" baby, ie, congenital malformation. **Loss** is a state of being deprived of, or being without, something one has had. The most serious loss is the loss of a loved one by death, but such a loss can also occur through divorce or separation. One can also lose an aspect of "self." Loss of health, body parts, pride, and independence are examples of loss of self.

**Grief** is an emotional state, a reaction to loss. Studies have shown that the grief reaction is similar whether the loss is of a loved one or a body part or function.

**Grief work** is the inner process of working through or managing the bereavement (Schoenberg et al 1974). There are five stages in the process:

1. *Disbelief*—In this stage, the person may say, "No, no . . . it can't be."

2. *Questioning*—The person who suffers the loss looks for reasons for the death, asking "What happened?" and "How?"

3. *Anger*—The person may express anger at God, asking "Why did this happen?"

4. *Anger combined with desperation*—The person seems resigned, dismayed, and in despair.

5. *Resolution*—The person accepts the loss.

The duration of the grief process may last up to a year, but the **acute grief** should be over in one or two months. The best indicator of the resolution of acute grief is a gradual return to the preloss level of functioning.

People who do not successfully complete the grief work may have prolonged or distorted grief reactions. For example, delayed grief may occur if affected persons are maintaining the morale of others and therefore are repressing their own reactions.

**Chronic grief** is a response that represents a denial of the reality of the loss. There can be no resolution if there is no acceptance. One manifestation of chronic grief is retaining the lost loved one's belongings as they were during his or her lifetime.

*Anticipatory grief reactions* are seen when there is a threat of death or separation (Lindemann 1944). Because the dynamics of anticipatory grief have much in common with those of acute grief, one might expect that working through anticipatory grief would diminish the acute grief when the loss finally does occur. This may be the case for some, but most people cannot work through the feelings of denial, and hope that the loss will not actually occur.

Those close to the dying person often have ambivalent feelings about the loved one that they find difficult to recognize or accept. The ambivalence may be interpreted as a death wish—which is too unacceptable to admit—and so these feelings are repressed.

Grief work can be helped or hindered by a person's emotional status and by the ability of family members or significant others to allow the expression of grief. The stable family, with healthy coping mechanisms and strong support, both within the family structure and from friends and other ties, can weather the crisis of loss. However, the high-risk family that does not have either the internal strength or support from extended family and friends may need help and support from other sources, including the health care team.

The maternity nurse may be involved with clients who are grieving for a loss. Parents grieve after the birth of an infant with a congenital anomaly and mourn the loss of the normal infant they dreamed would be theirs. Intense grief usually attends the death of a newborn. Even parents who had a strong preference for the sex of their unborn child may experience a brief period of sorrow after the birth of the "wrong sex" infant.

Occasionally a nurse may become frustrated with parents who mourn a minor anomaly or the gender of a child. The nurse may feel that the parents should be happy they have a healthy child. It is important to realize, however, that parents must mourn the idealized infant before they can begin to form a strong attachment with their actual infant. The nurse's acceptance and support promote attachment between the parents and child.

In the remainder of this chapter, selected high-risk perinatal situations are considered and methods of nursing management are described.

## ● LOSS OF NEWBORN

The loss of a newborn evokes intense mourning reactions whether the baby lives an hour, several days, or is stillborn; whether the baby is a nonviable 500-g fetus or a full-term 4000-g infant; whether the baby is planned or not. Both parents show the same grief reactions, although the father may have more difficulty expressing his grief. He may be suppressing his own feelings and delaying his grief work while supporting and comforting the mother.

The couple dealing with the loss of a newborn will feel anger, guilt, pain, and sadness. However, because they have had little or no time to know the child as a person, the soothing part of the mourning process—"identification" built on memories, shared experiences, and living together—is absent.

The following example of Mary, a woman who lost her newborn and then later had two healthy children, relates some of the feelings associated with the loss of an infant. Through experiences like Mary's nursing has become attuned to the needs of families undergoing this crisis. See p 822 for care of the family with fetal/newborn loss.

## One Family's Story

*One day I was working, feeling happy and healthy, and the next day I found myself in the hospital, having given birth to our baby almost three months early. There were no warning signs. On all my prenatal visits the doctor assured me "everything was fine." I started bleeding in the morning and when it didn't stop, the doctor advised that I be admitted to the hospital. I was terrified because I knew if I went into labor now, the baby might not live. As I lay there on the bed, with blood infusing in one arm and an intravenous line in the other, thoughts were racing through my head. Primarily I thought about whether the baby was going to die or live through all of this. Certain things in my environment seemed to fade into oblivion and other things became very intense. One of the nurses caring for me had a terrible cold, and I kept thinking "I wish she would leave the room" because I was sure that on top of everything else I would catch that cold. I was feeling very vulnerable.*

*The bleeding continued, and contractions started. After it became obvious that the baby would be born, my concerns changed. I began to worry about whether the baby would be all right if it lived. I thought that if the baby was going to be retarded or deformed, I wanted it to die instead. I remember feeling very guilty about these thoughts, especially after Beth did not live. I wondered if we could afford long hospitalizations and care if they would be needed. During the entire time, my husband was supportive and comforting, although seemingly overwhelmed by everything.*

*When I was taken into the delivery room, it was as if I were progressing through a normal delivery. After Beth was born, they let me look at her and touch her very briefly before rushing her off for special care. I remember saying "She's so beautiful." That moment was the highlight of the entire experience for me. I recapture the sight frequently. The next day the doctor told me that the baby's weight was a positive factor (slightly over 3 lb), but that her lungs were not well developed. It was too early for him to talk about her prognosis. When I asked if I could go in to see her, he said he preferred that I did not. How I wish I would have had the assertiveness to take the matter into my own hands and insist, but I had no self-direction and seemed to be waiting for others to tell me what to do next. This feeling was in sharp contrast to my normal way of functioning.*

*In the morning the woman who takes the baby pictures came in to get permission from mothers to photograph babies. I was very excited about the prospect, but when she learned the baby wasn't in the regular nursery, she said it probably wouldn't be possible to photograph her. I was so disappointed. The mother in the bed next to me was receiving her baby for feedings, and I felt so alone and so empty during those times. We named our baby and started hoping and believing that she was going to be all right. The ambivalence was overwhelming—wanting to hold and love her, but knowing that if we became too attached, the hurt would be greater if we lost her.*

(continues)

*I felt very angry that everyone else seemed to be having healthy babies. I was an intelligent, competent woman. Why was I so inadequate at this? When friends and relatives called I tried to tell them what a beautiful baby we had but that she was born early. My husband visited her, and I pried every bit of information out of him that I could about her progress.*

*Later that day, the doctor came in and told me that Beth had died. My husband came and we cried and cried. Other than having him there, nothing seemed to comfort. One of the staff came in and asked what we wanted to do with her body. That came as a shock. Somehow I never thought of having to make a decision like that. We decided to bury her near my grandparents. It was critically important to me that she had been baptized, and the nurses assured me that she had been baptized shortly after delivery.*

*My husband took me home from the hospital empty-armed. My feelings were very confusing. I felt guilty—thinking that perhaps if I had stopped working earlier or had called the doctor earlier things would have been different. I was angry. I was sad. I wondered if we would ever have other children. A neighbor had hand-crocheted some beautiful white baby clothes before I went to the hospital, and she told me to keep them—that was very meaningful and I got them out and looked at them many times. When I got back to work, people who knew I was pregnant but hadn't heard the outcome asked about the baby. I had to tell them.*

## ● CARE OF THE FAMILY WITH FETAL/NEWBORN LOSS

The death of an infant evokes powerful reactions in both parents and health care professionals. Sadness, shock, and anger may be felt by parents and staff alike. However, it is imperative that nurses learn to deal with their feelings so that they can be supportive of the family.

### ● Nursing Assessment

When a fetus or newborn dies, the nurse assesses the family's ability to adapt to their loss. Open communication between the mother, her partner, and the health team members contributes to a more realistic understanding of the medical condition and its associated treatments. The nurse may discuss prior experiences the family has had with stress and what they feel were their coping abilities at that time. Determining what social supports and resources the family has is also important.

Parents who have lost an infant suffer a devastating experience, precipitating an intense emotional trauma. During the pregnancy, the couple has already begun the attachment process, which now must be terminated through the grieving process. The behaviors that couples exhibit while mourning may be associated with the five stages of grieving described by Elizabeth Kübler-Ross

(1969). Often the first stage is *denial* of the death of the fetus. Even when the initial health care provider suspects fetal demise, the couple is hoping that a second opinion will be different. Some couples may not be convinced of the death until they view and hold the infant's body. The second stage is *anger*, resulting from the feelings of loss, loneliness, and perhaps guilt. The anger may be projected at significant others and health team members, or it may be omitted when the death of the fetus is sudden and unexpected. *Bargaining*, the third stage, may or may not be present depending on the couple's preparation for the death of the fetus. Bargaining is the person's attempt to postpone the inevitable, asking for additional time. If the death is unanticipated, the couple may have no time for bargaining. In the fourth stage, *depression* is evidenced by preoccupation, weeping, and withdrawal. Physiologic postpartal depression appearing 24 to 48 hours after delivery may compound the depression of grief. The final stage is *acceptance*, which involves the process of resolution. This is a highly individualized process that may take months to complete.

### ● Nursing Diagnosis

Nursing diagnoses that may apply to a family with a fetal/newborn loss may include:

- Dysfunctional grieving related to an actual loss
- Altered family processes related to loss of a family member
- Ineffective individual coping related to depression in response to loss of child
- Ineffective family coping related to death of a child
- Anxiety related to death of a child

### ● Nursing Plan and Implementation
#### PROVISION OF EMOTIONAL SUPPORT TO THE FAMILY

In some facilities, a checklist is used to make sure important aspects of working with the parents are addressed. The checklist becomes a communication tool between staff members to share information particular to this couple (Beckey et al 1985, Carr and Knupp 1985). Such a checklist might include the following items:

- When the fetal death is known before admission, inform the admission department and nursing staff so that inappropriate remarks are not made.
- Allow the woman and her partner to remain together as much as they wish. Provide privacy by assigning them to a private room.
- Stay with the couple and do not leave them alone and isolated.

● As much as possible, have the same nurse provide care to increase the support for the couple. Develop a care plan to provide for continuity of care.

● Have the most experienced labor and delivery nurse auscultate for fetal heart tones. This avoids the searching that a more inexperienced nurse might feel compelled to do. Avoid the temptation to listen again "to make sure" (Whitaker 1986).

● When fetal death is confirmed by ultrasound there may not be a need to ascertain fetal heart tone.

● Listen to the couple; do not offer explanations. They require solace without minimizing the situation.

● Facilitate the woman and her partner's participation in the labor and birth process. When possible, allow them to make decisions about who will be present and what ritual will occur during the birth process. Allow the woman to make the decision regarding whether to have sedation during labor and birth. Provide a quiet supportive environment; ideally the labor and birth should occur in a labor room or possibly a birthing room rather than the delivery room.

● Keep the woman comfortable, especially if she must go through labor and birth. Use breathing and relaxation techniques, medication.

● Give parents accurate information regarding plans for labor and birth.

● Provide ongoing opportunities for the couple to ask questions.

● Arrange for the woman to be assigned to a room that is away from new mothers and babies. Let the woman decide if she wants to be on another unit. If early discharge is an option, allow the family to make that selection.

● Encourage the couple to experience the grief that they feel. Accept the weeping and depression. A couple may have intense feelings that they are unable to share with each other. Encourage them to talk together and allow emotions to show freely.

● Give the couple an opportunity to see and hold the infant in a private quiet location. (Advocates of seeing the infant believe that viewing assists in dispelling denial and enables the couple to progress to the next step in the grieving process.) If they choose to see their infant, prepare the couple for what they will see by saying "the baby is cold," "the baby is blue," "the baby is bruised," or other appropriate statements.

● Some families may elect to bathe or dress their infant; support them in their choice.

● Take a photograph of the infant, and let the family know it is available if they want it now or some time in the future.

● Offer a card with footprints, crib card, ID band, and possibly a lock of hair to the parents. These items may be kept with the photo if the parents do not want them at this time (Beckey et al 1985).

● Prepare the couple for returning home. If there are siblings, each will progress through age-appropriate grieving. Provide the parents with information about normal mourning reactions, both psychologic and physiologic.

● Furnish the mother with educational materials that discuss the changes she will experience in returning to the nonpregnant state.

● Provide information about community support groups including group name, contact person if possible, and phone number. Use materials such as the book *When Hello Means Goodbye* by Schwiebert and Kirk (1985).

● Remember it is not so important to "say the right words." The caring support and human contact that a couple receives is important and can be conveyed through silence and your presence.

The nurse experiences many of the same grief reactions as the parents of a stillborn infant. It is important to have support persons and colleagues available for counseling and support.

## ● Evaluation

Nursing care is effective if:

● The family members express their feelings about the death of their baby.

● The family participates in decisions regarding whether to see their baby and in other decisions regarding the baby.

● The family has resources available for continued support.

● The family knows the community resources available and has names and phone numbers to use if they choose.

● The family is moving into and through the grieving process.

## ● CARE OF FAMILY WITH BIRTH OF AN AT-RISK NEWBORN

The birth of a preterm or ill infant or an infant with a congenital anomaly is a serious crisis situation for a family. Acute grief reactions follow the loss of the perfect baby they have fantasized. In the case of a preterm birth, the mother is denied the last few weeks of pregnancy that seem to prepare her psychologically for the stress of birth and the attachment process. Attachment at this time is fragile, and interruption of the process by separation can affect the future mother-child relationship.

Feelings of guilt and failure often plague mothers of preterm newborns. They may ask themselves "Why did labor start? What did I do (or not do)?" A woman may have guilt fantasies, and wonder "Was it because I had sexual intercourse with my husband (a week, three days, a day) ago?" "Was it because I carried three loads of wash up from the basement?" "Am I being punished for something done in the past—even in childhood?"

The birth of the newborn with congenital abnormalities also engenders feelings of guilt and failure. As in the birth of a preterm infant, the woman may entertain ideas of personal guilt: "What did I do (or not do) to cause this?" "Am I being punished for something?"

Parental reactions and steps of attachment are altered by the birth of a preterm infant or one with a congenital anomaly. A variety of new feelings, reactions, and stresses must be recognized and dealt with before the family can work toward the establishment of a healthy parent-infant relationship.

Although reactions and steps of attachment are altered by the birth of these infants, a healthy parent-child relationship can occur. Kaplan and Mason (1974) have identified four psychologic tasks as essential for coping with the stress of an at-risk newborn and for providing a basis for the maternal-infant relationship:

1. Anticipatory grief as a psychologic preparation for possible loss of the child, while still hoping for his or her survival.

2. Acknowledgment of maternal failure to produce a term or perfect newborn expressed as anticipatory grief and depression and lasting until the chances of survival seem secure.

3. Resumption of the process of relating to the infant, which was interrupted by the threat of nonsurvival. This task may be impaired by continuous threat of death or abnormality, and the mother may be slow in her response of hope for the infant's survival.

4. Understanding of the special needs and growth patterns of the at-risk newborn, which are temporary and yield to normal patterns.

Klaus and Kennell (1982), on the other hand, feel that with extra, sustained support and early contact with her infant a mother need not necessarily become involved in anticipatory preparation for her child's possible death.

Most authorities agree that the birth of a preterm infant or a less-than-perfect infant does require major adjustments as the parents are forced to surrender the image they had nurtured for so long of their ideal child.

Solnit and Stark (1961) postulate that grief and mourning over the loss of the loved object—the idealized child—mark parental reactions to a child with abnormalities. Simultaneously, parents must adopt the imperfect child as the new love object. Parental responses to a child with health problems may be viewed as a five-staged process (Klaus and Kennell 1982):

1. *Shock* is felt at the reality of the birth of this child. This stage may be characterized by forgetfulness, amnesia of the situation, and a feeling of desperation.

2. There is disbelief (*denial*) of the reality of the situation, characterized by a refusal to believe the child is defective. This stage is exemplified by assertions that "It didn't really happen!" "There has been a mistake; it's someone else's baby."

3. *Depression* over the reality of the situation and a corresponding grief reaction follows acceptance of the situation. This stage is characterized by much crying and sadness. Anger about the reality of the situation may also occur at this stage. A projection of blame on others or on self and feelings of "not me" are characteristic of this stage.

4. Equilibrium and *acceptance* are characteristic of a decrease in the emotional reactions of the parents. This stage is variable and may be prolonged because of a prolongation of the threat to the infant's survival. Some parents experience chronic sorrow in relation to their child.

5. *Reorganization* of the family is necessary to deal with the child's problems. Mutual support of the parents facilitates this process, but the crisis of the situation may precipitate alienation between the parental partners.

These stages of parental adjustment are similar to the stages of dying and of grieving. Indeed, reorganization is necessary to deal with a crisis concerning a newborn at risk.

In the birth of either an infant with an anomaly or a preterm infant, the process of mourning is necessary for attachment to the less-than-perfect child. Grief work, the emotional reaction to a significant loss, must occur before adequate attachment to the actual child is possible. Parental detachment precedes parental attachment.

## ● Nursing Assessment

Development of a nurse-family relationship facilitates information gathering in areas of concern. A concurrent illness of the mother or other family members or other concurrent stress (lack of hospitalization insurance, loss of job, age of parents) may alter the family response to the baby. Feelings of apprehension, guilt, failure, and grief that are verbally or nonverbally expressed are important aspects of the nursing history. These observations enable all professionals to be aware of the parental state, coping behaviors, and readiness for attachment, bonding, and care-taking. Appropriate nursing observations during interviewing and relating to the family include:

1. *Level of understanding.* Observations concerning the ability to assimilate information given and to ask appropriate questions; the need for constant repetition of "the same" information

2. *Behavioral responses.* Appropriateness of behavior in relation to information given; lack of response; "flat" affect

3. *Difficulties with communication.* Deafness (reads lips only); blindness; dysphagia; understanding only of foreign language

4. *Paternal and maternal education level.* Parents

unable to read or write; only eighth grade completed; mother an MD, RN, or PhD; and so on

Documentation of such information, obtained by the nurse through continuing contact and development of a therapeutic family relationship, enables all professionals to understand and use the nursing history in providing continuous individual care.

Visiting and care-giving patterns give an indication of the level or lack of parental attachment. A record of visits, caretaking procedures, affect (in relating to the newborn), and telephone calls is essential. Serial observations must be obtained, rather than just isolated instances of concern. Grant (1978) has developed a conceptual framework depicting adaptive and maladaptive responses to parenting of a preterm or less-than-perfect infant (Figure 28.1).

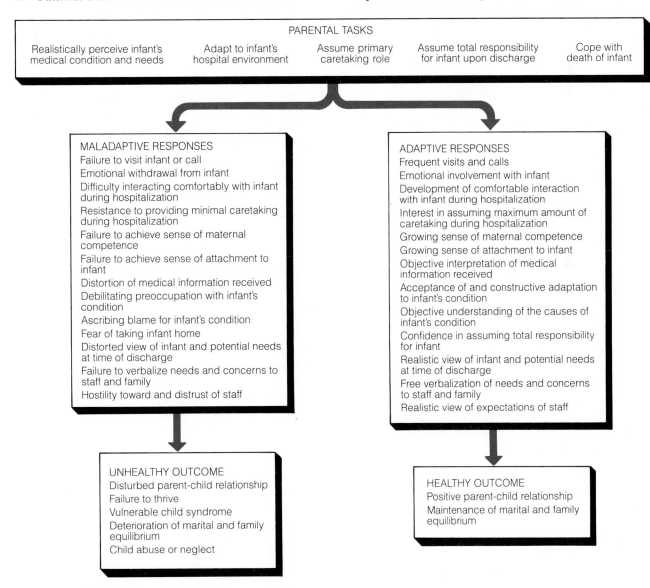

*Figure 28.1   Maladaptive and adaptive parental responses during crisis period, showing unhealthy and healthy outcomes (From Grant P: Psychological needs of families of high-risk infants. Fam Comm Health 1978; 11:93; by permission of Aspen Systems Corporation.)*

If a pattern of distancing behaviors evolves, appropriate intervention should be instituted. Follow-up studies have found that a statistically significant number of preterm, sick, and congenitally defective infants suffer from failure to thrive, battering, or other disorders of mothering. Early detection and intervention will prevent these aberrations in mothering behaviors from leading to irreparable damage or death.

## ● Nursing Diagnosis

Nursing diagnoses that may apply to the family of a newborn at risk include:

● Dysfunctional grieving related to loss of idealized newborn

● Fear related to emotional involvement with an at-risk newborn

● Altered parenting related to impaired bonding secondary to feelings of inadequacy about caretaking activities

## ● Nursing Plan and Implementation

### PREPARATION OF PARENTS FOR INITIAL VIEWING OF NEWBORN

Before parents see their child, the nurse must prepare them for the viewing. It is important that a positive, realistic attitude regarding the infant be presented to the parents rather than a pessimistic one. An overly negative, fatalistic attitude further alienates the parents from their infant and retards attachment behaviors. Instead of allowing attachment and bonding to develop, the mother will begin the process of anticipatory grieving, and once started, this process is difficult to reverse.

In preparing parents for the first view of their infant, it is important for a professional to have looked at the baby. The parents should be prepared to see both the deviations and the normal aspects of their infant. All infants exhibit strengths as well as deficiencies. The nurse may say, "Your baby is small, about the length of my two hands. She weighs 2 lb, 3 oz but is very active and cries when we disturb her. She is having some difficulty breathing but is breathing without assistance and in only 35% oxygen."

The equipment being used for the at-risk newborn and its purpose should be described before the parents enter the intensive care unit. Many intensive care units have booklets for parents to read before entering the unit. Through explanations and pictures, the parents can be better prepared to deal with the feelings they may experience when they see their infant for the first time.

### SUPPORT OF PARENTS DURING THEIR INITIAL VIEWING OF THE NEWBORN

Upon entering the unit, parents may be overwhelmed by the sounds of monitors, alarms, and respirators, as well as by the unfamiliar language and "foreign" atmosphere. It is more reassuring when parents are prepared and accompanied to the unit by the same person(s). The primary nurse and physician caring for the newborn should be with the parents when they first visit their baby. Parental reactions are varied, but there is usually an element of initial shock. Provision of chairs and time to regain composure will assist the parents. Slow, complete, and simple explanations—first about the infant and then about the equipment—allay fear and anxiety.

As parents attempt to deal with the initial stages of shock and grief, they may fail to grasp new information. The parents may need repeated explanations in order to accept the reality of the situation, procedures, equipment, and the infant's condition on subsequent visits.

Misconceptions about equipment and its placement on the infant and about its potential harm are common. Such statements as "Does the fluid go into the brain?" "Does the white wire on the abdomen go into the stomach?" and "Does the monitor make the baby's heart beat?" imply much fear for the infant's safety and misconception about the machines. These worries are easily overcome by simple explanations of all equipment being used.

Concern about the infant's physical appearance is common, yet may remain unvoiced. Parents may express such concerns as "He looks so small and red—like a drowned rat." "Why do her genitals look so abnormal?" "Will that awful looking mouth [cleft lip and palate] ever be normal?" Such questions need to be anticipated by the nurse and addressed. Use of pictures, such as of an infant after cleft lip repair, may be reassuring to doubting parents. Knowledge of the development of a "normal" preterm infant will allow the nurse to make reassuring statements such as "The baby's labia may look very abnormal to you, but they are normal for her maturity. As she grows, the outer lips of the labia will become larger and the clitoris will be covered and the genitals will then look as you expect them to. She is normal for her level of maturity."

The tone of the neonatal intensive care unit is set by the nursing staff. Development of a safe, trusting environment depends on viewing the parents as essential care givers, not as visitors or nuisances in the unit. Provision of chairs, privacy when needed, and easy access to staff and facilities are all important in developing an open, comfortable environment. An uncrowded and welcoming atmosphere lets parents know "You are welcome here." However, even in crowded physical surroundings, an attitude of openness and trust can be conveyed by the nursing staff.

A trusting relationship is essential for collaborative efforts in caring for the infant. Nurses must therapeutically use their own responses to relate on a one-to-one basis with the parents. Each individual has different needs, different ways of adapting to crisis, and different means of support. Professionals must use techniques that are real and spontaneous to them and avoid adopting words or actions that are foreign to them. Nurses must also gauge their interventions to match the parents' pace and needs.

Powell (1981) suggests several positive strategies that increase the effectiveness of nursing interventions with parents:

- Problem solve with the family rather than giving advice.
- View the baby as a total individual rather than emphasizing the problem.
- Observe the uniqueness of the newborn rather than stereotyping or labeling the newborn as slow, unmanageable, etc.
- Avoid labeling parents as inadequate, rejecting, or angry.
- Stress the baby's similarities to other babies.
- Stress strengths and competence of parents.
- Help parents realize that they are in charge of their children and themselves.
- Be aware of the needs of all members of the family, including siblings.

## FACILITATION OF ATTACHMENT

It is essential that the mother be reunited with her infant as soon as possible after birth so that:

1. She knows that her infant is alive.
2. She knows what the infant's real problems are. Early acquaintance between mother and infant allows a realistic perspective of the baby's condition.
3. She can begin the grief work over the loss of the idealized child and begin the process of attachment to the actual child.
4. She can share the experience of the infant's problems with the father, who may have already seen and touched the infant.

## FACILITATION OF ATTACHMENT IF NEONATAL TRANSPORT OCCURS

If the newborn must be moved to a regional center, the nurse should ensure that the mother sees the infant before transport.

Bringing the mother to the nursery or taking the infant in a warmed transport incubator to the mother's bedside will allow her to see the infant before transportation to the center. When the infant reaches the referral center, a staff member should call the parents with information about the infant's condition during transport, safe arrival at the center, and present condition.

Support of parents, with explanations from the professional staff, is crucial. Occasionally the mother may be unable to see the infant before transport, for example, if she is still under general anesthesia or experiencing complica-

tions such as shock, hemorrhage, or seizures. In these cases, before the infant is transported a photograph of the infant should be taken to be given to the mother, along with an explanation of the infant's condition, problems, and a detailed description of the infant's characteristics, to facilitate the attachment process until the mother can visit. An additional photograph is also helpful for the father to share with siblings and/or the extended family. With the increased attention to improved fetal outcome, prenatal maternal transports, rather than neonatal transports, are occurring more frequently. This practice gives the mother of an at-risk infant the opportunity to visit and care for her infant during the early postpartal period.

## PROMOTION OF TOUCHING

Parents visiting a small or sick infant may need several visits to become comfortable and confident in their abilities to touch the infant without injuring her or him. Barriers such as incubators, incisions, monitor electrodes, and tubes may delay the mother's confidence. Knowledge of this "normal" delay in touching behavior will enable the nurse to understand parental behavior.

Klaus and Kennell (1982) have demonstrated a significant difference in the amount of eye contact and touching behaviors of mothers of normal newborns and mothers of preterm infants. Whereas mothers of normal newborns progress within minutes to palm contact of the infant's trunk, the mother of a preterm infant is slower to progress from fingertip to palm contact and from the extremities to the trunk. The progression to palm contact with the infant's trunk may take several visits to the nursery.

Through support, reassurance, and encouragement, the nurse can facilitate the mother's positive feelings about her ability and her importance to her infant. Touching facilitates "getting to know" the infant and thus establishes a bond with the infant. Touching as well as seeing the infant helps the mother to realize the "normals" and potentials of her baby (Figure 28.2).

The nurse can also encourage parents to meet their newborn's need for stimulation. Stroking, rocking, cuddling, singing, and talking should be an integral part of the parents' caretaking responsibilities.

## FACILITATION OF PARENTAL CARETAKING

Bonding can be facilitated by encouraging parents to visit and become involved in their baby's care (Figure 28.3). When visiting is impossible, the parents should feel free to phone whenever they wish to receive information about their baby. A warm, receptive attitude on the part of the nurse is very supportive. Nurses can also facilitate parenting by personalizing a baby to the parents, by referring to the infant by name, or by relating personal behavioral characteristics to the parents. Remarks such as

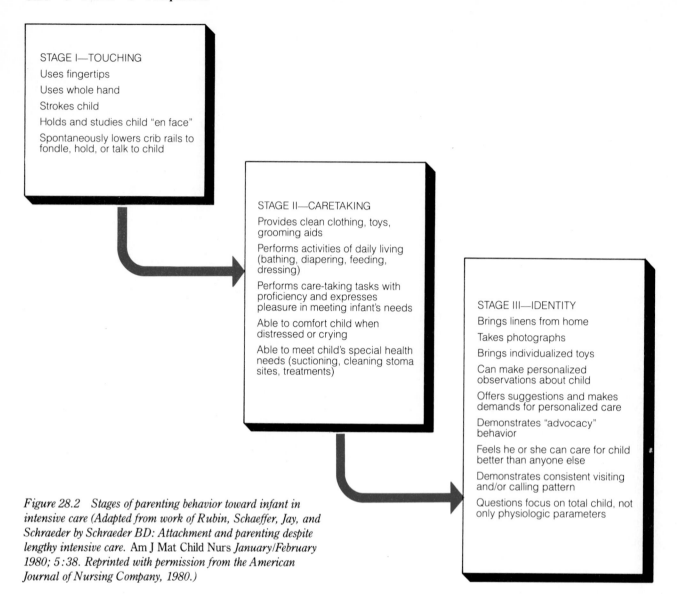

STAGE I—TOUCHING
Uses fingertips
Uses whole hand
Strokes child
Holds and studies child "en face"
Spontaneously lowers crib rails to fondle, hold, or talk to child

STAGE II—CARETAKING
Provides clean clothing, toys, grooming aids
Performs activities of daily living (bathing, diapering, feeding, dressing)
Performs care-taking tasks with proficiency and expresses pleasure in meeting infant's needs
Able to comfort child when distressed or crying
Able to meet child's special health needs (suctioning, cleaning stoma sites, treatments)

STAGE III—IDENTITY
Brings linens from home
Takes photographs
Brings individualized toys
Can make personalized observations about child
Offers suggestions and makes demands for personalized care
Demonstrates "advocacy" behavior
Feels he or she can care for child better than anyone else
Demonstrates consistent visiting and/or calling pattern
Questions focus on total child, not only physiologic parameters

*Figure 28.2   Stages of parenting behavior toward infant in intensive care (Adapted from work of Rubin, Schaeffer, Jay, and Schraeder by Schraeder BD: Attachment and parenting despite lengthy intensive care. Am J Mat Child Nurs January/February 1980; 5:38. Reprinted with permission from the American Journal of Nursing Company, 1980.)*

"Jenny loves her pacifier" help make the infant more individual and unique.

Caretaking may be delayed for the mother of a preterm, defective, or sick infant. The variety of equipment needed for life support is hardly conducive to anxiety-free caretaking by the parents. However, even the sickest infant may be cared for, if even in a small way, by the parents. As a facilitator of parental caretaking, it is the responsibility of the nurse to promote the parents' success. Demonstration and explanation, followed by support of the parents in initial caretaking behaviors, positively reinforce this behavior. Changing the infant's diaper, giving their infant skin care or oral care, or helping the nurse turn the infant may at first be anxiety-provoking for the parents, but they will become more comfortable and confident in caretaking and receive satisfaction from the baby's reactions and their ability "to do something." Complimenting

the parents' competence in caretaking also increases their self-esteem, which has received recent "blows" of guilt and failure. It is vitally important that the parents never be given a task if there is any possibility that they will not be able to accomplish it.

Often mothers of high-risk infants have ambivalent feelings toward the nurse. As the mother watches the nurse competently perform the caretaking tasks, she feels both grateful for the nurse's abilities and expertise and jealous of the nurse's ability to care for her infant. These feelings may be acted out in criticism of the care being received by the infant, manipulation of staff, or personal guilt. Instead of fostering (by silence) these inferiority feelings within mothers, nurses should recognize such feelings and intervene appropriately to enhance mother-infant bonding.

Nurses who are understanding and secure will be able

to support the parents' egos instead of collecting rewards for themselves. To reinforce positive parenting behaviors, professionals must first believe in the importance of the parents. The nurse can hardly convince doubting parents of their importance to the infant unless the nurse really believes it. Both attitudes and words must say: "You are a good mother/father. You have an important contribution to make to the care of your infant." Unless as much care is taken in facilitating parental attachment as in providing physiologic care, the outcome will not be a healthy family.

Verbalizations by the nurse that improve parental self-esteem are essential and easily shared. The nurse can point out that, in addition to physiologic use, breast milk is important because of the emotional investment of the mother. Pumping, storing, labeling, and delivering quantities of breast milk is time-consuming and a "labor of love" for mothers. Positive remarks regarding breast milk reinforce the maternal behavior of caretaking and providing for her infant: "Breast milk is something that only you can give your baby" or "You really have brought a lot of milk today" or "Look how rich this breast milk is" or "Even small amounts of milk are important, and look how rich it is."

If the infant begins to gain weight while being fed breast milk, it is important to point this out to the mother. Parents should also be advised that initial weight loss with beginning nipple feedings is common because of the increased energy expended when the infant begins active rather than passive nutritional intake.

Provision of care by the parents is appropriate even for very sick or defective infants who are likely to die. It has been found that detachment is easier after attachment, because the parents are comforted by the knowledge that they did all they could for their child while he or she was alive.

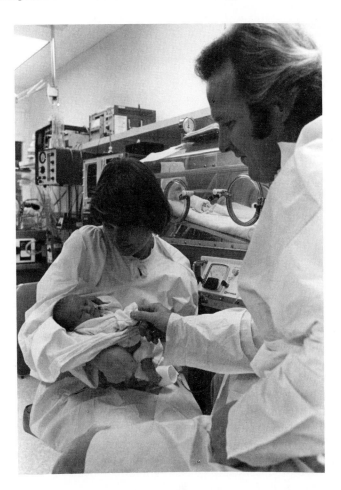

*Figure 28.3  It is important that the parents of high-risk infants be given the opportunity to get acquainted with their children. Physical contact is extremely important in the bonding process and should be encouraged whenever possible.*

## PROVISION OF CONTINUITY IN INFORMATION GIVING

During crisis, maintenance of interpersonal relationships is difficult. Yet in a newborn intensive care area, the parents are expected to relate to many different care providers. It is important that parents have as few professionals as possible relaying information to them. A primary nurse should coordinate and provide continuity in information giving to parents. Care providers are individuals and thus will use different terms, inflections, and attitudes. These subtle differences are monumental to parents and only confuse, confound, and produce anxiety. Several relationships with trusted professionals minimize unnecessary anxiety and concern and facilitate open communication. The nurse not only functions as a liaison between the parents and the wide variety of professionals interacting with the infant and parents but also offers clarification, explanation, interpretation of information, and support to the parents.

## USE OF THE FAMILY'S SUPPORT SYSTEM

The parents should be encouraged to deal with the crisis with help from their support system. The support system attempts to meet the emotional needs and provide support for the family members in crisis and stress situations. Biologic kinship is not the only valid criterion for a support system; an emotional kinship is the most important factor. In our mobile society of isolated nuclear families, the support system may be a next-door neighbor, a best friend, or perhaps a school chum.

The nurse must search out the significant others in the lives of the parents and help them understand the problems so that they can be a constant parental support.

## FACILITATION OF FAMILY ADJUSTMENT

The impact of the crisis on the family is individual and varied.

Information about the ability of the family to adapt to the situation is obtained through the nurse-family relationship. The birth of the infant (normal newborn, preterm infant, infant with congenital anomaly) should be viewed as it is defined by the family, and appropriate intervention can then be instituted.

Because the family is a unit composed of individuals who must deal with the situation, it is important to encourage open intrafamily communication. Secret-keeping should not be encouraged, especially between spouses, because secrets undermine the trust of their relationship. Well-meaning rationales such as "I want to protect her," "I don't want him to worry about it," and so on can be destructive to open communication and to the basic element of a relationship—trust.

The nurse should encourage open communication between family members, particularly between spouses. Open communication is especially important when the mother is hospitalized apart from the infant. The father is the first to visit the infant and relays information regarding the infant's care and condition to the mother. In this situation, the mother has had minimal contact, if any, with her infant. Because of her anxiety and isolation, she may mistrust all those who provide information (the father, nurse, physician, or extended family) until she can see the infant for herself. This can put tremendous stress on the relationship between spouses. The parents (and family) should be given information together. This practice helps overcome misunderstandings and misinterpretations and promotes mutual "working through" of problems.

The entire family—siblings as well as relatives—should be encouraged to visit and receive information about the baby. Methods of intervention in assisting the family to cope with the situation include providing support, confronting the crisis, and understanding the reality. Support, explanations, and the helping role must extend to the kin network, as well as to the nuclear family, in an attempt to aid them in communication and support ties with the nuclear family.

The needs of siblings should not be overlooked. They have been looking forward to the new baby, and they too suffer a degree of loss. Young children may react with hostility and older ones with shame at the birth of an infant with an anomaly. Both reactions make them feel guilty. Parents, preoccupied with working through their own feelings, often cannot give the other children the attention and support they need. Sometimes another child becomes the focus of family tension. Anxiety thus directed can take the form of finding fault or of overconcern. This is a form of denial; the parents cannot face the real worry—the infant at risk. After assessing the situation, the observant nurse could see that another family member or friend steps in and gives the needed support to the siblings of the affected baby.

Desires and needs of the individuals must be respected and facilitated; differences are tolerable and should be able to exist side by side. Eliciting the parents' feelings is easily accomplished with the question: "How are you doing?" The emphasis is on *you,* and the interest must be sincere.

Families with children in the newborn intensive care unit become friends and support one another. To encourage the development of these friendships and to provide support, many units have established parent groups. The core of the groups consists of parents who previously have had an infant in the intensive care unit. Most groups make contact with families within a day or two of the infant's admission to the unit, either through phone calls or visits to the hospital. Early one-on-one parent contacts help families work through their feelings better than discussion groups. This personalized method gives the grieving parents an opportunity to express personal feelings about the pregnancy, labor, and delivery and their "different than expected" infant with others who have experienced the same feelings and with whom they can identify (Elsas 1981).

## PROVISION OF PREDISCHARGE TEACHING

Predischarge planning begins once the infant's condition becomes stable and indications suggest the newborn will survive. Adequate predischarge teaching will help the parents to transform their feelings of inadequacy and competition with the nurse into feelings of self-assurance and attachment. From the beginning the parents should be taught about their infant's special needs and growth patterns. This teaching and involvement is best facilitated by a nurse who is familiar with the infant and his or her family over a period of time and who has developed a comfortable and supportive relationship with them.

The nurse's responsibility is to provide instructions in an optimal environment for parental learning. Learning should take place over time, to avoid the necessity of bombarding the parents with instructions in the day or hour before discharge.

Teaching and learning methods are used in assessment of parental readiness to learn. Parents often enjoy doing minimal caretaking tasks with gradual expansion of their role.

Many intensive care units provide facilities for parents to room-in with their infants for a few days before discharge. This allows parents a degree of independence in the care of their infant with the security of nursing help nearby. This practice is particularly helpful for anxious parents, parents who have not had the opportunity to spend extended time with their infant, or parents who will be giving complex physical care at home, such as tracheostomy care.

The basic elements of predischarge care are as follows:

1. Teaching parents routine well-baby care, such as

bathing, temperature taking, formula preparation, breast-feeding.

2. Training parents to do special procedures as needed by the newborn, such as gavage or gastrostomy feedings, tracheostomy or enterostomy care, medication administration, cardiopulmonary resuscitation (CPR), and operation of apnea monitor. Before discharge, the parents should be as comfortable as possible with these tasks and should demonstrate independence. Written tools and instructions are useful for parents to refer to once they are home with the infant, but these should not replace actual participation in the infant's care.

3. Referring parents to community health and support organizations. The visiting nurses' association, public health nurses, or social services can assist the parents in the stressful transition from hospital to home by providing the necessary home teaching and support. Some intensive care nurseries have their own parent support groups to help bridge the gap between hospital and home care. Parents can also find support from a variety of community support organizations, such as mothers of twins groups, trisomy 13 clubs, March of Dimes Birth Defects Foundation, handicapped children services, and teen mother and child programs. Each community has numerous agencies capable of assisting the family in adapting emotionally, physically, and financially to the chronically ill infant. The nurse should be familiar with community resources and help the parents identify which agencies may benefit them.

4. Helping parents recognize the growth and development needs of their infant. A development program begun in the hospital can be continued at home, or parents may be referred to an infant development program in the community.

5. Arranging medical follow-up care before discharge. The infant may need to be followed up by a family pediatrician, a well-baby clinic, or a specialty clinic. The first appointment should be made before the infant is discharged from the hospital.

6. Evaluating the need for special equipment for infant care (such as a respirator, oxygen, apnea monitor) in the home. Any extra equipment or supplies should be placed in the home before the infant's discharge. The nurse can be instrumental in helping the parents assess the newborn's needs and coordinate services.

Further evaluation after the infant has gone home is useful in determining whether the crisis has been resolved satisfactorily. The parents are usually given the intensive care nursery's telephone number to call for support and advice. It is suggested that the staff follow up each family with visits or telephone calls at intervals for several weeks to assess and evaluate the infant's (and parents') progress.

## • Evaluation

Nursing care is effective if:

- The parents are able to verbalize their feelings of grief and loss.
- The parents verbalize their concerns about their baby's health problems, care needs, and potential outcome.
- The parents are able to participate in their infant's care and show attachment behaviors.

## • CARE OF FAMILIES WITH ATTACHMENT PROBLEMS

During the past 20 years a body of evidence has grown that clearly demonstrates that the most common element in the lives of parents who neglect or abuse their children is a "lack of empathic mothering" in their own lives (Steele and Pollack 1982). This phrase describes inadequate responses of the caretaker to the infant, frequently beginning in the perinatal period and related to poorly developed maternal-infant attachment or insufficient bonding (Kempe and Helfer 1982). Because of this finding, attention has been given to the promotion of adequate parent-infant bonding to prevent malattachment and its related sequelae. Factors that may retard the formation of maternal-infant attachment include "an abnormal pregnancy, an abnormal labor or delivery, neonatal separation, other separation in the first six months, illnesses in the infant during the first year of life, and illnesses in the mother during the first year of life" (Kempe and Helfer 1982).

## • Nursing Assessment

In the prenatal period, warning signs that may indicate lack of acceptance and a potential for malattachment include the following (Kempe and Helfer 1982):

- Negative maternal self-perception
- Excessive mood swings or emotional withdrawal
- Failure to respond to quickening
- Excessive maternal preoccupation with appearance
- Numerous physical complaints
- Failure to prepare for the infant during the last trimester

At delivery, signs of maladaptive responses include:

- Lack of interest in seeing or holding the infant
- Withdrawal, sadness, or disappointment

- Negative comments ("She's so ugly.")
- Expressions of marked disappointment when told of the infant's sex

When shown the infant, the mother may avoid looking at the child or may regard the child without expression. She may decline to hold the infant, or if she does agree to do so, she may not touch or stroke the infant's face or extremities. The mother may also avoid asking questions or talking to the infant and may suddenly decide she does not want to breast-feed (Johnson 1986).

During the postpartal period, the following maternal behaviors are evidence of early maladaptive parenting:

- Limited handling of or smiling at the infant
- Lack of preparation or questions about the infant's needs and care
- Failure to snuggle the newborn to her neck and face
- Negative or hostile comments about the newborn, such as "He looks just like a withered old monkey to me."

The father also may exhibit signs of malattachment to his infant. Examples of maladaptive paternal behaviors are inattentiveness and indifference toward the child; rough or inappropriate handling; and tense, rigid posture. He may also show no protective behavior toward the infant (Johnson 1986).

A serious sign of malattachment may be exhibited by the infant in the form of nonorganic failure to thrive. Most authorities agree that nonorganic failure to thrive is caused by disturbed or lack of nurturing maternal behaviors (Yoos 1984).

## • Nursing Care

Promotion of healthy parent-infant attachment should begin during the prenatal period. The health history should include questions that provide care givers with some initial understanding of the parents' attitudes, support systems, fears, and knowledge. As the pregnancy progresses, the nurse can elicit further information and begin teaching. During the third trimester, care givers should look for evidence that the parents have started to prepare for the infant. After birth, mother, father, and newborn must have time alone together whenever possible to begin getting acquainted.

When maladaptive behaviors are identified, various interventions can be used. A team approach involving all three nursing shifts is advised. Any positive behaviors are communicated so that each staff member can continue to offer support and encourage further development of such behaviors.

Hospital practices should be examined for factors that may inhibit or exaggerate the maladaptive behaviors. Hospital practices such as strict adherence to four-hour feedings, discouraging the mother from unwrapping and looking at her newborn, or prolonged separation, although far less common today, may create a problem for some mothers.

When infants require lengthy intensive care, special efforts by the nurse may facilitate attachment. It is important that parents believe that the child "belongs" to them rather than to the medical team. They should be encouraged to participate in care and to give suggestions about that care. Schraeder (1980, p 38) suggests establishing a care plan and including specific nursing diagnoses such as "altered parenting" or "altered family processes." Nursing interventions are then established according to the stages of parenting behaviors outlined in Figure 28.2. For example, if the mother entered the nursery, lowered the crib rail, and established an *en face* position while talking to the infant, she would be ready to move into stage 2. If there is a specific problem, with the feeding schedule or technique, for example, the parents might be encouraged to work with the nurses to help establish the care plan.

Jenkins and Tock (1986) describe sending an informative letter to the parents "from the baby" on a weekly basis to promote proximity. The letter describes the competencies of the infant and behaviors such as "I like to open my eyes when I eat, but I get so tired that I soon close them" (p 34).

During the postpartal period, continued family interaction should be encouraged through supportive staff, liberal visiting policies, and educational offerings for both father and mother. Staff should be trained in assessment techniques and alert for evidence of malattachment, so that appropriate interventions may be initiated.

Parents need a supportive, understanding person they can interact with as they work through their feelings about the baby. Occasionally, in the presence of severe emotional disorders, a referral to a psychologist or psychiatrist may be necessary. Referral to community agencies such as the Public Health Department is advised so that follow-up can be established.

The referral should be accompanied by a summary of the hospital course, the identified strengths and maladaptive behaviors, the educational process that was accomplished in the hospital, and the mother's response.

Personal or telephone contact may be maintained after discharge so that the parents can continue to have contact with a supportive person with whom they are already acquainted. They should be encouraged to call the postpartal unit or newborn nursery if they have questions.

## • CARE OF WOMEN WITH UNWANTED PREGNANCY AND RELINQUISHMENT ISSUES

Sometimes a pregnancy is unwanted. The expectant woman may be an adolescent, unmarried, or economically restricted. She may dislike children or the idea of being a mother. She may feel that she is not emotionally ready for the responsibilities of parenthood. Her partner may disapprove of the pregnancy. These and many other reasons may cause the woman to continue to reject the idea of her pregnancy. An emotional crisis arises as she attempts to resolve the problem. She may choose to have an abortion, to carry the fetus to term and keep the baby, or to have the baby and relinquish it for adoption.

Many mothers who choose to give their infants up for adoption are young and/or unmarried. More young women choose to keep the child than to give it up, however. Approximately two thirds of children born out of wedlock are raised by their mothers alone.

The decision of a mother to relinquish her infant is an extremely difficult one. Harvey (1977) reports that there are social pressures against giving up one's child. Some women may want to prove to themselves that they can manage on their own by keeping their infants.

The mother who chooses to let her child be adopted usually experiences intense ambivalence. These feelings may heighten just before delivery and upon seeing her baby. After childbirth, the mother will need to complete a grieving process to work through her loss.

## ● Nursing Care

The woman with an unwanted pregnancy must make the difficult decision whether to have the child or have an abortion. If she decides to complete the pregnancy, she must decide whether to keep the baby. During this difficult time, the expectant woman may look to others, such as the nurse, for help in making these decisions. The woman should be given information rather than direct advice during this time, and be allowed to discuss her situation and problem solve.

The mother who decides to relinquish the child usually has made considerable adjustments in her life-style to give birth to this child. She may not have told friends and relatives about the pregnancy and so lacks an extended support system. During the prenatal period, the nurse can help her by encouraging her to express her grief, loneliness, guilt, and other feelings.

When the relinquishing mother is admitted to the maternity unit, the staff should be informed about the mother's decision to relinquish the infant. Any special requests for delivery should be respected and the woman encouraged to express her emotions (Harvey 1977). After the delivery the mother should be allowed access to the infant; she will decide whether she wants to see the newborn. Seeing the newborn often aids the grieving process. When the mother sees her baby, she may feel strong attachment and love. The nurse needs to assure the woman that these feelings do not mean that her decision to relinquish the child is a wrong one; relinquishment is often a painful act of love (Arms 1984). Postpartal nursing management also includes arranging ongoing care for the relinquishing mother.

Initial denial of pregnancy by women usually moves into acceptance of the pregnant state. Occasionally, however, a nurse may encounter a woman who denies she is pregnant even as she is admitted to the maternity unit. It may seem impossible that a woman who is obviously pregnant could maintain this delusion. Because of this denial, the woman has not sought prenatal care. Preparation for the birth experience may be incomplete, and the mother and infant may be at risk.

The nurse must establish a trusting relationship with this woman. While building rapport with the woman, the nurse should gently guide the mother-to-be to accept reality.

In the event that a woman decides to keep an unwanted child, the nurse should be aware of the potential for parenting problems. Families with unwanted children are more crisis prone than others, although in many cases, parents grow to love their child after attachment occurs. The nurse should be ready to initiate crisis strategies or make appropriate referrals as the need arises.

## ● CARE OF THE FAMILY AT RISK FOR CHILD ABUSE

Child abuse is the physical, emotional, or sexual harming of a child by parents, siblings, or other caretakers. Among the many serious effects of child abuse are physical handicaps, poor self-image, inability to love others, antisocial or violent behavior in later life, and death.

A small number of abusing parents have serious mental illnesses, but most abusing parents have less serious problems. The parents of an abused child rarely hate or bear the child ill will. Most often the abusing parents suffer from low self-esteem and guilt, and many have been victims of abuse as children.

It may be necessary to remove children temporarily from the parents' home during therapy, but the goal of treatment is to help parents and their children live together.

## ● Nursing Care

The health professional is required by law to report cases of suspected child abuse. The law not only protects the nurse who in good faith reports a case of suspected child abuse that is mistaken, but also holds an individual liable if a case of abuse is known and not reported.

Nurses who work in prenatal and postnatal settings are in a unique situation to help prevent child abuse by identifying families who show the potential for emotional and physical abuse. Some of the signs that can alert the nurse to the possibility of child abuse are:

● Parents express distaste or rejection the first time they see the infant.

- Mother seems unduly concerned about the "correct" appearance of the baby.
- Parents are extremely unhappy with the sex of the baby.
- Mother has extremely unrealistic views of motherhood.
- Parents give the child a derisive or cruel name or fail to name the baby for an extended period of time.
- Parents make many comments about "not spoiling" the baby or "controlling bad behavior."
- Mother repeatedly refers to her infant as "bad," "impossible," or other disparaging terms.
- Parents were abused as children or abuse each other.
- Parents abuse alcohol or drugs.

Once they have identified a family at risk for child abuse, primary care givers can develop an intensive interdisciplinary approach to prevention involving both public health nurses and social workers (Christensen et al 1984). The nurse can begin intervention by encouraging the parents to express their feelings about the situation. The nurse must understand the parents' emotional needs to provide the proper intervention. It is particularly valuable to involve the parents in planning the medical care for the child so they feel that they are doing something positive and perhaps "making up" for the harm.

The nurse's attitudes are critically important in the development of a therapeutic nurse-client relationship. Empathy, warmth, and understanding are essential. The nurse who is repulsed by the parents' behavior and projects blame or rejection will increase the parents' guilt and further lower their self-esteem. The child may bear the brunt of the parents' frustration and self-hate.

The nurse should explain to the parents the function of the child welfare authorities, pointing out that they are there to help the parents. The nurse can also help by referring the parents for appropriate counseling or to self-help groups such as Parents Anonymous.

## • CARE OF THE ADOLESCENT PARENT FAMILY

As mentioned in Chapter 6, pregnancy and the birth of a child are normal developmental crises for a family. When the parents are very young or immature, the crisis situation may be compounded.

The adolescent mother may be faced with many factors that complicate her situation. She may have used pregnancy to escape from an intolerable situation at home. She may come from a family in which emotional or physical abuse or incest took place. Economic conditions and poverty may be a problem. Emotional support may be lacking. The adolescent may not have told her parents about the pregnancy for fear of rejection. She may feel shame and lack of self-esteem. There may be pressure for her to marry the father. Career and education plans may be threatened by the responsibility and expense of being a parent.

The adolescent may view the new baby as an object—a toy or plaything—by which she can increase her own self-esteem and solidify her role identity. When the infant does not fulfill these needs, frustration and abuse may result.

## • Nursing Care

The nurse who plans to be involved with adolescent parents should develop a complete understanding of the developmental needs of both adolescents and infants. The teenager often lacks knowledge about normal infant growth and development as well as information about child care.

The nurse may use role modeling to demonstrate infant care to the mother, rather than merely telling her. Having the teenager repeat the procedure is important so that the nurse can give positive feedback about her skills and abilities. As the teenage mother's confidence in her ability to care for the infant increases, her self-esteem rises.

Whenever possible the father of the child should be involved both before and after the infant is born. The nurse may offer contraceptive counseling to the young couple. Referrals to community agencies may be appropriate, depending on the specific problems of the young parents. Supportive grandparents can also provide assistance. If possible, adolescent parents should be encouraged to finish high school.

## • CARE OF THE SINGLE-PARENT FAMILY

In the United States, about 11 million children live in single-parent homes—about 90% with their mothers and the remainder with their fathers (Tankson 1986). Single-parent homes most commonly are a result of divorce, desertion, or death of a spouse. Single-parent families also occur when the child's parents are unmarried and the child lives with either the mother or the father.

Some older unmarried women are choosing to have children without a partner. As these women near the end of their reproductive years, they decide that childbearing and childrearing are experiences they desire.

Single-parent homes may also occur as a result of adoption. This phenomenon, although still relatively rare, is increasing.

Hazards to successful childrearing do exist for single-parent families. As children pass through certain developmental stages, they must be provided with opportunities to relate to individuals of the same and opposite sex to learn sex roles. In a single-parent family, these opportunities may not be readily available, and substitute experiences must be provided. An additional drawback in a single-parent family is the lack of opportunities for the child to observe parental man-woman interactions. Furthermore, the parent in a single-parent situation is usually employed outside the home and must handle the demands of both job and family alone.

## • Nursing Care

Nurses will be able to counsel the single parent more effectively if they understand the stresses and demands of parenting a child. A single parent is more likely to have minimal support.

The nurse can begin by assessing the parent's educational needs and providing information as needed. Interventions may include investigation of the availability of child-care facilities and referral to single-parent support groups, such as Parents Without Partners.

## ESSENTIAL CONCEPTS

● **The counseling process used by the nurse follows the crisis intervention model because the survivor is in a situational crisis rather than being ill.**

● **Early identification of potential high-risk fetuses through assessment of prepregnant, prenatal, and intrapartal factors facilitates strategically timed nursing observations and interventions.**

● **Intrauterine fetal and newborn death poses a major nursing challenge to provide support and caring for the parents.**

● **Attachment can be systematically assessed.**

● **Interventions can facilitate attachment.**

● **Complications in parent-infant attachment can occur because of maternal illness or hospitalization of the infant.**

● **Fathers, siblings, and others also become attached to the fetus and newborn.**

● **The nurse is the facilitator for interdisciplinary communication with the parents, identifying their understanding of their infant's care and their needs for emotional support.**

● **Parents of at-risk newborns need support from nurses and health care providers to understand the special needs of their baby and to feel comfortable in an overwhelmingly strange environment.**

● **Parents who abuse their children often feel isolated, are unable to trust others, have few supports for coping with stress, or have unrealistic expectations for their children's behavior.**

## References

Aguilera DC, Messick JM: *Crisis Intervention: Theory and Methodology,* 5th ed. St. Louis: Mosby, 1986.

Arms S: *To Love and Let Go.* New York: Knopf, 1984.

Beckey RD et al: Development of a perinatal grief checklist. *J Obstet Gynecol Neonatal Nurs* May/June 1985; 14:194.

Carr D, Knupp SF: Grief and perinatal loss: A community hospital approach to support. *J Obstet Gynecol Neonatal Nurs* March/April 1985; 14:130.

Christensen ML, Schommer BL, Valasquez J: An interdisciplinary approach to preventing child abuse. *Am J Mat Child Nurs* March/April 1984; 9:108.

Elsas TL: Family mental health care in the neonatal intensive care unit. *J Obstet Gynecol Neonatal Nurs* May/June 1981; 10:204.

Grant P: Psychosocial needs of families of high-risk infants. *Fam Com Health* November 1978; 1(3):91.

Harvey R: Caring perceptively for the relinquishing mother. *Am J Mat Child Nurs* January/February 1977; 2:24.

Hoff LA: *People in Crisis: Understanding and Helping,* 3rd ed. Menlo Park, CA: Addison-Wesley, 1988.

Jenkins RL, Tock MKS: Helping parents bond to their premature infant. *Am J Mat Child Nurs* 1986; 11:32.

Johnson SH: *High-Risk Parenting: Nursing Assessment and Strategies for the Family at Risk,* 2nd ed. Philadelphia: Lippincott, 1986.

Kaplan, DM, Mason EA: Maternal reactions to premature birth viewed as an acute emotional disorder. In: *Crisis Interventions.* Parad HJ (editor). New York: Family Services Association of America, 1974.

Kempe CH, Helfer RE (editors): *The Battered Child,* 3rd ed. Chicago: University of Chicago Press, 1982.

Klaus MH, Kennell JH: *Parent-Infant Attachment,* 2nd ed. St. Louis: Mosby, 1982.

Kübler-Ross E: *On Death and Dying.* New York: Macmillan, 1969.

Lindemann E: Symptomatology and management of acute grief. *Am J Psychiatry* 1944; 101:141.

Powell ML: *Assessment and Management of Developmental Changes and Problems in Children,* 2nd ed. St. Louis: Mosby, 1981.

Schoenberg B et al: *Anticipatory Grief.* New York: Columbia University Press, 1974.

Schraeder BD: Attachment and parenting despite length of intensive care. *Am J Mat Child Nurs* 1980; 11:32.

Schwiebert P, Kirk P: *When Hello Means Goodbye.* Oregon Health Sciences University, 1985.

Solnit A, Stark M: Mourning and the birth of a defective child. *Psychoanal Study Child* 1961; 16:505.

Steele B, Pollack C: A psychiatric study of parents who abuse infants and small children. In: *The Battered Child,* 3rd ed. Helfer RE, Kempe CH (editors). Chicago: University of Chicago Press, 1982.

Tankson EA: The single parent. In: *High-Risk Parenting: Nursing Assessment and Strategies for the Family at Risk,* 2nd ed. Johnson SH (editor). Philadelphia: Lippincott, 1986.

Whitaker CM: Death before birth. *Am J Nurs* February 1986; 86:156.

Yoos L: Taking another look at failure to thrive. *Am J Mat Child Nurs* January/February 1984; 9:32.

## Additional Readings

Borg S, Lasker J: *When Pregnancy Fails: Families Coping with Miscarriage, Stillbirth and Infant Death.* Boston: Beacon Press, 1981.

Gustaitis R, Young EWD: *A Time to Be Born, A Time to Die.* Reading, MA: Addison-Wesley, 1986.

Janowski MJ: The road not taken . . . teenage mothers' courageous decision. *Am J Nurs* March 1987; 87:334.

Lake MF et al: Evaluation of a perinatal grief support team. *Am J Obstet Gynecol* November 1987; 157(5):1203.

Leander D et al: Parental response to the birth of a high-risk neonate: Dynamics and management. *Phys Occup Ther Pediatr* Fall/Winter 1986; 6:205.

Morris D: Management of perinatal bereavement. *Arch Dis Child* July 1988; 63(7):870.

Pate CMH: Care of the family following the birth of an infant with cleft lip and/or palate. *Neonatal Netw* June 1987; 5:30.

Sherwen LN: The nursing role in helping the high-risk mother in crisis master maternal tasks. *J Perinatol* 1986; 6:75.

Sommerfield DP et al: Do health professionals agree on the parenting potential of pregnant women? *Soc Sci Med* 1987; 24(3):285.

Trouy MB, Ward-Larson C: Sibling grief. *Neonatal Network* February 1987; 5:35.

Wagner P, Segall ML: The NICU graduate: A multidisciplinary approach to complex home care. *Perinatal/Neonatal* July/August 1987; 11:12.

Wilson AL et al: The next baby: Parent's responses to perinatal experiences subsequent to a stillbirth *J Perinat* Summer 1988; 8(3):188.

Zuskar DM: The psychological impact of prenatal diagnosis of fetal abnormality: Strategies for investigation and intervention. *Women Health* 1987; 12(1):91.

# Common Abbreviations in Maternal-Newborn and Women's Health Nursing

| | |
|---|---|
| ABC | Alternative birthing center *or* airway, breathing, circulation |
| Accel | Acceleration of fetal heart rate |
| AC | Abdominal circumference |
| ACTH | Adrenocorticotrophic hormone |
| AFAFP | Amniotic fluid alpha fetoprotein |
| AFP | $\alpha$-fetoprotein |
| AFV | Amniotic fluid volume |
| AGA | Average for gestational age |
| AID or AIH | Artificial insemination donor (H designates mate is donor) |
| AIDS | Acquired Immune Deficiency Syndrome |
| ARBOW | Artificial rupture of bag of waters |
| AROM | Artificial rupture of membranes |
| BAT | Brown adipose tissue (brown fat) |
| BBT | Basal body temperature |
| BL | Baseline (fetal heart rate baseline) |
| BMR | Basal metabolic rate |
| BOW | Bag of waters |
| BP | Blood pressure |
| BPD | Biparietal diameter *or* Bronchopulmonary dysplasia |
| BPM | Beats per minute |
| BSE | Breast self examination |
| BSST | Breast self-stimulation test |
| CC | Chest circumference *or* Cord compression |
| cc | cubic centimeter |
| CDC | Centers for Disease Control |
| C–H | Crown-to-heel length |
| CHF | Congestive heart failure |
| CID | Cytomegalic inclusion disease |
| CMV | Cytomegalovirus |
| cm | centimeter |
| CNM | Certified nurse-midwife |
| CNS | Central nervous system |
| CPAP | Continuous positive airway pressure |
| CPD | Cephalopelvic disproportion *or* Citrate-phosphate-dextrose |
| CPR | Cardiopulmonary resuscitation |
| CRL | Crown-rump length |
| C/S | Cesarean section (or C-section) |
| CST | Contraction stress test |
| CT | Computerized tomography |
| CVA | Costovertebral angle |
| CVP | Central venous pressure |
| CVS | Chorionic villus sampling |
| D & C | Dilatation and curettage |
| decels | deceleration of fetal heart rate |
| DFMR | Daily fetal movement response |

| | |
|---|---|
| DIC | Disseminated intravascular coagulation |
| dil | dilatation |
| DM | Diabetes mellitus |
| DRG | Diagnostic related groups |
| DTR | Deep tendon reflexes |
| ECHMO | Extracorporal membrane oxygenator |
| EDC | Estimated date of confinement |
| EDD | Estimated date of delivery |
| EFM | Electronic fetal monitoring |
| EFW | Estimated fetal weight |
| ELF | Elective low forceps |
| epis | Episiotomy |
| FAD | Fetal activity diary |
| FAS | Fetal alcohol syndrome |
| FBD | Fibrocystic breast disease |
| FBM | Fetal breathing movements |
| FBS | Fetal blood sample *or* fasting blood sugar test |
| FECG | Fetal electrocardiogram |
| FFA | Free fatty acids |
| FHR | Fetal heart rate |
| FHT | Fetal heart tones |
| FL | Femur length |
| FM | Fetal movement |
| FMAC | Fetal movement acceleration test |
| FMD | Fetal movement diary |
| FMR | Fetal movement record |
| FPG | Fasting plasma glucose test |
| FRC | Female reproductive cycle |
| FSH | Follicle-stimulating hormone |
| FSHRH | Follicle-stimulating hormone-releasing hormone |
| FSI | Foam stability index |
| G or grav | Gravida |
| GDM | Gestational diabetes mellitus |
| GFR | Glomerular filtration rate |
| GI | Gastrointestinal |
| GnRF | Gonadotrophin-releasing factor |
| GnRH | Gonadotrophin-releasing hormone |
| GTPAL | Gravida, term, preterm, abortion, living children; a system of recording maternity history |
| GYN | Gynecology |
| HA | Head-abdominal rates |
| HAI | Hemagglutination-inhibition test |
| HC | Head compression |
| hCG | Human chorionic gonadotrophin |
| hCS | Human chorionic somatomammotrophin (same as hPL) |
| HMD | Hyaline membrane disease |
| hMG | Human menopausal gonadotrophin |
| hPL | Human placental lactogen |

| | | | |
|---|---|---|---|
| HVH | Herpes virus hominis | OP | Occiput posterior |
| ICS | Intercostal space | p | Para |
| IDDM | Insulin-dependent diabetes mellitus (Type I) | Pap smear | Papanicolaou smear |
| IDM | Infant of a diabetic mother | PBI | Protein-bound iodine |
| IGT | Impaired glucose tolerance | PDA | Patent ductus arteriosus |
| IGTT | Intravenous glucose tolerance test | PEEP | Positive end-expiratory pressure |
| IPG | Impedance phlebography | PG | Phosphatidyglycerol *or* Prostaglandin |
| IUD | Intrauterine device | PI | Phosphatidylinositol |
| IUFD | Intrauterine fetal death | PID | Pelvic inflammatory disease |
| IUGR | Intrauterine growth retardation | PIH | Pregnancy-induced hypertension |
| JCAH | Joint Commission on the Accreditation of Hospitals | Pit | Pitocin |
| | | PKU | Phenylketonuria |
| LADA | Left-acromion-dorsal-anterior | PMI | Point of maximal impulse |
| LADP | Left-acromion-dorsal-posterior | PPHN | Persistent pulmonary hypertension |
| LBW | Low birth weight | Preemie | Premature infant |
| LDR | Labor, delivery and recovery room | Primip | Primapara |
| LGA | Large for gestational age | PROM | Premature rupture of membranes |
| LH | Luteinizing hormone | PTT | Partial thromboplastin test |
| LHRH | Luteinizing hormone-releasing hormone | PUBS | Percutaneous umbilical blood sampling |
| LMA | Left-mentum-anterior | RADA | Right-acromion-dorsal-anterior |
| LML | Left mediolateral (episiotomy) | RADP | Right-acromion-dorsal-posterior |
| LMP | Last menstrual period *or* Left-mentum-posterior | RDA | Recommended dietary allowance |
| LMT | Left-mentum-transverse | RDS | Respiratory distress syndrome |
| LOA | Left-occiput-anterior | REEDA | Redness, edema, ecchymosis, discharge (or drainage), approximation (a system for recording wound healing) |
| LOF | Low outlet forceps | | |
| LOP | Left-occiput-posterior | | |
| LOT | Left-occiput-transverse | REM | Rapid eye movements |
| L/S | Lecithin/sphingomyelin ratio | RIA | Radioimmune assay |
| LSA | Left-sacrum-anterior | RLF | Retrolental fibroplasia |
| LSP | Left-sacrum-posterior | RMA | Right-mentum-anterior |
| LST | Left-sacrum-transverse | RMP | Right-mentum-posterior |
| MAS | Meconium aspiration syndrome *or* Movement alarm signal | RMT | Right-mentum-transverse |
| | | ROA | Right-occiput-anterior |
| | | ROM | Rupture of membranes |
| MCT | Medium chain triglycerides | ROP | Right-occiput-posterior, or retinopathy of prematurity |
| mec | Meconium | | |
| mec st | Meconium stain | | |
| M & I | Maternity and Infant Care Projects | ROT | Right-occiput-transverse |
| ML | Midline (episiotomy) | RRA | Radioreceptor assay |
| MLE | Midline echo | RSA | Right-sacrum-anterior |
| MRI | Magnetic resonance imaging | RSP | Right-sacrum-posterior |
| MSAFP | Maternal serum alpha fetoprotein | RST | Right-sacrum-transverse |
| MUGB | 4-methylumbelliferyl quanidinobenzoate | SET | Surrogate embryo transfer |
| multip | Multipara | SFD | Small for dates |
| NANDA | North American Nursing Diagnosis Association | SGA | Small for gestational age |
| | | SIDS | Sudden infant death syndrome |
| NEC | Necrotizing enterocolitis | SMB | Submentobregmatic diameter |
| NGU | Nongonococcal urethritis | SOAP | Subjective data, objective data, analysis, plan |
| NIDDM | Noninsulin-dependent diabetes mellitus (Type II) | SOB | Suboccipitobregmatic diameter |
| NIH | National Institutes of Health | SRBOW | Spontaneous rupture of the bag of waters |
| NP | Nurse practitioner | SROM | Spontaneous rupture of the membranes |
| NPO | Nothing by mouth | STD | Sexually transmitted disease |
| NSCST | Nipple stimulation contraction stress test | STH | Somatotrophic hormone |
| NST | Nonstress test *or* nonshivering thermogenesis | STS | Serologic test for syphilis |
| NSVD | Normal sterile vaginal delivery | SVE | Sterile vaginal exam |
| NTD | Neural tube defects | TC | Thoracic circumference |
| OA | Occiput anterior | TCM | Transcutaneous monitoring |
| OB | Obstetrics | TNZ | Thermal neutral zone |
| OCT | Oxytocin challenge test | TORCH | Toxoplasmosis, rubella, cytomegalovirus, herpesvirus hominis type 2 |
| OF | Occipitofrontal diameter of fetal head | | |
| OFC | Occipitofrontal circumference | TSS | Toxic shock syndrome |
| OGTT | Oral glucose tolerance test | ū | umbilicus |
| OM | Occipitomental (diameter) | u/a | urinalysis |

| | |
|---|---|
| UA | Uterine activity |
| UAC | Umbilical artery catheter |
| UAU | Uterine activity units |
| UC | Uterine contraction |
| UPI | Uteroplacental insufficiency |
| U/S | Ultrasound |

| | |
|---|---|
| UTI | Urinary tract infection |
| VBAC | Vaginal birth after cesarean |
| VDRL | Venereal Disease Research Laboratories |
| WBC | White blood cell |
| WIC | Supplemental food program for Women, Infants, and Children |

*Appendix B*

# Conversion of Pounds and Ounces to Grams

## Conversion of Pounds and Ounces to Grams

| | OUNCES | | | | | | | | | | | | | | | OUNCES |
|---|---|---|---|---|---|---|---|---|---|---|---|---|---|---|---|---|
| | 0 | 1 | 2 | 3 | 4 | 5 | 6 | 7 | 8 | 9 | 10 | 11 | 12 | 13 | 14 | 15 |
| 0 | — | 28 | 57 | 85 | 113 | 142 | 170 | 198 | 227 | 255 | 283 | 312 | 340 | 369 | 397 | 425 |
| 1 | 454 | 482 | 510 | 539 | 567 | 595 | 624 | 652 | 680 | 709 | 737 | 765 | 794 | 822 | 850 | 879 |
| 2 | 907 | 936 | 964 | 992 | 1021 | 1049 | 1077 | 1106 | 1134 | 1162 | 1191 | 1219 | 1247 | 1276 | 1304 | 1332 |
| 3 | 1361 | 1389 | 1417 | 1446 | 1474 | 1503 | 1531 | 1559 | 1588 | 1616 | 1644 | 1673 | 1701 | 1729 | 1758 | 1786 |
| 4 | 1814 | 1843 | 1871 | 1899 | 1928 | 1956 | 1984 | 2013 | 2041 | 2070 | 2098 | 2126 | 2155 | 2183 | 2211 | 2240 |
| 5 | 2268 | 2296 | 2325 | 2353 | 2381 | 2410 | 2438 | 2466 | 2495 | 2523 | 2551 | 2580 | 2608 | 2637 | 2665 | 2693 |
| 6 | 2722 | 2750 | 2778 | 2807 | 2835 | 2863 | 2892 | 2920 | 2948 | 2977 | 3005 | 3033 | 3062 | 3090 | 3118 | 3147 |
| 7 | 3175 | 3203 | 3232 | 3260 | 3289 | 3317 | 3345 | 3374 | 3402 | 3430 | 3459 | 3487 | 3515 | 3544 | 3572 | 3600 |
| 8 | 3629 | 3657 | 3685 | 3714 | 3742 | 3770 | 3799 | 3827 | 3856 | 3884 | 3912 | 3941 | 3969 | 3997 | 4026 | 4054 |
| 9 | 4082 | 4111 | 4139 | 4167 | 4196 | 4224 | 4252 | 4281 | 4309 | 4337 | 4366 | 4394 | 4423 | 4451 | 4479 | 4508 |
| P 10 | 4536 | 4564 | 4593 | 4621 | 4649 | 4678 | 4706 | 4734 | 4763 | 4791 | 4819 | 4848 | 4876 | 4904 | 4933 | 4961 |
| O 11 | 4990 | 5018 | 5046 | 5075 | 5103 | 5131 | 5160 | 5188 | 5216 | 5245 | 5273 | 5301 | 5330 | 5358 | 5386 | 5415 |
| U 12 | 5443 | 5471 | 5500 | 5528 | 5557 | 5585 | 5613 | 5642 | 5670 | 5698 | 5727 | 5755 | 5783 | 5812 | 5840 | 5868 |
| N 13 | 5897 | 5925 | 5953 | 5982 | 6010 | 6038 | 6067 | 6095 | 6123 | 6152 | 6180 | 6209 | 6237 | 6265 | 6294 | 6322 |
| D 14 | 6350 | 6379 | 6407 | 6435 | 6464 | 6492 | 6520 | 6549 | 6577 | 6605 | 6634 | 6662 | 6690 | 6719 | 6747 | 6776 |
| S 15 | 6804 | 6832 | 6860 | 6889 | 6917 | 6945 | 6973 | 7002 | 7030 | 7059 | 7087 | 7115 | 7144 | 7172 | 7201 | 7228 |
| 16 | 7257 | 7286 | 7313 | 7342 | 7371 | 7399 | 7427 | 7456 | 7484 | 7512 | 7541 | 7569 | 7597 | 7626 | 7654 | 7682 |
| 17 | 7711 | 7739 | 7768 | 7796 | 7824 | 7853 | 7881 | 7909 | 7938 | 7966 | 7994 | 8023 | 8051 | 8079 | 8108 | 8136 |
| 18 | 8165 | 8192 | 8221 | 8249 | 8278 | 8306 | 8335 | 8363 | 8391 | 8420 | 8448 | 8476 | 8504 | 8533 | 8561 | 8590 |
| 19 | 8618 | 8646 | 8675 | 8703 | 8731 | 8760 | 8788 | 8816 | 8845 | 8873 | 8902 | 8930 | 8958 | 8987 | 9015 | 9043 |
| 20 | 9072 | 9100 | 9128 | 9157 | 9185 | 9213 | 9242 | 9270 | 9298 | 9327 | 9355 | 9383 | 9412 | 9440 | 9469 | 9497 |
| 21 | 9525 | 9554 | 9582 | 9610 | 9639 | 9667 | 9695 | 9724 | 9752 | 9780 | 9809 | 9837 | 9865 | 9894 | 9922 | 9950 |
| 22 | 9979 | 10007 | 10036 | 10064 | 10092 | 10120 | 10149 | 10177 | 10206 | 10234 | 10262 | 10291 | 10319 | 10347 | 10376 | 10404 |

# The Pregnant Patient's Bill of Rights*

The Pregnant Patient has the right to participate in decisions involving her well-being and that of her unborn child, unless there is a clearcut medical emergency that prevents her participation. In addition to the rights set forth in the American Hospital Association's "Patient's Bill of Rights," the Pregnant Patient, because she represents *two* patients rather than one, should be recognized as having the additional rights listed below.

1. *The Pregnant Patient has the right,* prior to the administration of any drug or procedure, to be informed by the health professional caring for her of any potential direct or indirect effects, risks or hazards to herself or her unborn or newborn infant which may result from the use of a drug or procedure prescribed for or administered to her during pregnancy, labor, birth or lactation.

2. *The Pregnant Patient has the right,* prior to the proposed therapy, to be informed, not only of the benefits, risks and hazards of the proposed therapy but also of known alternative therapy, such as available childbirth education classes which could help to prepare the Pregnant Patient physically and mentally to cope with the discomfort or stress of pregnancy and the experience of childbirth, thereby reducing or eliminating her need for drugs and obstetric intervention. She should be offered such information early in her pregnancy in order that she may make a reasoned decision.

3. *The Pregnant Patient has the right,* prior to the administration of any drug, to be informed by the health professional who is prescribing or administering the drug to her that any drug which she receives during pregnancy, labor and birth, no matter how or when the drug is taken or administered, may adversely affect her unborn baby, directly or indirectly, and that there is no drug or chemical which has been proven safe for the unborn child.

4. *The Pregnant Patient has the right,* if cesarean birth is anticipated, to be informed prior to the administration of any drug, and preferably prior to her hospitalization, that minimizing her and, in turn, her baby's intake of nonessential preoperative medicine will benefit her baby.

5. *The Pregnant Patient has the right,* prior to the administration of a drug or procedure, to be informed of the areas of uncertainty if there is NO properly controlled follow-up research which has established the safety of the drug or procedure with regard to its direct and/or indirect effects on the physiological, mental and neurological development of the child exposed, via the mother, to the drug or procedure during pregnancy, labor, birth or lactation—(this would apply to virtually all drugs and the vast majority of obstetric procedures).

6. *The Pregnant Patient has the right,* prior to the administration of any drug, to be informed of the brand name and generic name of the drug in order that she may advise the health professional of any past adverse reaction to the drug.

7. *The Pregnant Patient has the right* to determine for herself, without pressure from her attendant, whether she will accept the risks inherent in the proposed therapy or refuse a drug or procedure.

8. *The Pregnant Patient has the right* to know the name and qualifications of the individual administering a medication or procedure to her during labor or birth.

9. *The Pregnant Patient has the right* to be informed, prior to the administration of any procedure, whether that procedure is being administered to her for her or her baby's benefit (medically indicated) or as an elective procedure (for convenience, teaching purposes or research).

10. *The Pregnant Patient has the right* to be accompanied during the stress of labor and birth by someone she cares for, and to whom she looks for emotional comfort and encouragement.

11. *The Pregnant Patient has the right* after appropriate medical consultation to choose a position for labor

*Prepared by Doris Haire, Chair, Committee on Health Law and Regulation, International Childbirth Education Association, Inc., Rochester, N.Y.

and for birth which is least stressful to her baby and to herself.

12. *The Obstetric Patient has the right* to have her baby cared for at her bedside if her baby is normal, and to feed her baby according to her baby's needs rather than according to the hospital regimen.

13. *The Obstetric Patient has the right* to be informed in writing of the name of the person who actually delivered her baby and the professional qualifications of that person. This information should also be on the birth certificate.

14. *The Obstetric Patient has the right* to be informed if there is any known or indicated aspect of her or her baby's care or condition which may cause her or her baby later difficulty or problems.

15. *The Obstetric Patient has the right* to have her and her baby's hospital medical records complete, accurate and legible and to have their records, including Nurses' Notes, retained by the hospital until the child reaches at least the age of majority, or to have the records offered to her before they are destroyed.

16. *The Obstetric Patient, both during and after her hospital stay, has the right* to have access to her complete hospital medical records, including Nurses' Notes, and to receive a copy upon payment of a reasonable fee and without incurring the expense of retaining an attorney.

It is the obstetric patient and her baby, not the health professional, who must sustain any trauma or injury resulting from the use of a drug or obstetric procedure. The observation of the rights listed above will not only permit the obstetric patient to participate in the decisions involving her and her baby's health care, but will help to protect the health professional and the hospital against litigation arising from resentment or misunderstanding on the part of the mother.

*Appendix D*

# NAACOG's Standards for Obstetric, Gynecologic, and Neonatal Nursing

## • I: NURSING PRACTICE

**STANDARD:** Comprehensive obstetric, gynecologic, and neonatal (OGN) nursing care is provided to the individual, family, and community within the framework of the nursing process.

**INTERPRETATION:** The nurse is responsible for decisions and actions within the domain of nursing practice. Comprehensive nursing care includes assisting the person to meet physical, psychosocial, spiritual, and developmental needs. Systematic use of the nursing process which encompasses assessment, nursing diagnosis, planning, implementation, and evaluation will meet the patient's needs. Individualized nursing care is best achieved by collaboration with patient, family, and other members of the health-care team. Complete and accurate documentation of all nursing care and patient response is essential for continuity of care and for meeting legal requirements. The nurse must promote a safe and therapeutic environment for the individual, family, and community.

## • II: HEALTH EDUCATION

**STANDARD:** Health education for the individual, family, and community is an integral part of obstetric, gynecologic, and neonatal nursing practice.

**INTERPRETATION:** The nurse is responsible for providing pertinent information to the individual, family, and community so they may participate in and share responsibility for their own health promotion, maintenance, and restorative care. The nurse plans, implements, and evaluates health education based on principles of teaching and learning. To enhance health care and promote continuity of health education, the nurse uses the educational resources within the community and collaborates with other health-care providers.

Health education should be documented and evaluated. Evaluation is based on individualized goals and set criteria.

## ● III: POLICIES AND PROCEDURES

**STANDARD:** The delivery of obstetric, gynecologic, and neonatal nursing care is based on written policies and procedures.

**INTERPRETATION:** Policies and procedures define the boundaries of nursing practice within the health-care setting and indicate the qualifications of personnel authorized to perform OGN nursing procedures. The qualifications may include educational preparation and/or certification. The policies and procedures should be in accordance with the philosophy of the agency, state nurse practice act, governmental regulations, and other applicable standards or regulations.

A multidisciplinary framework should be used in writing policies and procedures. Policies and procedures should be evaluated on an ongoing basis and revised as necessary. The policies and procedures should be readily accessible to the health-care providers within the health-care setting.

## ● IV: PROFESSIONAL RESPONSIBILITY AND ACCOUNTABILITY

**STANDARD:** The obstetric, gynecologic, and neonatal nurse is responsible and accountable for maintaining knowledge and competency in individual nursing practice and for being aware of professional issues.

**INTERPRETATION:** Maintaining both the knowledge and skills required to achieve excellence in OGN nursing is incumbent upon the nurse. The nurse should be cognizant of changing concepts, trends, and scientific advances in OGN care. Updating knowledge and skills is achievable through formal education, professional continuing education, and the use of or participation in nursing research. Knowledge of specialty nursing can be recognized through certification.

The nurse should be aware of governmental policies and legislation affecting health care and nursing practice. Participating in legislative and regulatory processes is appropriate for the nurse.

Responsibilities defined in written position descriptions and performance demonstrated by the OGN nurse should be regularly evaluated and documented. In addition, criteria for the evaluation of OGN nursing practice should be drawn from applicable statutes, the ethics of the profession, and current standards of practice.

## ● V: PERSONNEL

**STANDARD:** Obstetric, gynecologic, and neonatal nursing staff are provided to meet patient care needs.
**INTERPRETATION:** The obstetric, gynecologic, and neonatal nursing management determines the staff required for the provision of individualized nursing care commensurate with demonstrated patient needs, appropriate nursing interventions, qualifications of available nursing personnel, and other factors which must be considered. These factors may include nursing care needs; number of deliveries; number and types of surgical procedures; average inpatient census; volume of ambulatory patients; percentage of high-risk patients; educational, emotional, and economic needs of the patients; provision for staff continuing education; medical staff coverage; ancillary services available; size and design of facilities; responsibilities of nursing staff; and ongoing research.

Personnel in each OGN unit should be directed by a registered nurse with educational preparation and clinical experience in the specific OGN area of practice. This nurse is responsible for management of nursing care and supervision of nursing personnel.

When nursing, medical, or other specialty students are assigned to the unit for clinical experience, their roles and responsibilities should be clearly defined in writing. Nursing students should not be included in the unit's staffing plan.

Written position descriptions which identify standards of performance for OGN nurses should be developed and used in periodic personnel evaluations. Documentation should reflect each nurse's participation in orientation and verify knowledge and expertise in those skills required for OGN nursing practice. Orientation and evaluation of personnel for whom the registered nurse is held accountable should be documented as well.

Written policies for the reassignment of OGN nursing personnel should exist to accommodate both increases and decreases of inpatient days and ambulatory visits. The policies should include a contingency plan for staffing during peak activity periods.

# Clinical Estimation of Gestational Age

Clinical estimation of gestational age. (Courtesy Mead Johnson Laboratories, Evansville, Ind.)

▶ **Examination First Hours**

**CLINICAL ESTIMATION OF GESTATIONAL AGE**
An Approximation Based on Published Data*

| PHYSICAL FINDINGS | | WEEKS GESTATION 20 21 22 23 24 25 26 27 28 29 30 31 32 33 34 35 36 37 38 39 40 41 42 43 44 45 46 47 48 |
|---|---|---|
| VERNIX | | APPEARS · COVERS BODY, THICK LAYER · ON BACK, SCALP, IN CREASES · SCANT, IN CREASES · NO VERNIX |
| BREAST TISSUE AND AREOLA | | AREOLA & NIPPLE BARELY VISIBLE NO PALPABLE BREAST TISSUE · AREOLA RAISED · 1-2 MM NODULE · 3-5 MM · 5-6 MM · 7-10 MM · ?12 MM |
| EAR | FORM | FLAT, SHAPELESS · BEGINNING INCURVING SUPERIOR · INCURVING UPPER 2/3 PINNAE · WELL-DEFINED INCURVING TO LOBE |
| | CARTILAGE | PINNA SOFT, STAYS FOLDED · CARTILAGE SCANT RETURNS SLOWLY FROM FOLDING · THIN CARTILAGE SPRINGS BACK FROM FOLDING · PINNA FIRM, REMAINS ERECT FROM HEAD |
| SOLE CREASES | | SMOOTH SOLES 3 CREASES · 1-2 ANTERIOR CREASES · 2-3 ANTERIOR CREASES · CREASES ANTERIOR 2/3 SOLE · CREASES INVOLVING HEEL · DEEPER CREASES OVER ENTIRE SOLE |
| SKIN | THICKNESS & APPEARANCE | THIN, TRANSLUCENT SKIN, PLETHORIC, VENULES OVER ABDOMEN EDEMA · SMOOTH THICKER NO EDEMA · PINK · FEW VESSELS · SOME DESQUAMATION PALE PINK · THICK, PALE, DESQUAMATION OVER ENTIRE BODY |
| | NAIL PLATES | APPEAR · NAILS TO FINGER TIPS · NAILS EXTEND WELL BEYOND FINGER TIPS |
| HAIR | | APPEARS ON HEAD · EYE BROWS & LASHES · FINE, WOOLLY, BUNCHES OUT FROM HEAD · SILKY, SINGLE STRANDS LAYS FLAT · ?RECEDING HAIRLINE OR LOSS OF BABY HAIR SHORT, FINE UNDERNEATH |
| LANUGO | | APPEARS · COVERS ENTIRE BODY · VANISHES FROM FACE · PRESENT ON SHOULDERS · NO LANUGO |
| GENITALIA | TESTES | TESTES PALPABLE IN INGUINAL CANAL · IN UPPER SCROTUM · IN LOWER SCROTUM |
| | SCROTUM | FEW RUGAE · RUGAE, ANTERIOR PORTION · RUGAE COVER · PENDULOUS |
| | LABIA & CLITORIS | PROMINENT CLITORIS LABIA MAJORA SMALL WIDELY SEPARATED · LABIA MAJORA LARGER NEARLY COVERED CLITORIS · LABIA MINORA & CLITORIS COVERED |
| SKULL FIRMNESS | | BONES ARE SOFT · SOFT TO 1" FROM ANTERIOR FONTANELLE · SPONGY AT EDGES OF FONTANELLE CENTER FIRM · BONES HARD SUTURES EASILY DISPLACED · BONES HARD, CANNOT BE DISPLACED |
| POSTURE | RESTING | HYPOTONIC LATERAL DECUBITUS · HYPOTONIC · BEGINNING FLEXION THIGH · STRONGER HIP FLEXION · FROG-LIKE · FLEXION ALL LIMBS · HYPERTONIC · VERY HYPERTONIC |
| | RECOIL · LEG | NO RECOIL · PARTIAL RECOIL · PROMPT RECOIL |
| | ARM | NO RECOIL · BEGIN FLEXION NO RECOIL · PROMPT RECOIL MAY BE INHIBITED · PROMPT RECOIL AFTER 30" INHIBITION |

20 21 22 23 24 25 26 27 28 29 30 31 32 33 34 35 36 37 38 39 40 41 42 43 44 45 46 47 48

*Brazie JV and Lubchenco LO. The estimation of gestational age chart. In Kempe, Silver and O'Brien. Current Pediatric Diagnosis and Treatment, ed 3. Los Altos, Calif: Lange Medical Publications, 1974, ch 4.

# Classification of Newborns (Both Sexes) by Intrauterine Growth and Gestational Age [1,2]

NAME _____  DATE OF BIRTH _____  BIRTH WEIGHT _____

HOSPITAL NO. _____  DATE OF EXAM _____  LENGTH _____

RACE _____  SEX _____  HEAD CIRC. _____

GESTATIONAL AGE _____

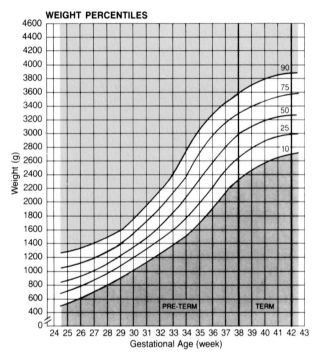

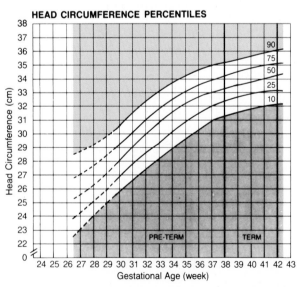

| CLASSIFICATION OF INFANT* | Weight | Length | Head Circ. |
|---|---|---|---|
| Large for Gestational Age (LGA) (>90th percentile) | | | |
| Appropriate for Gestational Age (AGA) (10th to 90th percentile) | | | |
| Small for Gestational Age (SGA) (<10th percentile) | | | |

*Place an "X" in the appropriate box (LGA, AGA or SGA) for weight, for length and for head circumference.

**References**
1. Battaglia FC, Lubchenco LO: A practical classification of newborn infants by weight and gestational age. *J Pediatr* 71:159-163, 1967.
2. Lubchenco LO, Hansman C, Boyd E: Intrauterine growth in length and head circumference as estimated from live births at gestational ages from 26 to 42 weeks. *Pediatrics* 37:403-408, 1966.

Reprinted by permission from Dr Battaglia, Dr Lubchenco, *Journal of Pediatrics* and *Pediatrics*.

# Actions and Effects of Selected Drugs During Breast-Feeding*

**Anticholinergics**
  *Atropine:*  May cause hyperthermia in the newborn; may decrease maternal milk supply

**Anticoagulants**
  *Coumarin derivatives (Warfarin):*  May cause bleeding problems; should be discontinued in mother or breastfeeding temporarily halted if infant to have surgery
  *Heparin:*  Relatively safe to use; check PTT
  *Phenindione (Hedulin):*  Passes easily into breast milk; neonate may have increased pro time and PTT

**Antihistamines**  May cause decreased milk supply; infant may become drowsy, irritable, or have tachycardia

**Antimetabolites**  Unknown, probably long-term anti-DNA effect on the infant; potentially very toxic

**Antimicrobials**
  *Ampicillin:*  Skin rash, candidiasis; diarrhea
  *Chloramphenicol:*  Possible bone marrow suppression; Gray syndrome; refusal of breast
  *Methacycline:*  Possible inhibition of bone growth; may cause discoloration of the teeth; use should be avoided
  *Sulfonamides:*  May cause hyperbilirubinemia; use contraindicated until infant over 1 month old
  *Penicillin:*  Possible allergic response; candidiasis
  *Metronidazole (Flagyl):*  Possible neurologic disorders or blood dyscrasias; delay breast-feeding for 12 to 24 hours after last dose
  *Aminoglycosides:*  May cause ototoxicity or nephrotoxicity if given for more than two weeks
  *Tetracycline:*  Long-term use and large doses should be avoided; may cause tooth staining or inhibition of bone growth

**Antithyroids**
  *Thiouracil:*  Contraindicated during lactation; may cause goiter or agranulocytosis

**Barbiturates**  May produce sedation
  *Phenothiazines:*  May produce sedation

**Bronchodilators**
  *Aminophylline:*  May cause insomnia or irritability in the infant

**Caffeine**  Excessive consumption may cause jitteriness

**Cardiovascular**
  *Propranolol (Inderal):*  May cause hypoglycemia; possibility of other blocking effects
  *Quinidine:*  May cause arrhythmias in infant
  *Reserpine (Serpasil):*  Nasal stuffiness, lethargy, or diarrhea in infant

**Corticosteroids**  Adrenal suppression may occur with long-term administration of doses greater than 10 mg/day.

**Heavy metals**
  *Gold:*  Potentially toxic
  *Mercury:*  Excreted in the milk and hazardous to infant

**Hormones**
  *Androgens:*  Suppress lactation
  *Oral contraceptives:*  Decrease milk supply; may alter milk composition; may cause gynecomastia in male infants
  *Thyroid hormones:*  May mask hypothyroidism

**Laxatives**
  *Cascara:*  May cause diarrhea in infant
  *Milk of magnesia:*  Relatively safe
  *Phenolphthalein:*  May cause diarrhea in infant

**Narcotic analgesics**
  *Codeine:*  Accumulation may lead to neonatal depression
  *Meperidine:*  May lead to neonatal depression
  *Morphine:*  Long-term use may cause newborn addiction

**Nonnarcotic analgesics**
  *Salicylates:*  Safe after first week of life
  *Acetaminophen:*  Relatively safe for short-term analgesia
  *Propoxyphene (Darvon):*  May cause sleepiness and poor nursing in infant

*Based on data from Hill WC: Drugs contraindicated during pregnancy and lactation. *Medical Times* 1987; 115(June): 132. Riordan J: *A Practical Guide to Breastfeeding*. St. Louis: Mosby, 1983, pp 140–145. Spencer RT, et al: *Clinical Pharmacology and Nursing Management*, 2nd ed. Philadelphia: Lippincott, 1986, p 1016.

## Radioactive materials for testing

*Gallium citrate (⁶⁷G):* Insignificant amount excreted in breast milk; no nursing for 2 weeks

*Iodine:* Contraindicated; may affect infant's thyroid gland

$^{125}I$: Discontinue nursing for 48 hours

$^{131}I$: Nursing should be discontinued until excretion is no longer significant; after a test dose, nursing may be resumed after 24 to 36 hours; after a treatment dose, nursing may be resumed after 2 to 3 weeks

$^{99}$*Technetium:* Discontinue nursing for 48 hours (half-life = 6 hours)

## Sedatives/Tranquilizers

*Diazepam (Valium):* May accumulate to high levels; may increase neonatal jaundice; may cause sedation

*Lithium carbonate:* Contraindicated; may cause neonatal flaccidity and hypotonia

*Chlordiazepoxide (Librium):* Use with caution after infant one week old

# Glossary

**Abdominal effleurage**   Gentle stroking used in massage.

**Abortion**   Loss of pregnancy before the fetus is viable outside the uterus; miscarriage.

**Abruptio placentae**   Partial or total premature separation of a normally implanted placenta.

**Abstinence**   Refraining voluntarily, especially from indulgence in food, alcoholic beverages, or sexual intercourse.

**Acceleration**   Periodic increase in the baseline fetal heart rate.

**Acini cells**   Secretory cells in the human breast that create milk from nutrients in the bloodstream.

**Acme**   Peak or highest point; time of greatest intensity (of a uterine contraction).

**Acrocyanosis**   Cyanosis of the extremities.

**Active acquired immunity**   Formation of antibodies by the pregnant woman in response to illness or immunization.

**Acute grief**   The most severe stage of the grief response; usually resolved within 1–2 months and followed by a gradual return to the pre-loss level of functioning.

**Adnexa**   Adjoining or accessory parts of a structure, such as the uterine adnexa: the ovaries and fallopian tubes.

**Adolescence**   Period of human development initiated by puberty and ending with the attainment of young adulthood.

**Afterbirth**   Placenta and membranes expelled after the delivery of the infant, during the third stage of labor; also called secundines.

**Afterpains**   Cramplike pains due to contractions of the uterus that occur after childbirth. They are more common in multiparas, tend to be most severe during nursing, and last two to three days.

**AIDS**   Acquired immune deficiency syndrome; a sexually transmitted viral disease that so far has proved fatal in 100 percent of cases.

**Allele**   One of a series of alternate genes at the same locus; one form of a gene.

**Amenorrhea**   Suppression or absence of menstruation.

**Amniocentesis**   Removal of amniotic fluid by insertion of a needle into the amniotic sac; amniotic fluid is used to assess fetal health or maturity.

**Amnion**   The inner of the two membranes that form the sac containing the fetus and the amniotic fluid.

**Amnionitis**   Infection of the amniotic fluid.

**Amnioscopy**   Visualization of the amniotic fluid through the membranes with an amnioscope in order to identify meconium staining of the amniotic fluid.

**Amniotic fluid**   The liquid surrounding the fetus in utero. It absorbs shocks, permits fetal movement, and prevents heat loss.

**Amniotic fluid embolism**   Amniotic fluid that has leaked into the chorionic plate and entered the maternal circulation.

**Amniotomy**   The artificial rupturing of the amniotic membrane.

**Ampulla**   The outer two-thirds of the fallopian tube; fertilization of the ovum by a spermatozoon usually occurs here.

**Androgen**   Substance producing male characteristics, such as the male hormone testosterone.

**Android pelvis**   Male-type pelvis.

**Antepartum**   Time between conception and the onset of labor; usually used to describe the period during which a woman is pregnant.

**Anterior fontanelle**   Diamond-shaped area between the two frontal and two parietal bones just above the newborn's forehead.

**Anthropoid pelvis**   Pelvis in which the anteroposterior diameter is equal to or greater than the transverse diameter.

**Apgar score**   A scoring system used to evaluate newborns at 1 minute and 5 minutes after delivery. The total score is achieved by assessing five signs: heart rate, respiratory effort, muscle tone, reflex irritability, and color. Each of the signs is assigned a score of 0, 1, or 2. The highest possible score is 10.

**Apnea**   A condition that occurs when respirations cease for more than 20 seconds, with generalized cyanosis.

**Areola**   Pigmented ring surrounding the nipple of the breast.

**AROM**   Artificial rupture of (amniotic) membranes through use of a device such as an amnihook or allis forceps.

**Artificial insemination**   Introduction of viable semen into the vagina by artificial means for the purpose of impregnation.

**Attachment**   Enduring bonds or relationship of affection between persons.

**Atony**   Lack of normal muscle tone.

**Attitude**   Attitude of the fetus refers to the relationship of the fetal parts to each other.

**Autosome**   A chromosome that is not a sex chromosome.

**Bacterial vaginosis**   A bacterial infection of the vagina, formerly called *Gardnerella vaginalis* or *Hemophilus vaginalis*, characterized by a foul-smelling, grayish vaginal discharge that exhibits a characteristic fishy odor when 10 percent potassium hydroxide (KOH) is added. Microscopic examination of a vaginal wet prep reveals the presence of "clue cells" (vaginal epithelial cells coated with gram-negative organisms).

**Bag of waters** The membrane containing the amniotic fluid and the fetus (BOW).

**Ballottement** A technique of palpation to detect or examine a floating object in the body. In obstetrics, the fetus, when pushed, floats away and then returns to touch the examiner's fingers.

**Barr body** Deeply staining chromatin mass located against the inner surface of the cell nucleus. It is found only in normal females; also called sex chromatin.

**Basal body temperature (BBT)** The lowest waking temperature.

**Baseline rate** The average fetal heart rate observed during a 10-minute period of monitoring.

**Baseline variability** Changes in the fetal heart rate that result from the interplay between the sympathetic and the parasympathetic nervous systems.

**Battledore placenta** Placenta in which the umbilical cord is inserted on the periphery rather than centrally.

**Bimanual palpation** Examination of the pelvic organs by placing one hand on the abdomen and one or two fingers of the other hand into the vagina.

**Biophysical profile** Assessment of five variables in the fetus that help to evaluate fetal risk: breathing movement, body movement, tone, amniotic fluid volume, and fetal heart rate reactivity.

**Birth rate** Number of live birth per 1000 population.

**Birth center** A setting for labor and delivery that emphasizes a family-centered approach rather than obstetric technology and treatment.

**Birthing room** A room for labor and delivery with a relaxed atmosphere.

**Bishop score** A prelabor scoring system to assist in predicting whether an induction of labor may be successful. The total score is achieved by assessing five components: cervical dilatation, cervical effacement, cervical consistency, cervical position, and fetal station. Each of the components is assigned a score of zero to three, and the highest possible score is 13.

**Blastocyst** The inner solid mass of cells within the morula.

**Blended family** Families established through remarriage; may include children from previous marriages of each spouse as well as children of the current marriage.

**Bloody show** Pink-tinged mucous secretions resulting from rupture of small capillaries as the cervix effaces and dilates.

**Brachial palsy** Partial or complete paralysis of portions of the arm resulting from trauma to the brachial plexus during a difficult delivery.

**Bradycardia** Slow heart rate.

**Bradley method** Partner-coached natural childbirth.

**Braxton Hicks contractions** Intermittent painless contractions of the uterus that may occur every 10 to 20 minutes. They occur more frequently toward the end of pregnancy and are sometimes mistaken for true labor signs.

**Brazleton's neonatal behavioral assessment** A brief examination used to identify the infant's behavioral states and responses.

**Breasts** Mammary glands.

**Breech presentation** A delivery in which the buttocks and/or feet are presented instead of the head.

**Broad ligament** The ligament extending from the lateral margins of the uterus to the pelvic wall; keeps the uterus centrally placed and provides stability within the pelvic cavity.

**Bronchopulmonary dysplasia (BPD)** Chronic pulmonary disease of multifactorial etiology characterized initially by alveolar and bronchial necrosis, which results in bronchial metaplasia and interstitial fibrosis. Appears in x-ray films as generalized small, radiolucent cysts within the lungs.

**Brown adipose tissue (BAT)** Fat deposits in neonates that provide greater heat-generating activity than ordinary fat. Found around the kidneys, adrenals, and neck; between the scapulas; and behind the sternum; also called brown fat.

**calorie** Amount of heat required to raise the temperature of 1 g of water 1 degree centigrade.

**Caput succedaneum** Swelling or edema occurring in or under the fetal scalp during labor.

**Cardinal ligaments** The chief uterine supports, suspending the uterus from the side walls of the true pelvis.

**Cardinal movements of labor** The positional changes of the fetus as it moves through the birth canal during labor and delivery. The positional changes are descent, flexion, internal rotation, extension, restitution, and external rotation.

**Cardiopulmonary adaptation** Adaptation of the neonate's cardiovascular and respiratory systems to life outside the womb.

**Caudal block** Regional anesthesia used in childbirth in which the anesthetic agent is injected into the caudal area of the spinal canal through the sacral hiatus, affecting the caudal nerve roots and thereby providing anesthesia to the cervix, vagina, and perineum.

**Cephalhematoma** Subcutaneous swelling containing blood found on the head of an infant several days after delivery, which usually disappears within a few weeks to two months.

**Cephalic presentation** Delivery in which the fetal head is presenting against the cervix.

**Cephalopelvic disproportion (CPD)** A condition in which the fetal head is of such a shape or size, or in such a position, that it cannot pass through the maternal pelvis.

**Cervical cap** A cup-shaped device placed over the cervix to prevent pregnancy.

**Cervical dilatation** Process in which the cervical os and the cervical canal widen from less than a centimeter to approximately 10 cm, allowing delivery of the fetus.

**Cervix** The "neck" between the external os and the body of the uterus. The lower end of the cervix extends into the vagina.

**Cesarean delivery** Delivery of the fetus by means of an incision into the abdominal wall and the uterus; also called *abdominal delivery*.

**Chadwick's sign** Violet bluish color of the vaginal mucous membrane caused by increased vascularity; visible from about the fourth week of pregnancy.

**Chloasma** Brownish pigmentation over the bridge of the nose and the cheeks during pregnancy and in some women who are taking oral contraceptives. Also called *mask of pregnancy*.

**Chorioamnionitis** An inflammation of the amniotic membranes stimulated by organisms in the amniotic fluid, which then becomes infiltrated with polymorphonuclear leukocytes.

**Chorion** The fetal membrane closest to the intrauterine wall that gives rise to the placenta and continues as the outer membrane surrounding the amnion.

**Chromosomes** The threadlike structures within the nucleus of a cell that carry the genes.

**Chronic grief** Grief response involving a denial of the reality of the loss, which prevents any resolution.

**Circumcision** Surgical removal of the prepuce (foreskin) of the penis.

**Circumoral cyanosis** Bluish appearance around the mouth.

**Circumvallate placenta** A placenta with a thick white fibrous ring around the edge.

**Cleavage** Rapid mitotic division of the zygote; cells produced are called blastomeres.

**Client advocacy** An approach to client care in which the nurse educates and supports the client and protects the client's rights.

**Clitoris** Female organ homologous to the male penis; a small oval body of erectile tissue situated at the anterior junction of the vulva.

**Coitus interruptus** Method of contraception in which the male withdraws his penis from the vagina prior to ejaculation.

**Cold stress** Excessive heat loss resulting in compensatory mechanisms (increased respirations and nonshivering thermogenesis) to maintain core body temperature.

**Colostrum** Secretion from the breast before the onset of true lactation; contains mainly serum and white blood corpuscles. It has a high protein content, provides some immune properties, and cleanses the neonate's intestinal tract of mucus and meconium.

**Conception** Union of male sperm and female ovum; fertilization.

**Conceptional age** The number of complete weeks since the moment of conception. Because the moment of conception is almost impossible to determine, conceptional age is estimated at 2 weeks less than gestational age.

**Condom** A rubber sheath that covers the penis to prevent conception or disease.

**Condyloma** Wartlike growth of skin, usually seen on the external genitals or anus. There are two types, a pointed variety and a broad, flat form usually found with syphilis.

**Conduction** Loss of heat to a cooler surface by direct skin contact.

**Conjugate** Important diameter of the pelvis, measured from the center of the promontory of the sacrum to the back of the symphysis pubis. The diagonal conjugate is measured and the true conjugate is estimated.

**Conjugate vera** The true conjugate, which extends from the middle of the sacral promontory to the middle of the pubic crest.

**Conjunctivitis** Inflammation of the mucous membrane lining the eyelids.

**Contraception** The prevention of conception or impregnation.

**Contraceptive sponge** A small pillow-shaped polyurethane sponge with a concave cupped area on one side, designed to fit over the cervix to prevent pregnancy.

**Contraction** Tightening and shortening of the uterine muscles during labor, causing effacement and dilatation of the cervix; contributes to the downward and outward descent of the fetus.

**Convection** Loss of heat from the warm body surface to cooler air currents.

**Contraction stress test** A method of assessing the reaction of the fetus to the stress of uterine contractions. This test may be utilized when contractions are occurring spontaneously or when contractions are artificially induced by OCT (oxytocin challenge test) or BSST (breast self-stimulation test).

**Coombs' test** A test for antiglobulins in the red cells. The indirect test determines the presence of Rh-positive antibodies in maternal blood; the direct test determines the presence of maternal Rh-positive antibodies in fetal cord blood.

**Cornua** The elongated portions of the uterus where the fallopian tubes open.

**Corpus** The upper two-thirds of the uterus.

**Corpus luteum** A small yellow body that develops within a ruptured ovarian follicle; it secretes progesterone in the second half of the menstrual cycle and atrophies about three days before the beginning of menstrual flow. If pregnancy occurs, the corpus luteum continues to produce progesterone until the placenta takes over this function.

**Cotyledon** One of the rounded portions into which the placenta's uterine surface is divided, consisting of a mass of villi, fetal vessels, and an intervillous space.

**Couvade** In some cultures, the male's observance of certain rituals and taboos to signify the transition to fatherhood.

**Crisis** Any naturally occurring turning point, such as courtship, marriage, pregnancy, parenthood, or death.

**Crisis intervention** Actions taken by the nurse to help the client deal with an impending, potentially overwhelming crisis, regain his or her equilibrium, grow from the experience, and improve coping skills.

**Crowning** Appearance of the presenting fetal part at the vaginal orifice during labor.

**Deceleration** Periodic decrease in the baseline fetal heart rate.

**Decidua** Endometrium or mucous membrane lining of the uterus in pregnancy that is shed after delivery.

**Decidual basalis** The part of the decidua that unites with the chorion to form the placenta. It is shed in lochial discharge after delivery.

**Decidua capsularis** The part of the decidua surrounding the chorionic sac.

**Decidua vera (parietalis)** Nonplacental decidua lining the uterus.

**Decrement** Decrease or stage of decline, as of a contraction.

**Desquamation** Shedding of the epithelial cells of the epidermis.

**Diagonal conjugate**   Distance from the lower posterior border of the symphysis pubis to the sacral promontory; may be obtained by manual measurement.

**Diaphragm**   A flexible disk that covers the cervix to prevent pregnancy.

**Diastasis recti abdominis**   Separation of the recti abdominis muscles along the median line. In women, it is seen with repeated childbirths or multiple gestations. In the newborn, it is usually caused by incomplete development.

**Dilatation of the cervix**   Expansion of the external os from an opening a few milimeters in size to an opening large enough to allow the passage of the infant.

**Dilatation and curettage (D and C)**   Stretching of the cervical canal to permit passage of a curette, which is used to scrape the endometrium to empty the uterine contents or to obtain tissue for examination.

**Diploid number of chromosomes**   Containing a set of maternal and a set of paternal chromosomes; in humans, the diploid number of chromosomes is 46.

**Down syndrome**   An abnormality resulting from the presence of an extra chromosome number 21 (trisomy 21); characteristics include mental retardation and altered physical appearance. Formerly called Mongolism or Mongoloid idiocy.

**Drug-dependent infant**   The newborn of an alcoholic or drug-addicted woman.

**Ductus arteriosus**   A communication channel between the main pulmonary artery and the aorta of the fetus. It is obliterated after birth by rising $PO_2$ and changes in intravascular pressure in the presence of normal pulmonary functioning. It normally becomes a ligament after birth but sometimes remains patent (patent ductus arteriosus), a treatable condition.

**Ductus venosus**   A fetal blood vessel that carries oxygenated blood between the umbilical vein and the inferior vena cava, bypassing the liver; it becomes a ligament after birth.

**Duncan's mechanism**   Occurs when the maternal surface of the placenta presents upon delivery rather than the shiny fetal surface.

**Duration**   The time length of each contraction, measured from the beginning of the increment to the completion of the decrement.

**Dysmenorrhea**   Painful menstruation.

**Dyspareunia**   Painful intercourse.

**Dystocia**   Difficult labor due to mechanical factors produced by the fetus or the maternal pelvis, or due to inadequate uterine or other muscular activity.

**Early decelerations**   Periodic change in fetal heart rate pattern caused by head compression; deceleration has a uniform appearance and early onset in relation to maternal contraction.

**Eclampsia**   A major complication of pregnancy. Its cause is unknown; it occurs more often in the primigravida and is accompanied by elevated blood pressure, albuminuria, oliguria, tonic and clonic convulsions, and coma. It may occur during pregnancy (usually after the twentieth week of gestation) or within 48 hours after delivery.

**Ectoderm**   Outer layer of cells in the developing embryo that give rise to the skin, nails, and hair.

**Ectopic pregnancy**   Implantation of the fertilized ovum outside the uterine cavity; common sites are the abdomen, fallopian tubes, and ovaries; also called oocyesis.

**Effacement**   Thinning and shortening of the cervix that occurs late in pregnancy or during labor.

**Ejaculation**   Expulsion of the seminal fluids from the penis.

**Embryo**   The early stage of development of the young of any organism. In humans the embryonic period is from about two to eight weeks of gestation, and is characterized by cellular differentiation and predominantly hyperplastic growth.

**Endoderm**   The inner layer of cells in the developing embryo that give rise to internal organs such as the intestines.

**Endometriosis**   Ectopic endometrium located outside the uterus in the pelvic cavity. Symptoms may include pelvic pain or pressure, dysmenorrhea, dispareunia, abnormal bleeding from the uterus or rectum, and sterility.

**Endometritis**   Infection of the endometrium.

**Endometrium**   The mucous membrane that lines the inner surface of the uterus.

**En face**   An assumed position in which one person looks at another and maintains his or her face in the same vertical plane as that of the other.

**Engagement**   The entrance of the fetal presenting part into the superior pelvic strait and the beginning of the descent through the pelvic canal.

**Engorgement**   Vascular congestion or distention. In obstetrics, the swelling of breast tissue brought about by an increase in blood and lymph supply to the breast, preceding true lactation.

**Engrossment**   Characteristic sense of absorption, preoccupation, and interest in the infant demonstrated by fathers during early contact with their infants.

**Epidural block**   Regional anesthesia effective through the first and second stages of labor.

**Episiotomy**   Incision of the perineum to facilitate delivery and to avoid laceration of the perineum.

**Epstein's pearls**   Small, white blebs found along the gum margins and at the junction of the hard and soft palates; commonly seen in the newborn as a normal manifestation.

**Erb-Duchenne palsy**   Paralysis of the arm and chest wall as a result of a birth injury to the brachial plexus or a subsequent injury to the fifth and sixth cervical nerves.

**Erythema toxicum**   Innocuous pink papular rash of unknown cause with superimposed vesicles; it appears within 24 to 48 hours after birth and resolves spontaneously within a few days.

**Erythroblastosis fetalis**   Hemolytic disease of the newborn characterized by anemia, jaundice, enlargement of the liver and spleen, and generalized edema. Caused by isoimmunization due to Rh incompatibility or ABO incompatibility.

**Estrogen replacement therapy (ERT)**   Use of estrogen and a progestin to decrease the symptoms of menopause and to help prevent osteoporosis.

**Estrogens**   The hormones estradiol and estrone, produced by the ovary.

**Ethnocentrism**   An individual's belief that the values and practices of his or her own culture are the best ones.

**Evaporation**   Loss of heat incurred when water on the skin surface is converted to a vapor.

**Exchange transfusion**   The replacement of 70 percent to 80 percent of circulating blood by withdrawing the recipient's blood and injecting a donor's blood in equal amounts, for the purpose of preventing the accumulation of bilirubin or other byproducts of hemolysis in the blood.

**External os**   The opening between the cervix and the vagina.

**Fallopian tubes**   Tubes that extend from the lateral angle of the uterus and terminate near the ovary; they serve as a passageway for the ovum from the ovary to the uterus and for the spermatozoa from the uterus toward the ovary. Also called oviducts and uterine tubes.

**False labor**   Contractions of the uterus, regular or irregular, that may be strong enough to be interpreted as true labor but that do not dilate the cervix.

**False pelvis**   The portion of the pelvis above the linea terminalis; its primary function is to support the weight of the enlarged pregnant uterus.

**Family-centered care**   An approach to health care based on the concept that a hospital can provide professional services to mothers, fathers, and infants in a homelike environment that would enhance the integrity of the family unit.

**Female reproductive cycle (FRC)**   The monthly rhythmic changes in sexually mature females.

**Ferning**   Formation of a palm-leaf pattern by the crystallization of cervical mucus as it dries at mid-menstrual cycle. Helpful in determining time of ovulation. Observed via microscopic examination of a thin layer of cervical mucus on a glass slide. This pattern is also observed when amniotic fluid is allowed to air dry on a slide and is a useful and quick test to determine whether amniotic membranes have ruptured.

**Fertility awareness methods**   Natural family planning.

**Fertility rate**   Number of births per 1000 women aged 15 to 44 in a given population per year.

**Fertilization**   Impregnation of an ovum by a spermatozoon.

**Fetal alcohol syndrome (FAS)**   Syndrome caused by maternal alcohol ingestion and characterized by microcephaly, intrauterine growth retardation, short palpebral fissures, and maxillary hypoplasia.

**Fetal death**   Death of the developing fetus after 20 weeks' gestation. Also called fetal demise.

**Fetal blood sampling**   Blood sample drawn from the fetal scalp (or from the fetus in breech position) to evaluate the acid-base status of the fetus.

**Fetal bradycardia**   A fetal heart rate less than 120 beats/minute during a 10-minute period of continuous monitoring.

**Fetal distress**   Evidence that the fetus is in jeopardy, such as a change in fetal activity or heart rate.

**Fetal heart rate (FHR)**   The number of times the fetal heart beats per minute; normal range is 120 to 160 beats per minute.

**Fetal position**   Relationship of the landmark on the presenting fetal part to the front, sides, or back of the maternal pelvis.

**Fetal presentation**   The fetal body part that enters the maternal pelvis first. The three possible presentations are cephalic, shoulder, or breech.

**Fetal tachycardia**   A fetal heart rate of 160 beats/minute or more during a 10-minute period of continuous monitoring.

**Fetoscope**   An adaptation of a stethoscope that facilitates auscultation of the fetal heart rate.

**Fetoscopy**   A technique for directly observing the fetus and obtaining a sample of fetal blood or skin.

**Fetus**   The child in utero from about the seventh to ninth week of gestation until birth.

**Fibrocystic breast disease**   Benign breast disorder characterized by a thickening of normal breast tissue and the formation of cysts.

**Fimbria**   Any structure resembling a fringe; the fringelike extremity of the fallopian tubes.

**Folic acid**   An important vitamin directly related to the outcome of pregnancy and to maternal and fetal health.

**Follicle-stimulating hormone (FSH)**   Hormone produced by the anterior pituitary during the first half of the menstrual cycle, stimulating development of the graafian follicle.

**Fontanelle**   In the fetus, an unossified space or soft spot consisting of a strong band of connective tissue lying between the cranial bones of the skull.

**Foramen ovale**   Septal opening between the atria of the fetal heart. Normally, the opening closes shortly after birth; if it remains open, it can be repaired surgically.

**Forceps**   Obstetric instruments occasionally used to aid in delivery.

**Frequency**   The time between the beginning of one contraction and the beginning of the next contraction.

**Fundus**   The upper portion of the uterus between the fallopian tubes.

**Gametogenesis**   The process by which germ cells are produced.

**Genotype**   The genetic composition of an individual.

**Gestation**   Period of intrauterine development from conception through birth; pregnancy.

**Gestational age**   The number of complete weeks of fetal development, calculated from the first day of the last normal menstrual cycle.

**Gestational age assessment tools**   Systems used to evaluate the newborn's external physical characteristics and neurologic and/or neuromuscular development to accurately determine gestational age. These replace or supplement the traditional calculation from the mother's last menstrual period.

**Gestational trophoblastic disease (GTD)**   Disorder classified into two types; benign (hydatidiform mole) and malignant.

**Goodell's sign**   Softening of the cervix that occurs during the second month of pregnancy.

**Graafian follicle**   The ovarian cyst containing the ripe ovum; it secretes estrogens.

**Gravida**   A pregnant woman.

**Grief**   An emotional state; a reaction to loss.

**Grief work**   The inner process of working through or managing the bereavement.

**Gynecoid pelvis**   Typical female pelvis in which the inlet is round instead of oval.

**Habituation**   Infant's ability to diminish innate responses to specific repeated stimuli.

**Haploid number of chromosomes**  Half the diploid number of chromosomes. In humans, there are 23 chromosomes, the haploid number, in each germ cell.

**Harlequin sign**  A rare color change that occurs between the longitudinal halves of the newborn's body, such that the dependent half is noticeably pinker than the superior half when the newborn is placed on one side; it is of no pathologic significance.

**Hegar's sign**  A softening of the lower uterine segment found upon palpation in the second or third month of pregnancy.

**Hemolytic disease of the newborn**  *Hyperbilirubinemia* secondary to Rh incompatibility.

**Herpesvirus**  A family of viruses characterized by the development of clusters of small vesicles. The infection is recurring and is frequently found about the lips and nares; a genital form also exists that is primarily sexually transmitted.

**Heterozygous**  A genotypic situation in which two different alleles occur at a given locus on a pair of homologous chromosomes.

**Homozygous**  A genotypic situation in which two similar genes occur at a given locus on homologous chromosomes.

**Human chorionic gonadotropin (HCG)**  A hormone produced by the chorionic villi and found in the urine of pregnant women; also called *prolan*.

**Human placental lactogen (HPL)**  A hormone synthesized by the syncytiotrophoblast that functions as an insulin antagonist and promotes lipolysis to increase the amounts of circulating free fatty acids available for maternal metabolic use.

**Hyaline membrane disease**  Respiratory disease of the newborn characterized by interference with ventilation at the alveolar level, thought to be caused by the presence of fibrinoid deposits lining the alveolar ducts. Also called *respiratory distress syndrome (RDS)*.

**Hydatidiform mole**  Degenerative process in chorionic villi, giving rise to multiple cysts and rapid growth of the uterus with hemorrhage.

**Hydramnios**  An excess of amniotic fluid, leading to overdistention of the uterus. Frequently seen in diabetic pregnant women, even if there is no coexisting fetal anomaly. Also called *polyhydramnios*.

**Hydrops fetalis**  See *erythroblastosis fetalis*.

**Hyperbilirubinemia**  Excessive amount of bilirubin in the blood; indicative of hemolytic processes due to blood incompatibility, intrauterine infection, septicemia, neonatal renal infection, and other disorders.

**Hyperemesis gravdarum**  Excessive vomiting during pregnancy, leading to dehydration and starvation.

**Hypnoreflexogenous method**  A combination of hypnosis and conditioned reflexes used during childbirth.

**Hypocalcemia**  Abnormally low level of serum calcium levels.

**Hypoglycemia**  Abnormally low level of sugar in the blood.

**Hysterectomy**  Surgical removal of the uterus.

**Hysterosalpingogram**  Instillation of radiopaque substance into the uterine cavity to visualize uterus and fallopian tubes.

**Icterus neonatorum**  Jaundice in the newborn.

**Inborn error of metabolism**  A hereditary deficiency of a specific enzyme needed for normal metabolism of specific chemicals.

**Increment**  Increase or addition; to build up, as of a contraction.

**Induction of labor**  The process of causing or initiating labor by use of medication or surgical rupture of membranes.

**Infant**  Child under one year of age.

**Infant death rate**  Number of deaths of infants under one year of age per 1000 live births in a given population per year.

**Infant of a diabetic mother (IDM)**  At-risk infant born to a woman previously diagnosed as diabetic, or who develops symptoms of diabetes during pregnancy.

**Inferential statistics**  Statistics that allow an investigator to draw conclusions about what is happening between two or more variables in a population and to suggest or refute casual relationships between them.

**Infertility**  Diminished ability to conceive.

**Informed consent**  A legal concept that protects a person's rights to autonomy and self-determination by specifying that no action may be taken without that person's prior understanding and freely given consent.

**Infundibulopelvic ligament**  Ligament that suspends and supports the ovaries.

**Innominate bone**  The hip bone, ilium, ischium, and pubis.

**Intensity**  The strength of a uterine contraction during acme.

**Internal os**  An inside mouth or opening; the opening between the cervix and the uterus.

**Intrapartum**  The time from the onset of true labor until the delivery of the infant and placenta.

**Intrauterine device (IUD)**  Small metal or plastic form that is placed in the uterus to prevent implantation of a fertilized ovum.

**Intrauterine growth retardation (IUGR)**  Fetal undergrowth due to any etiology, such as intrauterine infection, deficient nutrient supply, or congenital malformation.

**Introitus**  Opening or entrance into a cavity or canal such as the vagina.

**Involution**  Rolling or turning inward; the reduction in size of the uterus following delivery.

**Ischial spines**  Prominences that arise near the junction of the ilium and ischium and jut into the pelvic cavity; used as a reference point during labor to evaluate the descent of the fetal head into the birth canal.

**Isthmus**  The straight, narrow part of the fallopian tube with a thick muscular wall and an opening (lumen) 2–3 mm in diameter; the site of tubal ligation. Also a constriction in the uterus that is located above the cervix and below the corpus.

**Jaundice**  Yellow pigmentation of body tissues caused by the presence of bile pigments. See also *physiologic jaundice*.

**Karyotype**  The set of chromosomes arranged in a standard order.

**Kegel's exercises**  Perineal muscle tightening that strengthens the pubococcygeus muscle and increases its tone.

**Kernicterus**  An encephalopathy caused by deposition of unconjugated bilirubin in brain cells; may result in impaired brain function or death.

**Klinefelter syndrome**  A chromosomal abnormality caused by the presence of an extra X chromosome in the male; characteristics include tall stature, sparse pubic and facial hair, gynecomastia, small firm testes, and absence of spermatogenesis.

**Labor**   The process by which the fetus is expelled from the maternal uterus; also called childbirth, confinement, or parturition.

**Lactation**   Process of producing and supplying breast milk.

**Lacto-ovovegetarians**   Vegetarians who include milk, dairy products, and eggs in their diets, and occasionally fish, poultry, and liver.

**Lactose intolerance**   A condition in which an individual has difficulty digesting milk and milk products.

**Lactovegetarians**   Vegetarians who include dairy products but no eggs in their diets.

**La Leche League**   Organization that provides information on and assistance with breast-feeding.

**Lamaze method**   A method of childbirth preparation, also known as *psychoprophylaxis*.

**Lanugo**   Fine, downy hair found on all body parts of the fetus, with the exception of the palms of the hands and the soles of the feet, after 20 weeks' gestation.

**Large for gestational age (LGA)**   Excessive growth of a fetus in relation to the gestational time period.

**Last menstrual period (LMP)**   The last normal menstrual period experienced by the mother prior to pregnancy; sometimes used to calculate the infant's gestational age.

**Later decelerations**   Periodic change in fetal heart rate pattern caused by uteroplacental insufficiency; deceleration has a uniform shape and late onset in relation to maternal contraction.

**Leboyer method**   Birthing technique that eases the newborn's transition to extrauterine life wherein lights in the delivery room are dimmed and noise is kept to a minimum.

**Leiomyoma**   A benign tumor of the uterus, composed primarily of smooth muscle and connective tissue. Also referred to as a myoma or a fibroid.

**Leopold's maneuvers**   Series of four maneuvers designed to provide a systematic approach whereby the examiner may determine fetal presentation and position.

**Letdown reflex**   Pattern of stimulation, hormone release, and resulting muscle contraction that forces milk into the lactiferous ducts, making it available to the infant; milk ejection reflex.

**Leukorrhea**   Mucous discharge from the vagina or cervical canal that may be normal or pathologic, as in the presence of infection.

**Lie**   Relationship of the long axis of the fetus and the long axis of the pregnant woman. The fetal lie may be longitudinal, transverse, or oblique.

**Lightening**   Moving of the fetus and uterus downward into the pelvic cavity; engagement.

**Linea nigra**   The line of darker pigmentation extending from the umbilicus to the pubis noted in some women during the later months of pregnancy.

**Local infiltration**   Injection of an anesthetic agent into the subcutaneous tissue in a fanlike pattern.

**Lochia**   Maternal discharge of blood, mucus, and tissue from the uterus; may last for several weeks after birth.

**Lochia alba**   White vaginal discharge that follows lochia serosa and that lasts from about the tenth to the twenty-first day after delivery.

**Lochia rubra**   Red, blood-tinged vaginal discharge that occurs following delivery and lasts two to four days.

**Lochia serosa**   Pink, serous, and blood-tinged vaginal discharge that follows lochia rubra and lasts until the seventh to tenth day after delivery.

**Loss**   A state of being deprived of, or without, something one has had.

**L/S ratio**   The ratio of the phospholipids lecithin and sphingomyelin produced by the fetal lungs; useful in assessing fetal lung maturity.

**Luteinizing hormone (LH)**   Anterior pituitary hormone responsible for stimulating ovulation and for development of the corpus luteum.

**Macrosomia**   Condition seen in neonates of large body size and high birth weight, as those born of prediabetic and diabetic mothers.

**Malposition**   An abnormal position of the fetus in the birth canal.

**Malpresentation**   A presentation of the fetus into the birth canal that is not "normal," that is, brow, face, shoulder, or breech presentation.

**Mammogram**   Soft tissue radiograph of the breast without the injection of a contrast medium.

**Mastitis**   Inflammation of the breast.

**Maternal mortality**   Number of maternal deaths from any cause during the pregnancy cycle per 100,000 live births.

**McDonald's sign**   A probable sign of pregnancy characterized by an ease in flexing the body of the uterus against the cervix.

**Meconium**   Dark green or black material present in the large intestine of a full-term infant; the first stools passed by the newborn.

**Meconium aspiration syndrome (MAS)**   Respiratory disease of term, postterm, and SGA newborns caused by inhalation of meconium or meconium-stained amniotic fluid into the lungs; characterized by mild to severe respiratory distress, hyperexpansion of the chest, hyperinflated alveoli, and secondary atelectasis.

**Meiosis**   The process of cell division that occurs in the maturation of sperm and ova that decreases their number of chromosomes by one half.

**Menarche**   Beginning of menstrual and reproductive function in the female.

**Mendelian inheritance**   A major category of inheritance whereby a trait is determined by a pair of genes on homologous chromosomes; also called single gene inheritance.

**Menorrhagia**   Excessive or profuse menstrual flow.

**Menstrual cycle**   Cyclic buildup of the uterine lining, ovulation, and sloughing of the lining occurring approximately every 28 days in nonpregnant females.

**Mentum**   The chin.

**Mesoderm**   The intermediate layer of germ cells in the embryo that give rise to connective tissue, bone marrow, muscles, blood, lymphoid tissue, and epithelial tissue.

**Metrorrhagia**   Abnormal uterine bleeding occurring at irregular intervals.

**Middle adolescent**   The adolescent between 15 and 17 years of age.

**Milia**  Tiny white papules appearing on the face of a neonate as a result of unopened sebaceous glands; they disappear spontaneously within a few weeks.

**Miscarriage**  See *spontaneous abortion.*

**Mitleiden**  A phenomenon in which expectant fathers develop symptoms similar to those of the pregnant woman: weight gain, nausea, and various aches and pains.

**Mitosis**  Process of cell division whereby both daughter cells have the same number and pattern of chromosomes as the original cell.

**Modeling**  The process of teaching behaviors through role playing or having the client talk with a person who has mastered a similar crisis.

**Molding**  Shaping of the fetal head by overlapping of the cranial bones to facilitate movement through the birth canal during labor.

**Mongolian spot**  Dark, flat pigmentation of the lower back and buttocks noted at birth in some infants; usually disappears by the time the child reaches school age.

**Moniliasis**  Yeastlike fungus infection caused by Candida albicans.

**Mons pubis**  Mound of subcutaneous fatty tissue covering the anterior portion of the symphysis pubis.

**Moro reflex**  Flexion of the newborn's thighs and knees accompanied by fingers that fan, then clench, as the arms are simultaneously thrown out and then brought together, as though embracing something. This reflex can be elicited by startling the newborn with a sudden noise or movement; also called the startle reflex.

**Morula**  Developmental stage of the fertilized ovum in which there is a solid mass of cells.

**Mottling**  Discoloration of the skin in irregular areas; may be seen with chilling, poor perfusion, or hypoxia.

**Mucous plug**  A collection of thick mucus that blocks the cervical canal during pregnancy; also called operculum.

**Multigravida**  Female who has been pregnant more than once.

**Multipara**  Female who has had more than one pregnancy in which the fetus was viable.

**Multiple pregnancy**  More than one fetus in the uterus at the same time.

**Myometrium**  Uterine muscular structure.

**Nägele's rule**  A method of determining the estimated date of delivery (EDD): after obtaining the first day of the last menstrual period, one subtracts 3 months and adds 7 days.

**Natural childbirth**  Prepared childbirth, in which the couple attends a prenatal education program and learns exercises and breathing patterns that are used during labor and childbirth.

**Neonatal mortality rate**  Number of deaths of infants in the first 28 days of life per 1000 live births.

**Neonate**  Infant from birth through the first 28 days of life.

**Neonatology**  The specialty that focuses on the management of high-risk conditions of the newborn.

**Nevus flammeus**  Large port-wine stain.

**Nevus vasculosus**  "Strawberry mark"; raised, clearly delineated, dark red, rough-surfaced birth mark commonly found in the head region.

**Newborn screening tests**  Tests that detect inborn errors of metabolism that, if left untreated, cause mental retardation and physical handicaps.

**Nipple**  A protrusion about 0.5 to 1.3 cm in diameter in the center of each mature breast.

**Nipple preparation**  Prenatal activities designed to toughen the nipple in preparation for breast-feeding.

**Nonstress test (NST)**  An assessment method by which the reaction (or response) of the fetal heart rate to fetal movement is evaluated.

**Nuchal cord**  Term used to describe the umbilical cord when it is wrapped around the neck of the fetus.

**Nulligravida**  A female who has never been pregnant.

**Nullipara**  A female who has not delivered a viable fetus.

**Nurse-midwife**  A certified nurse-midwife (CNM) is an RN who has received special training and education in the care of the family during childbearing and the prenatal, labor and delivery, and postpartal periods. After a period of formal education, the nurse-midwife takes a certification test to become a CNM.

**Obstetric conjugate**  Distance from the middle of the sacral promontory to an area approximately 1 cm below the pubic crest.

**Older adolescent**  The adolescent between 17 and 19 years of age.

**Oligohydramnios**  Decreased amount of amniotic fluid, which may indicate a fetal urinary tract defect.

**Oogenesis**  Process during fetal life whereby the ovary produces oogenia, cells that become primitive ovarian eggs.

**Oophoritis**  Infection of the ovaries.

**Ophthalmia neonatorum**  Purulent infection of the eyes or conjunctiva of the newborn, usually caused by gonococci.

**Oral contraceptives**  "Birth control pills" that work by inhibiting the release of an ovum and by maintaining a type of mucus that is hostile to sperm.

**Orgasm**  Climax of the sexual experience.

**Orientation**  Infant's ability to respond to auditory and visual stimuli in the environment.

**Ortolani's maneuver**  A manual procedure performed to rule out the possibility of congenital hip dysplasia.

**Ovarian ligaments**  Ligaments that anchor the lower pole of the ovary to the cornua of the uterus.

**Ovary**  Female sex gland in which the ova are formed and in which estrogen and progesterone are produced. Normally there are two ovaries, located in the lower abdomen on each side of uterus.

**Ovulation**  Normal process of discharging a mature ovum from an ovary approximately 14 days prior to the onset of menses.

**Ovum**  Female reproductive cell; egg.

**Oxygen toxicity**  Excessive levels of oxygen therapy that result in pathologic changes in tissue.

**Oxytocin**  Hormone normally produced by the posterior pituitary, responsible for stimulation of uterine contractions and the release of milk into the lactiferous ducts.

**Oxytocin challenge test (OCT)**  See *contraction stress test* (CST).

**Papanicolaou (Pap) smear** Procedure to detect the presence of cancer of the uterus by microscopic examination of cells gently scraped from the cervix.

**Para** A woman who has borne offspring who reached the age of viability.

**Paracervical block** A local anesthetic agent injected transvaginally adjacent to the outer rim of the cervix.

**Parametritis** Inflammation of the parametrial layer of the uterus.

**Parent-infant attachment** Close affectional ties that develop between parent and child. See also *attachment.*

**Passive acquired immunity** Transferral of antibodies (IgG) from the mother to the fetus in utero.

**Pelvic cavity** Bony portion of the birth passages; a curved canal with a longer posterior than anterior wall.

**Pelvic cellulitis** Infection involving the connective tissue of the broad ligament or, in severe cases, the connective tissue of all the pelvic structures.

**Pelvic diaphragm** Part of the pelvic floor composed of deep fascia and the levator ani and the coccygeal muscles.

**Pelvic floor** Muscles and tissue that act as a buttress to the pelvic outlet.

**Pelvic inflammatory disease** An infection of the fallopian tubes that may or may not be accompanied by a pelvic abscess; may cause infertility secondary to tubal damage.

**Pelvic inlet** Upper border of the true pelvis.

**Pelvic outlet** Lower border of the true pelvis.

**Pelvic tilt** Also called pelvic rocking; exercise designed to reduce back strain and strengthen abdominal muscle tone.

**Penis** The male organ of copulation and reproduction.

**Perimetrium** The outermost layer of the corpus of the uterus; also known as the serosal layer.

**Perinatal mortality rate** The number of neonatal and fetal deaths per 1000 live births.

**Perinatology** The medical specialty concerned with the diagnosis and treatment of high-risk conditions of the pregnant woman and her fetus.

**Perineal body** Wedge-shaped mass of fibromuscular tissue found between the lower part of the vagina and the anal canal.

**Perineum** The area of tissue between the anus and scrotum in the male or between the anus and vagina in the female.

**Periodic breathing** Sporadic episodes of apnea, note associated with cyanosis, that lasts for about 10 seconds and commonly occur in preterm infants.

**Periods of reactivity** Predictable patterns of neonate behavior during the first several hours after birth.

**Persistant occiput posterior position** Malposition of the fetus in which the fetal occiput is posterior in the maternal pelvis.

**Phenotype** The whole physical, biochemical, and physiologic makeup of an individual as determined both genetically and environmentally.

**Phosphatidylglycerol (PG)** A phospholipid present in fetal surfactant after about 35 weeks' gestation.

**Phototherapy** The treatment of jaundice by exposure to light.

**Physiologic anemia of infancy** A harmless condition in which the hemoglobin level drops in the first 6 to 12 weeks after birth, then reverts to normal levels.

**Physiologic jaundice** A harmless condition caused by the normal reduction of red blood cells, occurring 48 or more hours after birth, peaking at the fifth to seventh day, and disappearing between the seventh to tenth day.

**Pica** The eating of substances not ordinarily considered edible or to have nutritive value.

**Placenta** Specialized disk-shaped organ that connects the fetus to the uterine wall for gas and nutrient exchange; also called *afterbirth.*

**Placenta accreta** Partial or complete absence of the decidua basalis and abnormal adherence of the placenta to the uterine wall.

**Placenta previa** Abnormal implantation of the placenta in the lower uterine segment. Classification of type is based on proximity to the cervical os: *total*—completely covers the os; *partial*—covers a portion of the os; *marginal*—in close proximity to the os.

**Platypelloid pelvis** An unusually wide pelvis, having a flattened oval transverse shape and a shortened anteroposterior diameter.

**Polar body** A small cell resulting from the meiotic division of the mature oocyte.

**Polycythemia** An abnormal increase in the number of total red blood cells in the body's circulation.

**Polydactyly** A developmental anomaly characterized by more than five digits on the hands or feet.

**Positive signs of pregnancy** Indications that confirm the presence of pregnancy.

**Postdate pregnancy** Pregnancy that lasts beyond 42 weeks' gestation.

**Postpartal hemorrhage** A loss of blood of greater than 500 mL following delivery. The hemorrhage is classified as *early* or *immediate* if it occurs within the first 24 hours and *late* or *delayed* after the first 24 hours.

**Postpartum** After childbirth or delivery.

**Postterm infant** Any infant delivered after 42 weeks' gestation.

**Postterm labor** Labor that occurs after 42 weeks of gestation.

**Precipitous birth** (1) unduly rapid progression of labor; (2) a delivery in which no physician is in attendance.

**Precipitous labor** Labor lasting less than three hours.

**Preeclampsia** Toxemia of pregnancy, characterized by hypertension, albuminuria, and edema. See also *eclampsia.*

**Pregnancy-induced hypertension (PIH)** A hypertensive disorder including preeclampsia and eclampsia as conditions, characterized by the three cardinal signs of hypertension, edema, and proteinuria.

**Premature infant** See *preterm infant.*

**Premenstrual syndrome (PMS)** Cluster of symptoms experienced by some women, typically occurring from a few days up to two weeks prior to the onset of menses.

**Prep** Shaving of the pubic area.

**Presentation** The fetal body part that enters the maternal pelvis first. The three possible presentations are cephalic, shoulder, or breech.

**Presenting part** The fetal part present in or on the cervical os.

**Presumptive signs of pregnancy** Symptoms that suggest but do not confirm pregnancy, such as cessation of menses, quickening, Chadwick's sign, and morning sickness.

**Preterm infant** Any infant born before 38 weeks' gestation.

**Preterm labor** Labor occurring between 20 and 38 weeks of pregnancy.

**Primigravida** A woman who is pregnant for the first time.

**Primipara** A woman who has given birth to her first child (past the point of viability), whether or not that child is living or was alive at birth.

**Probable signs of pregnancy** Manifestations that strongly suggest the likelihood of pregnancy, such as a positive pregnancy test, enlarging abdomen, and positive Goodell's, Hegar's, and Braxton Hicks signs.

**Progesterone** A hormone produced by the corpus luteum, adrenal cortex, and placenta whose function is to stimulate proliferation of the endometrium to facilitate growth of the embryo.

**Prolactin** A hormone secreted by the anterior pituitary that stimulates and sustains lactation in mammals.

**Prolapsed cord** Umbilical cord that becomes trapped in the vagina before the fetus is delivered.

**Prolonged labor** Labor lasting more than 24 hours.

**Prostaglandins** Complex lipid compounds synthesized by many cells in the body.

**Pseudomenstruation** Blood-tinged mucus from the vagina in the newborn female infant; caused by withdrawal of maternal hormones that were present during pregnancy.

**Psychoprophylaxis** Psychophysical training aimed at preparing the expectant parents to cope with the processes of labor and to avoid concentration on the discomforts associated with childbirth.

**Ptyalism** Excessive salivation.

**Pubic** Pertaining to the pubes or pubis.

**Pudendal block** Injection of an anesthetizing agent at the pudendal nerve to produce numbness of the external genitals and the lower one third of the vagina, to facilitate childbirth and permit episiotomy if necessary.

**Puerperal morbidity** A maternal temperature of 100.4F (38.0C) or higher on any two of the first 10 postpartal days, excluding the first 24 hours. The temperature is to be taken by mouth at least four times per day.

**Puerperium** The period after completion of the third stage of labor until involution of the uterus is complete, usually six weeks.

**Quickening** The first fetal movements felt by the pregnant woman, usually between 16 to 18 weeks gestation.

**Radiation** Heat loss incurred when heat transfers to cooler surfaces and objects not in direct contact with the body.

**Read method** Natural childbirth preparation centered on eliminating the fear-tension-pain syndrome.

**Reciprocal inhibition** The principle that it is impossible to feel relaxed and tense at the same time; the basis for relaxation techniques.

**Recommended dietary allowances (RDA)** Government-recommended allowances of various vitamins, minerals, and other nutrients.

**Regional anesthesia** Injection of local anesthetic agents so that they come into direct contact with nervous tissue.

**Relaxin** A water-soluble protein secreted by the corpus luteum that causes relaxation of the symphysis and cervical dilatation.

**Respiratory distress syndrome** See *hyaline membrane disease.*

**Retrolental fibroplasia** Formation of fibrotic tissue behind the lens; associated with retinal detachment and arrested eye growth, seen with hypoxemia in preterm infants.

**Rh factor** Antigens present on the surface of blood cells that make the blood cell incompatible with blood cells that do not have the antigen.

**RhoGAM** An anti-Rh (D) gamma-globulin given after delivery to an Rh-negative mother of an Rh-positive fetus or child. Prevents the development of permanent active immunity to the Rh antigen.

**Rhythm method** The timing of sexual intercourse to avoid the fertile time associated with ovulation.

**Risk factors** Any findings that suggest the pregnancy may have a negative outcome, either for the woman or her unborn child.

**Rooming-in unit** A hospital unit where the infant can reside in the same room with the mother after delivery and during their postpartal stay.

**Rooting reflex** An infant's tendency to turn the head and open the lips to suck when one side of the mouth or cheek is touched.

**Round ligaments** Ligaments that arise from the side of the uterus near the fallopian tube insertion to help the broad ligament keep the uterus in place.

**Rugae** Transverse ridges of mucous membranes lining the vagina, which allow the vagina to stretch during the descent of the fetal head.

**Rupture of membranes (ROM)** Rupture may be PROM (Premature), SROM (spontaneous), or AROM (artificial). Some clinicians may use the abbreviation RBOW (rupture of bag of water).

**Sacral promontory** A projection into the pelvic cavity on the anterior upper portion of the sacrum; serves as an obstetric guide in determining pelvic measurements.

**Salpingitis** Infection of the fallopian tubes.

**Scarf sign** The position of the elbow when the hand of a supine infant is drawn across to the other shoulder until it meets resistance.

**Schultze's mechanism** Delivery of the placenta with the shiny or fetal surface presenting first.

**Self quieting activity** Infant's ability to use personal resources to quiet and console him or herself.

**Semen** Thick whitish fluid ejaculated by the male during orgasm and containing the spermatozoa and their nutrients.

**Sepsis neonatorum** Infections experienced by a neonate during the first month of life.

**Sex chromosomes** The X and Y chromosomes, which are responsible for sex determination.

**Sexually transmitted disease (STD)** Refers to diseases ordinarily transmitted by direct sexual contact with an infected individual.

**Show** A pinkish mucous discharge from the vagina that may occur a few hours to a few days prior to the onset of labor.

**Simian line** A single palmar crease frequently found in children with Down syndrome.

**Sims Huhner test** Postcoital examination to evaluate sperm and cervical mucus.

**Sinusoidal pattern** A wave form of fetal heart rate where long-term variability is present but there is no short-term variability.

**Situational contraceptives** Contraceptive methods that involve no prior preparation, for instance, abstinence or coitus interruptus.

**Skin turgor** Elasticity of skin; provides information on hydration status.

**Small for gestational age (SGA)** Inadequate weight or growth for gestational age; birth weight below the tenth percentile.

**Spermatogenesis** The process by which mature spermatozoa are formed, during which the number of chromosomes is halved.

**Spermatozoa** Mature sperm cells of the male animal, produced by the testes.

**Spermicides** A variety of creams, foam, jellies, and suppositories, inserted into the vagina prior to intercourse, which destroy sperm or neutralize any vaginal secretions and thereby immobilize sperm.

**Spinal block** Injection of a local anesthetic agent directly into the spinal fluid in the spinal canal to provide anesthesia for vaginal delivery and cesarean birth.

**Spinnbarkeit** Describes the elasticity of the cervical mucus that is present at ovulation.

**Spontaneous abortion** Abortion that occurs naturally; also called *miscarriage*.

**Station** Relationship of the presenting fetal part to an imaginary line drawn between the pelvic ischial spines.

**Sterility** Inability to conceive or to produce offspring.

**Stillbirth** The delivery of a dead infant.

**Striae gravidarum** Stretch marks; shiny reddish lines that appear on the abdomen, breasts, thighs, and buttocks of pregnant women as a result of stretching the skin.

**Subconjunctival hemorrhage** Hemorrhage on the sclera of a newborn's eye usually caused by changes in vascular tension during birth.

**Subinvolution** Failure of a part to return to its normal size after functional enlargement, such as failure of the uterus to return to normal size after pregnancy.

**Surfactant** A surface-active mixture of lipoproteins secreted in the alveoli and air passages that reduces surface tension of pulmonary fluids and contributes to the elasticity of pulmonary tissue.

**Suture** (1) Fibrous connection of opposed joint surfaces, as in the skull. (2) The uniting of edges of a wound.

**Symphysis pubis** Fibrocartilaginous joint between the pelvic bones in the midline.

**Syndactyly** Malformation of the fingers or toes in which there may be webbing or complete fusion of two or more digits.

**Telangiectatic nevi (stork bites)** Small clusters of pink-red spots appearing on the nape of the neck and around the eyes of infants; localized areas of capillary dilatation.

**Teratogens** Nongenetic factors that can produce malformations of the fetus.

**Testes** The male gonads, in which sperm and testosterone are produced.

**Testosterone** The male hormone; responsible for the development of secondary male characteristics.

**Therapeutic abortion** Medically induced termination of pregnancy when a malformed fetus is suspected or when the woman's health is in jeopardy.

**Thermal neutral zone (TNZ)** An environment that provides for minimal heat loss or expenditure.

**Thrush** A fungus infection of the oral mucous membranes caused by *Candida albicans*. Most often seen in infants; characterized by white plaques in the mouth.

**Tonic neck reflex** Postural reflex seen in the newborn. When the supine infant's head is turned to one side, the arm and leg on that side extend while the extremities on the opposite side flex; also called the fencing position.

**TORCH** An acronym used to describe a group of infections that represent potentially severe problems during pregnancy. TO = toxoplasmosis, R = rubella, C = cytomegalovirus, H = herpesvirus.

**Toxic shock syndrome** Infection caused by *staphylococcus aureus*, found primarily in women of reproductive age.

**Transverse diameter** The largest diameter of the pelvic inlet; helps determine the shape of the inlet.

**Transverse lie** A lie in which the fetus is positioned crosswise in the uterus.

*Trichomonas vaginalis* A parasitic protozoan that may cause inflammation of the vagina, characterized by itching and burning of vulvar tissue and by white, frothy discharge.

**Trimester** Three months, or one-third of the gestational time for pregnancy.

**Trisomy** The presence of three homologous chromosomes rather than the normal two.

**Trophoblast** The outer layer of the blastoderm that will eventually establish the nutrient relationship with the uterine endometrium.

**True pelvis** The portion that lies below the linea terminalis, made up of the inlet, cavity, and outlet.

**Turner syndrome** A number of anomalies that occur when a female has only one X chromosome; characteristics include short stature, little sexual differentiation, webbing of the neck with a low posterior hairline, and congenital cardiac anomalies.

**Ultrasound** High-frequency sound waves that may be directed, through the use of a transducer, into the maternal abdomen. The ultrasonic sound waves reflected by the underlying structures of varying densities allow various maternal and fetal tissues, bones, and fluids to be identified.

**Umbilical cord** The structure connecting the placenta to the umbilicus of the fetus and through which nutrients from the woman are exchanged for wastes from the fetus.

**Uterosacral ligaments** Ligaments that provide support for the uterus and cervix at the level of the ischial spines.

**Uterus** The hollow muscular organ in which the fertilized ovum is implanted and in which the developing fetus is nourished until birth.

**Vagina** The musculomembranous tube or passageway located between the external genitals and the uterus of the female.

**Variable deceleration** Periodic change in fetal heart rate caused by umbilical cord compression; decelerations vary in onset, occurence, and waveform.

**Vasectomy** Surgical removal of a portion of the vas deferens (ductus deferens) to produce infertility.

**Vegan** A "pure" vegetarian; one who consumes no food from animal sources.

**Vena caval syndrome** Symptoms of dizziness, pallor, and clamminess that result from lowered blood pressure when a pregnant woman lies supine and the enlarged uterus presses on the vena cava; also known as supine hypotensive syndrome.

**Vernix caseosa** A protective cheeselike whitish substance made up of sebum and desquamated epithelial cells that is present on the fetal skin.

**Vertex** The top or crown of the head.

**Vulva** The external structure of the female genitals, lying below the mons veneris.

**Wharton's jelly** Yellow-white gelatinous material surrounding the vessels of the umbilical cord.

**Young adolescent** The adolescent less than 15 years of age.

**Zona pellucida** Transparent inner layer surrounding an ovum.

**Zygote** A fertilized egg.

# Credits

## Chapter Opening Quotations

Armstrong, Penny, and Feldman, Sheryl. *A Midwife's Story*. New York: Arbor House, 1986.

Baldwin, Rahima, and Palmarini, Terra. *Pregnant Feelings*. Berkeley, CA: Celestial Arts, 1986.

Borg, Susan, and Lasker, Judith. *When Pregnancy Fails*. Boston: Beacon Press, 1981.

Boston Women's Health Book Collective, Inc. *The New Our Bodies, Ourselves*. New York: Random House, 1985.

Drabble, Margaret, *The Millstone*. New York: William Morrow, 1966.

Klaus, Marshall, and Klaus, Phyllis H. *The Amazing Newborn*. Reading, MA: Addison-Wesley, 1985.

Peterson, Gayle, with contributions by Lewis Mehl, MD. *Birthing Normally: A Personal Growth Approach to Childbirth*, Berkeley, CA: Mind/Body Press, 1981.

Rich, Adrienne. *Of Woman Born*. New York: W. W. Norton, 1976.

Sorel, Nancy Caldwell, ed. *Ever Since Eve: Personal Reflections on Childbirth*. New York: Oxford University Press, 1984.

## Photographs

The endsheet photographs were submitted by the employees of Addison-Wesley Nursing and The Benjamin/Cummings Publishing Company; by those who reviewed the manuscript for this book; by those who contributed to the production of this book; and by the book's primary photographer, Suzanne Arms Wimberley.

The part opening photographs were taken by Barbara Miller, Cradle Pictures, Detroit, Michigan. Copyright © 1987. Courtesy of Memorial Hospital, Colorado Springs, Colorado.

The chapter opening photographs were taken mostly by Suzanne Arms Wimberley, with the following exceptions:

Chapter 1:   submitted by Jenny Hale Pulsipher
Chapter 2:   submitted by J. R. Przeslawski, Catherine McAuley Health Center, Ann Arbor, Michigan
Chapter 3:   taken by Karen Stafford Rantzman
Chapter 6:   submitted by Daniel Heller
Chapter 8:   submitted by Laura Kenney
Chapter 11:  submitted by Debra Hunter
Chapter 19:  submitted by Anne Emerson
Chapter 25:  submitted by Judith A. Geyer, Prince Georges Community College, Largo, Maryland

The origins of the photographs that appear within chapters are either given in the figure captions or are as follows:

Suzanne Arms Wimberley:
Figures 3.1, 3.12, 3.13, 7.3, 7.5, 8.1, 8.3, 8.6, 9.1, 9.2, 9.3, 10.1, 11.3, 12.1, 15.4, 15.8B, 16.1, 16.2, 16.3, 16.4A, 16.4B, 16.4C, 16.6 through 16.15, 16.19, 20.8, 21.20, 23.1, 23.3, 23.4, 23.5, 24.7, 24.11, 24.13, and 24.15; and Color Plate I.

Jeffry Collins:
Figures 21.4C, 21.5C, 21.6B, 21.12, 21.23, 21.28, 21.29, 22.1, 22.2, 22.3, 22.4, 22.6, 22.10, and 24.17.
(These photographs originally appeared in PL Swearingen: *The Addison-Wesley Photo-Atlas of Nursing Procedures* [Addison-Wesley Nursing, 1984].)

William Thompson, RN, Limited Horizons:
Figures 3.3, 3.5, 3.7, 8.4, 15.8A, 16.17, 22.7, 24.21, and 26.1.

George B. Fry III:
Figure 8.5.

# Index

Note: An *f* following a page number indicates a figure; a *t* following a page number indicates tabular material; and a *b* following a page number indicates boxed material. Drugs are listed under their generic names. When a drug trade name is listed, the reader is referred to the generic drug name.

## A

Abdomen
  of mother
    enlargement of as probable change of pregnancy, 168
    postpartal assessment of, 758, 761–763, 769
    postpartal changes in, 753
    prenatal assessment of, 188–189
  of newborn, assessment of, 588, 604
Abdominal breathing pattern cues, 427*t*
Abdominal effleurage, 281
  definition of, 847
Abdominal exercises during pregnancy, 219
ABO incompatibility, 324
ABO typing, on prenatal physical assessment, 190
Abortion, 62
  definition of, 180, 847
  ethical issues in, 10
  habitual, as high risk factor, 184*t*
  spontaneous, 305–307
    classification of, 305, 306*f*
Abruptio placentae, 310, 503–505
  definition of, 847
  differential signs and symptoms of, 504*b*
  as high-risk factor, 185*t*, 390*t*
Abstinence
  as contraceptive method, 56
  definition of, 847
Abuse
  child, care of family at risk for, 833–834
  substance. *See* Substance abuse; Drugs, addicting
  of woman, during pregnancy, 325
Accelerations, 407
  definition of, 847
Acceptance, fetal/newborn loss and, 822
Accessory glands, male, 44
Acetabulum, 32
Acetaminophen
  breast-feeding and, 845

  fetus/neonate affected by, 225*t*
Acidosis
  metabolic, in newborn respiratory distress, 702
  respiratory, in newborn respiratory distress, 702
Acini cells, definition of, 847
Acme of uterine contraction, 372
  definition of, 847
Acoustic stimulation test, 353
Acquaintance phase, 757
Acquired immunity
  active, 562
    definition of, 847
  passive, 562
    definition of, 855
Acquired immunodeficiency syndrome (AIDS), 81
  definition of, 847
  in newborn, 693–695
    and issues for caregivers, 694*b*
    teaching about, 693–695
  during pregnancy, 330–334
    care plan for, 332–333
Acrocyanosis
  definition of, 847
  in newborn, 440, 581, 597
Acrosomal reaction, 138
Acrosome of sperm, 44
Active acquired immunity, 562
  definition of, 847
Active phase of labor, 378, 380*b*, 429*t*
  characteristics of, 380*b*
  nursing care during, 24
Activity
  of fetus
    intrapartal assessment of, 394
    maternal assessment of, 348
    monitoring of during pregnancy, 216, 348
      teaching about, 348, 349–351
  of newborn, teaching parents about, 631
  postpartal resumption of, 785
  during pregnancy, 217–218
Acute grief, 820
  definition of, 847
Acyanotic congenital heart defects, 715*t*
Acyclovir, in herpes infections, 80
Addicting drugs. *See* Drugs, addicting
Admission to hospital
  for newborns
    AIDS and, 694*b*
    nursing care during, 617–620
    procedures for, 613–615

  nursing care during, 421–422
Adnexa, definition of, 847
Adolescence
  definition of, 847
  psychosocial effects of, 231
Adolescent
  middle, definition of, 231, 853
  older, definition of, 231, 854
  young, definition of, 231, 858
Adolescent pregnancy, 230–239
  care of parent family and, 834
  development tasks and, 232–233*t*
  father and, 234–235
  mother and, 231–233, 234*t*
  nursing process and, 236–239
  nutrition and, 262–263
  parents's reactions to, 235–236
  physiologic risks in, 231
  postpartum period and, 791–792
  pregnancy tasks and, 234*t*
  prenatal education in, 276–277
  psychologic risks in, 232
  sociologic risks in, 232
  and support during labor, 424
Adolescent spurt, 22
Adoption, 114
Adrenal gland, pregnancy affecting, 166
Advocacy, client, definition of, 849
Afterbirth, definition of, 847
Afterpains, 754
  definition of, 847
  relief of discomfort from, 783
Age (maternal), 16. *See also* Adolescent pregnancy; Older expectant couple
  as high-risk factor, 183*t*
  pregnancy affected by, 230–244
AIDS. *See* Acquired immunodeficiency syndrome
Airway, maintenance of in normal newborn, 617
Alcohol (alcoholism)
  fetus/neonate affected by, 335*t*
  as high risk factor, 183*t*
  newborn affected by, 688–689
  during pregnancy, 226, 336–337
Alert states of newborn, 564. *See also* Awake states of newborn
Alleles, 121
  definition of, 847
Altitude, as high risk factor, 183*t*
Alveoli, milk syntheiszed in, 36, 647
Ambulation during labor, 274*t*
Amenorrhea, 50
  definition of, 847